GEORGINA CAMPBELL'S
ireland

the guide

All the best places to eat, drink and stay

Georgina Campbell Guides

Editor: Georgina Campbell
Production Editor: Bob Nixon

Epicure Press,
PO Box 6173
Dublin 13
Ireland

website: www.ireland-guide.com
email: info@ireland-guide.com

11th Edition (2009/10), published October 2008.
Updates available from www.ireland-guide.com at all times

Front cover photographs:	Gregans Castle Hotel, Co Clare
	The Ritz Carlton Powerscourt, Co Wicklow
	Lakes of Killarney (Aghadoe Heights Hotel)
Back cover top, (left to right):	Roundwood House, Co Laois
	Kilpatrick House, Co Wicklow
	Ely Wine Bar, Dublin
	Irish Wolfhound (by W.M. Nixon)
	Mountain Biking in Kerry (Aghadoe Heights Hotel)
Back cover bottom, (left to right):	La Maison des Gourmets, Dublin
	Rathwood, Co Carlow
	The Hunting Lodge @ Castle Leslie, Co Monaghan
	Boqueria, Cork
	Fastnet Lighthouse (Heron's Cove, Co Cork)
Spine:	Tom Crean & friends, Co Kerry (by W.M. Nixon)

City and county introductions © W.M. Nixon
Design and Artwork by Brian Darling of The Design Station, Dublin
Printed and bound in Spain
First published 2008 by Georgina Campbell Guides Ltd.

ISBN: 978-1-903164-28-0

Georgina Campbell Guides Awards

Dromoland Castle, Co Clare
Hotel of the Year

Pearl Brasserie, Dublin
Restaurant of the Year

Richard Corrigan
Chef of the Year

Balloo House, Co Down
Pub of the Year

Mustard Seed @ Echo Lodge
Best Use of Fresh Ingredients

O'Connor's Seafood Restaurant, Co Cork
Seafood Restaurant of the Year

The full list of awards is on page 9

Georgina Campbell Guides Awards

The Lobster Pot, Co Wexford
Seafood Bar of the Year

Longueville House, Co Cork
Food EXTRA Award

Rathmullan House, Co Donegal
Natural Food Award

Carrig House, Co Kerry
Hideaway of the Year

Jaipur Group, Dublin & Wicklow
Ethnic Restaurant of the Year

Lisloughrey Lodge, Co Mayo
Irish Breakfast Award

The full list of awards is on page 9

GEORGINA CAMPBELL'S ireland

Restaurant of the Year

Pearl Brasserie
Dublin

See page 95

2008 WINNER:

Deanes Restaurant, Belfast

Chef of the Year

Richard Corrigan
Bentley's Oyster Bar & Grill, Dublin

See page 66

2008 WINNER:

Paul Flynn, The Tannery, Co Waterford

GEORGINA CAMPBELL'S ireland

Pub of the Year

Balloo House
Killinchy, Co Down

See page 674

2008 WINNER:
The Olde Glen Bar, Co Donegal

Bord Bía

Irish Food Board

The Best Use of
Fresh Ingredients Award

Mustard Seed at Echo Lodge
Ballingarry, Co Limerick

See page 465

2008 WINNER:

The Chart House Restaurant, Co Kerry

Fáilte Ireland
National Tourism Development Authority

Food EXTRA Award

Longueville House
Mallow, Co Cork

See page 281

2008 WINNER:
Enniscoe House, Co Mayo

Fáilte Ireland
National Tourism Development Authority

Natural Food Award

Rathmullan House
Rathmullan, Co Donegal

See page 316

2008 WINNER:
Jacques Restaurant, Cork

Fáilte Ireland
National Tourism Development Authority

Hideaway of the Year

Carrig House
Caragh Lake, Co Kerry

See page 368

2008 WINNER:

Coxtown Manor, Co Donegal

Bord Iascaigh Mhara
Irish Sea Fisheries Board

Seafood Bar of the Year

Lobster Pot
Carne, Co Wexford

See page 596

2008 WINNER:
Mary Ann's Bar & Restaurant, Co Cork

Bord Iascaigh Mhara
Irish Sea Fisheries Board

Seafood Restaurant
of the Year

O'Connors Seafood
Restaurant
Bantry, Co Cork

See page 249

2008 WINNER:
O'Grady's on the Pier, Co Galway

GEORGINA CAMPBELL'S ireland

Irish Breakfast Awards

— Hotel —
Lisloughrey Lodge
Cong, Co Mayo

— Country House —
Ballyvolane Country House
Fermoy, Co Cork

— Guesthouse —
Teach de Broc
Ballybunion, Co Kerry

— B&B —
Heron's Rest B&B
Galway

GEORGINA CAMPBELL'S ireland

Irish Breakfast Awards

— National Winner —

Lisloughrey Lodge
Cong, Co Mayo

See page 495

2008 WINNER:

Waterford Castle, Waterford

Ethnic Restaurant
of the Year

Jaipur Group
Dublin & Wicklow

Asheesh Dewan, proprietor

2008 WINNER:
Furama, Dublin

GEORGINA CAMPBELL'S ireland

Atmospheric Restaurant
of the Year

Chez Hans
Cashel, Co Tipperary

See page 548

2008 WINNER:

Hunter's Hotel, Co Wicklow

GEORGINA CAMPBELL'S ireland

Wine Award of the Year

The Twelve
Barna, Co Galway

See page 335

2008 WINNER:
Ashford Castle, Co Mayo

GEORGINA CAMPBELL'S ireland

Host of the Year

John Moriarty
Lord Baker's, Dingle, Co Kerry

See page 375

2008 WINNER:
Martina Sheedy, Sheedys Hotel, Co Clare

GEORGINA CAMPBELL'S ireland

Business Hotel
of the Year

Kingsley Hotel
Cork City

See page 230

2008 WINNER:
Clontarf Castle Hotel, Dublin

GEORGINA CAMPBELL'S ireland

Family Friendly Hotel of the Year

Renvyle House Hotel
Renvyle, Co Galway

See page 360

See page 360

2008 WINNER:

Ferrycarrig Hotel, Co Wexford

GEORGINA CAMPBELL'S ireland

Newcomer of the Year

Cliff House Hotel
Ardmore, Co Waterford

See page 560

2008 WINNER:
Inis Meáin Restaurant, Co Galway

GEORGINA CAMPBELL'S ireland

Country House of the Year

Ballyvolane House
Fermoy, Co Cork

See page 266

2008 WINNER:
Echo Lodge, Co Limerick

GEORGINA CAMPBELL'S ireland

Guesthouse of the Year

Ard na Bréatha
Donegal Town

See page 303

2008 WINNER:
Whitepark House, Co Antrim

GEORGINA CAMPBELL'S ireland

B&B of the Year

Heron's Rest
Galway City

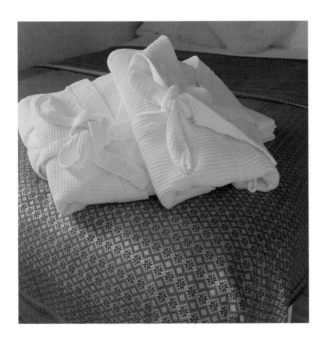

See page 325

2008 WINNER:

McMenamin's Townhouse, Co Wexford

GEORGINA CAMPBELL'S ireland

Farmhouse of the Year

Flemingstown House
Kilmallock, Co Limerick

See page 467

2008 WINNER:
Castle Farm Country House, Co Waterford

Waterways Ireland
Uiscebhealaí Éireann Watterweys Airlann

Waterways Hospitality Award

The Oarsman
Carrick-on-Shannon, Co Leitrim

See page 450

Irish Hospitality
...at its best

Visitors to today's Ireland will find a country of great contrasts. Yes, there's fast paced urban life and traffic laden streets, yet - despite the huge amount of development that has taken place in recent years - beyond the bustle of cities and large towns you will still find stunningly beautiful countryside: lakes, rivers, picturesque villages, and the gentler pace of life that has always been so special in rural Ireland. As in other modern societies, the pace of modern life does take its toll and the 'tiger years' of the last decade created a demanding cash rich/time poor generation of casual weekenders and frequent diners, who put unprecedented pressure on traditional hospitality. Yet that legendary hospitality has proved resilient, and rumours of its imminent demise have certainly been exaggerated: there are many, many people offering food, drink and accommodation all over Ireland who love nothing better than getting to know their guests, spending time with them, and helping them to get every last drop of enjoyment out of a visit to this country and - most particularly - to their own area. They say all politics is local and the same is true of hospitality - in a world of increasing sameness, it's the local differences that count and the most rewarding way to travel in Ireland is by visiting the people who care about the area they live in. The Irish themselves enjoy nothing better than sharing good food and breaks away with family and friends - and, in today's challenging economic climate, make a point of finding the places that offer the best quality and value.

Trends and News

A small island clinging to Europe's western seaboard could never be a low cost destination but, although prices may seem high in comparison with some other European countries, independent travellers visiting Ireland today will find good food, and standards of accommodation that are perhaps surprisingly high - too high, it could be said, as there's an exceptional number of five star hotels for the size of population; however, this generous supply has brought unexpected value at the higher levels, and special offers are frequently available, especially for stays of two or more nights with dinner included. And, as the wide-ranging entries in this guide show, quality and value are available at every level, whether you seek a luxurious place to stay, a budget hotel for a practical accommodation solution, a small but special retreat, a fine meal for a special occasion or a simple bite to eat based on the highest quality local and speciality foods. Welcome trends which have strengthened recently - in some cases dramatically, since the credit crunch started to bite - include a bringing together of environmental concerns and appreciation of quality food by consumers, which

is having unprecedented effects. Stiff competition is forcing many establishments to re-evaluate their offering, to the benefit of guests: with so much choice, it is the places offering something special that will thrive - so we find establishments raising standards all round and focusing on points of special interest including the activities and places to visit in their area and local artisan foods. The seismic changes currently going on in the world around us are beginning to change attitudes; this is seen in many ways including a renewed respect for traditional ways, which paves the way for eco-tourism. Who would have thought a decade ago that there would be a farmers' market in every other town in Ireland, or that organic foods would become so widely accepted? It's difficult to imagine that there could be a downside to such positive developments but farmers' markets have certainly had their (well chronicled) difficulties, and, as 'local', 'organic' and 'seasonal' have become the buzzwords for menu writers, there is a danger that some establishments are merely paying lipservice to a genuinely noble concept, so vigilance is definitely needed. But artisan food products are flourishing throughout the country and there is enormous genuine interest in Irish food, partly in reaction to the internationalism of food products and cooking styles that have brought a disappointing sameness to tables everywhere (and especially in many mid range restaurants) but also, increasingly, because of concerns over food miles and similar issues.

Over the last twenty years, the influence and strength of Euro-Toques (The European Community of Chefs, see below) has been a real force for good in reawakening interest and pride in the value of locally produced, traditional foodstuffs and the leading chefs have put a creative, often innovative, spin on traditional Irish dishes. The result is an attractive if, so far, limited contemporary Irish cuisine that is "entirely itself" - an Irish idiom that indicates our high regard for an individual approach to life and living.

On the other hand, Irish society has become increasingly cosmopolitan and this - plus the influence of international food fashion - has led to diverse cooking styles in restaurants, and rapid growth in the number and variety of ethnic restaurants and shops. All the main food cultures are well represented and the best restaurants - where you will find an emphasis on authenticity, rather than westernised versions of ethnic cuisines - are included in the guide. While Italian, Chinese and Indian/Pakistani restaurants are common in every corner of the island, you'll also find many others including regional French, Greek, Moroccan, Thai, Nepalese, Cuban, Filipino, Malaysian, and, since the enlargement of the European Union, an increasing number of Eastern European cuisines. Spanish food is enjoying a surge of popularity and influence - with tapas and other similar 'small bites' a fast growing trend, matching the growth of a new café-bar culture.

Style and Value

Some welcome current trends are resulting from the higher value placed on seasonal, naturally produced and local food - including a gradual move away from the very complex dishes that have been fashionable in recent years, towards a simpler style with more emphasis on the taste and flavour of top quality ingredients. Fine dining is far from dead, and there will always be a place for the skills of exceptional chefs and restaurant teams, but Irish diners have embraced the relaxed style of bistros and brasseries, offering shorter menus and simpler food. The wider availability of local speciality foods with real depth of flavour is gradually encouraging chefs to allow these ingredients to take pride of place instead of relying on fancy footwork in the kitchen for effect, and it is good to see a return to rustic cooking and 'cuisine grand'mère', with less usual ingredients and a growing number of slow cooked dishes appearing on menus. The growth of interest in wine also continues to be very noticeable, with many restaurants offering an extensive choice of good value house wines and half bottles on their wine lists - and, most interestingly, many more are now offering an increasingly wide selection of wines by the glass, sometimes a range of 50 or even more is offered. Giving value for money is also a high priority, and visitors who wish to eat well without breaking the budget will often find that the best value is offered on early dinner menus and fixed price two-course menus - and lunchtime remains the least costly way of enjoying a meal in our leading restaurants, where a stunning meal may often be found at a surprisingly reasonable price. A Sunday curiosity worth keeping an eye out for is the extended lunch hour, sometimes running from noon to seven in the evening.

The Irish Breakfast

Traditional Irish breakfasts, known as "the full Irish", are substantial and lingering over a leisurely breakfast remains an essential part of being on holiday. Providing a really good breakfast has become a point of pride in many of the best establishments (highlighted by our Irish Breakfast Awards) the traditional morning meal of porridge or cereals and fruit followed by bacon, sausage, black and white pudding, eggs, mushrooms, and tomatoes, accompanied by Irish soda bread and scones, has become just one choice from an elaborate menu, and you'll often also be offered fresh or smoked fish dishes, vegetarian dishes, local farmhouse cheeses, traditional cured hams and other cured meats and salamis.

Traditional Irish Breakfast

There's nothing like the 'full Irish' to set you up for the day. You could add other things - kidneys, liver, potato bread, baked beans - so maybe this is really a 'mini-Irish'. Serves 4

- ▶ *8 rashers of bacon, back or streaky*
- ▶ *8 sausages*
- ▶ *4 slices each of black and white pudding, or 8 slices of combination black & white pudding*
- ▶ *4 flat 'field' mushrooms, or 100g/4 oz button mushrooms*
- ▶ *2-4 tomatoes, as required*
- ▶ *4-8 eggs, as required*
- ▶ *Freshly ground black pepper to taste*
- ▶ *Fresh parsley sprigs to garnish.*

Image courtesy of Rudd's

Grill the bacon, sausages and pudding slices, or cook them in a dry non-stick pan until crispy; to avoid crowding the pan, use a very large one or cook in batches and keep warm until everything is ready. Cook the mushrooms and tomatoes with a little butter, in a separate pan, or under the grill. When everything else is ready, take the pan that was used for the bacon (or drain off any remaining fat from the grill pan, for flavour) and, adding a little extra oil or butter if necessary, cook one or two eggs per person in it. Arrange everything on heated plates, add a little grinding of black pepper and a sprig of parsley and serve with fresh brown bread or toast.

The Food Island

"Ireland the food island" is more than a clever sales slogan - we are a food producing nation and, in support of their mission to promote Irish food, Bord Bia (The Irish Food Board) has initiated programmes that have had a genuinely beneficial effect on the quality and diversity of Irish foods available to chefs and their customers. An initiative coordinated by Bord Bia to support the development of small food producers is the TASTE Council (acronym for traditional, artisan, speciality, trade expertise). Its main aim is to support the growing number of craft food producers to develop, distribute and market their products; also to offer a focus for small food producers that allows them to draw on expertise within the group itself. Membership of the council includes small food producers, organic growers, representatives of relevant organisations like Cáis (the Irish Farmhouse Cheesemakers Association), Euro-Toques (The European Community of Chefs), and retailers and distributors specialising in traditional, artisan and speciality foods. Bord Bia works with over 300 small speciality food producers (just part of a growing number of artisan food producers), a sector that continues to expand, driven by consumer demand at home and abroad. EU agricultural reform, particularly de-coupling, has concentrated farmers' minds on ways and means to survive in the leaner, meaner climate. Those who believe they have the capacity to expand profitably can do so without the need to acquire quotas, or rights to trade. Adaptable farmers see this as an opportunity to cut out the middle man and sell direct to the customer by turning their produce into consumer goods that can be sold locally and at food markets. Markets are a great place for producers and farmers to get mutual support from fellow producers, to get feedback on their produce and ideas for improvement, and just interact with consumers in a way that Irish farmers have not done for generations.

Baked Eggs with Smoked Ham and Mushrooms

Smoked ham and eggs are perfect partners and this versatile combination makes a great breakfast dish or starter. If you want to serve it as a main course for brunch or supper, allow 2 eggs per person. Especially delicious in the autumn, with real field mushrooms. Serves 4.

- ▶ *125g/5oz wild mushrooms, if available, or button mushrooms, sliced and sautéed*
- ▶ *80g/3oz smoked ham, diced*
- ▶ *2 tbs/30ml passata or tomato juice*
- ▶ *2 tbsp/20ml finely grated hard chese*
- ▶ *Salt & freshly ground black pepper*
- ▶ *4 eggs*

Preheat the oven 170°C, Gas Mark 3. Butter 4 ramekins and season lightly. Divide the mushrooms and ham between the 4 ramekins, reserving some mushrooms for garnish. Pour a little tomato juice into each one. Carefully break an egg into each dish, then sprinkle each one with cheese and seasoning. Place the dishes in a shallow roasting dish, pour boiling water around them to reach half way up the ramekins. Place the ramekins in the oven. Check the baked eggs after 10 minutes. The egg white should be just set with the yolk still runny but if you prefer your egg a little more cooked, bake for another 2-3 minutes. Garnish with the reserved mushrooms and serve with fingers of hot toast for dipping into the yolks. Simply delicious.

Irish Farmers' Markets

The widespread revival of local food markets has been one of the most exciting achievements of recent years. If you come from anywhere else in Europe you will wonder why they were in need of reviving. Although widespread and highly organised since Norman times, historical reasons led to all but a few local food markets dying out. Now, to the delight of food lovers, all that has changed and many towns all over Ireland have a weekly famers' market, sometimes even twice weekly. For a nation that treasures individualism there is a remarkable degree of mutual support between artisan food producers and other interested parties. The Irish Food Market Traders Association, whose aim is to promote and provide information on farmers markets, addresses the many and varied needs of food market traders; Bord Bia lend a helping hand with a web-based service offering advice and assistance for people wishing to establish a market and also (via the internet) promoting the all of the regular farmers' markets.

Although there has been a downside to the sudden proliferation of farmers' markets - notably that too much non-local food has found its way onto the stalls - this problem of success is being addressed and, rather than introducing yet more regulation, the focus is on creating incentives that will encourage self-regulation. Meanwhile, markets remain a wonderful way of experiencing Irish food - a chance to buy food for a picnic, to taste traditional and innovative food products from traditional smoked wild salmon, trout, mackerel, smoked mussels, or smoked scallops, fish patés, seafood soups and seaweeds (an ancient tradition in Ireland). Farmhouse cheeses are one of the glories of artisan producers and there are over 70 farmhouse cheesemakers, each producing cheeses that are unique to the family and farmland. Here, too, you will find distinctive Irish breads, biscuits and cakes. A surprising Irish speciality is handcrafted chocolates filled with cream and Irish liqueurs; fine examples are winners of Irish Food Writers Guild Chocolate Lovers' Awards: Gallwey's made in Co Waterford and Eve's made in Cork. Soft fruit and wild berries are often made into gorgeous preserves, chutneys and liqueurs. Traditional dry cures of bacon and ham are found alongside innovative smoked and cured meats, like the award-winning smoked Connemara lamb and smoked Irish beef, both creations of young craft butcher James McGeough of Oughterard, who has already won many awards including the top prizes at both The Irish Food Writers Guild Food Awards and The Craft Butchers Speciality Foods Competition.

The Bord Bia guide to farmers' food markets, held regularly in many cities, towns and villages:

Antrim
- City Food And Garden Market Belfast, St George's Street, Saturday 9-4pm
- Lisburn Market, Lisburn, Saturday
- Origin Farmers Market, Ballymoney, Castlecroft, Main St, Last Saturday of month 11-2pm
- The Park Shopping Centre, Belfast, Thursday 10-4pm
- Portadown Market, Last Saturday of month

Carlow
- Carlow Farmers Market, Potato Market, Saturday 9-2pm

Cavan
- Belturbet Farmers Market, McGowan's Garden, (Beside carpark) Fridays 4-7pm (May to October)
- Cavan Farmers Market, McCarren's, Farham Road, Saturday 10am-4pm

Clare
- Ballyvaughan Farmers Market, Village Hall Car Park, Saturdays 10am - 2pm
- Ennis Farmers Market, Car Park, Upr Main Street Friday 8-2pm
- Killaloe Farmers Market, Between the Waters Sunday 11-3pm
- Kilrush Farmers Market, The Square, Thursday 9-2pm
- Miltown Malbay Market, Miltown Business Centre Fridays 4.30-7pm
- Shannon Farmers Market, Town Centre, next to Skycourt Shopping Centrem Friday 12.30-7pm

Cork
- Ballydehob Food Market, Community Hall Friday 10.30-12pm
- Bandon Market, Bandon, Saturday 10.30-1pm
- Bantry Market, Main Square, 1st Friday of month
- Blackwater Valley Farmers Market, Nano Nagle Centre, Mallow, Every 2nd Saturday 10.30-1pm
- Clonakilty Farmers Market, McCurtain Hill Thursdays & Sundays 10-2pm
- Cobh Market, Sea Front, Friday 10-1pm
- Cornmarket Street Market, Cornmarket Street Saturday 9-3pm
- Douglas Food Market, Douglas Community Park Saturday 9.30-2pm
- Duhallow Farmers Market, Kanturk, Thursday and Saturday morning 10.30- 1.30p.m
- English Market Cork, Entrances on Princes St and Grand Parade, Daily
- Hosfords Food Market, Hosfords Garden Centre, Bandon-Clonakilty Rd (N71). 5 miles west of Bandon, First Sunday of every month April - September, 12-5pm
- Inchigeelagh Market, Creedons Hotel, Last Saturday of month
- Kanturk Food Market, Behind Supervalu Kanturk Thursday & Saturday, 10.30-1pm
- Macroom Farmers Market, The Square, Tuesday 9-3pm, UCD Office, Macroom
- Mahon Point Farmers Market, West Entrance, Mahon Point Shopping Centre, Thursday 10-2pm
- Midleton Farmers Market, Hospital Road, Saturday
- Schull Farmers Market, Car Park Near Pier, Sunday 10-3pm
- Skibbereen Farmers Market, Old Market Square Saturday 10-2pm

Derry
- Guildhall Country Fair, Last Saturday in month

Donegal
- Ballybofey Farmers Market, GAA grounds, Friday 12-4pm
- Donegal Town Farmers Market, Diamond, 3rd Saturday of Month

Down
- Castlewellan Farmers Market, Castlewellan Community Centre, Saturday 10am - 1pm
- Newry Dundalk Speciality Food and Craft Market, Marcus Square, Hill Street, Newry, Last Saturday of every month 9.30am-2pm

Dublin
- 12 Newmarket, Dublin 8, Newmarket, Thursday 2pm-8pm, Saturday 9.30am-4.30 pm
- Ballymun Farmers Market, Ballymun Plaza, beside the Civic Centre, Thursdays 11am - 4pm
- Citywest Market, Citywest Shopping Centre, Friday, 11-4pm
- Clontarf Farmer's Market, St Anthony's Church, Clontarf Rd, Dublin 3, Sundays, 10am -5pm
- Dalkey Market, Dalkey Town Hall, Friday 10-3pm
- Docklands Market, Mayor Square, IFSC, Wednesday 12-2pm
- Dun Laoghaire People's Park Market, People's Park, Sunday 11-4pm
- Farmleigh Food Market, Farmleigh House
- Fingal Farmers Market, Beside Swords Courthouse, Saturdays
- Fingal Food Fayre, Fingal Arts Centre, Last Sunday every month 12-5pm
- Howth Harbour Market, The Harbour, Howth Sunday 10-4pm
- Leopardstown Farmers Market, Leopardstown Racecourse, Friday 10-4pm
- Liffey Valley Shopping Centre, Quarryvale, D.22 Fridays 10-4pm
- Malahide Market, GAA facility, Church Rd Saturday 10-5pm
- Marley Park Food Market, Marlay Park Craft Courtyard, Saturday 10-4pm
- Monkstown Village Market, Monkstown Parish Church, Saturday 10-4pm
- Pearse Street Market, St Andrews Centre Saturday 9.30-3.30pm
- Ranelagh Marketm Multi Denominational School Sunday 10-4pm
- Smithfield Market, Smithfield Plaza, Dublin 1 Friday-Sunday, 10-6pm Weekly
- Temple Bar Market, Meeting House Square Saturday 9-5pm, Temple Bar Cultural Trust
- The Red Stables Food Market, St Anne's Park, Clontarf (beside the Rose Garden), Saturday 10am - 5pm

Galway
- Athenry Farmers Market -100% Organic Market Cross, Friday 930-4pm
- Ballinasloe Farmers Market, Croffy's Centre, Main Street, Fridays, 10-3pm
- Galway Marketm Beside St Nicholas Church Saturday, 8.30-4pm & Sunday 2-6pm
- Loughrea Market, Barrack Street, Thursdays 10am-2pm
- Oranmore, Behind Church, Thursdays 1pm-6pm
- Tuam Farmer's Market - 100% Organic Market Cross, Thursdays 930-4pm

Kerry
- Ballyseedy Farmer's Market, Ballyseedy Garden Centre, Saturday, 10-1.30 pm
- Caherdaniel Market, Village Hall, Friday 10-12am (Jun-Sept & Christmas

- Cahirciveen Market, Community Centre
  Thursday 10-2pm (Jun-Sept)
- Dingle Farm Produce & Craft Market (by the
  fishing harbour, opposite bus stop)
  Friday 10am-3pm
- Dunloe Farmers Market, Dunloe Golf Course
  Sundays 1-5pm
- Kenmare Farmers Market, on the Square,
  Wednesdays 10-6pm
- Listowel Farmers Market, The Square, Listowel
  Fridays 10am-2pm
- Milltown Market, Organic Centre, Saturday
  10-2pm
- Milltown Market, Organic Centre Tuesday-Friday,
  10-6pm
- Sneem Market, Community Centre, Tuesday
  11-2pm (Jun-Sept & Christmas)
- Valencia Island Market, The Royal, Knightstown
  Wednesday & Saturday 2-6pm

Kildare
- Athy Farmers Market, Emily Square, Sunday
  10-2pm
- Naas Farmers Market, The Storehouse Restaurant
  Saturday 10-3pm
- Whitewater Farmers Market, Whitewater Shopping
  Centre, Newbridge, Co. Kildare, Wednesdays &
  Saturdays 10-4pm

Kilkenny
- Callan Farmers Market, Main St. Callan, every
  Saturday 10am-12pm
- Kilkenny Farmers Market, The Parade, Kilkenny,
  every Thursday 9:30am-2:30pm

Laois
- Portlaoise Market Square, Portlaoise, Friday
  10-3pm

Leitrim
- Origin Farmers Market (Manorhamilton),
  Beepark Resource Centre, Friday 9am-2pm

Limerick
- Abbeyfeale Farmers Market, Parish Hall, Friday
  9am-1pm
- Kilmallock Farmers Market, The Kilmallock GAA
  Club, Friday 9am-1pm
- Limerick Milk Market, Limerick Milk Market ,
  Saturday 8am-1.30pm

Longford
- Longford Farmers Market, Market Sq, Friday
  9.30am-2:30pm

Louth
- Castlebellingham Farmers Market, Bellingham
  Castle Hotel, 1st Sunday of month
- Dundalk Town Producers Market, The Square,
  Dundalk, Friday 10am-2pm
- Newry Dundalk Farmers Market, The County
  Museum, Jocelyn Street, Dundalk, Saturday
  10am-2pm

Mayo
- Achill Country Market, Ted Lavelle's, Cashel,
  every Friday 11am-1pm
- Ballina Country Market, Community Centre,
  Teeling St., Every Friday 9am-1pm
- Ballina Farmers Market, Market Square,
  every Saturday 9am-2pm
- Charlestown Farmers Markets, Murphy's, Londis
  Car Park, every Thursday 9am-2pm
- Claremorris Country Market, Town Hall,
  Claremorris, every Friday 10am-2pm
- Foxford Woollen Mills Market, Woollen Mills,
  Foxford, every Saturday 10am-2pm
- Killala Farmers Market, Community Centre,
  every Sunday 9am-2pm
- Kiltimagh Farmers Market, Market Square,
  Kiltimagh, every Saturday 10am-1pm

- Louisburgh Market, Louisburgh,
  every Friday 9am-3pm
- Westport Country Market, Pete Callaghan Centre,
  off James St. Car Park, every Thursday
  8.30am-1pm
- Westport Food & Craft Market, The Mall, Westport
  every Saturday 9am-5pm (from March)

Meath
- Ashbourne Farmers Market, outside the County
  Council offices, every Saturday 10am-4pm
- Dunboyne Farmers Market (at the turn of former
  Emo petrol station on the N3), every day
  10am-6pm
- Kells Farmers Market, FBD Insurance Grounds,
  Saturday 10am-1pm
- Sonairte Farmers Market, Laytown, The Ecology
  Centre, 3rd Sunday in month, 10.30am-5pm

Monaghan
- Monaghan Farmers / Country Market,
  Castleblayney. Livestock Salesyard, last Saturday
  of month, 9am-1pm

Offaly
- The Full Moon Market, The Chestnut Courtyard,
  every 3rd Sunday
- Tullamore Country Fair, Millenium Square,
  Saturday 9am-4pm

Roscommon
- Origin Farmers Market (Boyle), grounds of King
  House, Saturday, 10am-2pm

Sligo
- Origin Farmers Market (Sligo), Sligo IT Sports
  Field Car Park, Saturdays 9am-1pm

Tipperary
- Cahir Farmers Market, beside The Craft Granary
  Saturday 9am-1pm
- Carrick-on-Suir, Heritage Centre, Main St.,
  Friday 10am-2pm
- Clonmel Farmers Market, St. Peter & Paul's
  Primary School, Kickham Street, beside Oakville
  Shopping Centre, Saturday 10am-2pm
- Nenagh Farmers Market, Teach an Lean, every
  Saturday 10am-2pm
- Templemore, Wednesdays 9am-3pm
- Thurles, Greyhound Stadium, Saturdays 9.30-
  12.30pm

Tyrone
- Origin Farmers Market, Strabane, The Score
  Centre, Dock Rd, last Saturday of month
- Tyrone Farmers Market, Tesco Carpark,
  Dungannon, 1st Saturday of month 8.30am-1pm

Waterford
- Ardkeen Producers Market, Ardkeen Quality Food
  Store, 2nd Sunday of every month
- Dungarvan Farmers Market, The Square,
  Thursday 9.30am-2pm
- Dunhill Farmers Market Parish Hall, last Sunday
  of month 11.30am-2pm
- Kilmacthomas, Friday 9.30am-2pm
- Lismore Farmers Market, Blackwater Valley
- Stradbally Community Market, 1st Saturday of
  month 10am-12.30pm
- Waterford Farmers Market, Jenkins Lane,
  Saturday 10am-4pm

Westmeath
- Athlone Co-Op Farmers Market, St. Marys Parish
  Hall, North Gate St., every Friday 10am-3pm
- Athlone Farmers Market, Market Square, Athlone
  Saturday 10am-3pm
- Mullingar Fairgreen (Adjacent to Lifestyle and
  Pennys), every Sunday 10.30am-2.30pm

Wexford

- Gorey Farmers Market, Gorey Community School, Car Park, Esmonde Street, Gorey, Saturday 9am-2pm
- New Ross Farmers Market, The Quay, New Ross Saturday 9am-2pm
- Wexford Farmers Market, Key West, Friday 9am-2pm
- Wexford Farmers Market Community Partnership,Enniscorthy, The Abbey Square Carpark, Saturday 9am-2pm
- Wexford Farmers Market Dunbrody, Dunbrody Abbey Centre 15th July, 19th August

Wicklow

- Aughrim Farmers Market, Aughrim Park Pavillion Saturdays 11am-2pm
- Blessington Farmers Market, Russbourough House, First Sunday of the month 10am-4pm
- Bray Farmers Market, outside Bray Heritage Centre, Main St., Saturday 11am-3pm
- Brooklodge Organic Market, Macreddin Village, 1st & 3rd Sunday of month
- Greystones Market, Meridian Point Shopping Centre, Saturday 10am-4pm
- Wicklow Town, Market Square, Main St., Saturday 10am-3pm

COUNTRY MARKETS

Carlow

- Bagenalstown, Church Road Com Centre Saturday 8.45 am
- Askea, Askea Community Centre,Friday 10am

Clare

- Ennis, Friary Car Park, Friday 8.30am

Cork

- Bandon, Weir Street, Friday & Saturday 10am
- Ballincollig, Community Centre, Friday 10am
- Carrigaline, G.A.A. Hall, Friday 9.30am
- Fermoy, Youth Centre, Friday 2.15pm
- Mallow, St.James` Hall, Friday 2pm
- Macroom, GAA Hall, Tuesday 11.30am
- Midleton Old School, Church Lane, Friday 10am
- Riverstown, Glanmire GAA Hall,Friday 9am
- Skibbereen, Abbeystrewry Hall, Friday 12pm

Donegal

- Inishowen, C of I Hall, Buncrana, 2nd & 4th Saturday 2-3 pm
- Ramelton Town Hall, Saturday, 11am
- Dunfanaghy*, Ozanam Centre, Saturday 11am

Dublin

- Kilternan, opp. Golden Ball, Saturday 10am
- Raheny, The Johnston Hall, Friday 1.30am

Galway

- Portumna Town Hall, Friday 8.30am

Kerry

- Killorglin, C.Y.M.S. Hall, Friday 10am
- Tralee, John Mitchells GAA Hall, Thursday 1.30pm

Kildare

- Naas, Town Hall, Friday 10am

Kilkenny

- Castlecomer, Community Hall, Friday 9am
- Freshford Community Centre, Saturday 11am
- Kilkenny, Market Yard, Friday / Saturday 9am

Laois

- Mountrath, Macra na Feirme Hall, Friday 8.30am

Leitrim

- Mohill, O'Malley's, Friday 10am
- Lonforsd, Granardz, Town Hall, Friday 8.30am

Louth

- Ravensdale, Communnity Centre, Saturday 11am

Mayo

- Ballina, Community Centre, Friday 9am
- Castlebar, Linenhall Art Centre, Friday 8am
- Westport, Town Hall, Thursday 8.30am

Meath

- Enfield, Community Hall, Friday 9.15am
- Kells Parish Hall, Friday 9.30am

Sligo

- Strandhill, Dolly`s Cottage, June wk/ends 2pm

Tipperary

- Cahir, Community Centre, Friday 8am
- Tipperary, Fethard Town Hall, Friday 8am
- Tipperary, Nenagh, New Institute, Friar Street Friday 8.30am
- Roscrea, Abbey Hall, Friday 2.15pm

Waterford

- Dungarvan, Causeway Tennis Club, Friday 10am
- Waterford, St. Olaf`s Hall, Friday 8am
- Tramore, Coastguard Station, 2nd Sunday of Month 2pm

Westmeath

- Ballynacargy, Parish Hall, Friday 5.30pm

Wexford

- Enniscorthy, I.F.A.Centre, Friday 8.30am
- Fethard-on-Sea, St Marys Hall**, Saturday 10am
- Gorey, Woodstock Hall, Saturday 9am
- Wexford, Wexford Bull Ring, Friday 9am
- Wexford, Wexford Bull Ring, Sat 10am

Wicklow

- Arklow, Arklow Pigeon Club, Saturday 10.30am
- Blessington, St.Kevins Com Centre, Saturday 2.30pm
- North Wicklow, Community Centre, Newcastle Saturday 10.30am

---

NB: Times, days and locations of markets do sometimes change; be sure to check locally or log on to: www.bordbia.ie/go/Consumers/Buying_Food/farmers_markets

Best Use of Fresh Ingredients Award

Bord Bia's 'Best use of Fresh Ingredients Award' aims to encourage chefs to support local and artisan producers by sourcing freshly available produce and highlighting this on their menus. Customers are increasingly looking for information on how their food is produced and

Bord Bia
Irish Food Board

where it comes from. The 'Best use of Fresh Ingredients Award' recognises a commitment to traceability and creativity in the use of local and speciality foods. Providing supplier and country of origin information on menus assures diners where the food on their plate has come from, it also credits the producer for their quality produce.

Bord Bia supports those restaurants who acknowledge that quality fresh ingredients (meat, eggs, fruit and vegetables) are a major contributing factor in creating a truly memorable meal, showing respect for ingredient sourcing and pride in the final dish delivered to their customers. By working closely with their food suppliers and providing customers with information and reassurance as to where their food comes from, chefs have an opportunity to use their menus as a valuable marketing tool.

Roast Rack of Pork with Fennel & Stuffed Apples

The pig was probably the first domestic animal to be brought to Ireland and, although its absolute supremacy as a source of meat was later to be challenged by cattle and sheep, its popularity has never waned. Until quite recently pork butchers specialising in every possible edible product of the pig were to be found in every town and village and, although the general butcher and supermarket have tended to supersede them, there is a healthy revival of interest in speciality butchers today – and also of rare breeds of pork. This roast makes a lovely, warming autumn or winter meal and is ideal for a big family Sunday lunch.
Serves 8-10

▶ *1 rack of pork, preferably free range,*
  2-3kg/4.5-6lb, chined and rind scored.

Marinade:
▶ *2 tbsp/30ml olive oil*
▶ *2-3 cloves garlic, chopped*
▶ *1 tsp/5ml fennel seeds, toasted*
▶ *Juice and rind of one lemon*
▶ *Freshly ground black pepper*

Other Ingredients:
▶ *8-10 red eating apples, cored*
▶ *16-20 prunes, stone removed*
▶ *Glass of dry cider, or white wine*
▶ *Selection of root vegetables - parsnips, carrots, potatoes - 8-10 of each*
▶ *8-10 red onions*
▶ *3 tbsp/45ml olive oil*
▶ *2-3/30-45ml runny honey*
▶ *Salt and freshly ground black pepper*

A day ahead, if possible, mix the marinade ingredients and spread over the pork joint. Leave in the fridge overnight.

To Cook: Pre-heat the oven to 200°C (400°F), Gas Mark 6. Place the pork on a roasting tray, season well and roast for 2 hours. Reduce the oven temperature, if necessary, when the crackling is crisp and well browned. Stuff the apples with prunes and add to the meat tray with the glass of wine. Continue cooking for another 35-40 minutes, or until the pork and apples are fully cooked. Roast the vegetables at the same time - toss them in pork fat or olive oil and seasoning, place them in another tray in the oven and cook for 45-50 minutes. 20 minutes before the end of cooking time, drizzle the pork, apples and vegetables with the runny honey.

To serve: Lift the pork and apples out of the roasting tray and keep warm. Boil up the juices with a knob of butter, and check the seasoning. Carve the pork and serve with the stuffed apples and roasted vegetables, and lightly cooked seasonal green vegetable.

Left-overs are very good cold in a sandwich with the stuffed apple mashed up!

Delicious Burgers with Melted Wicklow Blue Cheese & Tomato Salsa

Three secrets to making the best burgers: top quality mince, the onions sautéed till golden brown and cooked ahead of time - and a good splash of chilli oil in the mixture. And, for good measure, top it with a really interesting cheese, such as Wicklow Blue.
Serves 4

Burger Ingredients
- *450g/ 1lb minced beef or lamb*
- *1 large onion, finely chopped, sautéed in oil till golden and cooled*
- *1 tablesp. scallions, chopped*
- *1 tablesp. chilli oil, optional but nice (see recipe)*
- *Salt and black pepper*
- *Tomato Salsa*
- *16 approx. cherry tomatoes, chopped*
- *1-2 red onions, finely chopped*
- *Handful chopped coriander*
- *1 tablesp. chilli oil*
- *Lemon juice to taste*
- *Salt and black pepper*

To Serve
- *4 slices of Wicklow Blue or other cheese, eg a good Cheddar*

Mix the mince, onion, scallions, chilli oil and seasoning well together. With wet hands shape into 4 burgers. Flatten each one down with the palm of your hand until you have a nice even shape. This way they will cook more quickly and evenly. Keep in the fridge until ready to cook.

Grill, barbecue or cook on a black ridged pan, until fully cooked, 4-5 minutes on each side. Meanwhile mix all the salsa ingredients together. Then place a spoonful of salsa on top of each burger and top with a slice of cheese. Grill, or cover the barbecue or pan and continue to cook for another minute until the cheese has melted. Serve on a bap with some salad leaves and the remaining salsa.

Euro-Toques & Slow Food

Since the mid 1980s, **Euro-Toques** (The European Community of Chefs) has promoted local sourcing from small, artisan producers, in order to protect the quality, diversity and flavour of our food and to promote indigenous and traditional production methods. With over two hundred members and an energetic and vibrant organization, the Euro-Toque ethos has been of great value in working towards the creation of the contemporary Irish cuisine that many Irish people now take for granted. Creative and dedicated they may be, but they come out of their kitchens when needs be, and they are active in lobbying (and encouraging other organisations to lobby) against any threat to the diversity and quality of Irish food. At their annual Food Forum they tackle major issues, such as the dangers of introducing genetically modified food crops into Ireland, and have made calls on the government to make Ireland a GM-free zone. Euro-Toques are also diligent in developing young chefs, nurturing the particularly talented through the annual Bailey's/Euro-Toques Young Chef of the Year Competition and coaching Ireland's representatives at international cooking competitions including the prestigious Bocuse d'Or - an especially relevant involvement as that great chef, Paul Bocuse, was one of the founders of Euro-Toques (in 1986).

More recently, the international **Slow Food Movement** has caught the imagination of food lovers everywhere - despite the name it's a fast-growing movement and over the last few years many more local convivia have been established; it is open to both food professionals and members of the public, and the involvement of consumers helps make it a very potent force in the movement towards smaller production methods and artisan foods. Its emblem, the snail (a small, cosmopolitan and prudent animal), stands as the symbol of a movement that exists to spread awareness of food culture, to safeguard agricultural heritage techniques, to defend biodiversity in crops, craft techniques, food traditions, and eating places.

Members are free to attend international Slow Food events but, probably, what appeals even more to the Irish independence of spirit is that local activities are led from the bottom up - local convivia meet regularly to explore their own small corner with like-minded people. It provides a meeting ground with artisan food producers, with growers and traditional farmers, to share knowledge and support those who work in harmony with the principles of the movement. The Slow Food Terra Madre ('Mother Earth') Ireland event, held in Waterford City in September 2008, marked an important milestone for Ireland's commitment to the natural production of good food, and diversity.

Bord Iascaigh Mhara (BIM)

Bord Iascaigh Mhara / The Irish Sea Fisheries Board is dedicated to promoting the sustainable development of the Irish seafood industry at sea and ashore, working closely with all sectors from fisherman to fish farmer, processor, retailer and chef. BIM also plays a vital role in the development of aquaculture, supporting the trend towards environmentally friendly and organic fish farming, as well as the cultivation of shellfish like oysters, clams, scallops and mussels. For further information on the services provided by BIM visit www.bim.ie

Irish Seafood - Something Special

Luscious Dublin Bay prawns, succulent oysters, melt in the mouth mussels, tempting smoked salmon, mouth-watering mackerel, tantalising monkfish… just some of the delicious seafood you'll find on menus right round Ireland. Irish people love to eat seafood when dining out; in fact, unlike our European neighbours, we eat more seafood outside the home than in it (perhaps this is a testament to the quality of our restaurants). Visitors to Ireland also place a high value on the range and quality of Irish seafood. For many, a trip to Ireland wouldn't be complete without sampling a few oysters and sinking a pint of the black stuff.

Wonderful seafood is found in a vast range of establishments, from award winning restaurants to hotels, little bistros and pubs. Locally caught seafood is especially good and is often flagged on the menu. Seafood is incredibly versatile, allowing chefs to create innovative dishes suitable for all meal occasions whether it's a breakfast, light lunch, quick snack or gourmet dinner. Irish seafood is renowned for its quality and flavour and is much sought after in markets worldwide. Smoked Irish salmon finds a ready market in France, Italy and Germany while pub goers in Toyko are snacking on Irish crab, salmon and mussels and in Spain, monkfish and hake from Irish waters are snapped up.

Looking for delicious moules marinière in a seafront restaurant, a sumptuous seafood platter in a cosy pub or just a hearty bowl of chowder at lunchtime? For the best places to buy and enjoy seafood just look for the Seafood Circle.

Bord Iascaigh Mhara initially developed the BIM Seafood Circle initiative to encourage publicans to serve seafood dishes at lunchtime, a meal at which many people prefer to choose lighter, healthier dishes. This initiative has been further developed in conjunction with Georgina Campbell Guides to encompass not only pubs, but also restaurants and hotels. Seafood Circle membership is awarded on an annual basis and is subject to meeting the necessary criteria.

Check out the listings in this guide and you'll find top quality, innovative, delicious seafood dishes in the establishments carrying the distinctive Seafood Circle logo.

And if you fancy yourself as a seafood chef then watch out for the Seafood Circle specialist/seafood counter logos in fish shops around the country or check www.seafoodcircle.ie for a listing. Shops displaying the logo offer a range of top quality seafood and you'll be assisted by knowledgeable, professional staff.

Smoked Salmon Salad
with Horseradish crème fraîche

This is a delicious dish, perfect for a quick snack, or easy entertaining. Serves 4.
8 slices smoked salmon (You can also use smoked or peppered
mackerel or trout)

- ▸ *1 large bag mixed salad leaves*
- ▸ *12 cherry tomatoes – cut in half*
- ▸ *1 tablespoon wholegrain mustard*
- ▸ *1 tablespoon horseradish sauce*
- ▸ *4 tablespoons crème fraîche*
  or natural yoghurt
- ▸ *Handful of croûtons*
- ▸ *Handful chopped flat leaf parsley*

Mix horseradish and wholegrain mustard with the crème fraîche or yoghurt. Thin out with a little water until desired consistency. Place salad leaves in a large bowl, with the cherry tomatoes. Place slices of smoked salmon or flaked mackerel on top, with the croûtons. Pour over the dressing and sprinkle with chopped parsley.

Roast fish, creamed leeks and parsley mash

This simple, wholesome and very delicious dish depends on quality of ingredients - and the freshness of the fish - for its success. Serves 4

Ingredients

- *4 thick portions of any white fish*
- *2 handfuls chopped parsley*
- *4 large potatoes*
- *3 tablespoons olive oil*
- *300g/11oz leeks - finely sliced and washed*
- *150ml5 fl oz cream*
- *20g/1oz butter*
- *Salt and pepper*

Mix the parsley and 2 tablespoons of the olive oil in a processor until you have a fine purée. Peel the potatoes, boil until soft and mash. Whisk in the parsley purée with a fork and season to taste. Preheat the oven until very hot. Season the fish with a little salt and pepper. Heat a frying pan until very hot, add the remaining olive oil and sear the cod for 2- 3 minutes. Transfer into the hot oven and roast for another 3- 4 minutes. Meanwhile, place the cream and butter in a saucepan and boil, to reduce slightly. Add the finely sliced leeks and cook for just 30 seconds until slightly softened. To Serve: Place each piece of fish onto a mound of mash, and spoon over the creamed leeks.

Seafood, the healthy option

*Health professionals recommend that we eat seafood at least twice a week. Apart from tasting great, it is packed with protein, minerals, vitamins and essential Omega 3's, providing many of the nutrients we need for good health. BIM has developed a range of information materials on the health benefits of fish consumption. Visit **www.bim.ie/wellbeing**.*

DUBLIN CITY

As one of Europe's fastest expanding economic centres during the era of rapid expansion, Dublin's commercial and creative energy matched the vibrancy of its everyday life and hospitality. But if anything, the place is even more interesting in a time of marked economic adjustment, for within the modern development there is an old town where many meandering stories have interacted and combined to create today's busy riverside and coastal metropolis. Through a wide variety of circumstances, it has become an entertaining place suited to the civilised enjoyment of life in the 21st Century. And part of the fascination of the place is found in Dubliners' response to changed circumstances, for their city has known good times and bad.

With so much of it about, most Dubliners wear their city's history lightly in an environment where the past lives with the present in ancient monuments, historic buildings, gracious squares and fine old urban style that still manages to be gloriously alive. This if anything is emphasised by the city's modern architecture, seen particularly in the area around the International Financial Services Centre north of the river, and across the Liffey on George's Quay. Further impressive development has taken shape along both sides of the Liffey towards the Bay while the Port itself is busier than ever to add a touch of reality to the waterside glass towers. And though the city's official municipal spirit is expressed through The Spire in O'Connell Street, Dubliners themselves prefer to take their inspiration from the twin powerstation smokestacks of 1974 vintage – Laurel and Hardy - down at the rivermouth on the sea. Needless to say they caused disputation when they were being built, but now it seems most Dubs are quite fond of them.

The city and Ireland's spirit is also expressed in the Gaelic Athletic Association's impressive headquarters stadium at Croke Park which can accommodate over 80,000 spectators for several sports, while the legendary Lansdowne Road rugby stadium south of the river is being completely re-built as a 50,000 seater.

Dubliners may seem to take this dynamic interaction of ancient, classic and modern for granted, but then they have to get on with life. They've a vigorous appetite for it. So they'll quickly deflate any visitor's excessive enthusiasm about their city's significance with some throwaway line of Dublin wit, or sweep aside some highfalutin notions about legendary figures of supposed cultural importance by recalling how their grandfathers had the measure of that same character when he was still no more than a pup making a nuisance of himself in the neighbourhood pub. Dubliners are well aware that it's a good thing for writers to be unhappy, but you can have too much of a good thing.

The origins of the city's name are in keeping with this downbeat approach. From the ancient Irish there came something which derived from a makeshift solution to local inconvenience. Baile Atha Cliath - the official name in recent times - means nothing more exciting than "the townland of the hurdle ford". Ancient Ireland being an open plan sort of place without towns, the site of the future city was no more than a river crossing with several comfortable monasteries in the neighbourhood

But where the residents saw some inconvenience in the river, the Vikings sensed an opportunity. When they brought their longships up the River Liffey around 837AD having first raided at nearby Lambay in 795, they knew of a sheltered berth in a place which the locals of the hurdle ford called Dubh Linn - "the black pool". The Vikings settled along Wood Quay and around Dublin Castle. This living memory of this busy Viking capital was celebrated in 2006 with the arrival under sail and oar in Dublin from Denmark of the 29.4 metres longship Sea Stallion of Glendalough, which had been re-created at the ancient Viking central capital of Roskilde as a remarkably exact facsimile of the original, built in Dublin in 1042 with timber from County Wicklow

Exhibited in the impressive museum in Collins Barrack until July 2008, Sea Stallion represents a Dublin creation of the 11th Century in an 18th Century setting. With a rugged but successful voyage back to Denmark July and August 2008, the beautiful vessel's hull resemblance to a Venetian gondola was a tangible reminder of the enormous extent of the Viking world at its peak, though it was already declining in Ireland in 1042 as the raiders became absorbed into the population. Dublin was the Viking trading empire's western capital at a time when the eastern capital was to be found far into Russia, with sea power extended deep into the Mediterranean and through the Adriatic to the future location of Venice.

Although the name of Ireland's main Viking port was to go through mutations as the Vikings were succeeded in mnanagement by the Normans who in turn were in the business of becoming English and then more Irish than the Irish themselves, today's name of Dublin is the one the Vikings came upon - though the pre-Viking Irish would have pronounced it as something more like "doo-lin". With the Normans putting manners about the place, the descendants of Vikings and their Irish kinsfolk tended to move north of the Liffey where Oxmantown was Eastmantown – the Danes were the Eastmen while the Norwegian were the Northmen or Norsemen or Normans, and sometimes all three.

It was confusing for those who wanted to get on with day-to-day life in Dublin, but some sense of it was made with the Liffey divide which still prevails today in Dublin's northside-southside interface, though analysts suggest that it is now becoming more east-west, with the M50 and Dublin's coastal regions providing a barrier which the Normans knew as The Pale, a name which in itself has survived through various permutations of English power.

Be that as it may, the name Dublin still works best, for it was thanks to the existence of the black pool in the Liffey that Dublin became the port, trading base and cultural focus which evolved as the country's natural administrative centre. Thus your Dubliner may well think that the persistent official use of Baile Atha Cliath was an absurdity. But it isn't the business of any visitor to say so, for although Dublin came into existence through socioeconomic and historical pressures, it has been around for quite some time, and Dubliners have developed their own attitudes and their own way of doing things.

As for their seaport, it is still very much part of the city, and has never been busier – with forty major ship movements every day, sea and city are closely intertwined. However, Dublin Port is becoming a people-oriented transit focus, a giant ferry and cruise-liner port in the midst of residential, hospitality, administrative, business, service, entertainment and cultural centres. The opening of the Port Tunnel at the end of 2006 was at first seen as ultimately about providing convenient access for city folk to Dublin Airport north of the city. In time, it was thought, container freight will go to other developing purpose-built facilities, such as Bremore north along the east coast between Balbriggan and Drogheda, and several established ports to the southeast such as Rosslare, New Ross, and Bellview near Waterford. But at the end of 2008, Dublin Port was showing new vigour, and the realities of freight ships will be part of the scene for many years yet.

Located beside a wide bay with some extraordinarily handsome hills and mountains near at hand, the city has long had as an important part of its makeup the dictates of stylish living, and the need to cater efficiently for individual tastes and requirements. From time to time the facade has been maintained through periods of impoverishment, but even in the earliest Mediaeval period this was already a major centre of craftsmanship and innovative shop-keeping. Today, the Dublin craftsmen and shopkeepers and their assistants are characterful subjects worthy of respectful academic study. And in an age when "going shopping" had become the world's favourite leisure activity, this old city has reinvented herself in the forefront of international trends.

Dublin virtually shunned the heavier side of the Industrial Revolution, or at least took some care to ensure that it happened elsewhere. More recently, the growth of computer-related industries was a very Dublin thing – what better way to deal with the vagaries of the Irish weather than in a workplace which had to be climate-controlled? And in times past, the city's few large enterprises tended to be aimed at personal needs and the consumer market, rather than some aspiration towards heavy industry. Typical of them was Guinness's Brewery, founded in 1759. Today, its work-force may be much slimmed in every sense, but it still creates the black nectar, and if a new mash is under way up at the brewery and the wind is coming damply across Ireland from the west, the aroma of Guinness in the making will be wafted right into the city centre, the moist evocative essence of Anna Livia herself. Even when the main brewery is moved to an out-of-town location, the essence will still be created at St James's Gate, where the imaginatively renovated Guinness Storehouse - with its interactive museums, restaurants and bars - provides a visitor centre of international quality, and Dublin's most popular attraction.

Although some of the vitality of the city faded in the periods when the focus of power had been moved elsewhere, today Dublin thrives as one of Europe's more entertaining capitals. While it may be trite to suggest that her history has been a fortuitous preparation for the needs of modern urban life in all its variety of work and relaxation, there is no denying Dublin's remarkable capacity to provide the ideal circumstances for fast-moving people-orientated modern industries, even if those same people find at times that their movement within the city is hampered by weight of traffic. Nevertheless it's a civilised city where the importance of education is a central theme of the strong family ethos, this high level of education making it a place of potent attraction in the age of information technology.

Such a city naturally has much of interest for historians of all kinds, and a vibrant cultural life is available for visitors and Dubliners alike. You can immerse yourself in it all as much or as little as you prefer, for today's Dublin is a city for all times and all tastes, and if you're someone who hopes to enjoy Dublin as we know Dubliners enjoy it, we know you'll find much of value here. And don't forget that

Georgina Campbell's Ireland

there's enjoyment in Dublin well hidden from the familiar tourist trails.

History is well-matched by modernity, or a mixture of both. The glass palaces of the International Financial Services Centre point the way to a maturing new business district which is a village in itself. Upriver to the westward, the award-winning transformation of the Smithfield area encompasses the popular Old Jameson Distillery Visitor Centre, another magnet for the discerning visitor - particularly someone who enjoys a sense of the past interacting with the present, not least in the age-old story of the creation of whiskey. The revitalisation of the Smithfield area has succeeded in creating its own special dynamic, and it's clearly attractive for today's new Dubliners.

When Dublin was starting to expand to its present size during the mid-20th Century, with people flocking in from all over Ireland to work in the city, it was said that the only "real Dub" was someone who didn't go home to the country for the weekend. Nowadays, with Dublin so popular with visitors, the more cynical citizens have suggested that the surest test of a real Dub is someone who avoids Temple Bar, but here too the city's instinct for community has re-asserted itself.

It's rather unfair of any Dubliner to dismiss Temple Bar's bustling riverside hotbed of musical pubs, ethnic restaurants, cultural events and nightclubs as being no more than a tourist ghetto. After all, in addition to its many places of entertainment and hospitality, Temple Bar is also home to at least 1,300 people, and they've their own neighbourhood Food Fairs and Specialist Markets like all other Dublin villages, and these days a higher spirit of civic pride has resulted in cleaner streets and buildings.

So there's real life here too. And at the very least, it is Temple Bar which maintains Dubliners' international reputation as round-the-clock party animals, which they're quite happy to acknowledge - just don't expect them to do it themselves. Another thing they don't do is form an orderly queue. In fact, they don't queue at all. Any real Dub reckons that queuing is a clear sign of mismanagement of personal time and endeavour. They make alternative arrangements.

As to meeting them if you haven't made prior rendezvous arrangements, well – perhaps. Come nightfall, and your discerning Dubliner is more likely to be found in a pleasant pub or restaurant in one of the city's many urban villages, places such as Ranelagh or Rathmines or Templeogue or Stoneybatter or Phibsborough or Donnybrook or Glasnevin or Ringsend or Dundrum or Clontarf or Drumcondra or Chapelizod. And then there are places like Stepaside or Howth or Glasthule or Foxrock or Dalkey which are at sufficient distance as scarcely to think of themselves as being part of Dublin at all.

Or perhaps your Dubliner is into sport – nearly everyone is. If it's a stadium sport – fine, you pay your way in like everyone else. There's horse racing and greyhound racing too. That's where you'll find today's real Dubs enjoying their fair city every bit as much as city centre folk. That is, if they're not sailing on The Bay or playing golf. There are so many golf links and courses that it might be possible to play from one side of the city to the other, and as for boating and sailing – well, Dublin is only half of a circle, the other half is the sea, and the interaction between the two is mighty, as they'd say in Dublin.

Happy is the visitor who is able to savour it all, in and around this town for our times. If you do see it all, don't tell us – we haven't seen the most of it ourselves.

Local Attractions & Information

Abbey & Peacock Theatres Lower Abbey Street, Dublin 1	01 878 7222
The Ark Arts Centre Eustace Street, Temple Bar, Dublin 2	01 670 7788
Bank of Ireland (historic), College Green, Dublin 2	01 661 5933
Botanic Gardens Glasnevin, Dublin 9	01 837 4388 / 804 0300
Christchurch Cathedral Christchurch Place, Dublin 8	01 677 8099
City Arts Centre 23-25 Moss Street, Dublin 2	01 677 0643
Croke Park GAA Stadium and Museum, Dublin 3	01 819 2300
Drimnagh Castle (moat, formal 17c gardens) Longmile Road	01 450 2530
Dublin Airport	01 814 4222
Dublin Castle, Dame Street	01 677 7129 / 645 8813
Dublin Film Festival (April)	01 635 0290
Dublin Garden Festival, RDS (June)	01 668 0866
Dublin International Horse Show, RDS (August)	01 668 0866
Dublin International Organ & Choral Festival (June)	01 677 3066
Dublin Theatre Festival (October)	01 677 8439 / 677 8899
Dublin Tourism Centre (restored church) Suffolk Street	01 605 7700

Dublin Writer's Museum, Parnell Square	01 872 2077
Dublinia (living history) Christchurch	01 679 4611
Farmleigh House, Phoenix Park	01 815 5900
Farmleigh House, Boathouse Restaurant	01 815 7255 / 815 7250
Gaiety Theatre, South King Street	01 677 1717
Gate Theatre, Cavendish Row	01 874 4045
Guinness Brewery, St Jame's Gate	01 453 6700 ext 5155
Guinness Storehouse	01 408 4800
Helix DCU Performing Arts Centre, Collins Avenue, Dublin 9	01 700 7000
Hugh Lane Municipal Gallery, Parnell Square	01 874 1903
Irish Antique Dealers Fair, RDS (October)	01 668 0866
Irish Film Centre, Eustace Street	01 679 3477
Irish Museum of Modern Art/Royal Hospital Kilmainham	01 612 9900
Irish Music Hall of Fame, Middle Abbey Street	01 878 3345
Irish Tourist Board/Failte Ireland, Baggot Street Bridge	01 602 4000
Iveagh Gardens, Earlsfort Terrace	01 475 7816
Jameson Distillery Smithfield, Dublin 7	01 807 2355
Kilmainham Gaol, Kilmainham	01 453 5984
Irish Rugby Football Union, Ballsbridge	01 668 4601
Mother Redcaps Market, nr St Patricks/Christchurch (Fri-Sun 10am-5.30pm)	01 454 0656
National Botanic Gardens, Glasnevin	01 837 7596
National Concert Hall, Earlsfort Terrace	01 417 0077
National Gallery of Ireland, Merrion Square West	01 661 5133
National Museum of Ireland, Kildare Street	01 677 7444
National Museum of Ireland, Collins Barracks	01 677 7444
Natural History Museum, Merrion Street	01 677 7444
Newman House, St Stephen's Green	01 475 7255
Northern Ireland Tourist Board, Nassau Street	01 679 1977
Number 29, (18c House) Lower Fitzwilliam Street	01 702 6165
Olympia Theatre, Dame Street	01 679 3323
Pearse Street Market, (St Andrew's Cntr.) Sats 9am-3pm	01 087 630 3839
Point Depot (Concerts & Exhibitions), North Wall Quay	01 836 6777
Powerscourt Townhouse, South William Street	01 671 7000
Pro Cathedral, Marlborough Street	01 874 5441
Project Arts Centre, 39 East Sussex Street, Dublin 2	01 881 9613
RDS (Royal Dublin Society), Ballsbridge	01 668 0866
Royal Hospital Kilmainham	01 679 8666
St Michans Church (mummified remains), Dublin 7	01 872 4154
St Patrick's Cathedral, Patrick's Close	01 475 4817
Shaw birthplace, 33 Synge Street, Dublin 8	01 475 0854
Shelbourne Park, Greyhound Stadium	01 668 3502
Temple Bar Foodmarket (Saturday morning)	01 677 2255
Tivoli Theatre, Francis Street	01 454 4472
Trinity College (Book of Kells & Dublin Experience)	01 608 2308 / 896 1000
Viking Adventure, Essex Street W, Temple Bar	01 679 6040
Viking Splash (Amphibious Tours)	01 453 9185
War Memorial Gardens (Sir Edwin Lutyens), Islandbridge	01 677 0236
Zoological Gardens, Phoenix Park	01 474 8900

DUBLIN 1

DUBLIN 1 & IFSC

Good value in this area includes budget hotels **Belvedere Hotel** (formerly Comfort Inn, Parnell Square; 01 873 7700) and **Jurys Inn** (Parnell Street; 01 878 4900), and museum cafés at the Hugh Lane Gallery on Parnell Square, (**Brambles Café**, Tue-Sat 10-5.30 pm, Sun 10.30-5) and the Writers' Museum (Mon-Sat 10-5). The Moore Street/Parnell Street area is well known for its street markets and specialist food shops catering for an increasingly cosmopolitan population - it has become a hothouse of international flavours and is the city's best bet for authentic, keenly priced food from different cultures. There are so many Asian restaurants in the area now that it has recently been dubbed

'Dublin's Chinatown'. The choice of ethnic restaurants offering authenticity and value is wide - a stroll around the area is recommended to lovers of Asian food, who should find everything they could wish for and among the newer ones there are Chinese (eg **Charming Noodles**, **Sichuan House** and **Mandarin House**, all on Parnell Street, and **Abacus** at the Best Western Academy Hotel (see entry), Korean and Japanese (**Kimchi**, **Hop House**) and Mongolian. **China House** (Parnell Street, 01 873 3870) is a friendly, authentic, and very good value Chinese; **Hanyang** (Parnell Street 01 874 6144) offers authentic Korean cuisine & hospitality, beside the **Ice Bar** Asian pub; **Alilang** Korean Restaurant (Parnell Street; 01 874 6766) serves tasty and very reasonably priced food which is also endorsed by the local Asian community who frequent it. **Radha Govinda's** (Middle Abbey Street; 01 872 9861) Hare Krishna restaurant serving wholesome, inexpensive vegetarian food. There are plenty of mainstream ethnic offerings in the north city too, including: **Cactus Jack's** (Millennium Way; 01 874 6198): one of a small chain of above average Tex-Mex restaurants (also at Tallaght & Galway City). While in this part of town be sure to drop into the **Epicurean Food Hall** (see entry) on Middle Abbey Street, where you will find a great range of specialist food shops and cafés offering multicultural seated meals, food to go and meats, cheeses and other artisan products to take away - a picnic in one of the many parks nearby may be just the ticket. Alternatively **Soup Dragon** (Capel Street; 01 8723277) offers a stylish way to have a hot meal on a budget with a daily choice of soups and stews, or **Ristorante Romano** (Capel Street; 01 872 6868) is a simple cafe-style restaurant with great home cooking that is widely recognised as one of the best value Italian restaurants in town, especially at lunch. For those with a thirst that needs quenching in interesting surroundings, the **Church** (Mary Street; 01 828 0102) is in an old converted church with an impressive contemporary interior. The old has been meticulously restored and the new sits easily against it, a testament to brilliant design.

The **INTERNATIONAL FINANCIAL SERVICES CENTRE** (IFSC) is Dublin's relatively new banking and financial district that is situated between the River Liffey and Connolly Station. It is a bustling, lively area during the week with tens of thousands of people working there, and although at the weekends the area can be fairly quiet, it is frequently livened up by a concert at the nearby O2 (formerly Point Theatre) or through festivals and similar activities that are held around the Docklands. The area has seen many restaurants and pubs mushroom over the last few years including the characterful and busy **Harbourmaster Bar & Restaurant** (01 670 1688) that has a decked area outdoors for fine weather; **Il Fornaio** (Valentia House Square; 01 672 1852): new and equally informal branch of the long-established authentic Italian pizzeria/restaurant in Kilbarrack, Dublin 5. **Insomnia** (Lr Mayor St, Custom House Quay; 01 671 8651): one of an excellent small chain of speciality coffee outlets around Dublin (some under the Bendini & Shaw brand), whose complementary speciality is sandwiches. Also at: Charlotte Way, Dublin 1; Ballsbridge, Dublin 4; Main Street Blackrock, Co Dublin; Malahide. **Milano** (Clarion Quay; 01 611 9012): north quays branch of the stylish and reliable pizza & pasta restaurant chain. **Bar Italia IFSC** (Custom House Square; 01 670 2887) is the most recent arrival in the area; it is a little Italian café in the traditional trattoria style that is part of a popular small restaurant chain where prompt, efficient service and flavoursome food are the hallmarks. Recommended accommodation in the IFSC is in the **Clarion Hotel** (see entry) and **Jurys Custom House Inn** (see entry).

WWW.IRELAND-GUIDE.COM FOR ALL THE BEST PLACES TO EAT, DRINK & STAY

Dublin 1
RESTAURANT

101 Talbot Restaurant

100-102 Talbot Street Dublin 1 **Tel: 01 874 5011**
www.101talbot.com

Almost 18 years ago, 101 Talbot hit upon a winning formula of serving good, affordable food in relaxed surroundings. Today the restaurant, recently taken over by management, continues to pack its tables 5 nights a week, with the emphasis still very much on value and flavour. The decor remains decidedly modest, and the Talbot Street location still a little dreary, but the animated chatter that greets you as you enter the first-floor dining room should be enough to reassure you that this is one of the liveliest joints in town – even on a Tuesday night.

Given its proximity to the Abbey and Gate theatres, and the constantly changing art exhibitions on the walls, the crowd is a bohemian mix of theatre-goers, thespians and the artistic set. Mediterranean and Middle Eastern influences are evident across a large menu that caters especially well to vegetarians. Signature starters like baba ganoush, hummus and antipasti have been pleasing loyal diners for years, while mains may include heartier fare like pork belly, creative curries, pasta bakes or roast chicken, all with imaginatively used vegetables. Service is casual and efficient and dishes represent remarkably good value. A great place for a quick feed, or group get-together, but the bustle and basic decor rule it out for a romantic night out. **Seats 80**. Children welcome before 8pm. Open Tue-Sat, 5-11. A la carte. Early D 5-7.45pm, €21.95 (5-8, all evening Wed), Set D 2/3 course €30/35. House Wine €19.95. Closed Sun & Mon, Christmas. Amex, MasterCard, Visa, Laser. **Directions:** 5 minutes walk between Connolly Station and O'Connell Street. Straight down from the spire.

Dublin 1

HOTEL•RESTAURANT

Ⓝ Ⓥ

Best Western Academy Plaza Hotel

Findlater Place Off O'Connell Street Dublin 1 **Tel: 01 878 0666**

stay@academyplazahotel.ie www.academyplazahotel.ie

This newly refurbished hotel is tucked away just off busy O'Connell Street, and is within easy reach of nearby train, DART and bus stations. A bright and spacious foyer makes a good first impression, with white marble pillars, marble floor, and lightwood panelled reception conveying a stylish modern tone and setting the expectations for the rest of the hotel. Arriving guests are easily enticed into the comfortable contemporary bar which, with welcoming warm tones and smart leather seating set off against a polished bar top and gleaming beer taps, has a relaxed modern urban atmosphere. Guest rooms and suites in warm autumnal tones and neutral beiges are finished to a very high standard, offering maximum comfort with 'super comfort beds', glossy cream and black bathrooms and all the amenities today's travellers demand, including air conditioning, WI/FI internet access, a dressing table that doubles as a workstation and a flat screen plasma TV. Housekeeping is exemplary throughout the hotel, and well-trained hotel staff who clearly take pride in the newly refurbished interior are keen to ensure the comfort of all guests. Business guests are especially well catered for with facilities that include a number of conference suites and, for relaxation at the end of the day, there's a gym, games room and hair, beauty and massage salon (a spa is also planned). A buffet-style breakfast is served in a cosy retro dining room just off the bar, and later dining options include tempting contemporary pub grub in the bar. **Rooms 285** (6 suites, 6 executive, 51 family, 225 shower only, 235 no smoking, 11 single, 6 disabled); children welcome (under 5s free in parents room, cots available); lift; 24 hr room service. B&B €60-70 pps; ss €40. Fitness room, spa (massage, treatments). Closed 21 Dec - 26 Dec. **Abacus Restaurant**: An interesting choice for this new hotel restaurant, which opens onto Parnell Street - an area that is fast becoming known as Dublin's Chinese Quarter - Abacus offers fine Chinese dining in a smart setting, unusually for an hotel restaurant, is holding its own in an area renowned for authentic ethnic cooking. Head chef Jackie Lam is from Hong Kong, and offers an extensive Asian fusion menu based on Irish main ingredients, especially meats, with spices and vegetable supplied by the local Asian markets. With comfortable surroundings and polished service in addition to good cooking, this restaurant offers something different from its neighbours, which tend to lay the emphasis on keen pricing - being in an area that has become a destination for lovers of Asian food seems to be working well for all. Conferences/Banqueting (250/60); business centre, free broadband wi/fi. **Seats 80**; children welcome; toilets wheelchair accessible. D daily 5-10.30pm; early bird D €21.50, 5-7pm; also a la carte; house wine from €19; sc discretionary. Closed Dec 23-28. Amex, Diners, MasterCard, Visa, Laser. **Directions:** Off the top of O'Connell Street.

€89

BLOOMS LANE

Known variously as the Italian Quarter (reflecting the collection of Italian-inspired establishments that have congregated here), occasionally as 'Quartier Bloom', sometimes as 'Mick Wallaces' (after the inspired developer who created it), or, more usually, simply by its address, this stylish food court off the north quays is home to some interesting restaurants, cafés and shops. It's at its best on Friday night or Saturday lunchtime; on Saturday evening (unless the Italians have won a huge sporting event that day), it's more 'gloom' than 'Bloom', the street is dark and uninviting, and some atmospheric lighting is needed, to dispel a spooky 'Victorian Whitechapel' feeling. **Enoteca delle Langhe** (01 888 0834), an appealing shop-cum-wine bar, was one of the first to open; food, while not exactly incidental, plays second fiddle to the wines here. But they carry a good range of dried Italian meats, cheeses, panini etc, and you can sit at a sturdy wooden table and have something by the glass (or choose any bottle, plus 10%), and a bite from a limited but interesting selection of quality food. It's all very relaxed and sociable, prices are reasonable - and it's a pleasant way to shop for wine. Nearby you will also find other like-minded outlets like **Wallaces Italian Food Shop**, **Café Cagliostro** (great coffees), a juice café and **Taverna di Bacco** (01 873 0040), a dark and atmospheric restaurant, which offers an interesting menu and authentic ingredient-led Italian food, including great antipasta, unusual variations on risotto, handmade pasta dishes and really good coffees And many people head here specially to eat in **Bar Italia** (01 874 1000) chaotic, warm, real food, great coffee, it's the essence of Italy minus cheap local wine. With good restaurants, an excellent deli and the bustling daytime café, Blooms Lane makes a great addition to the atmospherics of Dublin.

WWW.IRELAND-GUIDE.COM FOR ALL THE BEST PLACES TO EAT, DRINK & STAY

Dublin 1

RESTAURANT

Chapter One Restaurant

18/19 Parnell Square Dublin 1 **Tel: 01 873 2266**

info@chapteronerestaurant.com www.chapteronerestaurant.com

In the former home of the great John Jameson of whiskey fame, Chapter One was our Restaurant of the Year way back in 2001 when everybody thought southside was the place to be. Since then many others have discovered that one of Ireland's finest restaurant resides in this arched basement beneath the Irish Writers' Museum and - despite being the darling of the media these days - it remains the Guide's favourite when dining out in Dublin. Together with an exceptional team including restaurant manager Declan Maxwell and sommelier Ian Brosnan, the proprietors - chef-patron Ross Lewis and front of house manager Martin Corbett - have earned an enviable reputation here, for outstanding modern Irish cooking and superb service from friendly and well-informed staff. It's an atmospheric room with original granite walls and old brickwork contrasting with elegant modern décor. A recent revamp has seen the comfy reception area halved in size: it's still a smart place for an aperitif but has made way for a larger dining room and a few

more tables - good news indeed for those struggling to get a booking. The cooking - classic French lightly tempered by modern influences - showcases specialist Irish produce whenever possible, notably on a magnificent charcuterie trolley, which showcases West Cork producer Fingal Ferguson, among others, and is a treat not to be missed. Another unusual speciality is a fish plate which is a carefully balanced compilation of five individual fish and seafood dishes, served with melba toast. Other specialities include slow cooked meat - a sweet-flavoured shoulder of spring lamb, for example, with creamed onion and curry spice, roast carrot and garlic, kidney, and boulangére potato - and, of course, a cheese menu offering farmhouse cheeses in peak condition. But many guests will stall at dessert, as an utterly irresistible choice of half a dozen delectable dishes is offered, each with its own dessert wine or champagne... An excellent wine list leans towards the classics and offers many fairly priced treats for the wine buff, and also carefully selected house wines and wines by the glass, including a range of dessert wines. Another special treat is the perfectly timed pre-theatre menu, for which Chapter One is rightly renowned: depart for one of the nearby theatres after your main course, and return for dessert after the performance - perfect timing, every time. Like the lunch menu, early dinner offers outstanding value. **Seats 85** (private rooms, 16 & 20); small conferences; air conditioning; children welcome. L Tue-Fri, 12.30-2, D Tue-Sat, 6-10.45. Set L €37.50. Pre-theatre menu €37.50 (6-6.15); also à la carte (Tasting Menu, for entire parties, €70). House wine €24.50. SC discretionary. Closed L Sat, all Sun & Mon, 2 weeks Christmas, 2 weeks August. MasterCard, Visa, Laser. **Directions:** Top of O'Connell Street, north side of Parnell Square, opposite Garden of Remembrance, beside Hugh Lane Gallery.

Dublin 1

HOTEL•RESTAURANT

Clarion Hotel Dublin IFSC

Excise Walk IFSC Dublin 1 **Tel: 01 433 8800**

info@clarionhotelifsc.com www.clariondublincity.com

This fine contemporary hotel on the river side of the International Financial Services Centre was the first in the area to be built specifically for the mature 'city' district and its high standards and central location have proved very popular - not only with business guests and the financial community, but also leisure guests, especially at weekends. This success is reflected in the recent addition of an extra floor and spa as well as further meeting room space. Bright, airy and spacious, the style is refreshingly clean-lined yet comfortable, with lots

of gentle neutrals and a somewhat eastern feel that is emphasised by the food philosophy of the hotel - a waft of lemongrass and ginger in the open plan public areas entices guests through to the Kudos Bar, where Asian wok cooking is served; the smart casual Kudos Restaurant also features world cuisine, but with more European influences. Uncluttered suites and bedrooms have everything the modern traveller could want, including a high level of security, air conditioning, generous semi-orthopaedic beds and excellent bathrooms with top quality toiletries. There is a sense of thoughtful planning to every aspect of the hotel, and helpful, well-trained staff show a real desire to ensure the comfort of guests. Clarion Hotel Dublin IFSC was our Business Hotel of the Year in 2002. **Rooms 179** (7 suites, 25 executive, 150 no smoking, 8 disabled, 5 family rooms). B&B €142.50 pps. Room rate €28. Kudos Bar & Restaurant: Mon-Fri,12-8; House wines, from €23. Kudos closed L Sun. Amex, Diners, MasterCard, Visa, Laser. **Directions:** Overlooking the river Liffey in the IFSC.

Dublin 1 ely chq

RESTAURANT•WINE BAR CHQ IFSC Dublin 1 **Tel: 01 672 0010**

chq@elywinebar.com www.elywinebar.ie

Ely CHQ (Customs House Quay) is a younger sister of the original Ely off St Stephen's Green and older one to Ely HQ on the south quay (see entries); the style reflects the dashing contemporary architecture of the IFSC and the (very large) space includes an authentic expansive vaulted basement area, as well as a bright, open ground floor space and a covered terrace where tables are in great demand in summer. The successful Ely theme of simple organic food appealingly presented (including meats from the Robson family farm in County Clare) is a feature of all three venues: the burger (providing you don't mind the house style, which is for half a bun) is quite simply the best in town: pure unadulterated prime organic meat - and €1 per burger is donated to Barnardo's children's charity. Seafood is zingingly sea-fresh and you could even be lucky enough to have a pleasant, efficient Italian waiter commandeer an 'espresso' with thick crema that would be appreciated in Naples or Milan, let alone Dublin's northside and there's a great tea menu offered too. But it is their great wine list and, especially, an unrivalled choice of nearly a hundred wines offered by the glass - that makes Ely such an exceptional dining destination. This allows diners to taste a huge range of wines that might otherwise be inaccessible - and every dish offered on the lunch and à la carte menus has a suggested glass of wine to accompany. The wine list, which is frequently revised and upgraded, runs to over 500 bottles and mirrors that of the original Ely, being both well thought out and comprehensive, with many old favourites available - indeed, 'with something to suit every taste and pocket', this twice-winner of our annual Wine Award also reflects the aims of this Guide. There is also a carefully selected beer list and you can even buy a Laguiole corkscrew ('guaranteed for life') and machine washable wine glasses to take home. Dine outside if the weather allows, with bright views of the dock and the Liffey it can be a magic spot. *Ely chq was the winner of our 2007 Wine Award of the Year. **Seats 250** (private room 35, outdoors, 120); children welcome before 7pm; Food served all day Mon-Sat 8am-11pm; L&D daily: Mon-Sat 12-3 & 5.30-11pm; Sun 1-8pm; a la carte; SC 12.5% on groups 6+. Closed Christmas week. Amex, Diners, MasterCard, Visa, Laser. **Directions:** On the banks of the Liffey in the IFSC, overlooking Georges Dock, 2 mins from Connolly Station.

Dublin 1 Eno Winebar & Restaurant

RESTAURANT•WINE BAR Mayor Square IFSC Dublin 1 **Tel: 01 605 4912**

 winebar@enowine.ie www.enowine.ie/winebar.asp

In a modern glass fronted building in Dublin's financial district, Eno started life as a wine shop, later expanding to include an al fresco dining area, a wine bar and a stylish restaurant. Due to its location, it can be very busy during the week, but over the weekend is one of the city centre's quieter restaurants. Subtly decorated with wine cases and floral motifs, the airy interior is divided into a restaurant area and less formal wine bar area (with comfortable velvet seats, and where food is also served). While good food is available at very reasonable prices (scallops were particularly enjoyed on a recent visit, and there is always a well-balanced and lively selection of dishes to choose from) wine is the raison d'etre of this establishment, and the exceptionally knowledgeable staff are keen to guide customers to a wine which suits their tastes and choice of food. The wine list - which covers all major regions and grape varieties, and offers many wines unavailable elsewhere in Ireland - is arranged by style rather than by region, which greatly assists decision making; the wines are reasonably priced too, with most at under €40 a bottle. Very few half bottles are offered, but there is a good choice of wines by the glass and also a well selected choice of champagnes and sparkling wines, dessert wines, ports and digestifs. The choice of seating areas allows for those just in for a drink, or a full meal with several different wines. Events such as food and wine evenings are held regularly. **Seats 65**; Mon-Fri 12-9pm (to 10pm Fri), Sat 6-10pm. **Directions:** In the heart of the IFSC.

Dublin 1

EPICUREAN FOOD HALL
Lr Liffey Street Dublin 1

On the corner of Liffey Street and Middle Abbey Street, The Epicurean Food Hall is a buzzy place bringing together a collection of small units with a common seating area where you will find a wide range of gourmet foods, cooked and uncooked - and the wines to go with them. The hall is open during the day every day (opens later on Sunday, remains open for late shoppers on Thursday evening); it's an enjoyable place to browse - there are lots of lovely little shops and cafés in the hall, including a good choice of ethnic ones, and they quite often change so these long-established tenants are just a taster: **La Corte** (01 873 4200) is one of the north river outposts of Stefano Crescenzi and David Izzo's smart Italian café (see entry). And, at **Layden Fine Wines**, you can buy a glass of good wine to accompany anything you're eating from one of the other shops/stalls - available by the glass or bottle (a modest corkage charge to consume on the premises, glasses supplied.) **Directions:** On the corner of Liffey Street and Middle Abbey Street.
WWW.IRELAND-GUIDE.COM FOR ALL THE BEST PLACES TO EAT, DRINK & STAY

Dublin 1
RESTAURANT

Floridita
Irish Life Mall Lower Abbey Street Dublin 1 **Tel: 01 878 1032**
info@floriditadublin.com www.floridita.co.uk/dublin

Located in the Irish Life Mall, probably the least likely spot for an exotic Cuban restaurant, Floridita is one of a successful Floridita chain with branches in London, Madrid, Moscow and Cuba. Marketed as a bar and music venue as well as a restaurant, the first floor dining room features a giant tilted mirror which reflects the live bands from downstairs to the restaurant above. The décor evokes some of the 1950's style of Cuba, and the atmosphere is high octane. The traditional cocktail of choice is the mojito criollo made with churned fresh mint, lime juice and sugar, although there are plenty of other cocktails on offer. Traditional Cuban cuisine tends to reflect its peasant history so the menu borrows from further afield with South American and Spanish influences; Cuban dishes to try include deep fried tostones (plantains pounded flat and deep fried) and moros y christanos (Moors and Christians) a mix of black beans and rice. A great venue for a celebration especially when visiting Cuban bands are playing. **Seats 100**. Average starter €9.60, average main course €20 and average dessert €7. House wines from €26; by the glass from €6.50; cocktails from €9. SC 12.5% added to all bills. Open L Mon- Fri 12 to 3, D Wed-Fri 5.30 to 10, Sat 6 to 10. Closed Sunday. Amex, MasterCard, Visa, Laser. **Directions:** In the Irish Life Mall off Abbey Street. ◇

Dublin 1
HOTEL•RESTAURANT

The Gresham
23 Upper O'Connell Street Dublin 1 **Tel: 01 874 6881**
info@thegresham.com www.gresham-hotels.com

At the centre of Dublin society since the early nineteenth century, the Gresham is one of the city's best business hotels. A recent makeover has transformed the ground floor, including the lobby lounge, a favourite meeting place renowned for its traditional afternoon tea; the Gresham and Toddy's bars are both popular meeting places and Toddy's, in particular, offers the kind of comfortable casual eating that was once the norm but is now increasingly hard to find in this busy city. Business guests will appreciate the refurbished bedrooms: 108 rooms have been transformed in executive contemporary style and all have good amenities. Charming and helpful staff ensure an above-average hotel experience, as does a very good breakfast in the Gallery Restaurant, an unappealing but comfortable dining room in the centre of the hotel, with no natural light. It is more attractive in the evening, when menus include an early dinner, useful when attending the various theatres nearby. Conference/banqueting (350/280). Business centre; secretarial services; video conferencing. Fitness suite. Wheelchair access. Secure multi-storey parking. **Rooms 288** (4 suites, 2 junior suites, 96 executive, 60 no-smoking, 3 disabled); Children welcome (u12s €40 sharing with parents); Lifts. B&B €170pps, ss up to €175; specials offered. Restaurant open daily 5.30-10pm. Early D €25.50, 5.30-7pm. Hotel open all year. Amex, Diners, MasterCard, Visa, Laser. **Directions:** City centre, on north side of the River Liffey. ◇

€ 107

Dublin 1
HOTEL

Jurys Custom House Inn
Custom House Quay Dublin 1
Tel: 01 607 5000

Right beside the International Financial Services Centre, overlooking the Liffey and close to train, Luas and bus stations, this hotel meets the requirements of business guests with better facilities than is usual in budget hotels. Large bedrooms have all the expected facilities, but with a higher standard of finish than most of its sister hotels; fabrics and fittings are good quality and neat bathrooms are thoughtfully designed, with generous shelf space. As well as a large bar, there is a full restaurant on site, plus conference facilities for up to 100 and a staffed business centre. **Rooms 239**. No room service. Adjacent multi-storey car park has direct access to the hotel. Room Rate from €142 (max 3 guests). Closed 24-26 Dec. Amex, Diners, MasterCard, Visa. **Directions:** IFSC, overlooking River Liffey. ◇

Dublin 1

The Morrison Hotel & Halo Restaurant

HOTEL•RESTAURANT

Lower Ormond Quay Dublin 1 **Tel: 01 887 2400**
reservations@morrisonhotel.ie www.morrisonhotel.ie

Centrally located on the north quays, close to the Millennium Bridge over the River Liffey, this contemporary hotel is within walking distance of theatres, the main shopping areas and the financial district. When it opened in 1998, it was a first for Dublin, with striking 'east meets west' interiors created by the internationally renowned designer, John Rocha, and the same team oversaw a recent development programme including extensive conference and meeting facilities - designed around a calm Courtyard Garden, which makes an

attractive venue for receptions, or pre-dinner drinks. Stylish public areas include the Café Bar - just the place for a cappuccino or cocktails - and there's a spa, offering holistic and relaxation treatments. Simple, cool bedroom design - the essence of orderly thinking - contrasts pleasingly with the more flamboyant style of public areas, and there is a welcome emphasis on comfort (Frette linen, Aveda toiletries, air conditioning); all rooms have complimentary broadband, Mac plasma screen with keyboard, wireless mouse and surround sound, iPod docking stations and CD players, safe and mini-bar. Exceptionally friendly and helpful staff make every effort to provide the best possible service for guests, and complimentary room upgrades to studios and suites are given when available. Conferences (240). Not suitable for children. Pets permitted by arrangement. **Rooms 138** (12 suites, 6 junior suites, 38 shower only, 5 for disabled, 80 no smoking). Lift. Room service (24 hours). Room rate €340 (SC incl). No private parking (arrangement with nearby car park). Closed 23-27 Dec. **Halo:** This popular restaurant is next to the riverside entrance of the hotel, allowing diners a view over the river and the busy thoroughfare on the quays. The décor sends mixed messages (minimalist oriental stools set beside Georgian style claw-footed tables), but it is a relaxed, informal space and head chef Richie Wilson offers well thought out and accomplished modern dishes, particularly fish - examples recently enjoyed by the Guide included a flavoursome dish of fillet of turbot with Iberico ham, truffle sauce and lentil stew. Menus are not too long, and top quality ingredients are a feature; breads are all home-made, and a signature dish of Irish Hereford beef with sautéed forest mushrooms, seared foie gras & tarragon mousse, indicates the sophisticated style. All the little niceties of a special meal are observed but without too much formality. The walk-in wine cellar is an unusual feature, where you can browse and take your pick. As elsewhere in the hotel, good service is a feature: all male staff are dressed in black, and are very courteous and knowledgeable. **Seats 110** (private room, 22). Air conditioning. D daily 6-10.30pm; à la carte; house wine from €23.50. Amex, Diners, MasterCard, Visa, Laser, Switch. **Directions:** Located on the quays in the city centre beside the Millennium Bridge.

Dublin 1

MV Cill Airne - Blue River Bar & Bistro and Quay 16

RESTAURANT

Quay 16 North Wall Quay Dublin 1 **Tel: 01 445 0994**
quay16@mvcillairne.com www.mvcillairne.com

The beautifully restored MV Cill Airne provides a uniquely atmospheric setting for this bar/bistro and restaurant on the fast developing north quays. A 1960's liner tender which once carried trans-Atlantic passengers, including Laurel and Hardy and President Eisenhower, ashore from the elegant liners to the ports of Dun Laoghaire and Cobh, it was later used as a training vessel for merchant navy officers. The small ship is now docked semi-permanently by the increasingly happening docklands area and looks as well as she must have looked in her glory days - and is especially attractive when lit up at night. There may be nobody present to greet arriving guests, but signage is clear and on the upper deck you will find the **Blue River Bar and Bistro**, which serves quite basic food at reasonable prices and has expansive outdoor seating on the afterdeck - a promising option, perhaps, for a sunny afternoon on the Liffey. A level below, on the main deck, is the fine dining restaurant, **Quay 16**. As on the upper deck, the finish is impeccable and, although the ambience is somewhat spoilt by loud music (which staff willingly turn down on request), tables are tastefully set up to make an attractive dining space - but the real star of this restaurant is the wonderful and authentic period timber interior. The restaurant offers a promising menu, albeit at prices which might not be charged in the same restaurant ashore; some additional touches are added to familiar fare (foie gras on fillet steak for example) and slightly unusual combinations (such as scallops with pork belly) work with varying degrees of success. Quay 16 also boasts an extensive wine list and, although this new arrival in Dublin may not overwhelm with amazing food, it offers something genuinely different - and the upstairs bistro is a great location for a drink and a quick bite to eat. **Blue River Bistro Bar:** 12-10pm, 7 days a week. **Quay 16 Restaurant:** L Mon-Fri 12-3pm; D Mon-Sat 6-10pm. **Directions:** On North Wall Quay, midway between the IFSC and the Point Theatre.

Dublin 1   Panem
CAFÉ   Ha'penny Bridge House 21 Lower Ormond Quay Dublin 1
                                                          Tel: 01 872 8510

Ann Murphy and Raffaele Cavallo's little bakery and café has been delighting discerning Dubliners - and providing a refuge from the thundering traffic along the quays outside - since 1996. Although tiny, it just oozes Italian chic - not surprisingly, perhaps, as Ann's Italian architect husband designed the interior - and was way ahead of its time in seeing potential north of the Liffey. Italian and French food is prepared on the premises from 3 am each day: melt-in-the-mouth croissants with savoury and sweet fillings, chocolate-filled brioches, traditional and fruit breads, filled focaccia breads are just a few of the temptations on offer. No cost is spared in sourcing the finest ingredients (Panem bread is baked freshly each day using organic flour) and special dietary needs are considered too: soups, for example, are usually suitable for vegans and hand-made biscuits - almond & hazelnut perhaps - for coeliacs. They import their own 100% arabica torrisi coffee from Sicily and hot chocolate is a speciality, made with the best Belgian dark chocolate. Simply superb. Open Mon-Sat, 9-5pm. Closed Sun, 24 Dec-8 Jan. **No Credit Cards**. **Directions:** North quays, opposite Millennium Bridge. ◊

Dublin 1   The Vaults
BAR•RESTAURANT   Harbourmaster Place IFSC Dublin 1 **Tel: 01 605 4700**
                                        info@thevaults.ie www.thevaults.ie

These ten soaring vaulted chambers underneath Connolly Station were built in the mid-19th century to support the railway and have since found many uses, including the storage of Jameson whiskey. In 2002 Michael Martin - previously known as head chef of the Clarence Hotel restaurant, The Tea Room - opened it as a multi-purpose venue. The atmosphere is intimate and welcoming and the vaults, which have been treated individually in styles ranging from sleek contemporary to neo-classical, also include some high tech audio visual equipment. Head chef Fraser O'Donnell ensures that everything is made from scratch - mainly grills, pizzas and pastas - and his food is skilfully executed and beautifully presented. This place encapsulates the dramatic changes that have been taking place north of the Liffey in recent years: simply stunning. **Seats 180** (private room 90); children welcome until 8pm. (All spaces available to hire, for business or pleasure). Reservations accepted. Food served Mon-Fri 12-8. Various menus - lunch, afternoon & evening - à la carte. Vegetarian dishes on main menu. SC 10% on groups 8+. House wine €21. Late night bar & club Fri/Sat to 02.30. Closed Sat & Sun, 24-26 Dec, Good Fri, Bank Hols. Amex, MasterCard, Visa, Laser. **Directions:** Under Connolly station; last stop on Luas red line.

Dublin 1
RESTAURANT

The Winding Stair

40 Lower Ormond Quay Dublin 1 **Tel: 01 872 7320**
www.winding-stair.com

This much-loved café and bookshop overlooking the Ha'penny Bridge re-opened in 2006 after a long closure and, to everybody's delight, it has turned out to be better than ever. Although now a proper restaurant with gleaming wine glasses and a fine new La Marzocco coffee machine, something of the old café atmosphere was carefully maintained and can still be found in the wooden floorboards, bentwood chairs and simple tables. There is a suitable amount of memorabilia from the café's heydays in the form of yellowing photographs and heaving bookshelves, and the view of the river and bridge continues to be one of the most atmospheric in town. General manager Elaine Murphy's strong vision for the reincarnation has happily held firm through various changes of head chef. Expect plenty of 'the organic and real' on menus that include superb signature starters such as an Irish charcuterie plate (Connemara dry-cured lamb and beef, salamis from the Gubbeen smokehouse in County Cork, accompanied by home-made chutney & capers), and main dishes including outstanding renditions of classics such as bacon and cabbage with parsley sauce. To finish, there's an excellent Irish farmhouse cheese selection and delicious seasonal desserts which, like the rest of the menu, are very fairly priced. Tim Sacklin's unusually interesting wine list, sourced from a variety of quality suppliers, is a pleasure to explore but should you wish to keep things simple, a blackboard with wines of the week offers a more focused choice. The Winding Stair is that rarity among Irish restaurants, serving simple, high quality food, and it has a lovely ambience. Aided by nostalgia, it also has loads of personality and has earned a loyal following - book a window table for a view of the river. **Seats 100**; children welcome; L&D served daily, 12.30-3.30, 6-10.30pm (to 9.30pm Sun); a la carte; house wine from €24. Closed 25-26 Dec, Bank Hols. MasterCard, Visa, Laser. **Directions:** On the north quays, beside the Ha'penny bridge.

Dublin 1
HOTEL

Wynns Hotel

35/39 Lower Abbey Street Dublin 1 **Tel: 01 874 5131**
info@wynnshotel.ie www.wynnshotel.ie

Traditionally a country people's hotel in Dublin city centre, this affordable, three-star hotel is just off O'Connell Street, with the Luas stopping just outside its door. There's a friendly welcome at reception, and they are accommodating, easily taking things like an early check-in in their stride. Rooms have recently been refurbished and are very comfortable for the price, with spotless bathrooms. The revamped dining room is bright and airy, with attentive staff and good, sensible food, which is also good value - and the bar also serves good coffee, and plates of food if you wish. While you may have to queue for breakfast if you come late, it's worth the wait, with very efficient service, good tea - and lovely eggs Benedict, and properly grilled rashers. The clientele is likely to be a mixture of continental families, Parish Priests up from the country, sisters on a shopping spree, elderly aunts and young ones on their first date. Visitors are surprised to find a place like this. No glitz, just a very comfortable stay - the perfect hideaway, without breaking the bank. Weekend and midweek breaks offer especially good value. Complimentary valet parking. B&B €90pps. MasterCard, Visa, Laser. **Directions:** Just off O'Connell Street. ◇

DUBLIN 2

DUBLIN 2 PUBS

Renowned for its pubs, Dublin is the home of Guinness - and of course, to countless famous literary, theatrical and artistic personalities. A good few of them spent many an hour in Dublin's pubs enjoying the legendary Irish banter over a pint of the black stuff, and these connections have added to the romance and intrigue of many of Dublin's finest drinking houses. We've chosen a selection of the finest 'must visit' establishments that represent the very best of Dublin pubs, and we've ordered them in the form of a convenient pub crawl. Alternatively they are all within a short walking distance of central areas such as Grafton Street: Sláinte! Just off the Eastern end of College Green across from the bottom of Trinity College is one of Dublin's oldest and best-loved pubs, **John Mulligan's** 'wine & spirit merchant' (Poolbeg Street; 01 677 5582) is mercifully un-renovated and likely to stay that way - dark, with no decor (as such) and no music, it's just the way so many pubs used to be. The only difference is that it's now so fashionable that it gets very crowded (and noisy) after 6pm - better to drop in during the day and see what it's really like. **The Palace Bar** (Fleet Street; 01 671 7388) is on the eastern edge of Temple Bar and has had strong connections with writers and journalists for many a decade. Its unspoilt frosted glass and mahogany are impressive enough but the special feature is the famous sky-lighted snug, which is really more of a back room. Many would cite The Palace as their favourite Dublin pub. **Brogan's** on nearby Dame Street (01 6793211) is another unspoilt bar, near the Olympia Theatre and opposite Dublin Castle, it's all about the old-fashioned art of conversation, and which is the best stout. **The International Bar** (Wicklow Street; 01 677 9250) is just a minute's walk towards Georges Street from Grafton Street and this unspoilt Victorian bar makes a great meeting place - not a food spot, but good for chat and music. Across from the International Bar, **The Old Stand** (Exchequer Street; 01 677 7220) is a fine traditional pub (a sister establishment to Davy Byrnes, see entry) that occupies a prominent position on the corner of Exchequer Street and St. Andrew's Street and lays claim to being "possibly the oldest public house in Ireland"! Named after the Old Stand at the Lansdowne Road rugby grounds, it has a loyal following amongst the local business community, notably from the 'rag trade' area around South William Street, and also attracts a good mixture of rugby fans and visitors, who enjoy the atmosphere. They offer no-nonsense traditional bar food (12.15-9 daily), but its warm and friendly atmosphere is the main attraction. **The Stag's Head** (Dame Court, 01 679 3701) between Dame Street and Exchequer Streets, is an impressive establishment that has retained its original late-Victorian decor and is one of the city's finest pubs. It can get very busy at times but this lovely pub is still worth a visit. Round the corner on George's Street **The Long Hall Bar** (South Great George's Street; 01 475 1590) is one of Dublin's finest bars: a wonderful old pub, it has magnificent plasterwork ceilings, traditional mahogany bar and Victorian lighting. Just off the top end of Grafton Street, **Neary's** (Chatham Street; 01 677 8596) is an unspoilt Edwardian pub which has been in the present ownership for over half a century and is popular at all times of day - handy for lunch or as a meeting place in the early evening and full of buzz later when a post-theatre crowd, including actors from the nearby Gaiety Theatre, will probably be amongst the late night throng in the downstairs bar. Traditional values assert themselves through gleaming brass, well-polished mahogany and classics like smoked salmon and mixed meat salads amongst the bar fare. A few steps down the road, just off the west side of Grafton Street, **McDaids** (Harry Street) was established in 1779 and more recently achieved fame as one of the great literary pubs - and its association with Brendan Behan, especially, brings a steady trail of pilgrims from all over the world to this traditional premises just beside the Westbury Hotel. Dubliners, however, tend to be immune to this kind of thing and drink there because it's a good pub - and, although its character is safe, it's not a place set in aspic either, as a younger crowd has been attracted by recent changes. A mere skip across Grafton Street takes you to **Kehoe's** (South Anne Street; 01 677 8312), which is one of Dublin's best, unspoilt traditional pubs. Kehoe's changed hands relatively recently and added another floor upstairs, but without damaging the character of the original bar. Very busy in the evening - try it for a quieter daytime pint instead. A short walk to the north is **The Bailey** (Duke Street; 01 670 4939), a famous Victorian pub just off the eastern side of Grafton Street that has a special place in the history of Dublin life - literary, social, political - and attracts many a pilgrim seeking the ghosts of great personalities who have frequented this spot down through the years. Although it's now more of a busy lunchtime spot and after-work watering hole for local business people and shoppers. Across the road is the fine, historic **Davy Byrnes** pub (see entry). Heading back up towards St. Stephen's Green just beyond the Shelbourne Hotel is **O'Donoghue's** (Merrion Row, 01 676 2807) which has long been the Dublin mecca for visitors in search of a lively evening with traditional music - live music every night is a major claim to fame - but a visit to this famous pub at quieter times can be rewarding too. Further up the road is **Toners** (Lower Baggot Street; 01 676 3090) which is one of the few authentic old pubs left in Dublin and is definitely worth a visit (or two). Among many other claims to fame, it is said to be the only pub ever visited by the poet W.B. Yeats. Across from Toners, **Doheny & Nesbitt** (Lower Baggot Street; 01 676 2945) is another great Dublin institution, but there the similarity ends. This Victorian pub has traditionally attracted a wide spectrum of Dublin society - politicians, economists, lawyers, business names, political and financial journalists - all with a view to get across, or some new scandal to divulge, so a visit here can often be unexpectedly rewarding. Although it has been greatly extended recently and is now in essence a superpub, it has at its heart the original, very professionally run bar with an attractive Victorian ambience and a traditional emphasis on drinking and conversation. Newly re-opened as the Guide goes to press, **The Lincoln Inn** (01 676 2978) has been a favourite haunt for staff and students at nearby Trinity College for many a year.

WWW.IRELAND-GUIDE.COM FOR ALL THE BEST PLACES TO EAT, DRINK & STAY

Dublin 2 is the heart of Dublin's tourist region with more pubs, restaurants, clubs and attractions than any other part of town. This is the home of Temple Bar (see entry), Trinity College, the shopping of Grafton Street and peaceful park walks in St. Stephen's Green and the Iveagh Gardens. **Coopers Restaurant** (see entry) offers a lot of the old favourites in an attractive old-cut stone coach house. **Papaya** (Ely Place, 01 676 0044) is a Thai restaurant serving all the usual Thai dishes, plus a few more unusual ones. **Leon** (Dawson Street and South William Street, 01 672 9044) is a café/crêperie useful to know about for its range of sweet and savoury pancakes, handy for a light meal and good value. **Chatham Brasserie** (Chatham Street, 01 679 0055) just off Grafton Street is popular for a break from shopping with indoor and outdoor seating and a slightly French elegance, although many people would opt instead for one of the little pizza restaurants that have clustered in this area - **Pizza Stop** (01 679 6712) on Chatham Lane, **Little Caesar** (Balfe Street, beside the Westbury, and branches) and **Steps of Rome** (Chatham Court, 01 670 5630) which are all cheap & cheerful places especially useful for families visiting the area; other great pizza places include **Cafe Toffoli** (Castle Street, 01 633 4022) and, down in Temple Bar, **Di Fontaine** (Crown Alley, 01 677 7959) is the place to look out for, for great New York style pizza. Beside the St. Stephen's Green shopping centre **Wagamama** noodle bar (South King Street; 01 478 2152) is not a place for those who seek comfort or privacy - but strikingly designed with high ceilings and kids love it. All food served in Wagamama noodle bars is GMO-free, portions are generous and the value is good. For a more grown-up style of Japanese, **Ukiyo** (Exchequer Street, 01633 40710) is known for its good food, sake and the karaoke booths. At the time of going to press, **Marks & Spencer** had just opened their first in-store restaurant in Ireland; on the top floor of the Grafton Street store, it offers a wide range of the meals for which they are well known - and a rooftop terrace with parasols, that is sure to become a popular place to meet. **Bobo's**, on Wexford Street (01 4005750; www.bobos.ie) has become something of a cult - with gourmet burgers all the rage, this retro neighbourhood restaurant serving fun food based on fresh local ingredients has really taken off; quoting Mark Twain 'Sacred cows make the best hamburgers' they say they take their grub seriously but not themselves. A lot of people really like that. For a great Lebanese experience head to St Andrew's Street - **The Cedar Tree** (see entry) is one of Dublin's oldest restaurants (here since 1986) and now also home to **Byblos/The Mezze House** (01 679 1517) which not only serves good food but there's belly dancing too, making for an unusual evening's entertainment. Also in St Andrew Street, another of Ireland's longest-established restaurants, the ever-reliable Italian **Le Caprice** (01 679 4050) and across Dame Street, another great blast from the past is the gloriously unchanging **Nicos Italian restaurant** (01 677 3062). Budget accommodation with above average facilities is available in the re-branded **Maldron Hotel**, formerly Quality Hotel Dublin City (Sir John Rogerson's Quay; 01 643 9500), which with a swimming pool and gym offers excellent value for money for business or pleasure guests within a short walk of the main city centre attractions.
WWW.IRELAND-GUIDE.COM FOR ALL THE BEST PLACES TO EAT, DRINK & STAY

Dublin 2
RESTAURANT

Acapulco Mexican Restaurant
7 South Great Georges Street Dublin 2 **Tel: 01 677 1085**
info@acapulco.ie www.acapulco.ie

You'll find reliable Tex-Mex fare at this bright, cheap and notably cheerful place on the edge of Temple Bar. Decorated in warm tones of red, pinks and green, the decor matches the food which is authentic Mexican - nachos with salsa & guacamole, enchiladas, burrito, sizzling fajitas - and good coffee. And deep fried ice cream is the house dessert... **Seats 70**; air conditioning; children welcome (high chair); Open 7 days: L 12-4pm (Sun 2-4pm), value L €5.75 12-4pm Mon-Fri; D 4-10.30pm (Fri/Sat to 11pm). Wines from €19. 12.5% SC on parties of 6+. Closed 24-26 Dec & 1 Jan. Amex, MasterCard, Visa, Laser. **Directions:** Bottom of South Gt George's St (Dame Street end).

Dublin 2
HOTEL
Alexander Hotel
Merrion Square Dublin 2 **Tel: 01 607 3700**
info@ocallaghanhotels.com www.ocallaghanhotels.com

Very well situated at the lower end of Merrion Square, within a stone's throw of the Dáil (Government Buildings), the National Art Gallery and Natural History Museum as well as the city's premier shopping area, this large modern hotel is remarkable for classic design that blends into the surrounding Georgian area. In contrast to its subdued public face, the interior is strikingly contemporary and colourful, both in public areas and bedrooms, all of which have been refurbished recently to a very high standard, in restful soft white, cream and brown colour combinations, and have good in-room amenities; suites have the additional attraction of a round seating area in the tower which is on the corner of this landmark building. Housekeeping is immaculate throughout the hotel. Perhaps its most positive attribute, however, is the exceptionally friendly and helpful attitude of the hotel's staff who, under the supervision of General Manager Declan Fitzgerald, immediately make guests feel at home and take a genuine interest in their comfort during their stay. Meals are offered at the hotel's Caravaggio's Restaurant and a bar menu at Winners contemporary cocktail bar. A popular choice for business guests, there is a business centre and gymnasium, and broadband throughout the hotel. Conference/banqueting (400/400); business centre; secretarial services; video conferencing. **Rooms 102** (4 suites, 40 no-smoking, 2 for disabled); children welcome (Under 2s free in parents' room; cots available). No pets. Lift. Gym. Room rate from €125(max. 2 guests). Open all year. Amex, Diners, MasterCard, Visa **Directions:** Off Merrion Square. ◊

Dublin 2   Avoca Café

RESTAURANT   11-13 Suffolk Street Dublin 2 **Tel: 01 672 6019**

info@avoca.ie www.avoca.ie

City sister to the famous craftshop and café with its flagship store in Kilmacanogue, County Wicklow (see entry), this large centrally located shop is a favourite daytime dining venue for discerning Dubliners. The restaurant (which is up rather a lot of stairs, where queues of devotees wait patiently at lunchtime) has low-key style and an emphasis on creative, healthy cooking that is common to all the Avoca establishments. Chic little menus speak volumes - together with careful cooking, meticulously sourced ingredients like Hederman mussels, Gubbeen bacon and Hicks sausages lift dishes such as smoked fish platter, organic bacon panini and bangers & mash out of the ordinary. All this sits happily alongside the home baking for which they are famous - much of which can be bought downstairs in their extensive delicatessen. **Seats 100**; toilets wheelchair accessible; opening hours: 10am-5.30pm Mon-Sat (hot food served until 4.30pm Mon-Fri), 11am-5pm Sun; à la carte. Bookings accepted but not required. SC 10%. Licensed. Closed 25/26 December, 1 Jan. Amex, Diners, MasterCard, Visa. **Directions:** Turn left into Suffolk St. from the bottom of Grafton St. ◊

Dublin 2   Aya Food Bar

RESTAURANT   49/52 Clarendon Street Dublin 2 **Tel: 01 677 1544**

mail@aya.ie www.aya.ie

This contemporary Japanese restaurant was Dublin's first conveyor sushi bar, restaurant and food hall - it's owned by the Hoashi family, who established Dublin's first authentic Japanese restaurant. Contemporary style is the order of the day - the menu includes a wide range of authentic Japanese sushi, Asian and Japanese tapas, tempura and teriyaki dishes and additions with broader Asian flavours to tempt a range of customers, and you will even find desserts on the conveyer. The sushi conveyor belt has stools and booths for communal diners, as well as restaurant seating for the à la carte. The early dinner ('Twilite Special') offers very good value. Some products are available to take away. **Seats 65** (sushi bar & restaurant); children welcome before 7pm; air conditioning. Open daily - Sushi Bar: 12.30-10 (to 11 Fri/Sat); Restaurant: L 12.30-3 (Sat to 4, Sun from 2pm), D 5-10 (Sat to 11, Wed to 9.30, Sun to 9). Set L €19; Set D €30. Also à la carte. House wine from €22. SC 12.5%. Closed 25-26 Dec. Amex, MasterCard, Visa, Laser. **Directions:** Directly behind Brown Thomas off Wicklow Street.

Dublin 2   Balzac

RESTAURANT   35 Dawson Street Dublin 2

Tel: 01 677 4444

Balzac is the latest incarnation in the distinctive building on Dawson Street, which formerly housed La Stampa and, with its grand Belle Epoque entrance, it never fails to impress. Having been given new life and credos under the consultancy of former head chef, Paul Flynn, the operation is now being led by chef Malcolm Starmer, who continues to deliver Flynn's assiduously thought out, refined take on classic bistro cooking. The transformation in recent years saw the decor in the bar area pared right back to a very subtle minimalism which helps to prepare the diner for the drama of what is still one of the most handsome dining rooms in the city, with its magnificent ceiling, faux-marble pillars, formidable flower pot centrepiece and impressive mirrors. The starkness of the brasserie aesthetic - black tables with linen runners and napkins, simple stainless cutlery and glasses, white tableware, wooden floor - has been somewhat softened of late by subdued lighting and billowing fabric punctuating the long banquettes, and the ongoing difficulty of incorporating the private dining area at the far end of the main room seems to have been solved by investing it with a cosy, parlouresque ambience all of its own. Service on a recent visit could have been considerably better informed and sharper focused, especially to warrant the standard 12.5% service applied to all bills. This is a room that needs to be worked, and demands a fully-attentive team capable of matching its sense of scale with a sense of the theatre it allows. However, the kitchen delivered well on a largely reduced but nonetheless varied menu which still boasts signature Flynn dishes such as crab crème brulée with pickled cucumber alongside good renditions of brasserie staples such as Provençal fish soup with rouille croûtons. Though the current menu offers less drama than previous offerings, it is admirably clear in intent, and the kitchen proved itself more than competent at delivering on its promise, especially when the path less travelled is chosen. The wine list is short, pragmatic and representative of old and new worlds, with a decent selection of wines by the glass and pichet. There is a sense that this is still an operation finding its groove, but it is well anchored by a confident kitchen. *Balzac is part of the La Stampa complex, overlooking the Mansion House in central Dublin. In addition to Balzac, the complex includes accommodation, a spa, Tiger Bec's restaurant and Sam Sara Café Bar. **Seats 200** (private room, 70); unsuitable for children after 8pm; reservations recommended; L Fri only, 12.30-3pm; D Mon-Sat, 6-11pm, early bird D about €28, 6-7.30pm, set D about €50, also a la carte. Closed all Sun, D 24 Dec, 25-27 Dec, Good Fri. Amex, MasterCard, Visa, Laser. **Directions:** Opposite the Mansion House on Dawson Street. ◊

Dublin 2
RESTAURANT

Bang Café

11 Merrion Row Dublin 2 **Tel: 01 676 0898**
www.bangrestaurant.com

Stylishly minimalist, with natural tones of dark wood and pale beige leather complementing simple white linen and glassware, this smart restaurant is well-located just yards from the Shelbourne Hotel, and continues to attract a young, well-heeled set. The handsome restaurant is on three levels with a bar in the basement, a semi-private dining room on the upper level, and in between, the main dining floor, where unstressed chefs can be seen at work in the open service kitchen: an air of calm, relaxed and friendly professionalism prevails. Head chef Lorcan Cribben recently served as Commissioner-General for the Irish branch of Euro-Toques, the chefs' organisation that is committed to defending quality local and artisan ingredients (Paul Bocuse's 'building blocks of good food'). Here, as would be expected, carefully sourced ingredients are the foundation for menus that offer innovative, modern food. The offering is broad, with uncomplicated crowd-pleasers such as bangers & mash (made with Hicks sausages) or seared scallops complemented by more complex dishes which demonstrate the considerable skill of the kitchen, whose strongest point is its unswerving consistency. This, together with a charming, professional front of house team, and a fun cocktail list, make Bang a popular party venue. A new raised terrace area cranks up this sense of fun, overlooking as it does two of the buzziest outdoor strips in town - the ever-lively terrace at The Unicorn, and the garden of the new Residence (a private member club also run by the Stokes twins). There is good value to be had too, especially at lunchtime. **Seats 99** (private room, 36; outdoors, 25 from 2009); reservations required; air conditioning; L&D Mon-Sat 12.30-3pm, 6-10.30pm; à la carte L&D. House wine €24. 12.5% sc on parties of 6+. Closed Sun, bank hols, 25 Dec-3 Jan. Amex, MasterCard, Visa, Laser. **Directions:** Just past Shelbourne Hotel, off St Stephen's Green.

Dublin 2
RESTAURANT•WINE BAR

Bar Pintxo

12 Eustace Street Temple Bar Dublin 2 **Tel: 01 672 8590**
info@porthouse.ie www.porthouse.ie

This younger sister of The Port House on South William Street follows the familiar formula of simple, well cooked hearty tapas served in atmospheric surroundings, with lashings of Spanish and Portuguese wine. Large streetside windows draped in tall curtains give an air of intrigue to the passer-by; on entering you are greeted by a lively buzz and character a-plenty. Exposed brick walls, white sanded wooden floors and rack upon rack of wine bottles set the tone, whilst the open kitchen and impressive wine bar provide the action. A classy worn feel is provided in old wooden leather covered chairs and shiny black tables, with the ground floor room providing a brighter dining experience than the cellar room, which offers a more intimate, candlelit ambience. Friendly staff are quick to seat customers and provide a menu of around two dozen dishes divided into hot and cold plates of tapas, in the Spanish and Basque style. You'll find the familiar dishes of patatas bravas, calamari, tortilla and paella, but there is also something for the more adventurous such as Galician octopus or seared foie gras. This is simple, uncomplicated food with big flavours, served in a smart cheerful style, for very acceptable prices. An extensive exclusively Spanish and Portuguese wine list includes an interesting selection of sherries. Some bottles are available by the carafe or glass, and a nice touch is to offer bottles being sold at a lower off licence price for those who want to take something home. Spanish and Basque beers are also offered, and an outdoor terrace opening onto Meeting House Square now gives an even more continental atmosphere in fine weather. **Seats 120** (private room, 30; outdoors, 30); open daily 11am-11pm; children welcome before 9pm; no reservations taken; free broadband wi/fi; air conditioning. SC discretionary. Closed 25 Dec. MasterCard, Visa, Laser **Directions:** Centre of Temple Bar, lower end of Eustace Street, off Main Street opposite Farringtons.

Dublin 2
RESTAURANT

Bentley's Oyster Bar & Grill
22 St Stephen's Green Dublin 2 **Tel: 01 638 3939**
info@bentleysdublin.com www.bentleysdublin.com

CHEF OF THE YEAR

Richard Corrigan made his name in London as a chef of tremendous skill and talent, earning international recognition for his two establishments Lindsay House, in Soho - and Bentley's Oyster Bar & Grill, a once-legendary London institution that he succeeded in returning to its former glories and fortunes. Now Corrigan has brought this winning formula to Dublin where he has opened an outpost of this classic seafood stalwart. An elegant Georgian townhouse overlooking St Stephen's Green seemed an ideal location for an Irish Bentley's, with Corrigan taking over the building that once housed Browne's Townhouse & Brasserie, a charming boutique hotel that was known for its luxury and class. This handsome building, with its impressive granite steps, fine staircase, ornate marble fireplaces and wonderful plasterwork, is a celebration of bygone craftsmanship, and a fitting home for this old but new venture. Diners at Bentley's will find the setting hugely appropriate, as the restaurant offers its signature blend of modern cuisine with traditional values and service. Waiters wear white dinner jackets, seats and banquettes are clad in deep blue leather with brass studs, large tables are covered in pristine linen, and the walls are lit by illuminated silver oyster shells. Dark parquet floors, pink walls (we much prefer the shade at the oyster bar to the fondant pink used in the front), large mirrors and a mix of downlighters and feature chandeliers break the space neatly into three 'rooms'. Despite the grand proportions, the acoustics are spot on in a room that buzzes with the hum of happy diners and the soft swish of efficient staff. The service is some of the finest on offer in the country. Waiting staff are highly knowledgeable, accommodating and friendly. Despite being a new venture, guests were all welcomed like old friends and regulars. The menu offers a seafood-heavy selection, although you needn't be a shellfish devotee, or even seafood fan, to enjoy the fare here. Meat eaters are well looked after with offerings like Wiener schnitzel, aged beef and native lamb. A circular oyster bar sits at the top of the room, with tall stools, and a selection of glistening bi-valves laid out to tempt. Of course, you can select these from the menu too, and have them served at your table. Particularly noteworthy are Bentley's signature dishes which all merit a sampling. The seafood cocktail is delicately dressed, so as to enhance the freshest and plumpest of native shellfish. Bentley's fish pie – a tasty mix of fish pieces and juicy prawns in a lemony sauce, and topped with creamy mash and golden crumbs – is a triumph. Do as chef suggests and liberally dash it with green Tabasco for a real taste sensation. Desserts are on the quirky-side – many taking their cue from tradition – and they taste and look superb. Wines can be ordered by the glass, carafe (in two thoughtful sizes) or bottle. Prices are a little expensive, but the selection is very good, and especially well chosen to complement the fish. If you don't have time for a pre-dinner drink in the delightful first floor bar, suggest taking your coffee or digestifs up here afterwards. Two generous adjoining reception rooms have been stylishly finished with grey walls, wooden floors and comfy striped armchairs. Large windows, stunning stucco ceilings and a marble fireplace add instant character, and the long and varied cocktail list is hard to resist. A baby grand is played throughout the evening, conveying a relaxing atmosphere that is matched by the peerless staff. At the time of going to press, the accommodation is not yet open, but the 11 glamorous bedrooms will be a real gem of an asset to this exciting new restaurant. **Directions:** North side of St. Stephen's Green.

Dublin 2
CAFÉ•RESTAURANT

Bewley's - Café Bar Deli

Bewleys Building 78-79 Grafton Street Dublin 2 **Tel: 01 672 7720**
info@mackerel.ie www.sherland.ie

Established in 1840, Bewley's Café had a special place in the affection of Irish people. Bewley's on Grafton Street was always a great meeting place for everyone, whether native Dubliners or visitors to the capital 'up from the country'. It changed hands amid much public debate in 2005 but, despite renovations, it has somehow retained its unique atmosphere together with some outstanding architectural features, notably the Harry Clarke stained glass windows. The popular Café-Bar-Deli chain has taken over most of the seating area now, but the coffee shop at the front remains, and also the in-house theatre (phone for details). Cafe Bar Deli: **Seats 350** open for food all day 8am-11pm (L from 12); from 9am Sun. Closed 25/6 Dec, Bank Hols. Amex, MasterCard, Visa, Laser. **Directions:** Halfway up Dublin's premier shopping street. ◊

Dublin 2
RESTAURANT
Ⓝ

The Blackboard Bistro

4 Clare Street Dublin 2
Tel: 01 676 6839

Tucked away in a tiny basement near the Lincoln Inn entrance to Trinity College, you'll find this unusual bistro offering modest French dining served with a personal touch. Steep cast iron steps lead promisingly down to a welcoming bright red door and, as you step through into the cosy restaurant, you could be mistaken for thinking you have entered a small Parisian neighbourhood restaurant, full of character and chic bistro charm. Deep moody tones of red and purple create a snug bohemian atmosphere and a smart darkwood panelled wine bar and bentwood chairs provide a little Parisian 'arrondissement' allure. A warmly informal tone is set by a friendly duo team of waiter and chef, who welcome guests to choose from a modest menu chalked onto a large blackboard. Both lunch and dinner menus change daily, offering a handful of enticing French starters, mains and desserts which focus on bold flavours in dishes that will satisfy any appetite: simple rustic cooking at its best. Begin, perhaps, with a soup or terrine, followed by a ragout of rabbit or pan-fried fillet of cod and a well-made fruit compote for dessert. Expect bold, no frills cooking in classic French style, and a modest wine list that confidently offers only French wines, all by the glass and bottle, including a rosé and a couple of champagnes. The Blackboard Bistro is run by people who take their food, wine and service seriously, and – by offering delicious, modest food in charming surroundings, served with the personal touch that only a small restaurant can deliver – has raised the bar for affordable city dining. Just the place for anyone who is tired of complicated, over-presented food, and longs for simple dishes with real flavour. Tuesday - Saturday 12-10pm. MasterCard, Visa, Laser **Directions:** In a basement near the Lincoln Inn entrance to Trinity College.

Dublin 2
RESTAURANT•WINE BAR

Bleu Café Bistro

Dawson Street Dublin 2 **Tel: 01 676 7015**
www.bleu.ie

A younger sister to Eamonn O'Reilly's excellent flagship restaurant One Pico (see entry), this modern bistro is now known generally as 'Bleu' or even 'Blue.' Smartly laid tables are rather close together and hard surfaces make for a good bit of noise - but the food is based on carefully sourced quality ingredients, and pleasingly presented on plain white plates. Well-located for a pleasant lunch break when shopping or visiting nearby galleries and museums, a two- or three-course set lunch offers excellent value and there's a range of pleasing choices on set menus and also a short lunchtime à la carte: dishes like pea & pancetta soup with crème frâiche and herbs, roast organic salmon with beetroot risotto & vine tomato beurre blanc, or a salad of rare beef with Cashel blue, watercress & sherry vinaigrette sum up the style. Evening menus are more extensive and a little dressier but include many of the lunchtime favourites too. Finish with good home-made desserts or a French & Irish cheeseboard with quince jelly and walnut & raisin bread. Long opening hours allow for a very nice little afternoon menu, which could make an enjoyable late lunch or early evening meal and there is an outdoor seating area for fine weather. Good wine list, with a dozen or so wines by the glass. **Seats 60** (outdoor seating

14); reservations advised; air conditioning. Open all day Mon-Sat 9am-midnight, L 12-5, D 5-12, Sun - L 12-4, D 5-10; Set L 2/3 course about €21.50/25. Early D about €29 (5-7.30), Set D about €20, also à la carte L&D. House wine from about €22. Closed bank hols. Amex, MasterCard, Visa, Laser. **Directions:** At top of Dawson St. off St. Stephen's Green.

Dublin 2   Brasserie Sixty6

RESTAURANT   66-67 South Great Georges Street Dublin 2 **Tel: 01 400 5878**
info@brasseriesixty6.com www.brasseriesixty6.com

Although it has a narrow street frontage, this is a large restaurant, high-ceilinged and extending way back into an old building. Décor is unfussy modern, for the most part, with wooden floors, simple bare-topped tables and leather 'bus seat' banquettes or chairs that would look at home in a country kitchen. Aside from a very large chandelier and some unusual artwork, the main decorative theme is a whole wall of mismatched plates, echoing the traditional kitchen dresser, a good idea that lends warmth and informality; it adds up to a comfortably stylish setting for menus that are strong on house specialities and offer something different from the standard fare. The signature main course is rotisserie chicken served with corn on the cob, coleslaw and cornbread or mash, a good retro idea, using top notch chicken that is cooked with a different marinade each day. Good steaks come with proper home-made chips, there are several versions of bangers and mash, or you might go mad with lobster, or even whole suckling pig for a group, on occasion - and follow with updated classic desserts. Service is pleasant and helpful. You may expect good coffee, a short but well-chosen wine list (plus beers, cocktails and freshly squeezed juices), plus a bill that won't break the bank. Cooking can sometimes be inconsistent, but all round this is a pleasant place for a meal that's bit out of the ordinary. *Cornerhouse Grill (see entry) is a younger sister establishment. Toilets wheelchair accessible; air conditioning; children welcome; open all day 8am-11.30pm (from 10am Sat & Sun), L 12-5, D 5-11.30, set L €14.95, also a la carte; house wine €19.50; SC 12.5% on groups 6+. Closed 25-26 Dec, 1 Jan, Good Fri. Amex, MasterCard, Visa, Laser. **Directions:** Opposite Georges Street arcade.

Dublin 2   Bridge Bar & Grill

RESTAURANT   The Malting Tower Grand Canal Quay Dublin 2 **Tel: 01 639 4941**
Ⓝ   reservations@bridgebarandgrill.ie www.bridgebarandgrill.ie

Ronan Ryan and Temple Garner have chosen a daring location, off the beaten track, for the third instalment in their growing collection of fine contemporary restaurants. The Bridge Bar and Grill's position right under the DART line on Grand Canal Quay makes for an authentic urban dining experience, whilst presented in the high standard of style and comfort that Dublin diners have come to expect from this successful duo. The restaurant is part of the Malting House, so from the outside there is lots of attractive stonework, and large windows giving an enticing view of the dining room, where sleek modern décor combines with darkwood panelling and comfortable leather seating to convey a feeling of contemporary bistro chic. The restaurant is split into two halves, the spacious front half allowing large groups to dine in comfortable leather booths, whilst surveying the gorgeous horse shoe bar - or, for a more intimate evening, couples will enjoy the low curved ceiling under the bridge arches; the odd rumbling train passing by overhead only adds to the metropolitan character of the place. The tone is smart, stylish, and relaxed, with simply laid tables of plain white linen and elegant silverware. Staff are quick to make guests feel welcome and provide a concise menu of enticing, uncomplicated dishes: the philosophy is to create focused dishes based on quality ingredients, resulting in uncluttered food, with big flavours and a nod to Italy. It is impossible not to enjoy this kind of cooking, with its emphasis on real flavour: good salads, crab cakes, excellent pasta, a house burger, fish, game in season, or a char grilled rib eye - and classic, comforting desserts like fruit crumbles or chocolate brownies. Ryan and Garner have yet again hit on a winning combination of well-executed delicious food in stylishly informal surroundings - the kind of place that lends itself equally to a relaxed family lunch or an intimate dinner for two, followed by cocktails. For this high standard of dining the value offered is excellent, and an extensive wine list has plenty of choice in the €20-€40 bracket, although there are also some expensive indulgences when the occasion demands. A Gaggia coffee machine supplies the perfect end to a meal that will leave you smiling as you think of an excuse to get back to the Bridge Bar and Grill as soon as possible. **Seats 70.** Reservations accepted; air conditioning; toilets wheelchair accessible; children welcome. L&D Mon-Sat, 12.30-3.30pm & 6-10.30pm; Sun L only, 1-5pm. Set 3 course L €29.95, Value D Mon-Thurs, €20.95, set D €44.95. House wine €22.95; SC 12.5% on groups 5+. Closed Sun D, 24-26 Dec, Good Fri. Amex, MasterCard, Visa, Laser. **Directions:** Just off Grand Canal Street beside the Treasury Holdings building. ◊

Dublin 2

HOTEL•RESTAURANT

Brooks Hotel & Francescas Restaurant

Drury Street Dublin 2 **Tel: 01 670 4000**
reservations@brookshotel.ie www.sinnotthotels.com

One of Dublin's most desirable addresses, especially for business guests, the Sinnott family's discreetly luxurious hotel is a gem of a place - an oasis of calm just a couple of minutes walk from Grafton Street. A ground floor bar, lounge and restaurant all link together, making an extensive public area that is quietly impressive on arrival - the style is a pleasing combination of traditional with contemporary touches, using a variety of woods, some marble, wonderful fabrics and modern paintings - and, while a grand piano adds gravitas, there's a welcome emphasis on comfort (especially in the residents' lounge, where spare reading glasses are thoughtfully supplied). Efficient service ensures you are in your room promptly, usually with the help of Conor, the concierge, who never forgets a face or a name. All bedrooms have exceptionally good amenities, including a pillow menu (choice of five types) and well-designed bathrooms with power showers as well as full baths (some also have tile screen TV), and many other features. Boardrooms offer state-of-the-art facilities for meetings and small conferences, and there is a 26-seater screening room. Fitness suite & sauna. Children welcome (under 2 free in parents' room; cots available without charge, baby sitting arranged). No pets. **Rooms 98** (1 suite, 2 junior suites, 3 executive, 87 no-smoking, 5 semi-invalid). Lift. Air conditioning throughout. 24 hr room service. B&B €160pps, ss €100. *Special breaks offered - details on application. Arrangement with car park. Open all year. *Brooks Hotel was our Business Hotel of the Year in 2007. **Francescas Restaurant:** Pre-dinner drinks are served in a lovely little cocktail bar, Jasmine, and the restaurant has a youthful contemporary look, and a welcoming ambience - an open plan kitchen has well positioned mirrors allowing head chef Patrick McLarnon and his team to be seen at work. Tables are elegantly appointed with classic linen cloths and napkins, and waiting staff, smartly attired in black, look after customers with warmth and professionalism. Patrick sources ingredients with great care (Clare Island organic salmon, organic chicken, dry-aged steak, speciality sausages), his cooking is imaginative and includes updated traditional themes, and there's a strong emphasis on fish and seafood. Starters may include a salad of natural smoked mackerel, with a chili apple relish, and there may be an an unusual main course of peat smoked Wicklow lamb - or pan-fried Finnebrogue venison, in season. Finish, perhaps, with an oatmeal and whiskey brulée and a classy individually packed infusion, or coffee. A nice wine selection includes good quality wines available by the glass. The early dinner offers good value, and breakfast offers a wide variety of juices, cereals and nuts, yogurt, pastries, meat, cheeses and fruit. A good range of hot dishes includes pancakes with maple syrup, kippers with poached egg and full Irish breakfast as you like it, although service can be slow. [*Informal meals also available 10 am-11.30 daily.] **Seats 30.** Reservations advised; children welcome; air conditioning; toilets wheelchair accessible. D daily, 6-9.30 (Fri/Sat to 10). Early D €18.50 (6-7); also à la carte & vegetarian menus. Closed to non-residents 24/25th December. Amex, MasterCard, Visa, Laser. **Directions:** Near St Stephen's Green, between Grafton and Great St. Georges Streets; opposite Drury Street car park.

Dublin 2

HOTEL•RESTAURANT

Buswells Hotel

23 Molesworth Street Dublin 2 **Tel: 01 614 6500**
buswells@quinn-hotels.com www.quinn-hotels.com

Home from home to Ireland's politicians, this row of 18th century townhouses has been an hotel since 1921. The location would be hard to beat and it's reasonably priced for the area; it remains a slightly old-fashioned hotel of character and it's a haven for politicians at the Dail (parliament) across the road and there's a special buzz in the bar, where food is served throughout the day and evening. Recent renovations made no fundamental changes and accommodation is comfortable in the traditional style, with the best rooms overlooking Kildare Street or Molesworth Street. The hotel offers a good range of services for conferences, meetings and private dining, and has a positive environmental policy (recipient of Green Failte Award - bronze medal). Conference/banqueting (85/50). Business centre, secretarial services, video conferencing. Children welcome (Under 3s free in parents' room; cots available free of charge). No pets. **Rooms 67** (2 junior suites, 6 single, 7 shower only, 59 no-smoking, 1 for disabled). Lift. B&B €150pps, ss about €75. 24 hr room service, Lift. **Trumans:** This elegant, well-appointed restaurant has a separate entrance from Kildare Street, or access from the hotel, and it offers a pleasing ambience and quite extensive menus featuring both modern and simpler dishes:

fillets of seabass with a brunoise of steamed vegetables wrapped in bok choi, with new potatoes and salsa verde is a speciality. A good wine list includes half a dozen house wines, a page of fine wines and a strong selection of half bottles. **Seats 60** (private room, 50); children welcome; reservations advised. L 12-2.30 (carvery), D 5.30-10 (Sun from 5.30pm). Set D about €42, also à la carte. House wine €19.50. SC discretionary. Closed 25-26 Dec. Amex, Diners, MasterCard, Visa, Laser. **Directions:** Close to Dail Eireann, 5 minutes walk from Grafton Street.

Dublin 2   # Butlers Chocolate Café
CAFÉ   24 Wicklow Street Dublin 2 **Tel: 01 671 0591**
chocolate@butlers.ie   www.butlerschocolates.com

Butlers Irish Handmade Chocolates combine coffee-drinking with complimentary chocolates - an over-simplification, as the range of drinks at this stylish little café also includes hot chocolate as well as lattes, cappuccinos and mochas and chocolate cakes and croissants are also available. But all drinks do come with a complimentary hand-made chocolate on the side - and boxed or personally selected loose chocolates, caramels, fudges and fondants are also available for sale. Open 7 days: Mon-Fri 8am-7pm, Sat 9am-7pm, Sun 11am-6pm. Closed 25-26 Dec, Easter Sun & Mon. Also at: 51 Grafton Street (Tel: 01 616 7004); 9 Chatham Street (Tel: 01 672 6333); 18 Nassau Street (Tel: 01 671 0772); Liffey Street (Tel 01 878 3402); Heuston Station; Dundrum Shopping Centre; Dublin Airport; 30 Oliver Plunkett St, Cork; 40 William St, Galway. All of the above have similar opening times to the Wicklow Street branch, except Nassau St, Grafton St & Henry St open at 7.30 am on weekdays. Amex, MasterCard, Visa, Laser. **Directions:** 5 city centre locations & Dublin Airport. ◇

Dublin 2   # Café Bar Deli
RESTAURANT   13 South Gt George's Street Dublin 2 **Tel: 01 677 1646**
georgesstreet@cafebardeli.ie   www.cafebardeli.ie

Despite its obvious contemporary appeal - paper place mat menus set the tone by kicking off with home-made breads and marinated olives - the friendly ghosts of the old Bewleys Café are still alive and well in this inspired reincarnation of this much-loved establishment. Tables are old café style, with bentwood chairs, the original fireplace and a traditional brass railing remain, but a smartly striped awning over the large street window signals the real nature of the place. Imaginative salads are packed with colourful, flavoursome treats with pizza and pasta menus continuing in the same tone, including daily specials. Spelt bread is available, all pasta dishes can be made with gluten/wheat free pasta and a dedicated children's menu was introduced in 2007. A sensibly limited wine list combines quality and style with value; service is friendly and efficient and prices remarkably moderate - an attractive formula for an informal outing. Branches at: Ranelagh, Dublin 6 (Tel 01 496 1886); Cork (Academy St); and Sligo (Garavogue). Children welcome; air conditioning. **Seats 160**; open 7 days: Mon-Sat, 12.30-11; Sun 2-10pm; A la carte. House wine €23 (litre). No reservations. Closed 25-27 Dec, Good Fri. Amex, MasterCard, Visa, Laser. **Directions:** Next door to the Globe Bar. ◇

Dublin 2   # Café en Seine
CAFÉ•PUB   40 Dawson Street Dublin 2 **Tel: 01 677 4567**
cafeenseine@capitalbars.com   www.capitalbars.com

The first of the continental style café-bars to open in Dublin, Café en Seine remains on top of the game - the interior is still impressive, in an opulent art deco style reminiscent of turn-of-the-century Paris. Not so much a bar as a series of bars (your mobile phone could be your most useful accessory if you arrange to meet somebody here), the soaring interior is amazing with a 3-storey atrium culminating in beautiful glass-panelled ceilings, forty foot trees, enormous art nouveau glass lanterns, and statues and a 19th century French hotel lift among its many amazing features. No expense has been spared in ensuring the quality of design, materials and craftsmanship necessary to create this Aladdin's cave of a bar. Lush ferns create a decadent atmosphere and the judicious mixture of old and new which make it a true original - and its many 'bars within bars' create intimate spaces that are a far cry from the usual impersonality of the superpub. Appealing food is a feature too: there's a sociable combination platter serving four people and hot dishes like steak sandwiches, scampi and quiches with salads are popular; everything is spotlessly clean and, while quite predictable, the food is really tasty. An informal range of contemporary dishes is available over lunchtime every day, also light bites all day - and there's a popular Jazz Brunch every Sunday. Little wonder that so many people of all ages still see it as the coolest place in town. Small al fresco covered section at front seats about 30. Lunch daily, 12-3; (Sun brunch 1-4). D daily: Sun-Wed, 5-9; Thu Small al fresco covered section at front seats about 30. Lunch daily, 11-3; (Sun brunch 12-3.30). Wheelchair access. Bar open 10.30am-2.30am daily. Snack menu 4-7pm daily. Closed 25-26 Dec & Good Fri. Amex, MasterCard, Visa, Laser. **Directions:** Upper Dawson Street, on right walking towards St Stephen's Green (St Stephen's Green car park is very close).

Dublin 2   Café Fresh
CAFÉ   Top Floor Powerscourt Townhouse Centre South William Street Dublin 2
                              Tel: 01 671 9669 info@cafe-fresh.com www.cafe-fresh.com

It's worth the trek up to the top of the Powerscourt Townhouse Centre for a bite at this aptly-named vegetarian restaurant, where you'll find wholesome home-made soups, good baking (and delicious desserts) great salads and some surprising main courses - their vegetarian lasagne is one of the most popular dishes, and with good reason. Carnivores seem to enjoy it just as much as vegetarians, and that includes their breakfasts. And they've recently published the attractive Cafe Fresh Cookbook too. Open Mon-Sat 10am-6pm and Thur, 10am-8pm. **Directions:** Top floor of the Powerscourt Townhouse Centre.

Dublin 2   Café Mao
RESTAURANT   2-3 Chatham Row Dublin 2 **Tel: 01 670 4899**
                                              chathamrow@cafemao.com www.cafemao.com

This popular and well-located Asian fusion restaurant has simple colourful décor, including some trademark oversized Andy Warhol style portraits which were reinstalled after a major refurbishment. The menu was slightly expanded to include more vegetarian options as well as a few light salads; however, the established favourites such as the chilli squid, Nasi Goreng, and the Thai green curry (vegetable or chicken) are as good as ever. Soups change regularly and, with their garlic and lemongrass naan, provide a filling snack. There is a good selection of genuine Asian beers (any of which complement the generally non-region specific cuisine), and an excellent English cider, as well as a number of cocktails and smoothies, and a small selection of wines by the glass. As fashionable and convivial as ever, Café Mao provides great value and very quick service and, while the specific dishes may not be completely true to the region's traditional cuisine, the flavours and use of ingredients certainly represents the potential of Asian food in general. Also at: Dundrum Town Centre and at The Pavilion in Dun Laoghaire. **Seats 110**; fully wheelchair accessible; children welcome; air conditioning. Open Mon-Tue, 12- 10pm; Wed-Sat, 12–11pm; Sunday 1.30-9pm. Menu à la carte. House wine from about €18; Asian beers from about €4.50. SC discretionary. MasterCard, Visa, Laser. **Directions:** City centre - just off Grafton Street at the Stephen's Green end. ◊

Dublin 2   Camden Court Hotel
HOTEL   Camden Street Dublin 2 **Tel: 01 475 9666**
                                 sales@camdencourthotel.com www.camdencourthotel.com

Complimentary secure parking and a leisure centre with swimming pool are among the main attractions of this conveniently located modern hotel. All bedrooms have neat bathrooms, practical fitted furniture and the usual facilities (plus satellite TV which can show your room bill, speeding check-out). Friendly staff, business and leisure facilities and fairly reasonable rates for the location make this a city centre base to consider. Conference/banqueting (115/100). **Rooms 246** (1 suite, 13 no-smoking, 13 for disabled); children welcome (under 2s free in parents' room; cots available without charge). No pets. Lift. 24 hr room service. Room rate from €105;no SC. Leisure centre (swimming pool, gym, sauna, steam). Closed 23-28 Dec. **Directions:** City centre, 10 minutes walk from St.Stephen's Green.

Dublin 2   Carluccio's Caffé
CAFÉ•RESTAURANT   52 Dawson Street Dublin 2 **Tel: 01 633 3957**
Ⓝ   www.carluccios.com

The familiar traditions of Graham O'Sullivan's long-running coffee shop on Dawson Street have recently been replaced by Carluccio's, a sleek Italian restaurant, café and deli, and the first outpost of this highly successful UK chain. Created by Antonio and Priscilla Carluccio, the winning formula of rustic Italian cooking, excellent coffee, great pastries and house ice creams has been quick to make its mark in the city centre. Open all day, serving breakfast through to light lunches and four-course evening meals, it has quickly attracted a following which sees regular queues forming, especially for their take-out coffee. A no-reservations policy means that you may have to wait around to dine (and many will choose to eat elsewhere for that reason), but there is a glorious little shop to peruse for distraction while you wait. Shelves packed with artisan pastas, quality olive oils and novelty chocolates hint at the Italian specialities on offer at the tables. Décor is bright and breezy with colourful stacking chairs in curved laminate, wipe clean tables and fabulous pendant lights. The atmosphere at meal-times is loud and bustling, ruling this out as a location for a romantic date; upstairs is especially family friendly, with an attractive children's menu on offer. Staff, many of whom are Italian, have been well trained to provide friendly, efficient and extremely attentive service. Menus change with the seasons and feature exciting regional favourites that your local Italian probably doesn't offer. Highlights include interesting antipasti plates and signature wild mushroom dishes. Prices are surprisingly reasonable and with 17 wines all offered by the glass, bills are easy to keep down. Although it is a franchise and unlikely to attract the same passionate following as nearby Dunne & Crescenzi, Carluccio's serves large numbers well and the food manages to have soul - finish with the house ice cream and an espresso, and you'll leave with a smile. **Seats 170**. Open: Mon-Fri 7am-10.30pm; Sat 8am-10.30pm; Sun 9am-10pm. **Directions:** On the corner of Duke Street and Dawson Street. ◊

Dublin 2

The Cedar Tree

RESTAURANT   11A South Andrew Street Dublin 2 **Tel: 01 677 2121**
Ⓝ   www.cedartree.ie

Right in the heart of the main shopping district, near the Tourist Information Office at St Andrew's Church, this basement restaurant does not have an eye-catching exterior (perhaps the way the regulars like it, a hidden oasis) but is easy to find, and it's Dublin's longest established Lebanese restaurant. Cosy and atmospheric, it's a popular spot and many of the regular customers are well known to the management, giving the restaurant a relaxed and welcoming atmosphere. The menu is extensive and should appeal to anyone with a taste for aromatic, mildly spiced minced lamb, beef and chicken dishes, and vegetable dishes with plenty of gentle spicy flavour. A huge choice of starters (about 25, all at about €6) ranges from grilled quail to pitta breads with simple dips or hummus, and there's a similar choice of main courses at about €18, including several vegetarian options and some combination/mixed offerings for the indecisive or curious (eg Mixed Meshwe, a combination of minced lamb, and lamb & chicken brochettes). Generous portions offer very good value and there's no real need for side dishes, but it's a pity there's a charge for bread, though, as it's the kind of food which calls for plenty of accompanying bread. Helpful staff have a good knowledge of the menu and there is a fair selection of Lebanese wines, in the €20 to €100 range, as well as a good choice of Old and New World wines. The house Lebanese wines at €20 are basic but very drinkable to complete the authentic experience. On Friday and Saturday nights there is oriental dancing in the restaurant, which may not be to everyone's taste but is in keeping with the style of the establishment. The main restaurant is in the basement and decorated in thoroughly ethnic style. Above on street level is Byblos restaurant which is open for lunch as well as dinner and serves similar fare but in smaller portions and with a tapas style approach to the menu and ordering.

Dublin 2

Chez Max

RESTAURANT   1 Palace St Dublin 2
👑 👁   **Tel: 01 633 7215**

Everyone loves Max Delaloubie's friendly brasserie, an almost-too-perfect reproduction of 1940s' Paris, opening onto a cobbled street at the entrance to Dublin Castle. The food, too, has that ring of Parisian authenticity - rillettes, frogs' legs - and early concern amongst devotees that such dishes may not survive in this essentially conservative city seem so far to be unfounded. And there is plenty there for everyone including lots of less contentious treats like Croque Monsieur and Croque Madame, Soupe a l'Oignon, Moules Frites, good pastries and a range of classic home-made desserts. Meanwhile, the proprietor continues to make people welcome and wannabe Parisians of every generation can groove to music that stretches from Henri Krein, Brassens and Piaf to St Etienne. The shortish wine list offers few surprises, but overall both wine and food offer very good value for money. **Seats 66** (outdoor, 25) reservations recommended; children welcome; open for breakfast from 7.30; tea/ coffee and pastries served all day; B, L & D daily;

B from 8am Mon-Fri, 10am Sat and 11am Sun; L 12-3.30 daily and D 5.30-10pm daily. House wine €22.50. Closed 25 Dec, 1 Jan. MasterCard, Visa, Laser. **Directions:** on the right of the Dame St. entrance to Dublin Castle. ◊

Dublin 2   # Chili Club

RESTAURANT   1 Anne's Lane South Anne Street Dublin 2 **Tel: 01 677 3721**

www.chiliclub.ie

This cosy restaurant, in a laneway just off Grafton Street, has great charm; it was Dublin's first authentic Thai restaurant and is still as popular as ever over a decade later. Owned and managed by Patricia Kenna, who personally supervises a friendly and efficient staff, it is small and intimate, with beautiful crockery and genuine Thai art and furniture. Don Pia-Kaen, who had been second chef for the previous six years, took over in 2008 from the original head chef Supot Boonchouy, who left a sound legacy: there has been no change of style and you will still find a fine range of genuine Thai dishes here, which are not 'tamed' too much to suit Irish tastes. Set lunch and early evening menus offer especially good value. **Seats 40** (private room, 16); children welcome. L Wed-Fri 12.30-2.30, D Tue-Sun 6-11pm. Set L €14. Early D from €14 (6-7pm), Set D €30. A la carte also available. House wine €20. SC discretionary (10% on parties 6+. Closed L Sat-Tue, all Mon, 25 Dec - 1 Jan. Diners, MasterCard, Visa, Laser. **Directions:** Off Grafton Street.

Dublin 2   # The Clarence Hotel, Tea Room Restaurant & Octagon Bar

HOTEL•BAR•RESTAURANT   6-8 Wellington Quay Dublin 2 **Tel: 01 407 0800**

reservations@theclarence.ie www.theclarence.ie

Dating back to 1852, this hotel has long had a special place in the hearts of Irish people - especially the clergy and the many who regarded it as a home-from-home when 'up from the country' for business or shopping in Dublin - largely because of its convenience to Heuston Station. Since the early '90s, however, it has achieved cult status through its owners - Bono and The Edge of U2 - who have completely refurbished the hotel, sparing no expense to reflect the the hotel's original arts and crafts style whenever possible. Now, however, the owners are planning a dramatic rede-velopment and expansion of the site in association with UK architects Foster & Partners, who are responsible for many of the world's most remarkable modern buildings; the proposed develop-ment would create a new landmark for the city, and include restoration of the quayside facade. Meanwhile, accommodation currently offers a combination of contemporary comfort and period style, with all the expected amenities including mini-bar, private safe, complimentary broadband and temperature control panels. Public areas include the clublike, oak-panelled Octagon Bar, which is a popular Temple Bar meeting place, and The Study, a quieter room with an open fire. Parking is available in several multi-storey car parks within walking distance; valet parking available for guests. Conference/banqueting (60/70); video conferencing on request; Secretarial service; Laptop-sized safe in rooms. Beauty treatments, massage, Therapy @ The Clarence (also available to non-residents). Children welcome (Under 12s free in parents' room, cots available without charge, baby sitting arranged). No pets. **Rooms 49** (5 suites, incl 1 penthouse; 21 executive, 4 family rooms, 6 no smoking, 1 for disabled). Lift. 24 hr room service, Turndown service. Room rate €340; SC discretionary. **The Tea Room:** The restaurant, which has its own entrance on Essex Street, is a high-ceilinged room furnished in the light oak which is an authentic period feature throughout the hotel. Pristine white linen, designer cutlery and glasses, high windows softened by the filtered damson tones of pavement awnings, all combine to create an impressive dining room; there is no separate reception area for the restaurant so you will be shown straight to your table. Head chef Mathieu Melin took the helm in the spring of 2007, and this respected kitchen continues to be a happy ship. An à la carte menu is the backbone of the food offering but the introduction of keenly-priced Market Menus at both lunch (daily) and dinner (Sun-Thu) has been a stroke of genius - at lunchtime, there's even an 'In-N-Out' guarantee that groups of up to four can have a 2-course Market Menu lunch in 45 minutes flat. The Market Menus have really livened up the dining scene at The Clarence, and Mathieu Melin shows his versatility in creating dishes for this menu. His combination plates ('a combination of 5 small dishes') offered as starter and as dessert are worth travelling for;

excellent home-made breads with pesto are also superb. A well-chosen, if expensive, wine list includes a selection of very good wines by the glass, and wine service is knowledgeable. *Lighter menus are also available in the hotel - an informal Evening Menu, for example, and Afternoon Tea; as well as a light à la carte and a number of classic main courses, The Octagon Bar Menu offers a great cocktail menu. **Seats 90**; toilets wheelchair accessible. L Sun-Fri 12.30-2.30, D daily 7-10.30 (Sun to 9.30). Special Market Menu - L €26 12.30-2.30pm (Sun-Fri); D €39 (Sun-Thurs 7-8pm); also a la carte L & D. House wine from €26. SC 12.5% on groups 8+. Octagon Bar Menu,12-10pm daily. Closed L Sat and 24 Dec-27 Dec. Amex, Diners, MasterCard, Visa. **Directions:** Overlooking the River Liffey at Wellington Quay, southside, in Temple Bar.

Dublin 2

CAFÉ•WINE BAR

Cobblers
Leeson Lane Dublin 2
Tel: 01 678 5945

This stylish and popular café and wine bar is located in an old cobbler's shop off Leeson Street with extensive seating on two levels, including sheltered outside seating which gets the lunchtime sun. Newspapers and wi-fi access are available, catering for the clientele consisting primarily of people working in the area. Lunch fare consists of excellent and varied pre-prepared sandwiches, salads and pasta dishes which can be heated up on the premises and assorted pizza slices. Some wine is available, although not of outstanding quality. Artisan crisps, excellent coffee and chocolate, and a pleasant secluded location are the other elements making this an extremely popular lunch spot. **Directions:** Leeson Lane is off St. Stephen's Green end of Leeson Street.

Dublin 2

HOTEL•RESTAURANT

Conrad Dublin & Alex Restaurant
Earlsfort Terrace Dublin 2 **Tel: 01 602 8900**
dublininfo@conradhotels.com www.conraddublin.com

Situated directly opposite the National Concert Hall and just a stroll away from St Stephen's Green, this fine city centre hotel celebrated its twentieth anniversary in 2005 with the completion of a €15 million refurbishment programme which saw the entire hotel renovated and upgraded. This is an extremely comfortable place to stay - friendly staff are well-trained and helpful, and many of the pleasantly contemporary guestrooms enjoy views of the piazza below and across the city; nice touches include providing an umbrella in each room - and also a laminated jogging map of the area with one- and three-mile routes outlined. The Conrad has particular appeal for business guests, as all of the bedrooms also double as an efficient office, with ergonomic workstation, broadband, dataports, international powerpoints and at least three direct dial telephones with voice-mail - and the hotel also has extensive state-of-the-art conference and meeting facilities, a fitness centre and underground parking. Public areas include a raised lounge, which makes an ideal meeting place, and the popular Alfie Byrne's Pub, which is home to locals and visitors alike and opens on to a sheltered terrace. **Rooms 191** (16 suites, 6 junior suites, 165 no-smoking, 1 for disabled). Lift. 24 hr room service. Turndown service. Room rate from €99 (high season €190) no SC. Open all year. **Alex:** The bright, spacious, split level restaurant offers a smart, modern dining experience, with vibrant décor and elegant comfortable furnishings set off by Elizabeth Cope paintings and low music, Impeccably professional staff are quick to show diners to tables smartly set with a white linen, stylish cutlery and gleaming glassware. A well-presented menu focuses on optimum freshness and seasonality, offering tempting contemporary dishes with a strong emphasis on seafood, although there are also attractive meat and vegetarian choices. Classic dishes such as whole Dover sole on the bone or a 10oz Irish rib eye are treated pleasingly simply, making for uncomplicated dishes that allow the sheer quality and clean flavours of the ingredients to shine through. A well-chosen wine list reflects the restaurant's demand for quality, and includes a special monthly wine selection which focuses on a particular country. Even though sometimes lacking in atmosphere, Alex makes up for this in faultless service and a good all-round dining experience. **Seats 92**; air conditioning, children welcome, live jazz on Saturday eve. B 7-10.30am; L 12.30-2.30pm, D 5.30-9.30pm daily. Set 2/3 course L €30/€35, set 2/3 course D €40/45; house wine from €26. Restaurant closed D 25 Dec, L 26 Dec. Amex, Diners, MasterCard, Visa, Laser. **Directions:** On the south-eastern corner of St Stephen's Green, opposite the National Concert Hall.

Dublin 2
RESTAURANT

Coopers Restaurant

62 Lr. Leeson Street Dublin 2 **Tel: 01 676 8615**
info@coopersrestaurant.ie www.coopersrestaurant.ie

Situated near Leeson Street Bridge in an attractive old cut-stone coach house, there's a large skylight providing plenty of natural light, and the old stone walls and the character of the building create a pleasing atmosphere. Noel Daly's style of cooking is refreshingly straightforward and reserved; you'll find a lot of the old favourites - prawns pil pil, Caesar salad and beef tomato & mozzarella salad are typical starters, for example, and you may expect steaks various ways (with the obligatory side order of Coopers fries), lamb cutlets, a fish dish of the day and a vegetarian pasta dish. Don't expect originality, but you should find pleasing versions of classic dishes that are full of flavour, sometimes with a contemporary slant, and presented with as little fuss as possible. An affordable wine list focuses on France and offers a handful of new world wines. An attractive al fresco dining area is pleasantly sheltered from the bustle of Leeson Street Bridge; with seating comfortably set up with plants around and an awning to protect diners from extremes of weather, it's pleasant spot to enjoy the light lunch menu (€15), perhaps, or the early evening menu (from €20) in summer. Toilets & public areas wheelchair accessible. **Seats 130** (outdoors, 30, private room up to 80); children welcome; L Mon-Fri, 12-3, Set L about €18.50/€22.50 2/3 course; D Mon-Sat, 5.30- "late," early D about €20/24.50, 5.30-7; set D about €37.95; also a la carte L&D; house wine about €19.50; 10% SC on groups 8+. Closed L Sat & L Sun, 25-27 Dec, Good Fri. Amex, Diners, MasterCard, Visa, Laser. **Directions:** Just before Leeson St. bridge coming from town centre.

Dublin 2
RESTAURANT
Ⓝ

Cornerhouse Grill

17 South Great Georges Street Dublin 2 **Tel: 01 707 9596**
info@cornerhousegrill.ie www.cornerhousegrill.ie

Located on the corner of South Georges Street and Exchequer Street, the Cornerhouse Grill is a younger sister of nearby Brasserie Sixty Six (see entry). The stylish dark green exterior and high windows set the tone for a smart, bustling interior which is every inch the classy urban steakhouse, evident in the dark wooden floors, quality furniture and wood panelled walls. The ground floor offers customers a spacious, high ceiling and lively dining room, whilst the lower dining area offers a more intimate ambience. A team of friendly and attentive staff, well turned out in white aprons, bring menus specialising mainly in different prime cuts of steak which are flame grilled to order. The Cornerhouse Grill takes pride in sourcing high quality cuts of Irish meat, and steps up to the mark by crediting suppliers on the menu. An extensive, exclusively old world, wine list provides a good selection in the €20 to €40 price range. This establishment is confident in the provenance and expert cooking of the meat, which makes for an authentic grill experience, with all the trimmings - and, for the most part, that confidence is justified although, like its stylish older sister, Brasserie Sixty Six, there's a tendency to inconsistency in some dishes. However, if you are looking for a perfectly cooked tender Irish steak in a sophisticated setting, and are willing to pay that little bit extra for the privilege, the Cornerhouse Grill is likely to be a good choice. **Seats 50**; open Mon -Sat, 11am - 11pm. **Directions:** Corner of Exchequer Street and South Great Georges Street. ◇

Dublin 2
RESTAURANT

Cornucopia

19 Wicklow Street Dublin 2 **Tel: 01 677 7583**
info@cornucopia.ie www.cornucopia.ie

You don't have to be vegetarian to enjoy this established wholefood restaurant, which is well located for a wholesome re-charge if you're shopping around Grafton Street. Originally a wholefood store with a few tables at the back, although it has now been a dedicated restaurant for some time, a waft of that unmistakable aroma remains. It may give out mixed messages in various ways - the smart red and gold frontage and pavement screen seem inviting in a mainstream way, but the atmosphere is actually quite student / alternative. It is very informal, especially during the day (when window seats are well placed for people watching), and regulars like it for its simple wholesomeness which - a rarity in restaurants - is pleasingly redolent of home cooking. Vegetarian breakfasts are a speciality and all ingredients are organic, as far as possible. Yeast-free, dairy-free, gluten-free and wheat-free diets are catered for, and no processed or GM foods are used. Organic wines too. And, at the time of going to press, a promising new cookery book is due to appear; called 'Cornucopia at home, The Cookbook' (Atrium Press), it will introduce a whole new generation of happy diners - vegetarian and otherwise - to this delightful restaurant and its philosophy. **Seats 48**. Mon-Sat 8.30am-9pm (to 8pm Sat), Sun 12-7. All à la carte (menus change daily); organic house wine €21.50 (large glass about €3.95). Closed 25-27 Dec, 1 Jan, Easter Sun/Mon, Oct Bank Hol Sun/Mon. MasterCard, Visa, Laser. **Directions:** Off Grafton St. turn at Brown Thomas. ◇

Da Pino

Dublin 2
RESTAURANT

38-40 Parliament Street Dublin 2
Tel: 01 671 9308

Just across the road from Dublin Castle, this busy youthful Italian/Spanish restaurant is always full - and no wonder, as they serve cheerful, informal, well cooked food that does not make too many concessions to trendiness and is sold at very reasonable prices. Paella is a speciality and the pizzas, which are especially good, are prepared in full view of customers. Although the restaurant came into new ownership in 2008, there are no obvious changes - and it remains an especially useful place for families to know about. **Seats 75**. Children welcome. Open 12-11.30 daily (to 11pm Sun-Tue). A la carte. Wine from €18.90. Closed Christmas & Good Fri. Amex, Diners, MasterCard, Visa, Laser. **Directions:** Opposite Dublin Castle. ◇

Darwins

Dublin 2
RESTAURANT

16 Aungier Street Dublin 2 **Tel: 01 475 7511**
darwinsrestaurant@eircom.net

Proprietor Michael Smith's own butchers shop supplies certified organic meats to this restaurant in an area known for its butchers but not, until recently, so much as a dining destination. But, together with a strong team, Michael offers discerning diners flavoursome cooking that pleases the eye as much as the taste buds and makes the most of well-sourced ingredients, including good vegetables and delicious fish. Given Michael's background, you may expect excellent meats - especially great steaks - but it may be more of a surprise to find that vegetarians are so well looked after, and that one of the house specialities is a vegetarian risotto of wild mushrooms and sun-dried tomato. Finish with a choice of gorgeous puddings - a well-made classic lemon tart perhaps - or mature farmhouse cheeses (attractively presented plated with fresh fruit and oatcakes) and a wack of irresistible Illy coffee. Good, reasonably priced house wines set the tone for a fair wine list - with interesting yet unpretentious food, great service and competitive pricing too, it is no surprise that this restaurant has earned a loyal following - and is doing very well. **Seats 50**; air conditioning; children welcome before 7; D Mon-Sat, 5.30 to 11; 2/3 course early D daily 5-7 €23.50/26.50; also à la carte. Closed Sun, 25-26 Dec & Bank Hols. Amex, MasterCard, Visa, Laser. **Directions:** Opposite Carmelite Church.

The Davenport Hotel

Dublin 2
HOTEL

Merrion Square Dublin 2 **Tel: 01 607 3900**
info@ocallaghanhotels.com www.ocallaghanhotels.com

On Merrion Square, close to the National Gallery, the Dail (Parliament Buildings) and Trinity College, this striking hotel is fronted by the impressive 1863 facade of the Alfred Jones designed Merrion Hall, which was restored as part of the hotel building project in the early '90s. Inside, the architectural theme is continued in the naming of rooms - Lanyon's Restaurant, for example, honours the designer of Queen's University Belfast, and the Gandon Suite is named after the designer of some of Dublin's finest buildings, including the Custom House. The hotel, which is equally suited to leisure and business guests, has been imaginatively designed to combine interest and comfort, with warm, vibrant colour schemes and a pleasing mixture of old and new in both public areas and accommodation. Bedrooms are furnished to a high standard with orthopaedic beds, air conditioning, voicemail, modem lines, personal safes and turndown service in addition to the more usual amenities - all also have ample desk space, while the suites also have fax and laser printer. Above all, perhaps, The Davenport is known for the warmth and helpfulness of its staff, and it makes a very comfortable base within walking distance of shops and galleries; it is the flagship property for a small group of centrally located hotels, including the Alexander Hotel (just off Merrion Square) and the Stephen's Green Hotel (corner of St Stephen's Green and Harcourt Street). Conference/banqueting (380/400). Business centre. Gym. Children welcome (Under 2s free in parents' room; cots available, baby sitting arranged). No pets. **Rooms 115** (2 suites, 10 junior suites). Lift. 24 hr room service. B&B about €80pps. Open all year. Amex, Diners, MasterCard, Visa. **Directions:** just off Merrion Square. ◇

Dublin 2
PUB

Davy Byrnes
21 Duke Street Dublin 2 **Tel: 01 677 5217**
www.davybyrnes.com

Just off Grafton Street, Davy Byrnes is one of Dublin's most famous pubs - references in Joyce's "Ulysses" mean it is very much on the tourist circuit. Despite all this fame it remains a genuine, well-run place and is equally popular with Dubliners, who find it a handy meeting place. But, although there are some concessions to food fashion these days (pasta and panini, a plate sharing menu - and, more promisingly, Frank Hederman's organic Irish smoked salmon), a modern gastro-pub this is not: the bar food offered is mainly traditional, providing 'a good feed' at reasonable prices. Irish stew is the house speciality and oysters with brown bread & butter, beef & Guinness pie and deep-fried plaice with tartare sauce are all typical; and there's always a list of daily specials like sautéed lambs liver with bacon & mushroom sauce, pheasant in season - and, in deference to the Joycean connections, there's also a Bloomsday Special (gorgonzola and burgundy). Not just a tourist pub, this is a popular meeting place for Dubliners shopping in nearby Grafton Street - and you can read a fascinating history of Davy Byrnes if you are kept waiting. Half a dozen wines are available by the glass, and about twice that number by the bottle. Not suitable for children under 7. Outside eating area. Bar food served daily, 12.30-9 (winter to 5). House wine €17.95. Eoin Scott - Irish roots, trad and contemporary songs 9-11pm Sun-Tue. Closed 25-26 Dec & Good Fri. MasterCard, Visa, Laser. **Directions:** 100 metres from Grafton Street.

Dublin 2
RESTAURANT

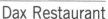

Dax Restaurant
23 Upper Pembroke Street Dublin 2 **Tel: 01 676 1494**
olivier@dax.ie www.dax.ie

Olivier Meisonnave named this appealing restaurant after his home town in Les Landes, and it was the culmination of a longheld ambition. Flagged floors, light-toned walls and pale upholstery set off simple contemporary darkwood furniture, and it all adds up to a tone of relaxed contemporary elegance with more than a hint of rustic chic. A welcoming bar area offers a post-work wind-down with hot and cold tapas and a broad, good-value choice of wines by the glass. The menu is concise at both lunch and dinner, but its solid offering is intriguing enough to warrant repeat visits. At lunch, the emphasis is on speedy and efficient service, with the ambience winding down considerably at dinner time. Expect fine ingredients delivered with interesting twists and an imaginative use of garnishes. The little extras such as an amuse bouche to start and home-made truffles with coffee add to the sense of being in excellent hands throughout. The largely French wine list is outstanding, and the whole front of house team share an obvious passion for and knowledge of the range on offer, which includes a broad and well-priced selection by the glass, and a good balance of affordable wines alongside the opportunity to spend some serious money. This is a well-oiled operation, one that is very comfortable in its own skin, making it as good for a dinner date as it is for a deal-brokering lunch. **Seats 65** (Private room seats 14); not suitable for children under 5 yrs; no wheelchair access; air conditioning; reservations recommended. Open Tue-Sat, L 12.30-2pm; D 6-10.30, Set L €28, Early 3 course D €35, 6-7pm, Tue-Thurs; also à la carte. SC 12.5%. Closed Sun, Mon, 25 Dec - 4 Jan. Amex, MasterCard, Visa, Laser. **Directions:** On Upper Pembroke Street.

Dublin 2
RESTAURANT

Diep Le Shaker
55 Pembroke Lane Dublin 2 **Tel: 01 661 1829**
info@diep.net www.diep.net

This fashionable two-storey restaurant is elegantly appointed, with comfortable high-back chairs, good linen and fine glasses and, with sunny yellow walls and a long skylight along one side of the upper floor creating a bright atmosphere, the ambience is always lively. This is a restaurant with many fans and, and at its best, the cooking is excellent; a team of Thai chefs has developed a new menu of Royal

Thai Cuisine: signature dishes include Lab Gai (spicy minced chicken salad), seafood dishes like Gaeng Goong Maprow Oon (red tiger prawn curry) and Pla Thod Kratiem Prik Thai (crispy whole sea bass). Special evening menus offered to groups of 6+ include A Taste of Bangkok, A Taste of Chiang Mai and A Taste of Phuket (approx €39.50-€54 per person); a less elaborate selection of special menus is also offered at lunchtime. Service is invariably charming and solicitous, and there's a great buzz that contributes to the popularity of this busy restaurant. **Seats 120**. Reservations accepted; not suitable for children after 9 pm; air conditioning; toilets wheelchair accessible. Jazz Tue & Wed night. L & D Mon-Thu 12-3 & 6-10, Fri – all day; Sat D only 6–10.30pm. L & D à la carte. House wine from about €21. SC 12.5% on parties 6+. Closed L Sat, Sun, bank hols, 25-29 Dec. Amex, MasterCard, Visa, Laser. **Directions:** First Lane on left off Pembroke Street. ◊

Dublin 2
RESTAURANT

Dobbins Wine Bistro

15 Stephens Lane Dublin 2 **Tel: 01 661 9536**
dobbinsbistro@gmail.com

This restaurant hidden away near Merrion Square is something of a Dublin institution, established since 1978 by the late John O'Byrne and manager Patrick Walsh. Recently a major revamp transformed the restaurant - gone were the famous old Nissen hut and sawdust-strewn floors of old, replaced with a sleek modern look with smart leather banquettes and chairs, and contemporary lighting. But fans were glad to find that the fundamentals remained in place. A visit to this unique oasis has always been a treat for great hospitality, food which was consistently delicious in a style that showed an awareness of current trends without slavishly following them, and a love of wine. Now, while old hands may miss the cosiness of the previous Dobbins, the hospitality and professionalism has not changed and, although the presentation may be slicker, the cooking should still please. Ingredients are sourced with care, and reflect the locality: Dublin Bay prawns (not the ubiquitous tiger prawns found in so many establishments that should know better), Castletownbere crab, organic salmon and pork that is served with crackling indicate the philosophy. And you'll find good value here too - although often described as 'expensive', Dobbins offers great value on their early dinner menu (€25 for 3 courses plus coffee or tea, with plenty of choice on each course) and lunch menus. Lovely wine list and good choice of wines by the glass. **Seats 120** (private room, 40); children welcome; air conditioning. L Mon-Fri 12.30-2.30, D Mon-Sat 6-9.30; Sun L only, 12-3pm. Set L about €23.50, early D Mon-Sat, 6-7pm, €25. L&D also à la carte, House wine from €20. SC discretionary. Closed L Sat, all Sun, D Mon, bank hols, Christmas week. Amex, Diners, MasterCard, Visa, Laser. **Directions:** Between Lower & Upper Mount Streets. ◊

Dublin 2
RESTAURANT

Dunne & Crescenzi

14 & 16 South Frederick Street Dublin 2 **Tel: 01 677 3815**
dunneandcrescenzi@hotmail.com www.dunneandcrescenzi.com

Always a delight for its unpretentiousness and the simple good food it offers at reasonable prices (for the high quality), this Italian restaurant and deli is very near the Nassau Street entrance to Trinity College, and the first of what is now a small family chain of restaurants in and around the city. It's the perfect place to shop for genuine Italian ingredients - risotto rice, pasta, oils, vinegars, olives, cooked meats, cheeses, wines and much more - and a great example of how less can be more. How good to sit down with a glass of wine (house wine is reasonably priced, and bottles on sale can be opened for a small corkage charge) and, maybe, a plate of antipasti - with wafer-thin Parma ham, perhaps, several salamis, peppers preserved in olive oil, olives and a slice of toasted ciabatta drizzled with extra virgin olive oil... There are even some little tables on the pavement, if you're lucky enough to get them on a sunny day. Indoors or out, expect to queue: this place has a loyal following. **Seats 50** (outdoor, 20); children welcome; air conditioning. Open Mon-Sat 8-11, Sun 10am-10pm. A la carte; wine from about €15. Amex, MasterCard, Visa, Laser. **Directions:** Off Nassau Street, between Kilkenny and Blarney stores.

Dublin 2   **Eden**

RESTAURANT   Meeting House Square Temple Bar Dublin 2 **Tel: 01 670 5372**

Ⓔ   eden@edenrestaurant.ie   www.edenrestaurant.ie

A veteran of the Temple Bar area, Eden has stood the test of time for a decade, though it may be beginning to show its age of late. The spacious two-storey restaurant, designed by Tom de Paor, opens onto its own outdoor terrace on Meeting House Square and continues to be one of the city's best outdoor dining options in summer months, especially on a Saturday when the daytime market makes way in the evenings for free movies screened in the Square itself. Generous hanging baskets with well-cultivated greenery emphasise this blurring of inside and outside, and the open kitchen adds to the buzz of the place. Menus change regularly to reflect the seasons, with lunch and early bird menus changing weekly. Signature dishes include the Eden smokies (smoked haddock with spring onion, crème fraîche and melted cheddar cheese), and the kitchen continues to champion organic meats and a down-to-earth, hearty culinary approach to cooking them. A three-course pre-theatre menu offers good value. The well-balanced and fairly priced wine list includes bubblies and interesting cocktails, and half a dozen wines by the glass. **Seats 96** (private room, 12-30; outdoor seating, 32); air conditioning; children welcome before 8pm. L daily,12.30-3 (Sun 12-3). D daily 6-10.30 (to 10 Sun). Set L €26, Early Bird D €25 (6-7, Sun-Thu), also à la carte. House wine from €23. SC 12.5% on groups 6+. Closed bank hols, 25 Dec - 2 Jan. Amex, Diners, MasterCard, Visa, Laser. **Directions:** Next to the Irish Film Theatre, opposite Diceman's Corner.

Dublin 2   **Ely HQ**

RESTAURANT•WINE BAR   Hanover Quay Docklands Dublin 2 **Tel: 01 633 9986**

 Ⓔ   hq@elywinebar.com   www.elywinebar.ie

This, the third and most recent of Erik and Michelle Robson's wine bar/cafés, is south of the river in the new Hanover Quay area of the city, which is nearing completion (see Hanover Quay round-up for details). On a corner site, it's an angular premises with huge windows and, with hard lines, drum lamp shades, canteen-style tables and (a few) large flower motifs on soft furnishings, there's a retro-60s' feel to the décor. It has a young, stylish atmosphere, a strong cocktail menu, the great wine list that has become the trademark of the Ely group, and large eating areas on two levels, ground floor and downstairs - and a fully heated covered terrace area. Smartly presented menus offer a choice of about a dozen starters and main courses, with the familiar emphasis on well-sourced ingredients, but with a rather more sophisticated tone than the other Ely menus. On the lunch menu, wine suggestions from Ely's phenomenal wines-by-the-glass list are made for every dish - and a euro from every order of organic bangers with sauerkraut mash goes to Barnardos. Good service is a strong point and ElyHQ is already proving a real winner in this fast-maturing and attractive area of the city. **Seats 200** (private room, 45; outdoors, 80); free broadband wi/fi; children welcome before 7pm (high chair); toilets wheelchair accessible; air conditioning. L & D Mon-Sat 12-3pm & 5.30-10.30pm. SC 12.5% on groups 6+. Closed Sun, Christmas week, bank hols. Amex, Diners, MasterCard, Visa, Laser. **Directions:** On the South Quays - Hanover quay is off Sir John Rogersons quay.

Dublin 2   **Ely Winebar & Café**

RESTAURANT•WINE BAR   22 Ely Place Dublin 2 **Tel: 01 676 8986**

         elyplace@elywinebar.com   www.elywinebar.ie

In an imaginatively renovated Georgian townhouse just off St Stephen's Green, this was the first of Erik and Michelle Robson's 'series' of Ely wine bar/cafés; it first opened in 1999 and, since then, they have built on their commitment to offer some of the greatest and most interesting wines from around the world - earning an unrivalled reputation for their unique list and, especially, for the quality and range of wines offered by the glass. And the exceptional wine offering is backed up by other specialities including a list of premium beers; on the food side, organic produce, notably pork, beef and lamb from the family farm in County Clare, is a special feature - and you will not only find premium cuts, but also products like home-made sausages and mince, which make all the difference to simple dishes like sausages and mash (from which a euro of every order goes to Barnardos) or beefburgers. Two much bigger sister establishments, 'ely chq' and 'ely hq', opened in the IFSC and on Hanover Quay in 2006 and 2007 respectively (see entries). Each has its own personality (and following) but all share the core values of commitment to an exceptional and constantly-evolving wine offering, with an unrivalled selection offered by the glass- and to quality food. **Seats 80**; children welcome before 7pm; free broadband wi/fi. Open Mon-Sat 12 noon-12.30 am. L 12-3 (1-4 Sat), D 5.30-10.30 (to 11 Fri/Sat). Bar open to midnight. Wines from €26. SC 12.5% on groups of 6+. Closed Sun, Christmas week, bank hols. Amex, Diners, MasterCard, Visa, Laser. **Directions:** Junction of Baggot Street/Merrion Street off St Stephens Green.

Dublin 2
RESTAURANT
♛ Ⓔ

Fallon & Byrne

11-17 Exchequer Street Dublin 2 **Tel: 01 472 1000**
restaurant@fallonandbyrne.com www.fallonandbyrne.com

This chic, contemporary French restaurant could easily be missed, given its location above their ground floor speciality grocery and food market (which simply begs you to browse). But once up the flight of stairs or lift, you'll find a bright and airy restaurant where diners are greeted promptly at the door. Except for large flower arrangements displayed against the rear wall, decoration is minimal - high ceilings, white walls, no paintings - but it has a definite buzz and that special French bistro ambience, so doesn't feel stark. Two islands of comfortable leather seating dominate the central area, surrounded by simply laid darkwood tables and chairs; arriving diners are swiftly escorted to their tables, or there's a bar/reception area along one end where you can have a drink (if you can find a free stool) while waiting for your table - an agreeable interlude, as you watch the attentive staff at work. At your table, breads, butter and water are presented, along with appealing menus offering a refreshingly simple and well-balanced choice. Authentic French cooking is what's on offer here: a deliciously sweet white onion soup with truffle crème frâiche, for example, or assiette of foie gras (done three ways) with cinnamon brioche to start, followed by main courses with an equally French tone such as a lean and succulent rabbit stuffed with a wild mushroom mousse and wrapped in pancetta, pan-fried sea trout with basil pappardelle, courgette, slow-roasted tomato & tomato coulis or a delicious vegetarian option of globe artichoke & roast tomato tart tatin. Even the long and mysterious trek to the toilets on the top floor (not an unusual experience in this area) will not dent enthusiasm for this place, with its simple and well planned menu, great tasting food, professional staff and good value on all menus, considering the quality of food and service. **Fallon & Byrne**, downstairs: Surrounded by bottles on the walls, you are in the cellar - clever idea; popular with the post-work crowd, who love the atmosphere and affordable menu - light bites (cheeseboard, salads, patés, olives) are also offered, and you can choose from the bottles around you (corkage €10). Before leaving, spend a little time looking around what has become Dublin's favourite food store - you are unlikely to leave empty-handed. **Fallon & Byrne Restaurant:** Open L Mon-Sun, 12.30-3pm (to 4pm Sun); D Mon-Thurs, 6-10pm; Fri-Sat, 6-11pm; Sun, 6-9pm. House wine €24. Wine Cellar: Over 600 wines, 70 by the glass; corkage €10 or €1 on Mondays. Open Mon-Sat 11am-10pm (Thurs-Sat to 11pm), Sun & Bank hols, 12.30-9pm. **Directions:** Central Dublin, just off lower end of Grafton Street. ◊

Dublin 2
RESTAURANT
Ⓝ

The Farm

3 Dawson Street Dublin 2 **Tel: 01 671 8654**
hello@thefarmfood.ie www.thefarmrestaurant.ie

Organic is the theme of this new addition to Dublin's dining scene. Situated prominently at the lower end of Dawson Street, its funky modern design and pavement tables attracts the attention of passers-by, and its popularity means that you may have to queue for a few minutes at the door before being seated in the main dining area. However, once seated, service is prompt and informative, with laminated menus offered immediately; well balanced and very clear on the origin and content of the dishes, they feature favourites such as pies, burgers, pastas and salads, but all with organic ingredients and an original twist: a crisp duck salad may come with with tangy Mediterranean fruits, and a dense chicken and mushroom pie well flavoured with tarragon - and have a beautifully crisp pastry top.

Children are more than welcome in this busy restaurant, where there should be something to suit all tastes and budgets. Open from mid morning to late night, The Farm's good, simple organic food has attracted a following in this busy commercial area. **Seats 70**; children welcome; open 11am-11pm (to midnight Fri/Sat). MasterCard, Visa, Laser. **Directions:** At the north end of Dawson Street.

Dublin 2
RESTAURANT

Fire

The Mansion House Dawson Street Dublin 2 **Tel: 01 676 7200**
enquiries@mansionhouse.ie www.mansionhouse.ie

The Mansion House has been the official residence of the Lord Mayor of Dublin since 1715 - it is the only mayoral residence in Ireland, and older than any mayoral residence in Britain. A very large room previously known as The Supper Room is now used as a restaurant and the room itself is of sufficient interest to be worth a look even if you haven't time to eat; the unusual Celtic themed contemporary décor of the restaurant, 'Fire', is unexpected in this graceful old room, but it offers well executed smart food, in classy surroundings served with a twist of chic. The cosmopolitan outdoor seating area at the front of Fire hints at the style that pervades throughout the impressive interior and the spacious dining room is slick, successfully blending a sophisticated modern feel within the historical setting of the building. The room's centrepiece of three Celtic spires, a beautiful wall mosaic at the rear of the building, and the elemental lighting sets an opulent atmosphere, without being too formal. Outstandingly polite staff are quick to make you feel very welcome, promptly providing enticing menus that offer uncomplicated contemporary and rustic European dishes based on the best of ingredients, notably the house speciality of flatbread pizzas - which are cooked in the restaurant's own wood burning stove - and delicious tender steaks of 100% prime dry-aged Irish beef. Deliciously moreish puddings end a meal here well, and a good wine list offers excellent value in the house wines selection and more adventurous options for those who wish to indulge. The popularity of Fire is well earned and easily explained, as it offers the right mix of unpretentious food cooked to a high standard, served with lashings of style at an affordable price. L Thu-Sat only, 12-3pm; D Mon-Sat 5.30-9.30pm (from 5pm Fri/Sat). Closed Sun. ◊

Dublin 2
RESTAURANT

Fitzers Restaurant

51 Dawson Street Dublin 2 **Tel: 01 677 1155**
eat@fitzers.ie www.fitzers.ie

A very popular meeting place after work or when shopping in town, Fitzers offers reliable Cal-Ital influenced cooking in a smart contemporary setting, and has a heated al fresco dining area on the pavement. **Seats 100** (outdoors, 20); Open daily 11am-11pm; set 3 course L €36.95; set 3 course D €43.95; house wine €22; SC 12.5% on parties 6+. Closed Dec 25/26, Good Friday. Amex, Diners, MasterCard, Visa, Laser. Also at: *Temple Bar Square, Tel: 01-679 0440(12-11 daily, cl 25 Dec & Good Fri) *National Gallery, Merrion Square Tel: 01-663 3500 Mon-Sat 9.30-5, Sun 12-4.30, closed Gallery Opening days). **Directions:** Halfway up Dawson Street, on the right heading towards St Stephen's Green.

Dublin 2
HOTEL
♥

The Fitzwilliam Hotel

St Stephens Green Dublin 2 **Tel: 01 478 7000**
enq@fitzwilliamhotel.com www.fitzwilliamhotel.com

If a comfortable city centre base is what you're after, you won't get more central than this stylish contemporary hotel, and, behind the deceptively low-key frontage (Luas station at the door), lies an impressively sleek interior - initially created by Sir Terence Conran's design group, the hotel recently celebrated its first decade by bringing the same team back to undertake a complete overhaul and refurb: this has been done with style and discretion and, although in some areas - notably the guest rooms - changes are fairly major, in others it feels more like a subtle freshen up. In tune with the hotel's reputation for understated luxury and discreet service, the public areas combine elegant minimalism with luxury fabrics and finishes, notably leather upholstery and a fine pewter counter in the bar, which is a chic place to meet in the Grafton Street area. In addition to the hotel's premier restaurant, Thornton's (see separate entry), breakfast, lunch and dinner are served daily in their smart informal restaurant Citron Brasserie, on the mezzanine level, which is ideal for Dubliners escaping from the full-on retail experience nearby. Some of the bedrooms over-look the Green and, while most are quite compact for a luxury hotel, the most desirable is a 2,000sq ft penthouse suite - and all are designed to an equally high standard with smart new decor, air-conditioning, safe, broadband, stereo CD player and minibar, and equal care has been lavished on the bathrooms too, including designer toiletries. There's an in-house hair & beauty salon, Free Spirit, and the hotel has a great hidden asset - Ireland's largest roof garden. Conference/banqueting (80/60). 3 conference rooms; secretarial services; children welcome; (under12s free in parents' room; cots available free of charge). 24 hour room service. **Rooms** 128 (2 suites, 128 executive, 90 no-smoking, 4 for disabled). Lift. B&B about €160pps. No service charge. Open all year. Amex, Diners, MasterCard, Visa, Laser. **Directions:** West side of St. Stephen's Green. ◊

Dublin 2
RESTAURANT•WINE BAR
Ⓝ

Georges Wine Bar and Bistro

29 South Frederick Street Dublin 2
Tel: 01 679 7000

This quiet and centrally located wine bar and restaurant has a whitewashed ground floor interior which is cool and spacious, as well as a cellar bar and a small outdoor terrace which makes the most of sunny afternoons. The wine list is relatively short for a wine bar but has some excellent choices at all price levels. The food menu is also quite short and simple and the style is hearty, with large portions of straightforward food, excellently prepared. Typically, from a choice of about ten dishes on each course, you might begin with tasty starters of crab or chicken salad, followed by simple main courses including steaks, burger and vegetarian/pasta dishes. And then old favourites - crumbles, cheesecakes and ice cream - to finish. There is some excellent seafood available, and all dishes are very reasonably priced with an early evening 20% discount on the total bill (including wine) which is available before 7pm on Thursday to Saturday evenings, offering excellent value. The service is relaxed but all staff know the wine list well. There is live music in the cellar bar every night from Thursday to Saturday. **Seats** 55; open Mon-Wed 7.30am (breakfast for nearby hotel) – 11pm; Thurs 7.30am-1am; Fri/Sat 7.30am-2am. Closed Sun. MasterCard, Visa, Laser. **Directions:** Frederick Street is parallel to Dawson Street in the city centre.

Dublin 2
RESTAURANT

Gotham Café

8 South Anne Street Dublin 2
Tel: 01 679 5266

This lively, youthful café-restaurant just off Grafton Street does quality informal food at reasonable prices and is specially noted for its gourmet pizzas - try the Central Park, for example, a Greek style vegetarian pizza with black olives, red onion & fresh tomato on a bed of spinach with feta & mozzarella cheeses and fresh hummus, which is just one of a choice of sixteen tempting toppings. Other specialities include Caesar salad, baby calzone and Asian chicken noodle salad. There's a good choice of pastas too - and it's a great place for brunch on Sundays and bank holidays. As part of a recent major renovation, a baby-changing facility was created and a children's menu was introduced too. Light breakfasts, including home-baked muffins, are offered, from 10.30am. Offering consistent quality at fair prices, it's no wonder this great café is such a long-standing success. **Seats** 65 (outdoor seating, 10); children welcome; air conditioning. Open daily: Sun-Thu 12 -11, Fri-Sat 12-12; (L 12-5, D 5-12). A la carte. House wine about €17.50. SC discretionary (10% on parties of 6+). Closed 25-26 Dec & Good Fri. Amex, MasterCard, Visa, Laser. Directions: Just off Grafton Street. **Directions:** Just Off Grafton Street.

Dublin 2
HOTEL

The Grafton Capital

Stephens Street Lower Dublin 2 **Tel: 01 648 1100**
info@graftoncapital-hotel.com www.capital-hotels.com

In a prime city centre location just a couple of minutes walk from Grafton Street, this attractive hotel offers well furnished rooms and good amenities at prices which are not unreasonable for the area. Rooms are also available for small conferences, meetings and interviews. The popular 'Break for the Border' night club next door is in common ownership with the hotel. Small conferences (25); wheelchair access; parking by arrangement with nearby carpark; children welcome (Under 12s free in parents' room; cots available; baby sitting arranged). No Pets. **Rooms** 75 (3 junior suites, 18 no-smoking, 4 for disabled). Lift. B&B about €100pps, ss €40. Short breaks offered. Closed 24-26 Dec. Amex, Diners, MasterCard, Visa, Laser. **Directions:** Near St. Stephen's Green.

HANOVER QUAY

The regeneration of Dublin's docklands has been ongoing over much of the last decade and the attractive mixed use development in the Grand Canal Dock area includes apartments with retail and commercial units overlooking Hanover Quay. The main attractions to the area are Dieter Bergman's **Riva Restaurant** and the longer established **Ely HQ** (see entries). Other establishments worthy of a mention include **Milano** (01 679 9579; Grand Canal Square), a new branch of the popular pasta and pizza chain which is best known for its wide range of excellent pizzas and **Herbstreet** (01 675 3875; Hanover Quay) which is becoming well known for its breakfast (and brunch at the weekend) while lunch time menus include soups, open sandwiches, burgers and salads. There are further restaurants planned at the time of going to press to keep an eye on www.ireland-guide.com for any new recommendations in the area.

WWW.IRELAND-GUIDE.COM FOR ALL THE BEST PLACES TO EAT, DRINK & STAY

Dublin 2 | **Harrington Hall**
GUESTHOUSE | 69/70 Harcourt Street Dublin 2 **Tel: 01 475 3497**

harringtonhall@eircom.net www.harringtonhall.com

Conveniently located close to St Stephen's Green and within comfortable walking distance of the city's premier shopping areas, Trinity College and the National Concert Hall, this four star guesthouse is now in common ownership with the neighbouring Harcourt Hotel. It was once the home of a former Lord Mayor of Dublin and has been sympathetically and elegantly refurbished, retaining many original features. Echoes of Georgian splendour remain in the ornamental ceilings and fireplaces of the well-proportioned ground and first floor rooms, which include a peaceful drawing room with an open peat fire. Although there are some smaller, more practical bedrooms at the back, the main guestrooms are beautiful and relaxing with sound-proofed windows, ceiling fans and marbled bathrooms. Staff could be more communicative (especially at check-in) but immaculate housekeeping is a strong point, and good breakfasts are served in a sunny yellow room with pictures of Dublin streetscapes to ensure a bright start to your day. All round this is a welcome alternative to a city-centre hotel, offering comfort and good value, handy to the Luas (tram), and with the huge advantage of guest parking behind the building; luggage can be stored for guests arriving before check-in time. **Rooms 28** (1 suite, 1 junior suite, 4 shower only, 7 executive, 9 family, 4 ground floor, 2 single, all no smoking); children welcome (under 14s free in parents' room, cot available without charge). Parking (10). Lift; room service (all day); free broadband wi/fi. B&B €60 pps, ss €35. Open all year. Amex, Diners, MasterCard, Visa, Laser. **Directions:** Off southwest corner of St Stephens Green (one-way system approaches from Adelaide Road).

Dublin 2 | **Hilton Dublin**
HOTEL•RESTAURANT | Charlemont Place Dublin 2 **Tel: 01 402 9988**

allan.myhill@hilton.com www.hilton.com/dublin

Overlooking the Grand Canal and set in well maintained shrubberies and seating areas, this attractive modern hotel is between Leeson Street and Charlemont Street bridges; with a Luas station just outside (and only a short walk from the city centre in fine weather), it caters well for both leisure and business guests. Underground parking gets arriving guests off to a good start (€10 per night to residents, lift to reception), followed by prompt efficient and friendly welcome in a bright reception area with comfortable seating, fresh flowers and a sociable atmosphere. Accommodation is very comfortable with kingsize beds, good desk space (with all the necessary technical items nearby) and work chair, safe, good lighting, mini-bar, tea/coffee making facilities iron and ironing board, all as standard, and well finished bathrooms. Public facilities include the Third Stop bar and a coffee shop (nice selection of freshly made sandwiches from 11 am to 3 pm), with main meals, including a good breakfast, served in The Waterfornt Restaurant. This is a lovely place to stay with excellent staff, who care about the customer. Conference/banqueting (400/260), business centre, broadband wi/fi; underground carpark; children welcome (Under 12s free in parents' room; cots available, high chair, baby changing facilities, childrens menu). No pets. Lift. **Rooms 193** (all no-smoking, 39 executive, 10 for disabled). Room rate €175-295 (max. 2 guests). Closed 24-26 Dec. **Waterfront Restaurant:** Located just off the reception area, this well-appointed restaurant is pleasant in the evening, when you can watch people strolling along the canal bank. Menus offer a well-balanced choice of modern dishes including starters like seared scallops with a basil mash or smoked salmon on chorizo rosti, and tried-and-trusted main courses such as fillet of beef (with roast aubergine, plum tomatoes and black pepper sauce, perhaps) or braised shank of lamb with mashed potatoes. Desserts are all home-made and tasty - a vanilla panna cotta with cardamom pineapple, perhaps, or deep apple pie with Chantilly cream; good coffee to finish. Although the choices are on the safe side, cooking is sound and - as elsewhere in the hotel - lifted by lovely service. A reasonably priced wine list is nicely laid out into groups of light, crisp, medium bodied and full flavoured groups. **Seats 78**; reservations recommended; children welcome (high chair, childrens menu, baby changing facilities); toilets wheelchair accessible; air conditioning. D daily, 6-10pm; a la carte; house wine from €28. Closed 24-26 Dec. Amex, MasterCard, Visa. **Directions:** Off Fitzwilliam Square.

Dublin 2

RESTAURANT

Hô Sen

6 Cope Street Temple Bar Dublin 2 **Tel: 01 671 8181**
timcostigan@hotmail.com www.hosen.ie

The shift of emphasis for Asian food may have moved over the river to the new 'Chinatown' in the Parnell Street area, but here in Temple Bar you'll find Ireland's first authentic Vietnamese restaurant. At Hô Sen, which was our Ethnic Restaurant of the Year for 2006, the chefs are trained in Vietnam and take pride in bringing their cuisine to this pleasingly simple restaurant - and in introducing this lighter, clear-flavoured Asian cooking style at prices which are very reasonable by Dublin standards, and especially for Temple Bar where restaurants are often over-priced. Dimmed lights and candles create an appealing atmosphere from the street and, with comfortably-spaced tables, gentle background jazz and chopsticks supplied as well as western cutlery, the scene is set for an interesting evening. Vietnamese cooking has a reputation for being among the healthiest in the world and, although the familiar Asian styles feature - fresh herb flavours of coriander and lemongrass are dominant - there is a light touch to both the flavours and the cooking. An extensive menu is shorter than it seems, as it includes many variations on a theme, and dishes are explained quite clearly. Specialities include Ka Kho Tho, a hotpot made with your choice of fish from the catch of the day, in which a generous amount of fish is cooked in a rich-flavoured 'pork marinade' with mushrooms, ginger root, lemongrass and a mixture of Vietnamese herbs and spices, including chilli. Choosing an appropriate wine might be a little problematic - a riesling might be the answer, or perhaps beer or tea would be a better choice. Although the presentation isn't fancy, everything is appetising, and service is lovely - pleasant, helpful and efficient. And, as the cooking here is as exciting as the welcome is warm, this place is a little gem - and its popularity indicates that Dubliners appreciate quality and value when they find it. **Seats 120** (private room available seats 20). L Sun only 12.30-3; D Tue-Sun 5-11 (to 9pm Sun), Early Bird D €17 (5-7pm). Wines from €16.95. Closed Mon, 25 Dec. MasterCard, Visa, Laser. **Directions:** In Temple Bar, behind the Central Bank.

Dublin 2

HOTEL•RESTAURANT

Holiday Inn Dublin

98-107 Pearse Street Dublin 2 **Tel: 01 670 3666**
info@holidayinndublin.ie www.holidayinndublincitycentre.ie

The Holiday Inn brand may possibly summon up the wrong images for independent travellers, but this centrally located hotel is not only a convenient place for visitors to stay, but has earned a particularly good reputation on several counts as a venue for business meetings and conferences (parking available), for food that is well above the standard expected from a mid-range hotel, and for its helpful staff. The accommodation offers all that would be expected (plus a gym for residents' use). Conferences/Banqueting (400), secure car parking, business centre, gym. **Rooms 101**; B&B from about €55pps to €150; open all year. **The Green Bistro:** This pleasant two-tier restaurant has tasteful décor, simple darkwood furniture and an outside area under a canopy where you can eat or just have a drink. It offers good straightforward fare in a central location until 10:30pm - appealing food, freshly cooked to order, includes pizza, pasta, fish and (excellent) steaks and is good value. Live music Sunday. 12.5% service charge for groups of 6 or more. MasterCard, Visa, Laser. **Directions:** CIty centre, near Trinity College.

Dublin 2

Hugo's

RESTAURANT•WINE BAR   6 Merrion Row Dublin 2 **Tel: 01 676 5955**

www.hugos.ie

Gina Murphy and Padraig McLoughlin's welcoming wine bar and restaurant is easily recognised by its bright turquoise façade and, although only open since 2007, its location very close to St Stephen's Green has attracted a lot of customers and they've already built up a clientele of regulars who enjoy the friendly atmosphere and informality. The interior is quite atmospheric, with rich wall-paper, plenty of mirrors and wine bottles on display; a downstairs area is similar in style and has additional tables, with less formal seating towards the front. Hugo's is popular with style-conscious Dubliners and can be a busy place in the evenings, making for a convivial atmosphere - and friendly staff contribute to this ambience. An extensive wine list offers a wide choice from €20 to €300; more choice by the glass would be welcome, although those offered are a good representation of the range available. Although the main appeal of Hugo's is as a wine bar, there's a growing emphasis on food, all of which is made fresh daily (there are no freezers on the premises). Varied menus offer plenty of small/starter dishes for nibbling with a glass of wine, and also some unusual French dishes such as frogs' legs, along with long-standing favourites including home-made patés, terrines and breads, steaks and fresh fish and home-made desserts. Although service can sometimes be a little disorganised, friendly staff ensure a good atmosphere. **Seats 70** (private room, 20); not suitable for children before 9pm; not suitable for wheelchairs, air conditioning; open noon-11pm daily (from 11am Sun); L 12-5pm (to 4pm Sat/Sun); D 5-11pm; early D 15% discount on food 5-7pm Mon-Thurs, a la carte. Closed 25-27 Dec, Good Fri, 1 Jan. Amex, MasterCard, Visa, Laser. **Directions:** Just off the Baggot Street corner of St. Stephen's Green.

Dublin 2

Il Posto

RESTAURANT   10 St Stephen's Green Dublin 2 **Tel: 01 679 4769**

info@ilpostorestaurant.com www.ilpostorestaurant.com

In a prime city centre location, directly opposite St Stephen's Green, head chef Sean Drugan offers an authentic Italian experience at Il Posto, in smart warm surroundings. Diners arriving down a leafy flight of steps from the busy Dublin pavement are swiftly whisked into the restaurant, and the welcoming sight of a smart granite topped bar and wine displayed in floor-to-ceiling wooden racks. Warm terra-cottas, polished wooden floor, soft lighting, and splashes of modern artwork make for a classy atmosphere in the dining area, and well turned-out professional staff are quick to seat guests and offer menus. Written in Italian (with detailed translations in English), the menu is promising, offering a full rang of appetising antipasti, pasta, fish and meat dishes. Old favourites such as Bolognese or Vongole are there, but they sit alongside more interesting dishes – try the risotto with gorgonzola, spinach, soy beans and peas, for example. Il Posto offers hearty, imaginative Italian food based on well-judged combinations of quality ingredients, simply presented and big on taste. The wine list is exclusively Italian, with plenty of choice in the mid range, and also offering some special bottles for when the occasion demands. This is not a budget outing – given the location, the setting and quality food, how could it be – but if you're not in a rush and willing to pay a little bit extra for the experience, Il Posto offers well executed Italian food, served with style. **Seats 60** (outdoors, 10); children welcome before 8pm; L Mon-Sat, 12-2.30pm; early dinner €20, 5-7pm, D Mon-Sun from 5pm. Live music Wed, 7-9pm. SC 12.5% on groups 5+. Closed Sun L; bank hols; 25, 26, 31 Dec. Amex, MasterCard, Visa, Laser. **Directions:** On the north side of St. Stephen's Green.

Dublin 2

Il Primo Restaurant

RESTAURANT   16 Montague Street Dublin 2 **Tel: 01 478 3373**

info@ilprimo.ie www.ilprimo.ie

This long established Italian restaurant changed hands in 2007, and re-opened with chef Anita Thoma and front of house man John Farrell as the new owners. They spruced up the restaurant into a smart continental style, but the old fashioned warmth remains - and the giant picture window, where customers can see and be seen, is still the most striking feature. The ever-friendly John Farrell welcomes Italianophiles into the tiny downstairs dining area, which looks through the service bar area to the kitchen. More seating is available upstairs in two other dining rooms, though downstairs is the popular choice with regulars. Il Primo specialises in rustic Italian food, matched by mostly Tuscan wines. The wine list has long been famed and is rightly renowned, with wine imported directly from the wineries offering some unique treats as well as good prices. The menu includes some of the restaurant's old favourites, such as seafood lasagne, along with some new ones - Barolo-braised oxtail with pappardelle, for example; pasta is home-made and the effort shows in the quality. Main courses are divided into a remarkable range of risottos (you may well find the best risotto in Ireland here - try the creamy smoked haddock & chive), creative pasta dishes (crab & leek lasagne, perhaps) and gourmet pizza. The many simple dishes often have a curious twist and are evidence of Anita Thoma's wide repertory of rustic Italian food. Il Primo's informally stylish atmosphere makes it a perfect venue for the casual foodie as well as those looking for a treat without formality. Just into their second year of operation under the new régime at the time of going to press, this restaurant has established itself as a firm favourite with the growing numbers who appreciate simple, stylish, quality ingredients-led cooking. **Seats 80** (private room, 35); reservations recommended at weekend; children welcome; air conditioning. L Mon-Sat, 12.30-3, D Mon-Sat 6-11; à la carte. House wines from €19. SC 12.5% for groups 5+. Closed Sun, Bank Hols. Amex, Diners, MasterCard, Visa, Laser. **Directions:** 5 mins from Stephens Green between Harcourt Street & Wexford Street.

Dublin 2
RESTAURANT

Imperial Chinese Restaurant
12A Wicklow Street Dublin 2 **Tel: 01 677 2580**
imperial@hotmail.com

Mrs Cheung's long-established city centre restaurant pre-dates the rush to the new Parnell Street 'Chinatown' by many a long year, during which time it has enjoyed enduring popularity. Although the '80s decor has dated (some might call it retro-chic, others simply old-fashioned), staff can seem more distant than is now the style, and the atmosphere lacks the buzz of its new wave competition, many Dubliners still enjoy it for its calm atmosphere and menus that offer the choice between westernised Chinese food or a more authentic style. And it has always had a clear vote of confidence from the local Chinese community, who flock here for the Dim Sum at lunchtime - a good selection of these delectable Cantonese specialities is available between 12.30 and 5.30 daily; beef tripe is very enjoyable and Fried Seafood Noodles also attract regular praise - lots of succulent prawns, scallops and squid with Pak Choi. Crispy aromatic duck is another speciality from a wide-ranging selection of Chinese dishes. *Imperial Chinese was our Ethnic Restaurant of the Year in 1999. **Seats 180**. Children welcome. Private room available. Open daily 12-11.30 (L12.30-2.30 Mon-Sat). Set 2/3 course L about €13.50/19, Set D about €30. Also à la carte. House wine about €17. SC 10%. Closed 25-26 Dec. Amex, MasterCard, Visa, Laser. **Directions:** On Wicklow Street near Brown Thomas. ◇

Dublin 2
RESTAURANT

Jaipur
41-46 South Great Georges Street Dublin 2 **Tel: 01 677 0999**
info@jaipur.ie www.jaipur.ie

This custom-built restaurant is named after the "Jewel of Rajasthan" and offered Dubliners one of the city's first contemporary images of ethnic dining. It's a cool and spacious place, with a large modern spiral staircase leading up to an area that can be used for private parties, with the main restaurant below it. Modern decor and warm colours send the right messages and it is a pleasing space. Head chef Mahipal Roma uses mostly Irish ingredients, while importing fresh and dried spices directly, and his menus offer an attractive combination of traditional and more creative dishes. Unless in a group, when it is easy to experience a selection of dishes, first time guests might get a broad view of the offering by ordering mixed plates - beginning, perhaps, with a Jaipur kebab platter (a tandoori assortment of prawn, chicken, lamb and fish) and then a main course selection, such as Chakra Mashaari Thaali - or, for vegetarians, Chakra Shakahari Thaali. Service is invariably attentive and discreet, adding an extra dimension to a visit here. And Jaipur was the first ethnic restaurant in Ireland to devise a wine list suited to spicy foods; under regular revision, it offers a wide choice of appropriate wines across a broad price range, including over a dozen by the glass. *There is a possibility that Jaipur may relocate to a new city centre premises in the near future. **Seats 100** (private room, 50). D daily, 5.30-11.30. Early D €22, 5-7pm; also A la carte. House wine from €18. Air con. Closed 25-26 Dec. *Also at: Dalkey, Malahide, Ongar & Greystones (see entries) Amex, MasterCard, Visa, Laser. **Directions:** At the corner of Sth Great Georges St. and Lower Stephens Street.

Dublin 2
CAFÉ•RESTAURANT

Kilkenny Restaurant & Café
5-6 Nassau Street Dublin 2 **Tel: 01 677 7075**
info@kilkennyshop.com

Situated on the first floor of the shop known simply as Kilkenny, with a clear view into the grounds of Trinity College, the Kilkenny Restaurant is one of the ost pleasant places in Dublin to have a casual bite to eat - and the experience lives up to anticipation. Ingredients are fresh and additive-free (as are all the products on sale in the shop's Food Hall) and everything has a home-cooked flavour. Salads, quiches, casseroles, home-baked breads and cakes are the Kilkenny Restaurant specialities, and they are reliably good. They also do an excellent breakfast: fresh orange juice to start and then variations combinations of the traditional fare. [Kilkenny was the Dublin winner of our Irish Breakfast Awards in 2003.] A range of Kilkenny preserves and dressings - all made and labelled on the premises - is available in the shop. **Seats 190**; air conditioning; children welcome. Open Mon-Sat, 8.30-5 (Thu to 7), Sun 11-5.30. Breakfast to 11.10, lunch 12-2.30. A la carte. Licensed. Closed 25-26 Dec, 1 Jan, Easter Sun. Amex, Diners, MasterCard, Visa, Laser. **Directions:** Opposite TCD playing fields. ◊

Dublin 2
RESTAURANT

L'Ecrivain
109a Lower Baggot Street Dublin 2 **Tel: 01 661 1919**
sallyanne@lecrivain.com www.lecrivain.com

Derry and Sallyanne Clarke's acclaimed city centre restaurant is the destination of choice for many of Dublin's most discerning diners, and equally popular with the social set. On two levels - spacious and very dashing, it has lots of pale wood and smoky mirrors, and the main seating level includes a conservatory complete with awning which also acts as an airy and comfortable smoking area. Lovely elegant table settings promise seriously good food, and the cooking style - classic French with contemporary flair and a strong leaning towards modern Irish cooking - remains consistent, although new ideas are constantly incorporated and the list of specialities keeps growing. Specialities change seasonally but dishes which this kitchen has made its own include a starter of baked rock oysters with York cabbage & crispy cured bacon, with a Guinness sabayon, a fine modern interpretation of traditional Irish themes - perhaps followed by a main course of loin & rack of spring lamb with organic leeks, aubergine schnitzel and lamb sweetbreads. Menus offered by Derry Clarke and Chef de Cuisine Stephen Gibson include set menus at lunch and dinner, an à la carte and a Tasting Menu (€120) that is available to whole tables only, between 7 and 8.30pm. Whatever the time and menu, all the thoughtful little touches of a special meal abound - and there are some major ones too, like the very welcome policy of adding the price of your wine after the 10% service charge has been added to your bill, instead of charging on the total as most other restaurants do: this is an expensive restaurant but a gesture like this endears it to customers who happily dig deep into their pockets for the pleasure of eating here. Seafood, lamb, beef and game, in season, are all well represented, but menus often include neglected ingredients like rabbit, which is always appealingly served, and vegetarian dishes are handled with style. Pastry chef Joyce O'Sullivan's wonderful puddings are presented with panache and might include Black Forest Gateau fondant (cherry ice cream with cherry & white chocolate mousse), or toffee apple semi freddo; a special wine is suggested for each dish on the dessert menu and an extensive tea and coffee menu is offered. Presentation is impressive but not ostentatious, and attention to detail - garnishes designed individually to enhance each dish, careful selection of plates, delicious home-made breads and splendid farmhouse cheeses - is invariably faultless. Lunch, as usual in top rank restaurants, offers outstanding value. Sommelier Martina Delaney is renowned for her fine, constantly changing wine list, and her warmth and enthusiasm when helping guests with their wine selection; the list, which includes an impressive selection available by the bottle, half bottle or glass, also offers many special bottles a tempting range of champagnes and digestifs. [L'Ecrivain was the winner of our Wine Award in 2002.] **Seats 104** (private room, 20. outdoor seating, 22); children welcome before 9pm; air con. L Tue-Fri 12.30-2, D Tue-Sat 7-10.30, Set L 2/3 course, €30/45. Set D €75 (Vegetarian Menu about €50).

Tasting Menu €120. House wine from €30. SC discretionary. Closed L Sat, all Sun, Christmas & New Year, Easter, bank hols. Amex, MasterCard, Visa, Laser. **Directions:** 10 minutes walk east of St Stephens Green, opposite Bank of Ireland HQ. ◇

Dublin 2
RESTAURANT

L'Gueuleton
1 Fade Street Dublin 2
Tel: 01 675 3708

This no-frills French restaurant took Dublin by storm when it opened in the autumn of 2004 - so much so that, in a very short time, it became necessary to extend. The format: simple premises and no-nonsense French bistro decor, with tightly packed tables and a few seats at the bar (with views into the kitchen), plus menus that offer a combination of less usual dishes (Catalan snails with fennel and mortea sausage, perhaps) and the classic (navarin of lamb, or Toulouse sausages with choucroute and lyonnaise potatoes), and delicious seasonal desserts. A plat du jour on the lunch menu, served with a glass of wine (or coffee or juice) is popular and great value. Add to this great cooking, a short, all-French wine list (by Simon Tyrrell), pretty efficient service and terrific value for money - and you have the kind of restaurant that Dubliners had been praying for. The original chef, Troy Maguire, left amidst much publicity in 2007, to set up the new Locks (see entry), but Warren Massey has stepped into the role with aplomb and the kitchen continues to please. The only downside is the continuing no reservations policy, although the queues seem to be less of a problem since the restaurant was extended. **Seats 75** (outdoor, 20). Open Mon-Sat, L 12.30-3, D 6-10 (Bank Hols, 1-3.30pm and 6-9pm). Closed Sun. A la carte. House wines from €20. No reservations; SC 12.5% on groups 5+. MasterCard, Visa, Laser. **Directions:** Off Georges St. ◇

Dublin 2
RESTAURANT•WINE BAR
V

La Cave Wine Bar & Restaurant
28 South Anne Street Dublin 2 **Tel: 01 679 4409**
lacave@iol.ie www.lacavewinebar.com

Margaret and Akim Beskri have run this characterful place just off Grafton Street since 1989 and it's well-known for its cosmopolitan atmosphere, late night opening and lots of chat. An excellent wine list of over 350 bins (predominantly French) includes over 15 bubblies, an exceptional choice of half bottles and a separate list of wines by the glass. With its traditional bistro atmosphere and classic French cooking, it's a great place to take a break from shopping, or for an evening out, or to hold a party. Classic menus with the occasional contemporary twist might include: paté de campagne, moules marinieres, West Coast oysters, rack of Wicklow lamb, warm salad of duck livers, and tarte tatin - all indicate the style. A private room upstairs (with bar) is suitable for parties and small functions - Christmas parties are a speciality, but it's ideal for any kind of party, family reunions or even small weddings. **Seats 28** (private room, 28); children welcome before 8pm; air conditioning. Open Mon-Sat 12.30-11, Sun 5.30-11. Set L €14.25. Early D €17.25, 4-7pm Set D 2/3+ course €17.25/€32.50. Also à la carte. House wine from €18. SC discretionary. Closed L Sun, 25 Dec, Good Fri. Amex, Diners, MasterCard, Visa, Laser. **Directions:** Just off Grafton Street.

Dublin 2
CAFÉ

La Maison des Gourmets
15 Castle Market Dublin 2 **Tel: 01 672 7258**
info@la-maison.ie

In a pedestrianised area handy to car parks and away from the hustle and bustle of nearby Grafton Street, this French boulangerie has a smart little café on the first floor and also a couple of outdoor tables on the pavement for fine weather. Home-baked bread is the speciality, made to a very high standard by French bakers who work in front of customers throughout the day, creating a wonderful aroma that wafts through the entire premises. You can begin with a classic French petit dejeuner - or something a little more substantial such as a croque monsieur or a ham and cheese croissant - and their award-winning sourdough bread is used as the base for a selection of tartines (French open-style sandwiches served warm) on the lunch menu: baked ham with thyme jus and smoked bacon cream, perhaps, or vegetarian ones like roast aubergine with plum tomato, fresh parmesan & basil pesto. Add to this a couple of delicious soups (typically, French onion with Emmental croûtons), a hot dish like classic beef bourguignon with potato purée, one or two salads - and a simple dessert like strawberries with balsamic reduction and fresh cream - and, accessorised by a very tempting drinks menu - the result is as tempting a little menu as any discerning luncher could wish for. Portions are on the small side, which suits most lunchtime appetites, and service can be a little slow; but everything is very appetising, the atmosphere is chic and you can stock up on bread and croissants from the shop as you leave - just don't think in terms of a quick bite. **Seats 18** (outdoors, 10); air conditioning; children welcome. Open Mon-Sat, 8-5 (L 12-3), Sun 11-5pm. A la carte. SC discretionary. House wine about €19. Closed bank hols, 4 days Christmas. Amex, Diners, MasterCard, Visa, Laser. **Directions:** Pedestrianised area between Georges Street Arcade and Powerscourt Shopping Centre.

Dublin 2   La Mère Zou
RESTAURANT   22 St Stephen's Green Dublin 2 **Tel: 01 661 6669**
info@lamerezou.ie www.lamerezou.ie

Eric Tydgadt's French/Belgian restaurant is situated in a Georgian basement on the north side of the Green. The style is now leaner-lined and fresh, but the essence of the restaurant hasn't changed since it opened in 2000. The popularity of this pleasing restaurant is based on its reputation for classic French/Belgian country cooking, as in rillette of pork with toasted baguette or steamed mussels with French fries and reasonable pricing - a policy carried through to the wine list too. The lunch menu - which offers a choice of three dishes on each course - also suggests six or seven more luxurious seafood dishes from the à la carte, or, at the other extreme, they offer a range of Big Plates, with a salad starter and a main course served together on a king-size plate. This is one of Dublin's most pleasant and reliable restaurants, with a sister establishment, La Péniche, on the Grand Canal (see entry). **Seats 55** (private room, 8, outdoor, 6); children welcome; Live jazz Fri-Sat 9-11; L Mon-Fri, 12-3pm. D 6-10.30 (to 11pm Fri-Sat; Sun to 9.30). Early D €26 (6-7pm), also à la carte. SC discretionary (10% on groups 6+). Closed L Sat, L Sun, Bank Hols, 25 Dec - 1st Fri Jan. Amex, Diners, MasterCard, Visa, Laser. **Directions:** Beside Shelbourne Hotel. ◊

Dublin 2   The Larder
RESTAURANT   8 Parliament Street Dublin 2
Ⓝ   **Tel: 01 633 3581**

With its admirable food philosophy founded on collecting the best of ingredients in order to create delicious no nonsense food, this smartly presented restaurant under the shadow of Dublin Castle, half way along Parliament Street, is indeed aptly named. A large, inviting street window draws the eyes of passers-by to both the sparkling deli counter, where friendly staff are busy taking orders, and an impressive floor-to-ceiling display of wine, Illy coffee and San Pellegrino sparkling water. Such early promise bodes well and, on entering, you will not be disappointed by the cosy, easy-going bistro atmosphere, presented in an authentic setting of exposed brick walls, worn wooden floorboards, bentwood chairs and whispers of jazz music at just the right level. Daytime at The Larder offers a lip-smacking breakfast menu, while lunch is a deli lover's paradise of gourmet sandwiches jam-packed with quality produce - and evening brings a modest menu of starters, charcuterie and cheese platters, salads, enticing mains and desserts, boosted by blackboards offering the daily specials. The Larder takes pride in straightforward, well-executed dishes that make best use of excellent ingredients and are full of flavour: think succulent home-made burgers, beef & Guinness pie, tender lamb shank or crab cakes. And you will be well advised to leave room for delicious desserts that include freshly-baked childhood favourites such as fruit crumbles or chocolate cake, washed down with an espresso or a speciality herbal tea? A short but well selected wine list offers old and new world in equal measure, with some by the glass. The Larder is an unpretentious place that punches above its weight, taking pride in getting the basics right, and it is sure to gain a reputation well beyond the immediate area for serving excellent food - whether it be breakfast, lunch, dinner or just an aromatic coffee and a piece of cake - at highly affordable prices. A great little find. **Seats 20**; Breakfast served 7.30am to 12pm, lunch 12pm to 5:30pm, Monday to Friday, dinner served from 5:30pm to 10:30pm, no dinner on Monday. Brunch served from 9:30am until 5:30pm Saturday and Sunday, dinner served from 5:30pm to 10:30pm Saturday and Sunday. All major credit cards accepted. **Directions:** On Parliament Street opposite Dublin Castle.

Dublin 2
RESTAURANT

Léon Bistro

33 Exchequer Street Dublin 2 **Tel: 01 670 7238**
www.cafeleon.ie

Having successfully recreated a corner of Paris in Dublin with their sophisticated brand of pastry cafés, Léon has now opened its first bistro with décor that's been cleverly devised to create a genuine Gallic ambience. Choose a table down at the back amongst the mismatched chairs, large gilt mirrors, showpiece chandelier and distressed panelling and you will soon believe you're somewhere in Montmartre. The menu enhances the illusion with its list of genuine French classics; perhaps a croque madam or omelette for lunch or maybe Toulouse sausage, beef bourguignon or duck confit for dinner. There's a vast choice of authentic dishes and, although they can be a little uneven, service is relaxed and informal, making this a good spot to meet friends for a glass of wine and laid-back meal. And be sure to leave room for dessert: order a classic from the menu or choose from the dazzling pastry display up front, where individual tarts and pastries, all made in-house, ensure a meal here will always end on a high note. Open 8am-10pm Mon-Sat (to 11pm Fri-Sat); 10am-10pm Sun. House wine €20.95. ◊

Dublin 2
RESTAURANT

Les Frères Jacques

74 Dame Street Dublin 2 **Tel: 01 679 4555**
info@lesfreresjacques.com www.lesfreresjacques.com

Although the number of French restaurants/bistros in Dublin has grown a lot of late, Les Frères Jacques - which opened beside the Olympia Theatre in 1986, well before the development of Temple Bar made the area fashionable - has retained its special place as one of the very few offering genuine French fine dining. Most of the staff are French, the atmosphere is French - and the cooking is classic French. But best of all, they do it with a light touch that Irish diners especially appreciate. The decor is soothing - all the better to enjoy seasonal menus that are wide-ranging and well-balanced but - as expected when you notice the lobster tank on entering - there is a strong emphasis on fish and seafood; game also features in season, although there will always be prime meats and poultry, and vegetarians will also be offered imaginative options. Lunch at Les Frères Jacques is a treat (and good value) but dinner is a feast. The à la carte offers classics such as West Coast oysters (native or rock) and grilled lobster, individually priced, and probably game in season. Finish with cheeses (perhaps including some Irish ones) or a classic dessert like warm thin apple tart (baked to order), with cinnamon ice cream and crème anglaise. The wine list, which naturally favours France, makes interesting reading - and reductions of as much as 50% per bottle are often offered on Mondays and Tuesday. **Seats 65** (private room, 40); reservation recommended; children welcome. L Mon-Fri, 12-2; D Mon-Sat, 7-10.30. Set 2/3 course L €18/23; Set 4 course D €39; also à la carte. House wine €22. SC 12.5%. Pianist on Fri/Sat nights. Closed L Sat, all Sun, 24 Dec-3 Jan. Amex, MasterCard, Visa, Laser **Directions:** Next to Olympia Theatre. ◊

Dublin 2
BAR

Market Bar & Tapas

Fade Street Dublin 2 **Tel: 01 613 9090**
info@tapas.ie www.tapas.ie

This large bar is located in the Victorian redbrick block best known for the George's Street Market Arcade. It's an attractive space with lofty ceilings, including a mezzanine floor and simple, stylish furnishings - unfortunately the wooden floor and hard surfaces bounce noise around and there's precious little to absorb it. It was an immediate hit with young Dubliners and the food, which is cooked in an open kitchen, has earned The Market Bar a reputation for serving some of the best tapas in Dublin. The menu is loosely Spanish, offering nibbles like olives, smoked almonds and anchovies, and more substantial dishes which can be ordered as small or large portions and include appealing renditions of Spanish classics like tortilla, morcilla inchos and patatas bravas. Allowing a little licence for local tastes, and providing you don't mind eating in a busy bar, this could be a good choice for casual eating while socialising - a great place for a group of friends, not recommended for a conversational twosome. Toilets wheelchair accessible, bar access via ramp; children welcome before 7pm; air conditioning. Food daily: Mon-Sat 12-10; Sun 4-10. Closed 25-26 Dec, Good Fri. Amex, MasterCard, Visa, Laser. **Directions:** Off Georges Street.

Dublin 2
RESTAURANT

The Mermaid Café

69-70 Dame Street Dublin 2 **Tel: 01 670 8236**
info@mermaid.ie www.mermaid.ie

Ben Gorman and Mark Harrell's unusual restaurant on the edge of Temple Bar is not large, but every inch of space is used with style in two dining areas and a wine lounge. Now nearly 15 years in business here, they've achieved well-earned recognition for a personal style of hospitality, imaginative French and American-inspired cooking and interesting decor. Innovative, mid-Atlantic, seasonal cooking can be memorable for inspired combinations of flavour, texture and colour - and specialities like New England crab cakes with piquant mayonnaise, the Giant Seafood Casserole (which changes daily depending on availability) and pecan pie are retained on daily-changing menus by popular demand. Vegetables, always used imaginatively, are beautifully integrated into main courses - roast rump of lamb with parsnip mash, broad beans, morels & marjoram is a good example. Then delicious desserts, wonderful Irish cheeses (like the deeply flavoured Gabriel and Desmond from West Cork, served with apple chutney) and coffees with crystallised pecan nuts: attention to detail right to the finish. Lunch menus are extremely good value, and Sunday brunch is not to be missed if you are in the area. Wines are imported privately and are exclusive to the restaurant. **Seats 95** (private room, 40); reservations required; air conditioning; toilets wheelchair accessible. L 12.30-2.30 (Sun brunch 12-3.30pm), D 6.00-11 (Sun to 9pm). All à la carte. House wine about €23. SC discretionary except tables 5+. Closed Christmas, New Year, Good Friday. *Next door, **Gruel** (Tel 01 670 7119), is a quality fast-food bistro (60 seats) under the same management, with a large and loyal following; open Mon-Sat 11-10.30; Sun 11-9. Amex, MasterCard, Visa, Laser.
Directions: Next door to Olympia Theatre, opposite Dublin Castle.

Dublin 2
HOTEL•RESTAURANT

Merrion Hotel

Upper Merrion Street Dublin 2 **Tel: 01 603 0600**
info@merrionhotel.com www.merrionhotel.com

Right in the heart of Georgian Dublin, opposite Government Buildings, this luxurious hotel comprises four meticulously restored Grade 1 listed townhouses built in the 1760s and, behind them, a contemporary garden wing overlooks formal landscaped gardens. Luxurious public areas include two interconnecting drawing rooms with log fires and French windows (giving access to the gardens), which are immensely popular for business meetings or afternoon tea, and an attractive cocktail bar for evening time. Irish fabrics and antiques reflect the architecture and original interiors with rococo plasterwork ceilings and classically proportioned windows - and the hotel owns one of the most important private collections of 20th-century art. Maintenance is immaculate - regular refurbishment of soft furnishings, for example, is so skilfully effected that it is completely unnoticeable. Discreet, thoughtful service is an outstanding feature of the hotel and staff, under the excellent direction of General Manager Peter MacCann, are exceptionally courteous and helpful - there's a pervading sense of comfort and warmth that's especially welcoming and appealing: every guest is made to feel like a VIP from the moment of arrival - and, passing through the magnificent reception rooms, buzzing with chatter, tinkling china and crackling fires, a sense of immediate calm takes over. In a world of indentikit hotels with bland service, The Merrion feels incredibly special. Beautifully furnished guest rooms and suites have sumptuous bathrooms (all with separate bath and shower) and all the extras expected in a hotel of this calibre, including broadband, cosy bathrobes and bespoke Irish Heather & Moss toiletries. The hotel's Tethra Spa, with its Romanesque styled pool and marble steam room is predictably luxurious, and offers a compact gym and extensive treatment menu using E'Spa products. Dining options match standards elsewhere in the hotel: choose between the elegant vaulted Cellar Restaurant (see below) and Restaurant Patrick Guilbaud (see separate entry), which is also on site. Breakfast is especially noteworthy with exquisite baked goods, an excellent buffet and tempting menu cooked to order. *The Merrion Hotel was our Hotel of the Year in 2008. Conference/banqueting (60/50). Broadband wi/fi; garden; fitness room; spa; steam room; swimming pool; guides available for walking. **Rooms 143** (20 suites, 10 junior suites, 80 no smoking, 5 for disabled, ground floor bedrooms suitable for less able). Children welcome (under 2s free in parents' room, cot available free of charge, baby sitting arranged). Air conditioning. Lift. 24 hr room service, B&B €180 pps. Underground valet parking, €20 per night. Open all year. **The Cellar Restaurant:** Warm, friendly staff swiftly seat arriving guests at beautiful classically appointed tables in this elegant vaulted dining-room, and explain Executive Head Chef Eddie Cooney's well-balanced menus, which are changed daily and have a refreshingly straightforward tone. With comfortable furniture and thoughtfully designed lighting and ventilation, this is a very relaxing room - and the philosophy is to source the best ingredients and treat them with respect in a simple style that shows the food to advantage without over-emphasis on display. Seasonality is key and the signature dish of seared Bantry Bay scallops with pea purée, crispy pancetta and foie gras foam highlights their respect for quality ingredients. Pair this ethos with a good wine list (which offers an impressive amount of wines by the glass), attentive service, sound cooking and imaginative menus and you have an accessible introduction to The Merrion's high standards. *In fine summer weather the hotel also offers dining outdoors on the terrace. **Seats 86**; air conditioning; children welcome; L Mon-Fri 12.30-2, Set L €24.95; D daily 6-10, early D 6-7 Mon-Thurs €32.50, also à la carte. Sun Brunch 12.30-2.30. **The Cellar Bar:** Much more than an ordinary bar, this atmospheric series of vaulted rooms is everything you could wish for in the bar of an outstanding hotel. In an interesting reverse of the usual procedure, an exciting new wine list offering a remarkable range of wines, sherries, champagnes and dessert wines by the glass or bottle has been the inspiration for new lunch and evening menus devised by the hotel's Executive Head Chef, Eddie Cooney. To the best of our knowledge, this is a new departure for an Irish hotel - changed times indeed. Open all year. Amex, Diners, MasterCard, Visa, Laser. **Directions:** City centre, opposite Government Buildings.

Dublin 2
HOTEL

Mont Clare Hotel

Merrion Square Dublin 2 **Tel: 01 607 3800**
info@ocallaghanhotels.com www.ocallaghanhotels.com

A few doors away from the National Gallery, this well-located and relatively well-priced hotel is in common ownership with the nearby Davenport and Alexander Hotels, and is a popular choice for business guests. The hotel is imaginatively decorated in contemporary style - except for the old stained glass and mahogany Gallery Bar, which has retained its original pubby atmosphere. Compact bedrooms are comfortable and have been recently refurbished - and executive rooms for business guests have full marbled bathrooms and good amenities, including air conditioning, three direct line phones, a personal safe, broadband and multi-channel TV with DVD. Conference/banqueting (200); business centre; use of gym (at Davenport Hotel). **Rooms 74** (40 no-smoking); children welcome (Under 2s free in parents' room; cots available free of charge). No pets. Lift. Parking. Room rate from €175. Closed 23-28 Dec. Amex, Diners, MasterCard, Visa, Laser. **Directions:** Corner of Clare Street, just off Merrion Square. ◊

Dublin 2
RESTAURANT

Montys of Kathmandu

28 Eustace Street Temple Bar Dublin 2 **Tel: 01 670 4911**
montys@eircom.net www.montys.ie

Shiva Gautham's long established and modest-looking restaurant opposite the Irish Film Centre is one of the few in Ireland to specialise in Nepalese cuisine - including his own new branch in Rathgar. The chefs are all from Nepal and, although all the familiar Indian styles are represented - tandoori, curry etc - the emphasis is on Nepalese specialities and varying standard dishes by, for example, using Himalayan spices. The menu is quite extensive and includes a platter of assorted starters which is a good choice for a group of four, allowing time to consider the rest of the menu without rushing; there's also a fair selection of vegetarian dishes, including a traditional Nepali mixed vegetable curry which can be served mild, medium or hot. Friendly and exceptionally helpful staff are an outstanding feature of the restaurant - service throughout is gently attentive and staff are happy to offer suggestions, or to choose a well-balanced meal for you, including specialities like Kachela (a starter of raw minced lamb with garlic, ginger, herbs and spices which is said to be a favourite amongst the Newars in Kathmandu, served with a shot of whiskey) and Momo - these Nepalese dumplings served with a special chutney require 24 hours notice and are 'the most popular dish in Kathmandu'. But you will also find sound renditions of old favourites here, including Chicken Tika Masala: moist pieces of tender boneless chicken cooked in the tandoori, and served in a creamy masala sauce. This can be a really rewarding restaurant; the food is invariably enjoyable - and at agreeably moderate prices. And, in addition to an extensive wine list (organised by price) and drinks menu, they even have their own beer, 'Shiva', brewed exclusively for the restaurant. **Seats 60** (private room, 30); children welcome. L Mon-Sat, 12-2; Set L about €20; D daily 6-11.30pm, (Sun to 10.30), Tasting Menu about €50. L&D à la carte available. SC 12.5% on groups 6+. House wine from €18. Closed L Sun, 25-26 Dec, 1 Jan & Good Fri. Amex, MasterCard, Visa, Laser. **Directions:** Temple Bar - opposite the Irish Film Centre(IFC).

Dublin 2 Morgan Hotel

HOTEL 10 Fleet Street Temple Bar Dublin 2 **Tel: 01 643 7000**

sales@themorgan.com www.themorgan.com

In deepest Temple Bar, this unusual boutique hotel is characterised by clean simple lines and uncluttered elegance. Bedrooms have beds in light beech, with classic white cotton bed linen and natural throws, while standard bedroom facilities include satellite TV and DVD, CD/hi-fi system, mini-bar, safe, voicemail and Internet access. Bathrooms in the better rooms are spacious and spare in style, although some less desirable rooms have shower only; some rooms also have a sound-proofing problem and it would be wise to ensure that your room is not over the bar. Staff are very helpful and there are nice touches about the hotel, such as having an umbrella available on loan for the duration of your stay. An excellent buffet breakfast offers lots of fresh fruit as well as yoghurts, muesli, good croissants and other breads, cheeses, charcuterie, good coffee and the usual full fry at about €18 per person. The stylish Morgan Bar is open all day and offers an oasis of comfort and relaxation amongst the hustle and bustle of Temple Bar - try an exotic Morgan Mai Tai, perhaps? Casual dining is available in the Morgan Bar, where an excellent (and extensive) tapas menu is served all day (12 noon until 10pm). Conferences/Banqueting (65); business centre, laptop sized safe in bedrooms, free broadband wi/fi. **Rooms 121** (16 suites, 30 no-smoking, 2 disabled). Children welcome (cots available without charge, baby sitting arranged). Lift. Room rate €160. Closed Christmas. Amex, Diners, MasterCard, Visa, Laser. **Directions:** off Westmoreland Street.

Dublin 2 Nude Café

CAFÉ 21 Suffolk Street Dublin 2 **Tel: 01 672 5577**

niamh@nude.ie www.nude.ie

Nude offers very fresh casual food - organic whenever possible - in a cool, youthful environment. Just off Grafton Street, it's a great place for a healthy breakfast or a quick snack, with plenty of room to sit down at long canteen-style tables. Queue up, order and pay at the till, then collect your food if it's ready or it will be delivered to your table. Just looking at the fresh fruit and vegetables hanging or racked up in the open kitchen should revive you while you wait! (And you may have to wait a while sometimes, as service can be a little slow). A choice of soups all come with with freshly baked breads; there are hot wraps - or try the chill cabinet for salads like Caesar or tomato & mozzarella, and cold wraps or soft bread rolls. Freshly squeezed juices, smoothies and organic Fair Trade coffees, teas and herbal teas are all very popular and the menu caters for vegetarians and other dietary requirements. **Seats 40.** Open daily 7.30am-9pm (to 10pm Thurs, 8pm Sun). *Also at: 38 Upper Baggot St 01 668 0551; George's Quay, 01 677 4661; Dublin Airport. MasterCard, Visa, Laser. **Directions:** Near Dublin Tourism office.

Dublin 2 Number 31

GUESTHOUSE 31 Leeson Close Lr Leeson Street Dublin 2 **Tel: 01 676 5011**

number31@iol.ie www.number31.ie

Formerly the home of leading architect, the late Sam Stephenson, Noel and Deirdre Comer's hospitable 'oasis of tranquillity and greenery' just off St Stephen's Green has undergone major refurbishment recently, and it makes a relaxing and interesting city centre base, with virtually everything within walking distance in fine weather. You approach the Georgian townhouse from the garden, and the welcome is warm and friendly (tea/coffee and cookies served as your car is being parked in their secure car park); public areas of the house are spacious and very comfortable, and the accommodation is in two different buildings - the elegant Georgian town-house on Fitzwilliam Place (decorated in deep tones) and the beautifully converted coach-house (much brighter), with an interconnecting patio garden. The elegant bedrooms have exceptionally comfortable beds, good bathrooms, and nice little extras including complimentary bottled water as well as phones, flat screen TV and DVD player. And breakfasts, served at communal tables inside, and in the conservatory, are a treat to treasure: juices, fresh fruit and cereals on display, freshly baked breads and delicious preserves, and lovely hot dishes like kippers, Eggs Benedict or scrambled egg with smoked salmon all cooked to order... it has a homely feel, as the kitchen is beside the breakfast room and there is no door, so you can watch as your breakfast is being prepared. Prices are moderate for central Dublin, and this is a lovely place to stay - in fact, with its stay-in-all-day atmosphere, you might find it hard to leave. **Rooms 21** (all en-suite & no smoking). Room rate from €240, ss €25; not suitable for children under 10; no pets; free broadband wi/fi. Rooms at the back are quieter. Secure parking. Open all year. Amex, MasterCard, Visa. **Directions:** From St. Stephens Green onto Baggot St., turn right on to Pembroke St. and left on to Leeson Street.

Dublin 2
PUB•GUESTHOUSE

O'Neill's Pub & Townhouse
37 Pearse Steet Dublin 2 **Tel: 01 671 4074**
oneilpub@iol.ie www.oneillsdublin.com

Established in 1885, this centrally located pub on the corner of Pearse Street and Shaw Street is easily recognised by the well-maintained floral baskets that brighten up the street outside. Inside, this cosy bar has kept its Victorian character and charm (two bars have lots of little alcoves and snugs) and serves a good range of reasonably priced home-cooked food - typically steak champignon with red wine sauce, served with French fries and an attractive salad; lamb filo parcels with mint yoghurt and chilli con carne - all good value. [B&B accommodation is available in en-suite rooms above the pub; quite expensive for simple accommodation (from €45-65 pps) but conveniently located and useful to know about.] Bar food: L 12.30-2.30, D 5.30-8. Closed Christmas & Good Fri. Amex, MasterCard, Visa, Laser. **Directions:** Opposite Pearse Street side of Trinity College.

Dublin 2
BAR•RESTAURANT

Odessa Lounge & Grill
13/14 Dame Court Dublin 2 **Tel: 01 670 7634**
info@odessa.ie www.odessa.ie

Tucked away just a few minutes walk from Grafton Street, this was one of the first places in Dublin to do brunch - a smart entrance gives way to a fashionably furnished restaurant and, downstairs, a more clubby room with comfy leather chairs, subdued lighting, and plenty of room to spread out and read the papers in peace, is an appealing place to be after a late night on the town. Menus, which were ahead of fashion when Odessa opened in 1994 and have changed little since, have an emphasis on seasonal ingredients - fresh seafood is a good bet and may include Galway Bay lobster and wild Irish crab, when available. Inconsistent cooking and disorganised service were weaknesses on a recent visit by the Guide, however. *The Odessa Club (www.odessaclub.ie) is a private Members Bar with screening facilities on the second floor, and is affiliated with Societe De Kring (www.kring.nl) in Amsterdam; wine tasting dinners are held regularly, and Odessa Club members are offered a special rate for accommodation nearby at **Grafton House** (www.graftonguesthouse.com; Tel 01 679 2041), 26/27 South Great George's Street. **Seats 190** (private room, 60); air conditioning. Sat & Sun open brunch 11.30-4.30; D daily 6-11, Early bird D about €20 (Sun-Fri, 6-7); Set D about €28/40 2/4 course. House Wine €20. SC 12.5%. Closed Bank Hols, 25/26 Dec. Amex, MasterCard, Visa, Laser. **Directions:** Just off George's Street / Exchequer Street. ◇

Dublin 2
RESTAURANT
😋 ★ ♟

One Pico Restaurant
5-6 Molesworth Place Schoolhouse Lane Dublin 2 **Tel: 01 676 0300**
www.onepico.com

Quietly located in a laneway near St. Stephen's Green, just a couple of minutes walk from Grafton Street, Eamonn O'Reilly's One Pico is one of Dublin's most popular fine dining restaurants. The surroundings are elegant, with crisp white linen and fine china and glassware, and the cooking is exceptionally good: sophisticated, technically demanding dishes are invariably executed with confidence and flair. The range of menus offered includes lunch and pre-theatre menus which, as usual in restaurants of this calibre, represent great value, an 8-course Tasting Menu, a vegetarian menu (on request), and an à la carte, with about ten quite luxurious dishes offered on each course, plus optional side dishes which should not be necessary as each main course is individually garnished. There is an occasional small nod to Irish traditions, but this is classical French cooking with a modern twist, albeit based for the most part on the very best local produce (suppliers are noted on the menu). Eamonn O'Reilly cooks with first class ingredients, turning them into classic dishes with lovely clean flavours, and his own unique style on each dish. Examples include creative seafood dishes - perfectly cooked pan-roasted bream with celeriac purée, celeriac fondant and red wine reduction, perhaps - and also upbeat versions of traditional meat dishes such as medallions of beef with asparagus and parma ham, fondant potatoes and béarnaise sauce. To finish, it is difficult to decide between an innovative and delicious cheese menu, or beautifully presented desserts that taste as good as they look - such as a gorgeous poached meringue with toasted nuts, lemon curd and vanilla cream, perhaps. Service - under the direction of restaurant manager, Andrew Scott, and sommelier, Arnaud Legat - is professional and friendly. A well chosen wine list offers some 80 bottles, with a dozen or so available by the glass. This is a fine restaurant and has earned its place among the city's best. *A sister restaurant is Bleu Bistro Moderne - see entry. **Seats 65** (private room, 46); air conditioning. L& D Mon-Sat: L12-3, D 6-11. Set 2/3 course L €29/35, Value D €45 (all evening Mon-Wed & 6-7.30pm Thurs-Sat); Set D €38, also à la carte. House wine €28. SC discretionary. Closed Sun, bank hols, 24 Dec-5 Jan. Amex, Diners, MasterCard, Visa, Laser. **Directions:** 2 mins walk off St Stephens Green/Grafton Street near government buildings.

Dublin 2

RESTAURANT•WINE BAR

Pearl Brasserie

20 Merrion Street Upper Dublin 2 **Tel: 01 661 3572**

info@pearl-brasserie.com www.pearl-brasserie.com

RESTAURANT OF THE YEAR

Just a few doors away from The Merrion Hotel, Sebastien Masi and Kirsten Batt's stylish basement restaurant has recently undergone a complete refurbishment - and very swish it is too. With the natural qualities of rough stone walls, an open fireplace, and a mixture of comfortable leather and softly floral highback chairs seen against sleek polished wooden floors, pale walls and subtle lighting, the ambience is of simple sophistication - smart, yet friendly. And romantic too, especially the dotey arched alcove for two, with padded upholstered ceiling... And the whole experience seems to have geared up a little in tune with the warmly sophisticated new décor. This has always been a delightful restaurant and very much 'itself,' but there is a new edge to it now that makes it a really outstanding dining destination. Sebastien - an excellent chef who is known for the assured contemporary international spin that he brings to a classic French base - lays a pleasing emphasis on clean flavours which highlight the quality of ingredients, many of which are local and occasionally give dishes an Irish bias. Several menus are offered, including an appealing vegetarian menu with four choices on each course; and - something which will make this restaurant especially attractive in the present economic climate - prices are very reasonable for a restaurant at this level, and in this area. There is a leaning towards fish and seafood, which Sebastien cooks with accuracy and flair - a beautifully simple main course of classic black sole fillet grenobloise with new potatoes, capers, lemon segments & fresh croutons, for example - while specialities from the land include luscious squab pigeon rossini - served with black truffle mashed potato...; other main courses include prime meats - pan-fried aged fillet of Irish beef with cèpe persillade and cèpe sauce, is a popular dish, and there are marginally less usual luxurious but equally enjoyable dishes such as seared organic salmon, aubergine caviar and baby courgette with pine kernel & herb ravioli. Desserts are a highlight and include particularly good ices, then coffee is served with home-made chocolates. And, under Kirsten Batt's direction, Sebastien Masi's delicious and beautifully presented meals are matched by exceptional service - from the moment you are greeted until saying goodbye, warm, friendly yet professional staff seem totally dedicated to making everyone feel at home and relaxed; equally, sommelier Julien Hennebert's interesting and informative wine list, is a good match for the food, favouring France and including a fine Sommelier's Choice selection and an unusual choice of half bottles. All round, an exceptional dining experience. **Seats 80** (private area, 10); children welcome; reservations recommended; air-conditioning. L Mon-Fri 12-2.30, D Mon-Sat 6-10.30. 'Value' L €24, D à la carte; also vegetarian menu. House wine €21. SC discretionary. Closed Sun, bank hols. Amex, MasterCard, Visa, Laser. **Directions:** Opposite Government Building, near Merrion Hotel.

Dublin 2 The Pembroke

PUB 31/32 Lower Pembroke Street Dublin 2 **Tel: 01 676 2980**
info@pembroke.ie www.pembroke.ie

This is a place with some character of its own and, along with some striking design features (notably the lighting), the atrium/conservatory area at the back brings the whole place to life, and there is space for a large number of outdoor tables. Meeting the needs of those who get in to work before the traffic builds up, good bar food begins with an impressive breakfast menu offering everything from cereals or muesli to the Full Irish, with all sorts of more sophisticated treats like scrambled egg with smoked salmon. Later menus offer appealing hot dishes and a range of bar snacks - lunch is basically a carvery/buffet, but better than that description implies; business people in the area find it a useful and reliable place to eat, and to bring their clients for lunch. **Seats 200** (private room 60, outdoor seating 80). Food served Mon-Sat, 7.30am-9pm (L 12-3pm). Closed Sun, Christmas & Good Fri. Amex, Diners, MasterCard, Visa, Laser. **Directions:** Near St Stephen's Green - off Lr Baggot Street.

Dublin 2 Peploe's Wine Bistro

RESTAURANT 16 St Stephen's Green Dublin 2 **Tel: 01 676 3144**

reception@peploes.com www.peploes.com

In the basement of the Georgian terrace than runs along the north side of St Stephen's Green, Peploe's is very handy to both the Grafton Street area and the nearby offices - perfect territory for a laid-back wine bar. The retro décor is reminiscent of a chic 1950s New York brasserie and creates a warm and inviting atmosphere, complete with neat table settings and stylishly-dressed staff. Although the dining room appears cramped, it is comfortable and the service is pleasant and professional. You can usually have an aperitif at the bar and the menu offers a good variety of dishes, which would be equally suitable for having an appetiser or two (from a choice of ten starters, or 'savouries') to accompany your wine or a full meal, and the dozen or so main courses are well-balanced between pasta, meat and fish, plus the chef's specials which are notified at the table. A choice of good breads gets your meal off to a good start, followed by quite unusual dishes such as pistachio crusted goat's cheese wrapped in parma ham and served with tomato berries (heart-shaped cherry tomatoes) or Morteau sausage (speciality pork sausage from Franche Comté) with horseradish potatoes and tartare sauce. Main courses might include rabbit 'en croûte' with a fricassée of vegetables in a champagne sauce while the chef's special is likely to be deliciously fresh fish. There's a fair sprinkling of luxurious ingredients on the evening menus, and prices aren't above average for the location. A generous seasonal crumble would be enough for two people and delightfully fruity, or you could finish with a choice of French and Irish cheeses, and good coffee. An extensive wine list includes a dozen or more champagnes and about thirty wines by the glass. Service is generally smart, the atmosphere is great and the cooking has style - all this and a fairly reasonable bill too. **Seats 90**. Reservations required; air conditioning; children welcome. Open 12.30-3.30pm & 6-10.30pm daily; L&D à la carte, also set L €39 and set D €55; house wine €22; SC 12.5% on groups 6+. Closed 24-29 Dec, Good Fri. Amex, MasterCard, Visa, Laser. **Directions:** North side of St. Stephen's Green.

Dublin 2 The Pigs Ear

RESTAURANT 4 Nassau Street Dublin 2 Dublin City **Tel: 01 670 3865**

bookings@thepigsear.ie www.thepigsear.ie

It may have served some of Dublin's finest food for years but Jacob's Ladder closed its doors in the summer of 2008, making way for an interesting newcomer, The Pig's Ear. With the same great upstairs location overlooking Trinity College's playing fields, diners can expect two bright and contemporary dining rooms, simply styled with pale varnished floorboards, dark wood furniture, and several smart feature mirrors. There's a few ornamental pigs dotted about the rooms too, which make a fun and cute feature. Tables are generously spaced and plainly set, but there's nothing plain about the food. Head chef Stephen McAllister, well known as a TV chef on RTE's The Restaurant programme and The Afternoon Show, has an impressive CV that's seen him work in the kitchens of many of Dublin's leading restaurants, including One Pico, L'Ecrivain and Restaurant Patrick Guilbaud. Here his menu takes traditional Irish favourites, presenting them in fresh, creative ways. Bacon and cabbage is served with creamy mashed potato and rich parsley sauce, signature lamb shepherds pie comes in a novel glass jar, while a starter of egg mayonnaise is made with hens eggs and served with smoked paprika. There are several creative seafood dishes too, all following the same principle of good ingredients, simply cooked. Desserts are tasty and traditional, maybe fruit crumble, sherry trifle or lemon tart, and there's the fun option of ordering a jar of Bourbon creams, custard creams or penny sweets with your coffee! The wine list offers plenty of choice across a wide price range, with 12 well-chosen wines by the glass, and there's Guinness, Budweiser and Carlsberg on tap. Service is very pleasant, there's a relaxed buzz to the place, and the cooking should please a wide audience. **Directions:** City centre overlooking Trinity College.

Dublin 2   # The Port House
RESTAURANT•WINE BAR   64a South William St Dublin 2 **Tel: 01 677 0298**

info@porthouse.ie www.porthouse.ie

This more recent Dublin venture by the team who created The Porterhouse (Parliament Street and other branches), bears all their hallmark attention to detail - the wine bottles on high shelves, warm brick walls, remains of an old fireplace, flagged floors and simple mismatched modern furniture make this basement wine bar highly atmospheric, especially when seen in candlelight. But, although that's a great start (and The Port House has been such a success that they've opened up a new floor above the original restaurant), there's more to this little place than atmosphere and they deliver well on the food side too, bringing a taste of Spain to South William Street. Menus offer a couple of dozen tapas-size items (think 'small starter'), divided into hot and cold 'pinchos'; order a few to share and see how it goes, depending on whether you're just having a drink and a nibble or want the equivalent of a light meal. There are some tempting items on offer, some more familiar than others: nibbles like toasted almonds with paprika, less usual offerings such as foie gras or mini sirloin steaks, and regional Spanish cheeses and tasty renditions of many of the well known tapas classics like calamares rabas (squid in batter), tostas de setas (mushrooms with garlic butter), tortilla (Spanish omelette) and patatas bravas (deep fried potato cubes with tomato sauce). Cooking is good and it's fun. There are some value wines, and also some interesting Basque bottled beers too (the ale and lager are perhaps better than the stout). **Seats 100** (private room, 6, outdoors, 6); no reservations accepted; not suitable for children under 10 yrs; air conditioning; Tapas served daily, all day 11-1am (Sun to 11pm); house wine from €3.50 per glass. Closed 25-26 Dec. MasterCard, Visa, Laser. **Directions:** A few doors up from the corner of Exchequer St and South William Street.

Dublin 2   # The Porterhouse
PUB   16-18 Parliament Street Temple Bar Dublin 2 **Tel: 01 679 8847**

www.theporterhouse.ie

Dublin's first micro-brewery pub opened here in 1996 and, although others have since set up, The Porterhouse was at the cutting edge. Ten different beers are brewed on the premises and connoisseurs can sample a special tasting tray selection of plain porter (a classic light stout), oyster stout (brewed with fresh oysters, the logical development of a perfect partnership), Wrasslers 4X (based on a West Cork recipe from the early 1900s, and said to be Michael Collins' favourite tipple), Porter House Red (an Irish Red Ale with traditional flavour), An Brain Blasta (dangerous to know) and the aptly named Temple Brau. But you don't even have to like beer to love The Porterhouse. The whole concept is an innovative move away from the constraints of the traditional Irish pub and yet it stays in tune with its origins - it is emphatically not just another theme pub. The attention to detail which has gone into the decor and design is a constant source of pleasure to visitors and the food, while definitely not gourmet, is a cut above the usual bar food. And, like the pub itself, the food combines elements of tradition with innovation: Carlingford oysters, Irish stew, beef & Guinness casserole are there, along with the likes of home-made burgers and a good range of salads. This is a real Irish pub in the modern idiom and was a respected winner of our Pub of the Year award in 1999. **Seats 50**; no children after 9pm. Open 11.30 - 12 daily (Thu-Sat to 2/2.30). Bar food served 12-9 daily (Sun 12.30-9.30). Closed 25 Dec & Good Fri. [*The original Porterhouse is located on Strand Road on the seafront in Bray, Co. Wicklow and, like its sister pub in Temple Bar, it offers bar food daily from 12.30-9.30. Tel/Fax: 01 286 1839. There is also a Porterhouse in London, at Covent Garden.] MasterCard, Visa.

POWERSCOURT TOWNHOUSE CENTRE

Built in 1774 as a Town House for Lord Powerscourt, it was extensively refurbished and opened as a Shopping Centre in 1981. It is right in the middle of the Grafton Street/Georges Street shopping area and, whilst offering interesting shops, Powerscourt Townhouse is also home to a selection of bars, restaurants and cafés, some within a lovely central atrium that can be particularly restful especially when there is a pianist playing. Promising places to drop into for a bite include **Café Fresh** (see entry), well known for its delicious vegetarian and vegan food; **La Corte** (01 633 4477), from the Dunne & Crescenzi stable (see entries), provides simple Italian food and great coffee; **Ba Mizu** (01 674 6712) is a stylish bar/restaurant serving an appealing contemporary menu, and **Mimo** (01 679 4160) - a sister establishment - is on the top floor, serving coffee, food and wine in an informal, relaxed and spacious environment. For more information on Powerscourt Townhouse see their website, www.powerscourtcentre.com.

Dublin 2   **The Purty Kitchen**
BAR•RESTAURANT   34/35 Essex Street Temple Bar Dublin 2 **Tel: 01 677 0945**
            info@purtykitchen.com www.purtykitchen.com

In the heart of Temple Bar, this younger sister of the popular Purty Kitchen in Monkstown offers some comfort and respite in a very busy part of the city. It's in a street corner pub with an authentic stone period frontage and, inside, a large high-ceilinged u-shaped room with an impressive bar in the centre, and large front windows which create a pleasing sense of space and lots of natural light. A dark wooden floor and polished darkwood furniture lend character to the relaxed, uncluttered space, and traditional booths offer a little privacy. An extensive bar menu features a good selection of appetisers, salads, open sandwiches (served on the Purty Kitchen's home-made seed bread), steaks, home-made burgers and chicken; there's an emphasis on fish and seafood, including specialities of Purty Seafood Chowder and the Purty Seafood Platter. In addition to a well-stocked, bar there is also a well-balanced wine list, with some offered by the glass. Staff are friendly but it can sometimes be difficult to get their attention. Although recent visits by the Guide suggest that the high standards set by the Purty Kitchen when it first opened are not always being maintained, at its best it offers tasty food, served in comfortable surroundings and at reasonable prices - plus a packed schedule of late night entertainment during the weekends - and can be a welcome refuge from busy Temple Bar. Mon-Wed: midday-12.30am, Fri-Sun: 12-3.30am. Food served daily from midday until 9pm. Closed Mon. All major credit cards accepted. ◊

Dublin 2   **Queen of Tarts**
CAFÉ   4 Cork Hill Dame Street Dublin 2
                              Tel: 01 670 7499

Behind Yvonne and Regina Fallon's quaint traditional shopfront near Dublin Castle lies an equally quaint traditional tea room, with warmly welcoming friendly and efficient staff, and wonderful smells wafting across the room as they struggle to make space for new arrivals to the comfortable, lived-in little room. Yvonne and Regina both trained as pastry chefs, but there's nothing 'cheffy' about the good home baking that you'll find here - the emphasis is on wholesomeness and real flavour. Service begins with breakfast (including a vegetarian cooked breakfast) which is served until the lunch/afternoon menu takes over at noon. Home-made scones, buttermilk brown bread, roast chicken & coriander tartlets, warm plum tarts with cream, chocolate fudge cake, orange chocolate pinwheel cookies and much else besides take their place on a surprisingly extensive menu, which includes some seriously good sandwiches and salads - most people pop in for a snack, but you could just as easily have a 3-course lunch. Inexpensive, consistently excellent food, lovely atmosphere and great service - what more could anyone ask? [*Also at: City Hall, Dame St. Tel 01 672 2925; and 3-4 Cow's Lane, Temple Bar]. **Seats 25**; air conditioning; toilets wheelchair accessible; children welcome. Open daily: Mon-Fri 7.30-7 (L12-7); Sat/Sun 8.30-7. Closed 24 Dec-02 Jan, bank hols. No Credit Cards. **Directions:** Opposite the gates of Dublin Castle.

Dublin 2
CAFÉ

The Reader's Café at Waterstones

Waterstones Bookshop 7 Dawson Street Dublin 2
Tel: 01 672 9932

Offering somewhere in a bookshop where you can relax over a good cup of coffee or a tasty bite to eat makes a great deal of sense, and the café upstairs at the back of Waterstones is a great spot for taking a break while reading a book from the shop, or from a browsing selection available on the tables. Although it may seem slightly confusing on arrival (it's a good idea to get the waiter's attention before getting settled) the food is simple, wholesome and reasonably priced - and there is some seating in the bookshop area proper, with communal tables in a pleasant room at the back. This is one of the few places you may expect to find Dublin coddle (aah...), and the menu also features good soups and patés and a choice of sandwiches, all for €8-€10. The service may be disorganised but for someone browsing in a bookshop time this is probably not a priority - and the good food and reasonable prices more than compensate. A handy place to know about. As bookshop, Mon - Sun, 9am - 7pm **Directions:** Bottom of Dawson Street in Waterstones Bookshop.

Dublin 2
RESTAURANT
⬛★★☆🍽

Restaurant Patrick Guilbaud

21 Upper Merrion Street Dublin 2 **Tel: 01 676 4192**
restaurantpatrickguilbaud@eircom.net
www.restaurantpatrickguilbaud.net

For over a quarter of a century this spacious, elegant French restaurant in a Georgian townhouse adjoining the Merrion Hotel has been the leading fine dining restaurant in Ireland. Approached from the street or directly from the hotel through a fine drawing room, where drinks are served, the restaurant is a bright, airy room, enhanced by an outstanding collection of Irish art (inspiration for the bespoke carpet which sets the tone for the new, improved restaurant which emerged after major refurbishment in 2007), and opens on to a terrace and landscaped gardens which make a delightful setting for drinks and al fresco dining in summer. Head chef Guillaume Lebrun has presided over this fine kitchen since the restaurant opened in its original premises in 1981, and is renowned for exceptional modern classic cuisine, based on the best Irish produce in season: his luxurious, wide-ranging menus include a wonderfully creative 9-course Tasting Menu (€150), themed as 'Sea & Land', perhaps, and celebrating traditional Irish themes with Gallic flair; at the other end of the spectrum, a daily table d'hôte lunch menu offers the best value fine dining in Ireland. Contemporary French cooking at its best, combined with the precision and talents of a team of gifted chefs, produces dishes of dexterity, appeal and exceptional flavour: a speciality starter of lobster ravioli, for example, is made from Clogherhead lobster coated in a coconut-scented lobster cream and served with hand made free range egg pasta, toasted almonds and lightly curry-flavoured olive oil. The main course house speciality is a magnificent dish of Challan duck (for two people) and, in due course, an assiette of chocolate ends your meal in spectacular fashion, with a plate of no less than five cold and hot chocolate desserts. Consistent excellence is the order of the day: cheeses are supplied by Sheridan's cheesemongers, breads are home-made, and the extensive and mostly French wine list includes some great classics, alongside some reasonably-priced offerings. A visit here is always an experience to treasure, each dish a masterpiece of beautiful presentation, contrasting textures and harmonious flavours, all matched by faultless service - under the relaxed supervision of Restaurant Manager Stéphane Robin, service is invariably immaculate, and Patrick Guilbaud himself is usually present to greet guests personally. Every capital city has its great restaurant and this is Dublin's gastronomic heaven: Restaurant Patrick Guilbaud continues to set the standard by which all others are judged. **Seats 80** (private room, The Roderic O'Conor Room is available for up to 25 people); children welcome; air conditioning. L & D Tue-Sat 12.30-2.15, D 7.30-10.15. Set L €35/45 for 2/3 courses. Vegetarian Menu (Main courses from €28). 9-course Tasting Menu €150. L&D à la carte available. House wine from about €38. SC discretionary. Closed Sun & Mon, bank hols, Christmas week. Amex, Diners, MasterCard, Visa, Laser. **Directions:** Opposite Government Buildings.

Dublin 2

RESTAURANT

Riva Restaurant

Unit 1 Hanover Quay Grand Canal Dock Dublin 2 **Tel: 01 675 3577**

rivarestaurant@gmail.com www.rivarestaurant.eu

Dublin's Dockland development has proven a magnet for eclectic eateries, with the southside Hanover Quay becoming something of a restaurant walkway. The waterside location is unrivalled in Dublin, tucked away from the traffic, yet with uninterrupted views of the Grand Canal Dock and flanked by handsome apartments. Riva, the latest venture from Dieter Bergman (former owner of the popular Il Primo), has maximised on the location, with a generous terrace packed with continental style café furniture. Vast plate glass windows wrap around the restaurant, allowing diners enjoy the views, no matter what the weather. (We love the thoughtful stack of soft blankets, ready to pass out to al fresco diners braving the elements.) The menu is pan-European, with heavy Italian leanings, and offers a vast range of dishes, from light salads to comforting casseroles and seafood to roasted joints. The vegetarian antipasti starter is large enough to share, its delicious Portobello mushrooms being especially good. A creative risotto section is followed by pasta dishes, all made with excellent homemade pasta, while carnivores have plenty of choice, including steak and chips, lambs liver or maybe duck confit. A plat du jour offers a different daily special, perhaps coq au vin or duck cassoulet. Riva was quite new as the guide went to press, and the menu, despite using good ingredients, may benefit from some fine-tuning. On the other hand Staff are enthusiastic, commendably well versed in the menu and attentive; the service is excellent, suiting the relaxed décor and continental food. Wine is a big deal here, with a room-length bar stylishly stacked with display bottles. The prices range hugely, so you can drink modestly or splurge on an old world name. It's a relaxing space for lunch or dinner, and an equally good choice for a date or with a larger group. **Seats 120**; children welcome (high chair); air conditioning; wheelchair friendly; reservations recommended. Open daily, 12-11pm (to 9pm Sun); house wine from €18. MasterCard, Visa, Laser. **Directions:** On Hanover Quay.

Dublin 2

RESTAURANT

Saagar Indian Restaurant

16 Harcourt Street Dublin 2 **Tel: 01 475 5060 / 5012**

info@saagarindianrestaurants.com www.saagarindianrestaurants.com

Meera and Sunil Kumar's highly-respected basement restaurant just off St Stephen's Green is one of Dublin's longest established Indian restaurants and, although it is an old building with an interesting history (Bram Stoker, author of Dracula, once lived here), it has a contemporary feel, with wooden flooring and restrained decor - and a music system featuring the latest Indian music. It is an hospitable place and you will be warmly welcomed - and probably offered a drink in the little bar while choosing from the menu. The cooking is consistently good, with menus (mainly à la carte although set menus are also available) offering a wide range of regional speciality dishes, all prepared from fresh ingredients and considerably coded with a range of one to four stars to indicate the heat level. Thus Malai Kabab is a safe one-star dish, while traditional Lamb Balti and Lamb Aayish (marinated with exotic spices and cooked in a cognac-flavoured sauce) is a three-star and therefore pretty hot. Beef and pork are not served but this is balanced by a good vegetarian selection, and the side dishes such as Naan breads, which are made to order in the tandoori oven, are excellent. Customer care is a high priority here, and service is always knowledgeable and attentive. The wine mark up is very moderate (unusually in Dublin) so the wine as well as the food offer good value – and, appropriately for the cuisine, beers are also offered. After a delicious and moderately priced meal this can be a hard place to leave – but fortunately the Kumars also have two other restaurants, in Athlone and Mullingar. **Seats 60**; children welcome, but not suitable for very young babies (under 1), or after 10pm; toilets wheelchair accessible. L Mon-Fri, 12.30-2.30; D 6-11 daily. L&D à la carte available. House wine about €16. SC discretionary. Closed L Sat, L Sun & Christmas week. Amex, Diners, MasterCard, Visa, Laser. **Directions:** Opposite Children's Hospital on Harcourt Street (off Stephen's Green). ◊

Dublin 2

RESTAURANT

Saba

26 -28 Clarendon Street Dublin 2 **Tel: 01 679 2000**

eat@sabarestaurant.com www.sabadublin.com

Saba, meaning 'happy meeting place' in Thai, offers a combination of Thai and Vietnamese cooking and this has become one of Dublin's most popular restaurants. The décor is black, modern and sophisticated, but staff are friendlier than such backdrops often deliver. There's some real culinary adventure here like the smoked trout mieng kam with ginger, shallots, lime and peanuts, served on betel nut leaves: you roll the mix of highly flavoured fish and spices into a cigar shape using the pungent betel leaves - an exciting marriage of the interesting and unusual with recognisable flavours. You'll find old favourites too such as tempura vegetables with a mustard and lime mayonnaise: a good selection of whole baby carrots, broccoli, asparagus and aubergine with a gentle sheet of crispy batter all well matched with the high tone of the citrus sauce. Main courses include cua lot, soft shell crab with birds eye chilli, galangal root and kaffir lime leaf - with a three star chilli warning. An unusual and interesting main course, it encompasses a cornucopia of flavours and textures, from the strong and sweet to rich and deep. Grilled lobster tail is also available with spinach, yellow beans and brown and red rice: the sweet white meat is given a spicy crust and served with gentler flavours from the rice. Less adventurous diners will be happy to find phad Thai and green chicken curry as well as classic Thai noodle soups such as tuk tuk soup of spicy egg noodles, Vietnamese parsley, chicken and peanuts. Refreshing desserts include plates of sorbets - mango, lychee and strawberry. They also have an interesting list of non-alcoholic drinks perhaps reflecting our changing times. There are now plenty of other places to get authentic cheap and cheerful Vietnamese and Thai food, but this is the smart version and well worth the culinary detour. **Seats 130**; wheelchair access to toilets; children welcome before 8pm; air conditioning; reservations recommended. Open daily noon-10pm (to 12 Fri/Sat); set L about €25; set D about €29.50; also a la carte L&D; coeliac & vegetarian options available; house wine from about €15.95. SC 10% added to groups 6+. Closed 25-26 Dec. Amex, MasterCard, Visa, Laser. **Directions:** Parallel to top of Grafton Street, behind Westbury Hotel. ◈

Dublin 2
RESTAURANT

Salamanca

1 St Andrew's Street Dublin 2 **Tel: 01 677 4799**
info@salamanca.ie www.salamanca.ie

The concept of tapas was new to Dublin when this atmospheric, informal bar and Spanish restaurant opened in the heart of Dublin several years ago, and it immediately struck a chord with Dubliners. It came into new ownership in 2008, but fans will be glad to know that there are no major changes. The entrance is pleasant - past a bar with flowers on the counter - and welcoming staff show you straight to a simple marble-topped table. The menu - which is in Spanish with English explanations - is flexible enough to suit anything from a light lunch to a full dinner and plenty of choices: three tapas plates will make a generous lunch for two. Spanish staples are generally well-handled: langoustines with serrano ham, squid in chilli butter and patatas bravas are all tasty and presentation is simple and traditional - and, on a recent visit by the Guide, the pmientos rellenos (peppers stuffed with spiced minced lamb) were particularly enjoyed. A handy location, tasty food, delightful staff and good value make this place busy at peak times, so be prepared to wait. The wine list includes a range of sherries by the glass, the traditional accompaniment for tapas, and there are a few excellent wines in the "premium" section of the wine list (€30 plus), particularly a wonderful Albarino. And their lovely frothy-topped mocha served in a tall glass is a great reviver. Meals: Mon-Thu, 12 noon-11 pm, Fri & Sat to midnight. Closed Sun. MasterCard, Visa. **Directions:** Near Dublin Tourism.

Dublin 2
RESTAURANT
Ⓝ

Seagrass

30 South Richmond Street Portobello Dublin 2 **Tel: 01 478 9595**
info@seagrassdublin.com www.seagrassdublin.com

Seen against the unkempt charm of the surrounding area, the smart awning and frontage of Seagrass, with its appealing outdoor tables, immediately sets it apart from other establishments on South Richmond Street, in the heart of southside's Portobello. It's a stylish new venture and the contemporary tone continues indoors, where diners can enjoy aquamarine shades and the relaxed bright, breezy atmosphere of the ground floor dining room - or opt for the more secluded basement lounge, with its classy wine bar and lots of exposed brick walls and dark leather sofas. Friendly staff are well turned out, busy taking orders and pouring wine, whilst the menu draws on Europe and the Mediterranean for inspiration, including a tempting brunch menu and an interesting shortlist of tapas-style tasting plates such as seared spiced tuna with Pernod & soy reduction, caramelised orange zest & beetroot balls, or braised lamb mini casserole with carrot & roasted baby onions. All the dishes sound appealing without being too complicated, rustic yet with a modern edge - this is a restaurant that could become known for its squid risotto and bread & butter pudding. Good ingredients and skilful cooking come together in delicious, well-crafted starters like ham, sweet onion & dill terrine with pear & lime jelly and mint mascarpone, and mains such as a perfectly cooked and flavoursome rustic lemon sole with clams & baked squid, tomatoes, shaved fennel, spinach, garlic & lemon. Well-executed versions of classic desserts will end a good meal well. An interesting wine list offers a balanced mix of old and new world wines, with useful tasting notes and a small selection by the glass and carafe. Seagrass has brought a new dining experience to Portobello, offering a high standard of food and service, in attractive, relaxed surroundings - at an affordable price. **Seats 65** (private room, 35, oudoor, 4); children welcome before 8pm; no wheelchair access; L Tue-Sat, 12-2.30pm, value L €15, 12-2.30pm; early bird D €20 Tue-Sun 5.30-7pm, brunch Sun 12-4pm, D Tue-Sun, 5.30 - 10pm. SC 12.5% on groups 5+. Closed Mon. Amex, MasterCard, Visa, Laser.

Dublin 2
RESTAURANT

Shanahan's on the Green

119 St Stephen's Green Dublin 2 **Tel: 01 407 0939**
sales@shanahans.ie www.shanahans.ie

This opulent restaurant was Dublin's first dedicated American-style steakhouse - although, as they would be quick to reassure you, their wide-ranging menu also offers plenty of other meats, poultry and seafood. However, the big attraction for many of the hungry diners with deep pockets who head for Shanahan's is their certified Irish Angus beef, which is seasoned and cooked in a special broiler, 1600-1800F, to sear the outside and keep the inside tender and juicy. Steaks range from a 'petit filet' at a mere 8oz/225g right up to The Shanahan Steak (24oz/700g), which is a sight to gladden the heart of many a traditionally-minded Irishman - and, more surprisingly perhaps, many of his trendier young friends too. Strange to think that steak was passé such a short time ago. There is much else to enjoy, of course, including a dramatic signature dish of onion strings with blue cheese dressing. The wine list includes many special bottles - with, naturally, a strong presence from the best of Californian producers. **Seats 100**; not suitable for children; reservations required; air conditioning. L Fri only (except for groups), 12.30-2. D daily, 6-10pm (to 10.30pm Sat). Set L about €45; otherwise à la carte. (SC discretionary, but 15% on parties of 6+). House wine €30. Closed Christmas period. Amex, Diners, MasterCard, Visa, Laser.
Directions: On the west side of St Stephen's Green, beside Royal College of Surgeons.

Dublin 2
BAR•RESTAURANT

Shebeen Chic

4 South Great Georges Street Dublin 2
Tel 085 118 6108

Chef Seamus O'Connell is best known for his avant-garde cuisine at Cork's eclectic Ivory Tower. Recently he's taken his creative genius to Dublin to team up with one of the capital's best-known restaurateurs and publicans, Jay Bourke. Together the pair has opened Shebeen Chic, a sassy eatery with unconventional décor and unconventional food. Decorated with junk shop finds, including traffic bollards, an old photo booth, toilet seats (new - we suspect!), net curtains, old books and mismatched furniture, it looks like a cross between a car boot sale and your grandmother's parlour. This edgy décor may be devised to cash in on the green movement zeitgeist, but it sits rather uncomfortably on the fence between clever and down right tacky. You need to be a laid back customer to appreciate the scuffed tables with wobbly legs and colourful chandeliers with (deliberately?) missing bulbs, but the menu proves a great distraction. Based on genuine Irish dishes, using genuine Irish ingredients, you'll find the likes of oysters, crubeens, tripe, black pudding, conger eel and lambs kidneys all on offer. A boxty menu delivers rosti-like potato cakes, made with exciting additions like seaweed and smoked mackerel. Less popular cuts, like beef skirt or ox cheek, deliciously braised in ale, give diners the opportunity to taste lost recipes that really deserve to be resurrected. Best of all, prices reflect the 'cheaper' ingredients, making dining here great value. Desserts are a quirky mix of Irish staples - apple pie with ice cream, jelly and ice cream, fruit crumble and blancmange all make appearances. Mercifully they've all been vamped up - the jelly bursting with fresh fruit purée, the blancmange singing with honey, lemon and carrageen moss. Service is relaxed and informal, with the staff eager and enthusiastic. A smaller dining room, off the ground floor, has one large table and its own kitchen sink, and is the perfect spot for a private party of about 15 guests. The wine list is short but varied, with most bottles very well priced at €25-30; these are bin ends so you can expect to find some real jewels at knockdown prices. As much of the food is hearty and robust it's a real plus to find the bar serves beer and Guinness on tap. Diners can eat and drink at the long bar upstairs, and there's a smaller bar and stage in the downstairs dining room where bands appear every night. Once the live music kicks in Shebeen Chic gains a real party buzz, and you'll leave with the sensation that this party may go on all night. **Seats 100**; L & D daily, 12-5pm & 5.30-10pm (to 11pm Thurs, Fri & Sat).
Directions: Dame Street end of South Great George's Street.

Dublin 2

HOTEL•RESTAURANT

The Shelbourne Dublin

27 St Stephen's Green Dublin 2 **Tel: 01 663 4500**

rhi.dubbr.res.supv@renaissancehotels.com www.theshelbourne.ie

The Irish Constitution was drafted here and the recent brief closure of this opulent 18th-century hotel overlooking St Stephen's Green (Europe's largest garden square) has served as a reminder to Dubliners that it is still central to life in the city today. Ranking among the world's great hotels, it emerged from its recent restoration and refurbishment with all the old grandeur intact, and the entrance creates an even stronger impression now that the lift has been relocated to allow the original staircase to take pride of place once again in the magnificent faux-marble entrance hall - now also enhanced by the creation of a new reception area. The Lord Mayor's Lounge - always a popular meeting place for Afternoon Tea - was treated with a light hand in the renovation and the famous Horseshoe Bar, renowned as a meeting place for local politicians and theatrical society and nothing short of a Dublin institution, was taken back to its old Sam Stephenson designed interior. New rooms added at the back of the hotel have increased the accommodation, and all are luxurious - but the older suites, named after famous people who have stayed there in the past, have all been refurbished to bring back the original glamour, and are very much in demand. Dining choices are between the stylish, No. 27 Bar & Lounge, and the opulent Saddle Room (see below). The hotel is in great demand for events and meetings, with a number of restored meeting/private dining rooms in the main building available, including The Constitution Room and The George Moore Suite - and also the state-of-the-art Great Room next door, for larger events. Conference/banqueting (500/350). Business centre, Broadband wi/fi, laptop-sized safe in rooms. Fitness centre, indoor swimming pool, jacuzzi, sauna, steam room, massage. Gift shop. 24 hour room service. Lift. **Rooms 265** (19 suites, 18 junior suites, 46 executive, 247 no smoking, 7 for disabled); Children welcome (under 12s free in parents room, cots available free of charge, baby sitting arranged); Dogs permitted to stay in bedrooms for a charge; B&B €192 pps. Open all year. **The Saddle Room:** Although there is no obvious sign over the door, hotel guests will spot this enticing looking restaurant within minutes of entering the large hotel foyer. The Saddle Room majors in seafood and steaks, with a large open plan kitchen putting the talented team on show for all to see. Divided in two by banquettes, the quieter side of the dining room features dark woods, moody lighting and cosy banquettes, creating a buzzy, clubby atmosphere. Tables, which are quite wide, are dressed with linen, beautiful Riedel glasses and flickering tea lights setting the scene for some serious food. The menu offers lots of interesting choices, with seafood and steak the obvious focus. The Oyster Bar serves four kinds of fresh oysters - it's interesting to order a combination and compare their individual characteristics - while a choice of Irish beef cuts fares well from The Grill. All dishes come with accompaniments, but side orders are usually required to make up a main course, pushing up the price of dining signif-icantly. An extensive and informative wine list is conveniently divided into drinking styles, and the friendly and knowledgeable sommelier helpfully guides guests towards further recommendations. Desserts offer a range of freshly interpreted classics, and there's a tempting cheese trolley too. And gone are the days of stiff, formal service - excellent staff provide a balance of informed and charming service that relaxes diners and enhances the dining experience. **Seats 135** (private room, 18); toilets wheelchair accessible; reservations recommended; air conditioning; L&D daily, L 12-2pm, D 6-10pm; a la carte L&D; house wine €30; SC discretionary. Open all year. Amex, Diners, Mastercard, Visa, Laser. Barfood also served 11-9pm daily. **Directions:** Landmark building on north side of St Stephen's Green in Dublin City Centre. ◊

Silk Road Café

CAFÉ•RESTAURANT Chester Beatty Library Dublin Castle Dublin 2 **Tel: 01 407 0770**
silkroadcafe@hotmail.com www.silkroadcafe.ie

In a fine location in the heart of the city centre, Dublin Castle provides wonderful gardens and historic architecture which greatly enhance the enjoyment of a visit to this unusual restaurant, which is in the clock tower beside the Chester Beatty Library (European Museum of the Year in 2002, and one of the few Dublin museums offering free entry). You will know that you're in the right place when you notice the uncharacteristic aroma of Middle Eastern spices wafting towards you on the Dublin air. Middle Eastern, Mediterranean, vegetarian and organic are the themes brought together by Abraham Phelan and his small but dedicated team, who create inspired versions of classics like Greek moussaka, Moroccan cous cous, falafel, spinach & feta pie and delicious salads to the delight of their many returning customers. Fresh organic herbs are used in all dishes and, in line with halal/kosher rules, all dishes are made without the use of pork or beef. Prices are very reasonable. **Seats 65** (private room 30); toilets wheelchair accessible; children welcome; air conditioning. Open Mon-Fri, 10-5; à la carte. No service charge. MasterCard, Visa, Laser. **Directions:** Beside Chester Beatty Library in Dublin Castle. ◈

The South William

BAR 52 South William Street Dublin 2 **Tel: 01 672 5946**
info@southwilliam.ie www.southwilliam.ie

Opened in January 2007 by brothers Marc and Conor Bereen, with Troy Maguire - who was well known from L'Geuleton at the time - involved as a food consultant, The South William was always going to do something different. And, although Troy Maguire has long since moved on (to Locks, see entry), it seems to be standing the test of time. A retro-style cocktail bar, with plastic seats, and worn leather couches lend the room a laid-back kitsch feel, and friendly staff add to the relaxed atmosphere. The food offering is deliberately restricted and kept to a theme - a short menu consists of six gourmet pies, which include traditional Irish staples such as bacon and cabbage or Guinness braised beef shin; the pies are good and come with a choice of side salads - but a bowl of mashed potato would be very welcome in addition. The wine list is short too, with a good mix of old and new world at a fair cost, with some offered by the glass, and there is a good selection of imported beers, bottled and on tap. In the evenings, the South William parks away its daytime chill and removes the bar stools 'to facilitate the art of dancing' as the lounge bar transforms to a funky night club with its own DJ. **Seats 110.** Open daily (normal bar hours Mon-Wed, to 2.30am Fri/Sat); food served 12-10pm daily (to 9pm Sat). Amex, MasterCard, Visa, Laser. Closed 25 Dec. **Directions:** On south end of South William Street on same side of street as Powerscourt Town House.

Stauntons on the Green

GUESTHOUSE 83 St Stephen's Green Dublin 2 **Tel: 01 478 2300**
stauntonsonthegreen@eircom.net www.stauntonsonthegreen.ie

Well-located with views over St Stephen's Green at the front and its own private gardens at the back, this guesthouse - which is in an elegant Georgian terrace on the south of the Green and has fine period reception rooms - offers moderately priced accommodation of a good standard, with all the usual amenities. Maintenance could be a little sharper and front rooms would benefit from sound-proofing from traffic noise, but it's in the heart of the business and banking district and the Grafton Street shopping area is just a stroll across the Green. Meeting rooms are available, with secretarial facilities on request - and there's private parking (valet parking service offered - it would be wise to phone ahead with your time of arrival to arrange this, as there is no parking at the door). **Rooms 57** (all en-suite, 24 shower only); children welcome. No pets. B&B €82.50 pps, ss €20. Closed 24-27 Dec. Amex, Diners, MasterCard, Visa, Laser. **Directions:** On south side of the Green. ◈

Stephen's Green Hotel

HOTEL St Stephen's Green Dublin 2 **Tel: 01 607 3600**
info@ocallaghanhotels.com www.ocallaghanhotels.com

This landmark hotel on a south-western corner site overlooking St Stephen's Green is the newest of the O'Callaghan Hotels group (Alexander, Davenport, Mont Clare, all in Dublin 2 - see entries).

Although it also incorporates two refurbished Georgian houses, the contemporary addition (a four-storey glass atrium) is its most striking feature. Public areas include an impressive foyer and, in memory of the writer George Fitzmaurice who used to live here, 'Pie Dish' restaurant and 'Magic Glasses' bar - both named after titles from his work. It's a great location and the very comfortable air-conditioned bedrooms have exceptionally good facilities, particularly for business travellers, including 3 direct line telephones, voice mail and modem line, desk, mini-bar as standard. The hotel offers a range of meeting rooms and wired and WiFi broadband is available throughout. Small conference/meeting rooms; business centre. **Rooms 75** (9 suites, including 2 studio terrace suites, 3 penthouse suites, junior suites; 40 no-smoking rooms, 2 for disabled); children welcome (Under 2s free in parents' room; cots available). No pets. Lift. 24 hour room service. Room rate about €245 (max. 2 guests). Open all year. Gym. Amex, Diners, MasterCard, Visa. **Directions:** Corner of Harcourt Street and St. Stephen's Green. ◊

TEMPLE BAR

The hub of the action for many visitors, the area others may wish to avoid. Whatever your feelings for the tourist centre of Dublin everybody should visit it once during daytime to judge it for themselves. Street performers and buskers ply their trade in and around Temple Bar Square which can be a great place to sit down and enjoy the atmosphere on a sunny day. There are many interesting places to visit - such as the Irish Film Centre - who host ever-changing exhibitions and Meeting House Square has weekly outdoor cinema screenings in the summer and a Farmers Market every Wednesday and Saturday. The whole area is full of bars and restaurants and one of the best known and amongst the first new-wave places in the area is the **Elephant & Castle** restaurant (Temple Bar, 01 679 3121) which is popular for large salads and bowls of chicken wings and its lively atmosphere. For reasonably priced accommodation **The Fleet Street Hotel** (Fleet Street; 01 670 8122) is conveniently situated in the heart of Temple Bar, within easy walking distance of all the city's main attractions, it is fairly small, allowing an intimate atmosphere and a welcome emphasis on service.

WWW.IRELAND-GUIDE.COM FOR ALL THE BEST PLACES TO EAT, DRINK & STAY

Dublin 2
HOTEL

Temple Bar Hotel
Fleet Street Temple Bar Dublin 2 **Tel: 01 677 3333**
reservations@tbh.ie www.templebarhotel.com

This pleasant hotel is relatively reasonably priced, and handy for both sides of the river. Spacious reception and lounge areas create a good impression and bedrooms are generally larger than average, almost all with a double and single bed and good amenities. Neat, well-lit bathrooms have over-bath showers and marble washbasin units. Conference/banqueting (70/60). **Rooms 129** (35 no-smoking, 2 for disabled); children welcome (Under 12s free in parents' room, cots available without charge). Lift. B&B about €120pps, ss €60. Wheelchair access. No pets. Room service menu (6-10pm). No parking, but the hotel has an arrangement with a nearby car park. Closed Christmas. Amex, Diners, MasterCard, Visa, Laser. **Directions:** Near Fleet Street car park. ◊

Dublin 2
RESTAURANT
◉★★✿

Thornton's Restaurant
128 St Stephen's Green Dublin 2 **Tel: 01 478 7008**
thorntonsrestaurant@eircom.net www.thorntonsrestaurant.com

With views overlooking St Stephen's Green, Kevin and Muriel Thornton's renowned restaurant is to be found on the top floor of the Fitzwilliam Hotel. You can take a lift up through the hotel, but it is best approached from its own entrance on the Green: mounting the wide staircase, deep-carpeted in dark blue, conveys a sense of occasion. The rather plain dining room has long been a subject of debate but most agree that recent renovation has created a more stylish space: the square room has been divided by panels of glass over-printed with sepia toned fish scales; Just like the arresting photography hanging on the walls, these were shot by Kevin, who is as adept with a camera as a sautée pan. The clever revamp has seen the addition of an intimate canapé bar with smart stools at the bar and comfy sofas, where diners can drop in for a more relaxed experience. Miniature creations - perhaps foie gras rolled in toasted almonds or goose with aubergine chips - can be individually ordered (€3.50 each) to accompany some exceptional wines by the glass, such as the celebrated dessert wine, Chateau d'Yquem (€40 per glass). For those who have come to dine, however, the understated linen-clad tables leave you in no doubt that the food is to be the star here. Given that Kevin Thornton is one of the most talented chefs in the country, lunch, with two courses costing just €45, represents outstanding value. Dinner is a full-on gourmet affair and although the à la carte offers just three choices per course, it's the tasting menus, available as 5, 8 or 14 courses (€95, €125, €185) that really showcase his genius. Most recently, in line with a number of other top restaurants, Thornton's has introduced a Chef's Table, so that guests can experience 'the heat of the kitchen'; not too literally in this case, as the designated table for six is set up beside a large round window that allows diners to see everything that's going on without disrupting the smooth flow of work. You can have a menu, with matching wines, designed especially for your table, and you will be talked through each course as it arrives. Kevin Thornton has a perfectionist's eye for detail with a palate to match, and he has passion for sourcing the very best seasonal ingredients – lucky for the diner that one of his signature ingredients is gold leaf, available all year. He has always had a name for generosity with truffles too, and he will not disappoint: a first course terrine of foie gras comes with truffle sauce (and warm brioche), for example, or you might try the truffle scrambled egg - and among the seafood dishes you will find a luxurious signature dish of sautéed prawns with prawn bisque, and truffle sabayon. Other signature dishes include roast suckling pig, and trotter served with glazed turnip and a light poitín sauce - and variations on these creations (braised pig head with poitín sauce, for example) may appear throughout an 8-course Surprise Menu (€125, available only to complete tables). Desserts, like a signature molten Valrhona chocolate, and imaginative petit fours, are always exquisite. Although beautifully presented, this is not show-off food - the cooking is never less than sublime and the emphasis is always on flavour; even the quartet of salts offered at table is not affection, as their different characteristics are quite distinctive. As one would expect for dining at this level, the wine list is extensive, featuring many great marques and a good choice of wines by the glass. Service is formal and never less than polished, and on recent visits the extreme professionalism found at this level has been lifted by some welcome humour, which is especially welcome at lunchtime, when the restaurant can be surprisingly quiet. The food is the star, of course, but if you want to experience this restaurant at its best, push out the boat and head in for dinner – then you will indeed find a restaurant experience with that real wow factor which could be missing at quieter times. **Seats 60**; reservations recommended; children welcome; air conditioning. L Thu-Sat, 12.30-2pm; D Tue-Sat, 6-10.30pm. L&D a la carte; Tasting Menu also offered, from €95-185 for 5-14 courses. House wine from €26. SC discretionary. Closed Sun, 24 Dec - 2 Jan. Amex, Diners, MasterCard, Visa, Laser. *Canapé Bar open from 1pm to midnight. **Directions:** On St Stephen's Green (corner at top of Grafton Street); entrance beside Fitzwilliam Hotel.

Dublin 2
RESTAURANT

Town Bar & Grill

21 Kildare Street Dublin 2 **Tel: 01 662 4800**
reservations@townbarandgrill.com www.townbarandgrill.com

Ronan Ryan and Temple Garner's New York/Italian style restaurant is doing just fine - the focus of public attention may have moved to their newer restaurants, South Bar & Restaurant and Bridge Bar & Grill (see entries) recently, but the city centre stronghold remains a favourite destination for foodies out on the town, not least because the range of menus offered is so well designed to suit every time and occasion. A delicate hand with the decor - warm floor tiles, gentle lighting and smart but not overly-formal white-clothed tables with promising wine glasses - creates a welcoming tone on arrival in the L-shaped basement, and professional staff are quick to offer the choice of a drink at the bar or menus at your table. Starters are likely to include a really excellent antipasti plate and dishes rarely seen elsewhere, such as slow cooked rabbit with gnocchi, while house versions of classics like grilled calf's liver with braised onions, nutmeg creamed spinach, confit pork belly & mash, appear among main courses which will also offer several interesting fish dishes and, in season, game such as crown of pheasant. An Irish and Italian cheese-board is offered and more-ish desserts may include classics like Town tiramisu; combinations are sometimes unusual, and flavours are delicious. Interested, well-informed staff add greatly to the enjoyment of a meal here, and the cooking is generally confident and accurate, set off handsomely by simple presentation on plain white plates. Prices are fair for the high quality of food and service offered, with lunch and pre-theatre menus offering very good value. There is also - perhaps uniquely in a city centre restaurant of this calibre - a special children's menu, offering healthy low-salt and low-sugar 'real' food such as char-grilled chicken breast bruschetta with buffalo mozzarella & tomato salsa, and home-made fish fingers with oven-roasted chips. Sunday lunch, available as a one-, two- or three-course menu (€18.95/24.95/29.95), offers a well-balanced choice that, while more adventurous than the usual Sunday lunch, includes the elements of tradition. The wine list offers many interesting selections, and some very special bottles, notably from Tuscany and the Napa Valley; a good choice is available by the glass. **Seats 80**; free broadband wi/fi; children welcome; air conditioning. Open daily: L 12.30-5.30, D 5.30-11 (to 10 on Sun); set L €18.95/24.95/29.95; pre-theatre menu €29.95, Mon-Thurs 5.30-7.15; Set 3 course D €59.95, also à la carte. Kids Menu €9.95. House wine €22.50. Pianist Thu-Sat from 8pm, Jazz on Sun from 8. SC 12.5% on groups 5+. Closed 25 Dec, Good Fri. Amex, MasterCard, Visa, Laser. **Directions:** Opposite side door of Shelbourne, under Mitchell's wine shop.

Dublin 2
HOTEL

Trinity Capital Hotel

Pearse Street Dublin 2 **Tel: 01 648 1000**
info@trinitycapital-hotel.com www.trinitycapitalhotel.com

A stylish hotel right beside the headquarters of Dublin's city centre fire brigade and opposite Trinity College. Very centrally located for business and leisure, the hotel is within easy walking distance of all the main city centre attractions on both sides of the Liffey and the lobby wine and coffee bar make handy meeting places. A multi-million euro redevelopment and refurbishment has greatly increased the size of the hotel recently and, although the hotel is mainly modern, accommodation now includes eight Georgian suites. All rooms have comfortable beds and good bathrooms (junior suites suites have jacuzzi baths) and are well equipped, with a safe, interactive TV, phone & data ports, hair dryer, trouser press, tea/coffee trays, hi-fi system and mini-bar. Café Cairo, extended in the recent renovations, offers an above-average experience for an hotel restaurant, providing an appealing alternative for guests who prefer to dine in (D daily, 6-9.30). Conference/banqueting (35/70); broadband wi/fi. **Rooms 172** (8 suites, 4 junior suites, 7 family, 10 disabled, 7 single, 160 no-smoking, 10 shower only); children welcome (under 12s free in parents' room; cots available without charge). Lift. Limited room service. Room rate €159. Closed 24-26 Dec. Amex, Diners, MasterCard, Visa, Laser. **Directions:** City centre.

Dublin 2
GUESTHOUSE

Trinity Lodge

12 South Frederick Street Dublin 2 **Tel: 01 617 0900**
trinitylodge@eircom.net www.trinitylodge.com

This well-signed and attractively maintained guesthouse offers an excellent location and a high standard of accommodation at a reasonable price, just yards away from Trinity College. As is the way with Georgian buildings, rooms get smaller towards the top so the most spacious accommodation is on lower floors. The reception area is a little tight, but guest rooms have air conditioning and are stylishly furnished in keeping with the age of the building, and most have bath and shower; as it is a listed building, it is not permissible to install a lift, a point worth bearing in mind if stairs could be a problem. An extensive breakfast is served in the stylish George's Bistro (see entry), where dinner is also available - and there are numerous good restaurants nearby. Air-conditioned rooms have a safe, direct-dial phone, tea/coffee making facilities, multi-channel TV, trouser press and iron; free broadband wi/fi. No private parking (multi-storey carparks nearby). **Rooms 16** (6 family, 1 ground floor, all shower only and no-smoking); children welcome, under 5 free in parents' room; cots available; children aged 5-11: €15 per child / night in parents' room, over 12 years old sharing room: €60 extra per night; free broadband wi/fi; no pets. Room service (limited hours). Room rate inc. breakfast €130. Closed 23-27 Dec. Amex, Diners, MasterCard, Visa, Laser. **Directions:** Off Nassau Street, near Trinity College. ◊

Dublin 2
RESTAURANT

Trocadero Restaurant

3/4 St Andrew Street Dublin 2 **Tel: 01 677 5545**
www.trocadero.ie

The Dublin theatrical restaurant par excellence - with deep blood-red walls and gold-trimmed stage curtains, black and white pictures of the celebrities who've passed through the place dimly lit, intimate tables with individual beaded lampshades and snug, cosy seating, the 'Troc' is one of Dublin's longest-established restaurants and has presided over St. Andrew Street since 1956. A new bar was added in 2007, but otherwise it remains much the same: it has atmosphere in spades, with food and service to match. Comforting menus reminiscent of the '70s offer starters like French onion soup, deep-fried brie, chicken liver paté and avocado prawn Marie Rose, followed by ever-popular grills - fillet steak (with Cashel Blue cheese perhaps), Wicklow rack of lamb and sole on the bone are the main-stays of the menu, also wild Irish salmon and Dublin Bay prawns from Clogherhead, naturally all with a sprinkling of freshly chopped parsley. Desserts include apple and cinnamon strudel and wicked chocolate and Baileys slice, and a better-value wine list will be hard to find. There's privacy too - sound-absorbing banquettes and curtains allow you to hear everything at your own table with just a pleasing murmur in the background. Lovely friendly service too: magic. **Seats 110**. Air conditioning. Children welcome (up to 9pm). D Mon-Sat, 5-11.30pm. Pre-theatre D 5-7pm €25, but table to be vacated by 7.45pm - also à la carte,. House wine from about €19. Closed Sun, 25 Dec - 2 Jan, Good Fri. Amex, Diners, MasterCard, Visa, Laser. **Directions:** Beside Dublin Tourism Centre.

Dublin 2 Tulsi Restaurant

RESTAURANT   17a Lr Baggot Street Dublin 2 **Tel: 01 676 4578**

      shamsul-haque06@hotmail.com www.tulsiindian.com

One of a small chain of authentic Indian restaurants, this bustling place has a compact reception area leading into an elegant restaurant with echoes of the Raj in the decor. Tables are set up with plate warmers, fresh flowers, sauces and pickles and service is brisk. There's a slight leaning towards Punjabi-style cooking, with its use of nuts and fruit in sauces, but also tandoori, tikka, biryani, balti and an extensive vegetarian menu. A selection of naan breads is offered and the food quality overall is consistently high; this, together with good value, make booking at both lunch and dinner advisable. Indian beer is available, in addition to a broad-based wine list helpfully arranged by style. **Seats 64** (outdoor,8). L Mon-Sat, 12-2.30, D daily, 6-11. Set L €10.95. Set D €25, also à la carte. House wine €17.95. Closed L Sun, L bank hols; 25-26 Dec, Good Fri. * Tulsi has a number of branches, including: 4 Olive Mount Terrace, Dundrum Road, Dundrum (01 260 1940); Lr Charles St., Castlebar, Co Mayo (Tel: 094 25066); Buttermilk Way, Middle St., Galway Tel: 092-564831). Sister restaurants 'Shanai Indian' at Cornelscourt S.C. and Old Bray Road, Foxrock, Co Dublin. Amex, Diners, MasterCard, Visa, Laser. **Directions:** 2 minutes walk east from St Stephens Green (Shelbourne Hotel side).

Dublin 2 Unicorn Restaurant

RESTAURANT   12B Merrion Court off Merrion Row Dublin 2 **Tel: 01 662 4757**

                            www.unicornrestaurant.com

In a lovely, secluded location just off a busy street near St. Stephen's Green, this informal and perennially fashionable restaurant is famous for its antipasto bar, piano bar and exceptionally friendly staff. It's particularly charming in summer, as the doors open out onto a terrace which is used for al fresco dining in fine weather - and the Number Five piano bar, which extends to two floors, is also a great attraction for after-dinner relaxation with live music (Wed-Sat 9pm-3am). Aside from their wonderful display of antipasto, an extensive menu based on Irish ingredients (suppliers are listed) is offered, including signature dishes such as risotto funghi porcini (which is not available on Monday), and involtini 'saltimbocca style' - pockets of veal stuffed with Parma ham, mozzarella and sage, braised in white wine and lemon sauce; good regional and modern Italian food, efficient service and great atmosphere all partially explain The Unicorn's enduring success - another element is the constant quest for further improvement. There is always something new going on - the 'Unicorn Foodstore' round the corner, on Merrion Row, is a relatively recent addition to the enterprise, for example, also the Unicorn Antipasto/Tapas Bar - and there is now a bar menu in the piano bar, which is a fair indication of the popularity of this buzzing restaurant. Many of the Italian wines listed are exclusive to The Unicorn: uniquely, in Ireland, they stock the full collection of Angelo Gaja wines and also the Pio Cesare range. **Seats 80** (private room 30; outdoor 30); not suitable for children after 9pm; reservations required; air conditioning. Open Mon-Sat, L12.30-4, D 6-10.30 (Fri/Sat to 11), open all day weekends. A la carte. House wine about €23. SC discretionary. Closed Sun, bank hols, 25 Dec-2 Jan. Amex, Diners, MasterCard, Visa, Laser. **Directions:** Just off Stephen's Green, towards Baggot Street. ◊

Dublin 2
RESTAURANT
Venu Brasserie
Annes Lane Dublin 2 **Tel: 01 670 6755**
www.venu.ie

Following in the footsteps of a father who has run the finest restaurant in Ireland for over a quarter of a century can't be easy, but Charles Guilbaud's brasserie has now established its own place in the city. Situated rather unglamorously in the basement of an office building, it aims to offer good, simple food at fair prices - and, whether or not you like the décor (just redecorated as we go to press), you're bound to love the affordable all-day menus and a concise, fairly priced wine list that includes four well-chosen house wines. Although by no means an exclusively French menu, head chef Denis Massey offers many dishes that will bring back the best kind of memories: think wholesome gratinated soup with croûtons, moules frites - and plenty of choice for vegetarians, including lovely salads. Main courses tread a carefully chosen path, offering a great choice from rib eye steak & chips or traditional fish & chips, to popular spicy dishes like grilled lamb skewers with cumin & coriander spices and seasonal seafood like Clogherhead crab salad. This is good simple food, and desserts like tarte aux pommes or home-made ice creams and sorbets mainly follow in the same vein, although there are some surprises too. Together with long opening hours and smart service, the great cooking and value here continues to earn many happy fans for Venu. **Seats 120**; toilets wheelchair accessible. children welcome; air conditioning. Open L Thu-Sat, D daily, 4.30-11pm; L a la carte; Early D €25, 4-6.30pm; set 3 course D €45. House wine €20. Closed L Sun-Wed, 25/26 Dec, 1 Jan, Good Fri, Bank Hols. Amex, MasterCard, Visa, Laser. **Directions:** From Grafton Street on to South Anne street, take 1st right.

Dublin 2
HOTEL•RESTAURANT
The Westbury Hotel
Grafton Street Dublin 2 **Tel: 01 679 1122**
westbury@jurysdoyle.com www.jurys-dublin-hotels.com/thewestbury_dublin

Possibly the most conveniently situated of all the central Dublin hotels, the Westbury is a very small stone's throw from the city's premier shopping street and has all the benefits of luxury hotels - notably free valet parking - to offset any practical disadvantages of the location. Unashamedly sumptuous, the hotel has recently undergone a major revamp which is similarly luxurious, with bedrooms that include penthouse suites and a high proportion of suites, junior suites and executive rooms. With conference facilities to match its quality of accommodation and service, the hotel is understandably popular with business guests, but it also makes a luxurious base for a leisure break in the city. Laundry/dry cleaning. Fitness Room. Conference/banqueting (220/220). Business centre. Secretarial services, video conferencing, broadband wi/fi. Children welcome (cots available free of charge; baby sitting arranged). No pets. **Rooms 205** (14 suites, 4 junior suites, 25 executive rooms, 155 no-smoking, 3 for disabled). 24 hr room service. Lifts. B&B from €219 pps. SC 15%. Car park. Open all year. **Wilde The Restaurant:** At last The Westbury Hotel has the destination restaurant it deserves - a sleek, sophisticated space that's taking classic cooking to a whole new level, matched by impeccable service with real charm and personality. The décor gives a nod to Art Deco, albeit with a modern, very glamorous twist - and there's an attention to detail that's carried through to the food. Before ordering, every table is brought a showcase tray of beautiful Irish Black Angus (the star attraction on the menu) in various cuts, from rib eye to sirloin, T-bone to fillet. Cooked to order, each cut is served with grilled Portobello mushrooms and a choice of six home-blended mustards, all offered in attractive glass jars. The house Caesar salad is a fun affair, tossed tableside with your choice of ingredients, including anchovies and pancetta. The prawn and crab cocktail, another signature dish, is served with a mini bottle of Tabasco, lime wedges and sea salt. Fish eaters are well catered for as well, with an appetising choice of mains, including grilled Atlantic lobster. Side dishes are unusual too and, in keeping with the classics, desserts combine retro favourites - Wilde banana split, perhaps - alongside modern treats like Valrhona white chocolate soup with berries. A broad-based wine list has plenty of choice in the €30-

40 range, 12 wines by the glass and several half bottles. Overall the food is excellent and, from the warm welcome on arrival to the excellent coffees and petit fours at meal's end, Wilde's attention to detail is impressive: a delightful asset to the Westbury that deserves to attract far more than resident guests. **Seats 120**; children welcome; air conditioning. SC 15%. L daily, 12.30-2.30; D daily 6.30-10.30 (Sun to 9.30). Set L about €34, Set D 2/3 course about €35/€55, also à la carte. House wine from €25. Open all year. Amex, Diners, MasterCard, Visa, Laser. **Directions:** City centre, off Grafton Street; near Stephens Green. ◊

Dublin 2

HOTEL•RESTAURANT

The Westin Dublin

Westmoreland Street Dublin 2 **Tel: 01 645 1000**
reservations.dublin@westin.com www.westin.com/dublin

Two Victorian landmark buildings provided the starting point for this impressive hotel, and part of the former Allied Irish Bank was glassed over to create a dramatic lounging area, The Atrium, which has a huge palm tree feature and bedroom windows giving onto it like a courtyard (effective, although rather airless). The magnificent Banking Hall now makes a stunning conference and banqueting room, and the adjacent Teller Room is an unusual circular boardroom - while the vaults have found a new lease of life as The Mint, a bar with its own access from College Street. It's an intriguing building, especially for those who remember its former commercial life, and it has many special features including the business traveller's 'Westin Guest Office', designed to combine the efficiency and technology of a modern office with the comfort of a luxurious bedroom, and the so-called 'Heavenly Bed' designed by Westin and 'worlds apart from any other bed'. For the ultimate in luxury, a split-level penthouse suite has views over Trinity College (and its own private exercise area). Very limited parking (some valet parking available, if arranged at the time of booking accommodation). Fitness room. Conferences/Banqueting (250/168); business centre, secretarial services, video conferencing, broadband wi/fi, laptop-sized safes in bedrooms. **Rooms 163** (17 suites, 7 junior suites, 67 executive, 163 no smoking, 19 for disabled). Lift. 24 hour room service. Room rate about €499 (max 2 guests). Children welcome (under 17s free in parents room, €45 for roll-away bed, cot available at no charge, baby sitting arranged). **The Exchange:** An elegant, spacious room in 1930s' style, the restaurant continues the banking theme and, with a welcome emphasis on comfort, it simply oozes luxury. Everything about it, from the classily under-stated decor in tones of cream and brown to the generous-sized, well-spaced tables and large carver chairs says expensive but worth it. And, in the Guide's experience, that promise generally follows through onto the plate in Executive Chef Darrin Parish's well-executed menus - a fairly contemporary style, and confident, unfussy cooking endear this restaurant to visitors and discerning Dublin diners alike. Fresh seasonal menus are a feature of The Exchange, and friendly service from knowledgeable young waiting staff enhances the dining experience. There is live music on Saturday night and at Sunday Brunch, which is quite an institution and, like the pre-theatre dinner menu, offers good value. **Seats 70**. Breakfast daily 6.30-10, L Tue-Fri 12-2, D Tue-Sat 6-10, set L €26; Early D €26, 6-7pm. Sun Brunch 12-4.30, €42.50; house wine €30. Restaurant closed L Sat, D Sun, L&D Mon. Hotel open all year. Amex, Diners, MasterCard, Visa, Laser. **Directions:** On Westmoreland Street, opposite Trinity College.

DUBLIN 3

CLONTARF / FAIRVIEW

Fairview and its more fashionable shoreside neighbour, Clontarf, are a few miles from central Dublin and convenient to attractions such as the Croke Park stadium; championship golf at the Royal Dublin Golf Club, walking, bird watching, kite surfing and many other activities on Bull Island, a large sand island in Dublin Bay. There are also sites of historical significance such as the Casino at Marino and Fairview Crescent, a former home of Bram Stoker, author of Dracula. A little further out, Clontarf is an affluent suburb, with all the shops, pubs, restaurants and cafés to be expected in such an area. **Picasso** (see entry) is an popular local Italian restaurant near the seafront on Vernon Avenue. The new **Restaurant Ten Fourteen** (01 805 4877), named after the date of the Battle of Clontarf, is on the

Clontarf Road almost opposite the Wooden Bridge; it is owned by the Caring & Sharing Association charity with Gaz Smith, formerly of The Chart House in Dingle amongst other well known restaurants, as Head Chef. However, as this pleasant brasserie style restaurant opened only shortly before the Guide went to press, our visit was perhaps premature. But it has potential and, with nice friendly staff and a welcoming attitude to young families, is already proving popular in the neighbourhood.
WWW.IRELAND-GUIDE.COM FOR ALL THE BEST PLACES TO EAT, DRINK & STAY.

Dublin 3   # Canters Restaurant
RESTAURANT   9 Fairview Strand Fairview Dublin 3 **Tel: 01 833 3681**
info@canters.ie www.canters.ie

This chic addition to urban Northside Dublin dining is a sister restaurant to the well-established Washerwoman's Hill Restaurant in Glasnevin (see entry) and it strikes a happy balance between the needs of those who simply want to 'eat out' and those who feel the need for a smarter dining experience. Starters such as garlic mushrooms with goat's cheese crumble and sun-dried tomato pesto offer a nod to older tastes with some modern twists; main courses tend towards the traditional and hearty - rack of lamb with dauphinoise potatoes, perhaps - but lighter, more contemporary options include good pasta dishes, which may also be vegetarian, such as red pepper and basil linguine with seared hollumi cheese. Ever-popular char-grilled steaks are here too, of course - and fish choices can include modern dishes like monkfish tail in pancetta, with marjoram and mushroom risotto & lemongrass dressing. An attractive dessert choice offers some refreshing dishes and might include old favourites like lemon posset - charming. Canters have structured their menu to appeal to the diversity of their local clientele, but this is definitely a notch above your usual neighbourhood restaurant. **Seats 90** (outdoor, 8; private room, to 56); broadband wi/fi; children welcome; toilets wheelchair accessible; air conditioning; reservation recommended. Open L daily, 12-3 (Sun L 12.30-3.30pm); set L about €19; D daily from 5.30-9.30pm (to 9 pm Sun); early D about €26, Mon-Thu, 5.30-7.30pm; also a la carte. Average starter €8, average main course €19, average dessert €6.50, house wines €17. SC of 10% for groups 7+. MasterCard, Visa, Laser. **Directions:** In the heart of Fairview, opposite Centra.

Dublin 3   # Clontarf Castle Hotel
HOTEL•RESTAURANT   Castle Avenue Clontarf Dublin 3 **Tel: 01 833 2321**

info@clontarfcastle.ie www.clontarfcastle.ie

This historic 17th century castle is located near the coast, and convenient to both the airport and city centre. Although it is a pity that the extensive grounds were given over to development some years ago so that special sense of space has been lost, the hotel itself has been sensitively developed, with each new development or update imaginatively incorporated into the old castle structure, retaining the historic atmosphere; some rooms, including the restaurant and the old bar, have original features and the atrium linking the old castle to the hotel is an impressive architectural feature. Recent major refurbishment and upgrade has resulted in a very stylish blend of the contemporary and traditional in all areas which, together with the hotel's longstanding reputation for professional and caring service, makes the Castle a seriously desirable venue for events of all kinds, both personal and corporate. The hotel is understandably popular with the business community, and their extensive conference and meeting facilities are regularly upgraded, to provide the latest technology for the benefit of anything from a single business guest to a conference for 600 - and with experienced, unobtrusive service to match. Luxurious, warmly decorated bedrooms are also furnished with pzazz, and equally well equipped for leisure and business guests with wireless broadband, voicemail and US electrical sockets, in addition to the many other amenities found in a hotel of this standard. Bathrooms are well-designed, and all south-facing rooms have air conditioning. Off duty, or for informal meetings, the hotel has two bars - the chic Indigo Lounge and, for traditionalists, Knights Bar - and dining in will be no hardship either (see restaurant, below). Well-trained and friendly staff greatly contribute to the atmosphere and comfort of a visit here, and recent investment has kept the hotel at the cutting edge for business guests. *Clontarf Castle was our Business Hotel of the Year for 2008. Conference/banqueting (600/380). Business centre; secretarial services; broadband wi/fi; laptop-sized safes in bedrooms. Children welcome (Under 12 free in parents' room; cots available free of charge, baby sitting arranged). No pets. **Rooms 111** (3 suites, 2 junior suites, 7 executive rooms, 97 no-smoking, 2 for

disabled, 9 ground floor). Lift. 24 hr room service. Turn down service. B&B €100 pps, SS €80.
Restaurant: Despite the labyrinth of narrow hotel corridors, Fahrenheit Grill, once reached, is a large, spacious restaurant comprising three interconnecting rooms. Décor is striking, and aside from one room with an impressively high ceiling and old wooden beams, it is modern and glamorous. Bold colours, darkwood furniture, black chandeliers, graphic banquettes and gold panelling all add up to create a chic, comfortable dining space. The menu is quite extensive, with steaks from the grill the focal point; several cuts of dry-aged Irish beef are offered, all having hung for 21 days. Seafood is dominant too, with the signature Dublin Bay Prawn Cocktail especially good. Vegetables have been given real consideration, and the exciting Mediterranean mix, served in gleaming copper pans, deserves serious attention. Service is genuinely friendly and professional, and despite a limited wine list, Fahrenheit Grill makes for a truly enjoyable dining experience. D Mon-Thurs, 5.30-10pm, Fri-Sun, 6-10.30 (Sun to 10pm); L Sun only, 1-3pm. Earl D €28, Mon-Thurs, 5.30-6.30pm; set D 2/3 course, €50/€60; house wine €25. Bar food available in **Knights Bar** all day, every day. Hotel closed 24-25 Dec.*There are sister hotels, the Crowne Plaza, at Dublin Airport & Dundalk (see entries). Amex, MasterCard, Visa, Laser. **Directions:** Take M1 from Dublin Airport, take a left on to Collins Avenue, continue to T junction, take left on to Howth Road. At second set of lights, take a right on to Castle Avenue, continue to roundabout, take right into hotel.

Dublin 3
CAFÉ•WINE BAR

Hemmingways
Vernon Avenue Clontarf Dublin 3
Tel: 01 833 3338

Fans of Hemmingways' quirky fish shop-cum-restaurant just off the seafront in Clontarf might miss the charming fishmonger vibe that formerly made this place so unusual. But, although the appealing fish counter, bar stools and bright lights have been replaced to double numbers, in their place sits a charming little dining room that's cosy, intimate and buzzy - and, although perhaps not as obvious as it once was, a nautical theme is still evident with fishing nets, portholes and boating memorabilia. The little wooden bar with four stools wouldn't look out of place on board a vessel, and is a great spot for a pre-dinner drink while waiting for your table. From here you can peer into the open plan kitchen at the back of the room, where a one-man show serves up dishes like clockwork - the busy kitchen porter is the only clue that anyone might be under pressure. Expect a hearty welcome from the owner, Brian Creedon, who strives to wait on his packed restaurant single-handedly and for the most part efficiently, somehow managing to make time for friendly banter with everyone. Many of the diners seem to know each other and good-sized tables, nicely spaced and set up with comfortable chairs, allow the legions of locals to chat to their neighbours. A short menu features Hemmingways' signature dishes like a smoky, silky fish chowder and juicy, piquant tiger prawn pil pil, while a supplementary blackboard of daily specials might include a starter of grilled sardines or perhaps fresh cod stuffed with seafood. The chef's strengths lie in his choice of ingredients and skilled seasoning - everything is cooked to perfection with deliciously fresh and clean flavours and rustic bistro-style presentation. A shortish wine list is fairly priced, although it would be good to see more wines by the glass. Portions are unusually large, which explains why there's only one daily dessert on offer. If you do feel the urge for something sweet, finish up with one of Hemmingways' legendary Irish coffees: they may slow down Brian's ability to tot up your bill at night's end, but at this stage the refreshingly informal vibe should have lulled you into a pleasantly relaxed state. This is what good neighbourhood restaurants are all about: honest, affordable cooking in a welcoming room. Open L & D Wed-Sat, L 12.30-3.30pm, D 6-9pm (to 11pm Fri/Sat), Sun Tapas, 3-8pm; house wine about €19. Closed Mon, Tue, 25 Dec. MasterCard, Visa, Laser. **Directions:** On the seafront in Clontarf, next to the Butler's Pantry. ◇

Dublin 3
HOTEL

Jurys Croke Park Hotel
Jones's Road Dublin 3 **Tel: 01 871 4444**
crokepark@jurysdoyle.com www.jurys-dublin-hotels.com/jurys_crokepark_hotel

The first major hotel to be built in this area, Jurys brings much-needed facilities and is very useful for business visitors, and fans attending events at Croke Park stadium just across the road. The design is pleasant and very practical, with extensive public areas including a very large foyer/reception with good seating arrangements and several sections conducive to quiet conversation - and the vast bar has a predictably large screen. An inner courtyard comes into its own in sunny weather, and a there's a gym for guests' use. A room card key is required to operate the lift (which can be annoying, but is a useful security measure), and accommodation is well-equipped with everything required by the business traveller; light sleepers should request a quietly-located room as some overlook the railway line, which may be disturbing. Staff make up in cheerfulness and willingness anything they lack in experience, and food in the hotel's Sideline Bistro is a step above the standard normally expected in hotels. Conferences/Banqueting; business centre, secretarial services, laptop-sized safes in bedrooms; Fitness room. **Rooms 232** (2 suites, 35 executive, 10 shower only, 5 family rooms, 4 ground floor, 12 for disabled); room rate €109 per night; 24 hr room service; lift; turndown service. Children welcome (cot available; baby sitting arranged); no pets. Open all year. Amex, Diners, MasterCard, Visa, Laser. **Directions:** From North Circular Road turn left onto Jones's Road, cross The Royal Canal and Jurys Croke Park Hotel is on your left.

Dublin 3
RESTAURANT

Kinara Restaurant

318 Clontarf Road Dublin 3 **Tel: 01 833 6759**
info@kinara.ie www.kinara.ie

This smart two-storey restaurant specialising in authentic Pakistani and Northern Indian cuisine enjoys a scenic location overlooking Bull Island - and is now firmly established as the area's leading ethnic restaurant (and one of the best in Dublin). Fine views are a feature at lunchtime or on bright summer evenings, and there's a cosy upstairs bar with Indian cookbooks to inspire guests waiting for a table or relaxing after dinner. A warm welcome from the dashing Sudanese doorman, Muhammad, ensures a good start, and the restaurant has a very pleasant ambience, with soft lighting, antiques, interesting paintings, the gentlest of background music and streamlined table settings. The menu begins with an introduction to the cuisine, explaining the four fundamental flavours known collectively as 'pisawa masala' - tomato, garlic, ginger and onions - and their uses. Each dish is clearly described, including starters like kakeragh (local crab claws with garlic, yoghurt, spices and a tandoori masala sauce) and main courses such as the luxurious Sumandari Badsha (lobster tails with cashew nuts, pineapple, chilli and spices). There is a declared commitment to local produce - notably organic beef, lamb and chicken - and a section of the menu devoted to organic and 'lighter fare' main courses (typically Loki Mushroom, a vegetarian dish of courgettes and mushrooms in a light spicy yoghurt sauce). The kitchen team have over 80 years experience between them and the quality of both food and cooking is exemplary: dishes have distinct character and depth of flavour, and everything is appetisingly presented with regard to colour, texture and temperature - and fine food is backed up by attentive, professional service under the supervision of restaurant manager, Anwar Gul, and fair prices. Care and attention marks every aspect of this comfortable and attractive restaurant, earning it a loyal following. *Kinara was the Guide's Ethnic Restaurant of the Year in 2004. **A sister restaurant, Kajjal, has recently opened in Malahide, Co Dublin (see entry). **Seats 77** (private room 20); air conditioning; children welcome. L & D daily, 12-4.30 & 5-11pm. Set L about €15; early D about €20 (Mon-Thu, 5.30-7.30pm); also à la carte L&D. House wine about €18.50. Closed 25-26 Dec, 1 Jan. Amex, MasterCard, Visa, Laser. **Directions:** 3km (1.5 m) north of city centre on coast road to Howth (opposite wooden bridge). ◇

Dublin 3
RESTAURANT
Ⓝ

Picasso Restaurant

1 Vernon Avenue Clontar Dublin 3
Tel: 01 853 1120

Just a stone's throw from the coast, Picasso is a family-run restaurant that's found favour with the locals for its quality Italian fare. The red brick and wood interior sets a warm tone that's carried through to the pleasant service and authentic cooking. Despite finding the tables a little too low for the chairs, both upstairs and downstairs rooms are comfortably and attractively laid out. The menu is extra long, and offers a vast selection of Italian classics, alongside interesting daily specials, many of which feature seafood. Highlights include polpette alla casalinga – stuffed meatballs with mozzarella in tomato and basil sauce – and linguine carbonara. Veal dishes are a popular choice, and regulars rate the gamberi piccanti – marinated fresh prawns in chilli, garlic and white wine. Many dishes are pricey, but the pasta offers good value. A broad dessert menu includes their hugely popular tirami'su. The mainly Italian wine list includes a few half bottles, but nothing is available by the glass, which seems an oversight. Reservations are recommended, especially at weekends when two sittings are in place. **Seats 60**; toilets wheelchair accessible. L Mon-Fri, 12.30-3pm; D Tue-Sun,6pm-11pm (Sunday, 5-10pm). **Directions:** On Clontarf seafront at the bottom of Vernon Avenue.

Tibors Bistro

Dublin 3
RESTAURANT
🅔 🅝 🅥

11b Vernon Avenue Clontarf Dublin 3 **Tel: 01 833 3989**
www.tibors.ie

Tibors is the quintessential bistro. Everything about this northside newcomer oozes appeal, and seems designed to please. Whether it's the cheerful welcome from several staff members as you step through the doors, the classy, intimate décor (which works equally well in the day or night), the charming service or the fabulous food, every detail has been carefully considered. Staff work hard to please, displaying impressive knowledge of the menu and wines while offering suggestions and recommendations. Starters eschew the obvious, and might include choices like a plate of Irish charcuterie or smoked coley and leek gratin. Salads are a speciality, with imaginative offerings like country beetroot salad with poached egg and salad cream, or warm salad of chicken livers with caramelised shallots and walnut oil dressing. Main courses are large and filling, and quality of ingredients is evident across all dishes. Chicken is organic, maybe served as a skewered, herb-stuffed fillet, or roasted on the leg with golden crisp skin and fragrant tarragon butter. A choice of homemade burgers includes a mushroom and chickpea patty served with tomato pesto, caramelised onions and home fries. The house steak, a 12oz rib eye, is a real star dish: marinated in mustard, oil and garlic to produce succulent, tender meat brimming with flavour, it's served with chunky onions rings, plump, skin-on chips and a salsa verde. Simple and perfect. This ethos of simplicity and quality is also reflected in the desserts, and service - although it is disappointing to find no vintages on the wine list. A relaxed, convivial atmosphere is created by the friendly waiters, the smooth jazz and comfortable seating - a roomy outside terrace should prove popular with the lunchtime crowd, especially for sunny Sunday brunch. The layout of the room means parties, families and couples can all be catered for in real comfort, which is a smart move in a neighbourhood restaurant. Tibors is more than a neighbourhood restaurant though: in many ways its standards are higher than some of our most popular city restaurants. **Seats 75** (outdoors, 30); children welcome before 7pm (high chair). L&D Mon-Thu, 12-3.30pm; 5.30-11.30pm. Fri-Sat, all day 12-11.30pm. Sun all day 11am-10.30pm; a la carte L&D; house wine from €20. SC 12.5% on groups 6+. Closed Christmas. Amex, MasterCard, Visa, Laser. **Directions:** At the bottom end of Vernon Avenue.

DUBLIN 4

Aberdeen Lodge

Dublin 4
GUESTHOUSE
🌕 🍴 🅥

53 Park Avenue Ballsbridge Dublin 4 **Tel: 01 283 8155**
aberdeen@iol.ie www.aberdeen-lodge.com

Centrally located (close to the Sydney Parade DART station) yet away from the heavy traffic of nearby Merrion Road, this handsome period house in a pleasant leafy street offers all the advantages of a hotel at guesthouse prices. Elegantly furnished executive bedrooms and four-poster suites have air conditioning and all the little comforts expected by the discerning traveller, including a drawing room with comfortable chairs and plenty to read, and a secluded garden where guests can relax in fine weather. Staff are extremely pleasant and helpful (tea and biscuits offered on arrival), housekeeping is immaculate - and, although there is no restaurant, a Drawing Room menu offers a light menu (with wine list). And you can also look forward to a particularly good breakfast, served in a dining room with floor-to-ceiling windows allowing a full view of the beautiful garden: fresh and stewed fruits, home-made preserves, freshly-baked breads and muffins, big jugs of juice are offered, and hot dishes cooked to order - including delicious scrambled eggs and smoked salmon, kippers and buttermilk pancakes with maple syrup, as well as numerous variations on the traditional Irish breakfast. Guests may join residents for breakfast - a useful service for early morning meetings - and the spa at the nearby sister property, Merrion Hall (see entry), is available for guests' use. [Aberdeen Lodge was the Dublin winner of our Irish Breakfast Awards in 2004.] *At the time of going to press another nearby sister property, Blakes Townhouse, is due to re-open after major redevelopment. Small conferences/banqueting (50/40); boardroom, business and fitness facilities for guests - and mature secluded gardens. **Rooms 17** (2 suites, 6 executive rooms, all no-smoking); children welcome. No pets. 24 hour room service. B&B €75 pps, ss €35. Residents' meals available: D (Drawing Room Menu) €22 + all-day menu. House wines from €30. Open all year. Amex, Diners, MasterCard, Visa, Laser. **Directions:** Minutes from the city centre by DART or by car, take the Merrion Road towards Sydney Parade DART station and then first left into Park Avenue.

Dublin 4   # Ariel House

GUESTHOUSE   50-54 Lansdowne Road Ballsbridge Dublin 4 **Tel: 01 668 5512**

ᗡᐧᐧᐧ   reservations@ariel-house.net www.ariel-house.net

This fine family-run establishment occupies three seamlessly adjoined Victorian houses beside the famous old rugby ground in leafy Ballsbridge. It makes a good impression from the outset, with tarmacadamed parking (plus extra parking to the rear), gardens laid out in lawn and shrubbery - making a pleasant place to sit with a book on a summer's day - and a sweep of granite steps leading up to the entrance. Inside, you'll find an elegant hallway, reception and a bay-windowed residents' lounge with antique furnishings, open gas fire, TV and a supply of daily newspapers. The 37 bedrooms are spread throughout the three storeys, including some at garden level, and a major refurbishment programme was completed in May 2008. Bedrooms offering a combination of period décor and modern comforts (all have TV and tea/coffee making facilities) vary in size - deluxe rooms and junior suites have four-posters and brass beds, and special attention is paid to the quality of beds in all rooms; bathrooms vary, standard rooms having compact, tiled bathrooms with bath and shower, heated towel rail, toiletries and hairdryer. Breakfast, served in an extended conservatory overlooking the garden, is a most pleasant experience: attentive staff, fresh flowers on white linen table cloths, clematis trailing outside the window and carefully cooked full Irish fry as well as an array of fruit and cereals. Under the management of Jennie McKeown, a daughter of the house and a professionally trained young hotelier, this is a well-run establishment. **Rooms 37** (3 junior suites, 10 executive, 3 family, 1 shower only, 10 ground floor, all no smoking); children welcome (under 6s free in parents' room, cots available free of charge); free broadband wi/fi; parking (25). B&B €60 pps or €99-150 for a single room. MasterCard, Visa, Laser. **Directions:** On Lansdowne Road off Ballsbridge.

Dublin 4   # Baan Thai

RESTAURANT   16 Merrion Road Ballsbridge Dublin 4

Tel: 01 660 8833

Delicious aromas and oriental music greet you as you climb the stairs to Lek and Eamon Lancaster's well-appointed first floor restaurant opposite the RDS. Friendly staff, Thai furniture and woodcarvings create an authentic oriental feeling and intimate atmosphere - and, as many of the staff are Thai, it's almost like being in Thailand. A wide-ranging menu includes various set meals that provide a useful introduction to the cuisine (or to speed up choices for groups) as well as an à la carte. The essential fragrance and spiciness of Thai cuisine is very much in evidence throughout, and there's Thai beer as well as a fairly extensive wine list. [*Also at: Leopardstown, 01 293 6996]. **Seats 64** (private room, 24); children welcome; air con. L Wed-Fri only; set L €10, 1 course. D daily 6-11, (to 11.30pm Fri & Sat); set 3 course D €30. MasterCard, Visa, Laser. Closed 24-26 Dec. **Directions:** Beside Paddy Cullens pub in Ballsbridge. ◊

Dublin 4   # Bahay Kubo

RESTAURANT   14 Bath Avenue Sandymount Dublin 4

Tel: 01 660 5572

Don't be put off by trains rumbling overhead as you approach this unusual Filipino restaurant - once you get upstairs past the rather worn carpeted entrance and stairway, you will find yourself in a spacious loft room. Friendly staff seat new guests immediately and bring iced water with menus that are well organised with explanations about the Filipino dishes. Several set menus are offered and an à la carte which is, by oriental standards, quite restrained; anyone who likes Chinese food should enjoy the Filipino versions, the fare here is very similar and offers good value for money. As in some other oriental cuisines, the weakness is in the dessert menu, so make the most of the excellent savoury dishes instead. The real selling point of this restaurant is the nightly live music by 'Manila Rhythm', a talented three piece of guitars and double bass performing a wide variety of music from Cuban songs to Frank Sinatra. The resulting atmosphere makes the restaurant ideal for larger groups seeking an informal night out for reasonable prices. Service is attentive, making up in willingness anything it may occasionally lack in training. **Seats 80**; reservations required. D Tue-Sat, 6-11 (Sun 5-10), L Thu & Fri, 12-2.30. Set Menu from about €29, also a la carte Live music Thu & Sat. Closed Mon Amex, MasterCard, Visa, Laser. **Directions:** Above Lansdowne Bar, at railway bridge.

Dublin 4   # BALLSBRIDGE HOTELS

www.D4hotels.com

The former JurysDoyle hotels in Ballsbridge, recently sold for development, have re-opened under new management pending planning decisions on the sites. The **Ballsbridge Inn** and **Ballsbridge Towers**

(previously Jurys Hotel Ballsbridge and The Towers) offer quality accommodation in a wonderful location; this is a room only operation with a lobby area and Food Hall serving continental style breakfast and day food. A full restaurant is available at its adjacent sister property **Ballsbridge Court** (see below). Full bar facilities from 5pm. Room rates: Ballsbridge Inn from €99; Ballsbridge Towers from €109.
Ballsbridge Court (formerly the Berkeley Court Hotel), offers fine accommodation with a good standard of service, and its wonderful bar loved by locals. Ballsbridge Court has a full restaurant/brasserie, open from 7am-11pm. Rooms from €129.00.

Dublin 4
RESTAURANT
V

Bella Cuba Restaurant

11 Ballsbridge Terrace Dublin 4 **Tel: 01 660 5539**
info@bella-cuba.com www.bella-cuba.com

Juan Carlos & Larissa Jimenez's bright, warm-toned restaurant is decorated with dramatic murals by a Cuban designer, providing a uniquely Cuban atmosphere - and Juan Carlos's cooking demonstrates the Spanish, Caribbean and South American influences on Cuba's food. Most dishes are slow cooked, with very little deep frying, and the flavours are of aromatic spices and herbs - predominantly garlic, cumin, oregano and bay. Informative menus give the names of dishes in two languages, with a full description of each, and it's well worth a visit to experience something genuinely different: begin with a famous Cuban cocktail like a Daiquiri or Mojito and then try a speciality of drunk chicken rice or roast pork with Cuban dressing. Service, under the direction of Omar Jiminez, is professional and friendly, adding to the appeal of this cheerful restaurant. The wine list, which offers a choice fairly balanced between the old and new, includes a pair of Cuban bottles. The early evening 'Value Menu' allows you to choose from a limited selection on the à la carte. **Seats 33**; not suitable for children after 7pm. D daily, 5 - 11 (to 10.30pm Sun). Early D €20 (5-7). Also à la carte. House wine €18.50. SC 10% on parties 6+. Closed Christmas. Amex, MasterCard, Visa, Laser. **Directions:** Middle of Ballsbridge.

Dublin 4
RESTAURANT

Berman & Wallace

Belfield Office Park Beaver Row Clonskeagh Dublin 4 **Tel: 01 219 6252**
bermanandwallace@eircom.net www.bermanandwallace.com

This smart pavilion-style restaurant, in a courtyard surrounded by office buildings, supplies the local business community with wide-ranging high quality brasserie-style daytime food. Choose from such all-time favourites as Irish Stew, fish and chips, bangers and mash (made with Hicks sausages) and baguettes filled with chargrilled steak and garlic mayonnaise, to pasta dishes, lamb passanda, chicken piri-piri with herb risotto and a great deal more. There are also several revitalising or detoxing juices and smoothies for the diet conscious, and there is a daily health lunch special on offer. Wines by the glass or by bottle. **Seats 80** (outdoor 20). Open Mon-Fri, 7.30-3. Parking for 20 cars. Closed Sat/Sun, Christmas, Easter, bank hols. Amex, MasterCard, Visa, Laser. **Directions:** From Donnybrook, turn at Bus Station up Beaver Road towards Clonskeagh. Turn left at second set of lights into business park.

Dublin 4
HOTEL
V

Bewleys Hotel

Merrion Road Ballsbridge Dublin 4 **Tel: 01 668 1111**
ballsbridge@bewleyshotels.com www.bewleyshotels.com

This modern hotel is cleverly designed to incorporate a landmark period building next to the RDS. Bedrooms are spacious and well-equipped, making a good base for business or leisure visits. Like its sister hotels at Newlands Cross, Leopardstown and Dublin Airport, you get a lot of comfort here at a very reasonable cost. Although it changed ownership in 2008 (and is now part of the Moran Hotel Group) there has been no obvious change - except that Tom O'Connell's renowned restaurant, O'Connells in Ballsbridge, no longer operates here and the hotel restaurant is now called The Brasserie. Conferences/Banqueting (250/180); business centre; free broadband. **Rooms 304** (10 shower only, 64 family rooms, 254 no smoking, 12 for disabled, 50 ground floor). No pets; garden; parking. Lift; limited room service. Room rate €119-299; children welcome (under 16s free in parents room, baby sitting arranged, cots available free of charge). Closed 24-26 Dec. Amex, Diners, MasterCard, Visa, Laser. **Directions:** At junction of Simmonscourt and Merrion Road.

Dublin 4
RESTAURANT

Brownes

18 Sandymount Green Sandymount Dublin 4
Tel: 01 269 7316

Peter Bark keeps raising the bar at his popular restaurant on Sandymount Green so that it's gone well beyond being a good daytime café and neighbourhood restaurant in the evening these days - the secret is well and truly out and it attracts growing numbers of diners from beyond the area too. During the day you'll find gourmet sandwiches, (crayfish tails; rare beef, horseradish and rocket) and, by night, simple, classical French-inspired food. Décor is minimal, with good paintings by local artists and simple bentwood chairs, but the chef here cooks up things like a mean moules marinière (starter or main - nice fat mussels in a wine and cream sauce), and great meats including aged sirloin (crusty on the outside and pink within, served with chunky, crispy 'real' chips) and pan-fried rack of lamb, served on a bed of flageolet beans, with tasty, slightly waxy, continental-style new potatoes. Finish with a well-made traditional dessert (crème brûlée, crumble) or excellent home-made ice creams and sorbets. BYO wine - a small corkage charge is levied "unless you offer us a glass of something nice". Coffee could be the weak point, so call for the (surprisingly modest) bill and have it at home. **Seats 22**; about €32-35 for 3 courses. D 6-10pm. **Directions:** Sandymount green. ◇

Dublin 4
HOTEL

The Burlington Hotel Dublin
Upper Leeson Street Dublin 4 **Tel: 01 618 5600**
info@burlingtonhotel.ie www.burlingtonhotel.ie

Ireland's largest hotel, the Burlington has more experience of dealing with very big numbers efficiently and enjoyably than any other in the country. All bedrooms have been recently refurbished and banquets for huge numbers are not only catered for but can have a minimum choice of three main courses on all menus. Good facilities for business guests: a high proportion of bedrooms are designated executive, with ISDN lines, fax machines and air conditioning. Conference/banqueting (1500/1200); business centre; secretarial services; video conferencing. No pets. Special offers often available. **Rooms 500**. B&B about €145 pps, ss €115. Open all year. Amex, Diners, MasterCard, Visa, Laser. ◇

Dublin 4
GUESTHOUSE

Butlers Town House
44 Lansdowne Road Ballsbridge Dublin 4 **Tel: 01 667 4022**
info@butlers-hotel.com butlers-hotel.com

On a corner site in Dublin's 'embassy belt' and close to the Lansdowne Road stadium, this large townhouse/guesthouse has been extensively refurbished and luxuriously decorated in a Victorian country house style and is a small hotel in all but name. Public rooms include a comfortable drawing room/bar and an attractive conservatory-style dining room where good breakfasts are served; an attractive all-day menu is also offered. Rooms are individually decorated and furnished to a high standard, some with four-poster beds. **Rooms 19** (3 superior, 1 disabled, all no smoking); not suitable for children. No pets. 24 hr room service. Private parking (15). Wheelchair accessible. Turndown service offered. B&B about €95, ss €45; no SC. Closed 21 Dec-5 Jan. Amex, Diners, MasterCard, Visa, Laser, **Directions:** Corner of Lansdowne Road and Shelbourne Road. ◇

Dublin 4
RESTAURANT
ⓣ

Canal Bank Café
146 Upper Leeson Street Dublin 4 **Tel: 01 664 2135**
info@tribeca.ie www.canalbankcafe.com

Trevor Browne and Gerard Foote's well-known almost-canalside restaurant is designed to meet the current demand for quality informal food or 'everyday dining', but the philosophy is to use only the best ingredients - organic beef and lamb, free-range chicken and a wide variety of fresh fish daily. The menu is user-friendly, divided mainly by types of dish - starters like crispy fried calamari with lemon mayonnaise, big salads (Caesar, niçoise) and, for those who need a real feed, steaks various ways and specialities like Brooklyn meatloaf with spinach, onion gravy & mashed potatoes, and there's also a good sprinkling of vegetarian dishes. A carefully selected, compact wine list includes a good choice of house wines - and a range of brunch cocktails too. **Seats 65**; children welcome; air conditioning. Open 10am-11pm daily. A la carte. House wine €19.95. SC 10% on parties of 6+. Closed 24-28 Dec & Good Fri. Amex, Diners, MasterCard, Visa, Laser. **Directions:** Ballsbridge side of the canal on Leeson Street. ◇

Dublin 4
RESTAURANT

The Courtyard Restaurant & Piano Bar
1 Belmont Avenue Donnybrook Dublin 4 **Tel: 01 283 0407**
info@thecourtyardcafe.ie www.thecourtyardcafe.ie

Set well back from the road and approached through the courtyard that inspired the name, Bert and Michelle Egan's popular neighbourhood restaurant is a relaxed spot with some style, where good food combines attractively with reasonable prices and a pleasing ambience. It's not a place that visitors are likely to find by chance, but useful to know about, especially as they are open from late afternoon every day so you can enjoy a leisurely early evening meal before going on to a concert or the theatre in town. Piano in the evening. **Seats 170** (private room, 70, outdoors, 40); air conditioning; children welcome; D Mon-Sat, 5.30-10.30; L Sun only, all day 12.30-8.30pm; Early D about €20, 5.30-7; Sun L about €25; House wine €18-20. SC 10%. Closed 25 Dec, Good Fri. Amex, Diners, MasterCard, Visa, Laser. **Directions:** Behind Madigans pub. ◇

Dublin 4   Donnybrook Fair Café
RESTAURANT   89a Morehampton Road Donnybrook Dublin 4 **Tel: 01 614 4849**
                           restaurant@donnybrookfair.ie www.donnybrookfair.ie

The sleek looks of the exterior of Dublin's chicest supermarket, Donnybrook Fair, are matched by some equally sleek products on the shelves: fine food produce from around the globe jostles with local producers' goods as well as delectable treats from the fish and deli counters. Up a spiral stairway from the shop floor you'll find Donnybrook Fair Café, a bright and airy space where the menu features plenty of old reliables, with starters including simple soups and salads, and chicken liver paté, while main courses include good meats - rack of lamb, rib-eye steak - and a wide choice of fish. Desserts will please lovers of golden oldies such as chocolate brownie cake, vanilla crème brûlée and mandarin cheesecake. The eclectic wine list contains plenty of moderately priced wines, as well as more expensive wines by the glass. Although it sometimes struggles to keep up with the high-end produce found below, this smart café remains a popular place to meet for a bite. **Seats 80** (private room, 25); children welcome; air conditioning; reservations accepted; food served all day, Mon-Sat, 8am - 9.30pm (L 12-5, D 5.30-9.30); Sun brunch only, 9-4pm; set Sun set meal about €23.95; early D about €23.95, Sun-Fri, 5.30-7pm, also a la carte L&D; house wine from €19; SC on groups of 10+. Closed Sun eve, Christmas. MasterCard, Visa, Laser. **Directions:** City side of Donnybrook village, AIB on corner. ◇

Dublin 4   Dunne & Crescenzi
RESTAURANT   11 Seafort Avenue Sandymount Dublin 4 **Tel: 01 667 3252**
                               dunneandcrescenzi@hotmail.com www.dunneandcrescenzi.com

Genuine Italian fare is what you'll find at this small restaurant, a younger branch of the well-known Dublin 2 establishment (see entry). Like its older sister, it's a quality ingredients-led place with tightly packed tables, an extensive Italian wine list and a menu that dispenses with the idea of courses, offering instead a selection of charcuterie plates, panini and other light dishes like insalata caprese, and some hot dishes so you can have a light bite or a full meal as appetite dictates. **Seats 80**; air conditioning; children welcome. Open all day from 8.30am. House wine about €15. MasterCard, Visa, Laser **Directions:** Next to O'Reilly's pub.

Dublin 4   Dylan Hotel Dublin
HOTEL•RESTAURANT   Eastmoreland Place Dublin 4 **Tel: 01 660 3000**
                                      justask@dylan.ie www.dylan.ie

It feels as if it's in a peaceful backwater, yet this splendid Victorian building is just yards from one of Dublin's busiest city centre roads. Arrival at the gates of Dylan is an experience in itself, especially in the evening, when it is magically lit by old fashioned lamps outside the main entrance, where doormen greet you. A modern wing sits comfortably with the original building and the lobby offers a fore-taste of the edgy design beyond: leather padded walls, over-sized floral motifs and tactile wallpaper along with ultra-modern seating and creative lighting are just some of the quirky elements that create an atmosphere of decadent elegance. The edgy look continues in the individually designed bedrooms, which are fitted to a very high specification. Standard rooms are laptop compatible and include a plasma screen TV, MP3 players, safes, cordless phones with voicemail and speakerphone, customised 7th Heaven Beds, Frette linen, air conditioning, under-floor heated bathrooms, power showers, robes & slippers, Etro toiletries, mini bar and twice daily housekeeping. Even the most demanding international traveller would be hard pressed to complain at this five star boutique hotel. Not suitable for children. Business centre, secretarial services, free broadband wi/fi. **Rooms 44** (6 suites, 38 executive, 15 shower only, 1 disabled, all no smoking); Lift; 24hr room service. Room rate from €199. Lifts. Non-smoking hotel. Open all year except 25-26 Dec. **The Still:** This bright, white dining room is filled with glittering chandeliers, luxurious cream and white chairs, wildly curved furnishings, a pale padded wall and a baby grand piano. The ambience is lavish 1940s Hollywood decadence and there are always plenty of big Irish names to be spotted here. Padraig Haydn's cooking is still as stylish and flavourful as ever, but the story at this fashionable restaurant is the more customer-friendly approach, with good value pricing and a nicely honed menu. The lunchtime line-up in The Still runs to a well structured choice of five starters and an equal number of main courses and desserts, all separately priced but comfortably within the €30 mark for two courses. Fresh gazpacho is poured from individual jugs into chilled bowls at the table, and citrus cured salmon comes with a soft boiled egg and micro salad leaves. Grilled mackerel fillet and summer vegetables are complemented with tiny pools of tapenade, and a golden-crusted mushroom pithvier garnished with a wreath of pickled wild baby mushrooms provides a non-meat choice. Décor in both reception areas and the restaurant has been tweaked as well, with some of the wilder designer seating modified to be more user-friendly, although the 18 crystal chandeliers still twinkle away cheerfully in the dining room. Dylan remains very much a place to be seen, and provides an opulent stage setting for an exciting dining experience. Bar food, which can also be served on the covered terrace, is now available from 12 noon to 5pm and includes some hot dishes like pan-fried cod fillet with ratatouille and herb sausages with potato purée and onion jus, as well as oysters, a cheese platter, open sandwiches and fresh soup of the day. The wine list is a huge encyclopaedic tome which requires long study, but there is a good choice in the €25-35 bracket as well as the stratospheric numbers. Five white wines, a rosé and five reds are well selected to cater for popular tastes, ranging from €6.40 to €12.70 by the glass; the Provençal rosé Ch. Vignelaure 'La Source' is particularly good, as is the Bisol prosecco, which appears alongside top label champagnes. **Seats 44** (private room, 12, outdoors, 20); air conditioning; L daily, 12.30-2.30pm, D daily 6-10.30pm (to 11pm Thu-Sat); set 3 course L €38, also à la carte L&D. Average starter €21, main courses €35, desserts €15. Tasting Menu of 8 courses €110. House wine from €20.95. SC discretionary. Amex, Mastercard, Visa, Laser. **Directions:** Just off Upper Baggot Street before St. Marys Road. ◇

Dublin 4

CAFÉ•RESTAURANT

Expresso Bar Café

1 St Mary's Road Ballsbridge Dublin 4

Tel: 01 660 0585

Great flavour-packed food, good value and efficient service invariably pleases the loyal following at Ann-Marie Nohl's clean-lined informal restaurant, which is renowned for carefully sourced ingredients that make a flavour statement on the plate. An all-morning breakfast menu offers many of the classics, often with a twist: thus a simple poached egg on toast comes with crispy bacon and relish, porridge is a class act topped with toasted almonds and honey, and French toast comes with bacon, or winter berries and syrup. Lunch and dinner menus tend to favour an international style, but the same high standards apply: whether it's a Dublin Bay Prawn pil pil with Chilli, coriander, char-grilled lime and crusty toast, or grilled balsamic chicken with a peach and baby spinach salad, or a vegetarian pasta such as fettucine with black olive, rocket, sundried tomato tapenade & oven-roasted vine tomatoes, it's the quality of the ingredients and cooking that make the food here special. Wines on display add to the atmosphere, and an informative and well-chosen wine list offers half a dozen by the glass, and a pair of half bottles. Weekend brunch is a must. **Seats 60** (outdoor, 14); not suitable for children after 5pm; air conditioning. Open Mon-Fri, 7.30am-9pm (B 7.30-11.30am; L 12-5.30, D 6-9pm), Sat 9am-9.30pm (L 9-5, D 6-9.30pm), Sun brunch 10am-5pm. Closed D Sun, 25 Dec, 1 Jan, Good Friday. MasterCard, Visa, Laser. **Directions:** Opposite Dylan Hotel, off Upper Baggot Street.

Dublin 4

Four Seasons Hotel

HOTEL•RESTAURANT

Simmonscourt Road Dublin 4 **Tel: 01 665 4000**

reservations.dublin@fourseasons.com www.fourseasons.com/dublin

Set in its own gardens on a section of the Royal Dublin Society's 42-acre show grounds, this luxurious hotel enjoys a magnificent site, allowing a sense of spaciousness while also being convenient to the city centre - the scale is generous throughout and there are views of the Wicklow Mountains or Dublin Bay from many of the sumptuous suites and guest rooms. A foyer in the grand tradition is flanked by two bars - the traditional wood-panelled Lobby Bar and the newer Ice, which is deliciously contemporary, and very popular with Dubliners. Accommodation is predictably luxurious and, with a full range of up-to-the-minute amenities, the air-conditioned rooms are designed to appeal equally to leisure and business guests. A choice of pillows (down and non-allergenic foam) is provided as standard, the large marbled bathrooms have separate bath and shower, and many other desirable features - and there's great emphasis on service, with twice daily housekeeping service, overnight laundry and dry cleaning, one hour pressing and complimentary overnight shoe shine: everything, in short, that the immaculate traveller requires. But the Spa in the lower level of the hotel is perhaps its most outstanding feature, offering every treatment imaginable - and a naturally lit 14m lap pool and adjacent jacuzzi pool, overlooking an outdoor sunken garden. Outstanding conference and meeting facilities make the hotel ideal for corporate events, business meetings and parties in groups of anything up to 550. Conferences/Banqueting (550/450), business centre, secretarial services, video conferencing (on request), broadband wi/fi. Children welcome (under 18s free in parents' room, cot available free of charge, baby sitting arranged). **Rooms 196** (16 suites, 26 junior suites, 178 no-smoking, 13 for disabled). 24 hr room service, Lift, Turndown service. Room rate €225 (max. 3 guests). No SC. Open all year. **Seasons Restaurant:** This spacious, classically-appointed restaurant overlooks a leafy courtyard and no expense has been spared on the traditional 'grand hotel' decor and, whether or not it is to your taste, this is an extremely comfortable restaurant and the service is usually exemplary. Executive Chef Terry White's contemporary international menus have their base in classical French cooking and offer a wide-ranging choice of luxurious dishes, with a considerate guide to dishes suitable for vegetarians, 'healthier fare' and dishes containing nuts. An unusual speciality dish to try is an Irish scallop tasting, prepared with Parmesan with creamy spicy sauce, jalapeno salsa or natural, with caviar. An extensive hors d'oeuvre buffet of hot and cold dishes has become a favourite feature of late, and a 7-course Tasting Menu is offered. The standard of cooking is high and, while it may not rival the city's top independent restaurants as a cutting edge dining experience, this is a fine hotel restaurant with outstanding service - and Sommelier Simon Keegan's excellent wine list includes some very good wines by the glass. *Informal menus are also available at varying times in The Café (daily), and in Ice Bar (Tue-Sat); Afternoon Tea, served daily in the Lobby Lounge, includes an extensive menu of classic teas and infusions. **Seats 90** (private room, 12); air conditioning. Breakfast 7-11 daily, L 12.30-3 daily, D 6.30-9.30 daily. Set L from €35; à la carte also available D. House wine from €33. Amex, Diners, MasterCard, Visa. **Directions:** Located on the RDS Grounds on corner of Merrion and Simmonscourt Roads. ◊

Dublin 4

The French Paradox

RESTAURANT•WINE BAR

53 Shelbourne Road Ballsbridge Dublin 4 **Tel: 01 660 4068**

pch@chapeauwines.com www.thefrenchparadox.com

On a busy road near the RDS, this inspired and stylish operation brings an extra dimension (and a whiff of the south of France) to the concept of wine and food in Dublin. French Paradox combines a wine shop, a large and atmospheric ground floor wine bar (where weekly wine tastings are held) and a dining room on the first floor, which gains atmosphere from the irresistible charcuterie on display close beside the tables. French Paradox is a former winner of our Wine Award and the main emphasis is on the wide range of wines available by the glass - perhaps 65 wines, kept in perfect condition after opening, using a wine sommelier, with inert gas. Pierre and Tanya Chapeau are renowned for their directly imported wines and food is, in theory, secondary here; but, although the choice is deliberately limited (a small à la carte offers a concise range of individual dishes and shared charcuterie plates), the quality is exceptional and - although the hot dinner dishes may be less successful - everyone just loves specialities like the foie gras, the smoked duck salad and the 'Bill Hogan', made with the renowned thermophilic cheeses from west Cork... and sitting outside on a sunny summer day, enjoying a plate of charcuterie with any one of the dozens of wines available by the glass, you could be lunching in the south of France. Classic desserts - tarte tatin, chocolate terrine, crème brûlée - and excellent coffees to finish. Wines offered change regularly (the list is always growing), and food can be purchased from the deli-counter to take home. **Seats 25** (+25 in tasting room, +12 outside); not suitable for children after 7pm; air conditioning; toilets wheelchair accessible. L&D Mon-Thu, 12-3 & 6-9.30; open all day Fri & Sat, 12-10. Set L about €16.95; value D about €25, 6-8.30pm. A la carte. House wines (6) change monthly, from €19. Closed Sun (except for "Rugby Match" Sundays), Christmas, Bank Hols. Amex, MasterCard, Visa, Laser. **Directions:** Opposite Ballsbridge Post Office.

Dublin 4
RESTAURANT

Furama Restaurant

G/F Eirepage House Donnybrook Dublin 4 **Tel: 01 283 0522**
info@furama.ie www.furama.ie

In the sleek black interior of Rodney Mak's long-established restaurant, Freddy Lee, who has been head chef since the restaurant opened in 1989, produces terrific food with an authenticity which has been unusual in Ireland until recently. The waiter stationed beside the entrance opens the door and welcomes customers on arrival, setting the tone for excellent service that is as friendly as it is technically correct. With the dining room reached over a curving bridge and water features, the interior is welcoming and quietly elegant. Customers here are largely locals and faithful regulars drawn here by the relaxed hospitality and reliably authentic take on classic Chinese dishes, which include faultless crispy duck, dim sum fried or steamed, and excellent seafood dishes like the seared scallops with ginger, spring onion and soy glaze beautifully presented in their shells. Although Chinese restaurants are notoriously weak in the dessert department, Furama's banana fritters are an exception, presented piping hot in feathery batter with toasted sesame seeds, a pool of caramel syrup and a scoop of vanilla ice cream; it is also extremely good value as desserts including the excellent fritters are only €3-3.50, which compares remarkably well with extra side dishes at about €6.50. House wines at about €20 are good value, and also available by the glass; more expensive wines on the list favour expense account diners, running to the €40-60 level. This restaurant is highly recommended for its consistency over the years, both in quality of food and impeccable service. A Special Chinese Menu can be arranged for banqueting with one week's notice (up to 30 people) and outside catering is also available. *Furama was our Ethnic Restaurant of the Year in 2008. **Seats 70**; air conditioning. Mon-Fri: L 12.30-2pm, D 6pm-11.30pm, Sat D only 6-11.30pm, Sun open 12.30pm-11pm; D Various set menus from about €35. A la carte available. House wine from about €19. SC 10%. Parking. Closed Sat L, 24-26 Dec & Good Fri. Amex, Diners, MasterCard, Visa, Laser. **Directions:** Opposite Bective Rugby Ground in Donnybrook, near town side of Donnybrook Bridge.

Dublin 4
GUESTHOUSE

Glenogra House

64 Merrion Road Ballsbridge Dublin 4 **Tel: 01 668 3661**
info@glenogra.com www.glenogra.com

Conveniently located for the RDS and within 3 minutes walk of the Sandymount DART station, this well-known guesthouse is run by the owners, Peter and Veronica Donohoe, who are doing an excellent job. The public areas have all been refurbished and, from the minute you arrive there is a great sense of welcome and hospitality - lovely fresh flowers in the large hall, someone to carry your bags to your room and explain the facilities, the security of knowing there is safe parking. Although regularly refurbished, the bedrooms are not furnished in the latest style - expect to find darkwood furniture, fringed lampshades and little dressing table mirrors - but they are comfortable and clean, and offer some welcome extras, including smart white bathrobes and portable radios. Moreover, you'll get a really good breakfast, with plenty of choice (including scrambled egg with smoked salmon) leaf tea, and exceptionally delicious home-made muesli. **Rooms 13** (2 shower only, 1 family room, all no-smoking); children welcome (under 10s free in parents' room, cots available free of charge). Free broadband WiFi, no pets. B&B €59.50 pps, ss €30. Closed 22 Dec - 10 Jan. Amex, Diners, MasterCard, Visa, Laser. **Directions:** Opposite Four Seasons Hotel, RDS.

Dublin 4   # Grand Canal Hotel
HOTEL   Grand Canal Street Dublin 4 **Tel: 01 646 1000**
reservations@grandcanalhotel.com www.grandcanalhotel.com

Smartly maintained and with a secure car park, this business hotel located in the up-and-coming Grand Canal area is ideal for anyone requiring fairly priced quality accommodation within walking distance of Dublin city centre and the Ballsbridge area. Reception is friendly and efficient, and public areas are bright clean and relaxing. The top floor is dedicated to executive rooms, but all rooms are spacious and have hospitality tray, cable TV, WiFi, direct dial telephone, iron, and hairdryer; bathrooms have large baths and quality towels, and the standard of housekeeping is good. A fairly standard but well-presented buffet breakfast is served in a pleasant breakfast room. The hotel has a range of meeting rooms, and food of various kinds is available in different areas during the day and evening; the useful Canal Express Bar serves coffee and snacks for people in a hurry, whether hotel guests or popping in off the street. Conferences/Banqueting (140/200); free parking for guests; broadband wi/fi. **Rooms 142**; children welcome (under 3s free in parents' room, cot available free of charge, baby sitting arranged); 24hr room service; Lift; B&B from €67 pps, single room only from €122. Closed 22-28 Dec. Amex, Diners, MasterCard, Visa, Laser. **Directions:** On Grand Canal Street: 50m from Grand Canal DART station, beside the north end of the Grand Canal.

Dublin 4   # Herbert Park Hotel
HOTEL   Ballsbridge Dublin 4 **Tel: 01 667 2200**
V
reservations@herbertparkhotel.ie www.herbertparkhotel.ie

This large, privately-owned contemporary hotel is attractively located in an 'urban plaza' near the RDS and the public park after which it is named. It is approached over a little bridge, which leads to an underground carpark and, ultimately, to a smart lower ground foyer and the lift up to the main lobby. Public areas on the ground floor make a popular meeting place - impressively light and spacious, with excellent light meals and drinks provided by efficient waiting staff. The bright and modern style is also repeated in the bedrooms, which have views over Ballsbridge and Herbert Park and are stylishly designed and well-finished, with a high standard of amenities. A good breakfast is served in the Pavilion Restaurant, a bright, elegant, contemporary room which overlooks a garden terrace (where tables can be set up in fine weather. Team building, jazz events, golf packages and special breaks are all offered. A good choice for the business guest or corporate events as well as private guests, this hotel is reasonably priced for the standard of accommodation and facilities offered, and staff are efficient, enthusiastic and warm. Conference/banqueting (160/220); business centre, video conferencing, broadband wi/fi, laptop-sized safes in bedrooms. **Rooms 153** (2 suites, 40 executive rooms, 138 no-smoking, 8 for disabled); children welcome (under 2 free in parents' room, cots available free of charge, baby sitting arranged, playground). No pets. Lift. 24 hr room service. Turndown service. B&B €120pps. SS €120. No SC. Open all year. Fitness room, garden, newsagent. Restaurant: **Seats 200**. Breakfast 8-10 (Sat & Sun to 10.30, Sun from 8); L 12.30-2.30; D daily 5.30-9.30. Set L €30 (Buffet Sun L €39.50); D à la carte. House wine €23.50. Amex, Diners, MasterCard, Visa. **Directions:** In Ballsbridge, shortly before RDS heading out of city.

Dublin 4

Itsa4

RESTAURANT

6a, Sandymount Green Sandymount Dublin 4 **Tel: 01 219 4676**
itsa4@itsabagel.com www.itsabagel.com

This smart contemporary place has a 'New York Diner' feel, appropriate given the American connections of Domini and Peaches Kemp, the talented and hard-working sisters who are already well known for the 'Itsa Bagel' cafés - but this is a fully-fledged restaurant and not an extension of the bagel concept. Quality ingredient-led menus have a strong emphasis on provenance and no obvious distinction between starters and main courses at lunchtime; you might start, for example, with a platter of Terry Butterly's excellent pale smoked salmon, served in a portion generous enough to serve two easily, or perhaps a portion of potato skins with cheddar, dry-cured bacon and a sour cream dip as another nibbling option to share. The daily pasta dishes are invariably excellent and specialities include superb dry-aged rib-eye beef, which is served with a gorgeously rich béarnaise sauce and great vegetables (from Gold River Farm, in Co Wicklow); many say that the house 'organic' chips (which are unpeeled) have 'more flavour but less crispness' than regular chips - an odd response as, given a suitable variety, organic chips will be just as crisp as any others. Excellent desserts include gorgeous home-made ice creams and sorbets, and matured Sheridans cheese is served simply on a wooden platter with warm biscuits and grapes. Java Republic organic Fairtrade coffees are good (and served with excellent breakfasts too - try the Eggs Benedict), service is friendly and efficient, and there's an interesting well-priced wine list which includes unusual bottles from specialist suppliers. **Seats 58** (outdoor, 10); toilets wheelchair accessible; air conditioning; free broadband wi/fi; children welcome before 9pm (high chair, children's menu, baby changing facilities); L & D Tue-Sat, 12-3 and 5.30-10; Sun all day 1-8pm; Junior Bites (under 12s) €10-12; pre-concert D 5.30-6.30pm, Tue-Fri, €23; house wine €17. Closed Mon (except Bank Hols); 25-26 Dec, Good Fri. MasterCard, Visa, Laser. **Directions:** On Sandymount Green.

Dublin 4

Juniors

RESTAURANT

Bath Avene Dublin 4
Tel: 01 664 3648

Squashed into a row of red brick shopfronts, Junior's is a laidback restaurant of the type more often seen in the side streets of Paris or Naples. Run by two brothers, Paul and Barry McInerney, one looks after front of house while the other produces satisfyingly hearty food in a tiny space separated from customers only by a deli counter and a classic Italian espresso machine. Style here leans towards rustic Italian granny cooking reflecting the chef's continental experience, with big fresh soups, antipasta plates heaped with first rate charcuterie and chunks of Parmesan, enormous bowls of bouillabaisse-style fish stew and melting roast pork belly, served with herby greens and creamy Tuscan white beans. Daily menus are written up on blackboards, while the small but admirably selective wine list is printed up for longer perusal, with a good choice available by the (generous) glass. Opened in July 2008, this buzzy spot doesn't take bookings - it's first come - first served, but intending diners don't mind waiting in the pub next door. Also open for lunch, which tends to be soup and hefty hand-cut sandwiches. **Seats 26**. **Directions:** Just off Grand Canal Street.

Dublin 4

Kites Restaurant

RESTAURANT

15-17 Ballsbridge Terrace Ballsbridge Dublin 4 **Tel: 01 660 7415**
kites@eircom.net

Lots of natural light with white painted walls, dark wooden fittings and a rich, dark carpet create a good first impression at this split-level Ballsbridge restaurant, and a mix of diners gives the place a nice buzz. The cuisine is a combination of Cantonese, Szechuan, Peking and Thai - predominantly Cantonese - and menus range from the standard set meals to a list of specials. For the indecisive, a house platter of appetisers makes a good beginning, offering a selection from about two dozen starters on offer you'll get some well-made popular dishes - spring rolls, samosa, chicken satay - along with some more unusual additions. Duckling and seafood are specialities: half a crispy aromatic duck comes with fresh steaming pancakes, while a combination dish of salt & pepper jumbo king prawns and stir-fry scallops is interesting. Stir-fried lamb with ginger & spring onion (one of the few Peking dishes) is to be recommended. Courteous, good humoured and charming service adds to the experience. **Seats 100** (private room, 40); air conditioning. L daily 12.30-2, D daily 6.30-11.30. Set L

€20.50, set D €36; also à la carte. House wine from €23. SC 10%. Closed 25-26 Dec. Good Fri. Amex, Diners, MasterCard, Visa, Laser. **Directions:** In the heart of Ballsbridge.

Dublin 4 La Péniche

RESTAURANT Grand Canal Mespil Road Dublin 4 **Tel: 087 790 0077**

info@lapeniche.ie www.lapeniche.ie

Dining afloat is an attraction in many European cities but, until recently, Dublin has remained stubbornly out of the loop, so perhaps it should come as no surprise that it is Eric Tydagt and his team at the popular French/Belgian restaurant 'La Mère Zou' who finally introduced the city to this entertaining experience. The barge is smartly got up with red velvet couches and seat covers, and gleaming varnished tables complete with a small lamp and button to call for service. It's quite a squeeze when fully booked, but that's all part of the fun. The menu is based on authentic French bistro dishes, and the idea is that you can have a full four-course meal, a simple charcuterie plate or just a dessert with coffee. Typical sharing dishes include Galway Oysters, a platter of duck rillette, saucisson, paté de campagne & cured ham), and a similar plate offering a combination of charcuterie and cheese. Homely hot dishes range from good soups and rustic classics such as flavoursome Toulouse sausage with basil pesto mash, to a prawn & smoked fish pie, with white wine sauce & pomme purée. There's a special too, and vegetarians can look forward to classic salads and hot dishes like mushroom vol-au-vent with mixed salad. The atmosphere is helped along by very friendly and helpful service and, as well as a good choice of (mainly French) wines, there's a small list of French beers and ciders. On Thursdays, dinner is even more fun, eaten under way as La Péniche cruises the canal. The barge is a great place for a party, and can be hired exclusively, with live music if requested. All round it's a hugely entertaining addition to the Dublin dining scene, and adds a new dimension to the city. *La Péniche was our Atmospheric Restaurant of the Year in 2007 - and has been such a success that a second boat is planned. **Seats 45** (outdoors, 40); children welcome; L Tue-Fri, 12-3pm; D Tue-Sat, 6-10.30pm; Sun L only, 2pm-5pm; set D €35; also a la carte L&D. SC 10% on groups 6+. Closed Mon, 1 Jan - 15 Jan. MasterCard, Visa, Laser. **Directions:** Boat on Grand Canal - Mespil Road.

Dublin 4 The Lobster Pot

RESTAURANT 9 Ballsbridge Terrace Ballsbridge Dublin 4 **Tel: 01 660 9170**

www.thelobsterpot.ie

On the first floor of a redbrick Ballsbridge terrace, conspicuously located near the Herbert Park Hotel - and just a few minutes walk from the RDS - this long-established restaurant has lost none of its charm or quality over the years, even with a total refurbishment in 2008, and now has a unique appeal as the experience is so different from contemporary restaurants. The whole team - owner Tommy Crean, restaurant manager (and sommelier) John Rigby and head chef Don McGuinness - have been working here together since 1980 and the system is running very sweetly. How good it is to see old favourites like dressed Kilmore Quay crab, home-made chicken liver paté and fresh prawn bisque on the menu, along with fresh prawns mornay and many other old friends, including kidneys turbigo and game in season. The menu is a treat to read but there's also a daily fish tray display for specials - dishes are explained and diners are encouraged to choose their own combinations. All this and wonderfully old-fashioned service too, including advice from John Rigby on the best wine to match your meal. If only there were more places like this - long may it last. L Mon-Fri 12.30-2pm. D Mon-Sat, 6.30-10.30. House wine about €22.50. SC 12.5%. Closed Sun, 24 Dec-4 Jan, bank hols. Amex, Diners, MasterCard, Visa, Laser. **Directions:** In the heart of Ballsbridge adjacent to the US Embassy.

Marble Hall

Dublin 4
B&B

81 Marlborough Road Donnybrook Dublin 4 **Tel: 01 497 7350**
marblehall@eircom.net www.marblehall.net

First time visitors have no idea of the delights that lie ahead as they arrive at Shelagh Conway's wonderful B&B, which is discreetly situated in a redbrick Georgian terrace, with no signage just a neatly presented frontage. But this warm and welcoming place will quickly work its charm. Shelagh herself is always on hand to look after guests, and her house is a gem. Everything is immaculate, with polished wooden floors and beautiful ceiling cornices throughout the ground floor; a little sitting room at the front of the house has a white marble fireplace and period armchairs - there's a TV/DVD player here for guests' use, along with a collection of DVDs, books and magazines. The period bedrooms are large and bright, with big comfortable beds, plenty of pillows, books, mineral water, television and hairdryer and a spruce little shower room. Double doors from the sitting room open on to a lovely breakfast room with round and oval tables, and antique lace cloths; here, although there are only three rooms, Shelagh sets up a sideboard of delicious things including fresh fruits, pineapple, perhaps compôtes of fresh and dried fruits, muesli, cereals and yoghurt, home-baked bread and honey, which guests can help themselves to while she is preparing delicious hot dishes including Cashel Blue pancakes with crispy bacon and grilled mushrooms as well as a perfectly cooked and well-presented version of the traditional Irish breakfast. This is Irish hospitality at its best, and very hard to leave. *Marble Hall was the winner of our B&B Breakfast of the Year award in 2008. **Rooms 3** (all non-smoking and en-suite); no wheelchair access; own parking (4). B&B €45-65 pps, ss€15. Closed 1 Dec-6 Jan. **No credit cards. Directions:** Located between Donnybrook and Ranelagh.

Merrion Hall

Dublin 4
GUESTHOUSE

54 Merrion Road Ballsbridge Dublin 4 **Tel: 01 668 1426**
merrionhall@iol.ie www.halpinsprivatehotels.com

This redeveloped Edwardian property opposite the RDS is one of the small group of privately owned Halpin guesthouses; handy to the DART (suburban rail), it makes a good base for business or leisure. New rooms have recently been completed, almost doubling the original accommodation, and all rooms are comfortably furnished with period furniture (some have 4-posters), fine original windows, TV, and bathrobes - and bathrooms are well-appointed, with in-bath jacuzzi and quality cosmetics. There's a well-stocked library, a comfortable big drawing room, and a fine, airy, spacious, basement dining room and outside patio, with tables set up in summer. In common with other Halpin establishments, good breakfasts are served here - an attractive buffet and well-presented fry. This is a very comfortable guest house and, although some rooms are susceptible to the late night/early morning rumble of the nearby DART, and jacuzzis in neighbouring bathrooms, it runs smoothly, without any sign of pressure from the extra rooms. *Next door, Blakes Spa & Suites is due to open at the time of going to press, offering a spa facility for the use of all Halpin guests, and 30 extra bedrooms. Small conference/private parties (50/50); off-street parking at the back; garden; children welcome (under 2s free in parents' room, cots available free of charge). No pets. **Rooms 34** (8 junior suites, 10 executive, 4 family rooms, 4 ground floor, 2 for disabled, all no smoking). Lift. 24 hr room service. Turndown service. B&B €75 pps, ss €35. Drawing Room/room service menu available 7am-9pm daily; set D €20; house wine €25. Open all year. Amex, Diners, MasterCard, Visa. **Directions:** Opposite the RDS in Ballsbridge.

Merrion Inn

Dublin 4
PUB

188 Merrion Road Dublin 4 **Tel: 01 269 3816**
themerrioninn@gmail.com

The McCormacks are a great pub family (see separate entry for their Mounttown establishment) and this attractive contemporary pub on the main road between Dublin and Dun Laoghaire makes a handy meeting place. It is a well-maintained and spacious place on two floors, with various quiet sections on the ground floor and an attractive covered outdoor section at the back to relax in relative peace, away from the busy bars. Expect to find above-average pub fare: a hot and cold buffet is served at lunch time and there's a well balanced dinner menu with vegetarian and gluten-free dishes marked up. This is a busy pub and everything is set up to serve large numbers efficiently, with glasses of chilled water among the extras you pick up on the way; main course choices offer quite an extensive range of popular dishes - salads, chicken dishes, omelettes, bangers & mash, several fish dishes, steaks various ways - then there are home-made desserts, which change daily. There's a large function room with bar upstairs, and a partially covered heated patio area is available for smokers. **Seats 150** (private room, 70); toilets wheelchair accessible; children welcome before 9pm (high chair, childrens menu, baby changing facilities). Bar food served daily 12-10 (L12-3, D 3.30-10). Buffet / à la carte. House wine €18.95. Closed 25 Dec & Good Fri. Amex, Diners, MasterCard, Visa, Laser. **Directions:** Merrion Road, opposite St. Vincent's Hospital.

Dublin 4
HOTEL

Mespil Hotel

Mespil Road Dublin 4 **Tel: 01 488 4600**
reservations@leehotels.com www.mespil.com

This attractive modern hotel enjoys an excellent location in the Georgian area of the city, overlooking the Grand Canal and within walking distance of St Stephen's Green and all the city centre attractions in fine weather. Public areas are spacious and elegant in an easy contemporary style, and the comfortable lobby makes a good meeting place. Bright, generously-sized bedrooms are comfortably furnished with good amenities including broadband, direct dial phones, tea/coffee facilities, iron/trouser press, and bathrooms with full bath and overbath shower. Dining options include the 200-seater Glaze Restaurant, which is open for lunch and dinner daily and offers a well-balanced choice of traditional and contemporary fare based on carefully sourced ingredients at fair prices, and the Terrace Bar, where lunch and light snacks are served. The hotel takes pride in the friendliness and efficiency of the staff and is moderately priced for the area; special breaks offer especially good value. Small meeting and seminars (25). **Rooms 255** (15 for disabled); children welcome (under 12s free in parents' room, cots available free of charge, baby sitting arranged); no pets. Lift. Room service (limited hours). Room rate €155 (max. 3 guests). Closed 24-26 Dec. Amex, MasterCard, Visa, Laser. **Directions:** On the Grand Canal at Baggot St. Bridge.

Dublin 4
HOTEL

The Montrose Hotel

Stillorgan Road Dublin 4 **Tel: 01 269 3311**
info@montrose.ie www.montrose.ie

This friendly south-city hotel, which is conveniently located near the University College Dublin campus and the RTE studios, has recently undergone extensive refurbishment, and changed ownership; most rooms are offered to executive standard, and there is also some wheelchair-friendly accommodation. All rooms have quite good facilities (direct dial phone, multi-channel TV, tea/coffee-making facilities and trouser press/iron), also 12-hour room service and laundry/dry cleaning services. It's popular with business guests, and executive rooms also have broadband, complimentary newspaper and business magazines. The hotel's Belfield Restaurant is open for lunch and dinner every day and offers traditional food such as roasts, sole on the bone and roast duck (pianist on Fridays). Although conference facilities are not extensive (max. 70 delegates), there's a business centre, seven meeting rooms and free parking, making this an attractive venue for small events. **Rooms 180** (3 suites, 36 executive); children welcome (under 12s free in parents' room, cots available free of charge). Lift, limited room service. B&B from €101pps, ss about €74; weekend specials available. Open all year. Amex, Diners, MasterCard, Visa, Laser. **Directions:** On Stillorgan dual carriageway near RTE studios, opposite UCD campus. ◊

Dublin 4
HOTEL

Mount Herbert Hotel

Herbert Road Sandymount Dublin 4 **Tel: 01 668 4321**
info@mountherberthotel.ie www.mountherberthotel.ie

Close to Lansdowne Road DART station and the RDS, this sprawling hotel is made up of a number of interconnecting houses and offers comfortable, well-priced accommodation with easy access to the city centre. It has been upgraded and refurbished many times over the years, and has good business and conference facilities; rooms are quite simple and on the small side, but its many regular guests like it for its friendliness and good value - and, with the uncertainty surrounding the future of other hotels in the area, many new guests will doubtless come to see it as a home from home in the near future. **Rooms 172.** Room rate from €69 to €220. MasterCard, Visa, Laser. ◊

Dublin 4

Ocean Bar

BAR   Charlotte Quay Dock Ringsend Road Dublin 4 **Tel: 01 668 8862**
info@oceanbar.ie www.oceanbar.ie

Dramatically situated on the water's edge with lots of glass on two sides, and extensive outdoor patio seating to take advantage of views over the Grand Canal Basin, Ocean has great atmosphere and makes an excellent meeting place for people of all ages. The waterside location, friendly staff, and comfortable lounging couches all make it a great place to relax - and a particularly good choice for visitors to the city. There's a choice of several bars and dining areas and, while menus offering a wide range of contemporary favourites may not contain many surprises, ingredients are well-sourced, and pleasant food is freshly prepared and competently cooked. Tables are laid with simple cutlery, paper napkins - and food is served modern bistro-style on big white plates. The Sunday jazz brunches are a particular success. Function rooms are available too, one on the ground floor next to the bar and two downstairs. **Seats 180** (private room, 80; outdoor seating, 80); children welcome; air conditioning; toilets wheelchair accessible. Food served daily, 12 -10. House wine about €21. Conference/banqueting. Closed 25 Dec, Good Fri. Amex, MasterCard, Visa, Laser. **Directions:** On Pearse Street/Ringsend Road bridge (Grand Canal Basin).

Dublin 4

Orchid Szechuan Chinese Restaurant

RESTAURANT   120 Pembroke Road Dublin 4
Tel: 01 660 0629

This long established restaurant has a faithful following - not surprisingly, as the food is high quality, and provides for both conservative and adventurous tastes, whilst the service is admirably efficient and friendly. Once you have braved the entrance (which can be a little off-putting) the interior is warm, welcoming and typically old-style Chinese with smoky mirrors and black-painted walls decorated with simple floral designs. Fresh flowers and linen napkins set the tone for clearly presented menus that offer many Szechuan specialities but also some Cantonese and a few Thai dishes. Try the light and crispy deep-fried scallops, served with a simple light soy dip, and follow with Yin-yang Prawn, two prawn dishes (one hot and spicy, the other a mild fresh flavoured stir-fry) served side-by-side, both delicious and pretty and popular roast duck in plum sauce, prettily garnished with an orchid. 'House dinners' are good-value; one is dedicated entirely to Dim Sum, which is served in the evening here and includes some eight dishes as well as jasmine tea or (very good) coffee. The wine list is on the pricey side, but offers a good choice. **Directions:** On Pembroke Road.

Dublin 4

Pembroke Townhouse

GUESTHOUSE   90 Pembroke Road Ballsbridge Dublin 4 **Tel: 01 660 0277**
info@pembroketownhouse.ie www.pembroketownhouse.ie

Conveniently located close to the RDS and Lansdowne Road, this fine guesthouse has all the amenities usually expected of an hotel. There's a drawing room and study for residents' use and the comfortably furnished rooms, which are individually designed, have recently been re-decorated; all have a safe and facilities for business guests (wi-fi is available in all areas), as well as direct dial phone and cable television (no tea / coffee making facilities, but will be delivered on request). Breakfast is the only meal served, but it offers a full buffet with dishes like French toast and omelettes as well as the traditional cooked breakfast. When arriving by car, it is best to go the carpark at the back, as you can then take a lift with your luggage (avoiding heavy traffic and steep steps to the front door). **Rooms 48** (1 suite, 2 family, 3 shower only, 2 disabled, 35 no smoking); broadband wi/fi (fee); private parking at rear; lift; limited room service. B&B €65-95 pps, single €95. Closed 22 Dec - 5 Jan. Amex, Diners, MasterCard, Visa, Laser. **Directions:** Pembroke Road leads onto Baggot St. On the right hand side going towards town.

Dublin 4

Poulot's Restaurant

RESTAURANT

Mulberry Gardens Donnybrook Dublin 4 **Tel: 01 269 3300**

reservations@poulots.ie www.poulots.ie

Lorna Jean and Jean Michel Poulot's restaurant is tucked away down a laneway and easy to miss. The L-shaped dining-room overlooks a pretty courtyard garden, floodlit at night, and the decor is simple - a warm neutral scheme opens the area up and creates a sense of space. Jean Michel brought with him a reputation for his time at Halo at the Morrison and, before that, at a number of other important kitchens including Ballylickey Manor in County Cork, where Lorna Jean was also working at the time. Large menus give detailed descriptions of a range of luxurious dishes, including French classics like seared duck foie gras (served with brioche and a fig compôte) and more unusual specialities such as a fennel and Parmesan risotto with yellow fin tuna and wasabi cream; among the main course specialities you may find a very refined loin of venison - little cylinders of tender, lean meat, served with celeriac cream, wild mushrooms and a game jus flavoured with juniper and black pepper. Classic desserts include an excellent crème brûlée,

and Valrhona chocolate fondant - served, perhaps, with a superb hazelnut ice cream. Presentation on huge white plates is dramatic and, like the over-sized menus, acts as a reminder that this is definitely fine dining, and not for those days when you're in the mood for something simple. The atmosphere, however, is relaxed, helped by service which has retained an old-style professionalism. An extensive wine list is Lorna Jean's special interest and, although it naturally leans towards France, it offers a careful selection from all over the world. * Cookery and wine courses available, details from the restaurant. **Seats 70**; toilets wheelchair accessible; children welcome; air conditioning. Open Mon-Sat, L12-3, D 7-10.30. Value D €29, 6-7.30pm. Closed Sun, Mon; Bank Hols. Amex, Diners, MasterCard, Visa, Laser. **Directions:** From city, first left after Victoria Avenue; to city, right turn opposite Ulster Bank in Donnybrook.

Dublin 4

Radisson SAS St Helen's Hotel

HOTEL•RESTAURANT

Stillorgan Road Dublin 4 **Tel: 01 218 6000**

info.dublin@radissonsas.com www.sthelens-dublin-radissonsas.com

Set in formal gardens just south of Dublin's city centre, with views across Dublin Bay to Howth Head, the fine 18th century house at the heart of this impressive hotel was once a private residence. Careful restoration and imaginative modernisation have created interesting public areas, including the Orangerie Bar and a pillared ballroom with minstrels' gallery and grand piano. Bedrooms, in a modern four-storey block adjoining the main building, all have garden views (some of the best rooms also have balconies) and air conditioning,

and are well-equipped for business guests. Accommodation is comfortably furnished to a high standard in contemporary style, although some rooms (and bathrooms) are less spacious than might be expected in a recent development. Conference/banqueting (350/220). Business centre, video conferencing, free broadband wi/fi. Fitness centre; beauty salon. Garden. Ample parking. Children welcome (under 18s free in parents' room, cots available without charge, baby sitting arranged). **Rooms 151** (25 suites, 70 no-smoking, 8 for disabled). 24 hr room service, Lift, Turndown service. Room rate from €170 (max. 3 guests). Open all year. **Talavera:** In four interconnecting rooms in the lower ground floor, this informal Italian restaurant is decorated in warm Mediterranean colours and, with smart wooden tables dressed with slips, modern cutlery, fresh flowers and Bristol blue water glasses, it is atmospheric when candle-lit at night. A well-balanced menu offers a choice of dishes inspired by tradition and tailored to the modern palate. A good atmosphere and caring service from friendly, efficient staff add to the attraction of a meal here. The wine list offers a strong selection of regional Italian bottles to match the food. *Lighter menus are also offered all day in the Orangerie Bar and Ballroom Lounge. Residents may expect the usual good Radisson buffet for breakfast. **Seats 140**. Air conditioning, toilets wheelchair accessible. D daily 6-10.30. Set menus from €35; also a la carte. Amex, Diners, MasterCard, Visa, Laser. **Directions:** Just 5.5km (3 miles) south from the city centre, on N11.

Dublin 4
RESTAURANT

Roly's Bistro

7 Ballsbridge Terrace Ballsbridge Dublin 4 **Tel: 01 668 2611**
ireland@rolysbistro.ie www.rolysbistro.ie

This bustling Ballsbridge bistro has been a hit since the day it opened. Today, head chef Paul Cartwright's imaginative, reasonably priced seasonal menus please a large number of appreciative regulars at lunch and an early dinner, and also an evening à la carte menu - and founding chef-patron Colin O'Daly's paintings adorn the walls and the menu card, which has a delightful reproduction of his "Sensitive study of a young dancer in morning light". A lively interpretation of classical French cooking gives more than a passing nod to Irish traditions, world cuisines and contemporary styles, and carefully sourced ingredients are the sound foundation for cooking that rarely disappoints. Breads (from the in-house bakery and also available to purchase), may include sliced yeast loaves, bacon & onion, tomato and pesto flavours, gluten-free bread and brown soda. Many specialities have evolved over the years: Dublin Bay Prawns are always in demand (and may be served with coriander scented wild rice), and an upbeat version of traditional Kerry lamb pie is another favourite. Service is usually efficient although staff can seem under pressure, and high demand can sometimes lead to a rush to turn around tables too quickly; but everyone loves the buzz, and Roly's has always given value for money - they offer a good range of wines at an accessible price. Offering quality with good value has been the philosophy of the restaurant from the outset; this it continues to do well on the whole, and the set menus - notably the pre-theatre - offer particularly good value. **Seats 220**; air conditioning. L daily 12-2.45 (to 3 Sun), D daily 6-10; Set L €20.95; Early D 2/3 course €22.95/€25.95 (Mon-Thu, 6-6.45), Set D €42; L&D also à la carte. SC10%. Closed Good Fri & 25-27 Dec inc. Amex, Diners, MasterCard, Visa, Laser. **Directions:** Heart of Ballsbridge, across the road from the American Embassy. ◊

Dublin 4
HOTEL•RESTAURANT

Schoolhouse Hotel

2-8 Northumberland Road Ballsbridge Dublin 4 **Tel: 01 667 5014**
reservations@schoolhousehotel.com www.schoolhousehotel.com

Dating back to its opening in 1861 as a school, this canalside building at Mount Street Bridge has seen many changes, and it is now one of Dublin's trendiest small hotels - and an ideal place to stay while exploring Dublin. A huge amount of business goes through the hotel and can show signs of wear and tear, but the spacious individually decorated bedrooms (all named after Irish writers) are well appointed, with king size beds, very good fabrics, air conditioning and power showers. Bedrooms have comfortable seating and a dining area, a necessary amenity as there are no public areas dedicated to residents. Booking is efficient and the reception staff are well organised and friendly in the Irish tradition. The bar is lively and offers a good bar menu which is popular with the locals, and has is a well furnished outdoor seating area where you can enjoy a drink and a smoke. **The Cellar Restaurant** is quieter, offers table service and a contemporary style à la carte menu in a lofty double-height room. Although the busy bar will be the main appeal for younger guests and it may not live up to any claims to be a ' special boutique hotel', this is generally a comfortable and calm place to stay. Small conference/banqueting (18/85). **Rooms 31** (30 no-smoking, 10 ground floor, 2 for disabled); children welcome (under 5s free in parents room; cots available with no charge). No pets. Lift. B&B from about €99 pps, SS €66. Wheelchair accessible. Parking (available for residents at no extra charge). SC discretionary. Closed 24-26 Dec. Amex, Diners, MasterCard, Visa. **Directions:** Southbound from Trinity College, at the end of Mount St. across the Grand Canal.

Dublin 4
GUESTHOUSE

Waterloo House

8-10 Waterloo Road Ballsbridge Dublin 4 **Tel: 01 660 1888**
info@waterloohouse.ie www.waterloohouse.ie

Evelyn Corcoran's pair of Georgian townhouses make a luxurious and reasonably priced base in a quiet location, which is very convenient to the city centre and also Lansdowne Road (rugby), RDS (equestrian & exhibitions) and some of the city's most famous restaurants. Excellent breakfasts are a high point of any stay. Equally attractive to the business or leisure traveller. **Rooms 17** (1 disabled); children welcome (under 4 free in parents' room, cot available). No pets. Lift. B&B about €60 pps, ss about €20. Conservatory & Garden. Wheelchair access. Own parking. Closed Christmas. MasterCard, Visa, Laser. **Directions:** South on St. Stephen's Green on Merrion Row for 1 mile. First turn right after Baggot Street Bridge. ◊

DUBLIN 5

DUBLIN 5 - RAHENY AREA

RAHENY is a pleasant suburb with some excellent amenities including St. Anne's Park, once home to the Guinness family; this is one of the finest parks in North Dublin - stretching from Raheny village down to the coast at Bull Island, and then along to the edges of Clontarf, it has extensive parkland walks, famous rose gardens and playing fields. A protected Victorian red brick stable yard (1885) has recently been renovated and converted into artists' studios, a gallery and the **Rose Café** (087 671 7791), which overlooks the park and offers wholesome home-made fare; it is situated in a spacious (if very bright and, perhaps, hot) first floor conservatory, and also has some tables out in the courtyard in fine weather. There is an artisan food market here every Saturday, and there is a monthly arts & crafts market (on a Sunday). Close to the park, at 23 Watermill Road, Raheny village, local residents enjoy **Mulino's** (01 831 3636), a smart and friendly Italian-style neighbourhood restaurant which is open daily from 12 noon onwards. At the Kilbarrack end of Raheny, just off the coast road to Howth, **Il Fornaio** (01 832 0277) is a great little restaurant/bakery serving simple, ingredient-led authentic Italian food in casual surroundings; their pizzas are renowned and it's the ideal place to pick up the makings of a picnic.
WWW.IRELAND-GUIDE.COM FOR ALL THE BEST PLACES TO EAT, DRINK & STAY

DUBLIN 6

DUBLIN 6

Dublin 6 is a mainly residential sector of the city and is made up of suburbs well-known for vibrancy such as Rathmines, Rathgar, Templeogue and Terenure. In Rathmines, **Wild Lily** (Upper Rathmines Road; 01 497 6870) is a small restaurant known for its charm, friendly staff and rather big ideas - high prices for a neighbourhood restaurant - but open long hours and the locals love it. The area has attracted a number of the city's best ethnic restaurant, especially Indian restaurants, and the line-up has recently been joined by **Monty's of Rathgar** (01 4920633) at 88 Rathgar Road, an outpost of the highly respected Nepalese restaurant of the same name in Temple Bar (see entry); the new, richly decorated, restaurant is on two floors and offers many of the specialities Monty's is famous for - and a choice between traditional low seating and western tables and chairs. **Diep Noodle Bar** (www.diep.net; 01 497 6550) is a younger Ranelagh sister to **Diep le Shaker** off Fitzwilliam Square (see entry). A colourful little place, it quickly gained a reputation as the in place for discerning young things to meet; it has a great atmosphere, chic, clean-lined decor and - as if a mixture of Thai and Vietnamese food weren't fashionable enough - a cocktail bar too. While the entrance to the cool modern restaurant **The Wild Goose** (Sandford Road, Ranelagh; 01 491 2377) is not obvious as it's somewhat concealed beside the doors to McSorley's pub (in the premises formerly occupied by Ouzo); once discovered however, you'll find yourself in a one-off restaurant where there's plenty of buzz - and where the wine list leads the food. *Shortly before the guide went to press an all day café/shop, **Pinocchio**, opened at the Luas Kiosk in Ranelagh, Dublin 6 (Tel: 01 497 0111; e-mail: info@pinocchio.ie www.pinocchiodublin.com; it's a sister to Campo dei Fiori in Bray, Co Wicklow, see entry).
WWW.IRELAND-GUIDE.COM FOR ALL THE BEST PLACES TO EAT, DRINK & STAY

Dublin 6
RESTAURANT

Antica Venezia

97 Ashfield Road Ranelagh Dublin 6
Tel: 01 497 4112

A real throw-back in time and refreshingly so: this entirely Italian-run restaurant has a classic Italian 70s' interior with stained wooden floors and ceiling beams, Venetian trompe-l'oeil scenes on the walls and candlewax-dripped Chianti bottles on every table. The food is also traditional Italian, with a menu that could easily date back to the Seventies too: old-fashioned favourites, like stuffed mushrooms and antipasto misto of Italian meats, are followed by classics like chicken breast with mushroom and white wine sauce, salmon with lemon butter sauce, pork with marsala sauce and a choice of pasta dishes and pizzas, with predictable but very typically Italian desserts such as banoffi, tiramisu and cassata as well as a selection of ice creams. Consistently good food, with great service that is laid back but attentive - a perfect recipe for a popular neighbourhood restaurant. **Seats 45**; reservations advised; air conditioning; children welcome. D daily, 5-11, L Fri only 12-2.30. A la carte. House wine €18.50. SC discretionary, but 10% on parties of 6+. MasterCard, Visa, Laser.

Dublin 6
RESTAURANT•CAFE•BAR

Bijou Bistro

47 Highfiield Road Rathgar Dublin 6 **Tel: 01 496 1518**
bijourestaurant@eircom.net

A distinctly French atmosphere prevails at this neighbourhood restaurant and, despite recent developments which have virtually doubled its size, it is still advisable to book a table. It's appealingly decorated in a gently modern style, with soft neutral tones and good lighting, and the well-tried system of casual dining is offered in a comfortably furnished area on the ground floor and there's a more formal restaurant upstairs. Well-made breads accompany an innovative menu with a dozen or so choices on each course and several fish specialities each evening (typically pan-fried fillet of monkfish with clam & mussel ratatouille, chargrilled potato and watercress salad); ingredients are well-sourced (if you're lucky you might get Connemara mountain lamb in season - late summer/autumn) and vegetarian dishes are imaginative. Cooking is accurate and stylish - and presented on plates decorated with a colourful art deco flourish. Finish with classic desserts or an Irish cheese selection with quince jelly. Good wine list too, plus a couple of weekly specials. **Seats 100** (private room, 12); children welcome; air conditioning. Open all day 7 days, 12-10.30pm; L 12-4pm, D 6-10.30pm. House wine from €20. SC discretionary. Closed 25 Dec. Amex, Diners, MasterCard, Visa, Laser. **Directions:** Rathgar crossroads.

Dublin 6
RESTAURANT
V

Eatery 120

120 Ranelagh Dublin 6 **Tel: 01 470 4120**
info@eatery120.ie www.eatery120.ie

Its impressive tiled frontage with picture window framed above a bright band of mismatched floral tiles (a theme continued in the chic interior) is reminiscent of an old-fashioned Spanish deli, the new waiting and smoking areas are Paris Metro themed and the interior is a stylishly comfortable international mix of velvet cushioned banquettes, bistro chairs and clusters of moon lamps... Eatery 120 is very much a restaurant of our times. The unattractive name may summon up all the wrong images, but this is a neighbourhood restaurant with a difference and has attracted fans from a wide area – not surprisingly, perhaps, considering head chef Eoin Lennon's background with both of Ireland's most talented chefs, Kevin Thornton and Michael Deane. Unpretentious nonetheless, the long opening hours and its 'where haute-cuisine meets home cooking' policy endear it to local followers, who love the seasonality of menus proudly based on local ingredients in season (and supporting the weekly Ranelagh farmers' market), the friendly atmosphere and brilliant, accurately cooked food which varies according to the time of day. Menus offered indicate respect for a wide customer base and include a very nice children's menu as well as weekend brunch, weekday lunch, early dinner, and an à la carte - a lot of thought has gone into the menus, and also into a compact but very interesting wine list that is organised in a friendly way by style, and offers a high proportion of the list by the glass. Cited specialities of smoked mackerel paté, glazed pork belly (served with mustard mash, savoy cabbage and apple sauce), dry-aged rib-eye (12-oz Fermanagh steak with classic béarnaise, pepper sauce or blue cheese butter and hand-cut chips) say a lot about the philosophy here too - a wide range is actually offered, yet this is not show-off cooking but real food for real people. Service can be a little slow at times, but staff are friendly - and all is forgiven once food as good as this arrives: bravo! **Seats 100** (private room to 60, outdoors 16); children welcome (high chair, childrens menu, baby changing facilities); reservations recommended; air conditioning. L daily 12-2.45pm (11am-3pm Sun); D daily 5.30-10pm (to 9.30pm Sun); early D Mon-Fri, €19.95, 5.30-6.45pm. Wine from €19. SC 12.5% on parties of 6+. Closed 25-26 Dec. Amex, Diners, MasterCard, Visa, Laser.

Dublin 6

Jo'Burger

RESTAURANT
137 Rathmines Road Dublin 6 **Tel: 01 491 3731**
info@joburger.ie www.joburger.ie

Noisy, loudly decorated, and busy – this informal restaurant is perfect for those looking for a fun atmosphere and excellent reasonably priced food. Jo'burger has quickly earned a reputation in the top rank of Dublin's new wave of gourmet burger joints, and offers quite a varied choice for a menu that concentrates almost exclusively on burgers. While the music and occasionally cramped communal seating might not appeal to everyone, those who enjoy the energy of a place like this can look forward to some excellent food. The menu (presented in old comic book annuals) consists of some 15 to 20 burger options, with beef, lamb, or chicken as the focus, with some quirky toppings. The current fashion for massively packed burgers, cooked to order, between fresh buns of real bread is seen here, and the sweet potato fries are developing a well-deserved cult following around town. Salads are also available (but no desserts), and several foreign beers and ciders are on offer as well as a few wines, by the glass and by the bottle. Jo'burger offers great value for money and this, along with excellent service, further explains the queues outside at weekends (no reservations). Mon-Sun,12 noon -11pm (Late on Fri and Sat). MasterCard, Visa, Laser **Directions:** Opposite the TraveLodge. ◇

Dublin 6

Mint

RESTAURANT
47 Ranelagh Village Dublin 6 **Tel: 01 497 8655**
★★
info@mintrestaurant.ie www.mintrestaurant.ie

Just over a year after taking over the reins at Mint, chef Dylan McGrath earned international recognition for this small Ranelagh restaurant in 2008. McGrath perfected his techniques in the kitchens of renowned chefs Paul Rankin, Conrad Gallagher, John Burton-Race and Tom Aikens, before returning to Ireland with some of the freshest, most original cooking the capital has ever seen. Despite being a small restaurant, it's classy and understated and has been cleverly designed to maximise on space. It's a shame there's no room for a reception area, or even a bar, but the lack of space means that you are whisked away to your table the second you arrive. Here you're encouraged to linger over aperitifs (they do a roaring trade in pre-dinner champagne) and graze on a tasting plate of amuse-bouches that couldn't fail to excite you, or alert you to the kitchen's impressive capabilities. Those who love fine dining without the pomp will enjoy Mint's atmosphere – cool jazz, leather banquettes, dark woods and the most beautiful tableware, much of it bespoke from an Irish ceramicist based in London. Tables are extremely close together, which you may find annoying, but are far more likely to see as an opportunity to enquire about the culinary work of art your neighbours are currently tucking into. Staff are extremely professional, congenial and knowledgeable, serving everything with pride and panache. The à la carte menu features just five starters (ranging from €28-40) and five mains (costing €46-48), making McGrath's seven-course Tasting Menu of €125 surprisingly good value. A signature starter of roasted scallops served with caramelised chicory, blood orange, peeled black grapes and olive oil is as exotic, colourful and exquisite as it sounds. A signature main course of hay-smoked loin of pork served with sweetcorn, pork belly, polenta and pearl barley is a triumph of flavours that showcases McGrath's creative daring. Desserts are memorable and elaborate confections that look and taste sensational, but cheese fans will find Mint's beautifully presented cheese trolley difficult to pass up. The wine list is weighty and extensive, but offers little under €35. Every item that leaves the kitchen has been prepared to the highest standards and with the highest level of attention to detail. Even the bread selection, offering seven or eight exquisite varieties – from rich black olive swirls, to floury foccacia or crusty red pepper and parmesan rolls – would make most bakers sigh in awe. Saucing is one of McGrath's strongest points, and something that puts his cooking into a league of its own. Every component, from hazelnut mayonnaise to beetroot juice or lemongrass soup, zings with purity, intensity and brilliance. The food here is creative, original and outstanding, ensuring you'll leave Mint feeling your money was well spent. **Seats 45**; reservations advised; wheelchair accessible; children welcome, but not suitable after 8pm. L Thu-Fri, 12.30-2pm; D Tue-Sat, 6.30-10pm. Closed Sun, Mon, bank holidays. Amex, MasterCard, Visa, Laser. **Directions:** Centre of Ranelagh Village. ◇

Dublin 6
RESTAURANT

Poppadom Indian Restaurant

91a Rathgar Road Dublin 6 **Tel: 01 490 2383**
www.poppadom.ie

Behind a neat but unremarkable frontage in a row of modern shops lies Poppadom, a colourful and airy new wave Indian restaurant, with linen-clad tables, comfortable chairs and a bar. The aim is to demonstrate the diversity of Indian cooking and offer some appealingly unusual dishes. Complimentary poppadoms with fresh chutney dips are brought before menus which offer regional specialities including a starter of Karwari Prawns - deep-fried jumbo prawns marinated in ginger, garlic, yoghurt, garam masala and barbecued in the tandoor - and main courses ranging in heat, including chicken and lamb specialities. Vegetarians have plenty of dishes available as main courses or side orders, and variations like garlic, onion & coriander naan and lime rice offer a subtle change from the norm. Food presentation matches the contemporary surroundings, and is backed up by solicitous service. Make a point of trying the masala tea, made with leaf tea and cardamom pods. A sound wine list helpfully gives advice on the styles that partner spicy food well. Also at: Newlands Cross, Dublin 22 (01 411 1144); Cornmarket St, Limerick (061 416644); and O'Connell St, Sligo (071 914 7171). **Seats 48**; children welcome; reservations advised; air conditioning. D daily, 6-12. A la carte. Wines from €19. SC discretionary. Closed 25 Dec. Amex, MasterCard, Visa, Laser. **Directions:** A minute away on the same side as Comans Pub, Rathgar. ◊

Dublin 6
RESTAURANT

TriBeCa

65 Ranelagh Village Dublin 6 **Tel: 01 497 4174**
info@tribeca.ie www.tribeca.ie

An outpost of the Canal Bank Café see entry, Ger Foote and Trevor Browne's bright and airy NY-style restaurant was a hit for its good fast food and relaxed feel, with smart-casual décor and wooden floors and tables. Carefully sourced burgers (made from 100% organic beef), salads, omelettes and chicken wings take their place alongside the oriental-inspired dishes that keep the more adventurous diners happy. Long before the current rush by mainstream restaurants to pay lip service to the concept of quality ingredients, Foote & Browne were out there sourcing the truly good product that makes it possible for simple food to stand out. It's not cheap, but it is wholesome, tasty fare - and portions are generous, making it good value for money. *Up on the first floor you will find **Wine Upstairs**, a wine bar offering carefully selected wines (over 200 wines, with 15 offered by the glass) and also some equally carefully chosen food to go with them - charcuterie plates, cheese and a couple of hot specials each night. **Seats 80** (private room, 30, outside seating 12); fully wheelchair accessible; children welcome (high chair, baby changing facilities); air conditioning; free broadband wi/fi. Open daily, 12-11. Set L €10/12 (12-5); otherwise à la carte, plus daily blackboard specials. House wine €19.50. Live Jazz every second Thursday. Closed Dec 25-26, Good Fri. MasterCard, Visa, Laser. **Directions:** Heading southbound from city centre, halfway along Ranelagh main street, on right.

Dublin 6W
RESTAURANT
Ⓥ

Vermilion

94-96 Terenure Road North Terenure Dublin 6W **Tel: 01 499 1400**
mail@vermilion.ie www.vermilion.ie

This is a purpose-built restaurant on the first floor above the Terenure Inn pub, and the decor - a contemporary, smart interior in soft primary colours - reflects an innovative food philosophy, which offers colourful, beautifully presented and updated versions of many Indian favourites. Interesting nibbles are provided, and the menu includes specialities from Kerala, Tamil-Nadu and Goa, with pride clearly taken in the quality of ingredients and cooking. Each summer, from June to September, Vermilion hosts an Indian Summer Festival, following a culinary trail around India - complete with Bollywood movie clips and belly dancing. Although the menu gives detailed explanations, this is not a traditional Indian restaurant, so don't expect the usual, familiar experience of 'popular' Indian food. Service is friendly and solicitous. Always innovative, the restaurant has a loyalty card, offer up to 15% credit back to returning customers - and they have recently introduce a 'Lighter for Less' menu, offering smaller portion sizes for a lower price - with starters from €4.95, mains from €14.95. **Seats 90**; children welcome (high chair, childrens menu); reservations advised; air conditioning. D daily 5.30-10.30 (to 8.30pm Sun), L Sun only, 2-5pm; set Sun L €15.95. Value menu all evening Mon-Thurs, €60 for 2 people inc. bottle of wine. Early D €20/24 Mon-Sat, 5-30-7pm (to 6.30 Fri/Sat and 2-5.30pm Sun); also à la carte; house wine from €19.50. SC 10% on groups 6+. Closed 25-26 Dec, Good Fri. Amex, Diners, MasterCard, Visa, Laser. **Directions:** 200 yards from Terenure crossroads.

Dublin 6

WINE BAR•RESTAURANT

Ⓝ

Wild Goose Grill

1st Floor 1 Sandford Road Ranelagh Dublin 6

Tel: 01 491 2377

Another of the growing number of Dublin restaurants that start with wine and make food a secondary element, this stylish first floor restaurant above McSorleys pub is the brainchild of former Ely manager, Kevin McMahon, so the emphasis on wine should come as no surprise. The predictably impressive wine list offers an exceptionally good choice at reasonable prices, and includes about two dozen by the glass. On the food side an eclectic selection of popular dishes is offered, including some available as starters or main courses (Greek salad; beetroot, green bean and goats cheese salad, both at 9/14); there's a good sprinkling of vegetarian and seafood dishes but the big crowd pleaser is the chargrilled dry aged rib-eye steak, offered with a choice of three types of potatoes and three sauces. With crisp white linen, generous wine glasses, attractive spoon back chairs - and lots of bottles - there's a stylish ambience and this, together with welcoming and helpful staff, and a different offering from other restaurants in the area, make it a popular place so reservations are recommended, especially at week-ends. **Seats 90**; reservations accepted; children welcome; air conditioning. D daily 5.30-10.30; L Sun only 1-3pm; house wine 22. Closed 25-26 Dec. Amex, MasterCard, Visa, Laser. **Directions:** Above McSorleys public house in Ranelagh.

DUBLIN 7

DUBLIN 7

Dublin 7 is in the north inner city on the banks of the River Liffey, and is within walking distance of all of the major sites and attractions in Dublin. It includes the well known city centre neighbourhood of Smithfield, tourist attractions include the Four Courts and the **Old Jameson Distillery** (01 807 2355; www.whiskeytours.com), where the whiskey tour is a 'must visit' while in the city; a popular attraction is their 'Shindig' evenings held on Thursday, Friday and Saturday nights from April to October (€60 per person, for tour, complimentary drink, 4-course dinner and musical entertainment; groups of 60+ only). The OJD has a bar and restaurant, open to the public daily; the bar is attractive, and the contemporary first floor restaurant, **The Third Still**, is open for lunch daily - the style is international, which seems a missed opportunity to introduce visitors to the best of real Irish food. Comfortable budget accommodation is available in the **Maldron Hotel** (Smithfield Plaza, 01 490 8200).

WWW.IRELAND-GUIDE.COM FOR ALL THE BEST PLACES TO EAT, DRINK & STAY

Dublin 7

RESTAURANT

Hanley at the Bar

The Distillery Building May Lane Dublin 7

Tel: 01 878 0104

Well-known caterer Claire Hanley's smart daytime restaurant near the Jameson Distillery has always been popular with the lawyers from the nearby Law Library and the Four Courts, but was otherwise a well-kept secret until this area began its recent phase of rapid development. High stools at the bar provide a comfortable perch if you are waiting for a table (it gets very busy at lunchtime), but it's worth a little patience as you may expect good contemporary cooking in very chic surroundings.

Dublin 7

RESTAURANT•PUB

The Hole in the Wall

Blackhorse Avenue Phoenix Park Dublin 7

Tel: 01 838 9491

PJ McCaffrey's remarkable pub beside the Phoenix Park is named in honour of a tradition which existed here for around a hundred years - the practice of serving drinks through a hole in the wall of the Phoenix Park to members of the army garrison stationed nearby. Today the Hole in the Wall also claims to be the longest pub in Ireland - and it is certainly one of the most interesting. They have always offered food too - a bar menu available throughout the afternoon and evening - but with the arrival of Damien Grey, who will be well known to viewers of RTE's 'The Restaurant', a while ago, the bar has been well and truly raised. With a new dining room opened in 2007, it's now as much a restaurant as a pub and the house speciality these days is free-range chicken breast with butternut squash, artichokes, shitake mushrooms & beurre blanc, it's a far cry from the Beef & Guinness Pie, Dublin Coddle, and Irish Stew of old. Even fish and chips are fresh cod with duck fat chips There's also a new wine shop in the pub, source of the extensive wine list offered in the restaurant. Children welcome.

Piano Fri & Sat night. Wheelchair access to toilets. Parking. Bar menu served daily (2-10). Closed 25 Dec & Good Fri. Amex, MasterCard, Visa, Laser. **Directions:** Beside Phoenix Park. ◇

Dublin 7
RESTAURANT

Rhodes D7

The Capel Building Mary's Abbey Dublin 7 **Tel: 01 804 4444**
info@rhodesd7.com www.rhodesd7.com

Gary Rhodes opened here in 2006, in a part of town which is only just beginning to blossom, and - although the choice of location seemed unwise to many Dubliners - his only Irish venture to date seems to be thriving. The restaurant is set back from the street a little, allowing for tables on a terrace along the front - perfect for smokers, although the space is tight for comfort and ease of service. Inside, the basic structure is modern but the designers have gone for a mixum-gatherum of styles which does little for the atmosphere: the interior is dominated by some specially commissioned and very colourful large modern paintings which you will love or loathe but, with an antique table here, trellis-back chairs there, modern table settings, and some vaguely old-fashioned light fittings, it doesn't add up to a 'look'. But it is on the food, wine and service that Rhodes is judged and, although essentially a franchise - Gary Rhodes was upfront from the start that he would not personally be cooking - head chef Paul Hargreaves worked with him as sous chef for six years before coming to Dublin, and his cooking is impressive. The menu is well-judged, offering plenty of choice from a dozen or so appealing starters and main courses. Based on a UK prototype, some feel that there's an 'Englishness' which seems stilted in Dublin but the Rhodes menus have been adapted carefully - of the specialities, haddock rarebit may sound a bit English (delicious nevertheless), and confit duck is French-inspired, but you'll also find a nod to Irish traditions in dishes like Baileys crème brûlée and Jameson oatmeal parfait, and - as can be seen on menus that are peppered with the names of respected Irish products (Ardsallagh goat's cheese, Clonakilty black pudding, Cashel Blue) there's a genuine commitment to using Irish produce where possible. Decent wines from an interesting and fairly priced list should certainly please, with a good choice by the glass. The cooking is generally excellent and, backed up by good service, Rhodes D7 has become an established favourite with Dubliners. **Seat 250** (private room, 50, outdoors, 50); air conditioning; pianist playing various times; children welcome (high chair, childrens menu, baby changing facilities); toilets wheelchair accessible. Food served Mon-Sat, 12-10.15pm (closed Mon D), Sun L only 12-4pm; set 2 course L €17.50, 12-3pm, value D €19.95, 5.30-7pm; also a la carte L&D. Closed Sun D & Mon D, Bank Hols. Amex, MasterCard, Visa, Laser. **Directions:** Junction of Capel St. and Mary's Abbey.

Dublin 7
RESTAURANT

Seven

73 Manor Street Dublin 7
Tel: 01 633 4092

Tightly packed with darkwood tables and dark leather highback chairs, this smart little restaurant is in a redbrick corner building in Stoneybatter, a pleasant residential area near the Phoenix Park. Aside from likely association with the address, the theme that inspired the name is the seven wonders of the world - illustrated in light boxes mounted on the wall, and also runs through the menu, which is sensibly restricted to seven starters and seven main courses. What draws people to this little spot is good simple food, i.e. carefully sourced quality ingredients and well-cooked unfussy food: begin with smoked haddock chowder with mussels and bacon, perhaps, or a simple, tasty starter of crisp calamari with a mixed leaf and sesame soy dressing. Choices are well-balanced, including fish and vegetarian dishes, but the most popular main course by far is a really good rib eye steak, perfectly caramelised on the outside and juicy inside, served with delicious mash and green beans. Flavour and texture combinations are carefully judged; this is particularly noticeable in the choice of accompaniments for each dish and therein lies the reason the food here is so delicious. Seven was an immediate hit with local residents, and the combination of small size and big popularity means there will be more than one sitting and your best chance of getting in without a reservation, on any day of the week, will be to arrive very early. **Seats 38**. L Mon-Fri 12-2.30; D Mon-Fri 6-9.30, Sat & Sun 5.30-9.30. ◇

DUBLIN 8

DUBLIN 8

Dublin 8 is the only postcode that crosses the River Liffey and is made up of areas on both sides of the river, at the western edges of the city centre. The best known areas/attractions in Dublin 8 for the visitor to Dublin are the Guinness Brewery, Kilmainham Gaol, The Irish Museum of Modern Art, Christchurch Cathedral, St. Patrick's Cathedral and the Phoenix Park. Heuston Station (serving the West and South West of Ireland) is also in Dublin 8. The atmospheric **Havana Tapas Bar** (Grantham Street ; 01 476 0046) is only just in Dublin 8 and has a newer branch down the road in South Great George's Street, Dublin 2 (01 400 5990). **The Brazen Head** (Lower Bridge Street; 01 677 9549) is Dublin's (possibly Ireland's) oldest pub and was built on the site of a tavern dating back to the 12th century - and it's still going strong. Full of genuine character, this friendly, well-run pub has lots of different levels and dark corners. Food is wholesome and middle-of-the-road at reasonable prices - visitors will be pleased to find traditional favourites like Irish stew. Live music nightly in the Music Lounge. **The Chorus Café** (Fishamble Street; 01 616 7088) is a small restaurant with a big heart. It is a bright and friendly little place near the site of the first performance of Handel's Messiah, hence the name - and some features of the decor. Interesting breakfasts are followed by an all-day procession of good things. It is a useful daytime place to know about if you're visiting anywhere in the Christchurch area. The Guinness Brewery (St. James Gate; 01 471 4261) is home to the modern glass-walled Gravity Bar which serves the most spectacular pint of Guinness in Dublin - indeed, in all Ireland from its unique position atop the impressive Guinness Storehouse, a handsome 1904 building. The Guinness Museum tells the story - using fascinating high tech exhibits - of the famous company's 250-plus years in business. It also includes (on Level 5) the traditional Brewery Bar, serving nourishing Irish fare (seafood chowder, beef & Guinness stew). NB: you have to pay in to use these bars. Down the road is Royal Hospital Kilmainham and the Irish Museum of Modern Art which is also home to the self service **Grass Roots Café** (01 612 9900) which is a pleasant place for an informal meal, whether or not you are visiting the museum - it has good parking facilities and the spacious room, which is attractively located overlooking a garden area, has a pleasingly cool modern ambience; a handier choice for a quick lunch than city centre venues, perhaps. On Thomas Street, look out for the unpromising but surprising **Piedescalso**, a café/gallery which is a hub of local activity and popular with NCAD students who appreciate both the tasty food and the value. Across the river Liffey **Nancy Hands** (Parkgate Street; 01 677 0149) is a newish pub with an old feel, but far from being a theme pub. It's a characterful place for a drink and the selection stocked is unusually extensive. Food was an important aspect of Nancy Hands from the outset and, on the whole, it is well done with menus successfully straddling the divide between traditional bar food (seafood chowder, steaks; lunchtime carvery) and lighter international fare. A couple of doors along, **Ryan's of Parkgate Street** (01 677 6097) is one of Ireland's finest and best-loved original Victorian pubs, with magnificent stained glass, original mahogany bar fixtures and an outstanding collection of antique mirrors all contributing to its unique atmosphere. Bar food is available every day except Sunday and, upstairs, there's a small restaurant, FXB at Ryans, serving food which is a step up from bar meals. For good budget accommodation try **Jurys Inn Christchurch** (01 454 0000) which is within walking distance of the main city centre areas on both sides of the Liffey and close to Dublin Castle and events in Temple Bar; large multi-storey car park at the rear has access to the hotel. New to the area are two more luxurious options, **Hilton Dublin Kilmainham** on the Inchicore Road - convenient to Heuston Station and the main road south (N4) - and **Radisson SAS Royal Hotel** (see entries) within walking distance of Trinity College and the Grafton Street area. **WWW.IRELAND-GUIDE.COM FOR ALL THE BEST PLACES TO EAT, DRINK & STAY**

Dublin 8   **Bar Italia Café**

CAFÉ•RESTAURANT   Lr Exchange Street Essex Quay Dublin 8 **Tel: 01 679 5128**
acrobat_ltd@yahoo.it www.baritalia.ie

In a modern office block on the edge of Temple Bar and close to the Civic Offices known disparagingly to Dubliners as 'The Bunkers', this little Italian-trattoria style restaurant has floor-to-ceiling glass to make the most of a splendid view across the Liffey towards the magnificent Four Courts - and there's plenty of space outside to enjoy lunch 'al fresco' when the weather's right. Attentive Italian waiters quickly seat new arrivals, service throughout is quick and professional and the banter lends a relaxed atmosphere - matched by colourful, flavoursome food, simply presented. The minestrone soup can be memorable, panini and pasta dishes are the business, and it's a place worth seeking out for their espressos alone. And it's great value too. **Seats 25**. Outdoor seating. Open every day: Mon-Fri, 8-6, Sat 9-6, Sun 12-6. A la carte. Closed Christmas/New Year. Also at: Bar Italia, 26 Lower Ormond Quay, Dublin, 1 (Tel 01 874 1000). MasterCard, Visa. **Directions:** South quays, west end of Temple Bar (near Dublin Corporation head office).

Dublin 8   The Cake Café
CAFÉ   The Daintree Building Pleasants Place (behind Camden Street) Dublin 8
                                Tel: 01478 9394   thecakecafe@gmail.com   www.thecakecafe.ie

A love of traditional food and recognition of the environmental impact of their business are the driving forces behind this paradise for cake lovers. But don't be fooled by the name, they've plenty of quality savouries too. A homely atmosphere is created with flower print table cloths, and dainty higgledy piggledy crockery and the open kitchen means you can watch staff merrily baking away. The cookies and cream with cardamom panna cotta and the 'adult jelly & icecream' made with wine and home-made ice cream are trademark products and expertly made with quality ingredients. As is the lemon curd cake, chocolate brownie and there's a wonderful array of beverages to go with the cakes from iced latte to sweet spiced milk, extra rich Valhrona hot chocolate and twenty different teas including liquorice mint. A substantial lunch, or breakfast, can be had too, including terrine of Cashel Blue cheese with hazelnut and crème fraiche; Portuguese sardines on toast with black pepper and lemon juice; or something simple from the breakfast menu like toast with proper butter and their own brown sugar marmalade. But their own home-made beans on toast are a marvel, made from scratch with cannellini beans, sausage and tomato, served on hot buttered toast. Faultless. May open in the evenings in the summer months. **Seats 16** inside and 25 outside, fully wheelchair accessible, children welcome, house wines about €19. No SC. Open 8.30am to 5.30pm Mon Fri, Sat 9-6, Closed Sun, Bank Hols, 2-3 weeks at Christmas, 3 days at Easter. Amex, MasterCard, Visa, Laser. **Directions:** Behind Daintree Shop on Camden Street.

Dublin 8   Enoteca Torino
CAFÉ•RESTAURANT   Grattan Crescent Inchicore Dublin 8
Ⓝ   **Tel: 01 453 7791**

A pleasant walk away from Kilmainham Gaol and associated attractions, this Italian café/restaurant is situated on the ground floor of a modern building but the atmosphere inside is cosy and the restaurant has an immediate feel of authenticity. The fare is typical of the many similar Italian restaurants which have sprung up around Dublin in recent years (Enoteca delle Langhe in Blooms Lane is a sister establishment, see entry.) The starters include mixed cheese and bread plates and crostinis and main courses are primarily pasta-based with one or two specials available every day. A small selection of wine is available by the bottle or by the glass and a varied selection of desserts are on display for diners to make their choice. This restaurant is a great addition to the area and offers good value. **Seats 40**; Mon-Sun, 10-am-11pm (from 12 Sun). ◇

Dublin 8   Gallic Kitchen
CAFÉ   49 Francis Street Dublin 8 **Tel: 01 454 4912**
                                                                    galkit@iol.ie

This little spot in Dublin's "antique" district has been delighting locals and visitors alike for some years now. Patissière Sarah Webb is renowned for quality baking (quiches, roulades, plaits, tartlets, wraps) and also salads and delicious little numbers to have with coffee. A judicious selection from an extensive range is offered to eat in the shop: sourcing is immaculate, cooking skilful and prices reasonable, so you may have to queue. Outside catering offered (with staff if required). Open Mon-Sat, 9-4.30.
*Sarah also has a stall at several markets: Temple Bar (Sat, 9-5); Dun Laoghaire (Thu, 10.30-5); Leopardstown (Fri, 11-5); Laragh, Co Wicklow (one Sun each month). MasterCard, Visa, Laser. ◇

Dublin 8   Hilton Dublin Kilmainham
HOTEL   Inchicore Road Kilmainham Dublin 8 **Tel: 01 420 1800**
Ⓝ ⓥ   reservations.dublinkilmainham@hilton.com www.hilton.com/dublinkilmainham

This new 4* standard hotel is just 5 minutes from Heuston Station (trains to south and west of Ireland) and a short distance from the city centre – Phoenix Park, Royal Hospital Kilmainham / IMMA, Collins Barracks Museum and Christ Church Cathedral and are all nearby. Designed to have equal appeal for leisure and business guests, large well-appointed rooms are well set up for business with generous desk space and broadband access, also comfortable seating and entertainment for time off. In-house bar and restaurant options include the contemporary Cinnamon Bar & Café or Cinnamon Restaurant (international food with an Irish twist), and the city centre restaurants are only a 10-minute taxi drive. **Rooms 120** (all no smoking); meeting rooms (60), business centre, secretarial service; children welcome (cots available); wheelchair friendly, lift. B&B €65pps, single €120. Fitness centre; hydrotherapy pool. Closed 24-27 Dec. Amex, MasterCard, Visa, Laser. **Directions:** On the Inchicore Road.

Dublin 8

Konkan Indian Restaurant

RESTAURANT

46 Upper Clanbrassil Street Dublin 8 **Tel: 01 473 8252**

info@konkan.ie www.konkan.ie

Near Harold's Cross Bridge, the homely red frontage and the fairy lights in Konkan's window convey an informal charm to passers by. Once inside, a small welcoming dining room is modestly decorated with red carpet and randomly placed Indian curios – you could be in the living room of a well travelled friend. Indian music drifts lightly across the cosy room, and there's a lived-in look that adds to the comfortable charm of this characterful neighbourhood restaurant. Warmly welcoming staff seat diners with a smile and promptly offer an extensive and well-organised menu which includes many old favourites such as Rogan Josh, Biriyani or Korma, as well as an appealing list of authentic regional dishes from Southern India. There is also an excellent range of vegetarian and low fat dishes, and a good choice of side dishes. An expert team of chefs demonstrates respect and deep understanding for a culinary tradition that produces dishes full of flavour and subtlety, taking pride in highlighting the variety and complexity that Indian cuisine has to offer. Delicious food provided by polite, warm staff in a relaxed setting full of character make this hospitable restaurant a must for anyone who enjoys Indian cooking - and all for a price that is hard to believe. A short wine list is offered, also soft drinks and Indian Cobra beer. Konkan is the Indian restaurant that everyone wishes they had around the corner. **Seats 50**; Mon–Sun 5.30-11pm, take away and delivery available. MasterCard, Visa, Laser. **Directions:** Near Harolds Cross Bridge. ◊

Dublin 8

Locks Restaurant

RESTAURANT

Number 1 Windsor Terrace Portobello Dublin 8 **Tel: 01 454 3391**

info@locksrestaurant.ie www.locksrestaurant.ie

Under the guidance of co-owners Kelvin Rynhart and Teresa Carr (formerly of Bang Café) and chef co-proprietor Troy Maguire (of L'Gueuleton) the 'new' Locks has succeeded in outshining the old Dublin haunt, asserting itself as a choicer, more relevant take on Dublin dining - and it has now settled in to its rightful place in the culinary life of the capital. Large feature windows overlook the canal, allowing diners watch the world go by in sheer comfort. Whitewashed tongue and groove walls create a relaxed Scandinavian ambience, while dark parquet floors and comfortable ochre bucket seats add a sophisticated city vibe. An open fronted kitchen allows diners to view the action, and a small bar area is popular for an aperitif or browsing the menu - the range offered is wide and includes a good value early dinner menu and a Feasting Menu, for groups. The ground floor dining room is bright and buzzy and the upstairs room was also coolly revamped, although the atmosphere is more subdued. The food is best described as bistro de luxe, featuring rustic French classics with gourmet accents. Luxurious ingredients, including truffles, foie gras and single estate chocolate are expertly handled alongside choice artisan produce from Ireland and the continent. Fans of L'Gueuleton will spot old favourites like snails, and Troy's signature black pudding and apple tarte tatin. Portions verge on the large side, leaving little room for dessert, which is a shame, as the short selection is strikingly original. The young, hip floor staff, gathered from some of Dublin's coolest eating places (including quite a few from L'Gueuleton), provide lively, informed service, as well as being well versed in the intricacies of the menu. They can offer help with the wine list too, which is broad and interesting but would benefit from added tasting notes. All round, Locks offers exciting, good value dining in vibrant surroundings and its growing success is well deserved. **Seats 80** (private rooms, 12/24); children welcome; reservations recommended. L daily, 12-3pm; D Mon-Sat, 6-11pm, set L €42.50, set 3 course D €55, early D from €37.50, 5.30-7.30 pm; also à la carte L&D; house wine from €28. SC 12.5% for groups 6+. Closed Sun D, bank hols, Christmas week. Amex, Diners, MasterCard, Visa, Laser. **Directions:** Half way between Portobello and Harold's Cross Bridges on the canal bank (city side).

Dublin 8
The Lord Edward

RESTAURANT•CHARACTER PUB

23 Christchurch Place Dublin 8 **Tel: 01 454 2420**
ledward@indigo.ie www.lordedward.ie

Dublin's oldest seafood restaurant/bar spans three floors of a tall, narrow building overlooking Christ Church Cathedral. Traditional in a decidedly old-fashioned way, The Lord Edward provides a complete contrast to the current wave of trendy restaurants that has taken over Dublin recently - which is just the way a lot of people like it. If you enjoy seafood and like old-fashioned cooking with plenty of butter and cream (as nature intended) and without too many concessions to the contemporary style of presentation either, then this could be the place for you. While certainly caught in a time warp, the range of fish and seafood dishes offered is second to none (sole is offered in no less than nine classic dishes, for example), and the fish cookery is excellent, with simplest choices almost invariably the best. There are a few non-seafood options - traditional dishes like Irish stew, perhaps, or corned beef and cabbage - and desserts also favour the classics. This place is a one-off - long may it last. Bar food is also available Mon-Fri, 12-2.30. **Seats 40**; children welcome. L Mon-Fri, 12.30-2.30, D Mon-Sat 6-10.15. 5 course D €35; also à la carte. House wine from €20. Reservations required; SC 12.5% on groups 8+. Closed L Sat and all Sun, 24 Dec-2 Jan, bank hols. Amex, Diners, MasterCard, Visa, Laser. **Directions:** Opposite Christ Church Cathedral.

Dublin 8
Nonna Valentina

RESTAURANT

1-2 Portobello Road Dublin 8 **Tel: 01 454 9866**
nonnavalentina@yahoo.ie www.nonnnavalentina.ie

One of the the Dunne and Crescenzi group of restaurants, this attractively located two-storey restaurant is named after Stefano Crescenzi's grandmother and enjoys a pleasant outlook over the Grand Canal. Stylishly simple rooms with hardwood flooring and white clothed tables are given a sense of occasion by neat chandeliers, gold picture frames and smart chair covers but, although this is at the fine dining end of the restaurants in the group, the main emphasis is on immaculately sourced ingredients, great service and the buzz created by rooms full of happy diners. Concise menus in Italian and English may include authentic versions of old favourites like bruschetta, buffalo mozzarella or breseola. Specialities include delicious home-made pastas, deeply-flavoured sauces, and a short choice of main courses including a perfectly cooked organic fillet steak, poultry and game - all beef, pork, lamb and chicken is supplied by the renowned organic butcher Downey's. And sweet-toothed diners would do well to leave a little room for delicious home-made desserts - Valentina's tiramisu' with Vinsanto sets a new standard for the Italian trifle, for example. All this plus excellent coffee, a short, carefully selected wine list, great service and very fair prices. **Seats 60** (private room, 20); children welcome (high chair); air conditioning; Food served all day 12-11; set L €22.50; early D €22.50, Mon-Fri, 4-7pm, also à la carte; House wine about €18. Closed 25 Dec. Amex, MasterCard, Visa, Laser **Directions:** On the banks of the canal.

Dublin 8
The Phoenix Café

CAFÉ

Ashtown Castle The Phoenix Park Visitors Centre Dublin 8 **Tel: 01 677 0090**
redhouselucan@hotmail.com

Hidden away next to the Aras an Uachtaráin Visitor Centre, you'll find the Phoenix Café. The modern building is sympathetic to the lush green surroundings and the first floor has a dramatic double height roof, floor-to-ceiling windows and a quirky antler chandelier. The vast majority of ingredients are organically sourced and café fare includes a wide range of hearty quiches, soups and a daily hot special. Salads change regularly but could include carrot with pumpkin and black onion seed, or broccoli and cauliflower, as well as leaf salads and potato salads. Dainty cakes can include lemon drizzle cake, hummingbird cake, flourless chocolate cake and muffins, always including flour-free options. Real care is taken in the preparation of the food and this, combined with the sylvan setting, makes The Phoenix Café a real hidden treasure. **Seats 80 inside, 70 outside.** Main course with three salads €9.50, hot daily special €10.50, desserts €2.80 to €4. Lunch only, 7 days. Open Summer 10 -5, Winter 10-4. Closed 10 days over Christmas. No SC. No credit cards. **Directions:** From Parkgate St in to Phoenix Park to second roundabout (Phoenix Monument) take 3rd exit and drive up avenue to car park.

Dublin 8

HOTEL

Ⓝ

Radisson SAS Royal Hotel

Golden Lane Dublin 8 **Tel: 01 898 2900**

info.royal.dublin@radissonsas.com   www.royal.dublin.radissonsas.com

This smart new hotel is in a developing area of the city centre, within walking distance of attractions (Dublin Castle, Trinity College), shopping and entertainment, and features a rooftop terrace that can be used for barbecues. With 15 meeting rooms, a large conference room (400 delegates) and, air conditioning and complimentary wireless broadband throughout, it caters particularly well for business guests – and a particularly desirable exeuctive meeting room on the seventh floor has its own bar and views across the city. Accommodation is predictably well-appointed and includes business class rooms, and various suites including a Presidential Suite. As well as the main bar ('SURE') , The Vintage Room offers somewhere for a quieter drink and there's a circular bar ('O') for private parties (30). The famous Radisson breakfast buffet is served in Verre en Vers, a stylish dining room which operates as a brasserie-style restaurant for other meals. Conference/banqueting (400/300); business centre; free broadband WiFi. **Rooms 150**; children welcome (under 17s free in parents room, additional bed €45, cots available free of charge). Lift. 24 hr room service. B&B €80 pps; ss €80. Underground parkng (60). Amex, MasterCard, Visa, Laser. **Directions:** At the crossroads of Golden Lane and Chancery Lane.

DUBLIN 9

DUBLIN 9

The Botanic Gardens (Botanic Road; 01 804 0300; www.botanicgardens.ie; open 9am daily) are in Glasnevin and provide a great (free!) morning or afternoon out for visitors to Dublin. They are only a few minutes bus or taxi ride from the city centre and guided tours are available at various times of the day; the tea rooms are not especially pretty, but well worth knowing about - everything is made freshly on the premises, and salads include fresh herbs form the walled garden when available. Further out from the city is DCU (Dublin College University) which is home to Ireland's newest and most exciting multi-venue performance space - The Helix (Collins Avenue, Glasnevin; 01 700 7000; www.thehelix.ie). The Helix is a multi-venue arts centre that comprises three auditoria serving a mixture of high quality music, drama and entertainment. Since its opening in 2002 by President Mary McAleese, The Helix has generated an impressive reputation for staging cutting edge and diverse theatre and music. If you have worked up a thirst at the gardens or fancy a pint after a show then the **John Kavanagh 'GraveDiggers' Pub** (Prospect Square, Glasnevin; 01 830 7978) lays claim to being the oldest family pub in Dublin - it was established in 1833 and the current family are the 6th generation in the business. Known as 'The Gravediggers' because of its location next to the Glasnevin cemetery and its associated folk history, this is a genuine Victorian bar, totally unspoilt - and it has a reputation for serving one of the best pints in Dublin. No music, "piped or otherwise". Theme pub owners eat your hearts out. **Porterhouse North** (Cross Guns Bridge, Glasnevin; 01 830 9922; www.porterhousebrewco.com) is a large white canalside building that was originally a garage and has been redeveloped to retain some of the original art deco features. Inside it is a very trendy pub with a buzzy atmosphere giving it obvious youth appeal. Menus offer a range of popular dishes but, although interesting as a bar, it's not really a food place (perhaps with the exception of pizzas), more a place to drop in for a drink.

WWW.IRELAND-GUIDE.COM FOR ALL THE BEST PLACES TO EAT, DRINK & STAY

Dublin 9
CAFÉ•WINE BAR

Andersons Food Hall & Café

3 The Rise Glasnevin Dublin 9 **Tel: 01 837 8394**
info@andersons.ie www.andersons.ie

Previously a butcher's shop, with its original 1930s' tiled floor, high ceiling and faccedilade, Noel Delaney and Patricia van der Velde's wonderful delicatessen, wine shop and continental-style café is quietly situated on a side road, so the unexpected sight of jaunty aluminium chairs and tables outside - and a glimpse of many wine bottles lining the walls behind the elegant shopfront - should gladden the hearts of first-time visitors sweeping around the corner from Griffith Avenue. Oak fittings have been used throughout, including the wine displays, and the chic little marble-topped tables used for lighter bites suit the old shop well - in the extension behind, there are larger tables and space for groups to eat in comfort. Now, where cuts of meat were once displayed, there's a wonderful selection of charcuterie and cheese from Ireland and the continent, with the choice of an Irish or Iberian plate offering a delicious selection of produce, all served with speciality breads. A short blackboard menu of hot dishes and specials, plus a daily soup, a range of salads, gourmet sandwiches, wraps, hot panini, pastries and classic café desserts complement the charcuterie and cheese which have the gravitas to balance the collection of wines lining the walls - and, in addition to the wine list, which changes regularly, you can choose any bottle to have with your food at a very modest corkage charge. There's also an extensive drinks menu, offering speciality coffees and teas, and some unusual beverages, like Lorina French lemonade. A weekend breakfast menu offers all kinds of treats including smoked salmon and scrambled eggs, and a number of dishes uses various Hicks sausages - Hicks wine & garlic sausage, for example, served on ciabatta with tomato, smoked applewood cheddar & sweet pepper relish. *Also at: **Andersons Crêperie** (01 830 5171), Carlingford Road, Drumcondra, Dublin 9, where the speciality is buckwheat pancakes, but they also offer charcuterie, cheeses etc. **At the time of going to press a new branch has opened in Drogheda, Co Louth (see Drogheda round-up.) **Seats 44** (outside seating 18); No reservations, children welcome (childrens menu, high chair, baby changing facilities), toilets wheelchair accessible. Open Mon-Sat, 9-7 (to 8.30 Thu-Sat), Sun 10-7; last food orders half an hour before closing. 14 House Wines (€18.95-€23.95) & 160 wines available from the wine shop at €6 corkage. Closed 1 week over Christmas, Good Fri & Easter Sun. MasterCard, Visa, Laser. **Directions:** Off Griffith Avenue, near junction with Mobhi Road.

Dublin 9
CAFÉ•WINE BAR

The Cheese Pantry

104 Upper Drumcondra Road Dublin 9
Tel: 01 797 8936 info@thecheesepantry.com www.thecheesepantry.com

Formerly the famous Youkstetter's pork butcher shop, this handsome tiled shopfront with dark green paintwork, matching awning and outside seating, is now home to Aidan and Karen McNeice's popular deli and café, The Cheese Pantry. With its custom-built temperature-controlled cheese room, shelves of 'foodie' pantry items and an impressive selection of wines, it looks like a deli and wine shop but breakfast, lunch and dinner are also served here. Providing simple, good food at fair prices, varied menus that cater to all tastes are cooked with flair. At breakfast you'll find the traditional Full Irish alongside the likes of home-made granola, scrambled eggs with smoked salmon, porridge with honey and Belgian waffles. Lunch choices can range from classic Caesar salad, linguini with smoked salmon and white wine cream sauce, to the house favourites of saffron scented seafood chowder and home-made fish pie. The ante is upped at dinner time with the appearance of all the old favourites with a twist - steak with grilled Cashel Blue or seared chicken fillet on chorizo mash perhaps – but Dover sole, Barbary duck, wood pigeon, fish dishes and game (in season) also feature. For a small corkage fee, you can choose any wine in the shop to have with your meal, making this an attractive option. Offering decently priced good food in casual surroundings, it's no wonder this neighbourhood bistro is a hit with the lucky locals. **Seats 35**; reservations recommended; children welcome (high chair, childrens menu, baby changing facilities); wheelchair friendly; air conditioning; free broadband wi/fi. Open daily 8.30am-10pm (10.30am-4pm Sun). House wine from €15. MasterCard, Visa, Laser. **Directions:** Across from the Skylon Hotel.

Dublin 9
GUESTHOUSE

Egans House
7-9 Iona Park Glasnevin Dublin 9 **Tel: 01 830 5283**
info@eganshouse.com www.eganshouse.com

Pat and Monica Finn's pleasant guesthouse is situated in a residential area near the Botanic Gardens at Glasnevin, and offers comfortable, well-maintained accommodation at a reasonable price. The location is extremely handy- not only is it within walking distance of the Botanic Gardens, but also conveniently close to Phibsborough, with all its shopping amenities. And an amazing number of places - the airport, north Dublin golf clubs, Dublin City University, The Helix (DCU Performing Arts complex), Dublin port and the city centre - are all very accessible from here. While the atmosphere is Edwardian, modern facilities are provided, including a PC with broadband in the resident's lounge, plus a giant television and a stereo system, while more old-fashioned entertainment can be had from the piano. Standards of comfort are high and guest rooms have tea/coffee trays, a desk, internet access, and a safe large enough to hold a laptop, which is useful; all are en-suite, although it should be noted that some bathrooms offer shower only. Breakfast consists of a generous buffet, and staff are friendly and helpful. Parking is available in front of the house, and there is also on-street parking without much difficulty. Wine licence. Parking. Children welcome (Under 3s free in parents' room; cots available). No pets. Garden. **Rooms 23** (22 shower only, 14 no-smoking, 13 ground floor, 4 family rooms). B&B €60, No SS. Closed 22-28 Dec. MasterCard, Visa, Laser. **Directions:** North of city centre - Dorset Street - St. Alphonsus Road- Iona Park.

Dublin 9
RESTAURANT

Independent Pizza Company
28 Lr Drumcondra Road Dublin 9 **Tel: 01 830 2044**
www.ilovepizza.ie

A sister restaurant of the popular Gotham Café just off Grafton Street (see entry), the Independent Pizza Company is in smart new premises and the menu includes many of the Gotham favourites, so you can expect to find designer salads and contemporary pasta dishes, for example, alongside the excellent range of gourmet pizzas for which they are best known. Family-friendly (crayons, colouring books provided) and a handy place for a meal on the way to the airport. Lunchtime specials are good value and there's a good drinks menu, including speciality coffees. *The Independent Pizza Company celebrates 25 years in business in 2009, and will be introducing new menus and decor to mark the occasion. **Seats 50** (Max table size 8). Wheelchair access to all areas; children welcome (high chair, children's menu, baby changing facilities); air conditioning. Open daily, 12 noon-11 (Fri/Sat to 12). House wine about €15; beer licence. A la carte; sc discretionary (except 10% on groups of 6+ adults). Closed 2 days Christmas, Good Fri. Amex, MasterCard, Visa, Laser. **Directions:** On the airport road - under the bridge at Drumcondra railway station.

Dublin 9
HOTEL•RESTAURANT

The Maples House Hotel
79-81 Iona Road Glasnevin Dublin 9 **Tel: 01 830 4227**
info@mapleshotel.com www.mapleshotel.com

Conveniently located near the Botanic Gardens and Dublin City University, this neat double-fronted Victorian redbrick hotel is well lit, with flags to help you find it in a largely residential street. Although not smart, it offers the kind of reliability and comfort that is welcome in a suburban setting. Cosy fires (log effect, but still cheering) and a relaxed atmosphere, plus the spacious bar and rather attractive ground floor restaurant all make the visitor feel welcome. Accommodation is spotlessly clean and comfortable, and rooms have not only the traditional facilities of tea and coffee making equipment and hair dryer, but also flat screen televisions and the computer connections that today's traveller requires. All bedrooms have a neat en-suite shower room, and the area is generally quiet, so you should be sure of a good night's sleep. The large hotel bar attracts non-residents and the restaurant, complete with fire, serves modern Irish food in a most pleasant setting, with white linen and modern crockery and glassware. All this, plus a decent wine list and attentive service from pleasant staff, makes a meal here a relaxing experience. Room rate from €49. MasterCard, Visa, Laser. ◊

Dublin 9
RESTAURANT

The Washerwomans Hill Restaurant
60a Glasnevin Hill Glasnevin Dublin 9 **Tel: 01 837 9199**
info@washerwoman.ie www.washerwoman.ie

Convenient to the Botanic Gardens and the airport area, first impressions of the outside of this popular neighbourhood restaurant may be a little dusty but a prompt welcome and the offer of a choice of tables should help new arrivals warm to it. Traditional, slightly country kitchen in style, this charming restaurant is quite dimly-lit and cosy, with simply-laid darkwood tables and local artwork displayed on the walls. Well-balanced traditional table d'hôte and à la carte menus offer the popular dishes, sometimes with a contemporary twist, and the cooking style is quite homely. Some suppliers are listed on the menu and special diets can be accommodated. The ambience on the ground floor is warmer and more relaxed than a first floor room, which has rather gimmicky decor. [*A more contemporary sister restaurant, Canters, is in Fairview (see entry)] **Seats 70** (private room, 35); children welcome (not after 10pm); air conditioning. L Mon-Fri 12.30-3.30 (Sun 1.30-4); D daily 5-9pm (to 9.30pm Fri/Sat); Sun all day 12-6pm. Set L about €20, Set Sun L about €26, early D about €26 (6-8). Set D about €35; also à la carte. House wine about €17.50. Closed Sat L, Sun D. 25-26 Dec, Good Fri. **Directions:** Past Bon Secours hospital, opposite the Met Office. ◇

DUBLIN 14

Dublin 14	Indian Brasserie
Restaurant	Main Street Rathfarnham Dublin 14
	Tel: 01 492 0261

For anyone who has been to India, finding a truly authentic restaurant which offers a similar experience is not easy: but the Indian Brasserie comes close. It is just a minute's walk from Rathfarnham Castle, at the Butterfield Avenue end of the village, and the water feature at the entrance is instantly therapeutic. This is carried through by the warmth of the reception, and the restaurant, which has functional seating and a comfortable atmosphere, is run as a buffet: Balwant Negi, who came to Ireland as diplomatic chef to the Ambassador 40 years ago, offers freshly prepared wholesome food, aiming to make it the nearest to home cooking that can be achieved in a restaurant. The selection usually includes around eight starters, five or six salads and seven or eight main courses, with each dish individually prepared from scratch and the selection worked out so that all the dishes complement each other. Breads - which are baked quickly at a very high temperature - are cooked to order. The hospitality is intended to make each guest feel as if they are visiting a private house - customers are encouraged to try a little of everything that has been prepared on the night. The Indian Brasserie has a loyal local clientèle, who appreciate both the high quality and moderate prices, and also offers a takeaway service. **Seats 70**; fully wheelchair accessible; children welcome (high chair, children's menu). D daily 5-11pm (to 10pm Sun). L Sun only 12.30-3pm. Early D, €20, Mon-Fri, 5-7pm; set 2/3 course D €23.50/€29; also à la carte; set Sun L €20. House wine about €15. SC 10% on groups 8+. Closed Good Fri, 25-27 Dec. Amex, MasterCard, Visa. **Directions:** At the Butterfield Ave. end of Rathfarnham village, under TSB Bank.

Dublin 14	The Yellow House
CHARACTER PUB	1 Willbrook Road Rathfarnham Dublin 14
	Tel: 01 493 2994

Named after the unusual shade of the bricks with which it is built, the landmark pub of Rathfarnham makes a perfect rendezvous, with no chance of confusion. The tall and rather forbidding exterior gives little hint of the warmth inside, where pictures and old decorative items relevant to local history repay closer examination. (Traditional bar food is served in the lounge and there's a restaurant upstairs serving evening meals and Sunday lunch.) Closed 25-6 Dec & Good Fri. Amex, Diners, MasterCard, Visa, Laser. **Directions:** Prominent corner building in Rathfarnham Village.

DUBLIN 15

Dublin 15	Castleknock Hotel & Country Club
HOTEL	Porterstown Road Castleknock Dublin 15 **Tel: 01 640 6300**
	reservations@chcc.ie www.towerhotelgroup.com

This large modern hotel just outside Castleknock Village has brought welcome accommodation and amenities in the area. With its own golf course, extensive conference facilities and countryside views, it makes a pleasant base for both business and leisure guests. Spacious, comfortably furnished bedrooms are not over-decorated and have cable TV, radio, telephone with voice mail, broadband internet access, in room safe, tea/coffee facilities and trouser press as standard, and bathrooms have separate shower and bath. Non-smoking bedrooms are available on request (subject to availability), and there are also a number of interconnecting rooms for families. The hotel offers formal dining in The Park restaurant, and an informal option in The Brasserie, where breakfast is also served. Conferences/Banqueting, golf, leisure centre. Ample parking. **Rooms 144**; B&B from €75 pps. Closed 24-26 Dec. MasterCard, Visa, Laser. ◇

Dublin 15
RESTAURANT

Cilantro

Above Brady's Pub Old Navan Road Castleknock Dublin 15
Tel: 01 824 3443

Brady's Inn - a large but pleasant pub - is a local landmark in Castleknock, and above it you will find this very agreeable owner-run Indian restaurant. Modern and clean lined, with black leather fireside seating in the reception area, and generous white-clothed tables set up with crisp linen napkins, generous fine wine glasses and fresh flowers, it creates a good first impression - enhanced by a warm welcome from friendly Indian staff. A balanced wine list (including some Indian beers) and menus are promptly presented, and aperitifs follow swiftly. Poppodums and an array of chutneys make tasty nibbles to begin with, while looking through menus that offer a wide range of dishes, including many of the traditional favourites, but also less known dishes. Tandoori specialities feature on the main course choices, and a mixed tandoori dish brings together pieces of lamb, chicken and beef, cooked over charcoal in the tandoor. Various creamier dishes are offered too, plus tempting naan breads and an unusual range of side vegetables. To finish, try a refreshing lassi (a traditional, slightly salty, mixture of yoghurt and water). Tasty food, friendly staff and giood value make this an ideal neighbourhood restaurant - and Cilantro has earned a loyal following. Sister establishments: Tulsi (Galway, Dublin), Kasturi. **Seats 90**; D daily 5-11.30pm. MasterCard, Visa, Laser. **Directions:** Over Brady's Pub. ◇

Dublin 15
RESTAURANT
Ⓝ

Jaipur Restaurant

Unit 35 & 39 Ongar Village Dublin 15 **Tel: 01 640 2611**
info@jaipur.ie www.jaipur.ie

This latest branch of the highly regarded Jaipur chain of Indian restaurants is a real asset to Ongar Village - conveniently located in the centre of the new village, it's well worth seeking out as it has set the culinary benchmark for the area. It looks a little out of place in a sparse office building, but this is quickly forgotten once inside as – like its sister restaurants - the interior is stylish and cosy, with an open dining area decorated sparingly with modern images of India, and atmospheric instrumental music playing quietly. Friendly staff provide a prompt welcome and offer enticing menus of tradi-tional Indian fare alongside dishes with a more unusual twist. Unusually for an Indian restaurant, desserts are a delight, especially the house variations on kulfi (Indian ice cream). The attention to detail which this chain is renowned for is evident in a wine list that is carefully matched to Indian food – and the King Cobra (beer) is an interesting option for the indecisive. And most attentive service is another highlight of this busy, delightful spot. **Seats 56**; children welcome; air conditioning; D daily, 5-11pm; early D €20, 5-7pm, also à la carte. Closed 25-26 Dec. Amex, MasterCard, Visa, Laser. **Directions:** Centre of Ongar village.

Dublin 15
RESTAURANT

La Mora

Luttrellstown Castle Resort Castleknock Dublin 15 **Tel: 01 860 9500**
lamora@luttrellstown.ie www.luttrellstown.ie

La Mora is the formal restaurant at Luttrellstown Castle Resort's clubhouse and its first floor location affords diners delightful views across the golf course to the mountains in the distance. The clubhouse is a handsome stone and wood-clad building that draws on mountain lodges for inspiration. This log cabin theme is wonderfully executed inside with heavy beams, walls clad in honeyed wood and a soothing palette of moody greys, browns and reds that draws on Ralph Lauren's distinctive interiors look. Non-members are welcome and diners can linger in the stylish Clubhouse Bar before moving to La Mora, the gorgeous restaurant that's a sophisticated mix of wood-clad walls, gigantic canvasses and muted furnishings. The large, bright room is especially family-friendly by day and justifiably popular for Sunday lunch with large tables, plenty of room and a good children's menu. While weekend lunch offers favourites like rack of lamb or roast rib eye, dinner menus might feature more unusual dishes like West Cork lobster salad or Thai baked sea bass; cooking is impressive, exact and beautifully presented. Service may sometimes be a little uneven, but La Mora (Italian for blackberry) provides extremely good food in a remarkable setting and a visit here is sure to be enjoyable. ***Luttrellstown Castle Hotel & Resort** is expected to re-open late in 2009, following an extensive refurbishment programme. See website for details (www.luttrellstown.ie). D Wed-Sat, 7-9pm; Sun brunch, 1-5pm. Closed D Sun, Mon, Tue. **Directions:** In Luttrellstown golf club. ◇

Dublin 15
HOTEL
Ⓝ

Park Plaza Tyrrelstown

Tyrrelstown Town Centre Tyrrelstown Dublin 15 **Tel: 01 827 2359**
info@parkplazatyrrelstown.com www.plazatyrrelstown.com

Within less than twenty minutes from the airport (the hotel will arrange collection and drop off), this modern four star hotel in a fast-developing suburb in north-west Dublin is comfortable and stylishly decorated, with excellent facilities including ample conference rooms of all sizes (boasting Ireland's biggest conference projector screen), a guest library, and a gym. All of the colourful and tastefully furnished guest rooms feature flat screen televisions and wireless internet access (internet is also available through the provided televisions). A good bar food menu is available in The Hourglass bar, where cocktails and an interesting wine list is offered in addition to the usual range of drinks; for main meals, the Maya Ché Restaurant serves the full Park Plaza Breakfast (€21) and offers well-priced lunch and dinner menus consisting primarily of traditional fare but also a selection of Asian dishes (3-course lunch €23, 3-course dinner €35). Primarily designed and located for conferences, this hotel also offers business travellers very comfortable accommodation close to Dublin airport. **Directions:** Approximately 8km from central Dublin between the N3 and N2 and 3km from Blanchardstown Town Centre. ◇

Dublin 15
HOTEL•BAR•RESTAURANT

The Twelfth Lock

Castleknock Marina The Royal Canal Castleknock Dublin 15
Tel: 01 860 7400 info@twelfthlock.com www.twelfthlock.com

The Twelfth Lock is a small hotel in a picturesque location beside the Royal Canal. It has a warm, friendly atmosphere and the main bar is modern, light and airy, with a variety of high and low wooden tables dotted around, and a fine fire that would warm up the coldest evening - and, there's also a sizeable heated deck with views out over the canal. Interesting bar menus offer a good range of quality, informal fare such as lamb chops or grilled salmon steak, with good vegetarian choices also. Attentive staff cope well even when the bar is busy but, as it is very popular but not very large, it's wise to get here early. *The Bar Bistro offers a slightly more formal evening dining experience, Wednesday-Saturday only. **Accommodation:** The ten guest rooms are on the lower ground floor and a little dark, but comfortably furnished. **Rooms 10** (1 disabled); children are welcome, but not allowed in bar after 7pm. Lift. Room service (limited hours). Room rate €85 (with breakfast); weekend rates available. Bar Meals Mon-Thurs, 12 noon-9pm; Fri-Sun 12 noon-8:30pm. Outside eating. Wheelchair accessible. Bar Bistro open Wed-Sat from 7pm(to 11.30pm). Amex, MasterCard, Visa, Laser. **Directions:** On Royal Canal, at Twelfth Lock near Brady's Castleknock Inn Pub. ◇

DUBLIN 16

DUNDRUM

Dundrum Shopping Centre has attracted a lot of restaurants, mostly casual - including **Milano, Café Mimo** (at House of Fraser) - and, at the time of going to press **Roly Saul** is due to re-locate here from Dun Laoghaire to open his latest venture Roly Saul The Restaurant (www.roly.ie).

Dublin 16
RESTAURANT
Ⓔ Ⓝ

Ananda

2-4 Sandyford Road Dundrum Town Centre Dublin 16 **Tel: 01 296 0099**
info@anandarestaurant.ie www.anandarestaurant.ie

Ananda was one of the most eagerly awaited restaurant openings of 2008. And with good cause: this partnership between Asheesh Dewan, owner of the outstanding Jaipur restaurants, and Atul Kochhar, the first Indian chef to receive a Michelin star for his renowned London restaurant Benares, promised a new benchmark for Indian food in Ireland and - open just weeks before The Guide went to press - that promise seems to have been fulfilled with éclat. Ananda's executive chef is Sunil Ghai, who has been working in the Jaipur restaurants for eight years, and is known for an impressive understanding of Indian cooking and remarkable finesse with spicing; prior to Ananda's opening, Sunil spent several months working in Benares, and, together with Atul, has developed a highly innovative and contemporary menu. Don't come to Ananda expecting standard samosas and chicken tikka - instead be prepared for culinary treats that challenge the broadest perceptions of Indian cooking. A vegetable korma might feature fragrant apricots and sage, seared scallops might come spice-crusted on polenta and coconut, lamb shanks might be slow cooked in Kashmiri chilli and pine extract. A great way to sample four dishes in one is to order Ananda's thaali, available as a vegetarian choice or with meat and seafood. This selection of four complimentary dishes, served with rice and excellent naan, showcases the breadth of skill in the kitchen, and is a knockout dish. Interestingly, each menu contains a wine list, which is a useful idea, although it would be more user-friendly to see the food up front, and the wine list at the back. There are 16 wines by the glass, followed by a choice of 75 bottles, most of which are accessibly priced between 23-40. Cobra and Tiger beers are available too, although not on the menu. The creative vision in the kitchen has been carried through to the glamorous dining room, which has taken the best of Indian design and given it a stylish contemporary twist. Flock fabric chairs in jewel colours sit beneath organically shaped lamps that seem to float like giant jellyfish. Alcoves are trimmed with subtle dark woodcarvings, evoking the palaces of Rajasthan; bright canvasses of rural scenes reference the colourful southern provinces; richly coloured walls evoke the vibrant saris that dot India's streetscapes. All these elements have been perfectly tied together on a pale striped carpet to create a stylish, comfortable and highly distinctive dining room.The purity of flavours, the wonderfully presented dishes, the smart service and the beautiful dining room make Ananda appealing on so many levels. For the quality of cooking on offer, it offers surprisingly good value too. **Seats 85**; children welcome (high chair); air conditioning. Open daily; L 12-3pm (to 5pm Sun); D from 5.30pm. Closed 25-26 Dec. MasterCard, Visa, Laser. **Directions:** 200m from main Dundrum crossroads.

Dublin 16

RESTAURANT

Café Mao

The Mill Pond Civic Square Dundrum Shopping Centre Dublin 16
Tel: 01 296 2802 dundrum@cafemao.com www.cafemao.com

This modern, airy two-storey restaurant is a younger sister of the well-known Café Mao restaurants in Dublin. Conveniently located in a restaurant piazza to the rear of the shopping centre, it's a handy place for an après shop bite. The atmosphere is bright and buzzy, and interesting food is based on seasonal ingredients; the standard of cooking is consistently good, offering simple, tasty food that is served quickly and at a reasonable price. Chilli squid, Nasi Goreng and Malaysian chicken are established favourites, vegetarians might try a starter of Jakarta salad followed by Thai green vegetable curry. Chilli strength is considerately indicated on the menu, also vegetarian and low fat dishes, dishes containing nuts. A compact but wide-ranging drinks menu includes cocktails, fresh juices and smoothies, a range of coffees and teas and speciality beers as well as wines. Café Mao Dundrum Shopping Centre is understandably popular for its healthy food, good value and friendly efficient service. **Seats 130** (outdoor, 50); fully wheelchair accessible; children welcome; serving food daily 12-10pm (to 10.30pm Fri/Sat); Value L about €9.95, value D about €15, 5-7pm; set 2/3 course D about €24/€28; House Wine €18. Closed 25/26 Dec. **Directions:** At the back of Dundrum shopping centre next to the Old Mill Pond. ◇

Dublin 16

RESTAURANT

Harvey Nichol's First Floor Restaurant

Dundrum Town Centre Sandyford Road Dublin 16
Tel: 01 291 0488 www.harveynichols.com

Before the arrival of Harvey Nichol's in Ireland, the concept of fine dining in a department store was quite alien to most Dubliners, but the First Floor Restaurant & Bar at Harvey Nichol's has a separate entrance and express lift so, having whizzed up, most find that the scene has been set pretty impressively. The interior - designed by French interior architect Christian Biecher - is contemporary cool, with vibrant pinks taking the lead in the popular bar (where in-house mixologists are at hand to create the perfect cocktail...) and a combination of warm, plummy pinks and yellows linking into the restaurant too, where glass walls, high-backed couches and banquettes are balanced by slouchy leather carver chairs and crisp, white-clothed classic modern table settings. Head chef Thomas Haughton arrived at Dundrum via a lot of prestigious kitchens, most recently Luttrellstown Castle, so his modern classic cooking comes as no surprise. A meal here comes with all the details that make a special occasion - gorgeous breads, chef's complimentary amuse bouche (pea & truffle panna cotta perhaps) - and dishes on a typical dinner menu could include luxurious starters such as pavé of foie gras with ginger marinated apple, cider meringue & toaste brioche, or a rillette of fragrant crab with tartare of avocado and tomato and thyme milkshake, and main courses like pot-roasted belly of pork with caramelised parsnip and turnip purée or pan-seared seabass with fennel confit, sauce vierge and black olive tapenade. Despite the initial hype, Thomas Haughton has maintained the high standards set from the outset and his clean-flavoured cooking is outstanding - and, whilst portions are on the small side, this sophisticated restaurant continues to offer one of south Dublin's most exciting dining experiences. The wine list is impressive too, offering treats for the connoisseur as well as a choice of eight good, well-priced house wines (although tasting notes would be welcome). Good value can also be found through a variety of inventive promotions which include pre-theatre dining, themed gourmet evenings and special value cocktail and wine events. **Seats 80** (private room, 12); toilets wheelchair accessible; children welcome before 9pm; air conditioning; L daily, 12.30-3pm; set 2/3 course L €19.50/24.50, set Sun L €27.50; D Tue-Sat, 6-10, 2/3 course value D €24.50/29.50, 6-7.30pm, also à la carte D; house wine €22. Live jazz Sun L. Closed Sun D, Mon D and 25/26 Dec. Amex, Diners, MasterCard, Visa, Laser. **Directions:** Above Harvey Nichol's department store in the Dundrum Town Centre.

Dublin 16
HOTEL

IMI Residence

Sandyford Road Dublin 16 **Tel: 01 207 5900**
reservations@imires.ie www.imi.ie/accommodation

Within easy access of the M50, (Sandyford Industrial Estate exit), 1 km from the Luas stop at Balally and on the local bus route to Dundrum less than ten minutes away, the residence is on spacious grounds surrounded by trees with lots of parking. It is a residence rather than an hotel, rather like upmarket university campus accommodation. The reception area is typical of the facility: modern, minimalist, high-ceilinged, high-windowed, with bare concrete walls covered here and there with modern paintings and wall hangings. There is a definite business air about the place - lots of light and no frills, yet good uncomplicated service by efficient, friendly staff. Comfortable bedrooms are decorated in smart, muted tones (blue/grey carpet, cream walls), with work space, TV, telephone and internet lines. Particularly neat, well maintained shower rooms have black and blue tiles and full length mirror. Only a continental, self-service breakfast is offered, with good coffee. The residence is an ideal base for the business traveller and its understated operation should appeal to a wider category of cost-conscious visitors to Dublin. Conferences (300); broadband; wheelchair friendly; laptop-sized safes in bedrooms; children welcome (under 6s free in parents' room, cot available free of charge). **Rooms 50** (all shower only, executive and no smoking, 25 ground floor, 2 for disabled); limited room service, Lift. B&B is excellent value, from as little as €70 per room. **Directions:** Sandyford Industrial Estate Exit from M50. Entrance where Clonard Road meets Sandyford Road at traffic lights. ◇

Dublin 16
RESTAURANT

L'Officina by Dunne & Crescenzi

Dundrum Shopping Centre Dundrum Dublin 16 **Tel: 01 216 6764**
dunneandcrescenzi@hotmail.com www.officina.ie

Located in an informal dining piazza to the rear of Dundrum Shopping Centre, this younger sister to the well-known Dunne & Crescenzi restaurants offers al fresco dining alongside the fountains in the Old Mill Pond. Decorated in tune with the style of food service - simple, no-fuss, efficient - there's a buzzy atmosphere, and an impressive display of wine contrasts with the simplicity of paper place mats and minimal table settings. Italian staff are quick to greet and seat arriving guests; menus and wine list are promptly presented, along with an outline of the mouthwatering daily specials. Impeccably sourced ingredients form the backbone of healthy menus at L'Officina, where the use of artisan products is proudly highlighted and there are plenty of simple classic Italian dishes on offer such as Caprese salad, panini, or minestrone soup. Menus also include platters that are particularly good for sharing and sampling several dishes. Evening menus are a little more extensive, including fish and organic fillet of beef, and plenty of choice for vegetarians. Finish with a treat from a selection of homemade desserts, partnered with some of Ireland's finest coffee. All round, L'Officina offers great quality at a fair price and the staff are terrific. **Seats 60**; children welcome; air conditioning. Open Mon-Sat, 10.30am-10pm; Sun 12-10pm. MasterCard, Visa, Laser. **Directions:** At the rear of the shopping centre - next to the fountain.

DUBLIN 18

DUBLIN 18

Bordering onto Stillorgan (sometimes Dublin 4, or Co Dublin) and Blackrock (Co Dublin), Dublin 18 is a chameleon area, with edges a little blurred and, it seems, sometimes shifting... but one thing is certain, and it's that the burgeoning business parks have ensured the choice of interesting places to eat and comfortable places to lay your head are on the increase: A lively business area, it now has the 352 bedroom **Bewleys Hotel Leopardstown** (01 293 5000; www.bewleyshotels.com), for example, offering a high level of comfort (and links to the airport) for as little as €89; and also the newer, designled 82-room contemporary **Beacon Hotel** (see entry).
WWW.IRELAND-GUIDE.COM FOR ALL THE PLACES TO EAT, DRINK & STAY

Dublin 18
HOTEL

The Beacon Hotel

Beacon Court Sandyford Business Region Dublin 18
Tel: 01 291 5000

In burgeoning south county Dublin, Sandyford has become the focus for extensive development, and the Beacon Hotel is a most welcome facility. Located within sight of the M50 motorway, five minutes walk from the Luas tramline, (15 minutes to the city centre) and about 20 minutes by car to the ferry at Dun Laoghaire, it looks no different to the neighbouring glass/concrete exteriors of a private hospital and office block, but that is just on the outside: internally the hotel is a model of cutting edge design. Although it resembles its sister hotel, The Morgan in Temple Bar (see entry), The Beacon is bolder, more designer-led. The open plan, light-filled foyer has the appeal of an art gallery with elegant candelabras, moulded wall sculpture and bizarre seating arrangements, as exemplified by a cleverly adapted four poster bed. It is unashamedly a business hotel with several air-conditioned meeting rooms equipped to the highest standards, also free underground parking for guests, accessible by lift from the lobby. Bedrooms are ultra modern, a happy amalgam of provocative lighting, both over and under the bed, beds set playfully at an angle and crimson velour "headboards"; pristine bathrooms are behind sliding, opaque glass doors, emphasising the streamlined experience, and housekeeping overall is excellent There is a ground floor bar and a Thai Restaurant which doubles as breakfast room - breakfast, as in the Morgan, is expensive at about €20 but not well done here. Sunday Brunch at The Beacon features a jazz band and well-known local artists. Reception is cool and uninvolved- and, despite the sexy ambience, it is not a place for lingering; very few guests are in the bar at night and breakfasts are speedily consumed. **Rooms 88**. Room only rate from €105. Breakfast about €20. My Thai restaurant D daily, 6-10.30 (takeaway also available). **Directions:** In the heart of the Sandyford business region. ◇

Dublin 18
RESTAURANT

Bistro One

3 Brighton Road Foxrock Village Dublin 18 **Tel: 01 289 7711**
bistroone@eircom.net www.bistro-one.ie

This popular neighbourhood restaurant can get very busy but there is a bar on the way in, where guests are greeted and set up in comfort, and the attitude throughout is laid back yet not without care. Ingredients are carefully sourced, with suppliers credited on the menu - fresh produce comes from Newfresh & Denis Healy (organic grower), John O'Reilly butchers supply the meats and cheeses from Sheridan's cheesemongers. Seasonal menus - which considerably indicate dishes containing nuts or nut oil - offer eight or ten tempting choices per course: starters will almost certainly include the ever-popular Bistro One's salad with pancetta, rocket & pine nuts - while the pasta and risotto selection can be starter or main course as preferred, typically, spaghetti with home-made meatballs, tomato & fresh basil, perhaps, or pea & parsley risotto. Main courses are mainly excellent renditions of the classics - in seafood dishes (fish & chips with tartare sauce & minted mushy peas) and and meats (dry-aged chargrilled ribeye with chunky chips and béarnaise sauce) - and that is the enduring appeal of this restaurant. There are generous side vegetables and a choice of French and Irish cheese; home-made ice creams or classic puddings to finish. **Seats 75**; children welcome. D Tue-Sat 6-10.30, L 12-2.30. Set L about €21; D à la carte. House wine €22. SC 10%. Closed Sun, Mon & 25 Dec - 2 Jan. MasterCard, Visa, Laser. **Directions:** Southbound on N11, first right after Foxrock church.

Stillorgan
RESTAURANT
😋 🍴

China Sichuan Restaurant

The Forum Ballymoss Road Sandyford Industrial Estate Dublin 18
Tel: 01 288 4817

This Dublin favourite recently moved to a new location opposite Stillorgan Luas station and is buzzing, even on weekday nights, with fans of the authentic Chinese cuisine. With smiling welcomes and friendly accommodating service, the Hui family have been presiding over what many rate as the best Chinese restaurant in the country for over 20 years. Old favourites like the tea-smoked duck, sizzling and shredded dishes and three styles of dumpling are still there along with an impressive range of seafood which includes scallops, squid and cuttlefish. Star dessert is the plate of toffee banana fritters, sent piping hot from the kitchen to the table, where the accomplished waiters deftly dip each toffee coated morsel into iced water and arrange the crisp fritter alongside vanilla ice cream. Brisk lunchtime business features a well-priced table d'hôte and fast service while the evening attracts a more leisurely mix of regular diners, celebratory groups and a fair representation of suits entertaining out-of-towners. Well selected wine list with a good price range. **Seats 100** (outdoor, 20); children welcome; reservations required; air conditioning. L Sun-Fri 12.30-2.30 (from 1pm Sun). D daily 6-10.30. Set L about €16 (Sun €17), Set D about €36; à la carte available; house wine about €20; SC10%. Closed L Sat, 25-27 Dec & Good Fri. Amex, MasterCard, Visa, Laser. **Directions:** Opposite Stillorgan Luas station. ◇

Dublin 18
RESTAURANT

The Gables Restaurant

The Gables Foxrock Village Dublin 18 **Tel: 01 289 2174**
value@mccabeswines.ie www.mccabeswines.ie

This imaginative venture by McCabes Wines, whose shop is part of the restaurant, offers a wine experience in addition to brunches and stylish contemporary food. The wine list offers quality wines at an unusually low mark-up - and you can have any wine from about 800 available in the shop at a moderate corkage charge (none at all when ordering from the table d'hôte menu). The list, which is organised by grape variety, offers a good range of wines by the glass - and a novel 'try before you buy' offer: you taste a wine before ordering it and, if you like it, you can add it to your bill and have a case put into your car (at a very favourable price) while dining at The Gables: easy peasy. The restaurant offers modern food with an international tone in congenial surroundings, and the cooking is consistent although service can be uneven. **Seats 70** (outdoor, 20). Open 8am-10pm daily (Sun 10-9). L 12.30-5pm; D 6-9.30 (Sun 5-7); à la carte. House wine from €18. SC discretionary. Closed 25 Dec, Good Fri. Amex, Diners, MasterCard, Visa, Laser. **Directions:** Travelling into the city on N11, turn off left for Foxrock Village.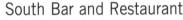

Dublin 18
RESTAURANT

South Bar and Restaurant

Unit a8 Beacon South Quarter Sandyford Dublin 18 **Tel: 01 293 4050**
reservations@south.ie www.south.ie

It may seem surprising to find Ronan Ryan and Temple Garner's brand of smart, contemporary dining in the middle of an industrial estate but the site - close to the Beacon Hotel and the Beacon Hospital - is well chosen, and it has become a popular destination for residents of the southern Dublin suburbs. It was built on the success of their hugely popular Town Bar and Grill, giving the new venture a great kick start, and this time they're serving classic bistro fare in a dining room so slick that you quickly forget about the location. Externally the green copper cladding and curving glass hint at the visual treat indoors: a dramatic sweeping staircase, huge slabs of bespoke terrazzo flooring, a cascade of silver pendant lights and a giant glass wall that floods the basement with natural light. While the ground floor dining room is spacious and handsome, it's the versatile basement room that's most atmospheric and unique. For Sunday lunch, request a table at the foot of the stairs where you can watch generations of families and smart young couples arrive and depart; by night cosy-up in a banquette across the room, where you'll enjoy moody lighting and views of the chic horseshoe-shaped cocktail bar. Comfy seats, large tables, fresh buds and crisp linen make it a sophisticated but relaxed affair. Menus featuring modern classics, simply cooked and attractively presented, have wide appeal. Favourites like beer-battered fish, Caprese salad, pork belly or the house burger, use the choicest ingredients and, as you'd expect, everything, from the bread to the tartar sauce and ice cream, is home-made. Portions are filling but sensible, allowing room for the excellent desserts, should you wish. Menus change regularly and, given the quality of the cooking, food here is good value. Choose from the interesting selection of house wines (the house champagne is especially affordable) and you'll keep your bill agreeably low. South's staff are friendly, obliging and efficient, making dining here a very pleasant experience. There's live music on offer Thursday to Saturday nights too, lending extra buzz to this impressive and atmospheric restaurant. **Seats 200** (private dining 55); toilets wheelchair accessible; children welcome (high chair, children's menu, baby changing facilities); free parking (40 cars), live music Thurs-Sat. Open L&D Tues-Sat, Sun L only; L 12-4 (to 5pm Sun), D 6-11. Set 3 course D €29.95/49.95. SC 10% on groups 5+. Closed D Sun, Mon, Good Fri, 25 Dec. Amex, Diners, MasterCard, Visa, Laser. **Directions:** N11 Stillorgan dual carriageway South, right at Newtownpark Avenue junction. At roundabout take 3rd exit, left at T-junction.

Dublin 18
HOTEL

Stillorgan Park Hotel

Stillorgan Road Stillorgan Dublin 18 **Tel: 01 200 1800**
sales@stillorganpark.com www.stillorganpark.com

A sister establishment to the famous Talbot Hotel in Wexford, this well-run hotel has seen regular renovations over the years and it is furnished in a lively modern style throughout. Public areas include stylish, recently refurbished reception and lounge areas, and spacious bedrooms - some with views of

Dublin Bay - are under renovation at the time of going to press and have well-finished bathrooms. Ample free parking is an attraction, and good facilities for business guests include work space and broadband lines in rooms. A regular airport coach service leaves from the front door. Conference/banqueting (500/370); business centre, video conferencing, free broadband wi/fi. Children welcome (under 12s free in parents' room, cots available without charge, baby sitting arranged). Fitness room, day spa, steam room. **Rooms 150** (8 junior suites, 132 executive rooms, 129 no-smoking, 6 for disabled) Lift. B&B from €65 pps, ss €44. No SC. **The Purple Sage Restaurant:** An attractive, informal restaurant with welcoming staff. Menus are appealing in a fairly contemporary style, including imaginative vegetarian cooking and healthy options, which have always been a feature. **Seats 120**; reservations recommended; air conditioning; toilets wheelchair accessible; children welcome (high chair, children's menu, baby changing facilities). L Mon-Fri, 12.45-2.30; D Mon-Sat, 5.45-9.30; Sun L 12.30-3.30pm. Set L €26; set Sun L €26; early D €25.50, Mon-Sat 5.45-7.30pm, Set D €37.50; à la carte D also available; house wine €22; no SC. Amex, Diners, MasterCard, Visa, Laser. **Directions:** Situated on main N11 dual carriageway.

DUBLIN 22

R R R   DUBLIN 22

Dublin 22, on the western edges of the city, is a busy commercial area known mainly for its industrial estates and business parks - and the huge Liffey Valley Shopping Centre. Hotels which service the needs of the area well include the landmark **Red Cow Moran Hotel** on the Naas Road (01 459 3650; www.moranhotels.com), with outstanding conference facilities; **Bewleys Hotel Newlands Cross** (01 464 0140; www.bewleyshotels.com), offering a lot of space and comfort at a modest price; and the newer **Clarion Hotel Liffey Valley** (01 625 8000; www.clarionhotelliffeyvalley.com), cleverly disguised as a warehouse but actually quite stylish within. On the Naas Road, at Kingswood, the new **Maldron Hotel Citywest** (1850 605 705) offers good accommodation and facilities for a budget hotel, and is well located for business travellers. The most recent addition to the area is the **Louis Fitzgerald Hotel** (01 403 3300; www.louisfitzgeraldhotel.com).
WWW.IRELAND-GUIDE.COM FOR ALL THE BEST PLACES TO EAT, DRINK & STAY

DUBLIN 24

DUBLIN 24

Tallaght is one of the fastest developing areas of western Dublin and lies at the foot of the Dublin - Wicklow mountains. Particularly well known for its shopping centre, its Luas (tram) line makes travelling to the city centre very easy. The large **Plaza Hotel** (Belgard Road; 01 462 4200; www.plazahotel.ie) serves the area well, with secure underground parking and extensive conference and banqueting facilities.
WWW.IRELAND-GUIDE.COM FOR ALL THE BEST PLACES TO EAT, DRINK & STAY

Dublin 24   Glashaus Hotel and Suites
HOTEL•RESTAURANT   Tallaght Cross Town Centre Belgard Square West Tallaght Dublin 24
N   Tel: 01 427 1200 info@glashaushotel.ie www.glashaushotel.ie

Situated in the new development of Tallaght Cross Town Centre, this modern hotel has underground parking (complimentary for residents 5pm-11am) and is only minutes from the Luas line - an ideal place to stay when on business in the area, or for visiting The Square Shopping Centre. Public areas are bright and welcoming – and, with very helpful staff at reception, check-in is an unusually pleasant experience. With just 48 rooms, it's on a more human scale than many of the bigger new hotels yet the attractively styled bedrooms are generously sized and well-equipped, with air conditioning, tea/coffee station, flat screen TV, iron and board, in-room safe and internet access. Smartly tiled bathrooms have marble units, full bath with overhead shower, and good towels and toiletries – you get a lot for a very competitive room rate. **Rooms 48** (4 family, all no smoking, 2 disabled); children welcome (under 5s free in parents room, cot available free of charge); free broadband, 24-hr room service, Lift. Room rate from €89. **Osten Square Bistro Bar:** All meals are served in this smart café-bar-style bistro with mezzanine, and both food and service are a cut above the average. It is well planned for different times of day, with lime walls, white topped round tables with simple good quality settings and a lot of glass making for a bright daytime atmosphere, softened by subtle lights in the evening. Well trained, courteous staff welcome guests and offer menus promptly – an à la carte offers a good choice of popular dishes, and a novel 'Gastro Menu' offers six dishes with a different selected bottle of premium imported beer with each one. Starters might include tasty sesame coated calamari with pickled ginger and aioli or warm confit duck noodle salad, and you'll find mains like slow-cooked belly of pork, or char-grilled sirloin steak with variations on the traditional accompaniments. Some dishes may need a little more work to perfect them but fresh, good quality ingredients are used and there's a feeling that someone in the kitchen is genuinely interested in cooking and presenting good food – and cooked dishes at breakfast are also freshly prepared, hot, appetizing and tasty. Here, as elsewhere, the value offered is good. **Seats 120** (private room, 12, outdoors, 18); children welcome before 9pm (high chair, children's menu, baby changing facilities). Hotel closed 24-27 Dec. Amex, MasterCard, Visa, Laser. **Directions:** Between Tallaght Hospital and the Square shopping centre just off Belgard Road.

COUNTY DUBLIN

Dublin County is divided into the three administrative "sub-counties" of Dun Laoghaire-Rathdown to the southeast, South Dublin to the southwest, and the large territory of Fingal to the north. However, although these regions are among the most populous and economically active in all Ireland, the notion of Greater Dublin being in four administrative parts is only slowly taking root - for instance, all postal addresses still either have a Dublin city numbered code, or else they're simply County Dublin.

Inevitably, it is in the countryside and towns in the Greater Dublin Region that some of the pressures of the success of the Irish economy are most evident. But although Dubliners of town and county alike will happily accept that they're part of a thrusting modern city, equally they'll cheerfully adhere to the old Irish saying that when God made time, He made a lot of it. Those with long family associations with the county certainly have this approach. But as the region has also experienced the greatest population changes in recent years, it has its own multinational dynamism.

The traditionally relaxed approach is good news for the visitor, for it means that if you feel that the frenetic pace of Dublin city is just a mite overpowering, you will very quickly find that nearby, in what used to be - and for many folk still is - County Dublin, there continue to be oases of a much more easy-going way of life waiting to be discovered.

Admittedly, the fact that the handsome Dublin Mountains overlook the city in spectacular style means that, even up in the nearby hills, you can be well aware of the city's buzz. But if you want to find a vigorous contrast between modern style and classical elegance, you can find it in an unusual form at Dun Laoghaire's remarkable harbour, where one of the world's most modern ferryports is in interesting synergy with one of the world's largest Victorian artificial harbours.

A showcase marina within the haven, expensively built so that its style matches the harbour's classic elegance, has steadily developed, while the harbour area of Dun Laoghaire town beside it continues to be improve in quality and vitality.

Northward beyond the city into Fingal, despite the proximity of the airport you'll quickly discover an away from-it-all sort of place of estuary towns, extensive farming, pleasant parkland, fishing and sailing ports, and offshore islands alive with seabirds. The large island of Lambay – a nature reserve – has Ireland and the world's newest gannetry, an offshoot of the previous global front-runner, the gannetry on the stack rock at Ireland's Eye eight kilometres to the south. This was established (almost within city limits, another world first) back in 1989, and served as a reminder that the gannet is not a seagull – it's a pelican.

Fingal is an easygoing environment of leisurely pace in which it's thought very bad form to hasten over meals in restaurants where portion control is either unknown, or merely in its infancy. It's interesting to note that connoisseurs of this intriguing region reckon that one of its long established features, the

Dublin-Belfast mainline railway first used in 1838, effectively creates a "land island" on the Donabate-Portrane peninsula, as there are only two road crossings into this sandy territory with its four golf courses. Add in the legendary Portmarnock links just across the estuary, and this is golfing heaven.

Local Attractions and Information

Balbriggan/Skerries	Ardgillan Castle	01 849 2212
Blackrock	Deepwell House & Gardens	01 288 7407
Donabate	Newbridge House, Park & Traditional Farm	01 843 6534
Dun Laoghaire	Farm Market (Harbour Plaza, Thurs 10.30am-4pm)	087 611 5016
Dun Laoghaire	Harbour Office (24 hours)	01 280 1130
Dun Laoghaire	National Maritime Museum, Haigh Terrace	01 280 0969
Dun Laoghaire	Tourist Information	1850 230330
Leopardstown	Racecourse	01 289 3607
Leopardstown	Farm Market Fri 11am-7pm	087 611 5016
Malahide	Malahide Castle & Demesne	01 846 2184
Malahide	Fry Model Railway (Malahide Castle)	01 846 3779
Malahide	Talbot Botanic Gardens (Malahide Castle)	01 846 2456
Malahide	Coffee shop (Malahide Castle)	01 846 3027
Naul (Fingal)	Seamus Ennis Centre (Traditional Music)	01 802 0898
Rathfarnham	Marlay Demesne gardens	01 493 7372
Sandycove	James Joyce Museum (Martello Tower)	01 280 9265
Sandyford	Fernhill Gardens (Himalayan species)	01 295 6000
Skerries	Skerries Mills - Working Windmills, Craft and Visitor Centre	01 849 5208
Tallaght	Community Arts Centre, Old Blessington Rd	01 462 1501

Blackrock
RESTAURANT

Dali's Restaurant

63-65 Main Street Blackrock Co Dublin **Tel: 01 278 0660**

info@dalis.ie

Just across the road from the Library, this appealing restaurant has a loyal local clientèle and a reputation beyond the immediate area. There's a chic little bar just inside the door and a gently contemporary dining area, up a few steps, beyond. Menus are light and colourful, including some unusual dishes - a starter of Gorgonzola tartlet with a rocket & Waldorf salad perhaps, or main courses like confit rabbit and black bacon linguine with girolle cream, or roast veal chop with lemon & anchovy butter and lyonnaise potatoes - and there's an emphasis on fresh seafood. Daily fish specials are offered and, at lunchtime, might include excellent main courses like pan-fried fillet of sea bream with roast garlic & olive oil mash, tomato & shallot compôte and salsa verde. Dinner menus also offer plenty of seafood, possibly including starters of mackerel fillet, skate & langoustine ravioli or seared scallops and main courses like seared tuna with crab spring roll, whilst meat lovers will enjoy pan-fried magret duck breast, loin of Finnebrodge Estate venison or rack of lamb. Desserts are more than tempting - warm grilled peaches with amaretto and crème fraîche or nougat and raspberry semifreddo are typically delicious examples. There is also an excellent cheese board offering a selection of Irish and French. Good value for money, and honest cooking based on quality ingredients, has them beating a path to the door, so booking is essential, especially at weekends. Set lunch menus offer a choice of half a dozen dishes on each course and, like the early evening menus, offer particularly good value. Professional, efficient service and a good wine list complete an appealing package. *Hartley's in Dun Laoghaire is in common ownership (see entry). **Seats 70**; children welcome; air conditioning. L Tue-Sat, 12-3, Sun L only, 12.30-3.30pm; D Tue-Sat 6-"late". Set L about €28; early D about €28, Tues-Thurs, 6-7pm, Sun L about €29; also à la carte L&D; house wine €20, sc discretionary except 10% on parties of 6+. Live classical guitar on Thursday evenings. Closed D Sun, all Mon, 25-27 Dec. Amex, Diners, MasterCard, Visa, Laser. **Directions:** Opposite Blackrock Library.

Blackrock
CAFÉ•BAR

Tonic

5 Temple Road Blackrock Village Co Dublin **Tel:** 01 288 7671
mail@tonic.ie www.tonic.ie

This smart designer bar brings some welcome style to Blackrock village with its cool walnut woodwork, cube seats, cream leather banquettes and artwork for sale on exhibition - all of which, plus a big screen upstairs, have made it the in place for the trendy young crowd. Informal menus are offered through the day - brunch, daytime and evening bistro - and there's a patio area for al fresco dining in fine weather; however, perhaps it's more a place to drop into for a drink in stylish surroundings. **Seats 100**; toilets wheelchair accessible. Open 12am-12pm; food served all day 12-11, L11-3, D 4-9 (to 10.30pm Fri/Sat). Closed 25 Dec & Good Fri. Amex, MasterCard, Visa, Laser. **Directions:** Centre of Blackrock village. ◊

DALKEY

Dalkey is named after its neighbouring island and grew up as a medieval port. After the construction of the railway, it thrived as a seaside suburb from the 19th century onwards until the present day where it has become a spot for the rich and famous to reside. It is well served by the DART and buses, with spectacular views of Killiney Bay and Dalkey Island, with many interesting shops, art galleries and restaurants. Dalkey Hill provides a pleasant wooded park to walk in and Dalkey Castle and Heritage Centre (+353 (0)1 285 8366, open all year) are a 'must see' for any visitor. Dalkey Island provides the opportunity for an interesting boat trip, and once on the island visitors can explore the ruins of a 17th century church, or try a spot of fishing or seal watching. Every Friday there is a farmers' market at the Dalkey town hall.

Dalkey
PUB
👑

Daniel Finnegan

2 Sorrento Road Dalkey Co Dublin **Tel: 01 285 8505**
www.finnegans

This is a pub of great character and is much-loved by locals and visitors alike. It's been in business for over 40 years and it's comfortable and cosy, with wood panelling and traditional Irish seating in 'snugs' - and the large extension built a few years ago has now 'blended in'. Food is served at lunchtime only - sandwiches or a full hot bar lunch, including starters such as baked Dalkey crab, brie fritters with apple coulis and main courses like roast stuffed pork steak, T-bone steak with pepper sauce and smoked cod, followed by traditional desserts like raspberry & apple crumble and vanilla cheesecake. The fresh fish (from the harbour nearby) is excellent, the vegetables predictable but tasty and good value. No reservations - get there early to avoid a long wait. Carpark nearby. Bar food 12.30-3pm Mon-Sun. Closed 25 Dec, Good Fri & & New Year. Amex, Diners, MasterCard, Visa, Laser. **Directions:** Near Dalkey DART station.

Dalkey
WINE BAR

IN

115-117 Coliemore Road Dalkey Co Dublin **Tel: 01 275 0007**
info@indalkey.ie www.indalkey.ie

This stylish contemporary café-bar in the centre of Dalkey has retained a special niche, offering something rather different from pubs and restaurants in the area. The atmosphere is relaxed and what you get here is informal dining in comfortable, pleasant surroundings: menus are offered for breakfast and lunch (including a 'mini' lunch of soup, warm open sandwich & small fries) as well as dinner, and there's a separate children's menu. Regular dishes range from the ubiquitous steak, and bistro dishes like beef & Guinness hotpot to crisp confit of duck; specialities include Kimchee prawns - fish is purchased daily from local markets - and you may even find home-raised Irish bison on the menu. Drinks include a fairly priced cocktail menu and there are some organic wines. **Seats 80** (+15 outdoors; private room 40); toilets wheelchair accessible; children welcome (high chair, children's menu, baby changing facilities); live piano jazz classics Thu - Sun 10pm-1am. Open 10 am-11pm (Fri & Sat to 1.30). Bar meals daily: 10-11. Meals Daily - B 10-12, L 12-4, D 5-10. Amex, Diners, MasterCard, Visa, Laser. **Directions:** At the end of Dalkey's main street, across from AIB bank.

Jaipur Restaurant

Dalkey
RESTAURANT

20 Castle Street Dalkey Co Dublin **Tel: 01 285 0552**
info@jaipur.ie www.jaipur.ie

This stylish south County Dublin branch of a privately owned group of highly-regarded progressive Indian restaurants (see associated entries under Dublin 2, Malahide, Greystones, Ongar and Dundrum) is well-established as a favourite in the area. The trademark modern decor (revamped in 2007) is a refreshing change from traditional Indian restaurants - warm colours send the right messages and it is a pleasing space. Menus offer an attractive combination of traditional and more creative dishes; Jaipur Jugalbandi, an assortment of five appetisers is a good choice for a group settling for a meal, to avoid indecision. Fresh and dried spices are directly imported but proprietor Asheesh Dewan and head chef Kuldip Kumar are keen to make the most of Irish ingredients, notably organic Wicklow lamb braised in yoghurt and spices and speciality seafood dishes. Jaipur is a fine restaurant - and was the first ethnic restaurant in Ireland to devise a wine list especially suited to spicy foods. Service is attentive and discreet. **Seats 70**; children welcome (high chair); air conditioning; D daily, 5.30-11; Early D €22, 5-7; also à la carte. House wine €18. Closed 25 Dec Amex, MasterCard, Visa, Laser. **Directions:** On Dalkey's main street.

Nosh

Dalkey
RESTAURANT

111 Coliemore Road Dalkey Co Dublin **Tel: 01 284 0666**
comments@nosh.ie www.nosh.ie

Samantha and Sacha Farrell's bright, contemporary restaurant is next to the famous Club Bar and, with its clean lines and lightwood furniture, no-nonsense menus and quality ingredients, it has a special place in the Dalkey dining scene. Padraig Rogers' contemporary seasonal menus have a slight bias towards fish and vegetarian food, and change throughout the day: their great weekend brunch menu, which includes traditional Irish and buttermilk pancakes and a wide range of coffees and other drinks is very popular. For lunch there's some overlap from dishes on the Brunch menu and a dozen or so other choices, ranging up to the "Posh Nosh" daily special. In the evening, you might begin with a prawn starter (prawn pil-pils is a long-standing speciality) and proceed to beer-battered cod with pea purée, home-made chips (another house speciality). Vegetarians are well looked after with an imaginative choice of dishes such as cajun roast butternut & feta filo parcel with chunky ratatouille & crème fraîche. Desserts are home-made and there's a limited but well-chosen wine list, with a few half bottles. A long running success story, and deservedly so. **Seats 45**; not suitable for children after 9pm; wheelchair accessible; air conditioning. L Tue-Fri, 12-4 (Sat & Sun, Brunch 12-4); D Tue-Sun 6-10; 2/3 course value D €21/24, 6-7.45pm, Tue-Fri & Sun; also a la carte. House wine €19.95. Closed Mon, bank hols. MasterCard, Visa, Laser. **Directions:** End of Dalkey town, take left.

The Queen's Bar & Restaurant

Dalkey
RESTAURANT•PUB

12 Castle Street Dalkey Co Dublin **Tel: 01 285 4569**
queens@clubi.ie

The oldest pub in Dalkey, and also one of the oldest in Ireland, The Queen's was originally licensed to 'dispense liquor' as far back as 1745, and renovations and improvements in recent years have been undertaken with due respect for the age and character of the premises. It's attractively done up, with dark wood, little alcoves and a raised level breaking up the space, and there's also a small section outside at the front to go if the weather's fine. Quiet traditional bar fare is available and the more contemporary Queen's Restaurant is busy, but it could be worth a wait. Food is generally reliable but can be spoilt by erratic service. A late evening drink in the outside front section is quiet and relaxed; earlier, it's lively, particularly in summer. Restaurant **Seats 70**; Wheelchair accessible. D daily from 6pm; early D 6-7.30. Bar menu Mon-Fri, 12-4 & 5-7.30; Sat 12-4; Sun 12.30-3.45. Closed 25 Dec & Good Fri. Amex, Diners, MasterCard, Visa, Laser. **Directions:** Centre of town, beside Heritage Centre.

Ragazzi

Dalkey
RESTAURANT

109 Coliemore Road Dalkey Co Dublin
Tel: 01 284 7280

Possibly Dublin's buzziest little bistro, this is the pizza place where everyone goes to have their spirits lifted by theatrical Italian waiters and great value. Lovely pastas, luscious bruschettas - but best of all the pizzas, renowned for their thin, crisp bases and scrumptious toppings. But it's the atmosphere that counts - every town should have a place like this. D served daily, 5.30-10.30pm. ◊

Dalkey
RESTAURANT

Thai House Restaurant

21 Railway Road Dalkey Co Dublin **Tel: 01 284 7304**
tony@thaihouse.ie www.thaihouse.ie

Established in 1997, Tony Ecock's bustling two-storey restaurant has earned a loyal following and offers dishes that do not pander too much to the western palate. In typical oriental style, a number of set menus are offered and there is also an extensive à la carte which offers a wider choice. After an aperitif in the wine bar/reception area, begin, perhaps, with the Thai House Special Starter Pack, a sampling plate of six starters, well-balanced in flavour and texture and including some vegetarian options; service can be under pressure at times, so it is a good plan to get your starters ordered promptly. After this you can relax and consider the options including authentic Thai soups and main courses which include a range of curries - a speciality is fresh monkfish dumplings in green curry sauce - and vegetarian dishes are listed separately. Groups of four can share a dessert platter. The wine list includes a page of house favourites and a Thai beer. **Seats 34**; not suitable for children after 8pm; air conditioning. D Tue-Sun, 5-10.30pm (to 11pm Sat/Sun). Closed Mon. Amex, Diners, MasterCard, Visa, Laser. **Directions:** 100 metres from Dalkey DART Station. ◇

Dublin Airport
HOTEL•RESTAURANT

Carlton Hotel Dublin Airport

Parkway House Old Airport Road Dublin Airport Co Dublin
Tel: 01 866 7500 info@carltondublinairport.com www.carltondublinairport.com

Although not actually in the airport complex, this purpose-built 4 star hotel is very close to it, and convenient to the M1 and M50 motorways. Just 200 metres from the entrance to the airport (shuttle to the main door every 10 minutes), it's ideally suited to the business traveller, or for conferences and meetings; 19 conference rooms have all the necessary ancillary technology including wired and wireless broadband, phone and video conferencing, and air conditioning. Well-appointed bedrooms and suites all have oversized beds and bathrobes, clothes press, complimentary broadband, flat-screen televisions, pay-per-view movies, quality complimentary reading material and good sound-proofing. (You can see the planes take off and land but the sound is very muted.) Those who need to make an exceptionally early start may miss the full breakfast, but you can arrange the night before for a continental breakfast to be brought to you in the lobby before you catch the complimentary shuttle bus, and staff are invariably cheerful, even in the hours around dawn. Secure parking (250). Conference/Banquets (500/300); business centre, secretarial services, laptop-sized safes in bedrooms, free broadband wi/fi. **Rooms 100** (1 suite, 6 junior suites, 20 executive, 10 family, 13 ground floor, 7 for disabled); children welcome (under 12s free in parents' room, cots available free of charge); lift; all day room service. **Clouds at the Carlton:** Few locations can rival the stunning views from this rooftop restaurant, and the dining room is decorated in a modern yet warm style which allows the dramatic views to take centre stage. Bar food is available elsewhere in the hotel, but the restaurant is the place to be, being large and spacious with comfortable chairs (if a little low), crisp table linen and staff who know what they're doing. The highly regarded chef Patsy McGuirk was a consultant at the time of opening, and it shows in many ways, including detail; your meal begins with an amuse bouche (perhaps a sliver of rabbit and hazelnut terrine), for example, setting a promising culinary tone from the outset. The menu is appetising, with clear respect for the seasons and imaginative notes are introduced into the food here without thee confusion of too many flavours - and the beautifully balanced dishes have great visual appeal. Things get off to a good start as soon as two kinds of delicious home-baked bread are brought to the table, and then you may begin, perhaps, with a perfectly judged dish of scallops with a parsnip mash and some elegantly thin slices of black pudding, or rocket and pumpkin salad with French fried egg as well as baked goat's cheese. Fish, such as hake served with leeks and a chive beurre blanc, features strongly on the menu, also a knock-out risotto, while meat lovers will go for dishes such as caramelised pork ribs served with a coriander and chilli salad and pomegranate jus, or the half duck, with pak choi and a sweet potato purée. Puddings are similarly tempting: perhaps a chocolate pyramid with framboise liqueur, raspberries and vanilla ice cream, or variations on the themes of crème brulée, cheesecake or homemade ices, accompanied by a home made chocolate chip cookie. The wine list does not let the side down , containing a knowledgeable selection of wines, with several available by the glass, including some pudding wines. All round, an unexpected pleasure - and, a curiosity: besides good food and a panoramic view of the city, this aptly named restaurant also boasts one of the capital's highest smoking areas, with dramatic views of landing aircraft. Above-average informal fare is available elsewhere in the hotel, and includes a children's menu. **Seats 120** (private room, 60; outdoors, 40); pianist on Saturday evenings; children welcome before 8pm. D daily 6.30-9.30pm (6-9 on Sun); house wine from €24.50; SC 10% on groups 8+; closed 24-26 Dec. Amex, MasterCard, Visa, Laser. **Directions:** Close to Dublin airport on the Swords/Santry road: M50 exit 4 (Ballymun) or M1 - Santry exit. ◇

Dublin Airport
HOTEL

Clarion Hotel Dublin Airport

Dublin Airport Co Dublin **Tel: 01 808 0500**
info@clarionhoteldublinairport.com www.clarionhoteldublinairport.com

This large, comfortable hotel is right at the airport and has recently undergone extensive refurbishment. It makes an ideal meeting place and there is complimentary wifi in the lobby, bar and restaurant. Bedrooms all have TV and pay movies, and mini-bar; guests may use the ALSAA Leisure Complex swimming pool, gymnasium and sauna free of charge. Well-equipped meeting rooms/conference suites available for groups of up to 300. Courtesy bus to and from the airport terminal (24 hr). In line with other Clarion hotels, Kudos bar and restaurant offers lively informal food in attractive surroundings. **Rooms 248** (15 executive rooms, 4 family rooms, 2 for disabled); children welcome (Under 12s free in parents' room; cots available without charge); wheelchair accessible. Lift. 24 hour room service. Room rate about €129. Parking. Closed 24-25 Dec. Amex, Diners, MasterCard, Visa, Laser. **Directions:** In airport complex, on the right when entering airport.

Dublin Airport
HOTEL

Radisson SAS Hotel Dublin Airport

Dublin Airport Co Dublin **Tel: 01 844 6000**
reservations@airport.dublin.radissonsas.com www.airport.dublin.radissonsas.com

This spacious modern hotel in the airport complex is just two minutes drive from the main terminal building (with a coach service available). Rooms are all double-glazed and include a high proportion of executive rooms. It's a good choice for business guests and, should your flight be delayed, the large bar and restaurant on the ground floor could be a welcome place to pass the time. Conference/banqueting (450/300); video conferencing; business centre; secretarial service. **Rooms 229** (2 suites, 3 junior suites, 116 executive rooms, 184 no-smoking, 2 rooms for disabled, 2 family rooms); children welcome (under 10s free in parents' room; cots available free of charge). Lifts. Room service (24 hr). Room rate about €270 (1 or 2 guests). Closed 24-25 Dec. Amex, Diners, MasterCard, Visa, Laser. **Directions:** Situated in airport complex. ◊〉

DUBLIN AIRPORT AREA

A number of new hotels have sprung up around Dublin airport recently, but they are not always as close as you might expect. The **Clarion** and **Radisson SAS hotels** are on site (see entries), and the following are in the locality. Budget accommodation is available at the **Premier Inn** (01 895 7777), and **Travelodge** (01 807 9400; www.travelodge.ie). Nearby hotels offering more extensive facilities and a higher level of service include: **Bewleys Hotel** (01 871 1000; www.bewleyshotels.com), **Carlton Dublin Airport Hotel** (see entry), **Crowne Plaza Hotel** (01 862 8888; www.cpdublin-airport.com), and **Hilton Dublin Airport** (01 866 1800; www.hilton.co.uk/dublinairport). **Roganstown Golf & Country Club Hotel** is also convenient to the airport (see entry). The nearest town is Swords (see entry), where you will find **Wrights** cafe bar (01 840 6760; bar food available) and **The Old Boro** Pub (01 895 7685), both centrally located, and you could eat at **Indie Spice** restaurant (see entry), or the owner-chef run **Cookers** (01 8409911) in an area of the town known as Applewood Village. The attractive coastal town of Malahide is also convenient to Dublin airport, and offers a wide range of restaurants and bars (see entries).
WWW.IRELAND-GUIDE.COM FOR ALL THE BEST PLACES TO EAT, DRINK & STAY

DUN LAOGHAIRE

Dún Laoghaire is a seaside town and ferry port situated some 12 km south of Dublin city centre. The name derives from its founder, Laoghaire, a 5th century High King of Ireland, who chose the site as a sea base from which to carry out raids on Britain and France. The harbour is notable for its two granite piers - one of which is the busiest pier for leisure walking in Ireland - and is home to four yacht clubs. On the way into Dun Laoghaire, tucked away on Monkstown Crescent, is **Seagreen** (Tel: 01 202 0130 www.seagreen.ie) a treasure trove store with modern furniture, distinctive artwork, fine fashion labels, luxury gifts - and **Ellen's Tea Rooms**, where a French chef cooks delicious home-made daytime food. And, nearby in Glasthule, **The Eagle House** (Glasthule Road; 01 280 4740) is a fine traditional establishment that is full of interest and a great local. The interior is dark, but has a fascinating collection of model boats, ships and other nautical bric-á-brac and is arranged in comfortably sized alcoves and 'snugs' on different levels. Bar meals, available at lunchtime and in the evening, can be very good. There are three farmers markets in Dun Laoghaire (Peoples Park on Sundays; Dun Laoghaire Harbour on Saturdays and at Dun Laoghaire Shopping Centre on Thursdays). There are garden visits at Grasse Cottage (Rochestown Avenue; 01 285 2396) or nearby in Carysfort Lodge (Blackrock; 01 288 9273) and Burton Hall (Sandyford; 01 295 5888). The best golf is found a little further south in County

Georgina Campbell's Ireland

Wicklow - Powerscourt Golf Club (Enniskerry, 01 204 6033) and Druids Glen Golf Club (Newtownmountkennedy, 01 287 3600). Both piers are popular for fishing and there are also charter boats available (Dun Laoghaire Boat Charter, Tel: 01 282 3426).
WWW.IRELAND-GUIDE.COM FOR ALL THE BEST PLACES TO EAT, DRINK & STAY

Dun Laoghaire
RESTAURANT
E

Alexis Bar & Grill

17-18 Patrick Street Dun Laoghaire Co Dublin **Tel: 01 280 8872**
info@alexis.ie www.alexis.ie

Tucked away on Patrick Street, off Dun Laoghaire's main drag, huge glass windows allow passers-by a promising glimpse inside Alexis, the bright bistro owned by respected Dublin chef Alan O'Reilly and his brother Pat, and named after the great French chef and humanitarian Alexis Soyer, who visited Ireland in the mid-19th century and created the soup kitchens which provided wholesome food for the needy during the Famine. Expect a warm, friendly welcome, generously spaced tables, comfy banquettes and bentwood seats - and a menu which is as notable for very fair pricing as for its appeal to the tastebuds. An open kitchen runs along the back wall of the large open dining room, while a long tongue and groove bar makes a chic focal point, dispensing drinks and coffees. Much of the cooking is rustic French and Italian in origin and the menu doesn't differentiate between starters and mains (small portions of many dishes can be ordered). Admirable pride in quality ingredients is seen first in a menu that lists the provenance of key produce and that promise follows through on the plate in flavoursome, precise cooking: food is handsomely presented with meat and seafood dishes all expertly cooked and wonderfully fresh. A keenly priced wine list offers a dozen wines by the glass. Although it is noisy, and service can sometimes let the food down, great cooking, attention to detail and (all too unusually for the Dublin area) great value make this one of the area's most highly regarded restaurants. **Seats 90**. Reservations required; toilets wheelchair accessible; children welcome; air conditioning. L Tue-Fri 12.30-2.30, Sun 12.30-2.30; D Tue-Sun 5.30-10pm. L&D à la carte; house wine €20. Closed Sat L, Mon, Bank Hols. MasterCard, Visa, Laser. **Directions:** Coming from Dun Laoghaire harbour - straight up Marine Road on to Patrick Street. ◇

Dun Laoghaire
RESTAURANT•WINE BAR

Bodega Wine & Tapas

Pavilion Centre Dun Laoghaire Co Dublin
Tel: 01 284 2982

Formerly the Forty Foot bar and restaurant, this ultra-modern two-storey premises in the Pavilion Centre is now part of the Jay Bourke/Stephen Pile empire - of the Eden, Market Bar and Café Bar Deli fame in partnership with Thomas Read. Experienced chefs from Eden quickly succeeded in making this one of Dun Laoghaire's most popular venues. Seating is designed to impress, with huge windows allowing views over the harbour and Dublin Bay. The bar area has comfortable sofas around the central polished wood bar and you can eat in any part of the room, although the dining area at one end is the most comfortable option and has tables simply laid with good linen and cutlery and handsome, plain glasses. The outdoor terrace, particularly on a warm day, is a delight. The best of the Market Bar menu has been imported: Fish Pie, with smoked salmon, coley and haddock; chorizo stew with potatoes and peppers; and calamari with lemon mayo, accompanied by a basket of bread, are typical of the colourful, tasty and good value food offered. The tapas menu here has become the fashionable food of this area and, with attentive and well-informed staff and a pleasing ambience, it's not at all surprising that this place is so popular. World wines are reasonably priced. **Seats 150** (private room, 100, outdoors, 60); toilets wheelchair accessible; children welcome before 9pm (high chair, baby changing facilities); Bookings only available for groups 8+. Broadband wi/fi. Food is available daily from 12-2.45pm and 5-10pm. Pub: normal hours, late bar Saturday and Sunday. Sc 10% on groups 8+. Closed 25 Dec, Good Fri. MasterCard, Visa. **Directions:** At Pavilion Centre.

Dun Laoghaire
RESTAURANT

Café Mao

The Pavilion Dun Laoghaire Co Dublin **Tel: 01 2148090**
dunlaoghaire@cafemao.com www.cafemao.com

This large, informal contemporary café-restaurant near the harbour is a sister of Café Mao in Dublin 2 and at Dundrum Shopping Centre (see entries). It is run on the same lines, with the philosophy of providing simple, quick and healthy food, with youthful appeal, at a reasonable price - and there's always a good buzz. Dishes with nuts are highlighted on the menu, also chilli strength, low fat and vegetarian dishes. House specialties include Goreng, Malaysian chicken and five spiced chicken; daily specials are particularly good value, and there's a daily cake selection - e.g. cappuccino with walnut gateau, toffee & apple gateau, pecan pie & Mississippi mud pie - and an interesting drinks menu. It's a good place for brunch, with tables outside for fine weather. **Seats 120**; fully wheelchair accessible; children welcome until 7pm; large parties welcome. Open daily 12 - 11 (to 10 Sun); Early D about €15 5-7; Bookings accepted. Closed 25 Dec, Good Fri. MasterCard, Visa, Laser. **Directions:** Dun Laoghaire seafront, near station. ◇

Dun Laoghaire   Cavistons Seafood Restaurant
RESTAURANT   59 Glasthule Road Dun Laoghaire Co Dublin **Tel: 01 280 9245**
info@cavistons.com   www.cavistons.com

Caviston's of Sandycove has long been a mecca for lovers of good food - here you will find everything that is wonderful, from organic vegetables to farmhouse cheeses, cooked meats to specialist oils and other exotic items. But it was always for fish and shellfish that Cavistons were especially renowned - even providing a collection of well-thumbed recipe books for on-the-spot reference. At their little restaurant next door, they serve an imaginative range of healthy seafood dishes influenced by various traditions and all washed down by a glass or two from a very tempting little wine list. Head chef Noel Cusack's food at Cavistons is simple, colourful, perfectly cooked - it speaks volumes for how good seafood can be. Start with Cavistons smoked salmon plate, perhaps, or tasty pan-fried crab and sweetcorn cakes with red pepper mayonnaise, then follow with seared king scallops with a saffron and basil sauce - or a more traditional pan-fried haddock fillet with tartare sauce. Gorgeous desserts include timeless favourites like chocolate brownies with chocolate sauce & cream, or you can finish with a selection of Caviston's cheeses (they sell a great range in the shop). Don't expect bargain basement prices though - this may be a small lunchtime restaurant, but the prime ingredients are costly - and it's a class act. **Seats 28**; children welcome; L 3 sittings: Tue-Fri - 12, 1.30 and 3pm, Sat 12, 1.45, 3.15pm A la carte; house wine from €19; SC 10% on groups 6+. Closed Sun, Mon & Christmas/New Year. Amex, Diners, MasterCard, Visa, Laser. **Directions:** Between Dun Laoghaire and Dalkey, 5 mins. walk from Glasthule DART station.

Dun Laoghaire   The Gastropub Company
RESTAURANT•PUB   6-7 Marine Road Dun Laoghaire Co Dublin **Tel: 01 214 5772**
www.gastropubcompany.com

Martin Connolly's pub on Marine Road is one of Dun Laoghaire's busiest and its covered terrace is very lively during the day. The interior is spacious and welcoming, with wood - all of which is salvage - the primary feature: Floorboards came from 300-year-old beams that supported the Dublin docks before steel came along; the mahogany bar top is from a school laboratory - look hard enough and you can still see some scratched initials. The mirrored back bar also has a long history - it comes from the refurbished Hill 16 pub near Croke Park. There's a dedicated restaurant space at the back, opposite the open kitchen, where not only are the chefs working hard, but obviously enjoying what they do. Menus change often but popular dishes include clam chowder, or tomato & mozzarella cheese salad to start, followed by choices like Wicklow lamb shank or rare steak, as well as burgers and fried fish. Delicious desserts might include poached pear with ice cream, glazed lemon tart or sticky toffee pudding. Service is friendly, with just the right amount of attention, and the wine list includes a good selection available by the glass (and there's an Orange Muscat to accompany desserts). Alternatively, you can buy wine in the shop next door and pay just €8 corkage. Sunday lunch is unusual - a whole roast chicken, accompanied by the usual trimmings, is brought to the table and you carve it yourself. A good atmosphere and reasonable prices makes this a very family-friendly restaurant. **Seats 160** (private room, 30, outdoors, 40); children welcome (high chair, baby changing facilities); toilets wheelchair accessible; live swing Saturday nights; food served all day, 12-10.30pm (to 10pm Sun), value L €10, value D 4-7pm, €19.95. House wine €19. Closed Good Fri, 25 Dec. MasterCard, Visa, Laser. **Directions:** 1 minute from the DART, on Marine Road, opposite the Pavilion.

Dun Laoghaire
RESTAURANT

Hartley's
1 Harbour Road Dun Laoghaire Co Dublin
Tel: 01 280 6767

Housed in a handsome cut-stone listed building (once the Kingstown train terminal, and a treat for railway buffs), Hartley's sits elegantly overlooking Dun Laoghaire's modern harbour in the premises previously occupied by Brasserie na Mara. The neo-classical masterpiece is a wonderful setting for a restaurant and since the end of 2007 it has been in common ownership with the popular Dali's in Blackrock (see entry) – and is notoriously difficult to get into, especially at weekends. The new proprietors have opened up the handsome dining room to make the most of its high ceilings and huge windows, with over-sized mirrors hanging high on the walls to reflect the smart cream seating, simple Corian-style tabletops and wooden floors. Efficient, welcoming reception sets a positive tone; to the right of the chic dining room a long, sleek bar faces the harbour, making a pleasant place to sip aperitifs, read the menu and enjoy the relaxing ambience. Menus offer a great selection of dishes for all palates including salads, pasta, steaks and char grilled burgers, with extra space given over to seafood - chowder and a daily mussel dish have taken their place as signature dishes, alongside fish dishes with international influences and more traditional choices such as textbook perfect whole black sole with lemon tarragon butter. Although, in the Guide's experience, cooking may be a little inconsistent, the food is attractively presented and the menu offers considerable value on many dishes. A carefully chosen wine list has many appealing bottles across a good price range too, and the overall experience offered in this stylish and well located restaurant should be enjoyable - especially since a recent extension, including a terrace, was completed. **Seats 80**; children welcome; L daily, 12-3pm (to 5pm Sun), D 6pm-"late" (Sun 5.30pm-9pm); L&D a la carte. Amex, Diners, MasterCard, Visa, Laser. **Directions:** Coast road, beside DART, opposite the Pavilion.

Dun Laoghaire
PUB

P. McCormack & Sons
67 Lr Mounttown Road Dun Laoghaire Co Dublin
Tel: 01 280 5519

This fine pub (and 'emporium') has been run by the McCormack family since 1960. It's one of the neatest pubs around, with trees and shrubbery between the car park and an imaginative conservatory extension at the back of the pub, effectively screening the car park and allowing for an attractive outdoor eating/drinking space beside the conservatory; with large tables and outdoor heaters, it is an appealing area. The main part of this well-run pub is full of character, and bar food cooked to order includes fresh fish available on the day as well as classics like home-made hamburger (with mixed leaf salad, fries & a choice of toppings), hot sandwiches and salads. At lunchtime there is a carvery but evening menus offer more interesting food including tasty light dishes like warm crispy bacon and croûton salad, and steak sandwiches alongside more substantial dishes including a fish special, a 10 oz sirloin steak or pasta dishes with fresh parmesan. Not suitable for children after 9pm; toilets wheelchair accessible. Bar food daily, 12-3 & 4-10. Closed 25 Dec, Good Fri. Amex, Diners, MasterCard, Visa, Laser. **Directions:** Near Dun Laoghaire at Monkstown end.

Dun Laoghaire
RESTAURANT

Rasam
18-19 Glasthule Road Dun Laoghaire Co Dublin **Tel: 01 230 0600**
info@rasam.ie www.rasam.ie

Above The Eagle pub in Glasthule, this is an appealing restaurant, impressively decorated in dark teak, with traditional Balinese furnishings and generous, well-spaced tables - and a new open air garden area has now been added at the back. Rasam offers something different from other Indian restaurants, as the cuisine is lighter and more varied - the menu is laid out like a wine list, with the name of the dish and a brief (but clear) description, and the name of the region it comes from alongside the price. Two head chefs are from Bengali and Kerala regions, so the food reflects that as well as other regions. You might begin with samosas which are delightfully served; main courses might include a relatively simple Kori Gassi, which is a long-established dish at Rasam - chicken is simmered in a spicy masala of brown onions and tomatoes, and other meats are well represented - Pork Sobotel, is an aromatic example. Shakahari Thali, is a memorable mixture of five lentils, cooked with spinach and other vegetables, tempered with spice. Many special ingredients are used in the cooking here, including rare herbs and spices unique to the restaurant, all ground freshly each day. Everything is made on the premises - great accompaniments include delicious naan bread and chapatti, and there is an extensive range of side dishes. Indian restaurants are not known for their desserts but, in addition to some western dishes like mille-feuille of strawberries & almonds and baked alaska, there's an interesting 'Falooda' kulfi with saffron & pistachio, which is served on a bed of sandalwood syrup - and an otherwise classic crème brûlée is 'easternised' with rose petal flavouring. An extensive wine and drinks menu is thoughtfully selected for compatibility with Indian food, and solicitous staff ensure that everything is as it should be. All round, for a great Indian dining experience, Rasam has earned its place right at the top of the league. *Rasam was our Ethnic Restaurant of the Year, 2007. **Seats 75**; children welcome; reservations recommended; D daily, 5.30-11.30 (Sun to 11); Early D €21.95, 5.30-6.30, Set 4 course D €44.95, also à la carte. Closed 25-26 Dec, Good Fri. MasterCard, Visa, Laser. **Directions:** Over The Eagle pub.

Dun Laoghaire
RESTAURANT

Real Gourmet Burger

The Pavilion Dun Laoghaire Co Dublin **Tel: 01 284 6568**
info@realgourmetburger.ie www.realgourmetburger.ie

With burgers the 'in thing' on the casual dining scene at the moment, smart informal restaurants specialising in this much-maligned dish have been among the most noticeable new arrivals in Dublin recently. And, with its handsome lean lined room and speciality organic burgers, the opening of Real Gourmet Burger in 2007 extended the quality options for eating out casually in the Dun Laoghaire area, especially for families looking for good food at a moderate price. The range of burgers offered includes beef, lamb, venison and chicken and there are options for vegetarians and children, plus simple side orders of salad or chips. All burgers are cooked medium or well done, due to health regulations which is fine for some, especially chicken, although this requirement is always a disappointment for those who like to sink their teeth into a real beefburger that's pink and juicy in the middle. Friendly service is usually a high point here, and - although the cooking can be a little uneven- it's reasonably priced and family-friendly. **Directions:** On the Pavilion in Dun Laoghaire. ◇

Dun Laoghaire
HOTEL

Royal Marine Hotel

Marine Road Dun Laoghaire Co Dublin
Tel: 01 280 1911

Having been closed for some four years, the Royal Marine Hotel in Dun Laoghaire re-opened to some acclaim in 2007 - the original Victorian building has been restored to its former glory, and The Dun Laoghaire Historical Society are very happy with all the refurbishments. New buildings on each side house conference facilities on the right, and very comfortable accommodation on the left. About a third (82) of the bedrooms are in the original building, the rest in the new area; all are air conditioned, spacious and comfortable, with double-quilted mattress and flat screen tv among the features. Many of the rooms have wonderful views over the harbour and Dublin Bay, the 52 executive suites have balconies and there are family rooms available (connecting doors). Now styled as a conference, destination and leisure spa, it boasts some welcome new facilities, combining well with the traditional warmth and friendliness that has always been present in this landmark hotel. The hotel has a restaurant, The Dune and two bars - the bright and airy Pavilion at the front and the Hardy, with a good cocktail menu, at the back. The hotel's sansanaSpa offers 9 treatment rooms, a hydrotherapy bath and a hammam. Conference/banqueting 800/550. **Rooms 228**. Amex, Diners, MasterCard, Visa, Laser. **Directions:** Town centre, 200 yards from ferry terminal. ◇

Dun Laoghaire
RESTAURANT

Tribes

57a Glasthule Road Glasthule Dun Laoghaire Co Dublin
Tel: 01 236 5971

The brown and beige colour scheme of Tribes may pay tribute to its earthy name, but the styling here is far more contemporary then ethnic, and the cooking very much French-style in its influences. A long narrow room is fitted with smart leather seats, wooden flooring, a few cosy banquettes and moody lighting, which sets a clubby theme by night. Staff are cheerful and friendly with service, for the most part, efficient. Diners should find their whole dining experience is pleasingly visual, from the gorgeous salt and pepper sets to the red candle lights and imaginatively presented food; the functional metal bread basket and lacklustre bread is the only weak link in the chain. Dishes are seasonal and feature tempting cheffy touches like pork with char-grilled apple and calvados sauce or roasted salmon with mascarpone and crab crushed potatoes. Risotti are something of a house speciality and use imaginative ingredients like Jerusalem artichokes or cauliflower with comte and pine nuts. The wine list is adequate, and fairly priced, and the room is pleasant to linger in after dinner. Early bird menus are understandingly popular with locals who enjoy the comfortable space and sheer quality and creativity of the cooking. **Seats 60** (outdoors, 10); children welcome; air conditioning; L Sun, 1-4pm, D Mon-Sun, 5.30-10pm; house wine €19; SC 10%. Closed 25-26 Dec, 1 Jan, Good Fri. Amex, MasterCard, Visa, Laser. **Directions:** Just past Dun Laoghaire heading South.

Glencullen
RESTAURANT•PUB

Johnnie Fox's Pub

Glencullen Co Dublin **Tel: 01 295 5647**
info@jfp.ie www.jfp.ie

Nestling in an attractive wooded hamlet in the Dublin Mountains, south of Dublin city, this popular pub dates back to the eighteenth century and has numerous claims to fame, including the fact that Daniel O'Connell was once a regular, apparently, and it's "undoubtedly" the highest pub in the land. A warm, friendly and generally well run place, it's just about equally famous for its food at the "Famous Seafood Kitchen" - which can be enjoyable - and its music "Famous Hooley Nights" (booking advisable). Unlike so many superficially similar pubs, it's also real. Kitsch, perhaps, but the rickety old furniture is real, the dust is real and there is a turf or log fire at every turn. It's a pleasant place to drop into at quieter times too, if you're walking in the hills or just loafing around, but its most useful function is that Dubliners find it an amusing place to take visitors from abroad. Recommended as an unusual outing rather than a meal out, but reservations are recommended if you wish to eat. **Seats 352** (private room, 55, outdoor 60); children welcome (under supervision, not after 7.30pm). Traditional Irish music and dancing. Reservations recommended for food. Own parking. Open daily, full hot menu Mon-Thurs, 12.30-2.30 & 5.30-9pm; soup/snacks available 2.30pm-5pm. Full menu Fri-Sun, 12.30-9.30; all menus à la carte, house wine €19.50. No SC. Closed 24-25 Dec & Good Fri. Amex, Diners, MasterCard, Visa, Laser. **Directions:** In Dublin Mountains, 30 minutes drive from Dublin city centre. 5 mins from junction 15 of M50. ◊

HOWTH

The fishing port of Howth is easily accessible by DART from Dublin, and is an interesting place to wander around. The fish shops along the west pier attract a loyal clientéle, and for many a year it's been a tradition to come out from town after work on a Thursday to buy fish for the fast day on Friday - while that is largely a thing of the past, the shops still stay open later on Thursday evenings, which gives the place a special buzz in summer, when people stay on for a walk around the harbour or a bite to eat before going home. There is a lengthy beach that stretches as far as Sutton and there is also a spectacular cliff top walk around the peninsula that overlooks Dublin Bay - this should not be missed on a fine day (at the top of the hill the popular **Summit Inn** (01 832 4615) provides a good stop-off point for a drink and/or a bite to eat). The area is also well-known as being home to Ireland's largest public golfing complex in Deer Park; this is also home to a castle and a lovely hill walk amongst the famous Rhododendron gardens, the spectacular sea and coastal views from the top are breathtaking and you can even see as far as the Mountains of Mourne in Northern Ireland on a clear day. A Farmers' & Fishermen's Market is held on the pier every Sunday, and there are several interesting food shops around the village too: up in the village, **Baily Wines** (01 832 2394) is not only an interesting owner-run wine shop but also offers a carefully selected choice of deli products, including some of the finest Irish artisan foods. Then up beside the church, there's **Main Street Country Market** (01 839 5575) for fresh produce and some specialist groceries. On the harbour front, is **Casa Pasta Restaurant** (01 839 3823), known for its great atmosphere and inexpensive food appealing to all age groups. There are a couple of ethnic restaurants: the long-established **El Paso** (01 832 3334) and a stylish Indian, **The Village Restaurant** (01 832 0444), which are on the front. Also on the harbour front you will find the local late night hotspot in **Wright's Findlater Bar** and the ever popular topfloor **Skyy Bar** which has a roof terrace with views over the harbour, music and late drinks. Further along the **Waterside Bar** might be the place to start your evening out (01 839 0555). Up in Howth village **Ella** (seen entry) is a chic restaurant/wine bar. For accommodation: the village centre **Baily Hotel** (01 832 2691; www.baily.com) has been re-styled as a boutique hotel (the large Bá Mizu next door is attached to the hotel). For garden lovers the Talbot Botanic Gardens in Malahide Castle (01 846 2456) and the National Botanic Gardens in Glasnevin (01 804 0300) are about 20 minutes drive away. Fishing is popular from the end of the west pier or off the rocks in Balscadden Bay. Championship golf (links) is available about 10-15 minutes drive away in The Royal Dublin Golf Club (01 833 6346) or the two golf clubs in Portmarnock (the famous Portmarnock Golf Club, 01 846 2968 & the newer Portmarnock Golf Links 01 846 0611).
WWW.IRELAND-GUIDE.COM FOR ALL THE BEST PLACES TO EAT, DRINK & STAY

Howth
RESTAURANT•CHARACTER PUB

Abbey Tavern

Abbey Street Howth Co Dublin **Tel: 01 839 0307**
info@abbeytavern.ie www.abbeytavern.ie

Just 50 yards up from the harbour, part of this famous pub dates back to the 15th century, when it was built as a seminary for the local monks. Currently owned by James and Eithne Scott-Lennon, this well-run and immaculately maintained pub retains authentic features including open turf fires, original stone walls, flagged floors and gas lights. In 1960 the Abbey started to lay on entertainment and this has brought the tavern its fame: the format is a traditional 5-course dinner followed by traditional Irish music. It's on every night but booking is essential, especially in high season. Daytime food is offered in the bar although, in the Guide's experience, the evening meals served upstairs tend to be better. At the time of going to press, the first floor restaurant is due to re-open as "The Loft". **Seats 70** (private room, 40); children welcome; reservations required; air conditioning. Restaurant open Fri-Sat D (extended opening days from March 08); 2/3 course D €35/39; house wine €18. SC discretionary. Bar food served daily, 1-9pm; carpark on harbour. Restaurant closed Sun, Mon; establishment closed 25 Dec & Good Fri. Amex, Diners, MasterCard, Visa, Laser. **Directions:** 15km (9 m) from Dublin, in the centre of Howth.

Howth
RESTAURANT

Aqua Restaurant

1 West Pier Howth Co Dublin **Tel: 01 832 0690 / 1850 34 64 64**
dine@aqua.ie www.aqua.ie

Formerly a yacht club, this is now a fine contemporary restaurant with plenty of window tables to take advantage of sea views westwards, towards Malahide, and take in the island of Ireland's Eye to the north. What was once a snooker room is now a characterful bar with a unique blend of original features and modern additions - with an open fire and comfortable seating, it has retained a cosy, clubby atmosphere and is a lovely place to relax before or after your meal. The restaurant is a large, bright room with white-clothed tables set up smartly, comfortable highback chairs and subtle decor inspired by the history of the building and maritime themes - constantly evolving, it is a source of pleasure to regular guests who frequently notice small changes. The kitchen is behind a glass screen, so you can see the team of chefs at work, adding to the interest of a meal. The style of cooking is strong, simple and modern; given the location, seafood is the natural choice but rib-eye beef is also a speciality. Menus offer a pleasing repertoire - deep-fried calamari on spiced tomato sauce with warm pesto; the house Caesar starter salad (served as a starter in the evening or with chicken as a main course at lunchtime); Aqua Fish & Chips; and good pasta dishes all make regular appearances. Although choices are restricted, the lunch and early dinner menus offer very good value and ensure a busy restaurant at off-peak times; they are understandably popular with the loyal local clientèle, who also love the jazz lunch on Sundays. The waterside location, well-sourced ingredients, cooking that is never less than enjoyable and interested service all make dining at Aqua a pleasure; à la carte menus offer a much wider choice of dishes, although they are pricey - it's the value of the set menus that keeps people going back. **Seats 80**; air conditioning; children welcome before 8.30pm (high chair). L & D Tue-Sun, 12.30-3.30pm (12-5pm Sun) & 5.30-10.30pm, Sun D 5-8.30pm. Early D €29.95, 5.30-7pm (Sat 5.30-6.30pm)., Set Sun L €29.95. Also à la carte. Live jazz Sun L. House wine €23, SC 10% on groups 6+. Closed Mon, 25-26 Dec, Good Fri. Amex, MasterCard, Visa, Laser. **Directions:** Left along pier after Howth DART Station.

Howth
RESTAURANT

Ella

7 Main Street Howth Co Dublin **Tel: 01 839 6264**
info@ellawinebar.com www.ellawinebar.com

Aoife Healy's chic little restaurant and wine bar is in the centre of Howth village, just across from the Baily Hotel, and it has a loyal following of local diners who enjoy the relaxed, intimate atmosphere, consistently good cooking and very obliging staff who always want to be sure that everyone is enjoying their meal to the full. Although plenty of seafood is offered (and seafood cooking is accomplished) Ella offers a good range of other foods - perhaps more so than other restaurants in the area; Pork Fillet wrapped in Prosciutto, with Calvados jus is a typically tempting speciality. Cooking is kept pleasingly simple and there's an emphasis on fresh local foods, with suppliers credited on the menu of (fish and seafood from Dorans on the west pier in Howth, and meats and poultry are from Ray Collier butchers, just a couple of doors away, and guaranteed Irish). Long opening hours make this a great neighbourhood restaurant, and the express lunch menu offers especially good value. **Seats 32**; not suitable for children after 8pm; reservations accepted; toilets wheelchair accessible. Open Mon- Sat L 12.45-2.45; D 6-10. Express L about €12, early D €26; also à la carte. Closed Sun, 1 Jan - 10 Jan. MasterCard, Visa, Laser. **Directions:** On the main street - opposite the Baily Hotel. ◇

Howth

The House

RESTAURANT

4 Main Street Howth Co Dublin **Tel: 01 839 6388**
info@thehouse-howth.ie www.thehouse-howth.ie

Located in one of the most attractive old buildings in Howth village, opposite the Baily Hotel, The House is run by proprietor Karl Dillon and head chef Ian Connolly, formerly of Gruel and The Mermaid Cafe respectively - and, true to form, the menu clearly states a commitment to local, organic and artisan produce. The smart casual interior is quietly stylish with effective lighting, bare tables with bentwood chairs and simple settings. Guests are promptly settled in and drinks offered before choosing from a modestly priced bistro-style menu that includes some unusual dishes. Starters might include a fish soup, or a selection of James McGeough's renowned charcuterie (from Connemara). Mains follow in the same style of quality ingredients cooked simply, such as a char-grilled rib-eye steak or a classic dish of beef & Guinness stew - and there may be less usual choices such as mussels with smoked pork, cider, garlic, cream and fries. A compact, informative wine list carries through the same philosophy of quality and value for money; beginning with interesting house wines at €20. Finish with a home-made dessert (maybe a yummy chocolate & prune cake with espresso syrup if you're lucky) and delicious Illy coffee. As well as great food and good cooking, caring service and long opening hours add to the appeal of a meal here, although it can be noisy - and it's a popular place for large groups too, so get there ahead of the crowd if you like to eat in peace. Reservations essential at weekends. **Seats 60** (outdoors, 50); children welcome (high chair, childrens menu, baby changing facilities); toilets wheelchair accessible; reservations recommended. Food served Mon-Sat, 9am-10pm, B 9-12, L 12-3.30pm, D 6-10pm; Sun L 11.30-4pm, D 6-10pm; house wine €20. Closed 25 Dec. Amex, MasterCard, Visa, Laser. **Directions:** In the centre of Howth village, opposite the Baily Hotel.

Howth

Ivans Oyster Bar & Grill

RESTAURANT

17-18 West Pier Howth Co Dublin **Tel: 01 839 0285**
info@ivans.ie www.ivans.ie

Synonymous with seafood, the Beshoff family have been high profile fishmongers in Ireland since 1914. (Ivan Beshoff, after whom the restaurant is named, was survivor of the 1905 mutiny on the Russian battleship Potemkin, and settled in Ireland in 1913.) Formerly best known for their fish and chips, this enterprising family now run a slick seafood bar and restaurant on Howth's West Pier where, with its folding glass windows and welcoming topiary trees at the entrance, a blocky modern building promises something different. Despite plenty of neighbouring competition, proprietor Alan Beshoff has quickly set Ivan's apart: next door to his ultra-modern dining room is an authentic oyster bar in the swishest fish shop in Dublin. The oyster menu includes both native and French bivalves along with delicious oyster shots in piquant liquids (try beetroot gazpacho or perhaps citrussy ponzu). A short shellfish menu is also available to customers who perch on tall stools surrounded by organic goodies, wonderful flowers and a dazzling seafood counter. Guests in the adjoining restaurant can still sample the oyster fare while choosing from a vast fish-rich menu. The dining room is the epitome of industrial chic, with exposed duct piping, over-sized glass lampshades, poured cement, a glass façade, dramatic grey wall and a muted metallic bar. But elegant seating, bunches of dried lavender in vases and warm, friendly service soften the room, making it a welcoming and sophisticated space. Good breads and a little amuse bouche - perhaps lobster and tomato concassé - set the tone for some quality cooking. Ivan's crab cakes are oh so fluffy and light, signature fish and chips come with sweet pea purée, while black sole with beurre noisette is textbook delicious. Daily specials like gambas ketaifi keep it interesting for regulars while real fish fiends will head straight for Ivan's Fruits de Mer, a man-sized platter of Dublin Bay prawns, crevettes, brown shrimp, crab, oysters, clams, crayfish, mussels and winkles at about €110. Dessert offerings are limited but you'll want for nothing after spotting Ivan's hot chocolate fondant. An expansive, imaginative wine list (with a good selection by the glass) and quality coffees highlight the attention to detail of this hip Howth haunt. Quality cooking, charming service and gorgeous décor make Ivan's a welcome addition to Northside dining. **Seats 100** (outdoors, 20); toilets wheelchair accessible; children welcome before 8pm (high chair, baby changing facilities), air conditioning; L daily, 12.30-2.45 (12-3 Sun); D daily 6-10pm (to 9pm Sun). Early D €23, 5.30-6.30pm. House wine from €19. SC 12.5% on groups 6+. Closed D 24 Dec, 25 Dec, D 31 Dec, 1 Jan, Good Fri. Amex, MasterCard, Visa, Laser. **Directions:** 2 mins walk from Howth DART station down West Pier.

Howth

RESTAURANT•RESTAURANT WITH ROOMS

King Sitric Fish Restaurant & Accommodation

East Pier Howth Co Dublin **Tel: 01 832 5235**

info@kingsitric.ie www.kingsitric.ie

Named after an 11th century Norse King of Dublin who had close links with Howth, Aidan and Joan MacManus' striking harbourside establishment is one of Dublin's longest established fine dining restaurants. The bright and airy first floor restaurant takes full advantage of the harbour views, especially enjoyable on summer evenings - and, from this East Pier site, chef-patron Aidan can keep an eye on his lobster pots on one side and the fishing boats coming into harbour on the other. Informative notes on menu covers state the restaurant's commitment to local quality produce - and gives a listing of Irish fish in six languages. Specialities worth travelling for include a luscious red velvet crab bisque, and classics such as sole meunière and Dublin lawyer. In winter, lovers of game are well looked after and farmhouse cheeses and desserts are always worth leaving room for. Aidan MacManus oversees one of the country's finest wine lists, with strengths in Chablis, Burgundy and Alsace, with the special feature of a temperature-controlled wine cellar on the ground floor. The house wine is outstanding for both quality and value, and a perfect match for delicious fish cooking. Aidan and Joan MacManus work hard to keep fine dining prices accessible - lunch is especially good value, also their Special Value Menu (D Mon-Thu, no time restriction). The King Sitric was the Guide's Seafood Restaurant of the Year in 2006, and received the Wine List of the Year Award in 2001; the restaurant operates a Food & Wine Club off-season. Banqueting (70). **Seats 70** (private room, 28); children welcome (high chair); air conditioning. L Mon-Fri, 12.30-2.15; D Mon-Sat, 6.30-10. Set L from €27. 'Value' D €35/40 (Mon-Thu evening all year, no time restrictions); 4-course Set D €58; also à la carte; house wine from €24; SC discretionary (12.5% parties 8+). Restaurant closed Sun, bank hols. **Accommodation:** The comfortable en-suite rooms have sea views - and a very nice breakfast menu is offered, including several fish dishes. **Rooms 8** (2 superior, 1 family room, 3 ground floor, all no-smoking). B&B €72.50 pps, ss €32.50; children welcome (under 12s free in parents' room, cots available free of charge; baby sitting arranged); limited room service. Amex, MasterCard, Visa, Laser. **Directions:** Far end of the harbour front, facing the East Pier.

Howth

RESTAURANT

The Oar House

8 West Pier Howth Co Dublin **Tel: 01 839 4562**

www.oarhouse.ie

Although a relative new-comer to Howth, the nautically-themed interior of The Oar House - an old smoke house on the West Pier - has a lived-in feel that makes you believe it's been sating diners for decades. A sister restaurant to the ever-popular Casa Pasta on the harbour front, the corrugated roof, fishing nets, buoys, old sailing masts and instruments give it an atmosphere that's at once vibrant and welcoming. Tables are dressed with paper cloths and the casual vibe makes it extremely relaxing and child-friendly. A vast menu features every manner of seafood, from chowder to shellfish to fish pie (many of which can be ordered as tapas) and is supplemented by a long list of daily specials written up on big boards. From grilled sardines to baked monkfish, or maybe succulent scampi to seafood platters everything is simply and cleverly prepared in the bustling open kitchen. Caring service, big portions, good desserts and a choice setting make this place a real treasure for fish fans. **Seats 50** (outdoors, 20); children welcome (high chair; baby changing facilities); parking outside on pier; reservations recommended; open all day 12.30-10.30 (to 10pm Sun). Value L about €22, 3-6pm; house wine abaouty €19. Closed Good Fri, 25 Dec. Amex, MasterCard, Visa, Laser. **Directions:** On the West Pier next to Doran's fish shop. ◈

Marine Hotel

Howth/Sutton Area
HOTEL

Sutton Cross **Tel: 01 839 0000**
info@marinehotel.ie www.marinehotel.ie

Well-located on the sea side of a busy junction, this attractive and well-run hotel has ample car parking in front and a lawn reaching down to the foreshore at the rear. Public areas give a good impression: a smart foyer and adjacent bar, an informal conservatory style seating area overlooking the garden and a well-appointed restaurant. Bedrooms, some of which have sea views, have recently been refurbished. A popular venue for conferences and social gatherings, especially weddings, the Marine is also the only hotel in this area providing for the business guest. Conference/banqueting (200/190); business centre; secretarial services. **Rooms 48** (1 junior suite, 6 shower only, 31 executive rooms, 12 no-smoking, 2 disabled); children welcome (under 3 free in parents' room; cots available without charge). No pets. Lift. Limited room service. B&B about €55-110 pps, ss about €30. Meridian Restaurant: L&D daily; bar meals available, 5-8pm daily. Golf nearby. Garden. Closed 25-26 Dec. Amex, Diners, MasterCard, Visa, Laser. **Directions:** Take coast road towards Howth from city centre, on right at Sutton Cross. ◈

Fitzpatrick Castle Hotel Dublin

Killiney
HOTEL
🏛

Killiney Co Dublin **Tel: 01 230 5400**
jenna.shortall@fitzpatricks.com www.fitzpatrickshotels.com

Located in the fashionable suburb of Killiney, this imposing castellated mansion overlooking Dublin Bay dates back to 1741. It is surrounded by landscaped gardens and, despite its size and grand style, has a relaxed atmosphere. Spacious bedrooms combine old-world charm with modern facilities, and a fitness centre has a 22 metre pool, jacuzzi, spa and relaxation deck. Although perhaps best known as a leading conference and function venue, Fitzpatrick's also caters especially well for business guests and 'The Crown Club', on the 5th floor functions as a 'hotel within a hotel', offering pre-arranged private transfer from the airport and a wide range of facilities for business guests. Five championship golf courses, including Druid's Glen, are nearby. **Rooms 113**. Room rate about €130. Garden. Lift. Closed 24-26 Dec. Amex, Diners, MasterCard, Visa, Laser. **Directions:** Take M50 from the airport, follow signs for Dun Laoghaire ferry port; south to Dalkey - top of Killiney hill. ◈

Courtney's Pub

Lucan
PUB
R R R

1 Main Street Lucan Village Co Dublin **Tel: 01 628 0251**
info@courtneyslounge.com www.courtneyslounge.com

The thatched roof, old-fashioned windows and hanging baskets of Courtney's Bar attract customers in and inside is every bit as pleasant. Comfortable seating, an optional dining area and friendly staff make eating here a pleasure. Bar food includes old favourites like steak sandwich and golfer's grill as well as a selection of salads including a very good Cajun Chicken Caesar. It's all reasonably priced and available from 12.30pm to 9pm. Outdoors at the back, there is a pretty terrace on two levels, within sound if not sight of the Griffeen river. Upstairs is a popular restaurant, Dukes (as in John Wayne), with dishes such as beef, monkfish and duck.

Finnstown Country House Hotel

Lucan
HOTEL
R R R

Newcastle Road Lucan Co Dublin **Tel: 01 601 0700**
manager@finnstown-hotel.ie www.finnstown-hotel.ie

Approached by a long tree-lined driveway, this fine old manor house is set in 45 acres of woodland and (despite a large, blocky extension), is full of charm. It may not be immediately obvious where the hotel reception is, but an open fire in the foyer sets a welcoming tone and all of the large, well-proportioned reception rooms - drawing room, restaurant, bar - are elegantly furnished in a traditional style well-suited to the house. Although quite grand, there is a comfortable lived-in feeling throughout. Bedrooms vary and include some studio suites, with a small fridge and toaster in addition to the standard tea/coffee making facilities; although most rooms have good facilities including full bathrooms (with bath and shower), some are a little dated, and the view can be disappointing if you are looking over the extension - and light sleepers should ensure a quiet room is allocated if there is a wedding or other function taking place. Residential golf breaks are a speciality. Conference/banqueting (300). Leisure centre; swimming pool; tennis. Children welcome (Under 3s free in parents' room; cots available without charge, baby sitting arranged). Pets permitted. Parking (200). Wheelchair accessible. *The hotel came into new ownership recently, so changes may be expected. **Rooms 77** (28 executive, 20 family, 10 no-smoking, 1 for disabled). B&B from about €89 pps. Limited room service. Closed Christmas. **The Dining Room:** As in the rest of the house, the decor of this comfortable room, is pleasantly quirky - and, with good lighting and piano playing, the atmosphere is relaxing. Rather small tables are nicely set up with fresh flowers, and menus are not over-ambitious, offering about five choices on each course; most are familiar but there are may be some surprises, and what arrives on the plate is far from the average hotel meal: quality ingredients are used and down to earth cooking has the emphasis on flavour - and food is attractively presented without ostentation, all making for an enjoyable meal that is also good value for money. **Seats 100** (private room, 30). L Sun-Fri, 12.30-3pm (Sun 12.30-6pm); D Mon-Sat 6-9.30; set L about €29.95. set D about €42. L&D also à la carte. House wine €21.50. House closed Christmas. *Long term accommodation also available in apartment suites. Amex, Diners, MasterCard, Visa, Laser. **Directions:** Off main Dublin-Galway Road (N4): take exit for Newcastle off dual carriageway. ◇

Lucan
RESTAURANT

R R R

La Banca

Main Street Lucan Village Co Dublin **Tel: 01 628 2400**
www.labanca.ie

This pleasant neighbourhood restaurant off Lucan's winding main street is well positioned near the Italian Embassy. Moving swiftly through the dark and distinctly tatty entrance area, you will be pleasantly surprised by a bright, modern and well presented restaurant, where arriving guests are welcomed by friendly Italian staff who show you to your table promptly and present a comprehensive Italian menu, good bread and gorgeous garlic-infused olive oil. A wide choice of antipasti dishes includes a delicious shared plate, a sociable choice if dining out with friends. Main course choices include all the Italian staples, including pasta dishes like cannelloni alla carne and pizza; fish is also well represented and, if you are lucky, you may have the opportunity to enjoy perfectly cooked sea bass and swordfish. As is often the case in Italian restaurants, service is good, with friendly Italian waiters always ready to be of assistance. *The Vault Bar is a small downstairs area (you have to brave the dark entrance area again to reach it or the toilets); it opens on Friday & Saturday nights and is available for private parties. Live music in Vault Bar Fri-Sat night. Opening hours Tue-Sat 4-10.30pm, Sun 2-9.30pm. ◇

R

MALAHIDE

The attractive coastal town of Malahide is only 15 minutes from the airport, and about 25 minutes into Dublin city by frequent direct trains (DART). There's no shortage of things to do: championship golf includes two courses in Portmarnock (the famous Portmarnock Golf Club, 01 846 2968 & the newer Portmarnock Golf Links 01 846 0611), the Christy O'Connor-designed Roganstown GC (01 843 3118) in nearby Swords, and The Island (01 843 6205) at Donabate, and there's good walking at Malahide and Portmarnock beaches, and Malahide Castle (01 846 2184), where you'll also find the Fry Model Railway and and tea rooms, there is extensive parkland and the Talbot Botanic Gardens (01 846 2456) - and the castle hosts concerts in the summer months. Plentiful accommodation includes the ever-growing **Grand Hotel** (01 845 0000; www.thegrand.ie), with every facility; there's quality shopping too and a Farmers' Market every Saturday - and the town is alive with bars, cafés and restaurants. In New Street, **Gibneys** pub (01 845 0863) is a first port of call for many; this characterful place has a large beer garden at the back and offers contemporary bar food and an interesting wine selection (including a blackboard menu by the glass); next door is their award-winning wine shop & off-licence. In a first floor premises on The Green, and overlooking the marina area, the relaxed **Ciao Ristorante** (01 845 1233) can claim one of the best views in town - rivalled perhaps by **Cruzzo Bar & Restaurant** (see entry).

WWW.IRELAND-GUIDE.COM FOR ALL THE BEST PLACES TO EAT, DRINK & STAY

Malahide
RESTAURANT

Bon Appetit

9 St James Terrace Malahide Co Dublin **Tel: 01 8450 314**
info@bonappetit.ie www.bonappetit.ie

Since 2006 chef-patron Oliver Dunne has been presiding over this four-storey Georgian building in a seaside terrace in the charming town of Malahide. Bon Appétit had long been the fine dining centre of the area under the direction of former owner Patsy McGuirk, and the town has welcomed this talented young chef, who made his name at Mint in Ranelagh after training in many of London's top restaurants. The entrance level now offers a smart reception area and bar (where a pianist plays at weekends), the lower floor is a bistro, Café Bon (see below), and the fine dining restaurant, Bon Appétit, is on the first floor. In the Guide's experience, reception may be disconcertingly off-hand but, once upstairs, expectations rise as the sensual palette of muted metallics and moody greens creates a real sense of luxury in two classically proportioned adjoining rooms. Silk lined walls, contemporary chandeliers, cream carver chairs, huge mirrors, fresh flowers and generous linen-draped tables all add to the sense of anticipation. Menus offered include a 3-course set dinner menu with six choices on each course (€75) and a Menu Prestige (€90) which offers less choice but comes with all the little niceties (amuse bouche, sorbet, pre-dessert, petits fours) and the option of a Sommelier Wine Selection (€60) to accompany each course. In both cases there are supplements on some dishes - ravioli of prawns (served, perhaps, with basil coulis, tomato fondue and lobster bisque) and fillet of Aberdeen Angus (typically with slow roast tomato and Bordelaise onion pomme purée) both incur a 5 supplement on the Set Menu for example, and a cheese selection, offered as an alternative to a pre-dessert on the Menu Prestige, costs an extra €10. Luxury ingredients like foie gras and, perhaps, turbot, lobster and prawns feature although, surprisingly, there is no mention at all of provenance - not so much as a 'Howth lobster' or a 'Wicklow lamb', less still the names of any artisan suppliers - which gives menus a strangely impersonal feel. The cooking, however, is highly sophisticated, with each plate served as a work of art - every dish is paired with thoughtfully considered accompaniments which, for the most part, work well and enhance the dining experience. The wine list is lengthy, with some value to be found, and, although service may not always match the expectations of professionalism in fine dining at this level, the overall experience is something that would not until recently have been expected outside Dublin city centre. The chic ground floor cocktail bar is a nice space for digestifs, or a pleasant way to kick start an evening in one of Dublin's most exciting new restaurants. Downstairs, Café Bon is an informal but equally stylish operation in the basement, with longer opening hours. Here head chef Andy Turner turns out smart modern dishes - quail and black pudding with poached egg on top, foie gras parfait, upscale steaks; it's much more accessible than the fine dining restaurant and the early bird offers good value. **Bon Appetit: Seats 100** (private room, 40); children welcome (high chair); pianist at the weekend, air conditioning. D daily 6-10.30pm (to 9.30 Sun); Sun 1pm-8pm inc.; gourmet menu €90; also à la carte; house wine €22; SC 10% on groups 8+. Closed 1st week Jan, 1st two weeks Aug. Amex, Diners, MasterCard, Visa, Laser. **Directions:** Coming from Dublin go through the lights in the centre of Malahide and turn left into St James's Terrace at Malahide Garda Station.

Malahide
RESTAURANT
R

Cape Greko

Unit 1 First Floor New Street Malahide Co Dublin **Tel: 01 845 6288**
info@capegreko.ie www.capegreko.ie

This friendly first floor restaurant offers a genuinely relaxed big Greek Cypriot experience and it's a fun, good value place for a group outing. It's a simple room decorated in cool blue and white to match the Greek flag that takes pride of place over the wine rack, with high-backed lightwood chairs and tables simply laid. You can be sure of a warm welcome, and friendly staff are quick to take orders from menus that offer a good selection of the classics - tzatsiki, hummus with pitta bread, grilled halloumi with tomato & onion salad and calamari. Favourites from the main courses include lamb kleftiko (meltingly tender slow-cooked lamb shank), or chicken kebabs served with tzatsiki. A range of side orders includes a Mediterranean salad, along with other staples such as couscous and roasted peppers, but it's worth checking whether you need to order extras as some dishes are very generous. There is live music on Friday nights too, which makes it a real night out. **Seats 54**; children welcome before 9pm (high chair); reservation recommended. Food served all day 12.30-11pm (to 10pm Sun); value D about €21.50, 5-7pm, Mon-Fri; 4-6.30pm Sat-Sun. House wine €18, SC 10% on groups 4+. MasterCard, Visa, Laser. **Directions:** At the corner of New Street above Mario's Pizzas.

Malahide
RESTAURANT
◉ R

Cruzzo Bar & Restaurant

The Marina Village Malahide Co Dublin **Tel: 01 845 0599**
info@cruzzo.ie www.cruzzo.ie

Built on a platform over the water, this attractive bar and restaurant is large and stylish in Florida style, with views over the marina. Approaching from the carpark over a little bridge creates a sense of antic-ipation, and the interior is dashing, with a large piano bar on the lower floor and a rather grand staircase rising to the main dining areas above, which are comfortable and well-appointed, with well-spaced tables in interesting groupings - although it is worth ensuring a table with a view when booking, as there is always something interesting going on in daylight, and the sea water all around is impres-sively lit at night; an elevated section at the front has the best tables in the house. Contemporary menus hold no great surprises (except, perhaps, the use of ingredients like lump crab and Canadian lobster) but offer a varied choice of perhaps eight or ten dishes on each course, including attractively presented starters and main courses that offer imaginatively dressed up versions of popular dishes (dry aged beef - sirloin or fillet - is a speciality). Cooking can be inconsistent, but the location and ambi-ence always give a sense of occasion - especially at weekends, when a band or pianist playing downstairs adds to the atmosphere. Although prices on the à la carte are quite high, the early dinner menu is very good value (although vegetables are charged extra), and there is a nice little 'grown up' children's menu too. *Proprietor Damien Molloy also operates Dublin Sea Tours - sightseeing coastal tours of Dublin Bay (www.dublinseatours.ie). **Seats 260**; children welcome before 9pm (high chair, children's menu, baby changing facilities); lift, toilets wheelchair accessible, air conditioning. L Tue-Sat 12-3 (Sun 12.30-3.30); D Mon-Fri 6-10pm, Sat, 5.30-10.30pm, Sun 6.30-9.30pm. Early D €18, Mon-Fri, 6-7pm; L & D also à la carte. Live music (Jazz & Sinatra) Fri, Sat evening. House wine from €21.50. SC 12.5% on parties 6+. Closed L Mon, D Bank Hol Mon, 25-26 Dec,1 Jan, Good Fri. Amex, Diners, MasterCard, Visa, Laser. **Directions:** From Malahide Village through arch into Marina.

Malahide
RESTAURANT
B R

Jaipur Restaurant

St James Terrace Malahide Co Dublin **Tel: 01 845 5455**
malahide@jaipur.ie www.jaipur.ie

This chic new-wave Indian restaurant is one of five Jaipurs - the others are in Dublin 2, Dalkey, Greystones and Ongar (see entries) and, although Malahide is particularly well-served with interesting eating places, it has earned a loyal following. The restaurant is in the basement of a fine Georgian terrace, accessed by a built-up pavement high above the road, which gives it a sense of calm and exclusivity - and, seen from the pavement above, the warm lights and richly coloured décor is very inviting. Here, head chef Anughau Srivastava creates colourful, well-flavoured dishes that have a lot of eye appeal, and the cooking is crisp and modern - a contemporary take on traditional Indian food that suits the setting and is typical of the Jaipur group. The range of dishes offered is wide but tandoori cooking is a specialty and, particularly Tandoori Jhinga - large prawns marinated with Indian spices, cooked in the tandoor and served with a citrus salad; variations include Jaipur Jugalbandi, a combi-nation dish of prawn, chicken, lamb and fish cooked in a tandoor. Another favourite with Irish diners is a Kashmiri dish of slow-roasted lamb shank flavoured with aromatic spices, and there's also a good range of appealing vegetarian choices (highlighted on the menu); Chakra Shakahari Thaali, for example, is a combination of lentils, greens, potatoes and vegetables, served individually with rice and bread. Many of the traditional Indian dishes take well to contemporary treatment, and even desserts - not usually a strength in ethnic restaurants - are worth leaving room for here. And, as at all the Jaipur restaurants, special care has been taken to offer a range of wines to complement the subtle spicing of the food. Good service from friendly and well-trained staff complete the picture. **Seats 80**; children welcome (high chair); air conditioning; D daily, 5-11. Early D, €22 (5-7pm). Gourmet menu €45, also à la carte. House wine from €20. Closed 25-26 Dec. Amex, MasterCard, Visa, Laser. **Directions:** In Georgian terrace facing the tennis club in Malahide.

Malahide
RESTAURANT
N E R

Kajjal - Pakistani & Eastern Cuisine

Unit 7 The Green Malahide Co Dublin **Tel: 01 806 1960**
info@kajjal.ie www.kajjal.ie

The smart, discreet frontage of this new restaurant fits in well with the neighbouring row of chi chi boutiques near Malahide marina. Kajjal is a sister restaurant of the highly-regarded Kinara

Indian/Pakistani restaurant on Clontarf's seafront and it offers the same qualities of style, delicious food and friendly, attentive staff. Billed as 'Pakistani and Eastern cuisine', the menu offers an exciting mix of regional cooking, accompanied by a few Indian staples; while ordering, guests are served fresh poppadoms with delicious home-made dips. The rich colour scheme seems inspired by the exotic spices and organically shaped lampshades, reminiscent of exotic flowers, enhance the interesting, moodily lit room. Circular booths opposite the long bar are great for families, while individual tables are well-sized for couples. Meltingly tender lamb dishes, featuring Irish lamb, are a speciality, perhaps simmered with spinach and garam masala or in a classic rice biryani. Seafood might appear in the guise of tandoori crab claws or piquant tiger prawns, and an appealing selection of vegetarian sides can be ordered as mains. Expert spicing and attractive presentation ensure each dish is a success, and diners who have visited the sub-continent will be pleased to find paratha (layered wholemeal bread) on offer alongside a choice of naan bread. A brief selection of appealing-sounding desserts strays from the usual shop-bought items that so often let ethnic restaurants down. The wine list is interesting, although it could offer more value at the lower end, and coffees are good, as is service, which is attentive and efficient. Despite Malahide having a good range of eating options, Kajjal has been warmly welcomed, with good reason, by savvy northside foodies. **Directions:** Part of the new Green development by Malahide Marina, it is around the corner at the back, opposite the bottom of Old Street. ◈

Malahide   Siam Thai Restaurant

RESTAURANT   1 The Green Malahide Co Dublin **Tel: 01 845 4698**

R   siam@eircom.net   www.siamthai.ie

One of Dublin's longest-established Thai restaurants, the popular Siam Thai is attractively located in a purpose-built modern building overlooking Malahide village green. A smart blue-covered heated terrace at the front is very appealing from the road and the spacious stylishly decorated interior has a full bar; the back is subtly lit and ideal for private parties, and the front area has pleasant views out over the marina. A typically warm Thai welcome gets guests into the mood, and there is a pianist on some nights, which adds to the atmosphere. Menus offer many of the Thai classics on an extensive à la carte as well as the set menus, so it is wise to order an aperitif and allow plenty of time to decide - or the indecisive might begin with Siam Combination Appetisers, followed perhaps by main courses like sizzling fillet beef with oyster sauce or crispy duck with tamarind. Outstandingly friendly staff are knowledgeable and efficient. **Seats 120** (private room, 45, outdoor, 30); children welcome; air conditioning. Live music (piano or live Thai band) most nights. L daily 11.30-5; D daily 5-12. Early D about €21 (5-7.30 Sun-Thu); Set D about €32/36 2/3 course; à la carte also available. House wine €20. Closed 25-26 Dec. Amex, Diners, MasterCard, Visa, Laser. **Directions:** In Malahide village, near marina overlooking the green.

Monkstown   The Purty Kitchen

CAFÉ•PUB   3-5 Old Dunleary Road Monkstown Co Dublin **Tel: 01 284 3576**

     info@purtykitchen.com   www.purtykitchen.com

Established in 1728 - making it the second oldest pub in Dublin (after The Brazen Head) and the oldest in Dun Laoghaire - this attractive old place has seen some changes, but its essential character remains, with dark wooden floors, atmospheric lighting, large mirrors and a good buzz. It's well set up for enjoyment of the bar food for which it has earned a fine reputation, with shiny dark wooden tables (a candle on each) and inviting menus which still have some old favourites like the famous Purty Seafood Chowder and traditional Mussels Marinière. But, although best known for seafood - and a wide range is offered, including Prawn and Crayfish Pil Pil, Caribbean-style Crab Cakes and tender calamari and Pacific Rock Oysters - there are other choices, including a separate vegetarian menu. Head chef Jacqueline Foster has brought her American experiences to the kitchen: butcher's block selections include char-grilled fillet steak, North Star short ribs and Hereford Beef Burger. Fresh food with a home-cooked flavour, presented attractively on different shaped plates, make this an unusually enjoyable informal dining experience. A list of House Favourites also includes some dishes that have stood the test of (considerable) time, such as a traditional breakfast, home-made beef burgers and seafood quiche, all at reasonable prices. A garden terrace offers a pleasing outdoor alternative in fine weather, and the Food

& Wine Emporium next door specialises in artisan Irish foods. Restaurant: D two sittings 7pm & 9pm, reservations advisable. No reservations in bar but names taken when you arrive and you can wait at the bar. *There is a newer Purty Kitchen in Temple Bar (see entry). *The Purty Café, next door to the pub, now offers coffee, cakes and sandwiches. à la carte menu available Mon-Fri 12-9.45, Sat-Sun, 12.30-9.45. Vegetarian menu also available. Purty Kitchen Food & Wine Emporium open every day (pub hours). Toilets wheelchair accessible. House wine from about €16.50 (€4.50 per glass). Live music Tue & Fri evenings. Closed 25 Dec, Good Friday. Amex, Diners, MasterCard, Visa, Laser.
Directions: On left approaching Dun Laoghaire from Dublin by the coast road. ◊

Seapoint

Monkstown
RESTAURANT

4 The Crescent Monkstown Co Dublin Tel: 01 663 8480
info@seapointrestaurant.com www.seapointrestaurant.com

Seapoint is one of a new breed of restaurant which aims, and manages, to tick many boxes. It is a suburban eatery that is built to survive these tighter times, and to maximise the potential for getting footfall through its cutesy courtyard off Monkstown's well-served strip of restaurants and into the bright and breezy space of its long dining room. It draws locals in with a range of offerings which include morning coffee, light lunches (from the charmingly titled 'afternoon dip' menu), antipasti with or without a glass/bottle of wine, and a dinner menu with impressively affordable choices (including several fish offerings under €20) alongside deliciously indulgent ones (rock oysters on ice perhaps). More importantly, Seapoint keeps the locals coming back thanks to the help of a strong team which include accomplished chef Nick Clapham, previously of Ernies in Donnybrook, leading the kitchen, and proprietor Shane Kenny, formerly of Wines Direct, guiding a cheerful front-of-house team. Shane's passion for small producers is evident in the well-priced, comprehensive list which is laid out according to wine style and from which many wines are offered by the glass. The kitchen's approach to ingredients is similarly unfussy and clear in focus: central ingredients are treated with respect and supported but not crowded by bold accompanying flavours, with a healthy leaning towards fresh herbs and vegetables. All in all, one of the more confident and assured new arrivals of 2008.

Michael's Food & Wine

Mount Merrion
RESTAURANT

57 Deerpark Road Mount Merrion Co Dublin
Tel: 01 278 0377

In fine weather, a few tables for alfresco dining set a welcoming tone outside Michael and Mary Lowe's wine shop, Italian deli and little trattoria-style restaurant. You'll notice bottles of wine in view as you arrive and, in the shop, find the walls lined from floor-to-ceiling with Michael's collection of specially imported Italian wine; a table displaying speciality foods (pastas, Italian sauces etc) takes centre stage and a deli counter at the back of the shop offers charcuterie, great cheeses, olives, and other treats to take home. At the back, a small room is simply furnished with wooden tables and chairs and small candles, and a blackboard notice sums up the philosophy of this little place very well: "No salt or sugar added, 99% ingredients & 1% skill"! A blackboard menu offers a small selection of dishes (some available in two sizes) including a must-try and totally delicious antipasta dish with bruschetta, sun-blushed tomatoes, salami, prosciutto, red and green pesto, olives, a pair of hand-made Italian cheeses and a choice of salads. Main dishes normally include a hot special such as pizzaiola - mozzarella, aubergine, bruschetta, red pesto, regato and parmesan, and vegetarians will also enjoy the 'veggie snack' of focaccia, courgette, aubergine, pesto, red peppers, mozzarella, layered and served with fresh rocket leaves wrapped in a slice of roasted aubergine. Tempting desserts are displayed in a glass cabinet in the wine shop where you may may choose a bottle to enjoy with your meal for a corkage fee of about €5.75 and, on bottles over €30, there is no corkage charge. The quality of ingredients used and generous portions makes for very good value, and friendly service and advice is always at hand. Cheese & Wine night on Wednesdays, 7pm onwards. **Seats 24**; D Thurs-Fri, 7-9.30pm, L Sat only 12-3pm. MasterCard, Visa, Laser. **Directions:** Situated off Fosters Avenue on Deerpark Road just past Kiely's of Mount Merrion. ◊

Portmarnock

Portmarnock
HOTEL•RESTAURANT

Portmarnock Hotel & Golf Links

Strand Road Portmarnock Co Dublin **Tel:** 01 846 0611
sales@portmarnock.com www.portmarnock.com

Originally owned by the Jameson family of whiskey fame, Portmarnock Hotel and Golf Links enjoys a wonderful beachside position overlooking the islands of Lambay and Ireland's Eye. Convenient to the airport, and only eleven miles from Dublin city centre, the hotel seems to offer the best of every world - the peace and convenience of the location and a magnificent 18-hole Bernhard Langer-designed links course. A recent extension has added a new wing to the hotel and, although this obstructs the views once enjoyed from public areas, it does afford them to many of the 40 new bedrooms. Décor in the original hotel and old house is a little tired and dated looking in places, and this is most obvious where the existing hotel joins up with the new accommodation. While all accommodation is imaginatively designed and furnished to a high standard of comfort, with good bathrooms, the new bedrooms are superior in many ways. The new rooms have unusual sea green colouring with bespoke headboards featuring enlarged images of grainy sand. The cool green colour scheme and contemporary styling are extremely appealing, so it's worth requesting a new room when booking. The Jameson Bar, in the old house, has character and there's also an informal Links Bar and Restaurant next to the golf shop (12-10 daily). Conference/banqueting (350/250) Business centre. Golf (18). Oceana, health & beauty: gym, sauna, steam rooms & a wide range of treatments. Children welcome (under 4 free in parents' room, cots available without charge, baby sitting arranged). No pets. Garden. **Rooms 98**. Lift. 24 hour room service. B&B about €169 pps, ss about €75; special offers often available. Open all year. **Osborne Brasserie:** Named after the artist Walter Osborne, who painted many of his most famous pictures in the area including the view from the Jameson house, the restaurant is in a semi-basement overlooking a garden courtyard at the centre of the hotel. First-time visitors may not find it easily, so inquire at reception. When it first opened in 1996 this restaurant was an important addition to a sparse north Dublin dining scene, and a succession of distinguished chefs put this formal dining room firmly on the map. Now it is less a culinary destination and more a semi-formal dining option for resident guests and a 'special occasion' restaurant for local residents - but those who have not eaten here for some time will be agreeably surprised by the smart new décor and more contemporary food currently offered. Menus feature imaginative combinations attractively presented, with about six dishes on each course – and, although the dinner menu still offers some sophisticated dishes, there's now a wider choice to include a range of salads (available as starters or mains) and grills, and more emphasis on offering value. Evening starters might include carpaccio of beef fillet with baby spinach, parmesan & truffle, or pan-seared scallops, both priced around €10-12. Apart from the salads, main courses range from around €16 (beef burger with mixed leaf salad and French fries) to about €34 (T-bone steak béarnaise), with several fish dishes around €28. Lunch menus are similar but with more bistro-style main courses offered. Service is friendly and not overly formal, making this a relaxed, comfortable space to dine. **Seats 80** (private room, 20); air conditioning. D only Tue-Sat, 7-10. Set D from about €47, Tasting Menu from €50-60. A la carte available; house wine from €19.85; SC discretionary. Closed Sun, Mon. Links Brasserie open 12-10 daily. Amex, MasterCard, Visa, Laser. **Directions:** On the coast in Portmarnock. ◇

Saggart

Saggart
RESTAURANT

Avoca Café Rathcoole

Naas Road Saggart Co Dublin **Tel:** 01 257 1800
rathcoole@shop.avoca.ie www.avoca.ie

Although it's right on a busy road and lacks the pretty setting associated with Avoca shops outside the city, this purpose-built lifestyle emporium is airy and colourful, with all the by now famous Avoca sections offering lovely shopping areas that are ideal for gifts and showcasing the best of Irish goods. A large enticing food hall with plenty of natural light looks out onto newly landscaped gardens, and upstairs there are two restaurants; **The Birdcage** which is self-service and the **Egg Café** (for reservations 01 257 1810) with table service. They share a large outdoor terrace, which is very popular when the weather allows - and has lovely views of the Dublin Mountains. Both restaurants tend to be very busy, but friendly staff and lovely food will compensate for any delays; as in the other Avoca cafés, you will be spoiled for choice of wholesome dishes from the well-designed self-service counters. A cut above an in-store café (even for Avoca), the Egg Café is making its mark as a destination restaurant, which is ideal for both the store and the neighbourhood. A perfect place to go for delicious food, with ample parking. **Seats 100**; Open daily 9.30-5pm (to 8pm Thurs). **Directions:** By edge of Naas Road, just west of Citywest campus. ◊

Saggart

HOTEL

R R R

Citywest Hotel Conference Leisure & Golf Resort

Saggart Co Dublin **Tel: 01 401 0500**
info@citywesthotel.com www.citywesthotel.com

Only about 25 minutes from the city centre and Dublin airport (traffic permitting), this enormous hotel was planned with the needs of the rapidly expanding western edge of the capital in mind. It is set in its own estate, which includes two 18-hole golf courses and a comprehensive leisure centre with a large deck level swimming pool and a wide range of health and beauty facilities. The other big attraction is the hotel's banqueting, conference and meeting facilities, which include a convention centre catering for 4,000 delegates, making Citywest one of the largest venues in the country. All round, a valuable - if awesome - amenity for West Dublin. Conference/banqueting (4,000/2,000); secretarial services, video-conferencing. Leisure centre, swimming pool. Hairdressing/beauty salon. Children welcome (under 6 free in parents' room, cots available free of charge). Restaurant: L Mon-Fri, D daily. **Rooms 1,317** (19 suites, 759 no smoking). Lift, room service 24 hr. B&B about €75 pps, ss €30. Open all year. Amex, Diners, MasterCard, Visa, Laser. **Directions:** Off Naas Road - N7 (from Dublin, take left after Independent printers & follow road for about a mile.

SKERRIES

So far remarkably unspoilt, Skerries is not completely undeveloped but its essential atmosphere has remained unchanged for decades (perhaps because it does not yet have a marina and all its attendant development) and it makes a refreshing break from the hurly-burly of Dublin city. The harbour is renowned for its fishing - Skerries is also a popular small boat angling centre in summer with the Skerries Islands and Rockabill grounds easily reached - notably Dublin Bay prawns (langoustine), and the surrounding area is famous for market gardening, so it has always been a good place for a very subtstantial bite to eat - and there are several pubs of character along the harbour front to enjoy a pint before your meal - or the **Coast Inn**, just across the road from the **Red Bank** (see entry), does a great line in cocktails. **Olive Coffee & Wine** (see entry) is a very attractive little place accross from Gerry's Supermarket. While in the area, allow time to visit Skerries Mills (working windmills (01 849 5208)) - which also hosts a Farmers Market every Saturday - and take a stroll in Ardgillan Castle and Victorian Gardens (Tel: 01 849 2212) nearby at Balbriggan which has a great children's playground, (both also have tea rooms). There are many testing golf courses in the area and there are plenty of coastal and parkland walks.

Skerries

CAFÉ•WINE BAR

Olive

86a Strand Street Skerries Co Dublin **Tel: 01 849 0310**
info@olive.ie www.olive.ie

Peter Dorrity and Deirdre Fahy's charming specialist food shop and café is in the centre of Skerries with a wide pavement at the front that allows space for an outside seating area - making a very pleasant place to enjoy a bite to eat while people-watching in fine weather. The shop sells a carefully selected range of artisan produce from Ireland and abroad, including their own home-made range of hummus, basil pesto, olive tapenade and sweet Harissa pepper oil; a range of unusual salads is also freshly prepared for the shop and may include lentil & roasted vegetables, lemon & mint couscous and mixed bean salad amongst many others. All these items make regular appearances on the café menu, along with other good things, including about ten types of muffins every day, home-made soups, panini and home-baked cookies. In July and August, they also open as a wine bar in the evening at weekends, offering simple fare like platters of meats and farmhouse cheeses - and, a novel idea, they recently introduced Picnic Baskets for rent in the summer; with the lovely beaches and Ardgillan Castle on the doorstep, there are lots of lovely places to picnic, with a basket full of goodies from the deli. All this, and keen, knowledgeable staff too - magic. **Seats 30** (outdoors, 18); toilets wheelchair accessible; children welcome (high chair). Open daily 8.30-7pm; house wine €17.50. Closed Christmas. MasterCard, Visa, Laser. **Directions:** Turn right at monument in town, on the right.

Skerries
RESTAURANT•GUESTHOUSE

Red Bank House & Restaurant

5-7 Church Street Skerries Co Dublin **Tel: 01 849 1005**
sales@redbank.ie www.redbank.ie

Golfing breaks are a speciality at Terry McCoy's renowned restaurant with accommodation in the characterful fishing port of Skerries. The restaurant is in a converted banking premises, which adds to the atmosphere (even the old vault has its uses - as a wine cellar) and Terry is an avid supporter of local produce, with fresh seafood from Skerries harbour providing the backbone of his menu. Menus, written in Terry's inimitable style, are a joy to read and a statement at the end reads: "All items on the menu are sourced from Irish producers and suppliers. There are too many items for us to list all ingredients after each dish but you can take my word for it, we use local Irish because it's the freshest & so the best." Dishes conceived and cooked with generosity have names of local relevance - grilled goat's cheese St. Patrick, for example, is a reminder that the saint once lived on Church Island off Skerries - and dishes suitable for vegetarians are marked on the menu. The dessert trolley is legendary - a large space should be left if you fancy pudding. An informative, fairly priced wine list includes a wide selection of house wines, and a good choice of half bottles - and the early dinner and Sunday lunch menus offer great value. **Seats 60** (private room,10). D Mon-Sat, 6.30-9.45; L Sun only, 12.30-4.30. Set Sun L €33; Set D €50/55. A la carte also available; house wines from €24.50; no sc. Children welcome (high chair). Closed D Sun and L Mon-Sat. Restaurant only closed 24-27 Dec. **Accommodation:** 18 fine, comfortably furnished guest rooms have all the amenities normally expected of an hotel. Facilities for private parties (50). Gourmet Golf breaks - up to 40 golf courses within 20 minutes drive. While in the area, allow time to visit Skerries Mills (working windmills (Tel: 01 849 5208)) and the beautifully located Ardgillan Castle and Victorian Gardens (Tel: 01 849 2212) nearby, where there are tea rooms. **Rooms 18** (all superior & no-smoking, ground floor bedroom, 1 for disabled). Free broadband; Children under 4 free in parents' room (cots available free of charge). Pets permitted in certain areas. B&B €60 pps, ss €15 (DB&B rate is good value at €90 pps). Accommodation open all year. Amex, Diners, MasterCard, Visa, Laser. **Directions:** Opposite AIB Bank in Skerries.

Skerries
Bar/Restaurant

Stoop Your Head

Harbour Road Skerries Co Dublin
Tel: 01 849 2085

After a quiet off-season drink a few doors along at Joe May's, there can be no greater pleasure in north Dublin than to slip into 'Stoops' for some of Andy Davies' mainly seafood cooking. 'Fresh, simple and wholesome' is how he describes his food, and who could want any more than that? If it's busy you may have to wait at the little bar - where you can opt to eat if you like, or have a look at the menu while waiting for a table (they seem to turn over fairly fast). The surroundings are simple - chunky wooden tables, closely packed - and the menu is not elaborate but there is plenty to choose from, and there are blackboard specials every day too; what could be more delightful than starters of dressed crab, or moules marinière - or perhaps a classic fresh prawn Marie Rose, as Dublin Bay prawns (langoustines) are landed in Skerries and a speciality; like the crab claws, they are offered as starters or main courses, in irresistible garlic butter. You don't have to eat seafood here - there are other choices like Asian chicken salad, or pasta dishes or even fillet steak medallions - but it would be a pity to miss it. Super fresh and deliciously simple, it's a treat. **Seats 50** (outdoor seating, 20); air conditioning; no reservations. Children welcome (high chair, children's menu, baby changing facilities). Toilets wheelchair accessible. L & D daily: L 12-3, D 5.30-9.30 (Fri/Sat to 10pm); Sun D 4-8pm. Afternoon menu Mon-Sat, 3-5pm. House wine about €17. Closed 25 Dec & Good Fri. Amex, MasterCard, Visa, Laser. **Directions:** On the harbour front in Skerries.

Stillorgan
RESTAURANT
Beaufield Mews Restaurant & Gardens
Woodlands Avenue Stillorgan Co Dublin **Tel: 01 288 0375**
info@beaufieldmews.com www.beaufieldmews.com

Dublin's oldest restaurant is located in a characterful 18th century coachhouse and stables - surrounded by beautiful mature gardens where guests can have an aperitif on the lawn before dinner, or take coffee afterwards, as the gardens are lit up at night. With its mature trees, spacious surroundings and old-fashioned feeling about the buildings and gardens, you could be forgiven for thinking you have been mysteriously transported to the country - there's even an antique shop where guests are encouraged to have a browse before dining (Open 3-9pm). In 2007 the Cox family, who have owned and run Beaufield Mews for over 50 years, surprised everyone by doing a revamp, changing the traditional, old-fashioned restaurant into a sophisticated contemporary one, with modern décor and furnishings. But, as original features like wooden beams, heavy old latch doors and bare brick walls have been retained, the end result isn't too much of a shock and the concensus is that it still has plenty of character and menus, although updated, also remain in tune with the old Beaufield Mews that so many people know and love - roast Irish duckling with caramelised orange sauce remains a speciality. The gardens are a very special feature, and becoming more precious to city dwellers all the time; a large outdoor patio area overlooking the gardens allows guests to relax with an aperitif or an after-dinner coffee in fine weather, and drink in the atmosphere. Good wine list. **Seats 200** (private room, 60; outdoor seating, 20); toilets wheelchair accessible; children welcome before 9pm (high chair, childrens menu, baby changing facilities). D Tue-Sat, 6.30-9.30; L Sun only, 12.30-2.30 (Sun L €24.95). Early D €24.95 (Tue-Thur, 6.30-7.30); set D €34.95, also à la carte. SC 12.5% Closed Mon, 24-26 Dec, Good Fri. Amex, Diners, MasterCard, Visa, Laser. **Directions:** 4 miles from city centre, off Stillorgan dual carriageway/ N11.

Swords
CAFÉ•RESTAURANT
Ⓝ Ⓡ
Gourmet Food Parlour
Unit 2 St Fintans North Street Swords Co Dublin **Tel: 01 897 1496**
info@gourmetfoodparlour.com www.gourmetfoodparlour.com

A newer and smaller cousin of the popular Dun Laoghaire establishment, the Gourmet Food Parlour offers good value and ingredients for a mostly lunch trade. Although lacking in character, the room is big and bright, with simple furniture, and chalkboards listing appetising sandwiches and daily specials. Breakfast is served until midday, with interesting choices ranging from muesli to the traditional cooked breakfast, albeit with a twist. Lunch, which can be eaten on the premises or for take away (a useful option for local businesses) offers choices between salads, gourmet sandwiches and more substantial dishes, with a daily special also available. A selection of various antipasti is also offered, along with a short but well chosen list of wines available by the glass. All round, a useful place to know about. **Seats 46**; open Mon-Sat 8am-5.30pm (from 10am Sat); Sun 12-6pm. MasterCard, Visa, Laser. **Directions:** North Street is at the Castle end of Swords Town.

Swords
RESTAURANT
Ⓝ Ⓡ
Indie Spice
Burgundy House Forster Way Swords Co Dublin **Tel: 01 807 7999**
indiespice@eircom.net www.indiespicecafe.com

Located above a shop, with a narrow door leading up steep stairs to the first floor dining room, arrival at Indie Spice may not seem promising - but, once you have walked past the open kitchen to your table, it quickly becomes obvious that the warm and stylish interior promises something a little special. The room is large, with striking contemporary décor, but divided into smaller sections and with low lighting giving a sense of intimacy. Service is prompt and courteous, with poppadoms and dips brought to your table right away. With a long and interesting menu, offering a wide variety of dishes in familiar styles (Tandoor, Biriyani etc), the chef's specialities are recommended, especially for first time visitors not familiar with the menu. Dishes enjoyed on a recent visit by the Guide included a well-flavoured starter of Salmon Gulnar, (fresh salmon rolled in ground herbs then baked with ginger and honey) and a main course of Moghlai Lamb with Sultana, a delicate yet richly flavoured dish with spices of cumin, coriander, cayenne pepper, cardamom and cinnamon, served with excellent Peshwaree Naan and Pilau Rice. This is a pleasing restaurant and, given the long opening hours, may be a useful place for travellers using the airport to know about. **Seats 130**; children welcome (high chair, children's menu); air conditioning. Open for L&D Mon-Fri, 12-2.30pm and 5.30-11.30pm. Open all day Sat 12-11.30pm; Sun 1-11pm; set 2 course L €8.95 (12-2.30pm); set Sun L €19.95; value D €15.95, Mon-Thurs, 5.30-7pm; also à la carte L&D; house wine €19.95; SC 10% on groups 8+. Amex, MasterCard, Visa, Laser. **Directions:** Behind the Plaza shopping centre, on the first floor.

Swords

Roganstown Golf & Country Club Hotel

HOTEL•RESTAURANT

The Naul Road Swords Co Dublin **Tel: 01 843 3118**

info@roganstown.com www.roganstown.com

Set in a 300 acre estate in north county Dublin and built around the original Roganstown House, this is primarily a golf hotel but its convenience to Dublin airport and the city make it an attractive destination for travellers who wish to avoid the big airport hotels, business guests and those seeking a weekend break from the capital without a long drive. It is a pleasant, well-managed hotel with a friendly can-do attitude, and very comfortable accommodation in well-appointed modern rooms which overlook the championship golf course, a Japanese-styled courtyard or mature front gardens; rooms, which are uncluttered and work well, have good facilities including a laptop safe, direct dial telephone, internet access, satellite TV, minibar, hairdryer, iron and ironing board, and tea & coffee making facilities. The hotel has earned a reputation for good food, both in the comfortable O'Callaghans Bar, and McLoughlins Restaurant, which offers fine dining in very pleasant surroundings and attracts diners from a wide area. Head chef Lewis Bannerman has been with the hotel since it opened, and he successfully balances the requirements of different kinds of guests. While not cutting edge, his food is imaginative and skilfully prepared, and the dining experience here is always enjoyable. Conference facilities include the wheelchair accessible Aungier Suite which has state-of-the-art facilities, its own bar and splendid views of the golf course, which is also ideal for banqueting, and can be subdivided into smaller groups as desired. An additional two dedicated boardrooms can each accommodate up to 16 delegates. For golf lovers, the Christy O'Connor Junior-designed golf course will be an exciting challenge. Conferences/banqueting (300/240), business centre, free Broadband wi/fi. **Rooms 52** (3 shower only, 16 executive, 1 junior suite, 43 no smoking, 20 groundfloor, 3 for disabled); children welcome (cots avail free of charge, baby sitting arranged). Room service limited hours; Lift. B&B €70 pps, ss €40. Midweek specials offered. Golf (18), leisure centre with 'pool, day spa, beauty salon. Closed 24-26 Dec. Helipad. Amex, Diners, MasterCard, Visa, Laser. **Directions:** Take Ashbourne road from Swords village, take right turn for Naul, 500m on the left. ◊

SWORDS AREA

For an interesting outing in North Dublin, take a trip to **The Grange** (01-807 8888) at Oldtown (near Ballyboughal Village), where you may be surprised to find a contemporary art gallery, a shop selling lovely things you won't find anywhere else, and a smart café offering homemade all day food 6 days a week (closed Mon); also working artists' studios to see, and room hire for meetings and small events. **WWW.IRELAND-GUIDE.COM FOR ALL THE BEST PLACES TO EAT, DRINK & STAY**

COUNTY CARLOW

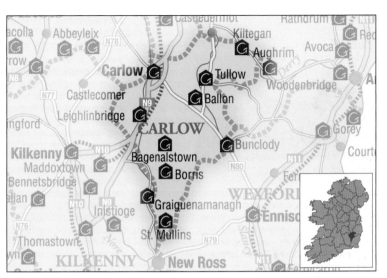

Carlow's character and charm is within easy reach of Dublin, yet the city influence is kept at bay with a lively sense of place. Although it is Ireland's second smallest county, it confidently incorporates such wonderful varieties of scenery that it has been memorably commented that the Creator was in fine form when He made Carlow. Whether you're lingering along the gentle meanderings of the waterway of the River Barrow, or enjoying the upper valley of the River Slaney while savouring the soaring outlines of the Blackstairs Mountains as they sweep upwards to the 793 m peak of Mount Leinster, this gallant little area will soon have you in thrall.

There's history a-plenty if you wish to seek it out. But for those who prefer to live in the present, the county town of Carlow itself fairly buzzes with student life and the energetic trade of a market centre which is also home to a micro-brewery that, among other admirable products, is the source of the award-winning O'Hara's Stout.

With the main roads much improved in recent years, a more leisurely pace can be enjoyed at riverside villages such as Leighlinbridge and Bagenalstown. Leighlinbridge - pronounced "Lochlinbridge" – has for many years been Carlow's most community-conscious riverside village, the holder of a Tidy Towns Gold Medal and an Entente Floriale winner. There are also welcome improvements taking place to fulfill Bagenalstown's potential as a proper miniature river port, while the hidden hillside village of Borris is an enchantment in itself.

Local Attractions and Information

Carlow	Eigse – Arts Festival (June)	059 914 0491
Carlow town	Tourist Information	059 917 0776
Carlow county	Carlow Rural Tourism	059 913 0411 / 913 0446
Carlow	Craft Brewery, Micro-brewery	059 913 4356
Grangeford	World Ploughing Championship 2006	059 862 5125
Tullow	Altamont Gardens	059 915 9444

BAGENALSTOWN

Situated in the Barrow Valley, located on a pleasant stretch of the River Barrow, Bagenalstown derives its name from Walter Bagenal, who founded the town in the 18th century. Visitors can enjoy riverside walks, or take in the historical aspect of the town from the 18th century courthouse, which is inspired by the Parthenon in Athens or perhaps visit the neo-classical railway station. Dunleckney Manor (059 072 1932, open April August) nearby is worth a visit, along with plenty of activities on offer such as coarse fishing on the River Barrow, cycling, or horse riding at the Carrigbeg Stables (059 972 1962).

Picnic tables and a picturesque lock and riverside walks all add to the visitor's enjoyment. Leisure boats and barges also cruise on the Grand Canal and the River Barrow.

Bagenalstown
COUNTRY HOUSE

Kilgraney House

Borris Road Bagenalstown Co Carlow **Tel: 059 977 5283**
info@kilgraneyhouse.com www.kilgraneyhouse.com

On a lovely site overlooking the Barrow Valley, Bryan Leech and Martin Marley's charming late Georgian house - which (encouragingly) takes its name from the Irish 'cill greíne', meaning 'sunny hill or wood' - is set in extensive wooded grounds. It is a serene and restful place with beautiful walks, and Altamont gardens nearby; Bryan and Martin have a great love of gardens - a recent project has been the development of their monastic herb gardens, and the kitchen garden provides plenty of good things for Bryan to transform into delicious dinners. His cooking style is creative and contemporary, making full use of local and artisan produce. Six-course menus begin with an amuse bouche and, although there are various influences at work, there's a leaning towards Japan, notably in specialities like their own home-smoked duck and a very beautiful dish of wild Slaney salmon wrapped in nori and wasabi. Your breakfast next morning will showcase local foods, including cheeses, more traditionally. But it is for the sheer sense of style pervading the house that it is most famous - Bryan and Martin's enjoyment in its restoration and furnishing is abundantly clear: elegant, yes, but with a great sense of fun too. Dinner can be shared with other guests at a communal table, or served at separate tables; a short, informative wine list is chosen with care - and non-residents are welcome by reservation. An Aroma Spa offers a range of therapies and massages, for both men and women, including pregnancy treatments. Self-catering accommodation is also available, in two courtyard suites, the gate lodge and a recently restored cottage. **Rooms 8** (2 suites, 3 shower only, 1 ground floor, all no smoking). Small conferences. Not suitable for children under 12. No pets. B&B about €65-120pps, ss about €35. D (non-residents welcome by reservation), 8 pm. Set 6-course D about €50. (Vegetarian meals or other special dietary requirements on request.) Wines from about €20. Herbal treatment room (massage & aromatherapy); hot tub. Closed Mon-Tue and mid Nov-Feb. Helipad. Amex, MasterCard, Visa, Laser. **Directions:** Just off the R705, halfway between Bagenalstown and Borris. ◇

Bagenalstown
COUNTRY HOUSE

Lorum Old Rectory

Kilgraney Bagenalstown Co Carlow **Tel: 059 977 5282**
enquiry@lorum.com www.lorum.com

Everybody loves staying at Bobbie Smith's mid-Victorian cut stone granite rectory - it was built for the Rev. William Smyth-King in 1864, and now makes a warm and welcoming family home. Elegant and homely, there's a library as well as a lovely drawing room where guests can gather around the fire and relax; spacious accommodation includes one particularly impressive guest room with a four-poster and all rooms are very comfortable, with big beds, phones and tea/coffee trays. But it is Bobbie Smith's easy hospitality that keeps bringing guests back. Bobbie, who is a member of the international chefs' association, Euro-Toques, is committed to using local produce and suppliers whenever possible and is renowned for delicious home cooking using mainly organic and home-grown ingredients; rack of local lamb is a speciality, cooked with a honey, mustard & rosemary glaze, and residents have dinner at a long mahogany table, where wonderful breakfasts are also served. This relaxed place was the Guide's Pet Friendly Establishment in 2000 and guests are still welcome to bring their own dogs, by arrangement. This area makes an ideal base for exploring the lush south-east of Ireland, and is close to many places of interest, including medieval Kilkenny, Altamont Gardens, New Ross (where river cruises are available, and you can see the famine ship Dunbrody), Kildare's National Stud and Japanese Gardens. Also close by is Gowran Park racecourse and activities such as golf and a riding school (offering both outdoor and indoor tuition). Dinner must be booked by 3 pm; a concise, well priced wine list with tasting notes is offered - and guests may bring their own wine if they wish (corkage €12, or €15 for champagne).

Private parties/small conferences (10). **Rooms 5** (all en-suite, all shower only and no smoking); not suitable for children under 12 years. B&B from €75 pps, ss €20. Dinner for residents by arrangement(8pm) €45. Cycling. Own parking. Garden. Closed Dec/Jan/Feb. Amex, MasterCard, Visa, Laser. **Directions:** Midway between Borris & Bagenalstown on the R705.

BALLON

Ballon boasts a rich history of stone masonry, one of Ireland's oldest crafts, whilst Ballon Hill provides excellent views of the surrounding countryside. A guided tour of Malone's 12 acre fruit farm (059 915 9477, open May to October) is well worthwhile. Within a short distance of the village is Altamont Gardens Tullow (059 915 1769), set in a small and uniquely beautiful estate, the gardens at Altamont are one of County Carlow's premier tourist attractions and touted as the 'most romantic gardens in Ireland'.

Ballon
HOTEL•RESTAURANT

Ballykealey Manor Hotel
Ballon Co Carlow **Tel: 059 915 9288**
ballykealeymanor@eircom.net www.ballykealeymanorhotel.com

Seat of the Lecky family for three centuries, the present house was designed by Thomas A Cobden, and built in the 1830s as a wedding present. Gothic arches and Tudor chimney stacks add unique character, and the house is set in well-maintained grounds and promising first impressions are well founded. Owners Edward and Karen Egan completely refurbished the hotel when they took over some years ago and new rooms recently added do not detract from the original house. Bold decorative touches in the entrance hall set a confident tone that is carried through into spacious reception rooms, furnished in an elegant mixture of contemporary style and period features, combining comfort with a friendly atmosphere. Individually designed bedrooms are luxuriously furnished, decorated in keeping with the character of the house and have all the expected amenities. Conferences/banqueting (20-260). Wheelchair access; **Rooms 12** (1 junior suite, 4 shower only, 2 non-smoking); children welcome (under 6 free in parents' room, cot available without charge). Pets by arrangement. B&B about €70pps, ss about €20; no SC. Closed 24 Dec. **The Oak Room:** This aptly-named restaurant is in what was previously the drawing room and library, and retains many original features including 10 foot solid oak dividing doors, hand-carved oak bookcases and fine cornices and mouldings - which, together with a welcome open fire on chilly days, makes a handsome setting for enjoyable food. Menus offer a good range of popular dishes, the cooking is good and service professional - a sound combination that makes this a favourite dining spot for both residents and non-resident guests. **Seats 32** (private room 32). D daily, 7-9.30; L Sun only 12.30-3.30. D A la carte, Set Sun L. House wines €18. A la carte bar menu available 12.30-9.30. Closed 24 Dec. MasterCard, Visa, Laser. **Directions:** 10 miles from Carlow on the N80. ◊

Ballon
RESTAURANT

The Forge Restaurant
Kilbride Cross Ballon Co Carlow **Tel: 059 915 9939**
theforgekilbride@eircom.net

'The Forge for home baking and local produce' is their motto and it sums up nicely the appeal of Mary Jordan's unpretentious daytime restaurant. Off the road but handy to it and with ample parking, the granite building dates back to the 1700s and it makes a great place to break a journey for a wholesome bite. Mary takes pride in sourcing local ingredients and her menus offer simple home cooking, fresh scones and jam, home-made vegetable soup, ploughman's sandwiches and comforting hot lunchtime favourites like baked ham or roast beef, and of course, tea and coffee. It's good to see seasonal produce used and local suppliers credited on the menu. There is also a tourist information point as well as local art and craft work for sale. Walkers are welcome and packed meals supplied on request. All round, a great little place for a break and known for its consistency. Small wonder then that, at the time of going to press, there are plans afoot for expansion. **Seats 60** (outdoor, 30, private room, 14); wheelchair friendly; children welcome (high chair, childrens menu, baby changing facilities); parking. Open 9.30-5 daily (Sun 12-5.30), L 12.45-2.30 (Sun, 12-5.30). Late opening by arrangement; Set 3 course L €15-20, also A la carte. House wine €21. Closed 10 days at Christmas. MasterCard, Visa, Laser. **Directions:** Off the N80, between Ballon and Bunclody.

Ballon
COUNTRY HOUSE

Sherwood Park House
Kilbride Ballon Co Carlow **Tel: 059 915 9117**
info@sherwoodparkhouse.ie www.sherwoodparkhouse.ie

Built around 1700 by a Mr Arthur Baillie, this delightful Georgian farmhouse next to the famous Altamont Gardens is listed by Maurice Craig, the foremost authority on Ireland's architectural history, and is beautifully located, with sweeping views over the countryside. Patrick and Maureen Owens, who have welcomed guests here since 1991, accurately describe it as "an accessible country retreat for anyone who enjoys candlelit dinners, brass and canopy beds, and the relaxing experience of eating out while staying in". Spacious accommodation is furnished in period style and thoughtful in the details that count - and Maureen takes pride in offering guests real home cooking based on the best of local produce, including "best locally produced Carlow beef and lamb, from Ballon Meats" and fish from Kilmore Quay. As well as having Altamont Gardens on the doorstep (just 5 minutes away on foot), there's a lovely garden on site and it's a good area for walking - and fishing the Slaney. Dinner is available by arrangement and is mainly for residents, although non-residents are welcome when there is room - it is served at 8pm and guests are welcome to bring their own wine and any other drinks. (Please remember to give advance notice if you would like dinner.) **Rooms 5** (all en-suite & no smoking); children welcome; pets permitted by arrangement. B&B €55 pps, ss €10. D €40 (BYO wine); non-residents welcome by reservation. Garden. Amex, MasterCard, Visa, Laser. **Directions:** Signed from the junction of the N80 and N81.

BORRIS

This captivating village is located in the shadow of the Blackstairs Mountains and offers beautiful scenery, excellent for either walking and scenic drives, or perhaps a visit to one of the many local craft workers. Interesting local sites include the fine old Borris House (059 977 1884). Anglers are well catered for on both the River Barrow and the Brandon lake and for those who are looking for a more active pursuit Borris offers cycling, canoeing, quad biking, clay pigeon shooting - or, for the really adventurous, Mount Leinster is a great spot for hang gliding.

Borris
PUB

M O'Shea
M O'Shea Borris Co Carlow
Tel: 059 97 73106

Halfway up the steep main street of Borris, this unspoilt old-world grocery-pub is well worth a visit. The old grocery section at the front links into a modern-day shop next door - a very practical arrangement that brings past and present together in a delightful way. Conversions and extensions towards the back allow for several larger rooms, where food can be served or music sessions held, and there's a paved area at the back for fine weather. Absolutely charming. Sandwiches, weekday lunches (12.30-2pm) available, snacks all day. Music every fortnight or so: "it's a bit random". Closed 25 Dec & Good Fri.

Borris
HOTEL

The Step House Hotel
66 Main Street Borris Co Carlow **Tel: 059 977 3209**
cait@thestephouse.com www.thestephouse.com

James and Cait Coady's lovely old house on the main street of this pretty village has offered some of the area's most appealing accommodation for many years and, further to a major redevelopment which has also taken in the family pub next door (in the Coady family for 5 generations), it has re-opened as The Step House Hotel. Cait has always had a good eye for interior design and the new hotel is stylishly decorated and furnished in upbeat period style, with a mixture of antiques and more contemporary touches. An impressive foyer sets the tone for handsome public areas that include a fine bar, 1808, (where excellent informal meals are served) with attractive terrace, and The Garden Room, a fine banqueting room that opens onto a landscaped garden and can also used at busy restaurant times, perhaps including Sunday lunch. Comfortable, very spacious bedrooms are elegantly furnished and include some with four-posters - all are furnished to a high standard with amenities including flat screen TV, tea/coffee facilities and lovely bathrooms with separate bath and shower; one room even has two bathrooms, one of them suitable for wheelchairs. The redevelopemnt of this fine old house has been accomplished beautifully, and is a great credit to the Coadys - who also own one of Ireland's finest classic pubs, Tynans Bridge Bar, in Kilkenny city. **Rooms 20** (2 suites, 2 family rooms, all no-smoking); not suitable for children. Pets permitted by arrangement. B&B €75pps, ss €10. Fishing, walking, garden. Closed 25 Dec. **The Cellar Restaurant:** The restaurant is in the kitchens of the old house and, spread through small interconnected rooms with archways and vaulted ceilings, it has great character and a sense of privacy. With natural lighting, sage green carpet, off white walls, and grape & vine stencils, it is a really pleasant space – and tables are promisingly set up with crisp white linen, smart tableware and fresh flowers. Head chef Alan Foley, formerly at Dublin's Chapter One restaurant (see entry), brings to this kitchen a philosophy of using the best local ingredients, organic where possible, in his classical cooking. His menus are short but full of interesting dishes, which are very well conceived and delivered. You might start with roast scallops, asparagus and lime with horseradish veloute (€14) for example, or a delicious open ravioli of veal with aubergine purée and parmesan glaze (€12), followed perhaps by Challons duck with pistachio pear, spinach purée and pepper & thyme jus (€30), or roast monkfish with parsnip mousseline, girolles and red wine sauce (€30), all perfectly cooked. Whilst, in the Guide's experience (shortly after opening), desserts might not quite live up to the promise of earlier dishes, the experience overall should be most enjoyable, enhanced by well-trained staff with a good knowledge of the menu and the short but well-chosen wine list. MasterCard, Visa, Laser. **Directions:** From main Carlow-Kilkenny road, take turning to Bagenalstown. 16km (8 miles) to Borris. ◇

CARLOW

Situated on the banks of the river Barrow about 80km from Dublin, Carlow (www.carlowtourism.com) is a friendly, bustling student town with good local transport and shopping facilities, plenty of sporting activities, banks, hotels and bars. The name Carlow is derived from the old Irish place name Ceatharloch, meaning 'four lakes' and today it is a youthful town, with a large student population attending the local Institute of Technology - recent growth has seen the population rise to about 20,000, approximately 4,000 of which are students. The countryside around the town is attractive, with many pretty towns and villages, scenic routes and places of historic interest to visit. Although not renowned as a dining destination in recent years, the town has a number of good informal eating places, notably the long-established **Lennon's Café Bar** (Tullow St; 059 913 1575) - which is closed for re-development as the Guide is going to press - and some new arrivals, including the popular **Rattlebag Café** (059 913 9568; see below) on Barrack Street - an ideal place to drop into for a snack (home baking is delicious), or maybe something more substantial. **Hennessy's Fine Foods** (059 913 2849) on Dublin Street, is a great deli and café, open all day Mon-Sat and now serving wonderful dinners on Sat. Garden lovers are spoilt for choice with four superb gardens all within 30km of Carlow town; Hardymount (Tullow; 059 915 1769); Ballon Garden (Ballon; 059 915 9144); Altamont (Tullow; 059 915 9444) and Heywood Gardens, Ballinakill, Co Laois; (057 873 3563). Golfers also have plenty to get excited about with three championship courses also within 30km [Carlow Golf Club (059 913 1695); Mount Wolseley Golf Club (Tullow; 059 915 1674) and Rathsallagh Golf Club (Dunlavin; 045 403 316)].
WWW.IRELAND-GUIDE.COM FOR ALL THE BEST PLACES TO EAT, DRINK & STAY

Carlow | # Barrowville Townhouse
GUESTHOUSE | Kilkenny Road Carlow Co Carlow **Tel: 059 914 3324**
| barrowvilletownhouse@eircom.net www.barrowville.com

Dermot and Anna Smyth's exceptionally comfortable guesthouse is just a few minutes walk from the town centre and has long been a favourite with discerning visitors to the area. It is a fine period house set in lovely gardens, and there is also a particularly pleasant and comfortable residents' drawing room, with an open fire and plenty to read. The house is immaculately maintained and bedrooms - which inevitably vary in size and character due to the age of the building - are comfortable and stylishly furnished with a mixture of antiques and fitted furniture, as well as direct dial phones, tea/coffee trays and television, and thoughtfully designed, well-finished bathrooms. Standards are consistently high and, continuing the tradition of the house under previous ownership, very good breakfasts are served in a handsome conservatory (complete with a large vine) overlooking the peaceful back garden. **Rooms 7** (2 shower only, all no-smoking). Not suitable for children. B&B €55pps, ss €20. Garden. Private parking (10). No pets. Closed 24-26 Dec. Amex, MasterCard, Visa, Laser. **Directions:** South side of Carlow town on the N9.

Carlow
RESTAURANT
Ⓝ Ⓡ

The Grill and Grape Steakhouse
Unit 1 54 Centaur Street Haymarket Carlow Co Carlow
Tel: 059 917 9717

This new steakhouse is in the ground floor of a modern complex of apartments and offices in Carlow Town. Attractively situated facing the River Barrow and a pleasant park area (well lit at night), the bright and airy restaurant has high glass walls on three sides allowing a view of swans on the river. An open grill kitchen with salad bar adds interest at the back, enlarged views of Carlow tourist attractions decorate the walls and discreet background music creates a relaxed ambience. Guests are greeted promptly and shown to a small bar area, or to tables set up simply but smartly. Menus offer a wide range of starters and salads, a few specials and fish dishes in addition to the main offering of grills, burgers and steaks - and a novel feature is the Hot Rock steaks, which are served to the table for you to cook yourself. Very good ingredients are seen at their best in simple dishes - classic starters like plump and delicious steamed mussels in white wine, or perfectly cooked scallop salad with crisp green asparagus and salad leaves. Typical main courses include perfectly cooked Tournedo Rossini (at a hefty €33.50), a large prime fillet with a generous slice of foie gras on top; or you might try the hot rock fillet (about €28.50), which is just seared and served on a volcanic rock heated to 420 degrees; you can then slice it and cook it as you like it in front of you; it comes with an excellent béarnaise sauce and side dishes of grilled onion steak (large slice of grilled Spanish onion) and baked potatoes. Only bought-in ice creams are offered for dessert, but there's an interesting wine list, and staff are knowledgeable about the menu and wine list, although some further training would improve service in general. Overall, although prices tend towards the special occasion bracket, an outing here should be a very enjoyable experience. Parking: Pay car park to the side of the restaurant. MasterCard, Visa, Laser. ◇

Carlow
RESTAURANT
Ⓝ Ⓡ

La Piccola Italia
144 Tullow Street Carlow Co Carlow **Tel: 059 914 0366**
elainemeaney@hotmail.com

Husband and wife team Adriano Lafrate and Elaine Meaney are cutting quite a dash with their informal modern Italian restaurant in Carlow Town. Simple and classy, with stripped wooden floors, exposed brick and cream walls, cream and white table linen, comfortable chairs and fresh flowers, it sets out to relax from the outset, with a bar in the front section giving it a welcoming, homely feel. A glass of complimentary Prosecco, along with a plate of fresh baked garlic and pesto foccacia, is served right away - and iced water quickly poured before guests are presented with the menus. The Italian menu, with explanations for all the dishes, offers a wide range of favourites: Antipasti dishes are followed by first course pasta, second courses of meat and fish, plus various pizzas. Finish with a delicious dessert and very good coffee. A carefully selected wine list offers both value and treats for those special occasions. A welcome addition to the Carlow dining scene, La Piccola Italia offers authentic Italian cooking based on fresh ingredients, a relaxing ambience, good service and good value: every town should have a place like this. **Seats 55**. Open daily, L Mon-Sat. 12-2.30pm; D Mon-Sat, 5-10pm (to 11pm Fri/Sat); Sun D 1-10pm. Early D Mon-Thurs, 5-7pm. Closed 25 Dec. MasterCard, Visa, Laser.

Carlow
CAFÉ
Ⓝ Ⓡ

Rattlebag Café
202 Barrack Street Carlow Co Carlow
Tel: 059 913 9568

This attractive cafe is pretty enough to make you stop the car when passing, and an ideal place to drop into for a snack - beautiful home baking for example - and coffee, or maybe something more substantial. It has a friendly atmosphere and is very popular with the local community. Specialities include a hot duck wrap with hoi sin sauce (which invariably attracts special praise), beef stroganoff, chicken and broccoli bake - and tasty light meals such as beef on a toasted bap with horseradish and caramelised onion. **Seats 36** (outdoors, 4); children welcome (high chair). Open Mon-Sat, 9am-5pm; Sun 11-4pm. Closed Easter, 25-26 Dec, 1 Jan. MasterCard, Visa, Laser. **Directions:** Located on main Dublin-Waterford Road.

Clonegal
RESTAURANT

Sha-Roe Bistro

Main Street Clonegal Co Carlow **Tel: 053 937 5636**
sha-roebistro@hotmail.com

The pretty and well-preserved village of Clonegal is on the borders of Wexford, Carlow and Wicklow, away from the main road to anywhere. But here, in a fine 18th century building, you will find chef Henry Stone, and his partner Stephanie Barrillier's small but beautifully appointed restaurant. A lovely sitting room acts as reception area, and simple décor throughout - warm cream walls, pale wooden floors, plain darkwood tables, comfortable chairs, the warm glow of night lights - provides a pleasing backdrop for the rather good paintings, which are for sale. Original features include a huge open stone fireplace, with a wood burning stove, there's a pretty courtyard used as a retreat for smokers, or for dining in fine weather - and a Chef's Table now allows parties of 4-6 to dine in the kitchen and observe the chefs at work. The warm welcome belies an impressive professionalism - this is a place where guests can relax in the confidence that everything will run smoothly. Deceptively simple menus based on seasonal foods might begin with grilled Dublin Bay Prawns (langoustines) with bisque risotto, or an Irish charcuterie plate served with red cabbage marmalade and crusty poppy seed bread, featuring artisan produce like venison salami, chorizo, air-dried Connemara beef and pork salami. Of the main courses, beef - matured for seven weeks - is a delight (a steak with flat mushrooms and oven-baked tomato, perhaps), also a gorgeously tender rump of Wexford lamb roasted with courgettes, aubergine, garlic and red onion. Although this is red meat country, seafood such as perfectly seared fresh scallops with a frothy chervil cream and wine sauce will also be offered, and there is always an an appealing vegetarian dish such as a richly delicious pea and asparagus risotto. Simple, perfectly cooked side dishes of seasonal vegetables might include sugar snap peas with sesame seeds and new potatoes with parsley butter, and many of the tempting desserts feature seasonal fruits - or you may want to try the local cheese plate. Suppliers are credited on the menu and a short but well chosen wine list includes a good fairly-priced house selection as well as a number of wines by the glass. Stephanie is an outstanding host and Henry - a talented and dedicated chef running a serious kitchen - has a well-earned reputation for enticing menus, faultless cooking and good value, making Sha-Roe well worth a detour. Space is limited so reservations are essential especially at weekends and for the €55.00 Chef's Table menu. After Sunday lunch, a visit to historical Huntington Castle (just around the corner) might be recommended. **Seats 25**. Not suitable for children after 8pm. D Wed-Sat, 6.30-9.30, a la carte; L Sun only, 12.30-3.30, set Sun L €32; house wine €19.50. Closed Sun D, Mon, Tue and Jan. MasterCard, Visa, **Directions:** Off N80 Enniscorthy-Carlow road, 8 km from Bunclody, on Main St.

Leighlinbridge
HOTEL•BAR•RESTAURANT

The Lord Bagenal Hotel

Main Street Leighlinbridge Co Carlow **Tel: 059 972 1668**
info@lordbagenal.com www.lordbagenal.com

The Lord Bagenal is beautifully situated on the River Barrow, with a fine harbour and marina right beside the inn and a pleasant riverside walk nearby. Although now a large hotel rather than the pub that is fondly remembered by many regular patrons, proprietors James and Mary Kehoe have taken care to retain some of the best features of the old building - notably the old end bar, with its open fire and comfortably traditional air - while incorporating new ideas. (A novel - and highly practical one - is a supervised indoor playroom, which is in the bar but behind glass so that, in time-honoured fashion, offspring can be seen and not heard). Bar meals include a popular lunchtime carvery/buffet which draws local diners, but it is the newer fine dining restaurant that will be of interest to visitors - and fortunately there is no need to travel far after dinner, as the bedrooms are just a few yards away. A large marbled foyer with a raised seating area and a fine selection of James Keogh's art collection, features a circular stairway with toughened glass steps leading to accommodation. All rooms are comfortably furnished in a modern hotel style with phones, TV and tea/coffee facilities, while the newer ones have extra features including flat screen TV and impressive bathrooms with roll tops baths - the spacious deluxe riverside rooms with views over the bridge and marina are especially desirable. Golf & equestrian nearby; fishing boats for hire. Marina (30 berths). Conferences/ banqueting (500/280). Garden, fishing, walking. Children welcome (under 3s free in parents' room, cot available free of charge, baby sitting arranged; playroom). No pets. **Rooms 39** (all en-suite, 1 for disabled). Lift, all day room service; B&B from €75 pps, ss €45.* Special breaks offered. **Waterfront Restaurant:** The restaurant is in a bright, high-ceilinged room opening on to a large covered deck area overlooking the marina and river. Set up smartly with generous well-spaced tables dressed classically in white linen, it has a partially open kitchen so diners can catch a glimpse of head chef George Keogh and his team at work - his style is contemporary, using well-sourced foods which he combines in an interesting and flavour-some way. Typical dishes from the repertoire might include a starter of breast of quail with wild mushroom risotto and salsify crisps, and a main course of confit belly of pork with apple, white asparagus and colcannon mash. George's good cooking, together with the renowned Lord Bagenal wine list and a very pleasing setting, makes a combination to savour. **Seats 90**. D Wed-Sat 6-10pm; à la carte. L Sun only, 12-4pm. House wine €18. Bar food 12-10pm daily. Closed 25 Dec. Amex, Diners, MasterCard, Visa, Laser. **Directions:** Just off the main N9 Dublin/Waterford Road in Leighlinbridge. 12km (8 m) Carlow/32 km (20 m) Kilkenny. ◇

Leighlinbridge   Mulberry's Restaurant
CAFÉ   Arboretum Garden Centre Kilkenny Road Leighlinbridge Co Carlow

                                 Tel: 059 972 1558 arboretum@eircom.net www.arboretum.ie

This pleasant self-service restaurant is in the garden centre at the Arboretum and offers an attractive selection of wholesome, freshly-prepared food. Tables are simply set up, but every second table has fresh flowers; in addition to a blackboard menu, a self-service counter presents an appetising display of salads and quick-serve dishes - everything is fresh and home-made with good ingredients, and there's a nice flair in the desserts (banoffi pie is a house speciality). Not really a wine place, but there's wine by the glass from the fridge, and a few quarter bottles, also fruit drinks (including apple juice) and minerals. A good place to break a journey, as there's a pleasant ambience and a browse around is relaxing. Ample parking (150). Wheelchair friendly. Children welcome. Wine licence. Open 9-5.50pm Mon-Sat, Sun 11-5pm. Closed 25 Dec & 1 Jan. Amex, Diners, MasterCard, Visa, Laser. **Directions:** From Carlow, take N9 towards Leighlinbridge.

St Mullins   Mulvarra House
B&B   St Mullins Graiguenamanagh Co Carlow **Tel: 051 424 936**
                                       info@mulvarra.com www.mulvarra.com

Noreen Ardill's friendly and well-maintained modern house is in a stunning location overlooking the River Barrow above the ancient and pictur-esque little harbour of St Mullins and, although it may seem unremarkable from the road, this relaxing place is full of surprises. Comfortably furnished bedrooms have balconies to take full advantage of views of the romantic Barrow Valley, for example, and not only is there the luxury of (limited) room service, but even a range of treat-ments (massage, mud wraps, refresher facials) to help guests unwind from the stresses of everyday life and make the most of this magical place. Noreen - a keen self-taught cook - prepares dinners for residents to enjoy in the dining room which also over-looks the river: quality produce, much of it local, is used in home-made soups, seafood paté, fresh Barrow salmon, stuffed loin of pork and Baileys bread & butter pudding, all of which are well-estab-lished favourites, although menus are varied to suit guests' preferences. Genuinely hospitable and reasonably priced, this is a tranquil place where the host wants guests to relax and make the most of every moment. Special breaks offered. **Rooms 5** (all en-suite & no-smoking, 1 family room); children welcome (under 3s free in parents' room; cot available without charge; baby sitting arranged). Room service (limited hours). B&B €40, ss €10. Residents D nightly, €30 (7.30pm, by reservation). House wine €20. Walking; fishing; treatments/mini spa (must be pre-booked). Pets permitted by arrange-ment. Garden. Closed Mid Dec-Mid Jan. MasterCard, Visa, Laser. **Directions:** 7km (4.5 m) from Graiguenamanagh; take R702 from Borris, turnright in Glynn; signposted from Glynn.

Tullow   Ballyderrin House
CAFÉ•B&B   Shillelagh Road Tullow Co Carlow **Tel: 059 915 2742**
                             ballyderrinhouse@eircom.net www.ballyderrin.com

The Holligan family offer comfortable B&B accommodation at their home near the market town of Tullow and, with Pamela Holligan's well-known cookery school on site, good food is sure to be part of the experience. Set on two acres and comfortably close to the capital for short breaks, the house dates back to 1869 and was extended in 2002 to provide all the modern comforts for guests. Log fires set a welcoming tone downstairs, and the individually decorated bedrooms have king-size beds and power showers. Home-grown and local produce features (in their cafe/shop as well as breakfast for residents); Pamela - who is Ballymaloe trained and a member of Euro-Toques - offers a range of day, evening and residential courses, which are held in a purpose-built cookery school for up to 20 students. (Contact Ballyderrin for details of courses.) There is plenty to do in the area including fishing in the River Slaney, golfing at the nearby championship course at Mount Wolseley, horse riding and visiting gardens, including Altamont, which is very close. **Rooms 4** (2 executive, 2 family, all shower only and no smoking); children welcome (under 5s free in parents' room, cots available free of charge). B&B €35 pps, ss €20; 25% discount for children. Dogs permitted (staying outside). Closed 25-26 Dec. MasterCard, Visa, Laser. **Directions:** From Tullow take R725 towards Shillelagh. About 0.5km (0.25m) from town on left hand side (well signed).

Tullow
HOTEL•RESTAURANT

Mount Wolseley Hotel Spa & Country Club

Tullow Co Carlow **Tel: 059 918 0100**
info@mountwolseley.ie www.mountwolseley.ie

In a lovely area of green and gently rolling hills and river valleys, the immaculate exterior of this modern hotel attached to the Christy O'Connor-designed championship course creates a good impression on arrival, a feeling quickly reinforced by friendly, helpful staff who set a welcoming tone that is noticeable throughout the hotel. You don't have to be a golfer to enjoy a visit here - the hotel also has special appeal for spa-lovers and it makes an attractive venue for weddings and other events - but it must help, as this is a picturesque and varied course to play. The hotel is only an hour and a half from Dublin and, with spacious public areas, well-finished accommodation and plenty of activities on offer both in the area and on site, it is understandably popular as a short break destination - and guests have the choice of fine dining in Frederick's Restaurant (see below) or eating more casually in the Aaron Lounge & Morrissey Bar. Conferences/Banqueting (750/550); Business centre, video conferencing, laptop-sized safes in bedrooms, free broadband wi/fi. Archery, clay pigeon shooting, cookery classes, garden visits nearby, golf (18), leisure centre (fitness room, pool, sauna, jacuzzi, steam room, spa), tennis, walking. Heli Pad. **Rooms 143** (3 suites, 8 junior suites, 4 executive, 4 family, 60 no smoking). B&B €75-115 pps; SS €30. Lift; 24-hr room service. Children welcome (under 12s free in parents' room, cot available free of charge, baby sitting arranged, playground, play room, kids club). **Frederick's Restaurant:** Named after Frederick York Wolseley, the original owner of the estate, the restaurant is in an airy dining room where smartly appointed tables with crisp white linen and fresh flowers provide an appropriate background for imaginative contemporary cooking backed up by helpful, well-informed service. Ever-popular braised shank of lamb is a speciality and the food standard is much higher than is usual in hotels. The set dinner menus offer good value, and there is live music on Friday and Saturday evenings. **Seats 180** (private room, 70, outdoors, 30); air conditioning; D 6.30-9.30pm. L daily in lounge, 12-9pm. Hotel closed 25-26 Dec. MasterCard, Visa, Laser. **Directions:** N7 from Dublin, left in Castledermot for Tullow. Take left at bridge, then right.

Tullow
RESTAURANT

Rathwood

Rath Tullow Co Carlow **Tel: 059 915 6285**
info@rathwood.com www.rathwood.com

This award-winning garden centre and shopping emporium near Tullow is a good place for a journey break (or even a day out) as, in addition to an exceptionally wide range of quality goods for garden and home (including classy gift items), there is good wholesome food available all day. It has always gone well beyond what might be expected in a garden centre, and the popular café has recently been completely revamped to emerge as a 'country restaurant ' with attractive outside seating areas on a heated patio, a new smoothie and juice bar, and even a function room. Menus based on seasonal fresh local Irish produce are quite extensive, but good home baking remains the strength and it would be a mistake to leave without a taste of their sinful Pavlova or Black Forest gateau - or perhaps a juicy apple tart or healthy carrot cake. Vegetarians and coeliacs are catered for (try the gluten-free lemon mousse), and they can supply cakes for special occasions too. A useful place to know about. **Seats 56** (+50 in conservatory); wheelchair friendly; children welcome (high chair, childrens' menu, baby changing facilities); country walks, outdoor play area, on site train. Open 7 days: Mon-Sat 9.30am-5pm (including bank hols); Sun 11-5; L daily 12-2.30 (to 3pm Sun); set 3 course L €25; Sun L €25; house wine (half bottle) €9.95. Closed 3 days at Christmas. MasterCard, Visa, Laser. **Directions:** Just over an hour from Dublin, take Blessington or Naas to Tullow road - well signed on R725 to Shillelagh.

COUNTY CAVAN

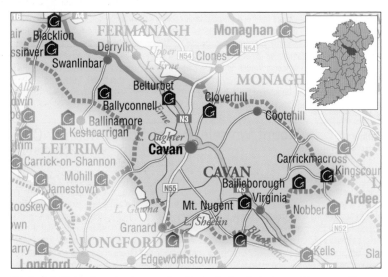

This is one of Ireland's most watery counties. It's classic drumlin landscape, interwoven with more lakes than they know what to do with. But the very fact that the meandering waterways dictate the way of the roads means that much of Cavan is hidden. In today's intrusive world, this is a virtue. It is a place best discovered by the discerning visitor. Much of it has quiet and utterly rural charm, seemingly remote. But it isn't so very far from Belfast or Dublin, and noted for its unique entrepreneurial flair.

Yet if you take your time wandering through this green and silver land - particularly if travelling at the leisurely pace of the deservedly renowned Shannon-Erne Waterway which has joined Ireland's two greatest lake and river systems - then you'll become aware that this is a place of rewardingly gentle pleasures. And you'll have time to discover that it does have its own mountain, or at least it shares the 667m peak of Cuilcagh with neighbouring Fermanagh.

No ordinary mountain, this - it has underground streams which eventually become the headwaters of the lordly River Shannon, while 47 kms to the southeast is the source of the River Erne near Bellanagh – it eventually flows northwest, so Ireland's greatest rivers are closely interwined, yet only connected by canal.

Cavan is much more extensive than is popularly imagined, for in the northeast it has Shercock with its own miniature lake district, while in its southeast it takes in all of Lough Ramor at the charming lakeside village of Virginia. It also shares Lough Sheelin, that place of legend for the angler, with Westmeath and Meath, while in the far northwest its rugged scenery hints at Donegal. And always throughout its drumlin heartlands you can find many little Cavan lakes which, should the fancy take you, can be called your own at least for the day that's in it.

Local Attractions and Information

Bailieboro	Tourism Information	042 966 6666
Ballyjamesduff	Cavan County Museum	049 854 4070
Ballyjamesduff	International Pork Festival (June)	049 854 4242 / 087 632 0042
Belturbet	Tourist Office	049 952 2044
Cavan town	Cavan Crystal	049 433 1800
Cavan town	Tourist Information	049 433 1942
Cootehill	Maudabawn Cultural Centre	049 555 9504
Cavan	Cavan Equestrian Centre	049 433 2017
Mullagh	Lakeview Gardens	046 924 2480
Shannon-Erne	Waterway (Ballinamore-Ballyconnell)	071 964 5124

Cavan Area

Radisson SAS Farnham Estate Hotel

HOTEL•RESTAURANT

Farnham Estate Cavan Co Cavan **Tel: 049 437 7700**
info.farnham@radissonsas.com www.farnhamestate.com

A winding driveway through lush parkland and a maturing golf course brings you to the dramatic entrance of Farnham Estate Hotel: the reception is in a giant glass atrium linking the classical building dating from 1810 to the striking 21st century extension - impressive by any standards although, after set-down, residents are asked to park several hundred metres from the entrance and use a courtesy bus which, while it leaves the front of the house clear of parking, may be less than amusing in bad weather. Although not univer-sally admired (especially by those who remember the old house as it was), most visitors see the hotel as an inspired marriage of the ancient and modern, and it has a warm, friendly atmosphere. There are three stunning drawing rooms in the house itself, and The Wine Goose Cellar Bar is atmospheri-cally situated underground, in tunnels. The old house also has eight suites which have been cleverly restored with a sensitive eye to the past and some real modern flair: traditional fabrics cover exotic seats and old-fashioned shapes are given quirky colours and patterns, an idea which has been over-done in Ireland recently, but this is an early example and it was achieved with a sure eye and quality materials. Rooms in the extension are sleek and modern and, although some rooms would benefit from sheer curtains for daytime privacy, they are very comfortable, with huge beds and wide-ranging facilities including WI/FI internet access, robes, irons, hairdryer, mini bar, coffee making facilities, simple heat control and complicated interactive flat screen TV & radio; fashion-led bathrooms may lack natural light (and insulation) but have both bath and shower. The long, low design of the hotel helps it to merge into its surroundings more comfortably, but this means long corridors which attract inevitable comparison with airports - if this could be problem, ask for a room near the reception area when booking. The 1,250 acre estate has a private lake for fishing, seven kilometres of walks (no dogs allowed though) and a partially constructed 18-hole golf course. The health spa offers nineteen treatment rooms, a thermal suite, a relaxation room, an indoor-outdoor infinity pool and its own restaurant. This is an appealing venue for business, conferences and weddings - The Redwood Suite, which has ten meeting rooms, can take up to 380 delegates theatre-style or seat 220 for a function. Conferences/Banqueting (380/220); business centre, secretarial services, video conferencing; free broadband wi/fi; laptop-sized safes in bedrooms. Archery, croquet, clay pigeon shooting, coarse fishing, equestrian nearby, golf (18), fitness room, swimming pool, sauna, steam room, spa (treat-ment rooms, hair dressing), meditation. Heli Pad. **Rooms 158** (8 suites in the old house, 4 new suites, 120 no smoking, 50 ground floor, 8 for disabled.) Children welcome (under 17s free in parents' room, cots available free of charge, baby sitting arranged.) Lifts; 24 hr room service; no pets. B&B €100-120pps, ss €95. **Botanica Restaurant:** Beside the Botanica Bar on the upper level of the impressive lobby/atrium area, smart casual is the tone in this spacious dining room, which is very attractively situated overlooking the lawns and mature trees around the old house. Breakfast (the good spread typical of Radisson hotels), lunch and dinner are all served here and in its evening guise it's the most sophisticated of several enjoyable dining experiences offered at the hotel, all of which, including The Pear Tree Restaurant at the Health Spa, have botanical themes inspired by the estate's abundant plant life. Menus offer many of the old favourites like steak and crispy duckling, albeit dressed up for dinner, and also a sprinkling of less usual choices that might be based on produce from the estate - although, disappointingly (especially as there are polytunnels in use and big plans for the kitchen gardens), menus offer no information on the provenance of ingredients. While sophis-ticated, the cooking is not unduly complicated, and flavoursome food and friendly staff make for an enjoyable dining experience. A vegetarian menu is also offered, and a balanced wine list offers half a dozen house wines, a similar number of half bottles, a pair of each of organic and de-alcoholised wines, and plenty to choose from under €30. **Seats 180** (private room, 40); children welcome; L served daily 12.30-3, D served daily 7-9.30. Set L €35, Gourmet D about €55, D also à la carte. House wine €22. Open all year. Amex, MasterCard, Visa, Laser. **Directions:** From Dublin, N3 to Cavan town, then take the Killeshandra Road for 3km to the gates of the estate. The hotel is a 1.7km drive from the gates.

Cloverhill
RESTAURANT WITH ROOMS

The Olde Post Inn

Cloverhill Co Cavan **Tel: 047 55555**
gearoidlynch@eircom.net www.theoldepostinn.com

Gearoid and Tara Lynch's restaurant is in an old stone building in a neatly landscaped garden which served as a post office until 1974 and, since then, has made an attractive and popular inn. Gearoid is a talented chef and, with Tara managing front of house, they make a good team - since their arrival here in 2002 they have earned a reputation beyond the immediate area for fine food and genuine hospitality. There's a pleasant rural atmosphere about the place, with a bar to enjoy your pre/post-prandial drinks and an old-world style throughout, with dark beams and simple wooden furniture - but, comfortably rustic as it may seem (and all the more welcome as the continuing rush to shiny modernism threatens to sweep away the oddly characterful throughout Ireland), that is far from the case in the kitchen, and elegantly-appointed tables with crisp white linen and gleaming glasses give a hint of the treats to come. Gearoid's route to Cloverhill has included time in some fine establishments - at least one of which lives on here, in a house speciality: 'Le Coq Hardi' chicken breast (stuffed with potato, apple, bacon & herbs, wrapped in bacon and served with an Irish whiskey sauce). A committed Euro-Toques chef, Gearoid sources ingredients with great care and shows respect for regional and seasonal foods, and the excellent cooking is made all the more enjoyable by the friendly, helpful local staff. The Olde Post Inn was our Newcomer of the Year in 2004. Ample parking. **Seats 80** (private room, 25); children welcome (high chair, baby changing facilities) toilets wheelchair accessible. D Tue-Sun, 6.30-9pm (Sun to 8.30), L Sun only, 12.30-2.30. Set D about €53, also à la carte, Gourmet Menu €75. Set Sun L about €28. Closed Mon. **Accommodation:** While not especially luxurious or large, the seven en-suite rooms at the inn are convenient for diners who don't wish to travel far from the dinner table, and most have full baths. **Rooms 7** (2 shower only, 1 family room, all no smoking); children welcome (under 4s free in parents' room, baby sitting can be arranged, cot available free of charge). No pets. B&B €50 pps, ss €10. Closed 24-27 Dec. Amex, MasterCard, Visa, Laser. **Directions:** 9km (6 m) north of Cavan town: take N54 at Butlersbridge, 2.5km (2 m) on right in Cloverhill village.

KINGSCOURT

An active market town, in the south east corner of Cavan, visitors can enjoy exploring the beautiful countryside of nearby Lough an Leagh Mountain or the Dun na Ri forest park. Kingscourt offers good coarse fishing at the local lakes such as Evrey and Greaghlone or the golfer can play 9 holes at Cabra Golf Course (028 966 7714). Nearby at Muff Rock, an annual horse fair is held on the 12th of August - it is the oldest horse fair in Ireland.

Kingscourt
HOTEL

Cabra Castle Hotel & Golf Club

Kingscourt Co Cavan **Tel: 042 966 7030**
sales@cabracastle.com www.cabracastle.com

Renamed Cabra Castle in the early 19th century, this impressive hotel is set amidst 100 acres of grounds, with lovely views over the Cavan countryside. Although initially imposing, with its large public rooms and antique furnishings (and even suits of armour in the foyer), the atmosphere is relaxing. The bedrooms vary in size and outlook, but all are comfortable and individually decorated; accommodation includes some ground floor rooms suitable for less able guests and, in addition to rooms in the main building, there are some rooms in an extension which are particularly suitable for families - and six cottages have recently been built, adding 27 rooms and allowing a self-catering option for some guests. There are also some romantic beamed rooms in a converted courtyard, providing modern comforts without sacrificing character. The combination of formal background and easy ambience make this a good venue for private and business functions; it is popular for both weddings and conferences (250/500 respectively). Conferences (500); business centre; broadband wi/fi. **Rooms 86** (2 suite, 2 junior suites, 26 shower only, 4 family rooms, 40 no smoking, 1 for disabled); children welcome (under 2s free in parents' room, cots available without charge, baby sitting arranged); pets permitted by arrangement. All day room service (7am-10pm). B&B €118pps, ss €25. Tennis, beauty salon, helipad; Equestrian, fishing and garden visits nearby. Golf (9), walking, massage, hair dressing, boutique. Off-season value breaks. Closed at Christmas. MasterCard, Visa, Laser **Directions:** Dublin - N2 - Navan - R162 - Kingscourt.

Kingscourt
CHARACTER PUB

Gartlans Pub

Main Street Kingscourt Co Cavan
Tel: 042 966 7003

This pretty thatched pub is a delightfully unspoilt example of the kind of grocery/pub that used to be so typical of Ireland, especially in country areas. Few enough of them remain, now that the theme pub has moved in, but this one is real, with plenty of local news items around the walls, a serving hatch where simple groceries can be bought, all served with genuine warmth and hospitality. The Gartlans have been here since 1911 and they have achieved the remarkable feat of appearing to make time stand still. Closed 25 Dec & Good Fri. **Directions:** On the main street in Kingscourt village.

Mountnugent
FARMHOUSE
R

Ross House

Mountnugent Co Cavan **Tel: 049 854 0218**
rosshouse@eircom.net www.ross-house.com

In mature grounds on the shores of Lough Sheelin, Peter and Ursula Harkort's characterful old house enjoys an excellent location and offers a good standard of accommodation at a modest price. Bedrooms, which are distinctly continental in style, have telephone, TV and tea/coffee trays and some unusual features: three have their own conservatories, four have fireplaces (help yourself to logs from the shed) and most have continental-style showers. Peace and relaxation are the great attraction, and there's a fine choice of activities at hand: a pier offers boats (and engines) for fishermen to explore the lake, there's safe bathing from a sandy beach, and also tennis. Ross House is also an equestrian centre, with all facilities including riding lessons, cross country riding, shows and breeding, outdoor arena and warm-up area and the most recent addition, completed in 2008, a very large indoor arena (60 x 40m). Ulla cooks for everyone, making packed lunches, sandwiches, high tea and a 4-course dinner (€22; wine list from about €11). **Rooms 6** (all en-suite & shower only); children welcome (playground, cot available, €5); pets permitted. B&B €38 pps, ss €10. SC discretionary. Equestrian, fishing (fly fishing & Coarse), tennis. Open all year. MasterCard, Visa, Laser. **Directions:** From Dublin Airport: M50, then N3 to Navan-Kells- Mountnugent. 5 Km from Mountnugent, signposted.

R

VIRGINIA

This attractive town is on the the northern side of beautiful Lough Ramor, which has wooded shores and a great reputation for coarse fishing. It makes a good base for a fishing holiday, or simply exploring an attractive and unspoilt part of the country. For travellers between Northern Ireland and Dublin, it's the ideal spot to take a break - up at **The Park Hotel** (049 854 6100), perhaps, which has character and very friendly staff and is set in well-maintained parkland and its own golf course and you can get a bite in the bar then take a stroll along the shore. Another option, in a waterside position right on the Dublin road, is the **Lakeside Manor Hotel** (049 854 8200; www.lakesidemanor.ie) which has been earning compliments for good food lately - but don't expect a manor house. The championship courses at Headfort Golf Club (046 928 2001) and The Nuremore Hotel & Country Club (042 966 1438) are within 30km of Virginia. Nearby, Loughcrew Historic Gardens (049 854 1356) is an intriguing place to spend a couple of hours and there are several more notable gardens within 20-30km of Virginia including - Rockfield House (Navan; 046 905 2135); Grove Gardens (Kells; 046 943 4276); Tullynally Castle & Gardens (Castlepollard; 044 61159) and Ballinlough Castle (046 943 3234).
WWW.IRELAND-GUIDE.COM FOR ALL THE BEST PLACES TO EAT, DRINK & STAY

COUNTY CLARE

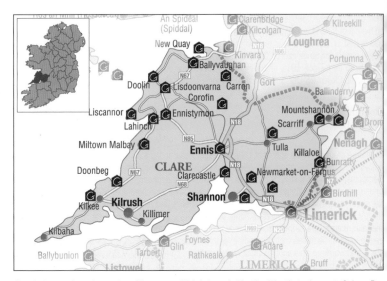

Clare is impressive, a larger-than-life county which is bounded by the Atlantic to the west, Galway Bay to the north, the River Shannon with Lough Derg to the east, and the Shannon Estuary to the south. Yet it's typical of Clare that, even with its boundaries marked on such a grand scale, there is always something extra added.

Thus the Atlantic coasts includes the astonishing and majestic Cliffs of Moher. Close under them in dangerous water is the majestic breaker known as Aileens, the surfer's Nirvana. Less challenging nearby, but still at the top of world standards, is one of Ireland's greatest surfing beaches nearby at Lahinch, which is also a golfer's Nirvana. As for that Galway Bay coastline, it is where The Burren, the fantastical North Clare moonscape of limestone which is home to so much unexpectedly exotic flora, comes plunging spectacularly towards the sea around the attractive village of Ballyvaughan.

To the eastward, Lough Derg is one of Ireland's most handsome lakes, but even amidst its generous beauty, we find that Clare has claimed one of the most scenic lake coastlines of all. As for the Shannon Estuary, well, Ireland may have many estuaries, but needless to say the lordly Shannon has far and away the biggest estuary of all. It is the port of call for the largest freight ships visiting Ireland, and on its northern shore is Shannon Airport. Yet the Estuary is also home to a numerous and remarkable friendly dolphin population, with Kilrush the most popular port for dolphin-watching.

The county town of Ennis has seen steady expansion, yet it is managing itself so well within its new bypass that it is the holder of a Gold Medal in the National Tidy Towns competition. Places like Ennistimon, Milltown Malbay, Corofin and Mountshannon - they all have a very human and friendly dimension. For this is a county where the human spirit defines itself as being very human indeed, in the midst of scenic effects which at times seem to border on the supernatural.

Local Attractions and Information

Ballyvaughan	Aillwee Cave	065 707 7036
Bunratty	Bunratty Castle & Folk Park C/O Shannon Heritage Centre	061 360788
Cliffs of Moher	Tourist Information	065 708 1171
Corofin	Clare Heritage Centre	065 683 7955
Corofin	Clare Heritage Centre	065 683 7955
Ennis	Tourist Centre	065 682 8366
Killimer	Killimer-Tarbert Ferry	065 53124
Kilrush	Kilrush Heritage Centre	065 905 1577
Kilrush	Scattery Island Interpretive Centre	065 905 2139
Kilrush	Vandeleur Walled Garden	065 905 1760

Quin	Craggaunowen (Celts & Living Past)	061 360788
Quin	Knappogue Castle	061 360788
Shannon Airport	Tourist Information	061 471664

BALLYVAUGHAN

This attractive little port is best known for its major attraction, the Aillwee Cave but, as it is in a leafy valley with a wide range of amenities close at hand, it makes a comfortable base for exploring the Burren. The Burren is a unique rocky landscape famed for the rare flowers and fauna that grow in profusion over the apparently barren limestone pavements. Ballyvaughan is surrounded by megalithic tombs such as Poulnabrone dolmen, Celtic ring forts, medieval churches and castles. The area is a haven for walkers and, in particular, hill walkers. Hotel accommodation is available in the village at **Hylands Burren Hotel** (065 707 7037; www.hylandsburren.com), who offer all day food (speciality: seafood) and off-season breaks. Of the pubs, the traditional **Monks Bar** (065 707 7059), on the pier, has open fires and, at its best, a name for good seafood, while those with a yen for a real old pub of character should drop in for a jar at nearby **O'Loclainn's**, family-run for generations. New to the village is **The Soda Parlour Coffee House and Crêperie** (Wed-Sun 10-5): nice menu of sweet and savoury crepes at fair prices plus enticing ice cream (sundae style). Outside Ballyvaughan (3km from the village on Lisdoonvarna Corkscrew Hill road), Cathleen Connole's **Burren Wine and Food** (065 707 7046), is a long-established wine and fine food shop which now opens for lunch, May-Sep; a delightful mother and daughter operation, it offers herbs and saladings from their own garden, local cheese etc. (including a magnificent St. Tola Feta cheese) plus excellent pizzas using local products. The local farmers market is held in the village hall car park on Saturday mornings (May to October). The nearest championship golf courses are the recently redeveloped Galway Bay Golf Club (Oranmore; 091 790 711) and Lahinch Golf Club (065 708 1003).
WWW-IRELAND-GUIDE.COM FOR ALL THE BEST PLACES TO EAT, DRINK & STAY

Ballyvaughan | **Aillwee Cave**
CAFÉ

Ballyvaughan Co Clare **Tel: 065 707 7036**
info@aillweecave.ie www.aillweecave.ie

Visitors to this 2-million-year-old cave will see more than the amazing illuminated tunnels and waterfalls, for there is also much of interest to food lovers. Cheese-making demonstrations show how the local Burren Gold cheese is made and, even if the process is in a quiet phase at the time of a visit, there is still plenty to see - and buy, thanks to a well-stocked food shop; free tastings of the cheeses and home-made fudge are available here, and other goodies to take home, including home-made preserves. Just inside the entrance to the cave there is a souvenir shop with a good book section (including travel and cookery books of Irish interest), and a café serving inexpensive, wholesome fare - typically baked potatoes with Burren Gold cheese. Fast food (coffee, panini etc) is also available - and there is now a garden centre as well as a mountain trail "guaranteed to work up an appetite". *The Liscannor Rock Shop is a sister enterprise. Children welcome. Café **Seats 60.** Wheelchair access (to building only, not the cave). Meals all day Mon-Sun (10-6.30). Closed mornings in Dec; Christmas. Diners, MasterCard, Visa, Laser. **Directions:** 4.5 km (3 miles) south of Ballyvaughan.

Ballyvaughan | **An Fulacht Fia**
RESTAURANT

Coast Road Ballyvaughan Co Clare **Tel: 065 707 7300**
reservations@anfulachtfia.com www.anfulachtfia.com

In a stunning location on the edge of Ballyvaughan village, this purpose-built new restaurant has spectacular views of Galway Bay. Owned and built by a local man, John Console, it is attached to a substantial two-storey house finished in local granite - and surrounded by a wonderful natural Burren landscape garden (An Fulacht Fia means 'Cooking Pit'). The restaurant is a delight: the entrance hall, which doubles as a reception and bar, is stunning with a welcoming contemporary look; a modern gas fire is a striking feature with its dramatic cherry red chimney piece reaching to a high apex above you – and, surrounding another fire at end of the dining room, is a huge granite relief of a Galway hooker. Luxurious embossed curtains and high velvet seats in pale green and cherry red are impressive, seen against linen cloths and sparkling ware highlighted by subtle recessed lighting. Head chef Rob Day uses locally supplied ingredients from the Burren area, which are sustainable, traceable and organic. His menus offer a choice of eight starters - a warm salad of wild mushroom and spinach, with pesto, parmesan crostini and sundried tomato perhaps (€7.25); or Atlantic scallops, pan-seared with grilled fennel and orange salad (€10) and twelve main courses, such as shank of Burren lamb, slow-cooked on the bone, served with fondant potato, red pepper purée and thyme jus (€26) and, for vegetarians, a Thai laksa in a chilli and lemongrass scented coconut broth, served with fragrant jasmine rice (€19.95). Finish, perhaps, with a refreshing yoghurt strawberry mousse, with mango & passion fruit sorbet & vanilla biscuit. A long and varied wine list starts at €22 for Rose d'Anjou A,C. "Premiere". Under the direction of restaurant manager Siobhan Forde, this is a welcoming restaurant and promises to be a great asset to the area. In summer they are open every day and serve early bird and Sunday lunch. Out of season they plan to open 4 days a week. Open 7 days from 5.30pm; Sun 1.30-9pm; early bird menu 5.30-7pm €24.95. MasterCard, Visa, Laser. **Directions:** On the coast road in Ballyvaughan.

Ballyvaughan
GUESTHOUSE

Drumcreehy House

Ballyvaughan Co Clare **Tel: 065 707 7377**
info@drumcreehyhouse.com www.drumcreehyhouse.com

Just along the shore road towards Galway, Armin and Bernadette Grefkes' attractive purpose-built guesthouse makes a comfortable and moderately-priced base for a break in this lovely area and is a delightful place to stay. The furnishing style is a mixture of old and new with antiques and newer country furnishings blending well; front bedrooms have sea views across Galway Bay while those at the back have a pleasant outlook over the Burren - and all have phones and television. There's also a comfortable sitting room with an open fire available for guests' use and everything is spotless and full of character. A very good breakfast includes local cheese, from Annaliese Bartelink in Kilnaboy, gravadlax, smoked salmon and unusual hot dishes such as herrings with horseradish sauce as well as the more usual options. Free broadband wi/fi. Beach nearby (10 minute walk). Garden. **Rooms 10** (all en-suite & no smoking, 2 family, 2 ground floor). Children welcome (cot available without charge, baby sitting arranged); Pets permitted. B&B €55 pps, ss €16. Closed 24-26 Dec. MasterCard, Visa, Laser. **Directions:** 2 km (1 mile) outside Ballyvaughan village - N67 in Galway direction; house on right.

Ballyvaughan
RESTAURANT•COUNTRY HOUSE

Gregans Castle Hotel

Ballyvaughan The Burren Co Clare **Tel: 065 707 7005**
stay@gregans.ie www.gregans.ie

Gregans Castle has a long and interesting history, going back to a tower house, or small castle, which was built by the O'Loughlen clan (the region's principal tribe) between the 10th and 17th centuries, and is still intact. The present house dates from the late 18th century, and has been added to many times; it has been run as a country house hotel by the Haden family since 1976, currently by Simon Haden and his wife Freddie, who have been proprietors since Simon's parents retired in 2003. Surrounded by trees and gardens, Gregans is an oasis of warmth, comfort and hospitality set in the lunar landscape of the surrounding Burren, and can be seen from miles around. It is a place with a uniquely serene atmosphere. Peace and quiet are the dominant themes: spacious rooms with lovely countryside views are luxuriously furnished with understated contemporary style by Freddie - and deliberately left without the worldly interference of television. Yet this luxurious hotel is not too formal or at all intimidating; non-residents are welcome to drop in for lunch or afternoon tea in the Corkscrew Bar - named after a nearby hill road which, incidentally, provides the most scenic approach to Ballyvaughan. In fine weather guests can sit out beside the Celtic Cross rose garden and watch patches of sun and shade chasing across the hills. In the morning, allow time to enjoy an excellent breakfast - a delicious buffet set up with fresh juices and fruits, organic cereals, freshly baked bread, home-made preserves and local produce including Burren Smokehouse organic smoked salmon, Burren Gold organic cheese and Limerick ham; the menu of hot dishes reads very simply - but the secret is in the quality ingredients, which sing with flavour. Small Conferences/Banqueting (15/65); free broadband wi/fi. Croquet, cycling, falconry, gardens, walking, wine courses. Golf and garden visits nearby. Pets permitted staying in outhousekennel. Children welcome (no concessions, but cot available, €20, baby sitting arranged). No pets. All day room service. No Pets. **Rooms 21** (3 premier suites, 3 junior suites, 7 ground floor) B&B €117.50 pps; ss €75. No SC. **The Dining Room** is well placed to take advantage of the lovely views over the Burren (where there can be very special light effects as the sun sets over Galway Bay on summer evenings) and, although it has always been elegantly furnished in keeping with the rest of the house, returning guests will find that Freddie has recently been casting her magic wand over this area too. The result is a contemporary classic, very calm and serene in beautiful tones; the atmosphere remains intimate yet feels fresh - a fitting setting for fine dinners that are often accompanied by a pianist or, more unusually, a hammer dulcimer. Gifted new head chef, Mickael Viljanen, cooks in a modern European style, and continues the commitment to using local and organic produce, when available, which has always been a key feature of Gregans Castle - all fish is caught locally around Galway Bay, and Burren lamb and beef come from local butchers. A skilled and creative chef, Mickael offers exciting menus, which include a daily changing nine course Tasting Menu (excellent value at €75, with half board guests only charged a €20 supplement) in addition to a seriously tempting à la carte: begin, perhaps, with Foie Fras x 3 (a petit pot with Madeira jelly; pressed terrine with cherry compôte, with almond foam), followed by a fish dish such as braised turbot with turbot cannelloni, cèpe sabayon and spinach - or, maybe, the perennial favourite, Burren lamb: a rack and shoulder, perhaps, served with a vegetable broth. Seriously seductive desserts might include a late summer berry tart with vanilla mousseline cream and local wild raspberries, and there is always a fine selection of local cheeses, with home-made biscuits. The wine list is an interesting read and includes an impressive selection of organic and biodynamic wines, leading off with the excellent Spanish house wines. Dinner is a treat at Gregans Castle - and people travel from miles around to enjoy it - but they also offer an attractive short à la carte lunch menu (very nicely served in The Corkscrew Bar) and delicious Afternoon Teas too. **Seats 50** (private room, 36); unsuitable for children under 5 years after 8pm. D daily, 6-8.30pm; set 3 course D €39, also à la carte. House wines from €25. Pianist 2 days a week. Short à la carte lunch is available in the Corkscrew Bar, 12-2.30pm daily. Afternoon Tea, 2.30-5pm daily. Hotel closed 1 Dec-12 Feb. Amex, MasterCard, Visa, Laser. **Directions:** On N67, 5km south of Ballyvaughan.

Ballyvaughan
GUESTHOUSE

Rusheen Lodge

Knocknagrough Ballyvaughan Co Clare **Tel: 065 707 7092**
rusheen@iol.ie www.rusheenlodge.com

John and Rita McGann swapped houses with their daughter Karen, who now runs Rusheen Lodge to the high standards for which it has always been well known, and they live next door so there's no shortage of experienced hands nearby for very busy times - and, as it was John McGann's father, Jacko McGann, who discovered the Aillwee Cave, an immense network of caverns and waterfalls under the Burren which is now a major attraction in the area, the McGanns understand better than most the popularity of Ballyvaughan as a visitor destina-

tion. Fresh flowers in both the house and garden create a riot of colour in contrast to the overall green-greyness of the surrounding Burren, suggesting an oasis in a wilderness - which is just what Rusheen Lodge aims to provide. Constant refurbishment is the policy here and accommodation includes a 3-room executive suite, which was quite recently added and has proved very popular; all of the generously proportioned, well-appointed bedrooms have phones, tea/coffee trays, TV, trouser press and good bathrooms. All this, plus spacious public rooms, good food and warm hospitality make Rusheen Lodge a particularly pleasant place to stay. While evening meals are not provided, the pubs and restaurants of Ballyvaughan are close by and breakfast - whether traditional Irish or continental - is a major feature of a stay. **Rooms 9** (2 suites, 1 executive, 2 family, 3 ground floor, all no-smoking). B&B €50pps, ss€20. Children welcome (under 3s free in parents' room, cot available without charge, baby sitting arranged); free broadband wi/fi; no pets; garden. Closed mid Nov-mid Feb. MasterCard, Visa, Laser. **Directions:** 0.75 km from Ballyvaughan village on the N67, Lisdoonvarna road.

BUNRATTY

With its famous medieval Castle and Folk Park, Bunratty attracts vast numbers of visitors and there is plenty of competition here when it comes to accommodation, restaurants and, of course, entertainment: of the hotels, the best known is the **Bunratty Castle Hotel** (061 478700; www.bunrattycastlehotel.com), a modern hotel on a rise overlooking Bunratty Castle and Folk Park which is attractively designed to reflect its Georgian origins. Both Blarney Woollen Mills and Avoca Handweavers (061 364029) have outlets at Bunratty (the latter due for reconstruction after a fire at the time of going to press) and, with wholesome daytime café food available, this can be a good place to break a journey. There is a farmers market nearby in Shannon every Friday (Skycourt Shopping Centre) and excellent championship golf is available on the parkland courses of Dromoland Castle Golf Club (061 368 444) and Adare Manor Hotel & Golf Resort (061 395 044). **WWW.IRELAND-GUIDE.COM FOR ALL THE BEST PLACES TO EAT, DRINK & STAY**

Bunratty

RESTAURANT•CHARACTER PUB

Durty Nelly's

Bunratty Co Clare **Tel: 061 364 861**

www.durtynellys.ie

Although often seriously over-crowded with tourists in summer, this famous and genuinely characterful old pub in the shadow of Bunratty Castle somehow manages to provide cheerful service and above-average food to the great numbers who pass through its doors. All-day fare is served downstairs in the bar (all day, noon-11pm) and the Oyster Restaurant (lunch and dinner); upstairs there is a more exclusive restaurant, The Loft, open in the evening only (5.30-10pm). Both areas offer à la carte menus. There was a change of ownership recently but, at the time of the Guide's last visit, all seemed much the same as usual. Closed 25 Dec, Good Fri. Amex, MasterCard, Visa, Laser. **Directions:** Beside Bunratty Castle.

Bunratty

RESTAURANT

The Red Door Restaurant

Bunratty House Hill Road Bunratty Co Clare **Tel: 061 466 993**

www.thereddoorrestaurant.com

This semi-basement restaurant is at the back of the Bunratty estate, overlooking Bunratty Park and the castle; as you drive through tall iron gates and up the drive to Bunratty House, you can't miss the smart banner signs proclaiming that you've arrived at The Red Door Restaurant. This hospitable and characterful restaurant's will to please quickly attracted a loyal following. You can sit outside in summer and there's a bar as you enter, with sofas to relax in and views across the park. The labyrinth of small rooms in the downstairs restaurant are well furnished, with red and cream brick walls subtly lit, and comfortable leather dining chairs, creating an intimate, relaxed ambience. The Early Bird menu offers hearty main courses such as roast stuffed pork steak; lunch is a similarly generous affair offering dishes like well-made fishcakes (with identifiable pieces of fish in them, plus the odd shrimp), with hand-cut chips and home-made tartare sauce - or big, meaty sausages with nicely made gravy. The dinner menu is more ambitious, and a note informs diners that the beef is raised nearby and sourced from a local butcher. A short wine list, grouped by country, is well-chosen and reasonably priced. L & D Tue-Sun, 12.30-3.30 & 5.30-9.30. Early bird D 5.30-6.45pm. Closed Mon. **Directions:** Behind Bunratty Castle, at Bunratty House - enter tall tall iron gates & follow signs. ◊

Carron

CAFÉ

Burren Perfumery Tea Rooms

Carron Co Clare **Tel: 065 708 9102**

burrenperfumery@eircom.net www.burrenperfumery.com

When touring Clare you will be pleased to find this charming spot - the perfumery is beautifully laid out, with a herb garden (where many native plants are grown - and later used in the organic herbal teas), pleasing old buildings and lovely biodynamic scents. The little tea rooms are beside the distillation room, where essential oils are extracted in a traditional still, and open on to a courtyard opposite the perfumery shop. Although small and simple, the tea rooms are pretty, with floral waxed tablecloths, fresh flowers and cups and saucers all creating a happy mismatch of pastels - and what they do is of high quality, made freshly on the premises, and uses local and organic produce. At lunchtime there might be summer minestrone & herbs soup with brown bread, or salad plates - a home-made organic goat's cheese & spinach quiche served with mixed salad - or, from a range of traditional home baking, you might just have a lavender flower muffin. There are all kinds of teas and tisanes, also natural juices - and coffee is served in individual cafetières. In July & August, Sunday lunch is offered, with special dishes available (booking required), and organic wines are now offered by the glass (€3.20-3.50) or bottle (€18-22). **Seats 20**; children welcome (high chair); open daily 10-4.15 (to 5 on Sun), Apr-Sep. Set 2 course L €15. Organic wine €18 a bottle or €3.20-3.50 per glass. Cafe closed Oct-Easter. [Perfumery open daily 9am-5pm all year (except Christmas); high season (Jun-Sep) open to 7pm.] MasterCard, Visa, Laser. **Directions:** In the Burren, east of Gort - off R480 & N67.

Fergus View

Corofin
FARMHOUSE

Kilnaboy Corofin Co Clare **Tel: 065 683 7606**
deckell@indigo.ie www.fergusview.com

Mary Kelleher's neat farmhouse was originally a teacher's residence (the theme is seen throughout) and now makes an hospitable and inexpensive base for exploring this fascinating area. The care taken to ensure guests enjoy their visit to the full is apparent in her attention to detail, with information packs in every room and specific directions given to the best places for walking. Locally sourced quality foods and home-grown fruits, vegetables and herbs are showcased in interesting breakfasts that include home-made yoghurt, freshly squeezed juice, home-made muesli, Anneliese Bartelink's excellent local Poulcoin cheeses and a wide range of teas as well as cooked breakfasts with free-range eggs. Although a little on the small side, in order to include en-suite facilities, bedrooms are comfortable and thoughtfully furnished. As well as a comfortable sitting room, there is a relaxing conservatory which opens on to the garden and has extensive views. There's also a lovely stone cottage next door, Tigh Eamon, which has been charmingly converted for self-catering accommodation. *No evening meals, but Mary will direct you to the best local choices. **Rooms 6** (5 en-suite,1 shower only,1 with private bathroom, all no-smoking); children welcome (cot available, €12); walking; garden. No pets. B&B €39 pps; ss €15. Closed end Oct-March. **No Credit Cards. Directions:** Follow R476 to Corofin - 3.25km (2 m) north, on Kilfenora Road.

DOOLIN

Most famous for its music, and as a ferry port for visits to the nearby Aran Islands, Doolin also makes a good base for exploring the area, or a journey break when touring the Burren. Useful places to know about include the Doolin Crafts Gallery (Tel 065 707 4309), which is just outside Doolin, beside the cemetery, and in new ownership; it has a pleasant café and garden as well as a shop selling quality crafts and home-made fare. Also on the edge of Doolin - at the top of the hill - the **Aran View House Hotel** (065 707 4061; www.aranview.com) is a family-run hotel with dramatic sea views across to the islands; new to the town, for those who prefer contemporary design, is the new 'boutique' **Tir gan Ean House Hotel** (065 707 5726; www,tirganean.ie). In the village, the friendly **O'Connors Pub** (065 7074168) is renowned for its traditional Irish music and also offers good food and, although it's looking a bit scruffy these days, everyone loves Deirdre Clancy & Niall Sheedy's **Doolin Café** (065 824 505460), which is open for lunch and dinner every day in summer. A short and very scenic drive away in Ballyvaughan, there is a farmers' market each Saturday morning May-October. Doolin is well suited to walkers as it is centrally located on the Burren Way Walking Route, a 42 km (26m) signposted walking trail from the town of Liscannor, along by the Cliffs of Moher, on to Doolin and into Ballyvaughan. Nearby Lahinch provides clean, safe beaches, is renowned for the quality of its surfing waves and is also home to one of the west coasts most challenging links golf courses (Lahinch Golf Club; 065 708 1003).
WWW.IRELAND-GUIDE.COM FOR ALL THE BEST PLACES TO EAT, DRINK & STAY

Ballinalacken Castle Country House & Restaurant

Doolin

COUNTRY HOUSE•RESTAURANT

Doolin Co Clare **Tel: 065 707 4025**
ballinalackencastle@eircom.net www.ballinalackencastle.com

Well away from the bustle of Lisdoonvarna, with wonderful views of the Atlantic and the West coast, Declan O'Callaghan's unusual property is easily identified from afar by the 15th century castle standing on it. With its welcoming fire, well-proportioned public rooms and antique furnishings, the house has retained a Victorian country house atmosphere, and comfortable accommodation includes some recently renovated suites - one with panoramic views, another an historic room with a fireplace. Children welcome (under 4s free in parents' room, cot available without charge, baby sitting arranged). Pets permitted by arrangement. Clay pigeon shooting and walking. Equestrian, fishing (fly, coarse & sea angling), hunting/shooting and scuba diving all nearby. **Rooms 12** (1 suite, 1 junior suite, 3 executive, 1 room shower only, 2 family; all no-smoking). B&B €80pps, SS €80. Limited room service. Closed 1 Nov-mid Apr. **Restaurant:** Michael Foley, formerly of Dromoland Castle, is the chef and the high ceiling Dining Room, with cream embossed paper and gentle Irish background music makes a fine setting for modern cooking, founded on the best local produce - and you are sure to meet many local diners and visitors who always come here for the lovely food. Menus offer a good choice of local seafood and meats, well-made soups, and interesting vegetarian options; the adventurous cooking may be a surprise - although there are clues in a full dining room (even on a cold, damp evening, as on a recent visit), and confident staff offering prompt and friendly service. Well-balanced flavours and accurate cooking make the most of prime ingredients like St Tola goat cheese, local crab and scallops, and Burren lamb. A wonderful starter, of open cannelloni of prawns with leek and tomato in a white wine sauce, topped with parmesan cheese, is made with homemade pasta and ultra fresh prawns; classic fillet of Irish beef is perfectly cooked and served with a white and red onion marmalade, and a rich Burgundy sauce; classic crème brulée comes with a seasonal rhubarb twist. The cooking has finesse and good coffee rounds off the evening nicely here. **Seats 32** (private room, 14); open to non-residents; reservations recommended; children welcome (high chair). D Wed-Mon, 7-8.45pm; A la carte. House wine €21; Service discretionary. Restaurant closed Tue. Establishment closed Nov-mid Apr. Amex, MasterCard, Visa. **Directions:** Coast road, R477 North of Doolin Village.

Doolin
COUNTRY HOUSE

Ballyvara House

Doolin Co Clare **Tel: 065 707 4467**
info@ballyvarahouse.ie www.ballyvarahouse.ie

Rebecca Flanagan's large guesthouse just outside Doolin village is smartly presented, and offers hotel standard accommodation. Public areas are impressively spacious and comfortable, and amenities for guests' use include a library and residents' bar (with wine licence), and a games room with pool table. Two suites have king-size mahogany sleigh beds and a private lounge area, and the other stylishly furnished bedrooms include double, triple and family rooms, with queen-size beds as standard where there is a double; some rooms have balconies, and all have well equipped bathrooms with spa or Jacuzzi bath, power showers and heated towel rails. Good in-room facilities include TV/radio, tea/coffee facilities, hairdryer, direct dial telephone, alarm clock and ironing facilities. An extensive breakfast menu is offered, and served in a bright and attractive room - or in your room if preferred. Outside there's a private courtyard garden and an outdoor sitting patio (for smokers), also plenty for children, including a multi-purpose astro turf playing court - lined for soccer, basketball and tennis - a play area (new playground equipment installed in 2008), and even resident donkeys and ponies. The atmosphere can seem a little impersonal, but Rebecca is a committed host - and, at the time of going to press, plans extensive landscaping, to include a historical/archaeological walk for guests. No dinner, but guests are referred to Tir gan Ean Hotel in Doolin, which is in common ownership. **Rooms 11** (all en-suite, 2 suites, 2 family, 1 shower only, 5 ground floor, 1 for disabled); limited room service; B&B €50-80pps; ss €40. Children welcome (under 3s free in parents' room, cot available free of charge, baby sitting arranged, playground). Free broadband wi/fi; pool table, tennis, garden, walking. Equestrian, garden visits and golf nearby. Closed Oct-Mar. Amex, MasterCard, Visa, Laser. **Directions:** In Doolin take the left at Fitzpatrick's Bar on left; up hill; 0.8km (0.5m) on left.

Doolin
RESTAURANT•GUESTHOUSE

Cullinan's Seafood Restaurant & Guesthouse

Doolin Co Clare **Tel: 065 707 4183**
cullinans@eircom.net www.cullinansdoolin.com

Proprietor-chef James Cullinan and wife Carol have earned a loyal following at their stylish and comfortable little restaurant overlooking the Aille river. Along with an à la carte, menus include an attractive early dinner offering great value with three or four choices (including vegetarian dishes) on each course. Menus showcase locally sourced seafood, including Burren smoked salmon, Doolin crabmeat and Aran scallops, in modern Irish cooking with a French influence - and carnivores are well looked after too, with a loin of Clare lamb among the specialities. To finish, there are tempting homemade desserts or Irish farmhouse cheeses. Quite an en extensive wine list favours France and includes half a dozen half bottles. **Seats 25**; D Thu-Tue, 6-9. A la carte; early D €30 (Mon-Fri, 6-6.45pm). Children welcome. House wines €22. SC discretionary. Closed Wed & Jan-Feb. **Accommodation:** Warm hospitality, comfortable beds and a tasty breakfast make this a good place to stay, at a reasonable price. **Rooms 8** (3 shower only, 2 family rooms, 3 ground floor, all no-smoking); all day room service. B&B €50 ss €20. Children welcome (under 3s free in parents' room, cot available without charge). Garden. No pets. Closed Jan & Feb. MasterCard, Visa, Laser. **Directions:** Centre of Doolin.

Doolin
RESTAURANT

Roadford House Restaurant
Killagh Doolin Co Clare **Tel: 065 707 5050**
roadfordhouse@eircom.net www.roadfordrestaurant.com

Located on the edge of the buzzy village of Doolin, Frank and Marion Sheedy's smart contemporary restaurant is an oasis of calm - a place where everything is operated in a personal and highly professional manner. A well-maintained exterior with attractive planting and plenty of parking makes a good impression from the start, and the restaurant is smart and comfortable, with well-chosen modern table settings hinting at the stylish cooking that Frank has in store. Marion Sheedy is a skilled hostess and offers a warm and professional welcome, setting the tone for what is to come - fine dining at very fair prices. The menu, in the modern Irish style, emphasises the very best local food prepared in an imaginative way: superb Burren lamb and tender beef, sparkling fresh seafood (including seared scallops, perhaps), local cheese, unusual vegetarian options, seasonal vegetables, and to round off the meal, delicious desserts. Everything comes to the table freshly cooked and in prime condition, and details, such as really good breads, are excellent - Frank Sheedy has a happy knack of choosing delightful accompaniments to his carefully sourced ingredients and he cooks with confidence and skill. You will dine in style. The wine list is fairly short but well chosen to match the food, and keenly priced. **Seats 34**; reservations recommended; children welcome before 7pm (high chair); D served Tue-Sun (high season, call to check low season), 6-8.30pm (to 9pm at weekends). Sun L winter months only, 12-3pm. Early D about €30, 6-6.45pm, also a la carte. House wine €19; SC 10% on groups 8+. Closed Mon (except Easter weekend), 24-26 Dec, 7 Jan to end Feb. MasterCard, Visa, Laser. Accommodation also available. **Directions:** In centre of village take slip road opposite Mc Dermotts pub, 50m up on right hand side ◇

Doolin
RESTAURANT
V

Stone Cutters Kitchen
Luogh North Doolin Co Clare **Tel: 065 707 5962**
stonecutterskitchen@eircom.net www.stonecutterskitchen.com

Karen Courtney and Myles Duffy's traditional thatched cottage between Doolin and the Cliffs of Moher is well-signed and, judging by the way they have been packing 'em in on the days the Guide came to call, they're finding that cosy traditional surroundings and Myles's good home cooking are just what families want when they're out and about in the area. A blackboard proclaims the specials of the day in addition to the main menu, and you can expect sound renditions of old favourites like fish pie, home-made fresh fish & chips, beef & Guinness stew, also very good home baking. A useful place to know about. Wheelchair friendly; children welcome (high chair, children's menu, baby changing facilities, playground). **Seats 70** (outdoor, 24, private room, to 26); reservations recommended; house wine €14.95. Food served 12.30-9.30pm daily Jun-Sept and Easter, weekends only Easter-Jun. Closed end Sept - Easter. Amex, Diners, MasterCard, Visa, Laser **Directions:** 1.6km (1 mile) north of the Cliffs of Moher on the R478 opposite Doolin Pottery.

DOONBEG
The historic village of Doonbeg grew up around Doonbeg Castle which was built by Philip Macsheeda Mor Mac Con in the 16th century for the Earl of Thomond. The village is an excellent base for the water sport enthusiast as there is surfing at Doughmore strand and Spanish Point, scuba diving nearby in Kilkee and sailing at Kilrush Marina. Anglers are well catered for with excellent shore angling and chartered deep sea angling, whilst the equestrian enthusiast can take a pony trekking trip. There are also scenic coast walks - and you might even be lucky enough to spot a dolphin.

Doonbeg
GOLF RESORT•RESTAURANT

Doonbeg Lodge

Doonbeg Co Clare **Tel:** 065 905 5600
reservations@doonbeggolfclub.com www.doonbeggolfclub.com

Although Doonbeg Golf Club is a private club, there is limited visitor access to both golf and accommodation when available. Whether or not you are a golfer, this is very good news because The Lodge offers accommodation which is not just very luxurious - but downright gorgeous. Located on Doughmore Bay in West Clare, the contrast between the wild landscape, the brooding sea and the classy interiors of The Lodge lends a distinctly romantic tone to the resort, which is on first approach appropriately reminiscent of a baronial Scottish castle; however, closer inspection reveals a cluster of more intimate buildings and, in acknowledgment of Irish tradition, all are slated-roofed and built in local stone. With an emphasis on natural materials (they even had their own tartan designed, an understated choice in gentle country colours) and respect for the environment (de-salinated sea water is used for watering the links), the quiet elegance of The Lodge may come as a surprise. It has an Irish 'great house' feel with an American opulence - 'a relaxed country house atmosphere with an unparalleled level of the service' is the aim and, with the apparent ease born of long experience, House Manager Bernie Merry (previously at nearby Moy House, Lahinch) ensures the atmosphere is always warm and service professional. And then there is the White Horses Spa, designed by the US-based Irish designer Clodagh: offering every possible kind of pampering, the design is inspired by the local environment (the walls of the fitness room, for example, feature a continuous image of the beach at Doonbeg) and non-golfers, especially, could pass many an agreeable hour here. To be honest, we did not expect to fall for The Lodge - but it really is wonderful. **Restaurants:** Good food is a high priority at The Lodge, and there are three choices: Darby's is for everybody, a great spacious pub-like bar where you can have straightforward food like fish and chips, prawn salads, and steaks. Meals are also offered in the Members' Bar, where the ambience is elegant yet clubby, in the old-fashioned style - and fine dining is offered in The Long Rooms, an intimate restaurant with its own bar, antique mirrors and a great bay window looking on to the ocean. Much-lauded American chef Tom Colicchio, the force behind New York City's Grammercy Tavern, is a consultant, and the kitchen team is led by Aidan McGrath, who set the bar high from the outset and has earned a reputation for this fine dining restaurant far beyond the golfing community. Spa; golf shop. Accommodation from €149-819 per suite (1-3 bedroom). Breakfast €15 pp. Amex, MasterCard, Visa, Laser. **Directions:** 16km (10 miles) north of Kilkee. ◈

Doonbeg
BAR•B&B•RESTAURANT

Morrissey's Seafood Bar & Grill

Doonbeg Co Clare **Tel:** 065 905 5304
info@morrisseysdoonbeg.com www.morrisseysdoonbeg.com

This attractive family-run bar in Doonbeg village has upped the ante over the last couple of years and it is now run by the energetic Hugh McNally. While retaining some of the charm of the old bar, he has given this lively seafood bar & grill a refreshing new look, with an extension on to the River Cree and a lovely decking area overlooking the river, which has brought excellent views and light to the dining room. The interior is all darkwood floors, cream walls and burgundy leather, a nice contrast to a collection of paintings and photographs, both new and old, of the village and local coastline. Simply presented menus are just the right length with dishes such as seafood chowder, Carrigaholt crab claws and Atlantic jumbo prawns for starters along with main fish courses such as home-made scampi or fresh fillet of salmon with warm baby potato salad. Main offerings from the grill include an Angus sirloin steak, whilst in winter, specialities include roasted monkfish and meat casseroles. Cooking is good, and well-trained staff are friendly and efficient. **Accommodation:** Seven bedrooms are bright and pristine, with good facilities - phone, TV, iron/trouser press. The difficulty here is getting a booking, as the rooms are understandably in great demand. Children welcome (under 3s free in parents room, cot available at no cost). **Rooms 7** (all en-suite, 2 Executive, 1 Junior Suite, all no smoking); B&B about €50, SS €20. **Restaurant:** No reservations accepted. **Seats 70** (private room, 30; outdoor dining for 30); toilets wheelchair accessible; children welcome before 10pm; L 12-2.30; D 6-9.30; House Wine about €18. Closed Mon and Nov, Jan, Feb. MasterCard, Visa, Laser.

ENNIS

The county town - and the main road junction of County Clare - Ennis has a venerable history, dating back to 1241 when Ennis Abbey was founded by Donough Cairbeach O'Brien for the Franciscans. It became a famous seat of learning so it is appropriate that this characterful old town with winding streets is equally notable for its progressiveness in some areas of enterprise. There is a farmers market every Friday morning in Upper Market Street car park. Comfortable hotels in the area include the **Best Western West County Hotel** (065 682 8421; www.bestwestern.ie) which is a short walk from the centre of town and known for its exceptional business and conference facilities; also a short distance from the town centre, **Auburn Lodge** (065 682 1247) is a pleasant owner-managed hotel, with traditional music in the bar every night. For lovers of Indian food, **Tulsi** (065 684 8065), next to ESB on Carmody Street, offers authentic cooking and friendly service. Ennis is home to two golf clubs (Woodstock Golf Club (065 682 9463) and Ennis Golf Club (065 682 4074)) and the championship courses of Dromoland Castle (061 368 444), Lahinch (065 708 1003) and Doonbeg (065 905 5600) are within a short drive of the town.

WWW.IRELAND-GUIDE.COM FOR ALL THE BEST PLACES TO EAT, DRINK & STAY

Ennis	Newpark House
FARMHOUSE	Ennis Co Clare **Tel: 065 682 1233**
Ⓥ	newparkhouse.ennis@eircom.net www.newparkhouse.com

Strange as it may seem to find an authentic farmhouse in a country setting within easy walking distance of Ennis, the Barron family home is a genuine exception. Now run by Declan Barron, this 300 year old house is of great historic interest and has large homely rooms furnished with old family furniture, and a quiet atmosphere. Bedrooms vary in size and character, but are comfortable and full of interest. The en-suite bathrooms also vary considerably, and first-time guests may need a fairly independent spirit in order to get into the ways of the house as information is not always forthcoming. However, regular guests adore the place and its exceptionally convenient location makes it a useful base for touring the area, following country pursuits (golf, horse riding, fishing, walking) or genealogy - there's a lot of useful material in the house and the Barrons can give advice on researching your roots. **Rooms 6** (all en-suite & no smoking, 1 shower only; 1 family room). Children welcome (under 4s free in parents' room, cot available free of charge, baby sitting arranged); pets permitted by arrangement. B&B €55 pps, ss €10. Closed 1 Nov-Easter. MasterCard, Visa, Laser. **Directions:** 1.6km (1m) outside Ennis; R352, turn right at Roselevan Arms.

Ennis	Old Ground Hotel
HOTEL●RESTAURANT	O'Connell Street Ennis Co Clare **Tel: 065 682 8127**
Ⓥ	sales@oldgroundhotel.ie www.flynnhotels.com

This ivy-clad former manor house dates back to the 18th century and, set in its own gardens, creates an oasis of calm in the bustling centre of Ennis. The Old Ground was bought by the Flynn family in 1995 and has been sensitively extended and renovated by them with due respect for the age and importance of the building. Despite the difficulties of dealing with very thick walls in an old building, major improvements were made to existing banqueting/conference facilities in the mid '90s, and extra storeys have since been added to provide fine new rooms; as the famous ivy-clad frontage continues to thrive, the external changes are barely noticeable to the casual observer, and major refurbishment has also taken place throughout the interior of the hotel, including all the older bedrooms. Guests who were finding that some of the older bedrooms and bathrooms rather cramped when occupied by two people will be pleased to know that 24 rooms have recently been extended and redecorated. A traditional style bar, Poet's Corner (bar menu 12-9) features traditional music on some nights. *Town Hall Café (see entry), is an informal contemporary restaurant in an historic building adjacent to the hotel. Conference/banqueting (120/180). Children welcome (under 2 free in parents' room, cot available without charge, baby sitting arranged). No pets. Garden. **Rooms 105** (6 suites, 6 junior suites, 89 executive rooms, 60 no-smoking, 4 family, 3 single, 1 for disabled.) Lift. 24 hour room service; turn-down service. B&B €60-85pps; ss €32. Closed 24-26 Dec. **O'Brien Room Restaurant:** The hotel's formal dining room is at the front of the hotel and has warmth and charm, in an elegant old-fashioned style. Today's kitchen team has been part of the hotel for many years, and they take pride in using local produce in enduring speciality dishes such as Carrigaholt mussels with shallots & garlic in a chive cream sauce, or Burren lamb with rosemary & honey glaze, and homely desserts like seasonal fruit crumbles. **Seats 60**; children welcome; toilets wheelchair accessible; air conditioning. L&D daily: L 12.30-2pm (to 2.30pm Sun), D 6.30-9.15 (to 9pm Sun); set L €19; set 5 course D €35; also a la carte L&D. Closed 25-26 Dec. Amex, Diners, MasterCard, Visa, Laser **Directions:** Town centre.

Ennis
HOTEL•RESTAURANT

Temple Gate Hotel

The Square Ennis Co Clare **Tel: 065 682 3300**
info@templegatehotel.com www.templegatehotel.com

This family-owned hotel was built in the mid '90s on the site of a 19th century convent, to a design that retains the older features including a church. Existing Gothic themes have been successfully blended into the new throughout the hotel, creating a striking modern building which has relevance to its surroundings in the heart of a medieval town, and succeeds in providing the comfort and convenience demanded by today's travellers, at a reasonable price. 'Preachers' pub offers a bar menu (10-9.30 daily) and traditional music every weekend - and the shops and many famous music pubs of the town centre are just a short walk across a cobble-stone courtyard. Conference/banqueting (190/160). 24hr room service. **Rooms 70** (2 suites, 39 no smoking, 3 family rooms, 13 ground floor). Lift. B&B from €75 pps, ss about €35. **Restaurant: JM's Bistro** is located in a high ceilinged room with lots of character. With comfortable seating and professional, attentive and friendly service, it's a relaxing place to linger after an active day sightseeing, or the hustle and bustle of the town. International influences are seen in starters such as woodland risotto (with mushrooms & black pudding), Thai fish cakes or local seafood chowder. Main courses may include a speciality of prime oven-roasted monkfish on spring onion colcannon, or Burren rack of lamb with fresh herb crust and tomato & mint chutney. An attractive dining-in option for hotel guests, and popular with non-residents too. Toilets wheelchair accessible; children welcome (high chair, children's menu, baby changing facilities). Open daily, 7am-9.45pm, L 12.45-3 & D 7-9.45 (to 9.15 Sun); set L about €19.95, set D about €35. Closed 25-26 Dec. Amex, Diners, MasterCard, Visa, Laser. **Directions:** Town Centre location - In Ennis, follow signs to tourist office: hotel is beside it. ◊

Ennis
RESTAURANT
Ⓥ

Town Hall Café

O'Connell Street Ennis Co Clare **Tel: 065 682 8127**
oghotel@iol.ie www.flynnhotels.com

Adjacent to (and part of) The Old Ground Hotel, the Town Hall Café has a separate street entrance and a contemporary feel. The old town hall has been well restored and the restaurant is in an impressive high-ceilinged room with sensitively spare decor - large art works which will be loved or loathed, big plant pots and simple table settings allow the room to speak for itself. Daytime menus offer a mixture of modern bistro-style dishes and tea-room fare - recently, it seems, with more emphasis on casual fare wraps, open sandwiches etc - just what people need to re-charge during a day's shopping. In the evening, it all moves up a notch or two, when an attractive à la carte menu is offered. Desserts from a daily selection. **Seats 60**; children welcome (high chair); reservations recommended except for snacks. Open from 10am daily: L 12-4.30pm, D 6-9.45pm (to 9.30pm Sun). House wines from €18. Closed 25 Dec. Amex, Diners, MasterCard, Visa, Laser **Directions:** On main street of Ennis town.

Ennis
RESTAURANT
Ⓥ

Zucchini Restaurant

7 High Street Ennis Co Clare **Tel: 065 686 6566**
reservations@zucchini.ie www.zucchini.ie

This first floor restaurant is spacious, comfortable and attractively designed, and hung with paintings by local artists. It's a friendly, buzzy restaurant that is popular with the locals and is a pleasant place to dine. The menu offers the standard international dishes so familiar in Ireland today, featuring local seafood, local beef and lamb, etc, and also vegetarian options, but what makes it different is that owner-chef Colm Chawke takes pride in showcasing local produce and he is a good chef, so the quality ingredients he seeks out are treated with respect and have real flavour. Pricing is fair and the early dinner menu offers good value. Staff are charming, although service can be slow and lacking in professional expertise. In addition to a fairly short but well chosen and fairly priced wine menu, a full bar and beer menu is also available and there is a pleasant, spacious lounge area dedicated for aperitifs and after dinner drinks. **Seats 80**. Children welcome before 8pm (high chair, children's menu); air conditioning. D daily, 5-9.30pm. Early D around €25, 5-7pm, also à la carte; house wine from €19.50. Closed 3 days Christmas. MasterCard, Visa, Laser. **Directions:** Just off main town square (O'Connell Monument).

ENNISTYMON

Ennistymon is unchanged since it was established in 1588 and retains its historical character with traditional shop fronts and a lack of modern high street outlets. A hilly town ideal for walking, with slender streets and the picturesque River Inagh running through it. The river provides excellent salmon and trout fishing - and the famous waterfalls, for which the town is probably best known.

Byrnes Restaurant

Ennistymon
RESTAURANT
V

Main Street Ennistymon Co Clare **Tel: 065 707 1080**
byrnesennistymon@eircom.net www.byrnes-ennistymon.com

Located in a fine period house at the top of this old market town, Byrnes is a stylish high-ceilinged restaurant with views of Ennistymon's famous cascading river from the airy restaurant and an extensive outdoor dining area at the rear of the house. The Byrne family offer genuine hospitality and this, when wedded to contemporary style and ambitious standards of food, should ensure that a visit here will not disappoint. The surroundings - stylish, airy and yet cosy, with gentle music - are conducive to relaxation, and a warm welcome from Richard Byrne gets guests off to a good start. Mary Byrne is a skilful chef and everything is freshly cooked to order - her fairly short but well-balanced menu offers contemporary Irish cuisine with an emphasis on fresh local seafood and local meat, and there are always interesting vegetarian options. Gravad lax is something of a signature dish and makes an excellent starter with home-baked bread; fish dishes are simple in style but very good to eat, and tender lamb shank may be served with delicious cabbage flavoured with bacon. Leave room for desserts such as a more-ish chocolate cake and delicious home-made ice creams. Prices are reasonable for the quality with an early bird and Dinner/B&B deals offering especially good value. A short but well chosen wine list includes plenty of half bottles and wine by the glass. **Seats 55** (outdoor, 40, private room, 15); air conditioning; not suitable for children after 8 pm. L in summer months only, 12-4.30pm. D, Mon-Sat, 6.30-9.30pm; Set D 2/3 course D €33/35, also à la carte. House wines from €20. Closed Sun (except bank hol weekends), Christmas, Nov and Feb. Phone to check opening at lunch time and off season. MasterCard, Visa, Laser. Call ahead to check opening times Nov-Feb as they may be closed. **Directions:** Large, prominent building at the head of the main street.

Holywell Italian Café

Ennistymon
RESTAURANT

Ennistymon Co Clare **Tel: 065 707 7322**
info@holywell.net www.holywell.net

In the centre of Ennistymon, this is one of four descendants of the much-loved Italian café, previously at Ballyvaughan (the others are at Fanore, Lahinch and Galway). You enter a tiny hall and there is a corridor-bar, with two spacious rooms to the right and left. It's a comfortable place to eat - the familiar Tyrolean-style interior has been reproduced, and both rooms have large windows letting in plenty of light - and wines offered by the glass are generous. The food is still all vegetarian, specialising in simple dishes like pastas and pizzas, and it is a useful place to know about, with long opening hours in summer. Open 11am-11pm daily. Phone to check opening off season. MasterCard, Visa. ◇

Holywell - Italian Trattoria

Fanore
RESTAURANT

Craggagh Fanore Co Clare
Tel: 065 707 6971

Another of several descendants of the well-known vegetarian Italian café, previously at Ballyvaughan, the menu here has moved away from the trademark pizzas, towards a more balanced trattoria menu - and it includes meat. Although there is still a strong leaning towards vegetarians, the minestrone now includes diced beef, the antipasti plate includes stuffed Parma ham rolls and chicken liver paté, and home-made pasta is offered with seafood bolognese sauce - and you can even have a grilled meats plate. Home-made ices are a speciality. It's a relaxed place, with wonderful views at sunset. Staff are friendly and efficient, there's a short, well-selected list of Italian wines (also beers and minerals), and coffees - and the long opening hours (11am-11pm in summer) make this a useful place to know about. Open in the summer only. ◇

KILFENORA

One of the most famous music centres in the west of Ireland, traditional Irish music and set dancing at **Vaughan's Pub** (Tel: 065 708 8004; www.vaughanspub.com) and (previously thatched) barn attract visitors from all over the world; it's been in the family since about 1800 and serves traditional Irish food (seafood chowder, bacon & cabbage, beef & Guinness stew) based on local ingredients. Discerning travellers looking for a snack head for the nearby Visitor Centre, which does a very nice line in good home baking. The area is a rambler's dream while golfers and surfers will be tested to the utmost by the nearby Lahinch Golf Clubs (065 708 1003) famous links and the challenging waves of Lahinch strand.

WWW.IRELAND-GUIDE.COM FOR ALL THE BEST PLACES TO EAT, DRINK & STAY

KILKEE

Aside from its appeal as a base for golfing holidays, Kilkee is a traditional family holiday destination located on the Atlantic coast facing a lovely beach which slopes very gently into the Bay - many would say there is nowhere else to be during the long Irish summer holidays. Kilkee is for walkers too. The walk along the coastline to the Diamond Rocks is one of the most breathtaking and exhilarating in Ireland and the local cliffs rival that of the famous Cliffs of Moher, but without the entrance fee and the large crowds. Golfers will enjoy the challenge presented by championship course at nearby Doonbeg Golf Club (065 905 5600). Other local attractions include Scuba Diving, Fishing, Horse Riding and Dolphin Watching. If staying in a large impersonal hotel is not your thing, consider **Halpins Townhouse Hotel** (065 905 6032; www.halpinsprivatehotels.com) where the Halpin family adapted the original Victorian building to provide en-suite bathrooms which means that bedrooms are neat rather than spacious, but they are comfortable and well-appointed. There's a characterful basement bar with an open fire and a restaurant called Vittles. Alternatively the **Stella Maris Hotel** (065 905 6455; www.stellamarishotel.com) is a long-established family-run hotel with a warm and friendly atmosphere that has recently been refurbished. Nearby Kilrush hosts a farmers market each Thursday morning and Kilrush is also home to the Vandeleur Walled Garden (065 905 1760) which was recently restored to its former glory and well worth a visit.

WWW.IRELAND-GUIDE.COM FOR ALL THE BEST PLACES TO EAT, DRINK & STAY

Kilkee
RESTAURANT

Murphy Blacks

The Square Kilkee Co Clare **Tel: 065 905 6854**
murphyblacks@hotmail.com

Although the restaurant is quite modern, it is in a Victorian building and proprietors Cillian Murphy and Mary Redmond have retained period features to keep the authentic atmosphere of the existing pub. Cillian is an ex-fishing skipper who ensures the freshest fish possible and the effort that goes into ensuring the best from suppliers shows in succulent, well-flavoured food. He is in charge of front of house and Mary is the chef - a winning combination that has earned Murphy Blacks a reputation well beyond the immediate area. Although menus have a leaning towards seafood - and specialities include crab tartlet, a delicious prawn tempura with chilli dip and a superb main course of cannelloni of plaice - meat eaters are well catered for too. You'll find classics like rack of lamb and steaks, and there is always a vegetarian choice. Desserts are home-made and the selection changes monthly. A balanced, accessibly priced wine list includes a good choice of half bottles. **Seats 36** (outdoors, 12); children welcome; D Mon-Sat, 6-9pm; reservations advised; SC 10% on groups 6+. Closed Sun. MasterCard, Visa, Laser. **Directions:** Centre of town.

Kilkee
PUB

Naughton's Bar

46 O'Curry St. Kilkee Co Clare **Tel: 065 905 6597**
info@naughtonsbar.com www.naughtonsbar.com

Painted dark grey and wine, Naughtons is an 1870's pub the on main street, with French doors opening out onto a patio with seating for fine days. Owned by Elaine Haugh and her husband, Robert Hayes who is the chef, it is a lovely comfortable and really elegant pub, with two bars and nooks leading into each other, with high settle-bed type seating in part of the bar. With natural brick wall finish, beautiful mahogany counter, lovely mirrors and large paintings of the local area, painted by Robert's mother, Anna St. George who has a studio in Castleconnell, it's full of atmosphere. The feeling is casual, with families at earlier sittings and a little more dressy later. Styled a Fish and Steak Bar, the accent is on seafood and on simplicity, with seven starters, seven seafood choices offered, plus five meat dishes, and more seafood specials each night. The main dishes tend to be pricier (pan-fried hake in cream chive sauce €21.95) but choices like smoked and white fish chowder (€5.95), tub of mussels in wine, butter and cream (€11) and Naughton's Seafood Salad (€13.95) are very accessible – the salad is a mix of crabmeat and prawns served on a bed of seasonal salad with garlic or soda bread – and come with good accompaniments like home-cut real chips or baked potato and seasonal vegetables. There's a children's menu (€6.95), and a small but carefully chosen wine selection. The only trouble with Naughtons is that it's so popular - it's almost impossible to get a seat (bookings are only taken from 9pm). Food 5pm-9.30. MasterCard, Visa, Laser. **Directions:** Down O'Connell Street towards the sea, left on to O'Curry Street before beach. ◊

Kilkee
RESTAURANT
Ⓝ

The Pantry

O'Curry Street Kilkee Co Clare **Tel: 065 905 6576**
info@thepantrykilkee.com www.thepantrykilkee.com

The Pantry is on the main street, painted teal green with a long double traditional Kilkee bay window – and it is probably one very good reason why so many families come to Kilkee for the holidays. Owned and operated by Imelda Bourke and her husband, Pat, baking starts at 5.30 each morning, and they produce the most amazing selection of breads, cakes and desserts. They've recently revamped the restaurant and business is booming. They use butter in everything and only the best of ingredients, quoting Darina Allen saying that "if everyone on the street is making scones, you just make sure yours are the best", that's what they have done for the last 20 years, and every year it gets better. You can come here at 8.30am before breakfast to collect freshly squeezed orange juice, fresh fruit salad with natural yoghurt, honey and walnuts, smoothies and the best ever mixed berry and cinnamon scones or a wee Irish breakfast. All day, 7 days a week from Easter until September, you can have wonderful morning coffee, lunches and afternoon tea until 6.30 each day. Imelda, who is a home economist, is helped by her one-time student Bernie Haugh who is restaurant manager and head chef Maureen King who creates wonders for lunch like salmon & cod pies, roast vegetable & goat's cheese quiche, seafood chowders rhubarb crumble, and carrot cakes, which are eaten in a large bright room in coffee and creams, with modern lights hanging from a high ceiling and a long self-service counter running the full length of the back wall. Staff are young and friendly, with bright orange aprons and pale green t-shirts. There is a marvellous and somewhat chaotic buzz here and it is constantly packed and adored by locals and visitors for years. They even have a separate loo for kids! Menus are coeliac friendly, and there's an early bird; wines available, including half bottles. Open 8am to 6.30pm. Children welcome. MasterCard, Visa, Laser. **Directions:** Down O'Connell Street towards the bay, take a left into O'Curry Street just before the sea.

Kilkee
RESTAURANT•GUESTHOUSE

The Strand Restaurant & Guesthouse

Strand Line Kilkee Co Clare **Tel: 065 905 6177**
thestrandkilkee@eircom.net www.thestrandkilkee.com

This long-established seafront restaurant has been in family ownership for 130 years, and is now run by Johnny Redmond, who is the chef, and his wife Caroline. An unassuming yellow exterior gives little hint of the friendly welcome, buzzing atmosphere and wonderful views that await guests who can begin with an aperitif in the recently extended bar and lounge looking out over Kilkee Bay and the Atlantic beyond. In the split level restaurant, a gentle colour scheme and simply laid tables allow the view to take centre stage, and floor to ceiling windows right along one side ensure a view for all tables. Menus - mainly seafood, plus favourites such as fillet steak, rack of lamb and a vegetarian dish - arrive promptly at your table, along with delicious home-baked breads and a jug of water, and there's a tempting list of daily specials for seafood lovers a big bowl of Atlantic Mussels to start, perhaps, then baked John Dory, whole seabass or Dover sole. Finish with a home-made dessert such as apple & rhubarb crumble or hazelnut toffee meringues (deliciously chewy)... Friendly, efficient service, great cooking and apparently effortless management by Johnny and Caroline make dining here a very enjoyable experience. Restaurant: Children welcome (high chair, children's menu); **Seats 46** (outdoor, 12); reservation recommended; D 6-9.30pm, à la carte. SC 10% on groups 6+. Closed Dec-Mar (open 2 weeks over Christmas). **Accommodation:** Six individually decorated en-suite bedrooms, some with sea views, offer comfortable accommodation above the restaurant. More rooms are planned. **Rooms 6** (all en-suite, 5 shower only); children welcome (under 3s free in parents' room, cot available free of charge); B&B €45 pps, ss about €10. Closed Jan & Feb. MasterCard, Visa, Laser. **Directions:** On the waterfront in Kilkee. ◊

KILLALOE / BALLINA

At the southern end of Lough Derg - a handsome inland sea set in an attractive blend of mountain and hillside, woodland and farm - Killaloe straddles the Shannon with two townships - Ballina in Tipperary on the east bank, and Killaloe in Clare, with the ancient cathedral across the river to the west. However, while it's all usually known as Killaloe (Co Clare), establishments of interest to the Guide happen to be mainly on the east (Tipperary) side of the river. The aptly named **Lakeside Hotel** (061 376122; www.lakeside-killaloe.com) is popular for its location and facilities, while **Liam O'Riain's** (061 376722) is a traditional unspoilt pub. Then there's **Gooser's**, an attractive almost-riverside pub; it gets very busy in summer but makes a pleasant off-season stop and, at its best, the food can be enjoyable. On the hill west of the bridge you'll find **Crotty's** atmospheric pub (see entry) and, on the busy through road on the Ballina side, a modern café/restaurant, **RiverRun Bistro** (061 374919; www.riverruncafe.com), offers wholesome food in an informal atmosphere - and with local artwork displayed for sale too. (See also entry for Cherry Tree Restaurant). On Sundays the farmers market (Between the Waters, 11am-3pm) makes a lovely place to wander around while sampling and buying the finest local produce.

WWW.IRELAND-GUIDE.COM FOR ALL THE BEST PLACES TO EAT, DRINK & STAY

Killaloe
RESTAURANT

Cherry Tree Restaurant

Lakeside Ballina Killaloe Co Clare **Tel: 061 375 688**
cherrytreerestaurant@gmail.com www.cherrytreerestaurant.ie

Harry McKeogh's impressive modern restaurant is a favourite weekend destination for discerning Limerick residents, who enjoy the waterside location and consistently excellent contemporary cooking. A high-ceilinged room with well-spaced, classically appointed tables and River Shannon views makes for a fine restaurant, although its exceptional spaciousness can make it seem a little short on atmosphere unless there is a buzzy crowd in. All is well on the plate however, as Harry himself is back in the kitchen alongside head chef Falk Hammca; as you arrive, you will notice the team at work, as you are shown to a small reception area nearby or straight to your table. Harry is well known for his commitment to using the best local ingredients, many of them organic. These special foods and their suppliers are highlighted on simply worded seasonal menus offering a well-balanced choice of dishes - perhaps three on each course on the set menu, five on the à la carte; although the food is stylish and menus offer all the treats of fine dining - amuse-bouche, sorbet (refeshing rhubarb and lemongrass perhaps), petits fours - and are peppered with luxurious ingredients like truffles, foie gras, crab and diver-caught scallops, Harry McKeogh's trademark is a direct cooking style, without too many cheffy twirls. And the simpler foods have always been especially good here - the Cherry Tree's salads are legendary, for example, and an outstanding ingredient that has inspired more than one speciality dish is their superb beef, especially perfectly cooked dry-aged steak - and the Comeragh Mountains 'black-faced' lamb has also provided the base for outstanding dishes. Excellent puddings, each with a suggested dessert wine to accompany, might include a Grand Marnier chocolate fondant with hazelnut ice cream and pomegranate coulis - delicious. There's a fine cheese plate too, and an interesting, carefully chosen wine list includes seven half bottles. Set menus - especially Sunday lunch - offer outstanding value, and a dedicated Children's Menu offers three delicious choices on each course. **Seats 60** (private room, 10). Toilets wheelchair accessible. Children welcome until 7pm (children's menu). D 6-10 Tue-Sat. Set D €48; also à la carte; Sun L only 12.30-3, Sun L €32; house wine €19.50. Closed Sun D, Mon, 24-26 Dec, last week Jan, 1st week Feb. Amex, MasterCard, Visa, Laser. **Directions:** At Molly's Pub in Ballina turn down towards the Lakeside Hotel, the Cherry Tree Restaurant is just before the hotel, on the left.

Killaloe
BAR

Crotty's Bar & Restaurant

Bridge Street Killaloe Co Clare
Tel: 061 376 965

Passing through tall wrought iron gates on Bridge Street, which looks down on to the Shannon at the crossing from Killaloe to Ballina, you walk into a leafy bower with picnic tables arranged for outdoor dining, and then on into the most appealing old-fashioned pub interior you'll see for many a mile. Crotty's offers walls loaded with pictures and photographs and old newspapers (did you hear about the Titanic?) and mirrors and adverts for long-disappeared farm implements and lots more. Wooden tables are lit by candles stuck unceremoniously into stone hot water bottles and the uileann pipes play quietly in the background. Crotty's is a pub and serves exemplary pints, but it is also a very popular dining destination (service is brisk and pleasant) offering simple, straightforward food whose provenance is proudly displayed on the menu where names of suppliers are given. Typical hearty dishes would be steak (nicely tender with a choice of 8oz or 12oz), home-made burgers and breaded cod, and each comes with a choice of potatoes, including their speciality- dauphinoise. Desserts include a delicious home-made rum cassata. Although Crotty's does not accept credit cards, there is a cashpoint nearby. **Seats 65.** Open Mon-Sat 5-10pm, Sun & bank hols 4-10pm. **No credit cards. Directions:** 50 metres from the bridge in Killlaloe.

KILRUSH

Formerly a significant Shannon, Kilrush town is built around a square with a large Market House in the centre of it, and a wide street runs from the square towards the harbour, where there is now an impressive marina facility. Boat trips are available to watch the Shannon bottlenose dolphins, and also to see the early Christian ruins on Scattery Island, now uninhabited. The town was planned by the local landlords, the Vandeleurs, whose most obvious legacy is the beautiful Vandeleur Walled Garden (065 905 1760, with café), once the forgotten garden of Kilrush house, and now an oasis of tender and tropical plants that thrive in the area's unique climate. For Irish traditional music enthusiasts, there is an unusual music festival, Eigse Mrs Crotty, which focuses on concertina-playing. The attractive modern **Harbour Restaurant** (065 905 2836, Creek Marina) overlooks the harbour and is popular with residents and visitors alike.

WWW.IRELAND-GUIDE.COM FOR ALL THE BEST PLACES TO EAT, DRINK & STAY

LAHINCH

This bustling seaside resort is especially popular with lovers of the great outdoors - one of Ireland's greatest surfing beaches is here, on Liscannor Bay, and it is equally renowned for golf (Lahinch Golf Club; 065 708 1003) while Doonbeg Golf Club (065 905 5600) which has earned an excellent reputation is also a short drive away. A long sandy beach and Seaworld, a leisure complex, also attract family holidaymakers to Lahinch. There's a branch of the Holywell restaurant group here, **La Taverna** (065 7082 755), on Church Street; the **Atlantic Hotel** on Main Street (065 708-1049) is a popular place to go for an informal bite to eat, and those who prefer to stay in large hotels will find all facilities at the centrally located 4* **Lahinch Golf & Leisure Hotel** (065 7081100; www.lahinchgolfhotel.com). Nearby Doolin is just a short scenic drive away and has ferries to the Aran Islands, while the wonderful Burren is on the doorstep.

WWW.IRELAND-GUIDE.COM FOR ALL THE BEST PLACES TO EAT, DRINK & STAY

Lahinch
RESTAURANT

Barrtra Seafood Restaurant

Lahinch Co Clare **Tel: 065 708 1280**
barrtra@hotmail.com www.barrtra.com

Thanks to pleasingly simple décor, large windows and a conservatory, views of Liscannor Bay to take centre stage from Paul and Theresa O'Brien's traditional, whitewashed cottage, on the cliffs just outside Lahinch - and it can be magic on a fine evening. In 2008 they celebrated 20 years in business with typical generosity, by offering guests a complimentary glass of red wine from their own vines in the south of France. Aside from the stunning location, local seafood is the other star attraction - Barrtra was our Seafood Restaurant of the Year in 2002 - and Theresa's excellent, unfussy cooking continues to make the most of a wide range of fish, while also offering a choice for those with other preferences. Several menus are offered in high season, and giving value has always been a priority here. Local seafood is all offered at customer-kindly prices; lobster is a speciality, when available, and is quite reasonably priced - on the dinner menu it only attracts a moderate supplement. Otherwise expect dishes like the richly flavoured Barrtra fisherman's broth, crab and grapefruit cocktail with chive crème fraîche, and perfectly cooked fish with excellent sauces; exact timing and perfect judgement of flavourings enhances the fish, while always allowing it to be "itself". Vegetarian dishes (and dishes suitable for coeliacs) are highlighted on menus, and vegetables generally are another strong point (note the large polytunnel), a deliciously flavoursome combination that will include beautiful Clare potatoes is served on a platter. Paul is a great host, managing front of house with easy hospitality, and is responsible for an interesting and keenly priced wine list, which includes a wide choice of house wines and half bottles, several sherries and a beer menu. Quality and value are the hallmarks of this great little restaurant - and frequent visits by the Guide invariably confirm that it remains as delightful as ever. **Seats 40**; not suitable for children under 6 yrs after 7pm. D only, Fri-Wed 6-10pm. Set D €45; also à la carte. House wines from €21; s.c. discretionary. Closed Thurs & Jan-Feb. Phone to check opening hours off season. MasterCard, Visa, Laser. **Directions:** 3.5 miles south of Lahinch N67.

Lahinch
COUNTRY HOUSE

Moy House

Lahinch Co Clare **Tel: 065 708 2800**
moyhouse@eircom.net www.moyhouse.com

This stunning house just outside Lahinch was our Country House of the Year in 2003 and, although many new properties have opened since then, it remains one of Ireland's most appealing (and luxurious) country houses. It's on a wooded 15 acre site on the river Moy and enjoys a commanding position overlooking Lahinch Bay, with clear coastal views and, although it appears to be quite a small, low building as you approach, its hillside position allows for a lower floor on the sea side - a side entrance below has direct access to the dining room and conservatory, and the lower bedrooms (useful for anyone who might have difficulty with the narrow spiral staircase which joins the two floors internally). A large drawing room on the entrance level has an open fire and honesty bar, where guests are free to enjoy aperitifs before going down to dine, or to relax after dinner. Decor, in rich country house tones, uses rugs and beautiful heavy fabrics to great advantage and bedrooms, which all have sea views, are wonderfully spacious and luxuriously appointed, and lovely bathrooms have underfloor heating; one extra-luxurious suite has a private conservatory overlooking the Atlantic. Bedrooms have recently been refurbished in a gently contemporary style, giving the house a new freshness, and this has also been applied in the dining room (also with a conservatory, allowing lovely views for everyone) where a 4-course residents' dinner and breakfast are served at separate tables - a lovely, stylish place to dine. There's a short but interesting wine list and, all round, this lovely house offers a unique experience. **Rooms 9** (3 shower only, 2 family rooms, 1 suite, 4 ground floor, 1 for disabled, all no smoking); children welcome (cot available at no charge; baby sitting arranged); B&B €125-140 pps, ss €40. D 7-8.45 (residents only, reservations required), €55. House wine about €24. Closed Jan. Helipad. Amex, Diners, MasterCard, Visa, Laser.
Directions: On the sea side of the Miltown Malbay road outside Lahinch.

Lahinch
HOTEL•RESTAURANT

Vaughan Lodge

Ennistymon Road Lahinch Co Clare **Tel: 065 708 1111**
info@vaughanlodge.ie www.vaughanlodge.ie

Michael and Maria Vaughan's hotel - purpose-built to high specifications, mainly with the comfort of golfers in mind - offers peace and relaxation within easy walking distance of the town centre. They see it as a 'designer country house hotel' and that is a fair description, especially given their own hospitality, which is a combination of genuine warmth and professional expertise. Pleasing contemporary design combines with quality materials and a great sense of space in large, clean-lined bedrooms and public areas - including a clubby bar with leather easy chairs and sofas which golfers, in particular, are sure to enjoy; the ambience throughout is of a comfortable gentleman's club. A drying room is available for golfers' or walkers' wet clothing. Children welcome (under 12 free in parents' room; cot available without charge). No pets. **Rooms 22** (1 junior suite, 4 executive, 6 ground floor, 1 shower only, all no smoking); B&B €125 pps, ss €40. All day room service. Lift. Ample parking space. **Restaurant:** Run as a stand-alone restaurant specialising in seafood, this is a large, spacious room and dark polished wood tables, crisp linen runners and elegant table settings set the tone for head chef Carol O'Brien's fine cooking. Refreshingly, her menus are to the point and written in clear, accurate English; although there is an emphasis on fresh local seafood, interesting artisan foods from area feature strongly, some of them from named producers - Inagh goat's cheese, excellent Burren lamb and beef. All are used in an interesting modern style, sometimes with an Irish tone as, for example, in Inagh goat's cheese in a warm hazelnut tart with garlic & aubergine caviar & rocket salad, seared scallops with citrus beurre blanc and roast rack of Burren lamb with chestnut purée, shallots and lardons of bacon. The dinner menu is good value and is presented in a series of beautifully cooked dishes including a lovely desserts, and a well chosen local cheese selection. The wide-ranging wine list (grouped by price) includes a strong house selection and useful tasting notes. Carol O'Brien is a confident chef and continues to produce top quality food, backed up by excellent hospitality and service, making this is one of the most highly regarded restaurants in the area. **Seats 60**. D daily Tue-Sun 6.30-9.30; set D €45. House wine €23. SC 10% on groups 8+. Closed Mon, Nov - Mar. Amex, Diners, MasterCard, Visa, Laser. **Directions:** On N85 just at the edge of Lahinch on the left.

Liscannor

CHARACTER PUB•RESTAURANT

Vaughans Anchor Inn

Main Street Liscannor Co Clare

Tel: 065 708 1548

The Vaughan family's traditional bar has great character, with open fires and lots of memorabilia - it was our Pub of the Year in 2006 and it's just the place for some seriously good seafood at fair prices, either in the bar or in a newer restaurant area at the back. Although famed locally for their seafood platters (and they are delicious - and great value) there's much more to the menu than that: Denis Vaughan is a creative chef who cooks everything to order and patience is quite reasonably requested on this score, as it gets very busy and everything really is fresh - they offer about twenty varieties of fish, and the menu may even be changed in mid-stream because there's something new coming up off the boats. However, you don't have to eat seafood to eat well here - vegetarian options are offered, also game in season, and they do excellent steaks too, and many other good meat dishes including roasted rack of lamb with shepherd's pie of shank & kidney, caramelised parsnip and lamb jus - and you can have sautéed foie gras with any of the meat dishes if you wish. Cooking combines old-fashioned generosity with some contemporary (and, in some cases, sophisticated) twists: succulent organic salmon, for example, may be served with tempura of smoked salmon, buttered cabbage & smoked bacon butter, a mixture of traditional Irish combinations and new cooking styles. It's understandably very popular and they don't take bookings so, get there early - lunch time (when some more casual dishes, like open sandwiches, are also offered) might be worth a gamble but, if you want to have a reasonably quiet dinner without a long wait, get there before seven o'clock. Good bread, good service - and great value. An interesting wine list offers a dozen or so house wines, and something for every budget and occasion. **Seats 106**; toilets wheelchair accessible; children welcome before 9pm (high chair, children's menu). Food served 12-9.30 daily; house wine from €18.95. Accommodation also available. Closed 25 Dec. (Open Good Fri for food, but bar closed.) MasterCard, Visa, Laser. **Directions:** 4km (2.5 m) from Lahinch on Cliffs of Moher route.

Lisdoonvarna

HOTEL•RESTAURANT

Sheedys Country House Hotel & Restaurant

Lisdoonvarna Co Clare **Tel: 065 707 4026**

info@sheedys.com www.sheedys.com

John and Martina Sheedy run one of the west of Ireland's best-loved small hotels - it offers some of the most luxurious accommodation and the best food in the area, yet it still has the warm ambience and friendly hands-on management which make a hotel special. The sunny foyer has a comfortable seating area - and an open fire for chillier days - and the cosy bar is just the place to snuggle down with an after dinner drink and explore the rather fine range of interesting Irish Whiskeys including Midleton Rare. All the bedrooms are spacious and individually designed to a high standard with generous beds, quality fabrics and elegant, quietly soothing colours; comfort is the priority, so bathrooms have power showers as well as full baths and there are bathrobes, luxury toiletries and CD music systems, in addition to the usual room facilities. Fine food and warm hospitality remain constant qualities however - and an original feature has already enhanced the exterior in a way that is as useful as it is pleasing to the eye: the gardens in front of the hotel have been developed to include a rose garden, fruit trees, and also a potager (formal vegetable and herb garden), which supplies leeks, Swiss chard, beetroot and cabbage to the kitchen: a delightful and practical feature. Not suitable for children, except babies (cot available free of charge). No pets. **Rooms 11** (3 junior suites, 2 with separate bath & shower, 1 for disabled, all no smoking). B&B €70 pps, ss €25. DB&B rate offers exceptional value at €120 pps. **Restaurant:** The combination of John Sheedy's fine cooking and Martina's warmth and efficiency front of house make Sheedy's a must-visit destination for discerning visitors to the area. The restaurant has recently been refurbished and a new carpet and curtains (the windows were previously curtainless, which was stylish but a little stark) have added a warmer tone which is welcome on cooler days. But thankfully there has been no change to John's carefully-presented meals; amuse-bouches sent out from the kitchen while you are choosing your dinner sharpen the anticipation of delights to come. And everything on John's well-balanced menus just seems so appetising. His cooking style reflects a pride in carefully sourced local foods (many of them named on the menu, along with their suppliers) and pleasing combinations of classic and modern Irish. Savour interesting dishes made from sparkling fresh seafood, tender and uniquely flavoured lamb and beef, and local farmhouse cheeses from the Burren: everything is cooked to order, every dish is beautifully presented, and vegetarian dishes are equally appealing. Finish with a gorgeous speciality dessert such as home-made ice cream or old-fashioned lemon posset with fresh fruit sorbet - raspberry perhaps - and crisp shortbread. Under Martina's direction, the service is gently paced, professional and unobtrusive, and a carefully selected wine list complements the cooking at prices that are very fair for the quality provided. The same high standards apply at breakfast when an extensive menu is on offer: delicious fresh fruit compôtes and juices; great home-made bread and pancakes; a cheese plate, a fresh fish dish, as well as classic Burren smoked salmon with scrambled eggs. A stay here is a treat by any standards. **Seats 25**; children welcome. D daily, 7-8.30. A la carte. House wine €21.50. SC discretionary. Establishment closed Oct-mid March. MasterCard, Visa, Laser. **Directions:** 200 metres from square of town on road to Sulphur Wells.

Miltown Malbay
GUESTHOUSE●RESTAURANT

The Admiralty Lodge

Spanish Point Miltown Malbay Co Clare **Tel: 065 708 5007**
info@admiralty.ie www.admiralty.ie

Golfers - and, outside the main holiday season when holidaymakers are staying in the adjacent campsites, anyone who seeks peace - will love Pat and Aoife O'Malley's luxurious guesthouse and restaurant just minutes away from Spanish Point Links Course, and very convenient to Doonbeg and Lahinch. A sweeping entrance leads to the smartly maintained building - there's an old 1830s' lodge in there somewhere, with various extensions in different finishes creating the rather pleasing impression of a cluster of buildings, now with a welcoming porch softening the slightly bleak exterior. Once inside, a large reception area with marble floor, mahogany desk, deep purple chaise longue and two huge elephant feet plants set the tone, and a spacious air of luxury takes over. Smart, comfortable and restful public areas continue in the same vein and large, airy bedrooms have a similar sense of style and generosity, with king-size four-posters and sumptuous marbled bathrooms with bath and power shower, flat screen TV and stereo. Children welcome (under 3s free in parents' room). Pets by arrangement. Garden, walking. Golf nearby. **Rooms 12** (1 superior, all no smoking, 1 ground floor, 1 disabled). Air conditioning. Room service (all day). Turndown service. B&B €90pps, ss about €60. Closed Nov-Mar. **Piano Room:** The restaurant is a long, warmly decorated room with beautiful crystal chandeliers, a grand piano, and French doors leading to a large garden. Immaculate table settings set the tone for Benjamin Martinetti's classic/modern menus which are interesting in their simplicity and match the style of cooking which is well thought out, with the main ingredient complemented by imaginative accompaniments. Complimentary pre-starters and really good breads arrive very promptly, and a nightly special starter (ballotine of fresh rabbit, served with a pea cream & thyme jelly perhaps) is offered in addition to the menu - a good idea for resident guests who may dine in each evening. Main courses offer a good choice and tend to favour local seafood (pan-fried fillet of turbot with white asparagus, and a beurre blanc sauce for example) and Irish meats cooked with French style (like roast rack of Irish lamb, with Provencal vegetable, black olive, tomato & garlic). Vegetarians are not overlooked, and might be offered a risotto of spinach and wild mushroom, with vintage Reggiano parmesan. Everything is perfectly cooked and elegantly presented - creative desserts, especially, are stunning to look at and a pleasure to savour: dome of chocolate mousse, with Baileys cream & coffee granité is a sinfully scrumptious example. Pat and Aoife are on hand throughout, backed up by lovely staff who are knowledgeable about the food. Although the seasonal aspect of the location tends to mean that chefs change from year to year, Benjamin Martinetti had been cooking for two seasons at the time of going to press; the standard of this restaurant has been consistently excellent from the outset, and it attracts diners from a wide area. An early bird menu offers particularly good value, and a recent addition - coinciding with a kitchen extension - is the introduction of a private Chef's Table: midweek demonstration 8-course dinners for groups of 12 are offered (€150, with wine). **Seats 55** (private room, 30); air conditioning; toilets wheelchair accessible. Pianist weekends or nightly in summer. D Tue-Sun 6.30-9pm (Mon residents only); Lounge Menu L daily, 12-3 (except Sun). Early D €30 (6-7), Set D €39. House wine €24. SC discretionary. Restaurant closed Sun L; also on Mon night (except for residents). Helipad. Amex, MasterCard, Visa, Laser. **Directions:** From Ennis take Lahinch road into Miltown Malbay, on to Spanish Point. ◇

Miltown Malbay
B&B•COOKERY SCHOOL

Berry Lodge

Annagh Miltown Malbay Co Clare **Tel: 065 708 7022**
info@berrylodge.com www.berrylodge.com

Near the coast of west Clare, between Kilkee and Lahinch, this Victorian country house has been run by Rita Meade as a restaurant with accommodation since 1994 and, more recently, as a cookery school. The restaurant, which is open for dinner every night in high season (for residents only, by reservation) and is available for small private functions, has an informal country style with pine furniture and a conservatory at the back of the house, overlooking the garden. Wide-ranging menus offer local seafood and exceptional meats from a local butcher, whilst a particular talent with poultry provides a speciality of slow roast spiced duckling with Guinness honey & orange sauce & red onion marmalade. *Golf breaks available (transfer available to Lahinch or Doonbeg Golf Clubs); brochure available on application, detailing cookery courses offered and other special features. **Seats 40.** D daily 7.30-9, residents only by reservation. Set D €35; house wines €20. SC discretionary. **Accommodation:** Neat en-suite bedrooms are furnished with an attractive country mixture of old and new. Children welcome (under 5s free in parents room). No pets. **Rooms 5** (all shower only). B&B €44-46 pps, ss €12. House Closed 1 Dec-Easter. MasterCard, Visa, Laser. **Directions:** N87 from Ennis to Inagh, R460 to Miltown Malbay, N67 to Berry Lodge over Annagh Bridge, second left, first right to Berry Lodge.

MOUNTSHANNON

The lakeside village of Mountshannon prospers in a sunny south-facing position. It is an attractive, relaxed village with plenty to recommend it: **Keane's** pub (061-927214) is a good traditional bar, lounge and shop, **An Cupán Caifé** (see entry) is an attractive little cottage restaurant (now being run by its original owner, Dagmar Hilty, once again), and the friendly **Mount Shannon Hotel** (061-927162); the hotel offers weekend music and bar food daily - an open fire is a welcome sight here in chilly weather. Mountshannon is a favourite haunt of anglers for the mayfly season on Lough Derg, with fishing boats available for hire. Mountshannon is also well placed for exploring the lake's western shores, with plenty of scope for walks and bicycle rides. The harbour offers a bathing area that is popular with families, and the area is a popular sailing centre.

WWW.IRELAND-GUIDE.COM FOR ALL THE BEST PLACES TO EAT, DRINK & STAY

Mountshannon
RESTAURANT

An Cupán Caifé

Main Street Mountshannon Co Clare **Tel: 061 927 275**
dhilly@eircom.net www.ancupan.com

In this charming Shannonside Village, Dagmar Hilty's welcoming café offers somewhere sympathetic to go for a cup of coffee or a casual lunch, as well as offering more ambitious meals in the evenings. Easily found on the main street, there is a Liechtenstein family interest in this simply decorated little place, so visitors from continental Europe are set at ease. Expect to find home-made soup, chicken Caesar salad, penne pasta and the like at lunchtime, while in the evenings there is a four-course dinner available, and also an à la carte menu, although prices might seem a little elevated for the surroundings. The wine list includes well chosen house wine by the glass. **Seats 24**; children welcome (high chair, children's menu); free broadband wi/fi. Open Wed-Sun, D Wed-Sun, 6-10.30pm, set 2/3 course D €24/28, also à la carte. L Fri-Sun only (& Bank Hol Mon), 12.30-3.30pm, set L €24. Afternoon tea served Fri-Sun, 3.30 -6pm. Closed Mon, Tue (open Bank Hols, 12.30-late) MasterCard, Visa, Laser. **Directions:** Main street Mountshannon.

Mountshannon

CAFÉ•WINE BAR

The Snug Café Winebar

Main Street Mountshannon Co Clare

Tel: 061 926 826

Those who remember Noel's popular restaurant on Mountshannon's main street should be happy to find this relaxed and cheerful little place in the same premises. The whitewashed building is instantly appealing, with a small garden to the front where a couple of tables are set out in fine weather, or candles in the windows gleaming out. Inside, there are deeply comfortable black leather chairs to sink into, books to read and another garden to the rear, also with tables. To a background of quiet jazz music, your order is taken and if things are busy you may be seated in the large room alongside, which is available for art exhibitions, concerts and other events. The menu is simple – starters consist of various types of toppings for crostini – pesto and toasted pinenuts, home-made pate, tapenade etc – and main courses are a choice of pizza ,or salads and pasta dishes. But although the range is limited, what they produce is very popular: the pizza is agreeably thin-based and cooked in a wood-burning oven. (Be warned, though, that they are cooked in pairs so, if ordering more than two, it's best to share and wait for the next delivery.) House wines are modestly priced and well chosen and, all round, The Snug is a welcome addition to this charming village. Café **seats 14** (plus private room, 26); children welcome; toilets wheelchair accessible; open Fri and Sat: 6pm till late; Sun: 2pm till 9pm Open by appointment for small events, groups etc. House wine €16.50. MasterCard, Visa, Laser. **Directions:** On the Main Street.

New Quay

HISTORIC HOUSE

Mount Vernon

Flaggy Shore New Quay Co Clare **Tel: 065 707 8126**

info@mountvernon.ie www.hidden-ireland.com/mountvernon

Set back from the flag-stone shore and looking on to the cliffs of Aughinish, you enter another place at Mount Vernon, a magical country house whose owners, Mark Helmore and Aly Raftery, seem to have a special empathy with it. Named after George Washington's residence in Virginia, it was built in the 18th century for his friend Colonel William Presse of Roxborough, who served in the American War of Independence. The three tall cypress trees in the walled garden are thought to be a gift from Washington. At the end of the 19th century it became the summer home of Sir Hugh Lane, the noted art collector, and then to his aunt Lady Augusta Gregory of Coole Park, County Galway. Many of the leaders of Ireland's cultural renaissance stayed and worked here, including WB Yeats, AE (George Russell), Sean O'Casey, Synge and GB Shaw. The lovely reception rooms have fine antique furniture, paintings and batiks and painted panels from Sir William Gregory's time as Governor of Ceylon; three fireplaces were designed and built by the Pre-Raphaelite painter Augustus John. The bedrooms are spacious and interesting with views to the sea, or the wonderfully tended gardens, which include lovely walled gardens to the side that provide a sheltered place to sit out in the sunshine. (And don't forget to ask about the cobweb clearing walks.) There is a leisurely feel here and meals are an event, with drinks and conversation at 7.30 and dinner at 8.00pm. There's an emphasis on organic and local foods, especially seafood like crab, lobster, salmon and monkfish in summer, moving towards game and other meats in the cooler months. Although conveniently located, only 20 miles from Galway city, this is a world apart. Golf links at Lahinch and Doonbeg are within comfortable driving distance. Guided walks on the Burren available locally. **Rooms 5** (4 en-suite, 1 with private bathroom, all no smoking); not suitable for children under 12; B&B €110 pps, ss €30. Residents D 8pm nightly, €55, must be booked by noon on the previous day, house wine €22. Dogs permitted by prior arrangement. Walking, equestrian, fly fishing, golf and hunting/shooting all nearby. Closed 1 Jan-1 Apr. MasterCard, Visa, Laser. **Directions:** New Quay is between Kinvara and Ballyvaughan.

NEWMARKET-ON-FERGUS/SHANNON

Useful places to know about in the Shannon / Newmarket-on-Fergus / Dromoland area include several hotels which are right at Shannon airport: **Oakwood Arms Hotel** (Tel 061 361500; www.oakwood arms.com) is a neat owner-managed hotel with good facilities, including conference facilities; **Shannon Court Hotel** (formerly Quality Hotel Shannon, Tel 061 364 588; www.irishcourthotels.com) offers modern accommodation at a reasonable price; the **Rezidor Park Inn** (061 471 122; www.rezidorparkinn.com) is directly accessible from the main terminal building at Shannon Airport, and is in an unexpectedly lovely location overlooking the estuary and, with its views and rather gracious atmosphere, it retains a little of the old romance of flight. Local attractions and activities include the enduringly popular Bunratty Castle, championship golf at Dromoland Castle Golf Club (061 368 444) and Adare Manor Hotel & Golf Resort (061 395 044) and a farmers market each Friday at the Skycourt Shopping Centre in Shannon.

WWW.IRELAND-GUIDE.COM FOR ALL THE BEST PLACES TO EAT, DRINK & STAY

Newmarket-on-Fergus
RESTAURANT•COUNTRY HOUSE

Carrygerry Country House
Newmarket-on-Fergus Co Clare **Tel: 061 360500**
info@carrygerryhouse.com www.carrygerryhouse.com

Only 10 minutes from Shannon airport and in a beautiful rural setting, Carrygerry is a lovely residence dating back to 1793. It overlooks the Shannon and Fergus estuaries and, peacefully surrounded by woodlands, gardens and pastures, seems very distant from an international airport. Owners Niall and Gillian Ennis have been here since 2003 and the ambience is very pleasant, with spacious, comfortable reception rooms, open fires and an hospitable atmosphere. Bedrooms in the main house are quite spacious and traditionally furnished in line with the rest of the house, while those in the coach yard are more modern but in need of refurbishment; although planned for 2008, this had not been completed at the time of going to press and we recommend guests to check when making inquiries about accommodation. Conference/banqueting (80/94). Children welcome (under 3s free in parents' room, cot available without charge, baby sitting arranged); No pets. **Rooms 11** (3 shower-only, 1 family room, all no-smoking). B&B €75 pps, ss €40. House closed 23-26 Dec. Amex, MasterCard, Visa, Laser. **Conservatory Restaurant:** The restaurant, which is open to non-residents, is shared between the dining room and a conservatory overlooking gardens at the front of the house. Set up classically with white cloths, fine glasses and fresh flowers, it's a pleasant spot to enjoy food cooked to order by Niall Ennis. He is a good chef, who changes menus monthly and takes pride in using local ingredients in season, especially herbs and vegetables - a main course of sea bass with white wine sauce may come with wild garlic, in season, or breast of Irish chicken might be stuffed with spinach. Good breads, and there may be some appealing dishes not often found on other menus - a starter of home-made gravadlax salmon, for example - and excellent local meats as, perhaps, in herb & Dijon mustard crusted rack of Clare lamb. Good vegetarian dishes are offered as well. Attractive surroundings, real food and pleasant, friendly service make for an enjoyable outing - and a good breakfast is served here too. **Seats 54** (private room, 12), not suitable for children after 8pm; D Tue-Sat, 6.30-9.30pm; set 2/3 course D about €35/€40; house wine €19. SC 10% on groups 10+. House closed 23-26 Dec, Restaurant closed Sun, Mon. MasterCard, Visa, Laser. **Directions:** Very close to Shannon airport, on old Newmarket-on-Fergus road.

Newmarket-on-Fergus
HOTEL/RESTAURANT/CASTLE

Dromoland Castle Hotel
Newmarket-on-Fergus Co Clare **Tel: 061 368 144**
sales@dromoland.ie www.dromoland.ie

HOTEL OF THE YEAR

The ancestral home of the O'Briens, barons of Inchiquin and direct descendants of Brian Boru, High King of Ireland, this is one of the few Irish estates tracing its history back to Gaelic royal families, and it is now one of Ireland's grandest hotels, and one of the best-loved. Today's visitor will be keenly aware of this sense of history yet find it a relaxing hotel, where the grandeur of the surroundings - the castle itself, its lakes and parkland and magnificent furnishings - enhances the pleasure for guests, without overpowering. It is an enchanting place, where wide corridors lined with oak panelling are hung with ancient portraits and scented with the haunting aroma of wood smoke, and it has all the crystal chandeliers and massive antiques to be expected in a real Irish castle. Guest rooms and suites vary in size and appointments, but are generally spacious, have all been refurbished recently and have luxurious bathrooms; although always refurbished in keeping with the castle, the range of rooms and suites offered now includes some more contemporary ones (with all the attendant technical bells and whistles) as well as the traditional style for which Dromoland Castle is best known. The Brian Boru International Centre can accommodate almost any type of gathering, including exhibitions, conferences, weddings and banquets, and the recently opened 'Spa at Dromoland' (which is really beautiful) is the perfect complement. Under the watchful eye of the warm and caring General Manager, Mark Nolan, for many years now, Dromoland Castle is an outstanding example of the best of Irish hospitality - and, particularly at a time when so many fine establishments are offering unrealistic packages that inevitably lead to compromises in terms of quality and service, it is a joy to experience the very best, and the steadfast dedication of the team here is something to be treasured. Conference/banqueting (450/300); business centre; secretarial services on request. Leisure centre (indoor pool, sauna, jacuzzi, masseuse, beauty salon, hairdressing); Spa; championship golf (18); tennis, cycling, walking, clay pigeon shooting, croquet, fly fishing, garden, pool table. Gift shop, boutique. No pets. Children welcome (under 12's free in parents' room, cot available free of charge, baby sitting arranged). **Rooms 98** (6 suites, 8 junior suites, 13 executive, 49 separate bath & shower, all no smoking, 1 disabled). Lift. 24 hr room service. Room rate €443 (max 2 guests), SC inc. Breaks offered. Closed 24-26 Dec. **Earl of Thomond Restaurant:** Dining here is always a treat by any standards - it is a magnificent room, with twinkling crystal, gilding and rich fabrics, and has a lovely view over the lake and golf course. Outstanding food and service invariably match the surroundings, and then some: begin with an aperitif in the Library Bar, overlooking the eighth green, before moving through to beautifully presented tables and gentle background music provided by a traditional Irish harpist. David McCann, who has been doing a superb job as Executive Head Chef since 1994, presents a wonderful selection of luxurious dishes on an à la carte menu, which is also available as a five course table d'hôte menu, and a separate vegetarian menu is also available. The offering is predictably glamorous with great attention to detail in both the sourcing of ingredients and the cooking, a commitment to the use of Quality Assured produce is highlighted on the menu; although the style is basically classic French some dishes highlight local ingredients and are more Irish in tone. Delicious desserts include a number of variations on classics (with a suggested wine to accompany each one) and there's an excellent range of Irish farmhouse cheeses. Lunch is only served in the Earl of Thomond Restaurant on Sunday, when an appealing menu offers a wide choice of interesting dishes - often including a special Dromoland version of Irish Stew - and very good value. The cooking here is invariably exquisite, and excellent service, under the warm direction of Restaurant Manager Tony Frisby, is a match for the food. The wine list - about 250 wines, predominantly French - is under constant review, (house wines from about €27), and Sommelier Pascal Venaut has a very nice way of gently guiding guests towards the best choices to accompany their meal. The breakfast menu includes a number of specialities - buttermilk pancakes with lemon & maple syrup, Limerick ham with mushrooms, poached eggs, toast & cheddar cheese - as well as a well-laden buffet, and the traditional Irish cooked breakfast. A treat indeed. **Seats 90** (private room 70); a 15% service charge is added to all prices. D daily, 7-9, L Sun only 12.30-1.30; Set Sun L €45; Set D €68; also à la carte. *The Gallery Menu offers a lighter choice of less formal dishes throughout the day (11.30-6.30), including Afternoon Tea. *Beside the castle, the Dromoland Golf and Country Club incorporates an 18-hole parkland course, a gym, a Health Clinic offering specialist treatments, also the Green Room Bar and Fig Tree Restaurant (6.30-9.30), which provide informal alternatives to facilities in the castle, including excellent food. Closed 24-26 Dec. Helipad. Amex, Diners, MasterCard, Visa, Laser. **Directions:** 26km (17 m) from Limerick, 11km (8 m) from Shannon. Take N18 to Dromoland interchange; exit & follow signage.

QUIN

Quin is an historic village about 15 km from Ennis, and is home to a heritage site, Craggaunowen (061 367 178; open daily in summer); telling how the Celts arrived and lived in Ireland, it includes replicas of dwellings and forts, and the ancient castle is also an attraction. A major feature is the Brendan Boat built using traditional methods and materials by Tim Severin, who sailed from Ireland to Greenland, re-enacting the voyage of St. Brendan, who was reputed to have discovered America centuries before Columbus. **The Gallery Restaurant** (065 682 5789; www.thegalleryquin.com) is located on the Main Street opposite Quin Abbey and operated by owner-chef Gerry Walsh, who takes pride in showcasing local produce (D Tue-Sun, also L Sun). **Zion Coffee House & Restaurant** (065 682 5417;www.zion.ie) is a more casual restaurant beside the Abbey, offering good breakfasts and lunches, and light refreshments throughout the day - also popular locally for informal evening meals. Championship golf is available just a few kilometres down the road, in Dromoland Castle Golf Club (061 368 444).
WWW.IRELAND-GUIDE.COM FOR ALL THE BEST PLACES TO EAT, DRINK & STAY

Scariff
RESTAURANT

MacRuaidhri's

The Square Scariff Co Clare **Tel: 061 921 999**
info@macruaidhris.com www.macruaidhris.com

On the square at the top of this hilly little country town you'll find the pleasant neighbourhood restaurant, MacRuaidhri's, which is run by local man Manus Rodgers and head chef Marcus Wren. Expect a warm welcome, friendly service and good value: a concise, keenly priced table d'hôte dinner menu offers a balanced choice including seafood and favourites like braised shank of lamb and pan-seared 10 oz steak (meats are 100% Irish and Quality Assured), and is very fairly priced. A more expensive, but still reasonably priced, à la carte menu offers a wide range of choice, and there's a short, but adequate, wine list. **Seats 50** (outdoors, 6); reservations required; air conditioning; reservations advised; children welcome; toilets wheelchair accessible. D Tue-Sat. 6-9.15pm (open Tue only in Jul-Sep), L Sun only, 2 sittings, 12.30 & 2.30pm; set D €39, also à la carte; house wine €19. Closed Sun D, Mon, and Tue off season. MasterCard, Visa, Laser. **Directions:** From Ennis follow signs for Tulla/Scariff until Bodyke village, turn right, 5km (3 miles), going straight through Tuamgraney. On Scariff square.

Tulla
RESTAURANT

Flappers Restaurant

Main Street Tulla Co Clare
Tel: 065 683 5711

The most remarkable thing about Jim and Patricia McInerney's small split-level restaurant in the village of Tulla is that it has been consistently enjoyable over such a long period. Patricia is the chef, and the dishes she sends out from the kitchen are a daily testament to her imagination, insistence on good ingredients and attention to detail. The room is simple - refreshingly free of decoration, except for a pair of striking pictures and fresh flowers on the tables, but there's always a prompt welcome and tables (which are covered in classic white linen in the evening) are nicely spaced. Lunchtime draws on hearty, good value home-cooked food from a simple menu. In the evening, there's a fairly priced à la carte menu offering a well-balanced choice of dishes which are a little out of the ordinary, with specialities including a starter salad of fresh crabmeat with coriander, chilli & lime and a main course of roast rack of lamb with scallion mash and (a rarity in Irish restaurants) fresh mint sauce; fish and vegetarian dishes are equally good, and delicious genuinely home-made desserts might include simple treats like crushed meringues with fresh fruit & passion fruit purée. Service is confident and pleasant, and a well-chosen wine list offers some good bottles at reasonable prices - and there's even a take-away service, a boon to self-catering holidaymakers. **Seats 40**; air conditioning; wheelchair access to toilets. Brunch Mon-Fri 9.30am-2.45pm, L Sat 12-3pm, D Fri-Sat, 7-9.30/10pm. A la carte; house wine about €17; SC discretionary (except 10% on groups of 8+). Closed Sun, bank hols; 2 weeks Nov & Jan. MasterCard, Visa, Laser. **Directions:** Main street Tulla village, 10 miles from Ennis. ◇

CORK CITY

It is Cork, of all Ireland's cities, which most warmly gives the impression of being a place at comfort with itself, for it's the heart of a land flowing in milk and honey. Cork is all about the good things in life. While it may be stretching things a little to assert that the southern capital has a Mediterranean atmosphere, there's no doubting its Continental and cosmopolitan flavour, and the Cork people's relaxed enjoyment of it all.

The central thoroughfare of St Patrick's Street is comfortably revitalised in a handsome and mainly pedestrianised style which is continued in the bustling urban network radiating from it. This fine thoroughfare was a river channel until 1783, as the earliest parts of Cork city were built on islands where the River Lee meets the sea. But for more two centuries now, it has been Cork's main street, affectionately known to generations of Corkonians as "Pana". Designed by Catalan architect Beth Gali, the regeneration project brought a flavour of Barcelona's Ramblas to a city which responded with enthusiasm and pride.

Oliver Plunkett Street has received the same improvement, and Grand Parade has responded to create a city centre with attractive pedestrian priorities. And the potential of the Port of Cork area in the city for sympathetic re-development is being actively progressed.

Cork's unique qualities, and its people's appreciation of natural produce, make it a favoured destination for connoisseurs. Trading in life's more agreeable commodities has always been what Cork and its legendary merchant princes were all about. At one time, the city was known as the butter capital of Europe, and it continues to be unrivalled for the ready availability of superbly fresh produce, seen at its best in the famous English Market where Grand Parade meets Patrick Street, while the Cork Free Choice Consumer Group (021 7330178) meets each month to promote the cause of quality food.

The way in which sea and land intertwine throughout the wonderfully sheltered natural harbour, and through the lively old city itself, has encouraged waterborne trade and a sea-minded outlook. Thus today Cork is at the heart of Ireland's most dynamically nautical area, a place world-renowned for its energetic interaction with the sea, whether for business or pleasure.

Local Attractions and Information

Cork Airport	021 431 3031
Cork Arts Society	021 427 7749
Cork City Gaol	021 430 5022
Cork European Capital of Culture	021 455 2005
Cork Farmers Market Cornmarket St Sats 9am-1pm	021 733 0178
Cork Tourist Information	021 425 5100
Cork Guinness Cork Jazz Festival (late October)	021 421 5170
Cork International Choral Festival (April/May)	021 421 5125
Cork International Film Festival (October)	021 427 1711
Cork Public Museum	021 427 0679
Cork Crawford Gallery, Emmett Place	021 480 5042
English Market (covered, with specialty food stalls), corner between Grand Parade & Patrick Street	021 427 4407
Firkin Crane Dance Centre Shandon	021 450 7487
Frank O'Connor House (Writers Cntr) 84 Douglas St	021 431 2955
Glucksman Gallery, UCC	021 490 1844
Good Food In Cork (Consumer Group) – Cork Free Choice	021 733 0178
Opera House	021 427 0022
Railway Station	021 450 4888
Tig Fili Arts Centre & Publishers, MacCreddin St	021 450 9274
Triskel Arts Centre Tobin St off Sth Main St	021 427 2022

CORK CITY

Visitors to Cork City with an interest in food and fresh produce have a treat in store at the famous English Market (open daily, see below), and should also visit Coal Quay Market, which is held in Cornmarket Street every Saturday. Of more general interest to visitors, there are museums and galleries including the **Crawford Gallery** (see entry for the Café), and Cork Opera House. The many wonderful gardens nearby include Lakemount Garden (Glanmire, 021 482 1052), Fota Arboretum & Garden (Carrigtwohill, 021 481 5543), Cedar Lodge Garden (Midleton, 021 461 3379), while golfers can play two of the best known golf courses in County Cork - Fota Island Golf Club (Carrigtwohill, 021 488 3710) and the Old Head of Kinsale Golf Club (Kinsale, 021 477 8444). A pleasant alternative to city centre accommodation is the 'new' **Montenotte** (021 453 0050; www.themontenottehotel.com, formerly the Country Club Hotel), perched high in a fashionable residential area with views over the city, with good leisure facilities. A good choice of budget accommodation to suit both leisure and business guests includes the **Travelodge Hotel** (Frankfield Road; 021 431 0722) near Cork Airport; **Jurys Inn** (Andersons Quay; 021 494 3000), in a convenient central location with all the features that Jurys Inns are well known for: room prices include comfortable en-suite accommodation for up to two adults & two children (including a sofa bed) and there is space for a cot (which can be supplied by arrangement). **The Maldron Hotel** (John Redmond Street; 021 452 9200), also in the city centre, has above average facilities including a good leisure centre (gym, pool, sauna and jacuzzi); dedicated meeting rooms for up to 100 delegates are serviced by a dedicated conference porter. For quick, quality Pan-Asian food noodle lovers could head for the local branch of the UK-based **Wagamama** (South Main Street; 021 427 8872) chain; it offers healthy, inexpensive meals, including an extensive choice of meat, seafood and vegetarian dishes, all cooked to order and promptly served. For those seeking a little more comfort on a budget **Milano** (Oliver Plunkett Street; 021 427 3106) might be a good option; like its Dublin sister restaurant (see entry) it offers good moderately priced Italian food - mainly, but not exclusively, authentic pizzas and pastas - in stylish surroundings. Its family-friendliness, consistency and good service are strong points; they're happy to cater for large parties, drinks receptions etc too; live jazz on Wednesday nights.

Cork City
RESTAURANT

Amicus

23 Paul Street Plaza Cork Co Cork
Tel: 021 427 6455

Right in the centre of the city, in Cork's Huguenot district, Ursula and Robert Hales' restaurant is a lot bigger than it used to be when it was tucked into a small site around the corner, but this lively place is still a very popular restaurant and - as they don't take bookings - you may have to wait for a table. An attractive old brick building with some tables outside for fine weather, it's bright and modern inside, with the main restaurant on the ground floor and a tapas bar/restaurant upstairs where an open kitchen allows you to watch the chefs at work. Arriving guests are promptly seated as soon as a table becomes available, and offered extensive menus which feature popular international dishes: salads, bruschetta, gourmet sandwiches, wraps and and pastas on the daytime menu with some overlap onto the evening menu which offers a smaller choice of more substantial dishes, notably seafood. Real, uncomplicated food, fair pricing and a youthful atmosphere add up to an attractive package which is clearly popular with locals and visitors alike. Service is friendly, although the pressure can sometimes show at busy times, and children are made welcome. **Seats 108** (+ outside seating). Open Mon-Sat 8am-10pm, Sun 12-10pm; L 12-6pm, D 6-10pm (till 11pm Fri/Sat); house wine about €18. Closed 25-26 Dec. MasterCard, Visa, Laser. **Directions:** Paul Street is off Patrick Street. ◈

Cork City
RESTAURANT

Bangkok 93 - A Taste of Thailand

8 Bridge Street Cork Co Cork **Tel: 021 450 5404**
maryan@iol.ie

Cork city's longest established restaurant specialising in Thai cuisine, Mary Anne and Jim Ryan's restaurant started off in 1993 as 'A Taste of Thailand' and soon earned a loyal following that kept it busy all the time. After a major refurbishment, they re-opened with a new name too, hence Bangkok 93 - A Taste of Thailand. Jim trained in Thailand and Australia, and freshness and authenticity are the key words here: everything is cooked to order with no artificial colours, flavours or additives used, and fresh ingredients are all Irish, except for exotics, and mainly come from the English Market. Many dishes are offered with a number of variations, including vegetarian options, but other special dietary requirements (vegan, diabetic etc) can also be catered for. Menus are quite extensive but organised in a user-friendly way by style - curry, grills and stir-fries, noodles and so on - and, for the undecided, there are a couple of the familiar banquet meals, offering a balanced selection of dishes on each course for groups of four or six. House specialities include traditional Thai curries, Thai beef salad and Pad Thai noodles, but the range offered is wide and some European dishes are offered too. Everything is made to order (mild, medium or hot to suit personal preference, or giving you 'fresh chillies on the side' so you can adjust your own meal to taste), and good food, service and value explain this restaurant's enduring popularity. The wine list offers a balanced choice of world wines, including some half and quarter bottles, also beers including Singha and Tiger. **Seats 60** (private room, 8); children welcome (high chair); air conditioning. D only Mon-Sun, 5-11pm (to 10.30pm Sun); Early D about €25 (6-7 pm); Set menus ('banquets') for min. 4 persons from about €30, otherwise à la carte. House wine from about €22 (beers, including Thai beers, available). Closed 24-26 Dec. MasterCard, Visa, Laser. **Directions:** 1 minute walk from city centre. ◇

Cork City
PUB•WINE BAR

Boqueria

6 Bridge St Cork Co Cork **Tel: 021 455 9049**
tapas@boqueria.ie www.boqueria.ie

Located in an attractive former pub in an old building, this welcoming place caused quite a stir when it first opened, and is now an established part of the Cork dining scene. A long, narrow premises with upholstered bar stools and comfortable seating at tables towards the back, the character of the original bar was retained, and improved with a new black marble topped bar, wine racks and large, unframed modern oil paintings. Aside from the breakfast menu (Mon-Sat, 9.30-12), the menu offers a mixture of genuine Spanish tapas dishes along with some Irish variations, such as smoked salmon, black pudding and Irish cheeses. Some of these little dishes are cold plates such as charcuterie or smoked fish, dependent on well-sourced artisan/organic products, whilst others are freshly cooked and served hot. Many of the familiars are here - tortilla espanola, patatas bravas, plus lots of interesting hybrids too. There's a full licence, and a list of about 40 Spanish wines includes quarter bottles, sherries by the glass and occasional specials; wine tastings are available for groups, and have proved very popular. **Seats 40**; free broadband wi/fi; not suitable for children under 7 yrs after 7pm; air conditioning; food served Mon-Sat, 9.30am - 11pm, Sun 5.30pm-10pm; house wine €19.50. Closed Good Fri, 25-26 Dec. MasterCard, Visa, Laser. **Directions:** Between Patrick St. and MacCurtain St. on Bridge St. ◇

Cork City
CAFÉ

Café Gusto

3 Washington Street Cork Co Cork **Tel: 021 425 4446**
info@cafegusto.com www.cafegusto.com

A smart blue and white frontage and neatly tiered bay tree at the door hint at the big ideas at work in this little designer coffee bar near Singer's Corner. The brainchild of Marianne Delaney, former manager of The Exchange on George's Quay, and her Ballymaloe-trained partner Denis O'Mullane, who take pride in sourcing the very best quality ingredients. They specialise in gourmet rolls, wraps and salads, either to go or to eat on the premises, and coffee is made by baristas trained to master standard, using 100% arabica beans from the Java Roasting Company. The same philosophy applies to the food, in a short menu ranging from Simply Cheddar (freshly baked Italian bread filled with Dubliner cheese, beef tomato, white onion & Ballymaloe relish) to The Flying Bacon (filled with chicken, bacon, Emmenthal, honey Dijon, lettuce & tomato). Food prices are not much more than supermarket sandwiches and the extensive range of coffees, teas, herbal teas etc is keenly priced too. Great value, popular local meeting place - if only there were more like this. *There's another café beside the Clarion Hotel on Lapps Quay, and a sister restaurant Liberty Grill, on Washington Street (see entry). **Seats 20**; air conditioning. Open Mon-Sat, 8am-6pm. Closed Sun, bank hols. **No Credit Cards. Directions:** On corner of Washington Street & Grand Parade. ◇

Cork City
RESTAURANT
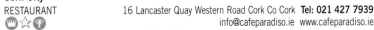

Café Paradiso

16 Lancaster Quay Western Road Cork Co Cork **Tel: 021 427 7939**
info@cafeparadiso.ie www.cafeparadiso.ie

Denis Cotter's ground-breaking vegetarian restaurant produces such exciting mainstream cooking that even the most committed of carnivores admit to relishing every mouthful and it attracts devotees from all over Ireland - and beyond. Seasonal specialities that people are happy to cross the country for include a beautiful beetroot mousse with orange scented yoghurt, served with fennel crispbreads and a rocket, pear & crisped beetroot salad, which is a brilliant example of the cooking style at this colourful little restaurant. It's a modest, slightly bohemian place with a busy atmosphere and, although it may have a persistently well-worn look these days, there is plenty to compensate for any downside in the surroundings - and staff are not only friendly and helpful but obviously enthusiastic about their work. Seasonal menus based on the best organic produce available are topped up by daily specials, which might include potato gnocchi or a vegetable risotto - and desserts, such as blackberry fool or a mountainous Strawberry Pavlova, which are also gorgeous. A well-priced global wine list features a strong representation from New Zealand and a number of organic wines; half carafes and glasses offer quality at a fair price. The cooking is never less than stunning - and significantly, in this era of "cheffy" food and big egos, the creator of this wonderful food describes himself simply as "owner cook" - and many of Denis Cotter's creations are featured in his acclaimed books: "Café Paradiso Cookbook", "Café Paradiso Seasons", and "Wild Garlic Gooseberries'... And Me. Café Paradiso may be small and a little tired around the edges, but it still packs a mighty punch. *Accommodation: three rooms are available over the restaurant for dinner guests, at a room rate of about €160. **Seats 45** (outdoor seating, 6); children welcome; toilets wheelchair accessible. L Tue-Sat, 12-3, D Tue-Sat 6.30-10.30. A la carte. House wines from €22. Service discretionary. Closed Sun, Mon, Christmas week. MasterCard, Visa, Laser. **Directions:** On Western Road, opposite Jurys Hotel.

Cork City   # Citrus Restaurant

RESTAURANT   Barrycourt House East Douglas Village Cork Co Cork **Tel: 021 436 1613**

Harold Lynch and Beth Haughton's restaurant is a lovely bright space, with windows on two sides and simple uncluttered tables - not a lot to absorb the sound of happy people enjoying Harold's cooking, but there's a good buzz. The style is international but as much as possible is based on local produce: meats and fish come from the English Market. Harold's menus read simply and are full of things you'd love to try - and a plate of anti-pasti makes a good start with your aperitif, while making the main choices. Starters might include a mildly spicy fish soup with rouille and there will usually be one or two tempting vegetarian dishes and updated classics such as salmon & potato cakes; excellent raw materials are generally allowed to speak for themselves. Tempting desserts tend to be variations on favourite themes and a well-chosen wine list is short but sweet. Service, under Beth's supervision, is charming and efficient. *Another restaurant, The Club Brasserie (see entry), opened on Lapps Quay in 2008. **Seats 60**; toilets wheelchair accessible; children welcome before 9pm. Mon-Sat: L12-3.30, D 5.30-10, Sun D only, 5-9. A la carte. House wine €18.50. SC discretionary. Closed L Sun, Christmas Day. Amex, MasterCard, Visa, Laser. **Directions:** Through Douglas village, 1st left after Bully's Restaurant.

Cork City   # Clarion Hotel Cork

HOTEL   Lapps Quay Cork Co Cork **Tel: 021 422 4900**

info@clarionhotelcorkcity.com   www.clarioncork.com

Those who like contemporary hotels and enjoy the buzz of the city centre will love the Clarion. In a brilliant central location with a wide terrace and boardwalk along the River Lee, this striking hotel embodies many of the best features of other recently built Clarion hotels and has excellent amenities including state-of-the-art conference facilities, spa, swimming pool, and gym. The entrance foyer is highly dramatic, with an atrium soaring right up to a glass roof, and rooms are arranged off galleries, which overlook the foyer; well-appointed accommodation includes riverside suites and a penthouse suite. A choice of dining is offered: Sinergie, a brasserie style restaurant, offers an international menu, good cooking and attentive service, while the Kudos bar provides an informal alternative and serves Asian fusion food to 10pm (weekends to 8pm). Conferences/Banqueting (350/270), business centre, free broadband wi/fi, secretarial services. **Rooms 191** (2 suites, 10 for disabled, 5 family, 95 no smoking); children welcome (under 12s free in parents' room, cots available at no charge, baby sitting arranged). Limited room service; Lift. B&B from €160 per room. Leisure centre with pool, fitness room, sauna, steam room, jacuzzi; beauty salon. Closed 24-27 Dec. Amex, Diners, MasterCard, Visa, Laser. **Directions:** Corner of Clontarf St. and Lapps Quay. Diagonally across from City Hall. ◇

Cork City
RESTAURANT

The Club Brasserie

Lapps Quay Cork Co Cork
Tel: 021 427 3987

This well-located restaurant is a second venture for Cork restaurateurs Harold Lynch and Beth Haughton - well known for their successful Citrus Restaurant in Douglas (see entry). It's in a new building on a pedestrianised riverside site and, beyond the modern glass-fronted exterior, lies a stylish high-ceilinged interior, with aged parquet floor, chandeliers and wall-bracket lamps. Even early in the week it has a good buzz and, with well-spaced white clothed tables and a mixture of comfortable chairs and banquettes and a friendly, welcoming atmosphere - it's a pleasant place to be. Harold is known for his commitment to quality ingredients, sourced locally where possible - and for cooking unfussy food with style. Menus offer a zesty take on a range of modern classics and many dishes are well-suited to appearing under various guises as different times of day. Lunch menus offer a combination of gourmet sandwiches (tartine of gravadlax and lamb burger with coriander, cumin & mint yogurt, for example); simple seafood like salmon & potato cakes or fish & chips with chunky fries & mint pea purée; classic salads (Caesar; seared beef; baked goat's cheese); homely mains (cottage pie, chicken curry, sirloin steak) and classic desserts. Evening brings a great value pre-theatre menu with a choice of three starters and mains (€20.50) and an appealing dinner à la carte which offers some smarter versions of lunch dishes and a lot else beside - starters like crab crème brulée; combo salads (available as starter or main) like Greek lamb (chargrilled lamb with feta, black olives, cucumber & red onions, with mint dressing); and serious mains like roasted pork belly with crackling and cider & rosemary cream. Desserts are suitably sinful and some, including old favourites like lemon meringue pie with passion fruit, are also on the lunch menu. An interesting wine list offers good quality with value - including a fair choice of half bottles. All round, an interesting choice of food and in attractive, comfortable surroundings and with good service makes for a pleasing dining experience. **Seats 85**; B 8-11am. L Mon-Sat 12-3pm, D Mon-Sun 5-10pm (Sun to 9pm). Pre-theatre set D 5-6.45pm, €20.50; house wine €19.50. Underground car park (shared with Clarion Hotel). Amex, Diners, MasterCard, Visa, Laser. **Directions:** Beside River Lee, front of next block to east of Clarion Hotel. ◇

Cork City
HOTEL

Cork International Airport Hotel

Cork Airport Cork Co Cork **Tel: 021 454 9800**
info@corkairporthotel.com www.corkinternationalairporthotel.com

Linked by a covered walkway leading to the door of the new Cork Airport terminal, this recently opened hotel could not be handier for the time-pressed traveller. More than just convenient, however, it also has an unusual and very funky style - and even humour; it is virtually an aviation museum - albeit with the exhibits arranged for continued use, and mixed with some very strange companion pieces - and the aviation theme that pervades the hotel extends to the rooms, which are available in Economy, Business and First Class categories. True to the original thinking behind this hotel, accommodation is designed to please, with the aim if making it an destination rather than just a convenient airport hotel - and the tone is calmer than in the public areas. Facilities are tailored to travellers' needs and include a Pullman Lounge where the business traveller can book a seat, take a shower, check emails, read in comfort and have a bite to eat - and an on-site spa where you could while away many an hour of delays. Special features include free Wifi throughout the hotel, and breakfast from 3.30am. Conference/banqueting (400). Park & Fly packages available. **Rooms 150**. B&B room rate about €105 (1-2 guests); about €85 without breakfast. Amex, MasterCard, Visa. **Directions:** Situated opposite the new Cork Airport terminal. ◇

Cork City
RESTAURANT•WINE BAR

The Cornstore Winebar & Grill

43 Cornmarket Street Cork Co Cork **Tel: 021 425 1888**
info@the-cornstore.com www.the-cornstore.com

In the buzzy Coal Quay renewal area, this new sister establishment to the highly regarded Aubars in Limerick (see entry) is in a stylishly converted two-storey granite mill building. Colourful Spanish tiles in the reception area lead to an expanse of polished wooden floors cleverly divided into areas of alcoves, flexible table and chair seating and more intimate booths, as well as a bar counter popular with singletons in for a quick drink or snack. Lobster is something of a speciality here, appearing as a starter with warm lemon butter; whole or half with hollandaise, pea purée and proper house chips as a main course, or the trencherman's surf & turf option of medallion of beef with half lobster and béarnaise sauce. Silky duck liver paté with Cumberland sauce is a popular starter, as is the generous fresh prawn cocktail served in a crushed ice coupe with real Marie Rose sauce. For sharing, there is a freshly baked country loaf served with tapenade, hummus, and pesto for dipping, and a range of stone-baked pizzas come straight from special ovens. The Cornstore's premium steaks are 100% Irish beef, hung 21-28 days - and choices range from the 10oz rib-eye to a 16oz T-bone. A short but irresistible list of home-made desserts features treats like pecan tart with mocha ice cream, crème brulée with short-bread biscuit and a different chocolate dessert each day - the molten-centred chocolate fudge cake is worth a detour. A well-balanced wine list leans towards the New World, and features 20 wines by the glass (€4.50-€9.95). Not surprisingly perhaps, The Cornstore has become one of Cork's hotspots, attracting customers with top class food, value for money and sharp service that manages to be both friendly and efficient. **Seats 170** (outdoors, 20); children welcome (high chair, children's menu, baby changing facilities); wheelchair friendly; air conditioning; reservations recommended. L & D daily, 12-4pm & 5-10.30pm; set L €15; early D 5-7pm, €21.95; set D €25.95. House wine from €19.95. SC 10% on groups 10+. Closed 25 Dec. Amex, MasterCard, Visa, Laser. **Directions:** Cornmarket Street is just off the top end of St. Patrick's Street in the middle of Cork.

Cork City
RESTAURANT

Crawford Gallery Café

Emmet Place Cork Co Cork **Tel: 021 427 4415**
crawfordinfo@eircom.net www.ballymaloe.ie

An excellent collection of 18th- and 19th-century landscapes is housed in this fine 1724 building and its large modern extension. And this is also home to the Crawford Gallery Café, one of Cork city's favourite informal eating places, which is managed by Fawn Allen, grand-daughter of Myrtle and the late Ivan Allen, founders of Ballymaloe House - and, by a remarkable coincidence, also a descendant of Arthur Hill, architect of a previous extension to the gallery, completed in 1884. Menus in this striking blue and white room reflect the Ballymaloe philosophy that food is precious and should be handled carefully, so Fawn Allen's freshly prepared dishes are made from natural local ingredients, and she also offers Ballymaloe breads and many of the other dishes familiar to Ballymaloe fans. Except for a few specialities too popular to take off (such as their spinach & mushroom pancakes), the menu changes weekly but the style - a balanced mixture of timeless country house fare and contemporary international dishes featuring carefully sourced meats, fish from Ballycotton and the freshest of seasonal vegetables - remains reassuringly constant. Substantial dishes, such as classic sirloin steak and chips, with béarnaise sauce - or a big vegetarian option like Mediterranean bean stew with coriander & basmati rice - are great for a real meal, and the home-made pickles, relishes, chutneys and preserves are delicious details. And, for a lighter bite, the home baking is outstanding. A short well-balanced wine list offers some half bottles. Conference/banqueting: available for private parties, corporate entertaining, lectures etc in evenings; details on application. **Seats 60**; no reservations (except for groups 6+); toilets wheelchair accessible. Open Mon-Sat, 8.30-3pm (from 9am Sat), B 8.30-11.30am, L 12.25-3pm; à la carte; house wine €19. Service discretionary. Closed Sun, 24 Dec-7 Jan, bank hols. Amex, MasterCard, Visa, Laser. **Directions:** City centre, next to Opera House.

Cork City
PUB

Dan Lowrey's Tavern

13 Mc Curtain Street Cork Co Cork
Tel: 021 4505071

This characterful pub beside the Everyman Palace Theatre was established in 1875 and is named after its founder. Long before the arrival of the "theme pub", Lowrey's was famous for having windows which originated from Kilkenny Cathedral, but it also has many of its own original features, including a fine mahogany bar. It has been run by Anthony and Catherine O'Riordan since 1995 and they lay emphasis on the fact that it's a family-run bar and always welcoming. Together with Eleanor Murray, who has been chef from the outset, Catherine oversees the kitchen herself and it's a good place for an fairly priced home-cooked meal - popular dishes like home-made quiche or lasagne served with salad or fries, for example, or seafood bake, filled with salmon, monkfish & cod, topped with creamed pota-toes and toasted breadcrumbs. It's popular with local business people at lunch time, and plain or toasted sandwiches are available to take away. **Seats 30** (plus outdoor seating for 10); not suitable for children after 9pm. L & D daily: 12-3.30 & 7-9, Sun L 12.30-5pm. (Sandwiches available all day). Closed 25 Dec & Good Fri. **No Credit Cards**. **Directions:** Next to Metropole Gresham Hotel, across from Isaacs Restaurant.

ENGLISH MARKET

It is hard to imagine a visit to Cork without at the very least a quick browse through the English Market (open daily) and - although it is most famous for its huge range of fresh food stalls selling everything from wet fish and almost forgotten vegetables to cheeses, freshly baked breads and, these days,

Georgina Campbell's Ireland

imported produce like olives - there's a growing choice of places to top up the browser's energy levels along the way. The premier spot is **Farmgate Café** on the first floor (see entry), but a growing number of stalls are offering nourishment on the go: Mary Rose's **Café Central** stall is well-known to regulars - she used to sell pork & bacon there but converted it to a coffee stall about 5 years ago, and now does a roaring trade in croissants, coffees and confectionery. Then **Fruit Boost** came along, serving fresh juices, soon followed by **The Sandwich Stall**, which serves filled rolls & coffee. And, more recently, there is **Joup** (www.joup.org), offering more substantial fare, including breakfast and lunches (mainly soups & salads) and also coffee & other beverages during the day.
WWW.IRELAND-GUIDE.COM FOR ALL THE BEST PLACES TO EAT, DRINK & STAY

Cork City
CAFÉ

Farmgate Café
English Market Cork Co Cork **Tel: 021 427 8134**
farmgatecafe@yahoo.ie

A sister restaurant to the Farmgate Country Store and Restaurant in Midleton, Kay Harte's Farmgate Café shares the same commitment to serving fresh, local food - and, as it is located in the gallery above the English Market, where ingredients are purchased daily, it doesn't come much fresher or more local than this. The atmosphere is lively and busy, as people come and go from the market below, giving a great sense of being at the heart of things. With its classic black and white tiles, simple wooden furniture and interesting art, work there's a combination of style and a comfortably down-to-earth atmosphere which suits the wholesome food they serve. Having highlighted the freshness of local ingredients for some time in dishes that were a mixture of modern and traditional, Kay Harte and her team now offer regional dishes using the food they buy in the market, and have introduced lesser known foods such as corned mutton to their menus alongside famous old Cork ones with a special market connection, like tripe & drisheen and corned beef & champ with green cabbage. Menus depend on what is available in the English Market each day, including "oysters to your table directly from the fish monger" and other fish - used, for example, in a chowder that is ever-popular with market regulars. And, however simple, everything is perfectly cooked - including superb breakfasts. Either full cooked or continental breakfast is offered, with self-service or table service available. All this and delicious home-baked cakes, breads and desserts too; whether as a bite to accompany a coffee, or to finish off a meal, a wonderfully homemade seasonal sweet is always a treat. This is an interesting and lively place to enjoy good food - and it's great value for money. *Farmgate Café was the winner of our Irish Breakfast Awards in 2007. **Seats 110**; children welcome. Meals Mon-Sat, from 9am - 5pm: B 9-10.30, L 12-4; house wine from €17. Closed Sun, bank hols, Dec 25-3 Jan. Diners, MasterCard, Visa, Laser. **Directions:** English Market - off Oliver Plunkett Street and Grand Parade.

Cork City
RESTAURANT

Fenns Quay Restaurant
5 Sheares Street Cork Co Cork **Tel: 021 427 9527**
www.fennsquay.ie

Housed in a 250-year old listed building, this is a bright, busy restaurant with a welcoming atmosphere and simple decor enlivened by striking modern paintings. Kate Lawlor (the head chef), her cousin Kevin Crowley and his partner Pennapa Wongsuwan recently bought Fenns Quay Restaurant from owners Eilish and Pat O'Leary and intend to continue in the same style. Kate's lunch and dinner menus both offer plenty of interesting choices, including a number of vegetarian options (highlighted) and daily specials, including seafood sourced daily from the nearby English Market. Carefully sourced ingredients are local where possible (especially meats, which are a point of pride), presented in a pleasing bistro style, with an emphasis on flavour. Specialities include char-grilled fillet steak "Wellie Style", an enduring favourite, which comes with roast flat cup mushrooms, red onion confit, house cut potato chips and a choice of sauces (béarnaise and peppercorn). A new wine list was in preparation at the time of the Guide's visit but the policy is to offer variety at reasonable prices, with several by the glass - good value is a feature of both food and drink. A comfortable outdoor seating area makes a pleasant extension to the restaurant, and recent renovations have enabled wheelchair access to the restaurant but not to toilets, unfortunately, as it is a listed building. **Seats 60** (outdoor seating, 10); children welcome; air conditioning. Open all day Mon-Sat 10am-10pm; L 12-3, D 6-10. L Deal about €10 (12-5), also à la carte; set 2/3 course D about €22.50/27.50; à la carte also available. House wine €17.95. SC 10% on groups 6+. On street parking can be difficult during the day, but is easy to find after 6.30. Closed Sun, 25 Dec, bank hols. Amex, MasterCard, Visa, Laser. **Directions:** Central city - 2 minutes from the Courthouse.

Cork City

RESTAURANT WITH ROOMS

Flemings Restaurant

Silver Grange House Tivoli Cork Co Cork **Tel: 021 482 1621**

info@flemingsrestaurant.ie www.flemingsrestaurant.ie

Clearly signed off the main Cork-Dublin road, this large Georgian family house is home to Michael and Eileen Fleming's excellent restaurant with rooms. On a hillside overlooking the river, the house is set in large grounds, including a kitchen garden, which provides fruit, vegetables and herbs for the restaurant during the summer. It is a big property to maintain and the entrance can seem a little run down, but this is quickly forgotten when you enter the light, airy double dining room, which is decorated in an elegant low-key style that high-lights its fine proportions, while well-appointed linen-clad tables provide a fine setting for Michael Fleming's classical, modern French cooking. Seasonal table d'hote and à la carte menus offer a wonderful choice of classics, occasionally influenced by current international trends but, even where local ingredients feature strongly, the main thrust of the cooking style is classical French - as in a superb speciality starter of pan-fried foie gras de canard with Timoleague black pudding & glazed apple. Less usual choices might include Roast Loin of Venison with Poached Pear, an imaginative combination and beautifully presented. Desserts may include a deep apple pie served with home-made ice cream - and a selection of cheese is served traditionally, with biscuits and fruits. Michael's cooking is invariably excellent, presentation elegant, and service both attentive and knowledgeable. A great antidote to the sameness of modern multicultural restaurants - a visit to a classic restaurant like this is a treat to treasure. Good wine list - and good value all round. *A converted basement into a comfortable bar/lounge seats up to 70. Banqueting (90). **Seats 80** (private room 30; outside seating, 30); children welcome. L&D daily, 12.30-3, 6.30-10; reservations not necessary. Set L €28.50, D à la carte; house wine about €22. Live music on Saturday nights in winter. SC discretionary. **Accommodation:** There are four spacious en-suite rooms, comfortably furnished in a style appropriate to the age of the house (B&B €55 pps, ss €33). Closed 24-27 Dec. Amex, MasterCard, Visa, Laser. **Directions:** Off main Cork-Dublin route, 4km from city centre.

Cork City

HOTEL

Gresham Metropole Hotel & Leisure Centre

MacCurtain Street Cork Co Cork **Tel: 021 4508122**

info@gresham-metropolehotel.com www.gresham-hotels.com

This imposing city-centre hotel next door to the Everyman Palace Theatre and backing on to the River Lee, celebrated its centenary in 1998. Always popular with those connected with the arts and entertainment industry, there are many displays (photos and press cuttings) of stars past and present in the public areas and the atmospheric, traditionally-styled Met Tavern. Many of the hotel's original features remain, including the marble facade, exterior carved stonework and plaster ceilings. Recent refurbishment has greatly improved the bedrooms, most of which now combine a period feel with modern facilities, and care has been taken to bring previously neglected areas back to their former elegance by, for example, correcting ceiling heights which had been changed in previous 'improvements'. The famous swimming pool remains, however, and can be viewed from part of the restaurant - an unusual accompaniment for your breakfast. Conference and meeting facilities have air conditioning and natural daylight. (450). **Rooms 113** (2 junior suites, 44 executive rooms,10 shower only, 55 no-smoking, 1 for disabled); children welcome (under 2 free in parents' room, cot available without charge, baby sitting arranged). No pets. Room rate from about €90. Leisure centre; indoor swimming pool. Arrangement with nearby car park. Open all year. Amex, Diners, MasterCard, Visa, Laser. **Directions:** City centre hotel.

Cork City

HOTEL•RESTAURANT

Hayfield Manor Hotel

Perrott Avenue College Road Cork Co Cork **Tel: 021 484 5900**

enquiries@hayfieldmanor.ie www.hayfieldmanor.ie

Set in two acres of gardens near University College Cork, the city's premier hotel provides every comfort and a remarkable level of privacy and seclusion, just a mile from the city centre. Although relatively new, it has the feel of a large period house, and is managed with warmth and discreet efficiency. Public areas include a choice of restaurants, both excellent of their type - the formal Orchids, which overlooks gardens at the back, and the smart-casual Perrotts - and a re-designed bar that skilfully links the contrasting traditional and contemporary styles of the interior. Spacious suites and guest rooms vary in decor, are beautifully furnished with antiques and have generous marbled bathrooms, all with separate bath and shower. On-site amenities include the unusual new Beautique spa, with indoor pool, and treatment rooms furnished with antiques. *Hayfield Manor was our Hotel of the Year in 2006. Conferences/Banqueting (110/120); business centre, secretarial service; free broadband wi/fi. 24 hr room service. Lift. Turndown service. Garden, golf nearby, leisure centre (fitness room, pool, jacuzzi); spa (treatment rooms, massage, hairdressing). **Rooms 88**. (4 suites, 4 interconnecting, 4 for disabled); children welcome (under 12s free in parents' room, cot available free of charge, baby sitting arranged). Lift. B&B about €110 pps, ss €90. **Orchids:** Since the refurbishment of Hayfield's Bar - a judicious blend of traditional and contemporary, resulting in the cosy atmosphere of a traditional bar, with chic modern touches - it has become an appealing place for an aperitif before going in to this fine dining restaurant, which overlooks the walled garden at the back of the hotel and has recently been completely refurbished in an elegant contemporary style that works well with the old style of the building. Well spaced tables are very comfortably arranged in three sections, with the main area opening onto the garden, and a raised section beside it. Emphasising the relative formality - Orchids is normally an evening restaurant, although open for lunch when there is demand - tables are set up classically, with pristine white linen and gleaming glasses. Menus are based on local produce where possible, and continue the tradition of fairly classical cuisine with an occasional contemporary twist for which this restaurant is well known - and a meal here is always enhanced by professional and caring service. **Perrotts:** In a conservatory area at the front of the hotel, this smart and relaxing contemporary restaurant offers an informal alternative to dining in Orchids. Open for lunch and dinner daily, it has a bright and airy atmosphere and plenty of greenery, and quickly became established as a favoured destination with discerning Corkonians who enjoy the ambience and stylish bistro cooking. The choice of dishes offered is wide, ranging from updated classics, to international lunchtime favourites like Perrotts homemade burger with bacon and Emmenthal cheese, spicy guacomole and tomato relish dip, and hand-cut chips. Stylish surroundings, varied menus, confident cooking and helpful, attentive service make for a very enjoyable dining experience. **Orchids: Seats 90**; children welcome; air conditioning. D Mon-Sat, 7-9.30. Set D about €45/55, 2/3 course, also à la carte. House wine from €31.75. SC in restaurant of 10% on parties of 10+. Perrotts Restaurant, 12-2.30 & 6-9.30 daily. Amex, Diners, MasterCard, Visa, Laser. **Directions:** Opposite University College Cork - signed off College Road. ◇

Cork City

HOTEL•RESTAURANT

Hotel Isaacs & Greenes Restaurant

48 MacCurtain Street Cork Co Cork **Tel: 021 450 0011**

cork@isaacs.ie www.isaacscork.com

Opposite the Everyman Palace Theatre and approached through a cobbled courtyard, this attractive hotel offers comfort in spacious rooms at a fairly reasonable price. Recent major renovations have made this a much more confident and comfortable hotel: new windows have reduced traffic noise, the fourteen newer superior rooms are quietly impressive and have set the standard for refurbishment of all the existing bedrooms, which is now complete so that all rooms have double glazing and air conditioning. A few of the rooms at the back have a charming outlook on to the waterfall, which is a feature from the restaurant - and destined to become the centrepiece of the new covered courtyard, which is to be glazed (and a new lift installed) shortly after we go to press. Small Conferences (50); broadband wi/fi; secretarial services available (from reception), video conferencing by arrangement. Children welcome (under 3 free in parents room, cot available free of charge, baby sitting arranged). All day room service. Car park nearby. No pets. Garden (courtyard). Self-catering apartments available (open all year). **Rooms 47** (14 executive, 4 shower-only, 37 no-smoking, 2 for disabled). Lift. Room service (all day). B&B €75 pps, ss €25. Closed 24-27 Dec. **Greenes:** Despite being next door to the well-known Isaacs restaurant (with the confusion of the hotel's similar name), Greenes is well-established as a successful stand-alone restaurant and has earned a following. The approach from the street is attractive, under a limestone arch to the narrow courtyard with the waterfall - which is floodlit at night - making an unusual feature when seen from the restaurant. The reception and the two restaurant areas have character and the atmosphere is definitely 'independent restaurant' rather than 'hotel dining room'. Head chef Frederic Desormeaux's menus are quite adventurous, offering modern renditions of classic dishes, sometimes with a French slant and often based on local ingredients, especially seafood. Starters might include air dried smoked Connemara lamb on salad leaves, with fresh figs, beetroot dressing & balsamic reduction, while main courses include classics like pan-fried T-bone steak with home-made chips and perhaps a speciality tajine of monkfish and Ballycotton mussels cooked in a fishy tomato broth with turned potatoes and rouille and garlic croûtons. Seasonal fruits feature strongly among the desserts (a dessert platter for two to share is an option) or, unusually, you can have a selection of Tipperary cheeses, with chutney, home-made biscuits and a shot glass of port. Accurate cooking, attractive presentation and friendly, helpful service - plus a lively atmosphere and quite reasonable prices - should ensure an enjoyable meal. The early dinner menu is especially good value. **Seats 100** (private room, 36, outdoor, 30); outdoor dining in heated courtyard; barbecues in summer; children welcome (high chair, children's menu, baby changing facilities). L summer only Mon-Sun, 12.30-3 (to 3pm Sun); D daily 6-10 (Sun & Bank hols to 9.30); value L €15; early D €30 (6-7pm); set 2/3 course D €38/45; also à la carte; set Sun L €30. House wine from €22. SC 10% on groups 10+. Closed D 24 Dec & 25-27 Dec. Amex, Diners, MasterCard, Visa, Laser. **Directions:** City centre - 400m down MacCurtain Street, on left; entrance opposite Everyman Palace Theatre, through cobblestone archway.

Cork City
CAFÉ

Idaho.Café

19 Caroline Street Cork Co Cork
Tel: 021 427 6376

This friendly and well-located little café hits the spot for discerning shoppers, who appreciate Mairead Jacob's wholesome food - this is that rare treat, good home cooking based on the best of ingredients. The day begins with breakfast, and a very good breakfast it is too: everything from lovely hot porridge with brown sugar and cream to warm Danish pastries, muffins, or Belgian waffles with organic maple syrup and the option of crispy bacon. You can choose from this menu up to noon, when they ease into lunch, with tasty little numbers like a house special of gratinated potato gnocchi with smoky bacon & sage or, equally typical of the treats in store, crispy duck, spring onion and Irish brie quesadillas or shepherdess's pie (using organic beef). But best of all perhaps, as baking is a speciality, are the 'Sweet Fix' temptations which are just ideal for that quick morning coffee or afternoon tea break - the coeliac-friendly 'orange almond' cake has developed a following, and there's a wide range of hot and cold drinks, including 'Hippy' specialist teas. Dishes which are vegetarian, or can be adapted for vegetarians, are highlighted on the menu at this great little place. Great service, and great value too: full marks. **Seats 30**; toilets not wheelchair accessible; children welcome. Open Mon-Sat, 8.30-5pm; B 8.30-12, L 12-4.30. House wine from about €16.50 or from 2.95 a glass, specialist beers from about €3.75. Closed Sun, Bank Holidays, 24-26 Dec. No Credit Cards. **Directions:** Directly behind Brown Thomas, Cork.

Cork City
HOTEL

Imperial Hotel

South Mall Cork Co Cork **Tel: 021 427 4040**
info@imperialhotelcork.ie www.flynnhotels.com

This thriving hotel in Cork's main commercial and banking centre dates back to 1813 and has a colourful history - Michael Collins spent his last night here, no less, and that suite now bears his name. However, it's the convenient location - near the river and just a couple of minutes walk from the Patrick Street shopping area - that has always made this hotel so popular for business and pleasure, also the free car parking available for residents. It has been run by the Flynn family (of

Georgina Campbell's Ireland

the Old Ground Hotel in Ennis, Co Clare) since 1998, and they have recently completed a major renovation and refurbishment of the hotel, which has brought new life to its fine old public areas and transformed others: the popular Pembroke Restaurant, for example, is now a more spacious and stylish contemporary restaurant, allowing for changing moods throughout the day, and Souths Bar has retained its character alongside the introduction of updated furnishings. As well as upgrading existing bedrooms, new superior rooms have been added and also a stunning 2-bedroom penthouse suite with wrap-around balcony and views over the city. Most recently, the Escape Lifestyle & Salon Spa became the first of its kind in Ireland. Live jazz in the bar on Friday nights is popular with guests and locals alike. Attractive weekend and off-season rates are offered. Conference/banqueting (280/230); business centre, video conferencing, free broadband wi/fi; private car park. **Rooms 126** (1 suite, 34 executive, 11 family, 4 single, 8 shower-only, 2 for disabled); children welcome (under 12s free in parents room, cots available without charge, baby sitting arranged). No pets. Lift. 24 hour room service. B&B €75-85 pps, ss €30. Spa, sauna, steam room, massage, beauty treatments, hair dressing, beauty salon. Closed 24-26 Dec. Amex, Diners, MasterCard, Visa, Laser. **Directions:** City centre location.

Cork City
RESTAURANT

Isaacs Restaurant

48 MacCurtain Street Cork Co Cork
Tel: 021 450 3805

In 1992 Michael and Catherine Ryan, together with partner/head chef Canice Sharkey, opened this large, atmospheric modern restaurant in an 18th-century warehouse and it immediately struck a chord with people tired of having to choose between fine dining and fast food, and became a trend-setter in the modern Irish food movement. The combination of international influences and reassuring Irish traditions was ahead of its time, and it quickly gained a following of people who enjoyed both the informal atmosphere, and the freshness of approach in Canice Sharkey's kitchen. In a quiet, low-key way, this restaurant has played a leading role in the culinary revolution that has overtaken Ireland over the last decade or two. Their original blend of Irish and international themes, together with a policy of providing quality food and good value in an informal, relaxed ambience has attracted endless imitations. Ingredients are carefully sourced, the cooking is consistently accomplished and menus are freshened by occasional inspired introductions (a plate of tapas, for example, which can be a starter or a lovely light lunch). A list of about seven specials changes twice daily, and most dishes are available with little oil and no dairy produce, on request. The service is terrific too, and a visit here is always great fun. The wine list which is considerately arranged by style ('dry, light and fresh', 'full bodied' etc), follows a similar philosophy, offering a good combination of classics and more unusual bottles, at accessible prices - and Isaacs coffee is organic and Fair Trade. **Seats 120**; toilets wheelchair accessible; children welcome (high chair, baby changing facilities). L Mon-Sat 12.30-2.30, D daily 6-10 (Sun to 9). Short à la carte and daily blackboard specials; vegetarian dishes highlighted. House wine from €20. Service discretionary. Closed - L Sun, Christmas week, L Bank Holidays. Amex, Diners, MasterCard, Visa, Laser. **Directions:** 5 minutes from Patrick Street; opposite Gresham Metropole Hotel.

Cork City
RESTAURANT

Ivory Tower

The Exchange Builldings Princes Street Cork Co Cork
Tel: **021 427 4665**

Seamus O'Connell, one of Ireland's most original culinary talents, runs this unusual restaurant upstairs in an early Victorian commercial building; the entrance to the dowdy building is uninspiring but as you arrive in the high-ceilinged room with its slightly faded decor, eclectic ornaments and modern paintings, you will receive a warm and friendly welcome. Guests are generally won over at this point, impressed by the efficient service and outstanding food and cooking. Recently, however - at least for the time being - Seamus has taken his creative genius to Dublin to team up with one of the capital's best-known restaurateurs and publicans, Jay Bourke, to open **Shebeen Chic** (see entry), a sassy eatery with unconventional décor and unconventional food. Meanwhile, he has left a team experienced in his ways in charge at the Ivory Tower and, at the time of going to press, it is really a question of watch this space - the creativity associated with this restaurant genuinely is a one-off, and developments wil be followed on our website, www.ireland-guide.com. **Seats 35**; not suitable for children under 5 private room available. D Wed-Sat, 6.30-9.15 (Tue is Sushi Night). 5-course D about €60; Surprise Menu about €75. House wine from about €18. SC discretionary. Closed Mon-Wed. Amex, MasterCard, Visa, Laser. **Directions:** Corner of Princes/Oliver Plunkett street. ◊

Cork City
RESTAURANT

Jacobs On The Mall

30A South Mall Cork Co Cork **Tel: 021 425 1530**
info@jacobsonthemall.com www.jacobsonthemall.com

Its location in the former Turkish baths creates a highly unusual and atmospheric contemporary dining space for what many would regard as Cork's leading restaurant. Head Chef Mercy Fenton does a consistently excellent job: modern European cooking is the promise and, with close attention to sourcing the best ingredients allied to outstanding cooking skills, the results are commendably simple and always pleasing in terms of balance and flavour. Details like home-made breads are good, and fresh local and organic produce makes its mark in the simplest of dishes, like delicious mixed leaf salads, or a house speciality of natural smoked haddock with potato, leeks, mussels, tomato & saffron sauce. Reflecting the availability of local produce, lunch and dinner menus change daily and are sensibly brief - with seafood and vegetables in season especially strong points: a simple meal of Ballycotton crab salad, and sirloin steak with lyonnaise potatoes could be memorable, for example. Creativity with deliciously wholesome and colourful ingredients, accurate cooking, stylish presentation and efficient yet relaxed service all add up to an outstanding dining experience. Finish on a high note - with a baked vanilla cheesecake, with delectable raspberry ice cream, perhaps, or farmhouse cheeses, which are always so good in Cork, served here with fruit and home-made oatcakes. An interesting and fairly priced drinks list includes cocktails, and a wide choice of spirits and after-dinner drinks; the wide-ranging wine list includes many interesting bottles, some organic wines and a good choice of half bottles and wines by the glass. *Development under way at the time of going to press will see Jacobs extended to become a 37-bedroom boutique hotel, Jacobs Mill (www.jacobsmill.com) in the near future. **Seats 130** (private room, 50, with own bar); air conditioning; toilets wheelchair accessible; children welcome; special diets willingly accommodated with advance notice. L & D Mon-Sat 12.30-2.30 & 6.30-10pm. Set L €35, set D €47.50, also a la carte. House wines from €22; SC 10% (excl L). Closed Sun, 25/26 Dec, L on bank hols. Amex, Diners, MasterCard, Visa, Laser. **Directions:** Beside Bank of Ireland, at the Grand Parade end of the South Mall.

Cork City
RESTAURANT

Jacques Restaurant

Phoenix Street Cork Co Cork **Tel: 021 427 7387**
jacquesrestaurant@eircom.net www.jacquesrestaurant.ie

An integral part of Cork life since 1982, sisters Eithne and Jacqueline Barry's delightful restaurant has changed with the years, evolving from quite a traditional place to a smart contemporary space. But, while the surroundings may go through periodic re-makes, the fundamentals of warm hospitality and great food never waiver and that is the reason why many would cite Jacques as their favourite Cork restaurant. There is always a personal welcome and, together with Eileen Carey, who has been in the kitchen with Jacque Barry since 1986, this team has always a put high value on the provenance and quality of the food that provides the building blocks for their delicious meals - and, appropriately, Jacque is now leader of the Cork Slow Food Convivium. Menus are based on carefully sourced ingredients from a network of suppliers built up over many years and, together with skill and judgement in the kitchen, this shows particularly as they have the confidence to keep things simple and allow the food to speak for itself. You could start your meal in delectably civilised fashion with a half bottle of Manzanilla, served with nuts and olives, while considering choices from menus that are refreshingly short, which allows this skilled team to concentrate on the delicious cooking that is their forte. There are also daily specials, which may include unusual items - lamb's tongue with mustard & breadcrumbs, with a fresh beet-root & carrot slaw, for example. Some of the moreish starters may also be available as a main course, and there are numerous wonderful speciality dishes, with a focus on fresh fish, such as fresh brill - typically served with hollandaise & buttered greens and Orla potatoes; delicious desserts or Irish cheeses are offered to finish. An interesting, informative wine list matches the food, and includes some organic wines, a wine of the month and a good choice of half bottles. Consistently good cooking in stylish, relaxed surroundings, genuinely hospitable service, and excellent value are among the things that make Jacques special. The early dinner menu offers particularly good value. *Jacques was the winner of our Natural Food Award, 2008. **Seats 62**; children welcome; air conditioning. An interesting, fairly priced wine list includes some organic wines and about ten half bottles. Open D only Mon-Sat 6-10pm. Early D, 6-7pm Mon-Wed, €25; also à la carte D. House wine about €20. SC discretionary. Closed Sun, Bank Hols, 24 Dec - 27 Dec. Amex, MasterCard, Visa, Laser **Directions:** City centre, near G.P.O.

Cork City
HOTEL

Jurys Cork Hotel

Western Road Cork Co Cork **Tel: 021 425 2700**
cork@jurysdoyle.com www.jurysdoyle.com/cork

Following complete redevelopment of their original riverside site on Western Road, Jurys Cork Hotel has now regained its place as one of the most popular Cork hotels, especially perhaps for business guests. Well-located, it is beside the university and within comfortable walking distance of the city centre in good weather, and also handy for those who wish to make a neat exit westwards on leaving. Although it doesn't have the wow factor of some of the showier new hotels, it is imaginatively designed to make the very most of its waterside location, with all the main public areas having balconies as well as acres of glass - and the relatively low key decor is designed to last. Informal dining is available in the Weir Bistro, a very pleasantly bright and airy room at the end of the hotel with a surprisingly away-from-it all feeling that belies its position just a river-hop away from the busy Western Road; where else in the city centre could you watch a man out fishing with his dog, just yards from your table? Jurys has always had a reputation for its lively bar, and The Weir Bar, which also takes full advantage of the riverside setting and has a large deck, looks set to continue the tradition. Also renowned as a business hotel, Jurys has a range of meeting rooms and a dedicated executive floor and lounge on the penthouse floor; executive extras include complimentary continental breakfast and drinks and canapés in the evening as well as turndown service, daily newspapers and business magazines. All bedrooms have been finished to a high specification, however, with air conditioning, 25" LCD TV, work desk, laptop safe, 'fair price minibar' as standard, and smart bathrooms all have separate bath and power shower and classy toiletries. Facilities include a leisure centre with 18m swimming pool, sauna, spa bath and a day spa, more recently opened. **Rooms 182**; business centre; complimentary broadband throughout the hotel. Laundry/dry cleaning. Complimentary guest parking. Room rate from €149 to €249. Open all year. **Directions:** On left, shortly before University College Cork. Watch closely for signs in one-way system. ◊

Cork City
HOTEL•RESTAURANT

Kingsley Hotel

Victoria Cross Cork Co Cork **Tel: 021 480 0500**
info@kingsleyhotel.com www.kingsleyhotel.com

BUSINESS HOTEL OF THE YEAR

Possibly the most attractively located hotel in the city, the Kingsley is conveniently situated alongside the River Lee, just minutes from both Cork airport and the city centre and has always been especially appealing to business visitors, for whom it quickly becomes a home from home. Major investment over the last two years has enlarged and upgraded the hotel yet, remarkably, it has retained the sense of intimacy and homely atmosphere that has been a special feature from the outset. A large, comfortably furnished foyer has a welcoming feel to it, with staff always on hand to assist guests - and there is an attractive linear lounge/informal restaurant area a few steps up from it (and overlooking the weir) which, like the River Bar beside it, makes a good meeting place; the recent redevelopment has focused on maximising the benefit of the riverside location, and greatly enhanced the appeal of both the lounge and bar - and longer term guests especially appreciate the long riverside walk that runs along the banks. A caring atmosphere is noticeable throughout the hotel, from the moment guests are greeted on arrival, and accommodation is personally decorated and well-planned to make a good home from home. Spacious rooms offer traditional comfort with a contemporary edge, and are designed with care: air conditioning, work station with complimentary broadband, interactive TV, personal safe, trouser press with ironing board, same day laundry and all of the small extras that make a difference. Executive suites at the back of the hotel include a room suitable for private entertaining or meetings (and especially luxurious bathrooms) and have river views - and an impressive 750 square metre 2-bedroom Presidential Suite built over two floors; with its own hot tub balcony, and spacious living area on the penthouse level, it is Cork's premier suite. The hotel's Business & Conference Centre is a top venue for small and medium-sized meetings has also been upgraded (see hotel website for full details); built for purpose, the hotel does not accept weddings. Good health and fitness facilities include the Yauvana holistic lifestyle spa, with exclusive Indian treatments. Conferences (230/127); business centre, broadband, secretarial services; video conferencing, on request; 24 hour room service. Leisure centre (recently refurbished & gym equipment renewed), swimming pool; treatment rooms, beauty salon. Children welcome (under 12s free in parents' room; cot available without charge, baby sitting arranged). Garden. Riverside walks. Pets permitted by arrangement. Parking. **Rooms 131** (71 separate bath & shower, 4 suites, 6 for disabled, all no smoking); 18 two-bedroom fully-serviced apartments, some with balcony, are also available for short or extended stay. Air conditioning. Lift. B&B €80 pps, ss €65. Open all year. **Otters Restaurant:** This lovely restaurant is on two levels, so different that it almost seems like two restaurants: the upper level is bright and airy and, overlooking the river and linear park with fishermen and joggers out on a summer's day, it has a wonderful ambience; the lower, which is darker, with more closely spaced tables, might be cosier in winter. As elsewhere in the hotel, attention from friendly staff is outstanding right from the beginning, when you are escorted courteously to your table, luxuriously set up with crisp linen, smartly polished cutlery and glassware; bread (made in-house) is brought immediately, together with chilled butter and iced water. Appealing menus may include starters like bruschetta of goat's cheese and crab mayonnaise, and fresh fish also features among the main courses, typically seared cod, garnished with roast cherry tomatoes and rocket salad. And desserts are likely to be the highlight of a meal here: an orange & polenta cake with berry compote and an elegant layered chocolate mousse are typical examples. And, with its elegant setting and such attentive staff, a meal here should always be enjoyable. **Seats 140** (private room 20). L & D daily: L 12.30-3, D 5.30-10 (Sun 6-10). Set L €30; Early Bird D 5.30-7.30 €26. set D €50; D also à la carte. House wine from around €17. SC discretionary. *Lounge and bar food also available through the day. Open all year. Amex, Diners, MasterCard, Visa, Laser. **Directions:** On main N25 Killarney road by Victoria Cross.

Cork City
GUESTHOUSE

Lancaster Lodge

Lancaster Quay Western Road Cork Co Cork **Tel: 021 425 1125**
info@lancasterlodge.com www.lancasterlodge.com

This large, modern purpose-built guesthouse is beside the newly re-opened Jurys Hotel, and there is secure parking in the grounds. Built to offer hotel quality accommodation at a moderate price, it is comparable to a budget hotel; public areas are not grand but reception is prompt and friendly, and there is bottled water on each floor, newspapers in the breakfast room and generally pleasing surroundings throughout, including original art works. Spacious guest rooms which include 9 new ones - are furnished to a high standard (with free broadband, safes, 12 channel TV, trouser press, tea/coffee facilities and room service as well as the more usual facilities) and the bathrooms, some with jacuzzi baths, are well-designed. Efficient double glazing helps to offset traffic and construction noise in rooms at the front (if you do not need to open windows), but rooms at the back may be a better option. Breakfast is served in a bright contemporary dining room. Small conferences (18); wheelchair friendly; children welcome (under 5s free in parents' room, cot available, baby sitting arranged, high chair); dogs permitted by arrangement. Free secure parking. 24 hour reception. **Rooms 48** (2 executive rooms, 5 shower only, 2 family, 3 ground floor, 2 for disabled, all no smoking). Lift; limited room service. B&B from €70 pps. ss €35 Closed 23-28 Dec. Amex, Diners, MasterCard, Visa, Laser. **Directions:** On Western Road, opposite Café Paradiso, between Cork University and Cork Courthouse.

Cork City
RESTAURANT

Les Gourmandises Restaurant

17 Cook Street Cork Co Cork **Tel: 021 425 1959**
www.lesgourmandises.ie

Just off South Mall, this little restaurant feels like an outpost of France - the menu at the entrance will draw you in, and you'll be glad you noticed it. It's run by Patrick and Soizic Kiely - both formerly of Restaurant Patrick Guilbaud but, although that says a lot about the key standards, this is far more reminiscent of family-run restaurants in France. There's nothing flash about the quiet style of this restaurant: a small reception area is cleverly arranged to make three compact seating areas with a bar, fresh flowers and stylish cushions; the welcome is cordial without being effusive, and the team under Soizic's guidance go about their business with quiet competence. The long, narrow, high-ceilinged room, formerly a Turkish bath, is a restrained, modern white space, with comfortable subdued lighting and low key music. The menu is not overlong, but changes daily to accommodate the day's market; there is usually a seafood platter, which varies and may contain 5 or so elements, each treated differently and with appropriate sauces/garnishes, arranged to please the eye as well as the palate. Outstanding dishes may include a 'crab sandwich' starter, of spanking fresh crab with remoulade sauce, layered in three tiers with toasted brioche & fresh dill. Presentation is stylish, and great attention is given to the marriage of complementary flavours - a tiny pink lamb rack, for example, comes with rosemary and black olive tapenade - and careful seasoning. To finish, there may be upbeat classic seasonal desserts and a good French & Irish cheese selection, and lovely coffee. The wine list is not long but very well chosen and includes some real finds, including the house wines. Terrific food and good value: this is one of the hidden treasures you'd like to keep a secret lest it become too popular. **Seats 30**; children over 6 welcome. D only, Tue-Sat, 6-9.30pm. Early D, 2/3 course: about €27.50/31.50. Also à la carte. House wine about €22. Closed Sun, Mon; Mar, Sep. MasterCard, Visa, Laser. **Directions:** City centre - access to Cook Street from South Mall. ◇

Cork City
RESTAURANT

Liberty Grill

32 Washington Street Cork Co Cork **Tel: 021 427 1049**
dine@libertygrillcork.com www.libertygrillcork.com

Liberty Grill is a sister establishment to Café Gusto (Washington Street & Lapps Quay, see entry), so you may expect the same food philosophy based on quality ingredients, where possible organic and locally sourced. It's situated on the renovated ground floor of an early Victorian block, with menus displayed on a lectern outside the door, and it's an attractive room, with some exposed stonework, darkwood floor and modern designer chairs. Lighting is well designed, and a brilliant white ceiling also reflects light, giving it a bright and spacious atmosphere. Comfortably spaced tables are set up bistro style and a youthful clientèle creates a buzz - sometimes it can be very noisy. Separate menus are offered for brunch, lunch and dinner. The extensive brunch menu is very appealing, especially if you are staying 'room only' in the area. Lunch and dinner menus major in a choice of burgers, steaks (including a vegetarian option) and salads, and fresh fish from the English Market. A small wine list is offered. Liberty Grill offers real, tasty food and good value in pleasant surroundings. **Seats 50**; children welcome before 9pm. Open Mon-Thu 8am-9pm, Fri-Sat 8-10. A la carte. House wine €16. Closed Sun, Bank Hols, 1st week in Aug. Amex, MasterCard, Visa, Laser **Directions:** On Washington Street in block between North Main Street and Courthouse.

Cork City
GUESTHOUSE

Lotamore House

Tivoli Cork Co Cork **Tel: 021 482 2344**
lotamore@iol.ie www.lotamorehouse.com

Sidney and Geri McElhinney's large period house is set in mature gardens and, although not overly grand, it was built on a generous scale. These old houses in Tivoli are large properties to maintain, but the approach and exterior maintenance is gradually improving and work was in progress on a fountain in the front garden on a recent visit. It is a generous, comfortable house and many regular guests prefer it to staying in an hotel - the spacious, airy rooms have air conditioning, phones, TV and trouser press (tea/coffee trays on request), and they're comfortably furnished, with room for an extra bed or cot; all have full bathrooms. A large drawing room has plenty of armchairs and an open fire and, although only breakfast and light meals are offered, Fleming's Restaurant (see entry) is next door. Meetings/Small conferences by arrangement (25). **Rooms 19** (All no-smoking, 1 family room); children welcome (cot available). No pets. B&B from about €65 pps, ss about €20. Own parking. Garden. Closed 22 Dec-5 Jan. MasterCard, Visa, Laser. **Directions:** On N8, 10 minutes drive from Cork City. ◇

Cork City
Market Lane Restaurant & Bar
BAR•RESTAURANT
5 & 6 Oliver Plunkett Street Cork Co Cork **Tel: 021 427 4710**
info@marketlane.ie www.marketlane.ie

This bustling two-storey restaurant and bar near the English Market is a friendly and welcoming place with a lively atmosphere. The premises was previously a pub - and, although now operated mainly as a restaurant, it has a full pub licence; there's a bar with old wooden furniture behind it along one side of the main dining area, which is set up simply but smartly with a mixture of banquettes and bent-wood chairs, plain-topped tables with simple, good quality cutlery and glasses, and menus that double as place mats. Fresh and artisan produce from the English Market is used as much as possible, with the aim of offering good quality food – and real value for money. This they do well, offering well cooked, unfussy food at moderate prices; varied menus offer plenty of choice and include sandwiches and salads, some unusual items (fish stew with seafood bisque, samphire and baby potatoes, for example, €14) and a good range of popular dishes. There's a small children's menu (including a home-made baby bowl, €2.95), plenty of vegetarian choices and a coeliac menu is available on request. Service is efficient, friendly and attentive, and a small wine list (38) offers a good selection from around the world, with a good number by the glass. This is a restaurant with its heart in the right place – no wonder it's always busy. **Seats 136** (outdoor seating available). Restaurant: Mon-Sat 12–10pm (to 10.30pm Sat), Sun 5–9pm (except bank hols); no reservations except for parties of 6+; a la carte menus; house wine from €23; sc 10% on groups 6+. Two car parks nearby. Amex, MasterCard, Visa, Laser. **Directions:** At Parnell Place end of Oliver Plunkett Street. ◇

Cork City
Maryborough Hotel & Spa
HOTEL•RESTAURANT
Maryborough Hill Douglas Cork Co Cork **Tel: 021 436 5555**
info@maryborough.ie www.maryborough.com

This hotel, which is quietly situated on the south of the city and very convenient to Cork airport and the Jack Lynch Tunnel, has a fine country house at its heart and is set in its own gardens. The main entrance is via the original flight of steps up to the old front door and as a conventional reception area would intrude on the beautifully proportioned entrance hall, guests are welcomed at a discreetly positioned desk just inside the front door. The original house has many fine features and is furnished in period style with antiques; spacious public areas now extend from it, right across to the new accommodation wing through the Garden Room, a spacious contemporary lounge furnished with smart leather sofas. The new section of the hotel - which is modern and blends comfortably with the trees and gardens surrounding it - includes excellent leisure facilities, the main bar and restaurant, and guest accommodation. Guest rooms and suites are exceptionally attractive in terms of design - simple, modern, bright, utilising Irish crafts: rooms are generously-sized, with a pleasantly leafy outlook and good amenities; compact, well-lit bathrooms have plenty of marbled shelf space, environmentally friendly toiletries, very small baths and towels, and suggestions on saving water by avoiding unnecessary laundry (the hotel's positive environmental policy has achieved recognition with a Green Failte Gold Award/Best in County). Conference/banqueting (500/400); business centre, secretarial services, video conferencing, free broadband wi/fi, laptop-sized safes in bedrooms. Leisure centre (swimming pool, jacuzzi, sauna, steam room); beauty salon; Spa. Children welcome (under 2s free in parents room, cots available without charge, baby sitting arranged). No pets. **Rooms 93** (2 suites, 3 junior suites, 88 executive rooms, 37 no-smoking, 8 for disabled). Lift. 24 hour room service. B&B €85 pps, ss €25. Closed 24-26 Dec. **Zings:** Creative use of lighting separates areas within this design-led dining area without physical divisions - and the tables are considerably spot lit (ideal for lone diners who wish to read). Gerry Allen, who has been head chef since the hotel opened in 1997 and has earned a local following, offers European cuisine with Mediterranean flavours on quite extensive menus. Although international influences dominate, local produce is used - pretty desserts that are worth leaving room for include a commendable number of choices using seasonal fruits, for example, and local farmhouse cheeses are also a strong option. A good selection of house wines is offered, also an unusually wide choice of half bottles, all moderately priced. **Seats 120**; not suitable for children after 7pm; air conditioning. L daily 12.30-2.30, D 6.30-9.30. Set L €30, D à la carte. House wines from €25. SC discretionary. Amex, Diners, MasterCard, Visa, Laser. **Directions:** Near Douglas village & adjacent to Douglas Golf Club; signed from roundabout where Rochestown Road meets Carrigaline Road.

Cork City   # Nakon Thai Restaurant
RESTAURANT   Tramway House Douglas Village Cork Co Cork **Tel: 021 436 9900**
V   www.nakonthai.com

Efficient reception by smiling staff gets guests off to a good start at this smart and consistently popular restaurant in Douglas village. The aim is to provide traditional Thai cuisine in a relaxed and friendly atmosphere and several menus offer a wide range of dishes, including all the popular Thai dishes - house specialities include hot & sour prawn soup - but also some lesser-known dishes. Everything is freshly cooked, without any artificial flavourings or MSG and, although the flavours typical of Thai cuisine - coriander, lime, chilli, saltiness - seem to have been tamed somewhat, authentic dishes always meet with approval. A simple dessert selection includes exotic Thai fruit salad for a refreshing finish. An informative fairly priced wine list deserves investigation (a gewurtztraminer partners Thai food exceptionally well, for example); imported Thai beers are also available. **Seats 42**; children welcome; air conditioning. D daily: Mon-Sat 5.30-11, Sun 5-10. Set menus from about €20; à la carte also available. House wine from €18. SC discretionary. Closed 24-28 Dec, Good Fri. Amex, Diners, MasterCard, Visa, Laser. **Directions:** Douglas Village opposite Rugby Club.

Cork City   # Radisson SAS Hotel & Spa
HOTEL   Ditchley House Little Island Cork Co Cork **Tel: 021 429 7000**
                                          info.cork@radissonsas.com www.radissonsas.com

Situated just east of Cork city, adjacent to an industrial estate, the location of this hotel is not attractive but it is near the Jack Lynch Tunnel, which gives easy access to the airport, and it is set in landscaped gardens. It follows the familiar Radisson practice of adding a well-designed modern build to an old property, with stylish contemporary interiors including spacious public areas. Designed to appeal to both leisure and business guests, the large Banks Bar is equally suitable for a relaxing drink and casual food, or for business meetings, and The Island Grillroom offers a more intimate dining area. Accommodation is to the usual high standard for new Radisson hotels, offering very comfortable rooms. In addition to other facilities expected of a hotel of this standard, wi/fi internet access is complementary throughout the hotel. 'The Retreat' leisure facilities include a Spa, with nine treatment rooms and a relaxation suite, and a Fitness Centre with hydrotherapy pool and state-of-the-art gymnasium. Conference/banqueting (450). **Rooms 129**. B&B from €60-80 pps. Open all year. **Directions:** Signed off main Cork-Midleton road. ◇

Cork City   # Radisson SAS Hotel Cork Airport
HOTEL   Cork Airport Cork Co Cork **Tel: 021 494 7500**
                                             res@corkairport-gsh.com www.gshotels.com

Formerly the Great Southern, this stylish modern hotel is very handily located, close to the terminal. Ideal for a first or last night's stay, it's also a useful meeting place and is well equipped for business guests. It aims to provide a tranquil haven for travellers amid the hustle and bustle of a busy airport; its success can be judged by its popularity with a discerning local clientéle as well as travellers passing through. Rooms have voice mail, fax/modem lines, desk space and TV with in-house movie channel as well as more usual facilities like radio, hair dryer, tea/coffee trays and trouser press. Conference/banqueting (100); business centre. **Rooms 81** (81 executive, 38 no smoking, 4 disabled). Lift. Room rate from €79 for a double or twin. Leisure centre. Parking (150). Amex, MasterCard, Visa, Laser. **Directions:** Off Cork-Kinsale road; situated within airport complex. ◇

Cork City   # Rochestown Park Hotel
HOTEL   Rochestown Road Douglas Cork Co Cork **Tel: 021 489 0800**
                                       info@rochestownpark.com www.rochestownpark.com

This large hotel stands in lovely grounds and at its heart is a fine old house that was formerly home to the Lord Mayors of Cork. The original parts of the building feature gracious, well-proportioned public rooms and guest rooms have always been furnished to a high standard with all the comforts - including air conditioning and safe in executive rooms - as well as the usual conveniences, making this popular for business guests. Facilities include a fine leisure centre with a swimming pool, sauna, steam room and computerised gymnasium, as well as a Thalasso therapy centre. (Although they rarely get the credit for it, this was the first Thalasso therapy centre in an Irish hotel and predated the current fashion for spas by many years.) The hotel's conference and meeting facilities are very highly regarded. *At the time of going to press, the hotel has just completed a major redevelopment and refurbishment plan. Conference/banqueting (700/500); business centre, video conferencing, free broadband wi/fi. Children welcome (under 6 free in parents' room; cots available free of charge, baby sitting arranged, creche). Leisure centre (swimming pool, sauna, fitness room, massage, spa), beauty salon. Garden. Parking (500). No pets. **Rooms 150** (10 junior suites, 90 executive rooms, 7 family, 132 no smoking, 23 ground floor, 5 for disabled). Lift. 24 hour room service. B&B €90 pps, ss €55. Thalassotherapy breaks offered, also short breaks. Long stay self-catering available. Open all year except Christmas. L&D daily 12.30-2.30 & 6.30-9.45 (Sun 5.30-8pm). Bar menu 10am-11.30pm daily. Amex, Diners, MasterCard, Visa, Laser. **Directions:** Second left after Jack Lynch Tunnel, heading in Rochestown direction.

Cork City
HOTEL

Silver Springs Moran Hotel

Tivoli Cork Co Cork **Tel: 021 450 7533**
silverspringsinfo@moranhotels.com www.moranhotels.com

A sister hotel of the Red Cow Moran Hotel in Dublin, this landmark hotel is situated in 25 acres of landscaped gardens about five minutes drive from the city centre; built on a steeply sloping site just above the main Cork-Dublin road, it has the natural advantage of views (albeit rather industrial) across Cork harbour from many public areas and bedrooms. Thanks to a major make-over (including modernisation of all bedrooms), which was overseen by John Duffy Design and completed without the hotel closing at any time, it has shaken off its blocky 1960s concrete image and this stylish "new" hotel is once again an attractive choice for both leisure travellers and the business community. Conferences/Banqueting (1,500/600); business centre, secretarial services, video conferencing, free broadband wi/fi. **Rooms 109** (5 suites, 2 mini-suites, 29 executive rooms, 16 no-smoking rooms and 5 for disabled); children welcome (under 5s free in parents' room, cot available free of charge, baby sitting arranged). B&B €60-70 pps, ss €30. Leisure centre (pool, sauna, jacuzzi, steam room, massage, beauty salon). Closed 25-26 Dec. Amex, Diners, MasterCard, Visa, Laser. **Directions:** At the Tivoli flyover above the main Cork Dublin road and clearly signed off it. (From Cork, take first left then right at the flyover.)

Cork City
RESTAURANT

Star Anise

4 Bridge Street Cork Co Cork **Tel: 021 455 1635**
staranise@eircom.net www.staranise-cork.com

A smartly painted frontage and cool frosted glass windows create a good impression on arrival at this chic contemporary restaurant - a feeling quickly confirmed by an attractive interior, with clean-lined modern table settings (linen napkins, gleaming glasses), mellow lighting, judiciously placed plants and some very attractive paintings and prints. Virginie Sarrazin's welcome is speedy, and the hospitality is genuine: a choice of table (if available), and tempting menus promptly presented. Proprietor-chef Lambros Lambrou's pleasingly seasonal, accurately described menus are well-balanced - with imaginative choices for vegetarians, and also some daily specials - and the reading is made all the more enjoyable by the arrival of a complimentary amuse-bouche and speedily delivered bread. Speciality dishes tend to favour seafood - Mediterranean fish stew, for example, and carnivores will love the slow cooked lamb, with classic desserts to finish. Imaginative food, sassy service, and an interesting wine list too; wines by the glass chalked up on a board start at about €5 and include a sparkling wine. **Seats 35**; children welcome (high chair); air conditioning. L & D Tue-Sat, 12-2.30; D, 6-10. Set 2/3 course D €23.95/28.95; also A la carte. House wine from €21. SC 10% on groups 6+. Open all year. Diners, MasterCard, Visa, Laser. **Directions:** Between Patrick's Bridge and McCurtain Street.

Cork City
RESTAURANT

Table

Brown Thomas Department Store 18-21 Patrick Street Cork Co Cork
Tel: 021 427 5106 table@itsabagel.com www.itsabagel.com

A younger cousin of sisters Peaches and Domini Kemp's highly regarded Dublin restaurants Itsabagel and Itsa4, Table is a stylish daytime restaurant on the second floor of Brown Thomas Cork, the chicest store in town. With smart modern décor contrasting with a neo-classical background, it's an appropriate setting for sassy food with a basic respect for tradition: the Kemps are renowned for their commitment to quality and meals here are based on local and organic products as much as possible, also Fair Trade tea and coffee. Breakfast, lunch and early supper menus are offered, with snacks (oatmeal & raisin cookies, chocolate brownies, freshly baked scones or any of their gorgeous desserts) in between, and special diets are catered for with dishes suitable for vegetarian, gluten-free, low fat and low salt diets, all of which may sound a bit 'worthy', but it's not like that at all. Fresh, colourful and tasty, this is classic Kemp fare and Itsabagel/Itsa4 fans will find many familiar dishes, including steak sandwiches and great salads - mixed leaves with Ardsallagh goat's cheese, perhaps, along with candied nuts, roasted red peppers and balsamic dressing. There's a junior menu too, offering things like home-made burger with hand-cut fries or penne with cream and roast cherry tomatoes, and lovely pressed juices or fresh orange juice to go with it and, of course, adults can choose from a nice little wine list, including a quartet of bubblies. **Seats 52**; children welcome (high chair, children's menu); air conditioning. Food served Mon-Sat, 9am-6.30pm (to 7.30pm Thurs), L 11.30-4pm; Sun L only, 12-5.30pm. Open same hours as BT. Visa, Laser. **Directions:** 2nd floor, Brown Thomas, Patrick Street. ◇

COUNTY CORK

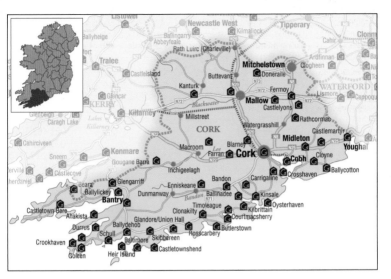

Cork is Ireland's largest county, and its individualistic people take pride in this distinction as they savour the variety of their territory, which ranges from the rich farmlands of the east to the handsome coastline of West Cork, where the light of the famous Fastnet Rock swings across tumbling ocean and spray-tossed headland.

In this extensive county, the towns and villages have their own distinctive character. In the west, their spirit is preserved in the vigour of the landscape. By contrast, East Cork's impressive farming country, radiating towards the ancient estuary port of Youghal, is invitingly prosperous.

The spectacularly located township of Cobh - facing south over Cork Harbour - asserts its own identity, with a renewed sense of its remarkable maritime heritage being expressed in events such as a Sea Shanty Festival, while the town's direct link with the Titanic – Cobh was the ill-fated liner's last port of call – is also commemorated in many ways.

Different again in character is Kinsale, a bustling sailing/fishing port which is home to many intriguing old buildings, yet is a place which is vibrantly modern in outlook, and it has long been seen as Ireland's gourmet capital.

The county is a repository of the good things of life, a treasure chest of the finest farm produce, and the very best of seafood, brought to market by skilled specialists. As Ireland's most southerly county, Cork enjoys the mildest climate of all, and it's a place where they work to live, rather than live to work. So the arts of living are seen at their most skilled in County Cork, and they are practised in a huge territory of such variety that it is difficult to grasp it all, even if you devote your entire vacation to this one county.

Local Attractions and Information

Ballydehob	Nature Art Centre	028 37323
Bantry	Bantry House	027 50047
Bantry	Murphy's International Mussel Fair (May) C/O Westlodge Hotel	027 50360
Bantry	Tourism Information	027 50229
Blarney	Blarney Castle	021 438 5252
Cape Clear Island	International Storytelling Festival (early September)	028 39157 / 087 971 1223
Carrigtwohill	Fota Estate (Wildlife Park, Arboretum)	021 481 2728
Castletownbere	Mill Cove Gallery (May to Sept.)	027 70393
Castletownroche	Annes Grove (gardens)	022 26145
Clonakilty	Lisselan Estate Gardens	023 33249

Cobh	The Queenstown Story	021 481 3591
Cobh	Sirius Arts Centre	021 481 3790
Cork	Airport	021 431 3131
Glanmire	Dunkathel House	021 482 1014
Glanmire	Riverstown House	021 482 1205
Glengarriff	Garinish Island	027 63040
Kinsale	Gourmet Festival (early October) c/o Jack Walsh	021 477 9900
Kinsale	Charles Fort	021 477 2263
Kinsale	Desmond Castle	021 477 4855
Kinsale	Tourism Information	021 477 2234
Macroom	Brierly Gap Cultural Centre	026 42421 / 41764
Mallow	Cork Racecourse	022 50207
Midleton	Farm Market Sats 9am-1.30pm	021 463 1096
	John Potter Cogan	021 463 1096
Midleton	Jameson Heritage Centre	021 461 3594
Millstreet	Country Park	029 70810
Mizen Head	Mizen Vision Signal Station	028 35115 / 35225
Shanagarry	Ballymaloe Cookery School Gardens	021 464 6785
Schull	Ferries to Sherkin, Cape Clear and Fastnet	028 28278
Schull	Schull Planetarium	028 28552
Skibbereen	Tourism Information	028 21766
Skibbereen	West Cork Arts Centre	028 22090
Youghal	Myrtle Grove 024 92274	
	Slow Food Ireland	
	(c/o Glenilen Farm, Drimoleague)	028 31179 / 086 814 1091

AHAKISTA

The small west cork village of Ahakista is near Bantry, on the Sheep's Head Way between Kilcrohane and Durrus villages. The nearest long sandy beaches are a short drive away, but there are small quiet beaches around Bantry Bay, where you will often have the beach to yourself and it is an ideal base for touring the Bantry Bay area. The village is well known for many reasons, including having one of the most relaxed bars in the country, known as **The Tin Pub** because of its corrugated iron roof; it has a lovely rambling country garden going down to the water at the back and, although between owners at the time of going to press, it is well worth a visit. The area offers enjoyable cycling routes and scenic walking routes, including the Sheep's Head Way and Beara Way. Visitors may also enjoy the West Cork Garden Trail, bringing together a number of private and public gardens open to the public in the summer months; Dereen Gardens (open April to September) to the north of the Beara Peninsula is especially worth a visit, and is famous for tree ferns, azaleas and rhododendron. The area is rich in historical sites including the Kealkil Stone Circle, the Breenymore Megaliths and the Ahakista Stone Circle. Golfers are spoilt for choice as the area offers an 18-hole course at Bantry Bay (027 50579), a challenging 9-hole course in Glengariff (027 63150) and there are three more courses within a 30km radius. There is lots to offer the angling enthusiast such as shore fishing, chartered deep sea boats, and also salmon and trout fishing in the many local lakes and rivers.

WWW.IRELAND-GUIDE.COM FOR ALL THE BEST PLACES TO EAT, DRINK & STAY

Ahakista

FARMHOUSE

Hillcrest House

Ahakista Durrus Bantry Co Cork **Tel: 027 67045**
hillcrestfarm@ahakista.com www.ahakista.com

Hospitality comes first at this working farm overlooking Dunmanus Bay, where Agnes Hegarty's guests - including walkers, who revel in the 88km "Sheep's Head Way" - are welcomed with a cup of tea and home-baked scones on arrival. It is a traditional farmhouse with some recent additions, and makes a comfortable base for exploring the area, or a traditional family holiday - there's a swing and a donkey on the farm, rooms are big enough for an extra child's bed and it's only five minutes' walk to the beach. There's a sitting room for guests, with television and an open fire, and bedrooms - either recently refurbished or in a new extension - have power showers or bath, very comfortable beds, electric blankets, hair dryers, tea/coffee making facilities and clock radios. Two newer rooms are on the ground floor, with direct access to a sheltered patio, and parking close by. Fine cooked-to-order breakfasts will set you up for the day and, for the evening, moderately priced evening meals are available for walking groups only; otherwise, there are plenty of good restaurants nearby, also pubs with traditional Irish music. Recent renovations have been well-planned, so that some rooms in the house can be used for self-catering instead of B&B if required. *Hillcrest House was our Farmhouse of the Year in 2001. **Rooms 4** (3 en-suite & no-smoking, 3 shower only, 1 with private bathroom, 2 ground floor) B&B €38 pps, ss €12; children welcome (under 3s free in parents' room, cot available without charge). Evening meals by arrangement (7 pm; €24); light meals also available. *Self-catering cottage and farmhouse also available, all year - details on the website. Closed 1 Nov - 1 Apr. MasterCard, Visa, Laser. **Directions:** 3 km from Bantry, take N71 and turn off for Durrus, then Ahakista - 0.25km to Hillcrest.

BALLYCOTTON

This hilly fishing village on the Atlantic coastline 40km from Cork has a busy fishing fleet and fantastic views over the harbour. There are wonderful views from the cliff walks and it is one of Europe's top bird watching sites. Attractions nearby include The Old Midleton Distillery (021 461 3594, open all year) where guided tours are available and golfers are spoilt for choice as there are 10 courses within a 20km radius of Ballycotton, including the Fota Island Golf Club (021 488 3700). Chartered deep sea angling is also easily available.

Ballycotton
HOTEL•RESTAURANT

Bayview Hotel
Ballycotton Co Cork **Tel: 021 464 6746**
res@thebayviewhotel.com www.thebayviewhotel.com

John and Carmel O'Briens' fine hotel overlooking Ballycotton Harbour enjoys a magnificent location on the seaside of the road, with a path down through its own gardens to the beach. The O'Briens completely rebuilt the hotel in the 1990s, keeping the building in sympathy with the traditional style and scale of the surrounding buildings and harbour, and its immaculate grounds, classy cream paintwork and smart black railings create an excellent first impression. Traditional, homely public areas include a pleasant bar with clubby leather furniture, a cosy atmosphere - and friendly staff. Accommodation is comfortable, and rooms are regularly refurbished; although they vary according to their position in the building, the bedrooms all except two of the ground floor rooms (which are quietly positioned on the side of the building) have sea views. Small conferences/banqueting (40/90). Children welcome (under 12 free in parents' room, cot available without charge, baby sitting arranged). No pets. Garden, tennis, fishing, walking. **Rooms 35** (2 suites, 5 no-smoking rooms, 5 ground floor). B&B €85pps, ss€32. Lift, all day room service, turndown service. Closed Nov-Apr. **Capricho at the Bayview:** Head chef Ciaran Scully has been at the Bayview since 1996 and his creative cooking has earned a loyal following. The restaurant is smartly furnished, with a nice traditional feel; the best tables have lovely harbour and sea views - and, in fine weather, light meals may be served in the garden. Ciaran is a committed chef, who takes pride in sourcing the finest ingredients, and gives over a page of his menu to crediting local produce and suppliers. Although based squarely on local produce, the cooking is classic French and there are contemporary international overtones and also some retro dishes and an element of fun, too. Unusual speciality dishes in the repertoire include three variations of 'Fishy, Fishy, Fishy', one of which is a trio of parcels of smoked salmon and crab with avocado salsa, slivers of smoked tuna with Asian salads and deep-fried Ballycotton prawn with crispy vegetables; another, based on braised pigs cheek and Gubbeen sausage, is called 'Three Little Pigs'. Vegetarian dishes are not always listed on the menu, so you may have to ask for a special dish to be made to order. Delicious desserts may include a 'Lemon Heaven' iced lemon soufflé, caramelised tangy lemon tart & lemon meringue ice cream, served on a ginger biscuit, and a selection of farmhouse cheeses is served with a terrine of dried figs and crab apple jelly. In lesser hands these fanciful dishes might sound worrying, but here they are well-founded. An informative wine list includes a good choice of half bottles. **Seats 45** (private room 28); children welcome (high chair, childrens menu). D 7-9 daily, L Sun only, 1-2. D à la carte. Wines from about €23. (Bar meals available daily 12.30-6). Amex, Diners, MasterCard, Visa, Laser. *The nearby Garryvoe Hotel is in the same family ownership and has recently undergone impressive redevelopment; its beachside location makes it a popular base for family holidays (see website above for details.) **Directions:** At Castlemartyr, on the N25, turn onto the R632 in the direction of Garryvoe - Shanagarry - Ballycotton. ◇

Ballycotton

RESTAURANT

Nautilus Restaurant
28 Silver Strand Ballycotton Co Cork
Tel: 021 464 6768

Ness and Lionel Babin opened this simple restaurant at The Inn by the Harbour (aka Lynch's) in the spring of 2008, and it wasn't long before the foodie wires were alive with it, quietly spreading the word about Lionel's good French cooking. The surroundings are quite plain and very appropriate, giving it a down-to-earth feeling about it that is reminiscent of so many small family-run French restaurants. Lionel, whose experience in Ireland includes nearby Ballymaloe House and Bang in Dublin (see entries), cooks good, simple French food at moderate prices. His customer-friendly menus offer a choice of five or six dishes on each course, with several – typically Ballycotton fish & chips with tartare sauce, Indian lamb curry with basmati rice & raita and risotto of broad beans and sweet peas with paremesan shavings – available as small or large portions. As elsewhere, there are some international influences at work, of course - chicken spring roll with a sweet & sour chilli & peanut dipping sauce, Thai seabass baked in banana leaves with coconut rice & sesame dressing, for example – but you'll also find classics like salmon gravadlax with vegetables à la grèque and honey & mustard dressing, and pork rillete with beetroot relish & toasted Ockham sourdough and main courses like steak & chips with Café de Paris butter; nobody makes these dishes like the French and the details (a real green salad, hand-cut chips or – what a treat – Ballycotton new potatoes, subtle sauces) are the business. Finish with gorgeously classic desserts – strawberry tartlette with strawberry jelly & cream, perhaps, or warm apple tart with vanilla ice cream (which, very properly, demands a 20 minute wait), and you should go home happy. Nessa is in charge front of house and there's a short reasonably priced wine list which, surprisingly, perhaps, offers choices from Spain, Italy and Germany as well as France. Children welcome. D Wed-Sat, 6.30-9pm; L Sun only, 1-4pm. House wine from €17.50. Mastercard, Visa, Laser. Closed Sun D, Mon, Tue, Jan. **Directions:** At The Inn by the Harbour.

BALLYDEHOB

Ballydehob – which, apparently, means 'where the sun always shines' – is said to be a microcosm of Irish local history, and legends and folklore certainly abound in the locality. The village is a pretty patchwork of pastel-painted buildings, and very typical of the area – and home to the renowned Skeaghanore duck, which feature on menus in all the area's best restaurants and are raised by Eugene and Helena Hickey on their farm nearby. Families self-catering in the area, especially, will be pleased to find a reasonably priced Italian restaurant **Antonio's** (028 37139), on the main street - a real Italian family offering real traditional food of the Romano region, all cooked to order (they also do takeaway, including pizzas, but have a full menu). Open for lunch and dinner.

WWW.IRELAND-GUIDE.COM FOR ALL THE BEST PLACES TO EAT, DRINK & STAY

Ballydehob

RESTAURANT

Annie's Restaurant
Main Street Ballydehob Co Cork
Tel: 028 37292

Anne and the late Dano Barry opened this legendary restaurant in 1983 - and, for many, a visit to West Cork is unthinkable without a meal here. Extending into the building next door a while ago allowed an upgrade of the whole restaurant so all facilities, including disabled toilets, are on the ground floor - but it's still the same Annie's, just a bit bigger. Annie is a great host, welcoming everybody personally, handing out menus - and then sending guests over to Levis' famous old pub across the road for an aperitif. Then she comes over, takes orders and returns to collect people when their meals are ready - there has never been room for waiting around until tables are ready, so this famous arrangement works extremely well. As to the food at Annie's, there's great emphasis on local ingredients and everything is freshly made on the day:

wild smoked salmon comes from Sally Barnes nearby at Castletownshend; fresh fish is delivered every night; meat comes from the local butcher; their famous roast boned duck is from nearby Skeaghanore Farm; their West Cork farmhouse cheeses include one of Ireland's most renowned cheeses, Gubbeen (made by Annie's sister-in-law, Giana Ferguson), smoked foods come from the Gubbeen Smokehouse, and all the breads, ice creams and desserts for the restaurant are made on the premises. Cooking was formerly in the hands of Dano, or Annie herself, but a new team is now in place - still overseen by Annie, but with local man Jason Smith (previously of The Rectory in Glandore and with experience in many top restaurants) as head chef; with another local man with experience in fine kitchens, Seamus Minihane, as second chef. This is a strong team - and regular customers will be pleased to find that they understand the value of simplicity and wholesome flavours. As always, prices are very fair - the 4-course dinner menu is priced by choice of main courses and there's a carefully chosen wine list, with plenty of bottles under €30; annual tasting sessions decide on the six wines selected as House Wines for the year - interesting choices, and great value too. **Seats 45**; not suitable for children after 9 pm; toilets wheelchair accessible; air conditioning. D Tue-Sat (open Mon Jul-Aug) 6.30-10pm, Set 2/3 course D €38.50/45, à la carte also offered; house wines €22. SC Discretionary. Closed Sun, Mon (open Mon Jul-Aug) & 31 Oct - 1 Dec. MasterCard, Visa, Laser. **Directions:** Street-side, midway through village.

Ballydehob
CHARACTER PUB

Levis' Bar

Corner House Main Street Ballydehob Co Cork
Tel: 028 37118

The Levis sisters ran this 150-year-old bar and grocery for as long as anyone can remember - sadly, Julia died in 2006 but, with help from younger members of the family, Nell is still welcoming visitors as hospitably as ever. It is a characterful and delightfully friendly place, whether you are just in for a casual drink or using the pub as the unofficial 'reception' area for Annie's restaurant across the road (see entry for Annie's above). Closed 25 Dec & Good Fri. **Directions:** Main street, opposite Annie's.

BALLYLICKEY

Ballylickey is positioned on Bantry Bay, midway between Bantry town and Glengarriff, know for its magnificent scenery. Visitors can take a ferry trip to the famour gardens on Garinish Island, or visit one of the many local archaeological sites. Other activities include cycling, golf, angling and sailing. Ballylickey is close to the West Cork Garden Trail which offers many beautiful private and public gardens.

Ballylickey
GUESTHOUSE

Ballylickey House

Ballylickey Bantry Bay Co Cork **Tel: 027 50071**
ballymh@eircom.net   www.ballylickeymanorhouse.com

Built some 300 years ago by Lord Kenmare as a shooting lodge, and home to the Franco-Irish Graves family for five generations, this fine house enjoys a romantic setting overlooking Bantry Bay, with moors and hills behind. Many will remember it when it was run as a country house by the present owner's parents, George and Christiane Graves, and known as Ballylickey Manor; since George and Christiane's retirement their son Paco now operates it along simpler lines, offering bed and breakfast in both the main house and a number of cottages and chalets in the wonderful gardens which were laid out many years ago by Paco's grandmother, Kitty. Guests with a literary turn of mind will be interested to know that the poet Robert Graves was a great-great uncle of Paco's, and visited the house on many occasions. **Rooms 11** (2 suites, 1 junior suites, 5 executive, 3 single, 6 ground floor, all no smoking). B&B €90 pps, ss €50; children welcome (under 4s free in parents' room, cot available); pets allowed in some areas by arrangement. Private parking. Garden, outdoor heated swimming pool, walking, fishing. Closed Nov-Mar. **Directions:** On N71 between Bantry & Glengariff.

Seaview House Hotel

Ballylickey
HOTEL•RESTAURANT

Ballylickey Bantry Co Cork **Tel: 027 50462**
info@seaviewhousehotel.com www.seaviewhousehotel.com

A warm welcome and personal supervision are the hallmarks of Kathleen O'Sullivan's restful country house hotel close to Ballylickey Bridge. Public rooms, which are spacious and well-proportioned, include a graciously decorated drawing room and a cocktail bar, both overlooking lovely gardens at the front of the house, and with outdoor seating for fine weather, also a cosy library and television room. Rooms vary, as is the way with old houses, and the most luxurious accommodation is in junior suites in a new wing; but many rooms have sea views, all are generously sized and individually decorated (six have just been refurbished) and most have good bathrooms. Family furniture and antiques enhance the hotel, and standards of maintenance and housekeeping are consistently outstanding. Small conferences/banqueting (20/75). Children welcome (under 4s free in parents room, cot available free of charge, baby sitting arranged). Pets permitted in some areas by arrangement (stay in bedroom). Garden. **Rooms 25** (6 junior suites, 2 family rooms, 5 ground floor rooms, 1 shower only, 2 for disabled, all no smoking). No lift. B&B €70 pps, ss €25. **Restaurant:** Overlooking the garden, with views over Bantry Bay, the restaurant is elegant and well-appointed with antiques, fresh flowers and plenty of privacy. Five-course dinner menus (with an option to have two or three courses if preferred) change daily and offer a wide choice on all courses; the style is country house cooking, with the emphasis firmly on local produce, especially seafood, in dishes like simple fresh Bantry Bay crab salad with Marie Rose sauce, or meats such as roast rack of lamb with rosemary. Choose from classic desserts or local cheeses to finish and then tea or coffee and petits fours may be served out of doors on fine summer evenings. A carefully selected and informative wine list offers an extensive range of well chosen house wines, a generous choice of half bottles - and many treats. Service, as elsewhere in the hotel, is always caring and professional. **Seats 50**; children welcome (high chair, childrens menu, baby changing facilities); toilets wheelchair accessible. D 7-10pm daily, set 2/3 course D about €35/45. House wines from €20. 10% sc. Hotel closed mid Nov-mid Mar. Amex, MasterCard, Visa, Laser. **Directions:** 10 mins drive from Bantry, on N71 to Glengarriff.

BALTIMORE AREA

Baltimore village has strong associations with the sea, and sailing, diving, angling and kayaking are among the most popular activities here. It's a place with a unique laid-back holiday atmosphere, but it's been all change in Baltimore village lately - and it's mostly down to Youen Jacob, who set up his famous Breton restaurant **Chez Youen** (028 20136; www.youenjacob.com) here in 1979, and his sons; between them they have now changed the heart of Baltimore completely with the completion of their new Waterside development (see entry) and, now that the construction phase is over, the feeling is that it is good for the town, especially as the popular **Baltimore Harbour Hotel** (www.baltimoreharbourhotel.ie) was closed at the time of going to press. For its size Baltimore offers a big choice of eating places, although the seasonal nature of west Cork means that opening times can be very variable and leases change from year to year; for example, visitors may spot an attractive restaurant, **The Mews** (028 20910), down a pretty laneway; it changed hands in the season before the guide went to press but, having been a favourite in the area for years, may be worth investigating. Just a 10-minute trip ferry from Baltimore harbour, **SHERKIN ISLAND** is a small island 5.5km long and 2.5km wide, with a population of only a hundred or so and three lovely safe beaches. There is an hotel on the island, **The Islanders Rest** (Tel 028 20116; wwww.islandersrest.ie), and **Horseshoe Cottage** (see entry) is an interesting and hospitable place to stay. Those taking the ferry to the island for the day will find **The Jolly Roger Tavern** (028 20598) useful to know about, for a bite to eat, and for music too. There are some lovely walks in the Baltimore area, and beautiful gardens to visit within 20km include Glebe Gardens, Baltimore (see entry), Lassanroe Garden (Skibbereen, 028 22563), Carraig Abhainn Gardens (Durrus, 027 61070) and Kilravock Garden (Durrus, 027 61111); as well as golf, horseriding and much more. Nearby Skibbereen hosts a farmers' market in the Old Market Square (opposite AIB Bank) on Saturday mornings.
WWW.IRELAND-GUIDE.COM FOR ALL THE BEST PLACES TO EAT, DRINK & STAY

Baltimore
CHARACTER PUB

Bushe's Bar

The Square Baltimore Co Cork **Tel: 028 20125**
tom@bushesbar.com www.bushesbar.com

Everyone, especially visiting and local sailors, feels at home in this famous old bar. It's choc-à-bloc with genuine maritime artefacts such as charts, tide tables, ships' clocks, compasses, lanterns, pennants et al - but it's the Bushe family's hospitality that makes it really special. Since Richard and Eileen took on the bar in 1973, it's been "home from home" for regular visitors to Baltimore, for whom a late morning call is de rigeur (in order to collect the ordered newspapers that are rolled up and stacked in the bar window each day). Now, the next generation - Tom, Aidan and Marion Bushe – have it running nicely. Simple, homely bar food starts early in the day with tea and coffee from 9.30, moving on to Marion's home-made soups and a range of sandwiches including home-cooked meats, salmon, smoked mackerel or - the most popular by far - open crab sandwiches (when available), served with home-baked brown bread. Although, like all pubs, it can get a little scruffy at busy times, this is a terrific place, at any time of year, and was a very worthy recipient of our Pub of the Year Award in 2000. Children welcome before 10pm (high chair, baby changing facilities). Bar food served 9.30am-8pm daily (12.30-8 Sun). Bar closed 25 Dec & Good Fri. *Accommodation: Although not ITB approved, there are three big, comfortable bedrooms over the bar, all with a double and single bed, bath & shower, TV and a kitchenette with all that is needed to make your own continental breakfast. There are also showers provided for the use of sailors and fishermen. Amex, MasterCard, Visa, Laser.
Directions: In the middle of Baltimore, on the square overlooking the harbour.

Baltimore
HOTEL

Casey's of Baltimore

Baltimore Co Cork **Tel: 028 20197**
info@caseysofbaltimore.com www.caseysofbaltimore.com

The Casey family's striking dark green and red hotel is just outside Baltimore and enjoys dramatic views over Roaring Water Bay to the islands beyond. It has been ingeniously developed over the years to add more accommodation and extend the ground floor public areas towards the back, taking advantage of the view over well-kept gardens - including a kitchen garden on the seaward side that supplies seasonal produce to the kitchen. Some bedrooms also have wonderful views and, although some may seem a little dated, rooms are quite comfortably furnished, with all the necessary facilities, and compact bathrooms have full bath and shower. Friendly staff create a relaxed atmosphere and, as well as a spacious restaurant with sea views, there are well-organised outdoor eating areas for bar food in fine weather; local seafood is the speciality, of course, but menus always offer other choices, including at least one vegetarian dish. Small conferences/banqueting (35/80). Incentive packages; short breaks. **Rooms 14** (1 shower only, 4 ground floor) B&B €87.50 pps, ss €20; children welcome (under 3s free in parents' room, cots available without charge, high chair, childrens menu, baby changing facilities), but not in public areas after 7 pm. No pets. Bar meals daily 12.30-3 & 6.30-9. **Restaurant Seats 80:** Air conditioning. L & D daily: L12.30-3, D 6.30-9. Set L (Sun) €25. à la carte L&D also available; house wine from €19; service discretionary. Closed 20-27 Dec. Amex, Diners, MasterCard, Visa, Laser **Directions:** From Cork take the N71 to Skibbereen & then R595 to Baltimore; on right entering the village.

Baltimore
RESTAURANT

Customs House

Baltimore Co Cork **Tel: 028 20200**
www.thecustomshouse.com

Gillian Oliva and her American husband Billy (who is the chef) have been running this well-known restaurant since 2006, and it continues to please with good cooking and value. You ring the door-bell to go into the restaurant which is in two interconnecting rooms and has a classy and relaxed feeling, with very low music, a subtle shade of yellow on the walls, oil paintings, venetian blinds and floorboards painted rather funkily with (sound-absorbent) red rubber. There's delicious home-made ciabatta bread on the table, water is brought without asking (efficient service is a strong point here) and two menus are offered: a very short menu offering just two dishes on each course, including a vegetarian option, for €35 and one with more choice for €45. Local seafood is dominant, of course - a seafood tapas plate is a speciality starter, and Dover sole on the bone is an ever-popular main course - but you'll also find alternatives including dry-aged Hereford beef and roast breast of local Skeaghanore duck, an all-Irish cheese selection may offer lesser known cheeses such as Ardagh Castle and Crozier Blue as well as some of the more famous local ones. Pride is taken in both the ingredients (local, where possible) and the cooking here; upbeat classic desserts and breads - are all home-made. The wine list offers a fair choice and includes some half bottles and pudding wines, but none by the glass, and you can round off your meal with artisan hand-roasted coffee, or one o' a choice of Dilmaha teas. **Seats 34.** D, 7-10pm. Set D €45; not suitable for children under 13 Opening times & days vary, please call in advance off season. Closed Oct-Apr. MasterCard, Visa, Laser. **Directions:** Beside the Garda Station, 50 metres from the pier.

Baltimore
CAFÉ

Glebe House Gardens

Glebe Gardens Baltimore Co Cork **Tel: 028 20232**
glebegardens@eircom.net www.glebegardens.com

Jean and Peter Perry's wonderful gardens just outside Baltimore attract a growing number of visitors each year and they have a delightful café for those in need of a restorative bite; it's all very wholesome - and they generously allow you to bring your own picnic too, if preferred. The menu is sensibly short but the food, using organically grown ingredients from the garden and from named local craft suppliers, is unpretentious, and cooked (to order) to a very high standard indeed. For example, you might try a four fish chowder, accompanied by delicious home-made brown bread and the lightest, fluffiest white scone you are likely to find anywhere followed, perhaps, by a scrumptious three cheese (Irish farmhouse) and tomato tart accompanied by a delicately dressed salad from the garden. Other possibilities include smoked mackerel pate with a green salad, breads and toasts, or a children's lunch of Rosscarbery sausage with pea & potato mash - and all this at a surprisingly reasonable cost. Simply delicious. In 2008 the food side of the business developed further with the addition of a new restaurant space and dinner was offered for the first time, featuring daily changed menus based on whatever is freshest and best on the day. The choice offered is limited to three main courses (which always include a vegetarian option) plus a selection of starters and desserts. Wine list available. Gardens open weekends Easter-June and Wed-Sun Jun-Aug. Café open daily from 10am for breakfast, lunch and afternoon tea; restaurant open Wed-Sun 7-10pm, in summer. **Directions:** Off Skibbereen-Baltimore road: entrance directly opposite 'Baltimore' sign as you enter the village. ◇

Baltimore
RESTAURANT WITH ROOMS•CAFÉ•WINE BAR

Rolf's

Baltimore Co Cork **Tel: 028 20289**
info@rolfsholidays.eu www.rolfsholidays.eu

The Haffner family have been at this delightful place for over 25 years, and the complex - which began as a holiday hostel and is now styled 'country house' - has been extensively upgraded. Now, in addition to self-catering accommodation with character and the popular restaurant and wine bar, all of their guest rooms are en-suite. Although not a country house in the conventional sense, it certainly has a great deal to offer, including a lovely garden terrace with a sea view, which is available for fine weather. The café is open during the day and serves an à la carte lunch, with a more extensive dinner menu offered in the Restaurant 'Café Art', which has a dedicated local following and delights visitors with its great food and atmosphere. Euro-Toques chef-owner Johannes Haffner uses as much home-grown, organic and local produce as possible - and, refreshingly, alongside popular specialities like loin of Slaney Valley lamb and free range supreme of chicken, his wide-ranging menus include quite a few classics and retro dishes (beef stroganoff made with vodka is a speciality), and all baked goods and desserts are home-made. A well-chosen wine list includes a range of champagne cocktails and aperitifs, and many treats among the main listing including an unusually good choice of half bottles - and many wines not listed are available by the glass in the Wine Bar. **Accommodation: Rooms 14** (all en-suite, all shower only, all no smoking); children welcome (cot available free of charge); B&B €40-50 pps; ss €10-20. Pets permitted by arrangement; garden; walking. **Restaurant: Seats 60** (also outdoor 40). Toilets wheelchair accessible. B 8.30-11, L 12-2.30, D 6-9.30 (to 9 off-season). A la carte. House wine from €20. Open all week. Reservations advised. Closed 24-26 Dec. MasterCard, Visa, Laser. *Self catering holiday cottages also available. **Directions:** On Baltimore Hill, 10 minute walk from village.

Baltimore

B&B

The Slipway

The Cove Baltimore Co Cork **Tel: 028 20134**

theslipway@hotmail.com www.theslipway.com

Quietly located away from the bustle around the square, but within easy walking distance of several excellent restaurants, Wilmie Owen's unusual house has uninterrupted views of the harbour and distant seascape from all the bedrooms, and also the first floor breakfast room, which has a balcony (a delightful room but, unfortunately, not available to guests, except at breakfast time). There's a lovely garden and a self-catering cottage is also available for weekly rental (sleeps 2); details on application. **Rooms 4** (all shower only & no-smoking, 1 family room, 2 ground floor); not suitable for children under 12; no pets, garden; B&B €40 pps, ss €16/€25 low/high season. Closed Nov-Mar officially, but phone to check, open over New Year. **No Credit Cards. Directions:** Through Baltimore village, to the Cove, 500 metres.

Baltimore

GUESTHOUSE•RESTAURANT•PUB

The Waterfront

The Square Baltimore Co Cork **Tel: 028 20600**

info@youenjacob.com www.youenjacob.com

When Youen Jacob acquired the pub next door to his long-established restaurant Chez Youen in 2004, this new venture turned out to be the beginning of something much bigger that would transform the centre of Baltimore. Youen and his sons, Youen Jacob Jnr. (manager) and Pascal Jacob (chef), have now linked their Baltimore Bay Guesthouse at the top of the square and The Waterfront pub – and, although registered as a 3* guesthouse at the time of going to press, this impressive development is well on the way to becoming an hotel. The Waterfront complex now includes a pub (Jacob's Bar), two restaurants (The Look Out and La Jolie Brise Pizza & Grill, on the square) and some fine new rooms, plus the existing ones in the previous Baltimore Guest House. The cheerful continental-style café La Jolie Brise Pizza & Grill (pizza made in authentic Italian way & fresh fish and shellfish – no pasta) still spills out on to the pavement and is also accessible from The Waterfront. Although still very new at the time of the Guide's visit, this is a stylish development marked by Youen Jacob's commitment to quality: the new building doesn't merely fit into the square, it completes it. And – like the rooms at the Baltimore Bay Guesthouse (under refurbishment at the time of going to press) which set a standard in space and comfort when they first opened, the stylish new rooms are extremely spacious and have lovely bathrooms – and even the rooms at the back have some very special features that will make them at least as desirable as those with a view. Small conferences/Banqueting (50/70); free broadband wi/fi. Children welcome (under 4s free in parents room, cot available free of charge; half price up to 12 yrs if bed required; baby sitting arranged); **Rooms 13** (all en-suite, 1 junior suite, 3 shower only, 3 family, 1 for disabled); lift; pets permitted by prior arrangement (stay in bedroom, no charge). B&B €60 pps, ss €20. Sea angling, walking & scuba diving all nearby. Accommodation open all year. MasterCard, Visa, Laser. Two doors along from The Waterfront, **Chez Youen** is still doing what it does best: simple but dramatic presentation of seafood in the shell; this is a pricey affair (a shellfish platter costs about €60) but different from other places, and Youen's wine list is also exceptional - he imports a wide range of wines directly from France (see his website for full details). This may seem very like a Jacob takeover of Baltimore but it seems to have been well received locally and, for the visitor, the town is the better for it. Bar: Open from 10.30 am. Bar meals from 12.30-9pm daily. Open all year. La Jolie Brise Pizza & Grill; **seats 50** (outdoors 60); children welcome (high chair, baby changing facilities); no reservations accepted; open Wed-Sun, May-Sept, 6-10pm (will open for private functions off season); house wine from €20.50. Closed Mon, Tue, bank hols, Oct-Apr. **Directions:** On the waterfront, overlooking the harbour.

Baltimore Area

B&B

Horseshoe Cottage

Sherkin Island Baltimore Co Cork **Tel: 028 20598**

joe@gannetsway.com www.gannetsway.com

Joe and Fiona Aston offer an authentic experience at their beautifully located island B&B, which is open for most of the year. Although small, it is well laid out, with a pretty sheltered garden that not only pleases the eye but also supplies organic vegetables for the table, and there's a comfortable sitting room with lots of books and games. There are three en-suite bedrooms, all simply but comfortably furnished with good quality beds and linen, and tea and coffee-making facilities. Fiona cooks dinner for guests - fresh fish, local meat, and soups and salads feature and, of course, seasonal vegetables from the kitchen garden too. The day begins with a hearty breakfast of fresh fruit or fruit compote, home-baked bread and, again, the best of local/artisan food including smoked salmon and scrambled eggs and fresh fish. And this is a B&B with a difference, as Fiona offers various therapies to guests and Joe has a 45' schooner, the Anna M, which he uses to take guests out on fishing/sight-seeing trips of Roaring Water Bay, mainly for dolphin and whale-watching. **Rooms 3**. B&B €40pps for the first night, reduced to €38 for subsequent nights. 2 nights B&B with full day's sailing is €300, all summer. **Directions:** On Sherkin Island within easy walking distance of pier and pubs, yet in a quiet position facing south above Horseshoe Bay.

Baltimore Area
RESTAURANT

Island Cottage

Heir Island Skibbereen Co Cork **Tel: 028 38102**
www.islandcottage.com

Just a short ferry ride from the mainland yet light years away from the "real" world, this place is unique. Hardly a likely location for a restaurant run by two people who have trained and worked in some of Europe's most prestigious establishments - but, since 1990, that is exactly what John Desmond and Ellmary Fenton have been doing at Island Cottage. Everything about it is different from other restaurants, including the booking policy: bookings are accepted for groups of 6 to 24 people; a basic advance booking for at least six people must be in place before other smaller groups of 2 to 4 can be accepted - not later than 3pm on the day; changes to group numbers require 24 hours notice and a booking deposit of €20 per head is required to reserve a table (you post a cheque or postal order). The no-choice 5-course menu depends on the availability of the fresh local, organic (where possible) and wild island ingredients of that day, which might include salmon, shrimp and crab. A typical menu might be: marinated salmon on a bed of mayonnaise, with home-made brown bread; breast of duck (made using hand-reared ducks "of exceptional quality" from Ballydehob) with red wine sauce & potato and carrot purée; green salad with French dressing and Gubbeen cheese; hot lemon crêpe soufflé with strawberry coulis; filter coffee. Changes to the menu of the day are not possible. Off-season cookery courses offered, also private dinner service; cottages for rent - details from the restaurant. **Seats 24** (max table size 10; be prepared to share a table). Set Menu - no choice, no exceptions D €40. Open May-Sept, Wed-Sun, 8.10-11.40 pm; one sitting served at group pace. Wine from €20. Off-season: groups of 16-24 by arrangement. Closed Sun- Tue, and mid Sep-May (please phone to check off season opening days/times). **No credit cards. Directions:** From Skibbereen, on Ballydehob road, turn left at Church Cross, signposted Hare Island and Cunnamore. Narrow winding road, past school, church, Minihan's Bar. Continue to end of road, Cunnamore car park. Ferry (blue boat) departs Cunnamore pier at 7.55 returns at 11.55 (journey: 4 minutes.) For ferry, contact John Moore/Richard Pyburn Tel: 086 809 2447. ◊

BANDON

Bandon, set deep in the valley of the Argideen River is an historic town, and home to West Cork Heritage Centre (023 41677); housed in the former Christ Church in Bandon's main street, it features a unique exhibition in which visitors are transported through time to experience Bandon town in years gone by. Nearby, at Timoleague Castle Gardens (023 46116), there is a working walled garden, a country house and a ruined Norman Castle - an interesting place to spend some time. Food and agriculture have always been important to Bandon town as products from the area such as meat, butter and corn were mainly exported through the nearby port of Kinsale and merchants imported wines, spices, sugar and tobacco. Today, with an increasingly close relationship between food and tourism as well as strong local interest, the town hosts a farmers' market every Saturday, and has a growing number of restaurants, cafés and specialist food shops, and also good accommodation. The fine old **Munster Arms Hotel** (023 41562) on Oliver Plunkett Street is the hub of local activities and popular with business visitors; on the same street, Daniele Quatrana's authentic modern Italian restaurant **Italistro** (023 52300) is gaining a name for good food and value - useful to know about, especially as it's open 7 days; for a more traditional take on Italian dining, **Sorrento** (023 29839) is on South Main Street. For Indian, head to **Anarkali** (023-29762) on North Main Street, who also do takeaway. Down by the river, on McSwiney Quay, you'll find the bright, contemporary **Marmatiece Restaurant** (023-42715) with river view, which is popular for its value and style. Visitors often need a good café rather than a restaurant - and, along the same stretch, the very special **URRU** food shop and café (see entry) is well worth seeking out and people travel miles for their artisan sandwiches. Other good cafés in the town include **The Early Bird**, an attractive modern continental style café/deli with outside seating on South Main Street, offering appealing informal food.
WWW.IRELAND-GUIDE.COM FOR ALL THE BEST PLACES TO EAT, DRINK & STAY

Bandon

HISTORIC HOUSE

Kilbrogan House

Bandon Co Cork **Tel: 023 44935**

kilbrogan.house@gmail.com www.kilbrogan.com

This elegant three-storey Georgian townhouse, built in 1818, faces out on to Kilbrogan Hill, a quiet, mostly residential street in Bandon town. In 1992, brother and sister Catherine and David Fitzmaurice bought it in a dilapidated state and, following sympathetic restoration, opened it as a guesthouse in 2004. You get the feeling that this listed house has changed little since it was built. At the back, a large lawn is surrounded by shrubs and tall trees and the stables, which have been converted into self-catering accommodation, add to the olde worlde atmosphere. Inside, a large hall is welcoming, with a polished wooden floor and a curving staircase leading up to bedrooms and a first floor sitting room with a piano - there is also a drawing room on the ground floor for guests' use, and a conservatory half way up the stairs at the back of the house. Some of the bedrooms look out on to Kilbrogan Hill and the hills beyond the rooftops, others onto the gravel parking area and the lawn and trees at the back; all have mod cons such as flat-screen TV, broadband internet connection and hairdryer, but are elegantly furnished with antiques (including very comfortable beds with lovely starched cotton sheets), and interesting prints decorate the walls; well-appointed bathrooms have full bath and power shower, and heated towel rails. Blue and white check cotton napkins and tablecloth on the breakfast table give a cheerful country feel, and David is a trained chef, so you can look forward to a delicious cooked breakfast. This is a lovely place to stay, and Catherine and David are great hosts, keen to ensure that their guests find all the best places to visit (and eat) during their stay in Bandon. **Rooms 4** (all no smoking); not suitable for children under 12 yrs; broadband. B&B €50 pps, ss €10. Closed Dec, Jan. *Self-catering also available, rates on application. Amex, MasterCard, Visa, Laser. **Directions:** Turn right at Methodist church, follow signs for Macroom, bear left at Post Office. Take 1st right 200 metres up hill on right.

Bandon

RESTAURANT•PUB

The Poachers Inn

Clonakilty Road Bandon Co Cork **Tel: 023 41159**

mclaughlinbc@hotmail.com

Barry and Catherine McLoughlin's roadside bar and restaurant just outside Bandon is a typical pub with the bar downstairs and restaurant above and, with dark wood, hunting prints, a fire-place corner with leather sofas, and other seating divided between banquettes and high tables with bar stools, it has a cosy ambience. But, although this place may be unremarkable in appearance, the kitchen is turning out wonderfully flavourful dishes based on fresh local seafood (from Castletownbere), and they have earned a great reputation in the locality and beyond for their fine food and hospitality. Barry is the chef and, once guests learn that he was previously at Fishy Fishy Café and Casino House (widely recognised as two of the finest restaurants in an area well known for its good food), expectations are immediately raised. And there should be no cause for disappointment here as top quality ingredients are deftly handled and, even when eating in the bar, the seafood is restaurant quality, both in taste and contemporary presentation on smart white plates. Crispy Dinish Island crab and prawn cakes come with spicy mango and plum salsa, and deep dish seafood pie is comfort food of the first order; dishes like West Cork seafood chowder at about €6.50, and, when available, fresh crabmeat open sandwiches at around €10.95, are popular with the many family groups who are attracted to this spot. Steak, a chicken dish and a vegetarian choice is also offered for non-fish eaters, and desserts are of the homely kind - hot-sticky toffee pudding, bread and butter pudding, and apple cinnamon & walnut crumble are all typical. The restaurant upstairs is open for dinner several nights a week, with menus that overlap to some extent with the bar meals, and also offer some extra dishes. Catherine manages front of house and service under her direction is informal, but pleasant and efficient. Wines are served by the glass from a dispenser, a choice of four or five each red and white, also a rosé. This new venture has proved a great asset to the area, and cookery courses are also available. **Restaurant: Seats 50** (outdoors, 10); children welcome before 9pm (high chair); reservations required, air conditioning, free broadband wi/fi, toilets wheelchair accessible. D Thurs-Sat only, 7-10pm; L Sun only, 12-3.30pm; house wine from €19. Pub food served daily, 12-7.30pm; weekend music sessions. Restaurant closed Sun D & Mon-Wed, house closed 25 Dec. MasterCard, Visa, Laser. **Directions:** On the main West Cork road heading out of Bandon, right hand side.

Bandon
URRU

CAFÉ•CULINARY STORE   The Mill McSwinney Quay Bandon Co Cork **Tel: 023 54731**

Ⓝ   info@urru.ie www.urru.ie

People come from all around the area (and a stop en route to holiday in West Cork has become de rigeur) to shop at Ruth Healy's stylish, modern culinary store on the river: a kitchen shop, deli, food-store and café, it offers a unique combination of quality products - and great coffees and teas too, to sip with your artisan snack. Whether you're looking for the very best of specialist Irish foods from producers like Ummera Smokehouse, Frank Krawczyk, James McGeough, Caherbeg and Gubbeen, a cookbook or that special something for your kitchen - or top drawer larder imports like single estate olive oil, balsamic vinegar, teas, coffees & wines; you'll find the very best of everything in this bright and colourful store, hand-picked because it's special. And, although the café is very informal, with a choice of high stools at the beechwood counter or seating at one large table at the back of the shop, the same principles apply to the fare offered here – a daily blackboard suggests simple but unusual combinations that include artisan products that are also on sale (smoked fish and meats, salamis, farmhouse cheeses, charcuterie, breads, preserves, pastries, ice creams, honey) and, if you wish, to take away. Wines are charged at the retail price plus €5 corkage – and, unusually, no tips are accepted. Well worth a look, so take the town route instead of the by-pass next time you're heading west. Also at: Mallow (see entry). **Seats 16**; children welcome; air conditioning. Open Mon-Sat 9.30am-6pm. Wine from shop plus €5 corkage. No SC. Closed Sun, Bank Hols, 25-28 Dec. Amex, MasterCard, Visa, Laser. **Directions:** On entering Bandon from Cork, turn right at Methodist church, then immediate left. River on right, shop on left at end of quay.

Bandon Area
Blue Geranium Café

CAFÉ   Hosfords Garden Centre Cappa Enniskeane Co Cork **Tel: 023 39159**

john@hosfordsgardencentre.ie www.hosfordsgardencentre.ie

Garden lovers travel from all over Ireland to visit Hosfords, which is one of the country's best garden centres and specialises in hardy geraniums hence the name of their attractive new cafe, which is proving popular with locals as well as garden centre customers. It's a large airy glasshouse-style space with modern pale wood, and large tubs of palms and tree ferns used as dividers; large sliding doors open on to an inviting outdoor patio area where tables and chairs are set up, and there is a children's playground alongside. The setting is attractive, with seasonal flowers such as a bunch of sweet peas on every table and the food, although self-service, is good quality. Typical of the best type of food now expected at lifestyle shopping outlets and top garden centres, with prices to match, you can expect to find dishes like quiche and salad (€10.50), chicken pie with mash (€13.50), and home-bakes such as freshly baked scones with jam and butter (€2.75). Staff take the self-service aspect of the operation a little too literally at times - no help appears to be available for elderly or incapacitated visitors taking food to their tables. Open Mon-Sat, 9am-6pm, Sun 12-5.30pm. **Directions:** On the Bandon-Clonakilty road (N71). ◈

BANTRY

Delightfully situated at the head of Bantry Bay, this historic town has much to offer the visitor - notably the mid-18th century Bantry House (027 50047; www.bantryhouse.com), which is still a family home; set in lovely grounds and gardens, it houses the French Armada Museum. The Beara peninsula is to the northwest, with Sheep's Head also nearby, on the peninsula south of Bantry Bay and all have many spectacular walks. Rowing, sailing and golf are popular past times for visitors to the area. The beautifully located championship course at Bantry Bay Golf Club (027 50579) will provide a stern test for the best of golfers while there are too many superb gardens in the area to name, but the following are within 20km (Carraig Abhainn Gardens, Durrus 027 61070; Illnacullin, Garinish Island, 027 63040; Kilravock Garden, Durrus, 027 61111; Lassanroe Garden, Skibbereen, 028 22563 & Cois Cuain Gardens, Bantry, 027 67070). Several hotels in the town include the (very) large new **Maritime Hotel, Spa & Suites** (023 20126) along the quay below Bantry House; the long-established **Westlodge Hotel** (027 50360; www.westlodgehotel.ie) on the edge of the town, which has extensive amenities, making it a weather-proof base for a family holiday; by contrast, the offering is modest at the O'Callaghan family's **Bantry Bay Hotel** (027 50062; www.bantrybayhotel.net) on Wolfe Tone Square, but there is warm family hospitality to compensate. Very useful to anyone self-catering in the area, the famous Bantry Friday Market sells every good thing you could possibly want to eat and draws shoppers from a wide area, so the many small restaurants and daytime cafés in the town are in great demand. There's the vegetarian café **Organico** (see entry) and on Main Street you'll find the long-established bakery and café, **Floury Hands** (027 52590); on New Street, there's **The Stuffed Olive** (027 55883) specialist foodstore and café. On the quay, the popular bistro and pizzeria

The Brick Oven (027 52500) has expanded recently, now extending into the premises next door - and with separate restaurant **The Mariner** (027 55399; a great place for a quick and honest meal, The Brick Oven is a good choice for families. **The Fish Kitchen** (027 56651; open Tue-Sat 12-9 (phone to check off season); no credit cards (yet). Is a great spot above The Central Fish Market on New street... not big on atmosphere, but real imagination and style in the cooking, reasonably priced, and lovely staff.

WWW.IRELAND-GUIDE.COM FOR ALL THE BEST PLACES TO EAT, DRINK & STAY

Bantry

HOTEL•RESTAURANT

Maritime Hotel

The Quay Bantry Co Cork **Tel: 027 54700**
info@themaritime.ie www.themaritime.ie

Although many questioned the wisdom of allowing a development including a large modern hotel to be built along the quay below Bantry House, it has brought welcome amenities and a standard of accommodation not previously available in the area. Smart and contemporary, it's a welcoming, colourful place with some funky features and a linear design following the shoreline that allows most interior areas to take advantage of the view. Stylish, luxurious accommodation includes some two-bedroom family suites with sitting room and kitchen - and leisure facilities include 19m swiming pool, gym, sauna, steamroom and Jacuzzi. B&B €60 pps, ss €35; free broadband; room service (24-hr). Leisure centre (swimming pool, gym, sauna, jacuzzi). **Oceans:** Informal meals are available in the Maritime Bar, but the restaurant has a definite sense of occasion. Decorated in sumptuous shades of burgundy and purple, with wooden structures reminiscent of an upturned keel echoing the maritime theme, the restaurant has wooden floors that are nicely complemented by comfortably upholstered chairs and plush banquettes beside the windows overlooking the harbour - and darkwood tables smartly laid with strips of white linen and simple, classy table settings. Menus feature locally sourced foods, such as Beara peninsula monkfish, Bantry lamb and the famous Bantry Bay mussels, and the emphasis is on Irish ingredients spiked with touches of more exotic ingredients, such as sundried tomato coulis and chick peas with chorizo. Service is pleasant and efficient and, although not adventurous, the wine list offers a fair range including half a dozen by the glass, and some half bottles. **Directions:** Below Bantry House on The Quay.

Bantry

BAR•RESTAURANT

O'Connor's Seafood Restaurant

The Square Bantry Co Cork **Tel: 027 50221**
oconnorseafood@eircom.net www.oconnorseafood.com

SEAFOOD RESTAURANT OF THE YEAR

Easy to spot by the three model yachts in full sail in the front window, Peter and Anne O'Brien's long-established seafood restaurant is right on the main square (site of Friday markets and the annual early-May mussel festival) and, although no longer directly in the O'Connor family, there's a very old family connection as Anne's great-grandmother was the original owner of the bar licence back in 1914 - pretty good continuity by any standards. A welcoming interior mingles chic décor with artefacts connected with the seafaring tradition of the town; the ambience is cool and relaxed, helped along by a friendly, courteous and knowledgeable service team, headed up by the owners, who are nearly always present to welcome customers personally. Naturally, fresh fish and shellfish is the big thing here. Local small boats supply some of it, especially local crab, lobster and prawns, and the renowned Bantry Bay mussels, cooked all ways, are a speciality - try their Mussels in Murphy's Stout (steamed in stout and cream), followed perhaps by lobster (when in season), and served with an abundance of fresh seasonal vegetables. There's a fair choice of non-fish dishes available too, all using local produce - roast rack of local lamb is another speciality (served with black pudding mash and a port & thyme jus), also roast Skeaghanore duck breast with rosemary flavoured butter beans - an unusual dish, it is served on a duck liver terrine. You'll also find a vegetarian dish of the day, although there's less choice for vegetarians than for meat or fish lovers. Since superlative fresh ingredients need little to enhance them, the ethos in the kitchen is to keep cooking simple, adornments complementary, and fuss to a minimum. You won't find towers of ingredients stacked cheffily high on the plate - just quality fresh local food presented with panache, and made for enjoying. The wine list is well structured and easy to browse - in sections according to taste. It's nice to see also a real seasonal choice of wines by the glass - including sparkling. Great value for money at lunch and on the Early Bird evening menu too. **Seats 48** (private room, 12); children welcome before 8 pm (high chair); air conditioning. L 12.15-3, D 6-10 (Sun to 9). Early D €29 (6-7pm); set D 2/3 course €27/29.50; also à la carte; house wine €20. SC discretionary. Closed L Bank hols, Good Fri, 25 Dec, Sun Oct-May, but telephone to confirm opening times off-season. MasterCard, Visa, Laser. **Directions:** Town centre; prominent location on square.

Bantry
CAFÉ•SHOP•BAKERY

Organico
2 Glengarriff Road Bantry Co Cork **Tel: 027 51391**
info@organico.ie www.organico.ie

Hannah and Rachel Dare's vegetarian café is situated above the Organico bakery and food shop, near the centre of the town. In a spacious room (with internet connection) they offer tasty snacks, breads and cakes from the bakery, and lunches including splendid salads. Rachel, a Ballymaloe-trained cook, is the force behind the menu, which is based on organic vegetables, salads, pulses, (spelt) flours and raw cane sugar - and even the milk in the Fair Trade organic latte is organic too. Local free range and artisan foods also feature farmhouse cheeses, butter, eggs and, for the non-vegetarian, the most interesting fact is that dishes such as minestrone soup, which are usually dependent on a good meat stock, are full of flavour. And yes, even their little wine list is organic. The staff are pleasant and efficient, and it's good value for money - well worth a visit. **Seats 50**; children welcome (high chair, childrens menu); broadband wi/fi. Open Mon-Sat, 9.30-5.30pm. L 12-3.30pm. House wine €20. Closed Sun, Bank Hols, 24 Dec - 15 Jan. Amex, MasterCard, Visa, Laser. **Directions:** On road from Main Square to Glengarriff, 3 mins walk from tourist office.

Bantry
PUB

The Snug
The Quay Bantry Co Cork
Tel: 027 50057

Maurice and Colette O'Donovans' well-named bar is a cosy and welcoming place, bustling with life and ideal for a wholesome bite at moderate prices. Maurice is the chef and takes pride in using local produce and giving value for money; his menus feature a wide range of popular dishes, many of which are in the house style. At lunch time, home-made soups and favourites like deep-fried mushrooms with garlic mayonnaise top the bill and are followed by a range of open sandwiches, panini, baguettes and fourly baps and specials such as roast lamb or goujons of fresh haddock. More extensive evening menus offer dressier dishes as well, including starters like Bantry Bay prawn cocktail or oak smoked salmon salad, and a good choice of main courses including steaks, home-made beefburgers and local Skeaghanore duck with orange sauce as well as a number of fish dishes - including Bantry Bay mussels, of course. This wholesome fare, together with good value, keeps 'em coming back for more. Children welcome (but not after 9pm). Food served daily, 11am-9pm (Sun 12.30-9). Closed 25 Dec & Good Fri. MasterCard, Visa, Laser **Directions:** Beside Garda Station, on the quay as you enter Bantry. ◇

Bantry Area
RESTAURANT WITH ROOMS

Larchwood House Restaurant
Pearsons Bridge Bantry Co Cork
Tel: 027 66181

The gardens are a special point of interest here, complementing the restaurant, which is in a relatively modern house with both the traditionally-furnished lounge and dining room enjoying lovely garden views. Sheila Vaughan, a Euro-Toques chef, presents seasonal dinner menus: warm duck salad with ginger, quite traditional main courses such as loin of lamb with lemon and mint, and classical desserts like lemon ice cream or warm chocolate cake with caramel sauce - good cooking and, while the pace is leisurely, the view of the garden is a treat. This is a haven for garden lovers, who often make it a base when visiting the many gardens in the locality; here, the Ouvane River flows through the three acre woodland garden, which includes an island accessible via a footbridge and stepping stones all created by Aidan Vaughan. **Seats 25**. D Fri & Sat only, 7-9pm. Set D about €45. House wine €23. SC discretionary. Gardens open Mon-Fri 9am-5pm, also several Sundays in June (phone to check dates). B&B accommodation is also offered about €40 pps, no ss. Closed Sun-Thurs; Christmas week; limited openings in winter, please call ahead to check. Amex, Diners, MasterCard, Visa. Laser. **Directions:** Take the Kealkil Road off N71 at Ballylickey; after 2 miles signed just before the bridge. ◇

BEARA PENINSULA

Aside from Castletownbere (see entry), a tour around the scenic BEARA PENINSULA has remarkably few places where you might be tempted to stop for a bite or - except for **Mossie's Ulusker House** at Adrigole (027 60606; www.mossiesrestaurant.com) - stay overnight. At Bunaw on Kilmacallogue Harbour, at the northern end of the Healy Pass, **Teddy O'Sullivan's** is a pleasantly traditional and hospitable pub offering good simple food (try a big bowl of the mussels the area is famous for); at Derreen Gardens, nearby at Lauragh, there is also a café serving teas and **Josie Corkery's B&B and Restaurant** (064 83155) has also been delighting visitors to Lauragh for many years. Further west at the village of Ardgroom, look out for **The Village Inn**, a well-maintained and friendly traditional pub serving home-cooked food. Should hunger strike way out west at Allihies, **O'Neill's** pub offers bar food (and a restaurant upstairs Thu-Sun evenings; 027 73008) and there's even simple Failte Ireland-approved accommodation at Mary O'Sullivan's **Seaview B&B** (027 73004). Championship golf is available about 30km away in Bantry Bay Golf Club (027 50579) and there are several excellent gardens less then 30km away - Derreen Garden (Kenmare, 064 83588); Cois Cuain Gardens (Bantry, 027 67070) and Kilravock Garden (Durrus, 027 61111) being the closest. There is a farmers' market in Castletownbere on the first Thursday of each month.
WWW.IRELAND-GUIDE.COM FOR ALL THE BEST PLACES TO EAT, DRINK & STAY

BLARNEY

Blarney, 8km (5m) north of Cork city, is world famous for its castle and the Blarney Stone, with its traditional power of conferring eloquence on those who kiss it... Although it attracts a lot of tourists, its convenience to the city also also make it a good base for business visitors. Those who prefer a smaller but lively establishment may like the **Muskerry Arms** (021 438 5200), a traditional pub and guesthouse with traditional music in the bar each evening. The nearest championhip golf course is Fota Island Golf Club (near Cobh, 021 488 3710), while garden lovers have plenty of visits worth noting within 30km including Lakemount Garden (Glanmire, 021 482 1052), Fota Arboretum & Gardens (Carrigtwohill, 021 481 5543), Cedar Lodge (Midleton, 021 461 3379) and Annes Grove Garden (near Mallow, 022 26145). If farmers' markets are of interest, then there are several in Cork City including the renowned English Market (open daily) and Coal Quay Market (Saturdays, Cornmarket Street).
WWW.IRELAND-GUIDE.COM FOR ALL THE BEST PLACES TO EAT, DRINK & STAY

Blarney
GUESTHOUSE

Ashlee Lodge

Tower Blarney Co Cork **Tel: 021 438 5346**
info@ashleelodge.com www.ashleelodge.com

Anne and John O'Leary's luxurious purpose-built guesthouse is just a couple of miles outside Blarney and within very easy striking distance of Cork city (a bus from the city will drop you outside their door). Everything is immaculate, beginning with the impressive reception area with highly polished floor and well-kept plants and fresh flowers in all the public areas, including the breakfast room. Bedrooms may not have views, but the exceptionally high level of comfort more than compensates: spacious rooms furnished with quality in mind have king size beds and all the latest technology - wide screen TV, radio and CD unit, direct dial phones with modem access, personal safe and individually controlled air conditioning - as well as tea/coffee facilities, trouser press, hairdryer, bathrobes and towelling slippers. But the most outstanding feature of Ashlee Lodge is the O'Learys themselves, who are exceptionally helpful hosts and genuinely wish to assist guests in every way possible - notably with local knowledge of all kinds, especially the many golf courses nearby; they arrange tee times, provide transport to and from golf courses and generally act as facilitators. They take great pride in giving a breakfast to remember too - an impressive buffet is beautifully laid out with lots of juices, cereals and fresh fruits in season, then there are freshly-baked breads, real honeycomb on every table, and a wide range of hot dishes including fish of the day, all impeccably cooked to order - and prettily presented too. Everything is pristine and the only small downside is that the hard flooring used throughout the house can be noisy. *Dinner is sometimes available, by arrangement - Anne is the chef, and she offers an appealing choice of about five starters and half a dozen main courses There's also a choice of 14 wines, all available by the glass and preserved by 'La Verre de Vin' system. **Rooms 10** (4 suites, 1 shower only, 6 ground floor, 1 for disabled, all no smoking). B&B €70 pps, ss €25. D daily (by arrangement only),

6-8.30pm. Free broadband wi/fi; mini-spa with hot tub, massage. garden, fishing nearby. Golf breaks. Closed 20 Dec - 31 Jan. Amex, MasterCard, Visa, Laser. **Directions:** Located on R617 Blarney-Killarney road: from Blarney village take road past Blarney Park Hotel, signed Killarney, for approx 2km; turn left at filling station - Ashlee Lodge is on left about 0.5km further on.

Blarney   # Blairs Inn
CHARACTER PUB   Cloghroe Blarney Co Cork **Tel: 021 438 1470**
Ⓥ   blair@eircom.net www.blairsinn.ie

John, Anne and Duncan Blair's pretty riverside pub is in a quiet, wooded setting. Sitting in the garden in summer, you might see trout rising in the Owennageara river, while winter offers welcoming fires in this comfortingly traditional country pub. It's a lovely place to drop into for a drink and they offer food in both the bar and a restaurant area – the long-established kitchen team working under head chef Hervé Remboure has recently been joined by Duncan Blair, who trained at Ballymaloe. Outdoor seating is provided in a covered patio area, with bar. **Seats 45** (restaurant/bar) & 100 in garden; children welcome before 7pm. Bar menu 12.30-9.30 daily (additional evening bar menu 4-9.30pm). Restaurant L 12.30-4, D 6.30-9.30; a la carte; house wine €21; service discretionary. Live traditional music Mon, 9.30pm, Jun-Sept. Closed 25 Dec & Good Fri. Amex, Diners, MasterCard, Visa, Laser. **Directions:** 5 minutes from Blarney village, on the R579.

Blarney   # Blarney Castle Hotel
HOTEL   Village Green Blarney Co Cork **Tel: 021 438 5116**
                               info@blarneycastlehotel.com www.blarneycastlehotel.com

This attractive family-run hotel overlooks the village green in the centre of Blarney, beside the castle. It has been in the Forrest family since 1837 but, with the exception of the restaurant, reception area and a very characterful old bar, they completely rebuilt the hotel a few years ago. The new accommodation includes spacious, bright bedrooms with excellent views and all have a double and single bed, wide screen TV, tea/coffee-making; and well-finished bathrooms. Helpful, friendly staff create a welcoming atmosphere and prices are reasonable. The adjacent Lemon Tree Restaurant may not carry through the anticipated Mediterranean theme, but offers meals that are above the standard expected in hotel dining rooms and staff are very hospitable. Short breaks available all year. Golfing breaks offered; numerous golf courses nearby, transport etc arranged for guests. **Rooms 13** (1 junior suite,1 shower only, all no smoking); children welcome (under 5 free in parents' room, cot available without charge, baby sitting arranged.) Pool table. Private parking. No lift. B&B €60 pps, ss €20. [Meals: The Lemon Tree Restaurant: D 6-9pm. Bar food 12-9.30 daily.] Closed 24-25 Dec. Amex, MasterCard, Visa, Laser. **Directions:** Centre of Blarney, on village green (next to Blarney Castle entrance). ◊

BUTLERSTOWN

Butlerstown is a pretty pastel-painted village, with lovely views across farmland to Dunworley and the sea beyond. At **Atlantic Sunset B&B** (Dunworley, 023 40115) Mary Holland provides comfortable accommodation and a genuinely warm welcome in her neat modern house with views down to the sea near sandy beaches and a coastal walk. The house is wheelchair accessible and the ground floor rooms are suitable for less able guests. **O'Neill's Pub** (023 40228) is as pleasant and hospitable a place as could be found to enjoy the local view - or to admire the traditional mahogany bar and pictures that make old pubs like this such a pleasure to be in. O'Neill's is now a popular stopping off point for the "Seven Heads Millennium Coastal Walk" so it may be useful to know that children (and well-behaved pets) are welcome. Nearby Clonakilty hosts a farmers' market on Thursdays (mostly food) and Saturdays (both food and crafts), 10am - 2pm, while in Clonakilty a visit to Lisselan Gardens (023 33249) is a must. Golfers will relish the challenge and scenic beauty of one of the most talked about golf courses in the world, The Old Head of Kinsale Golf Club (021 477 8444) which is a short drive away in Kinsale.

WWW.IRELAND-GUIDE.COM FOR ALL THE BEST PLACES TO EAT, DRINK & STAY

Carrigaline   # Carrigaline Court Hotel & Leisure Centre
HOTEL   Main Street Carrigaline Co Cork **Tel: 021 485 2100**
Ⓥ   reception@carrigcourt.com www.carrigcourt.com

This conveniently-located modern hotel is very much at the heart of the local community, and is known for hands-on management and attentive staff. Interesting contemporary furniture is an attractive feature in the bright, spacious public areas - and throughout the hotel - notably in the pleasing Collins

Bar; traditional Irish music sessions (local players) are held here on Monday nights, and there are large plasma screens for major sporting events. Accommodation includes several suites, and all bedrooms are attractively decorated and well-equipped for business guests with work desks, broadband and safes as well as the more usual amenities - and marbled bathrooms. International menus offer a wide range of popular dishes in the hotel's restaurant, The Bistro, where reliable food, good service and a pleasing ambience should make for an enjoyable meal. Conference/banqueting facilities (350/220), also smaller meeting rooms; secretarial services; free broadband wi/fi. Leisure centre (swimming pool, jacuzzi, sauna, steam room, massage), beauty salon. Children welcome (under 11s free in parents' room, cot available without charge, baby sitting arranged). Weekend offers and golf breaks offered. No pets. **Rooms 88** (2 suites, 1 junior suite, 2 family, 1 for disabled). Lift. 24 hour room service. Turndown service offered. B&B €95 pps, ss €20. Closed 25-26 Dec. **Seats 150** (private room, 50); children welcome (high chair, childrens menu, baby changing facilities); air conditioning, toilets wheelchair accessible. D Mon-Sat 6-9.45pm, D Sun 6-8.45pm, L Sun only 12.30-2.15pm. Set D around €40, also à la carte; set Sun L €25. House wine from €18. Closed 25 Dec. Amex, Diners, MasterCard, Visa, Laser. **Directions:** Follow South Link Road and then follow signs for Carrigaline.

Carrigaline
GUESTHOUSE

Glenwood House

Ballinrea Road Carrigaline Co Cork **Tel: 021 437 3878**
info@glenwoodguesthouse.com www.glenwoodguesthouse.com

This well-respected guesthouse is in purpose-built premises, very conveniently located for Cork Airport and the ferry and set in gardens where guests can relax in fine weather. Comfortable, well-furnished rooms (including five newer ones, and one designed for disabled guests) have all the amenities normally expected of hotels, including broadband, TV with video channel, trouser press/iron, tea/coffee facilities and well-designed bathrooms. Breakfast has always been a strong point - fresh fruits and juices, cheeses, home-made breads and preserves as well as hot dishes (available from 7am for business guests, until 10 am for those taking a leisurely break). A guest sitting room with an open fire makes a cosy retreat on dark winter evenings. **Rooms 15** (3 shower only, 1 for disabled, 13 no smoking, all ground floor); children welcome (Under 5s free in parents' room, cot available without charge); free broadband wi/fi; room service (limited hours). B&B €50pps, ss €9. No pets. Garden. Private parking (15). Closed mid Dec-mid Jan. MasterCard, Visa, Laser. **Directions:** Entering Carrigaline from Cork, turn right at Ballinrea roundabout.

Carrigaline
BAR•RESTAURANT

Hogans Bar & Restaurant

Main Street Carrigaline Co Cork **Tel: 021 437 5902**
info@hoganscarrigaline.ie www.hoganscarrigaline.ie

Returning visitors who are disappointed by the disappearance of the once-familiar Gregory's Restaurant in Carrigaline will be pleased to find Gregory Dawson's cooking very close by, at this stylish new bar and restaurant in the old post office premises on the main street. An impressive architect-designed interior by Duffy and MacCann has made the most of the long narrow building - beyond the smart contemporary entrance, exposed stone, traditional tiling and parquet in the full height entrance hall set the tone for a conversion that has many interesting modern features yet also echoes the past. Using height and good lighting to create a sense of space, feature wall wine storage and a balcony make a link between the comfortable bar and the restaurant above it - where you'll find a warm welcome from restaurant manager Ann-Marie Doyle and well spaced modern tables set up classily with good quality stainless cutlery, attractive glasses and white linen napkins. Well planned menus offer a good balance of about 10 dishes on each course but are not over-extensive; choices include several dishes available as starters or main course (warm crispy duck confit salad, perhaps, with rustic potatoes and apricot & peach chutney), highlighted vegetarian- and coeliac-friendly dishes and two daily fish specials (typically pan-fried John Dory with tomato & chive sauce. It's good to find classics like lamb's kidney and mushroom fricassee and chicken liver pate with Cumberland sauce and Melba toast alongside pan-fried crab cake and fresh herb salsa, and an interesting vegetarian main course (such as a Provencale bean stew with peppers, tomato, basil, basmati rice and tossed green salad) alongside a good choice of meat dishes and several steaks and burgers. Good quality ingredients are sourced locally as far as possible and the cooking is excellent, producing delicious dishes – and generous portions too. Although not a cheap place to eat, the quality and quantity match the prices and good food is backed up by friendly, attentive and professional service and a good wine list (although no vintages are given), so a meal here should be an enjoyable experience all round. **Seats 50**; children welcome (highchair, childrens menu); ground floor and toilets wheelchair accessible. D Tue-Sun 5.30-9.30pm; bar meals L Mon-Sat 12-3pm; D Tue-Fri 5-7; early D €19.95 Tues-Thurs, 5-7pm; house wine €19.95; SC 10% on groups 10+. Amex, Diners, MasterCard, Visa, Laser **Directions:** Travelling from Cork direction, on right-hand side of main street, beyond the bridge.

Carrigaline Area

Roberts Cove Inn

PUB   Roberts Cove Minane Bridge Nr Carrigaline Co Cork **Tel: 021 488 7100**
N   info@robertscoveinn.com www.robertscoveinn.com

Scenically located in located in a bay that looks out towards the famous Daunt Rock beacon, Roberts Cove Inn is built on the site of an old mill, where a community of monks once milled corn. Owned since 1988 by Denis Quinn, this warm and friendly place has character in spades – and a reputation for atmosphere and good food, in both the bar and restaurant. Soup and sandwiches are available at lunchtime during the week but full bar meals are available each evening and feature a good choice of popular dishes, including seafood but also a wide range of other dishes such as steaks various ways, lamb cutlets, curry and pasta dishes. In the restaurant, a reasonably priced table d'hôte and an à la carte menu overlap to some extent with the bar meals (a speciality of roast stuffed porksteak with wine & mushroom sauce features on both menus, for example), but restaurant menus are more structured and offer more prime dishes such as roast crispy duck à l'orange, rack of lamb with sherry & rosemary sauce and sole on the bone. Desserts are home-made and there's a choice of coffees or tea to finish. The hearty cooking suits appetites sharpened by a day on the water very well, and service is good humoured and efficient. Surprisingly, given its out-of-the-way location, this characterful inn is open all year, including the restaurant. **Seats 80** (outdoors, 14); children welcome before 8pm (high chair, childrens menu, baby changing facilities); toilets wheelchair accessible. L (soup & sandwiches) Mon-Sat, 12-3pm; bar food served all day Sun & Bank Hols; Sun L 12.30-3.30pm; D daily 6-10pm (4-9pm Sun). Set Sun L €23.50; set D €37.50. House wine €17.50. Open all year. MasterCard, Visa, Laser. **Directions:** From Carrigaline take R611 Kinsale road, left at Ballyfeard for Minane Bridge, follow signs to Roberts Cove.

Castlemartyr

Capella Castlemartyr

HOTEL   Castlemartyr Co Cork **Tel: 021 464 4050**
info.castlemartyr@capellahotels.com www.capellacastlemartyr.com

Built around a 17th century manor house and the ruins of an adjacent castle that belonged to the Knights Templar and dating back to 1210, this luxurious hotel opened to some fanfare in 2007. The entrance is through impressive old gates in the centre of Castlemartyr village, skirting the edge of the18-hole Ron Kirby-designed golf course, and gives a hint of the lush variety to be found in the 220-acre estate. The driveway leads past the ancient castle to the beautiful entrance of the old house which was once owned by Sir Walter Raleigh

(who later sold it to the Earl of Cork, Richard Boyle) and includes among its special features a ballroom declared 'the best room in Ireland' by the renowned 18th century travel chronicler Arthur Young, and now fully restored as Knights Bar. Just eleven of the hotel's 109 guestrooms and suites are in the old house and the rest are in a new section alongside it which is uncompromisingly modern, yet sits surprisingly comfortably beside the elegance of the old; however, due to the low-rise design, corridors are extremely long and any guest with mobility problems should ensure a room as near reception as possible. A porter greets you at your car and brings your luggage to your room, and the accommodation is predictably luxurious - the rooms are huge, ranging from a mere 500 sq ft to a Presidential Suite of over 3,000 sq ft and they sport correspondingly enormous beds and bathrooms – and all the expected technological bells and whistles, including a central computer system that controls all the room functions from the bedside. The Capella has luxurious amenities although, due to the fact that its opening coincided with the sudden economic downturn, the emphasis at the time of going to press is on value for money rather than service, and the hotel has gained fame for its special offers. In true country house style, however, guests can take the hotel's resident dogs - a beautiful pair of setters called Earl and Countess - for walks on the estate. Conferences/Banqueting; business centre, free broadband wi/fi secretarial services, video conferencing, laptop-sized safes in bedrooms. Archery, clay pigeon shooting, croquet, cycling, falconry, garden, golf (18 when complete), leisure centre (swimming pool, fitness room, jacuzzi, sauna, steam room), destination spa, beauty salon (masseuse, hair dressing), walking, wine courses. Equestrian and fishing (fly, coarse, sea angling) nearby. Children welcome (cot available free of charge, baby sitting arranged). **Rooms 109**; Lift; 24 hr room service; B&B €80-100pps. Heli-Pad. *In addition to the accommodation and amenities offered at the hotel, the Castlemartyr Resort offers guests the option of staying at Golf Lodges (42, built within the old walled garden, and with direct access to the golf course) and 10 cottagey Mews Residences in the 'Old

Bawn' area of the castle (see www.castlemartyrresort.ie for details). **Dining:** Given its location in an area internationally renowned for the range and quality of its produce, a welcome emphasis on cooking driven by the availability of seasonal produce was envisaged from the outset, applying in all areas from the Spa Café at the 24,400 sq ft Auriga Spa to the Bell Tower fine dining restaurant. At the time of going to press, however, it seems that the policy to emphasise value for money has led to menus that are more restricted than might be expected in an establishment at this level, and choices tend to be on the safe side. Aperitifs and after-dinner drinks can be taken in Knights Bar - complete with restored rococo ceiling and baby grand piano. **Bell Tower Restaurant: Seats 60** (private room, 8); children welcome (high chair, children's menu); air conditioning; L Sat & Sun, 12-2.30pm; D daily, 6-9.30pm. Open all year. Amex, Diners, MasterCard, Visa, Laser. **Directions:** On main N25 from Cork. ◇

CASTLETOWNBERE

Although it is currently rather run-down and could be described as a "place that time forgot", there are signs of regeneration in the fishing port of Castletownbere and it makes a good base for exploring the beautiful south-western tip of the Beara peninsula. Berehaven is a safe anchorage for yachts and is ideal for watersports, from sea angling to windsurfing. The area is also ideal for land-based outdoor activities with golfing, hiking, biking and hill walking all available nearby. Championship golf is available about 30km away in Bantry Bay Golf Club (027 50579) and there are several excellent gardens less then 30km away - Derreen Garden (Kenmare, 064 83588); Cois Cuain Gardens (Bantry, 027 67070) and Kilravock Garden (Durrus, 027 61111) being the closest. There is a farmers' market in Castletownbere on the first Thursday of each month. The 5* **Capella Dunboy Castle Hotel** (027 70294; www.dunboycastlehotel.com) was still under construction on the 40-acre waterside site of the original castle south-west of the town at the time of our summer 2008 visit and, although the project shows no immediate prospect of completion at the time of going to press, it is an amazing place and will undoubtedly bring a new focus to the area when it opens. Whether staying nearby or visiting Castletownbere for the day, visitors need food: in addition to **McCarthy's** (see entry) you could try **John Patricks Butcher & Restaurant**, a quirky, inexpensive place where you'll find wholesome lunches for walkers (simple Irish food - bacon and cabbage, Irish stew, steaks); **Gallagher's** offers generous fare too, including excellent home-made cakes. Also, Ciannit Walker's interesting food shop **Taste at the Pier** (027 71842; not actually at the pier at all, but just off the square) plans to introduce a daytime café. If you need something in the evening, you might try **Cottage Heights Seafood Restaurant** (027 71743; www.cottage-heights.com), on an elevated site at Derrymiham - or **The Old Bakery** (027 70869), which is well recommended locally; mainly seafood, as you'd expect, and reasonably priced.

WWW.IRELAND-GUIDE.COM FOR ALL THE BEST PLACES TO EAT, DRINK & STAY

Castletownshend
BAR•RESTAURANT

Mary Ann's Bar & Restaurant

Castletownshend Skibbereen Co Cork **Tel: 028 36146**
maryanns@eircom.net www.maryannsbarrestaurant.com

The pub is as old as it looks, going back to 1846, and has been in the energetic and hospitable ownership of Fergus and Patricia O'Mahony since 1988; they have loved it and maintained it well (it is not unusual to find Fergus up a ladder with a paintbrush in his hand), but any refurbishments at Mary Ann's have left its original character intact. The O'Mahonys have built up a great reputation for food in both the bar and the restaurant, which is split between an upstairs dining room and The Vine Room at the back, which can be used for private parties; alongside it there is a garden which has been fitted with a retractable awning over the tables, allowing for all-weather dining. Seafood is the star, of course, in both bar and restaurant and it comes in many guises, usually along with some of the lovely home-baked brown bread which is one of the house specialities. Another is the Platter of Castlehaven Bay Shellfish and Seafood - a sight to behold, and usually including langoustine, crab meat, crab claws, and both fresh and smoked salmon. Much of the menu depends on the catch of the day, although there are also good steaks and roasts, served with delicious local potatoes and seasonal vegetables. Desserts are good too, but local West Cork cheeses are an excellent option that may prove too difficult to resist. One of the most appealing things about Mary Ann's is that such a wide choice is available in the bar as well as the restaurant and that includes daily blackboard specials, which may offer real treats like lobster thermidor or lobster mayonnaise. Some bar food indeed! The O'Mahonys are hands-on owners and almost always present but, whether they are there or not, their outstanding friendly and helpful staff are always on hand and do an excellent job in making visitors feel at home and well looked after. The O'Mahonys also have a very successful art gallery on the first floor. *Mary Ann's was our Seafood Bar of the Year in 2008. **Restaurant Seats 30** (outside, 100, private room 30); toilets wheelchair accessible; children welcome. D & L daily in summer, 6-9pm; 12-2.30pm. A la carte. House wine from €18.95. SC discretionary. *Bar food 12-2.30 & 6-9 daily. Closed Mon Nov-Mar, 25 Dec, Good Fri & 3 weeks Jan. Amex, MasterCard, Visa, Laser. **Directions:** Five miles from Skibbereen, on lower main street.

CLONAKILTY

Clonakilty is a quaint town of narrow streets, brightly coloured houses and hanging baskets. For visitors to the area, there are several safe beaches nearby, walks in the countryside and local attractions such as The West Cork Model Railway Village and Lios-na-gCon Ringfort. Clonakilty hosts a farmers' market on Thursdays (mostly food) and Saturdays (both food and crafts), 10am - 2pm, and a visit to Lisselan Gardens (023 33249) is a must. Golfers will relish the challenge and scenic beauty of one of the most talked about golf courses in the world, The Old Head of Kinsale Golf Club (021 477 8444) which is a short drive away in Kinsale. The unlikely product that Clonakilty is most famous for today is black pudding - specifically, Edward Twomey's delicious grainy black pudding. It is now available from every supermarket and good food store throughout the country and, of course, you can buy it (and many other excellent meats) from their fine butchers shop, in Pearse Street. - a good choice if you are in self-catering accommodation in the area. You will, of course, find local black pudding on every breakfast menu in the area - including, no doubt, the traditional **Emmet Hotel** (023 33394; www.emmethotel.com), which is situated on a lovely Georgian Square and has a separate restaurant, **O'Keeffe's** attached (see entry) and **Quality Hotel & Leisure Centre** (Tel: 023 36400; www.choicehotelsireland.ie), which is a little out of the town and, with good facilities and activities for children, is an extremely popular destination for family holidays and short breaks.

WWW.IRELAND-GUIDE.COM FOR ALL THE BEST PLACES TO EAT, DRINK & STAY

Clonakilty
BAR•RESTAURANT

An Sugan

41 Wolfe Tone Street Clonakilty Co Cork **Tel: 023 33498**
ansugan4@eircom.net www.ansugan.com

The O'Crowley family has owned this characterful bar and restaurant since 1980: it's always been a friendly, well-run place and, although it can be very busy at times, their reputation for good food is generally well-deserved. Menus change daily and are very strong on seafood - specialities include Union Hall smoked salmon parfait, baked crab An Sugan, and seafood basket while daily fish specials could include a choice of ten, ranging from cod on a bed of champ to lobster An Sugan (fresh lobster flamed in a brandy & tomato sauce). If you're not in the mood for seafood you might try a terrine of the famous Clonakilty puddings or a prime Hereford sirloin steak. Lunch menus are shorter and simpler, but also offer a wide choice of seafood - and some traditional comfort food, like bacon & cabbage. A private dining room is available. **Seats 42**; reservations recommended. Food served 12-9.30 daily; L12.30-2.30, D 6-9.30. Set Sun L about €28, Set D about €30/35, also A la carte. House wine from €18. Service discretionary. No private parking. Closed 25/26 Dec & Good Fri. MasterCard, Visa, Laser. **Directions:** From Cork, on the left hand side as you enter Clonakilty.

Clonakilty
HOTEL

Dunmore House Hotel

Muckross Clonakilty Co Cork **Tel: 023 33352**
dunmorehousehotel@eircom.net www.dunmorehotel.com

The magnificent coastal location of the O'Donovan family's hotel has been used to advantage to provide sea views for all bedrooms and to allow guests access to their own stretch of foreshore. Comfortable public areas include a traditional bar and lounges, whilst the contemporary dining room is light, bright, and home to a fine collection of paintings. Bedrooms are furnished to a high standard and make a comfortable base for the numerous outdoor leisure activities in the area, including the hotel's own nine hole golf course, free to residents; packed lunches available on request. Hands-on owner-management, a high standard of maintenance and housekeeping, and professional, friendly staff make this a pleasing hotel. Conference/banqueting 200/250. **Rooms 23** (2 junior suites, 4 shower only, 1 for disabled); children welcome (under 3 free in parents' room, cot available without charge; junior evening meal 5.30-6.30). Wheelchair accessible. Dogs allowed in some areas. B&B €100 pps, ss €10. Bar food available all day (12-8.30). **Restaurant Seats 80** (only opens if sufficient bookings, if not then all eat in the bar); toilets wheelchair accessible; air conditioning D daily, 7-8.30

(c. €40), L Sun only, 1-2.30 (c. €25). Golf, fishing, walking. Closed Christmas; 19 Jan-11 Mar. Amex, Diners, MasterCard, Visa, Laser. **Directions:** 4 km from Clonakilty town, well signed. ◊

Clonakilty
RESTAURANT

Gleeson's

3 Connolly Street Clonakilty Co Cork **Tel: 023 21834**
gleesonsclonakilty@eircom.net www.gleesons.ie

Robert and Alex Gleeson's fine restaurant has a discreet, smartly-maintained frontage and rather mysterious interior, with dark woods and deep, rich tones in furnishings which exude quality and include many original touches (such as beautifully simple slate place mats). Robert's cooking style is modern French and his experience in famous kitchens - The Dorchester, for example - should give an idea of what to expect. His menus, which offer about seven choices on each course on the à la carte and three on the early dinner menu, are not over-elaborate but this is emphatically fine dining albeit with a pleasingly relaxed tone that makes it feel welcoming and accessible to all. Local produce, like Skeaghanore duck, from Ballydehob, is show-cased in dishes such as a crisp slow-roasted Skeaghanore duck leg with chorizo & white bean cassoulet and braised red cabbage - or you might try an updated classic main course of roast loin of monkfish wrapped in Parma ham served with herb cous cous, spinach tian and a light Indian cream sauce. Vegetarian dishes are imaginative (grilled vegetable, feta and pasta gateaux with red pepper & cherry tomato compote and crisp polenta, perhaps) and classical desserts include delicious home-made ice creams (a speciality of the house), or local farmhouse cheeses, served with home-made crackers, are a tempting alternative. Precise cooking and perfectly balanced flavours characterise the cooking throughout and a meal is a restorative experience; classically trained chefs are an increasingly rare treasure these days and cooking of this calibre is a treat, especially when accompanied by pleasing surroundings and friendly professional service, as it is here. This fine restaurant has deservedly earned a loyal following, and reservations are strongly recommended. Prices are fair throughout and the early dinner menu offers outstanding value. A carefully selected, wide-ranging and very informative wine list kicks off with champagnes and champagne cocktails and a lovely selection of wines by the glass; the main list is arranged by style, with tasting notes and the half bottle selection is well chosen. **Seats 45**; not suitable for children under 7 yrs. D Tue-Sat, 6-9.30. Set 2/3 course D with coffee €26.50/35 (6-7pm Fri/Sat & 6-9.30pm Tue-Thurs); also à la carte. House wine from around €20. SC 10% on groups 6+. Closed Sun (except bank hol weekends) & Mon; bank hols, 24-26 Dec. Amex, MasterCard, Visa, Laser. **Next door, on the first floor, Robert and Alex Gleeson have teamed up with another well-known chef, Mark Kirby, to open **Mio** (023 58571, a bright and confident pizza, pasta and steak restaurant; with an emphasis on quality ingredients and simplicity. Open for long hours (Wed-Sun, 12-10), this is a relaxed place that complements Gleesons and will have wide appeal. **Directions:** Town centre; next door to Scannels Pub.

Clonakilty
CAFÉ

Harts Coffee Shop

8 Ashe Street Clonakilty Co Cork **Tel: 023 35583**
hartscoffeeshop@gmail.com

For a decade, good home cooking has been the attraction at Aileen Hart and Tony O'Mahoney's friendly coffee shop in the town centre, and the consistently high standard they have maintained over that time has regulars making a beeline for this welcoming spot as soon as they hit town. A nifty little menu offers all kinds of healthy meals - ranging from a breakfast ciabatta with bacon, eggs & cheese, through warm baguettes (peppered steak strips, perhaps, with lettuce and mayo), sandwiches toasted and cool - all served with side salad & home-made vinaigrette dressing - to specials such as an Irish cheese plate with a choice of crackers or bread. A Specials board suggests additions to the regular menu - soups (vegetables, perhaps, or pea & mint) based on home-made stocks, which are also used in traditional stews (beef & Beamish, perhaps), available in regular or large portions. But best of all, perhaps, is the choice of home-baked scones just like your granny used to make, served with home-made jam, and tarts - everything from a vegetarian quiche to an old-fashioned apple tart served with cream - and cakes ranging from healthy carrot cake to gooey orange chocolate drizzle cake. Simple, wholesome, home-made: just lovely! Great selection of drinks too, including freshly squeezed juices teas and Green bean coffees. **Seats 30**; children welcome; wine licence. Open Mon-Sat, 10-5. Closed 3 weeks Christmas, Sun & Mon. **No Credit Cards**. **Directions:** Clonakilty town centre.

Clonakilty

Inchydoney Island Lodge & Spa

HOTEL•RESTAURANT

Inchydoney Island Clonakilty Co Cork **Tel: 023 33143**
reservations@inchydoneyisland.com www.inchydoneyisland.com

This hotel enjoys great views over the two 'Blue Flag' beaches at Inchydoney, which bring crowds to the area in summer, so many guests will prefer this as an off-season destination. The building is architecturally uninspired, but it has mellowed as landscaping of the large carpark on the seaward side matures - and once inside the hotel, that pampered feeling soon takes over. Dramatic artworks in the spacious foyer are impressive, and other public areas include a large, comfortably furnished first-floor residents' lounge and library, with a piano, extensive sea views, and a soothing atmosphere. Most of the generously sized bedrooms have sea views and all have been completely redesigned recently, so that they now have balconies in addition to air conditioning, safe and all the more usual amenities – and bold modern décor with a good seasoning of bling. The exceptional health and leisure facilities that make this a special destination for many returning guests include a superb Thalasso-therapy Spa, which offers a range of special treatments and makes Inchydoney a particularly attractive place for an off-season break. Special breaks are a major attraction - fishing, equestrian, golf, therapies - and its romantic location ensures its popularity for weddings. Conferences/banqueting (300/250); secretarial services. Self-catering apartments available (with full use of hotel facilities). Thalassotherapy spa (24 treatment rooms); beauty salon; swimming pool; walking; snooker; pool table. Children welcome (under 3s free in parents' room, cots available for €15, baby sitting arranged). **Rooms 67** (3 suites, 1 junior suite,2 for disabled). Lift; 24 hr room service. B&B €180 pps, ss €110. SC10%. Open all year except Christmas.
Gulfstream Restaurant: Located on the first floor, with panoramic sea views from the window tables, this elegant restaurant offers fine dining in a broadly Mediterranean style. Adam Medcalf, who has been head chef since 2006, uses fresh local produce, organic where possible, on seasonal menus that always include imaginative vegetarian options - and willingly caters for any other special dietary requirements. Lighter dishes for spa guests are also offered, with nutritional information outlined. **Seats 70** (private room 250); non-residents welcome by reservation; children welcome (high chair, childrens menu, baby cahnging facilities); toilets wheelchair accessible; air conditioning. D 6.30-9.45; set 5 course D €60, also à la carte. House wine €25. SC10%. [*Informal/ bar meals also available 11-9 daily.] Amex, MasterCard, Visa, **Directions:** N71 from Cork to Clonakilty , then causeway to Inchydoney.

Clonakilty

Malt House Granary Restaurant

RESTAURANT

30 Ashe Street Clonakilty Co Cork
Tel: 023 34355

Right in the heart of the town, Ian and Norma Steward's smartly painted restaurant tempts passers-by with a beckoning glow of candle light seen through large shopfront windows - a window table here is just the spot for people watching while you eat. Inside, the restaurant is divided into three section (including one with a large round table perfect for a family gathering), and special old stone walls hung with photographs of local scenes, low lighting and gentle background jazz make an atmospheric setting for meals based mainly on the area's best seasonal produce - fish and seafood from local ports, cured meats from nearby Gubbeen Smokehouse, and steak from Dan Lordan butchers in Ballinspittle. Under Norma's direction, friendly and knowledgeable staff are quick to offer drinks and Ian's thoughtfully constructed menus, which include two sociable tasting plates among the starters - one of local seafood and another of local cured meats - and also plenty of appealing mainstream vegetarian and coeliac friendly dishes. The choices are wide, offering eight or nine dishes on each course and perhaps including some unusual items (hare, for example, and MacSweens vegetarian haggis). Ian enjoys coming out and speak to customers about his menu and cooking, and his enthusiasm shines through;

he clearly takes special interest in showcasing the fine produce that West Cork is renowned for: his Seafood Tasting Plate, for example, comes on a large platter, with beautifully cooked warm local langoustines, a few slices of home cured gravad lax and mini crab cakes - accompanied by little ramekins of mustard sauce and Marie Rose sauce, and a crisp salad garnish. Another highlight is the 350g Irish Porterhouse Steak, cooked perfectly to order, very juicy and tasty - and served with some good old fashioned 'skirlie' potatoes and a side pot of Rioja beef Jus, with just a minimal splash of sauce decorating the plate. Finish with a lovely baked lemon cheesecake with whiskey soaked sultanas, perhaps, and a good strong espresso. Easy menu presentation, honest local foods aplenty, and staff with real knowledge of the ingredients are among the qualities that make The Malthouse stand out. Wines to match are well chosen and well priced; no half bottles but a good choice of wines by the glass. A great place for a special meal. **Seats 50** (private room 19); toilets wheelchair accessible. MasterCard, Visa, Laser. **Directions:** Town centre, on main street.

Clonakilty
HOTEL•RESTAURANT

O'Keeffe's of Clonakilty

Emmet Square Clonakilty Co Cork **Tel: 023 33394**
emmethotel@eircom.net www.emmethotel.com

Marie O'Keeffe's well-regarded restaurant is hidden away in the centre of Clonakilty, on a lovely serene Georgian square that contrasts unexpectedly with the hustle and bustle of the nearby streets - a most attractive location, although parking is likely to be difficult in high season. Although located in separate premises next door, O'Keeffe's also has direct access from the **Emmet Hotel** (www.emmethotelcom) and bookings are made through the hotel. The restaurant overlooks the square and, with bold decor that is unexpected in an old house, it has plenty of atmosphere. Marie O'Keeffe's reputation for creative modern cooking is well established in the area, and she is well known for her commitment to using seasonal local produce, much of it organic, when possible. Seafood tends to take the starring role on her concise, moderately priced menus, which are topped up with daily specials depending on the best produce available on the day; local meats and poultry always feature too, of course; breast of chicken stuffed with Clonakilty black pudding is a house speciality, served with a mustard mash and chicken jus. Several imaginative vegetarian dishes are offered (spelt lasagne with goat's cheese, semi-sundried tomatoes, spinach & ricotta is a speciality that is also suitable for coeliacs) and, given notice, other special dietary requirements can be met. A courtyard garden is pleasant for al fresco dining in fine weather; Sunday lunch is available in the restaurant, otherwise bar lunches are provided in the hotel. **Seats 50** (outdoor seating, 40); reservations advised; children welcome. D daily, 6.30-9.30; à la carte. House wine €17.40. SC discretionary. Bar L daily 12.30-2.30 with bar menu from 12-10pm (in the hotel). Restaurant closed 25 Dec. Amex, Diners, MasterCard, Visa, Laser, Switch. **Directions:** In the centre of Clonakilty - turn left into Emmet Square at the Catholic Church. ◈

Clonakilty
BAR•RESTAURANT

Richy's Bar & Bistro

Wolfe Tone St Clonakilty Co Cork **Tel: 023 21852**
richysbarandbistro@eircom.net www.richysbarandbistro.com

Situated in the centre of Clonakilty, close to a little park, Richy Virahsawmy's bar and bistro is one of those relaxed places where today's specials are chalked up on a blackboard and it attracts a real cross-section of people. It's spacious and appealingly furnished with smart window blinds and wooden floors giving a clean, modern feeling, softened by warm yellow walls and paintings well lit in little recessed alcoves. Well-spaced tables, banquettes along one wall and a bar in one of the two eating areas create a comfortable setting for food that ranges widely around the Mediterranean, with a leaning towards Spain - and locally sourced ingredients may include less usual food like samphire, as well as local lamb and fish. A thoughtfully selected, clear and reasonably priced wine list is organised by style and includes an interesting house selection (9, all available by the glass, and other drinks are available from the bar, which is handy for families with young children). A great place to know about, especially when on a family holiday. * Richy has published a cookbook, West Cork Fusion; and he also has plans to open in Cork city. **Seats 70** (outdoors, 16); children welcome before 9pm (high chair, childrens menu). Open daily; Summer 12 - 10pm; winter, 5-10pm. Early D Mon-Thu, 5-7, €25; also a la carte. House wine €19.95. Closed 25 Dec. Amex, MasterCard, Visa, Laser. **Directions:** Next to tourist office. ◈

Clonakilty Area

BAR•RESTAURANT

Deasy's Harbour Bar & Seafood Restaurant

Ring Village Clonakilty Co Cork

Tel: 023 35741

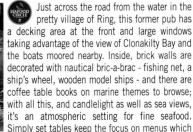

Just across the road from the water in the pretty village of Ring, this former pub has a decking area at the front and large windows taking advantage of the view of Clonakilty Bay and the boats moored nearby. Inside, brick walls are decorated with nautical bric-a-brac - fishing net, a ship's wheel, wooden model ships - and there are coffee table books on marine themes to browse; with all this, and candlelight as well as sea views, it's an atmospheric setting for fine seafood. Simply set tables keep the focus on menus which are a little international in style (no house or local specialities mentioned), but offer a wide range of seafood including less usual varieties such as shark, as well as fairly classic prime fish dishes - monkfish medallions wrapped in prosciutto with seared scallops and dill crème fraiche, perhaps. Piquant dips and sauces are out of the ordinary, adding a new dimension to familiar dishes - grilled John Dory fillets may come with a spicy local beetroot relish & celeriac purée, for example. Other than seafood, there are some token offerings of meat or poultry for carnivores, and vegetarians are always offered an interesting alternative. Good cooking is also seen in tasty vegetables and delicious desserts, and details like lovely breads and thoughtful presentation. With an informal relaxed atmosphere, interesting food and a lovely setting, this has become a popular spot so book well ahead, especially in high season. Service can be slow a little at busy times, but friendly staff are always good humoured and helpful. **Seats 50**; not suitable for children after 7pm; D Wed-Sat 6-9.30; L Sun only, 1-3; set Sun L €30; house wine €20. Closed Sun D, Mon, Tue and 24-26 Dec. MasterCard, Visa, Laser. **Directions:** 2km outside Clonakilty.

COBH

Seated on the historical island of Barrymore, Cobh is built on a hill meaning that the town is shaped in an appealing pyramid style, with the town houses rising on top of one another. The town itself provides great views of the harbour and the surrounding hills. Cobh's extensive maritime history is exhibited in the Cobh Museum (021 481 4240, open April to October) and is housed in a former Scots Presbyterian church on the main road into Cobh from Cork. The Sirius Arts Centre (021 481 3790), founded in 1988 includes galleries and exhibitions by local artists and the artist in residence. Golfers can enjoy the local 9-hole course (021 481 2399). Visitors can sample the freshest of local produce every Friday morning at the Cobh farmers' market.

Cobh

COUNTRY HOUSE

Knockeven House

Rushbrooke Cobh Co Cork **Tel: 021 481 1778**

info@knockevenhouse.com www.knockevenhouse.com

Clearly signed on the outskirts of Cobh, and at the end of a winding driveway overhung by tall trees, you will find John and Pam Mulhaire's large and peacefully situated 1840s' house. Its rather plain exterior, tarmac parking area and low-maintenance garden give no hint of the luxurious interior which is revealed when the front door opens on to a huge hall, where a deep red carpet and dramatic flower arrangement set on an antique desk set the tone for a house that offers guests the best of every world: lavish decor and facilities worthy of a top-class hotel, along with great hospitality, and reasonable prices. The Mulhaires have lived here for over 20 years, but only opened for guests in 2004 - Pam is very chatty, relaxed and friendly, a natural hostess who treats her guests to tea and home-made scones on a silver tray on arrival, and on request at any time. An impressive drawing room has plenty of comfortable seating and an open fire and, like the rest of the house, the bedrooms are also decorated with sumptuous good taste (although lovers of old houses may be disappointed by the practical PVC double-glazed windows). Accommodation is very comfortable, with generous beds and immaculate en-suite bathrooms that have power showers (no full bath) and many thoughtful details, including pristine white bathrobes and Molton Brown toiletries. A good breakfast served on white Villeroy & Boch china, with pristine white cotton napkins includes a delicious fresh fruit salad, fresh orange juice, good-quality cereals, yoghurts, ham and cheese as well as a sound rendition of the traditional hot breakfast. This is an exceptionally comfortable place to stay and, although no dinner is offered, the restaurants of Midleton (or Monkstown, just across the ferry) are not too far away. Children welcome (cot available). **Rooms 4** (all en-suite and no smoking); limited room service. B&B €60pps, single about €75. MasterCard, Visa, Laser. **Directions:** On the outskirts of Cobh.

Cobh   # Sheraton Hotel & Spa at Fota Island Resort
HOTEL•RESTAURANT   Fota Island Cobh Co Cork **Tel: 021 467 3000**
reservations.fota@sheraton.com www.sheraton.com/cork

A beautiful long tree-lined driveway, with glimpses of the water to the right, has always been the entrance to Fota Island Golf Club and – unless you had noticed an odd green box set into the countryside from a distance - it in no way prepares first time visitors for what awaits around the last corner: whilst the recently planted trees are beginning to soften the approach to this controversial building, it is easy to see why there was such local opposition to the development. However, as is often the case with new developments, things look different once you get inside. Guests are welcomed at the door, then you move through a large lobby/reception that opens into a spacious high-ceilinged area, with warm lighting, an open fire and lots of comfy seating. Off this, a bar overlooks lawns to the front, with a decking area for fine weather; this comfortable and appealing room has an open fire which is shared with the adjacent restaurant - also overlooking the grounds, it's a clean-lined room, with classic white linen softened by warm lighting. Accommodation is luxurious, with a high proportion of suites and superior rooms, and many rooms enjoying panoramic views over woodlands or golf course; all are spacious and extremely comfortable, with huge beds and big flat screen tv, in addition to the usual facilities, and beautiful bathrooms have double-ended bath with head rests and separate walk-in shower. Good food has been a feature in all areas of the hotel since it opened and dining choices include the Fota Restaurant, offering a smart option for all-day meals, The Cove seafood grill room for evening dining (see below), and The Amber Bar for light meals at any time. Complimentary wireless internet available in all public areas. *The Fota Spa is a big attraction, another is golf - it can sometimes be difficult to get enough tee times at the adjacent Fota Island Golf Club, but it is hoped that the new 9-hole course will allow more flexibility. Conferences/Banqueting (306/260), business centre, secretarial services, video conferencing, free broadband wi/fi. **Rooms 131** (6 suites, 2 junior suites, 7 disabled, all no smoking); children welcome (cot available free of charge, baby sitting arranged; B&B room rate about €165; 24 hr room service; Lift. Championship golf course (18), tennis, walking, resort spa (massage, treatments), leisure centre (swimming pool, fitness room, jacuzzi, sauna, steam room). Fly fishing, sea angling, watersports and equestrian nearby. **The Cove:** A more intimate choice than the bistro-style Fota Restaurant, the key focus of the fine-dining restaurant is fresh seafood, complemented by local meat and organic produce - and Executive Chef Neil Foster (who came here from the Sheraton at Park Lane, London) is in his element here, cooking dishes that allow him to flex his culinary muscles. His à la carte menus offer around half a dozen equally tempting choices on each course, including at least one vegetarian option, and are peppered with luxurious ingredients, most of them Irish and with suppliers credited: O'Connells in the English Market supplies fresh fish and seafood, for example, smoked and cured fish is from nearby Ballycotton whilst meat, poultry and game come from Ballyburden Meat. To start, try a subtly spiced dish of seared diver scallops, perhaps, served with slow roasted sumac spiced pork belly, cauliflower & lemongrass purée and sherry & raisin dressing (€18), followed by local black sole meunière, served on or off the bone, with Niçoise salsa and balsamic jus (€34, including parsley baby potatoes and vegetables). Although sophisticated this is not show-off cooking, and prices are reasonable for the standard of food and service. The thoughtfully constructed menu is balanced by an extensive wine list, which is indexed for easy reference and includes a respectable choice of wines by the glass and half bottles. **Seats 80** (outdoor, 30); children welcome (high chair, childrens menu, baby changing facilities); D daily 6-10pm (to 10.30pm Sat-Sun); "The Cove" seafood grill room, seats 44, open Tue-Sat, 7pm-10pm; Barfood served daily 12.30-8 (to 6pm Fri-Sat). Helipad. Hotel closed 25-26 Dec. Amex, Diners, MasterCard, Visa, Laser. **Directions:** N25 east from Cork. Approx. 8 km (5m) later take a left and follow signs for Fota island.

COURTMACSHERRY

43km (27 m) west of Cork City and just a few minutes off the R600 Kinsale-Clonakilty coast road, the unspoilt seaside village of Courtmacsherry is an attractive holiday destination with lots of activities – it is a tidal harbour and offers a variety of safe and sheltered sailing & leisure areas. Accommodation in the area includes the privately owned **Courtmacsherry Hotel** (023 46198; www.courtmachotel.com), where characterful lodgings and good food are to be found, and there are some atmospheric pubs in the village, including **The Pier House** and **Lifeboat Bar** - the fastest of the RNLI fleet of all-weather lifeboats is based at Courtmachserry – a real point of pride in the village. **WWW.IRELAND-GUIDE.COM FOR ALL THE BEST PLACES TO EAT, DRINK & STAY**

CROOKHAVEN

The small village of Crookhaven is almost at the end of Mizen Head, tucked snugly on the sheltered side of a narrow neck of land which creates a deep inlet - the 'crooked haven' which may have given the little settlement its name. Known for the excellent sandy beaches at nearby Barleycove and a laid-back holiday atmosphere, this away-from-it-all village somehow offers not just one but a choice of good pubs and eating places that open each summer for the families on holiday locally, and the many visitors who make a point of exploring the peninsula. **O'Sullivans Bar** (028 35319) run by Billy, Angela and Dermot O'Sullivan, has been a favourite for many a long year and is known for the seafood chowder, crab sandwiches and baskets of shrimp that can be eaten in the bar or out on the pier and are the stuff that holiday dreams are made of; there's music nightly and also a shop and post office. A few yards away you'll find **The Crookhaven Inn** (028 353509), where Emma Jepson and Freddy Olson serve good daytime food and dinner right through the summer season. **WWW.IRELAND-GUIDE.COM FOR ALL THE BEST PLACES TO EAT, DRINK & STAY**

CROSSHAVEN

On the west side of Cork Harbour, 17km from Cork city, Crosshaven is a favourite seaside resort for Cork people and an important yachting centre. The seasonal nature of the town means that restaurants tend to come and go but there are several pubs of character including **Cronin's** (see entry), where the Cronin family has a reputation for good seafood, and **The Moonduster Inn** (021 483 1610; www.moondusterinn.com), which also has an attractive first floor restaurant with views cross the water to Currabinny. There is a farmers' market in Crosshaven Village Square on Saturdays (9.30am – 1pm) and garden lovers and golfers have treats in store in the surrounding area including Fota Arboretum & Gardens (021 481 5543) and Fota Island Golf Club (021 488 3710) which are both in Carrigtwohill. **WWW.IRELAND-GUIDE.COM FOR ALL THE BEST PLACES TO EAT, DRINK & STAY**

Crosshaven
CHARACTER PUB

Cronin's Pub

Crosshaven Co Cork **Tel: 021 483 1829**
info@croninspub.com www.croninspub.com

The Cronin family's Victorian pub on the harbour front has oodles of character and, with its walls and high shelves crammed with maritime memorabilia, it serves as a sort of unofficial exhibition of local history. It has always had a good reputation for food, especially seafood, and now there's an enthusiastic new generation at work here, with Joeleen Cronin front of house and her brother Dennis (who is Ballymaloe-trained) as head chef. They're doing a good job with both the bar food and an evening restaurant, **The Shore Thing**, which is in a narrow high-ceilinged room off a passageway behind the bar. Tables are set up simply, and the menu is sensibly short; good ingredients, notably seafood, are mainly sourced locally, cooking is good and presentation unfussy. The popular lunchtime bar menu is more extensive and includes quite a lot of pub food staples as well as seafood. Ample free parking in public carpark across the road. **Restaurant seats 35**; children welcome; L&D Tue-Sat, 12-2.45pm & 6-9pm; house wine €19. Bar food served Mon-Fri, 11.45-2.45pm, Sat, 11.45-3.30pm. Restaurant closed Sun, Mon & Jan. Amex, Diners, MasterCard, Visa, Laser. **Directions:** Straight into village, at car park.

Doneraile
HISTORIC HOUSE

Creagh House

Main Street Doneraile Co Cork **Tel: 022 24433**
info@creaghhouse.ie www.creaghhouse.ie

Michael O'Sullivan and Laura O'Mahony left a perfectly normal home to take on this Regency townhouse in need of renovation in 2000; since then, they have been giving it enormous amounts of TLC on an ongoing basis and their efforts are now paying off, as it is reaching its full glory. A listed building, with notable historical and literary connections, stately reception rooms and huge bedrooms, its principal rooms are among the largest from this period outside Dublin, and have beautiful restored plasterwork. Yet it is a relaxed family home and place of work (Michael and Laura both have offices in restored outbuildings), and this hospitable couple have clearly thrived on the challenge of restoration. Accommodation is wonderful, in vast rooms with huge antique furniture, crisp linen on comfortable beds, little extras (bowls of fruit, bottled water, tea/coffee/hot chocolate making facilities), and bathrooms to match - bath and separate shower, and big, soft towels. All modern partitions have been removed to restore the original scale, and 19th century furniture is used throughout, with 18th and 19th century prints and modern paintings. Anyone interested in architecture and/or history is in for a treat when staying here and Doneraile is well-placed for exploring a wide area - Cork, Cashel, Lismore and Killarney are all within an hour's drive. Garden lovers will be fascinated by the 2-acre walled garden behind Creagh House, which is under restoration ("black topsoil four feet deep!") and the house is beside Doneraile Court, which has 600 acres of estate parkland, free to the public. **Rooms 3** (all en-suite, with separate bath and shower, all no smoking); children welcome (under 3s free in parents room, cot available free of charge). No pets. B&B €120 pps, no ss. Garden. Golf nearby. Closed Oct-Mar. Amex, MasterCard, Visa. **Directions:** Take N20 (Limerick road) from Mallow - 12.5km (8 m). ◇

DURRUS

Located in West Cork, 10km (6 m) from Bantry, at the head of the Sheep's Head and Mizen Head peninsulas, the village has begun to become more developed with tourist housing, but still retains its small pastoral atmosphere. Visitors may enjoy a trip to the Cool na Long Castle built by the McCarthy family, and the gardens of Cois Abhann and Kilvarock are nearby. Durrus is home to the award winning cheese of the same name made by Jeffa Gill, one of the many farmhouse cheeses that have made the West Cork region famous.

Durrus
COUNTRY HOUSE•RESTAURANT

Blairs Cove House

Durrus Bantry Co Cork **Tel: 027 61127**
blairscove@eircom.net www.blairscove.ie

Philippe and Sabine de Mey's beautiful Georgian property enjoys a stunning waterside location at the head of Dunmanus Bay, and it is a wonderful place to stay. Everything revolves around the courtyard, which has been beautifully restored with cobbled paths, shrubs and flowers, and its 250-year old stone outbuildings have been converted to make four stylish suites or small apartments that are offered for self-catering or B&B. Each one is totally individual (one large one has an open fire and is particularly appealing for a family, or for longer stays); they are furnished in very different but equally dashing styles - and there is also a romantic self-catering cottage for two in the grounds. **Rooms 4** (suites); children welcome (under 2s free in parents' room, cot available free of charge, baby sitting arranged). B&B €115 pps, ss €30. Dogs permitted in certain areas. **Restaurant:** Although Philippe and Sabine still manage the accommodation, the restaurant has now been leased and is run independently. **Seats 85** (private room, 40); children welcome (high chair); reservations required. L Sun only, 1-3pm; set Sun L €29. D Tue-Sat, 7-9.30pm. Set D €46/56, 2/3 course; house wine €20, SC discretionary. Closed Sun D (except bank hol weekends), Mon & 7 Jan - 14 Feb. Diners, MasterCard, Visa, Laser. **Directions:** 3km (1.5 m) outside Durrus on Mizen Head Road, blue gate on right hand side.

Durrus

Carbery Cottage Guest Lodge

B&B

Durrus Bantry West Cork Co Cork **Tel: 027 61368**

carberycottage@eircom.net www.carbery-cottage-guest-lodge.net

With well-maintained gardens, plenty of parking and beautiful views, this purpose-built B&B and adjoining self-catering cottage creates a great first impression and a warm welcome extends to your four-legged friends too, with kennels provided, and large grassed penned areas for dogs to run. Owners Mike Hegarty and Julia Bird will be known to many as former owners of the unique Tin Pub at Ahakista, and they have brought the unique laid-back charm associated with it to this venture, which offers a home-from-home with all sorts of hospitable gestures such as a well-stocked drinks fridge where you replace what you take, or use it to store your own. A very comfortable guest sitting room has lots of books, DVDs and games, and there's a sheltered patio for guests; tea and coffee is always available in the dining room where residents' evening meals are served at a big wooden table: seasonal seafood banquets are a speciality, but the menu also includes other choices including home-made soup (served with freshly baked yeast bread) and steak, perhaps, or a casserole, and various home-made puddings. Bedrooms are spacious, simply furnished and modern - not the height of luxury, but very comfortable; two are en-suite with separate bath and shower, the third has a similar bathroom across the corridor. Full breakfasts are available all morning, and packed lunches can be arranged. This is a real can-do place, and would make a wonderfully relaxed holiday base. **Rooms 3** (2 en-suite, 1 with private bathroom, 2 family rooms, 1 ground floor, 1 partially equipped for disabled); children welcome (under 12's free in parents' room). B&B €40 pps, no ss. Open all year. Residents D, Mon-Sat, 6-8, €30. Fishing nearby, walking, short breaks, free broadband wi/fi, dogs very welcome (stay in bedroom, no charge). *Self catering also avail. **No Credit Cards**. **Directions:** Between Durrus and Ahakista.

Durrus

Good Things Café

CAFÉ

Ahakista Road Durrus Co Cork **Tel: 027 61426**

info@thegoodthingscafe.com www.thegoodthingscafe.com

Great ingredients-led contemporary cooking is the magnet that draws those in the know to Carmel Somers' simple little café-restaurant just outside Durrus village. Well-placed to make the most of fine West Cork produce, she also sells some specialist foods from Ireland and abroad and a few books including Good Food in Cork, the great little guide to local producers written by Myrtle Allen and Caroline Workman. The daytime café menu offers a concise list including great salads, West Cork fish soup, West Cork Ploughmans (a trio of local cheeses served with an onion cassis compôte), Durrus cheese, spinach & nutmeg pizza... then there are irresistible desserts to choose from a display. Dinner brings a more formal menu, with a choice of four on each course, and will feature some of the daytime treats along with main courses like turbot with dill sauce with wilted spinach and local spuds, or beef fillet with pesto. Service is prompt and attentive from the moment a choice of breads and iced water is brought to your table to the arrival of home-made chocolate truffles with your coffee. Ingredients are invariably superb and a meal here can be memorable; this place is a one-off and it is well worth planning a stop when travelling in West Cork, especially during the day, when the bright atmosphere and white café furniture seems more appropriate. An interesting, well-priced wine list includes seven well-chosen house wines, and a good choice of half bottles. *Cookery classes also available; details from the restaurant. **Carmel plans to move into new premises so keep an eye on her website. **Seats 40** (plus 10 outdoor in fine weather); toilets wheelchair accessible; ample parking; children welcome. In summer, open all day (11-9) Wed-Mon (daily in Aug & during Bantry Music Festival), L 12.30-3; D (7-9). A la carte. House wine about €18. Closed Tue and Sep-Easter. Reservations advised for dinner; a call to check times is wise, especially off-season. MasterCard, Visa, Laser. **Directions:** From Durrus village, take Ahakista/Kilcrohane Rd.

Farnanes
PUB

Thady Inn

Farnanes Co Cork
Tel: 021 733 6379

Formerly a barracks for British soldiers, this small pub is set well back from the road and the present owners, Den and Martha O'Flaherty, have kept it simple, just as the previous generation did for 30 years before them. They offer a small menu and do a limited number of well-known dishes well: soups, paté, smoked salmon, cold meat plates (home-cooked roast beef, chicken, ham or tongue salad) and - the dish that has really made their reputation - great steaks, served with perfectly cooked crispy chips - rounded off with homely apple tart and cream or chocolate cake. Everything – soups, meats and desserts – is cooked from scratch, the meats are Irish and the roast beef is cooked rare. A good place to break a journey: it's refreshing to visit a pub that hasn't been done up and concentrates on the business of being an inn - looking after wayfarers well. **Seats 40**; not suitable for children after 7pm; Pub open 10.30am-11.30pm; food available Mon-Sat, 12-9.45pm, Sun 4pm-9.45pm; house wine €18. No Credit Cards **Directions:** Off N22 between Macroom and Cork.

R

FERMOY

If you need to break a journey in Fermoy, head for Jason and Fiona Hogan's **Munchies Eating House** (025 33653), on Lower Patrick Street - this simple café has an old-fashioned style, but food is carefully-sourced (including produce from their own organic plot) and freshly cooked with care – try the warm chicken salad and home-made apple pie! They have a great coffee and tea menu, too and a decked area for fine weather. Open all day Mon-Sat (9-5). Or, if you are in the mood for something spicier, you might try Brendan and Tina Moher's authentic **Thai Lanna** (025 30900) on McCurtain Street: everything is cooked to order by native Thai chefs and Nina, who is head chef, previously had her own restaurant in Thailand and teaches Thai cooking in Ireland. Open for dinner every evening and lunch Thu & Fri. For the sporting tourist, Fermoy's main attraction is the excellent salmon fishing on the Blackwater, and angling for trout in several of the tributary streams. Garden Lovers will have plenty to occupy them with several outstanding gardens within 30km including Ballyvolane House (Fermoy, 025 36349), Annes Grove Garden (near Mallow, 022 26145) and Lismore Castle Gardens (Lismore, 058 54424). Golfers relishing a challenge may try the Ron Kirby-designed links style championship golf course at nearby Castlemartyr Golf Club (086 042 0202). There is also a farmers' market held in Fermoy every Saturday.
WWW.IRELAND-GUIDE.COM FOR ALL THE BEST PLACES TO EAT, DRINK & STAY

Fermoy
RESTAURANT
R

La Bigoudenne

28 MacCurtain Street Fermoy Co Cork
Tel: 025 32832

At this little piece of France in the main street of a County Cork town, Noelle and Rodolphe Semeria's hospitality is matched only by their food, which specialises in Breton dishes, especially crêpes - both savoury (made with buckwheat flour) and sweet (with wheat flour). They run a special pancake evening once a month or so, on a Saturday night. But they do all sorts of other things too, like the salads that you only seem to get in France, soup of the day served with 1/4 baguette & butter, a plat du jour and lovely French pastries. Opening times are a little complicated, but it's worth taking the trouble to work them out as it's a lovely spot - and even the bill is a pleasant surprise. This is a place that deserves to be better known. **Seats 36**. D Tue-Fri, 5.45-9.30, D Sat-Sun, 6.45-9.30: Early D Tue-Thu 5.45-7 (about €21), later D €35 & à la carte; L Thu only, 12.30-3.30. Set D €35, also à la carte. House wine €16.80. Closed Mon & 1-15 Oct. Amex, MasterCard, Visa. **Directions:** On the main street, opposite ESB. ◇

Fermoy Area
COUNTRY HOUSE

Ballyvolane House

Castlelyons Fermoy Co Cork **Tel: 025 36349**
info@ballyvolanehouse.ie www.ballyvolanehouse.ie

COUNTRY HOUSE OF THE YEAR
COUNTRY HOUSE BREAKFAST AWARD

The Greene family's gracious mansion is surrounded by its own farmland, magnificent wooded grounds, a trout lake and formal terraced gardens - garden lovers will find a stay here especially rewarding. The Italianate style of the present house - including a remarkable pillared hall with a baby grand piano and open fire - dates from the mid-19th century when modifications were made to the original house of 1728. Jeremy and the late Merrie Green first welcomed guests to their home in 1983, and is now run by their son Justin and his wife Jenny; Justin has management experience in top hotels and they are an extremely hospitable couple, committed to ensuring that the standards of hospitality, comfort and food for which this lovely house is renowned will be maintained. Elegantly furnished and extremely comfortable, it has big log fires, and roomy bedrooms furnished with family antiques look out over beautiful grounds. Ballyvolane has private salmon fishing on 8km of the great River Blackwater, with a wide variety of spring and summer beats, so it is logical that delicious food should be another high point, and memorable modern Irish dinners are served in style at separate tables or around a long mahogany table, depending on the occasion. Tina Mahon, formerly at Buggy's Glencairn Inn near Lismore, took over the kitchen in 2008 and the style remains country house, with all ingredients home-grown or sourced from the local area, and organic where possible: wholesome house specialities include wild garlic soup, roast rib of McGrath's Hereford beef with béarnaise sauce, and carrageen moss pudding with walled garden rhubarb. A carefully chosen, evocative and very informative wine list complements the food; among the treats in store you'll find a clutch of lovely house wines (including an organic red), half a dozen champagnes, and a good choice of dessert wines. A lovely relaxed guest Drawing Room at the back of the house has recently been restored (and looks as if it has always been that way), and five extra 'retreat' bedrooms are under construction in one of the walled gardens at the time of going to press – also a weddings venue in the farm yard. There is much of interest in the area and the hospitality is wonderful, making this an excellent base for a peaceful and very relaxing break. A self-catering cottage is also available. French is spoken. Conferences/Banqueting (50). **Rooms 6** (all en-suite, 1 shower only, all no smoking). B&B €135 pps, ss €35; children welcome (under 3s free in parents' room, cot available, free of charge, baby sitting arranged); free Broadband wi/fi; dogs permitted (staying in bedrooms). Garden, croquet, fishing, walking, cycling. D daily at 8pm, non residents also welcome (all by reservation); 4 course D €60; house wine from €24. Closed 24 Dec - 1 Jan. Amex, Diners, MasterCard, Visa, Laser. **Directions:** Turn right off main Dublin-Cork road N8 just south of Rathcormac (signed Midleton), following house signs on to R628.

GLANDORE / UNION HALL

The attractive village of GLANDORE is beautifully situated in a sheltered location overlooking Glandore Harbour and its guardian rocks, Adam and Eve. The all-year population is small and it will never be a place for mass tourism but there is comfortable accommodation to be found at guesthouses in the area and at the family-run **Marine Hotel** (see entry), right beside the little harbour in the village. And the same family also own the beautifully located period house, **The Rectory** (028 33072; www.rectoryglandore.com), which is used mainly for weddings and private functions but is occasionally open as a restaurant as well, if not booked to capacity. Glandore is also fortunate in its pubs, which have different characters and are all special in their own way: **The Glandore Inn**, for example, acts as unofficial clubhouse for the local sailing community (and serves sound food), while the old-fashioned **Casey's** (at the 'top of the town') only opens in the evenings and is a place for impromptu sessions and late-night craic. Across the bridge, in **UNION HALL**, Dinty's Bar (028 33373) does good bar meals, and there is comfortable B&B accommodation to be found at **Shearwater** (028 33178), with sea views from all rooms. Those seeking fresh local produce might visit nearby Skibbereen Farmers' Market held on Saturdays (9am-1.30pm). As with all of West Cork, garden lovers are spoilt for choice with several superb gardens nearby including Lassanroe Garden (Skibbereen, 028 22563), Glebe Gardens & Café (Baltimore, 028 20232) and Lisselan Gardens (Clonakilty, 023 33249).
WWW.IRELAND-GUIDE.COM FOR ALL THE BEST PLACES TO EAT, DRINK & STAY

Glandore
PUB

Hayes' Bar

The Square Glandore Co Cork **Tel: 028 33214**
dchayes@tinet.ie www.hayesbar.ie

Hayes Bar is beautifully located overlooking the harbour and has outdoor tables - and Ada Hayes' famous bar food. The soup reminds you of the kind your granny used to make and the open sandwiches are stupendous. Everything that goes to make Hayes' special - including the wines and crockery collected on Declan and Ada's frequent trips abroad - has to be seen to be believed; their travels also affect the menu, inspiring favourites like Croque Monsieur and there's a tapas menu, offering Manchego cheese, Serrano ham, chorizo Pamplona and so on, with fino sherry and Spanish wines and beer. Wine is Declan's particular passion and Hayes' offers some unexpected treats, by the glass as well as the bottle, at refreshingly reasonable prices. Great reading too, including a lot of background on the wines in stock - and you can now see some of Declan's paintings exhibited, from June to August. By any standards, Hayes' is an outstanding bar. Meals 12-6pm, Jun-Aug; Tapas Menu 6-9; weekends only off-season. Closed weekdays Sep-May except Christmas & Easter. No Credit Cards. **Directions:** The square Glandore.

Glandore
HOTEL•RESTAURANT

The Marine

The Pier Front Glandore Co Cork **Tel: 028 33366**
info@themarine.ie www.themarine.ie

After a long closure, the O'Brien family's hotel down beside the harbour re-opened in 2007 as a compact yet very complete complex. There are 18 lovely 2- and 3-bedroom self-catering houses in addition to a totally revamped bar, an impressive new first floor restaurant and 11 of the original rooms in the pretty creeper-clad block across the car park, which were refurbished and retained. The family also own The Rectory (see Glandore round-up above), and they have always had a reputation for good food and hospitality, so the re-opening of the hotel has been a real boost to the village. Although it has changed so much, the old hotel was not completely demolished and returning guests will feel at home, especially in the stylish new bar which is totally different and yet retains the same friendly atmosphere, and helpful staff. A short bar menu offers wholesome fare and the surroundings - looking out at the harbour from the circular feature bar, perhaps, or sitting out on the deck - are relaxing. **Restaurant:** This fine high-ceilinged first floor room is tiered to take full advantage of the harbour and sea views, and stylishly furnished in warm tones, with comfortable contemporary seating and uncovered wooden tables that are set up attractively for smart-casual dining. Proprietor Shane O'Brien heads up the kitchen team and the aim is to present simple food with a bit of a twist to give a sense of occasion. Menus are well-balanced but local seafood tops the bill, of course, and an informative wine list is organised by style. Toilets wheelchair accessible; children welcome before 9 pm (high chair, childrens menu, baby changing facilities). **Seats 90**; reservations recommended. L Sun only, 12.30-3pm. D daily, 6-8.30pm. Amex, MasterCard, Visa, Laser. **Directions:** On the pier front in Glandore. ◇

Glanmire
RESTAURANT

The Barn Restaurant

Glanmire Co Cork
Tel: 021 486 6211

This long-established neighbourhood restaurant has a devoted local clientèle who love the old-fashioned atmosphere, good French/Irish cooking and professional service. An attractive entrance conservatory leads to a comfortable lounge/reception area, where the welcome is warm and you can choose from menus which offer a good choice of quite traditional dishes - starters like home-smoked salmon or chef's duck & chicken liver patés, and main courses of roast farmyard duckling, steaks various ways, and fresh seafood are all typical. This large restaurant is divided up into several comfortable dining areas, with well-spaced tables set up with fresh flowers. Everything is cooked to order, with the emphasis on flavour and wholesomeness - and professional, attentive service; all round a reassuringly old-style approach. Vegetarians are well looked after, saucing and presentation are good, and accompaniments are carefully selected. Sunday lunch is very popular and menus are similar in style. **Seats about 160**; reservations advised (essential at weekends). D daily, 6-9.30pm, L Sun only 12.30-2.30. Set D about €36, Set Sun L about €22. House wine about €22. Car park. Closed Ash Wed & Good Fri. Amex, Diners, Visa, Laser. **Directions:** On the edge of Cork city, on the old Youghal road at Glanmire. ◇

GLENGARRIFF

Famous for its mild Gulf Stream climate and lush growth - especially on nearby Garinish Island (Illnacullin Garden, 027 63040), with its beautiful gardens - Glengarriff has been a popular tourist destination since Victorian times and a little of that atmosphere still exists today. Golfers will be more than satisfied with the challenge posed by nearby Bantry Bay Golf Club (Bantry, 027 50579). The rather grand looking **Eccles Hotel** (027 63003; www.eccleshotel.com) overlooks the harbour and is perhaps most obviously associated with that era (although it actually dates as far back as 1745), while the smaller, moderately priced and very hospitable family-run **Casey's Hotel** (027 63010) nearby, was established in 1884 and has been run by the same family ever since. The new kid on the block is the **Glengarriff Park Hotel** (027 63000; www.glengarriffpark.com), a smartly presented modern hotel with a nice traditional bar and quite decent bistro-style food available during the day and evening in their **Blue Pool Bistro**. The attractive restaurant **Martello** (027 63860), on the main street, is open only for dinner on Friday and Saturday and lunch on Sunday.

WWW.IRELAND-GUIDE.COM FOR ALL THE BEST PLACES TO EAT, DRINK & STAY

Goleen
RESTAURANT WITH ROOMS

The Heron's Cove

The Harbour Goleen Co Cork **Tel: 028 35225**
info@heroncove.ie www.heronscove.com

When the tide is in and the sun is out there can be few prettier locations than Sue Hill's restaurant overlooking Goleen harbour. The Heron's Cove philosophy is to use only the best of fresh, local ingredients and in summer there's a natural leaning towards seafood - typically in wholesome starters like plump, perfectly cooked Bantry Bay moules marinières or, more unusually, West Cork smoked sprats. Main course specialities include fillet of John Dory with balsamic butter. If you're not in a fishy mood, there might be Goleen lamb cutlets (served on a bed of champ, with rosemary jus, perhaps) or crispy roast Skeaghanore duckling, and there's always at least one vegetarian dish. More-ish desserts include the Heron's Cove signature dessert, a baked chocolate & vanilla cheesecake, and a wide selection of home-made ice creams - passion fruit, blackcurrant, blackberry, rum & Michigan cherry (to name a few of the less usual ones). Great ingredients, pleasing cooking and friendly attentive service should make for an enjoyable meal - and, considering the quality of ingredients, a fairly priced one. An unusual Wine on the Rack system offers a great selection of interesting, well-priced wines that change through the season - they are listed but the idea is that you can browse through the bottles and make your own selection. **Seats 30**; children welcome. D daily in summer, 7-9 (bookings essential Oct-Mar); à la carte. House wine €22.50. SC discretionary. Closed Christmas & New Year. **Accommodation:** Comfortable en-suite rooms have recently been refurbished, making this an appealing place to stay. Some have private balconies, and all have satellite TV, phones, tea/coffee-making facilities and hair dryers. **Rooms 5** (4 shower only, all no smoking, 1 family room); children welcome (under 5s free in parents' room, cot available free of charge). B&B €55 pps, ss €35. Garden. Open for dinner, bed & breakfast all year except Christmas/New Year, but it is always advisable to book, especially off-season. Amex, Diners, MasterCard, Visa, Laser. **Directions:** Turn left in middle of Goleen to the harbour, 300m from village.

Gougane Barra
HOTEL●RESTAURANT

Gougane Barra Hotel

Gougane Barra Macroom Co Cork **Tel: 026 47069**
gouganebarrahotel@eircom.net www.gouganebarrahotel.com

In one of the most peaceful and beautiful locations in Ireland, this delightfully old-fashioned family-run hotel is set in a Forest Park overlooking Gougane Barra Lake (famous for its monastic settlements). The Lucey family has run the hotel since 1937, offering simple, comfortable accommodation as a restful base for walking holidays - rooms are comfortable and have recently been given a gentle upgrade but not over-modernised; all look out on to the lake or mountain, and there are quiet public rooms - also recently refurbished and now slightly more upbeat - where guests like to read. There has been very little real change over the years, and that's just the way people like it but, since Neil Lucey and his wife Katy took over management of the hotel from Neil's parents in 2005, their energy has brought a fresh approach. Walking holidays will remain an important part of the business, but there's now a new cultural edge too as Neil opened a little theatre in the hotel and they host a production each summer. And, while the spirit of the place will thankfully remain unchanged, the many improvements made recently include a stronger emphasis on food, and visitors are encouraged to drop in for informal meals - Katy's delicious bar menus include specialities like a moreish warm chicken salad, the superb house chowder which she brought from her father's kitchen in Lahinch, where her parents ran Mr Eamon's famous restaurant for many years - and her lovely rich walnut and treacle bread. It's a good place to bear in mind for afternoon tea too, a cup of tea with a freshly baked sultana scone, local strawberry jam and whipped cream goes down a treat when you're out and about. This is a magical place - as ever, the monks chose well. Intimate family weddings welcome (65). **Rooms 26** (all en-suite & no smoking, 8 shower only, 1 family room, 8 ground floor, all no smoking); children welcome (under 11s free in parents' room, cots available at no charge); free broadband wi/fi; B&B €75 pps, SS €10. Shop. Garden, walking. No pets. **Restaurant:** The formal meals, including breakfast, are served in the lakeside dining room which has also been gently upgraded to match Katy's good cooking. Smart linen-clad tables are welcoming, with gleaming glasses and fresh flowers, and menus are thoughtfully constructed to suit the varying needs of guests who can opt for a full 4-course dinner or two courses of their choice at a lower price. Dishes offered are also well chosen to include upbeat versions of old favourites (galia and honeydew melon with raspberry sorbet & mango coulis; grilled Muskerry sirloin steak with provençal tomato and a little red wine jus) alongside slightly more adventurous choices. Ingredients are carefully sourced, and a very nice Junior Menu is also offered. An informative wine list includes well-chosen house wines, a good choice of half bottles and a cocktail menu. **Seats 70**; L&D daily, 12.30-3 (Sun, 12.45-2.30) and 6-8.30pm (Sun to 8.45); set Sun L €27; set 2/3 course D €31/41; house wine from €17.50. Closed 20 Oct - 7 Apr. Amex, MasterCard, Visa, Laser. **Directions:** Situated in Gougane Barra National Forest; well signposted.

Kilbrittain
RESTAURANT

Casino House

Coolmain Bay Kilbrittain Co Cork **Tel: 023 49944**
chouse@eircom.net www.casinohouse.ie

Kerrin and Michael Relja's delightful restaurant is just a few miles west of Kinsale and it is well worth the effort of getting here, as it is one of the best in an area which takes great pride in the excellence of its food. It's a lovely old house and it has an unusually cool continental style in the decor, but Kerrin's hospitality is warm - and Michael's food is consistently excellent, in wide-ranging seasonal menus based on the finest local ingredients: Ummera smoked organic salmon, fresh seafood from nearby fishing ports (don't miss his wonderful speciality lobster risotto), Kilbrittain lamb and Ballydehob duck all feature - a starter dish of four variations of duck is another speciality. Tempting vegetarian dishes are listed ahead of the other main courses and nightly specials will include extra seafood dishes (turbot on lobster cream with purple champ, for example), all with individual vegetable garnishes and deliciously simple seasonal side vegetables. Variations on classic desserts are irresistible (a delectable chocolate cake on caramelised pineapple with red berry dressing, perhaps) and local cheeses are always seriously tempting in this area... An al fresco early summer dinner, or Sunday lunch, can be an especially memorable experience. A very nice wine list offers plenty of treats to match the food, and includes a well-chosen selection of half bottles. Casino House was our Restaurant of the Year in 2005, and it consistently offers some of the best food and hospitality in the country. *Casino Cottage: sleeps two €85 per night (or €155 for 2 nights), everything provided except breakfast - which can be supplied if needed. Longer stays discounted; weekly & winter rates available. Further accommodation is in the pipeline at the time of going to press. **Seats 35** (private room 22; outdoor dining 16). D Thu-Tue, 7-9, L Sun only,1-3; all à la carte; house wine from €20.90. Closed Wed, and 1 Jan-17 Mar. Amex, MasterCard, Visa, Laser. **Directions:** On R600 between Kinsale and Timoleague.

Kilbrittain
FARMHOUSE

The Glen Country House
The Glen Kilbrittain Co Cork **Tel: 023 49862**
info@glencountryhouse.com www.glencountryhouse.com

Although classified (correctly) as a farmhouse, Guy and Diana Scott's home is an elegant period house and they have recently renovated it to a high standard for guests. It is quietly located in a beautiful area, and the four large double bedrooms have lovely views across Courtmacsherry Bay. There's even a family suite (consisting of a double room and children's room, with interconnecting bathroom) and guests have the use of a comfortable sitting room with a welcoming open fire, and a dining room where lovely breakfasts are served - a buffet with fresh and poached seasonal fruits, freshly squeezed orange juice, organic muesli and organic yoghurt, and a menu of hot dishes including free range bacon from local pigs, and eggs from their own hens. It's a relaxed place, where dogs are welcome to join the two house spaniels (guests' horses are welcome too!) and, although there are no dinners, evening meals and baby sitting are offered for children, allowing parents to go out to one of the excellent local restaurants - Casino House and Dillon's of Timoleague are nearby. Unusually, the Scotts produce their own fuel (oats) for heating the house and water. **Rooms 5** (all en-suite & no smoking, 4 shower only, 1 family room); children welcome (babies free in parents' room, cot available without charge, baby sitting arranged); free broadband wi/fi; B&B €75 pps, ss €10. Garden. Pets permitted (stay in kennel/outhouse). Closed Oct-Easter. Heli-pad. *Self catering apartment also available, sleeps 4. MasterCard, Visa, Laser. **Directions:** Signposted off the R600, midway between Kinsale and Clonakilty.

Kilbrittain
BAR•RESTAURANT

The Pink Elephant
Harbour View Kilbrittain Co Cork **Tel: 023 49608**
info@pinkelephant.ie www.pinkelephant.ie

This low pink bungalow-style building is on a superb elevated site overlooking the sea and across the bay to Courtmacsherry and, as it is open for lunch as well as dinner in summer, it is a very useful place to know about. Picnic tables overlook a lawn towards the sea, or you can eat inside in a large room with a piano, which has been painted exuberantly in swirling shades of pink, and is put to good use in the evening when one of the staff tinkles the ivories and sings, along with one of the waitresses. Delicious food includes outstandingly good home-made bread, and menus naturally favour local seafood - lunch dishes are marked up on a blackboard in the bar (another lists wines available by the glass), and might include an excellent Provencal fish soup, or sausage and mash. Evening dishes depend on 'whatever the fishermen drop in', with prime seafood like lobster and brill offered if you're lucky. An unusual, informative and evocative wine list is illustrated with labels, and includes a pair of Fairtrade wines and a good choice of half bottles and dessert wines among many treats. Service is laid-back but efficient and charming. **Seats 80** (outdoors, 30); children welcome before 9pm (high chair, childrens menu); toilets wheelchair accessible; pianist in the evening; L daily 12-2.30 (Sun from 12.30), D daily 6-9, L&D a la carte; house wine from €20. Open 7 days in summer, phone for opening times in winter. MasterCard, Visa, Laser. **Directions:** On R600 coast road near Kilbrittain.

KINSALE
One of Ireland's prettiest towns, Kinsale sits at the mouth of the River Bandon and has the old-world charm of narrow winding streets and medieval ruins tucked in around Georgian terraces - all

contrasting with the busy fishing harbour and marina of today. It has excellent leisure activities including yachting, sea angling, and golf - most notably the Old Head of Kinsale Golf Club (021 477 8444) - for culture lovers the town also has several art galleries, while garden lovers should take in a visit to nearby Lisselan Gardens (Clonakilty, 023 33249). Kinsale was known several decades ago as the 'gourmet capital of Ireland' and, while that claim would now be hotly disputed by several other contenders, it is on the up and up again, offering a remarkable variety of good restaurants and and an exceptionally active programme of culinary activities - and, less widely recognised but of equal interest to the visitor, some of the best accommodation in the country. In the town, **The White Lady Hotel** (021 477 2737) offers moderately priced accommodation and a restaurant with pizzas, pastas and burgers as well as fresh seafood and steaks - a good choice for families. Kinsale also has a fine Eastern European restaurant **Jola's** (18/19 Lr O'Connell Street; 021 4773322); Jola, previously of Kensington's 'Wodka', has brought the flavours of Russia, Lithuania, Poland and Hungary to West Cork and her popular restaurant is open for lunch and dinner. Jean-Marc Tsai's mixture of French bistro and Asian food may no longer be available at **Le Bistro**, but fans will be pleased to know that he has opened the **Shanghai Express Asian Tapas Bar** (021 477 7100) on Lower O'Connell Street; although mainly a takeaway, there are a few tables where Jean-Marc serves his Asian Bites Menu, from 6pm every night except Tuesday; wine by the glass, full wine list and Asian beers available – magic! Outside the town, **Inishannon House Hotel** (Tel 021 477 5121; www.innishannon-hotel.ie) is a romantic riverside 'petit chateau' style house in lovely gardens and - also in the Innishannon direction - the recently restored 13-bedroom **Ballinacurra House** (087 2867443; www.ballinacurra.com) is a luxurious venue, available for private parties, small weddings, golfing groups and corporate events. The town's many pubs offer a judicious mixture of music and food - especially seafood; across the bridge, towards the west, **Castle Park** has a sandy south-facing beach and **The Dock Bar** (Tel: 021 477 2522) is a friendly pub. Kinsale Farmers' Market is held on Short Quay, in front of **Jim Edwards** restaurant (see entry) on Tuesdays (9.30am-1.30pm).

WWW.IRELAND-GUIDE.COM FOR ALL THE BEST PLACES TO EAT, DRINK & STAY

Kinsale
HOTEL

Actons Hotel

Pier Road Kinsale Co Cork **Tel: 021 477 9900**
information@actonshotelkinsale.com   www.actonshotelkinsale.com

Overlooking the harbour and standing in its own grounds, this attractive quayside establishment is Kinsale's most famous hotel, dating back to 1946 when it was created from several substantial period houses. It was sold in 2008 and is now in common ownership with The Trident Hotel. At the time of going to press, it is not clear what changes are likely; meanwhile the hotel continues to operate as before. A fine Health & Fitness Club offers a swimming pool with separate children's pool, hot tub, sauna, steam room and whirlpool spa; there's also a gym, aerobics room, solarium and treatment facilities. Good conference/banqueting facilities too (300/250). **Rooms 73** (2 junior suites, 14 executive, 1 shower only, 2 for disabled, 50 no smoking); children welcome (under 4 free in parents' room, cots available without charge, baby sitting arranged.) No pets. Wheelchair access. Lift. Garden. B&B €75 pps, ss €40 (wide range of special breaks available). **Captain's Table Restaurant**, L&D daily (speciality: the 'Derek Davis' steamed local seafood platter). Bar food available daily, 12-9.30. Closed 24-26 Dec, all Jan. Amex, MasterCard, Visa, Laser. **Directions:** On the waterfront, short walk from town centre.

Kinsale
GUESTHOUSE

Blindgate House

Blindgate Kinsale Co Cork **Tel: 021 477 7858**
info@blindgatehouse.com   www.blindgatehouse.com

Maeve Coakley's purpose-built guesthouse is set in its own gardens high up over the town and, with spacious rooms, uncluttered lines and a generally modern, bright and airy atmosphere, Blindgate makes a refreshing contrast to the more traditional styles that prevail locally. All bedrooms are carefully furnished with elegant modern simplicity, have full en-suite bathrooms and good facilities including fax/modem sockets as well as phones, satellite TV, tea/coffee trays and trouser press. Maeve is an hospitable host - and well-known in Kinsale for her skills in the kitchen, so breakfast here is a high priority: there's a buffet displaying all sorts of good things including organic muesli, fresh fruits and juices, farmhouse cheese and yoghurts, as well as a menu of hot dishes featuring, of course, the full Irish Breakfast alongside catch of the day and other specialities - so make sure you allow time to enjoy this treat to the full. **Rooms 11** (all en-suite & no smoking, 5 ground floor, 2 for disabled); room service (all day); children over 7 welcome (baby sitting arranged); broadband wi/fi; B&B €72.50 pps, no ss. No pets. Garden. Closed late Dec-mid Mar. Amex, MasterCard, Visa, Laser. **Directions:** From Fishy Fishy Café: Take left up the hill, keeping left after St Multose Church. Blindgate House is after St Joseph's Primary School, on the left.

Kinsale   # The Blue Haven Hotel
HOTEL   3/4 Pearse Street Kinsale Co Cork **Tel: 021 477 2209**
                          info@bluehavenkinsale.com www.bluehavenkinsale.com

 This famous hotel has an attractive exterior, with its name emblazoned in blue and white stained glass above the entrance and flags hanging from poles, giving it a cosmopolitan look. Under the current ownership since 2004, proprietor Ciaran Fitzgerald continues to do everything possible to restore and build on its once great reputation. Due to the nature of the building, public areas are quite compact, but a major refurbishment programme has seen a complete redesign of the bar, which now has a much more open contemporary feeling, and the lower deck of the restaurant, to create a cocktail lounge incorporating a residents' lounge where afternoon tea can be served during the day. All the bedrooms have double glazing to offset the street noise that is inevitable in a central location and, although not large, both the rooms and their neat bathrooms make up in thoughtful planning anything they lack in spaciousness - and there is extra accommodation available a few doors away at The Old Bank House (see entry), which is in common ownership. Conferences/Banqueting (80/70); free broadband wi/fi. Children welcome (unders 8s free in parents' room, cots available, baby sitting arranged). No pets. Street parking. **Rooms 17** (4 shower only, 3 single, 17 no smoking). B&B €100, ss €40. **Restaurant:** Now styled 'Restaurant Blu', the restaurant is a popular choice amongst Kinsale's dining options, and more than an hotel dining room. Like the rest of the public areas, the restaurant has had a makeover - and the cocktail lounge on the lower deck, plus the smart streamlined look of the new contemporary décor creates a more glamorous atmosphere. A lobster tank at the entrance to the restaurant sets the tone for menus that have the emphasis on seafood (offering perhaps half a dozen starters and a similar number of main courses based on local fish and seafood), balanced by steak, chicken and vegetarian dishes - and there is a separate children's menu too. Cooking is sound, care is taken with presentation, and an extensive wine list and good service add to the pleasure of a meal here. *A new café-bar, **Hamlets of Kinsale** (021 4772939) opened just before the Guide went to press; just around the corner at The Glen, it is in common ownership with The Blue Haven. **Seats 65**; children welcome before 9pm (high chair, childrens menu, baby changing facilities). L & D daily, set L €27.50, set D €45, à la carte also available. House wine from €22.50; sc 10%. Closed 25 Dec. Amex, Diners, MasterCard, Visa, Laser. **Directions:** In the centre of town.

Kinsale   # Chart House
B&B   6 Denis Quay Kinsale Co Cork **Tel: 021 477 4568**
Ⓥ   charthouse@eircom.net www.charthouse-kinsale.com

Billy and Mary O'Connor offer very appealing accommodation at this delightful 200-year old house, which they have completely renovated, with attention to period details. Beautifully furnished bedrooms have orthopaedic mattresses, phone, TV, hair dryer and a trouser press with iron; tea and coffee are served by the fire in a cosy reception/sitting room, and an imaginative breakfast menu is served communally on a fine William IV dining room suite. **Rooms 4** (2 suites with jacuzzi baths, 2 shower only, all no-smoking); not suitable for children; no pets. B&B from €60 pps (depending on room), single occupancy 75%; single room €50. Closed Christmas week. Amex, MasterCard, Visa, Laser. **Directions:** On Pier Road between Actons and Trident Hotels, turn right after Actons, last house on right.

Kinsale   # Crackpots Restaurant
RESTAURANT•WINE BAR   3 Cork Street Kinsale Co Cork **Tel: 021 477 2847**
Ⓥ   crackpots@iol.ie www.crackpots.ie

Carole Norman's attractive and unusual restaurant has had a make-over recently, but – except for the welcome addition of extra space and a new garden area - thankfully the basics remain the same: it's got a lot going for it - not only can you drop in for a glass of wine at the bar, as well as the usual meals, but all the pottery used in the restaurant is made on the premises so, if you take a fancy to the table-ware or any of the decorative pieces on the walls, you can buy that too. Menus are imaginative and considerate, with attractive options for vegetarians, and many of the specialities are seafood, notably shellfish: lobster, moules marinière, crab toes (in a coconut & lemongrass sauce), seared scallops, and whole sautéed prawns in their shells, and old favourites like chowder and smoked salmon are sure to make an appearance. If you feel like a change from fish there might be organic roast duck, or a classic fillet steak on the evening menu. **Seats 65** (outdoors 25); children welcome before 8.30pm (high chair); air conditioning. L & D Mon-Sat, 12.30-3.30pm & 6-10pm; Sun L only 12-3pm. Early D €25 (6-7); otherwise à la carte, house wines €20. Amex, MasterCard, Visa, Laser. **Directions:** Between Garda Station and Wine Museum.

Cucina

Kinsale
CAFÉ

9 Market Street Kinsale Co Cork **Tel: 021 470 0707**
ursula@cucina.ie www.cucina.ie

A little gem in the heart of Kinsale, you'll find Ursula Roncken's appealing all-day café behind a very attractive powder blue frontage with white lettering. Bright and attractive with a picture window onto Market Street, it's an all together kind of place with polished wood/blue & white tiled floor, modern paintings on cream painted walls and wooden-topped tables with attractive wooden seats - better still, it's friendly and welcoming, and serves great tasting food. Menus offer a very nice selection of dishes for both breakfast (eggs Benedict; roasted Portobello mushrooms on toasted muffin with herbed scrambled eggs and roast tomato; sourdough, wholemeal or fruit toast, with preserves and butter...) and lunch (crab & avocado salad; smoked chicken Caesar salad; blueberry cheesecake...), and the quality and flavour of all dishes is excellent. Great service too – friendly, knowledgeable and relaxed. Accommodation also offered. **Seats 38**. Open 8am-5pm (breakfast 8-11.30, lunch 12-4); food served to 4pm. **No credit cards. Directions:** In the heart of Kinsale Town.

Dalton's

Kinsale
PUB

3 Market Street Kinsale Co Cork **Tel: 021 477 7957**
fedalton@eircom.net

Frances and Colm Dalton's cheerful little red-painted town-centre bar - which was closed for refurbishment at the time of going to press - has a characterful, traditional-look interior with green & white floor tiles and lots of wood - and is well worth seeking out for good home cooking. It's a friendly spot and they make a good team - Colm is chef, while Frances is the baker - providing wholesome lunches which are more restaurant meals than usual bar food, five days a week. While there's plenty of choice, the menu is sensibly limited to eight or nine dishes, plus a couple of specials each day; there's an understandable emphasis on seafood - steamed mussels, crab cakes, smoked salmon with home-baked brown bread, warm seafood salad - and a sprinkling of other dishes. Good quality, fresh ingredients and real home cooking make for some delicious flavours - and desserts (apple & blackberry crumble perhaps) are all home-made. A short wine list offers a number of wines by the glass, and an above-average choice of quarter bottles. Outside lunchtime, Daltons operates normally, as a bar. **Seats 30**; new opening times were not yet known when going to press. Closed 25 Dec, Good Fri. No credit cards. **Directions:** Entering Kinsale from Cork, straight on past Blue haven Hotel, left at end; Daltons on left, opposite Market Place.

Fishy Fishy Café

Kinsale
CAFÉ•RESTAURANT

Crowley's Quay Kinsale Co Cork **Tel: 021 470 0415**
www.fishyfishy.ie

Martin and Marie Shanahan's Fishy Fishy Café mark two is a very big restaurant by West Cork standards, yet they've been full to capacity at peak times ever since opening in 2006, and they have kept the original Fishy Fishy (which has a wet fish bar) open too. The new premises was previously an art gallery and now has an atmospheric interior on two levels. It makes a design statement from the outset, with wooden gates opening onto a decking path leading to the front door - a bit like a zen garden, it is fitted into a neat rectangle with rounded beach stones filling the gaps. The interior is bright, airy and stylishly simple, with a smart bar, unpretentious café-style darkwood furniture and plenty of doors opening out on to the patio and balcony. A large paved outdoor seating area is enclosed by a hedge and, when it's warm enough to eat outside, is set up mainly with aluminium chairs and tables and seriously business-like parasols, giving it a continental air of dedication to the comfortable enjoyment of good food. The Shanahans' reputation for offering the widest possible range and freshest of fish is unrivalled throughout Ireland, and shellfish lovers might be lucky enough to feast on a lunch of oysters, mussels and perhaps even Christy Turley's crab cocktail - Christy is a local food hero, a third generation Kinsale fisherman who supplies much of Fishy Fishy's catch. Prices are very fair for the quality offered, and that includes the wine. Fishy Fishy is almost as famous for its celebrity spangled queues as for the fabulous fish and, true to their original style, no reservations are accepted. Fishy Fishy Café was our Seafood Restaurant of the Year in 2007. **Seats 150** (private room, 40, outdoors, 60); no reservations accepted; air conditioning; children welcome; open daily 12-4.30pm; a la carte menu. Closed Christmas 3 days. **No credit cards.** ◇

Kinsale
CAFÉ

Fishy Fishy Cafe @ The Gourmet Store

Guardwell Kinsale Co Cork
Tel: 021 477 4453

This delightful fish shop, delicatessen and restaurant has long been a mecca for gourmets in and around Kinsale and was our Seafood Restaurant of the Year in 2001. Although all sorts of other delicacies are on offer, seafood is the serious business here - and, as well as the range of dishes offered on the menu and a specials board, you can ask to have any of the fresh fish on display cooked to your liking. Not that you'd feel the need to stray beyond the menu, in fact, as it makes up in interest and quality anything it might lack in length - and vegetarian dishes available on request. [See also entry for the new Fishy Fishy]. **Seats 36**; not suitable for children under 7; wheelchair accessible; no reservations; Wed-Sat 12-3.30; à la carte; house wines from about €18. Closed Sun, Mon, Tue; 3 days Christmas. **No Credit Cards**. **Directions:** Opposite St Multose church, next to Garda station. ◇

Kinsale
GUESTHOUSE

Friar's Lodge

Friar's Street Kinsale Co Cork **Tel: 021 477 7384**
mtierney@indigo.ie www.friars-lodge.com

Maureen Tierney's friendly and exceptionally comfortable purpose-built guesthouse is very professionally operated, and offers an attractive alternative to hotel accommodation in the centre of Kinsale - it even has private parking, and there is a drying room for wet golfing gear. The style is a pleasing combination of traditional and modern and the spacious guest rooms have well-designed bathrooms - most with full bath and shower; as well as the more usual facilities, rooms also have computer/internet connection, safe and TV with DVD. Guests have use of an elegantly furnished sitting room with an open fire and, although evening meals are not offered, a good breakfast is served in a pleasant dining room. This is a very pleasing place to stay and offers good value too, in comparison with hotels. **Rooms 18** (2 executive, 2 shower only, 2 family rooms, 16 no smoking); children welcome (under 5s free in parents' room, cot available free of charge); lift; limited room service; B&B €65 pps, ss €15. Closed 22-27 Dec. MasterCard, Visa, Laser. **Directions:** Centre of Kinsale, next to parish church. ◇

Kinsale
GUESTHOUSE

Harbour Lodge

Scilly Kinsale Co Cork **Tel: 021 477 2376**
relax@harbourlodge.ie www.harbourlodge.ie

This waterfront guesthouse is extremely comfortable and the position, away from the bustle of the town centre, is lovely and peaceful; some bedrooms have balconies overlooking the marina, and there's a large conservatory "orangerie" for the leisurely observation of comings and goings in the harbour, also a sitting room with an open fire for chilly days. Thoughtfully furnished bedrooms have top of the range beds and luxurious bathrooms, and an extensive breakfast is served in the conservatory. The proprietors have recently opened The

Spinnaker Restaurant (see entry), which is next door, and guests can access it directly through the garden. **Rooms** 9 (1 suite, 1 family room, 1 shower only, 4 ground floor, all no smoking); children welcome (under 4s free in parents room, cot available free of charge, baby sitting arranged). Special breaks offered. B&B from €99 pps. Garden, walking, cycling. Golf and many other activities nearby. Open all year. Amex, Diners, MasterCard, Visa, Laser. **Directions:** Scilly waterfront: 1km (0.5 mile) from town centre, beside the Spinnaker.

Jim Edwards

Kinsale
RESTAURANT•PUB

Short Quay Kinsale Co Cork **Tel: 021 477 2541**
info@jimedwardskinsale.com www.jimedwardskinsale.com

This characterful old place in the heart of Kinsale is known for its atmosphere and the consistent quality of the hearty food served in both bar and restaurant. Its authentic cosy pub atmosphere is embellished with electric "oil" lamps above some of the tables, and the décor - a polished wood floor with inset patterned tiles, mustard and maroon colour scheme, and curios on display - works really well, for a relaxed pub atmosphere. Seafood is the speciality (try the medallions of monkfish with spring onion, ginger & lime dressing), but there's plenty to please everyone on all menus, from spicy chicken wings, or crab claws in garlic butter to sirloin steak, on the extensive bar menu and lunch menu - and then the treats of scampi or fresh lobster or rack of lamb on the à la carte; everything is carefully prepared and really tasty. Extensive wine list. Smartly dressed staff are very professional and efficient, and it's good value. *It's hard to imagine changes at Jim Edwards, but at the time of going to press plans are afoot to change the front of the building and have seating outside. **Seats 75**; children welcome; air conditioning; food served daily 12-10pm (from 12.30 Sun); L 12-3.30 (to 3pm Sun); set Sun L about €24.90; D 6-10pm; Set 2/3 course D, about €16/22, also a la carte L&D; house wine €21. Amex, MasterCard, Visa, Laser. **Directions:** Town centre.

Man Friday

Kinsale
RESTAURANT

Scilly Kinsale Co Cork **Tel: 021 477 2260**
www.man-friday.net

High up over the harbour, Philip Horgan's popular, characterful restaurant is housed in a series of rooms, and it has a garden terrace, which makes a nice spot for drinks and coffee in fine weather. Philip presents seasonal à la carte menus that major on seafood but offer plenty else besides, including several vegetarian choices and ever-popular duck, steak and lamb. While geared to fairly traditional tastes, the cooking is generally sound and can include imaginative ideas - and there's usually a good buzz, which adds hugely to the enjoyment of a meal. Simple, well-made desserts include good ice creams. Service is, for the most part, cheerful and efficient and, unlike many other restaurants in the area, which are seasonal, Man Friday is open in the winter. **Seats 130** (private room, 40). Not accessible to wheelchairs. D Mon-Sat, 6.30-10.30; gourmet D about €40; also à la carte, house wine from about €20; sc discretionary. Closed Sun (except bank hol weekends), Dec 24-26. Amex, MasterCard, Visa, Laser. **Directions:** Overlooking the inner harbour, at Scilly. ◈

Max's Wine Bar

Kinsale
RESTAURANT

48 Main Street Kinsale Co Cork
Tel: 021 477 2443

Run by a young couple, Olivier and Anne Marie Queva - the chef and restaurant manager respectively - Max's has a loyal following in the locality, and it's a happy find for visitors too. Returning visitors may remember it as a more cottagey place, with mirror-varnished tables and a pretty conservatory out at the back but, since major refurbishment, it has a new layout that allowed for a new kitchen and better use of space. Although the style is smarter, and more contemporary, something of the spirit of the old Max's lives on - and the food is as good as ever, so everyone is happy. Olivier's seasonal menus change regularly and offer a pleasing balance of luxurious ingredients and the more homely; seafood from the pier is the main feature - langoustines and oysters (in season), mussels, or black sole, less usual fish such as ling - with a balance of meats and poultry (roast rack of Irish lamb is a consistent favourite), and appealing vegetarian dishes offered too. An informative wine list offers a range of house wines (available by the glass), an above-average choice of half bottles and a range of aperitifs, dessert wines and ports. This is a lovely restaurant for an evening out, but the light snack lunch is also very useful for visitors exploring the town during the day. **Seats 30**; not suitable for children after 7.30pm. L Wed-Mon,12.30-3 (Sun 1-3), D Wed-Mon, 6.30-10. Set L/Early D (6.30-7.30) €21.90; also à la carte; house wine €19.50, SC discretionary. Closed Tue; mid Dec-1 Mar. Amex, MasterCard, Visa, Laser. **Directions:** Located parallel to tourist office, follow sign across from tourist office.

Kinsale
GUESTHOUSE

The Old Bank House

11 Pearse Street Kinsale Co Cork **Tel: 021 477 4075**
info@oldbankhousekinsale.com www.oldbankhousekinsale.com

This fine townhouse in the centre of Kinsale is in common ownership with the Blue Haven Hotel, and is a great asset to it. It has an elegant residents' sitting room and very comfortable, spacious bedrooms, with good amenities, and quality materials - all rooms are furnished with antiques and decorated to the same impeccable standard, with lovely bathrooms. Shortly before going to press, the former breakfast room was redeveloped and emerged as Café Blue, where casual food is available all day, seven days a week. **Rooms 17** (1 suite, 1 junior suites, 2 family rooms, all no smoking; children welcome (under 1 year free in parents' room, cot €20, baby sitting arranged); free broadband wi/fi. Lift. Room service (all day). B&B from €90 pps, ss €90. Golf-friendly: tee-off times, hire of clubs, transport to course, golf tuition can all be arranged; golf storage room. Closed 23-28 Dec. Amex, MasterCard, Visa, Laser. **Directions:** In the heart of Kinsale, next to the Post Office. ◈

Kinsale
B&B

The Old Presbytery

43 Cork Street Kinsale Co Cork **Tel: 021 477 2027**
info@oldpres.com www.oldpres.com

This old house in the centre of the town has provided excellent accommodation for many years and the current owners, Philip and Noreen McEvoy have kept up this tradition well. Bed and breakfast is offered in the original bedrooms, which have character - stripped pine country furniture and antique beds which have been refurbished, and the McEvoys have also added three self-catering suites, each with two en-suite bedrooms, sitting room, kitchenette and an extra bathroom. The new rooms are well-proportioned and furnished in the same style and to the same high standard; they can be taken on a nightly basis (minimum stay 2 nights), sleeping up to six adults. The top suite has an additional lounge area leading from a spiral staircase, with magnificent views over the town and harbour. **Rooms 6** (3 suites, 2 shower only, 2 family rooms, 1 ground floor, all no-smoking); children welcome (cot available without charge); free broadband wi/fi. B&B €80 pps, ss €80. Self-catering apartments, from €170 per night (min 2 nights). Closed mid Nov - mid Feb. Amex, MasterCard, Visa, Laser. **Directions:** Follow signs for Desmond Castle - in same street.

Kinsale
RESTAURANT

Oz-Haven Restaurant

Main Street Kinsale Co Cork **Tel: 021 470 0007**
www.ozhaven.com

This well-known restaurant has re-located from Oysterhaven to the premises formerly occupied by Jean-Marc Tsai and Jacqui St John-Jones' popular restaurant Le Bistro, in the centre of Kinsale. The lively revamped premises feature cartoon prints on the walls, chandeliers and simple bistro tables – and a large fish tank just inside the door. Predictably quirky menus offer the expected oddities (crocodile balls) and are strewn with comments that could be irritating; but underneath the baloney there's a good selection of dishes offered and – despite the Australian exotics – ingredients are good quality, mostly sourced locally, and organic where possible. In the Guide's experience, the cooking is good and food attractively presented, which – together with good service from professional staff, and attractive surroundings – makes for good value, although prices are quite high. The wine list offers reasonably priced house wines, and ten wines by the glass, otherwise prices rise rather steeply. **Seats 50**; children welcome (childrens menu, €10.95). L & D daily; all day grazing menu 12-5pm, dinner menu 7-9.30pm, Sun L 12-6pm. 2/3 course happy hour menu €24.95/29.95, Mon-Fri 6-7pm; set 5 course D €65, also à la carte. Set Sun L €26.95. House wine €19.95. Closed 24-26 Dec. Amex, MasterCard, Visa, Laser. **Directions:** Top of Main Street Kinsale, on the corner of Guardwell and Market Streets.

Perryville House

Kinsale
COUNTRY HOUSE

Long Quay Kinsale Co Cork **Tel: 021 477 2731**
sales@perryville.iol.ie www.perryvillehouse.com

One of the prettiest houses in Kinsale, Laura Corcoran's characterful house on the harbour front has been renovated to an exceptionally high standard and provides excellent accommodation only 15 minutes from the Old Head of Kinsale Golf Club. Gracious public rooms are beautifully furnished, as if for a private home. Spacious, individually decorated bedrooms vary in size and outlook (ones at the front are most appealing, but the back is quieter) and all have extra large beds and thoughtful extras such as fresh flowers, complimentary mineral water, quality toiletries, robes and slippers. The suites have exceptionally luxurious bathrooms although all are well-appointed. Breakfasts include home-baked breads and local cheeses; morning coffee and afternoon tea are available to residents in the drawing room and there is a wine licence. **Rooms 26** (5 junior suites, 8 superior, all no-smoking); not suitable for children. No pets. B&B from €65 pps, No SC. Closed Nov-1Apr. *Wireless internet throughout the house. Own parking. Amex, MasterCard, Visa, Laser. **Directions:** Central location, on right as you enter Kinsale from Cork, overlooking marina. ◊

The Spaniard Inn

Kinsale
RESTAURANT•CHARACTER PUB

Scilly Kinsale Co Cork **Tel: 021 477 2436**
info@thespaniard.ie www.thespaniard.ie

Who could fail to be charmed by The Spaniard, that characterful and friendly old pub perched high up above Scilly? Although probably best known for music (nightly), it offers bar food all year round and there's a restaurant in season. The popular traditional fare (Spaniard seafood chowder, smoked salmon platter, Oysterhaven mussels and oysters, beef & Guinness pie), for which The Spaniard is well known, is served informally in the bar alongside more contemporary dishes. Evening meals in the restaurant - which has its own separate bar - are more extensive. Live traditional music, Mon/Wed/Sat. Bar meals: L 12.30-3 (to 5.30 Fri/Sat/Sun); Restaurant D: 6-10 (from 6.30, Sun). Early D, €25 6-7pm. House wine, €20. Closed 25 Dec & Good Fri, (restaurant also closes 2 weeks Nov & Jan). Amex, MasterCard, Visa, Laser. **Directions:** At Scilly, about 0.5 kilometre south-east of Kinsale, overlooking the town.

The Spinnaker Restaurant & Bar

Kinsale
Bar/Restaurant

Scilly Kinsale Co Cork **Tel: 021 477 2098**
relax@harbourlodge.com

For those with long memories this well-known waterfront restaurant will always be associated with Heidi MacNeice, the colourful former owner who was once married to the poet Louis MacNeice. It's seen a few changes since then, and is now in common ownership with the Tiernans' Harbour Lodge, next door. It's a pleasingly traditional restaurant on three levels with a popular bar above at the back, and claims, probably quite rightly, to have the best views of any restaurant in Kinsale. With a lot of wood, Giles Norman photographs on the walls and old-style wooden tables with linen cloths and napkins and a fresh flower and nightlight on each table, it's a pleasant place to be. Chef Bernard Kronwald (formerly of Oz-Haven at Oysterhaven) offers a short early dinner menu which is good value at €25, but the later à la carte - which has an emphasis on locally sourced steaks and seafood - offers more appealing choices including lobster (served thermidor, Americaine or plain with butter) at €8 per 100g, and, perhaps, a special seafood platter offering a half lobster, oysters, prawns and mussels. The ubiquitous tiger prawn does make an appearance (and, at €24.95, an overpriced one at that) but for the most part this is good quality seafood, sourced locally and well cooked. Service is friendly, although staff can come under pressure as the restaurant gets busy. All round however, you'll find good food in very attractive surroundings here, if you're prepared to pay a little extra – and it is rapidly taking its place again, among Kinsale's best-liked restaurants. **Seats 110**; reservations recommended; children welcome. D Tue-Fri 5-10pm; Sat all day 12-10pm; early bird D €25, 5-7pm; house wine €19.95. Closed Sun, Mon; 23 Dec - 7 Jan. MasterCard, Visa, Laser **Directions:** Scilly waterfront: 1km (0.5 mile) from town centre, beside Harbour Lodge Guesthouse.

Kinsale
RESTAURANT

Toddies Restaurant

Kinsale Brewery The Glen Kinsale Co Cork **Tel: 021 477 7769**
toddies@eircom.net www.toddieskinsale.com

Pearse and Mary O'Sullivan's bustling downtown restaurant and bar is named after Pearse's grandfather, Toddie O'Sullivan, who was a legendary figure in Irish hospitality. The address may give the impression that it is 'out of town' but if you walk down Pearse Street (away from the harbour) and turn right at the T junction, you'll see their sign across the road, outside a fine limestone archway. It's above the Kinsale Brewery, with whom there is a strong working relationship as they pump their Kinsale lager, wheat beer and stout directly up to Toddies bar. From the courtyard, exterior stairs lead up to the restaurant, pausing at a large and stylish al fresco dining area provided by two terraces before arrival at the bar and a smart split-level dining room. It's an exciting place, and there's a growing fan club who love not only Pearse's fine modern Irish cooking, but also the inside-or-out table arrangements, great service by Mary and her bubbly staff, and the whole atmosphere of the place. Seafood is, of course, the star and fresh lobster risotto is one of many speciality dishes that had already established Toddies as a leading restaurant in the area - but Pearse's high regard for local meats (and many other local products, including West Cork cheeses), ensures a balanced choice. Toddies was our Atmospheric Restaurant of the Year in 2006 and many would cite it as their favourite Kinsale restaurant. **Seats 36** (terrace, 60); children welcome. D Tue-Sat 5-10.30pm (from 6.30 Sat & Sun). Gourmet menu €50, also à la carte. House wine from €25.50. SC 10% on groups 10+. Closed Mon, mid Jan- mid Feb. *Guests can eat at the bar, or in the restaurant. MasterCard, Visa, Laser. **Directions:** Drive to the end of Pearse St., take right turn, Toddies is second on the left through limestone arch and into courtyard.

Kinsale
HOTEL

Trident Hotel

Worlds End Kinsale Co Cork **Tel: 021 477 9300**
info@tridenthotel.com www.tridenthotel.com

This blocky, zinc-and-wood fronted waterside hotel enjoys the best location in town and, under the watchful management of Hal McElroy, has long been a well-run, hospitable and comfortable place to stay. Recent development has now seen major changes, including - most importantly from the guest comfort point of view - the addition of 30 new front-facing executive rooms, all with king-size beds and air conditioning as standard, and separate bath and shower. Older bedrooms are also fairly spacious and comfortable, with phone, TV and tea/coffee trays (iron and board available on request), and small but adequate bathrooms. The genuinely pubby Wharf Tavern is unchanged, and remains one of the town's most popular good meeting places. *Actons Hotel has recently come into common ownership. Conference/banqueting (220/200); video-conferencing on request. Sauna, gym, steam room, jacuzzi. Children welcome (under 3 free in parents room, cot available without charge, baby sitting arranged). No pets. Lift. Rooms 75 (2 suites, 2 wheelchair accessible). B&B about €95 pps, ss €33; no SC. **Pier One:** The restaurant, which has been refurbished and re-named, is well-located on the first floor with views over the harbour, which also makes it an exceptionally pleasant room for breakfast. The food is good and especially welcome in winter, when many of the smaller restaurants are closed. **Seats 80** (private room, 40); toilets wheelchair accessible. D daily, 7-9.30pm, L Sun only 1- 2.30. Set Sun L about €23; Set D about €28, D also à la carte; Bistro menu avail 4-9; Bar Menu 12-9. House wine from €19. SC discretionary. Amex, MasterCard, Visa, Laser. **Directions:** Take the R600 from Cork to Kinsale - the hotel is at the end of the Pier Road.

The Bulman

Kinsale Area
BAR•RESTAURANT

Summercove Kinsale Co Cork **Tel: 021 477 2131**
info@thebulman.com www.thebulman.com

Uniquely situated on the outskirts of Kinsale, near Charles Fort - it looks across towards the town and has a sunny western aspect - The Bulman is a characterful maritime bar. It's a great place to be in fine weather, when you can wander out to the seafront and sit on the wall beside the carpark, and it's cosy in winter when you can sip local beer from the Kinsale Brewery beside the fire in the downstairs bar. The first floor restaurant specialises in seafood, much of it locally caught, and possibly including less usual fish like sea bream. Portions are generous and you may wish the Asian/Mediterranean style could be a little simpler, but the overall dining experience should be enjoyable. **Restaurant: seats 54**; not suitable for children under 12; toilets wheelchair accessible, restaurant upstairs isn't. L Tue-Sun, 12.30-3pm, (Sun 1-4pm), D Tue-Sat, 6-9.30pm; set D €26.95, also a la carte; house wine about €20. Bar food also available Mon-Sat, 12.30-3pm. Own carpark. Restaurant closed D Sun, Mon (& Tues off season). Amex, MasterCard, Visa, Laser. **Directions:** Beside Charles Fort, short distance from Kinsale.

Carlton Kinsale Hotel & Spa

Kinsale Area
HOTEL

Rathmore Road Kinsale Co Cork **Tel: 021 470 6000**
info@carltonkinsalehotel.com www.carltonkinsalehotel.com

Entering through woodland down a narrow winding driveway with occasional passing places, first-time guests get no hint of what lies ahead and, even on arrival at set-down (and a rather confusing parking arrangement), the hotel presents an inscrutable, blocky exterior. But, on entering the lofty foyer backed by a wall of glass - all is revealed, as you catch your first view through to the sea beyond; and, when drawn over to the doors that open out on to a large decking area, even the weariest or most curmudgeonly check-in could hardly fail to be won over (on a fine day at least) by the beauty of Oysterhaven Bay. Although many will feel that the hotel itself does little to enhance its surroundings, it is well-designed to ensure that guests get the maximum benefit when looking out; the bright décor (intended to echo the colourful West Cork streetscapes perhaps?) won't be to everyone's taste, but it should be easy to let that go, as the view is the main focus in all of the public areas, including the aptly named Oysterhaven View restaurant on the second floor. Accommodation, in more restful tones, includes suites, sea view rooms and deluxe rooms, the latter overlooking gardens, and with doors opening on to private terraces to compensate for the lack of a view; all rooms are very comfortably furnished, with all the usual amenities, and separate bath and shower, although oddly for a new hotel, most rooms have only standard 4' 6" double beds. The hotel's C Spa, plus swimming pool, sauna and gym among other leisure facilities, will make this a popular short break destination, especially off-season, and there is a regular complimetary bus for transfers to Kinsale. **Rooms 70** (2 suites, 34 executive, 20 family rooms, 24 ground floor, 6 for disabled); children welcome (under 3s free in parents room, baby sitting arranged, cot available); free broadband WI/FI. Spa, leisure centre with 'pool, fitness room, garden. Lift; 24 hr room service; B&B €96 pps, ss €55. Closed 23-27 Dec. Helipad. **Directions:** 5km from Kinsale town centre.

Glebe Country House

Kinsale Area
COUNTRY HOUSE

Ballinadee nr Kinsale Bandon Co Cork **Tel: 021 477 8294**
info@glebecountryhouse.com www.glebecountryhouse.com

Set in two acres of beautiful, well-tended gardens (including a productive kitchen garden), this charming old rectory near Kinsale has a lovely wisteria at the front door and it is a place full of interest. The building dates back to 1690 (Church records provide interesting details: it was built for £250; repairs and alterations followed at various dates, and the present house was completed in 1857 at a cost of £1,160). More recently, under the hospitable ownership of Gill Good, this classically proportioned house has been providing a restful retreat for guests since 1989, and everybody loves it for its genuine country house feeling and relaxing atmosphere. Spacious reception rooms have the feeling of a large family home, and generous, stylishly decorated bedrooms have good bathrooms, phones and tea/coffee making facilities. The Rose Room, on the ground floor, has French doors to the garden. Dinner is not currently offered, but breakfasts are very enjoyable, and this can be a hard place to drag yourself away from in the morning although there are many things to do nearby, including golf, and it is well placed for exploring the area. The whole house may be rented by parties by arrangement and several self-catering apartments are also available. **Rooms 4** (2 shower only, all no-smoking); children welcome (under 10s free in parents' room, cots available without charge, baby sitting arranged.); B&B €55 pps, ss €15. Residents D to end in 2008. Pets permitted (stay in bedroom). Closed Christmas. Diners, MasterCard, Visa, Laser. **Directions:** Take N71 west from Cork to Innishannon Bridge, follow signs for Ballinadee 9km (6 miles). After village sign, veer left, 2nd on the right.

Macroom
HOTEL

The Castle Hotel & Leisure Centre

Main Street Macroom Co Cork **Tel: 026 41074**
castlehotel@eircom.net www.castlehotel.ie

In the ownership of the Buckley family since 1952, this well-managed hotel is ideally located for touring the scenic south-west and is equally attractive to business and leisure guests. Recent developments have added superior executive bedrooms and suites, an extensive new foyer and reception area, an impressive new bar and the more contemporary **'B's' Restaurant**. Extensive leisure facilities include a fine swimming pool (with children's pool, spa and massage pool), steam room, solarium and gym. Special breaks are offered, including golf specials (tee times reserved at Macroom's 18-hole course). Friendly staff take pride in making guests feel at home. Conference/banqueting (150); broadband wi/fi. **Rooms 60** (2 suites, 30 executive, 3 family, 4 disabled, 30 no smoking); children welcome (under 4s free in parents' room, cots available without charge; playroom; baby sitting arranged). B&B €75 pps; SS €25. No pets. Food available 9.30am-9pm. ('B's' Restaurant 12-3 & 6-8.45; 'Next Door Cafe Atilde' 9.30-5.30; bar food 12-9.30) Closed 24-28 Dec. Amex, MasterCard, Visa, Laser. **Directions:** On N22, midway between Cork & Killarney.

Macroom
BAR•RESTAURANT

The Mills Inn

Ballyvourney Macroom Co Cork **Tel: 026 45237**•
millinn@eircom.net www.millinn.ie

One of Ireland's oldest inns, The Mills Inn is in a Gaeltacht (Irish-speaking) area and dates back to 1755. It was traditionally used to break the journey from Cork to Killarney - and still makes a great stopping place as the food is good and freshly cooked all day - but is now clearly popular with locals as well as travellers. New owners took over in 2003 and they have continued to develop the premises ever since, while retaining its old-world charm and a genuine sense of hospitality. An atmospheric barn has been converted for use at busy times and for local events and, at the time of the Guide's 2008 visit, a large deli/wine & gift shop was about to open in old buildings alongside the inn. Accommodation is also offered; comfortable rooms have a strong sense of style. **Rooms 13** (some shower only, 1 for disabled). B&B €50pps, no ss. Amex, Diners, MasterCard, Visa, Laser. **Directions:** On N22, 20 minutes from Killarney. ◈

MALLOW

A century ago, Mallow was renowned as a spa, and is the oldest recorded warm spring in Ireland, discovered in 1724. Today this flourishing market centre is the largest town along the Blackwater Valley, and the nearby Doneraile Wildlife Park (022 24244), which includes 166 hectares of 18th century landscaped park in the 'Capability Brown Style', is a popular place for visitors. In the centre of the town, **The Hibernian Hotel** (Main Street; 022 58200; www.hibernianhotelmallow.com) is full of character and the hub of local activities and its traditional coffee shop, the **Coffee Dock**, is the place where everyone meets – a great contrast to new arrival **URRU** (Bank Place; 022 53292; www.urru.ie). This younger sister to the Bandon original (see entry) is tucked into a small courtyard just off the main street and this gem of a place is run on the same lines - bright and busy, it's a mix of all good things: fresh local foods, excellent coffees, olive oils, spices, a small kitchen equipment section, good quality book section, quality wines... and there are a few tables to relax and have coffee along with some excellent snacks. And a farmers' market is now held in the town every second Saturday, making it a newly foodie destination.

WWW.IRELAND-GUIDE.COM FOR ALL THE BEST PLACES TO EAT, DRINK & STAY

Mallow
RESTAURANT•COUNTRY HOUSE

Longueville House Hotel

Mallow Co Cork **Tel: 022 47156**
info@longuevillehouse.ie www.longuevillehouse.ie

FOOD EXTRA AWARD

When Michael and Jane O'Callaghan opened Longueville House to guests in 1967, it was one of the first Irish country houses to do so - and, today, it is one of Ireland's finest country house hotels. Its history is wonderfully romantic, "the history of Ireland in miniature", and it is a story with a happy ending: having lost their lands in the Cromwellian Confiscation (1652-57), the O'Callaghans took up ownership again some 300 years later. The present house, a particularly elegant Georgian mansion of pleasingly human proportions, dates from 1720, (with wings added in 1800 and the lovely Turner conservatory - which has been completely renovated - in 1862), and overlooks the ruins of their original home, Dromineen Castle. Very much a family enterprise, Longueville is now run by Michael and Jane's son William O'Callaghan, who is the chef, and his wife Aisling, who manages front of house. The location, overlooking the famous River Blackwater, is lovely. The river, farm and garden supply fresh salmon in season, the famous Longueville lamb, and all the fruit and vegetables. In years when the weather is kind, the estate's crowning glory is their own house wine, a light refreshing white, "Coisreal Longueville" - wine has always been Michael O'Callaghan's great love, and he now uses their abundant apple supply to make apple brandy too. Public rooms include a bar and drawing room, both elegantly furnished with beautiful fabrics and family antiques, and accommodation is equally sumptuous; although - as is usual with old houses - bedrooms vary according to their position, they are generally spacious, superbly comfortable and stylishly decorated to the highest standards. Dining here is always a treat (see below) and breakfast is also very special, offering a wonderful array of local and home-cooked foods, both from the buffet and cooked to order; Longueville was the National Winner of our Irish Breakfast Awards in 2003, and it's worth calling in even if you can't stay overnight - what a way to break a journey! (And the light lunch offered in the bar is ideal for travellers too.) As well as being one of the finest leisure destinations in the country, the large cellar/basement area of the house has been developed as a conference centre, with back-up services available. The house is also available for small residential weddings throughout the year. Conference/banqueting (50/120), secretarial services, free broadband wi/fi. Children welcome (under 2s free in parents' room, cot available free of charge, baby sitting arranged). Dogs permitted staying in outhouse/kennel. Garden, walking, hunting/shooting, fly fishing, clay pigeon shooting. Equestrian, golf and garden visits nearby. (Shooting weekends available in winter; telephone for details). **Rooms 20.** (6 junior suites, 1 superior, 3 family, 2 single, 2 shower only; all no-smoking). B&B €110 single room, from €235 - €360 for a double. Closed early Jan-mid Mar. **Presidents Restaurant:** Named after the family collection of specially commissioned portraits of all Ireland's past presidents (which made for a seriously masculine collection until Ireland's first woman president, Mary Robinson, broke the pattern) this is the main dining room and opens into the beautifully renovated Turner conservatory, which makes a wonderfully romantic setting in candlelight; there is a smaller room alongside the main restaurant, and also The Chinese Room, which is suitable for private parties. William O'Callaghan is an accomplished chef, and home- or locally-produced food is at the heart of all his cooking, in starters like house-smoked salmon, or salad of crab with dry-cured Longueville ham; main courses of Longueville lamb and home-reared pork – and, perhaps, wild rabbit; and a dessert trolley offers treats such as a croustade of caramelised apple with Longueville apple brandy ice cream - and it is hard to resist the local farmhouse cheeses. Delicious home-made chocolates and petits fours come with the coffee and as elsewhere in the house service, under Aisling O'Callaghan's direction, is outstanding. The shorter, simpler menus offered recently allow William more direct control in the kitchen - an improvement which has made for a more intimate, and even more enjoyable dining experience. A fine wine list offering many treats has particular strength in the classic French regions and includes a half a dozen champagnes, and a good choice of dessert wines and half bottles; it includes many wines imported directly by Michael O'Callaghan. **Seats 84** (private room 12). D daily, 6.30-9; children welcome (high chair, childrens menu). Set 2/3 course D €40/60, Menu Gourmand €85; light meals 12.30-5 daily; house wine €30, SC 10% added to parties of 8+. Mon & Tue in Nov and early Dec/Mar/Apr. House closed early Jan - mid Mar. Amex, MasterCard, Visa, Laser. **Directions:** 5km (3 m) west of Mallow via N72 to Killarney.

MIDLETON

Midleton is a busy market town and home of The Jameson Experience Midleton at the famous distillery (021 461 3594; www.whiskeytours.ie); here you can find out all you every wanted to know about Irish whiskey, and get a bite to eat at **The Malt House@The Jameson Experience** too, a place that's attracting local people as well as visitors. The first choice for accommodation in the town centre is **Midleton Park Hotel & Spa** (021 463 5100; www.mildletonpark.com), with all facilities, and food lovers will enjoy the Farmers' Market on Saturday mornings (one of the best in the country). Demand for daytime food in this busy shopping town is reflected in the number of restaurants offering good daytime menus, including the atmospheric **Le Bistro** (021 4638000) on Distillery Walk. Midleton is well-placed for visiting Cork city, and also exploring the whole of East Cork, including Cobh (last port of call for the Titanic), Fota Wildlife Park, Gardens & Arboretum (021 481 5543) and Youghal, famed for its connections with Sir Walter Raleigh. The pretty fishing village of Ballycotton merits a visit, and offers good coastal walking. Other gardens of note in the area include Cedar Lodge (Midleton, 021 461 3379). Ballymaloe Cookery School Gardens (Shanagarry, 021 464 6785), Lakemount Garden (Glanmire, 021 482 1052) and Ballyvolane House (Fermoy, 025 36349). Golfers should enjoy the championship course at nearby Fota Island Golf Club (Carrigtwohill, 021 488 3710).
WWW.IRELAND-GUIDE.COM FOR ALL THE BEST PLACES TO EAT, DRINK & STAY

Midleton
RESTAURANT

Farmgate

The Coolbawn Midleton Co Cork
Tel: 021 463 2771

This unique shop and restaurant has been drawing people to Midleton in growing numbers since 1985 and it's a great credit to sisters Maróg O'Brien and Kay Harte. Kay now runs the younger version at the English Market in Cork (see entry), while Maróg looks after Midleton. The shop at the front is full of wonderful local produce - organic fruit and vegetables, cheeses, honey - and their own super home baking, while the evocatively decorated, comfortable restaurant at the back, with its old pine furniture and modern sculpture, is regularly transformed from bustling daytime café to sophisticated evening restaurant (on Friday and Saturday) complete with string quartet. A tempting display of fresh home bakes is the first thing to catch your eye on entering and, as would be expected from the fresh produce on sale in the shop, wholesome vegetables and salads are always irresistible too. Maróg O'Brien is a founder and stall holder of the hugely successful Midleton Farmers' Market, which is held on Saturday mornings. *Farmgate was the winner of our Natural Food Award in 2007. **Seats 70** (outdoors, 30; private room, 30); children welcome. Open Mon-Sat, 9-5pm, L 12-3.30, D Thu-Sat, 6.30 - 9.30pm. Closed Sun, Bank Hols, 24 Dec-3 Jan. MasterCard, Visa, Laser. **Directions:** Town centre.

Midleton
BAR•RESTAURANT

Finíns

75 Main Street Midleton Co Cork
Tel: 021 463 1878

Finín O'Sullivan's thriving bar and restaurant in the centre of the town has long been a popular place for locals to meet for a drink and to eat some good wholesome food. The entrance is bright and cheery, painted in pillarbox red and white, and the theme is continued inside, where black topped tables are simply set up with the basics needed for a meal. This attractive, no-nonsense place offers a wide range of popular home-made dishes, mostly based on local produce notably fresh seafood from Ballycotton and harbour steaks, also old favourites like a well-made Irish Stew; evening menus are more extensive and include some more specialities including roast duckling. Good short wine list. Bar food available Mon-Sat 10.30am-10pm, specials available noon-6.30pm; Restaurant D Mon-Sat, 5-10pm. Bar menu à la carte; set D €40. House wine €18. Closed Sun, bank hols. **Directions:** Town centre.

Midleton
COUNTRY HOUSE

Loughcarrig House

Midleton Co Cork **Tel: 021 463 1952**
info@loughcarrig.com www.loughcarrig.com

Bird-watching and sea angling are major interests at Brian and Cheryl Byrne's relaxed and quietly situated country house, which is in a beautiful shore-side location. Comfortable rooms have tea/coffee making facilities and there's a pleasantly hospitable atmosphere. **Rooms 4** (all en-suite. shower only & no smoking); children welcome (under 2s free in parents' room); pets permitted by arrangement. Sea fishing, walking, Garden. Closed 16 Dec-16 Jan. B&B €40 pps, ss €10. SC discretionary. **No Credit Cards**. **Directions:** From roundabout at Midleton on N25, take Whitegate Road for 3.25km (2 m).

Midleton
RESTAURANT

O'Donovan's
58 Main Street Midleton Co Cork
Tel: 021 4631255

An attractive limestone-fronted building on the main street, Pat O'Donovan's highly-regarded restaurant blends traditional and modern decor - some features have been retained from its previous use as a pub, tables are elegantly set up with classic white linen tablecloths and napkins, and original modern oil paintings adorn the walls. But the most interesting feature is the hand-written mouthwateringly promising menu which, with a choice of 10 starters, and 7 main courses and desserts, offers a varied and adventurous meal and excellent value. Nothing but the best ingredients are allowed in this kitchen, and they are locally sourced where possible - fish comes from Ballycotton, mussels from Rossmore and scallops (when available) from Castletownbere. The cooking is excellent, and some dishes enjoyed on a recent visit will give the flavour - penne with wild mushroom and bacon to start, followed by a main course of salmon wrapped with Parma ham and a delicious dessert of clafoutis with ice cream: all perfectly cooked, well presented and full of flavour. Efficient, informative staff ensure that guests will enjoy their meal to the full, and a good wine list includes some interesting, unusual wines, and a fair choice of half bottles. An early dinner menu offers outstanding value at about €25 for three courses. **Seats 60**. D Tue-Sat, 5-9pm (from 6pm Sat). A la Carte; house wine about €21. Closed Sun, Mon. MasterCard, Visa, Laser. **Directions:** Travelling eastwards, at eastern end of Main Street, on right-hand side - opposite entrance to Midleton Distillery. ◇

Midleton
RESTAURANT

Raymond's Restaurant
Distillery Walk Midleton Co Cork **Tel: 021 463 5235**
raymondsrestaurant@eircom.net

Attractively situated on the quieter short stretch of road leading up to the gates of the Old Midleton Distillery, and opposite the river and a small park, this smart modern restaurant is an appealing place and especially convenient for visitors to the distillery. Raymond Whyte is originally from the area and, working now with head chef Stephen Lee (formerly at Jacobs on the Mall and Bayview Hotel Ballycotton), the style is broadly French/Mediterranean, although pride is taken in sourcing local produce for the kitchen, including seafood from Ballycotton, and meats from local farms. A good choice of about seven starters and main courses is offered on set menus (the early dinner is particularly good value), with an à la carte also offered at both lunch and dinner. All the usual bases are covered well – Caesar salad, steaks, pasta dishes – but there is much else beside, including the house speciality, Trio of Seafood – a grilled selection of three market day fish with red pepper sauce and lemon beurre blanc. Except for the possible annoyance of a tannoy system playing 'Happy Birthday' and 'Congratulations' to celebrating groups, this should be an enjoyable dining experience, offering good food and service in attractive surroundings. **Seats 55**; children welcome before 6.30pm (high chair, childrens menu); reservations recommended; L served daily, 12-3pm, D served Tue-Sat, 5-10pm; open all day Sun, 12-9pm. Early bird D, €28, 5.30-7pm; then a la carte; house wine €20. Closed Mon D & Bank Hol Mons. Amex, MasterCard, Visa, Laser. **Directions:** On Distillery Walk.

Midleton Area
RESTAURANT•GUESTHOUSE

Ballymaloe House
Shanagarry Midleton Co Cork **Tel: 021 465 2531**
res@ballymaloe.ie www.ballymaloe.com

Ireland's most famous country house, Ballymaloe was one of the first to open its doors to guests when Myrtle and her husband, the late Ivan Allen, opened The Yeats Room restaurant in 1964. Accommodation followed in 1967 and since then a unique network of family enterprises has developed around Ballymaloe House - including not only the farmlands and gardens that supply so much of the kitchen produce, but also a craft and kitchenware shop, a company producing chutneys and sauce, the Crawford Gallery Café in Cork city, and

Darina Allen's internationally acclaimed cookery school. Yet, despite the fame, Ballymaloe is still most remarkable for its unspoilt charm: Myrtle - now rightly receiving international recognition for a lifetime's work "recapturing forgotten flavours, and preserving those that may soon die"- is ably assisted by her children, and now their families too. The house, modestly described as "a large family farmhouse", is indeed at the centre of the family's 400 acre farm, but with over thirty bedrooms it is a very large house indeed, and one with a gracious nature. The intensely restorative atmosphere of Ballymaloe is remarkable and, although there are those who would say that the cooking is 'too homely', there are few greater pleasures than a fine Ballymaloe dinner followed by a good night's sleep in one of their thoughtfully furnished country bedrooms - including, incidentally, Ireland's most ancient hotel room which is in the Gate House: a tiny one up (twin bedroom, with little iron beds) and one down (full bathroom and entrance foyer), in the original medieval wall of the old house: delightful and highly romantic! Ground floor courtyard rooms are suitable for wheelchairs. Conferences/banqueting (60/120). Children welcome (cot available; baby sitting arranged). Pets allowed by arrangement. Outdoor swimming pool, tennis, walking, golf (nearby). Gardens. Shop. **Rooms 33** (5 ground floor, 1 single, 3 family, 1 disabled, 2 shower only, all no smoking). B&B €140pps, ss €60. SC discretionary. Room service (limited hours). No lift. Self-catering accommodation also available (details from Hazel Allen). **Restaurant:** The restaurant is in a series of domestic-sized dining rooms and guests are called to their tables from the conservatory or drawing room, where aperitifs are served. A food philosophy centred on using only the highest quality ingredients is central to everything done at Ballymaloe, where much of the produce comes from their own farm and gardens, and the rest comes from leading local producers. Jason Fahey has been head chef at Ballymaloe since 2004 and continues the house tradition of presenting simple, uncomplicated food in the 'good country cooking' style, which allows the exceptional quality of the ingredients to speak for themselves. This is seen particularly at Sunday lunchtime when - apart from the huge range of dishes offered, - the homely roasts and delicious vegetables are as near to home cooking you are ever likely to find in a restaurant, and what a joy that is. Then things move up a number of notches in the evening, when daily 7-course dinner menus, offer more sophisticated dishes, including vegetarian options, but there is still a refreshing homeliness to the tone which, despite very professional cooking and service, is perhaps more like a dinner party than a smart restaurant experience. Ballymaloe brown bread, French peasant soup, a selection of their own patés and terrines served with brioche and home-made chutney, grilled Ballycotton cod with prawns, sauce beurre blanc & garden sea kale, Irish farmhouse cheeses with home-made biscuits and an irresistible dessert trolley that includes country sweets like rhubarb compôte, and home-made vanilla ice cream are typical of simple dishes that invariably delight. The teamwork at Ballymaloe is outstanding and a meal here is a treat of the highest order. Finish with coffee or tea and home-made petits fours, served in the drawing room - before retiring contentedly to bed. And, then there is the wine: not only will wine lovers find Sommelier Colm McCan's list very interesting - but, at the time of going to press, work was in progress to develop a new wine cellar beside the Gate House; space previously used for storage is in a rocky area where the ambient temperature is naturally ideal and the rocky outcrops make for an authentic cellar atmosphere. And guests are to be encouraged to visit the cellar - yet another string to the amazing Ballymaloe bow. Children welcome at lunchtime, but the restaurant is not suitable for children under 7 after 7pm. (Children's high tea is served at 5.30.) Buffet meals only on Sundays. **Seats 110**; L daily 1-1.30pm, D daily 7-9.30pm (Sun 7.30-8.30pm); set D €70, set L €40; house wine from €24. Service discretionary. Reservations essential. House closed 23-26 Dec, 2 weeks Jan. Helipad. *Self Catering Accommodation also available. Amex, Diners, MasterCard, Visa, Laser. **Directions:** Take signs to Ballycotton from N 25. Situated between Cloyne & Shanagarry.

Midleton Area
CAFÉ

Ballymaloe Shop Café

Ballymaloe House Shanagarry Co Cork **Tel: 021 465 2032**
ballymaloeshop@eircom.net

At the back of Wendy Whelan's magnificent crafts, kitchenware and gift shop at Ballymaloe House, there is a delightful family-run café selling wholesome home-bakes and just the kind of light, nourishing fare that is needed to sustain you through a shopping expedition that may well be taking longer than you had planned. So take the weight off your feet, settle down with an aromatic cup of coffee or a glass of wine, or home-made lemonade - and a taste of this delicious home cooking. A simple menu of salads, light lunches, cakes and biscuits is offered - savoury bakes like goat's cheese, potato & mint tart, perhaps, and sweet treats such as chocolate tart, and pistachio macaroons. Everything is based on locally sourced fresh ingredients as far as possible, including smoked seafood from Frank Hederman in Cobh, local organic salads, Bill Casey's Shanagarry smoked salmon, and Gubbeen smoked bacon. *Wendy has a charming self-catering cottage, Rockcliffe House, in Ballycotton; details from the shop. Open 10-5 daily, L 12.30-4. House wine €4.90 per glass. Closed 23-27 Dec. Amex, MasterCard, Visa, Laser. **Directions:** 3.5km (2 m) beyond Cloyne on Ballycotton road.

Barnabrow Country House

Midleton Area
COUNTRY HOUSE●RESTAURANT

Barnabrow Midleton Co Cork **Tel: 021 465 2534**
barnabrow@eircom.net www.barnabrowhouse.ie

Geraldine Kidd's sensitively converted seventeenth century house has stunning views of Ballycotton, and the decor is commendably restrained. Innovative African wooden furniture is a point of interest and spacious, comfortable bedrooms are stylishly decorated. Some charming country bedrooms are in outbuildings at the back of the house, and a good breakfast is served in the main dining room, at a communal table. Derek Stewart has been cooking at the Trinity Rooms Restaurant since 2005 and continues the philosophy and cooking style that has earned it a fine reputation. Barnabrow caters exceptionally well for weddings (for which there is great demand) and other functions (up to 150) as well as normal private dining. Conference/banqueting (60/150); broadband wi/fi. **Rooms 19** (17 shower only, 2 family, all no smoking); children welcome (under 1s free in parents' room, cots available, free of charge, baby sitting arranged). Pets permitted in some areas. B&B €80pps, ss €25. D 7-9 Thu-Sun, L Sun Only 1-2.30; D à la carte; set Sun L €27; set 3 course D €50. House wine from €22; service discretionary (10% on parties of 10+). Restaurant closed Mon-Wed; house closed 23-27 Dec. Diners, MasterCard, Visa, Laser. **Directions:** From Cork N25 to Midleton roundabout, right for Ballinacurra, left for Cloyne, then on to Ballycotton road for 1.5 miles.

Wisteria Restaurant

Midleton Area
RESTAURANT
Ⓝ

Rock Street Cloyne Co Cork
Tel: 021 465 1444

Colm Falvey is a well respected chef in East Cork, and this friendly and welcoming restaurant is his latest venture, in premises on the main street of this historic village. Simple, but attractive and modern, the room has pale wood panelling to dado height and features modern painting and a striking wisteria mural. Well-spaced tables are set up with good quality cutlery, paper napkins and a single flower – and off-white wooden chairs (with cushions) are comfortable. A three-course early dinner offers great value with a choice of four dishes per course, while the à la carte (which, sensibly, is not too extensive) has some extra enticing dishes on each course, with vegetarian options - such as a starter of Ardsallagh goat's cheese salad with roast hazelnuts, or main course asparagus pea & fresh coriander risotto - included. A very high standard of cooking showcases ingredients of the highest quality, and mostly locally sourced: an excellent Ballycotton seafood chowder features among the starters, for example, and you may also find main courses such as fillet of hake with fresh crab & herb crust and beurre blanc sauce, and the meats that are so good in this area – a sirloin steak with chargrilled auberines & béarnaise sauce, for example, or roast rack of lamb with a plum tomato & fresh mint fondue. More-ish desserts could include almond meringue with a chocolate rum cream – and there's a farmhouse cheese selection. A concise, well-selected wine list offers a choice of about 24 mostly European wines. Service, under Kathy Falvey's direction, is friendly, efficient and attentive – all round, a very pleasing dining experience. **Seats 30**; children welcome (high chair, childrens menu); toilets wheelchair accessible. D Tue-Sun, 5-9pm (to 8.30pm Sun); early bird D €27.50, 5-7.30pm; also a la carte. House wine €18.50. Closed Mon. MasterCard, Visa, Laser. **Directions:** From Cork, in centre of village after left turn for Ballycotton, on right hand side.

O'Callaghan's Delicatessen, Bakery & Café

Mitchelstown
CAFÉ
Ⓥ Ⓡ

19/20 Lower Cork Street Mitchelstown Co Cork **Tel: 025 24657**
ocalhansdeli@eircom.net www.ocallaghans.ie

The ideal place to break a journey, O'Callaghans have an impressive deli and bakery as well as tasty fare for a snack or full meal in the café. This is the place to stock up with delicious home-baked breads and cakes, home-made jams and chutneys - and, best of all perhaps, there's a range of home-made frozen meals. They do a range of seasonal specialities too, including wedding confectionery and Christmas treats, made to order. There's also a great home-made gluten free range, offering everything from soda breads, to sweet and savoury tarts. For smokers, and anyone who prefers to eat out of doors, there is a sun deck which has a covered area. To avoid the busy main street, park around the corner on the road to the creamery - or, coming from Dublin, parking is also available on the new square (on right after second set of lights); but remember the square is not available for parking on Thursday - market day. **Seats 140** (outdoor 20). Food served Mon-Sat, 8.30 am- 5 pm; L 12.30-5pm. Closed Sun, bank hols, 24-27 Dec. Amex, Diners, MasterCard, Visa, Laser. **Directions:** On main street, right side heading towards Dublin.

Monkstown
BAR•RESTAURANT•GUESTHOUSE

The Bosun

The Pier Monkstown Co Cork **Tel: 021 484 2172**
info@thebosun.ie www.thebosun.ie

Nicky and Patricia Moynihan's waterside establishment close to the both the car ferry across to Cobh and the Ringaskiddy ferries (France and Wales) has grown a lot over the years, with the restaurant and accommodation becoming increasingly important. Bar food is still taken seriously, however; although including kangaroo among the starters may seem odd (the air miles don't bear thinking about), seafood takes pride of place and afternoon/evening bar menus include everything from chowder or garlic mussels through to real Dingle Bay scampi and chips, although serious main courses for carnivores such as beef with brandy & peppercorn sauce are also available. Next to the bar, a well-appointed restaurant provides a more formal setting for wide-ranging table d'hote and à la carte menus - and also Sunday lunch, which is especially popular. Again seafood is the speciality, ranging from popular starters such as crab claws or oysters worked into imaginative dishes, and main courses that include steaks and Aylesbury duckling as well as seafood every which way, from grilled sole on the bone to medallions of marinated monkfish. There's always a choice for vegetarians, and vegetables are generous and carefully cooked. Finish with home-made ices, perhaps, or a selection of Irish farmhouse cheeses. **Restaurant Seats 80** (private room, 30, outdoors, 20); children welcome before 7pm (high chair, childrens menu, baby changing facilities); air conditioning; toilets wheelchair accessible. D daily 6.30-9, L Sun 12-2.30, Set D €45.50, Set Sun L €31.50; à la carte also available; house wine about €22, sc discretionary. Bar food available daily 12-9pm. Closed 25-26 Dec, Good Fri. **Accommodation:** Bedrooms are quite simple but have everything required (phone, TV, tea/coffee trays); those at the front have harbour views but are shower only, while those at the back are quieter and have the advantage of a full bathroom. Fota Island Golf Course is only 12 minutes away, also Fota House and Wildlife Centre. **Rooms 15** (9 shower only, all no smoking). Lift. B&B €60 pps, ss €10; children welcome (under 5s free in parents' room, cot available without charge). No pets. Closed 24-26 Dec, Good Friday. Amex, Diners, MasterCard, Visa, Laser. **Directions:** On sea front, beside the Cobh ferry and near Ringaskiddy port ferry.

Oysterhaven
RESTAURANT

Finders Inn

Nohoval Oysterhaven Co Cork **Tel: 021 477 0737**
www.findersinn.com

Very popular with local people (but perhaps harder for visitors to find), the McDonnell family's well-named old-world bar and restaurant is in a row of traditional cottages east of Oysterhaven, en route from Crosshaven to Kinsale. It can look uncared for from the road, but it's a very charming place, packed with antiques and, because of the nature of the building, broken up naturally into a number of dining areas. Seafood stars, of course - smoked salmon, Oysterhaven oysters, bisques, chowders, scallops and lobster are all here, but there are a few other specialities too, including steaks, lamb and tender crisp-skinned duckling, and the cooking, by Cormac McDonnell, is excellent. Good desserts, caring service under the supervision of brother, Donagh, and a great atmosphere - well worth taking the trouble to find. **Seats 90** (private room, 70). D Tue-Sun, 7-9.30pm; not suitable for children under 7, or older after 10 pm; toilets wheelchair accessible. L Sun only, 2-7pm. A la carte; sc discretionary. Closed Mon; Christmas week. MasterCard, Visa, Laser. **Directions:** From Cork, take Kinsale direction; at Carrigaline, go straight through main street then turn right, following R611 to Ballyfeard; about 700 metres beyond Ballyfeard, go straight for Nohoval (rather than bearing right on R611 for Belgooly). ◈

Rathcormac
CAFÉ
R

Posh Nosh

Riversdale Rathcormac Co Cork
Tel: 025 37595

This upmarket deli, specialist food shop and café is a good place to take a break on a journey, serving a good range of in-house home baking, salads and hot dishes of the day, also good coffee. And, if you'd like to stock up while you're here, the food shop sells quality French and Italian imports and Irish artisanal and speciality foods such as Ditty's biscuits, farmhouse cheeses and preserves, and local free range eggs. You can eat in or take away and the delicious hot meals to go are clearly popular with the locals. Open all day, Tue-Sat. **Directions:** Just through Rathcormac village, heading south towards Cork on N8 Dublin-Cork road; on side turning, facing Murphy's pub. ◈

Rosscarbery

HOTEL

Celtic Ross Hotel, Conference and Leisure Centre

Rosscarbery Co Cork **Tel: 023 48722**

reservations@celticross.com www.celticrosshotel.com

This modern hotel is close to the sea, overlooking Rosscarbery Bay (although not on the sea side of the road), and well placed as a base for touring west Cork; the facilities in the leisure centre offer alternative activities for family holidays if the weather should disappoint. It's an attractive building with an unusual tower feature containing a bog oak, which is quite dramatic; public areas are spacious, and the bedrooms - many of which have sea views - have all the usual facilities. However, although currently in the hands of a proactive management team who aim to raise and maintain standards, shortage of accommodation in the area means that this hotel is always busy, and a fair degree of wear and tear is to be expected. Conference/banqueting (150). **Rooms 66** (1 shower only, 3 for disabled, 10 no smoking); children welcome (under 4s free in parents' room, cots available free of charge, baby sitting arranged). No pets. Wheelchair access. Lift. B&B from about €55 to €110 pps, ss about €25. Self-catering available with use of hotel leisure facilities. Leisure centre (swimming pool, therapies). Short breaks brochure available. **Directions:** Take N71 from Cork City, 10 minutes drive west of Clonakilty. ◇

Rosscarbery

RESTAURANT

O'Callaghan-Walshe

The Square Rosscarbery Co Cork **Tel: 023 48125**

funfish@indigo.ie

Well off the busy main West Cork road, this unique restaurant is on the square of the old village of Rosscarbery and has a previous commercial history that's almost tangible. Exposed stone walls, old fishing nets and glass floats, mismatched furniture, shelves of wine bottles and candlelight all contribute to its unique atmosphere - which is well-matched by proprietor-host Sean Kearney's larger-than-life personality. Then there's the exceptional freshness and quality of the seafood - steaks theoretically share the billing, but West Cork seafood 'bought off the boats at auction' steals the scene. Martina O'Donovan's menus change daily but specialities to look out for include the famous Rosscarbery Pacific oysters, of course, also a superb West Cork Seafood Platter, char-grilled prime fish such as turbot, and grilled whole lobster. Ultra-freshness, attention to detail in breads and accompaniments - and a huge dose of personality - all add up to make this place a delight. An interesting wine list includes a good choice of half bottles. O'Callaghan-Walshe was the Guide's Atmospheric Restaurant of the Year for 2004. **Seats 40**; not suitable for children after 7 pm. D Tue-Sun 6.30-9.15. D à la carte, house wine about €20, sc discretionary. Closed Mon, open weekends only in winter (a phone call to check is advised). MasterCard, Visa, Laser. **Directions:** Main square in Rosscarbery village. ◇

Rosscarbery

CAFÉ

Pilgrim's Rest

The Square Rosscarbery Co Cork

Tel: 023 31796

A charming café just across the square from O'Callaghan-Walshe, The Pilgrim's Rest gives out all the right vibes (delicious Illy coffee and lovely home-bakes) and is well worth checking out for a journey break. Off-season menus are quite restricted - just coffee and cakes in winter - but there is much more choice of wholesome light meals in summer. Open 6 days in summer, Tue, 12-5pm, Wed-Sun, 10-5pm; more limited opening off season, please call ahead to confirm. Closed Mon. MasterCard, Visa. **Directions:** Off N71, on main square of Rosscarbery village.

Rosscarbery Area

B&B

De Barra Lodge

Tineel Rosscarbery Co Cork **Tel: 023 51948**

info@debarralodge.com www.debarralodge.com

Heading west into Rosscarbery, you'll see a cluster of signs to the right off the N71 just before the bridge – turn right here even if you haven't time to read them, as one of them is for Sinead and Dan

287

Barry's purpose built B&B, De Barra Lodge. It's a bit of a hike up the road to find it, but well worth-while as Sinead has a background in hotels and has planned the accommodation offered here with the greatest of care. It's quite a large property as you approach, but broken up attractively into two sections, one stone and the other rendered; the two are joined by a glazed entry section, which gives the whole heart of the house a bright and spacious atmosphere. In contrast to other places in the area, the style is subtle and low-key contemporary decor, with pleasing pale colours and clean-lined modern furnishings. Bedrooms and their en-suite bathrooms or shower rooms have every comfort, with all the little details that make a room easy to settle into when away from home – what you are effectively getting here is hotel standard accommodation at B&B prices. Breakfast is served in a very pleasing room, with an attractive rural outlook – and the Barrys are hospitable people who really want their guests to get the most from their stay. It would make a good base for touring West Cork and the only downside could be that it's too far to walk to the coast or Rosscarbery village – but it's only a short run by car, and Dan is happy to assist with lifts to and from restaurants in the village if necessary. **Rooms 5** (all en-suite, 3 shower only, all no smoking); children welcome (under 3s free in parents room, cot available free of charge, baby sitting arranged); no wheelchair access; free broadband wi/fi. No pets. B&B €35-45 pps, single €60. Closed Christmas (and call in advance off season). **No credit cards. Directions:** From Clonakilty (N71) entering Rosscarbery turn right before bridge, travel to T-junction and turn right, further 8km on right.

SCHULL

Internationally known as a sailing centre, the seaside town of Schull attracts visitors from far and wide. The town includes some excellent craft shops, traditional pubs and restaurants including the **Courtyard Foodstore and Café**, now run by Katarina Runshe (see Grove House) and **Jagres** (formerly Adèle's). Visitors can sample the best of local produce at the Schull farmers' market every Sunday morning. Schull is home to Gubbeen farmhouse where Giana Ferguson makes the award winning Gubbeen cheese and her son Fingal cures his own delicious smoked bacon and other delicacies. Local attractions include the Schull Planetarium (028 28552, open June to September), which gives a detailed reproduction of the sky at night. Visitors can go on boat trips to the islands of Cape Clear and Sherkin Island, and other local activities include golf, sea angling, windsurfing, horse riding and cycling.

Schull
GUESTHOUSE

Corthna Lodge Country House

Air Hill Schull Co Cork **Tel: 028 28517**
info@corthna-lodge.net www.corthna-lodge.net

Situated up the hill from Schull, commanding countryside and sea views, Martin and Andrea Mueller's roomy modern house just outside the town is one of the best located places to stay in the area. Although fairly compact, bedrooms are comfortable with good amenities, and there's plenty of space for guests to sit around and relax - both indoors, in a pleasant and comfortably furnished sitting room and outdoors, on a terrace overlooking the lovely garden towards the islands of Roaring Water Bay. House computer available for guests' internet access; unusually, there's also a gym, a hot tub, a barbecue area - and a putting green. **Rooms 6** (all shower only & no smoking); children over 5 welcome. B&B about €42.50-47.50 pps, ss €22.50, triple room €115-125. Closed 15 Oct-15 April. MasterCard, Visa, Laser. **Directions:** Through village, up hill, first left, first right - house is signposted.

Schull
RESTAURANT

Grove House

Colla Road Schull Co Cork **Tel: 028 28067**
katarinarunske@eircom.net www.grovehouseschull.com

Overlooking Schull Harbour, this beautifully restored period house offers quality, relaxed surroundings and great food just a few minutes walk from the main street, and is now run by Katarina Runske and her son Nico Runske, who has taken over as chef from her late mother Catherine Noren. The approach is still less than immaculate, but landscaping has matured a little and slight untidiness around the house is not typical of the interior, where housekeeping is exemplary. There is plenty of parking, and a terrace overlooking the harbour and all the activity on the pier is set up attractively with garden furniture and parasols, so you can relax with a glass of wine or lunch. It is a pleasing house, and any period features have been retained in well-proportioned reception rooms. Katarina also teaches piano so there is music in the house, with a grand piano in the green room. A lovely dining room, set up stylishly with simple contemporary linen and cutlery, the restaurant has earned a following for unique ingredients-led cooking with a distinctive Swedish flavour, and is now regarded as the best place to dine in the area. About seven choices are offered on each course at dinner, and there are nightly seafood specials. The dishes offered are driven by the freshest produce available on the day, but the house signature dish - herrings three ways - is likely to be among the starters, and main courses may include other firm favourites like local duck in plum & red wine sauce, and Swedish meatballs. Puddings are a highlight, also local cheeses - and excellent home-made breads may include an unusual light rye style brown, and a white yeast loaf. Katarina is 'wine mad' and her informative list is extensive for a small place - you can sense the enjoyment she has had in making the selection, which includes real some treats, and wine service is also helpful. Restaurant L 12.30-3.30, D 6.30-10.30; house wine €17.50, closed L Sun - Open weekend only off season, but can be opened on request. Accommodation is also available all year. Amex, MasterCard, Visa, Laser. **Directions:** On right beyond Church of Ireland on Colla Road, 4 mins walk from village.

Schull
HOTEL

Harbour View Hotel

Main Street Schull Co Cork **Tel: 028 28101**
enquiries@harbourviewhotelschull.com www.harbourviewhotelschull.com

This attractive new family-run hotel overlooking Schull harbour has replaced the old East End Hotel, and is a real asset to the town. The exterior is traditional - cheerfully painted in true West Cork style and with colourful window boxes on the upper window ledges - and the interior has hit a nice level of contemporary style, which is smart and up to date but not making too obvious a statement. The hotel does not look very big from the outside and the main public areas, including the bar and restaurant, are just a comfortable size for a small town, so the extent of the amenities may come as a surprise - these include an impressive leisure centre with a swimming pool, gym and beauty rooms, which are all open to the local community as well as residents, and friendly, welcoming staff are on hand to deal with inquiries. The accommodation is a big change for the area too, as stylish and very comfortable bedrooms have been given a lot of TLC, including specially made local furniture, which is unusual and gives the rooms a feeling of being special; smart bathrooms all have a full bath too. Prices are very reasonable for the standard offered. **Rooms 30**. B&B €60-80 pps, ss €15. 50% reduction for children. Leisure centre (swimming pool, gym, beauty salon). **Directions:** Overlooking the harbour - On the right as you enter Schull from Ballydehob direction. ◈

Schull
B&B

Hillside House B&B

Hillside Schull Co Cork **Tel: 028 282 248**
mmacf@live.ie

Disregard the dull exterior of this warm and welcoming B&B just outside Schull - it has great views over the bay, is well away from any village noise and will make a homely and moderately-priced base for a stay in the area. The décor is a little dated too, but offset by good paintings, interesting old furniture and top rate beds. Everything works and the breakfast is good, with home-made breads and jams, plenty of fruit and the option of fish as well as the full Irish. And your hosts are generous with local information too - just what people need on holiday. Children welcome (under 3s free in parents' room, cot available free of charge); **Rooms 3**. B&B €35pps, ss€5. Closed Oct-May. No credit cards. **Directions:** Turn right at side of church coming from Skibbereen.

Schull
B&B

Stanley House

Schull Co Cork **Tel: 028 28425**
stanleyhouse@eircom.net www.stanley-house.net

Nancy Brosnan's modern house provides a West Cork home-from-home for her many returning guests. Compact bedrooms are comfortably furnished with tea/coffee making facilities and there's a pleasant conservatory running along the back of the house, with wonderful sea views over a field where guests can watch Nancy's growing herd of deer, and sometimes see foxes come out to play at dusk. Good breakfasts too. **Rooms 4** (all shower only, all no-smoking, 2 ground floor, 1 family); children welcome (under 3s free in parents' room, cots available without charge). No pets. Garden. B&B €35pps, single room €45, family room €95. Closed 31 Oct-1 Mar. MasterCard, Visa, Laser. **Directions:** At top of main street. follow signs for Stanley House.

Schull
CAFÉ•WINE BAR•CHARACTER PUB

T J Newman's / Newmans West
Main Street Schull Co Cork **Tel: 028 27776**
info@tjnewmans.com www.tjnewmans.com

Just up the hill from the harbour, this characterful and delightfully old-fashioned little pub has been a special home-from-home for regular visitors, especially sailors up from the harbour, as long as anyone can remember. The premises was bought by John and Bride D'Alton in 2003 but they kept the old bar much as it always has been and it remains the most popular pub in the town. Next door, the café/winebar, Newman's West, replaced the old off-licence, and offers lovely food and great value in immaculate premises. They have a second room on the first floor that doubles as an art gallery, and provide newspapers for a leisurely browse over an excellent cup of coffee. A cleverly thought out menu offers all sorts of tempting bits and pieces, notably the Newman's West Gourmet Choice and delicious desserts. **Seats 50**; children welcome; broadband wi/fi; toilets wheelchair accessible. Food served all day 9-12 (Sun, 10am-11pm). House wines (16), €15.90 (€4.50 per glass). Closed 25 Dec, Good Fri. **No Credit Cards. Directions:** Main West Cork route to Mizen Head.

Schull Area
COUNTRY HOUSE

Rock Cottage
Barnatonicane Schull Co Cork **Tel: 028 35538**
rockcottage@eircom.net www.rockcottage.ie

Garden-lovers, especially, will thrill to the surroundings of Barbara Klotzer's beautiful slate-clad Georgian hunting lodge near Schull, which is on a south-facing slope away from the sea, nearby at Dunmanus Bay. A fascinating combination of well-tended lawns and riotous flower beds, the rocky outcrop which inspired its name - and even great estate trees in the 17 acres of parkland (complete with peacefully grazing sheep) that have survived from an earlier period of its history - create a unique setting. The whole of the main house has been redecorated recently but it has always been known for its style and comfort, with welcoming open fires and bright bedrooms which - although not especially large - are thoughtfully furnished to allow little seating areas as well as the usual amenities such as tea/coffee making facilities, and en-suite power showers. There's a sheltered courtyard behind the house and also some appealing self-catering accommodation, in converted stables. And Barbara is an accomplished chef - so you can look forward to a dinner based on the best of local produce, with starters like fresh crab salad or warm Ardsallagh goat's cheese, main courses of Rock Cottage's own rack of lamb, or even lobster or seafood platters, beautiful vegetables and classic desserts like home-baked vanilla cheesecake or strawberry fool. Extensive breakfast choices include a Healthy Breakfast and a Fish Breakfast as well as traditional Irish and continental combinations - just make your choice before 8pm the night before. Barbara also offers laundry facilities - very useful when touring around. **Rooms 3** (all en-suite, 2 shower only, all no smoking); not suitable for children under 10. B&B from €70 pps, ss €30. No pets, garden, walking. Breakfast, 8.30-9.30 (order by 8pm the night before). Residents D Mon-Sat, €45, at 7.30pm; BYO wine. No D on Sun. Open all year. MasterCard, Visa, Laser. **Directions:** From Schull, 10km, at Toormore, turn into R591 after 2km. Sign on left.

SKIBBEREEN

This bustling market town on the River Ilen has plenty of shops, crafts and restaurants to interest the visitor. Skibbereen Heritage Centre (028 40900, open February to September) is an interesting port of call and is located in the beautifully restored gasworks building, housing 2 main exhibitions, one of which focuses on the effects the Famine had on Skibbereen; local attractions include the Skibbereen Trail which guides visitors around nearby sites which are linked to the Famine. The West Cork Arts Centre (028 22090) is also well worth a visit. The tradition of the market town is kept well alive with the cattle mart on Wednesdays, which gives visitors the chance to witness a glimpse of an authentic rural Ireland that is slowly disappearing. Visitors are also welcome at West Cork Herb Farm (028 38428) and on Fridays there is a Country Market in the town. A farmers' market is held in the town on Saturdays - and Skibbereen is also the venue for the Taste of West Cork food festival which showcases the best of local farmhouse produce every September. For holidaymakers self-catering in the area, **Skibbereen Food & Wine Market** (028 51500; 1, Ilen Street) is just the kind of place they need to know about: Charlie Costelloe's appealing delicatessen, wine shop and café beside the Heritage Centre offers a great choice of freshly prepared dishes based on artisan and fresh local produce and,

as well as food from the shop display, bulk orders are taken for 8 portions or more - ideal for evenng meals in a holiday cottge. Wines offered include some unusual bottles – organic perhaps – and Wines of the Month, which are a bargain at only €8.50. And there's free local delivery too.
WWW.IRELAND-GUIDE.COM FOR ALL THE BEST PLACES TO EAT, DRINK & STAY

Skibbereen   ## Kalbos
RESTAURANT   26 North Street Skibbereen Co Cork **Tel: 028 21515**
                                         kalbos@eircom.net

After over a decade in business, Siobhan O'Callaghan and Anthony Boyle decided to close their main restaurant and move across the road to the premises formerly occupied by their shop. Here they continue to do a great job on a smaller scale. Their simple food is wholesome and flavoursome - consistently delicious, their ingredients are well-sourced, accurately cooked, and appetisingly presented - and dishes have real flavour. Kalbo's is always a great choice - and good value too. **Seats 42**. Open daily in summer: L Mon-Sat, 12-3, D Fri & Sat only, 6-9. A la carte; house wine €17.95, sc discretionary. Closed Sun; 24-28 Dec & Good Fri. Amex, Diners, MasterCard, Visa, Laser. **Directions:** In town centre.

Skibbereen   ## Over the Moon
RESTAURANT   46 Bridge Street Skibbereen Co Cork **Tel: 028 22100**
   info@overthemoonskibbereen.com   www.overthemoonskibbereen.com

Husband and wife team Jennifer & Francois Conradie moved from Cork city in 2007 to open their own first restaurant in the centre of Skibbereen, and it made a big impact from the outset. Francois is the chef, and originally from South Africa; Jennifer is Irish and she is the host; they arrived in Skibbereen by a circuitous route, but both had worked in Jacobs on the Mall (see entry) for two years before setting up here. The season is short in West Cork but they don't waste a minute of the day offering a very attractive lunch menu from noon onwards and finally building up to a delicious dinner menu in the evening, when tables are set up formally with white linen to give a sense of occasion. But, regardless of the time of day, Francois' menus are based firmly on the best of local produce, and the names of valued suppliers are listed – Gubbeen cheeses and ham, Frank Krawczyk salamis, Sally Barnes' Woodcock Smokery, Skeaghanore ducks, Caherbeg organic meats and Alan Hassett of Baltimore Fresh Fish are among them. At lunchtime, you might try a crusty roll filled with Gubbeeen ham, Hegarty's cheddar & wholegrain mustard mayonnaise, for example - or Roaring Water Bay mussels with shallots, garlic, white wine & chorizo, which is one of the dishes that overlaps from lunchtime onto the evening menu. Short à la carte dinner menus offer a flexible choice, heavy on starters and with some dishes that can be a starter or main course – scallops & Rosscarbery black pudding, for example, which comes with spiced apple sauce and rocket salad. There are steaks too, of course (few Irish menus dare to ignore them) and meat lovers should also enjoy Dunmanway lamb with champ, summer vegetables & red wine jus. Dishes come fully garnished (no separate side orders) making them very good value as the most expensive main course is about €26. Service, under Jennifer's direction, is warmly efficient and there's a small but carefully chosen wine list, with France and South Africa especially well represented. **Seats 30**; reservations recommended; children welcome (high chair); no wheelchair access to toilets. L& D Wed-Sat & Mon 12-3pm and 6-10pm. Sun D only, 5.30-8.30pm. Set L/D for parties 10+ €30/35. Set D €40; also a la carte L&D. House wine €19. Closed Sun L, Tue & one month off season (various times, call to check). Amex, MasterCard, Visa, Laser. **Directions:** N71 from Cork, take 1st exit off second roundabout, pass West Cork Hotel, turn left, down the street on the right.

Skibbereen   ## West Cork Hotel
HOTEL   Ilen Street Skibbereen Co Cork **Tel: 028 21277**
          info@westcorkhotel.com   www.westcorkhotel.com

This welcoming hotel enjoys a pleasant riverside site beside the bridge, on the western side of the town. It came into new ownership in 2007 and, in addition to recent refurbishment, which had been completed with some style, the function room was extended to make a very pleasant room with river views. The main entrance is currently from the street (the main through road) and is quite small, but the hotel opens up behind the foyer, to reveal a bright and airy bar along the river side of the hotel, and a modern restaurant, where breakfast is served to residents, as well as main meals. Bedrooms are not especially large, but they are comfortably furnished in a neutral, modern style and have all the necessary amenities (phone, tea/coffee tray, TV) and neat, well-designed en-suite bathrooms, so this would make a good base from which to explore this beautiful area. Unless there is further redevelopment along the river, rooms at the back should be quieter and have a pleasant outlook over trees and river. Conferences/Banqueting (400/350); **Rooms 34** (2 family, 2 single, 10 shower only); B&B €75, SS €17. Garden. Private parking. Amex, Diners, MasterCard, Visa, Laser. **Directions:** Follow signs N71 to Bantry through Skibbereen. ◊

Timoleague
RESTAURANT

Dillon's

Mill Street Timoleague Co Cork
Tel: 023 46390

In the '90s, Dillon's traditional shopfront on the main street in Timoleague was a welcome sight for anyone needing a good food stop when heading west from Cork and, although they don't do daytime food any more, it's still something of an oasis in this area. The dining experience has moved up a few gears since then, but the informal café-style restaurant is much the same and, although Isabelle Dillon isn't in the kitchen herself these days, she's very much in evidence front of house. Vivien Toop is the chef now, but the philosophy of using the best local produce and making everything on the premises remains constant – breads, pasta and desserts are all home-made. Vivien's interesting menus offer about half a dozen choices on each course, and they change frequently, although some specialities (or variations) are always likely - de-boned roasted quail is a favourite, for example, and may be stuffed with bacon, almonds, prunes & raisins and served with a Muscat sauce. A well-chosen wine list is organised by style, and includes some interesting half bottles. This is an unusual restaurant and the slightly bohemian décor and background jazz make for an atmospheric outing. **Seats 30**; not suitable for children under 7 yrs after 7pm. Open for D Thu-Sun, 6.30pm-9.30pm; à la carte. Closed Mon-Wed (open Bank Hol Mon); first 2 weeks Mar, first 2 weeks Oct. Reservations recommended. No credit cards. **Directions:** On main street of village. On M71. ◊

YOUGHAL

Famous for its associations with Sir Walter Raleigh, Youghal is an historic town on the estuary of the Blackwater, and was once the second largest port in Europe, the many historic buildings and monuments within its walls have seen its designation as an Irish Heritage Port. Today, thanks to a recently opened by-pass, the town is more accessible for leisurely visits and it is well worth lingering a little to take in the historical walking tour which visits a number of diversely interesting old buildings, including the famous 1777 Clock Gate over the main street. **Old Imperial Hotel** with **Coachhouse Bar & Restaurant** (024 92435; www.theoldimperialhotel.com): at the front of this recently renovated town centre hotel is a wonderful old-world bar, previously known as D.McCarthy; while the rest of the hotel provides the usual facilities, this is a lovely little low-ceilinged bar of great character, with an open fire and a long history to tell - it's worth calling here for this alone. On the western end of the town, the popular **Tides Restaurant** (024 93127; www.tidesrestaurant.ie) is a useful place to know about, not least for its long opening hours; accommodation is also available. A more recent arrival is **Via@The Priory** (024 92574; 56 North Main Street), an Italian restaurant with an open kitchen and friendly staff, which is open every evening except Monday. Fishing in the River Blackwater (noted for salmon, trout and excellent coarse fish), golf (Youghal Golf Club, 024 92787), angling, pitch and putt and yachting are just some of the activities that are located either near or in the town. There is also a fine 5km blue flag beach. The Clock Gate Farmers' Market is held each Friday morning (10am-2pm).
WWW.IRELAND-GUIDE.COM FOR ALL THE BEST PLACES TO EAT, DRINK & STAY

Youghal

Aherne's Seafood Restaurant & Accommodation

RESTAURANT WITH ROOMS

163 North Main Street Youghal Co Cork **Tel: 024 92424**
ahernes@eircom.net www.ahernes.com

Now in its third generation of family owner-ship, one of the most remarkable features of Aherne's is the warmth of the FitzGibbon family's hospitality and their enormous enthusiasm for the business which, since 1993, has included some fine accommodation. But it is for its food - and, especially, the ultra-fresh seafood that comes straight from the fishing boats in Youghal harbour - that Aherne's is best known. While John FitzGibbon supervises the front of house, his brother David reigns over a busy kitchen. There are two bars – there's quite a large traditional one, with lots of wood and a timeless atmosphere, and the smaller one is beside the restaurant and also used for aperitifs – it has just been refurbished and is very chic. Wherever you choose to eat it, the bar food tends towards simplicity, and is all the better for that - oysters, chowder, Youghal Bay smoked salmon and oysters make for great snacks or starters (all served with the renowned moist dark brown yeast bread), and you'll find at least half a dozen delicious hot seafood main course dishes like baked cod wrapped in bacon and gorgeous prawns in garlic butter - its sheer freshness tells the story. Restaurant meals are naturally more ambitious and include some token meat dishes - rack of lamb with a rosemary jus or mint sauce, char-grilled fillet steak with mush-rooms and shallot jus or pepper sauce - although seafood is still the undisputed star of the show. Specialities like pan-fried scallops with spinach, bacon & beurre blanc sauce, or fresh crab salad can make memorable starters, for example, and who could resist a main course of hot buttered Youghal Bay lobster? These are, in a sense, simple dishes yet they have plenty of glamour too. It is well worth planning a journey around a bar meal at Aherne's - or, if time permits, have a relaxed evening meal followed by a restful night in their very comfortable accommodation. A wine list strong on classic French regions offers a good selection of half bottles and half a dozen champagnes. **Seats 60** (private room, 20); children welcome (high chair, baby changing facilities); toilets wheelchair accessible. D 6.30-9.30 daily; fixed price 2-course set D €35; 3-course €45; also à la carte; house wine €22, sc discretionary. *Bar food daily, 12-10. **Accommodation:** The stylish rooms at Aherne's are generously sized and individually decorated to a high standard; all are furnished with antiques and have full bath-rooms. Excellent breakfasts are served in a warm and elegantly furnished residents' dining room. Studio apartments are also available, equipped to give the option of self-catering if required. Conference room (20); free broadband wi/fi; safe & fax available at reception. **Rooms 13** (4 junior suites, 2 family rooms, 3 ground floor, 1 disabled); children welcome (under 5s free in parents' room, cot available without charge, baby sitting arranged). Dogs permitted (stay in bedrooms). B&B €105 pps, ss €25. Wheelchair friendly. Closed 23-29 Dec. Amex, MasterCard, Visa. **Directions:** on N25, main route from Cork-Waterford.

COUNTY DONEGAL

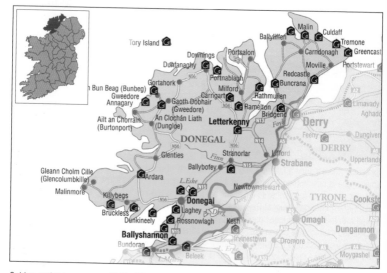

Golden eagles are no mere flight of fancy in Donegal. Glenveagh National Park in the northern part of the county is the focal point of a programme for the re-introduction of this magnificent bird to Ireland – it was last seen here in 1912. The first six Scottish-born chicks of the new wave were released at Glenveagh in June 2001. By the end of 2004, 15 adult birds were soaring over Donegal, with a further nine sightings to the south in Sligo and Leitrim. Over a five year period, 50 birds have been released, and the high expectations of success for the project began to be fulfilled with the first chick hatched and fledged in 2007.

Travel at sea level is also an increasingly significant element in visits to Donegal, one of Ireland's most spectacularly beautiful counties. It is much-indented by the sea, but the introduction of local car ferry services is shortening journeys and adding interest. The ferry between Greencastle and Magilligan across the narrow entrance to Lough Foyle has become deservedly popular, and another car ferry – between Buncrana and Rathmullan across Lough Swilly – adds to the travel options, albeit at a more leisurely pace.

For many folk, particularly those from Northern Ireland, Donegal is the holiday county par excellence. But in recent years, despite the international fluctuations of trading conditions, there has been growth of modern industries and the re-structuring of the fishing, particularly at the developing harbour of Killybegs, home port for the largest fishing vessels. This Donegal entrepreneurial spirit has led to a more balanced economy, with the pace being set by the county town of Letterkenny, where the population has increased by 50% since 1991. More recently, Letterkenny has become home to an impressive Arts Centre, a masterpiece of modern architecture. And if a more traditional townscape is preferred, Glenties in the southwest of the county has been national winner of the Tidy Towns competition five times in the past fifty years, and was the first title-holder in 1958.

But much and all as Donegal county is increasingly a place where people live and make a living, nevertheless it is still a place of nature on the grand scale, where the landscape is challenged by the winds and weather of the Atlantic Ocean if given the slighest chance. Yet at communities like Bundoran and Rossnowlagh, where splendid beaches face straight into the Atlantic, enthusiastic surfers have demonstrated that even the most demanding weather can have its sporting uses.

For most folk, however, it is the contrast between raw nature and homely comfort which is central to Donegal's enduring attraction. For here, in some of Ireland's most rugged territory, you will find many sheltered and hospitable places whose amenities are emphasised by the challenging nature of their broader environment. And needless to say, that environment is simply startlingly utterly beautiful as well.

Local Attractions and Information

Arranmore Ferry	Burtonport-Arranmore	074 952 0532
Buncrana	Lough Swilly Ferry	074 938 1901
Buncrana	National Knitting Centre	074 936 2355
Bundoran	Tourism Information	071 984 1350
Churchill	Glebe House & Gallery (Derek Hill)	074 913 7071
Donegal Airport	Carrickfin	074 954 8232
Donegal Highlands	Hillwalking/Irish lang.(adults)	074 973 0248
Donegal town	Donegal Castle	074 972 2405
Donegal town	Tourism information	074 972 1148
Donegal town	Waterbus Cruises	074 972 1148
Dunfanaghy	Workhouse Visitor Centre	074 913 6540
Dungloe	Mary from Dungloe Int. Festival (July/August)	074 952 1254
Dungloe	Tourism Information	074 952 1297
Glencolumbcille	Folk Museum	074 973 0017
Glencolumbcille	Tourism Information	074 973 0017
Glenties	Patrick Mac Gill Summer School (August)	074 954 6101
Glenveagh	National Park (Castle, gardens, parkland)	074 913 7090
Greencastle	Lough Foyle Ferry	074 938 1901
Greencastle	Maritime Museum	074 938 1363
Inishowen	Inishowen Tourism (Carndonagh)	074 937 4933
Letterkenny	An Grianan Theatre	074 912 0777
Letterkenny	Regional Cultural Centre	074 912 9186
Letterkenny	Earagail Arts Festival	074 916 8800
Letterkenny	County Museum	074 912 4613
Letterkenny	Newmills Watermill	074 912 5115
Letterkenny	North West Tourism	074 912 1160
Lifford	Cavanacor Historic House	074 914 1143
Rathmullan	Lough Swilly Ferry	074 938 1901
Tory Island	Ferry	074 953 1320 / 953 1340 / 913 5061

Annagry
RESTAURANT WITH ROOMS

Danny Minnie's Restaurant
Annagry Co Donegal **Tel: 074 954 8201**
www.dannyminnies.com

The O'Donnell family has run Danny Minnie's since 1962, and a visit is always a special treat. There's nothing about the exterior as seen from the road to prepare first-time visitors for the atmosphere of this remarkable restaurant. Hidden behind a frontage of overgrown creepers, a surprise: once through the door you are suddenly surrounded by antiques and elegantly appointed candle-lit tables and on summer evenings there may even be a harpist playing. Brian O'Donnell is a well-known chef (his recipes appear every month in Garden Heaven magazine) and his cooking matches the surroundings well - fine, with imaginative saucing, but not at all pompous. Menus are presented in both Irish and English and, on a wide-ranging à la carte menu; seafood stars in the main courses - lobster and other shellfish, availability permitting - but there is also a strong selection of meats including Donegal mountain lamb, typically served with honey, garlic and rosemary gravy, and Donegal beef, served various ways including classic Beef Wellington. Vegetables are a strength and gorgeous desserts, such as cardamom and lime pannacotta with a refreshing rhubarb and strawberry compôte, create an appropriately delicious finale. And the staff are lovely too - attentive waitresses provide warm and friendly service. There's nowhere quite like Danny Minnie's, winner of the Guide's Atmospheric Restaurant of the Year in 2000. **Seats 80**; not suitable for children after 9pm; reservations required. D Mon-Sat, 6.30-9.30pm. Set D about €50; also à la carte; house wine about €25; no sc. (Phone ahead to check opening hours, especially off peak season) Closed Sun D (except prior to bank hols), 25/26 Dec, Good Fri & early week off-season. [Accommodation is also offered in seven non-smoking rooms, five of them en-suite, two family rooms; B&B €65pps, ss€20]. MasterCard, Visa, Laser. **Directions:** R259 off N56 - follow Airport signs. ◇

ARDARA

This colourful and scenically located small town is a popular holiday destination, and recent prosperity has seen renovations to a lot of premises in the town and a certain amount of development. There are several successful festivals in the summer months, including the Ardara Walking Festival every March, and the 'Cup of Tae' traditional music festival held on the May bank holiday weekend. It is the home of hand-woven tweed and knitwear, and the Ardara Heritage Centre (075 41704, with tea rooms) tells the story of Donegal tweed. Nearby scenic points include the Glengesh Pass, the Maghera Falls and the views out over the Atlantic from Loughros Point.

Ardara
CHARACTER PUB

Nancy's Bar
Front Street Ardara Co Donegal
Tel: 074 954 1187

This famous pub, in the village renowned for its tweeds and handknits, is a cosy, welcoming place in its seventh generation of family ownership, with five or six small rooms packed with bric à brac and plenty of tables and chairs for the comfortable consumption of wholesome home-made food, especially seafood. Famed equally for a great pint of Guinness and the house chowder - maybe try it along with a "Louis Armstrong" (smoked salmon on brown bread topped with grilled cheese) and finish with an Irish coffee. Or there's "Charlie's Supper", a speciality of prawns and smoked salmon warmed in a chilli & garlic sauce. Things moved up a notch or two here recently, when another bar area was opened, and also an outdoor seating area with an awning, giving more room to enjoy everything this delightful pub has to offer. Great live music too. Children welcome before 9pm (high chair, baby changing facilities); wheelchair access to toilets. Bar food served daily 12-9, from Easter to September. Closed 25 Dec & Good Fri. **No Credit Cards. Directions:** In Ardara village; half an hour's drive from Donegal Town.

Ardara
RESTAURANT

O'Fabulous
Irish Habitué Front Street Ardara Co Donegal **Tel: 074 953 7791**
bookings@ofabulous.com www.ofabulous.com

Although passers-by might not notice much to mark it out from its neighbours, this glamorous new arrival on the main street of the very traditional village of Ardara has caused quite a stir locally, and introduced a new kind of visitor to an area which is mainly known for tweeds, hand knits, walking, music and craic. It's part of a small group of UK-based boutique properties (Swell Group International), all lavishly furnished to appeal to the well-heeled urban traveller. It may all seem a bit unlikely, like something out of a fashionable decorator's catalogue, but it's undeniably luxurious and has struck a chord with both local people and visitors to this small heritage town. Although it is not an hotel (and the accommodation is not officially approved), O'Fabulous is open to non-residents for meals, and home baking is speciality, so it would make an interesting diversion for morning coffee (from10.30am) or afternoon tea (from 2pm), featuring all the niceties - bone china, crisp linen, and a place by the drawing room fire. And dinner – styled 'Supper Club' - is served in an intimate dining room which seats only 12 -14 people (everything is on a domestic scale here). White-clothed tables are beautifully set with sparkling crystal, gleaming cutlery and fresh flowers, all of which contribute to the tranquil old-world ambience, and set the stage for a special dining experience. A limited menu offering four or five choices on each course changes weekly, and is surprisingly straightforward – starters of homemade chicken liver & bacon terrine with orange chutney, perhaps, the ubiquitous tiger prawn in a tomato & coriander salad, served with a lemon dressing; typical mains include roast half duckling with orange, cherry & port sauce, or sirloin steak with creamy pepper sauce and champ – bowing gracefully to local demand they have a Steak Night on Thursdays, great value at €19.95 too. Locally produced foods don't feature on the menu, although 'cultural heritage of the land' etc is highlighted on the brochure. But the ingredients are high quality, cooked well and simply served on delicate Vera Wang china by efficient and friendly local staff. As they say in Donegal, 'up here it's different'. **Seats 12-14**. Meals: D Thu (steak night) from 6pm; Fri & Sat 7pm and 9pm (2 sittings); Sat Early Bird Chef's Special 5pm; Sun 7 - 9. L Sun only 5- 7pm. Morning Coffee 10.30- 12.30 daily; Afternoon Tea 2- 4pm daily. MasterCard, Visa, Laser. **Directions:** On main street – just across from Nancy's. ◈

Woodhill House

Ardara
COUNTRY HOUSE•RESTAURANT

Woodhill Ardara Co Donegal **Tel: 074 954 1112**
yates@iol.ie www.woodhillhouse.com

Once the home of Ireland's last commercial whaling family, John and Nancy Yates' large house is on the edge of the village, overlooking the Donegal Highlands, and their years of restoration work are now bearing fruit. As well as the original rooms in the main house, which vary in position, size and character, and are now being refurbished, they offer lovely accommodation in converted outbuildings; overlooking the gardens; the rooms are all en-suite and slightly dearer than those in the house, but they are very spacious and appealingly furnished, with good en-suite bathrooms. As the rooms vary so much, it is advisable to discuss your requirements when booking. There's also a bar and restaurant (popular locally - booking recommended) offering quite traditional food based on local ingredients at reasonable prices: specialities include Donegal mountain lamb, and carrageen pudding. The gradual restoration of the gardens is perhaps Nancy's greatest achievement, and renovations on both the main house and outbuildings are still on-going. Small conferences/ private parties (50). **Rooms 14** (6 shower-only, 1 family room, 4 ground floor, 1 for disabled); children welcome (under 5s free in parents' room, cot available without charge). Pets permitted in some areas. B&B €48-65 pps, ss €10. Restaurant: **Seats 50** (private room, 15); children welcome; reservations accepted. D 6.30-10pm daily, Set D about €40; house wine €20; sc discretionary. Bar open normal hours (no food). House closed 20-27 Dec. Amex, Diners, MasterCard, Visa, Laser. **Directions:** 500m from Ardara village. ◈

Jackson's Hotel

Ballybofey
HOTEL
Ⓥ

Ballybofey Co Donegal **Tel: 074 913 1021**
enquiry@jacksons-hotel.ie www.jacksons-hotel.ie

This attractive family-run hotel is set in its own gardens and enjoys a tranquil position alongside the River Finn. A welcoming open fire in the followed through in other public areas including the restaurant, overlooking the garden. Recent development has seen the addition of 50 new rooms as well as an impressive conference and banqueting centre, meeting rooms, and an underground carpark. All bedrooms are furnished to a high standard, and are well-equipped with all the usual amenities (broadband, safe, ironing, tea/coffee trays, TV/DVD) and the best have river views. Special breaks offer good value. Conference/banqueting (1,500/550); business centre, broadband, secretarial services. **Rooms 138** (2 suites, 5 executive rooms, 50 no smoking, 10 disabled, 10 family rooms); children welcome (under 2 free in parents' room, cots available without charge, baby sitting arranged, playroom). Lift. 24 hour room service. Pets permitted in some areas. B&B about €80 pps, ss about €20. Leisure centre (22m pool), sauna, steam room, hot tub, jacuzzi, beauty treatments, Naturapathy/yoga/holistic treatments. Snooker, pool table, garden. Horse-riding, golf, fishing and bike hire all nearby. *Food available all day (9am-10.30pm); Restaurant: D 6-9.15 daily, Sun L 12.30-4. Open all year. Amex, Diners, MasterCard, Visa, Laser. **Directions:** Beside the river, in the centre of town.

Kee's Hotel

Ballybofey
HOTEL

Stranorlar Ballybofey Co Donegal **Tel: 074 913 1018**
info@keeshotel.ie www.keeshotel.ie

This centrally located, all-year hotel has been in the Kee family since 1892. Spacious public areas allow plenty of spaces for guests to relax, and good food has always been a feature of the hotel. The attractive fine dining restaurant has recently been refurbished, and head Chef Etienne Meyer's daily-changing menus are based on the best of local produce; he offers imaginative menus and good cooking – and appealing informal daytime food too. Rooms at the back have views of the Blue Stack Mountains and all bedrooms are regularly refurbished and have good bathrooms. Residents have direct access to a fine leisure centre, with swimming pool. Special breaks offered by the hotel, and offering very good value, include golfing holidays, bank holiday breakaways and a novel "Post Christmas Recovery Break". Conference/banqueting (200/250). **Rooms 53** (32 executive rooms, 23 family, 39 no smoking, 1 for disabled); children welcome (under 3s free in their parents' room; cots, high chairs available, baby sitting arranged); toilets wheelchair accessible. Lift. Room service (24 hr). No pets. B&B €85 pps, ss €15. **Seats 120**; food served 12.30-9.30pm (to 10pm weekends). SC discretionary. [Informal bistro style meals served in the Old Gallery, 12.30-3 and 5.30-9.30 daily.] Golf and fishing nearby. Amex, Diners, MasterCard, Visa, Laser. **Directions:** On the main street in the village of Stranorlar. ◈

BALLYLIFFIN

This small village near the coast of North Donegal is set in the spectacular rocky surroundings of Malin Head and the impressive Inishowen coastline. It is a popular base for walkers, and home to the world famous Ballyliffin Golf Club (074 937 6119), which offers two eighteen hole links courses on the Glashedy links and the Old links. The Old links course was designed by Nick Faldo and is amongst the choice few courses that always attract discerning golfers from Europe and America. Another attraction in Ballyliffin is the **Ballyliffin Lodge Hotel and Spa** (see entry), and good budget accommodation is available nearby at **Glen House Clonmany** (see entry); also at Clonmany, **The Rusty Nail** (074 937 6116) is friendly and characterful pub with a great view from the back and a good name for food.
WWW.IRELAND-GUIDE.COM FOR ALL THE BEST PLACES TO EAT, DRINK & STAY

Ballyliffin
HOTEL•RESTAURANT

Ballyliffin Lodge and Spa

Shore Road Ballyliffin Co Donegal **Tel: 074 937 8200**
info@ballyliffinlodge.com www.ballyliffinlodge.com

This impressive hotel in Ballyliffin village is a great asset to the area - with a beautiful view, space and comfort. Public areas include a traditional bar, Mamie Pat's, and the spacious guest rooms are finished to a high standard with many extras. General Manager Cecil Doherty, who is also a joint-proprietor of the hotel, has considered every detail including excellent on-site leisure facilities, with swimming pool and spa treatments. Discounts are available for hotel guests at Ballyliffin GC, and short breaks are offered. The hotel also accepts wedding parties (remember the Donegal catch-phrase is 'up here it's different'). Conference/banqueting 500/400; secretarial service. Children welcome (under 5 free in parents' room, free cot available). **Rooms 40** (12 junior suites, 4 superior, 4 disabled, all no smoking). B&B €95 pps, ss €20. Lift. Room service (limited hours). Open all year except 25 Dec & Good Fri. **Holly Tree Restaurant:** There is a classic and intimate feel to this rather small exclusive room: head chef Peter Sweetman is well known in the area for his commitment to local produce, notably fresh fish, and accomplished modern cooking - and people travel specially to eat here. Evening menus offer the choice of a set dinner or an à la carte, typically including pan-roasted fillet of Greencastle landed plaice on a buttermilk and scallion creamed potato, or the ever-popular roast rack of Irish lamb with a brioche and herb crust, roasted baby fennel, which is served with a lamb sausage and rosemary jus. Desserts may include a luscious and unusual Black Mission fig tart tatin. A well thought out wine list includes plenty of half bottles, and service is excellent. NB: A formal lunch is only available on Sunday, and is very different from the evening dining experience; as it is very popular, it is served in the much larger Aughrim Suite and a substantial carvery is provided. **Seats 55**; reservations required; children welcome; toilets accessible for wheelchairs; air conditioning; vegetarian menu available. D daily, 6.30-9.30. L Sun only, 12.30-4.30. Set D about €40, Set Sun L about €18. D also a la carte. Bar meals, 12.30-9.30 daily. House Wine €18. Closed 25 Dec, Good Friday. Residents can get a discount on local golf. Helipad. Amex, Diners, MasterCard, Visa, Laser. **Directions:** In Ballyliffin village (signed). ◊

Ballyliffin Area
GUESTHOUSE•RESTAURANT

Glen House

Straid Clonmany Co Donegal **Tel: 074 937 6745**
glenhouse@hotmail.com www.glenhouse.ie

Beautifully located and with an expansive view towards the sea, this large guesthouse has a charming 18th century house at its heart and would make a moderately priced and hospitable base for golf and the many other activities this lovely area offers - including visiting the nearby waterfall, a fine beach, hill walks (starting at Glen House), and summer festivals that highlight the music and culture of the area. Attentive staff are usually family, making guests feel at home, and there's a comfortable sitting room, with paintings by some young local artists on the walls. The eight spacious bedrooms are attractively furnished in quiet tones, and have tea & coffee facilities and good-sized bathrooms with power showers. Dinner is available all year, and the restaurant is also open during the day in summer. **Restaurant Seats 35** (Private Room available seats 16); D daily (non-residents welcome by reservation); Outdoor dining area (10); Toilets wheelchair accessible. Food usually served all day in summer (8am-9pm), D (5-9pm) but phone to check meal availability. Special hill walking breaks available. Closed 24-27 Dec. MasterCard, Visa, Laser.

BALLYSHANNON

R

On the southern shores of Donegal Bay, Ballyshannon is the gateway to County Donegal and is one of the oldest towns in Ireland, having been made a Borough by Royal Charter in 1613. The poet William Allingham was born here - his father was a ship-owner and merchant - and it is also the birthplace of Rory Gallagher, the rock guitarist (there's a Rory Gallagher festival every summer). Hungry visitors might head for the friendly restaurant/café/wine bar **Nirvana** (see entry). For golfers, the highly chal-lenging County Sligo Golf Club (071 917 7134) is a short drive down the N15.

WWW.IRELAND-GUIDE.COM FOR ALL THE BEST PLACES TO EAT, DRINK & STAY

Ballyshannon

RESTAURANT•CAFÉ•WINE BAR

N R

Nirvana Restaurant, Wine Bar & Café

The Mall Ballyshannon Co Donegal
Tel: 071 982 2369

A chic reception area, with soft seating and a smart designer bar where guests can relax both before and after dinner, sets the tone at Gerry and Brid Kelly's stylish restaurant which is off the beaten track on The Mall. Open since 2007, and ably assisted by their son Kevin, they have filled a niche in the local market by offering a variety of quality food in very pleasant surroundings. Evening menu choices include a comprehensive à la carte menu, and a tempting pizza menu with some interesting topping combinations; during the summer there may be special themed menus, such as one focused on Spanish cuisine. The contemporary dining area helps provide a very pleasant ambience in which to enjoy local chef David McCadden's special dishes using quality ingredients - venison steak on a bed of mash with a pink peppercorn sauce, perhaps, or baked fillet of codling infused with lemongrass and lime topped with a crispy dill stuffing and pesto dressing. Desserts are traditional with a selection of Irish cheeses also offered. The wine list is not long but suits the food well, and includes a fair number of choices under €20. Light meals are available during the day. With pleasing surroundings, a wide range of food to suit varying occasions and good value, this place looks set to be a success. **Seats 70**; children welcome; toilets wheelchair accessible. L & D daily, 12.30-5pm (to 4.30 Sun) and 6-9.30pm (to 9pm Sun). L Special €9.95; D a la carte; house wine €17.95. **Directions:** Turn left at The Mall, halfway up Main Street.

Bridgend

BAR•RESTAURANT

Harry's Bar & Restaurant

Bridgend Inishowen Co Donegal **Tel: 074 936 8444**
info@harrys.ie www.harrys.ie

Located just 10 minutes north-west of Derry, this landmark bar and restaurant looks modern and stylish, with a sleek stone grey exterior and plenty of parking spaces. Excellent food has earned a well-deserved local following for Harry's, served in a relaxed friendly atmosphere, in both the laid-back ambience of the bar and the smart contemporary restaurant. A stylish and spacious entrance bodes well, with a door leading off to the the bar – which has a nice 'pub' feel to it with a beautiful old carved wooden bar - and large double doors into the restaurant. Friendly welcoming staff swiftly take drinks orders and offer extensive menus, which are founded on meticulously sourced local produce, notably dry-aged Donegal beef and the freshest of local fish from nearby Greencastle, which are the special points of focus on the restaurant menu. An obvious understanding of quality ingredi-ents matched with skill in the kitchen creates enticing, down-to-earth food that delivers maximum flavour. Whether for casual meals or dressier occasions, Harry's offers a high quality dining experi-ence at a very modest price; a great dining option for the north-west – and very useful for a wholesome journey break. **Seats 110**; toilets wheelchair accessible; children welcome (high chair, children's menu, baby changing facilities); free broadband wi/fi. L in bar and restaurant daily, 12.15-4pm; D restaurant only Mon-Sun 4-9pm (to 10pm Sat/Sun); set Sun L about €21; house wine about €17. Various live music at weekends, see website for details. Open all year. Amex, MasterCard, Visa, Laser. **Directions:** At junction of Buncrana-Derry and Letterkenny-Derry roads, about 19km (12 m) north of Letterkenny, 5km (3 m) from Derry.

Bruckless
FARMHOUSE

Bruckless House

Bruckless Co Donegal **Tel: 074 973 7071**
bruc@bruckless.com www.bruckless.com

Clive and Joan Evans' lovely 18th-century house and Connemara pony stud farm is set in 18 acres of woodland and gardens overlooking Bruckless Bay - an ideal place for people who enjoy quiet countryside and pursuits like walking, horse-riding and fishing. The gardens are open to the public at certain times, as part of the Donegal Garden Trail; they are not too formal but beautifully designed, extensive and well-maintained - they really enhance a visit here, as does the waterside location: guests have direct access to the foreshore at the bottom of the garden. Family furniture collected through a Hong Kong connection adds an unexpected dimension to elegant reception rooms that have views over the front lawns towards the sea, and the generous, comfortably furnished bedrooms. Accommodation includes two single rooms and there is a shared bathroom; although the house is large, the guest bedrooms are close together, so the rooms sharing a bathroom are ideal for a family or a group travelling together. Home-produced eggs are a treat at breakfast, which is the only meal served - guests are directed to local restaurants in the evening. Self-catering accommodation is also available all year, in a two-bedroomed gate lodge. **Rooms 4** (2 en-suite, 2 single, all no-smoking) B&B €65pps, no ss. Weekly rates also offered. Garden, equestrian, walking, fishing. Pets permitted in certain areas. Closed 1 Oct-31 Mar. Amex, MasterCard, Visa. **Directions:** On N56, 18km (12 m) west of Donegal.

Bunbeg
HOTEL

Ostan Gweedore

Bunbeg Co Donegal **Tel: 074 953 1177**
reservations@ostangweedore.com www.ostangweedore.com

Although its blocky 1970s' architectural style may not be to today's taste, Ostan Gweedore was built to make the most of the location - and this it does exceptionally well. Spacious public areas, including the aptly named **Ocean Restaurant** and the **Library Bar** ("the most westerly reading room on the Atlantic seaboard") have superb views over the shoreline and Mount Errigal - as does the Sundowner Wine & Tapas Bar, which offers a wide range of wines by the glass and a menu of small tapas-style dishes to nibble while you watch the sun sinking in the west. The hotel takes pride in the restaurant - extensive menus offer a wide range of dishes based mainly on local produce, especially seafood and Donegal mountain lamb - and it has a strong local following. Most of the bedrooms have panoramic sea views and, although some may seem a little dated, they are all comfortable. It's a very relaxing place and in high season is ideal for families, with its wonderful beach and outdoor activities, including tennis, pitch & putt and day visits to nearby islands Tory, Gola and Arranmore. If you enjoy fresh air and exercise, ask at reception for the booklet Walks in the Bunbeg Area, which was specially commissioned by the hotel and details a variety of planned walks and cycle paths in the locality. Wet days are looked after too, with excellent indoor leisure facilities including a 19-metre swimming pool, Jacuzzi and gym, supervised by qualified staff, and a health & beauty spa which offers all the current pamper treatments. *Donegal Airport, Carrickfin is nearby. This romantic setting is predictably popular for weddings. Conferences/banqueting (300/350); broadband wi/fi. **Rooms 34** (3 suites, 6 family rooms, 1 ground floor, 1 for disabled); children welcome (Under 5s free in parents' room at managements discretion, cot available without charge, baby sitting arranged). B&B €120-150 per room, ss €20. **Ocean Restaurant:** D daily, 7-8.45, à la carte; Sundowner Tapas bar: 7pm-9.30pm daily. Leisure centre; spa. Fishing and golf (9-hole) available locally. *Self-catering apartments also available. Closed Nov-Feb (open for New Years). Amex, MasterCard, Visa, Laser. **Directions:** From Letterkenny, take coast road past hospital. ◇

BUNCRANA / INISHOWEN

Only a short distance from Derry City, BUNCRANA is a popular seaside resort on the eastern shore of Lough Swilly, and is the gateway to the INISHOWEN PENINSULA which extends between Lough

Swilly and Lough Foyle and is a favourite destination for golfers and walkers. It is a beautiful, mainly mountainous area and Ireland's most northerly point, Malin Head, is at its tip; a 100-mile (161 km) circular scenic drive known as the 'Inis Eoghain 100' is signposted around the peninsula and makes a lovely outing on a good day. There are stopping places en-route: **McGrory's of Culdaff** (see entry) is often the most convenient and, in Buncrana, **The Beach House Bar & Restaurant** (see entry) is near the ferry which links Buncrana with Rathmullan on the western shore of Lough Swilly in summer, and has long opening hours. Shortly before going to press one of the area's most famous establishments, re-opened at Fahan - **St John's Country House** (074 936 0289; www.stjohnscountryhouse.ie); now under new management - visit www.ireland-guide for an update. While in the area a visit to Glenveagh Castle & Gardens near Letterkenny (074 913 7090) is a must, and golfers have the fantastic champ-ionship courses at Ballyliffin Golf Club (Ballyliffin, 074 937 6119) within a short drive.
WWW.IRELAND-GUIDE.COM FOR ALL THE BEST PLACES TO EAT, DRINK & STAY

Buncrana
BAR•RESTAURANT
👁 N V

The Beach House Bar & Restaurant
The Pier Swilly Road Buncrana Co Donegal **Tel: 074 936 1050**
info@thebeachhouse.ie www.thebeachhouse.ie

Lovely views across the lough may be the trump card at this smart-casual restaurant but it has plenty else going for it too. A location beside the pier serving the Rathmullan car ferry must introduce it to a lot of happy visitors – who can walk off their meals on the beach afterwards. Welcoming signs at the door ensure that nobody passes unknowingly and, once inside, the stylish yet laid-back two-storey restaurant and Claire McGowan's friendly staff will have you hooked. Menus and water arrive promptly at your table, along with a bit of banter to make you feel at home. A good daytime choice ranges from soups, (including a seafood chowder) salads, sandwiches and bakes to tasty main courses like moules marinières pommes frites, whilst smartly presented evening menus up the ante a bit to include starters like pale smoked haddock & crab cakes alongside the ubiquitous tiger prawns and mains including several fish dishes, roast duckling and a choice of steaks. Appealing vegetarian dishes are included, and a proper Kids' menu is offered separately. Although not long, the wine list is appropriate. With nicely cooked popular dishes served by lovely staff in stylish surroundings, this is a pleasant place to eat. **Seats 100**; banqueting (100); Children welcome (high chair, childrens menu, baby changing facil-ities); Open all year: Open 7 days high season, L from 12, D from 5pm; Off Season - D Wed-Sun from 5pm; L Fri-Sun from 12pm; A la carte L & D; set Sun L €21.95. House wine €18; Live music on Saturday nights - see website for further detail. Closed Mon, Tue off season and Last 2 weeks in Jan. Amex, MasterCard, Visa, Laser, Switch. **Directions:** Located on Buncrana Pier about 40km (25 m) north of Letterkenny on R238. 23km (14m) from Derry city and 20km (12m) south of Ballyliffin.

BUNDORAN

A popular seaside resort on the southern shore of Donegal Bay, Bundoran looks across to the hills of Donegal in the north and is backed by the Sligo-Leitrim mountains to the south. Of the many hotels in and around the town, the best located by far is the **Great Northern Hotel** (071 984 1204; www.greatnorthernhotel.com) which is situated at the centre of an 18-hole championship golf course overlooking Donegal Bay; it also offers a new conference centre and good leisure facilities. And, if you enjoy traditional pubs, make a point of calling in at **Brennans / Criterion Bar** on Main Street - it's as fine an unspoilt Irish pub as you'll find anywhere: "no television, just conversation". The famous Lissadell House & Gardens (Ballinfull, Co Sligo, 071 916 3150) is within comfortable reach from here and the highly challenging County Sligo Golf Club (Rosses Point, 071 917 7134) is also short drive down the N15 in County Sligo.
WWW.IRELAND-GUIDE.COM FOR ALL THE BEST PLACES TO EAT, DRINK & STAY

BURTONPORT

BURTONPORT (Ailt an Chorrain) is a small fishing port and sea angling centre in The Rosses, renowned for its catches of salmon, lobster and crab in the summer months - fresh seafood which (along with many other varieties) finds its way on to menus in family-run pubs such as **Skippers Tavern** (074 954 2234) and **The Lobster Pot** (074 954 2012) both of which have a national reputation for fresh home-cooked food and warm hospitality; Skippers was undergoing major development at the time of going to press. Just off the town, the island of Arranmore is accessible by frequent car ferries; there is an hotel, **Arranmore House Hotel** (074 952 0918; www.arranmorehousehotel.ie), although it for sale at the time of going to press.
WWW.IRELAND-GUIDE.COM FOR ALL THE BEST PLACES TO EAT, DRINK & STAY

Carrigart

RESTAURANT•CHARACTER PUB

The Olde Glen Bar

Glen Carrigart Co Donegal
Tel: 074 915 5130

Just the sort of old pub advertising people dream about, the McLaughlin family's bar looks as it must have a hundred, maybe two hundred years ago. Low ceilings, ancient weathered bar and furniture, fires in winter, a big old room and then another behind. Then it got so popular they built on a further room, which is very light and bright, with paintings on the walls and this is also for drinking and sitting while you wait for a table to become available in The Restaurant. A dynamic young couple, Thomas & Maretta McLaughlin, run it; although working like mad all the time, Thomas has a word for everyone and is funny and relaxed and Maretta's the bubbly, glamorous and friendly wife who is front of house. Between them they've made such a roaring success of the place that they have to have two sittings every evening, and then go on beyond the summer proper into the end of October, as there are lots of golfers in the Rosapenna area until then. After that they do meals at weekends, maybe taking a break mid-winter. Why is it so popular? Because it provides just what you want: delicious, fresh, imaginative dishes served in an easy atmosphere, in a very basic but well thought out setting. And what might you eat? Tempura prawns, perhaps, served with a sweet chilli dipping sauce, and lovely halibut with dauphinoise potatoes, plaice with crab sauce and also local Hereford beefsteaks; good vegetables, local, meat and all fish brought in nearby. All this and a good wine list, great service and good value too. No wonder it's popular. *Olde Glen Bar was our Pub of the Year in 2008. **Seats 50**; children welcome before 9pm; toilets wheelchair accessible; D Tue-Sun, 6-9pm; house wine €16.50; SC discretionary. Closed Mon (May-Sept) and occasional weekends. MasterCard, Visa, Laser. **Directions:** 5 minutes from Carrigart village.

Culdaff

HOTEL•BAR•RESTAURANT

McGrory's of Culdaff

Culdaff Inishowen Co Donegal **Tel: 074 93 79104**
info@mcgrorys.ie www.mcgrorys.ie

In an area that has so much to offer in terms of natural beauty and activities like golf, angling and walking, McGrory's would make an ideal base. An inn in the true sense of the word, offering rest and refreshment to travellers, this north-western institution was established in 1924 and remains in the active care of the McGrory family, who set great store by the traditions of hospitality while also keeping an eye on changing tastes and the requirements of a fast-moving society. It is now a pleasing combination of old and new which is easy on the eye, and includes an evening restaurant as well as the bar where informal meals are served. Accommodation is offered in comfortable bedrooms that vary in size and outlook, but are all attractively furnished in a classic contemporary style, with well-planned bathrooms and all the necessary amenities (phone, tea/coffee tray, TV). For anyone touring the Inishowen peninsula this is a logical place to take a break, as popular bar food is available throughout the day. But it is probably for music that McGrory's is most famous - as well as traditional sessions in The Front Bar on Tuesday and Friday nights, Mac's Backroom Bar (constructed on the site of the old outhouses of McGrory's shop) is a major venue for live shows featuring international names. (Live music Wednesday and Saturday; events listings on the web.) Conference/banqueting (100/150); broadband wi/fi. **Rooms 17** (all en-suite, 4 shower only, 4 family rooms, 17 no smoking); children welcome (under 4 free in parents' room; cot available free of charge, baby sitting arranged); lift; room service (limited hours). No pets. B&B €55-75, ss €15. Special interest/off season breaks offered (midweek; weekend; golf - special rates with Ballyliffin Golf Club, early breakfast arranged). Restaurant: D Tue-Sun, L Sun. Bar meals daily, 12.30-8.30. Car park. Restaurant closed Mon; establishment closed 24-26 Dec. Amex, MasterCard, Visa, Laser. **Directions:** On R238 around Inishowen Peninsula.

DONEGAL TOWN

Donegal Town was originally a plantation town and is now best known as the main centre for the tweed industry and crafts. A visit to the area would be unthinkable without calling into Magee's on The Diamond, where there are hand loom weaving demonstrations; wholesome fare is available at the in-store restaurant, **The Weavers Loft**, and also at **The Blueberry Tea Room** (074 972 2933), just off The Diamond, on Castle Street. The Craft Village is on the edge of the town, and there's an excellent café, Aroma (see entry), serving great food, notably home baking. There is a farmers' market held monthly on a Saturday in The Diamond. A few miles west of the town, near

Mountcharles, Salthill Gardens (074 973 5387; www.donegalgardens.com) are open in the summer months and especially worth a visit.

WWW.IRELAND-GUIDE.COM FOR ALL THE BEST PLACES TO EAT, DRINK & STAY

Ard na Bréatha

Donegal
RESTAURANT•GUESTHOUSE

Drumrooske Middle Donegal Town Co Donegal
Tel: 074 972 2288 info@ardnabreatha.com www.ardnabreatha.com

GUESTHOUSE OF THE YEAR

In a slightly surprising location in what has become a mainly residential area on the edge of the town, Theresa and Albert Morrow's welcoming guesthouse is tucked into a quiet corner of their busy working farm and has a pleasant view out over an attractive garden to the countryside beyond. It is, as they say on their brochure, 'a place worth finding', and one of the first in Ireland to receive the EU flower award for Eco tourism. Their attention to detail, excellent customer service and concern for all things environmental has earned them a reputation of being exceptional and caring hosts from their many delighted guests. There is a very happy atmosphere and the house is planned with care to help people to relax, including a proper bar with bar stools, and a new contemporary residents' lounge with an open fire and a panoramic view of the Bluestack Mountains. A covered walkway links the house to accommodation in a separate building, just a few steps away: simple country style rooms are bright and comfortable, and all have phone, TV and full bath with shower. A lot of care also goes into breakfast, which is a very laid back affair, with all the treats people like to spoil themselves with on holiday, and a flexible attitude to timing. Small conferences/banqueting (20/45); free broadband wi/fi. Children welcome (under 3s free in parents' room, cot available free of charge, baby sitting arranged); wheelchair accessible; **Rooms 6** (1 family room, 3 ground floor, all no smoking); all day room service; dogs permitted to stay in bedrooms; B&B €40-55pps, ss €15. Closed 15 Nov - 15 Jan. **Restaurant:** The restaurant is open by reservation in the evening - tables in the attractive split level dining room are classically set up with white linen, and Albert offers a very reasonably priced full dinner menu with about five choices on each course; ingredients are locally sourced and organic where possible, and excellent specialities include Donegal rack of lamb and sirloin of Irish Angus beef. Cooking is good and the natural flavours of fine ingredients are allowed to take centre stage, in very enjoyable dishes that are served by staff who take pride in offering real Irish hospitality. Many guests opt to dine in on the first evening and never feel the need to go out for the rest of their stay, and it's easy to see why. A compact but well chosen wine list is reasonably priced and includes half and quarter bottles. **Seats 40.** D by reservation, 7-9.30 (Sun to 8.30); non-residents welcome. MasterCard, Visa, Laser. **Directions:** House is 1.5km (1 mile) from Donegal town, on the Lough Eske road. Take Killybegs road from Donegal town centre. First road to right for Lough Eske, continue to Vivo shop, take a right and go straight on.

Aroma

Donegal
CAFÉ

The Craft Village Donegal Co Donegal **Tel: 074 972 3222**
tomandarturo@yahoo.com

Tom Dooley's smart little café at the Craft Village just outside Donegal Town has won a lot of friends for its warm and friendly atmosphere and excellent freshly cooked food that offers much more than would be expected of a coffee shop. Tempting cakes, desserts and breads are all home-made and chef Arturo de Alba Gonzalez's menus include a frequently-changed blackboard, offering cooked-to-order dishes like real vegetable soups, fried polenta, prosciutto, garlic mushrooms and mixed leaves or white wine risotto with chargrilled chicken and seared asparagus, also salads like smoked chicken & avocado and, for the hungry young Mexican, the highly popular chimichangas. Ingredients are impeccably sourced and everything looks and tastes delicious - the quality of the food and good cooking both show on the plate. Service, under Tom's supervision is knowledgeable and efficient - with good espresso coffee and an extensive tea menu to go with the great home bakes, this makes a good daytime stop. And, although the coffee shop is small, there's a large outdoor eating area for fine weather. **Seats 30** (outdoors, 16); children welcome (high chair, childrens menu, baby changing facilities); open Mon-Sat, 9.30am-5.30pm (L 12-4); set L €17.50; SC disc. Closed Sun, 25-26 Dec, 1 Jan. MasterCard, Visa, Laser. **Directions:** 1.6km (1m) outside town on old Ballyshannon road.

Donegal

BAR•RESTAURANT

The Olde Castle Bar & Red Hugh's Restaurant

Donegal Town Co Donegal **Tel: 074 972 1262**

www.oldecastlebar.com

In a restored stone building directly overlooking the ruins of O'Donnell Castle in the heart of Donegal town, this traditional bar and restaurant is just the kind of place visitors are hoping to find - and, although it may seem a little touristy at first, the O'Toole family offer real Irish hospitality. In keeping with the old castle theme, the bar has flagged floors and lanterns on the arched walls, and some tables outside for fine weather. A compact but wide-ranging bar lunch menu offered daily includes favourites, with good seafood choices and traditional dishes including a hearty bowl of Traditional Irish Stew with perfectly cooked lamb and plenty of vegetables and potatoes in a tasty broth. Upstairs, above the bar, Red Hugh's is the evening restaurant, named after one of the town's most illustrious ancestors Red Hugh O'Donnell. The team of local chefs take pride in presenting an appealing à la carte menu, with local seafood the main speciality. A wholesome bowl of Seafood Chowder served with wheaten bread, and the hot and cold Seafood Platter for two are popular choices, and non-fish eaters have half a dozen dishes to choose from too, including local Ballintra steak. Food is natural, plentiful and reasonably priced, making it a popular choice for local clientele as well as visitors to this busy tourist town. Casual but very friendly service adds to the charm of good, flavoursome local foods simply cooked and presented in quite an atmospheric setting, and the wine list is sensibly pitched to match the food and surroundings. Bar lunch Mon-Sat. 12.30-4pm; The Red Hugh's Restaurant is open for D daily 6-9.45pm. **Directions:** In centre of Donegal Town, 1 minutes walk from the Diamond.

Donegal

HISTORIC HOUSE

Saint Ernan's House

Donegal Co Donegal **Tel: 074 972 1065**

res@sainternans.com www.sainternans.com

Set on its own wooded island, connected to the mainland by a causeway built after the Famine by tenants as a gesture of thanks to a caring landlord, Brian and Carmel O'Dowd's lovely Victorian country house on the edge of Donegal Town is remarkable for its sense of utter tranquillity. This atmosphere is due, in part, to its unique location - and also, one imagines, to the kindly ghosts who seem to reside here, especially the spirit of John Hamilton, that young landlord who built the house in 1826. That other-worldliness remains, and there is an almost tangible sense of serenity about the place that makes it the perfect retreat from the stresses of modern life. The spacious public rooms have log fires and antique furniture - plenty of space for guests to read, or simply to relax in front of the fire - and the individually decorated bedrooms echo that restfulness; as in all old houses, they vary in size and position but most also have lovely views and all are furnished to a high standard with antiques, and have good amenities including (surprisingly perhaps) television. If you can tear yourself away from the island, there is much to do and see in the area: the craft shops of Donegal Town are almost on the doorstep, for example, and Glenveagh National Park is just a short scenic drive away. The dining experience at Saint Ernan's follows the same philosophy of quiet relaxation and is only for resident guests; simple country house-style dinner menus offer two or three choices on each course and are based on local produce, with vegetarian dishes on request. **Rooms 6** (3 suites, 1 ground floor, all no smoking). B&B €120 pps, ss €40; not suitable for children under 6 yrs. Dining room seats 16, D Residents Only, 7-8pm Fri & Sat only, Set D €52 (semi-à la carte, priced by course); house wine €27. Closed end Oct-mid Apr. MasterCard, Visa, Laser. **Directions:** 1.5 mile south of Donegal Town on R267.

Downings

HOTEL

Rosapenna Hotel & Golf Resort

Downings Co Donegal **Tel: 074 915 5301**

rosapenna@eircom.net www.rosapenna.ie

Although local residents are understandably dismayed by the size and style of a new wing added in 2008 (20 new seaview suites with balconies), golfers may think they've died and gone to heaven when staying at Frank and Hilary Casey's renowned hotel on the shores of Sheephaven Bay. With comfortable and exceptionally spacious public areas, and guest rooms that have been thoughtfully designed down to the very last detail, it is a very hospitable and relaxing place to stay. And, of course, as virtually every guest is bound to be a golfer, residents make up a sociable community of golfers, either in the hotel, or at the superb new golf pavilion. The restaurant is open to non-residents but, in practice, it is usually filled to capacity by hotel guests; the wine list is carefully selected to complement the mainly traditional dishes and seafood on the menu. **Rooms 53** (1 suite, 5 junior suites, 4 family rooms, 3 shower only, 27 ground floor, all no smoking); children welcome (baby sitting arranged, cots available at no charge); all day room service; pets permitted in some area by prior arrangement. B&B €90pps, ss €20. Golf (18), residents' green fees €30, angling, snooker, indoor 'pool, sauna, steam room, gym, tennis. Equestrian, fishing and surfing nearby. **Restaurant: seats 100**; L daily, 11am-7pm; D daily 7.15-8.30, set D €55; children welcome, reservations required. Hotel closed end Oct-mid Mar. Amex, Diners, MasterCard, Visa, Laser. **Directions:** 36km (23m) northwest of Letterkenny, R425 to Carrigart then 2.5km.

DUNFANAGHY

Many people will have a soft spot for this traditional holiday area, often recalling family holidays spent at the famous old **Arnold's Hotel** (074 913 6208; www.arnoldshotel.com), which has been in the same family for three generations and is still a very comfortable, laid-back place to stay. Nearby at Marble Hill Strand, the **Shandon Hotel** (see entry) overlooks Sheephaven Bay, and is a popular family holiday destination. A little place that visitors will enjoy in the centre of the village is **Muck'n'Muffins** (074 913 6780), where you'll find a pottery studio on the ground floor and, upstairs, a coffee shop and wine bar overlooking the pier and the sea view across to Horn Head. The local Killyhoey Beach features on many of the 18 holes at the scenic Dunfanaghy Golf Club and Dunfanaghy makes an ideal base for touring Horn Head and the northern peninsulas. While in the locality, it is worth considering a visit to the Dunfanaghy Workhouse Visitor Centre (074 913 6504), a Famine Centre in the town that remembers the Great Famine in 19th century Ireland. The only place in Ireland where the corncrake can be heard in its natural habitat, Dunfanaghy is also a major centre for brown trout anglers and special interest holidays. Glenveagh Castle Gardens (074 913 7090) in nearby Glenveagh National Park (see round-up) is a 'must visit' while in the area, while golfers are spoilt for choice with several top championship courses within reach - Rosapenna Golf Links (Downings, 074 915 5301), Portsalon Golf Club (Fanad, 074 915 9459) are within a short drive and Ballyliffin Golf Club (Ballyliffin, 074 937 6119) is a little further away, on the Inishowen Peninsula.

WWW.IRELAND-GUIDE.COM FOR ALL THE BEST PLACES TO EAT, DRINK & STAY

Dunfanaghy

RESTAURANT WITH ROOMS

The Mill Restaurant

Figart Dunfanaghy Letterkenny Co Donegal **Tel: 074 913 6985**
themillrestaurant@oceanfree.net www.themillrestaurant.com

Beautifully located on the shore of the New Lake, which is a special area of conservation, the mill was the home of Susan Alcorn's grandfather and, as they are a family of accomplished painters, the walls are hung with wonderful watercolours. Susan and her husband Derek, who is the chef, have earned a dedicated following here, as the location is superb, the welcome warm and the cooking both imaginative and assured - and they also offer very good value. The split-level dining room has plenty of windows framing the views, fresh flowers on the tables, soft lighting and some well-placed antiques - a room of character and atmosphere. Seasonally influenced menus rely on the best ingredients, local where possible, and change every 4-6 weeks. While based on the classics, the Derek Alcorn's cooking style is his own - sometimes the ingredients may be unusual or under-used, but the originality is more in the way ingredients are combined, and in the detail, than in the choice of main ingredients. House specialities include an unusual upside down fish pie, which is filled with all manner of good things - lobster, crab claws and john dory in a brandy cream sauce, and gorgeous desserts might include a seasonal fruit crumble tart with custard & ginger ice cream, as well as a good Irish cheese plate. But the overall experience here is much more than the sum of its parts and, under Susan's direction, the hospitality and service is exemplary too. Overnight guests will also have a delicious breakfast to look forward to – a lovely buffet of fruits, juices, cereals etc, hot dishes cooked perfectly to order and all the little treats of home-baked breads and preserves. **Seats 50**; children welcome (high chair); air conditioning. D Tue-Sun 7-9pm, Set D €39 (+ side dishes); house wine €18; sc discretionary. Closed Mon, mid Dec-mid Mar. **Accommodation** is offered in six individually decorated rooms. The decor is simple but stylish, with good beds and some antique pieces, and there's also a lovely little sitting room off the dining room, with an open fire, and comfy big chairs and sofas to relax in. **Rooms 6** (all en-suite & no-smoking, 2 shower only); children welcome (under 5s free in parents' room, cot available without charge). Free broadband wi/fi; no pets. B&B €50 pps, ss €20. Garden; walking; cycling. Establishment closed mid Dec - mid Mar. Amex, MasterCard, Visa, Laser. **Directions:** N56 from Letterkenny to Dunfanaghy. 1km (1/2 m) outside Dunfanaghy on Falcarragh road on right hand side at the lake.

Dunfanaghy area
BAR•RESTAURANT

The Cove

Port na Blagh Dunfanaghy Co Donegal
Tel: 074 913 6300

Set well back from the road with plenty of parking at the front, there is no garden but some strategically placed plants soften the approach a little and, once inside, Peter Byrne and Siobhan Sweeney's restaurant is warm and welcoming. Peter shows arriving guests up to the first floor bar, where the luckiest guests will get seats at a corner table with big windows on both sides and views over the harbour. Waiting here for your table is no hardship, but once orders are taken from Siobhan's down-to-earth à la carte menu, offering nine or ten choices on each course, you'll be whisked away downstairs again, to an atmospheric dining room with a big open fire, lots of wood and good art on the walls. Specialities here include a really good house chowder served with home-baked brown bread and, along with a well-judged range of favourites, you'll find some less usual dishes too, such as crispy fried whitebait and whole boned quail. Main courses include a fair amount of seafood; pan-seared scallops served with a fino sherry & balsamic jus and organic mixed leaf salad is a house speciality but you'll also find delicious meat dishes such as slow cooked belly of pork, or shank of lamb, and imaginative vegetarian dishes too. Quite an extensive, informative wine list is broadly organised by price (Everyday Wines/Fine Wines) and offers plenty to encourage you to linger on a little after dinner. **Seats 42**; reservations recommended; toilets wheelchair accessible; not suitable for children under 10 yrs after 6.30pm. D Tue-Sun (& Bank Hol Mons), 6-9pm; early bird D, 2/3 course, €20/25; also à la carte; house wine €18. Closed Mon (except Bank Hols) and Jan - 16 Mar. Diners, MasterCard, Visa, Laser. **Directions:** On the main Creeslough-Dunfanaghy road (N56) in Portnablagh, overlooking the harbour. ◈

Dunfanaghy area
HOTEL

Shandon Hotel Spa & Wellness

Marble Hill Strand Port-na-Blagh Dunfanaghy Co Donegal **Tel: 074 913 6137**
shandonhotel@eircom.net www.shandonhotel.com

This large privately-owned hotel is in a prominent position overlooking Sheephaven Bay, and (although it's a bit of a climb up the hill on the way home) it's within walking distance of the famous beach. With excellent facilities for families, including a children's play centre, it's a popular family holiday destination and - with good food and plenty for older members of the family nearby too, including activities and treatments at the recently added Spa & Wellness Centre, golf, horseriding and walking, there is something for all age groups. Bedrooms vary in size according to their position in the building; the suites are especially desirable but all are comfortably furnished and have sea views. Staff are friendly and helpful and there are open fires and a very relaxed atmosphere, making for the best kind of traditional holiday. **Rooms 50**. Children welcome (baby sitting arranged, play room, playground). B&B from €75pps. Leisure Centre (swimming pool, children's pool, whirlpool spa, steam room, sauna), gym; Spa (treatments, hydrotherapy pool, heated loungers, themed showers, herb sauna, salt grotto, outdoor Canadian hot tub); pitch & putt, tennis courts, basketball, soccer pitch, snooker, table tennis, table football. Closed Nov-mid-Mar.

Dunkineely
HOTEL•RESTAURANT

Castle Murray House Hotel

St. John's Point Dunkineely Co Donegal **Tel: 074 973 7022**
info@castlemurray.com www.castlemurray.com

Martin and Marguerite Howley's beautifully located clifftop hotel has wonderful sea and coastal views over the ruined castle after which it is named. It is a comfortable and relaxing place to stay, with a little bar, a residents' sitting room and a large decked terrace that can be covered with an awning in a good summer, so meals may be served outside. A charming recent addition is an enclosed flower garden, supplying herbs to the kitchen and fresh flowers for the restaurant. Most of the bedrooms have sea views and all are quite large with a double and single bed, refurbished bathrooms (some with full bath) and all the necessary facilities including digital TV as well as phone and tea/coffee trays. Bedrooms have a mixture of modern and older pieces that give each room its own character, and are gradually being refurbished; the newer ones, which are more contemporary and gently stylish, feel more spacious but all are pleasing – and a sunny area on the sheltered flat roof at the back of the building has direct access from some bedrooms. Lovely breakfasts are served in the restaurant, and there's an appealing bar menu. Banqueting (60); free broadband wi/fi. Children welcome (under 5s free in parents room, cots available, baby sitting arranged). Pets permitted to stay in bedrooms by arrangement (no charge). Garden. Walking. Off-season value breaks. **Rooms 10** (6 shower only, 2 family, all no smoking). B&B €75pps, ss €20. **The restaurant** is on the seaward corner of the hotel overlooking the sea and the castle (which is floodlit at night), and an open fire makes for real warmth in this dramatic location, even in winter. Remy Dupuy has been head chef since 1994 and there is a consistent house style, with a strong emphasis on local produce. Menus are well priced and there is plenty to choose from, including vegetarian dishes. Seafood is the speciality of the house in the summer months - Remy has dedicated fishermen who fish lobster, monk, scallops and other fish for him. Mouthwatering menus open with starters like prawns & monkfish in garlic butter, and may also offer a choice of local oysters - and non-fishy treats like terrine of foie gras; main course choices are extensive, perhaps including less usual dishes like stuffed rabbit saddle with black pudding & Calvados, roast pheasant (in season), and at least one vegetarian option as well as seafood dishes - and it's good value too, even the supplement for lobster, from McSwynes Bay, is quite reasonable. In winter, when seafood is less plentiful, there are more red meats, poultry and game. Service, under the direction of restaurant manager Jorg Demmerer, is friendly and accommodating - and the wonderful location, helpful staff and interesting food make this a place people keep coming back to. The wine list leans towards the Old World, particularly France, and offers good house wines, a pair each of organic and non-alcoholic wines, an extensive selection of champagnes and plenty of half bottles. [NB: The Sunday lunch menu is quite traditional, with less emphasis on seafood.] **Seats 60** (outdoors, 20); not suitable for children after 8pm. D daily 6.30-9.30 (to 8.30 Sun), L Sun only 1.30-3.30; D from €34; house wine €21; No SC. Bar menu also available - phone to check times; also wise to check restaurant times off-season. Hotel closed mid Jan-mid Feb. MasterCard, Visa, Laser. **Directions:** Situated on the N56, 8km from Killybegs, 20km from Donegal Town on the coast road to St Johns Point; first left outside Dunkineely village.

GLENVEAGH NATIONAL PARK

Glenveagh National Park (Tel: 074 9137090; www.heritageireland.ie) is open to visitors all year, although visitor facilities are seasonal (mid March-early November). The Victorian castle, which is the focal point for visitors to the Park, was donated to the State by the last private owner, Henry Plummer McIlhenny, together with most of its contents - and the gardens are among the most interesting in Ireland, with many unusual and rare plants displayed in a series of garden rooms - the Pleasure Grounds, the Walled Garden, the Italian Garden and so on; garden tours are given regularly by experienced gardeners, but guests are also free to wander freely. The Interpretative Centre includes a restaurant, but there's a treat in store if you go to the **Tea Rooms** at the castle itself; they are in an attractive stone courtyard attached to the castle and specialise in excellent home baking.

WWW.IRELAND-GUIDE.COM FOR ALL THE BEST PLACES TO EAT, DRINK & STAY

GREENCASTLE

The ruins of the castle that this "typical" Donegal holiday village and commercial fishing port was named after still stand on a rock overlooking the entrance to Lough Foyle. There is an 18-hole golf course and an excellent bathing beach locally, and a maritime museum in the village close to the place where the Greencastle - Magilligan ferry leaves from the harbour. The Inishowen Maritime Museum is an interesting place to visit - it runs multiple themes and exhibitions of a maritime nature from Easter until October. **The Harbourside Café** (074 938 1835) is a nice little café next to the maritime museum that is open all day in summer and offers lots of tasty little bites - plain, toasted and gourmet sandwiches, plus homely bakes (scones, muffins and tray bakes, which change daily). Freshly squeezed orange juice is a tempting option on the drinks list - and there's delicious Illy coffee too. Overlooks the ferry, so you can be sure not to miss it.

WWW.IRELAND-GUIDE.COM FOR ALL THE BEST PLACES TO EAT, DRINK & STAY

Greencastle
BAR•RESTAURANT

Kealys Seafood Bar

The Harbour Greencastle Co Donegal **Tel: 074 938 1010**

kealys@iol.ie

The ferry between the fishing port of Greencastle and Magilligan Point in Northern Ireland brings many new visitors to an area that used to seem quite remote - and those in the know plan their journeys around a meal at Kealys excellent seafood restaurant. It's a low-key little place where simplicity has always been valued and, even if it's just to pop in for a daytime bowl of Tricia Kealy's Greencastle chowder and some home-baked brown bread, don't miss the opportunity of a visit to Kealys - if we did an award for seafood chowder, Kealys would take the prize! The approach to seafood is creative and balanced, seen in dishes, which are modern in tone but also echo traditional Irish themes, and in which delicious local organic vegetables are used with fish to make the most of both precious resources. A typical menu would include classic seafood dishes simply executed, such as lobster thermidor or whole sole on the bone and also dishes with a definite Kealys slant such as baked fillet of hake on braised fennel with a tomato & saffron butter sauce and, perhaps, a classic Irish partnership of baked salmon with a wholegrain mustard crust served on Irish spring cabbage and bacon. There will be at least one meat or poultry dish offered every day and there's always an imaginative vegetarian dish too - Gubbeen cheese & almond fritters, on a seasonal salad with honey & mustard dressing, for example. Breads are a speciality - perfect partners for the range of Irish farmhouse cheeses, as well as the famous chowder. Service is smart and friendly - and a compact but appealing wine list offers good value, and includes a small selection of half and quarter bottles. **Seats 65**; Toilets wheelchair accessible; children welcome until 9pm. L Fri-Sun, 12.30-2.45pm; D Wed-Sun, 7-9pm; Set D about €35, also à la carte. House wine €15. Bar food served 12.30-3pm daily. Closed Mon, Tue, 2 weeks Nov, 25 Dec, Good Friday. Amex, MasterCard, Visa, Laser. **Directions:** On the harbour at Greencastle, 32km (20 m) north of Derry City. ◊

KILLYBEGS

Killybegs is Ireland's premier deep sea fishing port and a popular sea angling centre. For comfortable modern town centre accommodation, try the well-established **Bayview Hotel** (074 973 1950; www.bayviewhotel.ie), with swimming pool and leisure centre, or the newer **Tara Hotel** (074 974 1700;www.tarahotel.ie). Dining options in the area include the 200-year old farmhouse restaurant, **Kitty Kellys** (074 973 1925; www.kittykellys.com), outside the town at Largy, which has special appeal for traditionalists - in both ambience and food.
WWW.IRELAND-GUIDE.COM FOR ALL THE BEST PLACES TO EAT, DRINK & STAY

Kincasslagh
CHARACTER PUB

Iggy's Bar

Kincasslagh Co Donegal

Tel: 074 954 3112

Just a short walk up from the harbour - it's also called the Atlantic Bar - Ann and Iggy Murray have run this delightfully unspoilt pub since 1986 and it's an all-year home-from-home for many a visitor. The television isn't usually on unless there's a match and Ann makes lovely simple food for the bar, mainly seafood - home-made soups, delicious crab sandwiches and Rombouts filter coffee. Children welcome. Bar open 10-12.30 daily, light food available 12-6, Mon-Sat. No food on Sundays. Closed 25 Dec & Good Friday. **No Credit Cards. Directions:** On the corner of the Main Street, where the road turns off to the harbour.

Laghey
RESTAURANT•COUNTRY HOUSE

Coxtown Manor
Laghey Co Donegal **Tel: 074 973 4575**
coxtownmanor@oddpost.com www.coxtownmanor.com

Just a short drive from the county town, this welcoming late Georgian house set in its own parkland is in a lovely, peaceful area close to Donegal Bay. Belgian proprietor, Edward Dewael - who fell for the property some years ago and is still in the process of upgrading it - personally ensures that everything possible is done to make guests feel at home. A pleasant wood-panelled bar with an open fire is well-stocked, notably with Belgian beers and a great selection of digestifs to accompany your after-dinner coffee - and it extends into a pleasant conservatory on one side and a comfortable drawing room, also with open fires, on the other. Accommodation is divided between a recently converted coach house at the back where the new bedrooms are very spacious, with plenty of room for golf gear and large items of luggage, and have excellent bathrooms to match - yet many guests still prefer the older rooms in the main house, for their character; some have countryside views and open fireplaces (turf, firelighters and matches supplied!) and they are large, comfortable and well-proportioned, with updated bathrooms, robes and Gilchrist & Soames toiletries. Children welcome (under 16 free in parents' room; cot available without charge, baby-sitting arranged). Walking; garden. No pets. **Rooms 9** (2 junior suites, all en-suite, 1 shower only, 5 no smoking, 2 ground floor). B&B €75-95 pps, ss €29. Breakfast buffet 8-10am; (cooked options include delicious Fermanagh dry-cured black bacon.) **Dining Room:** Although dinner is mainly for residents, the elegant and well-appointed period dining room is very much the heart of the house and is - like the food served here - attractive yet not too formal. Friendly staff promptly offer aperitifs and menus which are priced by course and offer mostly classic dishes with an emphasis on seafood (scallops from Donegal Bay, clams and mussels from Lissadell, for example), also Thornhill duck and local Charolais beef - a sound foundation for proficient cooking: starters will certainly include at least one shellfish dish (trio of Donegal Bay lobster, North Sea shrimps and prawns on filo pastry, perhaps); main course choices are also likely to favour seafood, but may also include less usual dishes like squab pigeon alongside Donegal lamb (with thyme jus). The produce is mostly local - and of superb quality - but the style is Belgian, offering a different experience from other dining options in the area. Belgian chocolate features strongly on the dessert menu but there are lighter options. Good food and lovely service from friendly, well-trained staff ensure that a meal here will be a special experience. Restaurant open to non-residents by reservation when there is room. **Seats 30**. D daily in high season, 7-9pm; set D about €50. House wine €22.50. Restaurant closed Sun, Mon in low season, house closed Nov - Feb. Amex, MasterCard, Visa, Laser. **Directions:** Main sign on N15 between Ballyshannon & Donegal Town. ◊

LETTERKENNY

The Letterkenny area - including Rathmullan and Ramelton - provides a good central location for exploring the county; a ferry between Rathmullan and Bundoran operates in summer (45 minutes), making the Inishowen peninsula very accessible. Originally a fishing village, which developed on the banks of Lough Swilly, Letterkenny town is now one of the largest and most densely-populated towns in Donegal - and one of the fastest-growing towns in Ireland. The Donegal County Museum is in the town and Letterkenny Farmers' Market is held on the 1st & 3rd Saturday of each month, 9am - 3pm (McGinley's Car Park, Pearse Road). You will also find some great wholesome, home-cooked and organic food amidst the gorgeous smell of herbs and spices in **Simple Simon's** (Oliver Plunkett Road; 074 912 2382 - opposite the library - other branches in Donegal Town and Glenties) - it is just the spot for lovers of herbal teas and home-made soups; while on Lower Main Street **The Yellow Pepper** (074 912 4133) is a bright and homely family-friendly restaurant located in an old shirt factory, offering wholesome food including home-grown vegetables, and cheerful service. For those who need accommodation in an hotel with leisure facilities, the new **Clanree Hotel** (074 912 4369; www.clanreehotel.com) is a useful choice, conveniently situated on the edge of town. For moderately-priced town centre hotel accommodation, try the **Letterkenny Court Hotel** (Main Street; 074 912 2977; www.letterkennycourthotel.com), or the new **Ramada Encore** (074 912 3100; www.encoreletterkenny.com), 5 minutes outside Letterkenny towards Ramelton. Travellers passing through the area who wish to avoid the town can get a bite at **The Silver Tassie Hotel** (074 912 5619; www.heblaneygroup.com), where bar food is available throughout the afternoon and evening. Nearby is the Glenveagh National Park, including Glenveagh Castle Gardens (074 913 7090) an elaborate series of gardens with tender specimens in a wilderness setting that are a 'must visit' when in County Donegal.
WWW.IRELAND-GUIDE.COM FOR ALL THE BEST PLACES TO EAT, DRINK & STAY

Letterkenny
HOTEL•RESTAURANT

Castle Grove Country House Hotel

Letterkenny Co Donegal **Tel: 074 915 1118**
reservations@castlegrove.com www.castlegrove.com

Parkland designed by "Capability" Brown in the mid-18th century creates a wonderful setting for Raymond and Mary Sweeney's lovely period house overlooking the lough. Castlegrove is undoubtedly the first choice for discerning visitors to the area, especially executives with business in Letterkenny; it is, as Mary Sweeney says, an oasis of tranquillity. Constant improvement is the policy and recent years have seen a number of additions, always carefully designed and furnished with antiques to feel like part of the main house. The original walled garden is under restoration as part of an on-going development of the gardens which will continue for several years. Public rooms include two gracious drawing rooms, each with an open fire, and a proper bar. Bedrooms are spacious and elegantly furnished to a high standard with antiques and, where practical, bathrooms have walk-in showers as well as full bath. Good breakfasts include a choice of fish as well as traditional Irish breakfast, home-made breads and preserves. Mary Sweeney's personal supervision ensures an exceptionally high standard of maintenance and housekeeping and staff are friendly and helpful. Two boats belonging to the house are available for fishing on Lough Swilly and there is a special arrangement with three nearby golf clubs. Conference/banqueting (25/50). House available for private use (family occasions, board meetings etc) Not suitable for children under 12. No pets. **Rooms 14** (1 suite, 2 junior suites, 2 shower only, 2 disabled, all no-smoking) B&B from €50 pps, no ss. *Weekends/ short breaks available. Open all year except Christmas. **The Green Room:** This large room is in a recent extension, but furnished in keeping with the original house, with generous classically appointed, well-spaced tables. Carefully sourced specialist and local ingredients are used: many of the herbs, vegetables and soft fruits are home-grown, the seafood - such as Swilly oysters - is local, and local meats are regularly used. **Seats 50** (private room, 15); reservations required; not suitable for children under 10 after 7pm. B 8-10 daily; snacks available all day; D 6.30-9pm daily. Closed 23-29 Dec. Amex, Diners, MasterCard, Visa, Laser. **Directions:** R245 off main road to Letterkenny. ◊

Letterkenny
RESTAURANT

Lemon Tree Restaurant

39 Lower Main Street Letterkenny Co Donegal
Tel: 074 912 5788

With its pretty lemon canopies, lemon painted and tiled frontage and colourful hanging flower baskets, this popular family-run restaurant in the centre of Letterkenny is easy to find. Inside it is warm and welcoming, with terracotta tiles, wooden furniture and peach sponged walls lending warmth, and an open kitchen adding buzz as you can watch brothers, Gary and Christopher Molloy at work. All meats are Irish sourced, fresh fish is a special feature and - unusually these days - everything is made freshly on site, including all breads, pastries, pastas and desserts. The house style is a mixture of traditional Irish and French classic, influenced by country house cooking: a wide choice of starters might include hand-made ravioli of Irish cheeses with roast vegetables and a fresh pepper coulis and, among the dozen or so main courses, there may be an unusual tasting plate of grilled fish. An early dinner menu offers good value and includes home-baked pizzas as well as a wide selection of seafood, poultry and meats. (*The Oak Tree**, on Port Road, is sister restaurant in the town and offers the same menu, but adds a bistro-style menu during the day). **Seats 40**; children welcome; reservations recommended. Open for D daily from 5-9.30pm (to 10pm Fri/Sat). Closed Good Fri, 24-26 Dec. Amex, MasterCard, Visa, Laser. **Directions:** Centre of town. ◊

Letterkenny
HOTEL

Radisson SAS Hotel

Paddy Harte Road Letterkenny Co Donegal **Tel: 074 919 4444**
info.letterkenny@radissonsas.com www.letterkenny.radissonsas.com

This modern hotel on the edge of Letterkenny town is well-placed for short breaks in one of Ireland's most beautiful areas, and within easy walking distance of the town; although it has been surrounded by building sites, new shops and other amenities have now opened nearby (Marks & Spencer is a useful landmark just opposite the entrance). It is a pleasing contemporary building: an atrium lobby with maple panelling and leather furniture lends a great sense of space and sets a smart tone for the rest of the hotel. There's a mix of suites and rooms, all featuring modern facilities and very nice bathrooms - Business Class rooms also have a desk area with broadband. At the hotel's TriBecCa Restaurant an early dinner menu offers great value and breakfast, which is also served here, is well above the usual hotel offering. This is a well-managed hotel, and a pleasant place to stay. Conference/banqueting (600/300); business centre, secretarial services, video conferencing, free broadband wi/fi. **Rooms 114** (1 suite, 21 executive, 5 family, 3 shower only, 3 disabled, 82 no smoking); children welcome (under 12s free in parents room, cot available free of charge, baby sitting arranged). Lift. 24 hr room service. B&B about €74.50, ss €14.50. No pets. **TriBeCa: Seats 80.** D Tue-Sat, 6-9.30; L Sun only 12.30-3. Set D about €32.50, also à la carte; Set Sun L about €21.50. House wine about €21. SC discretionary. Bar meals available 12.30-8 daily. Leisure centre (17m swimming pool, steam room, sauna, fitness room). Golf, gardens, walking, wind surfing etc nearby. Amex, MasterCard, Visa, Laser. **Directions:** Drive towards Letterkenny town, turn left at Tourist Office roundabout, turn left off roundabout (R250) - hotel is on right.

LOUGH ESKE

Lying beneath the Blue Stack Mountains with waterfalls at both the north and south ends, Lough Eske is a peaceful and picturesque area close to Donegal Town. The lough and the surrounding thickly-wooded mountains combine natural beauty with excellent fishing (for salmon, brown trout and sea trout) and a sense of history - Lough Eske has 12 islands, including the Isle of O'Donnell with the remains of an historic castle. Nearby Donegal Town offers the visitor much of interest including the 15th century Donegal Castle (074 972 2405, open March to October), the Old Franciscan Abbey and the Donegal Railway Heritage Centre (074 972 2655), with information on the history of the County Donegal railway. Visitors can also take advantage of the beautiful beaches at Rossnowlagh and Murvagh, just a short drive away.

Lough Eske
HOTEL•RESTAURANT

Harvey's Point Country Hotel
Lough Eske Donegal Co Donegal **Tel: 074 972 2208**
info@harveyspoint.com www.harveyspoint.com

Blessed with one of Ireland's most beautiful locations, on the shores of Lough Eske, this well-managed hotel was first opened by the Gysling family in the late 1980s, with chalet-style buildings linked by covered walkways and pergolas creating a distinctly alpine atmosphere reminiscent of their native Switzerland - a style that suited the site well, with the open low-level design allowing views of the lough and mountains from most areas of the hotel. Other than its location, the most outstanding feature of this hotel has always been the friendliness and helpfulness of the staff, and that is still its great strength. Otherwise, guests re-visiting today will find many changes, and a far more luxurious establishment: rooms in the new extension may not all have a lake view - but acres of space, six foot beds (or, in the latest batch of rooms, large twins) and huge baths will please many guests. However, the older rooms - which are tucked away in front of the extension, along the ground floor corridor - may be of more interest to those in the know, especially those travelling with their dog; although less luxurious, they have recently been refurbished and are very comfortable - and will appeal if you would enjoy being closer to the countryside, with access to the lough. *A swimming pool was nearing completion at the time of going to press. Conference/banqueting 300/350; video conferencing, secretarial services, free broadband wi/fi. Treatment rooms (hair, beauty, holistic), swimming pool. Children welcome (under 3s free in parents room, cots available free of charge, baby sitting arranged). Dogs permitted to stay in bedrooms (no charge). Garden. **Rooms 62** (4 suites, 38 junior suites, 20 ground floor, 14 disabled). Lift. Turndown service. Open all year. **Restaurant:** The bar and restaurant areas are still their old selves: a welcoming log fire sets the tone in the bar, where menus are promptly offered by friendly staff, and in the restaurant - a large room, extending right down to the foreshore – classically appointed tables are set up to take advantage of the beautiful view across the lough and, perhaps, watch the hotel's pet geese coming in from the water at feeding time. Paul Montgomery has been head chef since 2006 and he offers a number of menus, including a Celtic Trail dinner menu, with dishes inspired by all the Celtic regions, and the Green Garden Trail, for vegetarians; also a simpler but attractive Cuisine Art lunch menu. His classically toned menus offer an extensive choice and look a little complicated, but the cooking is assured and well up to the theatrical nuances of the fine dining experience laid on by attentive and well-trained restaurant staff. The restaurant is also open for lunch, every day except Saturday, and Room Service and Bar Snack menus are also offered. **Seats 100** (private room, 50); air conditioning; toilets wheelchair accessible. L 12.30-2.30pm (Sun 12-4) & D daily 6.30-9.30pm. Set D €65; Set L €35; set Sun L €32; house wine from €23; no SC. Off season (Nov-Mar), restaurant closed D Sun, all Mon & Tue. MasterCard, Visa, Laser. *A bar menu is also served daily, 12.30-5.30pm. MasterCard, Visa, Laser. **Directions:** N15 /N56 from Donegal Town - take signs for Lough Eske & hotel. (6km from Donegal Town.)

Lough Eske
B&B

Rhu-Gorse

Lough Eske Co Donegal **Tel: 074 972 1685**
rhugorse@iol.ie www.lougheske.com

Beautifully located, with stunning views over Lough Eske (and windows built to take full advantage of them), Grainne McGettigan's modern house may not be not architecturally outstanding but it has some very special attributes, notably the warmth and hospitality of Grainne herself, and a lovely room with picture windows and a big fireplace, where guests can relax. Bedrooms and bathrooms are all ship-shape and residents can have afternoon tea as well as breakfast, although not evening meals; however Harvey's Point is very close (see entry), and Donegal town is only a short drive. Animals are central to Rhu-Gorse, which is named after a much-loved pedigree dog bred by Grainne's father-in-law (a descendant now follows her around everywhere), and one of her special interests is breeding horses: not your average B&B, but a comfortable, hospitable and very interesting base for a walking holiday or touring the area. **Rooms 3** (2 shower only, 1 family room, all no smoking); children welcome (under 3s free in parents' room). B&B €42.50 (includes afternoon tea on arrival), ss €10. Pets allowed in some areas. Garden. Golf nearby. Closed 31 Oct-31 Mar. MasterCard, Visa, Laser. **Directions:** Take N15 /N56 from Donegal Town. Take signs for Lough Eske & Harvey's Point Hotel. Pick up signs for Rhu-Gorse. ◇

Lough Eske
HOTEL•RESTAURANT

Solis Lough Eske Castle Hotel

Lough Eske Donegal Co Donegal **Tel: 074 972 5000**
info@solishotels.com www.solislougheskecastle.ie

At the heart of this impressive new hotel, there is indeed a castle and, although it does not have views of Lough Eske, the setting should not disappoint as it is surrounded by beautiful woodland and formal gardens. With a history dating back to a castle built by the O'Donnells (founders of Donegal town) in the late 1400s, it is no stranger to add-ons and reconstructions, so the recent restoration of a Victorian castle (destroyed by fire in 1939) seems totally in keeping. And it has been very well done. Not only does the luxurious castle itself have great atmosphere and presence, with its spacious public rooms, impressive fireplaces and leaded windows, but the new sections are well conceived to be easy on the eye as well as being supremely practical in use. On arrival, for example, it's a pleasure to see how well-chosen sandstone subtly links the colour of new sections to the castle frontage, and there are similar examples everywhere – notably the leisure centre and spa, which is in the old walled garden and designed to look like the old lean-to glasshouses, with the swimming pool in a lovely bright garden setting. The 98 bedrooms and suites vary according to their position in the property, with most luxurious castle suites offering a sumptuous blend of antique charm and modern comfort, while others have a simpler, more contemporary feel; all are stylishly appointed, with lovely bathrooms and all the modern extras including wi/fi. Conference/Banqueting (250); small meetings (14-40); **96 Bedrooms**; Spa, Fitness Centre and Pool, Golf Nearby. **Cedars Restaurant:** Michel Flamme, well known in Ireland from his time at the Kildare Hotel & Country Club ('K Club'), joined the Castle team as Executive Head Chef in summer 2008 and wasted no time in putting his mark on the kitchen. The restaurant - which has woodland views and opens onto a large slate terrace - is bright and luxurious yet contemporary, with lots of deep buttoning in comfortable bucket chairs and matching wall coverings, and a combination of darkwood tables with dark moss green runners and others set with crisp white linen cloths and green linen napkins: a perfect backdrop for an exceptional dining experience. An à la carte menu offering about eight dishes on each course combines a wealth of fresh, locally sourced and sometimes organic produce – resulting in perfectly cooked and innovative dishes presented with flair. Begin, perhaps, with a beautifully balanced tomato and red pepper soup, or local Killybegs mussels with roasted garlic, fennel and Irish butter – followed by simply cooked main dishes such as seared rack of lamb with cabbage parcel, garlic potatoes and red wine jus; a great dish, the lamb beautifully pink and a big cabbage parcel with a filling of pepper, mushroom, courgette and shallots. An extensive list of world wines is offered to match the food. Staff are pleasant and helpful but, in the Guide's experience, slightly disorganised – a little extra training could make a big difference to the dining experience. Nevertheless, with its combination of exceptional cooking and reasonable prices, this restaurant is quietly taking its place as one of the most distinguished in Ireland. Not surprisingly Cedars is often fully booked, particularly during the summer months when hotel occupancy is high, so advanced reservation is strongly advised. *Informal meals are also available daily in the Gallery Bar, 11am-12 midnight. **Seats 110**. Children welcome. D daily 6-10, L Sun 1-3.

MALIN

As the northern-most point of Ireland, unspoilt Malin offers rugged coastal scenery and beautiful beaches, excellent for walking, swimming or horse riding. The area is rich in wildlife and is a favourite spot for birdwatchers, whilst anglers will enjoy fishing from the beach or from rocky coastal points. This is a great base for the golfer as you are in easy reach of Inishowen's five magnificent golf courses. Malin town is small and charming, with a village green and a lovely old church.

Malin	# Malin Hotel
HOTEL	Malin Co Donegal **Tel: 074 937 0606**
V	info@malinhotel.ie www.malinhotel.ie

Although it has been extensively upgraded since they took it over in 2003 (and extended to provide four new bedrooms and a lift), Patrick and Fiona Loughrey's attractive hotel overlooking the green has lost none of its charm. The pleasingly traditional bar is a popular meeting place, and the accommodation is appealing: neat, attractively decorated bedrooms have phones, tea/coffee and TV; the older rooms have been re-designed and, along with their bathrooms, completely refurbished. While some rooms are not very large, they are inviting and comfortable - offering a friendly and moderately priced base for exploring this beautiful area. The hotel's **Jack Yeats Restaurant** is earning a good reputation, both for the food and an informative and well selected wine list; however, food hours are variable due to the seasonality of the business (bar meals usually all day from 12 noon in high summer, with dinner daily from 6pm); the midweek dinner menu (Wed-Fri, 6-9.15) offers great value. Conference/banqueting (200/300); free broadband wi/fi; secretarial services. **Rooms 18** (1 suite, 7 executive, 11 shower only, 1 family room, 1 for disabled, all no smoking); children welcome (under 3s free in parents' room, cot available free of charge, baby sitting arranged). No pets. Lift. Limited room service. B&B €65-75 pps, ss €15. Walking. Closed 25 Dec. MasterCard, Visa, Laser. **Directions:** Overlooking the village green in Malin town.

Moville Area	# Carlton Redcastle Hotel & Spa
HOTEL	Redcastle Moville Inishowen Co Donegal **Tel: 074 938 5555**
	info@carltonredcastle.ie www.carltonredcastle.ie

Beautifully located overlooking Lough Foyle, on the shore side of the scenic route that runs up the eastern coast of the Inishowen peninsula, this 4* hotel is near the traditional holiday town of Moville yet, surrounded by extensive grounds and its own 9-hole parkland golf course, it's in a world of its own. Popular with locals as well as people on leisure breaks, it can be very busy at weekends but midweek short breaks offer good value and a much calmer atmosphere. It's an attractive hotel, with spacious public areas and good amenities, and the restaurant (Water's Edge) and Thalasso Spa, in particular, make full use of the lovely waterside location. Bedrooms and suites, which have wonderful views, are smartly decorated and finished to a high standard. **Rooms 93.** B&B €99pps, suites from €180. Midweek breaks offered. Open all year except Christmas. Helipad. MasterCard, Visa, Laser. **Directions:** On east side of Inishowen peninsula (R238 from Letterkenny or Derry City). ◊

RAMELTON

This beautiful old town, situated at the mouth of the River Lennon was built between 1609 and 1622. The O'Donnells had a castle here before the Gaelic chieftains were defeated in the 17th century and, in the Ulster plantation, the Stewarts built a town for the Scottish and English settlers; their history is evident in Ramelton's architectural heritage. The town was used as a backdrop to the fascinating 1995 TV drama 'The Hanging Gale.' There's an enjoyable walk from the tree-lined mall, following the river past the quay, then onto the guildhall and the ornate town hall, where country markets are held. Local attractions include the Ramelton Story exhibition (074 915 1266) housed in the recently renovated steamboat store, which portrays the story of Ramelton; the Donegal Ancestry Centre is also housed here. Nearby, the magnificent Glenveagh National Park (074 913 7090), offers some of the most breathtaking scenery in the country and includes wild deer, a castle and gardens. In nearby Gweedore, Ionad Cais Locha (074 953 1699, open March to November) is a two-storey farmhouse with a farm museum and a large collection of farm animals. Ramelton is an ideal base for exploring a wide area of this beautiful county, with walking, fishing, golf and horse riding all nearby, also shopping at Letterkenny.

Ramelton　　　　　　　　　　　　　　　　　　　　　　　　　　　　　Ardeen
COUNTRY HOUSE　　　　　　　　　　　　　Ramelton Co Donegal **Tel: 074 915 1243**
　　　　　　　　　　　　　　　ardeenbandb@eircom.net　www.ardeenhouse.com

Overlooking Lough Swilly, and set in its own grounds on the edge of the heritage town of Ramelton, Anne Campbell's mid-nineteenth century house is well-located for touring Donegal and Glenveagh National Park. It is not too grand and has the comfortable atmosphere of a family home - the drawing room and dining room are both furnished with antiques and have open fires, making this a very warm and comfortable place to return to after a day out. Individually decorated bedrooms with views over the lough or nearby hills all have their own character and are charmingly furnished (Anne is very handy with a sewing machine and time available in the winter is well used for guests' comfort). No dinners, but Anne can recommend pubs and restaurants nearby. **Rooms 5** (4 en-suite with shower, 1 twin has private bathroom, all no smoking, 1 family room); children welcome (under 2s free in parents' room, cots available free of charge, baby sitting arranged). B&B €40 pps, ss €10. Garden, tennis; free broadband wi/fi. No pets. *Self-catering also available in the 'Old Stables'; details on request. Closed Oct-Easter. MasterCard, Visa. **Directions:** Follow river to Town Hall, turn right; 1st house on right.

Ramelton　　　　　　　　　　　　　　　　　　　　　　　　　　　　　　Frewin
COUNTRY HOUSE　　　　　　　　　　Rectory Road Ramelton Co Donegal **Tel: 074 915 1246**
　　　　　　　　　　　　　　　　flaxmill@indigo.ie　www.frewinhouse.com

Thomas and Regina Coyle restored this large Victorian house with the greatest attention to period detail and guests have the opportunity to drink in the atmosphere on arrival while having a cup of tea in the little book-lined library, where the old parish safe is still set in the wall. Bedrooms vary, as is the way in old houses, but they are all beautifully furnished with antiques, and snowy white bedlinen - and a robe provided in case of night-time forays along the corridor (one bathroom is private, but not en-suite). A delicious breakfast, including freshly baked breads warm from the oven, is taken communally at a long polished table. This beautiful house is most unusual, notably because Thomas Coyle specialises in restoring old buildings and is a collector by nature - much of his collection finds a place in the house. *Dinner can be arranged €45pp, five courses. **Rooms 4** (3 shower only, 1 with private bath, 1 family room, all no smoking); not suitable for children under 8. No pets. B&B €85 pps, ss about €15. Garden. Closed 23 Dec-1 Jan. MasterCard, Visa. **Directions:** Take R245 from Letterkenny. Travel 7 miles approx and take right turn on approach to Ramelton. Located 400 yards on right. ◇

RATHMULLAN

An attractive small town on Lough Swilly, Rathmullan makes a good base for exploring the Fanad peninsula and as a ferry runs between the little harbour and Buncrana in summer (mid-May to September; from Buncrana every 1 hr 20 mins from 9am-7.40pm; from Rathmullan every 1 hr 20 mins from 9.40am - 8.10pm), the Inishowen peninsula, Derry city and the north Antrim coast are also accessible. Long sandy beaches and availability of holiday homes and other accommodation make it a popular choice for family holidays, and Portsalon Golf Club - one of Ireland's oldest golf clubs, founded in 1891 - is just a few miles up the coast. Other local attractions include the Flight of the Earls Heritage Centre (074 919 4277) or for those with an interest in cooking, Kathleen Loughrey's School of Home Baking (074 915 8122 may give you a few baking tips to take home. Rathmullan is only an hour's drive from Glenveagh National Park (074 913 7090), which offers magnificent scenery, walking, rich wildlife including deer, a castle and gardens. In Rathmullan village, the aptly named **Water's Edge** (074 915 8182; www.thewatersedge.ie) offers rooms and food with a wonderful view, making it a popular stopping place.

WWW.IRELAND-GUIDE.COM FOR ALL THE BEST PLACES TO EAT, DRINK & STAY

Rathmullan
RESTAURANT

An Bonnán Buí
Pier Road Rathmullan Co Donegal **Tel: 074 915 8453**
bonnanbui@yahoo.ie www.bonnanbui.com

Tucked into a side street in Rathmullan village, Martin Kelly and Monica Santos' informal restaurant has real draw-you-in appeal from the road – and if that doesn't work, their interesting menu will surely do the trick. A well-balanced variety of Irish, European and South American dishes means that pondering over the menu may take a little longer than usual in order to make your menu choices but will also allow you more time to soak up the atmosphere in this friendly, bustling restaurant - Monica is Brazilian and has an obvious influence, not only on the food offered (which is unique in this region), but the unusual artwork on the walls. Dishes such as the Portuguese dish of cod balls, Bolinho de Bacalhau, to start your meal, should whet your appetite for what is to follow - and you won't be disappointed with the range of fish dishes, the fine steak or the colourful Brazilian Moqueca De Frutos do Mar, with its plentiful variety of seafood in a fresh tomato and red pepper sauce. And, of course, it's impossible to leave without tasting Martin's "very good chocolate cake" with its world-wide reputation… A well-chosen wine list complements the menu. Offering a different dining experience, atmosphere and good value, it's easy to understand this restaurant's enduring popularity. Wine bar with tapas and outside balcony area. **Seats 48**; open Thu-Sun, 5.30-9.30; Sun 1-5 (L & light meals/snacks); children welcome (high chair, children's menu). Ring to confirm opening times off-season as reduced days and holidays taken. MasterCard, Visa, Laser. **Directions:** In Rathmullan village, on the road opposite the pier; on left when going away from the sea.

Rathmullan
GUESTHOUSE
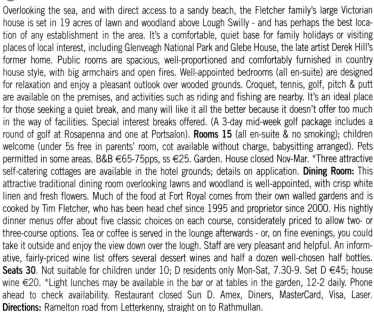

Fort Royal
Rathmullan Co Donegal **Tel: 074 91 58100**
fortroyal@eircom.net www.fortroyalhotel.com

Overlooking the sea, and with direct access to a sandy beach, the Fletcher family's large Victorian house is set in 19 acres of lawn and woodland above Lough Swilly - and has perhaps the best location of any establishment in the area. It's a comfortable, quiet base for family holidays or visiting places of local interest, including Glenveagh National Park and Glebe House, the late artist Derek Hill's former home. Public rooms are spacious, well-proportioned and comfortably furnished in country house style, with big armchairs and open fires. Well-appointed bedrooms (all en-suite) are designed for relaxation and enjoy a pleasant outlook over wooded grounds. Croquet, tennis, golf, pitch & putt are available on the premises, and activities such as riding and fishing are nearby. It's an ideal place for those seeking a quiet break, and many will like it all the better because it doesn't offer too much in the way of facilities. Special interest breaks offered. (A 3-day mid-week golf package includes a round of golf at Rosapenna and one at Portsalon). **Rooms 15** (all en-suite & no smoking); children welcome (under 5s free in parents' room, cot available without charge, babysitting arranged). Pets permitted in some areas. B&B €65-75pps, ss €25. Garden. House closed Nov-Mar. *Three attractive self-catering cottages are available in the hotel grounds; details on application. **Dining Room:** This attractive traditional dining room overlooking lawns and woodland is well-appointed, with crisp white linen and fresh flowers. Much of the food at Fort Royal comes from their own walled gardens and is cooked by Tim Fletcher, who has been head chef since 1995 and proprietor since 2000. His nightly dinner menus offer about five classic choices on each course, considerably priced to allow two- or three-course options. Tea or coffee is served in the lounge afterwards - or, on fine evenings, you could take it outside and enjoy the view down over the lough. Staff are very pleasant and helpful. An informative, fairly-priced wine list offers several dessert wines and half a dozen well-chosen half bottles. **Seats 30**. Not suitable for children under 10; D residents only Mon-Sat, 7.30-9. Set D €45; house wine €20. *Light lunches may be available in the bar or at tables in the garden, 12-2 daily. Phone ahead to check availability. Restaurant closed Sun D. Amex, Diners, MasterCard, Visa, Laser. **Directions:** Ramelton road from Letterkenny, straight on to Rathmullan.

Rathmullan
COUNTRY HOUSE

Rathmullan House
Rathmullan Co Donegal **Tel:** 074 915 8188
info@rathmullanhouse.com www.rathmullanhouse.com
NATURAL FOOD AWARD

Set in lovely gardens on the shores of Lough Swilly, this gracious nineteenth century house is fairly grand, with public areas which include three elegant drawing rooms, but it's not too formal - and there's a cellar bar which can be very relaxed. It was built as a summer house by the Batt banking family of Belfast in the 1800s, and has been run as a country house hotel since 1961 by the Wheeler family. Recently, under the energetic management of William and Mark Wheeler, and their wives Yvonne and Mary, an impressive extension was completed to a design that is admirably sympathetic to the surroundings. Here they have ten very desirable, individually decorated bedrooms, and The Gallery, a state-of-the-art conference facility for up to 80 delegates. Bedrooms in the original house vary in size, decor, outlook and cost, but all are comfortably furnished in traditional country house style. Donegal has an other-worldliness that is increasingly hard to capture in the traditional family holiday areas and, although now larger, Rathmullan House still retains a laid-back charm and that special sense of place - and it is greatly to their credit that the Wheeler family have developed their business (and extended the season) without compromising the essential character of this lovely place. And Rathmullan just goes on getting better; their latest venture is open-air theatre, with an ambitious production held in the grounds each summer – most recently The Tempest, no less. *Rathmullan House was our Country House of the Year in 2007. Conference/banqueting (80/60); free broadband wi/fi; video conferencing. Swimming pool, steam room, tennis, walking. Children welcome (free in parents room under 12 months, cot €10, baby sitting arranged, play ground, playroom). Pets permitted in bedrooms by arrangement (special pet-friendly room available). Gardens. **Rooms 32** (21 with separate bath & shower, 9 ground floor, 4 family, 1 for disabled, 10 no smoking). B&B €110-140 pps, ss €45, SC 10%. **The Weeping Elm:** The dining room was revamped and extended in the recent renovations, but the famous tented ceiling (designed by the late Liam McCormick, well known for his striking Donegal churches) has been retained. It is a pleasing room that makes the most of the garden outlook - including a formal garden beside the extension, which is maturing nicely - and provides a fine setting for Ian Orr's modern Irish cooking, as well as the tremendous breakfasts for which Rathmullan is justly famous. Cooking here is upbeat traditional and meticulously-sourced menus are based on the very best of local and artisan foods – and, working closely with organic gardener, Dennis Hawke, Ian uses fresh produce from their own lovely restored walled garden. There are many beautifully conceived combination dishes, and you can look forward to specialities like home-smoked Silverhill duck breast, with baked borlotti beans, Parmesan purée and garden rocket, or fillet of North Atlantic halibut with hand-made crab ravioli, garden spinach and cauliflower purée - and, perhaps, a fine farmhouse cheese selection or a refreshing compôte of garden fruits with carrageen pudding. (Both the cheeses and the carrageen are equally at home as part of the legendary Rathmullan breakfast too.) And a particularly attractive feature of Rathmullan is the Children's Menu - a proper little person's version of the adult menu, with lots of choices and no concessions to 'popular' fare, this is education on a plate. Like everything else here, the wine list is meticulously sourced and informative - unusually, the alcohol content is given along with other details; it also includes half a dozen organic & bio-dynamic wines, lots of lovely bubblies, a wide choice of half bottles and a section dedicated to wines selected to complement the menu, some of them available by the glass. All this plus caring service and a beautiful location... **Seats 80** (private room, 30; outdoors, 30); D daily 7-8.45 (to 9.30 Fri/Sat); Set D €47.50/52.50, 2/3 courses; house wine from €24; SC 10%. *Informal meals are available in The Cellar Bar, 12.30-7pm daily in summer and in Batts Bar 1-2.30pm daily. Children welcome at 7pm (children's menu, high chair and baby changing facilities available). Closed 25-26 Dec. Amex, MasterCard, Visa, Laser. **Directions:** Letterkenny to Ramelton - turn right to Rathmullan at the bridge, through village and turn right to hotel.

ROSSNOWLAGH
Situated on the south side of Donegal Bay, this busy seaside holiday spot is famous for its blue flag beach. Extending to the north northwest for over 2km, from the cliffs at Coolmore in the south to the rock outcrop at Carrickfad, it is one of the most popular surfing beaches in Ireland. Other attractions include La Verna House (071 985 1342), a Franciscan Friary with attractive grounds and gardens, and the Donegal Historical Society's Museum (074 972 2874) which has its home in Rossnowlagh.

Rossnowlagh
HOTEL•RESTAURANT

Sand House Hotel

Rossnowlagh Co Donegal **Tel: 071 985 1777**
info@sandhouse.ie www.sandhouse.ie

Perched on the edge of a stunning sandy beach two miles long, the Britton family's famous hotel lost its trademark crenellated roof-line some years ago, but emerged with an elegant new look, reminiscent of a French chateau. Wonderful sea views and easy access to the beach have always been the great attractions of The Sand House, which started life as a fishing lodge in the 1830s and completed its latest metamorphosis with a new floor of bedrooms, a panoramic lift (with the best view in the house), a new boardroom and a marine beauty spa. Existing bedrooms were also refurbished; all are very comfortable, with excellent bathrooms - and everyone can enjoy the sea view from the sun deck. Things that never change here include the welcoming fire in the foyer, exceptional housekeeping - and the excellent hospitality. Golf is a major attraction for guests at The Sand House, which is a member of The Emerald Triangle (three strategically-placed establishments offering great golf experiences: the other two are Rathsallagh, Co Wicklow, and Glenlo Abbey, Co Galway, see entries). Also partners in 'Play 3 Great Golf Courses in Ireland's North-West' (Donegal GC, Bundoran, Castle Hume). Spa; fishing, cycling, walking, tennis on site; horse riding, boating and many other activities available nearby. Details on application. Conferences (100). Children welcome (under 5s free in parents' room, cots available without charge, baby sitting arranged). Pets permitted by arrangement. **Rooms 50** (1 suite, 2 junior suites, 5 executive, 5 shower only, 25 no-smoking, 1 disabled). Lift. 24-hour room service. B&B €96pps, no ss. SC discretionary. Closed Dec & Jan. **Seashell Restaurant:** The restaurant is rather unexpectedly at the front of the hotel, so it has no sea view, but it is well-appointed, in keeping with the rest of the hotel. John McGarrigle, who has been with the hotel since 2000, presents seasonal 5-course dinner menus, changed daily; fresh seafood and locally sourced lamb and beef (also game, in season) provide the foundation for a traditional repertoire, with interesting side dishes an unusual strength. Finish with a choice of Irish cheeses or hotel-style desserts - if you ask very nicely you might be able to have them up in the conservatory, overlooking the sea. Staff are helpful and attentive. Good choice of wines by the glass. *Soup and sandwiches are also available in the bar at lunchtime, every day except Sunday. **Seats 80**; children welcome. D daily 7-8.30pm, L Sun only, 1-2pm. Set Sun L about €30; set D €50; house wines from €20. SC discretionary. Closed Dec & Jan. Amex, MasterCard, Visa, Laser. **Directions:** Coast road from Ballyshannon to Donegal Town. ◊

Rossnowlagh Area
RESTAURANT•GUESTHOUSE

Heron's Cove

Creevy Rossnowlagh Co Donegal **Tel: (071) 982 2070**
info@heronscove.ie www.heronscove.ie

For those who prefer to stay at a smaller place with a more intimate atmosphere, Seoirse and Maeve O'Toole's fine 10-bedroom guesthouse near the picturesque little harbour of Creevy Pier has offered a comfortable and hospitable base at a moderate price since opening in 2006, and could be just the ticket. Close to Rossnowlagh beach, and just 10 minutes drive from Donegal Golf Club at Murvagh, it has easy access to many other activities too, including sea angling, surfing and hillwalking; guests also have complimentary use of leisure facilities at the Mill Park Hotel in Donegal Town. Short breaks offered. **Rooms 10** (6 shower only, all no smoking); children welcome (under 3s free in parents room, cot available free of charge); free broadband wi/fi. B&B €75, ss €23. Closed 23-27 Dec, 3 weeks Jan. **Restaurant:** Having returned from Dublin to his native Donegal, local chef Peter Campbell takes pride in showcasing the best Donegal produce, notably steak and seafood, in this popular restaurant. Smartly decorated in black and cream, the modern split-level room has a sense of occasion, and an à la carte menu offers an appropriate choice of eight dishes on each course (mainly classics with a twist, with favourites including pan-fried fillet of Atlantic salmon coated in a herb couscous and served with a prawn and mussel butter sauce, and grilled sirloin of Irish beef with baby garlic potatoes and peppercorn sauce. With main courses ranging from €17.50 to €27 and side orders at €4.50, it is not inexpensive, but it's good value for money given the quality of ingredients, proficient cooking and pleasing surroundings. Friendly staff are a plus – and, on Fridays in summer, soft live music adds to the atmosphere. Wines produced by families with Irish roots are included on the wide ranging wine list, commemorating the Flight of the Earls from Donegal in 1607. **Seats 55**; children welcome before 7.30pm; toilets wheelchair accessible. D Mon/Tue/Sun 6- 9.30; Wed-Sat 6-10; L Sun only, 12.30 &

3pm. Early bird D €19.50. Closed Mon (& Tue in winter). MasterCard, Visa, Laser. **Directions:** On the main Ballyshannon to Rossnowlagh road, near Rossnowlagh beach. ◈

TORY ISLAND

The Gaeltacht (Irish-speaking) island of Tory lies eight miles off the north-west corner of Donegal and, in spite of its exposed position, has been inhabited for four thousand years. Perhaps not surprisingly, this other-worldly island managed quite well without an hotel until relatively recently, but once Patrick and Berney Doohan's **Ostan Thoraig** (074 913 5920) was built in 1994 it quickly became the centre of the island's social activities - or, to be more precise, **The People's Bar** in the hotel quickly became the centre. The hotel is beside the little harbour where the ferries bring in visitors from mainland ports. Although simple, it provides comfortable en-suite accommodation with telephone and television. The hotel is open from Easter to October. A special feature of the island is its 'school' of primitive art (founded with the support of well-known artist the late Derek Hill of nearby Glebe House and Gallery, Church Hill). It even has a king as a founder member: the present King of the Tory is Patsy Dan Rogers, who has exhibited his colourful primitive paintings of the island throughout the British Isles and in America. A tiny gallery on Tory provides exhibition space for the current group of island artists. Tory is accessible by ferry (subject to weather conditions) from several mainland ports: telephone 074 913 1320 for details, or ask at the hotel.

WWW.IRELAND-GUIDE.COM FOR THE BEST PLACES TO EAT, DRINK & STAY

Tremone
FARMHOUSE

Trean House

Tremone Lecamy Inishowen Co Donegal **Tel: 074 936 7121**
treanhouse@gmail.com www.treanhouse.com

Way out on the Inishowen peninsula, Joyce and Mervyn Norris's farmhouse is tucked into a sheltered corner in stone-walled countryside beside the sea. Surrounded by a large garden with mature trees and welcoming flowers, it is a substantial house and offers a comfortable base for a relaxing away-from-it-all holiday in a homely atmosphere. Guests have the use of a cosy sitting room with an open fire and simple country bedrooms have everything that is needed - the only room without an en-suite shower room has a private bathroom nearby - and, if any other guest prefers a bath, it can be used by arrangement. Joyce's home cooking is another attraction - she makes breakfasts that will really set you up for the day; no dinners but Joyce will advise on the best places to eat in the evening. **Rooms 4** (all en-suite, 1 with bath & separate shower, 3 shower only & all no smoking); children welcome (under 3s free in parents' room, cot available without charge); pets permitted in some areas by arrangement. Garden. B&B €32, ss €12. No SC. Open all year except Christmas. MasterCard, Visa. **Directions:** From Moville, follow R238 5kms, turn right & follow house signs.

COUNTY GALWAY

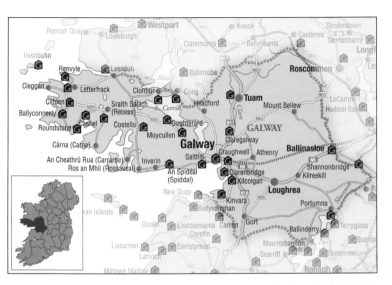

Galway surpasses many other parts of Ireland in the spectacular variety and charm of its many scenic routes. But it also has more to offer in the way of slightly offbeat expeditions and experiences, in addition to all the usual visual attractions of Ireland's Atlantic seaboard.

Visiting the Aran Islands across the mouth of Galway Bay, for instance, can be done by air as well as by sea. However, as the much-visited Aran Islands have shown, the presence of an air service doesn't seem to lessen the popularity of the ferries, and people often seem to think that you haven't properly visited an island unless you go there by boat. Then, too, there are many coastal boat trips, including an informative seaborne tour from Killary Harbour on the county's northwest coast, Ireland's only genuine fjord, while Lough Corrib is also served by miniature cruise liners.

As for sport ashore, the Galway Races at the end of July have developed into a six day meeting which is firmly established as Ireland's premier summer horse racing event, while the Ballinasloe International Horse Fair in the Autumn is simply unique. It dates back more than 280 years.

This has to be Ireland's most generous county, for in effect you get two counties for the price of one. They're neatly divided by the handsome sweep of island-studded Lough Corrib, with the big country of many mountains to the west, and rolling farmland to the east. As a bonus, where the Corrib tumbles into Galway Bay, we find one of Ireland's - indeed, one of Europe's - most vibrant cities. Galway is a bustling place which cheerfully sees itself as being linked to Spain and the great world beyond the Atlantic, and prides itself on annual theatrical, cinema and arts festivals.

The theme of double value asserts itself in other ways. As Autumn ripeness makes its presence felt, the county and city provide not one, but two, Oyster Festivals. Once September has ushered in the traditional oyster season, Galway's long and distinguished connection with the splendid bivalve mollusc is celebrated first with the Clarenbridge Oyster Festival on the southeast shore of Galway Bay, and then a week or so later, right in the heart of the city with the International Galway Oyster Festival itself.

Lough Corrib is both a geographical and psychological divide. East of it, there's flatter country, home to hunting packs of mythic lore. West of the Corrib - which used itself to be a major throughfare, and is now as ever a place of angling renown - you're very quickly into the high ground and moorland which sweep up to the Twelve Bens and other splendid peaks, wonderful mountains which enthusiasts would claim as the most beautiful in all Ireland.

Their heavily indented coastline means this region is Connemara, the Land of the Sea, where earth, rock and ocean intermix in one of Ireland's most extraordinary landscapes. Beyond, to the south, the Aran Islands are a place apart, yet they too are part of the Galway mix in this fantastical county which has its own magical light coming in over the sea. And yet, all its extraordinary variety happens within very manageable distances – Galway is a universe within one day's drive.

Local Attractions and Information

GALWAY CITY

Arts Centre 47 Dominick St	091 565886
Galway Airport	091 752874
Galway Arts Festival (July)	091 565886
Galway Crystal Heritage Centre	091 757311
Galway Races (late July/early August, Sept & Oct)	091 753870
Galway International Oyster Festival (late September)	091 527282 / 522066
Kenny's Bookshops & Art Galleries, High Street	091 562739
O'Brien Shipping (Aran Island Ferries)	091 563081
Tourist Information	091 563081
Town Hall Theatre	091 569755

COUNTY GALWAY

Aran Islands	Heritage Centre	099 61355
Aran Islands	Ferries from Rossaveal	091 568903 / 561767
Aran Islands	Flights from Inverin Airport	091 593034
Aughrim	Battle of Aughrim Centre	090 967 3939
Ballinasloe	International Horse Fair (Sept/Oct)	090 964 3453
Clarenbridge	Oyster Festival (September)	091 796342
Clifden	Connemara Pony Show (mid August)	095 21863
Clifden	Connemara Safari - Walking & Islands	095 21071
Gort	Thoor Ballylee (Yeats' Tower)	091 631436
Inishbofin	Arts Festival (Biennial, September)	095 45909
Inishbofin	Ferries (Cleggan)	095 44642
Inisheer	Duchas Inis Oirr (Arts Centre)	099 735576
Killary	Cruises on Connemara Lady	091 566736
Kinvara	Dungaire Castle	061 360788
Letterfrack	Connemara Bog Week (May)	095 43443
Letterfrack	Connemara Sea Week (October)	095 43443
Letterfrack	Kylemore Abbey & Gardens	095 41146
Loughrea	Dartfield Horse Museum	091 843968
Roundstone	Roundstone Arts Week (July)	095 35834
Roundstone	Traditional bodhran makers	095 35808
Tuam	Little Mill (last intact cornmill in area)	093 25486

GALWAY

Galway is a vibrant, youthful city with an international reputation for exceptional foods - notably the native Irish oysters, which are a speciality of the Clarenbridge area and celebrated at the annual Oyster Festival there in September. The area is renowned for its seafood, especially shellfish, and speciality produce of all kinds - including local cheeses, fruit and vegetables, and specialities that do the rounds of other markets around the country - is on sale at the famous city centre Saturday Market (beside St Nicholas Church; all day Sat & also Sun & Bank Hols, 2-6pm). Restaurants in the area showcase local produce, and - although there is at present no major dining destination here - there are many good places to eat in both city and county. Interesting restaurants in Galway are numerous, but some offering a different experience from those described separately include; the ever-popular **Da Tang Noodle House** (091 788638) on Middle Street; and **Vina Mara Restaurant & Wine Bar** (091 561 610; www.vinamara.com), also on Middle Street, which brings a flavour of Spain to the city and specialises in seafood. Good daytime cafés abound: for soup, sandwiches, good home baking, salads and desserts in an unfussy atmosphere, **Antons** (Father Griffin Road; 091 582 067) has been feeding a loyal lunch time trade for many years, so it's just the kind of place visitors need to know about. **Delight Gourmet Food Bar** (091 567823) on Upper Abbeygate Street lists delicious Illy coffee, smoothies and imaginative sandwiches among many options; **Revive Coffee & Rejuice** (Eyre Street; 091 533 779) is a popular day-time rendezvous offering a wide choice of quality snacks etc, based on fresh produce, cooked simply and served at tables, or at a counter - or in a covered courtyard with hanging baskets of flowers at the back. **Gourmet Tart Co.** (Lower Abbeygate Street; 091 5883840) is a French bakery & deli – no café, but they do such gorgeous food to take away, we have to recommend them. French bakers work through the night to have fresh croissants ready at 7.30am. Their Gourmet Salad Bar opened summer '08. Open 7 days a week from 7.30am to 7pm (9am on a Sunday morning; also at: 65 Henry Street, 8am – 6.30pm, and Upper Salthill (opposite Seapoint), 8am to 8pm. For good Indian

food, **Tulsi**, on Buttermilk Walk, Middle Street (091 564 831;www.tulsiindian.com) is a sister restaurant of the reliable Dublin restaurant of the same name; and, for style and informal fare (pizzas, pastas etc) at a reasonable price, head for **Milano** on Middle Street (091 568 488). For accommodation, it may be useful to know about the following in addition to the establishments described more fully: Mike and Breda Guilfoyle's hospitable guesthouse **Ardawn House** (College Road; 091 568 833) is convenient to the university and just a few minutes walk from Eyre Square; accommodation is comfortably furnished, with good amenities. For budget hotel accommodation, consider the city centre **Jurys Inn** (Quay Street; 091 566 444;www.jurysinn.com) which is in a superb riverside location beside Spanish Arch, and adjacent to a multi-storey carpark. East of the city, on the Tuam road, **Travelodge** (091 781 400; www.travelodge.ie) offers simple, clean, budget accommodation without service. Golfers staying in Galway who wish to play championship golf should take the short drive to Oranmore and the Galway Bay Golf Resort (091 790 711). Meanwhile garden lovers should make a point of visiting Ardcarraig (Bushypark, 091 524 336) and Brigit's Garden & Café (see entry for café, Roscahill, 091 550 905).
WWW.IRELAND-GUIDE.COM FOR ALL THE BEST PLACES TO EAT, DRINK & STAY

Galway City   Abalone Restaurant
RESTAURANT   53 Dominick Street Galway City Co Galway
                                                     Tel: 091 534 895

Round the corner from the Bridge Mills, an off-the-street entrance with a tiny porch leads to Alan Williams' smartly appointed little restaurant: gently minimalist décor, subdued lighting and gentle background music set a romantic tone and tables are promisingly set up with spotless white linen and simple glassware. A small dispense bar doubles as reception desk, where arriving guests are greeted and quickly settled in with menus and an aperitif. Alan Williams is a dedicated chef and, while his menu may be short and conventional, he is a good cook with a clear idea of what he wants to achieve, explaining his popularity with a loyal local clientèle. An amuse-bouche (a miniature prawn cocktail, perhaps) starts the ball rolling, then starters may include a good chicken liver & brandy paté with brioche and (very nice) wild plum sauce, and mains such as lovely seared scallops (complete with coral) served with a delicious truffle cream sauce and wonderfully light mashed potatoes, plus a tian of well-chosen vegetables. Pleasing desserts might include a wild berry crème brûlée or a well-made chocolate mousse. Good coffee to finish. Service is warm and enthusiastic, and a reasonably priced wine list includes a couple of half bottles. **Seats 20**; D Mon-Sun, 6-10pm; house wine €17.50; 10% sc on parties 8+. MasterCard, Visa, Laser. ◇

Galway City   Ard Bia & Nimmo's
CAFÉ•RESTAURANT•WINE BAR   Spanish Arch Galway City Co Galway **Tel: 091 539 897**
Ⓥ   ardbia@gmail.com www.ardbia.com

Ard Bia, literally High Food, is an appropriate moniker for this highly-regarded restaurant, which recently moved from cramped premises on Quay Street to an attractive riverside location - the stone-built medieval customs house overlooking the Claddagh Basin - which it now shares with sister restaurants Ard Bia Café and Nimmo's, plus a constantly changing exhibition of modern art. Proprietor Aoibheann MacNamara's enthusiasm, energy and commitment to quality are evident throughout the operation, which has become a favourite destination for both Galwegian food lovers and visitors to the city - who happen on it very easily in this central spot, and love its character and atmosphere, the quality and interest of the food, and the long opening hours offered between the three operations. With bare wooden floors, off-white painted walls, generously spaced tables and chairs and Aoibheann's trademark quirky art choices, the style is one of spare modernity, with a relaxed ambience (including simple table settings with paper napkins). The daytime **Ard Bia Café** is open from 10am, offering sandwiches and salads, soups (Galway Bay mussel and smoked haddock chowder with brown soda bread, perhaps) and day-long hot and cold specials including the generous Ard Bia hamburger and veggie burger; also speciality teas, freshly squeezed juices - and home-bakes (eg gluten free chocolate and orange cookies). **Nimmo's** is a lively evening restaurant on the ground floor, offering an eclectic à la carte menu with North African influences but – like all food served here – based on seasonal Irish food, mainly from local artisan suppliers. It's an atmospheric candle-lit space, with views of the river and the buzz of having the food served from an open kitchen. **The Supper Club** at Nimmo's offers a late night menu to private members, and opportunities for wine tastings, music events, parties and private screenings. Upstairs in the evening, **Ard Bia Restaurant** offers a more sophisticated experience (priced accordingly), with a very seasonal, broadly Mediterranean/Irish à la carte menu which, in summer, might typically include dishes like braised chicory & mustard tart, caramelised onions & organic leaves; roasted rack of Irish lamb with a creamy herb mash, wilted greens, rosemary jus and roasted baby beets, and a selection of Irish cheeses with home-made oatcakes & fig jam. There's an interesting wine list too, although without tasting notes. Service can perhaps be a little too laid back at times, but at all three operations you'll generally find good cooking, and good value for the quality offered. *As well as displaying exhibitions in the restaurants, Ard Bia Gallery Berlin offers artist residencies (www.ardbiaberlin.com). **Seats 80** (private room, 30, outdoors, 10); children welcome; reservations required; riverside deck; Upstairs Ard Bia: D only Wed - Sat 6.30- 10.30pm; a la carte. Downstairs at Nimmo's: D daily, 6-10.30pm; a la carte; house wine from €20. Ard Bia cafe menu served 7 days 10am-3.30pm (from 12 Sun). 10% sc on groups 10+. Closed Mon L (Nimmos), 25-26 Dec. Amex, MasterCard, Visa, LAser. **Directions:** Harbour front, beside the Spanish Arch and Galway City Museum.

Galway City

The Ardilaun Hotel

HOTEL

Taylors Hill Galway Co Galway **Tel: 091 521 433**
info@theardilaunhotel.ie www.theardilaunhotel.ie

This famous old hotel dates back to about 1840 and has been in the ownership of the Ryan family for over 40 years. Recent renovations have extended the hotel considerably, but without losing its gentle old-style atmosphere; everything about it confirms the feeling of a well-run establishment and, as ever, friendly staff make a good impression from the outset. The welcoming lobby/reception area is a convenient meeting place and pleasant spot to sit for a drink or a sandwich, and some of the spacious, traditionally furnished public areas overlook gardens at the back - including the restaurant, which is an elegant traditional dining room, with a lovely outlook and access to the garden. Bedrooms are traditionally furnished to a high standard and regularly refurbished. Excellent in-house leisure facilities include snooker and a leisure centre with 18m swimming pool. Off-season and special interest breaks are offered - an enjoyable prospect at an hotel that has character and a relaxed atmosphere. Understandably, it is one of the area's most popular wedding and conference venues. Conference/banqueting (600/400); business centre; free broadband wi/fi. Children welcome (under 3s free in parents' room, cots available without charge, baby sitting arranged, kids club). Pets permitted in some areas (charge to stay in bedrooms). Gardens. Leisure centre (fitness room, swimming pool, jacuzzi, sauna, steam room); beauty salon, treatments, massage. **Rooms 125** (4 suites, 3 junior suites, 32 executive rooms, 17 family, 9 shower only, 106 no-smoking, 8 groundfloor, 3 for disabled). Lift, 24 hr room service. B&B €150 pps, ss €25. No SC. Closed 22-27 Dec. Amex, Diners, MasterCard, Visa, Laser. Directions: 1 mile west of city centre (towards Salthill). **Directions:** 1.6km (1 m) west of city centre (towards Salthill).

Galway City

Cava Spanish Restaurant & Tapas Bar

RESTAURANT

51 Dominick Street Galway City Co Galway
Tel: 091 539 884

Even though Cava, Galway's new Spanish restaurant, a stone's throw from the main shopping/ restaurant area around Shop Street and Quay Street, was only open a short time at the time of the Guide's visit, it already had all the appearance of a confident, well-run business. Owner-operated by chef J P McMahon and his partner, Drigin Caffey, who supervises service, the ambience is authentically Spanish. Not a bull or toreador poster to be seen but the menu in the Spanish language, with English sub-titles, and an all-Spanish wine list (wines from Mad About Wine in Moycullen) leave one in no doubt about what's on offer. The tapas menu is available all day and there's a separate lunch and dinner menu, both à la carte. The tapas menu takes one on a 24-dish tour of Spanish cuisine in miniature, from shellfish soup with sherry to squid with garlic and parsley, salted cod cakes, sweet peppers with goat's cheese, braised tongue and kidneys in various guises. Dinner menu items of more substance include starters of Spanish cheeses and cured meats, warm duck salad with pears and raspberry vinaigrette and mains like Moorish couscous and braised fennel with potato omelette and lemon mayonnaise. The cooking is innovative, displaying knowledge and expertise that raises it above the average Galway dining experience. Desserts are simple, and again very Spanish: deep-fried churros with chocolate ice cream, for example, and a Spanish crème brûlée. The wine list covers the Spanish spectrum, brief but well chosen: Cava, naturally, featuring strongly by the glass for €6, rising to an expensive, aged Cava Mestres mas Via @ €120. And soft drinks get more than a cursory look in too, with elderflower bubbly, several fruit lemonades and lime crush, all at €4. The atmosphere is casual and bright: some exposed stone, high ceilings, aquamarine and caramel coloured walls, wooden floors and tables. And it is noisy - background music may well be impossible to decipher against the clamour of a full house of happy diners. **Seats 50**; reservations recommended; children welcome; toilets wheelchair accessible; air conditioning. Open daily 12-10.30pm (to 11.30 Thurs, 12.30 Fri/Sat, 10 Sun); a la carte menus; house wine from €18. SC 10% on groups 6+. Live Flamenco Fri nights. Closed 25 Dec. Mastercard, Visa, Laser. **Directions:** Lef Bank Galway city centre.

Galway City   Courtyard by Marriott
HOTEL   Headford Point Headford Road Galway City **Co Galway Tel: 091 513 200**
www.marriott.ie/gwycy

Located at Headford Point, well positioned for easy access to north County Galway and within walking distance of Eyre Square and Shop Street in fine weather, this new 4* hotel is a handsome building and an asset to an undistinguished area of the city. Aimed mainly at the business market, it has a large welcoming reception area with feature fireplace and plenty of varied seating, which makes a pleasant common area to meet people or work (complimentary wi/fi). Comfortable unfussy rooms have a large desk and an ergonomic chair, conveniently placed lighting and electrical outlets for working in comfort. All rooms also have a safe, mini fridge, tea/coffee making facilities, ironing facilities and pay per view movies. Facilities which will have equal appeal to the leisure market include the hotel's Absolute Spa and a fitness suite featuring state-of-the-art cardio vascular equipment and secure underground car parking. The Olive Tree Bistro offers popular Irish cuisine with a contemporary & Mediterannean influence. Breakfast offers a choice of healthy buffet or freshly prepared hot dishes cooked to order. Steam room, sauna, fitness room. Children welcome (under 16s free in parents' room, cot available); **Rooms 90**; B&B €75 pps, ss€45; 24hr room service, lift. Open all year. Amex, MasterCard, Visa, Laser. **Directions:** Off N84 on way into Galway city. ◊

Galway City   Da Roberta
RESTAURANT   161 Upper Salthill Galway Co Galway
Tel: 091 585 808

Roberta and Sandro Pieri's popular restaurant in Salthill moved (a little) recently, and it's now almost next to the sister restaurant Osteria da Roberta (see below), across from the Bank of Ireland. Although much bigger and brighter than the old da Roberta, the menus haven't changed and their 'piece of Italy' is still as popular as ever - and queues still regularly form at the door. Walls are hung with still life prints and posters of "Touring Club Italiano", tables sport linen cloths with paper covers, it's child-friendly and buzzes with the chatter of happy diners. Roberta smiles as she takes orders, Sandro moves from table to table with bottles of wine exchanging wry banter with customers as he pours wine, stuffing corks in his pocket. The menu offers many familiar Italian dishes such as prosciutto and salad leaves with soft cheese and pizzas with thin, crisp bases and a good choice of toppings. Bought-in desserts come with good coffee, and an appropriate all-Italian wine list also offers Italian beer. So what you get here is charming hospitality, an authentic Italian atmosphere and good value - a great recipe for success. *Nearby, **Osteria da Roberta**, (157/159 Upper Salthill) is run by the same family, and serves full meals - no pizza, so it is has less appeal for children and more for adults. (Open Mon-Sat 5-11, Sun 12.30-11). **Seats 46**; reservations required. Open daily 12-11.30. A la carte. House wine about €18.50. Amex, MasterCard, Visa, Laser. **Directions:** Central Salthill, opposite the Church. ◊

Galway City   The G Hotel
HOTEL•RESTAURANT   Wellpark Galway City Co Galway   **Tel: 091 865 200**
info@monogramhotels.ie www.monogramhotels.ie

A bad location - virtually on the Ffrench round-about and beside a large furniture retailer – and an unimpressive facade give no clues to the original interior of this new hotel, which is by internationally renowned milliner Phillip Treacy, a native of Galway. The proprietor, Galwayman Gerry Barrett, gave him free rein to indulge his quirky creativity, and he gave the western capital a stunning hotel. Eyecatching colour combinations, lighting, furniture, carpets, fireplaces make the public rooms both comfortable and delightfully varied. What might have been an intimidating (all black) lobby and reception area, is cleverly enlivened by a wall-mounted, exotic fish tank featuring the strangest creatures: sea horses, born and bred in Connemara. Accommodation is luxurious, as would be expected, and this is a fun place that brings a smile to people's faces. Boardroom/Banqueting (20/65), theatre facility next door for 40-150; media centre, broadband, secretarial services; Spa; Golf & equestrian nearby. Wheelchair accessible. **Rooms 101**

(3 suites, 26 junior suites, all others deluxe or superior); children welcome (baby sitting arranged); rooms from €200. Helipad. **Riva at the G:** The stylish restaurant offers refined Italian cooking that is a kind of hybrid of international hotel cuisine with Italian undertones and, although it does not reach the dizzy, stylish standards of the rest of the hotel, the theatrical surroundings in combination with competence in the kitchen and agreeable service should make for an enjoyable experience. **Seats 70.** Amex, MasterCard, Visa, Laser. **Directions:** From Oranmore - N6 for Galway East, at Skerrit roundabout take Dublin Road. Proceed to the Ffrench roundabout, take the 4th exit: the g is located immediately on the left. ◇

Galway City
HOTEL

Galway Bay Hotel

The Promenade Salthill Galway Co Galway **Tel: 091 520 520**
info@galwaybayhotel.com www.galwaybayhotel.com

This well-named hotel has clear views over Galway Bay to the distant hills of County Clare from public rooms on the upper ground floor as well as many of the large, well-equipped bedrooms - which have all been recently refurbished - and the rooftop garden. The large marbled foyer and adjacent public areas are very spacious and, although equally attractive for business or leisure (good leisure facilities make it a popular family holiday destination) it's a highly regarded conference centre and a good choice for business guests - as well as the usual facilities, all rooms have modem points and interactive TV for messages, internet and preview of the bill. Off-season and special interest breaks are offered - details on application. Conference/banqueting (1000/350). **Rooms 153** (4 suites, 2 junior suites, 2 executive, 50 no smoking, 13 ground floor, 2 for disabled); children welcome (under 2s free in parents' room, cot available free of charge, baby sitting arranged; creche, playroom) Rooftop garden. Ample parking (inc underground). No pets. Lifts. B&B €135 pps, ss €35. Leisure centre, swimming pool, gym; beauty salon. Open all year. Amex, MasterCard, Visa, Laser. **Directions:** Located on Salthill Road beside Leisureland, overlooking Galway Bay.

Galway City
HOTEL•RESTAURANT

Glenlo Abbey Hotel

Bushypark Galway Co Galway **Tel: 091 526 666**
info@glenloabbey.ie www.glenlo.com

Originally an eighteenth century residence, Glenlo Abbey is just two and a half miles from Galway city yet, beautifully located on a 138-acre estate, with its own golf course and Pavilion, it offers all the advantages of the country. Although it is not a very big hotel, the scale is generous: public rooms are impressive, and large, well-furnished bedrooms have good amenities and marbled bathrooms. The old Abbey has been restored for meetings and private dining, with business services to back up meetings and conferences. For indoor relaxation, the Oak Cellar Bar serves light food and, in addition to the classical River Room Restaurant - a lovely bright room with tables tiered to take full advantage of lovely views over Lough Corrib and the surrounding countryside. Conference/banqueting 180/160; business centre, secretarial services, video conferencing, free broadband wi/fi. Golf (9 & 18 hole); fishing, equestrian, cycling, walking. Children welcome (under 2s free in parents' room, cot available, baby sitting arranged). No pets. Garden. Boutique. **Rooms 46** (4 suites, 1 junior suite, 41 executive, 17 ground floor, 1 for disabled, all no-smoking). Wheelchair access. Lift. 24 hr room service. B&B €200pps (€125 low season). Ample parking. Helipad. Open all year except Christmas. **Pullman Restaurant:** This is the restaurant of choice at Glenlo Abbey - perhaps the country's most novel dinner venue, it was our Atmospheric Restaurant of the Year in 2005: four carriages, two of them from the original Orient Express that featured in scenes from "Murder on the Orient Express", filmed in 1974. Adapting it to restaurant use has been achieved brilliantly, with no expense spared in maintaining the special features of a luxurious train. There is a lounge/bar area leading to an open dining carriage and two private 'coupes' compartments, each seating up to six. Background 'clackity-clack' and hooting noises lend an authenticity to the experience and the romance is sustained by discreetly piped music of the 1940s and 50s. The view from the windows is of a coiffeured golf course, Lough Corrib and Connemara hills in the distance. Welcome by smart staff is pleasant, service throughout exemplary. Tables are set up as on a train, with silver cutlery, simple glassware and white linen (although napkins are paper); the food is suitably inclined to Asian influences and, while not cutting edge, it is very enjoyable. In line with the fun of the theme, you could begin your meal with a Pullman Summer Salad - and even end it with Poirot's Pie (apple tart); more typically, try an excellent 'Assiette of Oriental Appetisers' including sushi, sashimi, prawn tempura, smoked salmon, and mini spring roll, soy sauce and wasabi - and follow with a main course of 'Beijing Kao Ya', deliciously crisp-skinned roast half duck with a home-made barbecue & pomegranate sauce. Short, well-chosen wine list. Recommended as much for its unique, special occasion experience as for the fare - but the cooking is reliable and a visit is always enjoyable. *NB: There was a change of chef shortly before going to press, but no big change of style – and The Pullman is consistently seen as an attractive dining venue locally. **Seats 66**; open for D daily 7-9.30; house wine €22. Hotel closed 24-27 Dec. Amex, Diners, MasterCard, Visa, Laser. **Directions:** 4 km from Galway on N59 in the Clifden direction.

Galway City
CAFÉ

Goya's

2/3 Kirwans Lane Galway Co Galway **Tel: 091 567010**
info@goyas.ie www.goyas.ie

If only for a cup of cappuccino or hot chocolate and a wedge of chocolate cake, or a slice of quiche, a restorative visit to this delightful contemporary bakery and café is a must on any visit to Galway. There's something very promising about the cardboard cake boxes stacked up in preparation near the door, the staff are super, there's a great buzz and the food is simply terrific. What's more, you don't even have to be in Galway to enjoy Emer Murray's terrific baking - contact Goya's for her seasonal mail-order catalogues

"Fabulous Festive Fancies" (Christmas cakes, plum pudding, mince pies etc) and "Easter Delights" (simnel cake and others); wedding cakes also available. If you're wondering where to start, why not try a speciality: Goyas, 3-layer chocolate gateau cake. **Seats 56** (outdoor, 20), wheelchair accessible. Open all day Mon-Sat (L 12.30-3). MasterCard, Visa, Laser. **Directions:** Behind McDonagh's Fish Shop, off Quay Street.

Galway City
HOTEL

Harbour Hotel

New Docks Road Galway Co Galway **Tel: 091 569466**
info@harbour.ie www.harbour.ie

This contemporary-style hotel is conveniently situated at the heart of the city and offers comfortable, if expensive, accommodation with secure parking adjacent. Functional bedrooms with all the usual facilities (TV, trouser press) and well-fitted bathrooms have recently been refurbished and, even though still relatively new, an extension was required, to provide extra dining space, a separate breakfast room and a residents' lounge: a clear indication of Galway's current popularity as a holiday destination. Conference/banqueting 100/80; secretarial services, free broadband wi/fi. **Rooms 96** (14 executive, 4 for disabled, 55 no smoking); children welcome (under 16s free in parents' room, cot available without charge, baby sitting arranged). 24 hr room service, Lift. No pets. B&B €99 pps, ss €60. Spa, fitness room, steam room, sauna, jacuzzi, massage. Open all year except Christmas. Amex, Diners, MasterCard, Visa, Laser. **Directions:** Beside the docks in Galway, 5 mins from Eyre Square.

Galway City
B&B

The Heron's Rest B&B

Longwalk Spanish Arch Galway City Co Galway **Tel: 091 539 574**
theheronsrest@gmail.com www.theheronsrest.com

B&B OF THE YEAR
B&B BREAKFAST OF THE YEAR

The name of Sorcha Molloy's delightful B&B is far from fanciful - when looking for it along the Longwalk, you may well find it signed by Arthur the visiting heron, sitting on a car roof at her door. The location must be the best of anywhere you could stay in Galway - right in the centre of the city just seaward of Spanish Arch and with everything within easy walking distance, yet quietly situated with views across the river and out to sea. And it is a charming house, with lots of TLC lavished on the sweet waterside rooms, and a lot of care in everything Sorcha does, right down to the choice of natural toiletries and environmentally-friendly cleaning and laundry products. Having expanded into the adjoining house during 2008, Sorcha has been able to make many improvements in the overall style and service, with the addition of two single rooms and a new double ensuite master bedroom with stunning views of Galway Bay. She is a wonderful host and enjoys chatting to guests as she cooks breakfast - which used to be served in the kitchen and, even though it is now served in a dining room with a large oak table, she still prepares breakfast in the presence of her guests as this 'joyful banter' in the morning gives her a chance to pass on local information or discuss travel plans and offer tips and recommendations so it. To streamline the cooking and serving, Sorcha asks guests to order breakfast from a surprisingly extensive menu, and to choose a time, the night before. The menu is typically generous and unusual, offering about eight hot dishes (ranging from organic eggs with organic Connemara smoked salmon, grilled tomato and toasted caraway soda bread, to Lovely Lydia's sweet vanilla omelette stuffed with summer berries and marscapone, scattered with fresh toasted almonds), along with freshly baked bread or muffins, fresh orange juice, fruit salad and cheeses and a range of teas (including herbal teas) and espresso coffee. And, although there are no evening meals, afternoon tea and gourmet picnic baskets are both available on request - and some of the city's most interesting restaurants, including Ard Bia/Nimmo's and Sheridans on the Docks, are just a stone's throw away. Magic. **Rooms 5** (all en-suite, 3 shower only, 1 family room); children welcome (under 3s free in parents' room). free broadband wi/fi; masseuse; limited room service. B&B €75 pps. No evening meals but afternoon tea and gourmet picnic baskets are available on request. Street parking (pay & display). Closed Dec-Apr. Amex, MasterCard, Visa, Laser. **Directions:** On the Longwalk near the Spanish Arch.

Galway City
RESTAURANT
Ⓝ

Holywell Restaurant - Il Molino

Bridge Mills O'Briens Bridge Galway Co Galway **Tel: 091 566 231**
info@holywell.net www.holywell.net

One of a group of cafés descended from a famous beacon of excellence that was formerly in Ballyvaughan, this restaurant in the heart of Galway has a strong vegetarian ethos. It is in the basement of the restored Bridge Mills overlooking the Corrib river, and the careful restoration features interior stone walls, and the old mill wheel enclosed behind glass. Entrance via steps down from the street is quite dark but, despite the dominance of stone floors and walls, it is not a cold restaurant - with three separate dining areas, it has quite a cosy atmosphere. In summer, directly over the Corrib with views of the Clare hills in the distance across Galway Bay, Holywell is one of the city's most pleasant locations for an al fresco lunch. Inside, the change is emphasised by plain black tables and low table lamps and more suitable, perhaps, for dinner. A cheerful reception and service by staff of various nationalities, simple table settings and a clearly presented menu/wine list set a pleasantly casual tone which suits their offering – a simple package of pizza and half a dozen pasta dishes with limited starters and desserts, at a reasonable price. The simplicity and fresh flavours of the home cooked pasta or pizza here can make for a most enjoyable casual dining experience, especially given the exceptional location, attentive service and reasonable prices. Main course prices range from about €9.50 to €13.00 and the value is outstanding, especially as generous half portions are available – one pizza for two people makes a very acceptable lunch. Open daily from 12pm to 10pm.

Galway City
HOTEL
🏨

Hotel Meyrick

Eyre Square Galway Co Galway **Tel: 091 564 041**
reshm@monogramhotels.ie www.hotelmeyrick.ie

Formerly the Great Southern, this historic railway hotel overlooking Eyre Square right in the centre of Galway was built in 1845 and has always had a special place in the hearts of Galway people, who were sad to see the name change when it came into the Monogram Hotels group in 2006 - it is now a sister establishment to the famous g Hotel in Galway and the d Hotel in Drogheda (see entries). Prior to the sale, a major refurbishment programme had been undertaken, intended mainly to reinstate the grandeur and elegance of its 19th century heyday; this had been partially achieved, most notably in the public areas, where marble flooring, high ceilings, chandeliers and rich fabrics all contributed to re-creating the grandeur of old. However, all has since been changed, and a modern approach has seen it replaced with the currently fashionable 'nightclub' look. Since the takeover, further investment has also seen re-styling of the main restaurant overlooking Eyre Square, The Oyster Grill Restaurant, and the ground floor Oyster Bar, also the opening of a late night lounge TOSH. Accommodation has also had a make-over - the wide corridors (designed so that ladies in hooped dresses could pass without inconvenience) remain, of course, and are especially impressive in these days of compact modern buildings and, although standard rooms have been treated in a simple modern style, the best have period detail and are now superior rooms and junior suites - spacious and decorated in keeping with their stature, with bathrooms to match, and there are opulent 'Level 5' suites, with access to an executive lounge. The hotel's Square Spa & Health Club is on the top storey, with panoramic views over Galway city and harbour from the rooftop hot tub which, it has to be said, are interesting rather than scenic. Conference/banqueting (300/280); business centre, free broadband wi/fi. **Rooms 97**; children welcome (under 2 free in parents' room, cots available without charge, baby sitting arranged). No pets. 24-hour room service. Lift. B&B about €115 pps, ss €30; Leisure centre, indoor swimming pool, steam room, massage, beauty treatments. Closed 23-27 Dec. Amex, Diners, MasterCard, Visa, Laser. **Directions:** In heart of the city overlooking Eyre Square.

The House Hotel

Galway City
HOTEL

Spanish Parade Galway City Co Galway **Tel: 091 538 900**
info@thehousehotel.ie www.thehousehotel.ie

Cat lovers will immediately feel at home in this pleasant hotel near Spanish Arch, with cat motifs everywhere and a brochure image of a chilled-out ginger enjoying the best sofa, it's easy to see that this smart establishment is homely at heart. But you don't have to be feline-friendly to appreciate the excellent facilities and many thoughtful touches which aim to make this your Galway 'home away from home'. Even the names of the public areas are a reminder of this aim - The Parlour Bar & Grill; The Relax Lounge; The Den and, like home, the furniture doesn't all match. Although styled 'boutique' - and all rooms are individually designed - the hotel is bigger than it seems, with a range of accommodation options including comfy, classy and four suites overlooking Galway harbour; all have a high comfort factor including triple-glazed windows, air conditioning, mini-bar, LCD TV (with on demand movies, music and internet), laptop safe, complimentary broadband and bathrobe & slippers - even a complimentary hotel umbrella. All have smart en-suite bathrooms too, although about half have shower only (with rain dance shower head to compensate for lack of a good soak). There's free internet access throughout the hotel, and other services include in-room spa treatments by Absolute Spa, and same day laundry and dry cleaning service - just like home really. **Rooms 40**; lift, 24-hr room service; children welcome (cots available free of charge, baby sitting arranged); B&B €75pps. Closed 25-26 Dec. Amex, MasterCard, Visa, Laser. **Directions:** Centre city, a block away from the Spanish Arch.

The Huntsman Inn

Galway City
BAR•RESTAURANT•GUESTHOUSE

164 College Road Galway City Co Galway **Tel: 091 562 849**
info@huntsmaninn.com www.huntsmaninn.com

Within walking distance of the city centre and easily accessible by car, this busy spot looks like a pretty row of houses and, with its colourful hanging baskets, the façade cleverly disguises a large interior. Contemporary décor and muted colours complement an airy atmosphere, and it's a relaxed, comfortable place for flavoursome food at a reasonable price. Friendly, efficient staff, simple table settings and uncomplicated menus reflect a refreshingly down to earth philosophy. Varied menus begin with a good breakfast and later offer reliable favourites such as Huntsman fish cakes, char-grilled steak burger or chicken Caesar salad, with extra dishes on the evening menu including char-grilled escalopes of venison, perhaps, and Thai seafood curry; a separate children's menu doubles as a colouring competition. Everything is cooked with care and well presented, this is a very busy place and they manage the numbers consistently well. The New World dominates a compact fairly-priced wine list, which complements the food. **Seats 200** (outdoors, 50); air conditioning; toilets wheelchair accessible; children welcome before 9pm (high chair, childrens' menu, baby changing facilities); live music (Fri & Sat); broadband wi/fi. L daily 12.15-3, D daily 5.30-9.30. All menus a la carte. Bar food served daily, 12.30-9.30pm. Live Funky Jazz on Thurs from 6.45 pm. Closed Good Fri, 23 Dec - 29 Dec. **Accommodation:** The 12 smart, contemporary en-suite bedrooms offer all the usual conveniences plus satellite TV and computer facilities and a good breakfast. **Rooms 12** (2 suites, 3 shower only, 6 no smoking); children welcome (under 10s free in parents' room, cots available free of charge). Lift. B&B €60pps, ss €20. Amex, MasterCard, Visa, Laser. **Directions:** Follow signs for Galway East, just before Eyre Square.

Galway City
RESTAURANT

K C Blakes
10 Quay Street Galway Co Galway
Tel: 091 561826

K C Blakes is named after a stone Tower House of a type built sometime between 1440 and 1640, which stands as an example of the medieval stone architecture of the ancient city of Galway and the Caseys' restaurant, with all its sleek black designer style and contemporary chic, could not present a stronger contrast to such a building. Proprietor-chef John Casey sources ingredients for K C Blakes with care and wide-ranging menus cooked with skill offer something for every taste: traditional Irish (beef and Guinness stew), modern Irish (pan-fried scallops and black pudding), classical French (sole meunière) to global cuisine (a huge choice here - oriental duck with warm pancakes stuffed with cucumber and spring onion, perhaps). Professional service, creative cooking and smart surroundings make for quite a sense of occasion - yet this remarkably consistent operation is aimed at a wide market and is fairly priced. The upstairs dining room is a more cheerful choice - unless you prefer a people-watching window table downstairs. D daily, 5-10pm. Closed 25 Dec. Amex, MasterCard, Visa **Directions:** City centre, near Spanish Arch.

Galway City
RESTAURANT

Kirwan's Lane Restaurant
Kirwans Lane Galway Co Galway **Tel: 091 568 266**
clic@eircom.net

A stylish modern restaurant in common ownership with O'Grady's of Barna (see entry), Kirwan's Lane is a little oasis just off one of Galway's main shopping thoroughfares - on a fine day you can sit outside, and take time to breathe in the salt air away from the bustle of the city. Indoors, the airy two-storey restaurant is presented stylishly, with Georgia O'Keeffe-influenced oil paintings on white walls and quiet jazz hanging in the air. Smartly appointed tables have their white damask covered with paper tablecloths at lunchtime, when specials may include seafood risotto and fried fillets of plaice, or salads and other lighter dishes. Or you can choose from a well-judged à la carte that is not over-extensive, but takes on board the tastes of vegetarians and meat-eaters as well as having a strong showing of fish and shellfish. Outstanding breads set the tone for the smart cooking that is to come: a crispy julienne of ox tongue & pancetta, partnered with an orange & fennel cream to start perhaps, or flash-fried spicy prawns & bok choi – maybe followed by honey-glazed roast half duck with golden fried polenta and fresh figs. Finish with a tempting pudding (fresh raspberry meringue roulade, with mango coulis perhaps?) and really good coffee. With good cooking backed up by a relaxed ambience, attentive service, and an interesting wine list with well-chosen house wines, this is a pleasant place to eat. **Seats 90** (private room 60, outdoor seating 20); children welcome; air conditioning. L& D daily: L12.30-2.30, D 6-10. Set D about €42.50, also à la carte. House wine €19.50. No parking (multi-storey carpark nearby). Closed 24-29 Dec. Amex, MasterCard, Visa, Laser. **Directions:** Just off Cross Street and Quay Street. ◇

Galway City
RESTAURANT

The Malt House Restaurant
Olde Malt Mall High Street Galway Co Galway **Tel: 091 567 866**
info@themalthouse.ie www.themalthouse.ie

This old restaurant is in a quiet, flower-filled court-yard off High Street, an oasis away from the often frenetic buzz of modern Galway. Since a recent change of ownership the old-world character it was known for has changed - gone are the tablecloths (but not the white linen napkins) and the low lighting; in their place a more casual style, with cream walls set off by a series of colourful framed Reg Gordon photo-prints, bare black tables, comfortable cream and black chairs, stained wooden floor, banquette seating along one wall and lots of light from windows looking out on the little courtyard. Gone too is the charming bar, replaced with an extra dining space, in addition to the two other dining rooms. Menus have a contemporary bistro feel, in starters like Malbay crab toasties and Crozier Blue cheese quiche, and mains such as spiced lamb tagine and clam linguini. Long-serving head chef Brendan Keane is still in charge of the kitchen, however, and his trusted suppliers are acknowledged on menus which include vegetarian and gluten-free dishes; free-range chickens come from Justin Finnerty in Gort, Oyster Creek of Clarinbridge delivers shellfish, and organic vegetables are sourced from "Organic Joe" in Abbeyknockmoy. You might begin with half a dozen gorgeous meaty Gigas oysters; or a generous portion of crab claws in lots of garlic butter - although the 'in-house bread baked by Loretta' needed to mop it up is charged extra. Rack of Kinvara lamb was a highlight on a recent visit - terrific young lamb, cooked exactly as requested - although bland monkfish was less successful. Your choice of desserts might include strawberry tartelette with crisp pastry and lovely fresh berries, an expensive treat at €8 (the price of most desserts), but delicious all the same. Good service is provided by attentive young waiters and waitresses under manager Simon Marcus's busy eye. The biggest recent change is the wine list – The Malt House was formerly known for its exceptionally fine, in-depth list, now replaced by a short representative list of about 36 wines. Prices are quite high but the food quality is very good and, although the cooking can be uneven, this remains a pleasant place for a meal and it should be an enjoyable experience overall. **Seats 100** (private room, 20; also outdoor dining for 30). Children welcome. Air conditioning. Food served all day Mon-Sat: L 12-5, Set L €24.50 (value L €10.95). D 5-10, early bird €19.90 (5-7pm) Also à la carte L&D available, house wine from €19.90; no SC. Closed Sun, Bank Hols & Dec 25-Jan 2. Amex, MasterCard, Visa, Laser. **Directions:** Located in a courtyard just off High Street. ◇

Galway City
RESTAURANT•WINE BAR
Ⓝ

Martines Restaurant & Wine Bar

21 Quay Street Galway Co Galway **Tel: 091 565 662**
info@winebar.ie www.winebar.ie

This is one of Quay Street's longer established restaurants, owner-run by experienced restaurateur, Martine McDonagh, with the help of her two sons. The smart brown/black façade faces McDonagh's famous fish restaurant directly across the street, another McDonagh family venture, and - like most other Quay Street cafes and restaurants - Martine's has a few tables for on-street dining in the summer months. A small bar leads to the two separate dining rooms, the bright front one looking onto Quay Street or a darker one at the back with large mirrors and a motley assortment of furniture; bustling, with tables quite close together and low background pop/jazz music, there's a clubby feel to the place specially the back room. Popular with locals and tourists alike, it is middle-of-the–road establishment offering European-style fare – plenty of old favourites, well done. Pride is taken in ingredients – organic beef, free-range chicken and fish specials ranging from char-grilled mackerel to halibut and organic salmon - and you can expect predictable but tasty dishes like oysters, chicken liver pate, and breaded mussels; the cooking of local fish, lamb, duck and beef is consistently good, and the wine list carefully chosen. Service is friendly, and there's a good buzz. Many of the dishes are coeliac-friendly and the early evening 2-Course Menu at @ €19.95 is particularly good value. **Seats 80.** Open daily for dinner, L Fri & Sat only. Earlyburd D €19.95; also a la carte. Closed 25 Dec. Amex, MasterCard, Visa, Laser. **Directions:** City centre, near Spanish Arch.

Galway City
CAFÉ•RESTAURANT
Ⓝ

McDonaghs Seafood House

22 Quay Street Galway Co Galway **Tel: 091 565 001**
fish@mcdonaghs.net www.mcdonaghs.net

In Galway's busiest restaurant street, McDonagh's has been serving fish and chips long before this part of town became a magnet for tourists in search of food and drink. Nationally renowned as one of the best of its kind, it is today a thriving multi-faceted business: takeaway fish bar, indoor restaurant and boulevard seafood café in summer. Décor is decidedly nautical with stone floors, plain wooden tables and murals of traditional red-sailed Galway hookers and fishermen at work. It's renowned for the menu's extensive listing of fish species in more than a dozen different languages in confident confirmation of a cosmopolitan clientèle: everybody knows McDonaghs! The fish choice is wide and guaranteed fresh: you'll find McDonaghs Fish Soup, various fish in batter (cod, ray, whiting), local oysters (€12.90 per half dozen), spicy seafood pasta, grilled salmon, sea bass, scallops and mussels (3lbs for €12.50). For best value, choose the whiting or cod and chips at about €6.50 per portion. (There are even choices for carnivores - chicken & chips, striploin steak - but that misses the point of McDonagh's.) Desserts are few and simple: apple & rhubarb crumble, for example, or ice cream, all priced €4.50. The wine list of about twenty bottles has a chardonnay for €18 and includes Charles Heidsieck champagne €65. The fare itself is predictable enough - what you get here is a definite local flavour of a bustling chipper, offering a pleasant experience at fairly reasonable prices. Fish & Chips daily, 12-11pm (4-10pm Sun); Restaurant D Mon-Sat, 5-10pm. House wine €18. Closed Sunday. MasterCard, Visa, Laser. **Directions:** On Quay Street near Spanish Arch.

Oscars Bistro

Galway City
RESTAURANT

Dominick Street Galway Co Galway **Tel: 091 582 180**
oscarsgalway@eircom.net www.oscarsgalway.com

Located a short distance from the hectic bustle of the main beat, Oscars is endearingly eccentric and delivers far more than you might expect from the restrained exterior; an interior that is reminiscent of a theatre setting - from several different plays at once: the ceiling is luxuriantly draped like an Arabian tent, dark comfortable furniture could depict a gentlemen's club, the low level lighting a boudoir set for seduction and the music is gentle jazz supplemented by the chatter and buzz of happy customers. Service is efficient yet friendly and knowledgeable. But it's the menu and cooking that is the real star of Oscars. Closer to art cinema than mainstream Hollywood, Michael O Meara is creative, technically skilled and clearly not a chef who likes to be tied down to one food culture, style of cooking, or presentation. It's a wide ranging menu and you'll be spoilt for choice: whether your fancy takes you to choose modern Irish dishes, classic French, Eastern, or even Pacific rim, you'll find he's a serious cook who produces accurately cooked food and great flavour combinations. On a recent visit, the Guide enjoyed saddle of rabbit with a mousseline of guinea fowl and pistachio, roast parsnips, potato griddle cake and apricot and brandy jus; guinea fowl, with thyme infused roast sweet potatoes, seasonal greens accompanied by red wine and caramelised Dublin Bay Prawns marinated in garlic and chilli with a Malaysian vegetable selection in coconut, lemon and chilli sauce with Thai Jasmine rice; and traditional lambs kidneys with mustard and peppercorn sauce, mushrooms, leeks and colcannon. Other memorable dishes included boyzenberry sorbet, varied and gorgeous salads and rhubarb meringues. Portions are generous and everything is cooked to order. The wine list is extensive, strong on European wines and with a well-chosen New World selection. **Seats 45**. D Mon-Fri, 7-9.45pm (from 6pm Sat). D à la carte. House wines from about €19.50. Closed Sun (except Bank Hol weekends when they close Mon instead). MasterCard, Visa, Laser. **Directions:** 2 minutes across bridge from Jurys. ◈

Park House Hotel

Galway City
HOTEL

Forster Street Eyre Square Galway Co Galway **Tel: 091 564 924**
parkhousehotel@eircom.net www.parkhousehotel.ie

This hotel just off Eyre Square has the individuality that comes with owner-management and provides an exceptionally friendly and comfortable haven from the bustle of Galway, which seems to be constantly in celebration. Warmly decorated public areas include a well-run bar with lots of cosy corners where you can sink into a deep armchair and relax, and there is a choice of dining styles - The Park for formal dining, and The Blue Room for informal meals. Guest rooms are spacious, very comfortably furnished and well-equipped for business travellers, with a desk, internet access and safe; generous, well-planned bathrooms are quite luxurious, with ample storage space and Molton Brown toiletries. Good breakfasts include a buffet selection (with a delicious fresh fruit salad), plus a choice of hot dishes, including fish. And you know you're in Galway when you find oysters on the room service menu... If you want a thoroughly Irish welcome in the heart of Galway, you could not do better than stay at this cosy and central hotel: the prices are very reasonable - and private parking for residents is a real plus. **Rooms 84** (5 junior suites, 3 for disabled, 3 family rooms); children welcome (under 12s free in parents' room, cots available free of charge). No pets. Lift. All day room service. B&B about €115 pps, ss about €115. **Park Room Restaurant** (D & L Mon-Sat 12-3/6-9.30, D&L Sun 12.30-9); bar food L&D daily 12-9.30. Closed 24-26 Dec. Amex, MasterCard, Visa, Laser. **Directions:** Located adjacent to Eyre Square. ◈

Galway City
HOTEL•RESTAURANT

Radisson SAS Hotel & Spa

Lough Atalia Road Galway Co Galway **Tel: 091 538300**
sales.galway@radissonsas.com www.radissonhotelgalway.com

Ideally situated on the waterfront, overlooking Lough Atalia, this fine contemporary hotel is more central than its scenic location might suggest, as the shops and restaurants off Eyre Square are only a few minutes walk. An impressive foyer with unusual sculptures, audacious greenery and a glass-walled lift raise the spirits, and attractive public areas include the Veranda Lounge and a pleasant room in a sunny position looking over the roman-style leisure centre towards Lough Atalia. Guest rooms are furnished to a very high standard throughout with excellent bathrooms and facilities; luxurious 'Level 5' suites have secure members-only access, superb views, individual terraces and much else besides - all of which, plus services such as 3-hour express laundry, make this the ideal business accommodation. [*Radisson SAS Hotel Galway was our Business Hotel of the Year for 2005]. Excellent facilities for conferences and meetings are matched by outstanding leisure facilities, including a destination spa, Spirit One, which offers a range of beauty treatments, pamper programmes and spa break packages (details on application). Friendly, helpful staff are a great asset in every area of the hotel. Conference/banqueting (1000/570). Video-conferencing, business centre, secretarial services, free broadband wi/fi. Leisure centre (17m pool, children's pool, gym, sauna, steam bath, jacuzzi, outdoor hot tub); spa, beauty salon. No pets. Underground car park. Helipad. **Rooms 261** (2 suites, 2 junior suite, 16 executive, 9 family, 13 for disabled.) Lift. 24hr rooms service. B&B €95pps, ss €95. Children welcome (under 16s free in parents' room; cot available without charge, baby sitting arranged). **Restaurant Marinas:** The dining experience in this large split-level restaurant has an understandably Scandinavian tone (including a buffet option), but decor in blues and browns is inspired by Lough Atalia and there is a sense of style and confidence about the room that is reflected in capable, friendly service. An extensive à la carte menu is international in style and flavours, although non-fish eaters will find enduring favourites like char-grilled beef fillet, rack of lamb, and a vegetarian dish such as couscous-stuffed bell peppers. Although there is little mention of local produce, wheat-free and vegetarian dishes are highlighted, and also healthy eating options for guests attending Spirit One spa. But Marinas also offers the less usual option of a Scandinavian style buffet, which is an attractive choice if you are dining early, while everything is fresh. The best thing about the buffet is the varied selection of marinated salads and vegetables, cold meats, smoked fish, served with a wide choice of condiments and dressings; although some dishes will deteriorate while keeping hot, the buffet is good value and an enjoyable experience in such pleasant surroundings. The well-chosen wine list includes about a dozen wines by the glass and nine half bottles - a boon for business guests dining alone. The restaurant works equally well next morning for its famous Scandinavian buffet breakfast. *The Atrium Bar Menu has a more Irish tone, and offers an informal dining option, including a very reasonably priced 4-course buffet lunch. **Seats 220** (private room 80); air conditioning; toilets wheelchair accessible; children welcome (high chair, children's menu, baby changing facilities). D daily, 6-10.30pm, L Sun only, 12-3. D à la carte. House wines from €24. Guests dining in the hotel are entitled to a 35% discount on usual rates in the underground car park. Bar food also available daily. Amex, Diners, MasterCard, Visa, Laser. **Directions:** By lane from Lough Atalia, 3 minutes walk from bus & train station.

Galway City
CAFÉ

Sam Baileys Food Hall & Café

Eglinton Street Galway City Co Galway **Tel: 091 507 123**
info@sambaileys.com www.sambaileys.com

The large-windowed façade of Sam Bailey's looks out on Eglinton Street in the centre of Galway and, although it looks like a city centre franchise at first glance (and the shelves of the Food Hall just inside the door are stocked with rather ordinary goods), it deserves further investigation. Muted tones of wall panels and wallpaper, plain dark wood tables, comfortable high-backed chairs and background jazz vocals emphasise the franchise feel but the food, prepared in full sight of the customer, is above average, nicely presented in substantial portions and good value. Early opening makes this a good spot for breakfast, including the Full Irish, amongst other favourites like home-made pancakes with maple syrup and crisp fruit-filled scones. Later on there's a salad selection and an extensive range of gourmet sandwiches, which can be made to order. Desserts include New York-style cheesecake with berry coulis, home-made tiramisu, home-made pie and cupcakes. There are daily blackboard specials too and a long list of teas, coffees and cold drinks; this busy café is a valuable addition to the day time Galway scene. Open daily, 7am-7pm.

Galway City
PUB

Sheridan's on the Dock
Galway Docks Galway City Co Galway
Tel: 091 564 905

A lovely stone building on the corner of the docks nearest the city, this is one of Galway's oldest pubs dating back to at least 1882, when the writer Padraic O'Conaire was born there. A sailor's pub, it still has local clientele and is now owned by the Sheridans of cheese fame, and managed by Seamus Sheridan. It has been completely refurbished with black slate floors, white walls, pine tables, little stools and moss green window seats. It is a pub with - according to Seamus - the cheapest pint in Galway, the biggest selection of beers and the biggest selection of wines (at least 40 to date). Added to this is the best Honduras coffee and a small menu of some of the foods from their shop in the city, with plans for a restaurant upstairs (nearing completion at the time of going to press). A short menu might include a ham hock, chorizo & bean stew, a smoked seafood board, and of course, a fine cheese board. *Also at: Sheridans Shop & The Winebar, 14-16 Churchyard Street (091 564832; opposite St Nicholas' Church), where wine classes, readings, private parties and events can be held. Open Tue-Fri, 1-9pm; Sat 1-7pm. Food served daily. Closed Sun, Mon. Amex, Diners, MasterCard, Visa, Laser.

Galway City
CHARACTER PUB•RESTAURANT

Tigh Neachtain
Cross Street Galway Co Galway
Tel: 091 568 820

Tigh Neachtain (Naughton's) is one of Galway's oldest pubs - the origins of the building are medieval and it has been in the McGuire family for three generations – and the interior has remained unchanged since 1894. Quite unspoilt, it has great charm, an open fire and a friendly atmosphere - and the pint is good too. But perhaps the nicest thing of all is the way an impromptu traditional music session can get going at the drop of a hat. **Artisan:** Above the pub, a tight space overlooking busy Quay Street has cream/lime green walls to brighten it, along with attractive contemporary artwork and pretty table flowers. The lunch offering is divided into sections: freshly-made soup and seafood chowder both come with good speciality breads; there's an enticing array of sandwiches and salads (smoked duck, Cashel Blue & poached pear on ciabatta with walnut & spinach salad, and Mossfield cheddar with chorizo & pesto, among others); also appealing desserts. Dinner offers more with fillet of beef, lamb and chicken dishes in addition to several fresh fish, and pleasant, interested staff discuss the day's menu with enthusiasm. An unexceptional wine list offers some 30 wines. At the time of the Guide's visits, Artisan had not yet settled and the cooking was uneven; however it showed promise, and this is a useful place to know about. Closed 25 Dec & Good Fri. **Directions:** Situated on crossroads Quay Street/Cross Street/High Street.

Galway City
HOTEL

The Westwood
Dangan Upper Newcastle Galway Co Galway **Tel: 091 521 442**
resmanager@westwoodhousehotel.com www.westwoodhousehotel.com

A sister hotel to The Schoolhouse Hotel in Dublin and the Station House Hotel, Clifden (see entries) this 4* is well located, on the edge of Galway and convenient to both the city and Connemara. Set well back from the road, it has a pleasant almost-in-the-country atmosphere and has recently completed a major refurbishment programme, taking in all of the guest accommodation and the main public areas. Guest rooms, which include six junior suites and eight executive rooms, have been furnished to a very high standard in a contemporary classic style and some have fireplaces (a cheerful addition for business guests away from home); all feature locally handcrafted wooden furnishings as well as all the current technical features including individually controlled air-conditioning, entertainment system, wireless internet (through TV) and free wired broadband, iron & trouser press and tea & coffee making. The banqueting suites have also been refurbished and this is a popular venue for weddings and conferences. The Westwood offers a high standard of accommodation for business and leisure at fairly reasonable prices; a range of 2-3 night leisure breaks offers particularly good value. Conference/banqueting 350/275; free broadband wi/fi. **Rooms 58** (14 superior, 44 deluxe, 10 no smoking); children welcome (under 2s free in parents' room. cot available without charge, baby sitting arranged); Lift. 24 hr room service. No pets. B&B €99.50pps, ss €26. Closed 24-25 Dec. **Directions:** 1.5 km from Eyre Square (N59 for Clifden).

Galway City Area

Clayton Hotel

HOTEL

Ballybrit Galway Co Galway **Tel: 091 721 900**

www.claytonhotelgalway.ie

Convenient to both Galway city centre and Galway Airport, this new four star hotel is well located for business and leisure guests and, with Galway Race Course and Rosshill Golf Course very close by (and a good choice of other golf courses within a short distance), it is an especially attractive destination for sports lovers. An impressive entrance sets the tone for bright, spacious and well-appointed public areas which include the aptly-named Enclosure Bar and Tribes Restaurant, and - while all bedrooms have features such as underfloor heating, pillow-topped mattresses and plasma screens as standard - business guests in particular will be well looked after in the fourth floor executive accommodation, which includes a private executive lounge and a presidential suite with great views, a sheltered terrace and large sitting room with entertainment systems. Conference and business facilities include a very large ballroom/conference venue with natural daylight, which is designed for versatility; meeting rooms equipped for boardroom meetings, presentations and video conferencing have everything required including high definition plasma screens, wireless broadband, and audio-visual equipment. 20m swimming pool; fitness room, steam room, sauna. Conference/banqueting 800 (9 board rooms, 12 meeting rooms). **Rooms 200** (14 executive, 1 Presidential Suite) Room rate from €99. **Directions:** Off the N6; at the Lynch roundabout take the R339, hotel entrance is on the right.

Galway City Area

Connemara Coast Hotel

HOTEL•RESTAURANT

Furbo Galway Co Galway **Tel: 091 592 108**

info@connemaracoast.ie www.sinnotthotels.com

This beautifully located hotel is an attractive building which makes the best possible use of the site without intruding on the surroundings: set on the sea side of the road, in its own extensive grounds, it is hard to credit that Galway city is only a 10 minute drive away. An impressive foyer decorated with fresh flowers sets the tone on entering, and spacious public areas include a mezzanine and library, and a pleasant patio area on the sea side of the hotel. Facilities are particularly good too - a fine bar, two restaurants, a children's playroom and a leisure centre among them - and a policy of constant refurbishment and upgrading ensures that the hotel always has a warm, well-cared for atmosphere; spacious new bedrooms were recently added, and the older rooms have all been upgraded. This most likeable of hotels is understandably popular for conferences and weddings - the facilities and service are both excellent (the conference centre has also been refurbished), and the location is magic. A range of special breaks is offered both here and at its fine sister hotel, Brooks Hotel, in Dublin (details on application). Conference/banqueting (400/320); free broadband wi/fi; secretarial services, video conferencing. Children welcome (under 3s free in parents' room; cots available without charge, baby sitting arranged; playroom, playground, kids club). Leisure centre (swimming pool, jacuzzi, fitness room, sauna, steam room); masseuse; pool table, tennis, walking. **Rooms 141** (2 suites, 10 junior suites, 26 executive rooms, 7 ground floor, 25 family rooms, 1 for disabled, all no smoking). B&B €125pps, ss €40. 24 hr room service. **Restaurant:** Welcoming details such as proper butter curls and good nutty breads make a good first impression in this elegantly appointed sea view restaurant. Appealing menus are changed every day (a boon for regular diners and guests staying for several nights), and head chef, Ulriche Hoeche, offers a wide range of dishes, notably local seafood - a fish plate of smoked salmon and smoked mackerel with an herb crème fraiche makes a tasty starter, for example. Local meats are often represented by roast rack of Connemara lamb, or you might try beautifully crispy roast half boneless duckling with braised red cabbage and orange jus. When the hotel is full, the kitchen can come under pressure, and portions have increased in size recently – perhaps reflecting demand from large groups. **Seats 50**; D 7-9.30pm daily (children welcome), set D €40; informal D, Daly's 7-9.30pm daily; bar food daily 12.30-6.30 (1-4 Sat/Sun). Open all year. Amex, MasterCard, Visa, Laser. Heli-Pad. **Directions:** 9km (6 m) from Galway city on Spiddal road.

Galway City Area
PUB

Donnelly's of Barna
Barna Co Galway **Tel: 091 592 487**

Although recent developments have changed the shape and scale of Barna, Donnelly's of Barna is still a landmark at the crossroads, where a little road leads down to the small harbour. Established in 1892, this seafood restaurant and bar, serves food all day and always seems to be busy. It is a comfortable old world pub with little snugs, comfy corners and bric à brac as well as a more formal dining area. The same bar menu is served throughout the house, and the atmosphere is a casual friendly pub rather than formal dining. The menu offers a lot of seafood starters like moules marinière or pan-fried crab claws, and main courses of haddock mornay and fillet of salmon are all regulars - balanced by other favourites like oven roast duckling and sirloin steak. Although not inexpensive, the combination of good cooking, friendly attentive service and a relaxing ambience make this good value. Desserts - home-made chocolate brownie with vanilla ice cream & raspberry sauce and passion fruit crème brûlée among them - are enticing and the wine list is not too pricey. **Seats 150**. Mon-Sun 12-9.45pm (from 12.30 Sun). MasterCard, Visa, Laser. **Directions:** On road that leads to harbour.

Galway City Area
RESTAURANT

Mulberrys Restaurant
Unit 14 Barna Village Centre Barna Co Galway **Tel: 091 592 123**
Deirdre_Keaney@yahoo.com www.mulberrys.ie

In a line of pretty shops with ample parking, Mulberrys is one of the newer restaurants in the busy Barna suburb of Galway. Its contemporary black and cream shopfront is both inviting and welcoming, with clear signage declaring its Italian and Seafood style. Friendly staff welcome arriving guests in the spacious contemporary bar/reception area and, in the the restaurant plain dark wood tables are set simply with comfortable seating the tone, making for a relaxed atmosphere. A wide-ranging à la carte offers plenty of popular dishes, with starters like chowder or vegetable tartlet, while main courses offer a choice of pasta dishes such prawn & crab ravioli, fish dishes like halibut in beurre blanc plus several steak options and plus substantial mains such as roast half duck in plum sauce. Daily specials offer extra fresh fish dishes. Desserts offered tend to be old favourites - apple tart, crème brûlée - then good coffee and teas to finish. A modest wine list includes some half bottles. Overall, the quality of ingredients and cooking is good which, along with reasonable prices and the casual elegance of the place, makes Mulberrys a pleasant place to visit: a positive addition to the Barna restaurant stock. **Seats 78** (private room, 30; outdoors, 20); children welcome (high chair, childrens menu, baby changing facilities); wheelchair friendly; air conditioning. D only - Mon-Sun (Tue-Sun off season) from 5pm; L Sunday from 12.30. 2/3 course early bird D Mon-Fri, 5-7pm, €19.95/23.95; house wine €19.50. Closed Mon off-season. MasterCard, Visa, Laser. **Directions:** In the heart of Barna Village.

Galway City Area
RESTAURANT

O'Grady's on the Pier
Sea Point Barna Co Galway **Tel: 091 592 223**
kazgap@hotmail.com www.ogradysonthepier.com

In a stunning position, with views over the harbour and beach to distant mountains, Michael O'Grady's charming seafood restaurant is popular among Galway diners. It is a lovely spot on a fine summer's day, with tables set up outside the restaurant, and old boats around the harbour adding to the atmosphere. Inside, a low-key interior with simple table settings and nautical and seafood-related décor has character; there are some contemporary elements (especially on the first floor), but tradition has also been allowed its place - the old fireplace has been retained, for example, which bodes well for cosy sessions in wild weather - and Michael's aim is for his seafood to be "simply prepared and very fresh as my father did it years ago". This he and his team are doing very well, although world cuisine is given a little space too, notably among the daily blackboard specials. Interesting dinner menus offer a wonderful choice plus daily specials. Recent visits have found this charming place on top form - the cooking skill and style is impressive, and attentive, helpful staff back up the kitchen well, ensuring that the laid-back atmosphere is genuinely relaxing. The ubiquitous tiger prawn makes an appearance, but most of the fish and seafood is fresh local produce – and the best dishes are the simplest: a starter of Galway Bay lobster served with lemon & salad, perhaps, and main course of grilled whole dover sole on the bone with lemon & parsley butter. The cooking is skilfully judged, and one of the most delicious seafood dishes you are likely to encounter anywhere. (Ever innovative, Michael was winner of our Creative Seafood

Dish Award in 2001.) There's always some choice for non-seafood eaters (roast half duckling is a popular choice), and desserts are delicious too - if you can find room. Service, under the direction of the host, is attentive, and the wine list is well chosen to match the menu. *O'Grady's was our Seafood Restaurant of the Year in 2008. **Seats 85** (private room 25, outdoor seating 25); children welcome (high chair); air-conditioning. L & D daily, 12.30-5pm & 6-10pm, Sun L 12.30-2.45. Set Sun L €27.95, D à la carte; house wine €18.50. Closed 25/26 Dec. Amex, MasterCard, Visa, Laser. **Directions:** 7km (4m) west of Galway city on the Spiddal Road.

Galway City Area

HOTEL•RESTAURANT

The Twelve Hotel

Barna Village Galway City Co Galway **Tel: 091 597 000**
enquire@thetwelvehotel.ie www.thetwelvehotel.ie

WINE AWARD OF THE YEAR

Named after Connemara's famous Twelve Bens mountains, this new hotel has brought contemporary fashions to an area known until recently for its quiet, traditional style. It replaces a long-established hotel and the site has been well-used to create a sense of ample space, even though the building is right on the corner of two roads in Barna village, now a cramped suburb of Galway. You arrive through a small but quirky reception area, or directly from the car park through a covered seating area to the bar, which is a fine space with couch/seating and fire, and bookshelves full of books including some for children. The earthy mix of black tables, clay brown walls and wooden flooring is relaxing, and the sense of informality is emphasised by central raised counter-style tables and tall stools set up for parties of up to ten, as well as a spread of tables at normal height. The Pins bar has earned a great reputation for its food, and menus offer a wide range of appealing dishes, including unusual combinations in both salads and hot dishes, and many items are coeliac-friendly. A very tempting weekend lunch menu is offered in the bar, kicking off with a choice of reviving cocktails. Breads and baked goods and gourmet pizza are a speciality – the in-house bakery and shop is next door. The stylish guestrooms are quirky, but not at the expense of comfort; six room types are offered, most with separate bath and shower, some with their own cocktail bar; there's a suite to suit families or friends travelling together, a Funnymoon Suite – and, the ultimate, Suite X11, with an open fireplace used as a room divider. The dark tones continue among the bedrooms which have darkwood floors and subtle alterations of lighting and fabrics to make rooms distinctive from each other. Large old-fashioned gilt-framed, mirrors are a feature, especially leaning against the walls on the corridors – a design statement that also lends a homely touch. Conferencing/Banqueting (120/90); free broadband wi/fi. secretarial services, video conferencing. Fully wheelchair accessible; children welcome (under 5s free in parents' room, cots available free of charge, baby sitting arranged); Lift, all day room service. Dogs welcome (charge, stay in bedroom). **Rooms 48** (25 suites, 12 executive, 8 shower only, 22 family, 3 for disabled, all no smoking). B&B €85 pps, ss€30. **West At The Twelve:** The first floor restaurant, also predominantly black, has a variety of booths with leather banquette seating, mood lighting from ceiling lights and fat table candles. The focus is on wine, with wines visible on temperature-controlled racks behind glass and a champagne bar within the room. The restaurant has come on a lot since the Guide's last visit, shortly after opening - this time our peak season visit was to a restaurant showing healthy maturity under pressure. Reception and service now have an ease and confidence, totally customer-focused. Waiter, Kalman, who has been at the hotel since its opening, stands out in an above-average team; his unobtrusive way sets the tone for knowledgeable, attentive service, reflecting the relaxed sophistication throughout the hotel - a singular style that owes much, no doubt, to the management of proprietor Fergus O'Halloran, who is also responsible for the hotel's exceptional wine list. The à la carte menu changes regularly and, as before, its straightforward simplicity is appealing; it is reasonably priced and with no cheffy descriptions. Seafood is a strength, of course, but also imaginative vegetarian dishes, mature beef and less usual ingredients such as rabbit. The evening begins with a complimentary appetiser (a refreshing appetiser shot of pineapple and orange frappé, perhaps), possibly followed half a dozen local oysters or a crab salad, with very rich, fresh crab in a buttery salad. Main courses might include perfectly cooked fillet of lamb with a lightly spiced musky-tasting couscous timbale, and lovely lamb jus; or scallops and black pudding on mash potato - four plump scallops paired appropriately with gutsy pudding. Saucing is excellent (but could be more generous) and, accompaniments are good too - a dairy-rich potato gratin and a combination of steamed broccoli, stuffed tomato and carrot purée, perhaps. The cooking reaches a new high with desserts including excellent Ice creams and, perhaps, an intensely lemon, lemon tart that shows off the pastry chef's talent - also evident in superior breads such as tomato & olive or sesame and bacon. Since opening in 2007, The Twelve has become a respected rendezvous, an innovative destination with extra attractions such as The Sunday Feast with suckling pig, salads and flambé desserts for €39 and dinner in the kitchen at The Chef's Table for up to ten people – a gastronomic menu with "sensational" wines. The West's wine list has all the hallmarks of dedicated selection by a wine-loving hotelier. The twenty three pages outline in detail and with commentary, a range of wines and beverages across a wide range, subjected to monthly monitoring. A trademark of The West is wine with or without skins by the glass and bottle, red and white, old and new world, with informative tasting notes. Many areas and grape varieties are represented throughout the list, and trouble has been taken to collect a few rarities such as white Chateauneuf du Pape and a Sicilian white, from the Fiano grape, called Planeta. For further comment on the West's wine list see www.ireland-guide.com. **Seats 90** (private room, 96; outdoors, 30); children welcome before 7pm; air conditioning; pianist at weekends; D Tue-Sun, 6-10pm (6-9pm Sun); early D €25, 6-7pm only; set 3 course D €30, gourmet menu €125, also a la carte. L Sun only, 12-4; set Sun L €30. House wine €24. Closed Mon. Amex, Diners, MasterCard, Visa, Laser. **Directions:** At the crossroads in Barna Village, 10 mins from Galway City.

ARAN ISLANDS

Situated in Galway Bay, the Aran Islands of Inishmore, Inishmaan and Inisheer (Inis Mór, Inis Meáin and Inis Oirr), have a rugged splendour and a sense of time standing still, evident in the many thatch-roofed stone cottages that dot the landscape. Rich in history, the ruins of early Christian monasteries and fortifications dating back over 2000 years include the famous Dún Aonghusa ring fort. With sandy beaches, breathtaking cliffs, and twisting country lanes, the islands are well suited to walking or cycling. Visitors love the remoteness of the islands, the music and craic, and the glimpse of traditional island life that lies at the end of the short ferry trip. The largest of the islands, Inishmore, is also the most visited, so the true island experience may be more easily found on the smaller islands. The Aran Islands are easily accessible by ferry from Galway City, or the harbours at Rossaveal and Doolin, or by air from Galway (Aer Arann; www.aerarann.com; 091 541900).

Aran Islands   **An Dún**

B&B•CAFÉ•RESTAURANT   Inis Meain Aran Islands Co Galway **Tel:** 099 73047

anduninismeain@eircom.net   www.inismeainaccommodation.com

A short jump from Inis Mór, this interesting island is the most traditional of the group - very few cars, wonderful walks, and some people still wearing traditional clothes; by contrast the Inis Meain Knitting Co. factory and showroom offers great bargains on unique products only to be found in specialist outlets in Milan and Japan. At the foot of Dun Conchubhar (Connor's Fort) is Teresa and Padraic Faherty's restaurant and B&B, An Dún, which was the home of Padraig's grandfather and was the first restaurant on the island when it opened in 1989. In 2000 it was refurbished and extended to include en-suite bedrooms (modern, well fitted out, comfortable, great views), a new dining room and a mini-spa; Teresa is qualified in aromatherapy and can arrange packages for the new spa, especially off-season. More recently a neat garden has been added along the side of the house, which is almost next door to Synge's cottage, and their small shop has become a café/snack bar where seafood chowder, leek & potato soup, Aran smoked salmon and soda bread feature; this leads on to a deck in front, which adds to the atmosphere of leisure. The island's pretty traditional pub is just five minutes' walk. Mini-spa (sauna, steam shower, massage); aromatherapy. Shop. Children welcome (under 3s free in parents' room, cot available without charge). No Pets. Garden. Walking, cycling. **Rooms 5** (all en-suite, shower only and no smoking; 2 ground floor). B&B €50, ss €5-15 (advance booking only in winter). **Restaurant:** There are two dining rooms - the inner one is original and cottagey, while a modern extension has wooden floors and windows on two sides, with wonderful sea and mountain views. The style and atmosphere is homely and everything Teresa serves is made on the premises - some of the best traditional food on the islands is to be found here. Local foods star: fish straight from currachs, their own floury Inis Meain potatoes, fertilised in the traditional manner, with seaweed; scones, crumbles and tarts using local fruits. Specialities include fish dishes like home-made chowder or a trio of ultra-fresh mackerel, pollock and salmon on a lemony apricot sauce, and on cool days there will be stews, and home-cooked roasts of lamb, beef and gammon. And there will be interesting desserts like Baileys or brandy carrageen, or blackberry tart. A short wine list includes a Concannon, from the Livermore vineyard in California, which has local connections. **Seats 40** (outdoor seating 10); children welcome (high chair); reservations required (non-residents welcome); wheelchair accessible toilets. L 12-3.30pm; D daily in summer, 6.30-9.30. Set D available for residents, €25/30, otherwise à la carte. House wine from €18. Open all year except 1 week Oct & 1 week Jan. MasterCard, Visa, Laser. **Directions:** Centre of island, near church, next door to JM Synge cottage.

Aran Islands

HOTEL

Aran Islands Hotel

Kilronan Inishmore Aran Islands Co Galway **Tel: 099 61104**

info@aranislandshotel.com www.aranislandshotel.com

Just a short walk from the pier, this small cut-stone hotel overlooking Kileany Bay and Kilronan harbour has a homely appearance and it marks a change for the Aran Islands in that it is the islands' first regular modern hotel (it could be described as luxurious), and will operate throughout the year. The most popular spot in the hotel is Paitin Jack's with open stone fireplace, low ceilings, and a two tier layout; this bar often has traditional music played on one level and bar food served on the higher level. The dining room is also low ceilinged, and finished in wood and stone, with a view of the bay from 3 long small windows at one end; a communal balcony running along the front of the hotel will be decked with suitable sea hardy shrubs, and should be interesting and fun if you are in a holiday mood. Accommodation is very comfortable and five of the 22 en-suite bedrooms have good views of the bay and harbour; bedrooms are really cosy, with shades of gold, yellow and red, which would tempt you to holiday on the island even in winter time. There is a lift, power showers, seven TV channels, direct dial telephone, iron, hair-dryer, and tea/coffee stand, all contributing to a modern island. Head chef Declan Branigan, who is from Dublin and has married an islander, loves this new challenge; his food is modern Irish and he offers an à la carte, set dinner and an extensive bar food menu, which is available from 5pm to 11.30pm during the season. **Rooms 22** (all en suite, 2 family, 2 shower only, 5 ground floor, 2 for disabled, all no smoking); children welcome (under 5s free in parents' room, cots available free of charge, baby sitting arranged); wheelchair friendly; free broadband wi/fi; cycling, walking; Lift, Limited room service; B&B €55-115 pps, ss €25. Closed Dec 20-28. Diners, MasterCard, Visa, Laser. **Directions:** In Kilronan, Inishmore Island.

Aran Islands

CAFÉ

Fisherman's Cottage

Inishere Aran Islands Co Galway **Tel: 099 75073**

foodwise@eircom.net www.southaran.com

Inis Oirr, the smallest and most easterly of the Aran Islands is a tranquil place, perfect for quiet contemplation and relaxed walks and swimming in crystal clear waters. At the south end of the island and a 5 minute walk along the sea from the pier, you arrive at Maria and Enda Conneely's Fisherman's Cottage, a lovely white and blue cottage with half door, set among interesting herb and flower gardens. A pretty blue, green and white theme makes the dining room bright, and the conservatory has the same colour scheme, with lovely views of the bay. Enda and Maria are Slow Food members and feel that it is important that the food we eat does not have to travel too far, especially food that can be produced locally, so they try to use organically produced foods as well as locally caught wild fish and other produce from the Island - the aim is to do what they can to provide tasty local food that is unique to the island. Enda, a native of South Aran, has studied widely, including medicinal cooking in Switzerland, and cooking at the Cordon Vert Vegetarian School in Manchester, and Maria has studied Shiatsu and Macrobiotics, so the food reflects their love for a natural healthy lifestyle. Just don't expect big 'country portions' here: respecting the quality of food, portion sizes are healthy too. Next door to the café, they have built the cottage-style South Aran Centre. Yoga, cookery and Irish/English language classes are planned here - for further information contact Maria and Enda. **Seats 54** (private room, 20, outdoors, 35); not suitable for children; broadband wi/fi; cookery classes. L&D Tue-Sun, 10-4pm and 7-9pm; house wine €18-24. Closed Mon, Nov-Mar. MasterCard, Visa, Laser. **Directions:** Turn right at the pier and 400 metres on.

Aran Islands

RESTAURANT WITH ROOMS

Inis Meáin Restaurant & Suites

Inis Meain Aran Islands Co Galway **Tel: 086 826 6026**

post@inismeain.com www.inismeain.com

Inis Meain is the middle island of the group, and is the most tranquil and least visited; it is just 3 miles across and supports 150 inhabitants who appreciate this unique and special place. Ruairi de Blacam is a native of the island and a chef; he and his wife, Marie-Therese, who is from Cork and has a business and fashion background, decided to create a business on the island that would allow them live in this peaceful landscape of terraced limestone and traditional culture. Old traditions of farming, sport, and music are a large part of daily life here, and they are true to this in creating a haven of fine food and a peaceful place for rest. Although very modern, the long, low cut-stone building, designed by de Blacam & Meagher architects, blends into the surrounding limestone landscape. The dining space and kitchen are almost one and diners are given a view of the open simple kitchen, or an amazing panoramic 90% view of the island, sea and sky. The room is contemporary and spare; a great black and white photograph of a fisherman easing a periwinkle out of a shell, with a pint of stout beside him, gives real feeling to the whole place. The ingredients used are mainly sourced on the island: lobster and crab are caught by fishermen who use the local currachs, other fish comes from Rossaveal but they hope to get it landed at the new pier on Inis Meain soon (nearly completed at the time of going to press); periwinkles and carrageen moss are picked from the shore by Marie-Thérèse and Ruairi; potatoes, vegetables, fruit and herbs are home-grown on the restaurant site – an amazing range including spinach, broad beans, peas, scallions and onions, carrots, parsnips and radishes, fennel bulbs, rocket, lollo rosso, masses of herbs, rhubarb, pears and soft fruits like raspberries, strawberries gooseberries and blackberries – and even the elderflower cordial is hand-made in Cork by Marie-Thérèse's mum, Breda Leahy. The island is a fox-free zone so they're adding free-range chickens too. Ruairi's dinner menu offers a good choice and might include crab salad with aioli (freshest crab imaginable); steamed lobster with chilli garlic butter, fresh spinach and boiled potatoes (local potatoes in their skins), a magic crème brûlée... it will be a very simple meal but presented and cooked superbly. Catch of the day might very well be ling, once a staple food in these parts, simply fried with tiny macedoine of red and yellow peppers sprinkled on top. And Marie Thérèse is a great host – a visit here is sure to be a memorable experience. *This wonderful place was our Newcomer of the Year in 2008. **Seats 30**; restaurant & toilets wheelchair accessible; broadband wi/fi. D daily Apr-Sept; 7-9pm (opening times seasonal - please enquire in advance); house wine €20. Closed Sun, Mon D, Oct-Mar. **Accommodation:** There are just three suites and they are designed as large open spaces with a hall, living area, en-suite sleeping area, exterior door and outside sitting area. Fishing rods, bicycles and books of interest are provided instead of TV to help guests discover the peace and quiet of the island. (Failte Ireland approval pending). **Rooms 3** (all suites, en-suite, shower only and no smoking); B&B €100pps, ss €50. MasterCard, Visa, Laser. **Directions:** After passing only pub on your right, take next right, then take first left to Inis Meáin Restaurant & Suites entrance.

Aran Islands
GUESTHOUSE

Kilmurvey House

Kilronan Inis Mor Aran Islands Co Galway **Tel: 099 61218**
kilmurveyhouse@eircom.net www.kilmurveyhouse.com

Treasa Joyce's 150-year old stone house stands out as a beacon at the foot of the island's most famous attraction, Dun Aonghasa. It's a fine house and well kept, with a neatly manicured front garden and a walled vegetable garden at the back. It's steeped in history and has a large high-ceilinged hall and wide stairs giving a feeling of spacious grandeur. The spacious bedrooms are stylish and beautifully finished, with great views of fields, Dun Aengus and sea; four new rooms (and a conference room) were added in 2007 and two of the biggest rooms have king-sized beds. Residents' dinners are based on home-grown, local produce - guests love Treasa's baked cod, which she makes with an herb pesto crust or a tapenade, or beef and Guinness casserole on cool evenings - and there is a short, but well-chosen, wine list. Comfortable accommodation, good food, and warm hospitality make this an ideal place to stay. Conferences (60). **Rooms 12** (all en-suite, 4 shower only, 2 family, all no smoking); children welcome (under 5s free in parents' room, cots available free of charge, high chair). No pets. B&B €50pps, ss €15. Residents' D: €30, 7pm, by arrangement - please check when booking. House wine €22. *Café An Sunda Caoch (The Blind Sound) is a café at the Dun Aonghusa visitor centre, run independently by Treasa Joyce, which serves delicious home-made food - soups, cakes (don't miss the gorgeous fruit cake) sandwiches - every day in summer, 11am-5pm. Garden; walking. Closed 31 Oct-1 Apr. MasterCard, Visa, Laser. **Directions:** 7km (4.5 m) from Kilronan (take minibus from harbour, or rent bicycles). ◇〉

Aran Islands
RESTAURANT

Mainistir House

Inis Mor Aran Islands Co Galway **Tel: 099 61169**
mainistirhouse@eircom.net www.mainistirhousearan.com

It's over fifteen years since Joel d'Anjou opened this long single storey whitewashed building on a hill overlooking Galway Bay as a hostel and restaurant, and it is still the most talked about place on the islands. Despite the hostel atmosphere, Mainistir House provides guesthouse comfort at a hostel rate. But you don't even have to be staying here to experience Joel's famous 'Vaguely Vegetarian Buffet' (changes daily) which is served nightly and written on a blackboard. Six large tables are set up with checked cloths and everyone is served a starter - say a delicious lentil soup - then there are half a dozen dishes displayed on a big round table: prunes with onions & apple; tomato salad with pesto dressing & soft Boursin cheese; rice bulgur pilaf & canellini beans in a ragu sauce & vegetable stir-fry of cabbage, red peppers, carrots and mint are all possible, and delicious desserts are offered as extra. Service is prompt (and colourful), this is great food - and this fun and funky restaurant continues to give amazing value. Bring your own wine. Christmas and New Year packages available. **Restaurant Seats 45**. D daily, 8pm. Set Menu €15. BYO wine. Accommodation: (8 private rooms plus hostel accommodation for up to 70; all no smoking). B&B €25pps, ss €7.50 (includes a simple breakfast of porridge/cereals & freshly baked bread each morning). MasterCard, Visa. **Directions:** 1 mile along the main road from the harbour. ◇

Aran Islands    Man Of Aran Cottages

B&B•RESTAURANT   Kilmurvey Inis Mor Aran Islands Co Galway **Tel: 099 61301**

     manofaran@eircom.net www.manofarancottage.com

Despite its fame - this is where the film Man of Aran was made - Joe and Maura Wolfe make visiting their home a genuine and personal experience. The cottage is right beside the sea and Kilmurvey beach, surrounded by wild flowers, and Joe has somehow managed to make a productive garden in this exposed location, so their meals - for residents only - usually include his organically grown vegetables (even artichokes and asparagus), salads, nasturtium flowers and young nettle leaves as well as Maura's home-made soups, stews and freshly-baked bread and cakes. Dinner is served in the little restaurant but there are benches in the garden, with stunning views across the sea towards the mountains, where you can enjoy an aperitif, or even eat outside on fine summer evenings. The three little bedrooms are basic but full of quaint, cottagey charm and they're very comfortable, although only one is en-suite. Breakfast will probably be a well cooked full-Irish - made special by Joe's beautifully sweet home-grown cherry tomatoes if you are lucky - although they'll do something different if you like. Packed lunches are available too. **Rooms 3** (1 en-suite, all no smoking); children welcome (under 4s free in parents room, cot available). No pets. Garden, walking. B&B €45 pps, ss €15. Closed Nov-Feb. **No Credit Cards. Directions:** Mini bus or cycle from Kilronan, 6.5km (4 m).

Aran Islands   O'Malley's @ Bay View

RESTAURANT•WINE BAR   The Pier Kilronan Inishmor Aran Islands Co Galway
Tel:

The O'Malley brothers, who have earned a special reputation for their great cooking in Pier House Restaurant (see entry) have taken on a new challenge at Bay View which, like Pier House, occupies a very prominent position on the pier. As you approach by boat you'll see the large two-storey white building, with wooden benches on the terrace. Now totally refurbished, it has been converted to make a smart modern wine and tapas bar. There are three golden painted rooms with original coving and high ceilings, including a bright mirror-backed wine bar in the first room; paintings adorning the walls are for sale at the time of our visit, shortly after the restaurant opened in July 2007, the large and beautiful works were by local artists Cyril and Finuala Flaherty, and Jackie Rowantree. The main food offering is tapas (calamari with sweet chilli sauce, for example, and prosciutto roll, stuffed with rocket and cottage cheese, pizzas and gourmet burgers and wine by the bottle or glass (6) - but a full Irish breakfast is served till 5pm, and main courses include pan-fried mackerel with chorizo and potato salad, or Moroccan tagine with cinnamon and coriander couscous. Desserts like baked raspberry cheesecake with raspberry purée or chocolate tarte and rhubarb compôte alone should tempt the hundreds of day trippers to sample the food of these two passionate well-travelled and brilliant cooks. Open 10 am till 9.30pm (to 10pm Fri-Sun). MasterCard, Visa, Laser. **Directions:** Large two-storey white building on the pier in Kilronan. ◇

Aran islands   Pier House Guest House

GUESTHOUSE   Kilronan Inishmor Aran Islands Co Galway **Tel: 099 61417**
pierh@iol.ie www.pierhousearan.com

In a new building, right on the pier where the boats arrive, Maura & Padraig Joyce run this large well-kept guesthouse. As you walk from the ferry you will be offered tours of the island (mini-bus or pony and trap) or invited to hire one of the thousand or so bikes available on the island. Kilronan is the action centre of the island and Pier House is around the corner from pubs, cafés, a supermarket and the local hall; the attractive beach is round the next corner. While perhaps less characterful than some of the older houses, rooms are comfortable, with more facilities than most island accommodation (TV and phones as well as communal tea/coffee making facilities downstairs to use at any time) and views over sea and hills, and flag-stoned fields at the back. There's also a large residents' lounge and the house generally is comfortable and well-run. The restaurant is currently leased (see entry). *Four attractive self-catering apartments are also offered. **Rooms 10** (all en-suite & no smoking, 1 ground floor); children welcome (under 5s free in parents' room). B&B €60 pps, ss €20. MasterCard, Visa, Laser. **Directions:** Galway to Rosamhil then Ferry, 30 minutes to Island.

Aran Islands   Pier House Restaurant
RESTAURANT   Kilronan Inis Mor Aran Islands Co Galway **Tel: 099 61811**
info@aranrestaurant.com   www.pierhouserestaurant.com

Brothers Damien and Ronan O'Malley run this fine restaurant beside the pier, and it would be hard to imagine a better location for an island restaurant, as it so close to the ferry and all the life of Kilronan village, with beautiful views across the harbour. The setting is very relaxing and, with seating equally divided between inside and outdoor tables, it's a good place to be, whatever the weather. The cooking is modern Irish in style and, naturally enough, features locally caught fresh fish and seafood, with plenty of other choices - including an imaginative vegetarian dish, and meat such as braised Connemara lamb shank. Good home-made breads and delicious desserts are excellent. An extensive drinks menu offers spirits and beer as well as a wine list. The brothers have earned a loyal following and Pier House Restaurant is regarded by locals as 'the' place for a special evening out and since the opening of their newer place nearby, O'Malleys @ Bay View (see entry), food at The Pier House Restaurant continues to impress. **Seats 44** (+outdoor 40, private room 12); children welcome until 8pm. Open Daily L 12-5, D 6-9.30pm (to 10om Fri/Sat). Set Value D Sun-Thu about €32, also a la carte. House wine €19. Closed mid Oct - mid Mar. MasterCard, Visa, Laser. **Directions:** Overlooking pier and bay, 50 metres from the ferry point. ◊

Aran Islands   Radharc An Chlair
B&B   Castle Village Inis Oirr Aran Islands Co Galway **Tel: 099 75019**
bridpoil@eircom.net

Brid Poil's welcoming dormer house looks over the Cliffs of Moher, with views of Galway Bay on the left, and has had a great reputation for many years - she came over from Clare over twenty years ago when she married Peadar and thought this would be a nice thing to do. Her many regular guests clearly agree - when the ferry from Doolin started, all Clare came over and are still coming so you need to book a month ahead. A keen cook, Brid's philosophy is 'simple and in season' which should be the mantra of all on the islands: roast beef, baked ham with carrots and cabbage or hake baked with onion and bay leaf are among her most popular dishes, also Darina's bread and butter pudding. Brid only makes dinner for guests by arrangement, and there are treats for breakfast too, including prune and apricot compotes, freshly baked scones, and home-made grapefruit marmalade. **Rooms 6** (5 shower only, 1 bath, 2 ground floor, all no smoking); children welcome (under 5s free in parents' room); free broadband wi/fi. No pets. Garden; walking. B&B €35 pps, ss €10. Residents D by arrangement. **No Credit Cards. Directions:** At Castle Village, overlooking Cliffs of Moher.

Aran Islands   Tig Congaile
B&B•RESTAURANT   Moore Village Inis Meain Aran Islands Co Galway **Tel: 099 73085**
V   bbinismeain@eircom.net

Arriving on Inis Meain by boat, you will see Tigh Congaile on the hill above the little port. It is a lovely pale primrose-painted, green-silled house with a perfectly manicured lawn surrounding it, and it's just a 3-minute walk from the pier or the beach. Vilma Conneely worked in banking in California, met and married Padraic, came back home with him and opened Tigh Congaile 1993; so, on arrival, you are offered freshly brewed Guatemalan coffee to enjoy in the large dining room, which has a wonderful view and is hung with the work of local artists, displayed for sale. An all day/evening menu on the wall is ideal for the non-stop visitors coming on to the island from the various ferries. Vilma specialises in organic and sea vegetables, and uses as much seafood as she can get locally and from Galway - she is lauded quietly by many of the marine biologists in UCG for her interest in this, and her wonderful Sea Vegetable Soup is a speciality known well beyond the islands. Accommodation is in minimalist rooms with modern style wooden floor, comfortable beds and neat en-suite facilities - everything is immaculately clean and, of course, every room has a view to die for. If sitting outside on a fine day, the peace and the view make this the best spot on the island. Conference/meetings (45). **Seats 45**; children welcome (high chair, children's menu, under 2s free in parents' room, cot available free of charge); toilets wheelchair accessible. L&D daily, 11-4pm, 7-9pm; reservations required. A la carte. House wine about €16. Rooms 7 (all shower only, ground floor & no smoking, 1 family); B&B €38, ss €7. Fishing, cycling, walking, garden. Closed Oct-Easter. MasterCard, Visa, Laser. **Directions:** Five minutes walk from the pier.

Athenry
HOTEL
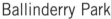

Raheen Woods Hotel
Athenry Co Galway **Tel 091 875 888**
info@raheenwoodshotel.ie www.raheenwoodshotel.ie

Conveniently located off the main Dublin - Galway road (N6), and only a short drive from Galway Airport and Galway City, this smart new hotel is within walking distance of the Heritage Town of Athenry town yet attractively situated in a woodland setting with landscaped gardens. It is an attractive hotel and has wide appeal but, with 'state of the art' conference and event facilities, complimentary wi-fi access throughout the hotel and a fine leisure centre, it has particular relevance to business travellers and conference /event planners. Useful for a journey break, as light meals and snacks are available throughout the day. Spa, gymnasium, 20m swimming pool, steam room, sauna, jacuzzi and yoga/meditation room. **Rooms 50**. B&B from €45pps. Open all year except Christmas. **Directions:** Off N6, about 15 minutes east of Galway city.

BALLINASLOE

Ballinasloe is County Galway's second largest town, after Galway City. Situated on the N6 National Primary route linking Dublin and Galway, it is one of the principal gateways to the West. Its position on the River Suck, a tributary of the Shannon, has historical importance and, in modern terms, allows access to the inland waterways – there is a marina in the town. The event the town is most famous for is the Ballinasloe Horse Fair; held every October, it is one of Europe's oldest and largest, dating back to the 1700s, and attracts up to 100,000 visitors from all over the world. Other equestrian activities also take place throughout the year. It is an interesting area to stay in but, because of its location, many visitors will stay only briefly. For lunch and evening meals, try the surprisingly named **Kariba's Restaurant** (090 964 4830) on Society Street, which provides honest food at fair prices and is well-supported by local people; a useful place to break a journey as food is available all day Mon-Sat. A new hotel, **The Carlton Shearwater** (www.carlton.ie) is at Marina Point – which, despite the name, is in the town centre; in line with other Carlton hotels, it offers a high standard of comfort and facilities. Ballinasloe Farmers' Market is held every Friday 10am-3pm (Croffey Centre, Main Street). **WWW.IRELAND-GUIDE.COM FOR ALL THE BEST PLACES TO EAT, DRINK & STAY**

Ballinasloe Area
COUNTRY HOUSE

Ballinderry Park
Kilconnell Ballinasloe Co Galway **Tel: 090 968 6796**
george@ballinderrypark.com www.ballinderrypark.com

At the end of a winding track, a smallish but perfectly proportioned early Georgian house comes into view. Recently rescued from dereliction, the house always demands more to be done, but George Gossip and his wife Susie have worked wonders, creating a comfortable home out of a ruin. All the interior walls are clad in panelling - not reclaimed, but new and designed by George. The effect is of timeless elegance and the palette of colours used in the various rooms is strikingly beautiful, especially the intense blue of the dining room. The bedrooms (two doubles with en-suite bathrooms, plus one twin room with shower only) are spacious, with comfortable beds and lots of light. While there are some eccentricities, these only add to the special nature of a stay at Ballinderry Park. The books and photographs, old framed silhouettes and antique maps that one finds throughout the house clearly speak of the owners' own taste, rather than that of some interior designer. In the evening, guests are invited to help themselves to a drink from a well-stocked cupboard then sit beside the log fire to peruse an interesting wine list that is both short and remarkably good value. George is not only a thoughtful host but well-known in

Ireland as a terrific cook, who seeks out the best ingredients (notably game, in season) and dreams up meals that are imaginative but don't strive for effect. And he will send you on your way with a wonderful breakfast as a warm memory of your stay. And, before you leave the area, there is a particularly fine ruined abbey awaiting your attention in nearby Kilconnell village. **Rooms 4** (2 shower only, all no smoking); children welcome (under 3s free in parents' room, cots available free of charge). Dogs permitted in certain areas by arrangement. B&B €75 pps, ss €20. Residents' D at 8pm, €50 (not always available Sun, Mon); house wine from €23. Cookery classes, fly fishing, walking, special interest breaks on site; Golf and hunting nearby. Closed 1 Nov - 31 Mar - but will open over winter for groups. Amex, MasterCard, Visa, Laser. **Directions:** R348 from Ballinasloe, through Kilconnell, take left for Cappataggle, immediately left & continue until road turns into one avenue. ◇

BALLYCONNEELY

Home to the world famous Connemara Pony, the tranquil, unspoilt village of Ballyconneely is situated on a peninsula jutting into the Atlantic between Clifden, to the north, and the pretty fishing village of Roundstone, to the South. The peninsula is ringed by beautiful beaches, which are ideal for both bathing and shore angling. Other local attractions include the Roundstone bog, rich in undisturbed wildlife and habitat, whilst golfers will enjoy a round at Connemara Golf Club (095 23 502/23 602). The seafood presented in the local restaurants and pubs is excellent, and there is an award-winning Irish smoked salmon producer, The Connemara Smokehouse (095 23 739), near Ballyconneely. The **Mannin Bay Hotel** (095 23120; manninbay.com); formerly known as Erriseask House, this famous small hotel re-opened in 2007 as Mannin Bay Hotel after development and refurbishment.

WWW.IRELAND-GUIDE.COM FOR ALL THE BEST PLACES TO EAT, DRINK & STAY

Ballyconneely

COUNTRY HOUSE

Ⓥ

Emlaghmore Lodge

Ballyconneely Co Galway **Tel: 095 23529**
info@emlaghmore.com www.emlaghmore.com

Built in 1862 as a small fishing lodge, Nicholas Tinne's magically located house is situated halfway between Roundstone and the 18-hole links golf course at Ballyconneely, in a Special Area of Conservation. It has been in the Tinne family for over 75 years and is quite a modest house in some ways, but it is comfortably furnished in keeping with its age. It feels gloriously remote and has its own river running through the garden with fly fishing, yet it is only a few hundred yards from sandy beaches and there are good pubs and restaurants nearby too. Nick also cooks dinner for residents: seafood treats and local meat prevail. **Rooms 4** (2 en-suite, 1 shower only; 2 with private bathrooms; all no smoking); not suitable for children. B&B €85, ss €30-40; single room €65. Residents D, €50 at 8.30pm (please book by 10am.); house wine €20. No pets. Golf, pony trekking& windsurfing nearby. Walking, fly fishing, garden. *Self-catering cottage also available nearby. Closed Nov-Easter. MasterCard, Visa. **Directions:** Turn inland off coast road 100 metres on Roundstone side of Callow Bridge. 10 km (6 m) from Roundstone, 4km (2.5m) from Ballyconneely.

CASHEL

Lying at the head of the beautiful Cashel Bay, the townland owes its name to the ring fort which borders the graveyard. Cashel Hill stands at the top of the bay; it is a pleasant walk to the top of this hill, where you will be rewarded by breathtaking views of the surrounding area. The area offers a number of historical sites, including a megalithic tomb, and the varied landscape offers walkers and pony trekkers some beautiful trails amid the many lakes and bogs, over the Twelve Bens and Maamturk Mountains, or along the secluded coves of Bertaghboy Bay. Activities in the area include golfing at Connemara Golf Club in Ballyconneely (095 23 502/23 602), horse riding, deep sea and also freshwater fishing - the area is known for its excellent salmon fishing. **Zetland Country House Hotel** (095 31111; www.zetland.com) is an early 19th century sporting lodge overlooking Cashel Bay, and could make a good base for fishing holidays; it came into new ownership shortly before the Guide went to press.

WWW.IRELAND-GUIDE.COM FOR ALL THE BEST PLACES TO EAT, DRINK & STAY

Cashel
HOTEL•RESTAURANT

Cashel House Hotel

Cashel Connemara Co Galway **Tel: 095 31001**
res@cashel-house-hotel.com www.cashel-house-hotel.com

Kay and the late Dermot McEvilly were among the pioneers of the Irish country house movement when they opened Cashel House as a hotel in 1968. The following year General and Madame de Gaulle chose to stay for two weeks, an historic visit of which the McEvilly family is justly proud - look out for the photographs and other memorabilia in the hall. The de Gaulle visit meant immediate recognition for the hotel, but it did even more for Ireland by putting the Gallic seal of approval on Irish hospitality and food. The beautiful gardens, which run down to a private foreshore, contribute greatly to the atmosphere, and the accommodation includes especially comfortable ground floor garden suites, which are also suitable for less able guests (wheelchair accessible, but no special grab rails etc in bathrooms). Relaxed hospitality combined with professionalism have earned an international reputation for this outstanding hotel and its qualities are perhaps best seen in details - log fires that burn throughout the year, day rooms furnished with antiques and filled with fresh flowers from the garden, rooms that are individually decorated with many thoughtful touches. Service (with all-day room service, including all meals) is impeccable, and delicious breakfasts include a wonderful buffet display of home-made and local produce (Cashel House was the Connaught winner of our Irish Breakfast Awards in 2001). Dermot McEvilly was an inspirational figure in Irish hospitality and he is much missed; but his legacy lives on in many ways – a current development that he actively encouraged, for example, is for the gardens to become a more active focus of interest; Kay McEvilly has taken this up with enthusiasm and the relaxed and informative short residential Cashel House Garden Courses with respected guest speakers have proved an immediate success. Similarly, there are plans for the hotel to work more closely with the equestrian side of the business. Conference/banqueting (15/80); children welcome (cot available (€10), baby sitting arranged, playroom). Pets permitted in some areas (stay in bedrooms). Walking, tennis. Gardens (open to the public). Well-located for local horse shows (Justice Connemara Pony & Irish Sport Horse Stud Farm is located within the hotel grounds; guests may view). **Rooms 32** (13 suites, 4 family rooms, 6 ground floor, 3 single, 1 shower only, all no smoking). B&B €135pps, no ss; SC12.5%. **Restaurant:** A large conservatory extension makes the most of the outlook on to the lovely gardens around this well-appointed split-level restaurant, which is open to non-residents. Arturo Amit who has been head chef since 2003, is known for cooking that showcases local produce, notably seafood. Despite occasional world influences - in a plate of warm Cleggan mussels with tomato chilli and garlic, for example - the tone of his five-course dinner menus is classic: roast Connemara lamb is an enduring favourite and there is an emphasis on home-grown fruit and vegetables, including some fine vegetarian dishes and homely desserts, such as rhubarb or apple tart, or strawberries and cream - then farmhouse cheeses come with home-baked biscuits. The personal supervision of Kay McEvilly and restaurant manager Ray Doorley ensures exceptionally caring service, and an extensive and informative wine list includes many special bottles for the connoisseur - yet there are also plenty of well-chosen, more accessible wines (under about €30), and a good choice of half bottles. *A short à la carte bar lunch menu offers interesting snacks and sandwiches, but also delicious hot meals, including Irish stew or even lobster, if desired; afternoon teas are also served daily in the bar. **Seats 85**. D daily 7-9, L 12-2.30. Set D €55. Set Sun L €30; also à la carte. House wine €30. SC 12.5%; (Bar food available, L 12.30-2.30, Afternoon Tea 2.30-5). Closed 2 Jan-2 Feb. Amex, MasterCard, Visa, Laser. **Directions:** South off N59 (Galway-Clifden road), 1 mile west of Recess turn left.

CLAREGALWAY

Just north-east of Galway on the junction of the N17 and N18 roads, Claregalway is now a fast-growing satellite town for Galway city; only 10km from the city, it is very convenient to Galway airport. Business guests visiting the area will find all the required facilities at the large **Claregalway Hotel** (091 738300; www.claregalwayhotel.ie), or at the smaller more intimate hotel, **The Arches** (www.arches-hotel.com). Visitors interested in history should see the ruins of a Franciscan abbey built by John de Cogan in 1290, among the most beautiful of its kind in the country; the church consists of nave, choir, north aisle and transept, surmounted by a graceful tower, of which parts remain in a good state of preservation. The area is also notable as the origin of the Irish ancestors of Che Guevara (Patrick Lynch). Garden enthusiasts will enjoy Ardcarraig (Bushypark, 091 524 336) and Brigit's Garden & Café (see

entry for café, Roscahill, 091 550 905), which are only a short drive away. Golfers will be challenged by the recently re-developed Galway Bay Golf Club (091 790 711) in Oranmore.
WWW.IRELAND-GUIDE.COM FOR ALL THE BEST PLACES TO EAT, DRINK

Clarinbridge
RESTAURANT
R

The Old School House Restaurant

Clarinbridge Co Galway **Tel:** 091 796 898
www.oldschoolhouserestaurant.com

Although it is beside the main road, this old schoolhouse restaurant is behind a high wall in its own garden, so it has a pleasantly rural feel. Happily it also still has the feel of a school, with the small desk with seat attached in the entrance hall a gentle reminder of schooldays – and terracota, crab-apple greens, honeys and lemon give it a dream-like school feel. It has the original plain school wooden doors, high ceilings, wooden wainscoting and wide-planked wooden floor, but a marble fire-place and old mirror in the spacious bar give it a homely feel. The restaurant was taken over by brothers Killian (chef) and Daire (restaurant manager) Hanrahan in 2008, and delighted local diners were quick to welcome this new talent: Local waitress Carol Finn looks after guests with warmth and charm – water is poured from a jug as soon as you sit at your table, and fresh white yeast bread with caraway and treacly brown arrive with a lovely grainy tapenade. A la carte menus offer a choice of eight starters and ten main courses, including two appealing vegetarian dishes and the remainder equally balanced between fish and meat. Begin, perhaps, with a generous and beau-tifully presented warm Bluebell Falls goat's cheese salad, with grilled Mediterranean vegetables, red pepper relish & pesto (also available as a main course) or a perfectly delicious cocktail of fresh crab with avocado, apple & tomato coulis (the crunch and fresh flavour of apple is a plus). To follow there might be oven-baked cod with chorizo & Spanish new potatoes & salsa verde, a gutsy dish with plenty of flavour, and meat choices could include dramatically presented tender honey roast pork belly with pork fillet, pickled red cabbage & pea purée. Service is efficient, under Daire's direction, the concise wine list is fairly priced and Killian knows his food - so a meal here should be a very enjoyable experience. **Seats 60** (private room, 30, outdoor, 16); toilets wheelchair accessible. D Wed-Sun, 5.30-9 (Sat, 6.30-10pm); L Sun only 12.30-5pm. Early D €25, 5.30-7. D à la carte. Set Sun L, about €24 (children's menu €10). House wine about €18.50. Closed Mon, Tue, 24-27 Dec, 31 Dec-3 Jan. Amex, MasterCard, Visa, Laser. **Directions:** 9km (6 miles) from Galway city, on N18 Galway-Limerick road. ◇

CLIFDEN

The main town of Connemara, Clifden nestles on the edge of the Atlantic with a dramatic backdrop of mountains. Although it has been somewhat over-developed recently, it remains an excellent base for exploring this exceptionally scenic area; the quality of food and accommodation available in and around the town is very high, and there is plenty to do: walking, horse riding, and bathing are all on the doorstep, the Connemara Garden Trail is relaxing and educational, and the island of Inishbofin (see entries) can be visited by ferry from Cleggan (sea angling charters are also available from Cleggan). For those who require a leisure centre and/or conference facilities, **The Clifden Station House Hotel** (095 21699; www.clifdenstationhouse.com) is built on the site of the old railway station and has everything required; the complex also includes a railway museum and a range of upmarket shops and boutiques. Outside the town, the beautifully located **Rock Glen Country House Hotel** (095 21035;www.rockglen-hotel.com) offers space and a peaceful atmosphere. There are several gardens of note within a short drive of Clifden including Ballynahinch Castle Hotel & Garden (Recess, 095 31006), Kylemore Abbey & Victorian Walled Garden (Letterfrack, 095 41155) and Cashel House Hotel & Gardens (Cashel, 095 31001). Golfers will relish the challenge posed by Connemara Golf Club (095 23502) which is just down the road in Ballyconneely.
WWW.IRELAND-GUIDE.COM FOR ALL THE BEST PLACES TO EAT, DRINK & STAY

Clifden
HOTEL

Abbeyglen Castle Hotel

Sky Road Clifden Co Galway **Tel: 095 21201**
info@abbeyglen.ie www.abbeyglen.ie

Set romantically in its own parkland valley overlooking Clifden and the sea, Abbeyglen is family-owned and run in a very hands-on fashion by Paul and Brian Hughes. It's a place that has won a lot of friends over the years and it's easy to see why: from the minute arriving guests meet Gilbert the parrot at recep-tion, it's clear that this place is different; it's big and comfortable and laid-back - and there's a charming generosity of spirit about the place. Complimentary afternoon tea for residents is a particu-larly hospitable speciality, served in a spacious drawing room or in front of an open peat fire in the relaxing bar, where many a late night is spent. A major building programme saw the addition of six new superior rooms, and the refurbishment of the existing bedrooms, which are all unusually spacious and have character. Most recently, a beauty and relaxation centre has been added, and the outdoor swimming pool that was a feature in the garden at the front of the hotel for many years has been re-designed - as a fountain and sun patio. **Rooms 45** (25 superior, 20 standard, all en-suite); not suitable for children; wheelchair accessible. Lift. Room service (limited hours). B&B €112pps, ss €30. No pets. **Restaurant: seats 70**; set D daily 7-9pm, €49; house wine €22.95. Garden, tennis, pitch and putt, snooker, jacuzzi, sauna, massage, treatments, walking. Fishing (sea, coarse & fly), equestrian and garden visits nearby. 12.5% s.c. Closed 6 Jan-1 Feb Amex, Diners, MasterCard, Visa, Laser. Helipad. **Directions:** About 300 metres out of Clifden on the Sky Road, on the left.

Clifden
HOTEL•RESTAURANT

Ardagh Hotel & Restaurant

Ballyconneely Road Clifden Co Galway **Tel: 095 21384**
ardaghhotel@eircom.net   www.ardaghhotel.com

Beautifully located, overlooking Ardbear Bay, Stéphane and Monique Bauvet's family-run hotel is well-known for quiet hospitality, low-key comfort and good food. Public areas have style, in a relaxed homely way: turf fires, comfortable armchairs, classic country colours, and a plant-filled conservatory area upstairs are pleasing to the eye and indicate that peaceful relaxation is the aim here. Bedrooms vary according to their position but are well-furnished with all the amenities required for a comfortable stay. Bedrooms include some extra large rooms, especially suitable for families and there are some single rooms at the back, with a pleasant countryside outlook. Children welcome (under 5s free in parents room, cot available without charge, baby sitting arranged). Pets permitted (stay in bedrooms, no charge). Garden, walking, pool table. Golf, fishing & beach all nearby. **Rooms 17** (2 suites, 4 shower only, 2 family rooms, all no smoking). Room service (all day). B&B €79 pps, ss €30. *Short/off-season breaks available. **Restaurant:** This long-established restaurant is a well-appointed light-filled room on the first floor, with wonderful sea and mountain views - and a warm reception is sure to set the tone for an enjoyable evening. Monique Bauvet's menus are wide-ranging and based on excellent ingredients including home grown organic vegetables and salads, and an extensive choice of local seafood, which may include oysters, mussels, scallops, squid, organic salmon, crab, lobster, and a variety of fish including black (Dover) sole, and there will be a fair choice of meats too, including local lamb - a roast rack, perhaps, with crushed celeriac and a red wine jus with rosemary & thyme - along with some poultry and at least one imaginative vegetarian choice. Cooking is reliably good and delicious home-made breads, well-flavoured soups (including the creamy house chowder), organic vegetables, home-grown salads and home-made ice creams are among the details that stand out, and there is also a good cheese selection, served with grapes, celery and crackers. Home-made petits fours will follow with your coffee (or tea/tisane). Relaxed service, under the direction of Stéphane Bauvet, contributes to an atmosphere of confident professionalism that greatly enhances a meal here. A fairly priced wine list strong on old world wines, especially Bordeaux and Burgundy, also has an interesting choice from South Africa and offers some half bottles. **Seats 55**. D 7.15-9.30pm daily, set D about €50, à la carte also available; house wine €22; sc discretionary. Closed Nov-Mar. Amex, Diners, MasterCard, Visa, Laser. **Directions:** 3 km outside Clifden on Ballyconneely Road.

Clifden
HOTEL•RESTAURANT

Foyles Hotel

Main Street Clifden Co Galway **Tel: 095 21801**
info@foyleshotel.com   www.foyleshotel.com

This handsome 19th century hotel in Clifden town centre has played a central role in the hospitality of the area for many a year - proprietor Eddie Foyle is related to a number of key players including brothers Paddy and Billy (Quay House and Dolphin Beach), and the hotel was their family home. Today, with design-led modern hotels appearing in virtually every part of Ireland, hotels like Foyles are becoming a rarity - and, one suspects, something that will seem increasingly precious with each passing year. Stepping in off the street into the old-fashioned foyer/lounge - a comfortable space with well-worn settees, gas fire, fussy florid carpet and a bavarian-style wooden staircase leading to bedrooms - is like stepping back in time, and it is a very calming experience. Upstairs, the hotel's Victorian origins are seen in pleasingly wide corridors (hooped dresses were in fashion at the time), and large, well-proportioned rooms - which are comfortably old-fashioned, with good beds and modern bathrooms. And, true to its roots, you'll find hands-on family management, and interested service from pleasant staff who are happy to help guests to get the most from their visit to the area. **Rooms 25**. B&B €70 pps. Closed Christmas & Jan. **Marconi Restaurant:** Welcoming window views of tables set up with white linen cloths and napkins, candles and pretty floral bouquets in old cups-as-vases are visible from the public footpath - and may well attract you in to this popular restaurant, which is accessible from the street or through the hotel. Barely audible jazz plays in a quirkily attractive and comfortable French-feeling room displaying memorabilia and arte-facts - the Marconi connection with the town, Alcock & Brown's remarkable trans-Atlantic flight and landing near Clifden and, right in the middle of the restaurant, a redundant merchant navy compass. Look out for the zany painting depicting famous former visitors to the hotel in chef's uniform - you may recognise Winston Churchill and Seamus Heaney, and perhaps be tempted to guess the identity of others. Warm, relaxed staff present an extensive à la carte menu offering plenty of local seafood (mussels steamed in chilli & coconut broth; crabmeat terrine with smoked salmon; lovely, simple fried fillets of lemon sole in parsley butter), balanced by meat dishes such as lamb shank with mustard mash or pork fillet with pear & apple crisps, and at least one vegetarian dish. The cooking can sometimes be a little uneven but excellent raw materials are used and it is very good value, especially the early dinner - 3 courses from the à la carte for about €25; available to 6.45pm only. A conservative, well-priced wine list includes 6 half bottles and a choice of house wines. Open from 6 to 9pm daily. Early D €24.95, also à la carte. Hotel closed Christmas & Jan. MasterCard, Visa. **Directions:** On the Main Street in centre of Clifden.

Clifden
COUNTRY HOUSE

Mallmore Country House

Ballyconneely Road Clifden Co Galway **Tel: 095 21460**
info@mallmore.com www.mallmore.com

Alan and Kathleen Hardman's restored Georgian home near Clifden is set peacefully in 35 acres of woodland grounds. Connemara ponies are bred here, and old woodland has been retained so the grounds are teeming with wildlife. The house has a warm and welcoming atmosphere, and there's a lovely drawing room for guests' use with an open turf fire and a beautiful sea view out over the gardens. Accommodation is spacious - individually decorated rooms in period style have superb views, and en-suite shower rooms. Tea and coffee is available all day, and the Hardmans take great pride in sending their guests off for the day with a really good breakfast, served in a formal dining room. **Rooms 6** (all en-suite, 2 family, all ground floor & no smoking); children welcome (under 2s free in parents room, cot available free of charge); free broadband wi/fi; B&B €40 pps. Fishing (fly & sea), golf, equestrian, garden visits & hillwalking all nearby. Closed 1 Nov- 1 Mar. **No credit cards. Directions:** 1.5 km from Clifden; signed off Ballyconneely road.

Clifden
RESTAURANT

Mitchell's Restaurant

Market Street Clifden Connemara Co Galway
Tel: 095 21867

This attractive and well-managed family-run restaurant offers efficient, welcoming service and very agreeably stylish "good home cooking" all day, every day throughout a long season - and they have been doing so, with admirable consistency, since 1991. An all-day menu offers a wide range of lightish fare - everything from sandwiches and wraps to seafood chowder; the international flavours are there but how refreshing it is to find old friends like deep-fried Gubbeen cheese and bacon & cabbage there amongst the home-made spicy fish cakes and fresh crab salad with home-made brown bread. There's some overlap on to an à la carte evening menu, which offers a judicious selection from the snack menu but the choice is much wider and includes half a dozen appealing meat and poultry dishes and a vegetarian dish of the day as well as eight or nine seafood dishes and a choice of main course salads. This is a very fair place, offering honest food at honest prices – and, in the Guide's recent experience, it is better than ever, the food really delicious and service outstanding. **Seats 70**; not suitable for children after 6 pm; air conditioning. Open daily, 12-10; set 3 course D about €27.50; also à la carte. House wine from about €18.50. Closed Nov-Feb. Amex, Diners, MasterCard, Visa, Laser. **Directions:** Across the road from SuperValu supermarket. ◊

Clifden
GUESTHOUSE

The Quay House
Beach Road Clifden Co Galway **Tel: 095 21369**
thequay@iol.ie www.thequayhouse.com

In a lovely location - right on the harbour, with pretty water views when the tide is in - The Quay House is the oldest building in Clifden and was built around 1820. Since then it has had a surprisingly varied usage: it was originally the harbourmaster's house, then a convent, then a monastery; it was converted into a hotel at the turn of the century and finally, since 1993, has been relishing its most enjoyable phase as a guesthouse, in the incomparable hands of long-time hoteliers, Paddy and Julia Foyle. It's a fine house, with spacious rooms - including a stylishly homely drawing room with an open fire. And the accommodation is exceptionally comfortable, in airy, wittily decorated and sumptuously furnished rooms that include not only two wheelchair-friendly rooms, but also seven newer studio rooms, with small fitted kitchens, balconies overlooking the harbour and, as in the original rooms, excellent bathrooms with full bath and shower. Breakfast is served in a charming conservatory, decorated with a collection of silver domes and trailing Virginia creeper criss-crossing the room on strings, and it is simply superb - treats include a buffet laid out to tempt you as you enter. Orders for your tea or coffee are taken even before you sit down at a table beautifully set up with individual jugs of freshly squeezed orange juice. Hot dishes, such as a perfectly cooked traditional Irish, or scrambled eggs with smoked salmon, are all served with crisp toast, and fresh top-ups of tea and coffee. Although officially closed in winter, it is always worth inquiring. *The Quay House was our Guesthouse of the Year for 2006, and also the national winner of the Irish Breakfast Awards. **Rooms 14** (all with full bathrooms, 2 ground floor, all no smoking, 1 for disabled); free broadband wi/fi; children welcome (under 12 free in parents' room, cots available without charge). No pets. B&B from €80pps, ss €40. Garden. Walking. Closed Nov-mid Mar. MasterCard, Visa, Laser **Directions:** 2 minutes from town centre, overlooking Clifden harbour - follow signs to the Beach Road.

Clifden
B&B

Sea Mist House
Clifden Connemara Co Galway **Tel: 095 21441**
sgriffin@eircom.net www.seamisthouse.com

Sheila Griffin's attractive house was built in 1825, using local quarried stone. Major renovations undertaken over the last few years have retained its character while adding modern comforts, allowing her to offer stylish and comfortable accommodation. A large conservatory makes a lovely, spacious room overlooking the garden, where guests can relax - and fruit from the garden is used in spiced fruit compôtes and preserves which appear at breakfast along with home-made breads, American-style pancakes with fresh fruit salsa and scrambled eggs with smoked salmon, plus a special of the day which brings an element of surprise to the menu each morning. The cottage garden adjacent to the house has been developing over the years and is now reaching maturity - guests are welcome to wander through it and soak in the tranquil atmosphere. There are also many other gardens to visit nearby (the Connemara Garden Trail). **Rooms 4** (all shower only & no-smoking, 1 family room); broadband wi/fi; private parking (3). No pets. Garden. B&B €60pps, ss €20. Closed Christmas, also mid-week off season. MasterCard, Visa, Laser. **Directions:** Left at square, a little down on right.

Clonbur
FARMHOUSE

Ballykine House
Clonbur Co Galway **Tel: 094 954 6150**
ballykine@eircom.net www.ballykinehouse-clonbur-cong.com

Comfortable accommodation and Ann Lambe's warm hospitality make this an appealing base for a peaceful holiday. There are guided forest walks from the house, angling on Lough Corrib, an equestrian centre (at nearby Ashford Castle) and bikes for hire locally. It's also well placed for touring

Connemara. Moderately priced rooms have TV, tea/coffee making facilities and hairdryers. No evening meals but the pubs and restaurants of Clonbur are all within walking distance, and so is Ashford Castle. On fine evenings, guests often like to walk to the pub or restaurant of their choice and get a lift back later. It's a sociable house with plenty of comfortable seating in the sitting room and conservatory for lounging and chatting, and a new patio/barbecue area was added in 2008 and guests enjoy sitting out there on fine evenings. There's also a library room for visitors, pool table - and a drying room for anglers. **Rooms 5** (4 with en-suite shower; 1 with private bath); not suitable for children under 6 yrs; B&B €35-40 pps, ss €15. Garden. Closed 1 Nov-17 Mar. No Credit Cards. **Directions:** 3km from Cong, on Cong/Clonbur Rd - R345.

Clonbur   # Fairhill House Hotel
HOTEL   Main Street Clonbur Co Galway **Tel: 094 954 6176**
V   fairhillhouse@eircom.net www.fairhillhouse.com

The Lynch family's friendly Victorian hotel in the centre of the pretty village of Clonbur dates back to 1830 and has recently been sympathetically refurbished, bringing it up to the standards demanded by today's travellers without spoiling its character. Accommodation is simple, but very comfortable for a country hotel. The new decor is gentle on the eye, most rooms have both single and double beds and all bathrooms have a full bath; many a swankier place pays less attention to these important basics. The heart of the hotel is the cosy bar, also accessible directly from the road, which has an open fire, lots of memorabilia and a sense that a lot of good nights are enjoyed here. A large restaurant at the back of the hotel also doubles as a small function room for local events. This would make a very pleasant base for a break in this exceptionally beautiful area. Conferences/Banqueting (260/200); free broadband wi/fi. **Rooms 20** (4 executive, 2 family, 6 single); children welcome (under 3s free in parents room, cot available free of charge, baby sitting arranged). B&B €55-65 pps. Limited room service; lift. Fishing (fly & coarse), equestrian, golf and walking all nearby. Closed 24-25 Dec. Mastercard, Visa, Laser. **Directions:** Clonbur is 4km from Cong.

Clonbur   # John J. Burke & Sons
PUB•RESTAURANT   Mount Gable House Clonbur Co Galway **Tel: 094 9546175**
V   tibhurca@eircom.net www.burkes-clonbur.com

Everybody loves Burkes pub - this characterful old family-run pub is one of this attractive village's greatest assets, well-known for atmosphere, music and homely food. It's a friendly, welcoming place no matter when you might drop in, and very much the heart of the community and sporting activities - and the business of feeding people with wholesome traditional meals is taken seriously both in the bar, during the day, and the more formal dining area overlooking the garden towards Mount Gable at the back of the pub in the evening. Bar meals are quite traditional - egg mayonnaise, spicy wedges, roasts, home-made lasagne, apple tart. There's a much wider range offered in the evening: starters like baked mussels or venison sausage, for example, followed by the likes of steaks, rack of lamb and fish from sea and river. Irish stew is a speciality - a unique version, using prime cuts of locally farmed lamb with herb dumplings and the friendly relaxed style (the food is kept refreshingly simple), with traditional music and dancing later in the evening, wins a lot of friends. Booking for the restaurant is essential in high season. **Seats 140** (private room 30; outdoors 20); Bar meals 10am-5pm daily; L 11-5pm (Sun 1-3pm), D 6.30-9pm; D daily 6.30-8.30. House wine from €19. Closed 24-26 Dec, Good Fri; open weekends only Oct-Feb. MasterCard, Visa, Laser. **Directions:** 48km (30 m) north of Galway city, between Lough Corrib & Lough Mask. 5km from Cong (R345).

Headford Area   # Lisdonagh House
COUNTRY HOUSE   Caherlistrane nr Headford Co Galway **Tel: 093 31163**
                                 cooke@lisdonagh.com www.lisdonagh.com

Situated about 15 minutes drive north of Galway city in the heart of hunting and fishing country, Lisdonagh House enjoys beautiful views overlooking Lake Hackett. Although the exterior maintenance and garden are sometimes less than pristine, it is a lovely property, with large well-proportioned reception rooms, and very comfortable bedrooms decorated in period style, with impressive marbled bathrooms to match. A five-course dinner menu is served in a handsome dining room, and offers fish and meat, although a vegetarian main course would be available on request; a pleasant breakfast is also served in the dining room. *Two villas in the courtyard are available, either for self-catering or fully serviced. The main house is often rented exclusively for private groups. Small conferences (50). **Rooms 9** (2 shower only, 1 family room, 4 ground floor, all no smoking); children welcome (under 2s free in parents' room, cots available free of charge, baby sitting arranged, creche). Dogs permitted in certain areas. B&B from €90-120 pps, ss about €30. 5-course residents' dinner, €49 is served between 7 and 9pm. House wine €29. Boat trips, walking, hunting/shooting and coarse fishing on site; golf and garden visits nearby. Closed 1 Nov-1 May. Amex, MasterCard, Visa, Laser. **Directions:** N17 to within 7km (4 m) of Tuam, R333 to Caherlistrane. ◊

INISHBOFIN

Inishbofin, 'the island of the white cow', is located 11km (7 miles) off the coast of Galway and it is estimated that it has been inhabited for as long as 6,000 years. The island is home to five small villages, where the main industries are farming, fishing and tourism. Ideal for an away-from-it-all holiday, the island is known for its sandy beaches and clear waters, which are ideal for shore angling, swimming, snorkelling and diving, and the interior of the island provides mountain walks and gentle hill climbing. Sailing is a popular activity too, and, as you sail into the harbour, you will see Oliver Cromwell's 16th century barracks, which were used a prison for Catholic priests. The Inishbofin Heritage Centre (095 45 861) houses an interesting exhibition, illustrating island life in bygone days.

Inishbofin   # The Dolphin Hotel & Restaurant
HOTEL•RESTAURANT   Inishbofin Co Galway **Tel: 095 45991**
info@dolphinhotel.ie   www.dolphinhotel.ie

Having run The Dolphin Restaurant here since 2000, there was delight all round when brother and sister, Pat and Catherine Coyne, developed it as a small hotel in 2006. Set in landscaped grounds, it is a wonderful addition to this beautiful unspoilt island: the building is a modern mix of slatted wood and brick and, in tune with the island's interest in the environment, solar panels and under floor heating were installed. There are eleven large, bright bedrooms, with thick deep blue carpets, walnut furniture, great beds, TV and tea-making facilities; all are en-suite, some with a bath. Upstairs rooms have sea and mountain views, and three special ground floor rooms have their own private sundeck on to the garden; one bedroom, and also the dining and lounge areas, have disabled access. There's also a lovely residents' lounge, with access to decking and great views. Banqueting (100); free broadband wi/fi. Walking, live music (trad.). Boat trips, angling, cycling and scuba diving all nearby. Children welcome (under 3s free in parents' room, cot available at no charge, baby sitting arranged). **Rooms 11** (8 shower only, 1 for disabled, all no smoking); B&B €85 pps. **Restaurant:** Menus change throughout the day at this versatile restaurant, which continues to be a great asset to the island. There are two dining rooms, which can be joined to accommodate large parties, with a deck for alfresco dining. Catherine cooks great food and now grows her own organic vegetables and herbs. At lunchtime - which considerably runs all afternoon - there's a range of drinks to comfort or refresh, depending on the weather, then made-to-order club or open sandwiches, or simple hot meals. Evening menus are more substantial - rack of lamb, steaks and fish of the day are typical, with lobster available to order. **Seats 100** (outdoor seating, 20). Open daily in summer: L 12.30-5; D 7-9.30. à la carte; house wine from €17.95. Establishment closed Nov-Mar. MasterCard, Visa, Laser. **Directions:** Travel from Galway to Clifden and on to Cleggan Pier where boat leaves to Inishbofin Island.

Inishbofin   # Doonmore Hotel
HOTEL   Inishbofin Island Co Galway **Tel: 095 45804 / 14**
info@doonmorehotel.com   www.doonmorehotel.com

The Doonmore Hotel was built on the site of the Murray family farmhouse in 1968; overlooking the sea and sand dunes, with geraniums along the front lounge, it looks more like a traditional guesthouse than an hotel, and offers old fashioned comfort. Traditional music is played regularly, and on cold days there are peat fires in the low-ceilinged sitting room and lounge. It is a very family-friendly place with a baby listening service in bedrooms, along with the usual facilities. 'Murray's' is well known for wholesome cooking - home baking, local produce like Connemara lamb and fresh seafood. There are fine sandy beaches on hand and there's a fitness room, cycling, sea angling, boat trips, scuba diving and walking. Small conferences/banqueting (40/80). **Rooms 20** (15 shower only, 5 family rooms, 16 ground floor); children welcome (under 3s free in parents' room, cots available at no charge, baby sitting arranged); toilets wheelchair accessible; broadband wi/fi. B&B €50-60 pps, ss €10. Restaurant seats 45 and opens daily for D to residents & non-residents 7-9pm. Bar food 12-9pm. Establishment closed Oct-Mar. Heli-pad. Amex, MasterCard, Visa, Laser. **Directions:** Ferry from Cleggan. ◊

Inishbofin

Inishbofin House Hotel & Marine Spa

HOTEL

Inishbofin Island Co Galway **Tel: 095 45809**

info@inishbofinhouse.com www.inishbofinhouse.com

For many years, the Day family's modest hotel on Bofin pier has been the first port of call for many visitors to the island and anyone returning after a few years will now be surprised to find a large modern hotel overlooking the inner harbour. Public areas include a large bright high-roofed entrance lobby and lounge with Spanish tiles, a smart and stylish bar and a dining room, on two levels, with great views to the sea and mountains. On the first floor, a truly lovely library/lounge with balconies off it is totally constructed in glass, allowing excellent panoramic views. Accommodation is luxurious for an island, and the bedrooms all have bath and shower. The Day family also operate a bar beside the pier (food available in summer). Banqueting (180). **Rooms 34** (2 with separate bath & shower, 2 disabled, all no smoking); children welcome (cot available, baby sitting arranged). Lift. Room service (limited hours). No pets. B&B €70-85 pps. Spa, beauty salon. Garden. Closed Jan-Feb. Visa, Laser. **Directions:** Ferries to the island run regularly from Cleggan, with ticket offices in Clifden (regular buses between Clifden and Cleggan) and also at Kings of Cleggan. For bookings and enquiries, phone: 095 44642 or 095 21520. Credit card bookings are accepted.

Kilcolgan

Moran's Oyster Cottage

RESTAURANT•CHARACTER PUB

The Weir Kilcolgan Co Galway **Tel: 091 796 113**

moranstheweir@eircom.net www.moransoystercottage.com

This is just the kind of Irish pub that people everywhere dream about. It's as pretty as a picture, with a well-kept thatched roof and a lovely waterside location (with plenty of seats outside where you can while away the time and watch the swans floating by). People from throughout the country beat a path here at every available opportunity for their wonderful local seafood, including lobster, but especially the native oysters (from their own oyster beds) which are in season from September to April (farmed Gigas oysters are on the menu all year). Then there's chowder and smoked salmon and seafood cocktail and mussels, delicious crab salads - and lobster, with boiled potatoes & garlic butter. Private conference room. The wine list is not over-extensive, but carefully selected, informative and fairly priced – and includes a good choice of half bottles. *Morans was the Guide's Seafood Pub of the Year in 1999. **Seats 120** (private rooms, 8 and 12; outdoor seating, 50/60); children welcome; air conditioning; toilets wheelchair accessible. Meals 12 noon -10pm daily. House wine from €19. Closed 3 days Christmas & Good Fri. Amex, MasterCard, Visa, Laser. **Directions:** Just off the Galway-Limerick road (N18), signed between Clarenbridge and Kilcolgan.

KINVARA

Situated in south County Galway, just on the edge of the Burren, this picturesque seaside village has become a lively community, with a strong pride in its heritage and culture. The village offers lots of local arts and crafts such as bog wood sculptures and ceramics, along with village festivals such as the Galway Hooker Festival and numerous music festivals. Local attractions include Dunguaire Castle (which hosts medieval banquets April to October, tel: 1800 269 811), which was built in the 1500s and is still in excellent condition today, whilst visitors have easy access to the Burren, the Cliffs of Moher and the Aran Islands. Golfers are spoilt with the 18-hole championship golf course at the Gort Golf Club (091 632 244), which is set in 160 acres of beautiful parkland on the outskirts of the Burren. Coole Park (091 631 804, open all year), near Gort, the famous meeting place of Irish literary figures from the 20th century, is only a short drive away too. Other activities available locally include walking, cycling and scuba diving, and the famous Oyster Festivals held in the Clarinbridge area each autumn are also within easy reach. Accommodation in the area includes the **Merriman Inn** (091 63822; www.merrimanhotel.com) in the village, and those who prefer somewhere smaller might try **Kinvarainn B&B** (091 638135), on Ardrahan Road.

WWW.IRELAND-GUIDE.COM FOR ALL THE BEST PLACES TO EAT, DRINK & STAY

Kinvara
BAR•RESTAURANT

Keogh's Bar & Restaurant

Main Street Kinvara Co Galway **Tel: 091 637 145**
mikeogh@eircom.net www.kinvara.com/keoghs

Michael Keogh's old pub in the picturesque village of Kinvara has a cosy bar with an open fire and a restaurant with character behind it, with wooden floors and benches and oilcloth-covered tables - and a large fireplace with a traditional black stove. The food style is modern Irish bar meals, served by charming international staff, and there are tables outside in summer. Local seafood is the main speciality - an informal bite of creamy fishy chowder, for example, or steamed mussels (both come with home-made brown bread), or more serious main courses like cod fillet with beurre nantais or pan-fried monkfish provençal. There are plenty of other choices too, including warm goat's cheese salad, or rack of Kinvara lamb; homely desserts might include a freshly-baked apple and rhubarb crumble. **Seats 50** (outdoor seating, 18); reservations accepted; children welcome, air conditioning. Weekly music sessions in summer. Food available daily 9.30am-10pm (Sun from 12), B 9.30, L 12-5, D 6-10. A la carte. House wine from about €15.95. Closed 25 Dec, Good Fri. Amex, MasterCard, Visa, Laser. **Directions:** Kinvara village - on the coast road to Doolin, 19km (12 m) from Galway.

Kinvara
RESTAURANT•PUB

The Pier Head Bar & Restaurant

The Quay Kinvara Co Galway
Tel: 091 638188

Mike Burke's well-located harbourside establishment has lots of maritime character and views out over the harbour to Dunguaire Castle. You'll find seafood like fat, tasty mussels, in moules marinière, with a milky onion and wine broth, and pan-fried skate, which is rarely seen on restaurant menus. Lobster is a speciality - served in the shell with garlic butter and a side salad - and something else they take pride in is top of the range steak, using local beef (totally traceable), which is slaughtered and butchered to order. And there's also music, all year: bands on Friday & Saturday nights usually, also traditional on Sunday afternoon. (Phone ahead to check availability). **Seats 100** (private room 50); children welcome. D Mon-Sat, 5-9.30pm; L Sun only, 12-3pm; a la carte; house wine about €15. Closed 25 Dec & Good Fri. Diners, MasterCard, Visa, Laser. **Directions:** Kinvara harbour front.

LEENANE

There can be few more spectacular locations for a village than Leenane, which is tucked into the shoreline at the head of Ireland's only deepwater fjord, backed by dramatic mountains. In the village you will find the delightful little **Blackberry Café** (see entry) and, just along the shore, is the **Leenane Hotel** (095 42249; www.leenanehotel.com), which is a budget-conscious establishment run by the same family as Rosleague Manor at Letterfrack (see entry). Nearby **Portfinn Lodge** (095 42265; www.portfinn.com), a seafood restaurant and guesthouse run by the Daly family since 1977 and recently taken over by Óran Daly, is a popular and reasonably priced base for fishing holidays. Leenane was the setting for the film of John B Keane's story, "The Field", (starring Richard Harris), a fact celebrated by several pubs in the village, which is also home to The Sheep & Wool Centre (095 42323) with sheep and wool museum, café and gift shop. And not far away - an eight mile scenic drive northwest of Leenane, on the Louisbourg road - is the recently re-opened **Delphi Mountain Resort & Spa** (095 42208; www.delphiadventureholidays.ie); an adventure centre also operates from the same site. **WWW.IRELAND-GUIDE.COM FOR ALL THE BEST PLACES TO EAT, DRINK & STAY**

Leenane
CAFÉ

Blackberry Café & Coffee Shop

Leenane Co Galway
Tel: 095 42240

Sean and Mary Hamilton's lovely little restaurant is just what the weary traveller hopes to happen on when touring or walking in this beautiful area. They're open through the afternoon and evening every day during the summer, serving reliably good food: home-made soups and chowders with home-baked bread, substantial snacks such as fish cakes and mussels, and delicious desserts like rhubarb tart and lemon meringue pie with cream. Extra dishes such as hot smoked trout and a chicken main course might be added to the menu in the evening, but the secret of the Blackberry Café's appeal is that they don't try to do too much at once and everything is freshly made each day. **Seats 40**. Open 12-4 and 6-9 daily in high season. A la carte. House wine about €15 (1/4 bottles also available). Closed Tue in shoulder seasons. Closed end Sep-Easter. Visa, Laser **Directions:** On main street, opposite car park.

Leenane
COUNTRY HOUSE

Delphi Lodge

Leenane Co Galway **Tel: 095 42222**
stay@delphilodge.ie www.delphilodge.ie

One of Ireland's most famous sporting lodges, Delphi Lodge was built in the early 19th-century by the Marquis of Sligo, and is magnificently located in an unspoilt valley, surrounded by the region's highest mountains (with the high rainfall so dear to fisher-folk). Owned since 1986 by Peter Mantle - who has restored and extended the original building in period style - the lodge is large and impressive in an informal, understated way, with antiques, fishing gear and a catholic collection of reading matter, creating a stylish yet relaxed atmosphere. The guest rooms are all quite different, but they have lovely lake and mountain views, good bathrooms, and are very comfortably furnished. Delphi has earned a reputation for good cooking that reaches far beyond the valley and dinner, for residents only, is taken house-party style at a long oak table - traditionally presided over by the person lucky enough to catch the day's biggest salmon. The set menu begins with a 'Tongue Tickler' (Irish goat's cheese beignets with beetroot salad, perhaps), and house specialities that delight happy fisherfolk include classic dishes like langoustine bisque, bouillabaisse and rib of beef, or Delphi's own lamb - and there are sometimes unusual ingredients, like the nephrops from Killary Bay, which might come with warmed rocket butter. Coffee and home-made chocolates round off the feast in the Piano Room, where the good company of other guests may well keep you from your bed. The famous Delphi Fishery is the main attraction, but many people come for other country pursuits, painting, or just peace and quiet. A billiard table, the library and a serious wine list (great bottles at a very modest mark-up) can get visitors through a lot of wet days. Delphi's 'abnormally modest' mark-ups reduce as the price (quality) rises; tasting notes are given for the wonderful house selection and, unusually, the main list has scores from Robert Parker, Wine Spectator and Wine Enthusiast magazines instead. *Delphi Lodge was our Country House of the Year in 2006. Small conferences/banqueting (20/28); free broadband wi/fi. **Rooms 12** (all executive standard). B&B €100 pps, ss €35. Residents D 8pm; D €50; L Sun only 1-2pm, €20. 8 well-chosen house wines, all €25; SC discretionary. Fly fishing, hunting/shooting, cycling, snooker, walking. Sea angling, golf and garden visits nearby. Closed 20 Dec - mid Jan. MasterCard, Visa, Laser. Heli-pad.
Directions: 13km (8 m) northwest of Leenane on the Louisburgh road.

Leenane
RESTAURANT

Portfinn Lodge

Leenane Co Galway **Tel: 095 42265**
orantaz@mac.com website www.portfinn.com

Run by the Daly family since 1977, Portfinn Lodge is located on a hill in the beautiful village of Leenane, overlooking the picturesque Killary harbour in the heart of Connemara. Portfinn includes a guesthouse with 11 comfortable rooms (each room is en suite and rooms catering to families or groups of fishermen are available), but it is mainly the restaurant that attracts visitors here. The views from the dining rooms - there are three of them leading on to each other - are wonderful; you might dine in an octagonal one, for example, with views of Killary, Maumtrasna and Maamturk mountains on either side. Outside the surrounding gardens are colourful with montbretia, fuchsia and nasturtiums, and the atmosphere is welcoming and warm on this house. Seafood has always been the speciality of the house and the current chef, Oran Daly, carries on that tradition with enthusiasm. Menus offer some choice for non-fish eaters - a beautifully cooked half roast organic duck served with a fresh orange & port reduction with a hint of cointreau, for example, or perhaps Connemara lamb, served with a lamb & rosemary jus, sirloin steaks, and chicken dishes - but you will find wide range of fish and seafood, and specials of the day depending on availability. Starers include mussels, crab and fish cakes, oysters and Portfinn Bisque - or you might begin with a (very) generous shrimp & crab cocktail (€9) served on a scallop shell. Main courses might include Mannin/Killary Bay scallops (delicious, €9 for a portion), beautifully cooked with a cream and white wine sauce served in a separate little dish. Afterwards, there's a large selection of Irish cheeses or you can finish with a classic dessert, such as sherry trifle or homemade chocolate torte. With a wonderful location, pleasant staff and good, generous food cooked by an experienced chef, a visit here should be very enjoyable. MasterCard, Visa, Laser. Opening times: open six days 6pm to 9pm. Early bird menu 6.00 to 7.30pm. Closed Mondays & Nov. to Mar.

LETTERFRACK

A visit to this part of the country would be unthinkable without a stop-off at the well-known Kylemore Abbey, Garden & Tea Rooms (see entry) whose beauty and tranquility is truly exceptional. Letterfrack is close to Connemara National Park (095 41 054), which offers 2,957 hectares of beautiful countryside and a rich habitat of wildlife. The park also includes an exhibition centre and visitors can take a guided walk along one of the many nature trails. Letterfrack is host to Connemara Bog Week, which is a varied festival held in June, including guided walks, fun runs and traditional music. Anglers will enjoy some of the best wild salmon fishing in the country.

Letterfrack
CAFÉ

Avoca Café Letterfrack

Letterfrack Co Galway **Tel: 095 41058**
www.avoca.ie

A very useful place to know about when you are exploring this beautiful area, the 'Possibly shop' ('possibly the most interesting craft shop in the west') is not huge, but it offers lovely clothing and crafts to buy - and wholesome light meals and refreshments in the well-known Avoca style, albeit on a smaller scale. Open daily high season 9.30am-6pm (Sun from 10.30); Sept-Apr open 9.30am-5.30pm. **Directions:** On main Clifden-Westport road overlooking Ballinakill Bay at Letterfrack, Connemara.

Letterfrack
RESTAURANT

Kylemore Abbey Restaurant & Tea House

Kylemore Letterfrack Co Galway **Tel: 095 41155**
info@kylemoreabbey.ie www.kylemoreabbey.ie

Providing you are tolerant of tour buses and high season crowds, this dramatically located Abbey offers a surprising range of things to see: a brief stroll from the abbey along the wooded shore leads to the Gothic church, a fascinating miniature replica of Norwich cathedral, for example, then there's a fine craft shop in a neat modern building beside the car park and also a daytime self-service restaurant, where everything is made on the premises, including traditional meals like beef & Guinness casserole and Irish stew. Big bowls of the nuns' home-made jams are set up at the till, for visitors to help themselves - beside them are neatly labelled jars to buy and take home. A short distance away, the nuns also run a farm and a restored walled garden, which supplies produce to the Garden Tea House. **Seats 200**; children welcome (high chair, baby changing facilities). Meals daily 9.30-5pm; L 12.30-2.30pm; set L €20. Closed Christmas Day & Good Fri. (The Garden Tea House, in the restored walled garden, is open Easter-Hallowe'en, 10.30-5.) Amex, MasterCard, Visa, Laser. **Directions:** 3km from Letterfrack, on the N59 from Galway.

Letterfrack
RESTAURANT

Pangur Bán Restaurant

Letterfrack Co Galway **Tel: 095 41243**
pban@indigo.ie www.pangurban.com

This pretty, 300 year-old whitewashed cottage, restored and run as a restaurant by John Walsh since 1999, has a perfect thatch roof and a smokers' lean-to with benches beside the entrance. The reception / bar area is unexpectedly bright and airy, with a raised wooden ceiling although, with whitewashed walls and an old fireplace, it retains its natural cottagey character, and windows offer a lovely summer view of roses and hydrangeas in the front garden. The name Pangur Ban, comes from the title of a poem by an 8th or 9th century Irish monk, the subject matter of which was ... "Pangur Ban, my cat..."; he might have worried about the elaborate witch mannequins hanging alongside a variety of locally produced paintings around the walls (all for sale) and would probably not have empathised with the music (a mix of '60s and '70s' pop – but very quietly played), but the table settings are appropriately simple. John's cooking style, however, is quite exotic, with a distinctly international tone to the menus. Local produce – possibly including game, in season - is included whenever possible, although dishes vary widely in style from those with international influences (Chinese chicken wings with sweet chilli sauce, fried mackerel fillets with Japanese coleslaw, barbecue lamb kebabs with couscous and baby spinach) to traditional dishes like pot roast rabbit with Toulouse sausage and garden herbs, half roast duck – and lobster, when available, which is served grilled with garlic butter. Rich home-made ice creams or seasonal fruits make a good ending, and there's a short mainly European, wine list. A relaxing summer meal is the aim here, and this is generally achieved well at Pangur Ban - portions are well-judged, staff are pleasant and a varied choice of food is offered at moderate prices. **Seats 45** (private room, 22). D Tue-Sun, 6-9.30; set 2/3 course D €27.50/€35.50, also A la carte. L Sun only, 12-3pm; set Sun L €22.50; house wine about €19. SC 12% on groups 8+. Ample parking. Closed Mon, Jan & Feb (a phone call to check opening times any time except high season is advised.) MasterCard, Visa, Laser. **Directions:** In Letterfrack village.

Letterfrack
COUNTRY HOUSE

Rosleague Manor Hotel

Letterfrack Co Galway **Tel: 095 41101**
info@rosleague.com www.rosleague.com

This lovely, graciously proportioned, pink-washed Regency house looks out over a tidal inlet through gardens planted with rare shrubs and plants. Although the area also offers plenty of energetic pursuits, there is a deep sense of peace at Rosleague and it's hard to imagine any better place to recharge the soul. The hotel changed hands within the Foyle family a few years ago and its energetic young owner-manager, Mark Foyle, is gradually working his way through a major renovation programme: the conservatory bar, restaurant and a number of bedrooms (and their bathrooms) have now been refurbished (two were actually demolished and re-built) and some have four-poster beds; and the gardens (already extensive, and listed in the Connemara Garden Trail) have been further developed to make new paths and establish a wild flower meadow. This is a very pleasant, peaceful place to stay and, with a choice of two lovely drawing rooms with log fires, as well as the bar, guests have plenty of space. And the restaurant - a lovely classical dining room, with mahogany furniture and a fine collection of plates on the walls - is open to non-residents by reservation. Head chef Pascal Marinot, who has been at Rosleague since 2000, offers a daily-changing dinner menu in a quite traditional style - starters like oysters with shallot vinegar & lemon, or Rosleague Caesar salad, a soup course, and straightforward main courses such as honey roast duckling or roast Connemara lamb. For dessert, Rosleague chocolate mousse is an inherited speciality - going back to Mark's uncle, Paddy Foyle's, time in the kitchen. In recent years, Rosleague has become very popular as a venue for small weddings. Small Conferences/Banqueting (16/85), free broadband wi/fi; **Rooms 20** (4 junior suites, 3 family, 2 ground floor). B&B €125pps, ss €35; children welcome (under 4s free in parents' room, cot available free of charge, baby sitting arranged). Garden, tennis, fishing, walking. Pets permitted (stay in bedroom free of charge). **Restaurant Seats 50** (Private Room seats 12). D 7.30-9 daily, non-residents welcome by reservation; Set D €48. House wine €21. Closed mid Nov-mid Mar. Amex, MasterCard, Visa, Laser. **Directions:** On N59 main road, 11km (7 miles) north-west of Clifden.

R

LOUGHREA

Loughrea is a substantial town in east Galway and takes its name from the adjacent lake, the second largest limestone lake in County Galway, after Lough Corrib. Growing fast, as a commuter town to Galway city, Loughrea has a number of hotels including the old family-run town centre **O'Deas Hotel** (091 841 611; www.odeashotel.com), popular as a base for fishing holidays, and the town has recently seen the opening of its first destination hotel **Lough Rea Hotel & Spa** (see entry) on the Galway Road (see entry). Although many travellers see it mainly as a convenient place to break a journey - **Weavers Restaurant** (091 841 783) on Main Street is useful to know about, with long opening hours – there is much of interest in the area. Loughrea Lake is an important bird sanctuary and popular for fishing, (trout, pike and perch), water-sports and swimming. The town centre Cathedral of St. Brendan is of interest, and The Turoe Stone, an important Celtic monument, is in nearby Bullaun, where you will also find Turoe Pet Farm and Leisure Park (091 841 580; www.turoepetfarm.com). Dartfield - Ireland's Horse Museum & Park (091 843 968) is a short distance east of the town, and horseriding and trekking are also available in the area.
WWW.IRELAND-GUIDE.COM FOR ALL THE BEST PLACES TO EAT, DRINK & STAY

Loughrea
HOTEL•RESTAURANT

Lough Rea Hotel & Spa

Galway Road Loughrea Co Galway **Tel: 091 880 088**
sales@loughreahotelandspa.com www.loughreahotelandspa.com

Located on the outskirts of Loughrea town, just off the N6 bypass, about 25 minutes drive from Galway city, this newly built, (opened July 08), locally owned offers a comprehensive range of facilities including the stunning Shore Island Spa and half a dozen conference/meeting/function rooms equipped with the latest technology. The somewhat institutional exterior belies the originality of the no-expense-spared interior design: smart contemporary furnishings, imaginative use of lighting and space. Swinging doors lead from the large front car park (there is another at the rear) to the reception/lobby, behind which an impressive glass-fronted lift can be seen ferrying guests to the upper floors. Almost all the luxurious bedrooms have a rural or lake view. The quality of carpets and fittings throughout is top of the range as is the attention to detail, a factor particularly apparent in the magnificent Bridal and 1236 A.D. suites. The hotel seems to have operated smoothly from the outset - due, no doubt, to hands-on management by General Manager Ken Bergin (formerly GM of the recently closed St. Clerans in nearby Craughwell), whose infectious enthusiasm for this new project is reflected by his pleasantly motivated, helpful staff throughout the hotel. The Lir Bar has an official capacity of 490 although clever design and comfortable seating give it a deceptively intimate air. It is a bar in the modern Irish sense where food is as important as drink; day-long service features Carvery Lunch from 12.30 to 4pm and a Bar Menu in the evening from 5 to 9.30pm, featuring soups, steaks, chicken, fish, desserts, teas and coffees. Conferences/banqueting (800/350); free broadband wi/fi, business centre, secretarial services, video conferencing, laptop sized safes in bedrooms. **Rooms 91** (all bath and shower); children welcome (cot available, baby sitting arranged, creche, kids club, playground, play room); fully wheelchair accessible; lift; B&B €45-60 pps; single €85. Spa ; leisure centre (gym, pool, jacuzzi); fishing (fly & coarse), golf and equestrian all nearby. **The Abbey Restaurant:** Burgundy dominates the colour scheme of the hotel's 85 seater restaurant: walls, floor- to-ceiling curtains and weighty, burgundy menu folders. Recessed banquettes, most comfortable chairs and inventive use of lighting and stained glass make for a relaxed ambience in contrast to the buzz of the Lir Bar. A compact à la carte menu is well balanced, offering six starters (including Thai-scented fish cakes, confit of duck leg with onion marmalade, and an unusual salad consisting of potatoes, halloumi cheese, roasted pumpkin seeds, pine and hazel nuts in citrus vinaigrette). a "Middle Course" choice of Soup of the Day or Salad of Stilton, Prosciutto, Tomato and balsamic vinaigrette, and eight main courses offering the usual range of meats (lamb, beef fillet, duck, chicken) a couple of fish dishes and a vegetarian pasta. At the time of the Guide's visit, the hotel had only been open a short time and it remains top be seen whether standards will be maintained. However, it was an very enjoyable meal, with many indications of expertise in the kitchen, and pleasant service. **Seats 85** (private room, 40); children welcome (high chair, children's menu, baby changing facilities); toilets wheelchair accessible; air conditioning. D daily 6.30-10pm; set D €35; also a la carte. House wine €18. Closed 24-25 Dec. MasterCard, Visa, Laser. **Directions:** Located on Dublin-Galway road.

Moycullen
RESTAURANT

White Gables Restaurant

Moycullen Village Moycullen Co Galway **Tel: 091 555 744**
info@whitegables.com www.whitegables.com

Since 1991, Kevin and Ann Dunne have been running this attractive cottagey restaurant on the main street of Moycullen and, although the village around them has seen unsympathetic development recently, this remains a charming place and is on many a regular diner's list of favourites. Arriving guests can have an aperitif in the bar before heading into the restaurant, where open stonework, low lighting and candlelight create a soothing atmosphere. Kevin sources ingredients with care and offers weekly-changing dinner and à la carte menus, with daily specials, and a set Sunday lunch which is in great demand. Cooking is consistently good in a refreshingly traditional style and features local meats including Connemara lamb (including the speciality smoked lamb) and excellent beef from the famous butchers McGeoughs of Oughterard; fresh fish and seafood, including lobster thermidor, is another speciality and many a guest wouldn't dream of ordering anything but the roast half duckling à l'orange. Good desserts and friendly, efficient service all help make this one of the area's most popular restaurants. An interesting wine list includes some classics and well-chosen house wines. **Seats 45**; children welcome; air conditioning. D Tue-Sat, 7-10; L Sun only, 12.30-3. Set D €46.50 (5 course), also à la carte; Set Sun L €28.50. House wine €22.50; sc discretionary. Closed Mon & 23 Dec-14 Feb. Amex, Diners, MasterCard, Visa, Laser. **Directions:** On N59 in Moycullen village, 11km (8 m) from Galway city.

ORANMORE

Between Galway city and Athenry, first impressions of Oranmore are that it is dominated by the N6; the **Quality Hotel & Leisure Centre** (091 792244; www.qualityhotelgalway.com) is right on the roundabout, so you can't miss it - has outstanding family facilities and is a popular place for business meetings. But there are two other newer hotels (**Ramada Encore** and **The Coach House Hotel**, 091 788367, on Main Street, both inexpensive). Oranmore itself is a pleasant place and it has the friendly Mary's Tea Rooms for breakfasts and scones etc. The area is renowned for its seafood, especially shellfish, and speciality produce of all kinds (including local cheeses, fruit and vegetables, and specialities that do the rounds of other markets around the country) is on sale at the famous Galway city centre Saturday Market (beside St Nicholas Church; all day Sat & also Sun & Bank Hols, 2-6pm). Golfers will enjoy a round in the Galway Bay Golf Club (Oranmore, 091 790 711).
WWW.IRELAND-GUIDE.COM FOR ALL THE BEST PLACES TO EAT, DRINK & STAY

OUGHTERARD

Oughterard is a charming riverside village, known as the Gateway to Connemara, an area of natural beauty renowned for outdoor activities notably fishing, but also horseriding, walking and water-sports - and Oughterard is famous for McGeough's butchers, who make the most wonderful air-dried meats, and other specialities well worth seeking out. On the Galway side of the village, **Brigit's Garden & Café** (see entry, 091 550 905) at Roscahill is an interesting place to visit, and their tea rooms specialise in home-baking; in the village itself, **The Yew Tree** (091 866 986), on the main street, is open all day, 9am-6pm, Mon-Sat and serves good home-cooked food - also including delicious home baking. The village is associable place, known for live music in the pubs at night. There are many interesting gardens to visit in the area; Connemara Garden Trail leaflets are widely available in tourist information offices and hotels; otherwise, for up to date details, contact the Connemara Garden Trail directly (095 21148).

WWW.IRELAND-GUIDE.COM FOR ALL THE BEST PLACES TO EAT, DRINK & STAY

Oughterard   Corrib Wave Guesthouse

GUESTHOUSE   Portcarron Oughterard Co Galway   **Tel: 091 552 147**

     cwh@gofree.indigo.ie   www.corribwave.com

A fisherman's dream, Michael and Maria Healy's unpretentious but neatly maintained waterside guest-house offers warm, family hospitality, comfortable accommodation, an open turf fire to relax by and real home cooking. Rooms are regularly redecorated and have phone, tea/coffee-making, TV, radio and a double and single bed; some are suitable for families. Maria cooks dinner for guests - fresh trout and salmon from the lake, Irish stew, bacon & cabbage - just the kind of thing people want. But best of all at Corrib Wave is the location – stunningly beautiful, with utter peace and tranquillity. Golf and horse riding nearby and everything to do with fishing organised for you. **Rooms 10** (all en-suite, 4 shower only, 2 family, 5 ground floor, all no smoking); children welcome. B&B €40-50 pps, ss €15. Breakfast 7.30-9.30. Residents D 7pm, about €25; house wine €19. Dogs permitted (staying in outhouse/kennnel). Fly fishing; garden; walking. Closed 1 Dec-1 Feb. MasterCard, Visa, Laser. **Directions:** From Galway, signed from N59, 1km before Oughterard.

Oughterard   Currarevagh House

COUNTRY HOUSE   Glann Road Oughterard Co Galway   **Tel: 091 552 312**

    mail@currarevagh.com   www.currarevagh.com

Tranquillity, trout and tea in the drawing room - these are the things that draw guests back to the Hodgson family's gracious, but not luxurious, early Victorian manor overlooking Lough Corrib. Currarevagh, which was built in 1846 as a wedding present for Harry Hodgson's great, great, great grandfather, is set in 150 acres of woodlands and gardens, with sporting rights over 5,000 acres. Guests have been welcomed here since 1890 (almost certainly making Currarevagh Ireland's oldest guesthouse, certainly the longest in contin-

uous family membership) and the present owners, Harry and June Hodgson, are founder members of the Irish Country Houses and Restaurants Association ('Ireland's Blue Book'), now joined by their son Henry and his wife Lucy. Yet, while the emphasis is on old-fashioned service and hospitality, the Hodgsons are adamant that the atmosphere should be more like a private house party than an hotel, and their restful rituals underline the differences: the day begins with a breakfast worthy of its Edwardian origins, laid out on the sideboard in the dining room; lunch may be one of the renowned picnic hampers required by sporting folk. Then there's afternoon tea, followed by a leisurely dinner. Fishing is the ruling passion, of course - notably brown trout, pike, perch and salmon - but there are plenty of other country pursuits to assist in building up an appetite again for dinner. And here there have been big changes lately, since Lucy joined the family, because she is a professional cook (Prue Leith-trained and with her own catering company Tindal O'Grady) and – to everyone's delight - has taken to the kitchen at Currarevagh with huge enthusiasm. Her dinner menus - all based on fresh local produce and maintaining the Currarevagh motto 'keep it simple, unfussy and ultimately delicious', as before – offer no choice, but they are changed daily and there is de finitely a new frisson of anticipa-tion as guests sit down to dinner. Typically, you might begin with Corrib smoked trout terrine with pickled cucumber and Dillisk seaweed; follow with poached loin of lamb with basil and spinach mousse, aubergine ratatouille and potato dauphinoise – and round off with chocolate mocha daquoise terrine … And there's an extensive, fairly priced wine list to accompany too. Very good news for guests at Currarevagh – and the area, too, as non-residents are welcome (by reservation). **Rooms 15** (all en-suite, 2 shower only, 1 family room, 1 single, all no smoking); children welcome (under 2s free in parents room, cot available at no charge). B&B €104pps, ss €35 or single room €90. Pets permitted. No sc. 4 course D €52, at 8pm (non-residents welcome by reservation). Wines from €19.50. Garden, walking, tennis, coarse fishing, pool table. Sea angling, equestrian and golf nearby. Closed Nov - mid-Mar (house available for private hire in winter). MasterCard, Visa, Laser. **Directions:** Take N59 to Oughterard. Turn right in village square and follow Glann Road for 6.5km (4 m).

Oughterard Area

CAFÉ

Brigit's Garden Café

Pollagh Roscahill Co Galway **Tel: 091 550 905**
info@galwaygarden.com www.galwaygarden.com

Jenny Beale's beautiful themed garden near Oughterard reflects the Celtic festivals and, in addition to woodland trails, a ring fort and a stone chamber has a café that is worth a visit in its own right. A pine-ceilinged modern room that also acts as reception/shop has a small kitchen open to view at one end, and is set up with tables covered in old-fashioned oil cloth; everything's very simple, with plain white crockery and stainless cutlery and paper serviettes and, in fine weather, there is seating outside too. A short (vegetarian) blackboard menu offers a daily soup - chunky, wholesome vegetable with thyme, perhaps - a meal in itself with brown bread & butter, and a special such as home-grown chard and blue cheese pasta. Lovely toasted sandwiches are generously filled with salad and a choice of fillings (egg mayonnaise, goat's cheese & herb, hummus & olive, cheese & scallion), and great home-bakes include delicious scones with jam & cream, a luscious, walnut & apricot carrot cake, which is nutty and moist. Good coffee, tea or tisanes, and soft drinks like cranberry or lemon juice - just the kind of place you need to know about when exploring the area. Good toilets too, including baby changing facilities, and environmentally friendly waste disposal including reed bed sewage treatment. Special events Summer Solstice Day, Summer Music in the Gardens, Elves and Fairies Day etc – held throughout the year. **Seats 50** (+35 outdoors); toilets wheelchair accessible; children welcome; children's playground. Open 10.30-5 daily (Sun 12-5). Closed Oct - mid Apr. MasterCard, Visa, Laser. **Directions:** Just off the N59 between Moycullen and Oughterard.

Oughterard Area

HOTEL

Ross Lake House Hotel

Rosscahill Oughterard Co Galway **Tel: 091 550 109**
rosslake@iol.ie www. rosslakehotel.com

Quietly located in six acres of beautiful gardens, this charming country house was built in 1850 and is now a protected building. The current owners, Henry and Elaine Reid, bought the property in 1981 and have gradually refurbished it, so the hotel now offers luxurious accommodation in spacious rooms and suites, all individually furnished with antiques - including some with four-poster beds. While graciously-proportioned and impressively furnished, hands-on management and the warm interest of the proprietors and their staff ensure a welcoming and surprisingly homely atmosphere. In order to allow guests to enjoy the quiet relaxation of the house and area to the full, the Reids have decided to discontinue holding weddings at Ross Lake. **Rooms 13** (1 suite, 1 junior suite, 3 superior, 1 shower only, 1 family room, 3 ground floor, all no smoking); children welcome (under 2s free in parents' room, cot available without charge). No pets. B&B €90 pps, ss €30. D 7-8.30 daily. Short breaks offered. Garden. Tennis. Walking, cycling, fishing. Closed 1 Nov-15 Mar. Amex, MasterCard, Visa, Laser. **Directions:** Signed off Galway-Oughterard road; 10km (6 m) from Moycullen village.

PORTUMNA

Portumna is a large town on the River Shannon in south-east Galway, with a bridge (opened periodically for river traffic to pass through) linking it to County Tipperary. It is a popular base for river cruising (there is an Emerald Star cruiser base near the bridge) and coarse fishing. The town is most famous for the 17th century Portumna Castle, which is scenically located near Portumna (or 'New') Harbour on Lough Derg, with Portumna Forest Park to the west of it. The castle was gutted by fire in 1826 and has recently been extensively restored and parts of it opened to the public; restoration included the 17th century walled kitchen garden, which has now been organically planted with fruit trees, flowers, herbs and vegetables, following the original plan.

Portumna
RESTAURANT

Dyson's Restaurant
Patrick Street Portumna Co Galway
Tel: 0909 742 333

Behind a smart marble frontage, John and Heather Dyson's restaurant in the centre of Portumna is an attractive premises on two floors, with a few tables in the ground floor reception area - used mainly for early dinners and anyone who finds stairs difficult - and the main dining room on the first floor, with a pleasant decked area off it for use in fine weather. The interior is bright and uncluttered - pale wood floor, darkwood tables, comfortable upholstered chairs in brown or cream leather and good modern seascapes on the walls - and the simplicity is effective. John, who had experience in some distinguished kitchens abroad before settling here, takes pride in sourcing the best of ingredients locally where possible, with an emphasis on organic foods and fish brought in daily from Galway; his menus offer about half a dozen starters (including a Galway Bay chowder, perhaps), and 10 main courses - which sensibly include several steak options as well as wide range of other choices, including some sophisticated fish dishes and perhaps some dishes with traditional influences as in rack of lamb grilled with cassoulet of bacon & cabbage. Portions are generous (as are the well-made sauces - it can be a good idea to ask for sauces on the side), so you may have to plan ahead to save room for classic desserts like molten chocolate pudding, crème brûlée with caramelised plums or lemon meringue pie. A short but well-assembled wine list also emphasises organic production and the house wines are great value. Good food, pleasing surroundings and friendly service make for an enjoyable outing and this restaurant is proving to be a great asset to the area. **Seats 40**; not suitable for children after 7pm; toilets wheelchair accessible; air conditioning. D Wed-Sat, 5-9.30pm; Sun 1-7pm. Set Sun L €28-35; early D €25/29.50, 5-7pm; also à la carte. Closed Mon, Tue, Bank Hols, last week Jan, 1st week Feb. MasterCard, Visa, Laser. **Directions:** Town centre, a couple of doors from the Post Office, opposite Credit Union.

Portumna
HOTEL

Shannon Oaks Hotel & Country Club
St. Josephs Rd Portumna Co Galway **Tel: 090 974 1777**
sales@shannonoaks.ie www.shannonoaks.ie

Situated near the shores of Lough Derg and adjacent to the 17th century Portumna Castle and estate, this spacious privately-owned hotel is the centre of local activities and a good choice for business and corporate events. Bedrooms have air conditioning as standard, and conference and meeting facilities are designed for groups of all sizes, with full back-up services. Off-duty delegates will find plenty to do too: a fine leisure centre on-site has an air-conditioned gymnasium as well as a swimming pool and ancillary services, and nearby activities include river cruising, fishing, golf, horseriding, cycling and clay pigeon shooting. Portumna Castle, with restored kitchen gardens, is worth a visit. Conference/banqueting (300/350); secretarial services. Leisure centre (swimming pool, fitness room, jacuzzi, sauna, steam room); beauty salon; walking. **Rooms 140** (39 two bed suites, 2 for disabled); children welcome (under 5s free in parents' room, cot available free of charge, baby sitting arranged, playground, kids' club). No pets. B&B €80 pps; ss €30. 24 hr room service, Lift. Amex, Diners, MasterCard, Visa, Laser. **Directions:** Located on the N65 on the edge of Portumna town.

RECESS

Home to the famous Connemara green marble, which has been quarried here for some 400 years, Recess is in an area of bog land, forest and lakes dominated by the mountain peaks of the impressive 12 Bens. Recess boasts the magnificent 18th century Ballynahinch Castle Hotel & Gardens (see entry), which is set in 450 acres of woodlands and salmon fishing rivers in the heart of Connemara. Local activities include golf at the Connemara Golf Club (095 23 502/23 602), fishing, horse riding and heritage centres.

Recess

HOTEL•RESTAURANT

Ballynahinch Castle Hotel

Recess Co Galway **Tel: 095 31006**

bhinch@iol.ie www.ballynahinch-castle.com

Renowned as a fishing hotel, this crenellated Victorian mansion enjoys a most romantic position in 450 acres of ancient woodland and gardens on the banks of the Ballynahinch River. It is impressive in scale and relaxed in atmosphere - a magic combination, which, together with a high level of comfort and friendliness (and an invigorating mixture of residents and locals in the bar at night), combine to bring people back. The tone is set in the foyer, with its huge stone fireplace and ever-burning log fire (which is a cosy place to enjoy afternoon tea) and the many necessary renovations and extensions through the years have been undertaken with great attention to period detail, a policy also carried through successfully in furnishing both public areas and bedrooms, many of which have lovely views over the river. A stay here is always a restorative treat - especially if you have one of the rooms on the top floor, which have recently been refurbished in a lovely gentle, ever-so-slightly-modernised classic style with bathrooms to match. And, after a restful night's sleep, a Ballynahinch breakfast will give you a good start ahead of a day's fishing, wilderness walks on the estate, or simply touring the area. (Ballynahinch was the Connaught winner of our Irish Breakfast Awards in 2002.) Fishing: 3 miles of private fly fishing for Atlantic salmon, sea trout and brown trout. Landscaped gardens and wilderness walks on 450 acres; members of Connemara Garden Trail; cycling, tennis. Golf nearby. Small conferences (12). Children welcome (under 3s free in parents' room; cots available without charge, baby sitting arranged). No pets. **Rooms** 40 (3 suites, all with separate bath & shower, all no smoking) No lift. 24 hr room service. B&B €150 pps, ss €40. Short/special interest/off season breaks offered - details on application. **Owenmore Restaurant:** This bright and elegant room has the classic atmosphere of a splendidly old-fashioned dining room, and is carefully organised to allow as many tables as possible to enjoy its uniquely beautiful river setting, where you can watch happy fisherfolk claiming the last of the fading daylight on the rocks below. Daily dinner menus have plenty of fine local produce to call on – smoked salmon, of course, also sea fish, Connemara lamb and prime Irish beef (supplied by the renowned butcher, McGeough's of Oughterard) - a great basis for specialities with enduring popularity like pan-fried scallops with fresh clam, roast Connemara rack of lamb, and baked Cleggan lobster. Vegetarians are well looked after too – steamed sprouting broccoli & asparagus brioche toast with roasted tomato, soft boiled egg & mustard emulsion, perhaps. Staff are hospitable and relaxed, and a thoughtfully-assembled wine list offers an unusual range of house wines and a good choice of half bottles – and expert advice on making the best choices for your meal. *Excellent meals are also served in the hotel's characterful bar - a mighty high-ceilinged room with a huge fireplace, and many mementoes of the pleasures of rod and hunt. An informal alternative to the Owenmore experience - and a great place for non-residents to drop into for a bite when touring Connemara. Owenmore Restaurant open daily, D 6.30-9 (Set D €60), house wines from €25.20. Bar meals 12.30-3 & 6.30-9 daily. SC 10%. Closed Christmas & Feb. Amex, Diners, MasterCard, Visa, Laser. **Directions:** N59 from Galway - Clifden; left after Recess (Roundstone road), 6 km.

Recess

HOTEL•RESTAURANT

Lough Inagh Lodge

Recess Connemara Co Galway **Tel: 095 34706**

inagh@iol.ie www.loughinaghlodgehotel.ie

Maire O'Connor's former sporting lodge on the shores of Lough Inagh makes a delightful small hotel, with a country house atmosphere. It has large, well-proportioned rooms, interesting period detail and lovely fireplaces with welcoming log fires, as well as all the modern comforts. Public areas include two drawing rooms, each with an open fire, and a very appealing bar with a big turf fire and its own back door and tiled floor for wet fishing gear. Bedrooms, which include one recently added room and several with four-posters, are all well-appointed and unusually spacious, with views of lake and countryside. Walk-in dressing rooms lead to well-planned bathrooms, and tea/coffee-making facilities are available in rooms on request.

Georgina Campbell's Ireland

While it has special appeal to sportsmen, Lough Inagh makes a good base for touring Connemara and is only 42 miles from Galway; in addition to fishing, golf, pony trekking and garden visits are all among things to do nearby. Off-season breaks offer especially good value. Small conferences/banqueting (15/50). Children welcome (under 3s free in parents' room, cots available without charge, baby sitting arranged). Pets permitted (stay in bedroom free of charge). Garden, walking, cycling, fly fishing. Equestrian, sea angling, garden visits and hunting/shooting all nearby. **Rooms 13** (5 junior suites, 1 family, 10 no smoking, 4 ground floor); room service (24 hr). B&B €140 pps, ss €20. **Finisglen Room:** This handsome dining room has deep green walls and graceful spoonback Victorian mahogany chairs, and non-residents are welcome for dinner by reservation. The food in both the restaurant and the bar is excellent; alongside the popular dishes like smoked salmon, pan-fried steaks, lobster (when available) you may find specialities including starters of pan-fried scallops with julienne of vegetables and cider dressing, or a main course of medallions of pork with apple & fig compôte and marsala jus. Desserts, including a wide range of ices, are home-made, service is friendly, and portions generous. The wine list includes a fair range of half bottles, some non-alcoholic wines and, unusually, a rosé among the house wines. *Tempting bar menus are also offered for lunch, dinner and afternoon tea. **Seats 36**; L 12.30-4; D daily 6.45-9pm (reservations required), Set D €49; also à la carte. House wine €22; Bar meals 12.30-4 & 6.30-9pm daily. SC10%. Closed mid Dec-mid Mar. Amex, Diners, MasterCard, Visa, Laser. **Directions:** From Galway city, travel on N59 for 64km (40 m). Take rght N344 after Recess; 5km (3 m) on right.

Renvyle

HOTEL•RESTAURANT

Renvyle House Hotel

Renvyle Co Galway **Tel: 095 43511**

info@renvyle.com   www.renvyle.com

FAMILY FRIENDLY HOTEL OF THE YEAR

In one of the country's most appealingly remote and beautiful areas, this famous Lutyens-esque house has a romantic and fascinating history, having been home to people as diverse as a Gaelic chieftain and Oliver St. John Gogarty - and it became one of Ireland's earliest country house hotels, in 1883. In good weather, it is best approached via a stunning scenic drive along a mountain road with views down into a blue-green sea of unparalleled clarity. Once reached, the hotel seems to be snuggling down for shelter and, although it has limited views, there is a shift of emphasis to the comforts within, a feeling reinforced by the cosy atmosphere of the original building, with its dark beams, rug strewn floors and open fires - and a snug conservatory where guests can survey the garden, and the landscape beyond. Photographs and mementoes recording visits from the many famous people who have stayed here - Augustus John, Lady Gregory, Yeats and Churchill among them - keep guests happily occupied for hours, but there is plenty to distract you from this enjoyable activity, including a heated outdoor swimming pool, tennis, trout fishing, golf (9-hole), and croquet - while the surrounding area offers more challenging activities including archaeological expeditions, horse riding, hill walking, scuba diving and sea fishing. Just loafing around is perhaps what guests are best at here, however, and there's little need to do much else. The hotel's bar food is excellent too - all this, plus the scent of a turf fire and a comfortable armchair, can be magic. The grounds and gardens around the hotel are a special point of interest at Renvyle, and come as a delightful contrast to the magnificently rugged surrounding scenery. Special breaks (midweek, weekend and bank holiday) are very good value and, with so much to do and good facilities, it is an excellent choice for a family break, especially with older children (and your dog). Renvyle also makes an excellent conference venue. *Renvyle House was selected for the one-off 'Spirit of Ireland Award' to celebrate the Guide's 10th anniversary in 2008. Conference/banqueting (200); secretarial services. Children welcome (under 2s free in parents' room, cots available without charge; crèche (seasonal), playroom, children's playground, children's tea, baby sitting arranged). Pets permitted by arrangement. Outdoor swimming pool (seasonal), archery, all-weather tennis court, clay pigeon shooting, croquet, lawn bowls, fly fishing, sea angling, snooker. **Rooms 68** (4 suites, 40 no smoking, 1 for disabled, 6 family rooms). B&B €95pps, no ss, no SC. **Restaurant:** Whilst bar lunches and light meals in the conservatory are very enjoyable during the day (and this is a great place to plan a break when touring the area), dinner at Renyle is an occasion to be relished. The large dining room - which is cannily organised with a window along one side where parents can see their children in the supervised playroom next door - is formally appointed and there is a pianist at the grand piano every night, adding to the sense of occasion. General Manager Ronnie Counihan is always on hand to chat with guests, and head chef Tim O'Sullivan looks after the inner man admirably. His menus feature local seafood and Connemara produce, including Renvyle rack of lamb, local lobster and vegetables in season - and not only is his cooking spot on, but he has written a cookery book, so you can try out his recipes at home.*Renvyle House was the winner of a Féile Bia Award in 2006. Restaurant open 7-9 daily (Set D about €45). Bar meals 11-5 daily (excl 25 Dec, Good Fri). Closed 1-21 Dec & 7 Jan - 8 Feb. Helipad. Amex, Diners, MasterCard, Visa, Laser. **Directions:** 18km (12 miles) north of Clifden.

ROUNDSTONE

This charming village is clustered around its traditional stone-built harbour, so seafood is very much the speciality in every bar and restaurant. The Conneely family's **Eldons Hotel** (095 35933; www.connemara.net) is a comfortable family-run hotel with its own seafood restaurant, **Beola**, next door, and there is also the Vaughan family's **Roundstone House Hotel** (095 35864; www.irishcountry-hotels.com). Both have a well-earned reputation with locals and visitors alike - and both offer golf and sea angling breaks. Nearby, Connemara Golf Club (Ballyconneely, 095 23502) will prove to be a stern test for any golfer, while garden lovers could spend some time in nearby Cashel House Hotel & Gardens (Cashel, 095 31001), and Ballynahinch Castle Hotel & Gardens (Recess, 095 31006). There are many other gardens interesting gardens to visit in the area too; Connemara Garden Trail leaflets are widely available in tourist information offices and hotels; otherwise, for up to date details, contact the Connemara Garden Trail directly (095 21148). Roundstone is also renouned for it's annual Connemara Pony Fare. The hill climber will also feel at home here, for Roundstone lies beneath Errisbeg Mountain, an easy climb for most, with fantastic views of sea, lakes and mountains waiting as a reward.

WWW.IRELAND-GUIDE.COM FOR ALL THE BEST PLACES TO EAT, DRINK & STAY

Roundstone
CHARACTER PUB•RESTAURANT

O'Dowd's Bar

Roundstone Co Galway **Tel: 095 35809**
odowds@indigo.ie www.odowdsbar.com

The O'Dowd family have been welcoming visitors to this much-loved pub overlooking the harbour for longer than most people care to remember. There are some new developments from time to time, but the old bar is always the same – or at least it was until recently, when the Guide was shocked to find a smart new façade and a new front door. Inside it was reassuring familiar, however, and it remains one of those simple places, with the comfort of an open fire and good pint, where people congregate in total relaxation - if they can get in (it can be very busy in the summer months). A reasonably priced bar menu majoring in seafood offers sustenance or, for more formal meals, the restaurant next door does the honours: seafood chowder, mussels, crab, hot buttered lobster, in-shell Aran Bay prawns in garlic butter etc; non-fish eaters will be pleased to find some other choices, including Connemara lamb; simple puds like blackberry & apple pie to finish. **Restaurant Seats 36**; children welcome before 7pm (high chair, children's menu). Meals 12-10 daily (to 9.30 in pub); reservations required in restaurant. A la carte. House wine from €19.50. SC 10% on parties of 6+. *Self-catering accommodation available - details on application. Closed 25 Dec. Amex, MasterCard, Visa, Laser. **Directions:** On harbour front in Roundstone village.

Roundstone Area
B&B

The Anglers Return

Toombeola Roundstone Connemara Co Galway **Tel: 095 31091**
info@anglersreturn.com www.anglersreturn.com

This charming and unusual house near Roundstone was built as a sporting lodge in the eighteenth century and, true to its name, fishing remains a major attraction to this day. But you don't have to be a fisherperson to warm to the special charms of The Angler's Return: peace and tranquillity, the opportunity to slow down in a quiet, caring atmosphere in this most beautiful area - this is its particular appeal. The house is set in three acres of natural gardens (open every day in spring and summer; best in late spring) and makes a good base for the Connemara Garden Trail - and, of course, for painting holidays. Bedrooms are bright and comfortably furnished in a fresh country house style, although only one is en-suite (the other four share two bathrooms between them); this is not a major problem and the overall level of comfort is high. However, bathroom arrangements are gradually being improved - one now features a restored

Victorian ball & claw cast-iron bath. As well as fishing, there is golf nearby, and riding and boat trips can be arranged for guests - and there are maps and information for walkers too. No television, but instead there are lots of books to read - and tea or snacks are available at any time during the day or evening, (out in the secluded back garden in fine weather, or beside the fire in the soothing drawing room, perhaps); dinner is available for groups staying several days, otherwise bookings can be made in nearby restaurants. Breakfast will include freshly-baked breads, home-made yoghurts, marmalade and jams, and freshly picked herb teas from the garden - and you are even invited to collect your own egg. **Rooms 5** (1 en-suite, 4 with shared bathrooms; all no smoking); not suitable for children. B&B €48, ss by arrangement. *Special interest breaks offered (painting, walking); details on application. Walking, fishing, garden. Closed 1 Dec-28 Feb. **No Credit Cards. Directions:** From Galway, N59 Clifden road; turn left onto R341 Roundstone road for 6.5km (4 m); house is on the left.

Tuam
BAR•RESTAURANT

Finns Bar & Restaurant

Milltown Tuam Co Galway **Tel: 093 51327**
johnfin.indigo.ie

John and Lucy Finn's attractive restaurant is on the river, in a charming little award-winning tidy town a few miles north of Tuam - a welcome sight for hungry travellers between Galway and Sligo. John cooks an eclectic mix of international and traditional dishes - reasonably priced and served in a relaxed atmosphere. The cooking is sound, it's good value for money and the small village setting - where everyone seems to know someone at another table - makes a welcome change from busy towns. On the down side, bookings are not accepted, which is a major disadvantage when diners may travel especially to eat here and then have the inconvenience of a long wait for a table. **Seats 80** (Private room, 14); no reservations; children welcome. D Tue-Sun, 5-9pm. A la carte; house wines from about €16. Service discretionary. Closed 3 days Christmas & Easter. Children welcome. MasterCard, Visa, Laser. **Directions:** 16km (10 miles from Tuam), on main N17 to Sligo. ◇

COUNTY KERRY

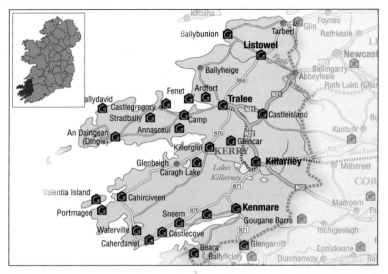

It's something special, being Kerry. This magnificent county in the far southwest has Ireland's highest and most varied mountains, and certain favoured areas also have our longest-lived citizens. Then, too, it's a region which has long been a global pioneer in the hospitality business - in 2004, the scenically-blessed town of Killarney celebrated 250 years in the forefront of Irish tourism, while its most senior hotel, the Great Southern, celebrated its own 150th anniversary.

So visitors inevitably arrive with high expectations. Kerry, however, can face the challenge. This magnificent county really is the Kingdom of Kerry. Everything is king size. For not only has Kerry mountains galore - more than anywhere else in Ireland - but there's a rare quality to Carrantuohill, the highest of all.

By international standards, this loftiest peak of MacGillicuddy's Reeks (try pronouncing it "mackilcuddy") may not seem particularly notable at just 1038 m. But when you sense its mysterious heights in the clouds above a countryside of astonishing beauty, its relative elevation is definitely world league. And all Kerry's mountains sweep oceanwards towards a handsome coastline which rings the changes between sheltered inlets and storm tossed offshore islands. Visually, Kerry has everything.

But these days, spectacular scenery isn't enough on its own. Like other leading visitor destinations, Kerry is well aware of the need to provide accessible entertainment and an increasing choice of places with cultural and historical interest. Here too, the Kingdom can oblige.

The oldest fossil footprints in the Northern Hemisphere are in Kerry, and they're about 350 million years old. You'll find them way down west, on Valentia Island, and they're reckoned one of the seven wonders of Ireland. In much more modern times, the Antarctic explorer Tom Crean was from Kerry. He came from the little village of Annascaul on the majestic Dingle Peninsula, and when he had finished with adventuring, he returned to Annascaul and opened the South Pole Inn.

The town of Killarney, among the lakes and mountains where they're re-establishing the enormous white-tailed sea eagle, has long been a magnet for visitors, but Killarney is determined not simply to rest on its laurels after more than a Quarter Millennium as Ireland's premier tourist destination, for it was in 1754 that its attractions were first internationally promoted. Meanwhile, on the more immediate question of keeping the place clean, Killarney scored well in the latest national Tidy Town contest, announced in September 2007 – it came in with a Gold Medal.

Across the purple mountains from Killarney, the lovely little town of Kenmare in South Kerry is both a gourmet focus, and another excellent touring centre. As one of the prettiest places in Ireland, Kenmare puts the emphasis on civic pride.

Away to the west, thrusting into the Atlantic, is the Dingle Peninsula where the harbour town of Dingle is the focal point for a thriving, highly individual and notably hospitable region. And in the far north-east of this large county, Listowel – famed for its writers and its Race Week in September – has the restored Lartigue Monorail, another award-winning attraction. It's unique. And if you want to know how unique, well, you'll just have to go and see for yourself.

Local Attractions and Information

Beaufort	Hotel Dunloe Castle Gardens	064 44583
Castleisland	Crag Cave	066 714 1244
Dingle	Ocean World	066 915 2111
Dunquin	Great Blasket Centre	066 915 6444 / 915 6371
Farranfore	Kerry International Airport	066 976 4644
Glencar	Into the Wilderness Walking Tours (May-Sep)	066 60104
Kenmare	Walking Festivals	064 41034
Kenmare	Heritage Centre	064 41233
Killarney	Muckross House, Gardens & Traditional Farm	064 31440
Killarney	Tourism Information	064 31633
Killorglin	Kerry Woollen Mills	064 44122
Killorglin	Puck Fair (ancient festival), mid-August	066 976 2366
Lauragh	Dereen Gardens	064 83103
Listowel	St John's Art Centre	068 22566
Listowel	Writers' Week (June)	068 21074
Tralee	Kerry County Museum	066 712 7777
Tralee	Rose of Tralee Festival (late August)	066 712 3227
Tralee	Siamsa Tire Arts Centre	066 712 3055
Valentia Island	The Skellig Experience	066 947 6306
Valentia Island	Valentia Heritage (Knightstown)	066 947 6411
Waterville	Craft Market	066 947 4212

Ardfert
PUB

Kate Browne's Pub
Ardfert Co Kerry
Tel: 066 713 4055 / 4030

 Situated on the main road but with parking to the side, this friendly and attractive pub has an old world ambience, with roughly plastered walls and country pine. The main dining area is a large, bright and airy room with an unusual slate bar and an old solid fuel stove, and another eating area off the main bar has an inviting open fire which makes guests feel at home. This is not a place to expect cutting edge cooking, but you'll find wholesome fare at all times of day, and with generous portions. Local seafood features in popular dishes like chowder (with excellent home-baked bread), prawn cocktail made with fresh prawns, which is very often not the case, and baked mussels, as well as main course fish dishes; but a wide ranging menu is offered to suit all tastes and the restaurant is very popular with families - a special children's menu is available too. **Seats 100** (outdoors, 20, private room, 50); toilets wheelchair accessible; children welcome (high chair, children's menu, baby changing facilities); food served daily, 12-10pm; house wine €20. Closed 25 Dec, Good Fri. Amex, Diners, MasterCard, Visa, Laser. **Directions:** 5km north of Tralee, on the left as you enter Ardfert.

BALLYBUNION

Situated in north County Kerry, at the mouth of the River Shannon estuary, Ballybunion faces west to the north Atlantic and across the Shannon to the shores of County Clare. The first transatlantic telephone transmission was made from the Marconi wireless station here in 1919 to Louisbourg, Cape Breton, Nova Scotia, by W. T. Ditcham, a Marconi Engineer. Ballybunion is in an unspoilt area of great natural beauty, with a wide range of flora and fauna, resident and migratory birds and marine animals, including sea otters, seals, porpoises and dolphins, which can be observed along the coast. The clean waters of the area also make it ideal for harvesting sea vegetables, such as dulse (dillisk/sea grass/Palmaria palmata) and Irish moss (carrageen moss/Chondrus crispus). To many visitors, Ballybunion is synonymous with golf - the links courses here are ranked among the top golf courses in the world (Ballybunion Golf Club, 068 27146), and attract many famous visitors including President Bill Clinton of the United States of America (August 1999). Quality accommodation is a feature of the area and, in addition to the establishments listed below, others useful to know about include **Cliff House Hotel** (068 27777; www.cliffhousehotel.com), an old family-run hotel of character which is in common ownership with the famous Listowel Arms Hotel (see entry); accommodation is modest but pleasant, and the bar/restaurant area is atmospheric - an enjoyable place to be, and with a local following. Much newer is David and Doreen Walsh's fine owner-run guesthouse on the edge of the town, **The Tides** (068 27980); designed with the comfort of golfers in mind, it has very spacious and comfortably furnished accommodation, a friendly atmosphere and an emphasis on hands-on service. In summer, visitors to Ballybunion take advantage of the blue flag sandy beaches, some of which are popular for surfing. The cliffs nearby offer walkers spectacular scenery and sometimes dolphins can be spotted in the clear waters.

WWW.IRELAND-GUIDE.COM FOR ALL THE BEST PLACES TO EAT, DRINK & STAY

Ballybunion
GUESTHOUSE•BAR•RESTAURANT

Harty-Costello Townhouse Bar & Restaurant
Main Street Ballybunion Co Kerry **Tel: 068 27129**
hartycostello@eircom.net www.hartycostellos.com

Although styled a townhouse, Davnet and Jackie Hourigan's welcoming town centre establishment is really an inn, encompassing all the elements of hospitality within its neatly painted and flower-bedecked yellow walls. The spacious bedrooms have television, phones, tea & coffee-making facilities and hair dryer, and also comfortable chairs and curtains thoughtfully fitted with blackout linings to keep out intrusively early light in summer; all have been completely refurbished recently, in a contemporary and uncluttered style. There's a choice of three bars and an evening restaurant where seafood is the speciality, complemented by an extensive wine list. It all adds up to a relaxing and hospitable base for a golfing holiday, or for touring the south-west. Golfing breaks and short breaks are offered: details on application. **Rooms 8** (all en-suite and no smoking); children welcome (under 12s free in parents' room, cot available); broadband wi/fi; no pets.. B&B €60 pps, ss €20. Room service (all day). Meals available Tue-Sat, 12-4 (bar); 6.30-9 (restaurant). No food on Sun & Mon; establishment closed 30 Oct-30 Mar. Walking. Amex, MasterCard, Visa, Laser. **Directions:** 50 miles from Limerick N69; 40 miles from Killarney.

Ballybunion
RESTAURANT•COUNTRY HOUSE•PUB

Iragh Ti Connor
Main Street Ballybunion Co Kerry
Tel: 068 27112 iraghticonnor@eircom.net www.golfballybunion.com

The name, which translates as "the inheritance of O'Connor", says it all: what John and Joan O'Connor inherited was a 19th century pub, and thanks to their scrupulous attention to detail, their inheritance has now been transformed into a fine establishment. The rooms are all generous and have been carefully refurbished and furnished with antiques, and bathrooms with cast-iron tubs and power showers. Public areas are also furnished with style and individuality and, in addition to good bar food in the character old pub (which is very popular), there's a fine dining restaurant with a well-deserved reputation for good cooking. Golfing holidays are a serious attraction and this is one of the best places for discerning golfers to stay. Small conferences (60). **Rooms 17** (2 junior suites, 15 superior rooms, all no smoking); free broadband; children welcome (under 3s free in parents' room, cot available without charge). No pets. B&B €105 pps, ss €60. No SC. Food served daily, 12.30-9.30pm. Garden. *Golf breaks offered, with tee times arranged at Ballybunion Old Course. Closed Christmas week. Amex, MasterCard, Visa, Laser. **Directions:** Top of main street, opposite statue of Bill Clinton.

Ballybunion
RESTAURANT•GUESTHOUSE

Teach de Broc
Links Road Ballybunion Co Kerry **Tel: 068 27581**
info@ballybuniongolf.com www.ballybuniongolf.com

GUESTHOUSE BREAKFAST OF THE YEAR

You don't have to play golf to appreciate this highly popular guesthouse, but it certainly must help as it is almost within the boundaries of the famous Ballybunion links. Aoife and Seamus Brock offer an extremely high standard of comfort, with satellite television in all rooms, and there is a commitment to constant upgrading and improvement: fairly recent additions include a new guest lounge and a wine/coffee bar, more fine bedrooms, and an electric massage chair for easing golfers' aches and pains after a long day on the links. Yet, however comfortable and well-located this exceptional guesthouse may be, it's the laid-back and genuinely hospitable atmosphere created by this energetic and dedicated couple that really gets them coming back for more. Always keen to provide the best possible service for the discerning golfer, an excellent breakfast is served from 6am, with freshly baked scones and croissants among the good things offered. **Rooms 14** (all en-suite, 4 with separate bath & shower, 2 shower only, all no-smoking, 1 for disabled); free broadband wi/fi; not suitable for children. B&B €80pps, ss €50. Masseuse on call; laundry service; horse riding nearby; own parking; garden; no pets. Lift. Turndown service. All day room service. *Stay & Play golf breaks offered; details on application. Closed 1 Nov - 15 Mar. **Strollers Bistro:** The wine bar idea, originally intended to offer just a light bite, has developed a little each year and it is now a fully-fledged restaurant offering an appealing à la carte menu. The choice is wide, with starters ranging from creamy seafood chowder to a sophisticated terrine of duck foie gras with brioche, frisée and beetroot relish, and main courses that include good vegetarian and seafood choices (including whole pan-fried black sole, and maybe even lobster if you're lucky) and meat dishes such as rack of Kerry lamb as well as the various chargrilled steaks that are de rigeur for golfers. Home-made desserts may include a speciality pecan pie, and you can take your coffee out to the new outside seating area beside the bar, where there is an open stove. The wine list has also grown and is well chosen to match the menu. Service, as elsewhere is delightful – professional, yet very warm and friendly. **Seats 30**; air conditioning. D daily, 6-10pm; sc discretionary. MasterCard, Visa, Laser. Helipad. **Directions:** Directly opposite entrance to Ballybunion Golf Club.

CAHERDANIEL

The small village of Caherdaniel is beyond Westcove, near the shore of Derrynane Bay and is an excellent base for visitors to explore the Ring of Kerry route, which includes breathtaking scenery, incorporating mountains, beaches and fantastic views over Kenmare Bay. In the vicinity of Caherdaniel, there are sites of historical interest including the curious hermitage of St Crohane, made out of solid rock, and an ancient stone fort a mile away. There are excellent walking routes in the nearby Derrynane National Park (066 947 5113), where a visit to Daniel O'Connell's house is a must, and pony trekking is available in the mountains, woodlands or on the beach. Golfers are well catered for by both the Waterville (066 947 4102) and Skellig Bay Golf Clubs (066 947 4133). During the summer months, visitors have the opportunity to sample the best in local farmhouse produce at the farmers' market, which is on every Friday. **The Blind Piper** (066 947 5346) is a popular pub in Caherdaniel village, offering moderately priced food in a good atmosphere - ideal for familes.
WWW.IRELAND-GUIDE.COM FOR ALL THE BEST PLACES TO EAT, DRINK & STAY

Caherdaniel
HOTEL•RESTAURANT

Derrynane Hotel
Caherdaniel Co Kerry **Tel: 066 947 5136**
info@derrynane.com www.derrynane.com

If only for its superb location, this unassuming 1960s-style hotel would be well worth a visit, but there is much more on offer. The accommodation is quite modest but very comfortable and the food is good - and, under the excellent management of Mary O'Connor and her well-trained staff, this hospitable, family-friendly place provides a welcome home from home for many a contented guest. Activity holidays are a big draw - there are beautiful beaches, excellent fishing, Waterville Golf Course offers special rates at certain times - and the hotel has published its own walking brochure. Don't leave the area without visiting Daniel O'Connell's beautiful house at Derrynane or the amazing Ballinskelligs chocolate factory. *Derrynane Hotel was our Family Hotel of the Year in 2005. Children welcome (under 4s free in parents' room, cots available without charge, baby sitting arranged; playroom) Heated outdoor swimming pool, tennis, pool table, fitness room, steam room, walking, garden. Equestrian and fishing (coarse, sea angling) nearby. **Rooms 70** (all en-suite, 15 family rooms, 32 ground floor, 50 no smoking). B&B €60-70 pps. *Special breaks offered: details on application. Closed Oct-Easter. **Restaurant:** Overlooking the heated outdoor swimming pool and the hotel's gardens, the restaurant enjoys stunning sea views - be sure to ask for a table by the window, as the view is a major part of the experience. While not a fine dining experience, good food has always been a feature of the hotel and there is a commitment to high quality ingredients, local where possible. The 4-course dinner menus offer a good choice of simply presented popular dishes like smoked salmon, chicken liver mousse, Kerry lamb or beef, and duckling - and a very reasonably priced children's menu is offered. Attentive staff do everything possible to make a meal here a pleasant experience - and a helpful wine list is clearly presented. *A light bar menu is also available every day, 11am-9pm. **Seats 100**. D 7-9 daily, Set D about €42. Also à la carte, sc discretionary. House wine €19.90. *All day salad bar available for light meals. Hotel closed Oct-Easter. Amex, Diners, MasterCard, Visa, Laser **Directions:** Midway on Ring of Kerry.

Caherdaniel
COUNTRY HOUSE

Iskeroon

Caherdaniel Co Kerry **Tel: 066 947 5119**
info@iskeroon.com www.iskeroon.com

Geraldine Burkitt and David Hare's beautiful property is in a secluded position overlooking Derrynane Harbour, and the effort taken to get there makes it all the more restful once settled in. Approaching it down the winding little road is an adventure and, once inside the gate, one can only marvel at the four and a half acres of sub-tropical gardens, which were laid out in the 1930s and are remarkably well-kept - amazing in this wonderfully wild place. Recently, the Hares undertook major renovation of outbuildings beside the house, and the result is two beautiful new suites with lovely kitchens which are available for self-catering or B&B and overlook the harbour and the islands of Deenish and Scarriff. The Hares are very hospitable (tea and homemade cakes on arrival, as much or as little conversation as you like at breakfast) but the aim is to provide peace and privacy for guests, which they are now doing even better than before. The private pier at the bottom of the garden joins an old Mass Path which, by a happy chance, leads not only to the beach but also to Keating's pub (known as Bridie's) where a bit of banter and, perhaps, some good seafood is also to be had in the evenings, although it's wise to check on this beforehand. In keeping with the caring philosophy of this lovely house, solar panels are used to heat the water. **Apartments 2** (both suites and no smoking). B&B €85 pps, ss €75. Unsuitable for children; free Broadband wi/fi; no pets. Fishing (fly, coarse, sea angling), walking and scuba diving nearby. Garden. *Self-catering studio apartment for two also available. Closed end Sept-1 May. MasterCard, Visa, Laser. **Directions:** Between Caherdaniel and Waterville (N70), turn off at the Scariff Inn, signed to Bunavalla Pier. Go to the pier and left through "private" gate; cross beach and enter through white gate posts.

CAHIRCIVEEN

Cahirciveen is a small market town half way round the Ring of Kerry; situated on the River Feale, at the foot of Benetee mountain, it overlooks Valentia Harbour and is the shopping centre of South Kerry - traditional fair days are still held on the street. Attractions of interest include the Heritage Centre (066 947 2777) - situated in the old Royal Irish Constabulary Barracks adjacent to the town centre - which has craft workshops, an audio-visual display and archaeological remains on view, and the 15th century Ballycarbery Castle (066 947 2777) is also worth a visit. On the main Ring of Kerry road, it is useful to know about Pat Golden's family-run "one stop shop", **The Quarry** (066 947 7601; www.patscraftshop.com): not only will you get good home cooking at the restaurant here, but there's also a post office and foodstore, filling station, tourist information point, bureau de change, a fine craft shop, with quality Irish clothing and gift items - and the unique 'Golden Mile Nature Walk'. As well as **QCs**, in the town (see entry), other handy places to take a break on the Ring of Kerry include Michael & Bridie O'Neill's **'The Point Bar'** (066 947 2165) at Renard Point, just beside the car ferry to Valentia island: this immaculately maintained pub is well-known for its fresh seafood (phone ahead to check times). The **Oratory Art Gallery & Café** is also recommended. New to Cahirciveen town, although its future is uncertain at the time of going to press, **The Watermarque Hotel** (066 947 2222; www.watermarquehotel.ie) has brought welcome facilities, including a spa. Cahirciveen hosts a Farmers' Market in the community centre on Thursdays (11am - 2pm June - Sept). Families staying anywhere in this area will love visiting the amazing Skellig Chocolate Factory (066 947 9119), off the Ring of Kerry at Ballinskelligs. Garden lovers should make a point of visiting Glanleam House & Sub-Tropical Gardens (066 947 6176) on nearby Valentia Island (exotic woodland gardens with bamboo forests and ferns), while golfers have the challenge of the world famous Waterville Golf Club nearby (Waterville, 066 947 4102). Other local activities include sailing (there is a marina at Cahirciveen), mountaineering, windsurfing, water skiing, walking, cycling and horse riding - and deep sea anglers are well catered for with the many charter boats available.

WWW.IRELAND-GUIDE.COM FOR ALL THE BEST PLACES TO EAT, DRINK & STAY

Cahirciveen
BAR•RESTAURANT

QC's Seafood Bar & Restaurant
3 Main Street Cahirciveen Co Kerry **Tel: 066 947 2244**
info@qcbar.com www.qcbar.com

Kate and Andrew Cooke's sensitively renovated bar and restaurant has some great original features that give it character, including a rugged stone wall and an enormous fireplace; the bar counter is also over a century old and there are numerous pictures of local interest and nautical antiques, reflecting Andrew's special love affair with the sea (he runs a yacht charter service* as well as the bar). The sea is fundamental here anyway, as local fish is the main feature - supplied by the family company, Quinlan's Kerry Fish at Renard's Point (one of their shops is just across the road). And there's a big Spanish influence, so expect delicious chargrills, with lots of olive oil and garlic: fresh crab claws and crabmeat are a speciality, also sizzling prawns, and pan-seared baby squid. Menus are flexible - any of the starters can be served in a main course size, and, although it undoubtedly helps to like seafood, there are plenty of other choices. Main courses include excellent meats to balance up all that fresh seafood, especially on evening menus, rack of Kerry lamb and char-grilled fillet steak (supplied by a local butcher). The most pleasing aspect of the food is its immediacy - everything is ultra-fresh, simply prepared and full of zest and, given the quality, it is also good value. At the back of the restaurant, there's a charming sheltered outdoor dining area and landscaped garden, carved from the hillside by their own sheer willpower - and, as Andrew is quick to point out, a hired digger. An interesting wine list leans strongly towards Spain, especially the reds, although house wines are from France & Chile; it is good to see sherry listed as a mainstream wine rather than relegated to aperitif status. [*For yacht charter information, see www.YachtCharterKerry.com]. **Seats 50** (outdoors, 40); children welcome. Meals: L 12.30-2.30 in Summer (Jun-Aug) only; D 6-9.30pm, 7 days in Jul-Aug, 6 days shoulder season (closed Mon), Winter Thu-Sun. Closed 25 Dec, Good Fri; annual closure 8 Jan - mid-Feb. Minimum credit card charge, €25. MasterCard, Visa, Laser. **Directions:** In the centre of Caherciveen.

CARAGH LAKE

Beautiful Lough Caragh – or Caragh Lake as it is usually called - is near Killorglin, on the Ring of Kerry. Its clear waters originate in the MacGillycuddy Reeks and provide an ideal environment for healthy fish for game anglers, with salmon and trout being the most predominant. The hills and rugged countryside provide some impressive scenery for walkers, while golfers will enjoy the tranquil 18-hole links course at Dooks (066 976 8205), which is close to nearby Glenbeigh, where the blue flag Rossbeigh beach is ideal for families, and popular with sea anglers too. Both the lake and the nearby strand provide the opportunity for water sports such as canoeing, windsurfing and swimming. Special events held in the area in the summer include the Puck Fair in Killorglin in August, and the summer races on Glenbeigh beach.

Caragh Lake
COUNTRY HOUSE•RESTAURANT

Carrig House Country House & Restaurant
Caragh Lake Killorglin Co Kerry **Tel: 066 976 9100**
info@carrighouse.com www.carrighouse.com

HIDEAWAY OF THE YEAR AWARD

At the heart of Frank and Mary Slattery's sensitively extended Victorian house lies a hunting lodge once owned by Lord Brocket - and he chose well, as it is very attractive and handsomely set in fine gardens with the lake and mountains providing a dramatic backdrop. The house is welcoming and well-maintained, with friendly staff (Frank himself carries the luggage to your room) and a relaxed atmosphere, notably in a series of charming sitting rooms where you can chat beside the fire or have a drink before dinner. This is a place where you can lose yourself for hours with a book, or playing chess, cards or board games in the games room, or boating out on the lake. Some of the large, airy bedrooms have their own patios, and all are furnished with antiques, and have generous, well-designed bathrooms with bath and shower - an impressive Presidential Suite has a sitting room with panoramic views across the lake to the Magillicuddy Reeks, two separate dressing rooms and jacuzzi bath. The extensive gardens are of great interest too - a map is available, and personalised tours can be arranged. This is a lovely serene place to stay – a perfect escape from the modern world. Not suitable for children under 8 except small babies (under 1 free of charge, cot available, baby sitting arranged). Dogs allowed in some areas (stay in kennel). Swimming (lake), fishing (ghillie & boat available), walking, garden, croquet. **Rooms 17** (1 suite, 1 junior suite, 14 no smoking, 1 single, 4 ground floor) B&B €90-125 pps, ss €50. Closed Dec-Feb. **Lakeside Restaurant:** Beautifully situated overlooking the lake, the restaurant is a fine room with well-spaced, elegantly appointed tables and a relaxed atmosphere. With a piano playing softly, a great sense of hospitality and the promise of chef John Luke's delicious food to come, this is a very pleasing place to be - and it is open to the public as well as resident guests, which makes for a livelier atmosphere. An extensive à la carte menu offers a balanced selection but, although the many tempting choices include some unusual dishes (a starter of roasted lamb sweetbreads, for example, or a main course of pan-seared veal liver), it is hard to resist the fresh Kerry seafood. A refreshing tartar of Kerry salmon with cucumber crème fraîche and pickled grapefruit, and a warm filo tartlet of Dingle crab with watercress and red onion vinaigrette make wonderful starters, for example, and main courses may include Arctic char (one of Ireland's earliest known fish, now farmed in a very natural way in Co. Sligo). But Kerry lamb is equally appealing, and a roast rack, served with puy lentils, smoked bacon and red wine jus, is an exceptionally enjoyable dish. Vegetarian choices are also interesting (a tian of cous cous, perhaps, with delicious summer vegetables). It will pay to plan ahead for dessert, as it would be a shame to miss out on treats like rum pannacotta with caramelised pineapple & cracked black pepper, or pears poached in white wine with sablé biscuits and cinnamon fig ice cream... There's a very nice wine list (and helpful advice offered) and, after dinner, it's lovely to be able to have your coffee or tea in a comfy sofa at the fireside. **Seats 50** (private room, 15; outdoors, 20); not suitable for children under 8. D daily, 7-9. Extensive à la carte. House wine from €28.50. SC 10% on groups 6+. Non-residents welcome (booking essential). Establishment closed Dec-Feb. Diners, MasterCard, Visa, Laser. **Directions:** Left after 4km (2.5 m) on Killorglin/Glenbeigh Road N70 (Ring of Kerry), then turn sharp right at Caragh Lake School (2.5km), 1km on the left.

Caragh Lake

HOTEL•RESTAURANT

Hotel Ard na Sidhe

Caragh Lake Killorglin Co Kerry **Tel: 066 976 9105**
reservations@ardnasidhe.com www.ardnasidhe.com

Set in woodland and among award-winning gardens, this peaceful Victorian retreat is in a beautiful mountain location overlooking Caragh Lake. Decorated throughout in a soothing country house style, very comfortable antique-filled day rooms provide plenty of lounging space for quiet indoor relaxation and a terrace for fine weather, all with wonderful views. Bedrooms shared between the main house, and some with private patios in the garden house, are spacious and elegantly furnished in traditional style, with excellent ensuite bathrooms. This is a sister hotel to the Hotel Europe and Dunloe Castle (see entries), whose leisure facilities are also available to guests. Dooks, Waterville, Killeen and Mahony's Point golf courses are all within easy reach. **Rooms 18** (3 suites,1 family room, 5 ground floor, 6 no smoking). Children welcome (Under 2s free in parents' room; cots available free of charge). No pets. B&B €75 pps (ss €75), SC included. Limited room service. **Fairyhill Restaurant:** Like the rest of the hotel, the dining room has intimacy and character and, after a fireside drink and a look through the menu, this is a delightful place to spend an hour or two. There's an emphasis on local ingredients and updated interpretations of traditional Irish themes on menus that may offer aromatic Kerry mountain lamb, and may include several fish dishes, although there is a stronger emphasis on meats than is usual in the area. Finish with imaginative desserts, or the Irish cheese plate. Coffee and petits fours can be served beside the drawing room fire. **Seats 32** (private room, 10, outdoors, 16); non-residents are welcome by reservation. D only, 7-8.30pm, usually closed on Mon; hotel closed mid Oct- May. Amex, Diners, MasterCard, Visa, Laser **Directions:** Off N70 Ring of Kerry road, signed 5 km west of Killorglin.

Castlegregory
PUB

Spillanes

Fahamore Maharees Castlegregory Co Kerry **Tel: 066 713 9125**
marilynspillane@tinet.ie   www.spillanesbar.com

It's a long way down from the main road to reach the Maharees, but many would make the journey just for a visit to Marilyn and Michael Spillane's great traditional pub – it's been in the family since 1875 and they work hard at both the food and hospitality, earning a loyal following as a result. After many years of informal self-service, the Spillanes recently decided to upgrade their system and offer full table service instead, and to accept reservations – so get there early if you plan to drop in without a booking. This is a very popular place and the wide-ranging menu is designed to suit all tastes and age groups, offering a selection of starters/light dishes, pizzas and burgers, and vegetarian dishes – but its strengths lie in great steaks and seafood, as always. In addition to the main menu, a daily specials list usually offers at least two fish dishes and a meat dish each evening. You'll find Cromane mussels, crab claws and Dingle prawns (in prawn cocktail or scampi, for example), maybe even crayfish, along with smoked haddock fishcakes and, perhaps, grilled hake fillet or whole baked seabass. The pub is full of character and it can get very busy, but the full dinner menu is available from 4pm which is ideal for families. *Self-catering accommodation also offered, in two new 2-bedroom apartments opposite the pub (beside beach); each sleeps 5. **Seats 90**; toilets wheelchair accessible; children welcome (high chair, children's menu, baby changing facilities). Meals daily in high season, 1-9.30 (Sun to 9); L 1-3pm & D 4-9pm; low season from 6pm. Closed Nov-Mar. MasterCard, Visa, Laser. **Directions:** Dingle Peninsula, 5.5km north of Castlegregory, between Brandon and Tralee bays.

Castleisland
RESTAURANT

Ⓝ **ⓥ**

Crag Cave

Castleisland Co Kerry   **Tel: 066 714 1244**
info@cragcave.com   www.cragcave.com

A short distance east of Tralee, this limestone show cave is one of Kerry's biggest attractions - and not only is it a wonderful outing for families, but it is weatherproof too. The million year-old limestone cave is a treasure trove of dramatically-lit stalactites and stalagmites and, regardless of age, a visit to see these would be enough on its own. However, the Cave Centre has been ingeniously developed to offer much more, including an impressive children's indoor adventure centre, a large gift shop – and a very pleasant restaurant offering good home cooking in attractive surroundings. Closed Mon & Tue in Jan & Feb. **Directions:** Crag Cave is located 2km outside Castleisland town just off the N21.

DINGLE PENINSULA - ANNASCAUL & CASTLEGREGORY

The Dingle Peninsula, dividing the bays of Tralee and Dingle, is one of the most popular leisure destinations in Ireland for both visitors and residents, who enjoy it for many reason including the rugged scenery, history, away from it all atmosphere, outdoor activities, music and good accommodation, food and drink - and, despite its remote location, it is an all-year destination. The area is particularly good for walking, hill walking and diving and dolphin watching (see Dingle Town, below). **Annascaul** on the southern side of the peninsula is a much-photographed village and features on many postcards and travel guides. It was also the birthplace of the Antarctic explorer Tom Crean, who was part of Robert Scott's ill-fated attempts to reach the South Pole; **The South Pole Inn** (066 915 7388; www.south-poleinn.ie) at the lower end of the street is named in honour of Crean and his connections with the great Irish explorer Sir Ernest Shackleton. On retiring in 1920, Crean returned to Annascaul, married and ran the South Pole Inn with his wife; today, it is a delightful, well-run pub, full of fascinating Shackleton and Crean memorabilia, and there is a statue in honour of Annascaul's most famous son in the centre of the village. **Castlegregory** is directly across from Annascaul, on the northern side of the Dingle Peninsula; it is the only real village in a large and unspoilt area, which gives it special appeal to those who prefer a quiet destination, especially outside the main holiday season. North of Castlegregory, **The Maharees Peninsula** is famous for its long sandy beaches and clean water, making it popular for family holidays, and there is a group of islands off the peninsula, known simply as "The Maharees". Activities offered in the area (bookable through Castlegregory Visitor Centre, 066 7139422) include golf, horseriding, cycling, fishing, windsurfing and, especially, diving. Waterworld dive centre is located at Pat & Ronnie Fitzgibbon's **Harbour House Guesthouse & Islands Restaurant** (066 713 9292; www.maharees.ie) at Scraggane Pier; they run diving courses (and their facilities include a swimming pool) and, aside from offering comfortable accommodation (8 rooms), this is a useful place to know about when touring as the restaurant is open to non-residents and they are usually open for lunch as well as dinner (a phone call is advised). Further west, underneath Mount Brandon and shortly before the road runs out at Brandon Point, **Mullallys Bar** (066 7138154), in the hamlet of Brandon, is as pleasant a traditional pub as you'll find anywhere, neat as a new pin and with a welcoming fire and good food offered.

WWW.IRELAND-GUIDE.COM FOR ALL THE BEST PLACES TO EAT, DRINK & STAY

DINGLE PENINSULA:
Dingle Town / Ventry / Slea Head Areas

The main town in Kerry's most northerly peninsula, Dingle is a lively all-year destination renowned for its music, crafts, fishing and, for over twenty years, for its most famous inhabitant, Funghie the friendly dolphin who is the area's best-loved resident and shows every sign of enjoying the attention of the many visitors who go out by boat from the harbour every day to watch him. This Gaeltacht (Irish-speaking area) is of great historical interest, and there are many ancient remains, especially in the Ventry / Slea Head / Ballyferriter / Ballydavid area west of the town. In Dingle Town, **Goat Street Café** (066 915 2770), on the main street, does lovely zesty food, including delicious sandwiches (also to take away), and **Global Village** (066 915 2325) on Main Street offers daily-changed menus cooked by proprietor-chef Martin Bealin. West of Dingle on the Slea Head Drive: **The Stone House** (066 9159970) is a restaurant inspired by the nearby Gallarus Oratory; this extraordinary grey building even has a stone roof – and, fortunately for the hungry visitor, good food too; opening hours vary, so a phone call is advised. Near Smerwick Harbour, and on the Kerry Way walking route, **Tig Bhric** (066 915 6325; www.tigbhric.com) is beside the early Christian monastic settlement Riasc (7 miles west of Dingle); it's a delightful bar, B&B and shop offering lovely home-made soups and sandwiches in the daytime, and dinner every evening except Friday - when there is traditional music. Nearby, the **Smerwick Harbour Hotel** (066 915 6470; www.smerwickhotel.com) offers all the usual facilities and makes an unusual conference venue. **Tig Áine** (Tel: 066 9156214; www.tigaine.com) in Ballyferriter overlooks Clogher Strand and offers good food, pleasant service and the most spectacular views.

WWW.IRELAND-GUIDE.COM FOR ALL THE BEST PLACES TO EAT, DRINK & STAY

Dingle
BAR•RESTAURANT WITH ROOMS

Ashe's Seafood Bar
Main Street Dingle Co Kerry **Tel: 066 915 0989**
ashesbar@eircom.net www.ashesseafoodbar.com

This old pub in the centre of Dingle has a smart traditional frontage, and lots of warm mahogany that makes for a warm and cosy feeling in the friendly bar. The pub goes back to 1849, and is now owned by Sean Roche and Anna Scanlon, who specialise in seafood. Lobster, langoustine (Dublin Bay prawns) and scallops are among the treats, but they also offer a wide range of other fish and seafood, and some appealing choices for non-fish eaters, including homely traditional dishes like braised shank of lamb. Lunch menus focus on lighter dishes, many of them seafood – a range of salads, for example, may include prawns or seared squid, there's a seafood chowder, of course, and perhaps Thai-style mussels and warm grilled oysters; main courses have less emphasis on seafood, although you may find a (pricey) treat like seared scallops alongside traditional stews (Irish lamb or beef & Guinness) and ever-popular chicken Caesar salad. Evening menus are more extensive, offering seven seafood dishes, with more of the luxurious choices (lobster is good value at €25 per 500g), and some prime meats. An early evening menu offers great value, and separate vegetarian and children's menus are offered too. Good cooking, great staff and a relaxed atmosphere make this an excellent choice for informal dining. A compact and contemporary wine list includes five house wines, also available by the glass. **Seats 52**; toilets wheelchair accessible; children welcome (high chair, children's menu, baby changing facilities). L&D Mon-Sat, 12-3 & 6-9; Sun D only in Jul-Aug; à la carte L&D; early 2/3 course D €21.50/27.50, 6-7pm; house wine €19.50. Closed Sun (Sept-Jun), 25 Dec, Good Fri. MasterCard, Visa, Laser. **Directions:** Lower Main Street, Dingle.

Dingle
GUESTHOUSE

Bambury's Guesthouse

Mail Road Dingle Co Kerry **Tel: 066 915 1244**
info@bamburysguesthouse.com www.bamburysguesthouse.com

Just a couple of minutes walk from the centre of Dingle, Jimmy and Bernie Bambury's well-run, purpose-built guesthouse has spacious modern rooms with tea/coffee trays, phone, satellite TV, hair dryer and complimentary mineral water. Bernie Bambury's breakfasts include griddle cakes with fresh fruit and honey a house speciality and vegetarian breakfasts are offered by arrangement. **Rooms 12** (all shower only & no smoking, 1 family, 3 ground floor); not suitable for children under 4; no pets. B&B €60, ss €20. Own parking. Open all year. MasterCard, Visa, Laser. **Directions:** On N86, on the left after the Shell garage, on entering Dingle.

Dingle
GUESTHOUSE

Castlewood House

The Wood Dingle Co Kerry **Tel: 066 915 2788**
castlewoodhouse@eircom.net www.castlewooddingle.com

This luxurious new purpose-built guesthouse on the western edge of Dingle town is run by Brian and Helen Heaton - Brian's parents, Nuala and Cameron, run the well-established Heaton's guesthouse next door and a little gate connects the two. Although it is on the land side of the road, the house is built on a rise and, from the many rooms with sea views, all you are aware of is the view across Dingle Bay. The scale is generous throughout: public rooms include an impressive dining room where a good breakfast is served, and a drawing room with views across the bay for guests' use. Guest rooms are spacious and individually decorated to a very high standard, with smart bathrooms and a lot of attention to detail. **Rooms 12** (2 junior suites, 3 family, 1 for disabled, 4 ground floor, all no smoking); children welcome (under 2 free in parents' room, cots available free of charge). Lift. Limited room service. B&B €65 pps, ss €21. Free broadband wi/fi; masseuse. Closed Dec-mid Feb (open few days over New Years day). MasterCard, Visa, Laser. **Directions:** Take Milltown road from Dingle, located around 500m from town centre on the right.

Dingle
RESTAURANT

The Chart House

The Mall Dingle Co Kerry **Tel: 066 915 2255**
charthse@iol.ie www.charthousedingle.com

Jim McCarthy's attractive stone-built restaurant has been one of Dingle's favourite dining destinations for over a decade. Right from the time of opening, in 1997, they set the bar high and - even in an area so well-endowed with good eating places - their well-earned reputation consistently holds good. There's a smart little bar just inside the door - where Jim, ever the perfect host, always seems to be meeting, seating and seamlessly ensuring that everyone is well looked after and generally having a good time. And head chef Noel Enright has led the talented kitchen team for over five years: his menus are steadfastly based on the best of fully traceable local ingredients, sometimes in dishes with an international tone. A superb speciality starter of Annascaul black pudding, for example, is wrapped in filo pastry and served with apple and date chutney and hollandaise sauce; other dishes are just gently updated – another favourite dish is rack of Kerry mountain lamb, which may be simply accompanied by a fondant potato, and redcurrant & rosemary jus; accurate, confident cooking lends these traditional foods a special character, and a large selection - perhaps half a dozen or more - of simple, perfectly cooked side vegetables are the ideal complement. Seafood is well represented, of course, and mainstream vegetarian dishes have wide appeal, but it tends to be the meat dishes that stay in the memory. Desserts include classics like a basket of home-made ice creams, or luscious lemon-scented pannacotta. But those with a savoury tooth will still feel that the smart money is on the Irish cheeses, which are cannily offered with a glass of vintage port and served with delicious home-made oat biscuits and two varieties of grapes. Terrific hospitality, top class ingredients and gimmick-free creative cooking all add up to a great restaurant, which is also moderately priced. An interesting wine list includes South African wines imported directly, and has helpful tasting notes as well as a clear layout of country of origin and vintages - and, of course, there's always a Chateau MacCarthy in stock. *Jim McCarthy was our Host of the Year in 2003 and The Chart House won the Féile Bia Award, in association with Bord Bia, in 2008. **Seats 45**; toilets wheelchair accessible; children welcome; air conditioning. D 6.30-10, daily in summer (Jun-Sep), restricted opening in winter - please phone ahead to check; all evening value D €35, also à la carte. SC discretionary. House wine €19.50. Closed 6 Jan-13 Feb. MasterCard, Visa, Laser. **Directions:** Left at the roundabout as you enter the town.

Dingle
HOTEL

Dingle Benners Hotel

Main Street Dingle Co Kerry **Tel: 066 915 1638**
info@dinglebenners.com www.dinglebenners.com

This 300-year old centrally-located hotel makes a very comfortable base within easy walking distance of the whole of Dingle town. Public areas include the streetside Mrs Benners Bar which has a welcoming fire and a lot more personality than would be expected of an hotel (food available from 12 noon daily), and a large, bright, dining room, where breakfast is served. Bedrooms in the older part of the hotel have a lot of character (some have four-posters) but the spacious newer bedrooms at the back of the hotel are quieter, and convenient to the car park at the rear. Banqueting (100); **Rooms 52** (33 superior, 9 no smoking, 4 suitable for less able guests); children welcome (under 3 free in parents' room, cot available without charge, baby sitting arranged). No pets. Lift. B&B €107 pps, ss €25. Golf nearby. Private parking (50). *Short breaks offer good value - details on application. Closed 20-26 Dec. Amex, Diners, MasterCard, Visa, Laser. **Directions:** Town centre, half way up Main Street on left beside Bank of Ireland.

Dingle
HOTEL

Dingle Skellig Hotel

Dingle Co Kerry **Tel: 066 915 0200**
reservations@dingleskellig.com www.dingleskellig.com

It may be modest-looking from the road, but this 1960s' hotel enjoys a superb shoreside location on the edge of the town and has won many friends over the years. It is a well-run, family-friendly hotel, with organised entertainment for children - and an attractive feature of the hotel is their policy of dedicating floors for family use to avoid disturbing those without children. There is a good leisure centre, also a health and beauty centre, the Peninsula Spa. Public areas in the hotel are roomy and comfortably furnished with some style - and

good use is made of sea views throughout. Constant improvement and refurbishment has always been the policy here and, while there are still some standard bedrooms, there are now more executive rooms and junior suites. Although best known as a family holiday destination, the Dingle Skellig also has good conference and business meeting facilities. Golf nearby. *Dingle Skellig Hotel was the winner of our Family Friendly Hotel Award in 2007. Conference/banqueting (250/230); video conferencing by arrangement; broadband wi/fi. Children welcome (under 3s free in parents' room; cots available free of charge, baby sitting arranged; crèche, playroom, children's playground). Garden, fishing, leisure centre, swimming pool, spa. [*Dingle Benner's Hotel (see entry) is in the same ownership.] **Rooms 111** (8 suites, 5 junior suites, 28 executive, 31 ground floor, 1 for disabled, 1 shower only, 76 no-smoking). Lift; 24-hr room service. B&B €125, ss €20. **Coastguard Restaurant:** Attractively located on the sea side of the hotel, this recently refurbished restaurant is in a large conservatory area and, while not a fine dining destination to compare with some restaurants in this exceptionally well-endowed town, you may be sure of a pleasant dining experience here - there is a commitment to using fresh local ingredients and the cooking is sound; there's always local seafood, but well-balanced menus offer plenty of choice for everyone, and friendly, solicitous staff do everything possible to ensure that all is well. NB: Parents wishing to eat in the main restaurant with children should inquire about available times for family dining. D daily in summer, 7-9; set 2/3 course D, €38.50/45. Bar meals also available, 12.30-9pm. *Short breaks (e.g. golf, spa, off-season) offer good value; details on application. Self-catering also available, in the hotel's Dingle Marina Cottages. Hotel open weekends only in winter (Nov-mid Feb); closed 17-27 Dec. Amex, Diners, MasterCard, Visa, Laser. **Directions:** On the sea side of the road as you approach Dingle from Tralee & Killarney.

Dingle
GUESTHOUSE

Greenmount House

Upper John Street Dingle Co Kerry **Tel: 066 915 1414**
info@greenmounthouse.ie www.greenmounthouse.ie

Just five minutes walk from the centre of Dingle, John and Mary Curran have run one of Ireland's finest guesthouses since the mid-70s. It's an exceptionally comfortable place to stay, quietly located on the hillside, with private parking and uninterrupted views across the town and harbour to the mountains across the bay. The spacious, well-appointed bedrooms are mainly junior suites, with generous seating areas and particularly good amenities, including fridges as well as tea/coffee-making trays, phone and TV (and, in most cases, also their own entrance and balcony); all bathrooms have recently been upgraded and a hot tub installed. The older part of the house was demolished in 2006 and has since been rebuilt to provide five new superior rooms, which have been completed to a predictably high standard, adding further to the appeal of this outstanding guesthouse. There's also a comfortable residents' sitting room with an open fire, and a conservatory overlooking the harbour, where wonderful breakfasts are served. Greenmount won our Irish Breakfast Award for the Munster region in 2001, and it has always been a point of pride: the aroma of home baking is one of the things that gives this house a special warmth, and all the preserves are home-made too; there's a wonderful buffet - laden down with all kinds of fresh and poached fruits, juices, yogurts, cheeses, freshly baked breads - as well as an extensive choice of hot dishes, including the traditional full Irish breakfast. The wonder is that anyone ever leaves this place of a morning at all. **Rooms 14** (10 junior suites, 3 shower only, 2 ground floor, all no smoking); children welcome (cot available free of charge, baby sitting arranged); free broadband wi/fi; no pets; B&B €85pps, ss €45. Garden, walking. Parking (15). SC discretionary. Closed Dec. MasterCard, Visa, Laser. **Directions:** Turn right and right again on entering Dingle.

Dingle
RESTAURANT

The Half Door

John Street Dingle Co Kerry **Tel: 066 915 1600**
halfdoor@iol.ie

Denis and Teresa O'Connor's cottagey restaurant is one of the prettiest and consistently popular in town, and well-known for great seafood. Menus go with the seasons but whatever is available is perfectly cooked and generously served without over-presentation. An outstanding speciality of the house is the seafood platter, available hot or cold as either a starter or main course with (depending on availability of individual items) lobster, oysters, mussels, Dublin Bay prawns, scallops, crab claws and all attractively presented and served with garlic or lemon butter. Good traditional puddings or Irish farmhouse cheeses to follow. **Seats 50**. Air conditioning. D Mon-Sat, 5.30-10. Early D 6-6.30 only; later, à la carte. Closed Sun; Christmas. MasterCard, Visa. **Directions:** On entering Dingle, turn right onto The Mall at roundabout, then right onto John Street.

Dingle
GUESTHOUSE

Heatons House

The Wood Dingle Co Kerry **Tel: 066 915 2288**
heatons@iol.ie www.heatonsdingle.com

Cameron and Nuala Heaton's fine purpose-built guesthouse is set in well-maintained gardens just across the road from the water and, although convenient to the town, it's beyond the hustle and bustle of the busy streets. An impressive foyer-lounge area sets the tone on arrival and spacious, bedrooms confirm first impressions: not so much regularly refurbished as completely redesigned, they all have bathrooms finished to a very high standard and phones, TV and hospitality trays - and the junior suites and superior rooms are not only luxurious, but also very stylish. Getting guests off to a good start each day is a point of honour, and breakfast includes an extensive buffet (everything from fresh juices to cold meats and Irish cheeses) as well as a full hot breakfast menu. *See also Castlewood House, which is in the same family ownership. **Rooms 16** (2 junior suites, 5 superior, 2 family rooms, 5 ground floor, 1 for disabled, all no smoking); not suitable for children under 8; free broadband wi/fi. No pets. B&B €69 pps, ss €32. Room service (limited hours). Fishing, walking, garden. Closed 1 Dec-26 Dec. MasterCard, Visa, Laser. **Directions:** 600 metres beyond marina, at front of town.

Dingle
BAR•RESTAURANT

Lord Baker's Restaurant & Bar

Dingle Co Kerry **Tel: 066 915 1277**
info@lordbakers.ie www.lordbakers.ie

HOST OF THE YEAR AWARD

Believed to be the oldest pub in Dingle, this business was established in 1890 by a Tom Baker. A popular businessman in the area, a colourful orator, member of Kerry County Council and a director of the Tralee-Dingle Railway, he was known locally as "Lord Baker" and as such is now immortalised in John Moriarty's excellent bar and restaurant in the centre of Dingle. Tables are set up in front of a welcoming turf fire in the front bar, where speciality dishes include a very good chowder with home-baked soda bread, and crab claws in garlic butter - and, at the back, there's a more formal dining set-up in the restaurant proper (and, beyond it, a walled garden). Seafood (notably lobster from their own tank) stars, of course, along with main courses like monkfish wrapped in bacon, with garlic cream sauce, and pan-fried sole on the bone with lemon butter; but there's also a good choice of other dishes using local mountain lamb (roast rack or braised shank, perhaps), also Kerry beef, chicken, and local duckling, all well-cooked and served in an atmosphere of great hospitality. In addition to the main menu, there are chef's specials each evening - and an unusual house speciality often features on the dessert menu: traditional plum pudding with brandy sauce! Sunday lunch in the restaurant is a particularly popular event and very well done (booking strongly advised); on other days, the lunchtime bar menu, plus one or two daily specials such as a roast, can be taken in the restaurant. An informative wine list includes a Connoisseur's Selection of ten wines. John is an excellent host, caring and watchful - no detail escapes his notice, ensuring that every guest in Dingle's largest restaurant will leave contented. **Seats 120**; children welcome. L Fri-Wed, 12.30-2; D Fri-Wed, 6-10. Early set D €26, 6-7pm, also à la carte; light lunch around €10. House wine about €22. Rest. closed Thurs, house closed 24-26 Dec. Amex, MasterCard, Visa, Laser. **Directions:** Town centre.

Dingle
GUESTHOUSE

Milltown House

Dingle Co Kerry **Tel: 066 915 1372**
info@milltownhousedingle.com www.milltownhousedingle.com

Set in immaculate gardens running down to the water's edge and with beautiful views of the harbour and distant mountains, the Kerry family's attractive guesthouse on the western side of Dingle enjoys the best location in the town. Day rooms include an informal reception room, a comfortably furnished sitting room and a conservatory breakfast room overlooking the garden - breakfast is quite an event, offering everything from fresh juices and fruit, through cold meats and cheeses, freshly baked breads and an extensive cooked breakfast menu. The bedrooms - all very comfortable and thoughtfully furnished with phone, TV with video channel, tea/coffee making facilities and iron/trouser press - include two with private patios. Constant upgrading is the policy here: a number of rooms have recently been increased in size and a new lounge, with sea and mountain views, was added to the front of the house. **Rooms 10** (6 junior suites, all with full bath en-suite, all no smoking, 3 ground floor); not suitable for children under 10. No pets. Garden. B&B €80 pps, ss €50. Room service (limited hours). Closed 28 Oct-27 Apr. Amex, MasterCard, Visa, Laser. **Directions:** West through Dingle town, 0.75 miles from town centre.

Dingle
CAFÉ

Murphys Ice Cream & Café

Strand Street Dingle Co Kerry **Tel: 066 915 2644**
dingle@murphysicecream.ie www.murphysicecream.ie

Many would make the trek to Dingle solely for the pleasure of tucking into one of the treats on offer at this cheerful blue and white fronted café down near the harbour. The Murphy brothers, Kieran and Séan, have been making ice cream with fresh Kerry milk and cream here since 2000 and have earned a national reputation in the meantime - now they supply a network of discerning restaurants and specialist outlets around the country and have a second café in Killarney. The café is unusual in that it only offers coffees and ice cream (the range of flavours is growing all the time), scooped in time-honoured fashion from a freezer cabinet in the shop and available in little tubs to take away if you like; also milk shakes and and ice cream desserts (sundaes, banana split). The only exception to this rule is German baker Wiebke Murphy's collection of superb utterly irresistible gateaux, which are displayed in a cabinet and would be very difficult to ignore. There's also a Murphy's Ice Cream Cake, the perfect party piece, and some of the Murphy's own favourite chocolates.* Kieran and Séan Murphy have recently published their 'Book of Sweet Things', available from the cafés and bookshops. **Seats 25** (outdoors, 8); toilets wheelchair accessible; children welcome. Open 7 days a week - high season, 11-10pm; low season, 11-6.30pm. No credit cards. **Directions:** In town centre.

Dingle
B&B

Number Fifty Five

55 John Street Dingle Co Kerry **Tel: 066 915 2378**
stelladoyledingle@gmail.com www.stelladoyle.com

Stella Doyle's charming B&B in the centre of Dingle offers accommodation with character - and a high level of comfort at a very affordable price. Although the frontage seems small from the road, it is larger than it looks: the two guest bedrooms are on the ground floor and delightfully furnished in a fresh country house style, with television and full bathrooms (bath and power shower). But there is a surprise in store when you go upstairs to the first floor and find a light and spacious open plan living room, which has great style and, like the rest of the house, is furnished with antiques and original art. There's a large seating area at one end and, at the other, a dining area with large windows looking out to fields at the back of the house; here Stella, who spent most of her working life as a chef, serves delicious breakfasts for guests; no menu - 'anything you like, really'. Guests are welcomed to this hospitable haven with a cup of tea on arrival - and breakfast is sure to send them happily on their way. **Rooms 2** (both en-suite with full bath & no smoking); not suitable for children. No pets. B&B €37.50 pps, ss €17.50. Closed 30 Sep-mid Apr. **No Credit Cards.** **Directions:** At main road roundabout, turn right up the mall; turn right up John Street - the house is at the top on the left side.

Dingle
RESTAURANT

Out of the Blue

Waterside Dingle Co Kerry **Tel: 066 915 0811**
timmason@eircom.net www.outoftheblue.ie

Tim Mason's deli and seafood restaurant is an absolute delight. Discerning locals know how lucky they are to have such an exciting little place on their doorstep and it's just the kind of place that visitors dream of finding - it is not unusual to find a different language spoken at every table. You can't miss the brightly-painted exterior from the road, an attractive decked area encloses the outside seating area and, once you get inside, it is obvious that this is a highly focused operation, where only the best will do: there's a little wine bar at the front and, in the simple room at the back (slightly extended recently, which makes it much more comfortable), seriously delicious seafood cookery is the order of the day for those lucky enough to get a table. Everything depends on the fresh fish supply from the boats that day and if there's no fresh fish, they don't open. Head chef Seamus MacDonald changes the menu every lunch and dinner time and cooks wonderful classics, sometimes with a modern twist - examples might include starters like squid flash-fried in garlic butter or smoked mackerel fillet with balsamic & shallot vinaigrette and potato salad and mains ranging from homely dishes such as pollock in a potato crust with chive cream to treats like pan-seared scallops flambéed in calvados and served with apple compôte. At €39 per kilo, lobster has got very expensive here, but there is plenty else to choose from. A short but skilfully assembled wine list - largely sourced by restaurant manager Irene Grobbelaar and Tim's brother, Ben Mason, of the Wicklow Wine Company, complements the food perfectly, and you will find a dozen fish named in five languages on the back: this place is a little gem. *Tim has plans to move to a new location at some stage - watch www.ireland-guide.com for details. **Seats 34** (+ 24 outdoors); children welcome before 8pm; air conditioning. L & D Thu-Tue, L 12.30-3pm, D 6.30-9.30pm (Sun 6-8.30). Reservations accepted (required for D). A la carte. House wines from €18. Closed Wed ('usually'), also days when fresh fish is unavailable & mid Nov-mid Mar. MasterCard, Visa, Laser. **Directions:** Opposite the pier on Dingle harbour.

Dingle
GUESTHOUSE

Pax House

Upper John Street Dingle Co Kerry **Tel: 066 915 1518**
paxhouse@iol.ie   www.pax-house.com

Just half a mile out of Dingle, this modern house enjoys what may well be the finest view in the area, and it is also one of the most comfortable and relaxing places to stay. John O'Farrell took over as proprietor in 2007 and, although no major changes were necessary, he has re-decorated throughout. Thoughtfully furnished bedrooms have every amenity, including a fridge and safe, and most of the well-finished bathrooms have full bath; two suites have their own terraces where guests can lounge around and enjoy that stupendous view – and there's a cosy sitting room with a fire for guests' use too. Breakfast is an enjoyable event with lots of home-made goodies; it is served in a bright and airy dining room overlooking the bay – and with a terrace outside for fine weather – where you can watch the free-range chickens that supplied the eggs for breakfast strutting their stuff. No dinners are offered at the time of going to press but that may change – and, meanwhile, the restaurants of Dingle are only a short distance away. **Rooms 13** (3 superior, 5 shower only, 1 family room, 6 ground floor, all no-smoking); children welcome (under 3s free in parents room, cots available at no charge). Pets permitted by arrangement. B&B €60-80 pps, €30 ss. Wine licence. Garden, walking. Closed 1 Nov-1Apr. MasterCard, Visa, Laser. **Directions:** Turn off at sign on N86. ◊

Dingle Area
RESTAURANT•GUESTHOUSE

Gorman's Clifftop House & Restaurant

Glaise Bheag Ballydavid Dingle Peninsula Co Kerry
Tel: 066 915 5162

info@gormans-clifftophouse.com   www.gormans-clifftophouse.com

Beautifully situated near Smerwick Harbour on the Slea Head scenic drive and Dingle Way walking route, Sile and Vincent Gorman's guesthouse is, as they say themselves "just a great place to relax and unwind". Natural materials and warm colours are a feature throughout the house, and open fires create a welcoming laid-back atmosphere. The bedrooms – which include some on the ground floor, with easy access from the parking area - all have sea or mountain views and are attractively furnished in a pleasingly simple style with thoughtfully finished bathrooms; four superior rooms have jacuzzi baths and other extra facilities, but all are very comfortable. The Gormans are knowledgeable and helpful hosts too, advising guests on everything they need to know in the area – all guests get the loan of a guide book and ordnance survey map during their stay. Breakfast - an excellent buffet with hot dishes cooked to order - is a treat that will set you up for the day. *Gorman's was our Guesthouse of the Year in 2002. Children welcome (under 3s free in parents' room, cot available free of charge). No pets. Garden, cycling, walking. **Rooms 9** (2 junior suites, 2 superior, 1 for less able, 1 shower only, all no smoking). B&B €75-85 pps, ss €35. Short breaks offered - details on application. **Restaurant:** With large windows commanding superb sea views, this is a wonderful place to enjoy Vincent Gorman's good cooking. Begin with a warm Dingle Bay prawn salad with fresh basil, perhaps - or an attractive speciality of potato cake & Annascaul black pudding with glazed apples, and grainy mustard sauce. Main courses include several seafood dishes (roast fillet of monkfish with roasted peppers, balsamic vinegar & olive oil dressing is a speciality) and the ever-popular sirloin steak (Irish Hereford beef); vegetarian choices are always given too, Sile's garden salad, perhaps, of tossed leaves and summer vegetables with toasted walnuts and seeds (their own organic garden is under development – quite an achievement in this location). Desserts, including home-made ice creams and a wicked chocolate nemesis, are a strong point too, or you can finish with an Irish cheese plate. Sile, who is a warm and solicitous host, supervises front of house. An interesting and informative wine list offers plenty of good choices for all pockets and includes Fair Trade house wines and about eight well-chosen half bottles; there is also a Summer Special Drinks List. *Visitors exploring the area will be glad to know that Gormans is now offering an à la carte menu from 12 noon every day in summer. **Seats 35**. Food served daily, 12-9pm. D daily, 7-9pm. Set D €32.50/39.50; gourmet menu €49.50. House wine from €20. House open Oct-Mar by reservation only; Closed 1 Jan-10 Feb. MasterCard, Visa, Laser. **Directions:** 12.5km (8 m) from roundabout west of Dingle Town - sign posted An Fheothanach. Keep left at V.

Dingle Area   The Old Pier
RESTAURANT•GUESTHOUSE   An Fheothanach Ballydavid Dingle Co Kerry
                              Tel: 066 915 5242 info@oldpier.com www.oldpier.com

Situated on the edge of the world overlooking the Atlantic and the Blasket Islands, Padraig and Jacquie O'Connor's friendly restaurant is extremely popular – and no wonder. Padraig has access to the very freshest of fish and seafood and his extensive menus may include lobster, black sole, and prawns (langoustine) when available, and all at very fair prices. There's a house 'Smerwick Harbour' chowder, mixed fish dishes based on the available catch – selection of seafood Mornay is a speciality - succulent bakes such as fresh cod in breadcrumbs and also good steaks and local lamb dishes, or roast duckling. Good cooking, together with generous portions, moderate prices and efficient, good-humoured service have all earned a following for this big-hearted restaurant. **Seats 40** (private room, 10, outdoors, 20); reservations required; D served Wed-Mon, 6-7.15pm; a la carte; house wine from €15.95. Restaurant closed Tue, Nov-Feb. **Accommodation:** The five pine-furnished en-suite rooms are offered in various combinations (single, twin, double, family) and have tea/coffee facilities, hair dryer and sea or mountain views. Special offers apply all year round. **Rooms 5** (1 family room, all en-suite, shower only and no smoking); children welcome (under 8s free in parents' rooms, cot available free of charge, baby sitting arranged, high chair, childrens menu); dogs permitted by arrangement (stay in bedrooms, no charge); limited room service. B&B €40-50 pps. *Two self-catering houses also available. MasterCard, Visa, Laser. **Directions:** 11.5km (8m) west of Dingle.

Fenit   The Tankard
BAR•RESTAURANT   Kilfenora Fenit Tralee Co Kerry **Tel: 066 713 6164**
                                                            tankard@eircom.net

Easily spotted on the seaward side of the road from Tralee, this bright yellow pub and restaurant has a great reputation, especially for seafood. An imaginative bar menu, which overlaps to some extent with the restaurant à la carte, is available from lunchtime to late evening, serving a good range of food. Seafood chowder with delicious hi-fibre home-made brown bread, salads like smoky 'Boxty' (smoked salmon with potato cake & salad), cold seafood dishes such as fresh crab and apple salad (a house speciality) and hot snacks including steamed mussels Tankard-style, plenty of non-seafood dishes too, including warm chicken salad, home-made burgers, pastas and sandwiches. **Restaurant:** Except on Sunday this is an evening restaurant, although lunch is available by arrangement. A phone call is always worthwhile to get the best of seafood cooking, which can be exceptional: the restaurant style is traditional, mainly classic French with Irish overtones. Simple well-cooked food, based on the finest local ingredients with excellent saucing and unfussy presentation give hardly a passing nod to fashion, which makes a refreshing change from the ubiquitous 'world cuisine'. Seafood is undoubtedly at the centre of the menu, much of it sourced through the owners' connections with the local fishing community, and the choices range from very simple monkfish to lobster and oysters. A good selection of other dishes is offered too, including duckling and lamb. There are sea and mountain views from the restaurant, which has a patio area and a path down to the sea. A very good wine list, well matched to the menu, completes the experience in this seafood-focused restaurant. **Seats 130**; toilets wheelchair accessible; children welcome (high chair, children's menu, baby changing facilities). D daily 6-10, L daily, 12-4. Set Sun L €22, D à la carte. House wines from about €18; sc discretionary *Bar meals daily, 2-10pm. Closed Good Fri. Amex, Diners, MasterCard, Visa, Laser. **Directions:** 8km from Tralee on Spa/Fenit road.

Fenit   West End Bar & Restaurant
PUB•RESTAURANT WITH ROOMS   Fenit Tralee Co Kerry **Tel: 066 713 6246**
                                                            westend@hotmail.com

The O'Keeffes have been in business here since 1885, and the present pub - which is exactly seven minutes walk from the marina - was built by chef Bryan O'Keeffe's grandmother, in 1925. Good food is available in both the cosy bar and the restaurant, which has earned a sound reputation in the area and includes an attractive conservatory dining area at the harbour end of the building. Bryan is a member of the Panel of Chefs of Ireland and his style is "classic French with Irish popular cuisine", with seafood and meats billed equally as specialities. Hand-written menus offer over a dozen starters ranging from Tralee Bay seafood chowder, to classic mussels 'Ernie Evans' style, and main courses also include old favourites - steaks, half roast duckling - and a very wide range of seafood dishes, leading off with lobster or grilled black (Dover) sole on the bone. Unpretentious, moderately priced accommodation is offered in ten en-suite rooms (B&B €35, no ss). Bar/restaurant Meals 5.30-10pm daily in season. A la carte; house wines from €19.50. Phone ahead to check food service off-season. Closed Jan-Mar. MasterCard, Visa, Laser. **Directions:** 11km (7 miles) from Tralee, well signposted.

KENMARE

Renowned for its fine restaurants and outstanding accommodation (the range and quality is exceptional for a town of its size), the Heritage Town of Kenmare (Neidín/'little nest') is pleasingly designed and ideally sized for comfortable browsing of its quality shops and galleries. It also has a full complement of characterful pubs, and makes an excellent base for exploring both south Kerry and the near parts of west Cork. At **Prego** (Henry Street, 064 42350), Gerry O'Shea's team offer a wide range of tasty dishes throughout the day beginning with a lovely breakfast menu; their formula using best local produce in simple, casual food with an Italian slant has been so successful that they've extended both menu and opening hours (now 9am-10.30pm in season) and opened a second restaurant, **Bácús** (see entry). Just across the bridge, the Arthur family's spacious country house **Sallyport House** (064 42066; www.sallyporthouse.com) is in a quiet and convenient location overlooking the harbour, with a garden and mountain views at the rear. A little further out, on the Castletownbere road, Peter & Amanda Mallinson offer comfortable, moderately priced accommodation at their Killaha East home, **Sheen View Guesthouse** (064 42817; www.sheenview.com). High up at the famous Moll's Gap viewing point on the Ring of Kerry, **Avoca Handweavers** (064 34720; www.avoca.ie) is an outpost of the County Wicklow weaving company, selling its fine range of clothing and crafts - and offering wholesome and appealing home-made fare with that amazing view, to sustain the weary sightseer (10-5 daily mid-Mar-mid-Nov). Kenmare Farmers' Market is held on Bridge Street, Wednesday-Sunday (10am - 6pm) and every day during July and August. For golfers, Kenmare Golf Club and Ring of Kerry are the closest but the nearest recommended championship golf courses are a little over 20km away - Killarney Golf & Fishing Club (Killarney, 064 663 1034) and Bantry Bay Golf Club (Bantry, 027 50579). The exceptional climate means that garden lovers are in for a treat in this area, with wonderfully exotic sub-tropical gardens to visit – Derreen Garden (064 83588) at Lauragh, off the Kenmare-Castletownbere road, is exceptional, and if you're doing the Ring of Kerry, it's worth allowing time to look at Glanleam Sub-Tropical Garden (066 947 6176; www.glanleam.com) on Valentia Island. Illnacullin on Garinish Island (027 63040) is a magnificent island garden combining formal and informal elements. For families, the Star Sailing & Adventure Centre (064 41222; www.staroutdoors.ie) is bit out of town at Dauros; it offers courses or just a good family day out all year round – and their first floor Con's Bar & Seafood Restaurant is open to everyone. Walking is particularly good in the Kenmare area, with Glen Inchaquin Park nearby and the both Kerry Way and the Beara Way in the wider area. It also has a very pretty harbour from where you can swim, fish or take boat trips on the Seafari (064 42059) to view the sea life in the area. There's a good Tourist Information Office on the square in Kenmare, and it's worth calling in to find out everything that's going on.
WWW.IRELAND-GUIDE.COM FOR ALL THE BEST PLACES TO EAT, DRINK & STAY

Kenmare
RESTAURANT

An Leath Phingin Eile
35 Main Street Kenmare Co Kerry **Tel: 064 41559**
www.leathphingineile.com

Eddie and Gaelen Malcolmson opened their lovely restaurant here in 2007, in the premises previously occupied by the veteran Kenmare restaurant An Leath Phingin, and it is now well established as one of the best restaurants in a town that has earned renown for the quality of its food and hospitality. The building has a lot going for it in terms of atmosphere - on two floors with lots of wood and open stone in view, it has a warm and welcoming feeling even on a wet night. The back room was changed to allow for more seating and the tables are close - but not too close for comfort, and friendly, well-briefed waiting staff work well under Gaelen's direction to make a visit here a real pleasure. Eddie is a fine classical chef in the modern European style, and his wide-ranging menus are the kind that make you want try everything. There's a balanced choice of eight equally desirable dishes on each course, based mainly on local ingredients and including produce from Billy Clifford's organic farm - char-grilled fillet of Irish Angus beef with peppered pommes frites, button mushrooms and red wine jus, is a favourite example. You'll find plenty of treats among the starters, including speciality dishes like a perfect twice-baked crab soufflé with hazelnut crust and a crab & tomato bisque, while main courses with a leaning towards seafood may include gently spiced pan-fried monkfish, with creamy coconut & coriander rice and a light curry cream. Classically delicious desserts might include home-made ices and sorbets, and perhaps a just-set vanilla pannacotta with fresh raspberries & confit orange zest - or there are farmhouse cheeses with home-made digestive biscuits (and, perhaps, a glass of LBV port). A carefully selected wine list includes eight interesting house wines (one of the reds is Massaya from Lebanon, another is Moillard organic pinot noir; and, unusually, there's a Spanish house rosé, Cristo Vega), offering excellent value at €19.50-30, and all available by the bottle, 1/2 litre or litre, and there are lovely dessert wines too. Prices are very fair, but a 2/3 course Value Menu at €24.95/29.95 is especially accessible. Consistently excellent cooking, lovely service and a good atmosphere make this restaurant stand out – everybody loves it. **Seats 40** (private room, 16); children welcome (high chair). D only Wed-Mon, 6-10. A la carte; also early value 2/3 course D €24.95/29.95 daily except Sat. House wine from €19. Closed Mon & Tue; call ahead to check opening times off season. MasterCard, Visa, Laser. **Directions:** Town centre.

Kenmare   # Bácús Bistro

RESTAURANT   Main Street Kenmare Co Kerry **Tel: 064 48300**
                                                         www.bacuskenmare.com

In a small room along the 'restaurant mile' at the top of Main Street, this is a sister restaurant to Gerry O'Shea's popular Prego on Henry Street. It's open all day and is equally known for good casual food through the day, including excellent breakfasts, and for bistro-style evening meals, when you will find tempting house specialities such as bouillabaisse and steak frites on the menu. As at Prego, fresh, local and organic ingredients are the starting point for everything they do and the cooking is good; its popularity is simply explained: generous food, well served in a good atmosphere and very keenly priced. What more could you want? **Seats 36** (outdoors, 8); children welcome; toilets wheelchair accessible. Food served daily, all day, 9am-10pm; L 12-4, D 6-10pm; à la carte; house wine €16.95. Amex, MasterCard, Visa, Laser. **Directions:** Top of Main Street Kenmare, on left hand side.

Kenmare   # Brook Lane Hotel

HOTEL   Kenmare Co Kerry **Tel: 064 42077**
                               info@brooklanehotel.com www.brooklanehotel.com

Situated just outside Kenmare on the Ring of Kerry Road (take the turn off for Sneem), this smart boutique hotel is sleek and modern, offering all the flair and comfort of a custom-built hotel but with the service and intimacy of the very best kind of B&B. Public areas include the smart-casual Casey's Bar and a restaurant, The Bistro, open for dinner and Sunday lunch. The stylish and very comfortable bedrooms are decorated in soothing warm neutrals in a clean and contemporary style, and business guests will find plenty of workspace. Treatment rooms, 'Me Time', have recently opened and make a very nice addition to the hotel. Brook Lane offers comfort, excellent service, and great value for money - so booking well in advance is advised. *Brook Lane Hotel has become known for traditional Irish music, details on application. Conferences/Banqueting (50/100), secretarial services, free broadband wi/fi. **Rooms 20** (1 junior suite, 8 executive, 2 family rooms, 9 ground floor, 1 for disabled, all no smoking); children welcome (under 4s free in parents' room, cots available free of charge, baby sitting arranged); 24 hr room service; air conditioning; Lift; B&B about €80 pps, ss €25. Special/off-season offers available. Casey's Bar & Bistro: meals 12.30-9.30 daily; live music in bar at certain times. Restaurant D 6-9.30 daily, L Sun only 12.30-3.30. Cycling, equestrian, fly fishing, sea angling, garden visits and golf all nearby. Closed 24-26 Dec. MasterCard, Visa, Laser. **Directions:** A short walk from the centre of town.

Kenmare   # D'Arcy's Oyster Bar & Grill

RESTAURANT   Main Street Kenmare Co Kerry **Tel: 064 41589**
                                 keatingrestaurants@ownmail.net www.darcys.ie

Situated at the top of Main Street opposite the Landsdowne Hotel, this well known restaurant was previously a bank and is now owned by John and Georgina Keating, who specialise

in local seafood, particularly oysters. A bank interior always lends gravitas and, with timeless jazz, understated décor and crisp white linen, it provides a pleasingly neutral setting. A new head chef, Wayne Seberry, took over the kitchen at D'Arcy's in the summer of 2008 and, although the Guide's visit was made prior to his arrival, it is clear that this confident young man is determined to put both himself and D'Arcy's on the Irish culinary map. Following UK experience with several top chefs, he has come to Kenmare via such esteemed kitchens as Paul Flynn's Dungarvan restaurant The Tannery and, most recently, the iconic Nick's Seafood Restaurant in Killorglin (see entries), so the scene seems to be set for a great dining experience - and, especially, a great seafood experience - here in the coming seasons. The service at D'Arcy's is very professional, and the well laid out seasonal menus are promptly presented, offering a wide range of oyster dishes, also other fish and seafood - including treats like lobster and black sole - some prime meats such as rack of Kerry lamb and rib-eye steak, and vegetarian dishes too. Desserts tend towards the classic - summer pudding, crème brulée, hot chocolate fondant. Aside from general expertise in the kitchen which makes for a special all-round experience, the offering at D'Arcy's is different from other restaurants as its focus on oysters is interesting. **Seats 60**; restaurant not suitable for children under 7. Serving food Tue-Sun 12-10 May-Sept, Thu-Sun 6-10 Oct-Apr; à la carte. House wine €19.50; sc discretionary. Closed Mon in summer, Mon-Wed Oct-Apr & mid Jan - mid Feb. Amex, MasterCard, Visa, Laser. **Directions:** Top of Main Street on left.

Kenmare   The Horseshoe
BAR•RESTAURANT   3 Main Street Kenmare Co Kerry **Tel: 064 41553**
thehorseshoe@eircom.net

Everyone loves the atmosphere at this pleasingly old-fashioned bar and restaurant at the bottom of Main Street; it is a cosy place and has always been known for unpretentious and wholesome good food, served in the informal oil-cloth-tabled restaurant at the back, with an open fire and original cattle stall divisions. You'll find pleasing meals of steaks, rump of lamb and prime fish, including black sole, and all sauces used are fresh and home-made. This cosy bar is especially attractive when visiting out of season, and it's open all year. **Seats 35**; children welcome before 10pm; air conditioning. Open for L & D daily, 12.30-2.30pm & 5-10pm; à la carte; sc 12.5% on groups 10+. Open all year. MasterCard, Visa, Laser. **Directions:** Centre of Kenmare.

Kenmare   Jam
CAFÉ   6 Henry St Kenmare Co Kerry **Tel: 064 41591**
    info@jam.ie   www.jam.ie

James Mulchrone's delightful bakery and café has been a great success since the day it opened in March 2001 and, unlikely as this may seem in a town that has some of the best eating places in Ireland, it brought something new and very welcome. Affordable prices, friendly service and an in-house bakery have proved a winning combination; everything is made on the premises using the best of local produce and you can pop into the self-service café for a bite at any time all day. Lovely main course choices may include salmon & spinach baked in pastry with horseradish, and there's always a selection of quiches. If you're planning a day out, they have all you could want for a delicious picnic here, including a wide range of sandwiches and salads, terrines and all sorts of irresistible cakes and biscuits. The café menu changes daily and party platters and celebration cakes are made to order (48 hours' notice required for special orders). The stated aim is "to provide fresh, quality, imaginative food at affordable prices in nice surroundings"; this they are doing very well both here and at their Killarney branch. *Also at: Old Market Lane, Killarney (see entry). **Seats 55**; air conditioning. Open Mon-Sat, 8am-6pm; house wine €4.75 per glass. Closed Sun, 4 days Christmas. MasterCard, Visa, Laser. **Directions:** Lower Henry Street on the left.

Kenmare
RESTAURANT

Lime Tree Restaurant

Shelburne Street Kenmare Co Kerry **Tel: 064 41225**
limetree@limetreerestaurant.com www.limetreerestaurant.com

This atmospheric restaurant has been one of the most consistently popular dining choices in the area for over fifteen years, and has recently moved into a new phase with former head chef Gary Fitzgerald back in the kitchen and, together with restaurant manager Maria O'Sullivan, heading up a dynamic team. It's a landmark in the town - an attractive cut stone building built in 1832 and set well back from the road - and an open log fire, exposed stone walls, original wall panelling and a minstrels' gallery (which provides an upper eating area) all give character to the interior. And a contemporary art gallery on the first floor adds an extra dimension to a visit here - fine original artwork in the restaurant gives a hint of what may be for sale. A la carte menus have quite an international tone but you'll find plenty of local produce, especially among the starters – the House Salad, for instance, is an unusual dish with Sneem black pudding wontons, sliced potato, melon, shaved parmesan and maple dressing, and a tian of smoked salmon, shrimp and crab is made with freshwater shrimp and crab topped and tailed with Kenmare smoked salmon and served with cucumber carpaccio and an orange nut dressing. There's a little less emphasis on local seafood than might be expected - but that allows for a wider choice (including vegetarian dishes) and, among several fish dishes, an enduring speciality is a selection of seafood cooked 'en papillotte' with white wine, herb butter and julienne vegetables: when cut open at the table, the aromas released are delicious. Other main courses include imaginatively updated traditional combinations – popular supreme of chicken, for example, may come with sage & onion stuffing, bacon and peperonata and parsley pesto. Desserts tend to be tweaked classics (rhubarb tartlet topped with gingernut crumble, served with raspberry ice cream and vanilla custard, for example) and Munster cheeses are served with water biscuits & fig chutney. Service, under Maria's direction, is professional and relaxed; a user-friendly wine list is organised by style ('light, crisp and appealing', 'soft bodied and fruity'...) and includes some interesting bottles. And remember that it might be wise to budget a little extra for dinner here - you could be taking home a modern masterpiece; gallery open from 4pm. **Seats 60** (private room, 18); not suitable for children after 7 pm; toilet wheelchair accessible; air conditioning. D daily 6.30-10pm; à la carte (average main course about €23). House wine €20; sc discretionary. Closed-Nov-Mar. MasterCard, Visa, Laser. **Directions:** Top of town, next to Park Hotel.

Kenmare
GUESTHOUSE

The Lodge

Killowen Road Kenmare Co Kerry **Tel: 064 41512**
thelodgekenmare@eircom.net www.thelodgekenmare.com

Rosemarie Quill's large, purpose-built guesthouse is just 3 minutes walk from the centre of town, offers hotel-style accommodation in spacious rooms which have king size beds, everything you could possibly need - including controllable central heating, phone, TV, safe, iron/trouser press and tea/coffee facilities, as well as well-finished bathrooms - at guesthouse prices. There is also plenty of comfortable seating and even a bar. **Rooms 10** (all en-suite & no smoking; 4 ground floor, 1 disabled); children welcome (under 3 free in parents' room, cot available without charge); 24-hour room service. No pets. B&B from €50 pps, ss about €30. Garden. Closed Nov- Mar. MasterCard, Visa. **Directions:** Cork road, 150m from town opposite golf course.

Kenmare
RESTAURANT

Mulcahys Restaurant
36 Henry Street Kenmare Co Kerry
Tel: 064 42383

If you are ever tired of finding the same old dishes on every menu, just head for Kenmare and refresh your palate at Bruce Mulcahy's original and friendly contemporary restaurant. A light-filled room is spacious and stylish, with smart modern table settings, and delicious breads presented on a pretty little bamboo tray. Far from being yet another copy-cat chef playing with world cuisines, Bruce has gone to the source to learn his skills - he learned about fusion food in Thailand, for example, and studied the art of sushi making in Japan; but the secret of this restaurant's great success is that, although many dishes are highly unusual, exciting menus cater for conservative tastes as well as the adventurous palate. Choices offered may include adventurous starters such as sushi & sashimi, carpaccio of beef, or tempura of crab dumplings, while main courses are a little nearer the traditional comfort zone, so you may find Kerry lamb with a cep & pistachio crust, paupiettes of sole with seafood colcannon or corn-fed chicken with chorizo and thyme aioli. All produce used is local and certified organic, where possible, and vegetarians get a dish of the day on the blackboard. Bruce's inspired cooking is backed up by charming and knowledgeable staff, working under Laura Mulcahy's direction. The early dinner menu is great value - and there's also a magical wine list to match the food. **Seats 45**; children welcome before 9pm (high chair); toilets wheelchair accessible. D Wed-Mon, 6-10pm; set 2/3 course D about €30/45, also à la carte. House wines from €21.50. SC 10% on groups 8+. Closed Tue; 23-26 Dec. MasterCard, Visa, Laser **Directions:** Top of Henry Street.

Kenmare
COUNTRY HOUSE

Muxnaw Lodge
Castletownbere Road Kenmare Co Kerry **Tel: 064 41252**
muxnawlodge@eircom.net www.muxnawlodge.com

Within walking distance from town (first right past the double-arched bridge towards Bantry), Hannah Boland's wonderfully cosy and homely house was built in 1801 and enjoys beautiful views across Kenmare Bay. This is very much a home where you can relax in the TV lounge or outside in the sloping gardens (you can even play tennis on the all-weather court). A building programme brought a couple of superior new rooms on stream recently but, while the original ones now seem old-fashioned by comparison, all the bedrooms are tranquil and comfortable, individually furnished with free-standing period pieces and pleasant fabrics - and have cleverly hidden tea/coffee-making facilities. **Rooms 5** (all en-suite & no-smoking); not suitable for children. B&B €35-40 pps. Residents D about €20. Garden. Closed 24-25 Dec. MasterCard, Visa. **Directions:** 2 minutes drive from Kenmare Town.

Kenmare
BAR•RESTAURANT

P F McCarthys
14 Main Street Kenmare Co Kerry
Tel: 064 41516

This fine establishment, previously known as the Fáilte Bar, goes back to 1913 and is now run by Paul and Breda Walsh, who took over in 2006. The renovated premises now brings natural light into bright rooms - it has a spacious feeling and a dining area separated from the bar by low partitions, topped by wine bottles for privacy. Everyone loves it, whether for a snack lunch or more leisurely dinner. Breda is known for her wholesome, fresh-tasting food: at lunchtime there's an extensive choice of home-made soups, salads, light snacks and a wide range of sandwiches. Evening menus are more selective, offering a full dinner menu, plus daily specials of fresh fish and steak dishes. Ingredients are carefully sourced and there's a home-made flavour to the food, including desserts. There's a great buzz, a friendly atmosphere and efficient service under Paul's direction. * Live music – usually Fri, Sat & Mon. **Seats 60**; outdoor seating available (garden); children welcome before 9pm; toilets wheelchair accessible. Food served Mon-Sat 12-9pm. No food on Sun. A la carte; house wine from €18.95; SC discretionary. Closed 25 Dec, Good Fri. MasterCard, Visa, Laser **Directions:** First Pub/Restaurant on the right hand side as you travel up Main Street.

Kenmare
RESTAURANT

Packie's

Henry Street Kenmare Co Kerry
Tel: 064 41508

In a town blessed with an exceptional choice of wonderful eating places, the Foley family's buzzy little restaurant has long been a favourite for returning visitors. The long main room has a tiny reception bar with a couple of stools shoehorned into it, and a dividing stone feature wall with foliage-filled gaps in it provides privacy and, along with candlelight, mirrors and framed pictures, makes for a warm, relaxed atmosphere - an impression immediately confirmed by welcoming staff, who are exceptionally friendly and efficient, keeping everyone at the closely packed tables happy throughout the evening. Head chef Martin Hallissey's menus (plus each evening's specials) are based mainly on local ingredients, notably organic produce and fish - and, although there's clear interest in international trends, combinations tend to be based on traditional themes, such as classic Irish stew with fresh herbs, which is a speciality. Close examination of menus will probably reveal more dishes that have stood the test of time than new ones, but what remains impressive is the basic quality of the food, especially local seafood, and the satisfying skill with which simple dishes are cooked, which is very pleasing. And there is no shortage of treats, including, perhaps, real prawn cocktail and roast lobster with garlic or citrus butter (fairly priced at €31.50). Finish with Irish farmhouse cheeses or good desserts, including unusual dishes like lemon posset with shortbread: gorgeous. An interesting and well-priced wine list offers plenty to choose from, with some available by the glass. This little restaurant punches above its weight - and consistent excellence keep people coming back. **Seats 35**; children welcome (high chair); air conditioning. D Mon-Sat, 6-10; set 2/3 course D €30/45; also à la carte. House wine from €18; sc discretionary. Reservations advised. Closed Sun; mid Jan- end Feb. MasterCard, Visa, Laser. **Directions:** Town centre.

Kenmare
HOTEL•RESTAURANT

Park Hotel Kenmare

Kenmare Co Kerry **Tel: 064 41200**
info@parkkenmare.com www.parkkenmare.com

This renowned hotel is only a short stroll to the Heritage Town of Kenmare - yet it enjoys a magnificent waterside location in the midst of Ireland's most scenic landscape, with views over gardens to the ever-changing mountains across the bay. Many travellers from all over the world have found a home-from-home here since the hotel was built in 1897 by the Great Southern and Western Railway Company as an overnight stop for passengers travelling to Parknasilla, 17 miles away. The current proprietor, Francis Brennan, re-opened the hotel in 1985, and has since earned international acclaim for exceptional standards of service, comfort and cuisine; it is a most hospitable and relaxing place, where a warm welcome and the ever-burning fire in the hall set the tone for a stay in which guests are discreetly pampered by outstandingly friendly and professional staff. And, since 2004, that pampering has been taken to new heights in the hotel's deluxe destination spa, Sámas, which translates from the Gaelic as 'indulgence of the senses'. Unlike anything else offered in Ireland, Sámas adjoins the hotel on a wooded knoll and is designed to rejuvenate the body, mind and spirit; there are separate male and female areas (also two day suites for couples) and guests can choose from over forty holistic treatments, designed by a team of professionals to meet individual needs. Sámas has recently been joined by an incredibly beautiful new stainless steel pool, which is available to residents of the new residences alongside the hotel, The Retreats, as well as hotel guests. Lifestyle programmes incorporating spa treatments with other activities in the area - walking on the Kerry Way, golf, fishing, horse trekking - offer a unique way to enjoy the deeply peaceful atmosphere of this luxurious hotel. As for the guest accommodation, spacious suites and bedrooms are individually furnished to the highest standards, with antiques, fine linen and home-baked cookies. And, in line with the excellence which prevails throughout the hotel, the outstanding breakfasts served at the Park start the day in style. [Park Hotel Kenmare was the national winner of our Hotel Breakfast of the Year Award in 2005.] Garden, tennis, croquet, cycling, walking, snooker on site. Destination Spa, 25m lap pool. Reel Room (12-seater cinema). Horse riding, fishing (fly, coarse, sea), mountain walks and stunning coastal drives are all nearby. Golf club adjacent (18 hole). **Rooms 46** (9 suites, 24 junior suites, 8 family, 8 ground floor, 3 single, 3 disabled, 46 no smoking). Lift. 24-hour room service. Children welcome (under 4s free in parents' room, cots available without charge, baby sitting arranged). Dogs may stay in kennels on grounds. B&B about €249 pps; off-season holistic retreats offer very good value. Hotel open for weekends only in Nov and 9 Feb - 1 Apr; open for Christmas & New Year; closed Jane - early Feb. **Restaurant:** The more that contemporary restaurants become the norm in Ireland, the more precious the elegance of this traditional dining room seems - and the views from window tables are simply lovely. Ensuring that the food will match the surroundings is no light matter but a stylishly restrained classicism has characterised this distinguished kitchen under several famous head chefs, and Mark Johnston - who has been with the hotel since 2006 - maintains this tradition admirably. A table d'hôte menu that is concise, yet allows sufficient choice, leans towards seafood, including lobster; there will always be a vegetarian choice, and Kerry lamb and local Skeaghanore duck are also enduring specialities. Superb attention to detail - from the first trio of nibbles offered with aperitifs in the bar, through an intriguing amuse-bouche served at the table, well-made breads, presentation of each dish for inspection on a tray before service, punctilious wine service and finally the theatrical little Irish coffee ritual and petits fours at the end of the meal - all this contributes to a dining experience that is exceptional. The wine list, although favouring the deep-pocketed guest, offers a fair selection in the €30-40 bracket and includes a wine suitable for diabetics. Service is invariably immaculate. A short à la carte lounge menu is available, 12-6pm. **Seats 80** (private room, 30, outdoor dining 20); not suitable for children under 7 yrs; a short à la carte lounge menu is available, 12-6pm. D, 7-9 daily; set D menu about €55; gourmet menu about €75; also à la carte. House wine from €37.50; sc discretionary. Amex, MasterCard, Visa, Laser. **Directions:** Top of town.

Kenmare
BAR•RESTAURANT

The Purple Heather

Henry Street Kenmare Co Kerry **Tel: 064 41016**
oconnellgrainne@eircom.net

Open since 1964, Grainne O'Connell's informal restaurant/bar was among the first to establish a reputation for good food in Kenmare, and is a daytime sister restaurant to Packie's (see entry). It's a traditional darkwood and burgundy bar that gradually develops into an informal restaurant at the rear, as is the way in many of the best Kerry bars - and what they aim for and achieve, with commendable consistency, is good, simple, home-cooked food. Start with refreshing freshly squeezed orange juice, well-made soups that come with home-baked breads, or salad made of organic greens with balsamic dressing. Main courses include a number of seafood salads, vegetarian salads (cold and warm), patés including a delicious smoked salmon paté plus a range of omelettes, sandwiches and open sandwiches (Cashel Blue cheese and walnut, perhaps, or crabmeat with salad) or Irish farmhouse cheeses (with a glass of L.B.V. Offley port, if you like). This is a great place, serving wonderfully wholesome food in a relaxed atmosphere - and it's open almost all year. *Grainne O'Connell also has self-catering accommodation available nearby. **Seats 45.** Meals Mon-Sat, 11-5.30pm; house wine €19. Closed Sun, Christmas, bank hols. Visa, Laser. **Directions:** Town centre - mid-Henry Street (on right following traffic flow).

Kenmare
FARMHOUSE•GUESTHOUSE

Sea Shore Farm Guest House

Tubrid Kenmare Co Kerry **Tel: 064 41270**
seashore@eircom.net www.seashorekenmare.com

The O'Sullivans' well-named farm guesthouse is beautifully situated overlooking the Beara peninsula, with field walks through farmland down to the shore - and, despite its peace and privacy, it's also exceptionally conveniently located, just a mile from Kenmare town. Mary Patricia O'Sullivan provides old-fashioned Irish hospitality at its best, with welcoming and efficient reception and spotlessly clean accommodation. A pleasant guest lounge has stunning views and plenty of tourist information and Irish heritage books - and Mary Patricia is herself a veritable mine of local information. Spacious, comfortably furnished bedrooms have the considerate small touches that make all the difference to the comfort of a stay. No dinner is offered, but breakfast is a feast of fruit salads, yoghurt, cereals etc as well as a choice of scrambled eggs draped with locally smoked salmon, pancakes or traditional Irish. *Glen Inchaquin Park is nearby and should not be missed. **Rooms 6** (all en-suite & no smoking, 4 shower only, 2 family rooms, 2 ground floor, 2 for disabled); children welcome (under 2s free in parents' room); free broadband wi/fi; jacuzzi; no pets. B&B €65 pps, ss €20. Garden, walking. Closed 15 Nov-1 Mar. MasterCard, Visa. **Directions:** Off Ring of Kerry N70 Kenmare/Sneem road; signposted at junction with N71.

Kenmare
HOTEL•RESTAURANT

Sheen Falls Lodge

Kenmare Co Kerry **Tel: 064 41600**
info@sheenfallslodge.ie www.sheenfallslodge.ie

Set in a 300-acre estate just across the river from Kenmare town, this stunning hotel made an immediate impact from the day it opened in April 1991; it has continued to develop and mature most impressively since. The waterside location is beautiful, and welcoming fires always burn in the handsome foyer and in several of the spacious, elegantly furnished reception rooms, including a lounge bar area overlooking the tumbling waterfall. Decor throughout is contemporary classic, offering traditional luxury with a modern lightness of touch and a tendency to understatement that adds up to great style; accommodation in spacious bedrooms - and suites, which include an extremely impressive presidential suite - is luxurious: all rooms have superb amenities, including video/DVD and CD players, beautiful marbled bathrooms and views of the cascading river or Kenmare Bay. Outstanding facilities for both corporate and private guests include state-of-the-art conference facilities, a fine library (with computer/internet), an equestrian centre (treks around the 300-acre estate) and The Queen's Walk (named after Queen Victoria), which takes you through lush woodland. A Health & Fitness Spa includes a pretty 15-metre pool (and an extensive range of treatments) and, alongside it, there's an informal evening bar and bistro, 'Oscars', which has its own separate entrance as well as direct access from the hotel. But it is, above all, the staff who make this luxurious and stylish international hotel the home-from-home that it quickly becomes for each new guest. *Two luxuriously-appointed self-contained two-bedroomed thatched cottages, Little Hay Cottage and Garden Cottage, and a 5-bedroomed house on the estate, are available to rent - and have recently been joined by a range of new properties available for rental, some of them fully serviced. Details on application. Conference/banqueting (120/120); free broadband wi/fi, business centre, secretarial services, video-conferencing. Health & Fitness Spa (swimming pool, jacuzzi, sauna, steam room, treatments, beauty salon), boutique, walking, gardens, croquet, clay pigeon shooting, tennis, cycling. Fishing (coarse, fly) and equestrian nearby. Heli-pad. Children welcome (cots available, €25, baby sitting arranged; playground). Dogs permitted to stay in outhouse/kennels. **Rooms 66** (1 presidential suites, 12 suites, 8 junior suites, 14 ground floor rooms, 10 no-smoking bedrooms, 1 disabled). Lift. All-day room service; turndown service. Room rate €256.50 pp (max 2 guests). **La Cascade:** This beautifully appointed restaurant is designed in tiers to take full advantage of the waterfalls - floodlit at night and providing a dramatic backdrop for an exceptional fine dining experience. Philip Brazil has been head chef since 2005, and continues the high standard of cooking which is the hallmark of this lovely restaurant, backed up by faultless service under the supervision of restaurant manager Benoit Roustaing. His menus are not over-extensive yet allow plenty of choice and, whilst there's an understandable leaning towards local seafood - including lobster and crab from Castletownbere, perhaps, also scallops, Dover sole and turbot - Kerry beef and lamb and local Skeaghanore duck are equally enduring specialities; a vegetarian menu is available on request, and also a six-course Tasting Menu. Cooking is consistently impressive and, although local ingredients feature, the tone is classic, with just an occasional nod to Irish cuisine. Speciality desserts include updated classics like warm chocolate truffle cake with white chocolate ice cream, or traditional sherry trifle with vanilla anglaise, and the farmhouse cheese selection is served with scrumptious parmesan biscuits. The atmospheric wine cellar is a particular point of pride - guests can visit it to choose their own bottle, and port may also be served there after dinner - deep-pocketed wine buffs will enjoy the wine list and should make a point of seeing it well ahead of dining if possible, as it details around 950 wines, with particular strengths in the classic European regions, especially Burgundy and Bordeaux, and a fine collection of ports and dessert wines. *Light lunches and afternoon tea are available in the sun lounge, 12-6 daily, and the informal Oscar's Bistro offers an extensive à la carte dinner menu, including a children's menu, Wed-Sun, 6-10pm. **Restaurant Seats 120** (private room, 20; outdoor seating, 12). Pianist, evenings; toilets wheelchair accessible. D daily 7-9.

Set D €65, gourmet D €90, vegetarian menu €55. House wines from €36.80. SC discretionary. Hotel closed Jan 2 - Feb 1. Amex, Diners, MasterCard, Visa, Laser. **Directions:** Take N71 Kenmare (Glengariff road); turn left at Riversdale Hotel.

Kenmare

COUNTRY HOUSE•GUESTHOUSE

Shelburne Lodge

Cork Road Kenmare Co Kerry **Tel:** 064 41013
shelburnekenmare@eircom.net www.shelburnelodge.com

Tom and Maura Foley's fine stone house on the edge of the town is well set back from the road, in its own grounds and lovely gardens. It is the oldest house in Kenmare and has great style and attention to detail; spacious day rooms include an elegant, comfortably furnished drawing room with plenty of seating, an inviting log fire and interesting books for guests to read - it is really lovely, and the feeling is of being a guest in a private country house. Spacious, well-proportioned guest rooms are individually decorated and extremely comfortable; everything (especially beds and bedding) is of the highest quality and, except for the more informal conversion at the back of the house, which is especially suitable for families and has neat shower rooms, the excellent bathrooms all have full bath. But perhaps the best is saved until last, in the large, well-appointed dining room where superb breakfasts are served: tables are prettily laid with linen napkins and the menu offers all kind of treats, beginning with freshly squeezed juices, a choice of fruits (nectarine with strawberries, perhaps) with extras like natural yoghurt, honey and nuts offered too, lovely freshly-baked breads, home-made preserves, leaf tea and strong aromatic coffee, and - as well as various excellent permutations of the full traditional Irish breakfast - there's fresh fish, and Irish farmhouse cheeses too. Simply delicious. [Shelburne Lodge was our Guesthouse of the Year in 2005, and also winner of the Best Guesthouse Breakfast Award.] No evening meals are served, but residents are directed to the family's restaurant, Packie's (see entry). **Rooms 10** (3 shower-only, 1 family, 1 ground floor); children welcome (under 2s free in parents' room, cot available without charge). B&B €55-70, ss €40. Garden, tennis. Own parking. No pets. Closed Dec 1-mid Mar. MasterCard, Visa. **Directions:** 500 metres from town centre, on the Cork road R569.

Kenmare

GUESTHOUSE

Virginia's Guesthouse

36 Henry Street Kenmare Co Kerry **Tel:** 064 41021
virginias@eircom.net www.virginias-kenmare.com

Mulcahy's restaurant and Virginia's guesthouse share an entrance, but are run quite separately. Neil and Noreen Harrington are superb hosts and guest comfort comes first with them, so each winter sees regular refurbishment – new mattresses and bedding, paintwork, whatever is necessary. Guestrooms have big comfortable beds, and everything you could need including phone, television, safe and tea/coffee trays - and en-suite power showers. And their breakfasts are a point of honour, offering amongst many delights a fresh orange juice cocktail with ginger, melon with feta cheese, a compôte of organic rhubarb with blueberries, natural yogurt, organic porridge (with or without whiskey cream), and banana pancakes along with all the usual egg dishes (free range eggs) and fries, simply delicious. **Rooms 8** (all shower only & no smoking, 1 family, 1 single); not suitable for children under 12 yrs; B&B €45-50 pps, single €60-85. Closed 24-26 Dec. MasterCard, Visa, Laser. **Directions:** Second building on right-hand side as you go down Henry Street in the town centre.

KILLARNEY

Famous throughout the world for its romantic beauty (Lakes of Killarney, Killarney National Park, the Ring of Kerry), the Killarney area has long been a source of inspiration for poets, painters and writers. Despite the commercial tone of the town itself - which has been a centre of tourism since the days of the Victorian Grand Tour - the surroundings are stunning and, with a number of the country's finest hotels are in the town and immediate area, it remains an excellent base for exploring the area, or for leisure activities, notably golf (Killarney Golf & Fishing Club, 064 663 1034), walking and fishing. When visiting Muckross House at the National Park, **The Garden Restaurant** (064 663 1440; www.muckross-house.ie) is open 9-5 daily, all year except Christmas/NewYear, and offers just the kind of good, wholesome food that's welcome, in attractive surroundings. Nearby, in the Muckross area, the Huggard family's **Lake Hotel** (064 663 1035; www.lakehotel.com) is romantically located right on the lakeshore, and combines the old-world charm of the original building and its welcoming log fire, with the luxury of recently added accommodation. And, convenient to the Killarney Golf & Fishing Club, the family-run guesthouse **Sheehan's 19th Green** (064 663 2868; www.the19thgreen-bb.com) offers a moderately-priced haven for golfers. **The Quality Hotel** (Cork Road; 064 663 1555) has exceptional leisure facilities for a budget hotel, including an indoor heated pool, sauna, hot tub, steam room and exercise room. The hotel also has a crèche, kids and teens clubs and outdoor activities for children including miniature golf. For those who want to be in the town centre and like a hotel of character however, the Buckley family's charming and moderately-priced **Arbutus Hotel** (064 663 1037; www.arbutuskillarney.com) on College Street could be the answer. For a casual bite in town, try **Panis Angelicus** (New Street; 064 663 9648), a stylish contemporary café and bread shop that has a tempting display of freshly baked breads, scones and gateaux and aromas of freshly brewed Italian coffee, or **Murphys Ice Cream** (066 915 2644; www.murphysicecream.ie) on Main Street (see Dingle entry for details). There is a country market in the Parish Hall on Anne's Road on Fridays (11.30am - 1.30pm).

WWW.IRELAND-GUIDE.COM FOR ALL THE BEST PLACES TO EAT, DRINK & STAY

Killarney
HOTEL

The Brehon

Muckross Road Killarney Co Kerry **Tel: 064 30700**
info@thebrehon.com www.thebrehon.com

Appropriately enough, as it is so close to the Irish National Entertainment Centre (INEC), everything at this 5* hotel, conference centre and spa is on a grand scale - and, while the exterior of the vast five-storey building may be overpowering, most would agree that the contemporary interior matches the official description of 'tasteful splendour'. Everything seems larger than life and - although it tends to show signs of the heavy wear it is subjected to - the design, decor and furnishings of the public spaces are striking, and feature some interesting modern art and sculpture. This house style continues through bedrooms and suites, which are extremely comfortable, with air-conditioning as well as more usual features, and luxurious marble bathrooms with separate shower and bath. The restaurant is airy and bright, and a wide ranging breakfast menu is offered. The hotel takes pride in its spa: developed by the Banyan Tree Spa, it is Europe's first Angsana spa and based on holistic Asian healing customs. Conference facilities include four meeting rooms and a large function space, which is also available for weddings. Conferences/Banqueting (250/200); free broadband wi/fi; business centre, Secretarial services; **Rooms 123** (4 suites, 5 junior suites, 30 superior, 3 family, 7 for disabled, all no smoking); children welcome (under 3s free in parents' room, cot available free of charge, baby sitting arranged). Lift, 24 hr room service. B&B €145 pps, ss €35. Spa, beauty salon, hairdressing; Leisure Centre (swimming pool, gym, sauna); walking, tennis, cycling; Golf, fishing and equestrian nearby. Open all year. *Special interest breaks each Spring & Autumn, contact for details. Amex, MasterCard, Visa, Laser. **Directions:** Located opposite the national park (N71) 1.5km from town centre.

Killarney
RESTAURANT

Bricín

26 High Street Killarney Co Kerry **Tel: 064 34902**
www.bricin.com

Upstairs, over a craft shop (which you will find especially interesting if you like Irish pottery), Paddy & Johnny McGuire's country-style first-floor restaurant has been delighting visitors with its warm atmosphere and down-to-earth food since 1990. It's a large area, but broken up into "rooms", which creates intimate spaces - and the country mood suits wholesome cooking, in menus offering a good range of popular dishes. Salmon & crab bake is an enduring favourite, for example, and there are traditional dishes like boxty (potato pancakes) which are not seen as often as they should be in Irish restaurants, and are the house speciality here - you can have them with various fillings - chicken, lamb vegetables - and salad. An interesting range of desserts includes good home-made ice creams. This is a welcoming restaurant that never disappoints, and it has an old-fashioned character which is becoming especially attractive as so many others adopt a contemporary style. An informative wine list offers a wide range in the €20-30 range, but no half bottles. **Seats 29**; air conditioning; children welcome. L & D Mon-Sat, 12-3pm & 6-9.15. Value D about €21 daily 6-7; Set D from about €27; also a la carte. House wine from €20. Closed Sun, Mon and Feb. Amex, Diners, MasterCard, Visa, Laser. **Directions:** On the High Street, Killarney. ⬦

Killarney
HOTEL

Cahernane House Hotel

Muckross Road Killarney Co Kerry **Tel: 064 31895**
info@cahernane.com www.cahernane.com

This family-owned and managed hotel is in a lovely quiet location, convenient to Killarney town yet - thanks to a long tree-lined avenue and parkland which stretches down to the water - it has a charmingly other-worldly atmosphere. The original house was built by the Herbert family, Earls of Pembroke, in the 17th century, and accommodation is divided between fine old rooms (including some suites and junior suites) in the main house, and more contemporary rooms in a recent extension; an atrium joining the two sections makes a pleasant conservatory seating area, opening onto the lakeside grounds. The hotel has many attractive features, not least its generous period sitting rooms and open fires, and a characterful cellar bar (spoilt a little by noise and bright downlighting) with a real old-fashioned wine cellar. Banqueting (80). Free broadband wi/fi. Children welcome (under 3s free in parents' room, cot available without charge, baby sitting arranged.) No pets. Garden, walking, fishing, tennis. Golf nearby. **Rooms 38** (28 with separate bath & shower, 15 no smoking). B&B from €80 pps. **The Herbert Room Restaurant:** This classically elegant dining room is situated on the lake side of the house and the setting is perfect for fine dining. Classical table d'hôte and à la carte menus are offered – almond & buttermilk risotto and tian of Dingle Bay crabmeat with ginger, spring onion and coconut are typical starters, and main courses might include roast rack of lamb with sweet potato fondant and pan-fried fillets of turbot with citrus fruits salad. Cheeses are offered with plum chutney, in addition to delicious desserts. A vegetarian menu is also available on request. Farmhouse Breakfast is a highlight, and a quite an extensive bar menu is offered for those who would prefer to eat informally. D daily 6.30-9.30; set L €35, set 5 course D about €55; also bar food, 12.30-9.30pm; house wine €24.* Off-season breaks offered. Closed mid Dec-mid Jan. Amex, Diners, MasterCard, Visa, Laser. **Directions:** Outskirts of Killarney, off the N71 near Muckross Park.

Killarney
RESTAURANT

Chapter 40

40 New Street Killarney Co Kerry **Tel: 064 71833**
info@chapter40.ie www.chapter40.ie

One of Killarney's most popular dining destinations, this smart high-ceilinged restaurant feels spacious and is attractively set up, with simple darkwood tables echoing the polished wooden floor, and contrasting cream leather used on high-backed chairs and bar stools. Menus with an emphasis on sociability are international in style, and include an early dinner which is very good value, a wide ranging à la carte and daily specials for all courses. Sharing dishes, like Chapter 40's Tasting Plate, duck confit pancakes or the Tapas Board, get a meal off to a lively start or you could begin with the seafood chowder (thickened with potato and carrageen moss and therefore gluten-free), followed perhaps by the seafood plate which is always good and includes a wide range of fish and seafood such as baked salmon, sautéed garlic crab claws and mussels, pan-fried brill, tempura of prawns, and brochette of monkfish; for dessert, the chocolate plate is a favourite. A lively atmosphere and good honest cooking along with value (all main courses include vegetables) and friendly service are the reasons for this restaurant's success; as it's always busy, reservations are essential, especially at weekends. **Seats 72** (private room, 16); toilets wheelchair accessible; children welcome (high chair, baby changing facilities); air conditioning; D Mon-Sat, 5-10pm; à la carte; house wine €22. Closed Sun. Amex, MasterCard, Visa, Laser. **Directions:** A few minutes walk from car park beside the Tourist Office, near Dunnes Stores.

Coolclogher House

Mill Road Killarney Co Kerry **Tel: 064 35996**
info@coolclogherhouse.com   www.coolclogherhouse.com

Killarney
HISTORIC HOUSE

Mary and Maurice Harnett's beautiful early Victorian house is just on the edge of Killarney town and yet, tucked away on its 68-acre walled estate, it is an oasis of peace and tranquillity. The house has been extensively restored and has many interesting features, including an original conservatory built around a 170 year-old specimen camellia - when camellias were first introduced to Europe, they were mistakenly thought to be tender plants; it is now quite remarkable to see this large tree growing under glass. It is an impressive yet relaxed house, with well-proportioned, spacious reception rooms stylishly furnished and comfortable for guests, with newspapers, books, fresh flowers - and open fires in inclement weather - while the four large bedrooms have scenic views over gardens, parkland and mountains. Gazing out from this peaceful place, it is easy to forget that the hustle and bustle of Killarney town is just a few minutes' drive away; it could just as well be in another world. Mary and Maurice enjoy sharing their local knowledge with guests to help them get the most of their stay at what they quite reasonably call 'perhaps the most exclusive accommodation available in Killarney'. **Rooms 4** (all en-suite, all no smoking); not suitable for children under 8; B&B €120 pps, ss €50. No pets. Garden, walking. Golf, fishing, garden visits nearby. *Coolclogher House is also offered as a weekly rental (from €5,500) for special occasions; suits groups of 10-12; staff can be arranged if required. *Golf breaks offered (B&B or rental). MasterCard, Visa, Laser. **Directions:** Leaving Killarney town, take Muckross Road; turn left between Brehon and Gleneagle hotels, onto Mill Lane; gates on right after 1km (0.5 m). ◇

Earls Court House

Woodlawn Junction Muckross Road Killarney Co Kerry **Tel: 064 663 4009**
info@killarney-earlscourt.ie   www.killarney-earlscourt.ie

Killarney
GUESTHOUSE

Although Roy and Emer Moynihan's purpose-built guesthouse quite near the town centre is now classified as an hotel, its essential qualities of hospitality, professionalism, comfort and character remain unchanged. A welcoming open fire burns in the large beautifully furnished foyer which, together with an adjoining guest sitting room, has plenty of comfortable seating for guests - an ideal rendezvous, or simply a place to relax - and, as elsewhere in the house, antiques, books, paintings and family photographs are a point of interest and emphasise the personality of this spacious home-from-home. Emer's personal attention to the details that make for real comfort - and the ever-growing collection of antiques that guarantees individuality for each room - are the hallmarks of the exceptionally comfortable accommodation offered, which includes a number of rooms with canopy beds. All the bedrooms are well-planned and generously-sized, with double and single beds, well-finished bathrooms, phone and satellite TV; tea/coffee-making facilities are available on request. Guests are directed to restaurants in the town for evening meals, but superb breakfasts are served in a newly-refurbished antique-furnished dining room, where guests are looked after with charm and efficiency. *Earls Court was our Guesthouse of the Year for 2004. **Rooms 30** (4 suites, 4 family, 2 for disabled, all no smoking); fully certified for disadvantaged access; children welcome (under 3s free, cot available without charge, baby sitting arranged). Pets allowed in some areas; broadband wi/fi. Lift. Room service (limited hours). B&B €70 pps, ss €30. Parking. Garden; jacuzzi; walking; golf nearby. Closed mid Nov-mid Feb. Amex, MasterCard, Visa. **Directions:** Take the first left at the traffic lights on Muckross road (signed), then 3rd premises.

Killarney
RESTAURANT

Gaby's Seafood Restaurant
27 High Street Killarney Co Kerry
Tel: 064 32519

One of Ireland's longest established seafood restaurants, Gaby's is expensive, but it has a pleasantly informal atmosphere. There's a cosy little bar beside an open fire just inside the door, then several steps lead up to the main dining area, which is cleverly broken up into several sections to make more intimate dining spaces. Chef-proprietor Gert Maes offers well structured seasonal à la carte menus in classic French style and in three languages. This is one of the great classic Irish kitchens and absolute freshness is clearly the priority; there are specials on every evening and a note on the menu reminds guests that availability depends on daily landings; but there's always plenty else to choose from, with steaks and local lamb among the favourites. Specialities include Atlantic prawns on a bed of tagliatelle in a light garlic sauce and lobster "Gaby": fresh lobster, cognac, wine, cream and spices - cooked to a secret recipe! Lovely desserts include "my mother's recipe" - an old-fashioned apple & raspberry crumble - or you can finish with an Irish cheese selection and freshly brewed coffee. An impressive wine list offers about fifteen interesting house wines by the bottle or glass, and many special bottles, although vintages are not always given. **Seats 75**; toilets wheelchair accessible; air conditioning; children welcome (high chair). D only, Mon-Sat 6-10; gourmet menu about €50, also à la carte; house wine €25; sc discretionary. Closed Sun (& Mon, Tue - Jan-Mar). Amex, MasterCard, Visa, Laser. **Directions:** On the main street.

Killarney
CAFÉ

Jam
Old Market Lane Killarney Co Kerry **Tel: 064 37716**
info@jam.ie www.jam.ie

James Mulchrone's highly regarded bakery, delicatessen and café has found a new home behind a smart frontage in an attractive pedestrianised laneway between Main Street and the Glebe public car park. It is good to see this delightful establishment in spacious new premises that allow for greater comfort and make a visit here all the more enjoyable and, at the time of going to press, refurbishment is underway which will include wheelchair access and outdoor seating. And, of course, the same basic principles apply here, so you may expect affordable prices, friendly service and real home-made food using the best of local produce (see entry under Kenmare for details). *There is also a third café just outside Tralee at Ballyseedy Home & Outdoor Living. **Seats 70**; children welcome; air conditioning. Open Mon-Sat, 8am-5pm. menu changes daily. Closed Sun, 4 days Christmas. MasterCard, Visa, Laser. **Directions:** Town centre.

Killarney
GUESTHOUSE

Kathleens Country House
Madams Height Tralee Road Killarney Co Kerry **Tel: 064 32810**
info@kathleens.net www.kathleens.net

Quietly situated off the main Killarney-Tralee road, Kathleen O'Regan Sheppard's long-established guesthouse is just a mile from the town centre – and well situated for some of the country's most beautiful scenic drives, as it's just at the beginning of the Ring of Kerry route. It's convenient for a wide range of outdoor pursuits too, and would make an especially handy base for golfers playing any of the nearby courses – Killarney Golf & Fishing Club, Beaufort GC and Dunloe GC are all very close by. When Kathleen opened here in 1980, she was one of the first to offer what was effectively hotel standard accommodation at guesthouse prices - and, today, this family-run business continues to give good value, hospitality and comfort. Guests tired of the sameness of modern rooms enjoy the fact that the décor is a little set in time, and an ongoing programme of maintenance and refurbishment ensures that everything is immaculate, including spacious public areas that provide plenty of room for relaxing. Individually decorated rooms are furnished to a high standard, with orthopaedic beds, phone, TV, and tea/coffee-making facilities, and the fully tiled bathrooms all have bath and shower. Excellent breakfasts are served in an attractive dining room overlooking the garden, setting you up for the day: everything served at breakfast is based on the finest produce, local where possible, and beautifully presented. **Rooms 17** (all no smoking, 2 ground floor, 3 single); free broadband wi/fi; children welcome (under 3s free in parents' room, cot available). B&B €65 pps, ss €15; wheelchair access ground floor only. Turndown service offered. Garden, walking. Closed 20 Oct-15 Mar. Amex, MasterCard, Visa, Laser. **Directions:** 1.6km (1m) north of Killarney Town off N22 (Tralee road).

Killarney
GUESTHOUSE
ⓥ

Killarney Lodge

Countess Road Killarney Co Kerry **Tel: 064 36499**
klylodge@iol.ie www.killarneylodge.net

Catherine Treacy's fine purpose-built guesthouse is set in private walled gardens just a couple of minutes walk from the town centre and offers a high standard of accommodation at a fairly moderate rate. Large en-suite air-conditioned bedrooms have all the amenities expected of an hotel room and there are spacious, comfortably furnished public rooms to relax in. Run by a member of one of Killarney's most respected hotelier families, this is a very comfortable place to stay; you will be greeted with complimentary tea and coffee on arrival - and sent off in the morning with a good Irish breakfast, including home-baked breads and scones. A good choice for the business traveller, and short breaks are available in conjunction with Killarney Golf & Fishing Club - accommodation and green fees are offered at preferential rates. **Rooms 16** (2 junior suites, 2 family, 1 shower only, 6 ground floor, all no smoking); children welcome (under 12s free in parents room; cot available without charge); free broadband wi/fi. B&B €70 pps, ss €30; no sc. No pets. Garden. Own secure parking. Room service (all day). Closed Nov-Feb. Amex, Diners, MasterCard, Visa, Laser **Directions:** 2 minutes walk from town centre off Muckross Road.

Killarney
HOTEL•RESTAURANT
🔲🏨🏚★🍸

Killarney Park Hotel

Kenmare Place Killarney Co Kerry **Tel: 064 35555**
info@killarneyparkhotel.ie www.killarneyparkhotel.ie

Situated in its own grounds, a short stroll from the town centre, the Treacy family's luxurious, well-run hotel is deceptively modern - despite its classical good looks, it is only fifteen years old. However, it has already undergone more than one transformation - indeed, constant improvement is so much a theme here that it is hard to keep up with developments as they occur. The exceptionally welcoming atmosphere strikes you from the moment the doorman first greets you, as you pass through to a series of stylish seating areas, with fires and invitingly grouped sofas and armchairs; the same sense of comfort characterises the Garden Bar and also the quiet Library. Elegant public areas are punctuated by a sweeping staircase leading to bedrooms luxuriously furnished in two very different styles. Spacious traditional suites have a private entrance hall and an elegant sitting area with a fireplace, creating a real home-from-home feeling; all the older rooms are also furnished in a similar warm country house style. However, the junior suites offer a dramatically contemporary style - thoughtfully and individually designed with a real wow-factor, they have air conditioning, well-planned bathrooms and the many small details that make a hotel room really comfortable. Housekeeping is impeccable and the staff are committed to looking after guests with warmth and discretion. Amenities include not only a health & fitness club with 20m swimming pool, but also one of Ireland's most highly regarded health spas, offering eight treatment rooms, outdoor hot tub, plunge pool and jacuzzi; the menu of treatments offered is seriously seductive and it may well happen that some guests never feel the need to leave the hotel at all during their stay. [Park Hotel Killarney was our Hotel of the Year in 2002.] *The nearby hotel, **The Ross** (see entry) is a sister hotel. Conference/banqueting (150/150); free broadband wi/fi; secretarial services, video conferencing. Spa. Leisure centre (swimming pool, sauna, plunge pool, jacuzzi, gym). Library; billiard room. Garden, walking, cycling. Children welcome (under 2s free in parents room; cots available without charge, playroom, crèche, baby sitting arranged). No Pets. **Rooms 72** (3 suites, 30 junior suites, 3 family rooms, 1 for disabled, all no-smoking). Lift. 24 hour room service. Turndown service. B&B €200 pps, ss €200; no sc. Closed 24-27 Dec. **The Park Restaurant:** This large and opulent room has the essential elements of grandeur - the ornate ceiling, glittering chandeliers - but has been lightened by a contemporary tone in the furnishings. Odran Lucey, who has been head chef since 1999, has earned a reputation for this restaurant as a dining destination in its own right, making it a great asset to this fine hotel. His menus are appealing and, although not overlong, they offer plenty of choice from which to make up a five course dinner or, as dishes are priced individually, make à la carte choices if preferred. The underlying style is classical but this is creative food, cooked with panache. Although the style is broadly international, it's very much food with an Irish flavour - seen in named ingredients like Dingle crabmeat, Kerry lamb and suppliers credited on the menu. A main course of pan-fried fillet of Irish beef, wild mushroom pithivier, red onion marmalade and sauce béarnaise demonstrates skilful blending of traditional partnerships and innovative thinking, and good judgment comes into play when it comes to a real classic - Dover sole - which is cooked classically, 'meunière'. Courteous, knowledge-able service and the presence of a pianist, who plays throughout dinner, add to the sense of occasion. A wide-ranging wine list includes many of the classics, and not only a fair choice of half bottles but also a sommelier's choice of the week, offering half a dozen good wines by the glass. An interesting feature of the restaurant is an open wine cellar, which guests are free to browse. *Odran Lucey is also responsible for the excellent bistro-style food served in The Garden Bar where - as elsewhere in the hotel - children are made very welcome. **Seats 150** (private room, 40); children welcome (high chair, children's menu, baby changing facilities); reservations required; air conditioning; toilets wheelchair accessible. D daily 7-9.30; Set D €65; also à la carte. House wines from about €28. SC discretionary. *Food is also served in the bar, 12 noon-9pm daily. Hotel closed 24-27 Dec. Amex, MasterCard, Visa, Laser. **Directions:** Located in Killarney town - all access routes lead to town centre.

Killarney
HOTEL

Killarney Plaza Hotel

Kenmare Place Killarney Co Kerry **Tel: 064 21100**
info@killarneyplaza.com www.killarneyplaza.com

In seeking to regain the glamour of the grand hotels, this new hotel offers an alternative to the modernism that has taken over in Irish hotels of late. The scale is large, but the proportions are pleasing and, although undoubtedly glitzy - miles of polished marbled floors and a great deal of gold - quality materials have been used and it will age well. Meanwhile, it has a lot to offer: a central loca-tion with underground parking; luxurious accommodation at prices which are relatively reasonable; a choice of three very different dining experiences (see separate entry for Mentons); and good leisure and relaxation facilities, including a Molton Brown Spa. *Short/off-season breaks are available - details on application. **Rooms 198** (5 suites, 27 executive, 12 disabled, 140 no smoking); children welcome (under 4s free in parents' room, cot available free of charge, baby sitting arranged). Lift. 24 hour room service. Turndown service. Pets permitted by arrangement. B&B €95 pps, ss €40. Leisure centre (swimming pool, sauna, steam room, jacuzzi, gym); Spa. Secure parking (125); valet parking. Restaurant Grand Pey (250); D daily 6-9pm. Open all year. Amex, Diners, MasterCard, Visa, Laser **Directions:** Town centre. ◊

Killarney
HOTEL

Killarney Royal Hotel

College Street Killarney Co Kerry **Tel: 064 31853**
info@killarneyroyal.ie www.killarneyroyal.ie

Another of Killarney's unrivalled collection of fine hotels, this family-owned establishment is a charming older sister to the luxu-rious Hayfield Manor Hotel in Cork city (see entry). Proprietors Joe and Margaret Scally have lavished care and investment on it, resulting in a beautifully furnished hotel in an elegant period style that is totally appropriate to the age and design of the building. No expense was spared on the highest quality of materials and work-manship, air conditioning was installed throughout the hotel and individually-designed rooms all have sitting areas and marbled bathrooms. But what is most remarkable, perhaps, is the warm and friendly atmosphere that prevails throughout the hotel, conveyed through the soft warm tones chosen for furnishing schemes, and the attentive attitude of friendly, caring staff. A combination of light contemporary food and heartier fare is offered throughout the day in the informal bar/bistro area, which is a popular meeting place, while the main restaurant – which has recently been smartly refur-bished – is more formal, and reservations are required. Conference/banqueting (50/110); secretarial services; free broadband wi/fi; laptop-sized safes in bedrooms. **Rooms 29** (5 junior suites, 5 family rooms, 20 no-smoking, 1 single, 1 disabled); children welcome (under 7s free in parents room, cots available without charge, baby sitting arranged). Dogs permitted by arrangement (stay in bedrooms, no charge). Lift. 24 hour room service. B&B €80-110 pps, ss €40. No on-site parking (arrangement with nearby car park). Golf, hunting, walking and horse racing all nearby. Closed 23-26 Dec. Amex, Diners, MasterCard, Visa, Laser. **Directions:** In Killarney town centre on College Street, off the N22.

Killarney
RESTAURANT

Lord Kenmare's Restaurant

College Street Killarney Co Kerry **Tel: 064 31294**
info@lordkenmares.com www.lordkenmares.com

This cosy first floor restaurant has elegant black furniture, polished floors, bare tables and blinds - a lot of hard surfaces all add up to a good bit of noise, but nobody seems to mind. Barbary duck breast is their stated speciality, served, perhaps, with pineapple, orange & salsa, but this does not do the restaurant justice as menus offer many more appealing dishes - tender whiskey & Calvados braised pork belly, for example, outstanding steaks and a beautifully presented hot seafood platter, a selection that may include prawns (probably of the tiger variety, alas) fresh salmon, monkfish, scallops, crisp fried calamari, mussels & grilled oysters. Good food, together with great service and value ensure that this cheerful place is always packed - even on weekdays, when other restaurants may not be busy, there's lots of buzz, so reservations are strongly advised. A la carte. House wine about €20. **Directions:** Town centre, above Murphy's Bar and Squire's Pub. ◇

Killarney
HOTEL•RESTAURANT

The Malton

Town Centre East Avenue Road Killarney Co Kerry **Tel: 064 38000**
res@themalton.com www.themalton.com

The pillared entrance and ivy-clad facade of this classic Victorian railway hotel still convey a sense of occasion, but guests who remember it of old will find that a recent change of ownership has brought more than a change of name - and, although the building itself is protected, the interior has had a modern makeover. The fine old inner doors have gone (hopefully resting somewhere safe until there is a change of heart) but the welcoming open fire at the entrance remains and still draws guests through to the spacious grandly-pillared foyer, which has had all of its traditional furniture removed and now, perhaps intentionally, feels very like a railway station. However, it has softened a little since the first round of modernisation took place - some much-needed seating has found its way into the foyer, and the smaller drawing rooms off it have – at least for the time being - been allowed to retain their elegant old furnishings. Accommodation in the newer section of the hotel has been upgraded in a style appropriate to its age and, in the original building, the bedroom corridors (built wide enough 'to allow two ladies in hooped dresses to pass comfortably'), still set the tone for generously-proportioned suites and executive rooms, furnished to individual designs. The bar has also been modernised, but with a fairly light hand (the famous Malton prints feature), and its convenience to Killarney town (and, of course, the station) is unchanged, so it is still a pleasant place to stay. There are two restaurants: the great gilt-domed Garden Room Restaurant is a prime example of Victorian opulence - contrasting with the smaller contemporary restaurant, Peppers (see below). Conferences/Banqueting (900/750); broadband wi/fi; business Centre, secretarial services. **Rooms 172** (2 suites, 34 junior suites, 69 superior rooms, family 10, 4 disabled). Lift. 24 hour room service. B&B €75 pps; no SC. Open all year.
Peppers: This is the hotel's bistro-style restaurant, and tables are very much in demand. Situated quietly in a corner position, behind the bar and overlooking the gardens, it is dashingly decorated in a modern style that works well with the room, and has been upgraded within that successful overall scheme since the hotel changed hands. The ambience, Mediterranean menus, consistently sound cooking and professional service make an appealing combination. It is well established as one of Killarney's leading eating places. **Seats 150**; reservations recommended; children welcome. D Tue-Sat, 6.30-9.30pm; house wine from €24. Amex, Diners, MasterCard, Visa, Laser. **Directions:** In the heart of Killarney town beside Railway Station.

Killarney
RESTAURANT

Mentons @ The Plaza

Killarney Plaza Hotel Kenmare Place Killarney Co Kerry **Tel: 064 21150**
info@mentons.com www.mentons.com

Gary Fitzgerald's first-floor restaurant in bustling downtown Killarney has two entrances - one up a rather grand flight of steps from the street (asserting its independence), the other through the hotel (up stairs or on the lift). It's a bright contemporary space on two levels and several areas, with classy modern table settings and quite a luxurious atmosphere - aided by welcoming and helpful staff. It appeals to all ages and is a popular lunch spot, when informal menus offer a range of light dishes such as Mentons chicken and bacon Caesar salad, and more substantial choices like Cronin's jumbo herb sausages with roast garlic mash, apple relish and thyme gravy. An early dinner offers good value, and more structured evening menus are sprinkled with house dishes - a layered starter salad, or homemade rustic agnollotti filled with confit duck leg, sundried tomato and sesame dressing, pecorino & rocket - and include local ingredients such as Cromane mussels. Gary Fitzgerald leads a good team, and the Guide has always found Mentons to be consistently enjoyable. **Seats 65**; air conditioning; children welcome. L daily 12.30-2.30pm, D daily 6-9; à la carte; house wine from €19.90. Closed last 2 weeks Jan. MasterCard, Visa. **Directions:** Killarney town centre - up steps beside main entrance to Plaza Hotel.

Killarney
HOTEL

Randles Court Hotel
Muckross Road Killarney Co Kerry **Tel: 064 35333**
info@randlescourt.com www.randlescourt.com

This well located, family-owned and managed hotel has been developed around an attractive house originally built in 1906 as a family residence, and extensively refurbished before opening as an hotel in 1992. Despite recent extension (23 new bedrooms), period features have been retained and it still has some of the domesticity and warmth of the family home. The hotel's very pleasant Conservatory Bar offers a full lunch menu daily and opens onto terraced gardens, allowing for al fresco meals with views of the mountains and lakes in fine weather. Spacious, comfortable bedrooms are individually furnished to a high standard, with the usual amenities and well-appointed bathrooms (some with separate bath and shower). A good breakfast is served and, for evening dining, there are two restaurants, Checkers and The Court Restaurant, both of which are very agreeable. *The neighbouring **Dromhall Hotel** (064 39300; www.dromhall.com) is a sister establishment and shared leisure facilities, including a 20-metre pool, sauna, steam room, gym and spa/treatment rooms, are accessible from both hotels. Conference/banqueting (80/30); business centre, secretarial service, video conferencing. **Rooms 78**; children welcome (under 5s free in parents' room, cot available without charge, baby sitting arranged). Pets permitted by arrangement. Lift. 24 hour room service. Turndown service. B&B from €60 pps, ss €30, SC inc. **Checkers Restaurant:** D daily, 7-9.30; bar meals 1-7pm. Special breaks offered - details on application. Underground car park. Closed 22-27 Dec. Amex, Diners, MasterCard, Visa, Laser. **Directions:** 5 mins walk out of Killarney centre on Muckross Road.

Killarney
HOTEL•RESTAURANT

The Ross Hotel
Town Centre Killarney Co Kerry **Tel: 064 31855**
info@theross.ie www.theross.ie

Lovers of contemporary style will adore the Treacy family's impressive new boutique hotel, which replaces their original much-loved property, which was a sort of 'Queen Mother' of the hotel world; all that now remains is the lovely bow-windowed frontage, which still gives a hint of the warmth that lay behind. Today an assertively design-led experience begins in a highly theatrical reception area, where bemused visitors in trainers perch on leather seats in the electric-green light of a standard lamp and wonder at it all; the Pink Lounge is indeed shocking pink - after that things calm down but it prepares the first-time guest for a funky stay. Accommodation, in the thirty rooms and five suites, is exceptionally comfortably appointed as would be expected, but much quieter in tone, the style and many of the details will be familiar to guests who know the Treacys' Killarney Park Hotel (see entry), just across the road; some spacious rooms at the front look across to the waiting jarveys with their jaunting cars and horses and two bay-windowed suites at the top have views across the town to the National Park, but most rooms are notable for comfort rather than outlook. Public areas include the aptly-named and stylish Lane Café Bar; with glass all along one wall and quirky furnishings, it's the coolest place in Killarney to meet for cocktails and they serve very good bar food and tapas all day. Broadband wi/fi, secretarial services. Children welcome (under 2s free in parents' room, cot available free of charge); **Rooms 30** (5 suites, 1 for disabled, all no smoking); B&B €110 pps; Lift; Closed 24-26 Dec. **Cellar One:** Undoubtedly the jewel in this stylish hotel's crown, this stunningly theatrical restaurant is on two levels - a 20-seater mezzanine and a 4-seater lower dining room and, although a lift is also available, the grand entrance down a curving glass and steel staircase is the stuff that dreams are made of. Everything about it is larger than life, including the brilliant lime green and shocking pink furnishings (tempered by sober greys and browns of the main stage set); but there is definitely method to this mad creativity as it is not only a delightful place to eat but - except that the head waiter's desk is not handy to arriving guests, which can cause a small delay on arrival - it's an exceptionally well-designed restaurant from the working angle. Head chef Ian McMonagle has responsibility for all food operations in the hotel, and his à la carte menus in Cellar One are smart and modern, with strong world influences but also a few classics and plenty of named local ingredients: Cromane mussels, Skeaghanore duck, St Tola goat's cheese all feature, for example, and a starter plate of charcuterie is served with home-made chutney, and includes Coolea cheese as well as five cured meats; a signature main course is Tequila prawn & firecracker rice (two rices flavoured with chilli and vanilla) and Tequila butter but you could also choose the house variation of an old favourite, such as char-grilled fillet of Kerry beef with sautéed wild mushrooms, baby onions & red wine jus. And then you could finish in high retro style with an individual Baked Alaska. The stunning setting and great cooking is backed up by friendly, professional staff and both food and wine are good value. A great night out, in fact. **Seats 60** (private room, 60); air conditioning; children welcome (high chair); D served daily, 6.30-9.30pm; à la carte; house wine €28. *Bar food also available daily, 12.30-8pm. Visa. **Directions:** Situated in the town centre on Kenmare Place.

Killarney

RESTAURANT

Treyvaud's Restaurant

62 High Street Killarney Co Kerry **Tel: 064 33062**
info@treyvaudsrestaurant.com www.treyvaudsrestaurant.com

Brothers Paul and Mark Treyvaud opened this attractive and friendly town-centre restaurant in 2003, and it has earned a well-deserved local following and a reputation well beyond the area. The decor is gently contemporary, and daytime menus are carefully constructed to allow anything from a tasty little bite to a full-blown meal. You could start with a delicious bowl of seafood chowder, perhaps, which comes with excellent home-made bread, and then something from the 'Nibbles' section of the menu, such as tasty Treyvaud's fish cakes, or one of their speciality Sambos (the famous Club Sambo bears little resemblance to the usual); hot main courses include warm salads and Mark's Specials - their beef & Guinness pie with mashed potatoes is one of the best you'll find anywhere. The dinner menu takes over at 5 o'clock, and includes some items from the day menu - the soups and the speciality fish cakes, for example, with smoked haddock, wholegrain mustard & chives - plus a wide range of appealing and fairly-priced dishes including favourites like braised shank of Kerry lamb, and some less usual (ostrich, for example, which is farmed in Ireland), several seafood choices and at least two for vegetarians (one of which is likely to be a pasta dish). A short mid-range wine list offers a couple of half carafes and half a dozen fine wines. Good cooking, moderate pricing, long opening hours and well-trained staff with a clear desire to send customers away happy with their meal have proved a winning formula for this deservedly popular restaurant. The early dinner and (very popular) Sunday lunch offer especially good value. **Seats 80** (private room, 50); children welcome before 8pm; reservations recommended; air conditioning; L Tue-Sun, 12-5; D daily 5-10pm (to 10.30 Fri/Sat); L & D à la carte (early D 10% discount on food & drink, 5-7pm); also gourmet D €75. Set 4 course Sun L €22.95. House wine €17.95. Closed Mon & Tue off season (Nov-Feb). MasterCard, Visa, Laser. **Directions:** 500 yards up main street, on the left. ◇

Killarney

RESTAURANT

West End House

Lower New Street Killarney Co Kerry
Tel: 064 32271

Josef and Edel Fassbenders' unusual restaurant has a Tyrolean atmosphere and a most unusual history, having once been (very appropriately) one of Ireland's oldest schools of housewifery. Today it ranks as one of the "old guard" in Killarney hospitality terms as it has been serving wholesome, hearty fare at lunch and dinner without fuss or ostentation for many years and has maintained an enviable reputation for reliability and good value. The surroundings are simple but comfortable - a fireplace set at an attractively high level in the wall at the end of the bar casts warmth across the room, which can be very welcome on chilly evenings - and Josef's cooking is comfortingly traditional in a strong house style untroubled by fashion. Local produce is used to advantage, typically in good home-made soups that come with freshly-baked bread (try the West End chowder, a meal in itself, full of chunky pieces of white fish, some mussels and the odd prawn), main courses such as rack of Kerry lamb or tender well-hung steaks that taste like good steaks should. (B&B accommodation is also available.) L Wed-Sun, 12.30-2pm, D Tue-Sun, 6-9.30pm. Set D & à la carte; starters from about €5, main courses from about €19. Wine from €23. Closed Mon, L Tue. MasterCard, Visa. **Directions:** Opposite St Mary's Church. ◇

Killarney Area
HOTEL•RESTAURANT

Aghadoe Heights Hotel & Spa
Lakes of Killarney Killarney Co Kerry **Tel: 064 31766**
info@aghadoeheights.com www.aghadoeheights.com

A few miles out of town, this famous low-rise hotel, dating from the '60s, enjoys stunning views of the lakes and the mountains beyond and also overlooks Killarney's two 18-hole championship golf courses. It is now one of Ireland's most luxurious hotels and, under the caring management of Pat and Marie Chawke and their welcoming staff, it is a very special place. While the controversial exterior remains a subject of debate, the interior - which includes 24 recently added junior suites, a palatial glass-fronted two-bedroom penthouse suite and a luxurious spa & wellness centre - is superb. Stylish, contemporary public areas are airy and spacious, with lots of marble, original artwork, and a relaxed, open ambience and, from the foyer, hints of the stunning view that invite exploration - perhaps into the chic bar which links up with a terrace and the swimming pool area (lots of lounging space for sunny days), or up to the first floor open-plan Heights Lounge, where a day menu is available, and a delicious traditional Afternoon Tea is served (2-5.30pm). Accommodation is seriously luxurious, in spacious rooms with balconies and lake views, large sitting areas, plasma screen televisions, video, DVD player (library available) and a host of extras. Bathrooms are equally sumptuous, with separate shower and all the complimentary toiletries you could wish for. The 10,000 sq ft spa is among Europe's best and offers couples' suites, and some unique treatments - including 'Ayervedic Precious Stone therapy' in a custom-built Aromatherapy cabin. But at the heart of all this luxury it is the caring hands-on management of Pat and Marie Chawke who, with their outstanding staff, make everyone feel at home. And you will leave on a high too, as breakfast is another especially strong point. [*Aghadoe Heights was our Hotel of the Year in 2005.] Conference/banqueting (100/75); business centre, secretarial services, video conferencing, laptop-sized safes in bedrooms, free broadband wi/fi. Destination Spa. Leisure centre (swimming pool, jacuzzi, steam room, sauna, fitness room), hair salon. Garden, tennis, walking. Children welcome (Under 2s free in parents' room; cot available, €20, baby sitting arranged). Pets may be permitted by prior arrangement. **Rooms 74** (25 suites, 6 junior suites, 10 family rooms, 10 ground floor rooms, 1 disabled, all non smoking). Lift. Turn down service. 24 hour room service. B&B €185 pps, ss €70. Closed mid-week Nov-Feb. **The Lake Room:** The restaurant is on an upper floor, integrated into the Heights Lounge area, with distant views over the lakes and mountains; it is a bright and elegant space, with beautifully appointed tables and fresh flowers providing an appropriate setting for dining in a hotel of this standard. Head chef Gavin Gleeson - with experience at a number of top kitchens, including Dromoland Castle, before he joined the team at Aghadoe Heights - has developed new menus, which continue in the classical tradition of the hotel but with a lighter, more contemporary tone which is more in keeping with the atmosphere today. But updated versions of the classics are creeping back, especially in the main course choices - so you may find, for example, braised sole duglère with creamed leeks sitting happily alongside glazed breast of magret duck with tonka bean sauce, and fashionable confit belly of pork & milk-fed veal, with peach jus. A pianist sets the scene each evening and, under the direction of Restaurant Manager Padraig Casey, service is solicitous, as ever. An extensive and informative wine list includes a champagne menu, a strong range of classics, a good choice of wines by the glass and plenty of half bottles. **Seats 120** (private room, 75); reservations accepted; children welcome before 7pm (high chair, children's menu, baby changing facilities). D daily, 6.30-9.30pm; L Sun only 1-2.30pm. Set D about €70, also à la carte. House wines from €28. 12.5% SC on groups of 10+. *Informal menus also offered in The Heights Lounge and The Terrace Bar & Patio (from 10am-9.30pm daily in summer). Helipad. Amex, Diners, MasterCard, Visa, Laser. **Directions:** 3.2km (2 m) north of Killarney; signposted off N22.

Killarney Area
BAR•RESTAURANT

The Beaufort Bar & Restaurant
Beaufort Killarney Co Kerry **Tel: 064 44032**
beaurest@eircom.net www.beaufortbar.com

In the fourth generation of family ownership, Padraig O'Sullivan's attractive establishment near the Gap of Dunloe is always a pleasure to visit. The old tree at the front was left safely in place during renovations which, together with other original features like the stonework and an open fire, all contribute to the genuine character. The family take pride in running this fine pub, and the upstairs restaurant is a logical extension of the bar business. Head chef Tim Brosnan, has been cooking here since 1999, and takes pride in crediting local suppliers on his menus. Quite extensive, well-balanced à la carte and set dinner menus have a generous, traditional tone: starters may include seafood salad Marie Rose, and chicken liver paté, for example, and speciality main courses include Beaufort seafood platter, roast rack of Kerry lamb and Skeaghanore duck; finish with classic desserts or farmhouse cheeses. Pricing is fair, especially Sunday lunch which is very popular and good value. *A short traditional bar menu is offered, Tue-Thu evenings. **Restaurant Seats 60** (private room, The Kalem Room, seats 20); children welcome (high chair, childrens menu, baby changing facilities). D Tue-Sat, 6.30-9.30, à la carte; L Sun only, 1-3. House wine €21. Bar food served Tue-Thurs, 6-9pm. SC discretionary. Restaurant closed D Sun, all Mon; establishment closed Bank Hols, Nov. MasterCard, Visa, Laser **Directions:** N72 to Killorglin, left at Beaufort bridge.

Killarney Area
HOTEL

The Europe Hotel & Resort
Fossa Killarney Co Kerry **Tel: 064 71300**
sales.kih@liebherr.com www.theeurope.com

Although now around thirty five years old, this impressive hotel was exceptionally well built and has been so well maintained through the years that it has continued to outshine many a new top level hotel. However, never satisfied with anything but the absolute best, the proprietors decided to close the hotel in 2007/8 for major renovations, including a 50,000sq ft spa (ESPA at The Europe Hotel & Resort) and a new conference and events centre. Although work was still in progress at the time of the Guide's 2008 visit, most of the impressively spacious public areas – which make full use of the hotel's wonderful location - had received their makeover, and returning guests will be pleased to find that the style is contemporary, but also elegant, comfortable and not in any way in competition with the setting, which is emphatically the star here. Bedrooms – which have lots of space, quality furnishings, beautiful views and balconies all along the lake side of the hotel – had not changed at the time of our visit and, as they are so comfortable and well-planned, all that is needed is light refurbishment. A few new contemporary rooms completed shortly before the closure have now been opened, however, so there is a choice of style; they are handsome, if a little less practical. Leisure facilities include the new spa and leisure facility (with 20 metre swimming pool) and the hotel has two indoor tennis courts and their own Austrian Halfinger ponies for use within the hotel grounds, both complimentary to guests. Golf is, of course, a major attraction: the three Killarney golf courses - Killeen, Mahony's Point and Lackabane – adjoin the grounds, and the two nine-hole courses, Dunloe and Ross, are nearby. The hotel's continental connections show clearly in the style throughout but especially, perhaps, when it comes to food - breakfast, for example, is an impressive hot and cold buffet. Head chef Willie Steinbeck has responsibility for food in all areas of the hotel, including the smart new Brasserie Bar (with new terrace for outdoor dining) and the large and aptly-named Panorama Restaurant. Housekeeping is exemplary and, perhaps unexpectedly, this is a very family-friendly hotel. Conferences/Banqueting (550/380); business centre, broadband wi/fi. **Rooms 188** (8 suites, 38 junior suites, 21 family, 26 ground floor, 1 for disabled); children welcome (under 3s free in parents room, cot available without charge, baby sitting arranged; playroom, playground). No pets. Lift. 24 hr room service. B&B €105-120 pps, ss €80. No sc. Equestrian, fishing (coarse & fly), tennis, snooker, garden, leisure centre (pool, fitness room, sauna, steam room); Destination Spa. Closed 10 Dec - early Feb. Amex, Diners, MasterCard, Visa, Laser. **Directions:** On main Ring of Kerry road, N72.

Killarney Area
HOTEL

Hotel Dunloe Castle
Beaufort Killarney Co Kerry **Tel: 064 44111**
reservations@thedunloe.com www.thedunloe.com

Sister hotel to the Hotel Europe, Fossa and Ard-na-Sidhe, Caragh Lake (see entries), this beautifully located hotel is mainly modern (although the original castle is part of the development) and has much in common with the larger Europe: the style is similar, the scale is generous throughout, and standards of maintenance and housekeeping are exemplary. Like the Europe, the atmosphere is distinctly continental; some of the exceptionally spacious guest rooms have dining areas, and all have magnificent views, air conditioning and many extras. The surrounding park is renowned for its unique botanical collection, which includes many rare plants. Golf is, of course, a major attraction here and there is an equestrian centre on site (they breed Halfinger ponies, known for their gentle natures and great for trekking), also fishing on the River Laune, which is free of charge to residents. The space and relaxed atmosphere make it a good choice for families - and an impressive new outdoor play area has recently been completed. Informal meals are offered at The Garden Café, which is open all day and caters for everything from light snacks to hearty main courses. For fine dining the hotel's Oak Room Restaurant offers a classic à la carte menu, complemented by an extensive, well-balanced and informative wine list which - along with plenty of treats - includes a good choice of interesting affordable wines and an exceptional number of half bottles. Conference/banqueting (250/180). **Rooms 102** (2 suites, 29 executive, 10 family rooms, 1 for disabled, 18 ground floor); children welcome (under 2s free in parents' room, cot available without charge, baby sitting arranged; playroom; playground). No pets. Lift; 24 hr room service. B&B €145pps, ss €75 (weekend specials from about €210). Leisure centre (swimming pool, sauna, fitness room); pool table. Garden, fishing, walking, tennis, equestrian. Closed 1 Nov- 6 April. Amex, Diners, MasterCard, Visa, Laser. **Directions:** Off main Ring of Kerry road.

Killarney Area
HOTEL•RESTAURANT

Killeen House Hotel

Aghadoe Killarney Co Kerry **Tel: 064 31711**
charming@indigo.ie www.killeenhousehotel.com

Just 10 minutes drive from Killarney town centre and 5 minutes from Killeen and Mahoney's Point golf courses, this early nineteenth century rectory is now Michael and Geraldine Rosney's "charming little hotel". You don't have to be a golfer to stay here but it must help, especially in the pubby little bar, which is run as an "honour" bar with guests' golf balls accepted as tender; most visitors clearly relish the bonhomie, which includes addressing guests by first names. There's a comfortable traditional drawing room with an open fire for guests, furnished with a mixture of antiques and newer furniture, and the bedrooms vary in size but all have full bathrooms (one with jacuzzi) and are freshly-decorated, with phone and satellite TV. The hotel is popular with business guests as well as golfers; secretarial services are available, also all-day room service. **Rooms 23** (all en-suite). B&B €65 pps, ss €20; sc 10%. **Rozzers:** Resident guests see no need to go out when a good dinner is offered under the same roof as their (very comfortable) beds, and this charming restaurant is also popular locally. You can have an aperitif in the friendly little bar while browsing 5-course dinner menus that offer a wide choice on each course, plus specials each evening. The range offered is well-balanced, allowing for conservative and slightly more adventurous tastes, and some of the more luxurious dishes, such as oysters, chateaubriand steak or lobster, attract a supplement. Like the rest of the hotel, the dining room has a cosy charm and the owners' hospitality is outstanding. **Seats 50** (private room, 28);non-residents welcome; D daily, 6.30-9.30pm; Set D about €52, house wines from about €22, restaurant sc discretionary. Closed mid Oct-mid April. Amex, Diners, MasterCard, Visa, Laser. **Directions:** 6.5km (4 m) from Killarney town centre - just off Dingle Road. ◇

Killarney Area
HOTEL

Muckross Park Hotel & Cloisters Spa

Muckross Village Lakes of Killarney Co Kerry **Tel: 064 23400**
info@muckrosspark.com www.muckrosspark.com

At the heart of this large, well-executed development lies a fine Victorian house and, although the newer areas have an elegant contemporary style, an atmosphere of timeless quality prevails throughout. With a large conference centre, break-out meeting rooms and medieval-style banqueting suite, it is a popular choice for business and weddings, but it also makes a convenient and luxurious base for the independent traveller. It is located within the Killarney National Park, near Muckross House and Garden, handy to all the championship golf courses in the area, and ideally situated for exploring south Kerry. Beautifully furnished accommodation offers all that would be expected of an hotel of this calibre - ranging from romantic four-poster suites to spacious contemporary rooms, all featuring luxurious fabrics and many extras - and food and service to match. A good breakfast here will set you up for the day, and a particularly attractive feature of the hotel is the warm 'Irishness' of the staff. The adjacent Molly Darcy's pub is in common ownership with the hotel. **Restaurants:** Dining options are between the Blue Pool restaurant (named after the nearby Cloghreen Blue Pool Nature Trail), and the newer GB Shaw's, which is earning a following for fine food and service. Conferences/Banqueting (300/160); **Rooms 69** (6 suites, 42 double/twin bedrooms with separate seating areas that can be combined to create family rooms). B&B from €85 pps. Spa, walking, hill-walking, cycling, holistic healing, yoga, tai-chi; Championship golf and equestrian nearby. MasterCard, Visa, Laser. **Directions:** On main Kenmare/Ring of Kerry road, almost opposite entrance to Muckross House. ◇

Killorglin
RESTAURANT

Nick's Seafood Restaurant & Piano Bar
Lr Bridge Street Killorglin Co Kerry **Tel: 066 976 1219**
info@nicks.ie

This is one of the famous old restaurants of Ireland and Nick Foley's is clearly thriving. It consists of two attractive stone-faced townhouses - one a traditional bar with a piano and some dining tables, where arriving guests can linger over a drink and place their orders, the other the main dining area. With quarry tiles, darkwood furniture, heavily timbered ceiling, wine bottles lining a high shelf around the walls - and piano playing drifting through from the bar - the dining room has great atmosphere. Nick's cooking style of classic French with an Irish accent has earned a special reputation for his way with local seafood and - although there are always other choices, notably prime Kerry beef and lamb - it is for classic seafood dishes like grilled Cromane mussels, and lobster thermidor that his name is synonymous throughout Ireland. House cultivated oysters from the family farm are a speciality, and if you want to see what that much-maligned item 'the speciality seafood plate' is like at its best, make the journey to Nick's. It's unbeatable Irish seafood, and very good value. Desserts are all home-made and changed weekly, and there's a good cheeseboard too. Although it would be a shame to come here without enjoying such exceptional seafood, vegetarians aren't forgotten either and the service is outstanding, and the music and great atmosphere as beguiling as ever. An extensive wine list, hand-picked by Nick and with many bottles imported directly, includes interesting house wines and an unusual choice of half bottles. **Seats 60** (private room, 40); children welcome; air conditioning. Live Piano nightly (7.30-close). D Wed-Sun 6.30-9.45 in winter, daily in summer (to 9.30 Sun); 2 sittings at 6.45 and 9.15. Set D €50. Extensive wine list; house wine from €20; sc discretionary. Closed all Nov and Feb, Mon-Tue in Dec-Mar & Christmas. MasterCard, Visa, Laser.
Directions: On the Ring of Kerry road, 20 km from Killarney.

Killorglin
RESTAURANT•WINE BAR

Sol y Sombra Wine & Tapas Bar
Old Church of Ireland Lower Bridge Street Killorglin Co Kerry
Tel: 066 976 2347 info@solysombra.ie www.solysombra.ie

Atmospheric is one of the things they do best in the Foley family and this younger sister restaurant to Nick's (see entry), run by Clíodhna Foley, is no exception. Located in a former Church of Ireland premises just up the hill a little behind Nick's, it's an impressive place with a long bar, several seating areas and loads of character - the name means 'sun and shade' and one inspiration for the choice was the way the light from the stained glass windows plays on the interior. The menu very sensibly leads off with a definition of 'tapa' and explains that what's on offer here is actually 'raciónes' which are larger tapas portions, served on or with bread, and perfect for sharing with friends - a good decision that suits Irish tastes and is proving very popular. The food varies with the seasons and is based mainly on local Irish produce, with speciality foods imported from Spain for authenticity; an extensive range of little dishes is offered, with calamari a la plancha, roquetas de jamón Serrano, piquillo peppers and Spanish black pudding among the specialities. Desserts include one that will definitely put sherry trifle in the shade - a home-made zesty orange ice cream drizzled with medium sweet sherry. The Foleys have been importing wine for many years and their carefully selected, mainly Spanish, list includes a lot of specially imported bottles; you'll also find a good choice of wines by the glass, including three sherries. Live music is also an important feature here - check the website for details. **Seats 80** (private room, 25, outdoors, 20); children welcome before 9pm (high chair); toilets wheelchair accessible; air conditioning. D Wed-Mon, 6-10pm (to 9.30pm Sun, also closed Mon in winter); house wine from €19. Live music (various) on Thurs. 10% sc on groups 8+. Closed Feb, Tue (& Mon in winter). MasterCard, Visa, Laser. **Directions:** On left as you drive through town. Set back from road next to Nick's Restaurant

Killorglin Area

BAR•RESTAURANT

Jack's Coastguard Station Bar & Seafood Restaurant

Water's Edge Cromane Killorglin Co Kerry

Tel: 066 976 9102

Just a stone's throw from the sea at Cromane, where the mussels that the area is famous for are landed, this handsome stone building is smartly maintained and sends out all the right signals from the outset. Entrance is through an attractive traditional bar at the front, then through to a big, bright split level dining room with big windows overlooking a landscaped garden and sea at the back; the décor is basically simple but, with quirky details and bright turquoise accents in fun cushions and lovely fish-themed murals, the effect is quite wacky. But well-spaced tables, crisp white linen and gleaming glasses augur well and, after a warm welcome, menus are promptly presented. Head chef Helen Vickers is well known in the area and her background is classical, including working at the Ryan family's late lamented Arbutus Lodge Hotel in Cork, where some of Ireland's finest food was once served. So it should come as no surprise to find an angel in the kitchen here, weaving her own special magic with a superb range of seafood including, when available, hake, black sole, prawns, lobster, plaice on the bone, turbot, and scallops, although the ubiquitous tiger prawn finds its way in, even here, in a speciality tempura dish, served with a zucchini salad and sweet chilli sauce. But Cromane mussels also star, of course, typically in classic marinière style. The cooking is really excellent and everything beautifully presented, with generous servings of lovely fresh vegetables, and irresistible puddings - vanilla crème brûlée with almond biscotti comes highly recommended. A well-chosen wine list complements the food, and staff are pleasant and knowledgeable. This restaurant is a great asset to the area and it's well worth building a visit into your plans. Booking is strongly advised, especially at weekends. Be prepared for Dublin prices. **Directions:** Waterside in Cromane. ◇

LISTOWEL

A lively traditional market town on the banks of the River Feale in north Kerry, Listowel is probably most famous for its writers, notably John B. Keane and Brian MacMahon, and the Writers Week literary festival held in the town in June; the famous **John B Keane** pub in William Street is now run by his son Billy, also an author, who keeps on the family traditions. Interesting features of this Heritage Town include a beautiful five arch bridge over the River Feale, which dates back to 1829, Listowel Castle (086 385 7201, open May to September) and The Garden of Europe, located in the town park, where more than 2,500 trees and shrubs from all over Europe are grown. Local activities include golfing at the Listowel Golf Course (068 21592), excellent salmon and trout fishing on the River Feale, and horse riding at the Listowel Equestrian Centre (068 23 734, open six days a week, closed Mondays). The famous Listowel Races horse-racing festival takes place in September. The town offers interesting shopping including local crafts of pottery, candles, jewellery and knitwear. There's a farmers' market every Friday in the square, and an annual Listowel Food Fair is held in the town in November.

Listowel

RESTAURANT•BAR

Allo's Restaurant, Bar & Bistro

41/43 Church Street Listowel Co Kerry

Tel: 068 22880

Named after the previous owner, Helen Mullane and Armel Whyte's café-bar seems much older than it is, as the whole interior was reconstructed with salvaged materials (the flooring was once in the London Stock Exchange). It is brilliantly done, with the long, narrow bar divided up in the traditional way, with oilcloth-covered tables, now extending into a restaurant in the house next door. It is the type of contemporary, self-confident Irish eating house that visitors hope for but do not always find in every provincial town. Helen is an impressive hostess, buzzing about, dealing with orders and queries with grace and efficiency, backed up by an organised kitchen playing to its strengths: great raw materials, careful cooking by a mix of old hands and new recruits, well led by Armel. Pub/bistro lunch dishes executed with flair include the most delightfully fishy chowder, quiches, a tasty filo parcel of goat's cheese with mixed leaves and Mediterranean vegetables and crispy potato skins, fresh fish and crab and simple but excellent home-made desserts, such as a citrus tart and an innovative courgette and chocolate gateau. You could have a quick lunch here for less than €12 and not feel that your low spend was in any way resented. A different à la carte at dinner offers mains ranging from €19 to €32, highlighting the day's fresh fish and seafood from Fenit and with some good meat dishes - a perfectly cooked stuffed pork fillet with braised cabbage, for example, at €28.95.. Theme nights are often held. **Seats 50** (private room, 20, outdoor, 20); children welcome before 7pm. Open Tue-Sat, 12-9, L12-7, D 7-9 L & D à la carte; House wine from €22. Closed Sun & Mon, 25 Dec & Good Fri. D reservations required. Amex, MasterCard, Visa, Laser. **Directions:** Coming into Listowel on the N69, located half way down Church Street on the right hand side (almost opposite Garda Station).

Listowel
HOTEL

Listowel Arms Hotel

Listowel Co Kerry **Tel: 068 21500**
info@listowelarms.com www.listowelarms.com

This much-loved old hotel is rich in history and especially famous as the main venue for the annual Listowel Writers Week. Since 1996, the hotel has been in the energetic and discerning ownership of Kevin O'Callaghan, who has overseen a major extension and overhaul of the whole premises during the last few years and also added new bedrooms. Improvements are invariably done with great sensitivity, bringing greater comfort throughout the hotel without loss of its considerable character. A very attractive banqueting area and bedrooms all overlook the River Feale - and the race course, so these areas are at a premium in Listowel Race Week. Non-residents find this a handy place to drop into for a bite in the bar, where they serve traditional dishes like braised beef & stout casserole (12.30-9.30) and you can have tea or coffee in the lounge at other times. Conference/banqueting (500/400); video-conferencing, broadband wi/fi. **Rooms 42** (all en-suite, 2 suites, 10 executive, 1 family); children welcome (under 5s free in parents' room, cots available without charge). Wheelchair accessible. Lift. No Pets. All day room service. B&B about €70 pps, ss €15. (Higher rates apply to Festival weeks, incl Irish Open & Listowel Race Week.) Closed 25 Dec. Diners, MasterCard, Visa, Laser. **Directions:** In the corner of the historic old square in Listowel town centre. ◇

Portmagee
GUESTHOUSE•RESTAURANT•PUB
◉ Ⓥ

The Moorings

Portmagee Co Kerry **Tel: 066 947 7108**
moorings@iol.ie www.moorings.ie

Overlooking the harbour in this attractive little fishing port, The Moorings has been run by Gerard & Patricia Kennedy since 1994 - and it's pretty much the one-stop shop in Portmagee these days, as they work hard to provide everything the visitor could need. The Bridge Bar is a popular place to drop in to for a wholesome bite to eat when touring this beautiful area - meals are usually available all day, but a phone call to check times is advised. It's also well known for music and craic, with traditional Irish music (Fri & Sun), set dancing and Irish songs on various evenings. Bar food served noon-8.30pm daily. Then there's the Moorings Guesthouse, which offers appealing accommodation including four superior rooms and some family rooms; many rooms have a sea view and all are very comfortably furnished with phone, TV, tea/coffee making facilities and full bathrooms. They offer attractive packages, notably a 2-night Skelligs Package (April-September) which includes a pre-booked boat trip to the islands with packed lunch, then dinner in the evening, and an Irish Weekend with traditional music, set-dancing and traditional Irish food. **Rooms 16** (all en-suite, 4 junior suites, 1 shower only, 8 family, 2 ground floor, all no smoking); children welcome (under 3 free in parents' room, cot available without charge, baby sitting arranged). B&B from €50 pps, ss €15-20. No pets. Evening meals are served in **The Moorings Restaurant**, where there's a natural emphasis on fresh local seafood - starters like Skellig crab cakes, Cromane mussels and oysters, Caherciveen smoked salmon, for example, and main courses often including a hot seafood platter, pan-fried scallops monkfish with mussels and, perhaps, lobster (at a reasonable €30 per lb); non-fish eaters don't do badly either, with fillet steak and rack of Kerry lamb among the choices (also vegetarian specials), and the unpretentious 'good home cooking' style suits the cosy atmosphere and maritime theme very well. **Seats 50**; reservations recommended; children welcome (high chair, childrens menu, baby changing facilities); D Tue-Sun, 6-9.30pm. Closed Mon. And, most recently, they have a lovely gift shop, Cois Cuain, next door, selling unusual quality items that you won't see elsewhere. Establishment closed 19 Dec - 9 Jan. Amex, MasterCard, Visa, Laser. **Directions:** Turn right for Portmagee 5km outside Caherciveen on the Waterville Road (N70) onto R565, bear left after 10km before bridge.

SNEEM

Situated on the Ring of Kerry between Kenmare and Waterville, Sneem is "a knot" in Irish, and this colourful, immaculately kept village is divided in two by the River Sneem, creating an unusual "hourglass" shape ("The Knot in the Ring"). The first week of August sees Sneem at its busiest with the "Welcome Home Festival", in honour of those who emigrated from Ireland. Moderately-priced accommodation and stunning views make a good combination at the O'Sullivan family's hospitable **Old Convent House B&B** (064 45181), and the new **Sneem Hotel** (064 75100; www.sneemhotel.com) at Golden's Cove has brought much needed extra accommodation and facilities to the area. In the village, **Sacré Coeur** (064 45186) offers good plentiful food and value for money and, like **The Blue Bull** (064 45382) pub and restaurant, is a place favoured by locals and enjoyed by visitors. Of several other good pubs in the village, try Garbhagh and Mary Kavanagh's much-photographed bar **D O'Sheas** (064 45515), on North Square, which has been singled out as the best food enterprise in the Geopark area (Sneem to Kells) for taking sustainable and local development issues on board; as a novel way to put the area on the map, they created five 'Geopark' drinks - and they serve local food where possible: not 'fine' food, but hearty, country food in generous portions and they're open all year. There is a farmers' market on Tuesdays (11am - 2pm, June - September; also at Christmas). Golfers shouldn't miss out on the challenge posed by the world famous Waterville Golf Club (Waterville, 066 947 4102).
WWW.IRELAND-GUIDE.COM FOR ALL THE BEST PLACES TO EAT, DRINK & STAY

Sneem
HOTEL•RESTAURANT

The Parknasilla Hotel

Parknasilla Sneem Co Kerry **Tel: 064 45122**
info@parknasillahotel.ie www.parknasillahotel.ie

Set in 300 acres of sub-tropical parkland, overlooking Kenmare Bay, this classic Victorian hotel is blessed with one of the most beautiful locations in Ireland. Formerly the Parknasilla Great Southern Hotel, it came into new ownership in 2007 and, following major renovations to some areas, re-opened for the 2008 season. The most obvious change on arrival is the newly constructed holiday villas, set well back from the driveway in woodland between the gates and the hotel; they have caused a bit of a stir but are not too obtrusive and add mixed accommodation that is useful for families and groups of friends on golfing holidays etc. Villa guests have full use of all the hotel facilities, including the impressive new swimming pool and spa, all unobtrusively re-built above the little harbour and with huge windows taking advantage of the stunning sea and mountain view. In the hotel itself, there has been no significant change in public areas, which remain spacious and relaxing, with open fires and plenty of comfortable lounging furniture (although the wonderful Great Southern art collection is missed). The best bedrooms and suites in the main houses have been refurbished in luxurious period style, and there are some new more contemporary rooms (Parknasilla Suites and Courtyard Suites); much of the older accommodation (standard rooms, West Wing junior suites) had not been refurbished at the time of the Guide's 2008 visit but, in our experience, that was no hardship and a badly dated bathroom was the only serious disadvantage. Staff are very pleasant and helpful, and this gracious hotel remains a lovely place to stay. A wide range of activities is offered on the 500 acre estate, including walking, horse riding, tennis, golf (12), cruising, fishing, and cycling. **Rooms 95**. Room rate from about €320; offers available. **Pygmalion Restaurant:** A very large and beautifully appointed formal dining room, this is an impressive restaurant by any standards and diners are left in no doubt that this is dining in a style that befits the age and history of the building. The best tables, in a large semi-circular conservatory style area, have views over the gardens (and an extensive outdoor seating area) to the sea and mountains; even at breakfast there is a sense of occasion and, although it is not a destination restaurant, it serves residents guests very well. Executive Head Chef, Mr Andrea Crippa, makes good use of local ingredients, notably seafood, and although the cooking style is international, it is appropriate to the setting. Language difficulties can cause mis-communication, but service is friendly and helpful nevertheless – and, with one of the most beautiful views in Ireland to enjoy, a meal here will always be a treat. Family meals available, 5-6pm (babysitting arranged so parents may dine later). D 7-9 daily. A la carte. Amex, Diners, MasterCard, Visa, Laser. **Directions:** 25 km west of Kenmare, on Ring of Kerry. ◊

Sneem
GUESTHOUSE

Tahilla Cove Country House

Tahilla Cove Sneem Co Kerry **Tel:** 064 664 5204
tahillacove@eircom.net www.tahillacove.com

Although it has been much added to over the years and has a blocky annexe in the garden, this family-run guesthouse has an old house in there somewhere. There's a proper bar, with its own entrance and this, together with quite an official looking reception desk just inside the front door, makes it feel more like an hotel than a guesthouse. Yet this is a refreshingly low-key place, with two very special features: the location, which is genuinely waterside; and the owners, James and Deirdre Waterhouse. Tahilla Cove has been in the family since 1948, and run since 1987 by James and Deirdre who have the wisdom to understand why their many regulars love it just the way it is and, apart from regular maintenance, little is allowed to change. Comfort and quiet relaxation are the priorities. All the public rooms have sea views, including the dining room and also a large sitting room, with plenty of armchairs and sofas, which opens on to a terrace, overlooking the garden and cove. Accommodation is divided between the main house and the annexe; rooms vary considerably but all except two have sea views, many have private balconies, and all are en-suite, with bathrooms of varying sizes and appointments (only one single is shower-only). Although dated (this is part of the charm), all are very comfortable and have phone, TV, hair-dryer and individually controlled heating. It's also a lovely place to drop into for a cup of tea over-looking the little harbour – and that's the beautiful view that will begin each day as you enjoy breakfast in the dining room. **Rooms 9** (1 shower only, 3 family rooms, 3 ground floor, all no smoking); children welcome (under 2s free in parents' room, cot available without charge). B&B about €75 pps, ss €30. Pets allowed in some areas by prior arrangement. Free broadband wi/fi; Garden; walking; fishing. Closed for D Tue-Wed; house closed mid Oct-Easter. Amex, MasterCard, Visa, Laser. **Directions:** 16km (11 miles) west of Kenmare and 8km (5 m) east of Sneem (N70).

Ⓡ   # TRALEE

Situated at the point where the River Lee flows into Tralee Bay, Tralee is the main town of County Kerry and is the gateway to the rugged Dingle Peninsula. Although perhaps most famous for the Percy French song The Rose of Tralee - an association celebrated each August at the international Rose of Tralee Festival (071 23227) - this busy commercial centre has much else to offer in and around the town, including the town park which covers 80 acres and includes an award-winning rose garden; Siamsa Tíre (the National Folk Theatre of Ireland); and horse racing, great beaches (with the Jamie Knox Surfing/Wind Surfing/Kite Surfing School, 066 713 9411, a short distance away at Brandon). Nearby, the impressive restored working Blennerville Windmill (066 712 1064, open April to October) is well worth a visit and a restored steam train runs between Tralee and Blennerville, which adds to the fun. Quite near the windmill, you will find **The Station House** (066 714 9980; www.thestation-house.ie), where casual food is available all day, and fine dining offered at their restaurant Conway's (reservations advised). There are also rooms available at The Station House, although they may seem pricey for the standard offered. Local activities in the Tralee area include horse riding, hill walking (walkers are well accommodated as both the Dingle Way and the North Kerry Way begin in Tralee) and historical sites; some of the best golf courses in Kerry are just a short drive from Tralee, including Tralee Golf Club (066 713 6379), Killarney Golf & Fishing Club and Ballybunion Golf Club (068 27146) while sailing enthusiasts can enjoy the 100-berth marina at nearby Fenit. Food lovers will enjoy the Tralee farmers' market on Fridays (9am-5pm), and there are plenty of places of interest in and around the town, including the newest branch of the great deli baker and café **Jam** (066 7192580; www.jam.ie) at Ballyseede Home & Outdoor Living just off the Tralee-Killarney Road (N21). In the town, **The Grand Hotel** (066 712 1499; www.grandhoteltralee.com) on Denny Street has old world charm and, with its dark mahogany furniture and open fires in cold weather, the atmosphere is cosy; locals in the know just love this homely hotel for its bar food: everything is freshly prepared and service is quick and efficient - a good place to enjoy a cheerful and inexpensive meal, and suited to people of all ages (very popular for families). Visitors (and locals) of all ages also enjoy **Gringo's Restaurant** (066-7118808) on Princes Street, near the Brandon Hotel. Mexican and Western Steakhouse menus are offered (with separate kid's menu) and, with a lively atmosphere and whole-some, authentic food cooked by Latin American chefs, it's the kind of place that gives Tex-Mex a good name; open Mon-Sat 5pm-late; Sun from 1pm. Moderately-priced accommodation in Tralee is avail-able at **Benners Hotel** (066 712 1877; www.bennershoteltralee.com) on Upper Castle Street; **The**

Cooperage (066 7194347) restaurant at Benners Hotel is a dining destination in its own right and, although not quite settled at the time of the Guide's visit, this stylish operation is earning a following in the town and promises to match the popularity it previously enjoyed in Killarney.
WWW.IRELAND-GUIDE.COM FOR ALL THE BEST PLACES TO EAT, DRINK & STAY

Tralee

Ballygarry House Hotel & Spa

HOTEL•RESTAURANT

Killarney Road Tralee Co Kerry **Tel: 066 712 3322**

R

info@ballygarryhouse.com www.ballygarryhouse.com

This pleasant privately-owned hotel just outside Tralee presents a neat face to arriving guests and also has extensive landscaped gardens at the back; recent improvements to the main Tralee-Killarney road have worked in the hotel's favour as a slip road has been created, making access much easier and easing traffic noise. Now in the third generation of ownership by the McGillicuddy family, the hotel's 50th anniversary fell in 2008, and it's greatly to the credit of the management that so many features of the original 18th century Ballygarry House, and the traditions of hospitality that were established in the early days, have been maintained. It is held in affection locally and recent refurbishment, which has brought a more contemporary tone to the furnishing style, has been undertaken with due respect, with warm colours creating a welcoming atmosphere in the smart public areas. Accommodation is very pleasing, with many thoughtful details adding to the comfort of a stay - rooms overlooking the gardens at the back are particularly attractive and should be quieter. This is an appealing hotel, with exceptionally friendly and helpful staff, and it is moderately priced for the high standard offered. It is understandably popular for weddings. Conferences/Banqueting (600/400); free broadband wi/fi. Children welcome (under 4s free in parents' room; cot available without charge, baby sitting arranged). Spa (jacuzzi, steam room, beauty salon, hairdressing, massage, treatments). Walking, garden. Golf & fishing (sea angling, coarse) nearby. **Rooms 64** (2 suites, 9 junior suites, 11 family, 12 ground floor, 2 disabled, all no smoking) Lift. 24 hour room service. Turndown service. B&B €75-95pps, ss€30, no sc. No pets. Heli-pad. Closed 23-27 Dec. **Brooks:** This well-appointed restaurant is pleasingly set up overlooking the gardens at the back of the hotel and the modern classical food is appealing. Quite an extensive à la carte menu is offered, and its strength is in the presentation of traditional dishes with a successful modern twist. Cooking is sound, presentation attractive - and, best of all, staff are attentive and hospitable. **Seats 80**; children welcome (high chair, childrens menu, baby changing facilities). L & D daily, 12.30-2.30pm & 6.30-9.30pm. D à la carte; set L €27.50. House wine from €24. SC discretionary. Bar meals also available 11am-10pm daily). MasterCard, Visa, Laser. **Directions:** 1.6km (1 m) from Tralee, on the Killarney road.

Tralee

Ballyseede Castle

HOTEL•CASTLE

Ballyseede Tralee Co Kerry **Tel: 066 712 5799**

N R

info@ballyseedecastle.com www.ballyseedecastle.com

Now in common ownership with Cabra Castle in Co Cavan (see entry), this is a very likeable hotel of character with 15th century origins. Set in 35 acres of parkland and garden on the edge of the town, it is spacious, and comfortable, with quirky features that give a sense of fun - you may well be greeted by the resident Irish wolfhound (or a less prestigious but equally friendly canine companion). There's a relaxed and airy country house feeling about the place and it would make a good base for playing the championship golf courses in the area, or visiting the nearby Dingle Peninsula and the Ring of Kerry. They have a good reputation for weddings, although the small number of rooms means that most guests have to stay in other accommodation locally. **Rooms 23** (all en-suite). B&B from €75pps. Closed early Jan-mid Mar. MasterCard, Visa, Laser. **Directions:** Just off the Tralee-Killarney Road (N21).

Tralee

The Brandon Hotel

HOTEL

Princes Street Tralee Co Kerry **Tel: 066 712 3333**

R

www.brandonhotel.ie

Overlooking a park and the famous Siamsa Tíre folk theatre, and close to the Aquadome, Tralee's largest hotel is at the heart of activities throughout a wide area. A major refurbishment programme has recently been completed and all areas of the hotel have now been completed. Spacious public areas are impressive and, although some of the standard bedrooms are on the small side, all have direct-dial phone, radio and TV (no tea/coffee-making facilities) and en-suite facilities with both bath and shower. Equally well known as a business hotel, the Brandon has excellent conference facilities and fitness and relaxation facilities to match, including a well-equipped leisure centre with 17m pool and the Sanctuary spa. Conference/Banquets (950/650); free broadband wi/fi. **Rooms 185**; children welcome (under 12s free in parents room, cot available free of charge, baby sitting arranged). Private parking, lift, 24 hr room service. B&B from €80 pps. Leisure centre, swimming pool, gym. Closed 15-28 Dec. Amex, Diners, MasterCard, Visa. Directions **Directions:** Town centre.

Tralee
Brook Manor Lodge
GUESTHOUSE
Fenit Road Tralee Co Kerry **Tel: 066 712 0406**
v R
brookmanor@eircom.net www.brookmanorlodge.com

Set back from the road, in 3.5 acres of grounds, Sandra and Jerome Lordan's large purpose-built guesthouse offers immaculate and particularly spacious accommodation. Public rooms and bedrooms are large and very comfortably furnished - bedrooms are elegantly furnished and have generous beds and all the usual modern facilities - TV, phone, trouser press, tea/coffee making, hair dryer and radio/alarm - everything, in short, that the traveller (and, specifically, the golfing traveller) could need. Breakfast is cooked to order from an extensive menu, and served in a big conservatory that has been thoughtfully fitted with blinds for those mornings when the sun is just too bright. Sandra and Jerome are genuinely hospitable, making it a sociable place with a friendly can-do atmosphere. **Rooms 8** (1 suite, 1 junior suite, 2 superior rooms, 2 shower only, 2 family rooms, 3 ground floor, all no smoking); children welcome (under 3s free in parents' room, cot available free of charge). B&B €70 pps; (ss €20). Free broadband wi/fi; No pets. Closed 1 Nov - 1 Feb. MasterCard, Visa, Laser. **Directions:** 2 km from town centre on Fenit road (R558).

Tralee
Castlemorris House
GUESTHOUSE
Ballymullen Tralee Co Kerry **Tel: 066 718 0060**
R
castlemorris@eircom.net www.castlemorrishouse.com

Tony and Ciara Fields' attractive creeper-clad Georgian house makes a lovely place to stay. They really enjoy sharing their home with guests who, in turn, appreciate the space and comfort they offer and the friendly atmosphere of a family home. Afternoon tea with home-baked cake or scones is offered in the drawing room on arrival (in front of the fire on chilly days), and guests can use this room at any time, to watch television or relax with a book - and, in fine weather, there is a pleasant garden to sit in too. Bedrooms are spacious and well-furnished to provide comfort with style, and breakfast is a speciality. No dinner is offered, but there are restaurants nearby. **Rooms 6** (4 shower only, 2 family rooms, all no smoking); children welcome (under 4s free in parents room, cot available at no charge, baby sitting arranged); B&B €50 pps, ss €10. No pets. Garden. Closed Christmas. MasterCard, Visa, Laser. **Directions:** On south Ring Road/Killorglin road (Ring of Kerry) leaving Tralee/Dingle direction.

Tralee
Jewel of India
RESTAURANT
65 Boherbee Tralee Co Kerry
R
Tel: 066 711 7125

Occupying a recently refurbished building in the quieter business area of the town of Tralee, and within walking distance of town centre hotels and bars, this Indian restaurant offers a typically extensive and well-organised menu including a choice of set menus for parties of 4 - 6 people, and a number of house specials. Although strict authenticity may not be a priority, all dishes are well prepared with tender meat and flavoursome ingredients; sauces are very distinctive, which is not always the case in ethnic restaurants, and the kitchen is flexible when it comes to requesting hotter or milder dishes or variations on the menu. Some very fine vegetable dishes were particularly enjoyed on a recent visit by the Guide, notably the usually humble onion bajji and a wonderful aloo saag (potato and spinach). The selection of wines is basic, including a choice of quarter bottles, and there is also a choice of Indian beers. Staff are friendly and helpful and the service is very good - and the uninspiring, but spacious, interior (which features a few Indian adornments but is not overly decorated) allows for a calm atmosphere even when the restaurant is busy. Offering good food, value and service in comfortable surroundings, Jewel of India looks set to earn recognition as the leading Indian restaurant in Tralee and the surrounding area. Open for D only, daily. Amex, Mastercard, Visa, Laser. **Directions:** Off Boherboy Road.

Tralee
Meadowlands Hotel
HOTEL•RESTAURANT
Oakpark Rd Tralee Co Kerry **Tel: 066 718 0444**
R
info@meadowlandshotel.com www.meadowlandshotel.com

This hotel in a peaceful part of the town is set in 3 acres of grounds and landscaped gardens, yet within walking distance of the town centre. Open since 1998, the high quality of materials and workmanship has paid off as the building has mellowed and taken on its own personality - and this, together with caring service from well-trained staff, ensures its position as one of the area's leading hotels. The interior layout and design of the hotel are impressive; notably the whole hotel is wheelchair friendly and furniture, commissioned from Irish craft manufacturers, is interesting, well-made and practical. Stylish, well-designed bedrooms are spacious and comfortable, with strikingly original decor - and the suites have jacuzzis. In addition to the main restaurant, An Pota Stóir, informal meals, including seafood from the proprietor's fishing boats, are available in Johnny Franks bar, (12-9 daily). Conference/banqueting (200/180); free broadband wi/fi; business centre. Golf, equestrian, fishing and walking nearby. Garden. Children welcome (under 3s free in parents' room, cots available free of charge, baby sitting arranged). Wheelchair accessible. No pets. **Rooms 58** (2 suites, 10 superior rooms, 25 no smoking, 1 family, 5 ground floor, 2 for disabled). Lift. 24 hour room service. B&B €105 pps, ss €20. Off-season value breaks available. **An Pota Stóir Restaurant:** The dining room is finished in timber and decorated in a rustic style, with fishing and farming memorabilia - which , together with a high standard of service, makes for a relaxed atmosphere. The hotel has its own fishing boat (operated by the owner), and offers a short, regularly updated menu consisting of local seafood and some excellent non-seafood dishes; the cooking is fairly traditional but the chef uses local foods imaginatively, and to good effect; the welcome is very friendly too, and efficient and knowledgeable staff take pride in the quality of food. The wine list is simple but perfectly adequate and offers very good value. Probably not ideal for children, with the exception of Sunday lunch, although the staff would be very accommodating in any situation. **Seats 100** (private room 40); air conditioning; pianist Sat D; D Mon-Sat 7-9.30pm, L Sun only 12-2pm; set 3 course D €35; set Sun L €21.95; house wine from €19.50. SC Disc. Restaurant closed Sun D. Closed 24-25 Dec. Amex, MasterCard, Visa, Laser. **Directions:** 1km from Tralee town centre on the N69, but usually accessed by N21/N22: go straight through the last two roundabouts and turn right at each of the next two traffic lights; the hotel is on the right.

Tralee

RESTAURANT

Restaurant David Norris

Ivy House Ivy Terrace Tralee Co Kerry **Tel: 066 718 5654**
restaurantdavidnorris@eircom.net   www.restaurantdavidnorris.com

Restaurant David Norris has earned wide recognition as Tralee's leading fine dining restaurant, and it never disappoints. Although located on the first floor of an unprepossessing modern building, it has a nice little reception area with a sofa and stools at a small bar, and well-spaced tables are dressed with quality linen, plain glasses and white china, relieved by fresh flowers. A Euro-Toques chef, David Norris sources food with care; the ingredients used are organic wherever possible and everything served is hand-made on the premises. The emphasis is on taste, with beautiful yet not over-elaborate presentation - and the aim is to offer the best of food at reasonable prices. This he achieves well: seasonal menus are simply written and, while very promising, are not over-ambitious. About seven choices are offered on each course of an à la carte menu: seafood is well-represented, as would be expected in this area, but the range of foods offered is wide - Kerry beef may top the bill, also local lamb - and imaginative vegetarian dishes have mainstream appeal. Speciality dishes include a starter of crispy duck confit with Parmesan polenta and a chilli-garlic oil, and ever-popular breast of Irish chicken may be lifted into a different class by basting it with a mushroom and foie gras butter and serving it on Savoy cabbage with walnuts. Classic desserts, which include speciality hand-made ice creams, round off the meal in style, or there are Irish farmhouse cheeses, served with fresh fruit, home-made preserves and biscuits. Thoughtful detail is evident throughout, from the complimentary amuse-bouche that arrives with your aperitif to the home-made fudge served with your tea or coffee. Consistently good cooking, professional service, an informative but sensibly limited wine list and good value for money have all won this fine restaurant many friends - and visits by the Guide consistently confirm yet again David Norris's position as the premier restaurant in the area. **Seats 40**; children welcome. D Tue-Sat 5.30-10 (Sat 6.30-10); early D about €27, Tue-Fri 5.30-7; also à la carte. House wine from about €20; sc discretionary, except 10% (charged on food only) on parties of 10+. Closed Sun, Mon, all bank hols, 1 week Oct, 1 weeks Jan, 1 week Jul. Amex, MasterCard, Visa, Laser. **Directions:** Facing Siamsa Tire, across the road from the Brandon Hotel. ◇

Tralee Area
The Oyster Tavern
RESTAURANT•PUB

The Spa Tralee Co Kerry
Tel: 066 713 6102

This well-maintained bar and restaurant halfway between Tralee and the village of Fenit (a busy fishing port and excellent base for sailing), is easily spotted by its large roof sign. The Oyster has a strong local following, due to the convivial atmosphere in the bar and large selection of seafood in the restaurant. The dining room is basically a large extension to the small bar, with a view of the mountains across Tralee Bay on fine days. The menu is essentially traditional and everyone should find something to suit their tastes: an extensive seafood menu sits alongside a balanced choice of non-seafood dishes offering prime meat and poultry and a couple of vegetarian dishes. All food is skilfully prepared, and the service is both efficient and friendly. Children are welcome and the restaurant is popular with families, particularly for Sunday lunch. A fair selection of wines starts at €20. Bar open usual hours (no food served in the bar). **Seats 140.** D daily, 5.30-10pm, Winter hours 6-9.45pm (Sun to 8.45pm), L Sun only all year, 12.30-2pm. Set Sun L about €20, D à la carte. House wine from €20. Bar open usual hours (no food served in the bar). *Times not confirmed at time of going to press - a phone call to check is advised. Closed 25 Dec, Good Fri. Diners, MasterCard, Visa, Laser. **Directions:** 6.5km outside Tralee, on the Fenit road. ◊

Tralee Area
The Phoenix
RESTAURANT

Shanahill East Castlemaine Co Kerry **Tel: 066 976 6284**
phoenixtyther@hotmail.com www.thephoenixorganic.com

This unusual vegetarian restaurant has grown somewhat of late but it still exudes charm with its rambling gardens - you can choose whether to eat beneath trailing honeysuckle and fairy lights, or inside in the relaxed and cheerful dining area. The menu promises organic wines and the best of local and organic produce: a delicious salad or home-made soup, and interesting mains such as a house speciality of oven-grilled polenta & spinach cake served with goat's cheese crouton & apricot salsa – or an aubergine, sweet pepper & tofu curry. Dining at the Phoenix is an earthy experience, based on a strong respect for nature: guests are offered an opportunity to explore the natural garden, where most of the kitchen produce is picked fresh daily. This is a little gem, with a touch of magic adding an extra dimension to a relaxing evening. Live music brunches and dance nights sometimes, too. *The Phoenix offers accommodation including gypsy caravans and chalet rental, and has ample garden space to pitch a tent; packed lunches and airport transfers are also available. **Seats 45**; children welcome (high chair, childrens menu); reservations recommended. Open all day Tue-Sun 11am-11pm in high season; low season Wed-Sun 11am-6pm and also D Fri-Sun. D from about €25. Closed Mon (& Tues low season); Nov & Jan (may open by arrangement). Visa. **Directions:** 7km (4 m) west of Castlemaine on the R561 coastal road to Dingle. (N70 from Killarney or Tralee).

VALENTIA ISLAND

Valentia is a small island just off the 'Ring of Kerry' route and the most westerly point of Europe; the island's main claim to fame is that the first transatlantic cable was laid from here in 1857 (visit the Heritage Centre in Knightstown for details, 066 947 6411) and it is well worth a detour as you can take the ferry from Renard's Point to Knightstown, drive the length of the island and rejoin the mainland at the other end by crossing the bridge to Portmagee (or vice versa). But it is far better to allow more time, to capture the away-from-it-all beauty of the island - preferably on foot; the roads are very narrow and twisting, and there is much more to be seen when walking. Valentia combines a rich history with natural beauty and includes many Celtic church remains, standing stones, tombs and forts. A walk around the island could take you to much of interest including Glanleam House & Gardens (066 947 6176), famous for their subtropical gardens (and accommodation available), the wonderful **Lighthouse Café** (see entry) and the unique tetrapod track, which is an important geological site dating back 365 million years and one of only four in the world. A must-visit on the island is The Skellig Experience (066 947 6306, open April to November) which is one of Kerry's most important visitor attractions, an audio-visual exhibition about Skellig regions, the sea birds and the monks who used to live on the islands. Valentia Island is a popular spot for scuba diving, with three diving centres, and other activities available include cycling, canoeing, deep sea angling and shore fishing. Nearby Cahirciveen hosts a farmers' market on Thursdays in June - September (11am - 2pm) while a world-class links golf is available a short drive down the coast in Waterville Golf Club (Waterville, 066 947 4102).

WWW.IRELAND-GUIDE.COM FOR ALL THE BEST PLACES TO EAT, DRINK & STAY

Lighthouse Café

Valentia Island
CAFÉ•RESTAURANT

Dohilla Valentia Island Co Kerry
Tel: 066 947 6304

This unusual little restaurant is well signposted from Knightstown although, if travelling by car, the road becomes ever smaller and windier and you may wonder if the signs have been turned by some mischievous spirit; but no, you are not lost, and when you arrive you will even find space for parking. Then you walk up a grassy track, past flowers wild and planted, and a wonderful organic vegetable garden that has been claimed from the land sloping down to the cliffs. The café, a cheerful little building with a blackboard menu at the entrance and a large polytunnel tucked away behind the outdoor seating area, is a simple room set up in no-nonsense style for comfortable eating - there are no frills here, but what you get is exceptional in its simplicity and goodness. It's worth a visit even if just for cup of tea, served cheerfully with mismatched crockery to one of the outdoor tables, where you can sit and drink in the stupendous view. But there's plenty more on offer, from home-made soups served with delicious soda bread fresh from the oven to more substantial dishes and home-bakes for after or for tea. And, should you have time afterwards, you'll find the tetrapod trackway just along from the café... This place is magic. Open Tue-Sun 11am-7pm (to 10pm Fri-Sun); L 12-5.30pm. Call to check opening times off-season. Closed Mon. **Directions:** Follow the signs from Knightstown.

Sea Breeze - Knightstown's Coffee Shop

Valentia Island
CAFÉ

Knightstown Valentia Island Co Kerry **Tel: 087 783 7544**
grainneseabreeze@hotmail.com

Gráinne Houlihan's bright and funky coffee shop in Knightstown village is a great place to break a journey when touring the area. There's outdoor seating at the front for fine days and, inside, there's a pleasingly old-fashioned café with oilcloth-covered tables; aside from terrific coffees, good home cooking is the great strength, especially baking (warm scone with jam, butter & fresh cream, chocolate fudge cake...). You can have something as simple as a mug of soup and some home-made bread, a speciality sandwich, or one of half a dozen substantial savoury platters, including a vegetarian one, and there's a small wine list. At the back, a long corridor down to the loos is decorated with an eclectic collection of old mirrors - an inspired way to brighten up a long corridor. Toilets wheelchair accessible; children welcome (high chair, childrens menu); house wine from €4 per glass; Open weekends from Easter, 12noon-6pm; open daily in high season (June-end Sep). Closed Jan-Easter. **No Credit Cards. Directions:** On right in main street of village, coming from ferry.

WATERVILLE

This traditional village lies at the very south-west of Kerry between Currane and Ballinskelligs Bay. Waterville remains largely untouched from development with breathtaking scenery and a rich list of historical sites such as Staigue Fort (066 947 5127), Cill Rialaig and nearby Derrynane House (066 947 5113). With such close proximity to the sea, water sports such as canoeing, sailing and diving are easily accessible, while other activities on offer include horse riding and golf. Walkers will enjoy the scenic walk up to Coomakista Pass, or a quiet meander along the sandy beach of Skelligs Bay. The town includes attractive craft shops such as Waterville Craft Market (066 947 4212), and a treat that familes visiting the area should not miss is a visit to the famous Skelligs Chocolate Factory (0669479119; www.skelligschocolate.com) at Ballinskelligs (between Waterville and Portmagee). In this unlikely location the most exquisite (and beautifully packaged) hand-made chocolates are produced.

Brookhaven House

Waterville
GUESTHOUSE

New Line Road Waterville Co Kerry **Tel: 066 947 4431**
brookhaven@esatclear.ie www.brookhavenhouse.com

Overlooking the Atlantic Ocean and Waterville Championship Golf Course, Mary Clifford's family-run custom-built guesthouse lays the emphasis on comfort and personal service and, although it may initially seem a little stark from the road, it's all change as you turn into the drive and see the house properly, set in an attractive garden. The setting is peaceful and colourful and there's a little river that runs along the length of the garden, making an attractive feature. The spacious en-suite bedrooms are very comfortable and have all the necessary amenities; twin, double and triple rooms are all available, some with seating areas, all with direct dial phone, TV, hairdryer and tea & coffee-making facilities and most with lovely views over the bay - so book a room with a view of the sea if possible. And, as Mary is keen to point out, there's more to Waterville than golf - hill walking, watersports, angling and horse riding are all nearby. **Rooms 6** (2 junior suites, 1 shower only, 1 family room, 1 ground floor, all no smoking); children welcome (under 5s free in parents room, cot available at no charge). B&B €60 pps, ss €40. Free Broadband wi/fi. Drying room. MasterCard, Visa, Laser. **Directions:** Less than 1km from Waterville on the north side.

Waterville
HOTEL•RESTAURANT

Butler Arms Hotel
Waterville Co Kerry **Tel:** 066 947 4144
reservations@butlerarms.com www.butlerarms.com

Peter and Mary Huggard's hotel dominates the seafront at Waterville; it is one of several to have strong links with Charlie Chaplin and is one of Ireland's best-known hotels. Like many hotels that have been owner-run for several generations, it has established a special reputation for its homely atmosphere and good service. Improvements are constantly being made and public areas, including two sitting rooms, a sun lounge and a cocktail bar, are spacious and comfortably furnished, while the beamed Fisherman's Bar has a livelier atmosphere and can be a useful place for a break on the Ring of Kerry route. Bedrooms vary from distinctly non-standard rooms in the old part of the hotel (which many regular guests request) to smartly decorated, spacious rooms with neat en-suite bathrooms and uninterrupted sea views in a newer wing. Off-season value breaks; shooting (woodcock, snipe) Nov-Jan. Golf nearby. Garden; fishing; tennis. Snooker. Wheelchair accessible. Own parking. Children welcome (free cot, baby sitting arranged). No pets. **Rooms 40** (12 junior suites, 34 no-smoking rooms, 1 disabled). Lift. Room service (limited hours). Turndown service. B&B from €80 pps, ss about €30. SC discretionary. **Fishermen's Restaurant:** On the sea side of the old building, the restaurant is relaxing, and has a pleasant ambience, well-appointed linen-clad tables and friendly staff. The menu is flexible, priced as a full 5-course meal or à la carte, and offers a wide-ranging selection of dishes - main courses have an understandable leaning towards local seafood, including lobster, but Kerry mountain lamb, beef, and duckling are also likely choices, and there will be at least one for vegetarians. The house style is quite traditional and will please those who rate good, well-cooked food (with lots of flavour) above fashion. And do save a little room for delicious home-made desserts - or a trio of Irish cheeses, served with home-made tomato chutney. Restaurant **Seats 70**; reservations accepted (non residents welcome); children welcome; toilets wheelchair accessible. D daily, 7.30-9.30. Set D about €45, also à la carte. Bar food daily, 12-3 & 6-9pm. Hotel closed late Oct-end Mar, except for special bookings. Amex, MasterCard, Visa, Laser. **Directions:** On Ring of Kerry road. ◇

Waterville
B&B•RESTAURANT
🔲

The Old Cable House
Milestone Heritage Site Old Cable Station Waterville Co Kerry
Tel: 066 947 4233 interestingstay@iol.ie www.oldcablehouse.com

Alan and Margaret Brown's Old Cable House has Victorian character and the added interest of its transatlantic cable history. It is set high above the town to give clear Atlantic views, and the simply furnished rooms have everything necessary (including en-suite facilities) but with the emphasis on home comfort and Victorian atmosphere; the pine floors, original sash windows and the feeling of spending time in someone's treasured home are the real plus for those who appreciate vernacular architecture. Three disability-friendly rooms were recently added on the ground floor, and a restaurant extension was almost complete at the time of our 2008 visit. It is open to non-residents, and offers what the Browns correctly describe as unpretentious good food with character: Alan, who is the chef, lays the emphasis on seafood and locally sourced meats served in an hospitable atmosphere. Waterville Golf Club is on the doorstep, of course, and there are many interesting things to do when staying here. **Rooms 13** (4 family, 3 ground floor, 3 for disabled, all no smoking); children welcome (under 2s free in parents' room, cot available free of charge, baby sitting arranged; playground); free broadband wi/fi; B&B €42 pps; ss€15. Pets permitted (stay in bedroom, charge). **Restaurant Seats 32** (high chair, childrens menu); D daily in summer, 6-9.30pm; early D €20, 6-7pm; house wine from €17. Cycling, fishing, equestrian, golf and walking all nearby. Closed 24-25 Dec. MasterCard, Visa. **Directions:** In Waterville town.

Waterville

BAR•RESTAURANT WITH ROOMS

The Smugglers Inn

Cliff Road Waterville Co Kerry **Tel: 066 947 4330**
thesmugglersinn@eircom.net www.the-smugglers-inn.com

Lucille and Henry Hunt's famous clifftop inn enjoys a remarkable location right beside the world famous championship Waterville Golf Links. Gradual refurbishment of the premises has seen big improvements over the last few years; most recently the whole frontage has been upgraded and, together with colourful window boxes, it makes a welcoming first impression. This is an attractive place for an informal meal in the comfortable bar or, in fine sunny weather, at garden tables that overlook a mile of sandy beach to the sea and mountains beyond. The popular restaurant is in a large conservatory dining area which is shaded to avoid glare, and has magnificent views of the golf links and clubhouse, Ballinskelligs Bay and the McGillycuddy Reeks. Henry Hunt is a talented and dedicated chef, and local ingredients star in cooking which has a classical foundation, but includes modern dishes too, most noticeably on the bar menu. Seafood is the speciality, but non-seafood lovers have plenty of other choices, including Kerry lamb and beef, also some good vegetarian dishes. Lunch is served every day (the set lunch menu is good value, as is the early dinner), and bar snacks are available throughout the day, making this an ideal place to take a break when on the Ring of Kerry - although a phone call to check availability of food is advisable. Restaurant/Bar **Seats 90**. Children welcome before 7.30pm (high chair; children's menu); air conditioning. Restaurant: L 12-3 (to 4 Sun), D 6-9.30; bar food 12-8.30, (snack menu only 3-6 pm). Set Sun L €30. Early D €30 (6-7pm). Set D €41, also à la carte; house wine €18.50. NB - Minimum credit card transaction is €50. **Accommodation** is also offered, in pleasant rooms which have all been recently redecorated; they vary in size, outlook and facilities (one has a balcony) and price, but all are comfortably furnished in a homely style. There's a large first-floor residents' sitting room with sofas and armchairs, books, television - and magnificent sea views. **Rooms 14** (9 shower only, 1 family, 3 ground floor); children welcome (under 4s free in parents' room, cots available without charge); free broadband wi/fi; pets allowed in some areas by arrangement. B&B €55, ss €30. Garden, walking, fishing. Closed Nov-Mar. Amex, Diners, MasterCard, Visa, Laser **Directions:** Before village of Waterville, on coast road next to Golf Club.

COUNTY KILDARE

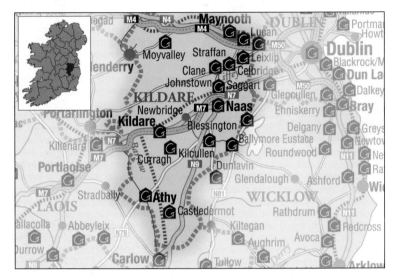

As would be expected of an area which includes the famed racecourses of The Curragh, Punchestown and Naas among its many amenities, Kildare is the horse county par excellence. The horse is so central and natural a part of Irish life that you'll find significant stud farms in a surprisingly large number of counties. But it is in Kildare that they reach their greatest concentration in the ultimate equine county. Thus it's ironic that, a mere 400 million years ago, Kildare was just a salty ocean where the only creatures remotely equine were the extremely primitive ancestors of sea horses.

But things have been looking up for the horse in County Kildare ever since, and today the lush pastures of the gently sloping Liffey and Barrow valleys provide ideal country for nurturing and training champions. Apart from many famous private farms, the Irish National Stud in Kildare town just beyond the splendid gallops of The Curragh is open for visitors, and it also includes a remarkable Japanese garden, reckoned the best Japanese rock garden in Europe, as well as the Museum of the Horse.

Another cornerstone of Kildare life is golf – the 2006 Ryder Cup between Europe and the US was staged in the county at the K Club, with the home team winning this "most passionate golf experience".

The gradual development of Ireland's motorway network has been particularly beneficial to Kildare, as it has lightened the traffic load through the county's towns. In fact, getting off the main roads is what enjoyment of life in Kildare is all about. The county's proximity to Dublin means that in the most recent population survey, Kildare was second only to neighbouring Meath in its increase, the numbers growing by 21.5% to 164,000. Yet it is surprisingly easy to get away from the traffic, and you'll quickly find areas of rural enchantment and unexpected swathes of relatively untamed nature.

In the north-west of the county is the awe-inspiring Bog of Allen, the largest in Ireland, across whose wide open spaces the early engineers struggled to progress the Grand Canal on its route from the east coast towards the Shannon. Such needs of national transport are intertwined through the county's history. But between the arterial routes, railroads and canals, there is an easier pace of life, and gentle country with it.

A southern leg of the Grand Canal curves away to become the Barrow Navigation, winding its way to Waterford. Beyond Athy, it goes near Kilkea, birthplace of Antarctic explorer Ernest Shackleton, whose growing fame is increasingly celebrated in his native county where his ancestors were involved in building the meeting-house which is now the Quaker Museum in Ballitore.

Local Attractions and Information

Athy	Heritage Centre	059 863 3075
Ballitore	Quaker Museum & Library	059 862 3344

Carbury	Ballindoolin House & Garden	046 953 1430
Celbridge	Castletown House	01 628 8252
Curragh	The Curragh Racecourse	045 441 205
Edenderry	Grange Castle & Gardens	046 973 3316
Kilcock	Larchill Arcadian Gardens (follies)	01 628 7354
Kildare (Tully)	Irish National Stud	045 521 617
Kildare (Tully)	Japanese Gardens	045 521 251
Kildare	Tourism Information	045 522 696
Kill	Goff's Bloodstock Sales (frequent)	045 886 600
Naas	Kildare Failte	045 898 888
Naas	Naas Racecourse	045 897 391
Newbridge	Riverbank Arts Centre	045 433 480
Punchestown	Punchestown Racecourse	045 897 704
Straffan	Lodge Park Walled Garden	01 628 8412
Straffan	Steam Museum	01 627 3155
Timolin-Moone	Irish Pewtermill	059 862 4164

R

ATHY

Athy is pleasantly situated alongside the River Barrow and the Grand Canal, which has three locks in the town, descending to the river. Two hotels have fairly recently opened in the area: **Carlton Abbey Hotel** (059 863 0100; www.carltonabbeyhotel.com) is the most central; it was once a convent and has many original features retained, including an impressive high-ceilinged bar with stained glass windows which is in the old abbey itself. **Clanard Court Hotel** (059 864 0666; www.clanardcourt.ie), set in large grounds a mile out side the town, is a popular hotel locally with good business and conference/banqueting facilities. In the town, Triona and Brid Edgar's **Gargoyles Café** (059 864 1482) at Grand Canal House beside the bridge, is a useful canalside place to know about; everything is sourced locally where possible and they take pride in good home cooking, offering lunches and casual food featuring home baking throughout the day and evening meals on Fridays and Saturdays (Mon-Sat, 9am-6pm (from 10 am Sat); D Fri & Sat only, 7-11pm. Closed Sun). Athy Farmers' Market and Craft Fair is held on Heritage Square each Sunday (10am - 3pm). A short distance away, at Ballitore, the Quaker Museum & Library (059 862 3344) is of interest for a number of reasons, including a connection with Antarctic explorer Ernest Shackleton who was born nearby at Kilkea; nearby also is the Timolin-Moone Irish Pewtermill (0507 24 164). Garden lovers will enjoy a visit to Heywood Gardens (Ballinakill, 057 873 3563), a landscaped estate with formal gardens designed by Sir Edwin Lutyens, and there are numerous other gardens to visit in nearby County Carlow. Golf courses abound in this part of Ireland and three of our recommended championship courses are within 30km; Rathsallagh Golf Club (Dunlavin, 045 403 316; also with gardens); Carlow Golf Club (Carlow Town, 059 913 1695) and The Heritage (Killenard, 0502 45500).
WWW.IRELAND-GUIDE.COM FOR ALL THE BEST PLACES TO EAT, DRINK & STAY

Athy
COUNTRY HOUSE

Coursetown Country House

Stradbally Road Athy Co Kildare **Tel: 059 863 1101**
www.coursetown.com

Jim and Iris Fox's fine 200-year old house just off the Stradbally road is attached to a large arable farm. The house is welcoming, immaculately maintained and very comfortable, with some unusual attributes, including Jim's natural history library (where guests are welcome to browse) and extensive, well-tended gardens stocked with many interesting plants, including rare herbaceous plants, and old roses and apple trees. Bedrooms vary according to their position in the house, but all are thoughtfully furnished in a pleasantly homely country house style and have direct dial phones, tea/coffee facilities and hair dryers. Iris takes pride in ensuring that her guests have the comfort of the very best beds and bedding - and the attention to detail in the pristine shower rooms is equally high, with lots of lovely towels and quality toiletries. (A bathroom is also available for anyone who prefers to have a good soak in a tub.) Another special feature is a ground floor room near the front door, which has been specially designed for wheelchair users, with everything completed to the same high standard as the rest of the house. Then there is breakfast - again, nothing is too much trouble and the emphasis is on delicious healthy eating. The wide selection offered includes fresh juices and fruit salad, poached seasonal fruit (plums from the garden, perhaps) pancakes, French toast with banana & maple syrup, Irish farmhouse cheeses, home-made bread and preserves - and the traditional cooked breakfast includes lovely rashers specially vacuum-packed for Iris by Shiel's butchers in Abbeyleix. **Rooms 4** (all with en-suite shower, all no smoking, 1 for disabled); not suitable for children under 8 and older children must have their own room. B&B €65pps, single €85. 10% discount on breaks of 2 nights or more. Small weddings catered for (20). No smoking house; pets allowed in some areas by arrangement. Garden. Closed 3 Nov- 12 Mar. MasterCard, Visa, Laser. **Directions:** Just outside Athy, on R428. Turn off N78 at Athy, or N80 at Stradbally; well signposted.

Ballymore Eustace

Ardenode Hotel

HOTEL

Ⓡ

Ballymore Eustace Co Kildare **Tel: 045 864 198**
info@ardenodehotel.com www.ardenodehotel.com

Fitzers Catering (see entry in Dublin 2) took over this small country hotel in 2006. It is not an hotel in the usual sense and customers hoping to drop in for a cup of coffee or a bar lunch will be disappointed but they are open for Sunday lunch and for private functions, particularly weddings. However, it is useful to know about this place as they will accommodate guests who are dining at the **Ballymore Inn** (see entry) and wish to stay nearby, and can arrange transport if necessary. Conferences/Banqueting (300/250); tennis court; garden; walking. Children welcome (cots available free of charge, baby sitting arranged); **Rooms 17** (5 shower only, 2 family, all no smoking); B&B €75pps, ss €20. MasterCard, Visa, Laser. **Directions:** From village square take a right at Paddy Murphy's pub, take right after the bridge, follow road and veer to right at fork, located on right.

Ballymore Eustace

The Ballymore Inn

RESTAURANT•PUB

Ballymore Eustace Co Kildare **Tel: 045 864 585**
theballymoreinn@eircom.net www.ballymoreinn.com

It's the fantastic food that draws people to the O'Sullivan family's pub and it's wise to book well ahead to get a taste of the wonderful things this fine country kitchen has to offer. The neatly painted cream and navy exterior, the clipped trees in tubs flanking the front door, all bring a sense of anticipation, confirmed by the warm interior with welcoming open fires. Hospitality is a strong point at this stylish bar - arriving guests are greeted at a reception area at the door, and you will either be given a table in the front Café Bar area, or you can go through to the 'Back Bar', a big open plan bar with a vibrant atmosphere. There are bar specials and a 'pizza & snack' menu offering home-made soup, delicious salads, warm panetella with various fillings and the famous Ballymore Inn speciality pizzas, based on artisan products and baked in a special pizza oven. An Express Lunch Menu, offers real food for customers in a hurry: a delicious home-made soup, and their renowned Kildare sandwich, or a simple hot dish, and a fish dish of the day (Duncannon cod with organic greens and yogurt, olive oil & lime dressing, for example); for a more leisurely lunch, a full menu is available. Evening Café Bar menus are a little more formal, offering a well-balanced choice, but this is beef country and the inn is renowned for its steaks - char-grilled aged sirloin or fillet - and rack of Slaney lamb is almost equally popular. Nobody understands the importance of careful sourcing better than Georgina O'Sullivan does and, as a matter of course, producers and suppliers are credited on dishes - and the policy of using only the very best ingredients, careful cooking and a relaxed ambience have proved a winning formula. And a concise, very carefully chosen wine list includes five bubblies, a couple of dozen available by the glass and eight wines by the half bottle. **Seats 100** (+16 outside); children welcome to 10pm (baby changing facilities); air conditioning. Reservations advised for Café Bar; Back Bar no reservations. Food served daily, L 12.30-3, D 6-9. House wines from €21.50; sc discretionary. Bar food also served daily 12.30-9. Live music Fri & Sat from 9.30pm. Closed 25 Dec & Good Fri. Amex, MasterCard, Visa, Laser. **Directions:** From Blessington, take Baltinglass road. After 2.5km (1.5 m), turn right to Ballymore Eustace.

Castledermot
HOTEL•RESTAURANT

R

Kilkea Castle Hotel
Castledermot Co Kildare **Tel: 059 914 5156**
kilkea@iol.ie www.kilkeacastle.ie

The oldest inhabited castle in Ireland, Kilkea dates back to the twelfth century and, as an hotel, has lost none of its elegance and grandeur. Many of the guest rooms have lovely views over the formal gardens and surrounding countryside, and some are splendidly furnished while incorporating modern comforts. Public areas include a hall complete with knights in armour and two pleasant ground floor bars - a cosy back one and a larger one that opens on to a terrace overlooking gardens and a golf course. Some of the bedrooms in the main castle are very romantic, and it is understandably popular for weddings. The adjoining (architecturally discreet) leisure centre has an indoor swimming pool, saunas, jacuzzi, steam room, well-equipped exercise room and sun bed. Outdoor sports include clay pigeon shooting, archery, tennis and fishing. There is an 18-hole championship golf course with informal meals served in the golf club. Special weekend breaks at the castle are good value. Conferences/banqueting (300/200). Leisure Centre, swimming pool. Garden. Tennis, Golf (18). Children welcome. No pets. **Rooms 36** (1 suite, 3 junior suites, 8 executive, 2 shower only). 24 hour room service. B&B from about €130 pps, ss about €40. SC 12.5%. Open all year. **De Lacy's:** Named after Hugh de Lacy, who built Kilkea Castle in 1180, this beautiful first-floor restaurant has a real 'castle' atmosphere and magnificent views over the countryside. Large tables sport crisp white linen, and there are fresh flowers and candles on every table. The restaurant overlooks the delightful formal kitchen garden (source of some ingredients on the table in summer) and has a bright, airy atmosphere: there is a sense of occasion here. Menus offer a wide choice, with no surprises but good quality ingredients providing a sound base for enjoyable meals. An updated classic of ever-popular fillet steak is usually on the menu, accompanied by pleasingly simple side dishes. A middle course offers soup or sorbet, and desserts may include old favourites like apple and raisin crumble with ice cream. Afterwards, it is pleasant to take coffee on the terrace in summer and wander around to see the old fruit trees, vegetables and herbs. Smartly dressed, well-trained waitresses give very good service and, although the cooking can be inconsistent, dining here should be a pleasant experience and lunch, especially, is good value. **Seats 60** (private room 40). L (daily by reservation) 12.30-2, D 7-9.30. Set L about €30. Set D about €55. House wine about €21; sc 12.5%. Toilets wheelchair accessible. Closed 3 days at Christmas. Amex, Diners, MasterCard, Visa, Laser. **Directions:** 5km (3 m) from Castledermot (off M9); signed from village. ◇

R R R

CELBRIDGE

Celbridge is attractively situated on the River Liffey, 22 kilometres (13 miles) from Dublin, and is the third largest town in Kildare. The town is of historical interest for many reasons, ranging from Celbridge Abbey (and its association with Jonathan Swift) to Castletown House. Castletown House (01 628 8252; www.heritageireland.ie) is the largest and most significant Palladian style country house in Ireland and the attraction that brings most visitors to Celbridge. It was built in about 1722 for the speaker of the Irish House of Commons, William Connolly (1622-1729) and, in recent history, it was purchased by the Hon. Desmond Guinness in 1967 and, together with the Castletown Foundation (who acquired the house in 1979), he set about preserving the house and restoring the principal rooms. Since 1994, Castletown has been in the care of the State and, following recent conservation work, re-opened to the public in 2007. The café, **CHC** at The West Wing is in the original double-height kitchens of the house and is run by Claire Hanley (see entry for **Hanley At The Bar**, Dublin 7, and www.clairehanley.ie); as well as the usual soups, sandwiches, salads and pasta dishes, you'll find updated versions of the some of the food that would have been familiar on Georgian tables including delicious syllabubs and trifles. There is a wealth of golf courses in the area and the closest include The K Club (Straffan, 01 601 7200); Palmerstown House (Johnstown, 045 906 901); Carton House (Maynooth, 0505 2000) and Castleknock Golf Club (Castleknock, 01 640 8736). Garden lovers will find plenty of interest in this part of Ireland too, including Larchill Arcadian Gardens (01 628 7354, Kilcock), Lodge Park Walled Gardens (Straffan, 01 628 8412) and Primrose Hill (Lucan) which are all nearby.

WWW.IRELAND-GUIDE.COM FOR ALL THE BEST PLACES TO EAT, DRINK & STAY

Celbridge

RESTAURANT

♛ ⚆ Ⓔ Ⓡ Ⓡ Ⓡ Ⓡ

The Village @ Lyon's Demesne - Restaurant la Serre

The Village Lyons Demesne Celbridge Co Kildare
Tel: 01 630 3500 info@villageatlyons.com www.villageatlyons.com

Beautifully situated alongside the Grand Canal, with the entrance - guarded by stone lions and a new lodge which sports the trademark soft Lyons green - just beside the 14th lock, the Lyons Demesne opened to some acclaim in 2007. The two restaurants - the fine dining Mill Restaurant, and informal Café La Serre – were originally envisaged as the first stage of an unusual project, The Village at Lyons, to include some small specialist shops, a cookery school and accommodation, and the completed sections sit well in their imaginatively landscaped setting with delightful little gardens and ever-present water. Following the untimely death of proprietor Dr Tony Ryan in 2008 and Richard Corrigan's move to Dublin (see **Bentley's,** Dublin, for details of his new venture), there was a noticeable slowdown and the stunning fine dining restaurant, The Mill, was closed. However, at the time of going to press the return of the venue's original chef, Paul Carroll is anticipated, following his recent work on the opening of Gordon Ramsay at the Ritz Carlton Hotel in Wicklow. Paul brings back his trademark style to the La Serre Restaurant (formerly Café La Serre) and sees the opening of The Mill as Ireland's premier Wedding and Corporate Venue. The Mill, (and several other areas, including The Garden Room and The Shackleton Room) makes a delightful venue for private gatherings, including exclusive weddings - there is a tiny chapel (it has to be seen to be believed), and the accommodation, in luxurious 2-bedroom 'cottages' (complete with Aga in their bespoke kitchens, amongst many other unexpected features), will delight all who stay here. **Restaurant La Serre** (formerly Café La Serre): You approach the main entrance past stone statuary and a bed of box balls, over a little bridge (pausing to admire the mill race below) and in through a massive front door which leads straight into the bar; known as The Lyons Den, it's a welcoming room with a huge fireplace, plenty of comfortable well-worn leather furniture and a full figure portrait of a lady to welcome arriving guests. The former Café La Serre is along a corridor towards the back of the building, and it's a very relaxed and informal space, with a covered courtyard area, an oyster bar and a high-windowed Turner-style conservatory that offers tables in a bright space alongside the maturing gardens. At the time of going to press, the previous casual style looks like changing, however, as Paul Carroll's new menus are currently being introduced and offer starters in the €16-20 range, with main courses at €34-40 and desserts at €10. **Seats 80** (outdoors, 20); open Wed-Sun for L&D, L 11-3.30pm, D 6-9.30pm (to 8.30pm Sun); reservations are advisable; house wine €27. Closed Mon (except bank hols) & Tues, 25-26 Dec, Good Fri. Heli-pad. Amex, MasterCard, Visa, Laser.
Directions: Left turn just before bridge in Celbridge village for Ardclough. Follow road for a couple of miles, you will come to a part in the road that has some really tight bends with warning signs. Shortly after that there is a left turn (as signed by a small pale green sign opposite turn). Drive over the hump back bridge and it is immediately on the right with two big lions on pillars flanking a gate. ◈

Ⓡ Ⓡ Ⓡ Ⓡ   CLANE

Clane is a fast-growing small town halfway between Maynooth and Naas; via the motorway which is accessed in Maynooth (about 10 minutes drive), it is about an hour from Dublin city centre at off-peak times. The River Liffey, the Grand Canal and Mondello Racing Circuit (045 860 200), home to Irish Motor Racing, are all close by. **The Westgrove Hotel & Conference Centre** (see entry) offers much-needed facilities . Abbeyfield Equestrian Centre (045 868 188) in Clane caters for people of all ages and for all levels; the nearby Donadea Forest Park, on the road to Kilcock, offers a variety of forest walks and facilities including parking, picnic site and toilet. There is a wealth of golf courses in the area and the closest include The K Club (Straffan, 01 601 7200); Palmerstown House (Johnstown, 045 906 901); Carton House (Maynooth, 0505 2000) and Castleknock Golf Club (Castleknock, 01 640 8736). Garden lovers, too, are very well catered for in this part of Ireland, with Lodge Park Walled Gardens (Straffan, 01 628 8412) nearby; and Primrose Hill (Lucan); Larchill Arcadian Gardens (01 628 7354, Kilcock); Hunting Brook Gardens (Blessington, 01 458 3972) and June Blakes Garden & Nursery (Blessington, 01 458 2500) all within a reasonable distance.
WWW.IRELAND-GUIDE.COM FOR ALL THE BEST PLACES TO EAT, DRINK & STAY

Clane
HOTEL
N R R R

Westgrove Hotel & Conference Centre

Clane Co Kildare **Tel: 045 989 900**
info@westgrovehotel.com www.westgrovehotel.com

In the outskirts of the village, near a small shopping centre, this friendly and well-run 4* hotel makes a good base for business, or for the many activities in the area - notably golf and horse racing. With a striking fresh floral arrangement in the large lobby as you enter, and a reception table set to the side with comfortable seats for guests, it makes a good impression from the outset – a feeling confirmed by a genuine welcome from very informal and informative staff. The hotel has contributed much-needed facilities to the town, offering excellent facilities including meeting and function rooms, a leisure club with 20m pool (free to residents) and an Elemis spa. Rooms are spacious and very comfortable, and the smart well-lit bathrooms all have bath and overbath shower; housekeeping is good, as elsewhere in the hotel. The main restaurant, Kirbys, was closed for refurbishment at the time of the Guide's most recent visit, but the busy bars are well-run and they do a very nice breakfast. Most of all, however, this hotel is notable for friendly and helpful staff who do everything possible to make guests feel at home and ensure a comfortable stay. **Rooms 99**. B&B from about €50, suites from €200. Closed 24-26 Dec. MasterCard, Visa, Laser.

Clane
CAFÉ•RESTAURANT
R R R

Zest Café

Unit 6/7 Clane Shopping Centre Clane Co Kildare
Tel: 045 893 222

Mark Condron's well-named lunch-time café and evening restaurant has earned a following for its relaxed atmosphere, friendly staff and fresh home-cooked food. Menus change constantly, but delicious starters might include unusual home-made soups, or classic options like chicken liver terrine. For the most part, the style of food is informal, offering a range of interesting pasta dishes, and gourmet pizzas, but more serious main courses are likely to include good steaks - a 10oz sirloin, or a char-grilled fillet - several good fish dishes, and imaginative chicken dishes. Lunch menus are much simpler than dinner - vegetable soup and home-made quiche topped with goat's cheese and salad, perhaps, or a succulent chicken wrap - but everything is done well here and even the simplest meal is sure to be enjoyable. The wine list is not extensive but offers a surprising range; four wines are available by the glass and there are a couple of half bottles. **Seats 54**; children welcome; toilets wheelchair accessible; air conditioning; café open Mon-Sat, 8.30am-4pm; restaurant open daily for D 5.45-10pm and for L Sun, 1-9pm; L&D à la carte; house wine from about €18. Amex, MasterCard, Visa, Laser. **Directions:** Off Main Street - turn at AIB, left hand side.

Curragh
COUNTRY HOUSE
W E V R R R

Martinstown House

Curragh Co Kildare **Tel: 045 441 269**
info@martinstownhouse.com www.martinstownhouse.com

Just on the edge of the Curragh, near Punchestown, Naas and The Curragh race courses, this delightful 200-year old house was built by the famous architect Decimus Burton who also designed the lodges in the Phoenix Park, Dublin, and is the only known domestic example of this 'Strawberry Hill' gothic architectural style in Ireland. It is on a farm, set in 170 acres of beautifully wooded land, with free range hens, sheep, cattle and horses, an old icehouse and a well-maintained walled kitchen garden that provides vegetables, fruit and flowers for the house in season. It is a lovely family house, with very nicely proportioned rooms - gracious but not too grand - open fires downstairs, and bedrooms that are all different, each with its own special character and very comfortably furnished, with fresh flowers. Meryl Long has welcomed guests to this idyllic setting for many years, aiming to offer them 'a way of life which I knew as a child (but with better bathrooms!), a warm welcome, real fires and good food.' Now Meryl has handed over the reins to her hotelier son, Edward Booth, and his wife Roisin, who both love the place and the work. A stay here is sure to be enjoyable, with the help of truly hospitable hosts who offers a delicious afternoon tea on arrival - and believe that holidays should be fun, full of interest and with an easy-going atmosphere. Small conferences/banqueting (12); **Rooms 4** (3 en-suite, 1 with private bathrooms, all no smoking); not suitable for children under 12. B&B from €110 pps, ss €35. Residents

D 7-9pm, about €55 (by arrangement - book the previous day). House wine from €28. No pets. Croquet lawn. Golf and equestrian activities nearby. Closed Christmas. Amex, MasterCard, Visa. **Directions:** Kilcullen exit off M9 then N78 towards Athy. Sign at 1st crossroads.

Johnstown
RESTAURANT
R R

The Morrell Restaurant

PGA National Ireland Palmerstown House Johnstown Co Kildare
Tel: 045 906 923 info@palmerstownhouse.com
www.themorrell.ie

This rather grand dining experience at Jim Mansfield's Irish PGA National/Palmerstown House remains a surprisingly well-kept secret, and it could repay investigation, especially if you are looking for an unusual place for a business outing. Having got off the busy N7, you'll be rewarded by a scenic contrast: an impressive great curved entrance gate, then a bridge, a long winding driveway past a walled garden and paddocks with horses and rolling green fields and a gracious mansion in the distance... The Golf Club is a luxurious modern two storey building, with a winding balustrade on each side, balconies, gazebo, water features, and tall lantern lights, all surrounded by immaculately tended gardens with wonderful topiary, a putting green, and a magnificent golf course. A very spacious lounge bar and casual dining space for golfers is on the ground floor, with amazing views across the 18th green and a man-made lake; upstairs, The Morrell Restaurant has an unexpectedly old fashioned, comfortable feel about it, with dark red walls, cream wainscotting, cream high backed leather chairs, crisp white linen and walls covered in all styles of pictures (not originals, alas, they are all in the main house). Head Chef Ciaran Cunningham was formerly at The St. Stephens Green Club and the food style is traditional fine dining, with some nice twists in presentation. Only an à la carte menu is offered, with starters probably including a speciality sauté of Dublin Bay Prawn with tartare of salmon, pickled cucumber and wasabi crème fraiche, and perhaps a twice baked goat's cheese soufflé with warm baby brioche and black olive tapenade); mains may include a protein-rich treat of seared fillet of prime Irish beef, with savoy cabbage and oxtail, beef & oyster pie, and a fish dish such as roulade of sole and scallop with a scallion fondue, spiced apple purée. Finish with a delicious dessert such as pinacolada crème brulée with passion fruit ice cream - and, of course, petits fours with your coffee. Service is attentive and very friendly. Extensive wine list to match the food. **Seats 76** (private room 16); unsuitable for children. D Tue-Sat 6-close; set D €60. House wine from €26. Closed Sun-Mon. Amex, Diners, MasterCard, Visa, Laser. **Directions:** Junction 8 off N7 Naas road.

Kilcullen
CAFÉ•BAR
⬛🍷R R

Fallons Café & Bar

Main Street Kilcullen Co Kildare **Tel: 045 481 063**
info@fallonb.ie www.fallonb.ie

Formerly Bernies Bar & Restaurant, this well known premises in the attractive village of Kilcullen was taken over by Brian Fallon (of Fallon & Byrne, see entry) quite recently, after his much-loved old family hotel, the Red House Inn at Newbridge, was destroyed by fire - and he brought the whole team with him, including chef Rose Brannock, who had made such a success of Café Tomat at The Red House. Following major renovations, the delightful result throughout the building is a mixture of old and new - a stylish blend that will be familiar to anyone who knew The Red House - with a very relaxing atmosphere. The neat brown exterior is cheered by colourful window boxes, a promising sign for first-time visitors, who will also warm to the welcoming fire and prompt greeting from pleasant staff, who guide you to the restaurant or to one of several eating areas in the buzzy bar - which is smartly and comfortably set up for dining, with wooden-topped tables and a mixture of aubergine banquettes and painted chairs. Rose Brannock's style of really good, simple bistro food is well-established, and her menus mainly offer a slightly modern taken on old favourites - starters of smoked salmon bruschetta with avocado & tomato salsa, and tiger prawns in batter with sweet chilli sauce are typical, also a main course of roast fillet of hake with baby potatoes and fillet of beef with béarnaise sauce and home-made chunky chips; in themselves there is nothing remarkable about these dishes but the high quality of ingredients and cooking skill lift them into a special league. Portions are generous, as befits this sporting area, and the value is good. A well-chosen list of about 40 wines features top producers and is fairly priced. **Seats 65**; food served daily 12.30-10pm. MasterCard, Visa, Laser. **Directions:** Centre of village. ◇

Kilcullen

RESTAURANT

N R R

Paul's Restaurant

Market Square Kilcullen Co Kildare

Tel: 045 482 966

Situated at ground level in a new office/apartment complex beside the River Liffey, this smart new restaurant is run by well-known local restaurateurs Paul and Freda Mullens. With a boardwalk set up for al fresco dining, and a canopy allowing for changeable weather, it's a very pleasant setting, and a stylish and comfortable seating area with contemporary couches and chairs confirms the good impression. Young waiting staff are smartly dressed in light pink shirts and dark trousers and guests can view the chefs at work, when seated in the impressive restaurant. An à la carte menu offers an interesting range of dishes with unusual ingredients and combinations although, at €9-18 for starters and €28.50-42 for main courses, the bar is set very high. All the little niceties are observed - three excellent fresh breads, olives, butter twirls and tomato pesto are offered, followed by an amuse bouche (chilled watermelon and vodka juice in a shot glass, perhaps, very refreshing). You might begin with whole roast quail with cauliflower cream, followed by of rack of lamb (four cutlets) with roast garlic and garden vegetables - perfectly cooked, although the Guide's experience suggests it may be under seasoned and a little bland. But, with an excellent pre-dessert (rhubarb crumble with mascarpone ice cream, perhaps), and a delicious dessert (flourless chocolate cake with Madagascar pepper ice cream) and a good espresso which comes with a little wooden box of petit fours - the waitress takes off the wrapping and opens it at the table for you – a meal here should end on a high. Cooking and service may be a little uneven, but Paul's has brought fine dining to Kilcullen and has the potential to overcome any teething problems - definitely one to watch. **Directions:** Beside the River Liffey on the Dublin side of the bridge. ◇

Kildare

RESTAURANT

R R

L'Officina by Dunne & Crescenzi

Kildare Retail Village Kildare Town Co Kildare **Tel: 045 535 850**

dunneandcrescenzi@hotmail.com www.dunneandcrescenzi.com

Although it is in the Kildare Village designer shopping outlet, this outpost of the small chain of high quality Italian restaurants run by Dunne & Crescenzi (see Dublin entries) is the only Italian restaurant in Kildare town and attracts diners who may not necessarily be on a shopping spree at all. Warmly lit and with lots of wood, the restaurant has a comfortable casual-chic ambience and is well-located within the village, with views of the Grey Abbey ruins, giving it a good atmosphere as a dining destination rather than just a place for a quick bite. You may expect the usual Dunne & Crescenzi signatures - although simple, the food is based on the best authentic Italian ingredients, and it is consistently high quality that has earned these restaurants a loyal following: D.O.P. products (EU certified authentic artisan produce) are used, notably cheese, salumi (cured meats), olive oils and vinegar. Open throughout the day, you can have anything from a wholesome snack (panini, bruschetta or their famous antipasti) to a relaxed dinner: among many delicious dishes offered, risotto con radicchio e salsiccia al vino rosso (risotto with radicchio, Italian sausage & red Tuscan wine) is one speciality. The wine list is not a weighty tome – but well chosen, and offers many treats; very reasonably priced house wines are available by the bottle, half carafe or glass. **Seats 150** (also outdoor seating); children welcome (high chair); air conditioning. Mon-Thurs, 10-6pm (to 8pm Thurs), Fri-Sat, 10-10pm, Sun 10.30-6pm. House wine from €16. MasterCard, Visa, Laser. **Directions:** Within walking distance of Kildare town, exit 13 M7.

Leixlip

HOTEL•RESTAURANT

R R R

Becketts Hotel

Cooldrinagh House Leixlip Co Kildare

Tel: 01 624 7040

A handsome property that is actually on the County Dublin side of the river that divides Leixlip, although the address is Kildare, this large house was once the home of Samuel Beckett's mother and it is now an unusual hotel, offering contemporary style and a high level of service for business guests. Imaginatively converted to its present use, luxurious accommodation includes four boardroom suites and six executive suites, all furnished to a high standard with a workstation and complimentary wi/fi. Public areas, including a bar and an attractive modern restaurant, have a far less business-like atmosphere. Cooldrinagh House overlooks the Eddie Hackett-designed Leixlip golf course, for which golf tee-off times may be booked in advance. Conference/banqueting (350/250) Business centre/secretarial services. Golf. Wheelchair accessible. No pets. **Rooms 10** (4 suites, 6 executive rooms) B&B from about €75. Open all year except Christmas. **Restaurant:** Atmosphere is the trump card in this stylish conservatory restaurant, with its stone walls, old wooden floors and soft lighting - and an exceptionally warm and genuine welcome. Pristine white tablecloths, gleaming silverware and glasses, and candlelit tables create a romantic atmosphere. Arriving guests are shown to their table promptly, and menus quickly follow, along with a basket of home-made breads. The à la carte - which is expensive - is available every night (the signature dish is Beckett's aromatic duck, with sultana, ginger & sage stuffing, and classic orange sauce), but it is worth getting here in time for the early dinner, which offers great value. An impressive range of wines (seen across the back wall as you enter the restaurant) is another attractive feature - and all this, plus the warm and efficient service that is part of the charm at Beckett's, ensures a strong local following, so booking is advisable. **Seats 130**. L Mon-Fri 12.30-2.15 & Sun 12.30-6; D daily: Early D Mon-Fri 6-7.30, Sat 6-6.30 €29; à la carte D daily 6-10. Closed L Sat. Amex, Diners, MasterCard, Visa. **Directions:** Take N4, turn off at Spa Hotel, next left after Springfield Hotel. ◇

Leixlip
HOTEL
R R R

The Courtyard Hotel
Main Street Leixlip Co Kildare **Tel: 01 629 5100**
info@courtyard.ie www.courtyard.ie

The restored stone walls of the original 18th century building are impressive at this privately-owned 4* hotel, which is best entered through an arch from the car park at the back, beside the River Liffey. The reception area is comfortably set up with comfy armchairs and a fireplace and both the Piano Bar and the Riverbank Restaurant - attractive rooms with high arched ceilings and big wooden beams - have views out over the Liffey. Accommodation is warmly furnished in a simple contemporary style and will appeal to business guests, with air conditioning, desk with data/fax lines and Wi-Fi internet; suites have balconies overlooking the gardens and river. Arthur Guinness established his first brewery here in 1759, four years before the world famous St. James' Gate Guinness Brewery, and it seems appropriate that the 'black stuff' should now be served here in the cosy and friendly 'Arthur's Bar'. Conferences/Banqueting (150/150); Free broadband wi/fi; business centre, secretarial services, video conferencing, laptop-sized safes in bedrooms. **Rooms 40** (8 executive, 16 ground floor, 2 disabled) Children welcome (under 12s free in parents' room, cots available). B&B €75pps, no ss. Lift. 24hr room service; garden; golf, equestrian, fishing and walking nearby. Open all year. Amex, Diners, MasterCard, Visa, Laser. **Directions:** Centre of Leixlip.

Leixlip
HOTEL•RESTAURANT
R R R

Leixlip House Hotel
Captains Hill Leixlip Co Kildare **Tel: 01 624 2268**
info@leixliphouse.com www.leixliphouse.com

Up on a hill overlooking Leixlip village, just eight miles from Dublin city centre, this fine Georgian house was built in 1722 and is furnished and decorated to a high standard in period style and, with gleaming antique furniture and gilt-framed mirrors in thick carpeted public rooms decorated in soft country colours, the atmosphere is one of discreet opulence. Bedrooms include two suites furnished with traditional mahogany furniture; the strong, simple decor particularly pleases the many business guests who stay here and there is a welcome emphasis on service - all-day room service, nightly turndown service with complimentary mineral water and chocolates - and a shoe valet service. The hotel is a popular wedding venue, and the banqueting suite had recently undergone complete refurbishment. Hotel guests have complimentary use of a nearby gym. Conference/banqueting (100/140). Secretarial services. Children welcome (cot available, baby sitting arranged). No pets. **Rooms 19** (5 executive, 14 shower only, 2 family). B&B from €80 pps, ss €40. **The Bradaun Restaurant:** The commitment to quality evident in the hotel is continued in the restaurant, a bright, high-ceilinged dining room, elegantly appointed with candles and fresh flowers on well-spaced tables. Head Chef Bryan McCarthy proudly credits his suppliers and devises menus that combine carefully sourced ingredients with imagination, creativity and flair, and food arrives beautifully presented, with wonderful attention to detail. Specialities include starters of baked Clonakilty black pudding with a compôte of rhubarb and fresh berries, or an unusual dish of Connemara smoked lamb, served with rocket, Desmond cheese, strawberry and aged balsamic. Slow cooking is a favoured technique and you may fine 24-hour braised ox cheek with artichoke purée and broccoli tempura among the choices - the à la carte, especially, is definitely not your average menu. Seafood choices are equally unusual, and sometimes combined with meat. Choices on the set menu tend to be simpler, and desserts are worth saving a little space for – a millfeuille of Wexford strawberries in season, perhaps, or a cocktail glass of home-made ice cream.

A customer-friendly wine list offers a wide range of wines by the glass, a dozen Wines of the Month and a similar number of half bottles as well as the main listing. **Seats 50**; children welcome. Food served daily 12-10. D Tue-Sun, 6.30-10 (Sun 12-8pm); Value D €32.50, 5.30-6.30pm; A la carte 6.30pm Fri/Sat; set L/D €32.50; house wine €22. Restaurant closed Mon (except for group bookings). Hotel closed 25-26 Dec. Amex, Diners, MasterCard, Visa, Laser. **Directions:** Leixlip exit off M4 motorway. Take right in Leixlip village at traffic lights.

🆁🆁🆁   MAYNOOTH

Attractively situated beside the Royal Canal, Maynooth is a busy university town and the centre for the training of Catholic diocesan clergy in Ireland. The grounds of St. Patrick's College run parallel to the canal and there are attractive waterside walks. The ever-expanding **Glenroyal Hotel** (01 629 0909; www.glenroyal.ie) has outstanding conference/business and leisure facilities and a branch of the popular Asian restaurant franchise, **Lemongrass**. Reflecting its youthful population, there are plenty of places to eat in Maynooth, including a good bar and informal restaurant **No 21 / The Roost** (01 628 9843) on Leinster Street (near the harbour). For accommodation in the town, something which is not generally known is that there are splendid Georgian and Neo-Gothic en-suite rooms at Maynooth Campus, which are available for public use - Tel: 01 708 3726 for further details. There is a wealth of golf courses in the area and the closest include Carton House (Maynooth, 0505 2000), The K Club (Straffan, 01 601 7200); Castleknock Golf Club (Castleknock, 01 640 8736) and Palmerstown House (Johnstown, 045 906 901). Garden lovers have plenty to visit in the area, including Lodge Park Walled Gardens (Straffan, 01 628 8412); Primrose Hill (Lucan); Ballindoolin House & Garden (Carbury, 046 973 1430); Larchill Arcadian Gardens, with follies (Kilcock, 01 628 7354); and Grange Castle & Gardens (Edenderry, 0405 33 316). Maynooth also has horse riding and pitch & putt facilities.
WWW.IRELAND-GUIDE.COM FOR ALL THE BEST PLACES TO EAT, DRINK & STAY

Maynooth
HOTEL•RESTAURANT
🍽️🏨☺ 🆁🆁🆁

Carton House Hotel
Maynooth Co Kildare **Tel: 01 505 2000**
reservations@carton.ie   www.carton.ie

Once the residence of the Dukes of Leinster, Carton House is an imposing mansion designed in classic style by the renowned architect Richard Castles, and built around 1740. It is set in one of Ireland's finest country estates - now home to two championship golf courses. No guest could fail to be impressed by the building itself, which is vast yet very elegant - and it has now been skilfully adapted to its new use through a stimulating combination of old and new. It is a natural choice for major corporate events and meetings, and would make a wonderful venue for special occasions of all kinds - these are, after all, uses that are not so very far from its previous life of entertainment on a grand scale. Public areas include a whole series of grand rooms, including The Duke's Study and The Gold Salon, each more impressive than the last, and the old kitchen - with its vast cast-iron stoves still in place - is now a bar, furnished rather surprisingly (but comfortably) in a very modern style. The accommodation has been designed and built in sympathy with the main house; the style is luxurious and contemporary, pleasingly bold in scale and with some appropriately regal colours - and, of course, rooms have all the little luxuries including robes and slippers and a minibar, as well as king-size beds, LCD screen television, DVD and CD player. Sporting activities are central to Carton House, and are a major attraction at this stylish destination so close to the capital - as is the hotel's leisure centre which has a full range of beauty and health treatments, an 18m pool, children's pool, jacuzzi, sauna & steam room, gym with cardiovascular & strength equipment and a juice bar. There are also two outdoor tennis courts, personal training and a wide range of specific training lessons. Prices are not unreasonable for a hotel of this calibre, and promotional offers are often attractive. Conferences/Banqueting (multiple rooms available to max. 480), broadband wi/fi; Spa, golf (36); **Rooms 165**; B&B from €85 pps. **The Linden Tree:** In a famous and beautiful room overlooking the golf course and gardens – and designed with very large windows to take full advantage of the setting - the fine dining restaurant has been allowed a classical style, with pristine white linen and simple, elegant table settings. The Linden Tree is mainly an evening restaurant and a visit here will always be worthwhile for the overall experience. Although the restaurant is not open for lunch, Irish High Tea is somewhat unexpectedly served here in the afternooons (2-4.30). *An informal dining option is also available (to members and visitors) in the Clubhouse, which is some distance from the house in renovated stables. **Seats 160**. Reservations necessary, held for 15 minutes only. D Mon- Sun, 7-9.45. A la carte. SC discretionary. Lunch for pre-booked groups only. **Directions:** 20 km west of Dublin's city centre (about 30 minutes from Dublin airport), Carton House is just east of Maynooth and signed from the town. ◇

Moyvalley   Fureys Bar
PUB   Moyvalley Co Kildare
R R R   **Tel: 046 955 1185**

Down a slip road off the M4 and insulated from traffic noise by thick hedges, this charming and immaculately maintained bar and informal restaurant has something of the best kind of Victorian country railway station about it, with its neat brickwork, jaunty flowers and wooden floors. Although by no means huge, a welcoming bar divides informally into cosy sections, and an area towards the back has a stove and views over the Royal Canal giving it the best of every world. Menus posted beside the front doors don't give too much away - soups, sandwiches, steaks, burgers, salads - but references to home-made 'house paté' and 'home-cut chips' hint at the good home cooking for which they are renowned, and one of their famous steaks, with 'all the trimmings' should be just the ticket for whether you're breaking a journey or coming up off a boat. Do call ahead, though, especially if numbers in your party are large, as 'groups can only be fed by arrangement'. Meals Mon-Sat, 12-7.50pm; no food Sun. MasterCard, Visa, Laser. **Directions:** Signed off M4 just west of toll booths. Located where the road, railway & canal meet between Enfield & Moyvalley.

Moyvalley   Moyvalley Hotel & Golf Resort
HOTEL•RESTAURANT   Balyna Estate Moyvalley Co Kildare
🏛 R R R   **Tel: 046 955 1009** info@moyvalley.com www.moyvalley.com

The long, curving driveway to this new hotel takes you through open meadows surrounded by mature trees, all part of the 530-acre Balyna Estate and a great mental divider, as you leave behind the busy road (and life) and look forward to the relaxation ahead. Although you pass the luxurious 10-bedroom Victorian manor Balyna House first, (available for exclusive use), the hotel is uncompromisingly modern. It looks a little stark (with new apartments directly opposite the front door, which seems a strange decision with so much space available), but it is quite a low building and not unattractive so it should soften with landscaping in due course - the gardens around the back of the hotel are interesting, which bodes well. Staff are very friendly and relaxed, setting a welcoming tone from the moment you arrive, and an impressively spacious, comfortably furnished reception area is hung with large atmospheric artwork and has access to the Waterways Restaurant. Up a fine staircase, the stylish first floor Sundial Bar, offers a casual menu; with large windows overlooking the golf course and plenty of comfortable seating, it's a very pleasant place to relax and enjoy a bite. Accommodation is mainly in the new hotel, in comfortable understated rooms with easy-on-the-eye coffee and cream décor, clean, simple bathrooms and, perhaps, access to a patio; however, in addition to the ten period rooms in Balyna House (house parties/events only), there is some very appealing accommodation in 2- and 3-bedroom units behind the hotel, in converted outbuildings. These little gems are like tiny townhouses and can be used as hotel rooms or for self catering - and only just across a sweetly landscaped courtyard from the hotel. With its lovely location so near to Dublin, this promises to be a great short break destination and a leisure centre is due to open shortly after the Guide goes to press. Conferences/Banqueting (250/180); free broadband wi/fi; laptop-sized safes in bedrooms; golf (18), archery, clay pigeon shooting, croquet, cycling, fly fishing, garden, walking. Equestrian nearby. Children welcome (under 12s free in parents' room, cot available, baby sitting arranged). **Rooms 64** (2 suites, 6 shower only, 21 ground floor, 2 disabled, all no smoking); Lift, 24hr room service; B&B €72.50 pps, ss €35. Closed 25 Dec. Heli-pad. **Waterways Restaurant:** This pleasing ground floor restaurant is set up in an attractive contemporary style and it opens on to the pretty courtyard, where Caribbean barbecues are held on Friday nights in July & August. With crisp white linen and comfortable high back chairs, good lighting and gentle music, it has a pleasant atmosphere and quite extensive à la carte menus offer upbeat versions of many favourites - the house speciality is surf'n'-turf and there is a choice of four other steaks, served with hand-cut chips, home-made onion rings, mushrooms and bake stuffed tomatoes; other choices are well balanced between fish, meats and poultry, with at least one vegetarian dish included. Sunday lunch is very popular, and an early dinner menu is especially good value. Service is friendly and willing. A wide-ranging wine list offers several half bottles and some quarter bottles. **Seats 100** (private room, 70, outdoors, 50); children welcome; reservations recommended; air conditioning. Food served daily 12-10pm (from 12.30 Sun); set L €25, set Sun L €25, also L & D à la carte; house wine from €24. Amex, Diners, MasterCard, Visa, Laser **Directions:** Just off the M4 near Enfield. ◇

R R R

NAAS

Although the casual visitor may not be especially aware of it, as this bustling town turns its back on its most attractive amenity - Naas is attractively situated on a branch of the Grand Canal and has a proper little harbour. It's a fast-growing place and the youthful **Osprey House Hotel & Spa** (045 881111; www.osprey.ie), in the Devoy Quarter, provides conference/business and leisure facilities. A wide choice of eating places includes a branch of the popular Dublin restaurant **Pasta Fresca** (045 901542), which is very close to the harbour and, in the town centre, **Lemongrass** (045 871544; www.lemongrass.ie) is behind the Town Hall (just off the main street); this smart modern place is the parent restaurant of a growing chain that now has franchises offering reliable Asian food in many other places and, like Pasta Fresca, has the great advantage of long opening hours (about 12.30/1pm-10pm, daily). At the other end of the main street (behind **Lawlors Hotel**, which had just re-opened after renovations at the time of going to press), **The Storehouse** (045 889333) restaurant has character - and if you want real place of character, make a point of dropping into one of Ireland's finest unspoilt old pubs, **Thomas Fletcher** (045 897 328) on the main street, if they are open - it's not a morning place. The Naas farmers' market is held next to The Storehouse restaurant in Friary Lane on Saturdays (10am-3pm). Naas is well located for many of the county's sporting activities including horse racing (three courses nearby - Punchestown 045 897704, The Curragh 045 441 205 and Naas 045 897 391). There's also golf at The K Club (Straffan, 01 601 7200); Palmerstown House (Johnstown, 045 906 901); Carton House (Maynooth, 0505 2000)), car racing (Mondello Park, 045 860 200) and attractions such as the Wicklow Mountains are not far away. The Japanese Gardens (045 521 617) and The National Irish Stud (045 521 251) are at nearby Kildare Town.

WWW.IRELAND-GUIDE.COM FOR ALL THE BEST PLACES TO EAT, DRINK & STAY

Naas
HOTEL
R R R

Killashee House Hotel & Villa Spa

Old Killcullen Road Naas Co Kildare **Tel: 045 879 277**
reservations@killasheehouse.com   www.killasheehouse.com

Set in an impressive 80 acres of gardens and woodland just outside Naas, this hotel is approached along an attractive driveway, with striking entrance and lobby areas, and a fine inner courtyard planted attractively with Virginia creeper. A grand staircase leads to a large traditionally furnished lounge on the first floor, with pleasant views and a pianist at certain times. Conference and business events are well catered for, and it is a popular wedding venue; bedrooms, which are well appointed for business guests and have all the usual amenities, include a number of suites, some with four-poster beds. Formal dining is offered at the beautifully appointed main restaurant, Turners. On site facilities include the Villa spa and leisure centre, with 25m pool; games room; archery, cycling, walks. *An 18-hole golf course with extensive leisure facilities is planned for 2010. Conference/banqueting (750/700). Business centre; broadband wi/fi; secretarial services, video conferencing. Children welcome (under 4s free in parents' room, cot available without charge, baby sitting arranged). No Pets. Garden, walking, cycling, leisure centre (pool, fitness room), Spa. **Rooms 141** (27 suites, 11 junior suites, 9 shower only, 4 family rooms, 70 no smoking, 6 for disabled). Lift. Room service (24 hrs). B&B from €99 pps, ss €45. Closed 24-25 Dec. MasterCard, Visa, Laser. Heli-pad. **Directions:** 45 minutes from Dublin on N7 to Naas, then 2km (1.5m) on R448, Kilcullen road.

Naas
RESTAURANT
R R R

La Primavera

27 South Main Street Naas Co Kildare **Tel: 045 897 926**
info@lap.ie   www.laprimavera.ie

An attractive frontage, with well-maintained hanging baskets in summer, makes this town centre restaurant easy to spot - and good first impressions are carried through into a pleasant split-level dining room, and a warm welcome from friendly staff who show arriving guests to simply-laid tables. Menus offer a wide-ranging, fairly contemporary, collection of dishes, including some seafood but mainly showcasing Irish meats, beef, in particular - their steaks are renowned. There are some interesting and unusual dishes offered, and a welcome emphasis on house specialities including starters like a good beef carpaccio, and unusual mains such as house-smoked loin of pork. A speciality 'Charcoal Combo' - fillet steak, smoked pork & rosemary-skewered prawns, shows originality and skill; side orders like crème fraîche mash, and fresh tossed vegetable strips in herbs and olive oil work well. Well-made desserts and good coffee to finish. Well-balanced wine list, although otherwise well-trained staff seem less knowledgeable in this area. All round: imaginative food, good cooking, caring service and good value. **Seats 60**; reservations accepted; air conditioning. D Tue-Sun, 5-10pm (Sun to 9.30). Early D about €15 (5-7), otherwise à la carte. House wine about €16. Closed Mon. Amex, Diners, Visa, Laser. **Directions:** At traffic lights on Limerick/Kilcullen junction.

Naas
RESTAURANT

Vie de Chateaux

The Harbour Naas Co Kildare **Tel: 045 888 478**
www.viedechateaux.ie

Just beside the canal harbour in Naas town, this small French restaurant and wine bar has simple décor and tightly packed tables, but it has struck a chord with local diners who like its warm atmosphere and the big blackboard menu offering unusual dishes that you won't find in other restaurants in the area. It's a sociable place, and there are platters of charcuterie or (mainly French) cheeses that can be order for one or to share, also a chargrilled rib of beef on the bone for two - and cheerful bistro classics like snails in garlic butter, moules frites and tarte tatin. As well as the blackboard menu, an à la carte menu simply priced by course is available as four individual courses (including a cheese course) or to make up a 3-course seasonal menu, which is very reasonable at about €30. Tasty food, friendly service and good value should prove to be a recipe for success. An informal lunch menu offers French classic of a different kind – tartines and soups, dishes of the day and 'big plates' with a starter and a main course served together for a quick meal. A mainly French wine list includes a good choice of wines by the glass, and there's a range for sale online too. **Seats 50;** Open daily, L Mon-Fri 12-2.30pm; D Mon-Sun 6-10pm (to 9pm Sun). MasterCard, Visa, Laser. **Directions:** Beside the canal harbour.

Newbridge
HOTEL
R R

Keadeen Hotel

Newbridge Co Kildare **Tel: 045 431 666**
info@keadeenhotel.ie www.keadeenhotel.ie

Centrally located and easily accessible from the M7 motorway, the O'Loughlin family's popular owner-managed hotel is set in ten acres of fine landscaped gardens just south of the town (and quite near the Curragh racecourse). The hotel undergoes regular refurbishment and generously spacious accommodation is furnished to a high standard. A fine romanesque Health & Fitness Club has an 18-metre swimming pool and aromatherapy room among its attractions, plus a staffed gymnasium. Extensive conference and banqueting facilities (1,000); secretarial services; video conferencing can be arranged. **Rooms 75** (1 suite, 3 junior suites, 20 executive, 1 for disabled); children welcome (under 3s free in parents rooms; cots available). No Pets. B&B €87.50 pps. Weekend specials available. Leisure centre, swimming pool. Garden. Parking. Closed 24 Dec - 4 Jan. Amex, Diners, MasterCard, Visa. **Directions:** From Dublin take N7 off M50, take sliproad sign posted Curragh race course & follow signs for Newbridge.

Straffan
HOTEL•RESTAURANT
🏰 ⛲ 𝒱 R R R

Barberstown Castle

Straffan Co Kildare **Tel: 01 628 8157**
info@barberstowncastle.ie www.barberstowncastle.ie

Steeped in history through three very different historical periods, Barberstown Castle has been occupied continuously for over 400 years. It now includes the original keep in the middle section of the building, a more domestic Elizabethan house (16th century), a 'new' Victorian wing added in the 1830s by Hugh Barton (also associated with nearby Straffan House, now The K Club, with whom it shares golf and leisure facilities) and, most recently, a large new wing added by the current owner, Kenneth Healy, which is built in keeping with its age and style. Some of the individually decorated rooms and suites are in the oldest section, the Castle Keep, but most are more recent - stylish and spacious, some with four-posters. Public areas include an elegant bar and two drawing rooms, and, there are big log fires everywhere - a cosy scenario for enjoying their delicious afternoon teas. Conference/banqueting (200/270); free broadband wi/fi, business centre. Garden, walking, archery, clay pigeon shooting. Fly fishing, golf & equestrian nearby. Spa. Children welcome (cot available) No pets. **Rooms 59** (16 junior suites, 17 premier rooms, 21 ground floor, 1 shower only, 3 disabled, all no smoking.) Lift. B&B €120 pps, ss €40. Closed 24-26 Dec. **Castle Restaurant:** Fine dining of character is offered here, and head chef Bertrand Malabat presents a number of menus including a six-course Tasting Menu (served to complete parties only) and a seasonal à la carte with about six choices on each course. The style is classic French with the occasional nod to international fashions; local beef or lamb usually feature, also game in season, and there will be several appealing fish dishes and at least one imaginative vegetarian dish. Finish with a classic sweet like vanilla crème brûlée - or a selection of Irish farmhouse cheeses and home-baked breads. Service is friendly and very professional. **Seats 100** (private room 32); not suitable for children after 8pm; reservations advised. D Wed-Sat, 7-9.30; à la carte. House wine about €23.50; sc discretionary (but 10% on parties of 7+). Fine dining restaurant closed Sun, Mon, Tue. Light meals are available in the Tea Rooms, 10am-4pm daily. Closed 24-26 Dec, Jan and Easter week. Amex, MasterCard, Visa, Laser. **Directions:** West M4 - turn for Straffan, exit at Maynooth - follow signs for Naas/Clane.

Straffan

HOTEL•RESTAURANT

R R R

K Club - Kildare Hotel & Golf Club

Straffan Co Kildare **Tel: 01 601 7200**

hotel@kclub.ie www.kclub.ie

The origins of Straffan House go back a long way - the history is known as far back as 550 AD - but it was the arrival of the Barton wine family in 1831 that established the tone of today's magnificent building, by giving it a distinctively French elegance. Current co-owners, the Smurfit Group, opened it as an hotel in 1991. Set in lush countryside, and overlooking formal gardens and its own pair of championship golf courses, the hotel boasts unrivalled opulence; the interior is magnificent, with superb furnishings and a wonderful collection of original paintings by famous artists, including Jack B.Yeats, who has a room devoted to his work – weekend art/history tours are offered. All suites and guest rooms are individually designed in the grand style, with sumptuous bathrooms, superb amenities and great attention to detail. Ahead of the 2006 Ryder Cup, major developments were undertaken by the hotel, including a new bedroom extension, an extension to the Byerley Turk Restaurant, and a spa. Although most famous for its golf, the hotel also offers river fishing for salmon and trout and coarse fishing with a choice of five stocked lakes (equipment bait and tackle provided; tuition available). For guests interested in horticulture, there is a mapped garden walk, with planting details, and there are weekend tours of the wine cellar, led by the hotel's highly-respected sommelier, Lisa O'Doherty. On-site amenities include: swimming pool; spa; tennis; walking; fishing; cycling; equestrian. Snooker; pool table. 24-hour concierge; 24-hour room service; twice daily housekeeping. **Rooms 92**. Lift. Room rate from about €280. **The Byerly Turk:** This is the K Club's premier restaurant and, beside it, a pleasantly clubby bar opens onto an elegant terrace with a distinctly French tone - here, on fine summer evenings, guests can consider menus over an aperitif and admire the golf course across the river before heading in to the restaurant, where tall, dramatically draped windows, marble columns, paintings of racehorses, tables laden with crested china, monogrammed white linen, gleaming crystal and silver are all designed to impress. Executive Head Chef, Finbarr Higgins, is commited to using the best of local and estate-grown produce, and all the little touches - a complimentary amuse-bouche, home-made petits fours with the coffee - that make a special dining experience memorable will be in place. He offers a Tasting Menu (€160 per person, served to a full table), based on The Market, The Sea, The Land and The Season, and a wide-ranging à la carte offers many luxurious dishes - a starter of slow-poached terrine of foie gras with Banyuls reduction and baby brioche is typical, for example, and a special main course, 'An beef Tuath', is The Ryder Cup signature dish: 2 medallions of Irish beef, shallot and wild mushroom crown, organic carrot with garlic and potato foam, mead sauce (€56). Unusually, there are two dessert menus, a normal one and a special soufflé menu (takes 20 minutes to prepare). Service is professional and friendly - and, given the intertwined history of Straffan House and the Barton family, it is appropriate that the Bordeaux Reserve from Barton and Guestier should be the label chosen for the hotel's house wine, heading up a signature list of 250 wines. **Seats 115** (private room 14); children welcome; air conditioning. Pianist in the evening. D 7-9.30 (Tue-Sat). tasting menu €160; also à la carte. House Wine from about €26; sc discretionary. *The River Room** is also in the main building and offers an informal dining option, which is especially suitable for families and larger groups. There is no dress code (other than the smart casual rule that applies throughout the hotel) and menus are more like sophisticated bar food. Breakfast is served here and it is also open daily 12-5 and 6-9.45. *Legends Restaurant** offers stylish European cuisine at the clubhouse of the Arnold Palmer Course, (Mon-Sat 4-9.30; Sun, from 1.30; light bar lunches available daily). There is also an Asian restaurant, the **Oriental**, at the Smurfit Clubhouse. Amex, Diners, MasterCard, Visa, Laser. **Directions:** 29km (18 miles) south west of Dublin airport and city (M50 - N4).

COUNTY KILKENNY

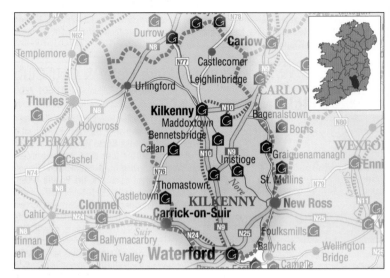

Kilkenny is a land of achingly beautiful valleys where elegant rivers weave their way through a rich countryside spiced by handsome hills. So naturally it's a place whose people care passionately about their county, and the miniature city at its heart. For Kilkenny - the Marble City - is one of Ireland's oldest cities, and proud of it. Its array of ancient buildings is unrivalled. But, by today's standards of population, this gem of a place is scarcely a city at all. Yet it's a city in every other way, with great and justified pride in its corporate status.

Civic pride is at the heart of it, and the city is benefitting from the refurbishment of its ancient quay walls along the River Nore, and the increase in pedestrian zones. Enjoying its reputation as a major centre for civilisation and culture for well over 1500 years, Kilkenny city thrives on a diverse mixture of public debates about conservation, arts festivals, and a comedy festival of international standing.

Rivers define the county. Almost the entire eastern border is marked by the Barrow, which becomes ever more spectacularly lovely as it rolls gently through the beautiful Graiguenamanagh, then thrusts towards the sea at the tiny river port of St Mullins. The southern border is marked by the broad tidal sweep of the Suir, and this fine county is divided diagonally by the meandering of the most beautiful river of all, the Nore.

Invaders inevitably progressed up its tree-lined course past what is now the lovely river village of Inistioge, towards the ancient site of Kilkenny city itself. They quickly became Kilkenny folk in the process, for this is a land to call home.

Local Attractions and Information

Callan	Edmund Rice House	056 772 5993
Gowran	Gowran Park Racecourse	056 772 6225
Inistioge	Woodstock Gardens	056 52699
Graiguenamanagh	Cushendale Woollen Mills	059 972 4118
Kilkenny	Kilkenny Castle	056 772 1450
Kilkenny	Cat Laughs Comedy Festival (May)	056 776 3416
Kilkenny	Rothe House (16c house, exhibitions)	056 772 2893
Kilkenny	City Tourist Information	056 7751 5000
Thomastown	Jerpoint Abbey	056 772 4623
Thomastown	Kilfane Glen & Waterfall	056 772 4558
Thomastown	Mount Juliet Gardens	056 777 3000
Tullaroan	Kilkenny GAA Museum	056 69202

Bennettsbridge

CAFÉ

Nicholas Mosse Irish Country Shop

The Mill Bennettsbridge Co Kilkenny **Tel: 056 772 7505**
sales@nicholasmosse.com www.nicholasmosse.com

One of the best reasons to venture out from Kilkenny city to nearby Bennettsbridge is to visit the Nicholas Mosse Pottery in their old mill which is located in a lovely rural setting on the banks of the River Nore. The restored mill is beautifully situated and very spacious, with three floors of pottery, including a large seconds area where some great bargains are to be found, and a 'decorate-it-yourself' studio where you can create something unique to take home. The full range of products is wide, including hand-blown glass and table linens, blankets, quilts and knitwear - as well as acres of the famous spongeware. Their café is on the first floor, overlooking the river, and a lovely spot for lunch or teas; the food offering has been widened of late and you can now choose from a concise list of about ten appealing savoury dishes including ever-popular cottage pie and lasagne, quiches and a pork and apricot terrine; served with good home-made breads, salads and chutneys, these make a tasty meal, and wine is now available too. But good home baking has always been their big thing, including cakes and desserts like sticky toffee pudding and chocolate brownie - and, of course, delicious freshly-baked scones made with the local Mosse's flour, and sold with good coffee or tea. Parking is easy and free and there's a lift in the store, also friendly staff who are always pleased to help. Worldwide shipping is offered, also mail order, gift wrapping, and a wedding service. **Seats 40**; children welcome (high chair, baby changing facilities); toilets wheelchair accessible. Opening hours: Mon - Sat 10am - 6pm; Sunday 1.30 - 5pm. Closed 25-27 Dec & 1 Jan. Amex, Diners, MasterCard, Visa, Laser. **Directions:** 7km (4 miles) south of Kilkenny, just before bridge turn off.

Callan

COUNTRY HOUSE

Ballaghtobin

Ballaghtobin Callan Co Kilkenny **Tel: 056 772 5227**
catherine@ballaghtobin.com www.ballaghtobin.com

Set in parkland in the midst of a five hundred acre working farm, this immaculately maintained house has been in the Gabbett family for three hundred and fifty years. Graciously proportioned rooms are beautifully furnished and the spacious bedrooms - which Catherine Gabbett has decorated stylishly - all have antique furniture and every comfort, including lovely bathrooms with bath and overbath shower, and tea/coffee trays. The house is surrounded by large gardens, with a hard tennis court, croquet lawn - and even a ruined Norman church - for guests' use. No dinners, but Catherine will direct you to one of several good restaurants within a short drive. **Rooms 3** (all en-suite & no smoking, 2 family rooms); children welcome (under 3s free in parents' room; cot available without charge). B&B €45 pps, ss €10. Pets allowed by arrangement. Garden, walking, tennis, croquet. Fly fishing, golf and hunting/shooting nearby. Closed Nov-Feb. MasterCard, Visa. MasterCard, Visa. **Directions:** Past Callan Golf Club on left, 4km (2.3 m), bear left; bear left at junction, entrance on left opposite Gate Lodge.

CASTLECOMER

An attractive town with wide tree-lined streets, Castlecomer takes its name from the local castle which was built by the Normans in 1171 on the mound opposite the present gates in to the Castlecomer Demesne. Today it is a thriving town with two annual festivals (one on the August Bank Holiday weekend, the other the famous Wellie race on New Year's Day, which has been running for over 25 years. With an 18 hole championship golf course among the activities, and many fine old buildings including the recently renovated Estate Farmyard at Castlecomer Discovery Park (www.discoverypark.ie), there is much of interest in the town. Originally part of the demesne of the 17th Century Castlecomer House owned by the Prior Wandesforde family, the Park attracts many visitors for a day out and has woodland walks, two fishing lakes (rainbow trout), a collection of wooden sculptures, picnic areas, a children's adventure playground among its attractions. Many people come especially to visit the design craft yard; refreshments are available here at **Jarrow Café** (056 444 0707), and, in the village, wholesome cooking is also to be found at **The Lime Tree** (056-4440966), a well established restaurant on The Square, which is very handy for a journey break.

WWW.IRELAND-GUIDE.COM FOR ALL THE BEST PLACES TO EAT, DRINK & STAY

GRAIGUENAMANAGH

Situated in the Barrow Valley, an area of outstanding natural beauty, Graiguenamanagh offers the visitor beautiful walks along the tow paths, boating and there's even a swimming place along the quay. In fact, the perfect little river port of Graiguenamanagh has everything, even including a book market - a collection of booksellers sharing premises on the main street - and an annual Book Festival. This charming place also has several hostelries of character, notably the legendary pub and general merchants **Doyle's** (059 972 4203), with its old shop at the front and cosy fire in the back bar, and comfortable accommodation and homely fare is offered at the aptly-named **Waterside** (see entry below), right on the quay. The beautiful old stone bridge marks the boundary between counties Kilkenny and Carlow and on the opposite quay, on the Carlow side, is Tinnahinch; here a new restaurant, **Boat's Bistro** (059 972 5075) opened on the quayside shortly before the Guide went to press and quickly began to build a following. And near Graiguenamanagh, in the New Ross direction, you will find Fran and Robert Durie's charming country house B&B **Ballyogan House** (059 9725969; www.ballyoganhouse.com), peacefully set in extensive gardens. Points of interest in Gariguenamanagh include Duiske Abbey (059 972 4238), a fully restored Cistercian church, with original medieval floor tiles still available to view, and the eel fishery at Graiguenamanagh, which dates back to the Cistercian monks who built the town and weirs on the river, and has been active again in recent years. It's not really a shopping place but Cushendale Woollen Mills (059 972 4118; www.cushendale.ie) is of particular interest - one of Ireland's oldest woollen mills, this family-run business goes back to the 17th century; the Mill Shop is open all year.

WWW.IRELAND-GUIDE.COM FOR ALL THE BEST PLACES TO EAT, DRINK & STAY

Graiguenamanagh | **Waterside**
GUESTHOUSE•RESTAURANT | The Quay Graiguenamanagh Co Kilkenny **Tel: 059 972 4246**
🏠 € | info@watersideguesthouse.com   www.watersideguesthouse.com

An attractive old stone warehouse on the quayside of this charming village on the River Barrow makes a characterful setting for Brian and Brigid Roberts' well-run guesthouse and restaurant. Gradual upgrading of the accommodation has been taking place for several years and this is a very pleasant, reasonably priced, place to stay in an interesting location, well off the road. The rooms are quite simple but comfortable, with direct dial phones, tea/coffee making facilities and TV in all rooms; some rooms at the top of the building are more spacious, and all overlook the river – this is a wonderful place to wake up in. Book lovers may be interested in weekend book sales at Waterside, which is the home of the Graiguenamanagh Book Festival and booktown project – ask Brian when you are there, and he will tell you all about it. Hillwalking holidays for small groups are offered. **Rooms 10** (all shower only & no smoking, 4 family rooms); children welcome (under 3s free in parents' room, cot available without charge, baby sitting arranged). No pets. B&B €49-59pps, ss €13.50. *Weekend packages/short breaks from €89 pps. No lift. **Restaurant:** On fine summer days there are tables outside on the quayside, and a comfortable reception area leads into the simply stylish restaurant, where Brigid offers varied menus and good home cooking - in very pleasant waterside surroundings. She uses fresh local produce wherever possible, sometimes including a speciality starter of rare Graiguenamanagh smoked eel. Braised lamb shank with mint jus is a more predictable speciality and, aside from a range of mainstream choices, game might be offered in season and interesting vegetarian choices are always included. Finish with a nice homely dessert such as pineapple, apple & almond pudding with crème anglaise. There's always an Irish cheese plate too, with home-made tomato chutney and a choice of half a dozen ports to accompany. Service is friendly under Brian's supervision - and the wine list, which is extensive for a country restaurant, is interesting and fairly priced. The early dinner and Sunday lunch menus are extremely reasonable, although the low price inevitably restricts choice. **Seats 42**. Outdoor Dining available in the Summer. D daily, 6.30-

9.30pm; L Sun only 12-3. Set Sun L €23, Early D €23 (6.30-7.45). D à la carte. House wine from €19.75. No SC. *In summer there's also a light Daytime Menu available, 11-4. Restaurant open weekends only in winter. Establishment closed Jan, 25 Dec. Amex, MasterCard, Visa, Laser. **Directions:** 27km (17 m) south east of Kilkenny on Carlow/Kilkenny border.

Inistioge   # Bassett's at Woodstock
RESTAURANT   Woodstock Gardens Inistioge Co Kilkenny **Tel: 056 775 8820**
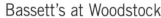   info@bassetts.ie   www.bassetts.ie

John Bassett grew up in Inistioge and returned with his partner Mijke Jansen to run this scenically located contemporary restaurant at the historic and beautifully restored Woodstock Gardens & Arboretum. In a modern building overlooking the Nore valley, and conveniently situated beside the visitors' carpark, this is not just a 'garden visits café' but a fully fledged restaurant which has become a destination in itself. Assuming you can take your eyes off the magnificent Kilkenny countryside for a moment, you'll first suspect that something special awaits you when you notice saddleback pigs in a small pen near the car park. Mijke and John welcome you personally, and you can have a drink in the little bar or go straight to your table in a room where the view seen through large windows takes centre stage - the other star of the show is Mijke Jansen's food, which is really excellent. The menu during the week is à la carte, with a tasting menu at weekends – and, although the choice may be limited, the quality, presentation and the delicate touch in the kitchen is wonderful. An early summer menu might include starters like roast boned quail with salad of puy lentils, and sautéed foie gras, with rhubarb chutney and melba toast - followed perhaps by perfectly cooked sirloin of Kilkenny beef, served with a gorgonzola sauce, green asparagus, gratin potato and red wine jus, or a fish dish such as fillet of seabass en papillotte, with champagne and seasonal vegetables - carefully folded and wrapped in string, with a sprig of rosemary on top. Everything is cooked and served correctly and very carefully presented, but not all cheffy. Eating a sublime chocolate truffle tart with vanilla ice cream - or a portion of Helen Finnegan's local Knockdrinna cheese - while you enjoy the rolling south Kilkenny countryside makes a wonderful ending for a memorable meal. Very good espressos too, and an interesting small wine list, including some organic wines. **Seats 34** (outdoors, 40); L wed-sun, 12-4 (to 6 on Sun); D Wed-Sat from 7. Closed Mon & Tue. MasterCard, Visa, Laser. **Directions:** Follow signs for Woodstock Gardens. ◊

Inistioge   # The Motte Restaurant
RESTAURANT   Plas Newydd Lodge Inistioge Co Kilkenny **Tel: 056 775 8655**
                                   rodneydoyle@eircom.net

On the edge of the picturesque village of Inistioge, with views of extensive parklands and the River Nore, Rodney & Deirdre Doyle's restaurant is situated in the classically proportioned Plas Newydd Lodge, named in honour of the famous ladies of Llangollen, who eloped from Inistioge in the late 18th century. Although small in size, this unique country restaurant has great charm. An L-shaped room with a Kilkenny marble fireplace and simple, effective decor makes a good setting for Rodney Doyle's accomplished cooking, and many will welcome the slightly retro feel to the menu, which offers dishes now seen less often and makes a change from the modern multi-national menus which are currently almost universal. Expect delicious home-made breads, starters like ham hock terrine with orange & apple chutney and a mustard seed dressing, and main courses such as delicious crispy stuffed duckling, or fillet of beef with their trademark cracked pepper & brandy cream sauce. Menus are sensibly limited, but always include an imaginative vegetarian dish, and classic desserts like strawberry Pavlova or Grand Marnier crème brûlée are delicious. It's good to see suppliers credited on the menu, and very hospitable service adds to the enjoyment. Small weddings or private parties can be catered for. **Seats 40** (private room 16); reservations recommended. D Thurs-Sat 7-9.30 (also Sun of bank hol weekends). Set 2/3 course D €36.50/42.50; L Sun only, 1-3.30pm, €28.50; house wine €19.95. SC discretionary (except 10% on groups of 6+). Closed Sun D (except bank hol weekends), Mon-Wed; 1 week June, 1 week Jan. Amex, MasterCard, Visa, Laser. **Directions:** Opposite village "name sign" on Kilkenny side of village.

KILKENNY

R

Ireland's smallest city both in area and population - Kilkenny is located on the River Nore and is famed for its history and, more recently, for its crafts, music, festivals and nightlife. There are many medieval buildings and the city has been referred to for centuries as the "Marble City", for the black stone with distinctive white oyster fossils which was quarried locally and known as Kilkenny Marble or Black Marble; it was exported to all corners of the world and is seen in many of Kilkenny's fine buildings and on the footpaths. Every visitor to the city wants to see Kilkenny Castle (056 772 1450), equally worth a visit is Kilkenny Rothe House (056 772 2893), 16th century house with exhibitions. Kilkenny hosts the annual Cat Laughs Comedy Festival in early June when the city becomes the "Comedy Capital of the World", and it also holds a very successful annual Arts Festival in late August, when the city is flooded with traditional and foreign music, beautiful paintings and sculptures and much more. For those seeking outdoor activities, this is good walking, golfing (Mount Juliet Golf Club, Thomastown, 056 777 3064) and fishing country and there is also horse racing at nearby Gowran Park (0)56 772 6225); however, the sport that the locals live and die by is hurling - Kilkenny are in the top echelons of the game and losing a match is unthinkable. Getting to see a hotly contested hurling match against arch rivals Cork in Nolan Park would be the memory of a lifetime. Every Thursday Morning there is a Farmers' Market selling local and regional foods in the Market Yard. A rich vein of hospitality runs throughout Kilkenny city and county and, in addition to those selected here, there are numerous places that may be of interest to visitors. **The Newpark Hotel** (056 776 0500; www.newparkhotel.com), for example, has recently changed ownership but it remains very much at the heart of local activities, and is a popular venue for conferences and meetings. Opposite the Newpark, **Rosquil House** (056 772 1419; www.rosquilhouse.com) is a 4* guesthouse offering hotel standard accommodation and home style breakfast at a reasonable price. In the city centre, **The Hibernian Hotel** (056 777 1888; www.kilkennyhibernianhotel.com) is in an old banking building and has character as well as a degree of luxury; nearby, **The Left Bank Bar** (formerly the Bank of Ireland) is in the same ownership and opened just before the Guide went to press. For details of a variety of eating places for every budget and occasion, including daytime snacks, the Kilkenny Good Food Circle Guide is available from Tourist Information Offices (Kilkenny City Tourist Information 056 77515000; www.kilkennytourism.ie). Outside the city, should your travels take you to the Callan area - perhaps to visit the Edmund Rice House (056 772 5993) - you may be glad to find the **Old Charter House** (056 775 5902), a village pub offering reliable bar lunches during the week (12-3pm) and moderately-priced accommodation. **WWW.IRELAND-GUIDE.COM FOR ALL THE BEST PLACES TO EAT, DRINK & STAY**

Kilkenny | **Butler House**
GUESTHOUSE | 16 Patrick Street Kilkenny Co Kilkenny **Tel: 056 776 5707**

res@butler.ie www.butler.ie

Located close to Kilkenny Castle, this elegant Georgian townhouse was restored by the Irish State Design Agency in the 1970s - and the resulting combination of what was at the time contemporary design with period architecture leads to some interesting discussions. However, bedrooms are unusually spacious - some have bow windows overlooking the gardens and Kilkenny Castle - and the accommodation is very adequate, with all the amenities now expected of good guesthouse accommodation. Bathrooms have been refurbished and upgraded, and most rooms now have full bath. Three magnificent bow-windowed reception rooms are available for receptions and dinners. An excellent breakfast is served at the Kilkenny Design Centre (see entry), which is just across the gardens in the refurbished castle stables. Conferences/banqueting (120/70); broadband wi/fi, business centre, secretarial services. Children welcome (under 2s free in parents' room; cot available without charge, baby sitting arranged). Parking (20). Walking, garden. No pets. **Rooms 13** (1 suite, 4 executive, 3 family, 1 shower only). B&B €100 pps, ss €40, sc discretionary. Off-season breaks offered. Closed 23-29 Dec. Amex, Diners, MasterCard, Visa, Laser. **Directions:** City centre, close to Kilkenny Castle.

Kilkenny

Campagne

RESTAURANT · The Arches 5 Gashouse Lane Kilkenny Co Kilkenny **Tel: 056 777 2858**

info@campagne.ie · www.campagne.ie

Set in the corner of a paved area adjacent to the old arches of the disused Kilkenny/Portlaoise railway line (effectively back lit at night), a smart sage green canopy over sage green woodwork and half frosted full-length glass windows will lead you to this eagerly-awaited new restaurant – Garrett Byrne, former head chef at Dublin's celebrated Chapter One, has now returned home to Kilkenny and opened his own restaurant with his partner and restaurant manager, Brid Hannon. Although it is on the ground floor of a new building, Garrett and Brid have chosen a rustic style - in tune with a passionately held food philosophy that will ensure the involvement of local food producers in the cooking - for their well-named, French-inspired restaurant. The dark oak floored room is almost triangular in shape, with an open kitchen and a small bar along one light oak-panelled wall, and a set of striking abstract landscape paintings on another. A third wall in deep aubergine features a trio of oval mirrors, and the curves are repeated stylishly through the centre of the restaurant, where three semi-circular banquettes enclosing tables for four to six create a serpentine loop that dominates the room. Seriously set up for the relaxed enjoyment of good food, generous tables sport crisp white linen, comfortable leather chairs or banquette seating, and smart cutlery and glasses, but no flowers. The welcome is warm and professional, the complimentary home-baked breads are lovely, and Garrett's predictably interesting à la carte menu offers a wide range of tempting dishes that balance the luxurious with the rustic - starters may include a celeriac soup with pancetta and mustard cream (€8) alongside a terrine of foie gras and suckling pig with beetroot purée & walnut dressing (€12), for example, and other choices include a beautifully presented gravadlax (€11), served with pickled cucumber and shaved fennel & potato salad, whilst deep-fried haddock (perfectly cooked with very crisp batter) comes with organic poached egg and scallion hollandaise. Mains are focused firmly on rusticity, with slow cooking a feature in dishes like slow-cooked beef, with mushrooms, caramelized shallots and smoked bacon (€28), and slow roast breast of veal, with lentils, organic carrots and pesto (€27); Irish traditions are seen in a dish of free range pork chop, with black pudding, creamed cabbage and mustard (€26) and, although the balance offered reflects the rural traditions of the area, there will be some fish too (sea bream, perhaps €26, or fillet of brill €29). Everything is beautifully cooked and full of flavour and - despite the rustic theme – presentation is sophisticated. Desserts might include a decadent Gateau Opéra with ice cream, and luscious Sauternes custard and Agen prunes (both €9). A compact, well-chosen wine list suits the style and the menu, but there are no half bottles and the mark-up is steep. House wines €25. Although only recently open at the time of our visit, there was a lovely ambience and, under Brid Hannon's direction, the delicious food was served efficiently by well-trained and friendly staff. The style may be informal here, but it's an extremely professional operation and there are many little details to give a sense of occasion – all of which should ensure good value. **Directions:** Just off John's Square.

Kilkenny

Chez Pierre

RESTAURANT · 17 Parliament Street Kilkenny Co Kilkenny **Tel: 056 776 4655**

chezpierrerestaurant@hotmail.com

Tucked behind a traditional red and cream painted shopfront on Parliament Street, Pierre Schneider's cosy little daytime restaurant has long been popular with Kilkenny people for serving honest, well- sourced and simply cooked bistro fare. But it is when he opens for dinner that his talent really shows through - his evening menus are known for excellent fish dishes that are a joy to eat, and accompanied by a hotpot of excellent vegetables which is left on the table. Until recently Chez Pierre only opened for dinner at the end of the week but, since the arrival of joint head chef Emilio Martin Castilla (formerly of Lacken House and, more recently, Bassetts of Inistioge), the restaurant is now open five nights a week. "Fresh is best" is Pierre's mantra and this is plain to see as the simple, clearly described, blackboard dishes emerge from the kitchen perfectly cooked and without any unnecessary frills. Dishes recently enjoyed by the Guide include a simple but delicious starter of naturally smoked haddock, marinated and served as a tian with chopped vegetables, a lovely mustard dressing and home-made bread. A main course of fresh turbot - a fine fillet, simply pan-fried and served with a fondue of tomatoes and herbs - was equally impressive.

Simple, flavoursome vegetables accompany and you may finish with French cheeses, in perfect condition. For those not in the mood for fish, other equally tempting choices might include a velvety duck liver mousse, served with chutney and salad – and, perhaps, a main course of Toulouse sausage. Willing service by staff smartly dressed in black, and a short wine list complete the picture. **Seats 25**; D Tue-Sat 6.45-9.30pm. Closed Sun, Mon; 24 Dec - 2 Jan. MasterCard, Visa, Laser. **Directions:** On Parliament Street.

Kilkenny Fléva
RESTAURANT   84 High Street Kilkenny Co Kilkenny **Tel: 056 777 0021**
V R   info@fleva.ie www.fleva.ie

Located over shops, beside Kilkenny's Town Hall, a bright red door will attract you to this bright and spacious first floor restaurant, which is in three interconnecting rooms overlooking High Street - and it is just the kind of place that visitors enjoy finding. Well-appointed in a slightly funky style, with cheerful Mediterranean colours, white-clothed tables and exhibitions by local artists, its most obvious asset initially is friendly and welcoming staff, who go out of their way to make arriving guests feel at home (iced water promptly offered with very good brown bread). Talented young head chef Michael Thomas continues the house style of 'international food with a contemporary Irish twist' and is committed to using the best of local produce; the famous Kilkenny beef is always on his menus of course, but you will also find less likely choices such as game, in season, and a good choice of seafood including less usual items like hand-dived scallops when available, and he is proud to support small local producers. He sources Kilkenny lamb from Dick Dooley at Ballyragget and a house speciality is delicious roast rack - with rosti potatoes, crunchy beans and lamb jus with redcurrants, perhaps. Home-made desserts are a highlight too - a mixed plate of three small desserts (bread & butter pudding, baklava and tiramisu), or a classic pavolva, crunchy and soft in the centre. With a lively atmosphere and creative cooking, backed up by good service and an extensive wine list (although some with no vintage and no shipper named), this is a great place to watch the world go by (book a window table). *An unusual and innovative feature at Fléva is a monthly Slow Food Sunday, when Slow Food is the theme for the set lunch menu, children's menu and an afternoon Slow Art Workshop. **Seats 60**; children welcome before 8pm (high chair, childrens menu). Open Tue-Sun, L&D Tue-Sat, 12.30-3pm & 6-10pm (Sat D 5.30-10.30); Sun L & D, 12.30-3pm & 5.30-9pm. Set Sun L €26.50; early 3 course D €26.50, 6-7.15pm (Sat 5.30-6pm). House wine from €22.50. SC 10% on groups 8+. Closed Mon, 25 Dec. Amex, Diners, MasterCard, Visa, Laser. **Directions:** Beside the Tholsel, Kilkenny's historical town hall on High Street.

Kilkenny Hotel Kilkenny
HOTEL   College Road Kilkenny Co Kilkenny **Tel: 056 776 2000**
R   kilkenny@griffingroup.ie www.griffingroup.ie

Dubbed 'the four star with flair', Hotel Kilkenny begins impressively in the spacious contemporary foyer, which has a very large modern reception desk and relaxed seating areas. Very comfortable accommodation includes about a hundred original rooms, which were refurbished recently in a smart contemporary style that is not too hard-edged, and a further 36 newer deluxe rooms. Public areas include a modern bar 'Pure', which is notable for an exceptional speciality drinks menu, and the restaurant 'Taste Italy', offering Tuscan-inspired cuisine. Set in award-winning gardens, the hotel is a popular wedding venue and offers extensive banqueting facilities and a state-of-the-art conference centre. A special feature is the 5-star Active Health and Fitness club. Conference/banqueting 400/380; children welcome (under 2s free in parents' room; cots available without charge). Ample complimentary car parking. No pets. **Rooms 103** (24 executive rooms, 5 no smoking, 2 disabled). B&B from about €60 pps. Open all year. Amex, Diners, MasterCard, Visa, Laser. **Directions:** On ring road at Clonmel roundabout exit. ◇

Kilkenny
RESTAURANT

Kilkenny Design Centre

Castle Yard Kilkenny Co Kilkenny **Tel: 056 772 2118**
info@kilkennydesign.com www.kilkennydesign.com

Situated in what was once the stables and dairy of Kilkenny Castle - and overlooking the craft courtyard - this deservedly popular first floor self-service restaurant is situated above temptations of a different sort, on display in the famous craft shop. Wholesome and consistently delicious fare begins with breakfast for guests staying at **Butler House** (see entry), as well as non-resident visitors. The room is well-designed to allow attractive and accessible display of wonderful food, all freshly prepared every day: home baking is a strong point, and there is plenty of hot food to choose from aswell - seafood chowder with home-made soda bread, for example, and beef & pepper casserole with button mushrooms or a speciality chicken & broccoli crumble with local Lavistown cheese. The lovely crumbly Lavistown cheese is also used in great salads, which are always colourful and full of life - fresh beetroot, asparagus, spinach, red onion, coriander & Lavistown, for example, combine to make a salad worth travelling for, and the selection changes all the time. A short carefully chosen wine list offers seven wines by the bottle or half bottles, and gourmet coffees and herbal teas are offered. Very reasonably priced too - well worth a visit. **Seats 150**; children welcome; toilets wheelchair accessible. Lift. Meals daily 11-7. Self service. Closed Sun & banks hols off-season (Jan-Mar). Amex, Diners, MasterCard, Visa, Laser. **Directions:** Opposite Kilkenny Castle.

Kilkenny
HOTEL•RESTAURANT

Kilkenny Ormonde Hotel

Ormonde Street Kilkenny Co Kilkenny **Tel: 056 772 3900**
info@kilkennyormonde.com www.kilkennyormonde.com

Kilkenny city's leading hotel enjoys an outstandingly convenient central location for both business and leisure guests, beside (but not adjacent to) a multi-storey carpark and within walking distance of the whole city. Following a major upgrade, the 'new' hotel has emerged impressively, with a much brighter and smarter lobby entrance and lovely high back seating in the Ormonde Lounge, a popular meeting place where excellent coffee is served. The bar has had a complete makeover, now with a decking area at the front. Accommodation is particularly spacious – rooms range from standard up to a Presidential Suite and include family and wheelchair friendly rooms; all are very well-appointed in a pleasingly low-key modern style, some with panoramic views of Kilkenny city. The hotel has always had an excellent reputation as a business and conference venue and, whether for an international conference for 450 delegates or a meeting for 15 or 20 people, the facilities are very impressive. Business/conference guests as well as local members will appreciate the expanded Health Club, which has a 21m deck level pool among the facilities ,and also the new KO Elemis Spa with 6 treatment rooms opened in summer 2008. Good food has always been a point of pride here too and there is a choice between the informal O'Reilly's Steak House (see below) and the main restaurant, Savour (formerly Fredricks) which is open for all meals, including breakfast; an early dinner offers outstanding value (6-7.30, €25). *The smaller **Pembroke Hotel** (www.pembrokekilkenny.com) on Patrick Street is a sister hotel. Conference/banqueting (450/500). Business centre, video conferencing. Leisure centre, 21m swimming pool, crèche. **Rooms 118** (6 suites, 6 executive rooms, 59 no smoking, 4 disabled). Lift. 24-hour room service. B&B from about €64 pps, ss €31; suites from €228. Children welcome (under 12s free in parents' room, cots available without charge, baby sitting arranged). **O'Reilly's Bar & Steak House:** Formerly Earls Bistro, this new informal steak bar is likely to be the restaurant of choice for many residents, and should also be popular with local diners. Brighter than before, with two new windows as well as contemporary light fittings, raised seating adds interest and the room is promisingly set up with sturdy mahogany tables, comfortable chairs and banquettes, good cutlery and glasses and crisp napkins. 100% Irish beef is the speciality and a typical steak house menu is offered, beginning with old favourites like buffalo wings and Caesar salad among about a dozen starters, and six steak variations among the main courses; flavoursome, accurately-cooked steaks come with traditional garnishes (steak/baked potatoes, onion rings and a choice of well-made sauces – béarnaise or an excellent blue cheese sauce, for example). Pleasing classical desserts and good coffee to finish. There's a good atmosphere and this, together with unfussy presentation on contemporary white plates and professional service, from smartly-dressed well-trained staff with good menu knowledge, adds to the enjoyment of a meal here. The wine list may not be especially exciting but, like the food served here, house wines are good value. **Seats 75**; toilets wheelchair accessible. Open D daily 6.30-9, L Sun only 12.30-2.30. Set D from €38/42. House wine about €25. sc discretionary. Amex, MasterCard, Visa, Laser. **Directions:** Kilkenny city centre off the parade opposite castle.

Kilkenny
HOTEL•RESTAURANT

Kilkenny River Court Hotel

The Bridge John Street Kilkenny Co Kilkenny **Tel: 056 772 3388**
reservations@rivercourthotel.com www.rivercourthotel.com

Beautifully situated in a courtyard just off the narrow, bustling streets of the city centre, with only the River Nore separating it from Kilkenny Castle, this fine hotel enjoys the city's premier location, and has a lovely big riverside terrace at the front. While equally attractive for business or leisure - bedrooms and public areas have all been recently refurbished to a high standard and the Health & Leisure Club provides excellent facilities for health, fitness and beauty treatments - the hotel has established a special reputation for conferences and incentive programmes, with state-of-the-art facilities for groups of varying numbers and plenty to do when off duty in the city, as well as outdoor pursuits - golf, fishing, equestrian - nearby. Conference/Banqueting (260/180); free broadband wi/fi. Leisure centre (swimming pool, fitness room, sauna). Children welcome (under 3s free in parents' room, cot available without charge, baby sitting arranged). Limited private parking (access can be a little difficult). Short breaks/special interest breaks offered. **Rooms 90** (2 suites, 20 executive, 4 family, 4 for disabled). Lift. 24hr room service; turndown service. B&B €130pps, ss €50. Closed 24-25 Dec. **Riverside Restaurant:** This aptly named restaurant takes full advantage of the riverside setting and has lovely views of Kilkenny Castle and the River Nore; it is an elegant room, with tall windows, beautifully appointed tables, and very comfortable high-back leather chairs. The atmosphere is that of a restaurant rather than a hotel dining room, and both the menus and chef Gerard Dunne's good cooking reinforce that impression. A frequently changed dinner menu begins with an amuse-bouche and a choice of popular starters, but main courses are more interesting - a dish of braised breast of duck, carved from the bone and served with wilted Asian greens and clementine & star anis marmalade is a speciality, for example, and there are many other unusual dishes, some making imaginative use of local foods; side dishes are also excellent, and desserts may include less usual treats like delicious rhubarb syllabub. The early dinner and Sunday lunch menus are particularly good value, and charming service adds to the occasion. **Seats 80** (private room 40, outdoor, 50). D daily 6-9.30, L Sun only 12.30-2.30. Early D €29.95 (6-7pm); also à la carte. Set Sun L €29.95. [Food is also served in the Riverview Bar, 12.30-8pm daily.]. Amex, Diners, MasterCard, Visa. **Directions:** Follow city centre signs, directly opposite Kilkenny Castle. Two archways on Dublin side of bridge - use the castle as a landmark.

Kilkenny
HOTEL

Langton House Hotel

69 John Street Kilkenny Co Kilkenny **Tel: 056 776 5133**
reservations@langtons.ie www.langtons.ie

Langtons is mainly famous for its maze of bars, with seating areas and restaurants that stretch right through this substantial building to a garden and private car park. Although the fine classic frontage remains, the old traditional bar at the front has been modernised, an outdoor bar and dining area has been added and, beyond the bar, the big Langton Ballroom has also been renovated. Viewed as an hotel, first impressions are mixed as the reception area is small (although an extension is planned) and arrival can seem a bit disorganised. However, this is a slightly wacky hotel of some character and good-sized rooms are furnished to a high standard with well-appointed bathrooms, making it a good place to stay if you want to be in the city centre. Langton's also offers a lively middle-of-the-road dining experience - good food without frills, friendly service and good value for money. Conferences/Banqueting (200/250). Private car park. Children welcome (under 5s free in parents room, cot available at no charge, babysitting arranged). **Rooms 30** (2 suites, 4 family rooms, 8 ground floor, 22 no smoking). B&B from €100 pps, ss €25. L & D daily, 12-5.30 & 5.30-10.30. Closed 25 Dec. Amex, MasterCard, Visa, Laser **Directions:** Town centre. ◊

Kilkenny
GUESTHOUSE
R

Laragh House

Waterford Road Kilkenny Co Kilkenny **Tel: 056 776 4674**
info@laraghhouse.com www.laraghhouse.com

John and Helen Cooney's modern two-storey white plastered guesthouse was only built in 2005, but is now well-established as one of the most popular in the area as it is within walking distance of Kilkenny city centre in fine weather (15 minutes), has off-street parking and, with all the modern amenities, offers a very reasonably priced alternative to an hotel. The eight bedrooms are individually styled, with multi-channel TV, direct dial telephone and internet access, and all have whirlpool bath or power showers. There's also a comfortably-furnished lounge for guests to relax in, and a smoking area is provided. **Rooms 8** (all en-suite & no smoking, 5 shower only, 2 ground floor, 2 disabled); children welcome (under 10s free in parents' room, cots available free of charge); broadband wi/fi. B&B €40-50 pps, ss€10. Limited room service. Closed 24-26 Dec. MasterCard, Visa, Laser. **Directions:** Easily reached from any direction via the city by-pass. ◊

Kilkenny
RESTAURANT
N R

Lombardis Italian Restaurant & Pizzeria

22 Parliament Street Kilkenny Co Kilkenny **Tel: 056 777 1666**
lombardiskilkenny@gmail.com

A new addition to the dining scene in Kilkenny, this large, bright burgundy-painted room is very relaxing, and is serving well-sourced and carefully prepared dishes. Very popular with families (behind reception is a stack of 6 baby chairs), there are plenty of crowd pleasers on the menu but all dishes are cooked with care and nicely presented. A very good version of Chicken Caesar salad comes in a large bowl, and king prawns in garlic butter comprise seven large specimens, with a nice balanced garlic and flat parsley sauce. Classic 'Pollo all'Italiano' (stuffed breast of chicken with roast pine nuts and sun-dried tomato stuffing, wrapped in bacon and served with a tarragon and wholegrain mustard sauce) is served sliced, with a mixture of al dente vegetables, and home-made fries. Steak lovers abound in Kilkenny, and you'll find good steak cooked perfectly here - and served with roasted baby potatoes flavoured with rosemary and pepper sauce, perhaps. Short but adequate wine list. Pleasant service from young Irish waitresses, family-friendliness and good value make this cheerful Italian/Irish restaurant a welcome addition to the city's burgeoning dining scene. **Seats 60**; children welcome (high chairs). Open daily, L&D Mon-Fri 12.30 - 3pm & 5-10pm; all day Sat & Sun 12.30-"late". Early 2/3 course D €17.95/21.95, Mon-Fri 5-7pm. House wine €19. Closed 25 Dec. MasterCard, Visa, Laser **Directions:** On Parliament Street.

Kilkenny
HOTEL
R

Lyrath Estate Hotel - Spa & Convention Centre

Dublin Road Kilkenny Co Kilkenny **Tel: 056 776 0088**
info@lyrath.com www.lyrath.com

Set in 170 acres of mature parklands on the outskirts of Kilkenny city, this modern hotel has a 17th century house at its centre, now extended to become a large hotel with a state-of-the-art conference centre and a spa. It is an unusual hotel and has character; a huge marbled foyer joins the old house and the new extension, and public areas include the comfortable Tupper's Bar and an adjacent conservatory, which offer informal food and open on to a sheltered terrace and interesting gardens at the back. The large first floor restaurant Reflections, where breakfast and dinner are served, overlooks the same area and has picture windows running the length of the room; the old Wine Cellar is open to diners to browse or have an aperitif but it is awkwardly positioned (you have to go through the restaurant and downstairs again) and it is used mainly for functions and groups. Most people opt for a drink in Tupper's or the X Bar, which is on the first floor between Reflections and the hotel's popular ethnic restaurant, Yindees, which offers a cross-section of Asian dishes. Accommodation is spacious and well-appointed in a modern classic style; there are several grades of rooms, soothingly decorated in tones of brown and cream - this could be a pleasant place to stay. There are extensive conference and banqueting facilites, also a spa, a leisure centre with swimming pool and gym. Conferences/Banqueting (1,500/950), 7 board rooms, 3 business centres; Spa; Private club floor. **Rooms 137** (1 penthouse suite, 9 suites, 28 executive). Room rate from €200. MasterCard, Visa, Laser. **Directions:** Just before Kilkenny on the Dublin/Carlow road. ◊

Marble City Bar

Kilkenny
PUB

66 High Street Kilkenny Co Kilkenny **Tel: 056 776 1143**
reservations@langtons.ie www.langtons.ie

The Langton family's historic bar was re-designed a few years ago by the internationally acclaimed designer, David Collins and, although initially controversial (especially the ultra-modern stained glass window which now graces an otherwise traditional frontage), it is a wonderful space to be in and attracts a varied clientèle. Everyone enjoys the vibrant atmosphere, and the excellent ingredients-led contemporary European bar food: a dish like confit of pork sausages with creamy potatoes and red wine onion gravy or black cherry jus, for example, will probably be based on the superb lean sausages hand-made nearby by Olivia Goodwillie (who also makes Lavistown cheese), and the fresh cod'n'chips in a crispy beer batter will be just in from Dunmore East. More recently the bar has re-invented itself again and the Marble City Tea Rooms, below the main bar/restaurant area, offer lighter food like coffees, teas and pastry, 9-7 daily - there's outdoor seating for a couple of dozen people and has access to a lane at the back of the building. There are also further plans to extend the seating - this place is incredibly popular. Good service, even at busy times; well chosen small wine list. *Tea rooms seating 50 downstairs. Bar food served daily. Food service begins with breakfast, from 10am; main menus from 12 noon-10 pm (Sun: L 12-3; D 5-10). A la carte. House wine about €20 (€5 per glass). Closed 25 Dec & Good Fri. Ample car parking at rear. Amex, Diners, MasterCard, Visa, Laser. **Directions:** Ample car parking at rear. Main Street, city centre.

Restaurant Café Sol

Kilkenny
CAFÉ•RESTAURANT

William Street Kilkenny Co Kilkenny **Tel: 056 776 4987**
info@cafesolkilkenny.com www.cafesolkilkenny.com

Noel McCarron's popular daytime café and evening restaurant is easy to find, just off the High Street. A small interior porch leads in to a large room warmly decorated in yellow and terracotta giving it a sunny, Mediterranean feeling. The house style is colourful and punchy, showing international influences but based on the best local produce. Daytime menus offer informal dishes like open sandwiches and salads, and some hot dishes. Evening menus offer the more predictable dishes (local beef, of course), but also include some unusual choices - a tasting plate of cured meats and Lavistown cheese. Vegetarians always do well here, too - and the lovely homely desserts are delicious. This is an interesting restaurant, offering something different from the 'sameness' of so many menus, and at reasonable prices. **Seats 45**; not suitable for children after 6pm; air conditioning; free broadband wi/fi. Open all day Mon-Sat, 12-10, Sun 12-9; early bird D to 7.15pm, €27; also à la carte. Wines from €20. SC 10% on parties 6+. Closed 25/26 Dec, 1 Jan. Amex, MasterCard, Visa, Laser. **Directions:** Coming from castle - up High St. - 2nd turn left opposite Town Hall.

Rinuccini Restaurant

Kilkenny
RESTAURANT

1 The Parade Kilkenny Co Kilkenny **Tel: 056 776 1575**
info@rinuccini.com www.rinuccini.com

Antonio and Marion Cavaliere's well-known Italian restaurant is in a semi-basement in the impressive terrace opposite Kilkenny Castle and the closely packed tables are an indication of its popularity, with the room quickly filling up. The cooking style is mainly classic Italian, with quite an extensive à la carte evening menu plus a shorter one available as an option at lunchtime. Service is prompt, and food is characterised by freshness of ingredients and a high standard of cooking: excellent minestrone, a superb plate of house antipasti, delicious seafood and memorable pasta, which includes a luxurious house speciality of spaghetti with lobster. Great service and outstanding value for money can sometimes be let down by a slightly frantic atmosphere, as so many people want to eat at this popular restaurant. **Seats 100** (private room, 60, also outdoor dining); not suitable for children after 8pm. L daily 12-2.30 (to 3pm Sun), D daily 5.30-10pm (to 9.30pm Sun). Reservations accepted. Early D €27.50 (5.30-7), otherwise à la carte. House wines from €19.95 Amex, Diners, MasterCard, Visa, Laser. **Directions:** Opposite Kilkenny Castle.

Kilkenny
RESTAURANT

Swans Chinese

101 High Street The Parade Kilkenny Co Kilkenny **Tel: 056 772 3088**
info@swansrestaurant.com www.swansrestaurant.com

Situated on the corner of High Street and Rose Inn street over Ladbrokes bookie office, with the entrance from High Street, Swans has been through a slightly inconsistent period but is now back on form and is once again a pleasant venue for enjoying well-prepared and presented oriental cuisine. The room is bright and very relaxing, with red alcoves, comfortable dark brown leather chairs and Chinese wall hangings; charming Chinese waitresses contribute to the ambience and the food has great flavour, bringing nicely served classics like crispy spring rolls, chicken chow mein and szechuan-style dishes to life. With good espressos to finish, this is a useful place to know. **Seats 56**; children welcome; air conditioning; L & D Mon-Fri, 12-2.30 & 5-11.30pm; Sat/Sun & Bank Hols all day, 12.30-11.30pm; set Sun L about €16.50; value D avail 7 days about €18.50, also à la carte; house wine €16. Closed 25 Dec, Good Fri. MasterCard, Visa, Laser. **Directions:** Kilkenny centre, 2 mins walk from Kilkenny Castle.

Kilkenny
RESTAURANT•HOTEL

Zuni Restaurant & Boutique Hotel

26 Patrick Street Kilkenny Co Kilkenny **Tel: 056 772 3999**
info@zuni.ie www.zuni.ie

Although Zuni is an hotel ('boutique' style, and offering a more youthful style of accommodation than other comparable establishments), the atmosphere is more restaurant with rooms: an oasis of contemporary chic in this bustling city, it is well established as an in-place for discerning Kilkenny diners. The room is large and airy, overlooking a courtyard (alfresco dining in fine weather) and there's a separate restaurant entrance so you don't have to go through the hotel. Although Maria Raftery's wide-ranging menus offer international dishes, use of local ingredients lends a distinctive Irish tone - Lavistown cheese gives relevance to a starter of Waldorf salad with green apple sorbet, for example, and the meat antipasti slate offers cured meats from Gubbeen Smokehouse in west Cork. And you can be sure of finding a variation on everyone's favourite - char-grilled Irish sirloin with chunky chips, mushroom duxelle, and béarnaise sauce. Attractively presented food is always full of flavour: smart salads make tasty starters and Maria, who cooks with panache in view of diners, is a cool and accomplished chef. Menus to note include an early dinner menu which offers a good choice and gives great value for money - and an upbeat contemporary variation on the traditional lunch which packs them in on Sundays. **Seats 70** (outdoor seating, 24); toilets wheelchair accessible; children welcome before 7pm. (Breakfast); L Tue-Sun 12.30-2.30 (Sun 1-3), D daily 6.30-10 (Sun 6-9). Early D about €25 (6.30-7.30). Otherwise à la carte. House wine from about €22. SC 12.5% added to parties 6+. **Accommodation:** Rooms have direct dial phones, air conditioning, iron/trouser press, TV, tea/coffee-making facilities; the minimalist décor - recently refurbished in pale tones - is difficult to keep immaculate. Breakfast is served in the restaurant. **Rooms 13** (8 shower only, 5 no smoking, 1 family room, 1 for disabled, all no smoking); children welcome (under 12s free in parents' room; cot available without charge, baby sitting arranged). Lift. B&B about €50ps, ss €20. No pets. Private parking, but guests must get the receptionist to open the security bar (best to use the mobile phone, perhaps). Hotel closed 23-27 Dec. Amex, MasterCard, Visa, Laser. **Directions:** On Patrick Street - leads to Waterford road; 200 yards from Kilkenny Castle.

Maddoxtown

Blanchville House

COUNTRY HOUSE

Dunbell Maddoxtown Co Kilkenny **Tel: 056 772 7197**
mail@blanchville.ie www.blanchville.ie

Monica Phelan's elegant Georgian house is just 5 miles out of Kilkenny city, surrounded by its own farmland and gardens. It's easy to spot - there's a folly in its grounds. It's a very friendly, welcoming place and the house has an airy atmosphere, with matching well-proportioned dining and drawing rooms on either side of the hall, and the pleasant, comfortably furnished bedrooms in period style all overlook attractive countryside. Dinner is available to residents, if pre-arranged, and, like the next morning's excellent breakfast, is taken at the communal mahogany dining table. The Coach Yard has been renovated to make four self-catering coach houses, and the house can also be rented - an ideal arrangement for groups of 12-20 people, for family get-togethers or other special occasions, where guests may have exclusive use of the house and coach yard. More recently, a small spa and holistic centre has been added in the coach yard, with a resident therapist. Blanchville is well-situated for golfers (5 great courses within half an hour's drive, including Mount Juliet). Special breaks offered include art workshop weekends, and bridge breaks. Small conferences/private parties (25). **Rooms 6** (5 en-suite, 1 with private bathroom, 2 shower only, all non-smoking, 1 family room); children welcome (under 5s free in parents' room; cot available without charge; baby sitting can be arranged). Pets permitted by arrangement. B&B €60 pps, ss €10. No SC. Turndown service offered. Residents D €50 by prior arrangement only. Walking, garden, cycling. Horse-riding, hunting, fishing, shooting and garden visits nearby. Closed 1 Nov-1 Mar. Amex, MasterCard, Visa, Laser. **Directions:** From Kilkenny take N10 (Carlow-Dublin road), 1st right 1km after 'The Pike Pub'. Continue 3km to crossroads (Connolly's pub). Take left, large stone entrance 1.5km on left.

THOMASTOWN

Thomastown is an early medieval town with charming streets and picturesque views of the River Nore, and also happens to be the birthplace of the 18th century philosopher George Berkeley. Local attractions include Jerpoint Abbey (056 772 4623, open March to November), a Cistercian abbey established in the second half of the 12th century. The abbey has Romanesque details; an impressive sculpted cloister arcade features unique carvings. There is also an informative visitor centre and exhibition. Visitors will enjoy a trip to Kilfane Glen and Waterfall (0772 4558; www.kilfane.com), a recently discovered romantic era garden featuring a superb waterfall and a cottage orné. Garden lovers should also make a point of seeing Mount Juliet Gardens (056 777 3000), and the restored Woodstock Gardens (056 779 403) at Inistioge are not far away. Golfers, of course, are well catered for with the championships golf course at Mount Juliet (056 777 3000).

Thomastown

Ballyduff House

COUNTRY HOUSE

Thomastown Co Kilkenny **Tel: 056 775 8488**
ballydhouse@eircom.net www.ballyduffhouse.com

Set in fine rolling countryside in its own farmland and grounds, Breda Thomas's lovely 18th century house overlooking the River Nore is blessed with an utterly restful location. Breda is a relaxed host who enjoys sharing her home with guests, and offers exceptionally spacious and comfortable accommodation in large period bedrooms with generous bathrooms and beautiful views over the river or gardens. Guests also have the use of large well-proportioned day rooms furnished with family antiques - and many return often, finding this rural retreat a warm and welcoming home from home. Beautiful walks on the estate. Fishing (salmon, trout). Riding, hunting and other country pursuits can be arranged. **Rooms 3**; children welcome. B&B €50 pps, no sse. Pets permitted by arrangement. Garden visits nearby. *Self-catering accommodation also offered at Ballyduff Castle, adjoining Ballyduff House (2-4 bedrooms). Open all year. No Credit Cards. **Directions:** 5km (3 m) south of Thomastown.

Thomastown
CAFÉ•RESTAURANT
R

Ethos

Low Street Thomastown Co Kilkenny **Tel: 056 775 4945**
cathal@ethosbistro.com www.ethosbistro.com

Cathal O'Sullivan and (chef) Paul Cullen's attractive restaurant has earned a local following, and its situation on the main street means that visitors find it very easily. It's an inviting spot and the set-up - café by day and bistro by night - is very customer friendly. Paul's lunch menus are casual - soup, salads, sambos, panini, bagels - and a more structured evening menu in a French/Asian style offers half a dozen starters, and about eight main courses. Specialities include seafood dishes like mussels with Thai green curry, and – more unusually - peppered Tipperary ostrich fillet, with crushed new potatoes, sautéed wild mushrooms, spinach & sweet red wine jus. There will always be good local meats too, including Kilkenny beef and pork; duck also features, vegetarian dishes too - and there's a lovely choice of desserts. Quality ingredients, good cooking and value have spelt success for this well-run restaurant and there are plans to extend it at the time of going to press. **Seats 40** (outdoors, 16); children welcome before 7pm; toilets wheelchair accessible; L Mon-Sun, 12-3.30pm (to 5pm Sun), D Wed-Mon 6.30-9.30pm; house wine €20; SC 10% on parties 8+. Closed D Tue, 25-26 Dec. Amex, MasterCard, Visa, Laser. **Directions:** N9 from Dublin/Waterford - just off Main St.

Thomastown
HOTEL•RESTAURANT

Mount Juliet Conrad

Thomastown Co Kilkenny **Tel: 056 777 3000**
mountjulietinfo@conradhotels.com www.conradhotels.com

Lying amidst 1500 acres of unspoilt woodland, pasture and formal gardens beside the River Nore, Mount Juliet House is one of Ireland's finest Georgian houses, and one of Europe's greatest country estates. Even today it retains an aura of eighteenth century grandeur, as the elegance of the old house has been painstakingly preserved - and it has a uniquely serene and restful atmosphere. Suites and bedrooms in the main house have period decor with all the comfort of modern facilities and there's additional accommodation in the Club Rooms at Hunters Yard, which is where most of the day-to-day activities of the estate take place, and very close to the main house. There is also self-catering accommodation offered, at the Rose Garden Lodges (close to Hunters Yard) and The Paddocks (at the tenth tee). Mount Juliet is highly respected as a golfing destination, and considerable investment has gone into upgrading the golf course, which now offers an 18-hole putting course in addition to the Jack Nicklaus-designed championship course. But there is much more to this wonderfully relaxing hotel than golf: it is well located for exploring one of Ireland's most beautiful areas and there is no shortage of things to do on the estate - gardens and woodlands to wander, new sports to try, the Spa & Health Club for pampering. The hotel is a top destination for activity breaks - there's a brand new equestrian centre (opened in 2008) and a range of Master Classes is offered in a number of disciplines, including fishing, painting, salsa and wellness. The hotel offers a choice of fine dining in the Lady Helen Dining Room (see below), or an attractive contemporary option in the stylish Kendals restaurant at Hunters Yard. Conference/banqueting (140/140). Children welcome (under 12 free sharing with 2 adults, but with extra bed is about €65; cot available €50, baby sitting arranged; children's play area). No pets. Gardens. Equestrian; Angling. Clay pigeon shooting, Archery, Tennis, Croquet, Cycling, Walking, Trails. Spa and Health Club (15m Swimming Pool; Treatments; Hair Dressing). Banqueting (romantic wedding venue, in large marquees set up outside the front of the house, overlooking the river.) **Rooms 58** (2 suites, 8 junior suites, 8 superior, 1 disabled; all no smoking). No Lift. B&B from €120 pps; sc discretionary. Open all year. **Lady Helen Dining Room:** Although grand, this graceful high-ceilinged room, softly decorated in pastel shades and with sweeping views over the grounds, is not forbidding and has a pleasant atmosphere. To match these beautiful surroundings, classic daily dinner menus based on local ingredients are served, including regional Irish farmhouse cheese. Service is efficient and friendly, and there is an extensive international wine list. **Seats 60** (private room 30); toilets wheelchair accessible. D daily 7-9.30. A la carte. L Sun only, 1-2.30pm. House wine from €32. *Reservations required. Alternatively, the contemporary restaurant Kendals, in Hunters Yard, is open for breakfast & dinner (6-10) daily, *Informal dining is also available in The Club, Presidents Bar (12noon-9pm). Amex, Diners, MasterCard, Visa, Laser. **Directions:** M7 from Dublin, then M9 towards Waterford, arriving at Thomastown on the N9 via Carlow and Gowran. (75 miles south of Dublin, 60 miles north of Rosslare).

COUNTY LAOIS

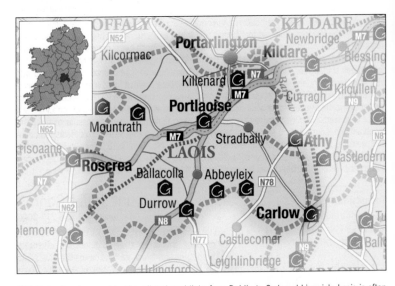

With its territory traversed by the rail and road links from Dublin to Cork and Limerick, Laois is often glimpsed only fleetingly by inter-city travellers. But as with any Irish county, it is a wonderfully rewarding place to visit as soon as you move off the main roads. For Laois is the setting for Emo Court and Heywood, two of the great gardens of Ireland at their most impressive.

And it's a salutary place to visit, too. In the eastern part, between Stradbally and Portlaoise, there's the Rock of Dunamase, that fabulous natural fortress which many occupiers inevitably assumed to be impregnable. Dunamase's remarkably long history of fortifications and defences and sieges and eventual captures has a relevance and a resonance for all times and all peoples and all places.

But there's much more to Laois than mournful musings on the ultimate vanity of human ambitions. With its border shared with Carlow along the River Barrow, eastern Laois comfortably reflects Carlow's quiet beauty. To the northwest, we find that Offaly bids strongly to have the Slieve Bloom Mountains thought of as an Offaly hill range, but in fact there's more of the Slieve Blooms in Laois than Offaly, and lovely hills they are too. And though the River Nore may be thought of as quintessential Kilkenny, long before it gets anywhere near Kilkenny it is quietly building as it meanders across much of Laois, gathering strength from the weirdly-named Delour, Tonet, Gully, Erskina and Goul rivers on the way.

Along the upper reaches of the Nore in west Laois, the neat little village of Castletown has long been a tidy place. Castletown has for the past seventeen years climbed steadily up the rankings in the annual Tidy Towns contest. Having been the tidiest village in all Ireland in 2001, Castletown repeated the performance and then some in 2002, and at the annual awards ceremony in Dublin Castle, it was announced that Castletown was both the tidiest village, and the national overall winner in all categories. This high standard has been maintained, and the most recent National Awards ceremony saw Castletown very much in the frame.

Local Attractions and Information

Abbeyleix	Abbeyleix Heritage House	0502 31653
Abbeyleix	Sensory Gardens	0502 31325
Ballinakill	Heywood (Lutyens gardens)	0502 33563
Donaghmore	Castletown House Open Farm	0505 46415
Donaghmore	Donaghmore Workhouse Museum	0505 46212
Emo	Emo Court (Gandon house & gardens)	0502 26573
Portlaois	Dunamaise Theatre & Arts Centre	0502 63356
Portlaois	Tourist Information	0502 21178
Slieve Bloom	Slieve Bloom Rural Development Assoc.	0509 37299
Stradbally	National Steam Traction Rally (August)	0502 25444

R # ABBEYLEIX

Founded in the 18th century by Viscount de Vesci, as an estate town, Abbeyleix takes its name from a 12th century Cistercian abbey and today it is an attractive Heritage Town with tree-lined streets and plenty to interest the visitor, including Abbeyleix Heritage House (057 873 1653) and the Sensory Gardens (057 873 1325). A few doors beyond the entrance to the Sensory Gardens on the Main Street as you head to Cork, **Café Odhrain** (057 855 7380) is a clean and pleasant place to break a journey, with efficient, friendly service and lovely wholesome food all day (about 8-5); it can be awkward to find a place to stop near the traffic lights here, as the road is very busy, but you'll be rewarded with fresh & healthy food: breakfast (fruits salad with Greek yoghurt, honey & oats; maple syrup pancakes; toasted bagels), panini, hand-cut doorstep sandwiches made to order, salads, home-made soups, hot dish of the day and excellent home baking. Apple & rhubarb tarts, scones and jams are delicious, and available to take away too. Also on the main street you'll find one of Ireland's best-loved old pubs, **Morrissey's** (0502 31281); it first opened as a grocery in 1775 and, true to the old tradition, 'television, cards and singing are not allowed'. Across the road, don't miss **Bramley** (Tel: 057 873 0996); this stylish gift shop and furniture store is an offshoot of **Castle Durrow** (see entry) and the perfect place to buy wedding presents. A short distance below Morrissey's on the right, **Preston House** (057 873 1432), for so many years a favoured place to break a journey, has re-opened under new management; open 12-5 daily at the time of going to press, with dinner opening and accommodation to follow. At the Cork end of the village **Abbeyleix Manor Hotel** (057 873 0111; www.abbeyleixmanorhotel.com) offers practical modern facilities. The town has a golf course (057 873 1450), a tennis club, a Polo Club - that offers great entertainment in the summer - and many delightful walks including one starting from the grounds of St. Michael & All Angels Church of Ireland, known as The Lords Walk. There are also many beautiful gardens to visit close to hand including Heywood Gardens (Ballinakill, 057 873 3563) and Gash Gardens (Portlaoise, 057 873 2247), and wonderful fishing on the internationally renowned River Nore.

WWW.IRELAND-GUIDE.COM FOR ALL THE BEST PLACES TO EAT, DRINK & STAY

Abbeyleix

B&B•COUNTRY HOUSE

Sandymount House

Oldtown Abbeyleix Co Laois **Tel: 057 873 1063**
avrilbibby@gmail.com www.abbeyleix.info

A charming mid-19th century house set quietly in mature woodlands on the de Vesci estate, Avril Bibby and Robin Scott's country house B&B is just outside Abbeyleix village and offers all the advantages of the relaxed rural life that is typical of the area, yet is within easy distance of shops, pubs and restaurants too. Recently restored, with all the original features retained and a contemporary approach giving freshness to the furnishings, this is a very pleasant place to stay, with all the advantages of old and new – bedrooms have smart en-suites and broadband and as well as television, phones, tea/coffee making and clothes pressing facilities. There are masses of things to do nearby – golf, horseriding, fishing, walking, historical sites and gardens to visit among them – and Avril and Robin are great hosts, who enjoy helping guests to get to know the area and to get the most out of their stay. They'll see you off with a good breakfast in the morning – and how nice to come back to a welcoming open fire in the comfortable guest sitting room or TV lounge after a long day out and about. **Rooms 4** (all en-suite, shower only and no smoking); children welcome (under 2s free in parents room, cot available free of charge); broadband wi/fi. B&B €50pps, ss €15. Dogs permitted (stay in kennel, no charge). Closed 20 Dec - 2 Jan. MasterCard, Visa, Laser. **Directions:** 2km down Ballacolla/Rathdowney (R433) road from Abbeyleix, on right hand side.

Ballacolla

B&B•PUB

Foxrock Inn

Clough Ballacolla Co Laois **Tel: 057 873 8637**
marian@foxrockinn.com www.foxrockinn.com

Sean and Marian Hyland run a very friendly, relaxed little place here for lovers of the country life. Hill walking, fishing (coarse and game), golf and pitch & putt are all in the neighbourhood (golf and fishing packages are a speciality) and they'll make packed lunches to see you through the day. An open fire and traditional music (days & times on inquiry) make the pub a welcoming place to come back to and there is accommodation just up the stairs, in simple but comfortable rooms. **Rooms 5** (all en-suite, shower only & no smoking); children welcome (under 2s free in parents' room, cot available without charge). B&B €45 pps, ss €19. Closed 1 Dec-7 Jan & bar closed Good Fri (accommodation open). Visa, Laser. **Directions:** On the R434, which links Durrow (N4) and Borris-in-Ossory (N7). Sign-posted off N7 and N8.

Durrow

HOTEL•RESTAURANT

Castle Durrow

Durrow Co Laois **Tel: 057 873 6555**
info@castledurrow.com www.castledurrow.com

Peter and Shelley Stokes' substantial 18th century country house midway between Dublin and Cork is an impressive building with some magnificent period features, and offers comfort and relaxation with style. A large marbled reception area with lovely fresh flowers gives a welcoming impression on arrival, and public rooms include a large drawing room/bar, where informal meals are served (a useful place to break a journey), and a lovely dining room with a gently pastoral outlook at the back of the house (see below). Very spacious, luxurious accommodation is in high-ceilinged, individually-decorated rooms and suites in the main house (some with four posters), with views over the surrounding parkland and countryside; some more contemporary but equally pleasing ground floor rooms are in a wing - particularly suitable for guests attending the weddings which have become a speciality, as they are convenient to the banqueting suite and avoid disturbing other guests. Conversion of stables in a second wing in 2008 has brought onstream a new set of rooms, this time in a simpler country style – not luxurious, but very charming. Conference/banqueting (160/170); secretarial services. Children welcome (under 5s free in parents' room, cot available without charge, baby sitting arranged, children's playroom). Pets permitted by arrangement. Spa, garden, walking, tennis (all-weather, floodlit), cycling, snooker. Golf, fishing, equestrian all nearby. Hairdressing, beauty salon. **Rooms 32** (10 junior suites, 3 ground floor, 4 family rooms, all no smoking and with bath & shower). B&B about €100 pps, ss €40. 24-hr room service. Turn down service. Closed 31 Dec-15 Jan. **Castle Restaurant:** Candles are lit in the foyer and restaurant at dusk, giving the whole area a lovely romantic feeling. Head chef David Rouse's policy is for careful sourcing of all food, and the quality shows. Fish cookery is especially impressive and wild Irish venison served with beetroot purée, potato rosti, braised fog, kohlrabi and aged balsamic vanilla jus - is a speciality in season; it sounds complicated but works well on the plate. A well-balanced cheese plate might include the delicious local Lavistown cheese from Kilkenny. Staff are very pleasant and helpful. **Seats 60** (private room, 18); reservations accepted; toilets wheelchair accessible. Breakfast 8-10, D daily, 7-8.45 (Sun D, 6-7.45pm). Bar meals also available, 12-7 daily. Set D about €50; Bar L à la carte. SC discretionary. House wines €20. Closed 31 Dec-15 Jan. Amex, MasterCard, Visa, Laser. **Directions:** On main Dublin-Cork road, N8, entrance from village green.

Killenard

HOTEL•RESTAURANT

The Heritage Golf & Spa Resort

Killenard Co Laois **Tel: 057 864 5500**
info@theheritage.com www.theheritage.com

This new luxury hotel and golf resort is set in the Laois countryside, just off the main Dublin-Cork road (N7). It is a very large development and as time progresses the landscaping is softening the hard edges. An impressive atrium sets the tone as you enter the hotel and, with a bifurcated staircase, crystal chandeliers and marbled floors, this lobby is designed to impress; other public areas are spacious and furnished in a similar style. Generous accommodation is in sumptuously furnished suites and guest rooms, which are extremely comfortable - and have beautiful bathrooms with separate shower and bath - although, surprisingly, some rooms do not have a view. But exceptional leisure facilities are the trump card at this hotel - as well as golf, there is a health club & spa (linked to the hotel by a tunnel), indoor and outdoor bowls, tennis, a 4-mile floodlit walking and jogging track around the golf course - and much more; new facilities are being added all the time. Fine dining is offered in The Arlington Room (see below), and an informal option is available at the very popular Soloriens Steakhouse & Italian Restaurant. Conferences/Banqueting (500/400); business centre, free broadband wi/fi. Children welcome (under 5s free in parents' room, cot available free of charge, baby sitting arranged, playroom). Destination Spa; leisure centre (pool, fitness room, jacuzzi, sauna, steam room); championship golf (18); coarse fishing; walking. **Rooms 98** (3 suites, 10 junior suites, 10 junior suites, 5 family rooms, 5 disabled, 88 no smoking). B&B €162.50 pps, ss €100. Wheelchair-friendly. **Arlington Room Restaurant:** Generous tables, crisp white linen and fine porcelain set the tone for a relaxing experience in this comfortable and well-appointed restaurant. Head chef Robert Webster offers a wide-ranging and luxurious à la carte menu which includes some less usual dishes, such as a starter of venison and caramelised onion pie with baby salad leaves and black truffle vinaigrette, and interesting vegetarian choices. A house speciality is grilled brill with prawn risotto, with spinach purée & morel cream, but Irish beef and poultry is also well represented. Excellent home-baked breads are a highlight, also delicious desserts including a hot 'Heritage Soufflé' with your choice of liqueur - and lovely petits fours and attentive service add to the occasion. A good, if rather expensive, wine list offers plenty of choice by the glass, and seven half bottles. **Seats 100** (Private room available seats 45), D daily 7-10 (Sun to 9.30); Set D €65 (Also priced by course). Piano Sat 8-11, air conditioning; House Wine about €23. Children welcome but not after 8. *Food also available in: **Greens** golf club restaurant (High season 7 days 7-9.30); **Soloriens Italian Restaurant & Steakhouse** (Wed-Sun 6.30-10) and The Hotel Bar 12-7 daily, includes outdoor seating on patio for 40. 12 Self catering houses available. *The Heritage Hotel Portlaoise** (see entry) is an older sister to the Killenard hotel in Portlaoise town centre. Hotel closed 24-26 Dec. Amex, MasterCard, Visa, Laser. Heli-pad. **Directions:** M7 exit no. 15 to Killenard.

Mountrath
COUNTRY HOUSE

Roundwood House

Mountrath Co Laois **Tel: 057 873 2120**
roundwood@eircom.net www.roundwoodhouse.com

It is hard to see how anyone could fail to love this unspoilt early Georgian house, which lies secluded in mature woods of lime, beech and chestnut, at the foot of the Slieve Bloom mountains - a sense of history and an appreciation of genuine hospitality are all that is needed to make the most of a stay here, so just relax and share the immense pleasure and satisfaction that Frank and Rosemarie Kennan derive from their years of renovation work. Although unconventional in some ways, the house is extremely comfortable and well-heated, and all the bathrooms have been renovated; each bedroom has its particular charm, although it might be wise to check if there is a large group staying, in which case the bedroom above the drawing room may not be the best option. Restoration is an ongoing process and an extraordinary (and historically unique) barn is in progress; this enterprise defies description, but don't leave Roundwood without seeing it; and do allow time to visit the top floor where Frank's latest venture is a Library of Civilisation, no less. Children, who always love the unusual animals and their young in the back yard, are very welcome and Rosemarie does a separate tea for them. Dinner is served at 8 o'clock, at a communal table, and based on the best local and seasonal ingredients (notably locally-reared beef and lamb); Rosemarie's food suits the house - good home cooking without unnecessary frills - and Frank is an excellent host. An informative and surprisingly extensive wine list includes a generous choice of half bottles. Small conferences/Banqueting (25/40); free broadband wi/fi. **Rooms 10** (all en-suite, 3 family, 6 no-smoking, 2 ground floor); children welcome (under 3 free in parents' room, cot available without charge; playroom, baby sitting arranged). No pets. B&B €85 pps, ss €25. No sc. D at 8pm (7pm Sun); set D, €35 (non-residents welcome by reservation if there is room); please book by noon. House wine €16.50. Garden, croquet, boules, walking - there is a mile-long walk in the grounds and garden renovation is ongoing. Stabling available at the house; horse riding nearby. Golf nearby. Establishment closed 25 Dec & month of Jan. Amex, Diners, MasterCard, Visa, Laser. **Directions:** On the left, 5km (3 m) from Mountrath, on R440.

PORTLAOISE

Not a lot of people know this, but the county town of Laois was previously called Maryborough (it was first established by Queen Mary in 1556 as "the Fort of Maryborough") and was only renamed 'Portlaoise' in 1922. Today it is a major commercial, retail, and arts centre for the Midlands and there is much of interest to visitors, including the old jail which is now an Arts Centre (057 866 3355), the ruins of an 800-year old hill-top castle at Dunamaise, a large

Georgian estate home and surrounding gardens at Emo (057 862 6587), a Georgian square at Mountmellick, and especially - the unspoilt Slieve Bloom Mountains & Forest Park. In addition to the recommendations below, it may be useful to know that budget accommodation is available at the **Comfort Inn** (057 866 6702) on the Abbeyleix road, and other good restaurants in the town include **The Lemon Tree** (057 866 2200) (above Delaney & Sons Bar/The Hare and Hound Bar, and **Palki Indian Restaurant** (059 863 8227) both on Main Street. The championship golf course nearby at The Heritage (Killenard, 0502 45500) provides a particularly tough challenge, and garden lovers would be interested to visit the nearby Gash Gardens (Castletown, 057 873 2247) or Heywood Gardens (Ballinakill, 057 873 3563).
WWW.IRELAND-GUIDE.COM FOR ALL THE BEST PLACES TO EAT, DRINK & STAY

Portlaoise   Ivyleigh House
GUESTHOUSE   Bank Place Church Street Portlaoise Co Laois **Tel: 057 862 2081**
🏆🏛️🍷 📺 🆅 🆁 🆁   info@ivyleigh.com www.ivyleigh.com

This lovely early Georgian house is set back from the road only by a tiny neatly box-hedged formal garden, but has a coachyard (with parking), outhouses and a substantial lawned garden at the back. It is a listed building and the present owners, Dinah and Jerry Campion, have restored it immaculately and furnished it beautifully in a style that successfully blends period elements with bold contemporary strokes, giving it great life. Two sitting rooms (one with television) are always available to guests and there's a fine dining room with a large communal table and a smaller one at the window for anyone who prefers to eat separately. Bedrooms are the essence of comfort, spacious, elegant, with working sash windows and everything absolutely top of the range including real linen. Large shower rooms have power showers and many excellent details, although those who would give anything for a bath to soak in will be disappointed. But it is perhaps at breakfast that this superb guesthouse is at its best. An extensive menu shows a commitment to using quality local produce that turns out to be even better than anticipated: imaginative, perfectly cooked and beautifully presented. As well as a full range of fresh juices, fruits, yogurts, cereals and porridge, speciality hot dishes include Cashel Blue cheesecakes - light and delicious, like fritters - served with mushrooms and tomatoes. And through it all Dinah Campion (who must rise at dawn to bake the bread) is charming, efficient and hospitable. This is one of Ireland's best guesthouses, and was Leinster winner of our Irish Breakfast Awards in 2002. No evening meals, but the Campions direct guests to good restaurants nearby. **Rooms 6** (all shower only & no smoking); not suitable for children under 8. B&B €75, ss €20. No pets. Garden. Golf & garden visits nearby. Closed Christmas period. MasterCard, Visa. **Directions:** Centre of town, follow signs for multi-storey car park, 30 metres from carpark.

Portlaoise   Kingfisher Restaurant
RESTAURANT   Old AIB Bank Main Street Portlaoise Co Laois **Tel: 057 866 2500**
🆁 🆁   www.kingfisherrestaurant.com

Situated in the centre of Portlaoise in the old AIB bank, this atmospheric and highly regarded Indian restaurant specialises in Punjabi cuisine. The welcome from immaculately attired staff is genuinely friendly and the large, high-ceilinged room (the former banking hall), is unusual, with decor portraying the crumbling sandstone walls of an ancient Indian temple. Simple table presentation and long menus may send out warning signals, but poppadoms with dipping sauces see you through the decision-making phase and, once food appears it has the fresh flavours of individual ingredients and authentic spicing creating satisfying combinations - in dishes that vary from creamy styles with almonds, to very spicy dishes with 'angry' green peppers. Tandoori, balti, biryani, 'exquisite' dishes and old favourites like korma, rogan josh, do piaza are all there, but they are skilfully executed, without recourse to elaborate presentation. Food is served with professionalism and charm, and reasonably priced - with a relaxed ambience and people of all ages enjoying themselves, this is a pleasant place to eat. **Seats 80.** L Wed-Fri 12-2.30, à la carte; D daily, 5.30-11.30; Set L menus from about €15 per person; set D menus from about €30 pp; also à la carte. House wine €16.95. Parking (15). Closed L Sat-Tue; 25 & 26 Dec, Good Fri. Amex, MasterCard, Visa, Laser. **Directions:** Town Centre.

Portlaoise
RESTAURANT

The Kitchen & Foodhall

Hynds Square Portlaoise Co Laois **Tel: 057 866 2061**
jimkitchen@eircom.net

Jim Tynan's excellent restaurant and food shop is definitely worth a little detour. Delicious home-made food, an open fire, relaxed atmosphere - a perfect place to break a journey or for a special visit. The food hall stocks a wide range of Irish speciality food products (and many good imported ones as well) and also sells products made on the premises: home-made terrines and breads for example (including gluten-free breads - which are also available in the restaurant) lovely home-bakes like Victoria sponges, crumbles and bread & butter pudding, and home-made chutneys and jams. You can buy home-made ready meals too, and any of the extensive range of wines from the shop can be bought for the restaurant without a corkage charge. The restaurant offers a great choice of wholesome fare, including at least three vegetarian dishes each day - old favourites like nut roast, perhaps and others like feta cheese tart and broccoli roulade. Hereford premium beef is typical of the Irish produce in which such pride is taken - and self-service lunches come with a wholesome selection of vegetables or salads. It's well worth making a special visit here in the autumn, to stock up their home-made and speciality Christmas food. *The restaurant - always notable for its original art - is officially home to 'The Tynan Gallery', with regular art exhibitions featuring both local and national artists. **Seats 200** (also outdoor 50+). Open all day Mon-Sat, 8.30-5.30; L12-3/3.30pm. A la carte & vegetarian menu. House wine from about €11.99; wheelchair access. Closed Sun, 25 Dec-1 Jan. Amex, MasterCard, Visa, Laser **Directions:** In the centre of Portlaoise, beside the Courthouse. ◊

Portlaoise
HOTEL

Portlaoise Heritage Hotel

Portlaoise Co Laois **Tel: 057 867 8588**
info@theheritagehotel.com   www.theheritagehotel.com

This very popular hotel is an older sister to the Heritage at Killenard (see entry) and it offers particularly good facilities for conferences and business travellers. Although situated right in the town centre, the hotel's proud claim is that guests never have to leave the premises during their stay, and public areas certainly offer a lot of choices to suit both off-duty business/conference guests and leisure guests; there are three dining options, for example - Spago Italian Bistro for informal meals, fine dining at The Fitzmaurice and casual eating at Kellys Foundry Grillhouse, which is a fun place where the speciality is dry-aged Irish Hereford beef, cooked on 'Black Rock' (volcanic stone). Accommodation, in several grades of room, is very comfortable and offers all the facilities expected of a good hotel. A dedicated conference wing offers excellent facilities for everything from small meetings to large conferences and events, and there is a fine health & fitness club with 22m pool, sauna, Jacuzzi, steam room and gym; personal trainer available; beauty therapies. Conferences/Banqueting (500/350), free broadband wi/fi, business centre, video conferencing. Spa (beauty treatments & massage). **Rooms 110** (4 suites, 4 junior suites, 28 executive, 90 no smoking, 4 disabled); Lift; 24 hr room service; Children welcome (under 5s free in parents room, cot available at no charge). Closed 24-27 Dec. Amex, Diners, Visa, Laser. **Directions:** Centre of Portlaoise.

COUNTY LEITRIM

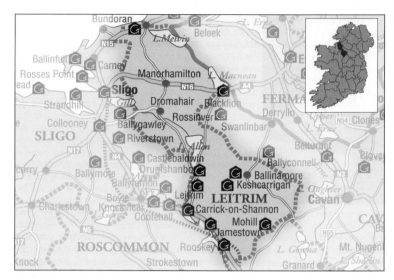

If you seek a county which best symbolises the resurgence of Ireland, you need look no further than Leitrim. In times past, it was known as the Cinderella county. Official statistics admitted that Leitrim did indeed have the poorest soil in all Ireland, in places barely a covering of low fertility. Back in the sad old days of the 1950s, the county's population had fallen to 30,000. It was doubted that it was still a viable administrative entity.

You'd be hard put to visualise those gloomy times now, more than fifty years on. Today, Leitrim prospers. The county town, Carrick-on-Shannon, is one of Ireland's brightest and best, a bustling river port. Admittedly, there are drawbacks. The town's very first traffic lights came into action in the summer of 2004. Formerly, there were no traffic lights in all Leitrim county. Or at least, not on the roads. The modern automated locks on the restored Shannon-Erne Waterway – whose vitality has contributed significantly to Leitrim's new prosperity – may have had their own boat traffic lights since the waterway was re-opened in 1994. But it took another ten years before the roads followed suit.

Yet despite the new energy, Leitrim is rightly seen as a pleasantly away-from-it-all sort of place which has many attractions for the determined connoisseur, not least enthusiasts for traditonal music, though "traditional" is scarcely the proper word – in Letirm, it's vibrantly alive and developing all the time. However, with some of Ireland's better-known holiday areas suffering if anything from an excess of popularity, the true trail-blazers may still be able to find the relaxation they seek in Leitrim.

But is it really so remote? Popular perceptions may be at variance with reality. For instance, Leitrim shares the shores of Lough Gill with Sligo, so much so that Yeat's legendary Lake Isle of Innisfree is within an ace of being in Leitrim rather than Sligo of Yeatsian fame. To the northward, we find that more than half of lovely Glencar, popularly perceived as being one of Sligo's finest jewels, is in fact in Leitrim. As for the notion of Leitrim being the ultimate inland and rural county - not so. Leitrim has an Atlantic coastline, albeit of only four kilometres, around Tullaghan.

It's said this administrative quirk is a throwback to the time when the all-powerful bishops of the early church aspired to have ways of travelling to Rome without having to cross the territory of neighbouring clerics. Whatever the reason, it's one of Leitrim's many surprises, which are such that it often happens that when you're touring in the area and find yourself in a beautiful bit of country, a reference to the map produces the information that, yes indeed, you're in Leitrim, a county which also provides most of the land area for Ireland's first Ecotourism 'Green Box'.

Leitrim's significance within this scheme achieved additional recognition when the first An Taisce National Awards were announced. The prize for the most appropriate building in the countryside – a concept which is surely central to An Taisce's very existence – went to Rossinver Organic Centre, whose buildings in North Leitrim near Lough Melvin were designed by Colin Bell.

Local Attractions and Information

Ballinamore	Shannon-Erne Waterway	071 964 4855
Ballinamore	Slieve an Arain Riverbus Cruises	071 964 4079
Carrick-on-Shannon	Moonriver Cruises	071 962 1777
Carrick-on-Shannon	Tourism Information	071 962 0170
Carrick-on-Shannon	Waterways Ireland	071 965 0898
Dromahair	Parke's Cas. (restored 17c fortified hse)	071 916 4149
Drumshanbo	Sliabh an Iarainn Visitor Centre	071 964 1522
Manorhamilton	Glens Arts Centre	071 985 5833
Mohill	Lough Rynn House and Gardens	071 963 1427
Rossinver	The Organic Centre (Ecotourism)	071 985 4338

BALLINAMORE

Ballinamore is a small town beside the Shannon-Erne Waterway, in a lovely area that's great for a family holiday as there's lots to do. Teresa Kennedy's farm guesthouse **Glenview House** (071 964 4157), for example, is attractively situated overlooking the waterway, and has a tennis court and an outdoor play area as well as an indoor games room; there's even a little agricultural museum in the outbuildings, and Teresa runs a popular restaurant too. Nearby, also overlooking the canal, **Riversdale Farm Guesthouse** (071 964 4122; www.riversdale.biz) is another homely place to stay, also with lots to do on site: no restaurant, but there's a small leisure complex, with swimming pool and squash - and barges at the bottom of the garden, available for holidays afloat. Nearby in Keeldrin a visit to **Swan Island Open Farm** & **Davy's Cottage Restaurant** (049 433 3065) is a real treat for all the family with both rare and traditional farm animals to see and feed, and also a children's play area. The farm is open Easter to October and a floating jetty at the farm ensures secure and easy mooring for cruisers; Davy's Cottage Restaurant is open year round from midday (daily, L 12-6; à la carte D 6-9pm); there's a friendly bar and the restaurant has an intimate ambience with a homely feeling and lovely simple home-cooked food with real flavour. This, of course, is wonderful fishing country, and golfers might relish the chance to play the championship course at the nearby Slieve Russell Golf Club (Ballyconnell, 049 952 5090).
WWW.IRELAND-GUIDE.COM FOR ALL THE BEST PLACES TO EAT, DRINK & STAY

R CARRICK ON SHANNON

An ideal location on the River Shannon has resulted in Carrick-on-Shannon becoming one of the most popular destinations for cruise holidays and fishing in Ireland and there is also a golf course (071 966 7015) on the outskirts of the town and just a short drive away the wonderful Strokestown Park House & Gardens (Strokestown, 071 963 3013) is a historic house and estate, with restored walled gardens and famine museum. This thriving town is cosmopolitan in its outlook, with a growing range of restaurants and some fascinating shops: with an interesting range of little shops around the central square, the characterful old Market Yard Centre is always a good browsing spot; it's right at the heart of this vibrant town, and the hub of local activities including Farmers' Markets (Thursdays), Crafts Markets (Saturdays), and many special events. **Vitto's** (see entry) is a bright and airy Italian here, casual in style and serving tasty casual food. Beside the bridge, **Cryan's Bar & Restaurant** (Tel: 071-962 0409) is well-known for steaks and music. For accommodation, don't overlook **Glencarne Country House** (071-966 7013) which is across the bridge along the Boyle road, with a Co Roscommon postal address, and **Caldra House** (071 962 3040; www.caldrahouse.ie), which is about 3km (2 m) out of town off the R280. The Dock (071 9650828; www.thedock.ie) is Carrick's cultural centre - housed in the beautiful 19th century former Courthouse building, overlooking the River Shannon, it has been wonderfully restored into Leitrim's first integrated centre for the arts, with a 100+ seat performance space, three art galleries, artists' studios, an arts education room; it is also home to The Leitrim Design House. Outside Carrick-on-Shannon, at Kilclare, **The Sheermore** (071 964 1029) is a friendly traditional bar, grocery and hardware shop on the Shannon-Erne Waterway and can be a pleasant pub to visit, well away from the bustle of the town; not really a food place (although snacks are available) but you can sit outside at the back in fine weather and watch the boats going by.
WWW.IRELAND-GUIDE.COM FOR ALL THE BEST PLACES TO EAT, DRINK & STAY

E99

Carrick-on-Shannon

Bush Hotel

HOTEL•RESTAURANT

Carrick-on-Shannon Co Leitrim **Tel: 071 967 1000**

info@bushhotel.com www.bushhotel.com

R

One of Ireland's oldest hotels, the Bush is known for its old-fashioned hospitality and staff are exceptionally pleasant and helpful. It has undergone considerable refurbishment in recent years and, while rooms will vary in size and comfort (and the 40 newer rooms are more luxurious), this hotel has personality. Public areas have character and a pleasing sense of history, and there are two bars, one of which has been given a contemporary make-over and is now a bistro bar, and a TV lounge with an open fire which is very appealing in chilly weather. A new conference room offers a full range of business and conference facilities and The Orchard Ballroom makes a bright and inviting venue for large events. Informal meals are available at the self-service coffee shop/carvery, with bar food also offered at lunchtime and in the evening. Conference/Banqueting (350/300); free broadband wi/fi; business centre, secretarial services. **Rooms 60** (1 suite, 3 family rooms); children welcome (under 2s free in parents' room, cot available without charge); B&B €89.50pps, single €99.50. The hotel has a gift shop, tourist information point and bureau de change and can arrange car, bicycle and boat hire and supply fishing tackle and golf clubs. Golf nearby. Tennis; garden. Parking (180). *Short breaks offered - details on application. Closed Christmas. **Restaurant:** The hotel's pleasant restaurant is notable for its traditional style and courteous service, and remains a popular destination. In addition to a set menu, they offer a Bistro Menu which is also available in the bar. Expect the comfortingly familiar kind of food that used to be more typical of Ireland: starters like egg mayonnaise and Irish oak-smoked salmon salad, and main courses that will almost certainly include steak - Irish sirloin steak au poivre, perhaps - baked fillet of salmon and roast crispy duckling. Finish off with profiteroles or lemon cheesecake. The food is well cooked, traditional and reliable, the service is delightful and it's great value. House wines are good value at € 19.95. **Seats 100** (private room, 50); children welcome (childrens menu); air conditioning. L&D daily, 12.30-2.30pm (to 4.30 Sun) & 6-9pm (to 8 Sun). Set L €23.95; set Sun L €28.95; house wine €19.95. MasterCard, Visa, Laser. **Directions:** Town centre - signed off the N4 bypass.

Carrick-on-Shannon

Ciúin House

GUESTHOUSE•RESTAURANT

Hartley Carrick-on-Shannon Co Leitrim **Tel: 071 967 1488**

info@ciuinhouse.com www.ciuinhouse.com

Quietly situated on the edge of the town but within comfortable walking distance of all its amenities, Fiona Reynolds' stylish new purpose built guesthouse is effectively a small hotel. Bedrooms are simply but warmly furnished to a high standard and are very well-appointed, with orthopaedic beds and all the in-room facilities expected of an hotel, and some of the pristine bathrooms have Jacuzzi baths. A private sitting room is comfortably furnished with style, and has a gas fire and a surround sound music system and plasma screen multi-channel television for guests' use. A high level of comfort and amenities, immaculate housekeeping, hands-on management and an emphasis on genuine hospitality and service all make this a great place to stay. **Restaurant:** An extensive breakfast is served in a bright and airy restaurant, which opens on to a paved area with outside seating in fine weather and is open to the public for breakfast and snacks, lunch and dinner. [*The restaurant was closed at the time of the Guide's most recent overnight visit, but a delicious informal evening meal was most hospitably prepared, and we look forward to revisiting in the near future; see www.ireland-guide.com for updates.] Small conferences/banquets (36); broadband wi/fi. **Rooms 15** (2 deluxe, 2 family, 2 shower only, 1 ground floor, 1 for disabled); children welcome (under 3s free in parents' room, cots available free of charge, baby sitting arranged). B&B €65pps. Closed Good Fri, 24-26 Dec. MasterCard, Visa, Laser. **Directions:** From Carrick-on-Shannon take the R280 Letirim road. Follow signs for Cootehall. Left for Hartley at Leitrim Observer offices, signed from road.

Carrick-on-Shannon
COUNTRY HOUSE

Hollywell Country House

Liberty Hill Cortober Carrick-on-Shannon Co Leitrim **Tel: 071 962 1124**
hollywell@esatbiz.com

After many years as hoteliers in the town (and a family tradition of inn-keeping that goes back 200 years), Tom and Rosaleen Maher moved some years ago to this delightful period house on a rise across the bridge, with its own river frontage and beautiful views over the Shannon. It's a lovely, graciously proportioned house, with a relaxed family atmosphere. Tom and Rosaleen have an easy hospitality (not surprisingly, perhaps, as their name derives from the Gaelic "Meachar" meaning hospitable), making guests feel at home very quickly and this, as much as the comfort of the house and its tranquil surroundings, is what makes Hollywell special. Bedrooms are all individually furnished in period style, with tea and coffee making facilities, and delicious breakfasts are worth getting up in good time for: fresh juice, fruits and choice of teas, coffees and herbal teas, freshly-baked bread, home-made preserves, lovely choice of hot dishes - anything from the "full Irish" to Irish pancakes with maple syrup or grilled cheese & tomato with black olive pesto on toast. No evening meals, but Tom and Rosaleen advise guests on the best local choices and there's a comfortable guests' sitting room with an open fire to gather around on your return. A pathway through lovely gardens leads down to the river; fishing (coarse) on site. Lots to do in the area - and advice a-plenty from Tom and Rosaleen on the best places to visit. Open mainly at weekends - please call for opening times. **Rooms 4** (2 junior suites, 2 shower only); not suitable for children under 12. B&B about €60 pps, ss about €30. Pets allowed by arrangement. *There are plans afoot for a chanhe of management within the family. Closed early Nov- early Feb. Amex, MasterCard, Visa, Laser. **Directions:** From Dublin, cross bridge on N4, keep left at Ging's pub. Hollywell entrance is on left up the hill. ◇

Carrick-on-Shannon
HOTEL•RESTAURANT
R

The Landmark Hotel

Dublin Road Carrick-on-Shannon Co Leitrim **Tel: 071 962 2222**
reservations@thelandmarkhotel.com www.thelandmarkhotel.com

This aptly-named hotel just across the road from the river has a dramatic lobby with a large marble and granite fountain feature - and an imposing cast-iron staircase creates a certain expectation. Bedrooms, many of which have views over the Shannon, are spacious and comfortable, with individual temperature control as well as the more usual amenities (direct dial phone, TV, tea/coffee facilities, trouser press) and well-finished bathrooms. Informal daytime meals are offered in Aromas Café, and the balcony dining area previously known as Ferrari's is now the Boardwalk Café, (aptly-named after the new boardwalk across the road) and the trademark wall-mounted Ferrari has gone. Very modern, with a marine theme, neon blue lighting and a cobblestone floor (the latter can be difficult for ladies in high heels) it also features 8 large screen televisions, which are less obtrusive than one would think. The smart-casual food is very well presented and excellent value There is also an outdoor seating area in front of the hotel. *A new confrence centre and meeting rooms are planned at the time of going to press. Conference/banqueting (500/320); secretarial services; broadband wi/fi. Golf nearby. Off-season breaks. Children welcome (under 4s free in parents' room; cots available without charge, baby sitting arranged). No pets. Parking. Heli-pad. **Rooms 60** (2 suites, 6 family rooms, 2 shower only, 2 for disabled). Lift. B&B €119 pps, ss €30. **CJ's Restaurant:** The hotel's elegant fine dining restaurant, CJ's, has earned a local following with discerning diners who enjoy the setting the welcoming ambience, comfortable surrounds and good cooking. Head chef Eunan Campbell's menus match the surroundings, with many treats to choose from - a seafood dish of Dublin Bay prawns in katifi with confit of aubergine, chilli jam and cucumber pickle is a speciality, but the range is wide and you will also find dressed-up versions of homely dishes like ever-popular double cut lamb chops with braised fennel, spinach whipped potato and minted balsamic sauce. A meal here has all the extra little touches that add a sense of occasion, and professional service. This is not an inexpensive restaurant, but it does give good value - and diners have the choice of moving out to the conservatory, to dine there if preferred, which can be very enjoyable on a fine summer evening. **Seats 58** (private room, 30), D 6-10 daily; house wine from €24; SC discretionary; closed Sun; Aromas Café, 9-5; Bar food served daily. Hotel closed 25 Dec. Amex, MasterCard, Visa, Laser. **Directions:** On N4, 2 hours from Dublin.

Carrick-on-Shannon

PUB

The Oarsman Bar & Café

Bridge Street Carrick-on-Shannon Co Leitrim **Tel: 071 962 1733**
info@theoarsman.com www.theoarsman.com

WATERWAYS HOSPITALITY AWARD

This attractive and characterful pub is run by brothers Conor and Ronan Maher, sons of Tom and Rosaleen Maher (see entry for Hollywell), and it will be very clear to anyone who visits that they've inherited "the hotelier's gene": everything is invariably spick-and-span, very welcoming and efficiently run, even at the busiest times. The bar - which is very pleasantly set up in a solidly traditional style with two welcoming fires, comfortable seating arrangements for eating the excellent bar meals, and occasional contemporary tastes in the decor - leads off towards a sheltered beer garden at the back, which makes a spot for a sunny day. A strong kitchen team produces consistently excellent food, offered on appealing lunchtime bar menus and more extensive à la carte evening menus offered upstairs. Here you might have a great meal, beginning with seared Kilkeel scallops with spring onion potato cake, minted pea purée and lime crème fraiche, followed by any one of half a dozen terrific main courses, say slow braised Tom Beirne's pork belly with ginger & herb marinated pork fillet, roast apple, colcannon mash, and balsamic reduction. And, desserts have always been a speciality here, so don't forget to save a space for a wonderful ending - delicious iced pineapple soufflé, with caramelised pineapple pieces, coconut & oatmeal cookies; and a chocolate plate - composed of warm dark chocolate torte, white chocolate & brandy mousse and organic truffle ice cream – both came in for special praise on a recent visit. This is one of the country's most pleasant pubs and it just goes on getting better - definitely worth a detour. Bar food: L Tue-Sat 12-3; snack menu 3-5pm; evening menu 5-8pm. **Restaurant seats 40**; not suitable for children after 9pm; free broadband wi/fi; D Thu-Sat 6.45-9.15pm. A la carte. House wine from about 17. Closed Sun, Mon, 25 Dec, Good Fri. MasterCard, Visa, Laser. **Directions:** Town centre: coming from Dublin direction, turn right just before the bridge.

Carrick-on-Shannon

RESTAURANT

Shamrat Restaurant

Bridge Street Carrick-on-Shannon Co Leitrim
Tel: 071 965 0934

Although the entrance is small from the street, first-time visitors to this appealing Indian restaurant may be surprised to find a spacious L-shaped first floor dining area and enough room for a comfortable reception area at the top of the stairs. Menus are wide-ranging, offering a varied selection of Indian and Bangladeshi dishes; the familiar ones are all there - onion bahjee, chicken tikka or pakora, biryani dishes and perhaps a dozen tandoori specialities. Uncluttered contemporary decor and well-spaced tables with comfortable high-back chairs make a pleasing setting for interesting, authentic and well-cooked food - and attentive service from friendly and helpful staff adds to the enjoyment. Children welcome. L&D daily; Mon-Sat: D 6-11.30; Sun, special family lunch 1-4, à la carte 4-11.30. Set D about €25.95, D also à la carte; Vegetarian Menu about €20.95. House wine about €17.50. Closed 25 Dec. Amex, MasterCard, Visa, Laser. **Directions:** Near the bridge, on right-hand side walking into town.

Carrick-on-Shannon

RESTAURANT

Victoria Hall

Quay Road Carrick-on-Shannon Co Leitrim **Tel: 071 962 0320**
info@victoriahall.ie www.victoriahall.ie

This stylish contemporary restaurant is in an imaginatively restored and converted, almost-waterside Victorian building beside the Rowing Club. Bright, colourful and classy, it has great appeal (chic minimalist table settings, well-spaced tables, good lighting) with a first floor dining space that is especially attractive. Menus offer a wide range of broadly Asian and European dishes, translating into meals that are well-executed and good value - and served by smart, attentive staff. Various menus are offered at different times of day, and an innovative feature is a range of boxty wraps: boxty is a traditional potato pancake associated with north-west Ireland, especially Leitrim, and the selection of fillings offered here - including Thai beef with garlic, chicken saté and vegetable tofu – makes an interesting blend of traditional and modern styles. *Associated accommodation is offered at **Caldra House**, quietly located 2 miles outside the town (096 23040). **Seats 70** (outdoors, 25); children welcome (high chair, childrens menu); reservations accepted. air conditioning; toilets wheelchair accessible. Braille menu available. Open daily, 12.30-10. L, 12.30-5, D 5-10. Value L €10.50; set L €15.50; Early D €23/30, Sun-Thur, 5-7.30pm, also à la carte. Gluten-free menu available. House wine from €19.65. SC 10% on groups 8+. Closed 25 Dec, Good Fri. MasterCard, Visa, Laser. **Directions:** On Boathouse Quay, behind the Rowing Club.

Carrick-on-Shannon ## Vittos Italian Restaurant & Wine Bar

RESTAURANT•WINE BAR — Market Yard Centre Carrick on Shannon Co Leitrim

R — **Tel: 071 962 7000** vittosrestaurant@yahoo.com www.vittosrestaurant.com

This attractive stone-built restaurant is on the corner of Market Yard, with access from the yard or the main street, and run by husband and wife team Jason (head chef) and Jo (restaurant manager) O'Brien. They chose the location for well as, like the Market Yard Centre itself, Vitto's aims to cater for a wide range of visitors, times and occasions, so this friendly place offers an extensive menu including pizza, pasta, salads and char-grilled steaks, chicken dishes, burgers and more traditional Irish dishes, plus a full bar. Everything is freshly prepared in-house and cooked to order - and all meats are char-grilled. Planned to be equally suitable for a group booking or a table for two, Vitto's is also very family friendly, with a special menu, crayons and colouring books provided for children, and outside seating available in summer. And all items on the menu are also available to take away - very useful to know if you're holidaying on a Shannon cruiser. **Seats 65** (outdoors, 25); children welcome (high chair, childrens menu, baby changing facilities); toilets wheelchair accessible. Open for D Tue-Sat, 5.30-9pm and Sun 12.30-8.30pm. SC 10% on groups 6+. Closed Mon. MasterCard, Visa, Laser **Directions:** Centre of town.

Dromod ## The Brandywell

PUB — Dromod Co Leitrim
Tel: 071 96 38153

The McGuinness family's large pub with accommodation on the main road through 'County Leitrim's tidiest village' has a relaxed atmosphere and a reputation for wholesome food - and daily specials are marked up on the blackboard. Wheelchair accessible. Hearty food for hungry travellers available all day (booking advisable for evening meals and Sunday lunch). Amex, MasterCard, Visa, Laser.

Dromohair ## Riverbank Restaurant

RESTAURANT — Dromohair Co Leitrim **Tel: 071 916 4934**
declan@riverbank-restaurant.com www.riverbank-restaurant.com

Formerly Cuisto Perigord, this fine restaurant is now run by returning native John Kelly (the chef), and Cavan man Declan Campbell (restaurant manger). John was introduced to cooking by Neven Maguire (see entry for MacNean Bistro) so you can expect refined modern cooking with an emphasis on tiptop ingredients, locally produced where possible - a list of suppliers is included with the menu. The restaurant is in a lovely leafy setting, in what was once an orchard, and it's an impressive building, with a big central feature fireplace and lots of character; tables, many of which are windowside, are set up smartly with white cloths and napkins, and staff are very hospitable. Menus are presented promptly, along with the offer of a drink, and you can choose between an à la carte with six or seven choices per course, plus a couple of unusual vegetarian dishes, and the set dinner, which is a selection from these. A sophisticated house speciality of pan-flashed turbot with crab & dill ravioli, ratatouille and asparagus velouté may well be among choices that will almost certainly include local beef, and local Thornhill duckling. Desserts tend to be classic with a twist - roasted rhubarb, for example, might come with toasted brioche and walnut ice cream. The wine list includes plenty of choice at around €25 and under, and several half bottles. Dining here is a pleasant experience, and Sunday lunch offers very good value. **Seats 70** (private room, 30, outdoors, 20); children welcome (high chair, childrens menu); reservations recommended. D Wed-Sun, 6.30-10pm (from 7pm Sun); set D about €40; L Sun only, 12.30-3pm; set Sun L about €40; house wine about €19; SC 10% on groups 10+. Closed Mon, 24-26 Dec. Visa, Laser. **Directions:** 3rd exit for Dromohair from Dublin roundabout in Sligo, follow signs. ◊

Drumshanbo

Ramada Lough Allen Hotel & Spa

HOTEL

Drumshanbo Co Leitrim **Tel: 071 964 0100**

R

info@loughallenhotel.com www.loughallenhotel.com

Although the exterior is not appealing, the interior of this bright and interesting contemporary hotel just outside the characterful village of Drumshanbo will quickly win you over - an attractive foyer area with an open fire and a collection of striking paintings, has glazed doors at the far end - allowing a tantalising glimpse into a high-ceilinged bar; beyond this, a clear lake view is seen through a wall of glass, with a deck for fine weather. It's also a fine place for a winter trip when, after long walks or a cycle, you can return to the warmth of the fire. Rushes Restaurant - which, strangely, is not in a water-side position - offers pleasing food, and good bar meals are also served. Accommodation - in spacious, comfortable rooms (some with balcony), furnished in an understated, modern style with fine views - includes some suites and family rooms, and self-catering apartments. *Although there is a possibility of name/management changes here after we go to press, the hotel was open normally at the time of the Guide's summer 2008 visit. Conference/banqueting (220/160). **Rooms 64** (5 junior suites, some family rooms, 4 shower only, 4 for disabled, all no smoking); children welcome (under 2s free in parents' room, cot available without charge, baby sitting arranged). No pets. Lift. 24 hr room service. B&B €70-80 pps, ss about €23. Leisure centre (lakeview swimming pool, hot tub, gym), spa. Garden, walking, cycling, equestrian. Open all year. Amex, Diners, MasterCard, Visa, Laser. **Directions:** 15 km from Carrick-on-Shannon, on Drumshanbo-Sligo road.

Jamestown

The Cottage Restaurant

RESTAURANT

Jamestown Carrick on Shannon Co Leitrim **Tel: 071 962 5933**

N **V** **R**

thecottagerestaurant@yahoo.com

Formerly a well-known Lebanese restaurant (Al Mezza), new proprietor chef, Shamzuri Mohd Hanifa, now offers modern European and Asian food at this cheerful white-washed restaurant on the edge of the pretty village of Jamestown. Bright red paintwork, window boxes and hanging baskets give it an attractive cottage appearance; inside it's cosy and uncluttered, with subtle lighting, simple, classically linen-clad tables and smartly turned out staff waiting to show you to your table. Suppliers are credited on simply worded à la carte menus that offer six or seven appealing dishes on each course. Begin, perhaps, with delicious pan-seared scallops, served with a garlicky potato & leek hotpot, or an organic mixed leaf salad with cajun-spiced chicken - typically followed by pan-fried Slaney rump of lamb with herb polenta cake, or pan-fried seabass with braised pak choy, and then good ice creams or farmhouse cheeses to finish. A concise wine list is well-priced and includes a wine of the month. Perfectly-cooked and well-presented food is served promptly by friendly staff which, together with pleasant surroundngs and good value, make for an enjoyable meal. For those arriving in Jamestown by boat, it's about half a mile from the quay, but it's a pleasant walk through the village - pavement all the way and past two particularly enticing pubs for a visit in each direction, perhaps. Reservations are not essential, but this is an understandably popular little restaurant and it can be very busy, especially at weekends. **Seats 40** (private room, 18, outdoor 16); children welcome (high chair, childrens menu); reservations recommended. L & D daily, 12-4pm & 6.45-10pm; a la carte L&D. House wine from €19. MasterCard, Visa, Laser. **Directions:** On right just before entering Jamestown village.

KESHCARRIGAN

This attractive canalside village has craic and music a-plenty at Des Foley's famous friendly pub **Gertie's** (071 964 2252), which has open fires, plenty of character and music on Thursdays (and limited food too). Just along the canal a little way, the well-known **Canal View House & Restaurant** (071 964 2404), which has its own berthing just across the road - is currently run by the partnership of French duo Vincent Maillard and chef Alexander Jourdan.

WWW.IRELAND-GUIDE.COM FOR ALL THE BEST PLACES TO EAT, DRINK & STAY

Keshcarrigan

Julianos Italian Grill

RESTAURANT

13 Ceislawns Keshcarrigan Co Leitrim **Tel: 071 964 2698**

N

julianos_italian@eircom.net www.julianos.ie

The end unit of a new terrace of shops about 200m from Gertie's on the way out of the village, Juliano's is neatly presented in a café style rather than a restaurant. A small porch, which has a serving hatch for take-away orders, opens directly into the restaurant, a simply furnished room with soft white and light olive green décor, and an open kitchen along one wall. The welcome is warm, and pleasant staff offer a restaurant menu similar to the take-away menu, with the addition of a few steak dishes and a stir-fry. They also have a small, but very adequate wine list, including some quarter bottles. The speciality is pizza but there's plenty else to choose from - you might share a bowl of excellent buffalo chicken wings to start and follow with mains such as fettuccine Alfredo (available with prawns or chicken) and a side salad (green or Caesar), or a mixed spicy stir-fry, all well cooked and presented. A nice touch is having a bowl of freshly grated Parmesan cheese on the table, rather than the usual quick sprinkling. A light, moist and delicious hot chocolate fudge cake features among the desserts, also a selection of ice creams. Everything is freshly made using fresh, quality ingredients, and this is very apparent. Juliano's would be ideal for boaters staying in the nearby marina, who can have a pint in Gertie's on their way back to the boat. **Seats 30** (outdoors, 8); children welcome (high chair, childrens menu). Open daily in summer, Mon-Sat, 4.30-11pm, Sun 3-10.30pm. House wine €19.50. Parking (20). Closed Mon & Tue off season; Good Fri, 25-26 Dec. MasterCard, Visa, Laser. **Directions:** In the heart of Keshcarrigan.

Kinlough
RESTAURANT

The Courthouse Restaurant
Main Street Kinlough Co Leitrim **Tel: 071 984 2391**
thecourthouserest@eircom.net www.thecourthouserest.com

In the old courthouse of the attractive village of Kinlough, Piero Melis's little restaurant is a welcoming place and offers good contemporary cooking in the Mediterranean style, with some local influences. A wide-ranging menu includes specialities like the perennially popular Linguini di Mare, flat spaghetti with clams and crab in a tomato sauce, and there are always daily specials; other favourites include starters like seafood risotto and there is a wide range of main course specialities including Thornhill duck. Highlights of a recent visit included excellent garlic mushrooms; lovely fresh, light seed bread; and (although some are bought in) really delicious desserts: a properly wobbly panncotta with summer berries and – especially – a superb house tiramisu. Good food and helpful, professional service all encourage return visits - and the main room has an open fire, making it especially appealing. **Seats 40** (private room 12). D Wed-Mon, 6.30-9.30, L on Sun only 12.30-2.30; set Sun L €21; set 2/3 course D, about €28/38; also à la carte. House wines from €18; SC 10% on parties of 6+. Closed - Tue, 2 weeks after Feb 14, Christmas. MasterCard, Visa, Laser. **Directions:** Off main Donegal-Sligo road (N15), 5 km towards Sligo from Bundoran. Take turning directly opposite Tullaghan House.

R

LEITRIM

Although the traffic seems to race through at breakneck speed, and it has recently suffered from over-development, this village near Carrick-on-Shannon remains an attractive little place, with a harbour and a towpath walk. There is a new waterside hotel, the **Leitrim Marina Hotel** (071 9623628; www.leitrimmarinahotel.ie) and numerous pubs, the **Leitrim Inn** (071 96 20460) having a reputation for homely traditional food, while **The Barge Steakhouse** (071 962 0807) is an inviting stone bar and restaurant with a welcoming open fire in the characterful bar; behind it, a large restaurant opens onto a garden where there is plenty of seating - steaks are the speciality and they hold barbecues in summer.

WWW.IRELAND-GUIDE.COM FOR ALL THE BEST PLACES TO EAT, DRINK & STAY

Mohill
HOTEL•CASTLE

Lough Rynn Castle Hotel & Estate
Lough Rynn Mohill Co Leitrim **Tel: 071 963 2700**
enquiries@loughrynn.ie www.loughrynn.ie

Set amongst 300 acres of rolling countryside, historic Lough Rynn Castle has seen major investment and a great deal of TLC to restore it to its former glory for its new use as an hotel. Aside from structural restoration, original furnishings were located and refurbished before being reinstated in their former home, and many other luxurious items, including hand-painted silk wallpaper from Paris, were carefully sourced to complement the property. Approached via a winding wooded road, it is now entered through an impressive manned black and gold wrought iron gate, and guests are welcomed at the door. Opulently appointed lounges, drawing rooms and a library (with memorabilia connected with author John McGahern, who was from the area) are remarkably private and intimate for public rooms in an hotel, and have views out over the lawns and lake: a peaceful and comfortable place to read, or have a light lunch or afternoon tea. Bedrooms – 43 of the planned 52 at the time of going to press - include luxurious castle rooms offering unique accommodation, with wonderful views of the estate and surrounding countryside. The aim is to make Lough Rynn a perfect country haven, and no expense or effort has been spared; there is over a square mile of lake, with a marina, and the gardens - which are also of significant historical interest - are under restoration too, together with the nature trails and lakeside walks. What has been achieved so far is remarkable, but this is still a work in progress: more new rooms, a leisure centre and spa, and a Nick Faldo-designed golf course (due 'late 2009') are all planned. However, this is a lovely place and there is plenty to keep visitors occupied here already. Banqueting (320). Rooms 43 (including suites and standard & deluxe lake view rooms); children welcome. Room rate from about €215. Fishing, walking, garden; equestrian nearby. Open all year. MasterCard, Visa, Laser. **Directions:** Signed from Mohill village. ◇

Rooskey   # Shannon Key West Hotel
HOTEL   The Waters Edge Rooskey Co Leitrim **Tel: 071 963 8800**
R   info@shannonkeywest.com   www.shannonkeywest.com

This well-run riverside hotel on the Leitrim/Roscommon border provides valuable facilities to the area and recent road improvements have taken the main through traffic away from Rooskey village, making it a more attractive destination – and, as the hotel is open all year it is a useful venue for off-season short breaks, meetings and conferences. Comfortably furnished bedrooms have all the usual amenities - direct dial phones, TV with video channel, tea & coffee-making facilities and trouser press; some rooms also have business facilities. On-site amenities include a gym, jacuzzi, solarium and steam room (but no swimming pool) and there is plenty to do and see in the area. Conference/banqueting (500/360), broadband, secretarial services available. **Rooms 40** (17 shower only, 5 family rooms, 15 no smoking, 13 ground floor, 1 for disabled); children welcome (cots available without charge, baby sitting arranged). B&B €60-70 pps. Fitness room, tennis, walking. Open all year. Amex, MasterCard, Visa, Laser. **Directions:** On N4, main Dublin-Sligo route, midway between Longford and Carrick-on-Shannon. ◇

Rossinver   # The Grass Roof Café
CAFÉ•RESTAURANT   The Organic Centre Rossinver Co Leitrim **Tel: 071 985 4338**
     organiccentre@eircom.net   www.theorganiccentre.ie

County Leitrim is at the heart of the 'greening' of Ireland and, as the momentum grows, more and more people are interested in visiting The Organic Centre, either to attend one of the wide variety of courses they offer (free annual booklet available on request), or just to have a look around. The organic display gardens are very interesting, showing how organic food can be grown by everyone, and they include many attractive features including a children's garden with willow sculptures and witches' houses. There's also an Eco-shop stocking all kinds of eco-friendly and ethical products ranging from foods (vegetables, home bakes, Fairtrade) to seeds, books and home products. Inspired by the ultrafresh, seasonal (and, otherwise, often hard to source) produce available to them, the cooks at The Grass Roof Organic Café create great vegetarian meals to feed the staff, people attending workshops and the public. There's even a weekly 'béile gaeilge' (Irish speaking lunch) on Tuesdays and all Irish speakers, even beginners, are very welcome. This is an unusual and rewarding place to visit and outside catering is offered too, for 'anything from a picnic to a banquet'. **Seats 50** (outdoors, 20); toilets wheelchair accessible; children welcome (high chair, baby changing facilities). Food served daily, 10-4pm (snacks during the week, full menu at weekends); house wine €20-22. Closed 20 Dec-10 Jan. MasterCard, Visa, Laser. **Directions:** 15 mins from Manorhamilton on R282.

COUNTY LIMERICK

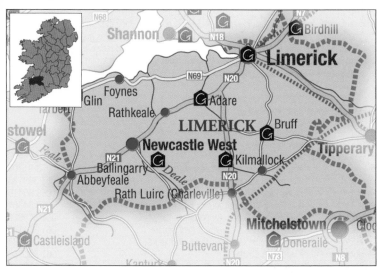

The story of Limerick city and county is in many ways the story of the Shannon Estuary, for in times past it was the convenient access provided by Ireland's largest estuary - it is 80 kilometres in length - which encouraged the development of life along the estuary's sea shores, and into the fresh water of the River Shannon itself.

Today, the area's national and global transport is served by air, sea and land through Shannon International Airport, the increased use of the Estuary through the development of Foynes Port and other deepwater facilities, improvement and restoration of rail links, and a rapidly expanding but inevitably busy road network which is being augmented by a tunnel under the Shannon Estuary immediately seaward of Limerick city.

In Limerick city in recent years, the opening of improved waterway links through the heart of town has seen the welcome regeneration of older urban areas continuing in tandem with the attractive new developments. But significant and all as this is, there's much more to the totality of Limerick county than the city and its waterways.

Inland from the river, the very richness of the countryside soon begins to develop its own dynamic. Eastern Limerick verges into Tipperary's Golden Vale, and the eastern county's Slieve Felim hills, rising to Cullaun at 462 m, reflect the nearby style of Tipperary's Silvermine Mountains.

Southwest of Limerick city, the splendid hunting country and utterly rural atmosphere of the area around the beautiful village of Adare makes it a real effort of imagination to visualise the muddy salt waters of the Shannon Estuary just a few miles away down the meandering River Maigue, yet the Estuary is there nevertheless.

Equally, although the former flying boat port of Foynes - with its evocative Flying Boat Museum well worth a visit - is seeing expansion of the nearby jetty at Aughinish to accommodate the most modern large ships, just a few miles inland we find ourselves in areas totally remote from the sea in countryside which lent itself so well to mixed farming that the price of pigs in Dromcolliher (a.k.a. Drumcolligher) on the edge of the Mullaghareirk Mountains reputedly used to set the price of pigs throughout Ireland.

The growth of the computer industry in concert with the rapid expansion of the energetic University has given Limerick a new place in Irish life in tandem with its established role as a leading manufacturing centre. The city's vitality and urban renewal makes it an entertaining place to visit, while the eclectic collection on stunning display in the unique Hunt Museum in its handsome waterside setting has a style which other areas of Limerick life are keen to match.

Georgina Campbell's Ireland

With newfound confidence, Limerick has been paying greater attention to its remarkable heritage of Georgian architecture, with Limerick Civic Trust restoring the Georgian house and garden at 2 Pery Square. It acts as the focal point for an area of classic urban architecture which deserves to be better known.

That said, rugby-mad Limerick still keeps its feet firmly on the ground, and connoisseurs are firmly of the opinion that the best pint of Guinness in all Ireland is to be had in this no-nonsense city, where they insist on being able to choose the temperature of their drink, and refuse to have any truck with modern fads which would attempt to chill the rich multi-flavoured black pint into a state of near-freezing tastelessness aimed at immature palates.

Local Attractions and Information

Adare	Heritage Centre	061 396666
Adare	May Fair	061 396894
Ballysteen	Ballynacourty Gardens	061 396409
Bruree	Heritage Centre and de Valera Museum	063 91300
Croom	Waterwheel and Heritage Centre	061 397130
Foynes	Flying Boat Museum	069 65416
Glin	Glin Castle Pleasure Grounds & Walled Garden	068 34364
Limerick	Belltable Arts Centre, 69 O'Connell St	061 319866
Limerick	Georgian House & Garden, 2 Pery Square	061 314130
Limerick	Hunt Museum, Customs House, Rutland St	061 312833
Limerick	King John's Castle	061 360788
Limerick	Limerick City Art Gallery, Pery Square	061 310633
Limerick	Limerick Museum, John's Square	061 417826
Limerick	Tourism Information	061 317522
Limerick	University of Limerick	061 333644
Lough Gur	Interpretive centre, 3000BC to present	061 360788
Patrickswell	Limerick Racecourse (Greenmount Park)	061 355055

R # LIMERICK

Of great historical and strategic importance, Ireland's fourth city is also renowned for its rich cultural tradition, with many excellent museums, galleries and theatres to visit - and Ireland's first purpose-built concert hall. The city also offers a wide range of accommodation, restaurants and pubs, many of them in attractive waterside locations. The famous old restaurant & bar **Moll Darby's** (Tel 061 411522; www.mhm.ie), is on George's Quay, for example, and the wholesome good food served there pleases many a visitor. Another long-established city centre restaurant with character is **Freddy's Bistro** (061 418749) on Glentworth Street; it's in an atmospheric old stone and brick building, and offers quite straightforward flavoursome food at a reasonable price. Fairly new to the city is a branch of the 'almost-nationwide' quality family dining restaurants **Café Bar Deli** (061 485 1865; www.cafebardeli.ie), see Dublin entries. **Poppadom** (061 446644) on Limerick Street is a branch of the Dublin 6 restaurant (see entry), and **Munchy Munchy** (061 313113) is the Chinese where you'll find the city's Chinese residents tucking in. The **Wild Onion** (061 440055; www.wildonioncafe.com) on High Street, is an American-run bakery and café well known for their great simple daytime food, especially breakfasts, and delicious homebakes (closed Sun & Mon). Vegetarians, especially, will enjoy **Ciaran's Café** (061 338787; www.ciarans.ie) on the University of Limerick campus at Castletroy; fresh juices, unusual vegetarian dishes and moreish desserts are on the menu and it has a following beyond the student community. Several smart new hotels have recently opened in the city (see below) and a promising newcomer due to open in the not-too-distant future is **No. 1 Pery Square** (061 311182; www.privateireland.com); this fine owner-run townhouse forms part of the Tontine buildings on leafy Pery Square, and will offer 20 bedrooms (including 2 suites), garden, cocktail bar, brasserie dining and 'health & wellness' treatments. For good budget city centre accommodation try the old reliable, **Jurys Inn** (061 207000; www.jurysdoyle.com), on Lower Mallow Street; this no-frills hotel is comfort-able and gives a lot for a little - some rooms even have views across the Shannon. **The Quality Hotel** (061 426100; www.qualityhotellimerick.com), on the Southern Ring is useful to know about, eg when breaking a journey with a family, for value and good leisure facilities including swimming pool. Limerick city is home to Ireland's first purpose-built Concert Hall (contact Tourist Information Office, 061 317 522, for details of events): other attractions in the city centre include King John's Castle

(1212), St. Mary's Cathedral (1168), The Hunt Museum (Rutland Street; 061 312 833), several (seasonal) walking tours including Angela's Ashes walking tour (from Arthurs Quay, 061 317 522), hop on-hop off sightseeing tour, and boat tours along the River Shannon. There is a Farmers' Market in the Milk Market every Saturday (8am-2pm) and golfers might like to try the championship course at nearby Adare Manor Hotel & Golf Resort (061 395 044) which has been home to the Irish Open for the last few years.
WWW.IRELAND-GUIDE.COM FOR ALL THE BEST PLACES TO EAT, DRINK

Limerick
HOTEL

Absolute Hotel

Sir Harry's Mall Limerick Co Limerick **Tel: 061 463 600**
info@absolutehotel.com www.absolutehotel.com

Located on the far side of the River Shannon where the Abbey River flows into it, this stylish modern hotel enjoys a great site with a waterside bar and restaurant, decked outdoor seating area and views of the hills - and a peaceful situation in what is still a city centre area. A roof garden is also promised. Absolute is a pleasing combination of an old stone building and contemporary interiors; giant blown-up photographs of Limerick in former times make the link, dominating the vast lobby and public areas on all floors. Accommodation is in Comfy (standard), Cosy (deluxe) and Chic (suites) plus three special business suites with boardroom, accommodating meetings for up to 12; Comfy rooms are smaller, but there's no shortage of style at any level with standard features including good lighting (although a wall-mounted bed light would be useful), a giant wall-mounted flat screen where you may choose between music, television, pay film and internet; generous storage space; ironing facilities; black-out curtaining; safe; mini-bar and state-of-the-art coffee and tea makers. And, for a surprisingly small premium, the larger Cosy rooms also offer free access to the sauna/wellbeing room in the spa as well as internet and movie deals. Fashion-led bathrooms are spacious but, with frosted glass door compromising privacy, no bath (only a power shower with rain dance shower head in all rooms) and a 'Belfast-sink' washbasin, they may not be to everyone's taste. Dining and socialising options are between the very spacious first floor Riverside Restaurant and bar, which overlook the river and leafy bank opposite, with a decking area for sitting out, and the Refuel Café. With its fine location and facilities, complimentary underground car parking and surprisingly reasonable room rates, Absolute represents real value for money for anyone visiting Limerick city. Conference & banqueting; business facilities; complimentary high speed internet access; laptop-sized safes in bedrooms; spa; hot tub; fitness suite; same day laundry/dry cleaning. **Rooms 99** (includes 3 business suites with boardroom & 12 Chic suites; all rooms shower only). B&B from €57.50pps; Room rate only about €100. Open all year. All major credit cards. **Directions:** Limerick city centre, on the N7 just north of the junction between the N7 & N20. ◇

Limerick
BAR•RESTAURANT
R

Aubars Bar & Restaurant

49-50 Thomas Street Limerick Co Limerick **Tel: 061 317799**
linda@aubars.com www.aubars.com

Padraic Frawley's modern city centre bar and restaurant is on the pedestrianised Thomas Street. What was once an old pub is now a dashing contemporary bar and restaurant; the layout is on several levels, with no hard divisions and a mixture of seating in various areas, which is attractive but can sometimes lead to confusion between customers coming in to eat and those having a drink. While the style is uncompromisingly modern, chef Maura Baxter's values are quite traditional, based on sound cooking. Appealing, well-balanced menus change frequently and offer a number of different options for bar food (Aubars) and more structured meals in the casual value dining café/bar (The Grill @ Aubars); rib eye steak with béarnaise sauce, rocket salad & chunky chips is a sound speciality. Vegetarians are well looked after, with appealing dishes marked clearly on menus and, all round, a visit here should be an enjoyable experience - and good value too. **Seats 45** (outdoors, 24). Open from 8 am; all day brunch menu. L 12-5.30 daily (Sun from 12.30). Set L about €15 (12-3); D Mon-Sun 5.30-9.30 (to 8.30pm Sun); early D about €20, Mon-Sat, 5-7pm; A la carte L & D. House wines from €19.95. SC discretionary. Bar meals: 12-8.30 daily. Establishment closed 25 Dec & Good Fri. Live Cuban/Latin music Fri D. Amex, MasterCard, Visa, Laser. **Directions:** Off O'Connell Street, second on the left, opposite Brown Thomas.

Brûlées Restaurant

Corner of Henry St & Mallow St Limerick Co Limerick **Tel: 061 319 931**
brulees@eircom.net

Donal and Teresa Cooper's restaurant is on a busy corner, with window tables catching a glimpse of the River Shannon and County Clare across the bridge. The interior is well-appointed, with little dining areas on several levels that break groups up nicely, and are elegantly furnished in a simple classic style that makes the most of limited space. For some years this has been the first choice in the city, for discerning local diners and visitors alike. A soothing ambience and nice details - real linen napkins, olives and freshly baked breads to nibble - make a good start, and Teresa's appealing menus show pride in using the finest of ingredients, both local and imported; vegetarian dishes are invariably imaginative, also fish and seafood, which will always include daily specials - and which Donal describes to guests very accurately, with prices. Donal's hospitality and thoughtful, professional service are an important part of the experience here, and Teresa's colourful modern Irish cooking is as good as it sounds. Begin, perhaps, with a tian of Skellig crab with ginger and wasabi crème fraîche and, from a balanced choice of main courses, maybe try a speciality dish of loin of Burren lamb with a pistachio crust. Side dishes are simple, there's a good cheese selection - and puddings always include, of course, a classic crème brûlée, served with a crunchy brandysnap. Cooking is accurate, presentation is attractive without being fussy and you'll get good value for the high quality of food served- lunch and early dinner menus offer especially good value. An interesting and informative wine list is fairly priced and includes some lovely wines by the glass, also well-chosen half bottles. **Seats 30**. L Thu-Fri only, 12.30-2.30; D Mon-Sat, 5-10pm. Early Bird D €30 (5-6.15pm), also à la carte. House wine €20; SC discretionary (12.5% of food on groups of 6+). Closed Sun, Mon; 25 Dec-1 Jan. Amex, MasterCard, Visa, Laser. **Directions:** On the corner of Henry Street and Lower Mallow Street, near Jurys Inn roundabout.

Castletroy Park Hotel

Limerick
HOTEL

Dublin Road Limerick Co Limerick **Tel: 061 335 566**
sales@castletroy-park.ie www.castletroy-park.ie

Immaculately maintained gardens, a large and warmly furnished foyer and welcoming staff create a good first impression at this 4* hotel near the university. Very popular with business guests and as a conference venue, it also has excellent leisure facilities (including a 1 km jogging track) and, offering a change of scene at the end of the day's business, The Merry Pedlar pub has more character than the usual hotel bar. Public areas are spacious, with plenty of pleasant seating area, and McLaughlins Restaurant offers international fine dining in a comfortable well-appointed room with a pleasant outlook. Bedrooms are thoughtfully furnished with the business guest in mind, and regularly re-furbished. Conferences/Banqueting (450/260); free broadband wi/fi; secretarial services; video conferencing. Leisure centre (pool, fitness room, jacuzzi, sauna, steam room); beauty salon - Celia Larkin 'Beauty at Blue Door'. Children welcome (under 6s free in parents room, cot available without charge, baby sitting arranged). Conservatory. Garden. **Rooms 107** (7 suites, 5 junior suites, 5 junior suites, 11 executive, 2 shower only, 1 disabled). Lift. 24 hour room service. Turndown service. B&B from €85pps. No SC. Open all year. **McLaughlin's Restaurant Seats 70** (private room, 16). Air conditioning. L & D daily. Amex, Diners, MasterCard, Visa, Laser. **Directions:** Dublin road, directly opposite the University of Limerick.

Clarion Hotel Limerick

Limerick
HOTEL

Steamboat Quay Limerick Co Limerick **Tel: 061 444 100**
info@clarionhotellimerick.com www.clarionlimerick.com

This dramatic cigar-shaped 17-storey hotel right on the River Shannon waterfront in the centre of Limerick enjoys panoramic views over the city and the Shannon region. Clean-lined contemporary elegance is the theme throughout and a semi-open plan arrangement of foyer, bars and dining spaces, takes full advantage of the location. Business facilities are excellent and bedrooms - which vary more than is usual in hotels due to the unusual shape of the building - are offered in several pleasingly simple, modern colour schemes. All rooms have striking maple furniture, air conditioning, and everything that makes an hotel room a comfortable retreat although, oddly, the lower level of windows is too high to allow you to savour the view while sitting down; the top two floors offer suites and penthouses for long lets. Residents have unlimited use of leisure facilities, and several decked balconies and terraces at different levels encourage guests to enjoy fine weather. Apart from the Malaysian/Thai all-day menu offered in the hotel's **Kudos Bar**, all meals are served in the well-appointed **Sinergie Restaurant**, an attractive contemporary room with river views. Menus are lively and generally well-executed; at its best, a meal here can be a most enjoyable experience. Although this landmark building is easily located, gaining access to the hotel can be tricky for those unfamiliar with the city's one-way system; a nearby car park is used by the hotel and it is advisable to get clear instructions before arrival. (There is a moderate charge for parking.) Conference/banqueting (240/170); secretarial services, business centre, video conferencing, free broadband wi/fi. **Rooms 158** (3 suites, 80 no smoking, 6 disabled, 5 family rooms); children welcome (under 12 free in parents' room; cot available without charge). Lift; room service (limited hours). B&B €130pps. Leisure centre; swimming pool, sauna, steam room. **Sinergie Restaurant:** L Sun-Fri,12.30-2.30; D daily, 7-9.45; (closed L Sat). Set Sun L about €25; Set D about €25; also à la carte. Kudos Bar serves Asian food, 12-9 daily. Short breaks (inc golfing breaks) offered; details on application. Closed 24-26 Dec Amex, Diners, MasterCard, Visa, Laser. **Directions:** Take Dock Road exit off the Shannon Bridge Roundabout, then first right.

Limerick   Copper & Spice
RESTAURANT   2 Cornmarket Row Limerick Co Limerick **Tel: 061 313 620**
[R]   brian@copperandspice.com www.copperandspice.com

Well situated near the restored Milk Market buildings, this attractively named restaurant would be hard to miss; you have to ring a bell to get in, so you are assured of immediate attention from agreeable staff. Indian background music creates atmosphere and the spicy theme is seen in the warm tones of the stylish modern decor and on promptly presented menus, which offer an unusual combination of Indian and Thai cuisine; however, there is a stronger leaning towards authentic Indian food than Thai, with a wide range of vegetarian dishes and, unusually, there are home-made ethnic Asian desserts. This stylish restaurant offers a different experience from other ethnic restaurants in the city, and gives value for money. A fairly priced wine list offers a balanced selection of world wines, and Asian beers. *A sister restaurant just off the main Dublin-Limerick road is above **The Mill Bar at Annacotty**, in a restored mill overlooking the Mulcair River (Tel: 061 338791). **Seats 75**; children welcome; toilets wheelchair accessible. air conditioning; D Mon-Sat, 5-10.30. (L Sun, Annacotty branch only, 12.30-4.30). Value D inc. drink €24.50 (5-7); house wine €19; sc 10% on groups 10+. Closed Sun, 24-25 Dec, 1 Jan, Good Fri. Amex, MasterCard, Visa, Laser. **Directions:** Near Milk Market buildings.

Limerick   The French Table
RESTAURANT   1 Steamboat Quay Limerick Co Limerick **Tel: 061 609 274**
[W][E][N][R]   frenchtable@yahoo.co.uk

This welcome newcomer to the city is a riverside restaurant just a short distance along from the Clarion Hotel. Run by Thomas Fialon and his wife Deirdre, who is from Limerick, it is an airy and spacious place, with tones of dark wood and aubergine seating lifted by touches of crisp white linen and gleaming glassware, plus the light streaming in through the windows. Views over the river add to the calm ambience, and welcoming staff are quick to make arriving guests feel at home. A la carte menus are offered at both lunch and dinner and, although Thomas Fialon sounds the odd rustic notes – braised farmed rabbit in a mustard and white wine sauce, for example – he really likes to take classic French dishes and interpret them with some finesse, as in his warm tartlet of goat's cheese with oak-smoked duck and a walnut dressing, where the pastry is as light and crisp as you could wish and the pieces of duck are dense with flavour. Details, such as salad dressings, are exemplary. From a classic dessert selection finish, perhaps with orange flavoured craqueline, with raspberries and Chantilly cream – a very attractive dish served with an outstandingly good raspberry sorbet, clearly made in house. Excellent service too – efficient, informative and courteous. The all-French wine list is of special interest, containing some real bargains, including a fine 1er cru Meursault for a mere €65, and a decent number of wines available by the glass. Open in the evenings and for lunch, when the roast beef sandwich with sautéed potatoes (€9) has to be the best value meal in town. **Seats 52**; children welcome (high chair); air conditioning; L Tue-Fri, 12-3pm; D Tue-Sat 6-10.30pm; a la carte L&D; house wine €25. Closed Sat L, all Sun & Mon, last 2 weeks in Jan & Jul. Amex, MasterCard, Visa, Laser. **Directions:** On riverbank by Dock Road, near the Clarion Hotel.

Limerick

George Hotel

HOTEL
R

O'Connell Sreet Limerick Co Limerick **Tel: 065 682 3000**
reservations@lynchotels.com www.lynchotels.com

This boutique hotel is right in the heart of Limerick's commercial and shopping centre, and makes a convenient meeting place. It is a warm and welcoming place in a relaxed modern style, and a pleasant bar off the lobby has plenty of sofas and easy chairs as well as bar seating and makes a good place to meet friends when shopping, or sit and read the papers between meetings. Stylish contemporary bedrooms have some nice touches including Egyptian cotton sheets, 26-inch flat screen TV, and tea & coffee facilities offering choice of teas and coffee. There are no leisure facilities on site but guests have concessional use of the nearby Quay Fitness leisure club, pool and gym at adjacent Howley's Quay. The first floor restaurant is casual, looking on to the busy street below and has a relaxed atmosphere; while there are no surprises on the menu (bruschetta, chicken Caesar, lamb shank are all typical), it offers very acceptable food and pleasant service. **Rooms 125**. Room rate from about €99. Meeting rooms. Free overnight parking in adjacent Howley's Quay multi-storey car park (and favourable rates for business delegates).MasterCard, Visa, Laser. **Directions:** Town centre on O'Connell Street. ◊

Limerick

Limerick Marriott Hotel

HOTEL
R

Henry Street Limerick Co Limerick **Tel: 061 448 700**
www.limerickmarriott.com

The new Limerick Marriott is not the largest hotel in the city but it is one of the most luxurious and scores highly where service is concerned. Although starkly modern from the street, the interior is gentler with warm colours and with a mixture of styles, the tone is set in the entrance, where an elegant brass-railed staircase suggestive of old-fashioned hospitality rises from a mainly crisply contemporary lobby, and friendly staff immediately do everything possible to make guests feel at home. Mainly aimed at the business guest, spacious warm-toned and very comfortably furnished rooms have high-speed internet (free wi/fi is available throughout the hotel), a spacious work desk and chair, desk-level power sockets, voice mail, safe and complimentary newspaper in addition to all the usual in-room facilities. Other features of the hotel are of equal interest to business and leisure guests, including terraced gardens with views of the city and the River Shannon; Savoy Aqua and Fitness club, with swimming pool, jacuzzi and spa treatments; and the very pleasant Savoy Bar on the ground floor, which reflects the site's previous life as a cinema. The Savoy Restaurant is open for all meals and light food is also available throughout the day in the Liszt Lounge. 10 conference, banqueting and private dining suites accommodating up to 220 guests. Fully serviced business centre. Meeting rooms (10). **Rooms 82** (includes 12 business suites). B&B from €80pps. Pets allowed; contact hotel for details. Swimming pool; spa. Complimentary valet parking (complimentary overnight parking for residents). Garden. MasterCard, Visa, Laser. **Directions:** Town centre. ◊

Limerick

Lynch South Court Hotel

HOTEL
R

Raheen Roundabout Adare Road Limerick Co Limerick **Tel: 061 487 487**
southcourt@lynchotels.com www.lynchotels.com

Ideally located for Shannon Airport and the Raheen Industrial Estate, the South Court Hotel presents a somewhat daunting exterior, but it caters especially well for business guests. In addition to excellent conference and meeting facilities, comfortable bedrooms are spacious and well-equipped. Executive bedrooms have a separate work area providing a 'mini-office' - and 'lifestyle suites' have an in-room gym, designed by Irish designer Paul Costelloe. Leisure facilities include the 'Polo Lifestyle Club', designed with international rugby player Keith Wood. Paul Costelloe was also involved in the design of the stylish café bar, The Cream Room, which is a popular meeting place. Bar lunches are available every day and the 100-seater Boru's Bistro offers dinner every evening. Conference/banqueting (1250/1000); business centre; video conferencing. Gym, sauna, solarium. Hairdressing. Shop. Children welcome (under 2s free in parents' room, cot available without charge, baby sitting arranged). No Pets. **Rooms 127** (1 suite, 15 junior suites, 55 executive, 14 no-smoking). Lift. 24-hour room service. B&B about €80 pps, ss about €26. Amex, Diners, MasterCard, Visa, Laser. **Directions:** Located on the main N20 Cork/Killarney road, 20 minutes from Shannon Airport. ◊

Market Square Brasserie

Limerick
RESTAURANT
N R

74 O'Connell Street Limerick Co Limerick
Tel: 061 316 311

This basement restaurant is popular for both its cosy, romantic décor – all gilt-framed mirrors, red velvet curtains and soft lighting – and precisely cooked food, where the quality of the basic ingredients is pre-eminent. In an addition to an appealing menu offering a good range of upbeat classic dishes, four or five specials are given – a nice feature, although it can be hard to remember them later. Dishes especially enjoyed on a recent visit include a starter of chicken liver with which was a great combination – the soft creamy liver and the crisply fried chorizo, both nicely relieved by well-dressed salad; and a main course of monkfish served with a prawn risotto, where a generous and spanking fresh chunk of the fish was cooked until just firm and set atop a terrific risotto with the seafood, the creamy rice and a buttery Parmigiano Reggiano kept in perfect balance. Special attention is paid to the accompanying vegetables, which reflect the season and speak of a kitchen where the chef cares about seasonality. A white chocolate and raspberry tiramisu may be more like a trifle than a tiramisu, but is none the worse for that. Slightly disorganised and impersonal service can let the kitchen down a little, but perfectly cooked food and great flavours mean that a meal here is likely to be very enjoyable nevertheless. A well-stocked wine list is offered, although some bottles are very pricey. D only, Tue-Sat from 6pm. **Directions:** City centre, on O'Connell Street.

Radisson SAS Hotel & Spa

Limerick
HOTEL
R

Ennis Road Limerick Co Limerick **Tel: 061 456 200**
sales.limerick@radissonsas.com www.limerick.radissonsas.com

Although just a short drive from the city centre, this hotel enjoys an almost rural setting and views of the Clare mountains. The original building dates back to the 1970s but has recently been re-designed. Public areas, notably the large open-plan foyer/lounge, have a great sense of space and style, with luxurious furnishings. Accommodation is also notable for its spaciousness: all rooms are styled deluxe, with the comfort and amenities that implies, but the spaciousness is the main attraction. The hotel's Rain Spa & Wellness Clinic includes cosmetic treatments, gym, pool, and outdoor Canadian hot tub among the features. Fine conference and business facilities have ample free parking. Conference/banqueting (500/325); free broadband wi/fi, business centre, secretarial services, video conferencing. **Rooms 154** (2 suites, 4 junior suites, 14 executive, 4 family, 3 disabled); children welcome (cots available; baby sitting arranged). Lift. 24-hour room service. Turndown service. B&B €72.50 pps, ss €52.50. Destination Spa. Leisure centre (indoor swimming pool, steam room, sauna, fitness room). Tennis courts, garden. Parking *Short breaks offered - details on application. Porters Restaurant: L 12.30-2.30 daily (from 1pm Sun), D daily, 5.45-9.30pm. Set L €20.50, early D €22.50 (5.45-7pm), set D from €23.50, also à la carte. Bar food also available daily, 12-9.30pm. Amex, MasterCard, Visa, Laser. Heli-pad. **Directions:** On N18, 5 km from Limerick city centre, 20 minutes from Shannon.

The Sage Café

Limerick
CAFÉ
R

67/68 Catherine Street Limerick Co Limerick **Tel: 061 409 458**
info@thesagecafe.com www.thesagecafe.com

On most days, this centrally-located café near the Milk Market has queues of people waiting to lunch on their healthy food, and it's easy to see why. From the green and white striped awning (which has tables underneath on fine days) to the cool greeny-white of the interior, there is an air of clean, green calm about the place. It's roomy and light, with some banquette seating around the walls, a few contemporary oil paintings and wooden tables. They do lovely fresh-flavoured lunch dishes (an eclectic collection, including samosas, aromatic Indian dishes, good steaks – and a great fish bake) and, through the afternoon when the savoury choices will have run out, there will be great home bakes, including scones, iced carrot cake, gooey chocolate cake, baked orange cheesecake, banana and walnut cake and almond cake, maybe served with a dollop of whipped cream and a giant strawberry and there are some gluten-free choices. **Seats 50**; children welcome (high chair); toilets wheelchair accessible; air conditioning. Food served Mon-Sat, 9-5.30pm; L 12-4pm. Closed Sun, Bank Hols, Christmas week. MasterCard, Visa, Laser. **Directions:** Centre of town.

Limerick
HOTEL
R

The Strand Hotel
Ennis Road Limerick Co Limerick
Tel: 061 421 800

Just across the Sarsfield bridge from the main commercial heart of Limerick, this blocky new seven-storey hotel was recently re-branded (Hilton Hotel Limerick) and takes full advantage of views from the upper floors with picture windows, balconies and terraces and has glass-fronted lifts which allow guests with key cards to enjoy the city sights and the distant views of the Galtee Mountains, and are blue-lit at night. Suites with balconies at the top of the hotel are especially desirable, but accommodation throughout is pleasant and comfortable, and the smart bathrooms all have bath and shower. Although equally attractive for leisure breaks, the Hilton is especially well-equipped for business guests - an executive floor has a dedicated lounge, and all rooms have laptop safe, high-speed internet access, plus cable and on-demand tv and individual air conditioning. There's a choice of 14 meeting rooms for groups of various sizes, and cutting edge conference technology. Leisure and off-duty business guests will all appreciate the Living Well Health Club, which has a 20m pool, plus children's pool, sauna, steam room and Jacuzzi, also a gym and beauty therapy rooms for both men and women. Food is available at either the River Restaurant, or the Terrace Café and Bar, with a large heated terrrace. Conference/banqueting 420/400; business centre (staffed). **Rooms 184** (1 Presidential Suite, 18 suites). Room rate from €85. **Restaurant:** L Mon Fri 12.30 2.30, Sun1-3; D Mon Thu 5.30 10, Fri & Sat 6- 11, Sun 9; closed L Sat. Bar open for snacks from 7am Mon-Fri and 9am Sat & Sun; all-day menu 12 10pm daily. Parking (fee applies). All major credit cards accepted. **Directions:** In the city centre on the north side of the River Shannon, on the Ennis Road next to the river. ◈

R

ADARE

The chocolate-box village of Adare is not only an interesting and well-located destination in its own right, but also an excellent place to break a long journey. Useful places to know about include **Fitzgeralds Woodlands House Hotel** (Tel 061 605 100; www.woodland-hotel.ie) which is a little way out of the village on the Limerick side; especially popular for weddings and large gatherings, they offer special breaks and have excellent leisure/health facilities including a wide range of therapies and treatments (a €5m redevelopment of their Revas spa was recently completed). Of the many cafés in the village, **The Food Room** (formerly the Inn Between, 061 396633) is especially appealing. Places of interest in and around the village include the Norman Desmond Castle and Bridge, a Trinitarian Abbey, an Augustinian Friary and the Town Hall – information available from Adare Heritage Centre (061 396666; www.adareheritagecentre.ie). An extensive paved River Walk along the River Maigue is most enjoyable, with sounds of the river and wildlife quickly taking over from nearby traffic. The area is renowned for its country sports, especially horse riding and hunting, and the **Dunraven Arms Hotel** (see below) is a focal point of equestrian activities. Golfers will enjoy a round on the championship course at Adare Manor Hotel & Golf Resort (061 395 044) or the older Adare Manor Golf Club (061 396 204). Garden enthusiasts might take the 35km (20 m) trip out to Glin Castle & Pleasure Grounds (appointment only, Glin, 068 34173).

WWW.IRELAND-GUIDE.COM FOR ALL THE BEST PLACES TO EAT, DRINK & STAY

Adare
HOTEL•RESTAURANT
R

Adare Manor Hotel & Golf Resort
Adare Co Limerick **Tel: 061 396 566**
reservations@adaremanor.com www.adaremanor.com

The former home of the Earls of Dunraven, this magnificent neo-Gothic mansion is set in 900 acres on the banks of the River Maigue. Its splendid chandeliered drawing room and the glazed cloister of the dining room look over formal box-hedged gardens towards the Robert Trent Jones golf course. Other grand public areas include the Gallery, named after the Palace of Versailles, with its unique 15th century choir stalls and fine stained glass windows. Luxurious bedrooms have individual hand-carved fireplaces, fine locally-made mahogany furniture, cut-glass table lamps and impressive marble bathrooms with powerful showers over huge bathtubs. A clubhouse in the grounds has full conference facilities, and there's a "golf village" of two and four bedroom townhouses which provide a comfortable accommodation option for longer stays, large groups and families; similarly, "The Villas" deluxe serviced residences sleep up to eight guests. Conference/banqueting (200/160); business centre, free broadband wi/fi. Leisure centre, swimming pool, spa treatments; beauty salon; hairdressing. Shop. Golf (18), equestrian; fishing; walking; cycling. Garden. Children welcome (under 12s free in parents room, cots available without charge, baby sitting arranged). No pets. **Rooms 62** (1 state room, 5 suites, 8 junior suites, 15 ground floor rooms, all no smoking); also townhouses, carriage house & villas (total 246). Lift. 24 hour room service. Room rate from about €296. No SC. Open all year. **Oak Room Restaurant:** This beautifully-appointed restaurant provides a fine setting for Mark Donohue's modern classical cuisine, which is cooking based on seasonal produce, including vegetables from the estate's own gardens. Irish artisan and other local ingredients feature, and Mark (a recent Féile Bia Chef of the Year) offers enticing à la carte menus, including some imaginative vegetarian dishes such as deep-fried Bluebell Falls goat's cheese with vegetable picalilli salad, and a main course of butternut squash gnocchi with a smoked Gubbeen soufflé, offered on the main menu along with well-balanced selection of treats. Medallions of rabbit and black pudding with seared scallop, parsley mash & shallot cream is an unusual speciality starter, for example, and main course choices may include a duo of Irish pork, fillet and braised belly, served with sweet potatoes and roast apples. An 8-course Tasting Menu (€72) features favourites from the à la carte and includes some surprises too; an accompanying wine pairing is also offered (and good value at €38). A predictably high-end wine list includes some unusual wines (a Pomerol Pétrus 1970, at about €4,450, for example) but there's a sprinkling of affordable bottles, and quite a few by the glass and half bottle. Overall, for the quality of food and service, and the beautiful surroundings, the Oak Room offers good value – especially when compared to high-end Dublin restaurants. **Seats 70**; D (6.30-9.30) daily; Set D about €65; 8-course Tasting Menu about €75. House wine from €25; SC discretionary. *More informal bistro style dining is offered all day at the Carriage House Restaurant, daily, 7am - 9.30pm. Open all year. Amex, Diners, MasterCard, Visa, Laser. **Directions:** On N21 in Limerick.

Adare

HOTEL•RESTAURANT

Dunraven Arms Hotel

Adare Co Limerick **Tel: 061 605 900**

reservations@dunravenhotel.com www.dunravenhotel.com

Established in 1792, the Murphy family's large hotel has somehow retained the comfortable ambience of a country inn. A very luxurious inn nevertheless: under the personal management of Bryan and Louis Murphy, the furnishing standard is superb throughout, with antiques, private dressing rooms and well-planned bathrooms, plus excellent amenities for business and private guests (interconnecting family rooms have recently been added), all complemented by an outstanding standard of housekeeping. It's a great base for sporting activities - equestrian holidays are a speciality and both golf and fishing are available nearby - and also ideal for conferences and private functions, including weddings (which are held beside the main hotel, with separate catering facilities). The hotel has earned an unrivalled reputation for the quality and value of short breaks offered, and there is an ongoing determination to combine personal service and quality with value, which makes Dunraven Arms an outstanding example of contemporary Irish hospitality at its best. A new path from the hotel to the beautiful nearby riverside walk was completed in 2008, and makes an enormous difference to the enjoyment of a stay here. *Dunraven Arms was the our Hotel of the Year in 2004. Conferences/Banqueting (180/280); free broadband wi/fi throughout hotel; business centre; secretarial services; laptop-sized safes in bedrooms. Equestrian, hunting, fishing, shooting, archery and golf nearby. Bike hire; walking. Leisure centre (swimming pool, steam room, fitness room), beauty salon, massage. Garden. No pets. Children welcome (cots available free of charge, baby sitting arranged). **Rooms 86** (6 suites, 24 junior suites, 56 executive, 30 ground floor, 2 family, all no smoking). Lift. 24-hour room service. Turndown service. B&B around €100pps, no ss. Room-only rate €195. SC12.5%. Open all year. Heli-pad. **Maigue Restaurant:** Named after the River Maigue, which flows through the village of Adare, the restaurant is delightfully old fashioned - more akin to eating in a large country house than in an hotel. Head chef, Laurent Chabert, continues the tradition of pride in using the best of local produce. Menus offer a balanced selection of about half a dozen dishes on each course and, although particularly renowned for their roast rib of beef (carved at your table from a magnificent trolley), other specialities like River Maigue salmon and local game in season, especially pheasant, are very popular. Menus are not overlong but may offer some dishes not found elsewhere, and little homemade touches add an extra dimension - farmhouse cheeses are served with home-made biscuits as well as grapes and an apple & date dressing, for example. Service, under the direction of John

Shovlin, who has been restaurant manager since 1980, is exemplary - as elsewhere in the hotel. A wide-ranging wine list offers some treats for the connoisseur as well as plenty of more accessible wines. **Seats 50** (private room 40); not suitable for children under 12 after 7pm; reservations recommended. D daily 7-9.30, L Sun only 12.30-1.30. Set Sun L about €27.50, also à la carte; D à la carte. House wine €22, SC 12.5%. Amex, MasterCard, Visa, Laser. **Directions:** First building on right as you enter the village coming from Limerick (18 km).

Adare

RESTAURANT

👑 Ⓔ Ⓝ Ⓡ

White Sage Restaurant

Main Street Adare Co Limerick **Tel: 061 396 004**

thewhitesagerestaurant@hotmail.com www.thewhitesagerestaurant.com

Adare is blessed with more than its share of hotels and eating establishments, and Tony Schwarz's White Sage Restaurant has added an exciting dimension since the spring of 2008. Ably assisted front of house by his wife Bobby, Tony demonstrates all the expertise one would expect from a chef of his pedigree; he has trained and worked in some of the country's leading restaurants and hotels, including a six year stint as head chef in Dan Mullane's Mustard Seed in nearby Ballingarry. The cooking is the primary focus here but without pretension, a mood sustained in the delightful cottage surroundings: plain white stone walls hung with colourful seascapes and woodland scenes, light green woodwork, cushioned banquettes, sugan chairs, varnished wood tables, creating a bright, cheerful atmosphere. The main room, with bar and dispense counter, looks out through glass doors onto an open-air patio with tables and umbrellas, and there are two small dining rooms to the front of the cottage. The regularly changing menu keeps a close eye on what is seasonal and fresh: salads come from Springfield House garden in nearby Dromcollogher and there is always something wild like local pigeon and preserves of seasonal berries. The best chefs display their talent in subtlety rather than flashy concoctions, and so it is here in deft touches: gently piquant piccalilli with pressed ham terrine; the crispest melba toast and home-made breads; sweetcorn puree as an accompaniment to organic salmon; tender, slow-cooked daube of beef with oysters bacon and Guinness; yogurt and cream cheese ice cream. This is modern Irish cooking with a dash of individuality at very reasonable prices; the Early Bird three course menu (5.30 to 7pm) particularly good value for €30.00, two courses €25.00. Service is competent and pleasantly relaxed. Open 5.30-10.30pm, Tue-Sat and on bank holiday Sundays. Amex, MasterCard, Visa, Laser. **Directions:** On Adare's main street, across the road from The Dunraven Arms. ◈

Adare

RESTAURANT

👑 ◉ Ⓥ Ⓡ

The Wild Geese Restaurant

Rose Cottage Main Street Adare Co Limerick **Tel: 061 396 451**

wildgeese@indigo.ie www.thewildgeese.ie

David Foley and Julie Randles' restaurant is in one of the prettiest cottages in the prettiest village in Ireland - and, with consistently good modern Irish cooking and caring service, it's an irresistible package. David Foley is a fine chef who sources ingredients with care - seafood comes from West Cork, there are local meats, poultry and game in season; everything comes from a network of small suppliers built up over the years. Menus offered include an early dinner, a semi à la carte which is considerately priced by course, and a separate vegetarian menu, on request. All the niceties of a special meal are observed - delicious home-baked bread (mustard seed, perhaps) is delivered with an amuse-bouche, such as a shot glass of asparagus soup. The cooking style is sophisticated - a luxurious main course example is pan-fried Castletownbere scallops on potato & chive pancakes, with champagne cream sauce, although a more homely rack of Adare lamb with traditional accompaniments such as potato & garlic gratin and rosemary jus is an enduring favourite. Like everything else in your meal, desserts (including ice creams) are freshly made on the premises. Friendly staff and a carefully selected, informative wine list add greatly to the dining experience. **Seats 60** (private room, 30, outdoor, 10); not suitable for children after 8pm. D Mon-Sat 6.30-10, Sun 6-9 summer only. Earlybird D €35 Sun-Fri to 7.30pm (to 7pm Sun); also à la carte & vegetarian menu. House wines €22. Closed Mon (& Sun Oct-Apr). Closed 24 Dec-2 Jan. Amex, Diners, MasterCard, Visa, Laser. **Directions:** From Limerick, at top of Adare village, opposite Dunraven Arms Hotel.

Ballingarry
COUNTRY HOUSE•RESTAURANT

The Mustard Seed at Echo Lodge

Ballingarry Co Limerick **Tel: 069 68508**
mustard@indigo.ie www.mustardseed.ie

BEST USE OF FRESH INGREDIENTS AWARD

Dan Mullane's famous restaurant The Mustard Seed started life in Adare in 1985, then moved just ten minutes' drive away to Echo Lodge, a spacious Victorian country residence set on seven acres of lovely gardens, with mature trees, shrubberies, kitchen garden and orchard - and very luxurious accommodation. Elegance, comfort and generosity are the hallmarks - seen through decor and furnishings which bear the mark of a seasoned traveller whose eye has found much to delight in while wandering the world. In addition to accommodation in the main house, the conversion of an old schoolhouse in the garden now provides three newer superior suites, a residents' lounge and a small leisure centre with sauna and massage room - this stylish development offers something quite different from the older rooms, and is in great demand from regular guests who make Echo Lodge their base for golf and fishing holidays. *Echo Lodge was our Country House of the Year, 2008. Small conferences (20); banqueting (70). Children welcome (under 4s free in parents' room, cots available without charge, baby sitting arranged). Pets allowed by arrangement. Garden, walking. Sauna, massage room. **Rooms 16** (2 suites, 4 shower only, 2 family, 2 ground floor, 1 for disabled, all no smoking). Turndown service. B&B €95 pps, single €130. Special winter breaks offered, depending on availability. Closed Christmas week, 2 wks Feb. **Restaurant:** Food and hospitality are at the heart of Echo Lodge and it is in ensuring a memorable dining experience, most of all, that Dan Mullane's great qualities as a host emerge (he was our Host of the Year in 2001). The evening begins with aperitifs in the Library, prettily served with a tasty amuse-bouche - and this attention to detail is confirmed in the beautiful dining rooms, where fresh flowers on each table are carefully selected to complement the decor. David Rice took over as head chef in 2007 and has continued the house tradition of excellent modern Irish cooking; the wonderful organic kitchen gardens supply him with much of the produce for the restaurant - do allow time to see them before dinner and, perhaps, hazard a guess as to what will be on the menu - while other ingredients are carefully sourced from organic farms and artisan food producers. Menus are wide-ranging and very seasonal - the components of a delicious salad will be dictated by the leaves and herbs in season. Plum tomatoes and asparagus, in mid-summer perhaps, accompanied by a Parmesan, basil and a balsamic reduction, and the soup course - typically of roast vegetable - is also likely to be influenced by garden produce. Main courses such as an unusual fillet of pork dish (rolled in soft herb and cooked in olive oil, then served with buttered Swiss chard, broad bean risotto, beetroot and cider jus) are based on the best local meats, seafood just up from the south-western fishing ports and seasonal game. Each dish has its own thoughtfully considered garnish and, with such an abundance of garden produce, vegetarians need have no fear of being overlooked - every course features an unusual vegetarian offering. Finish with Irish farmhouse cheeses at their peak of perfection, or gorgeous puddings, which are also likely to be inspired by garden produce. Finally, irresistible home-made petits fours are served with tea or coffee, at the table or in the Library. All absolutely delicious - and, with service that is professional and efficient, yet always relaxed and warm, the hospitality here is truly exceptional. After dinner, take a stroll through the lushly planted pleasure garden; there is even a special route - of just the right length - marked out for smokers. *(The Mustard Seed was our County House of the Year in 2008. An interesting wine list includes an unusually wide range of half bottles, a couple of magnums and a wine of the month. **Seats 70** (outdoors, 6); not suitable for children; reservations required; non residents welcome. D 7-9.30 (to 9pm Sun). Earlybird D €42 (Mon-Thurs,7-8); 4-course D about €65. House wine €26. Closed 24-26 Dec and 1st 2 weeks Feb. Amex, MasterCard, Visa, Laser. **Directions:** From top of Adare village, take first turn to left, follow signs to Ballingarry - 11km (8 miles); in village.

Bruff
B&B

Old Bank House

Bruff Co Limerick **Tel: 061 389 969**
info@theoldbank.ie www.theoldbank.ie

This refurbished, modernised nineteenth century former bank building has an impressive façade and now makes a substantial B&B. A high standard of accommodation is offered, and, some rooms have four-poster beds. Most rooms have a full bath with overbath shower and all have TV, tea/coffee facilities and clothes pressing. Although some of the internal refurbishment would not be to everybody's taste, it would make a comfortable place to stay at reasonable price for the standard offered. A fitness suite, sauna and de-humidifier room will be available for the 2009 season. No evening meals, but guests are directed to The Old Bake House Restaurant or Clancy's pub. **Rooms 9**. B&B €45-55 pps, ss€10. MasterCard, Visa, Laser. **Directions:** Bruff is located southeast of Limerick City (on the R512 road).

Glin Castle

Glin
CASTLE

Glin Co Limerick **Tel: 068 34173**
knight@iol.ie www.glincastle.com

Surrounded by formal gardens and parkland, Glin Castle stands proudly on the south bank of the Shannon; the FitzGeralds, hereditary Knights of Glin, have lived here for 700 years and it is now the home of the 29th Knight and his wife Madame Fitzgerald. The interior is stunning, with beautiful rooms enhanced by decorative plasterwork and magnificent collections of Irish furniture and paintings. But its most attractive feature is that everything is kept just the same as usual for guests, who are magnificently looked after by manager Bob Duff. Guest rooms and suites are decorated in style, with all the modern comforts, plus that indefinable atmosphere created by beautiful old things; accommodation was originally all in suites - huge and luxurious, but not at all intimidating because of the lived-in atmosphere that characterises the whole castle - but there are now "smaller, friendly, rooms with a family atmosphere". And there are many small thoughtfulnesses - the guests' information pack, for example, lists possible outings and itineraries under different interests (gardens, historical etc) and how much time you should allow. When the Knight is at home, he will take visitors on a tour of the house and show them all his pictures, furniture and other treasures; interested guests will also relish the opportunity to enjoy the famous gardens, including the 2-acre walled kitchen garden, which provide an abundance of seasonal produce for the castle kitchens. There is tennis on site, also an interesting shop - and make sure you fit in a visit to O'Shaughnessy's lovely old pub, just outside the castle walls (see entry). Head chef Seamus Hogan's menus change daily with the seasons, but a favourite dish is roast rack of lamb with puy lentils, wilted spinach & rosemary jus. *Glin Castle was our Country House of the Year in 2005. The garden and house are open to the public at certain times. Small conferences/private parties (20/30). Not suitable for children under 10 except babies (cot available without charge, baby sitting arranged). Pets permitted by arrangement in certain areas. Gardens, walking, tennis. **Rooms 15** (3 suites; all no-smoking). B&B €155pps. Dinner is available by reservation (non-residents are welcome if there is room); an attractive menu with about four choices on each course is offered. Dining Room **Seats 30**. D 7-9.30, Set D €60. House wine from about €25; sc discretionary. Closed 30 Nov - 1 Mar. Amex, Diners, MasterCard, Visa, Laser. **Directions:** 50km (32 miles) west of Limerick on N69, 6km east of Tarbert Car Ferry; drive up main street of Glin village, turn right at the top of the square.

O'Shaughnessy's

Glin
PUB

Glin Co Limerick
Tel: 068 34115

Not to be missed while in Glin is O'Shaughnessy's pub, just outside the castle walls; one of the finest pubs in Ireland, it is now in its sixth generation of family ownership and precious little has changed in the last hundred years. Gorgeous garden at the back too. Open Thu-Tue: Thu & Fri, 10.30-2.30 & 5.30-10.30/11pm; Sat 10.30am-11pm, Sun, 12-3, Mon & Tue 10.30-2.30. **Directions:** Up into village, take right turn; pub is on your left before the gates to Glin Castle.

KILMALLOCK

In south County Limerick, near the border with County Cork, Kilmallock (Cill Mocheallóg in Irish) is a town of historic and sporting interest in the foothills of the Ballyhoura Mountains. **Deebert House Hotel** (063 31200; www.deeberthousehotel.com) is an early 19th century flour mill that has recently been renovated and redeveloped as a 20-bedroom hotel. Walking holidays are a speciality in 'Ballyhoura country' and this will be a welcome new addition to the accommodation choices in the area.
WWW.IRELAND-GUIDE.COM FOR ALL THE BEST PLACES TO EAT, DRINK & STAY

Kilmallock
FARMHOUSE

Flemingstown House
Kilmallock Co Limerick **Tel: 063 98093**
info@flemingstown.com www.flemingstown.com

FARMHOUSE OF THE YEAR

Imelda Sheedy King's welcoming farmhouse is on the family's dairy farm just two miles from the medieval village of Kilmallock; well-signed at the entrance, it sits well back from the road up a long drive flanked by fields of grazing cattle, and leading to an immaculately maintained garden in front of the house. The original house dates back to the 18th century and has been sympathetically extended down through the years, to make a large and well-proportioned family home with pleasingly spacious, comfortably furnished reception rooms - and huge bedrooms, furnished with antique furniture and unfussy neutral decor that contrasts well with the dark furniture. En-suite facilities don't include baths, but have power showers - and, like the rest of the house, everything is well maintained and immaculate. Imelda is a great host, offering genuinely warm and welcoming hospitality - and she's also a great cook, as guests discover at a wonderful breakfast spread. Communal breakfast at the huge antique mahogany table helps guests to relax and communicate easily, as does Imelda's constant attention. The menu offers prepared fresh seasonal fruit (much of it home-grown, of course), a choice of cereals, home baking and preserves, and the "full Irish" breakfast which is cooked to order (along with a choice of other hot dishes including kippers, scrambled eggs with smoked salmon, and pancakes with fruit)... all this, and tea and coffee served in silver pots and the fine local cheeses, has guests oohing and aahing with pleasure. Dinner is also available, by prior arrangement - there's a choice of two or three dishes on each course, including treats like chicken liver paté, Slaney Valley leg of lamb (carved at the table), and apple tart with crème anglaise. Aside from the many things to do and see nearby, Flemingstown House is well placed to break a journey to or from the south-west, and it is a lovely place to stay - the standards of housekeeping, service and breakfast are remarkable, and it is representative of the very best rural Irish welcome. [*A 2-bedroom self-catering apartment has recently been added, available by the week.] **Rooms 5** (all shower only & no smoking, 1 family room); children over 2 years welcome (2-4 yrs free in parents' room). B&B €60 pps. ss €10. Pets permitted by arrangement. D €45 (residents only). Packed L on request. Likely to be closed Nov-Mar. MasterCard, Visa. **Directions:** R512 to Kilmallock from Limerick; then towards Fermoy for 3.5km (2 m). House set back from road, on left.

COUNTY LONGFORD

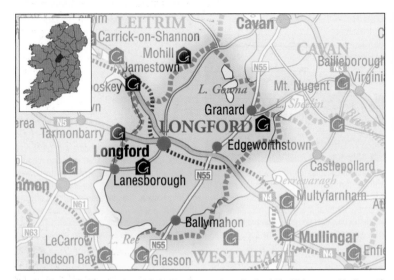

Longford is mostly either gently undulating farming country, or bogland. The higher ground in the north of the county up towards the intricate Lough Gowna rises to no more than 276m in an eminence which romantics might call Carn Clonhugh, but usually it's prosaically known as Corn Hill. The more entertainingly named Molly Hill to the east provides the best views of the lake in an area which arouses passionate patriotism. A few miles to the north is Ballinamuck, scene of the last battle in the Rising of 1798 in a part of Longford renowned for its rebellions against foreign rule.

To the southeast, there is even less pulling of the punches in the name of the little market town in its midst, for Granard - which sounds rather elegant - may be translated as "Ugly Height". Yet this suggests a pleasure in words for their own sake, which is appropriate, for Longford produced the novelist Maria Edgeworth from Edgeworthstown, a.k.a Mostrim, while along towards that fine place Ballymahon and the south of its territory on the Westmeath border, Longford takes in part of the Goldsmith country.

Goldsmith himself would be charmed to know that, six kilometres south of the road between Longford and Edgeworthstown, there's the tiny village of Ardagh, a place of just 75 citizens which is so immaculately maintained that it has been the winner of the Tidiest Village in the Tidy Towns Awards. Another award-winner is Newtowncashel in the southwest of the county, atop a hill immediately eastward of Elfeet Bay on northern Lough Ree, where the scenery becomes more varied as County Longford has a lengthy shoreline along the Shannon's middle lake.

West of Longford town at Clondra, the attractive Richmond Harbour is where the Royal Canal - gradually being restored along its scenic route from Dublin - finally reconnnects with the Shannon during 2009, having been closed since 1954. And as for Longford town itself, they're working on it, with an urban regeneration landmark in the restoration of a watermill on the Camlin River, providing the power for the ornamental lamps along the riverside walkway.

Local Attractions and Information

Ardagh	Heritage Centre	043 75277
Ballinamuck	1798 Memorial & Visitor Centre	043 24848
Ballymahon	Bog Lane Theatre	0902 32252
Kenagh	Corlea Trackway (Bog Road) Visitor Centre	043 22386
Longford	Backstage Theatre & Arts Centre	043 47885
Longford	Carrigglas Manor (Gandon stableyard, lace museum)	043 41026
Longford	Tourism Information	043 46566
Newtowncashel	Heritage Centre	043 25021

Granard

FARMHOUSE

ⓥ 🄡🄡

Toberphelim House

Granard Co Longford **Tel: 043 86568**

tober3@eircom.net www.toberphelimhouse.com

Dan and Mary Smyth's Georgian farmhouse is on a rise about half a mile off the road, with lovely views of the surrounding countryside. Very much a working farm, it is an hospitable, easy-going place. There's a guests' sitting room and three bedrooms: two en-suite (shower) with a single and double bed in each and one twin room with a separate private bathroom, all are comfortably furnished and well-maintained. Always improving, the Smyths gave the house a facelift for their 25th wedding anniversary a year or two ago - solid mahogany interior doors, re-tiling the bath and shower-rooms, re-painting the hall, stairs and landing - and an ongoing programme of maintenance continues. Families are welcome and light meals and snacks can usually be arranged. **Rooms 3** (2 en-suite shower only, 1 private bath-room, all no smoking); children welcome. B&B €50 pps, ss €5. Minimum stay 2 nights; prior booking advisable. Garden, walking. No pets. Closed 20 Sep-1 May. MasterCard, Visa. **Directions:** Take the N55 at the Cavan end of Granard, turn off at the Lir petrol station taking a right at the next junction. The house is situated about a km towards Abbeylara, to the left.

LONGFORD

Longford is situated in the low-lying central plain of Ireland and is well-known for its excellent game fishing and hunting. Longford is rich in heritage and is home to one of Ireland's first churches, St Mel's Cathedral, which was built in the 1800s. Other local heritage attractions include the ruins of the ancient Rathcline Church, the Battle of Ballinamuck Centre (043 24 848), which houses an exhibition in the former Royal Irish Constabulary barracks, and the Corlea Trackway Visitor Centre (043 22 386, open April to September), which interprets an Iron Age bog road which was built in the year 148 BC. The bog has contemporary significance too, providing the materials and inspiration for number of talented local artists who work with bogwood to create beautiful sculptures, which can be bought locally. Golfers are well catered for at County Longford Golf Club (043 46 310), an 18-hole championship course with mature trees and water features.

Longford

RESTAURANT

🄡🄡

Aubergine Gallery Café

1st Floor The White House 17 Ballymahon Street Longford Co Longford

Tel: 043 48633

Brother and sister Stephen and Linda Devlins' popular restaurant, above The White House pub on the main street, is up steep stairs in a smart, light-filled room. It has a lovely curved bar as the focal point as you arrive, with informal seating that allows extra space at lunchtime and is transformed into a reception area in the evening. Lightwood tables and a variety of coloured banquettes and comfortable chairs, together with some interesting artwork, create a vibrant, youthful atmosphere. Stephen Devlin is an accomplished chef and his menus are Irish/Mediterranean with delicious, fresh-flavoured dishes, placing an emphasis on vegetarian dishes. The cooking here is invariably creative, and seafood is well represented - and some things never change, so a good steak is de rigeur in these parts, as well as delicious poultry. Friendly staff, a warm relaxed atmosphere, stylish cooking and good value explain the success of this popular restaurant. So popular indeed, that it is now open for lunch and dinner every day. **Seats 45** (+ 20 in lounge area); children welcome; no reservations. Open daily, L Mon-Sat, 12-4pm; D Fri/Sat, 6-9.30 & Sun L 2-7.30pm. Set D about €32, also à la carte. House wine €16.50. Closed last week May, Dec 24-Jan 2. MasterCard, Visa, Laser. **Directions:** On main street (left as you're heading west), over the old White House pub (entrance on right of ground floor shop).

Longford

Viewmount House

COUNTRY HOUSE•RESTAURANT

Dublin Road Longford Co Longford **Tel: 043 41919**

info@viewmounthouse.com   www.viewmounthouse.com

James and Beryl Kearney's lovely 1750s' Georgian house just on the edge of Longford town was once owned by Lord Longford, and is set in four acres of beautiful wooded gardens, designed as a series of rooms. It really is a delightful house and has been sensitively restored with style, combining elements of grandeur with a human scale that makes guests feel very comfortable. Its warmth strikes the first-time visitor immediately on arrival in the hall, which has a welcoming open fire and a graceful white-painted staircase seen against warm red walls. An elegant period drawing room and the six guest bedrooms in the main house all have their particular charm (one is especially large, but all are delightful); but perhaps the handsomest room of all is the unusual vaulted dining room, where an extensive (and very delicious) breakfast menu is served. This is a most appealing house, with old wooden floors, rugs, antique furniture - and, most importantly, a great sense of hospitality; and we have been watching it with great interest in recent years - it has gradually been growing, as the Kearneys have joined the house to restored outbuildings alongside, providing some fine new bedrooms, and a restaurant (see below) which has been created in one of the classic stone outbuildings. **Rooms 13** (4 suites, 1 executive, 2 family, 3 shower only, 1 disabled, all no smoking); children welcome (under 4 free in parents' room, cot available). No pets. B&B €75, ss €10. Gardens. Golf nearby. Open all year. *Self-catering also available - details on application. **VM Restaurant:** Converted stables with exposed stonework make a fine restaurant of character which overlooks a Japanese garden with water features, and has an abundance of candles giving a cosy atmosphere at night. Whether entering from the car park or the house itself, guests arrive in a 'new' bar and restaurant reception area with a fire, where Beryl explains the menu while you enjoy a pre-dinner drink. 4-course dinner menus begin with an interesting cover note giving the history of the house, and Chef Gary O'Hanlon offers about half a dozen dishes on each course, with a slight leaning towards poultry (duck, guinea fowl, free range chicken) and two imaginative vegetarian main courses; as befits the surroundings, the tone is special occasion - the restaurant is beautifully set up with white linen, elegant white crockery and different flowers on each table, making a lovely setting for well-presented food. All the little niceties are observed, beginning with a complimentary amuse bouche (hoi sin duck in choux pastry, perhaps) before starters, which may include a particularly tasty dish of pan-roasted quail with bacon, cabbage & foie gras, served with a fresh berry jus. Main courses include the mandatory steak, of course (rib eye with colcannon, straw potatoes & green peppercorn Courvoisier sauce, for example), and there may be a special fish dish such as pan-seared artic char, which is served on marquis potato croquette with fried shitake and a watercress salad. Ingredients are sourced locally where possible and a few specialist products are mentioned, eg Boilié goat's cheese and arctic char (farmed in Co Sligo), although it would be interesting to see more information on local produce. Rather glamorous desserts might include brûlée three ways (ginger & vanilla bean, Valrhona chocolate and berry, served with a tuile disc) and coffee comes with petits fours. Overall, a meal here is a delightful experience, enhanced by attentive service and, especially Beryl Kearney's caring interaction with guests. An informative wine, helpfully organised by style, includes a fair choice under €30 and four half bottles. **Seats 55**; children welcome; reservations advised. D daily 6.30-9.30 (Sun 6-8), L Sun only 12.30-3. Set D €55, Sun L €29. House wine €20. Restaurant closed Mon, Tue. Amex, MasterCard, Visa **Directions:** From Longford R393 to Ardagh. 1km (0.5 m), up sliproad to right following signs. Entrance 200m on right.

COUNTY LOUTH

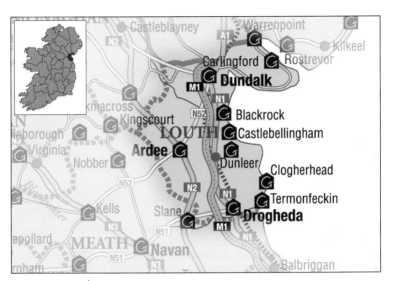

Strategically located in the middle of the main East Coast corridor between Dublin and Belfast, Louth is enthusiastic about the opportunities provided by the opening of the M1 motorway which now runs smoothly west of Dundalk. To the south, it crosses to Meath over the River Boyne near Drogheda on a handsome modern structure which is the largest cable-stayed bridge of its type in Ireland, a much admired and award-winning structure designed by Joe O'Donovan. With traffic pressure removed from its other roads, Louth begins to find itself. Though it may be Ireland's smallest county at only 317 square miles (it's just an eighth the size of Cork, the largest), Louth still manages to be two or even three counties in one, yet the locals cheerfully call it "the wee county".

Much of it is fine farmland, and this is celebrated with an annual Cooley Vintage Festival with a tractor world rally which in early August 2007 assembled at least 2,212 vintage tractors from 22 countries. The farmland is at its most productive in the area west of the extensive wildfowl paradise of Dundalk Bay, on whose shores we find the attractive village of Blackrock, one of Ireland's better kept secrets. But as well there are the distinctive uplands in the southwest, whose name of Oriel recalls an ancient princedom which is also remembered in Port Oriel, the busy fishing port at Clogherhead.

In the north of the county, the Cooley Mountains sweep upwards in a style which well matches their better-known neighbours, the Mountains of Mourne, on the other side of the handsome inlet of Carlingford Lough. Its name might suggest that this is a genuine fjord, but it isn't. However, its beauty is such that there's more than enough to be going along with, and on its Louth shore the ancient little port of Carlingford town used to be a best-kept secret. It was a quiet little place imbued with history, but today it is happily prospering both as a recreational harbour for the Dundalk and Newry area, and as a bustling visitor attraction in its own right.

The county's three main townships of Ardee, Dundalk and Drogheda each have their own distinctive style, and all three have been finding fresh vitality in recent years. The historic borough of Drogheda is the main commercial port with its harbour authority adding a new facility across the county border at Bremore in Meath. Drogheda's river valley is crossed by the Boyne Railway Viaduct of 1855 vintage, a remarkable piece of engineering work that it is reckoned one of the seven wonders of Ireland. Dundalk is the county town, and home to the Louth Museum, where a recent acquisition is the riding jacket worn by William of Orange at the Battle of the Boyne in 1690.

Local Attractions and Information

Ardee	(Tallanstown) Knockabbey Castle & Gardens	042 937 4690
Carlingford	Carlingford Adventure Centre	042 937 3100
Carlingford	Carlingford Sea School	042 937 3879
Carlingford	Heritage Trust	042 937 3888
Carlingford	Tourism Information	042 937 3033
Castlebellingham	Farm Market	0404 43885
Drogheda	Beaulieu House and garden	041 983 8557
Drogheda	Droichead Arts Centre	041 983 3946
Drogheda	Millmount Museum	041 983 3097
Drogheda	(Tullyallen) Old Mellifont Abbey	041 982 6459
Drogheda	Tourism Information	041 983 7070
Dundalk	Louth County Museum	042 932 7056
Dundalk	Tourism Information	042 933 5484
Termonfeckin	Irish Countrywomens Assoc. College	041 982 2119

R R

ARDEE

County Louth is rich in rural folklore and Ardee, the principal town of the rich farming countryside of mid-Louth, takes its name from the Irish Ard Fhirdia, the ford on the River Dee where the legendary hero in Irish folklore, Cúchulainn, fought and defeated and killed his friend Ferdia in the course of the Táin Bo Cuailgne. Places of interest in the area include Knockabbey Castle & Gardens (01 677-8816; www.knockabbeycastle.com) at Gallanstown, where 30 acres of gardens and grounds include meadows, herbaceous borders, a Victorian Flower Garden, restored glasshouse and other garden buildings, open May-Sep. A very different kind of castle is the 14th century **Smarmore Castle** (041 6857167; www.smarmorecastle.com) about 6.5 km south of Ardee, towards Collon; this extraordinary place offers accommodation, an Italian restaurant (run separately) and, most unlikely of all, an impressive leisure centre with 22m swimming pool, sauna, steam room, jacuzzi and fully equipped gym. On the northern edge of Ardee village, on the Dundalk road, **Fuchsia House & The Gables Bar** (041 685 8432) offers an unusual combination of Indian and international food; the uncared-for exterior can be off-putting however, at its best, the food – especially the Indian specialities - can be impressive (L&D Tue-Sat, Sun open all afternoon; closed Mon); Fucshia House also offer a delivery service and have a second establishment, **Indish Indian Takeaway** (041 687 1111) on Bridge Street.

WWW.IRELAND-GUIDE.COM FOR ALL THE BEST PLACES TO EAT, DRINK & STAY

Blackrock

RESTAURANT•PUB

R

The Brake

Main Street Blackrock Co Louth
Tel: 042 932 1393

There is little about the neat but plain exterior to prepare first-time visitors for the warmth and country charm of The Brake - all old pine and rural bric-à-brac, it has open fires and friendly staff. It's a great place to stop just for a late afternoon cup of tea but even better if you're hungry. It has a well-deserved reputation for good bar meals, and not just the usual pub staples, but a very wide choice including proper home-made chicken kiev, and all kinds of seafood especially Dundalk Bay prawns. There are plenty of meat dishes, too, especially steaks, and accompaniments are particularly good, all arranged buffet style, all for a moderate price. Beware of the unusual opening hours though, this is a late afternoon into evening place. **Seats 120**; not suitable for children under 12; air conditioning; toilets wheelchair accessible. Bar open 5-11.30. D daily 6-9.30pm. A la carte; house wine €18; sc discretionary. *The Clermont Arms, a few doors along the front, is in the same family ownership. Closed 25 Dec, Good Fri. MasterCard, Visa, Laser. **Directions:** Turn off the main Dublin-Belfast road 5km (3 m) south of Dundalk.

CARLINGFORD

This delightful medieval village is set amongst spectacular scenery with views across Carlingford Lough to the Mountains of Mourne in County Down. It is a small place and, although off the beaten track, is gradually being 'discovered' so it is best to avoid busy times like festivals, if you want to see it at its best. In the village, the 59-room **Four Seasons Hotel** (042 93 73530; www.4seasonshotel.ie) has good leisure and business facilities, including a leisure centre and function room; it is unconnected with the international brand. The village is very compact and visitors looking around can easily compare the prices, menus and style of the various restaurants and bars: **O'Hares** (042 937 3106) in the centre of the village is a renowned tradition pub/grocery shop and, although it has expanded in recent years (and, now having full restaurant facilities, serves a lot more food than the speciality Carlingford oysters and brown bread of old), the old back bar and open fire remain intact. Around the corner, opposite the pleasantly old-fashioned **McKevitt's Village Hotel** (042 937 3116; www.mckevittshotel.com), and **The Oystercatcher Lodge & Bistro** (042 937 3989; www.theoystercatcher.com) offers spacious, clean-lined accommodation; (the bistro, not listed by the Guide, is run separately). Around the corner at the heritage centre the small restaurant **Kingfisher Bistro** (042 937 3716) has a loyal local following and booking is essential; nearby **Food For Thought** (042 938 3838) is a very nice little deli with a few tables perfect for a quick bite or collecting food for a picnic. Back down on Newry Street, is **The Baytree Restaurant** (042 938 3848), formerly Capitano Correlli; they have a B&B next door. It might also be of interest to know that the bar and restaurant at **Carlingford Marina** (see entry) are open to the public; they serve excellent seafood. A little way outside Carlingford - signed off the Dundalk road - **Lilly Finnegans** (042 937 3730) is a pretty, traditional pub (open evenings only). The local area is excellent for walkers, hill walkers, golfers, sailing, fishing & other watersports and for people with an interest in history, architecture and natural beauty.

WWW.IRELAND-GUIDE.COM FOR ALL THE BEST PLACES TO EAT, DRINK & STAY

Carlingford
GUESTHOUSE

Beaufort House

Ghan Road Carlingford Co Louth **Tel: 042 937 3879**
michaelcaine@beauforthouse.net   www.beauforthouse.net

Michael and Glynnis Caine's immaculate property is well-placed to maximise on the attractions of a quiet and beautiful waterside position with wonderful sea and mountain views, while also being just a few minutes walk from Carlingford village. All areas are spacious and furnished to high specifications: hotel standard bedrooms have phone, TV with video channel and tea/coffee making facilities. The Caines were previously restaurateurs, and dinner is available by arrangement for parties of eight or more. (Set D about €40). Associated activities include a sailing school and yacht charter - corporate sailing events (team building and corporate hospitality), including match racing on Carlingford Lough, are a speciality. Small conference/banqueting (20). **Rooms 5** (2 shower only, 2 family rooms, 1 ground floor, all no smoking); children welcome (under 2s free in parents' room). B&B €50 pps, ss €25. D by arrangement only. Fishing, cycling, hill walking, bird watching, walking, garden. No pets. Golf nearby. Ample car parking. Closed 25 Dec. MasterCard, Visa, Laser. **Directions:** Approaching from Dundalk, turn right just before the village and harbour; house on shore. ◇

Carlingford
BAR•RESTAURANT

Ⓝ

Carlingford Marina Bar & Restaurant

North Commons Carlingford Co Louth **Tel: 042 937 3073**
www.carlingfordmarina.ie

Many visitors would assume that this marina is private and, like many other buildings of its type, this one is not especially impressive or welcoming from the land – entrance is from the carpark at the front, and you go up stairs to find a bright and spacious first floor bar and restaurant. It's all one room, in the modern style, broken into three areas with a bar seating area, a restaurant/dining area and a cosy section with couches beside a stove. The welcome is prompt and efficient, and the menu – presented simply on a single A4 page - is not overlong, but offers a carefully thought-out selection of appealing dishes, many of them featuring local seafood. Seafood lovers will find a seafood chowder, a seafood platter, and Carlingford mussels with chorizo cream among the starters, while main courses include a seasonal fish selection that varies according to availability, an unusual dish of smoked haddock & smoked salmon with lemon & prawn cream, fillet of beef with oyster and Guinness (a great traditional combination) and a fantastic, unfussy dish of whole dressed crab, served "hot'n'cold" with a vegetable garnish – what a change to find a whole crab used instead of the ubiquitous crab claws. And non-seafood eaters can do very nicely here too, with starters like a salade tiède of chicken liver with fruit vinegar (a rarity these days, but delicious) or a charcuterie selection, and main courses including rack of lamb with roast tomatoes, anchovy cream & basil oil. Attentive service from knowledgeable staff makes a meal here very relaxing, and a small but appropriate wine list is offered. **Directions:** Carlingford marina is on the Newry side of Carlingford town.

Carlingford
COUNTRY HOUSE•RESTAURANT

Ghan House

Carlingford Co Louth **Tel: 042 937 3682**
ghanhouse@eircom.net www.ghanhouse.com

Conveniently located just an hour from Dublin or Belfast airports, the Carroll family's 18th century house is attractively situated in its own walled grounds on the edge of Carlingford village, with views across the lough to the Mountains of Mourne. A proper little bar offers a relaxing space where guests can mingle - in a more convivial atmosphere, perhaps, than beside the drawing room fire, although that too has its moments; it's very pleasant for residents to return to, and especially welcoming for non-residents just coming in for dinner. Accommodation is in four rooms of character in the main house, each with sea or mountain views, and eight newer bedrooms in a separate building, which have been finished to a fairly high standard. And there's even more to it than comfortable accommodation and the delicious meals you will enjoy for dinner or breakfast, as the Carrolls also run a cookery school on the premises. Conference/banqueting (55/85); house available for exclusive use. Garden; walking. Children welcome (under 5s free in parents' room; cots available without charge; baby sitting arranged). No pets. Rooms 12 (1 shower only, 3 superior, 2 family). B&B Double Room €95 pps, single €75. (Discounts applied on stays of 2 or more nights.) Open all year except Christmas & New Year. **Restaurant:** Dinner is, of course, a high priority at Ghan House. You can be sure of a pleasant meal here – it's a nice dining room, and people enjoy the overall experience. The cooking style is quite contemporary, based mainly on quality home-grown (vegetable, fruit and herbs), home-made (breads, ice creams, everything that can be made on the premises) and local produce, notably Cooley lamb and beef, dry cured bacon, free range eggs. And, of course, seafood: oysters are synonymous with Carlingford (there are also mussels from the lough and lobster from Ballagan, while smoked salmon and crab come from nearby Annagassan). A user-friendly set dinner menu with about five choices on each course is also priced by course, allowing considerable flexibility without having a separate à la carte, and there's a fairly priced wine list. Seats 55 (private room 55); non-residents are welcome by reservation. D only, "most days" 7-9.30; Set D €42.50; L Sun only 12.30-3.30, €49.50 (5 course). House wine €18.50; sc discretionary. Children welcome. House closed 24-26 Dec and 31 Dec & 1 Jan. Amex, MasterCard, Visa, Laser **Directions:** 15 minutes from main Dublin - Belfast Road N1.10 metres after 30 mph sign on left hand side after entering Carlingford from Dundalk direction. ◇

Carlingford
RESTAURANT

Magees Bistro

Tholsel Street Carlingford Co Louth **Tel: 042 937 3751**
info@mageesbistro.com www.mageesbistro.com

Right in the heart of Carlingford village, just across the road from O'Hare's pub, this lively restaurant is a first choice for many coming to Carlingford. Its ancient walls with castle windows are a part of the old Heritage Town, and the interior is divided into two informal sections with plain wooden tables and chairs, with candlelight adding to the atmosphere. Most tables have views looking into the busy kitchen, and there's a small bar where you can wait for your table if it is not ready. A varied bistro menu includes some unusual choices - seafood gratin & frogs legs perhaps - alongside popular dishes like cajun chicken Caesar. Beef and lamb come from local farms in the Cooley peninsula, and main course favourites include a 10oz sirloin steak, chicken supreme and surf & turf, also a lot of local seafood including fresh lobster (which is fairly priced), a grilled seafood platter and various fresh fish of the day specials, all served with baby potatoes and al dente vegetables. Classic desserts to finish - sticky toffee pudding, crème brulée and a delicious vanilla & vodka pannacotta with marinated balsamic berries are all typical. Well-priced wine list, also some draught beers. With a good atmosphere, good simple cooking and good value, it's not hard to see why this restaurant is so popular. Opening hours: L Tue-Fri, 10-3.30pm (from 1pm on Sun), D Tue-Sun 7-9. Closed Sat L and Mon. **Directions:** On the paved street of Tholsel, near the gate tower. ◇

R # CLOGHERHEAD

The fishing village of Clogherhead is about 12km south of Drogheda, and easily accessed from the M1 Dublin-Belfast motorway. From the Clogherhead peninsula just north of the village (designated a Natural Heritage Area under the 1997 Louth County Development Plan), there are clear views of the Cooley and Mourne Mountains to the north and to Lambay Island to the south; it is popular for many activities including, fishing, walking, sightseeing and water-based activities. The village is close to the historic town of Drogheda, the Boyne Valley and Newgrange Heritage site, and the standing stones around Newgrange are made of Clogherhead rock. Clogherhead is mainly known for fishing - the harbour, known as Port Oriel, was built in 1885 and recently extended; in the village, **Little Strand Restaurant** (see entry) specialises in local seafood.

WWW.IRELAND-GUIDE.COM FOR ALL THE BEST PLACES TO EAT, DRINK & STAY

Little Strand Restaurant

Clogherhead
RESTAURANT

Strand Street Clogherhead Co Louth **Tel: 041 988 1061**
food@littlestrand.com www.littlestrand.com

Catherine Whelahan's popular restaurant is in a neat modern building, on the right hand side as you go through the village of Clogherhead to the beach, set back a little from the road, with steps up to the front door. The fairly large ground floor restaurant is more formally appointed than might be expected for the location and, upstairs, there's a large lounge area, used for aperitifs and coffee at busy times. You don't have to be a fish-lover to enjoy a meal here - menus offer a range of meat, vegetarian dishes – although local seafood, brought in to the nearby fishing harbour of Port Oriel is, of course, the speciality and very good it is too. House specialities include crab claws in garlic/lemon butter, lobster thermidor and sole on the bone with lemon, lime and dill butter; an exceptional dish is Clogherhead scampi, cooked and served the traditional way with sauce tartare. **Seats 60** (Private room 12-16); air conditioning. D Wed-Sun (high season) and Bank Holidays, 6pm-"late"; Sun 3-8/8.30pm (depends on demand); à la carte; special value menus offered; house wine about €18, sc discretionary. Closed Mon, Tue (& Wed/Thurs off-season). MasterCard, Visa. **Directions:** 7 miles from Drogheda, 3 miles from Termonfeckin village.

Forge Gallery Restaurant

Collon
RESTAURANT

Church Street Collon Co Louth **Tel: 041 982 6272**
info@forgegallery.ie www.forgegallery.ie

This charming restaurant has been providing good food, hospitality and service for over twenty years now. The building is full of character, and has been furnished and decorated with flair which - together with the art exhibitions which are always an interesting feature - makes a fine setting for food that combines country French and New Irish styles. Menus are a little flowery in places (the speciality of the house is Forge Rendezvous of Clogherhead prawns & scallops); seasonal produce stars, much of it local, especially seafood, but there is also game in season, vegetables and fruit - and the cooking is creative and accomplished. This not an inexpensive restaurant (starters on the à la carte rise to around €30 for a 'symphony of prawns, claws and smoked salmon rouille', main courses to as much as €40) but there is a shorter, more moderately priced daily menu which is also priced by the course, and Sunday lunch offers very good value. Seafood leaps from the menu but there's plenty else to choose from, including great steaks and delicious roast Aylesbury duckling. A short vegetarian menu is also offered, and there may be a difficult choice between tempting desserts and Irish cheeses. Sound cooking with a contemporary flair, excellent service and an unusual ambience make for enjoyable dining. An interesting wine list includes a wide choice of half bottles. **Seats 60**; not suitable for children after 6pm; private parking (9); air conditioning. Bar. D Tue-Sat (& bank hol Sun), 6-9.30pm. D à la carte. House wine from €24; sc discretionary (except 10% on parties of 6+). Closed Sun (except bank hols), Mon; 24-25 Dec & 2nd week Jan. Amex, Diners, MasterCard, Visa, Laser. **Directions:** On N2, 56km (35 m) from Dublin due north, mid-way between Slane and Ardee, in centre of village.

DROGHEDA

A bustling town straddling the River Boyne, Drogheda is one of the most historically interesting towns in Ireland, as many groups of settlers (pre-historic, Celtic, Vikings, and Norman) were instrumental in its formation, and it is associated with many of Ireland's most significant events, the most famous being The Battle of the Boyne. Although now a Dublin commuter town, the street plan has not changed significantly since the 13th century; today it is an excellent, compact shopping town, especially since the riverside Scotch Hall complex opened, and all amenities are within easy reach of each other. The fast-growing population brings business to the growing number of bars and restaurants in the town, including **Romanza Italian Restaurant** (041-980 4800) next to the back entrance to the town centre shopping centre, this restaurant and piano bar is run by the same family as the popular **George's Wine Bar** in Dublin (see entry); at the Bryanstown Centre, on the Dublin road, there is a branch of the reliable franchise **Lemongrass** (041-9877233; www.lemongrass.ie). And, at the time of going to press, a really interesting new restaurant with specialist foods has opened in the Highlanes Gallery on Laurence Street: for a taste of what to expect at **Andersons at Highlanes** (041 930 3295), see the entry for Andersons in Dublin 9. Visitors who prefer a small hotel may enjoy the family-run **Scholars Townhouse Hotel** (041 9835410; www.scholarshotel.com) on King Street, a renovated 19th century redbrick building formerly belonging to the Christian Brothers. Local attractions that may be of interest to visitors to Drogheda include the Martello Tower and St Peter's Church, which contains the preserved head of St Oliver Plunkett, kept as a shrine to the Saint who was martyred for his faith at Tyburn, England, in 1681. Two miles east of Drogheda, on the road to Baltray, is Beaulieu House and Garden (041 983 8557, open May to September), which is a Jacobean manor house constructed in 1628, with an elegant garden open to the public - an exceptionally interesting place to visit, not least because it is still a family home.

WWW.IRELAND-GUIDE.COM FOR ALL THE BEST PLACES TO EAT, DRINK & STAY

Drogheda
HOTEL
R

Boyne Valley Hotel & Country Club

Drogheda Co Louth **Tel: 041 983 7737**
reservations@boyne-valley-hotel.ie www.boyne-valley-hotel.ie

Set in large gardens just on the Dublin side of Drogheda town - and handy to the motorway - this substantial hotel has an 18th century mansion at its heart. Graciously proportioned rooms contrast well with later additions, including 34 new rooms added several years ago. Owner-run by Michael and Rosemary McNamara since 1992, it has the personal touch unique to hands-on personal management and is popular with locals, for business and pleasure, as well as making a good base for visitors touring the area. While rooms in the old building have more character, the new ones are finished to the high standard demanded by today's travellers. Fine conference facilities and an excellent leisure centre add greatly to the hotel's attraction. Conference/banqueting (450/450); secretarial services. **Rooms 72** (1 suite, 13 shower only, 35 no-smoking, 1 disabled). Pets allowed by arrangement. B&B from about €80 pps. Leisure centre, indoor swimming pool; beauty salon. All weather tennis; pitch & putt. Garden. Open all year. Amex, Diners, MasterCard, Visa, Laser. **Directions:** On southern edge of Drogheda town. From Dublin turn off M1 to N1 at Julianstown; from Belfast turn off M1 to N1 at Drogheda north.

Drogheda
BAR•RESTAURANT•WINE BAR
N **R**

Brú Bar Bistro

Northbank 1 Haymarket Complex Drogheda Co Louth
Tel: 041 987 2784 info@bru.ie www.bru.ie

Whether development out over the river in Drogheda town centre should have been allowed is a point of debate, but it could have been a lot worse as this big building on stilts is not only rather handsome but it's a very popular meeting place - and, with its long hours and accessibility, has become a focal point for the community. Stylish in a comfortable, casual way, it has a large bar and informal restaurant on the ground floor - opening onto extensive decking for fine weather - and an exclusive cocktail and Martini bar upstairs. A range of menus is offered, varying through the day and depending on the day of the week, but with the emphasis always on giving quality, variety and value for money in pleasing surroundings - which is no doubt the reason for its popularity. Head chef Michael Collier values his trusted suppliers and uses local produce where possible; the cooking style is colourful, modern and family-friendly - good salads, home-made burgers, pasta dishes and fresh fish all feature and, of course, a house favourite is the 10oz fillet steak, served stylishly with marinated Portobello mushrooms, red onion marmalade, garlic mash and red wine jus. The main evening menus are the more adventurous, but the early bird and Sunday lunch menus offer great value. **Seats 120**; children welcome (high chair, childrens menu, baby changing facilities); air conditioning. Food served daily, 12-10.30pm (to 10pm Sun). 2/3 course early bird D €19.50/22.50, 5.30-7pm; also a la carte; house wine €22. SC 10% on groups 8+. Closed 25-26 Dec, Good Fri. MasterCard, Visa, Laser. **Directions:** On north bank of river.

D Hotel

Drogheda
HOTEL
R

Scotch Hall Drogheda Co Louth **Tel: 041 987 7700**
reservethed@monogramhotels.ie www.thed.ie

This cool new hotel is part of an impressive waterfront development in Drogheda, about 30 minutes from Dublin Airport, and is now setting the benchmark for high standards of rejuvenation in the centre of Drogheda. The hotel's contemporary lines contrast pleasingly with the old town, and the interior is bright, clean-lined, spacious and easy on the eye; it has a friendly atmosphere and helpful staff. A huge foyer with some very modern seating divides into the reception/lounge area, and a smart bar and restaurant overlooking the river. Comfortable bedrooms, many with superb views over the river and Drogheda's town centre, all have comfortable chairs and standard amenities. With seven meeting and event suites, this is an ideal place to host business meetings, or for private gatherings, and a new function room seats 300. The 'd restaurant' is well located to take advantage of the river views and, although not quite matching the ambitious style of the hotel as a whole, and a meal here should be enjoyable. Conferences/Banqueting (300); free broadband wi/fi, business centre, secretarial services. Fully wheelchair accessible. Children welcome (under 12s free in parents room, cots available free of charge, baby sitting arranged); pets permitted in some areas. **Rooms 104** (2 superior, 6 for disabled), 24hr room service; lift; complimentary guest parking. B&B about €110. Open all year except Christmas. Amex, MasterCard, Visa, Laser. **Directions:** The entrance to the hotel is c. 300 metres on the left adjacent to the Scotch Hall Shopping Complex. ◊

R

DUNDALK

The county town of Louth ('the wee county'), Dundalk is in an area rich with historical folklore, and is convenient to the Cooley Peninsula and the charming medieval town of Carlingford on the southern shore of Carlingford Lough. Local activities abound, and include greyhound and horse racing (042 933 4438), swimming, soccer, ice-hockey and ice-skating (042 933 7256), walking, salmon & trout fishing, horse riding and golf (Nuremore Hotel & Country Club, Carrickmacross, 042 966 1438). There is a Farmers' Market on the Square, Fridays (10am-2pm) and at the County Museum, Saturdays (10am-2pm). Garden Lovers should take a trip out to Knockabbey Castle & Gardens (01 677 8816) at Tallanstown, Victorian gardens with medieval fish ponds, herbaceous borders and a visitor centre. Architecturally, Dundalk town was until recently dominated by a massive seven-storey windmill, which begs restoration; however the recent opening of the 14-storey **Crowne Plaza Hotel** (see entry) has changed all that: with views over the Cooley Mountains and Irish Sea from the top floor, it can be seen from miles around. Good reasonably priced accommodation nearer the ground is available at **Park Inn Dundalk** (042 939 5700; www.dundalkparkinn.ie), which is just north of the town on the Armagh road and also has leisure and conference facilities. In the town centre, the familiar old **Imperial Hotel** (042 933 2241) has undergone extensive renovations and, with secure free parking and a location adjacent to the new shopping centre, The Marshes, it is a convenient place to meet. And also in the town, on the Dublin road, a colourful garden ablaze with masses of home-raised flowers will lead you to the Meehan family's spick and span B&B, **Rosemount** (042 933 5878).
WWW.IRELAND-GUIDE.COM FOR ALL THE BEST PLACES TO EAT, DRINK & STAY

Ballymascanlon House Hotel

Dundalk
HOTEL
R

Carlingford Road Dundalk Co Louth **Tel: 042 935 8200**
info@ballymascanlon.com www.ballymascanlon.com

Set in 130 acres of parkland, this hotel just north of Dundalk has developed around a large Victorian house. It has been in the Quinn family ownership since 1948 and major improvements have been completed with panache, lifting the hotel into a different class; bright and stylish public areas are furnished and decorated in a warm, comfortably contemporary style, with a homely atmosphere. Spacious and very attractive new bedrooms share the same qualities, with specially commissioned furniture - and, in many cases, views over lovely gardens, the golf course or the attractive old stable yard. A good breakfast is served in the hotel restaurant, which is comfortable but lacks the style of other public areas. Corporate facilities include three versatile meeting rooms, with back-up business services available. Impressive leisure facilities include a 20-metre deck level pool and tennis courts. Special interest and off-season deals available. Conference/banqueting (300/250). **Rooms 90** (3 suites, 87 executive rooms, 51 no smoking, 1 for disabled); children welcome (under 3s free in parents' room; cots available without charge, baby sitting arranged). Lift. Room service (limited hours). B&B about €85 pps, ss €30. Leisure centre, swimming pool, Canadian hot tub; golf (18); garden, walking. Open all year. Amex, Diners, MasterCard, Visa, Laser. **Directions:** M1 from Dublin; on the Carlingford road, 5km (3 miles) north of Dundalk. ◊

Dundalk
HOTEL
Ⓝ Ⓡ

Crowne Plaza Dundalk

Green Park Dundalk Co Louth **Tel: 042 939 4900**
enquiries@crowneplazadundalk.ie www.crowneplazadundalk.ie

Open since September 2007, this striking 4-star hotel is conveniently located close to the M1 motorway, halfway between Dublin and Belfast, and - although there is plenty in the area to attract leisure visitors - it has particular appeal for business guests. A bright and spacious foyer sets the tone, and pleasant and helpful staff are quick to make arriving guests feel at home, and to help with information about the area. Public areas include the Fourteen Below bar, and the remarkable top floor Fahrenheit Grill - with views over the Cooley Mountains and Irish Sea, this is a destination restaurant and booking is necessary, especially at weekends. Rooms are fairly spacious and have king-size beds and all the usual facilities, including mini-bar and wall-mounted plasma screen television; well set up for business guests, there is a safe, desk with phone and free internet connection, although lighting could be improved throughout. Conferences/Banqueting (800/600); business centre, free broadband wi/fi. **Rooms 129** (2 suites, 7 shower only, 7 disabled, 106 no smoking); children welcome (under 13s free in parents room, cots available, baby sitting arranged); 24-hr room service; lift; dogs may be permitted by prior arrangement. B&B €55 pps, ss€30. Fahrenheit Grill: Seats 140; children welcome (high chair, childrens menu); reservations accepted; air conditioning; D daily, L Sun only. 2/3 course early bird D €23/29; also a la carte; house wine from €21. Amex, Diners, MasterCard, Visa, Laser. **Directions:** M1 Dundalk South exit (jct 16), continue towards Dundalk and hotel is on the left.

Dundalk
CHARACTER PUB
Ⓡ

McKeown's Bar & Lounge

16 Clanbrassil Street Dundalk Co Louth
Tel: 042 933 7931

This well-run pub of character has a great atmosphere and friendly staff - just the place for a pint and welcome reassurance that the great Irish pub is alive and well in Dundalk. Open Mon-Wed, 10.30-11.30; Thu-Sat, 10.30-12.30. Food (soup & freshly made sandwiches) served daily, 10.30-6.30. Closed 25 Dec, Good Fri. **No Credit Cards. Directions:** Town centre - middle of the main street.

Dundalk
BAR•RESTAURANT
Ⓥ Ⓡ

Quaglinos at The Century

The Century Bar 19 Roden Place Dundalk Co Louth **Tel: 042 933 8567**
info@quaglinosrestaurant.com

Well-known restaurateurs Pat and Eileen Kerley run The Century Bar, which is a listed building on a corner site opposite St Patrick's Cathedral, and Quaglino's restaurant. It's a romantic building dating back to 1902, with an ornamental turret on the corner, above the front door - and it has retained many features of historical interest, including the original bar counter and hand-carved bar backdrop. The restaurant is above the bar and here Pat Kerley - a committed Euro-Toques chef - takes great pride in the active promotion of Irish food and uses as much local produce as possible, including oysters, lobster and lamb. As in most Louth restaurants, generosity remains the keynote and providing good service with good value is a priority. Quaglino's has always had a strong following and loyal customers (plus many new ones) like this reliable restaurant very much, so reservations are essential. The early dinner menu offers outstanding value, and the wine list is carefully selected to match the food. **Seats 30** (private room, 12); children welcome. D Wed-Mon, 5.30-10.30 (to 10pm Mon, Wed, Thurs, to 9pm Sun). Early 2/3 course D €20/26 (Sun-Fri, 5.30-7.30); mid-week special Wed, Thurs night all night €52 per couple for meal inc. bottle of wine; also à la carte; no SC. House wine €17.50. Bar meals Mon-Sat, 12-3pm. Closed Tue, 25 Dec, Good Fri. Amex, Diners, MasterCard, Visa, Laser. **Directions:** Just off town centre almost opposite St. Patrick's Cathedral.

Dundalk
RESTAURANT
Ⓡ

Restaurant Number Thirty Two

32 Chapel Street Dundalk Co Louth **Tel: 042 933 1113**
no.32@ireland.com www.no32.ie

Attractively situated in a leafy corner of town near the museum, Susan Heraghty's great little place is the neighbourhood restaurant par excellence and a great asset to Dundalk. It occupies a two-storey corner site, with windows all along one side giving it a sense of space, the smart simplicity of the decor and table settings is appealing, and menus are written in an admirably down-to-earth style - and the same can be said of the prices, notably an exceptional early evening "Express" menu, and the later set menu is not far behind. Menus may include tian of crab & celeriac, grilled lamb burger, and pan-seared gurnard with bell pepper escabèche. There has always been a terrific generosity of spirit here, in quality of food and service; the later menu is like the Express but with a little more choice and slightly more sophisticated dishes - but prices are still very reasonable. Would that every town in Ireland had a place like this. **Seats 60**; reservations recommended; children welcome. D Mon-Sat, 5.30-10. Early 'Express' D €17 (Mon-Thu 5.30-6.30), Set D €26. House wine from €18.95. SC 12.5% on parties 6+. Closed Sun, bank hols. Amex, MasterCard, Visa, Laser. **Directions:** First left turn after courthouse at "home bakery". ◇

Dundalk
RESTAURANT
R

Rosso Restaurant
5 Roden Place Dundalk Co Louth **Tel: 042 935 6502**
enquiries@rossorestaurant.com www.rossorestaurant.com

Just opposite St Patrick's Cathedral, in Dundalk's new 'dining quarter', this smart contemporary restaurant has positioned itself at the leading edge of local cuisine and is decked out in minimalist style with a striking coffee and cream colour scheme. On arrival one might relax and enjoy an aperitif in the open bar and reception area, while reading the menu in the particularly comfy sofas and soft chairs. Two sleek dining areas feature effectively positioned light-reflecting mirrors, recessed lighting and polished wood tables, and there's a cheerful lively ambience, especially as the tables fill up. Proprietors Raymond McArdle, acclaimed executive chef of the Gilhooley family's Nuremore Hotel (see entry) in Co Monaghan, and Louisa Gilhooley, have assembled a strong team at Rosso and head chef, Conor Mee, uses carefully sourced, mainly local, produce and cooks with flair - and, one detects, much enjoyment. The result is a mix of innovative ideas and re-interpreted classics such as pressed foie gras and duck terrine, served with toasted brioche and fig chutney; and fillet of Irish Angus beef with baked miniature oxtail pie, creamed parsnips and red wine sauce. Desserts may include a speciality hot Valhrona chocolate fondant, with fresh vanilla ice cream or Baked Alaska. Lunch offers great value; dinner menus are rather grander and offer more choice, but the high standard of cooking and presentation is a constant factor. A well-chosen wine list includes a short choice of wines by the glass, and service is friendly and professional. **Seats 75** (private room, 40); children welcome; air conditioning; L Tue-Fri, 12.30-2.30; D Tue-Sat, 6.30-9.30 (Sat, 6-10pm); L&D a la carte; Sun, 12.30-7pm; Value meal Sun all day, 3 courses about €27; house wine €20. Closed Sat L, Mon, 25 Dec, 1 Jan. MasterCard, Visa, Laser. **Directions:** Opposite St. Patrick's Cathedral.

Dundalk
BAR
R

The Spirit Store
George's Quay The Harbour Dundalk Co Louth **Tel: 042 935 2097**
info@spiritstore.ie www.spiritstore.ie

This pub of great character and friendliness is right on the quay, where coasters dock, so you never know what country visiting sailors in the bar may come from. But everyone mixes well in the wackily-furnished bars downstairs and - although a youthful place best known for its music (regular events are held in the upstairs bar, often famous names) - people of all ages and backgrounds are welcomed here, even if only for a cup of tea to break a journey. The music venue is being extended to 200, all seated. Closed 25 Dec, Good Fri. MasterCard, Visa, Laser. **Directions:** On the quayside, beside the bridge.

Dundalk Area
BAR•RESTAURANT
R

Fitzpatrick's Bar & Restaurant
Rockmarshall Jenkinstown Dundalk Co Louth **Tel: 042 937 6193**
fitzpatricksbarandrestaurant@eircom.net www.fitzpatricks-restaurant.com

Masses of well-maintained flowers and a neat frontage with fresh paintwork always draw attention to this attractive and well-run establishment. It has plenty of parking and is well organised for the informal but comfortable consumption of food in a series of bar/dining rooms, all with character and much of local interest in pictures and artefacts. Prompt reception, friendly service and traditional home-cooked food (sometimes with a modern twist) at reasonable prices, all add up to an appealing package - and its obvious popularity with locals and visitors alike is well deserved. Well-balanced menus always include a good selection of fresh seafood – the evening à la carte might offer a tian of fresh crabmeat to start perhaps, with a chilled tomato & red pepper fondue and avocado & chilli brunoise, main courses like fillet of turbot with risotto milanaise, katalfui lamgoustine and parmesan wafer - and delicious informal meals from the Grill Menu including proper scampi, made with fresh Dublin Bay prawns (langoustine), coated in home-made breadcrumbs and served with a trio of dipping sauces, and a range of char-grilled steaks and organic burgers; a separate vegetarian menu is also offered. This is not inexpensive food (some main courses may be over €30), but it is real food, and the quantities are generous. It's also a pleasant place to drop into for a cup of tea or coffee. **Seats 90** (private room 40, outdoors 150); wheelchair friendly; children welcome before 9pm (high chair, childrens menu, baby changing facilities); air conditioning. Open daily in summer, otherwise Tue-Sun 12.30 -10pm (Tue-Wed to 9pm), Sun 12.30-3.30 & 5.30-9pm). D 6-10. A la carte menus, also vegetarian menu; house wine from €19.95. Closed Mon Oct-Apr (except bank hols), 24-27 Dec, Good Fri. MasterCard, Visa, Laser. **Directions:** Just north of Dundalk town, take Carlingford road off main Dublin-Belfast road. About 8km (5 m) on left.

Dunleer
RESTAURANT
R

Carlito's

Main Street Dunleer Co Louth
Tel: 041 686 1366

You can't miss the orange frontage and bright blue canopy of this unassuming Italian restaurant in the centre of Dunleer village, and it is very popular, so it is wise to book well ahead, especially at weekends. Although quite unremarkable from the street, it is a welcoming place, with a comfortable seating area just inside the door where groups can assemble over a drink before heading for their table. Tables are simply set (night light, cutlery and a paper napkin), but friendly and efficient local staff will make sure that you're quickly settled into a menu that is well planned to please everyone. Expect home-baked bread, good minestrone soup, mixed leaf salads with creamy home-made dressing, crisp thin-based pizzas, and a range of pasta dishes and daily specials - such as herb-crusted cod, served with local vegetables (choice of boiled or chipped potatoes). Finish with a real tiramisu perhaps. A useful place to know about if travelling with a family. D Tue-Sat, 6pm-9.30pm, Sun 5-8.30pm. MasterCard, Visa, Laser. **Directions:** On main street.

TERMONFECKIN

Termonfeckin is a picturesque little village 8km (5 miles) north-east of Drogheda, and the nearby Baltray and Seapoint golf courses attract many visitors. The long-established **Triple House Restaurant** (see entry) is in the village, and both accommodation and good food are available at the very pleasantly refurbished **Waterside Hotel** (www.watersidehotellouth.com), which is ideal for people with business in Drogheda and Dundalk as well as leisure visitors.
WWW.IRELAND-GUIDE.COM FOR ALL THE BEST PLACES TO EAT, DRINK & STAY

Termonfeckin
RESTAURANT
R

Triple House Restaurant

Termonfeckin Co Louth
Tel: 041 982 2616

In the pretty village of Termonfeckin, Pat Fox's long-established restaurant is in a 200-year-old converted farmhouse set in landscaped gardens surrounded by mature trees. The rather neglected exterior is off-putting and the décor is overdue a makeover, but the food here is produced from a kitchen that knows what it is doing – and you can settle in front of a log fire in the reception area on cold evenings with the menu and a glass of wine (there's also a conservatory, for use in summer). Pat's menus are based on the best of local produce, with daily blackboard seafood extras from nearby Clogherhead including fresh Clogherhead prawns, Annagassan crab, and a dish intriguingly entitled Port Oriel Pot-Pourri. Locally-reared meats feature too, in roast Drogheda smoked loin of pork with a nectarine & Calvados sauce, for example. Good starters may include spinach-filled crêpes (baked with cream sauce, tomato sauce and Parmesan), delicious and sweetly cured gravadlax, and delicate tomato and cream tortellini. Main courses tend to be less successful, although haddock with herb butter was a highlight on a recent visit - fresh and crisply crumbed, and served with excellent garlic potatoes. Not for the first time desserts, like the starters, redeemed the meal on this occasion – the house speciality, a chewy meringue dacquoise that varies with the season's fruits, never fails to please and ice creams are also very good. Plated farmhouse cheeses are also offered, typically including Cashel Blue, Cooleeney and Wexford Cheddar. This is very much a neighbourhood restaurant, giving a feeling that all the guests know each other – and the wine list reflects Pat's particular interests (wine evenings are held in winter). **Seats 40**; children welcome; toilets wheelchair accessible. D Tue-Sun 6.30-8.30 (to 8pm Sun), L Sun only 1-2.30; Set D about €30, à la carte available; early D about €22, 6.30-7.30 only; Set Sun L €22. House wines about €17-20; sc discretionary. Closed Mon, Christmas. MasterCard, Visa. **Directions:** 8km (5 m) north east of Drogheda. ◇

COUNTY MAYO

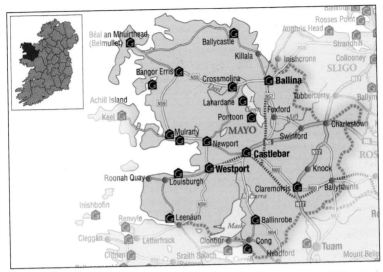

Mayo - far Mayo - might have been a byword for remoteness and declining population in times past. But now it is thriving, with the recent six-year Census showing a population increase of 5.3% (to 118,000). However, Mayo is so spacious that it still seems totally uncrowded. And they are a people who enjoy the present as much as savouring the past. No more so than at Westport on Clew Bay, near the famed Holy Mountain of Croagh Patrick. Westport is a neatly-planned town which responds to loving care, a frequent winner of Gold Medals in the annual Tidy Towns awards in Ireland, and the Entente Florale in France.

Five kilometres east of Mayo's bustling county town of Castlebar, the Museum of Country Life is at Turlough Park House. The first fully-fledged department of the National Museum to be located anywhere outside Dublin, it celebrates Irish country life as lived between 1850 and 1960 in an intriguing display of artefacts which were in regular everyday use, yet now seem almost exotic. As often, indeed, does Mayo itself - for Mayo is magnificent.

All Ireland's counties have their devotees, but enthusiasts for Mayo have a devotion which is pure passion. In their heart of hearts, they feel that this austerely majestic Atlantic-battered territory is somehow more truly Irish than anywhere else. And who could argue with them after experiencing the glories of scenery, sea and sky which this western rampart of Ireland puts on ever-changing display, particularly over Achill Island.

Yet among Mayo's many splendid mountain ranges we find substantial pockets of fertile land, through which there tumble fish-filled streams and rivers. And in the west of the county, the rolling hills of the drumlin country, which run in a virtually continuous band right across Ireland from Strangford Lough, meet the sea again in the island studded wonder of Clew Bay.

Along Mayo's rugged north coast, turf cutting at Ceide Fields near Ballycastle has revealed the oldest intact field and farm system in existence, preserved through being covered in blanket bog 5,000 years ago. An award-winning interpretive centre has been created at the site, and even the most jaded visitor will find fascination and inspiration in the clear view which it provides into Ireland's distant past. A few miles eastward, the charming village of Ballycastle is home to the internationally-respected Ballinglen Arts Foundation, creative home-from-home for artists worldwide.

Nearby, the lively town of Ballina is where the salmon-rich River Moy meets the sea in the broad sweep of Killala Bay. It takes a leap of the imagination to appreciate that the sheltered Moy Valley is in the same county as the spectacularly rugged cliffs of Achill Island. But leaps of the imagination is what Mayo inspires.

Local Attractions and Information

Ballina	Street Festival/Arts Week (July)	096 70905
Ballina	Tourism Information	096 70848
Ballycastle	Ballinglen Arts Foundation	096 43184/43366
Castlebar	Linenhall Arts Centre	094 902 3733
Castlebar	Tourism Information	094 902 1207
Castlebar	Turlough House (see entry under Turlough)	094 903 1589
Ceide Fields	Interpretive Centre	0996 43325
Clare Island	Ferries	098 27685
Foxford	Woollen Mills Visitor Centre	094 925 6756
Inishkea Island	Tours Belmullet	097 85741
Inishturk Island	Ferries	098 45520/45541
Killasser	(Swinford) Traditional Farm Heritage Centre	094 925 2505
Kiltimagh	Glore Mill Follain Arts Centre	094 82184
Knock	Interational Airport	094 936 7222
Moy Valley	Holidays	096 70905
Turlough	Turlough Park House. Museum of Country Life. Open Tuesday to Saturday 10am to 5pm, Sundays 2pm to 5pm, closed Mondays	094 903 1589
Westport	Clew Bay Archaeological Trail	087 293 5207
Westport	Westport House & Children's Zoo	098 25430/27766
Westport	Tourism Information	098 25711

ACHILL ISLAND

Achill island is the largest island in Ireland so don't forget to top up with fuel as you're driving on to it; there's a large service station, Lavelle's Esso Garage, on the right - and it is open on Sundays. It is a place of great beauty, with mountains, lakes, valleys, magnificent sea-cliffs, wild moors and spectacular scenery. It has a number of small attractive villages, several unpolluted sandy beaches ideal for bathing, excellent deep sea, shore and lake angling and opportunities for all kinds of outdoor activities. An interesting place that is also useful to know about is Seasamh O'Dalaigh's workshop and gallery, **Dánlann Yawl** (098 36137), at Owenduff (on the right coming from the mainland); it has a teashop during gallery hours, making a pleasant place for a break - and also a 2-bedroom apartment with magnificent views. On the island, the McNamara's family-run **Achill Cliff House Hotel** (098 43400; www.achillcliff.com) is at Keel; quiet, purpose-built, it is especially useful to know about as it is open all year except Christmas. Across at Dugort, **The Cottage** is a charming daytime restaurant offering really delicious home-made food including quiches and salads (dressed Achill salmon salad and homemade brown bread, perhaps), wraps, panini and baps – and gorgeous homemade desserts. **WWW.IRELAND-GUIDE.COM FOR ALL THE BEST PLACES TO EAT, DRINK & STAY**

Achill Dugort
GUESTHOUSE
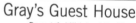

Gray's Guest House
Dugort Achill Island Co Mayo
Tel: 098 43244

Vi McDowell has been running this legendary guesthouse in the attractive village of Dugort since 1970, and nobody understands better the qualities of peace, quiet and gentle hospitality that have been bringing guests - especially artists and writers - here for the last hundred years. Mrs McDowell is very involved with the cultural life of the island - especially the Desmond Turner Achill Island School of Painting, and the cottage where Nobel prize-winning author Heinrich Böll once lived, which now offers a haven for artists and writers - and is an extraordinarily interested and hospitable hostess. This is an unusual establishment, occupying a series of houses, and each area has a slightly different appeal: there's a large, traditionally furnished sitting room with an open fire, comfortable leather lounge furniture, and several conservatories for quiet reading. Bedrooms and bathrooms vary considerably due to the age and nature of the premises, but the emphasis is on old-fashioned comfort; each of the three houses now has a fitted kitchen with everything you need to rustle up a light lunch, also a washing machine and tumble dryer, and the rooms all have tea & coffee-making trays; there are extra shared bathrooms in addition to en-suite shower facilities and phones for incoming calls. Children are welcome and have an indoor playroom and safe outdoor play area, plus pool and table tennis for older children. Dinner for residents is served in a large, quite formally-appointed dining room, where lovely old-fashioned menus offer dishes like smoked mackerel with gooseberry sauce, home-made celery and apple soup, local salmon or a traditional roast, and to finish, blackberry & apple pie with custard; there are several choices on each course and menus change daily. Packed lunches are also available on request. **Rooms 14** (13 en-suite, 1 with private bathroom, 13 shower only, 1 family room, 1 ground floor). Children welcome (under 3s free in parents' room). B&B €55 pps, ss €6, SC discretionary. D 7pm. Set D €32, house wine €18. Pets permitted in some areas by arrangement. Garden, fishing, walking. Pool table. Wheelchair accessible. Stair lift. Closed 24-26 Dec. Personal cheques accepted. **No Credit Cards. Directions:** Castlebar, Westport, Newport, Achill Sound - Dugort!

Achill Keel

CAFE•BAR

The Beehive

Keel Achill Island Co Mayo
Tel: 098 43134/43018

At their informal restaurant and attractive craft shop in Keel, husband and wife team Michael and Patricia Joyce take pride in the careful preparation and presentation of the best of Achill produce, especially local seafood. Since opening in 1991, they have extended both the menu and the premises more than once and now offer great all-day self-service food, which you can have indoors, or take out to a patio overlooking Keel beach. Everything is home-made, including delicious soups such as seafood chowder and traditional nettle soup (brotchán neantóg) all served with home-made brown scones. As baking is a speciality, there's always a tempting selection of cakes, bracks, teabreads, fruit tarts, baked desserts and scones with home-made preserves or you can simply have a toasted sandwich, or an Irish farmhouse cheese plate. You may want to allow a little extra time here as the shop is interesting, with quality gift items and clothing lines not found elsewhere. The restaurant is now fully licensed and the Joyces are considering extending the opening hours to develop an evening restaurant in the not too distant future - details on inquiry. **Seats 100** (outdoor seating, 60; private room, 50); toilet wheelchair accessible; children welcome (high chair, baby changing facilities). Meals 9.30-6pm daily, Easter-early Nov. A la carte. No sc. Closed Nov-Easter. Amex, Diners, MasterCard, Visa, Laser. **Directions:** Situated in the centre of Keel village overlooking beach and Minuan cliffs.

Achill Keel

RESTAURANT

Ferndale Restaurant

Crumpaun Keel Achill Island Co Mayo **Tel: 098 43908/9**
achillfinedining@eircom.net www.ferndale-achill.com

Located on a hillside overlooking Keel Village and Bay, right across to the cliffs, Ferndale must have some of the most stunning and ever-changing views in the West of Ireland, as the big waves roll in from the Atlantic. The interior of the restaurant is unusual and the decor, light beige fleck tiles, a swag of net curtain across the top of the huge main window and burgundy drapes adorned with small lights hanging from the ceiling and walls gives one a Turkish or Arabian feeling, which is also carried on in the style of the tables, chairs and napery. Swiss Chef Jon Fratschol's menu is truly a global affair comprising 7 pages, each one representing major ethnic cooking styles, such as South America, the Indian sub-continent, the Arabian Peninsula, Scandinavia and Mexico with the Caribbean among others. Typical examples are: Rack of Irish Lamb Chilli'n Lime (Caribbean style), Springbok and Venison Lapland (Scandinavia) or Bengali Seabream with nuts and a mustard marinade from India. Main courses are priced from around €19 to €32 served with vegetables and potatoes. Desserts are also wide-ranging such as Mango Cheesecake Bushfire, an Aussie invention, and Beghrir Pancakes, Arabian. Wines are also from around the world with house wines at about €19 and a couple by the glass. This unusual restaurant will not be to everyone's taste – and one can't help wishing there could be less choice and a bit more focus - but it is certainly different. **Seats 40**; reservations required; toilets wheelchair accessible. D daily in summer, 6-10.30; after Hallowe'en open weekends only (Thu-Sun) except fully open over Christmas. A la carte (main courses about €15-25). House wine from about €16. Accommodation is also offered. Amex, MasterCard, Visa, Laser. **Directions:** Signed up the hill from Keel village. Take a right at the Annexe Inn, signposted on the left after 400m.

BALLINA

St Muredach's Cathedral is an impressive river bank landmark in Ballina, (gaelic Béal an Átha), which is Mayo's largest town, and has the famous River Moy flowing through it, which creates a particularly pleasant atmosphere. Ballina has become a busy commercial and tourist centre, but is rich in heritage and the area is renowned for its many stone age tombs. It's a great base for a fishing holiday (the River Moy is world-famous for its salmon and trout fishing), or for exploring this beautiful and unspoilt part of the west of Ireland, and there is plenty of good food and accommodation to be found in and around the town, including one of the area's longest-established hotels, the **Downhill House Hotel** (see entry), which is quietly situated in a riverside location just a short walk from the town centre. Ballina holds a Street Festival in July (096 70905); this includes a heritage day when traders transform their shopfronts to recreate their Victorian look; the festival also showcases traditional foods, crafts, and there is open air entertainment. Ballina Farmers' Market is held on Friday mornings (9am-1pm, Community Centre) and on Saturdays (Market Square, 9am-2pm). And, even if this isn't the time to be buying fresh fish, foodie visitors should make a point of seeing Clarke's Salmon Smokery (096 21022; www.clarkes.ie), next to **Gaughan's** (see entry) on O'Rahilly Street – for some prime smoked salmon to take home, perhaps; branches also in Westport and Longford. While in the area, a trip out to Enniscoe House & Gardens (Crossmolina, 096 31112) is very worthwhile; as well as restored walled gardens and a lovely tea room, this fine property has woodland walks, a genealogy centre, a small rural museum (and even blacksmith working art certain times) and, most recently, a short working run of an old bog train. There is plenty of historical interest to visit nearby, including St Muredach's Cathedral; the ruins of Moyne Abbey; the Father Peyton Memorial Centre (a multimedia presentation telling the story of the Rosary Priest; 0964 5374); the Céide Fields near Ballycastle; and the Museum of Country Life, Castlebar. For relaxation, there is a lot of good walking in the area, Enniscrone Seaweed Baths to chill out in, and Foxford Woollen Mills for shopping. Golfers, meanwhile, face a mighty challenge on the links at nearby Enniscrone Golf Club (Enniscrone, 096 36297).

WWW.IRELAND-GUIDE.COM FOR ALL THE BEST PLACES TO EAT, DRINK & STAY

Ballina
HOTEL

Belleek Castle

Ballina Co Mayo **Tel: 096 22400**
belleekcastlehotel@eircom.net www.belleekcastle.com

Situated just outside Ballina amidst 1,000 acres of woodland and forestry, on the banks of the River Moy, Marshall and Jacqueline Doran's castle was the ancestral home of the Earl of Arran and, with a 16th century armoury, big open fires and massive chandeliers among many quirky features, it now makes an unusual small hotel. This is a wacky place for those who enjoy something out of the ordinary and it would be great fun for a group get-together. The Armada Bar is a recreation of the Captain's Ward Room from a galleon in the Spanish Armada - partly constructed from timbers salvaged from the galleons of the ill-fated Castile Squadron wrecked off County Mayo four centuries ago, it should provide plenty of talking points to pep up your drink. Belleek Castle is as different from a standard modern hotel as it is possible to be (it is registered as a one star hotel), but it manages to combine old world charm with modern comforts - bedrooms will vary according to their position in the house, but the best are bright and spacious, with four-poster beds and views out over the grounds. It makes a romantic wedding venue (the banqueting room is in medieval castle style), and the many activities to choose from nearby include championship golf, walking, surfing, and salmon and trout fishing on site; or, with its informal and friendly ambience, the castle simply makes an unusual base to explore this beautiful area. **Rooms 15**. B&B from €80-160 pps, ss €20. **Directions:** Follow signs on way into Ballina for Belleek. ◇

Ballina
BAR•RESTAURANT

Crockets on the Quay

Ballina Co Mayo **Tel: 096 75930**
info@crocketsonthequay.ie www.crocketsonthequay.ie

This well-known hostelry is attractively situated on the quay in Ballina, overlooking the River Moy, with seating outside for fine weather and a pleasant old-style bar. Extending behind the traditional bar is a series of contemporary bar areas, finishing up with a stylish big bar right at the back, with access to a car park behind the building. Interesting bar meals are served all day by friendly staff and, although the dim lighting seems quite surreal when coming in from the sunshine on a bright summer's day, it's a hospitable place - and it leaps into life at night. More formal evening meals and Sunday lunch are available in the restaurant, which is attractively situated overlooking the river. *There are plans to reconstruct the premises as an hotel, possibly in 2009. **Seats 60** (outdoor seating, 40); toilets wheelchair accessible; not suitable for children after 9pm; pool table, broadband wi/fi. Parking (30). Food available 12.30-9.30pm daily. House wine €19. Closed 24-26 Dec, Good Fri. Amex, MasterCard, Visa, Laser **Directions:** On the edge of Ballina; from town, take main Sligo road, turn left at first traffic lights.

Ballina   # Downhill House Hotel
HOTEL   Downhill Road Ballina Co Mayo **Tel: 096 21033**
 info@downhillhotel.ie www.downhillhotel.ie

One of the area's longest-established hotels, the Downhill House Hotel has been in the Moylett family for three generations and is known for its hands-on hospitality and relaxed, friendly atmosphere. Formerly a country house, it first opened in 1938 and, quietly situated on the banks of the River Brosna, still enjoys an almost-rural location just a short walk from the town centre. Following major renovations, the hotel re-emerged in 2008 with a smart new facade and a spacious new lobby and reception, along with more seating areas and a conservatory overlooking the gardens. While giving the hotel a major face-lift, it hasn't lost the comfortable old-fashioned feeling enjoyed by the guests who keep coming back year after year. It's a good base for fishing holidays with golf also nearby, good on-site leisure facilities and Children's Club (and even a Children's Check-in Desk), and plenty of interesting places for family outings, it's not surprising that it's so popular for traditional family holidays. The pretty setting also makes it popular for weddings. Short break offers are often available. Conferences/Banqueting (450/400); secretarial services, free broadband wi/fi. **Rooms 60** (1 suite, 5 shower only, 4 family, 50 no smoking, 1 single, 2 disabled); children welcome (under 4s free in parents room, cot available free of charge, baby sitting arranged, kids' club; playground nearby). No pets; all day room service; lift. B&B €85-105pps; ss€26. Garden, walking, snooker, pool table; Leisure centre (indoor pool, fitness room, jacuzzi, steam room, sauna). Fishing (fly, coarse & sea angling), equestrian, golf (3 championship courses less than 50 minutes drive), surfing all nearby. Closed 22-27 Dec. Amex, Diners, MasterCard, Visa, Laser. **Directions:** 1.5km (1 m) from Ballina on the main Sligo road (N59).

Ballina   # Gaughans
WINE BAR   O'Rahilly Street Ballina Co Mayo **Tel: 096 70096**
              edgaug@eircom.net

This is one of the great old bars of Ireland and has a gentle way of drawing you in, with the menu up in the window and a display of local pottery to arouse the curiosity. It's a fine old-fashioned place, with everything gleaming and a great sense of the pride taken in its care. Michael Gaughan opened the premises as a pub in November 1936 and his son, Edward, took over in 1972. Edward's wife Mary is a great cook and, once they started doing food in 1983 they never looked back; everybody loves the way they run the place and Mary still does all the cooking. Although they sold the pub licence a few years ago and now operate as a wine bar, Mary's specialities have not changed and her good home cooking includes home-made quiche Lorraine with salad, lovely old-fashioned roasts - roast stuffed chicken with vegetables and potatoes, perhaps, or baked gammon. Local seafood features, when available: smoked salmon is offered all year round, but fresh crab is only served from May to the end of August - such respect for seasonality is rare enough these days, and it is good to see it. There's always a daily special and old favourites like lemon meringue pie and pineapple upside-down pudding for dessert. Lighter options on the menu include open smoked salmon or crab sandwich (in season), smoked salmon salad, and ploughman's lunch - it's all unpretentious, wholesome fare. And, charmingly listed along with the Bewley's tea and coffee, the wine and Irish coffee "Glass of spring water: Free." Now that's style. **Seats 40**; children welcome. Food served Mon-Sat, 10am-6pm. Closed Sun, bank hols, 23 Dec - 2 Jan. Amex, Diners, MasterCard, Visa, Laser. **Directions:** Up to the post office, on the left.

Ballina

HOTEL•RESTAURANT

The Ice House Hotel

The Quay Ballina Co Mayo **Tel: 096 23500**
chill@theicehouse.ie www.theicehouse.ie

Bring your binoculars when heading for this quirky hotel, as the wildlife in the River Moy and wooded banks beyond the huge sliding windows of your room is perhaps its most fascinating feature - and could well keep you ensconced there in a comfy chair for longer than expected. Once the heart of Ballina's salmon industry, the 150-year old ice house is a lovely building but – right on the river and backed by the road – the challenging site called for some creative thinking. The result is a funky mix of traditional - some 'heritage' rooms in the original house have little balconies – and bold contemporary design in public areas, notably successful in Pier Restaurant (see below), perhaps less so in the main body of the hotel which features a lot of (rather utilitarian) fully-tiled surfaces in stairways, and reception and seating areas which are stylish but somewhat impersonal. But there is some outstanding artwork to please the eye and another high point is the Chill Spa, which has already earned an enviable reputation amongst intrepid spa-goers and includes a riverside hot tub (a mixed blessing when the river is low). Staying here is certainly a very different experience from the old-fashioned comforts that tend to be associated with this part of the country, and it will make an intriguing base for those who like to break with tradition and is certain to introduce many new visitors to the town. There is no carpark, but off-street parking spaces are available beside the hotel. Conferences/Banqueting (70/100); secretarial services, free broadband wi/fi. **Rooms 32** (7 suites, 3 executive, 4 shower only, 1 disabled); children welcome (under 7s free in parents room, cot available free of charge, baby sitting arranged); 24-hr room service, Lift, ample parking. Fly fishing, steam room and spa on site. Equestrian and golf nearby. **Pier Restaurant:** An ingeniously designed and atmospheric light-filled space, with an extensive decked area leading off it, the restaurant incorporates the original vaulted ice store which is set up with smartly laid tables and has a raised area at the back, allowing a river view even from the furthest tables. Head chef, Gavin O'Rourke, who may be remembered for his time at Dublin's Peacock Alley (which was famous for dramatic presentation), has a keen eye for the way food looks on the plate although not, these days, at the expense of simplicity. A la carte menus are divided by Sea and Land, offering a total choice of perhaps eight or nine dishes on each course; the dearest starter – home-made papardelle pasta with lobster, baby asparagus, roasted tomato & fresh basil (€25) – may prove irresistible and comes with plenty of luscious lobster, although some may find the sauce too spicy for the delicate lobster flavour; better, we think, is the Ice House Tasting Plate, a delicious assembly of unusual meats including smoked ox tongue, devilled lamb kidney, beef rillettes, and McGeough's black pudding (€19) from nearby Connemara. Baked fillets of halibut (perhaps in the singular – in the Guide's experience, the portion may be very tiny) makes a tasty main course, served with baby spinach, peas and sauce Albufeira, or meat lovers might go for an upmarket variation of steak & chips: a very generous dry-aged sirloin of Irish beef with Cashel Blue sabayon and pomme paillasson. Prettily presented desserts offer contemporary versions of classics (pecan brownie with lemon curd ice cream, perhaps), or there's an Irish cheese selection. A compact wine list is appropriate for the food, and – although some staff may seem to be better trained than others - service is pleasant. Seen overall, Pier Restaurant is a delightful place to be, and brings a very welcome addition to the dining options in the area. A good breakfast is also served in the restaurant. **Seats 70** (outdoors, 40; private room, 15); children welcome (high chair, childrens menu, baby changing facilities). Food available all day, 12.30-9.45pm. L&D daily, 12.30-3.30pm (from 12 Sun) and 6.30-9.45pm (6-9pm Sun). Closed 25-26 Dec. Amex, Diners, MasterCard, Visa, Laser. **Directions:** N59 to Ballina, through town, turn down by the river.

Mount Falcon Country House Hotel & Estate

Ballina
HOTEL•RESTAURANT

Foxford Road Ballina Co Mayo **Tel: 096 74472**
info@mountfalcon.com www.mountfalcon.com

Mount Falcon will be fondly remembered by many for its lovable eccentricity under the previous owner, Connie Aldridge (whose late husband Major Robert Aldridge, a keen archaeologist, helped discover the Ceidhe Fields) and it is now owned by the locally based Maloney brothers, who fell in love with it when visiting in 2002 and bought the estate when she retired. They have since been working on a multi-million euro building and refurbishment plan that included extending the original house and erecting a selection of luxurious courtyard houses and woodland lodges. Mount Falcon is now a 32-bedroom luxury hotel and it is a welcoming place, first seen in a series of ground floor drawing rooms and lounges with comfy sofas, open fires and coffee tables scattered with books and magazines about fishing, hunting and country life in general. Accommodation includes six deluxe rooms on the upper floors of the original house (including two suites, the Wallpool and Connor's Gap, which are named after famous pools on the Mount Falcon Fishery); they have been restored with pitch-pine shutters and floors, original cornices and marble fireplaces whilst integrating all the modern comforts. The other rooms are new and spacious, with custom-designed furniture, television and radio, direct dial phone, personal safe and hairdryer as standard. The estate enjoys more than 2 miles of double bank salmon fishing on the River Moy, and the 100 acres of grounds have been redeveloped and landscaped to incorporate lakeside and woodland walks. Other local activities include championship golf, at nearby Enniscrone Golf Club, and horse riding - and there are many beaches nearby. Conferences/Banqueting (250/180), broadband wi/fi, video conferencing. Spa, leisure centre with indoor 'pool, steam room, sauna, jacuzzi and gym. **Rooms 32** (2 suites, 4 junior suites, 2 for disabled); Children welcome (under 2s free in parents' room, cots available free of charge, baby sitting arranged); Lift; 24 hr room service. B&B €110pps, ss €85. Self catering also available. Helipad. **Restaurant:** Orders are taken over an aperitif in the Bolthole Bar, before you go through to the classically-appointed restaurant, in the original kitchen and storeroom and pantry of the main house; well-spaced tables set up with pristine white line and comfortable chairs create a sense of anticipation for a good dining experience to follow - and, with highly regarded executive head chef Philippe Farineau in the kitchen, you should have a treat in store. His motto of "Irish Produce, French Heart" is used to good effect, in frequently changed menus based mainly on locally sourced produce: there is a strong emphasis on seafood – Clare Island salmon, Clew Bay scallops and crab, beef and lamb from Tolans and Heffernans respectively, both butchers in Ballina. A typical Table d'Hote dinner (€64) offering half a dozen choices on each course might include a Clew Bay crab plate or warm Co Clare goat's cheese among the starters, followed perhaps by local black sole, plain grilled, with lemon & almond butter or Mayo rack of lamb, and desserts like warm dark chocolate fondant with amaretto ice cream – and round this off with petit fours and chocolates with your tea or coffee. All the little treats of fine dining are offered including a complimentary pre-starter (a little parfait of smoked mackerel, perhaps) as luxurious packaging for a memorable meal that could include local lobster 'Thermidor', and Irish venison. Service is professional and friendly, and a well- chosen and informative wine list includes four house wines (€28) and eight half bottles. **Seats 72** (private room 10). L&D daily 12.30-2.30 (to 2 Sun) & 6.30-9.30pm (Sun 7-9pm). Set Sun L €35; set D €64. Bar menu also available daily, 12.30-7pm. House wine €28. Hotel closed 24/25 Dec, Jan. Amex, Diners, MasterCard, Visa, Laser. **Directions:** Look out for discreet black and white signage on the right, about 6.5km (4 m) outside Ballina on the N26 to Foxford.

Ballina Area

Enniscoe House

HISTORIC HOUSE

Castlehill Crossmolina Ballina Co Mayo **Tel: 096 31112**
mail@enniscoe.com www.enniscoe.com

In parkland and mature woods on the shores of Lough Conn, Enniscoe can sometimes seem stern and gaunt, as Georgian mansions in the north-west of Ireland tend to be, but with family portraits, crackling log fires, warm hospitality and good home cooking, this hospitable house has great charm. It was built by ancestors of the present owner, Susan Kellett, who settled here in the 1660s, and is a very special place for anglers and other visitors with a natural empathy for the untamed wildness of the area. Large public rooms include a fine drawing room, with period details and plenty of seating, and a more intimate dining room, where Susan's delightfully simple dinners are served. Her menus change daily and make good use of home-grown and local produce in dishes like pan-fried scallops with Madeira dressing and rocket salad and a delicious house speciality of roast free-range pork; homely desserts like rhubarb and orange crumble to finish, and cheeses laid out on the sideboard - as they are again next morning, as part of an excellent breakfast. Traditionally furnished bedrooms are large, very comfortable and, like their en-suite bathrooms, regularly refurbished. There is much of interest around converted outbuildings at the back of the house, including a genealogy centre (The Mayo North Family History Research Centre, Tel: 096 31809), a small agricultural museum with working blacksmith, and conference facilities. The house is surrounded by beautiful woodlands, with a network of paths, and there are restored walled gardens (both ornamental and productive - one is run commercially as an organic market garden), which are open to the public and have tea-rooms and a shop. The latest addition, open since 2008, is a working run of an old bog railway; the first section with its little platform was about to open on the Guide's most recent visit, and the plan is to extend it, making an impressive tour around the grounds. There is brown trout fishing on Lough Conn and other trout and salmon fishing nearby; boats, ghillies, tuition and hire of equipment can be arranged. *Enniscoe has been selected for a number of the Guide's awards at different times, most recently the Food eXtra Award in 2008, for an outstanding all-round contribution to the hospitality of the area, with special emphasis on food. Small conferences (50). **Rooms 6** (all en-suite & no smoking, 2 family rooms) B&B €110 pps, ss €20. Turndown service. Restaurant: Seats 20. D daily, 7.30-8.30pm; reservations accepted; non-residents welcome by reservation. 3-course Set D about €50; house wines €18-24. Closed 1 Nov-1 Apr. MasterCard, Visa, Laser. **Directions:** 3km (2 m) south of Crossmolina on R315.

Ballinrobe

JJ Gannons Hotel

HOTEL•RESTAURANT•WINE BAR

Main St Ballinrobe Co Mayo **Tel: 094 954 1008**
info@jjgannons.com www.jjgannons.com

Right in the heart of the thriving town of Ballinrobe, JJ Gannon's goes back to 1838 but it's now in the third generation and rather funky from the outside - preparing first-time visitors for a mainly modern style, which is unusual for the area and reflects the taste of an energetic and very committed young couple, Niki and Jay Gannon, who are developing it as a 'green' hotel. (A geo-thermal heating system converts energy from the river, and a wood pellet burner provides back up.) A contemporary bar with a more traditional area at the back caters for all age groups and, impressively, a blackboard offers a wide selection of wines by the glass. The eleven bright bedrooms offer a range of standards including a junior suite, the rooms have been individually furnished with care, and include luxurious touches such as tailor-made linen and goose down duvets to fit the huge (6'6") beds, also velour bathrobes and slippers. Residents' breakfast is served in the bright and airy restaurant, (offering freshly squeezed orange juice, pressed apple juice, a JJ Gannon's smoothie or seasonal fruit kebabs to start you off) and a breakfast menu is also offered in the bar. With such committed owners, lovely friendly staff and good food, this is a place that's worth a detour. Conferences/Banqueting (50/80), business centre, secretarial services, video conferencing, free broadband wi/fi. Fishing, golf and equestrian nearby, walking, massage, short breaks. Children welcome (under 2s free in parents' room, cot available at no charge, free baby monitors, baby sitting arranged). **Rooms 11** (1 suite, 4 junior suites, 1 shower only, 4 family rooms, 1 for disabled, all no smoking); lift; limited room service; B&B €60 pps, ss €15. **Restaurant:** What was previously The Red Restaurant is now known as the Red Room – indicating a move away from fine dining to a more informal 'gastro pub' style. Cian Mulholland, formerly with Mint in Dublin, is now head chef and a new menu has been introduced comprising about half a dozen choices on each course, all reasonably priced. These include a creamy home-made chowder, steamed mussels in garlic, shallots, white wine and cream and an excellent duck liver paté. Main courses offer a choice of local butcher Martin Jennings' fillet and sirloin steaks, a must in Ballinrobe, pork, and perhaps a deliciously moist slow-roasted crispy duck with a celeriac and cardamon mash in an orange and balsamic jus. A new feature on the menu is a 'Specials' list which changes nightly and might offer a choice of turbot, monkfish, Dublin Bay prawns, brill and whole black sole on the bone, pan-roasted with lemon and caper butter. A well-priced, informative wine list includes plenty of wines served by the glass. Cian Mulholland - who is only in his early '20s and whose father was for many years Head Chef in the Connemara Coast Hotel - is rapidly making a name for himself in the south Mayo area, with locals and visitors alike. **Seats 50** (private room, 50, outdoor, 20); air conditioning; reservations recommended; children welcome; L Mon-Sat, 12.30-3.30; D Mon-Sat 6-9.30; Sun, 12.30-9.30; set Sun L €25; early D €30, 5-7pm; also a la carte L&D; house wine €21. *Bar food served daily 8am - 9.30pm. Closed 25 Dec. MasterCard, Visa, Laser. **Directions:** Southern Mayo, off N84.

BALLYCASTLE

Ballycastle, 'the town of the stone fortress', is on the scenic rugged coast of north Mayo, where sandy beaches and towering cliffs are exposed to the force of the Atlantic Ocean. An unspoilt small town, with a rich history going back 5000 years and many historical sites including megalithic tombs, early Christian and medieval ruins, its special attraction is the nearby Ceide Fields Interpretive Centre (096 43325) which was built at the world's most extensive stone age monument; here, preserved beneath the wild blanket bog, is a 5000-year old landscape of farms, stone dwellings and megalithic tombs. The surrounding area of Ballycastle lies largely untouched, with a variety of natural habitats including bog, mountains, meadows, rocky shores, cliffs and beaches. Simplicity, natural beauty and remoteness are the unique attractions of this area, which has attracted a vibrant artistic community (Ballinglen Arts Foundation; 096 43184/43366) but there are plenty of active pursuits too, including swimming, scuba diving, excellent shore angling, bog rambling and hill walking, and horse riding at the Heathfield Stables (096 43350). Golfers can play world class championship links golf to the east at Enniscrone Golf Club (096 36297) or to the west in Belmullet (Carne Golf Links, 097 82292).

Mary's Bakery & Tea Rooms

Ballycastle
RESTAURANT

Main Street Ballycastle Co Mayo
Tel: 096 43361

Mary Munnelly's homely little restaurant is the perfect place to stop for some tasty home cooking. Baking is the speciality but she does "real meals" as well - a full Irish breakfast, which is just the thing for walkers, home-made soups like mushroom or smoked bacon & potato, and free-range chicken dishes. And, if you strike a chilly day, it's very pleasant to get tucked in beside a real fire too. There's also a garden with sea views for fine weather - and home-made chutneys and jams on sale to take home. **Seats 30** (also outdoor seating for 12); toilets wheelchair accessible; children welcome. Open 10am-6pm daily in summer (may open later - to 8-ish - in high season; shorter hours off season); Closed Sun off-season (Oct-Easter), & first 3 weeks Jan. **No Credit Cards. Directions:** From Ballina - Killala - main road to Ballycastle, on way to Ceide Fields.

Polke's

Ballycastle
CHARACTER PUB

Main Street Ballycastle Co Mayo
Tel: 096 43016

This lovely old general merchants and traditional pub is just across the road from Mary's Bakery, and well worth a visit. It was established in 1820 and has remained in the family since then - the present proprietor, Brian Polke, has had responsibility for this national treasure since 1962. Not much has changed it seems: the long, narrow bar behind the shop is completely unspoilt, friendly and a joy to find yourself in. The whole place is immaculate too (including the outside loo in a whitewashed yard at the back), giving the lie to the widely-held view that "character" pubs are, by definition, scruffy. A nice touch of modernity which reflects the close-knit nature of the local community is the collection of pictures donated by artists from the nearby Ballinglen Arts Centre, which are exhibited in the bar and make a fascinating talking point for new arrivals. Open 10.30am-11.30pm. Closed 25 Dec & Good Fri. **Directions:** On main street.

Ballycastle
HOTEL•RESTAURANT

Stella Maris Country House Hotel

Ballycastle Co Mayo **Tel: 096 43322**
info@stellamarisireland.com www.stellamarisireland.com

Built in 1853 as a coastguard regional headquarters, this fine property on the edge of the wonderfully away-from-it-all village of Ballycastle was later acquired by the Sisters of Mercy, who named it Stella Maris, and it now makes a very special small hotel, restored by proprietors Terence McSweeney and Frances Kelly, who have created a warm and stylish interior where antiques rub shoulders with contemporary pieces. There's a welcome emphasis on comfort throughout public areas, including a cosy bar - but the location is this hotel's major asset and a conservatory built all along the front takes full advantage of it, allowing guests to relax in comfort and warmth while drinking in the majestic views of the surrounding coastline and sea. Accommodation blends understated elegance with comfort in uncluttered rooms that have magnificent views and are furnished with antiques but - with complimentary broadband, modern bathrooms and power showers - offer the best of both worlds. Children welcome (under 4s free in parents' room, cot available free of charge). Walking; fishing. Garden. Equestrian and golf nearby. No pets. **Rooms 12** (1 suites, 6 shower only, 1 ground floor, 1 disabled, all no smoking). B&B €112.50 pps, ss €50.
Restaurant: Dinner - cooked under Frances' direct supervision - is a very enjoyable experience, based on local ingredients as far as possible, including organic produce from nearby Enniscoe House (see entry) and also from the hotel's own new gardens. Strongly seasonal à la carte menus are well-balanced and imaginative, without being over-influenced by fashion and the cooking is admirably simple: toasted organic St Tola goat's cheese on a pesto croûton over garden greens, with raspberry purée, roast rack of spring Ballycastle lamb with sweet potato purée & minty jus, are typical and there is usually a choice of two fish dishes, perhaps including local organic salmon from Clare Island (vegetarian option on request). Classic desserts include refreshing seasonal fruits – warm stewed organic rhubarb with Chantilly cream, perhaps - and there will always be an Irish farmhouse cheese plate; then it's back to the conservatory for a digestif... The wine list, while relatively short, has been chosen with care. Residents also have a treat in store each morning, as the Stella Maris breakfast is worth lingering over: lashings of freshly squeezed juice, a beautiful fruit plate, gorgeous freshly-baked brown bread, handmade preserves and perfect hot food cooked to order, be it a traditional Irish or a special like creamy scrambled eggs with smoked salmon; not a grand display, but exceptionally delicious. Stella Maris was the Connaught winner of our Irish Breakfast Awards in 2004 and was our Hideaway of the Year in 2005. This is indeed a wonderful retreat. Short breaks offered - details on application. Banqueting (40). Restaurant **Seats 26**. Reservations recommended; non-residents welcome. D 7-9 (Mon residents' only), D à la carte, house wine €24. Short breaks offered - details on application. Restaurant closed Mon (to non-residents); hotel closed Oct-Mar. Closed Oct-Apr. MasterCard, Visa, Laser.
Directions: West of Ballina on R314; 2km (1.5 m) west of Ballycastle.

BELMULLET

Positioned on the strip of land between Blacksod and Broadhaven bays, Belmullet is the entrance to the Mullet peninsula, a district of untouched beauty with many secluded beaches and coves and a number of islands off its coast. (Inishkea Island Tours; 097 85741) The town is a centre for shopping, serving the Erris region, and **An Chéibh** (097 81007) on Barrack Street, is a friendly and comfortable bar and lounge, offering hearty food, especially local fish and seafood. It is one of the leading sea angling centres in Europe with both excellent shore and deep sea fishing available, and also excellent fresh water angling in the many local lakes and rivers, all with healthy stocks of salmon and trout. Nearby heritage sites of interest to the visitor include megalithic tombs, Iron Age cliff forts and castles from the 16th, 17th, and 18th century. Golfers relish the challenge of the 18-hole championship links course at Carne (097 82292), whilst other local activities on offer include walking, abseiling, pony trekking, scuba diving, windsurfing, sailing and canoeing.

Belmullet
HOTEL

Broadhaven Bay Hotel

Ballina Road Belmullet Co Mayo **Tel: 097 20600**
info@broadhavenbay.com www.broadhavenbay.com

This large new hotel enjoys commanding views over Broadhaven Bay and offers not only accommodation but also extensive bar, restaurant and banqueting facilities - all much needed services in the area. Comfortably-appointed bedrooms look over the bay to the front and a courtyard to the rear, and all have a safe, tea/coffee-making facilities, direct dial phone, iron and plasma tv as standard. Friendly, helpful staff are more than happy to help guests arrange any of the many activities in the area, including championship golf at the world famous Carne Golf Links, canoeing, walking, fishing, diving, cycling and horse riding. With a leisure centre and spa (and even in-house hairdressing), this is a comfortable place to be based when visiting one of the most beautiful and remote parts of Ireland. Conferences/Banqueting (600/500); **Rooms 70**. B&B €70-95 pps, ss around €10. **Directions:** On the road into Belmullet. ◇

R # CASTLEBAR

This bustling market town is one of the fastest growing in the country, and was originally a garrison town, deriving its name from a settlement around the De Barra Castle in the 11th century. Its central location is ideal for touring the county and visiting local attractions such as Ballintubber Abbey (094 903 0934), the Céide Fields (096 43325), Croagh Patrick mountain and the Foxford Woollen Mills (094 925 6756, open all year). Visitors can take a guided historical walk around the town or can pay a visit to the 18th century Turlough Park House (094 903 1755), which is home to the National Museum of Country Life and the grounds include formal gardens and an artificial lake. Reflecting the area's strong artistic tradition, the Castlebar Linenhall Arts Centre (094 9023733) is an interesting place to visit, and the energetic will find plenty of outdoor pursuits available locally, including cycling, horse riding, walking, golf and fishing. After a tiring day of exploring the area, visitors could consider a trip to the Kachina Natural Spa in Mayo Leisure Point (094 902 7110).

Castlebar
RESTAURANT
R

An Carraig

Chapel Street Castlebar Co Mayo
Tel: 094 902 6159

Louis and Ines Fourie took over this popular restaurant recently, and have maintained the style, quality and local following of the previous owners, the Horan family. In a quiet street just off the town centre, it's an attractive, quite traditional restaurant with cut stone walls and a nautical theme with lots of wood, portholes and an arch that links smaller dining areas and also provides visual interest, and a cosier more intimate atmosphere - a feeling enhanced by gentle lighting and candles. Menus are updated traditional, with steaks and seafood taking the starring roles - many of the old favourites are there, but most will have some kind of twist in the presentation, bringing them up to date. Finish, perhaps, with a shared dessert platter for two. Healthy options are offered and there's willingness to provide for special diets and allergies (advance notice preferred). Good customer care and home cooking is the aim, achieved very successfully - and they give good value too. With friendly, helpful service under the supervision of Berliner Ines, and South African born Louis' sound cooking, all the markers are for continued success. **Seats 55**. D Tue-Sun, 6-10pm (Sun 5.30-9.30). Early D €22 (6-7.15); also à la carte House wine, about €20. Closed Mon, last 2 weeks Jan. MasterCard, Visa. **Directions:** Town centre, opposite Church of the Holy Rosary. ◇

Castlebar
PUB•CAFE/BAR
R

Bar One Gastro Pub

Rush Street Castlebar Co Mayo
Tel: 094 903 4800

In the same family ownership as Dublin's stylish Saba (see entry), Mark and Alan Cadden's gastropub is the busiest bar food venue in the Castlebar area - and that is as it should be, as their parents, Mary and Michael, were pioneers of the catering industry west of the Shannon and were for many years owners of the Asgard Bar & Restaurant in Westport. Together with their brother Paul (owner of Saba), it is pleasing to see this generation of Caddens also at the forefront of the industry. Bar One is a very modern and well-designed bar, with dark timber floors, tables chairs, and with plenty of smart upholstered stools and areas suitable for standing when in for a drink at night. The welcome is warm and friendly, under the watchful eye of Michael, with menus promptly produced and specials explained: not to be missed is the cod in a crispy beer batter, mushy peas and home-cut fries, and an excellent seafood pie also comes highly recommended. Daytime specials change daily, and extras including steaks and prime seafood are added in the evening; gluten-free and vegetarian versions of several dishes are offered, and children are well catered for. The high standards established from the outset at Bar One are being maintained, and this well-run bar is notable for its very friendly service. At the weekend queues form for the night time D.J. and live music sessions, open till late, so be on time as this is Castlebar's night-time hotspot. **Seats 80**; toilets wheelchair accessible; children welcome (high chair, childrens menu); food served all day Mon-Sat, 12-8pm (to 2am Thurs-Sat). No food on Sun, Bank Hol Mon. Live music Thurs night. MasterCard, Visa, Laser.

Castlebar
RESTAURANT
🔲 🕭 € R

Café Rua

New Antrim Street Castlebar Co Mayo **Tel: 094 902 3376**
info@caferua.ie www.caferua.ie

Well-located near the Linenhall Arts & Exhibition Centre, you can't miss this attractive little restaurant, with its cheerful red frontage. Ann McMahon set up here over 10 years ago and is still very involved although Aran and Colleen McMahon now look after the day-to-day running. They are very serious about the food they serve, but the tone is light-hearted - it's not a very large room but pine tables (some covered in red oilcloths) are quite well-spaced, and most have a good view of the large blackboard menu that lists all kinds of good things to raise the spirits of weary shoppers and culture vultures. Wholesome, home-made fresh food is the order of the day here, and careful sourcing of ingredients is a point of pride - so pasta dishes are based on the excellent Noodle House pastas from Sligo, Irish farmhouse cheeses and other speciality ingredients are supplied by Sheridan's cheesemongers, fish comes from Clarkes of Ballina and pork from Ketterichs of Castlebar. Organic vegetables are supplied by a nearby organic scheme in summer, Macroom stoneground oats go into the porridge that is served with home-made apple compôte in winter - and ingredients for 'the full Irish' (sausages, puddings) come from the renowned butchers, Kelly's of Newport. Regular dishes like home-made chicken liver paté, warm chicken salad with garlic mayonnaise and ratatouille crostini are announced on one blackboard, while another gives hot specials like potato & lovage soup, grilled pork chops with carrots, new season potatoes & mushroom à la crème and Cashel Blue potato croquettes with beetroot chutney. There's an interesting drinks menu (wines, juices, hot chocolate with marshmallows) and 'because we know that they love food too', there's also a special children's menu, one of many thoughtful touches. Luscious desserts (rhubarb trifle, for example) and good home bakes too: great little place. *Shortly before the Guide went to press a second branch of Café Rua opened in Castlebar: **Rua**, a two-storey café, deli and bakery on Spencer Street, offers salads, sandwiches and artisan and specialist food products, freshly baked breads, cakes and scones - and many of the favourite dishes from Café Rua. **Seats 35**; children welcome. Open all day Mon-Sat, 9.30-6pm. Closed Sun; Bank Hols, 1 week at Christmas. MasterCard, Visa, Laser. **Directions:** Near Welcome Inn, opposite Supervalu carpark.

Castlebar
HOTEL
R

Lynch Breaffy House Hotel & Spa

Castlebar Co Mayo **Tel: 094 902 2033**
www.lynchotels.com

This handsome hotel set in its own grounds just outside Castlebar town dates back to 1890 and retains some of its original country house atmosphere in some areas, although it can be very busy at times. It has undergone major redevelopment in recent years and its principal attraction is the exceptional sports and leisure facilities offered. An impressive leisure complex and health spa, Life-Spa and Ku'dos Aqua & Fitness Club, have made the hotel an all-year destination for short breaks: facilities include a gymnasium, 20 metre pool, Café West (for refreshments at the leisure complex), also an exhaustive range of treatments, some of which are not available elsewhere in Ireland. And, with sports facilities that are unique in Ireland, including the Paul McGrath Soccer Academy on site, it now styles itself Breaffy International Sports Hotel. Renovation and considerable refurbishment has also been undertaken recently in public areas and accommodation, and a large number of deluxe bedrooms (including two presidential suites and 20 interconnecting family rooms) have been added recently. Conference/banqueting (500); business centre. **Rooms 125** (10 suites, 40 executive, 10 no smoking, 2 disabled); children welcome (under 2 free in parents' room, cots available without charge, baby sitting arranged). No pets. Lift. 24 hr room service. B&B €100-130pps, ss about €26. Leisure centre, swimming pool; spa. off-season value breaks. Garden, walking. Preferential local golf rates. Open all year. Amex, Diners, MasterCard, Visa, Laser. **Directions:** 4km outside Castlebar on the Claremoris Road. ◈

An Grianán Museum Café

Castlebar Area
CAFÉ
R

National Museum of Ireland for Country Life Turlough Castlebar Co Mayo
Tel: 094 928 9972 info@leonardcatering.com www.leonardcatering.com

The National Museum of Ireland's Museum of Country Life is a great place to spend an afternoon with the family and, although the grounds would be most enjoyable in sunshine, it's a useful haven if you happen to strike a bad spell of weather. The old house has some rooms restored to their 19th century glory and a rolling lawn leads down to a large tree-lined lake where, by contrast, the eye is drawn to the straight lines of the large, modern museum, housing three floors of photos and exhibits from the last two centuries. After building up a healthy appetite mooching around the museum, the courtyard Café in the old house is the place to go: a short but appealing menu offers a limited choice of wholesome dishes including home bakes such as a freshly made quiche, served with a selection from a varied salad bar. **Seats 85** (private room, 40, outdoors, 20); children welcome; toilets wheelchair accessible. air conditioning; food served during museum opening hours, Tue-Sun, 10-5pm, L 12-2.30pm. Closed Mon and Bank Hols. MasterCard, Visa, Laser. **Directions:** In National Museum of Ireland for Country Life in Turlough, off N5 Castlebar road.

Old Arch Bar & Bistro

Claremorris
BAR•RESTAURANT
V

James Street Claremorris Co Mayo **Tel: 094 936 2777**
www.theoldarchbistro.com

Fergus and Anne Maxwell's bar and informal restaurant in this recently by-passed town has an inviting black and white frontage with well-maintained window boxes, and there's a welcoming atmosphere in the comfortable, low-ceilinged reception area and bar. The restaurant is informal and friendly, and neatly uniformed staff present large, cheerful dinner menus offering a wide selection of popular dishes; arranged by section there are light dishes, soups & salads, fish & poultry, meat and vegetarian, and there is a separate children's menu. Typical dishes include crispy mushrooms with a garlic chive mayonnaise to start, and perhaps a main of Old Arch chicken supreme (stuffed with black pudding, wrapped in bacon and served with mushroom & brandy sauce). Portions are generous, the cooking is generally good and prices are moderate: ideal for a family-friendly restaurant in a growing town. At lunchtime, sandwiches get a menu of their own, and the main lunch menu changes daily. There's a large garden area too, with gas heaters, barbecue and plenty of seating. **Seats 80** (private room, 55; outdoors, 30); toilets wheelchair accessible; children welcome before 9pm (high chair, childrens menu, baby changing facilities). L &D daily: L 12-4, D 6-9 (to 10pm Fri/Sat). House wine €19. Pub food served 12-6pm daily. Closed 25-26 Dec, Good Fri. MasterCard, Visa, Laser. **Directions:** 10km fron Knock, on Galway-Sligo/Derry road. Beside railway bridge, on the main street.

CONG

This picturesque village on the edge of Connemara is beautifully situated on Lough Corrib, and world-famous as the setting for the John Wayne film 'The Quiet Man'. Guided tours and memorabilia associated with the film are an inevitable feature today, but there is more to Cong than The Quiet Man: historical sites include Cong Abbey, the remnants of the Augustinian abbey founded in the 12th century by Turlough O'Connor, King of Connaught and High King of Ireland. Ashford Castle & Gardens south of Cong is worth a visit just to see the beautiful estate, and informal food is available beside the castle, at **Cullen's at the Cottage** (see entry). You will also find a number of places offering casual daytime food in the village, including **Hungry Monk Café**, Abbey Street (094 954 5842). Cong is an excellent base for golfers who want to play some of the best golf courses in the west of Ireland, not only the course at Ashford Castle, but Westport Golf Club (098 28262), and also championship links at Connemara (095 23502/23602), Enniscrone Golf Club (096 36297) and Galway Bay Golf Club (098 36262). For non-golfers, there is a wealth of activities on offer including boat cruises, horse riding, canoeing and walking in the rich diverse landscape of the west taking in rivers, lakes, mountains and forests. Cong River also provides the keen angler with excellent salmon and brown trout fishing.

WW.IRELAND-GUIDE.COM FOR ALL THE BEST PLACES TO EAT, DRINK & STAY

Cong

HOTEL•RESTAURANT•CASTLE

Ashford Castle

Cong Co Mayo **Tel: 094 954 6003**
ashford@ashford.ie www.ashford.ie

Ireland's grandest castle hotel, with a history going back to the early 13th century, Ashford is set in 350 acres of beautiful parkland. Grandeur, formality and tranquillity are the essential characteristics, first seen in immaculately maintained grounds and, once inside, in a succession of impressive public rooms that illustrate a long and proud history - panelled walls, oil paintings, suits of armour and magnificent fireplaces. Accommodation varies considerably and each room in some way reflects the special qualities of the hotel. The best guest rooms, and the luxurious suites at the top of the castle - many with magnificent views of Lough Corrib, the River Cong and wooded parkland - are elegantly furnished with period furniture, some with enormous and beautifully appointed bathrooms; others have remarkable architectural features, such as a panelled wooden ceiling discovered behind plasterwork in one of the suites during renovations (and now fully restored). The hotel's exceptional amenities include a neo-classical fitness centre, and the extensive activities/outdoor pursuits available on the estate are detailed in a very handy little pocket book. The castle has three restaurants: The Connaught Room, which is mainly for residents, is the jewel in Ashford Castle's culinary crown and one of Ireland's most impressive restaurants; the George V Dining Room offers fine dining for larger numbers; the new Cullen's Cottage, in the grounds, offers accessible all-day informal dining. In addition, The Library and Drawing Room menus offer informal meals including Afternoon Tea. Executive Head Chef, Stefan Matz (who was the Guide's Chef of the Year in 2007) oversees the cooking for all food operations in the castle, and Cullen's Cottage; since joining the team in 2003, this highly-skilled and modest chef has worked wonders to introduce some gentle modernisation of menus, to bring the varying dining operations together and ensure high standards in each (see below). An impressive recent addition to the range is an extensive Children's Menu that invites younger guests to 'join Lord Ardilaun and his friends inside for some fun-filled activity...' and is packed with games, puzzles and colouring pages as well as healthy and delicious things to eat and drink. Conference/banqueting (110/166); business centre; free broadband wi/fi. Archery, boat trips, clay pigeon shooting, equestrian, walking, garden, fishing (fly & coarse), golf (9), fitness centre, sauna, steam room, massage, beauty salon, hairdressing. Children welcome (under 12s free in parents' room, cot available without charge). No pets. Heli-pad. **Rooms 83** (11 suites, 5 junior suites, 61 executive, 21 ground floor, 6 for disabled, all no smoking). Lift. 24 hour room service. Turndown service. Room rate about €485 (max 2 guests, with breakfast), room only €430; SC 15%. Short/off-season breaks offered - details on application. **The Connaught Room:** This small room is one of Ireland's most impressive restaurants. The style is broadly classical French, using the best of local ingredients notably seafood and Connemara lamb, and speciality produce like James McGeough's wonderful cured Connemara lamb from Oughterard. A wonderful à la carte is offered and, if at least two people (preferably a whole party) are agreed, a seasonal 5- / 7-course Menu Dégustation tasting menu is available; at €130/155 including wines selected to match each course, this is outstanding value - and after dinner you will be presented with a souvenir copy of the menu. Attention to detail is superb throughout, and caring service by Thomas Ponson and his team is at the heart of this theatrical experience, with commentary on the various dishes as they are served with perfect, silver-domed timing. The wine list is a stunning example of an old-fashioned grand hotel list, and has been sommelier Robert Bowe's responsibility for nearly 20 years; during that time, he has developed it from 250 listings to over 600, carefully sourced from about 15 suppliers. The Castle's wine programme includes a series of winemaker dinners held each winter (which may involve Irish winemakers from around the world. *Ashford Castle was the winner of the Guide's Wine Award in 2008. **Seats 34** (max table size 14). D only, Wed-Sun, 7-9.30pm (seasonal); reservations essential (usually residents only); Menu Dégustation 5/7 courses €80/95, also à la carte. **George V Dining Room:** This much larger but almost equally opulent dining room also offers a combination of fine food and attentive service, under the direction of Maître d'Hôtel and Sommelier Robert Bowe, whose constant, caring presence adds greatly to an outstanding dining experience. A five-course dinner menu offers a choice of about nine dishes on the first and main courses, including some tempting vegetarian suggestions; the choice is wide, with a suggested wine (by the glass or by the bottle) with each starter and main course. You might begin with the Ashford Castle version of Caesar Salad (with Connemara ham), and for the main course there's a slight leaning towards seafood, but game will be offered in season, and a speciality that may surprise is the daily roast, served from a carving trolley. Irresistible desserts, or a superb cheese trolley, to finish. Although unarguably expensive, the dining experience at Ashford Castle gives value for money. In addition to the main wine list (see above), there are also wines of the month, and recommendations by the glass to accompany individual dishes. *All meals in the castle are by reservation. *A light daytime menu is available in The Gallery. **Seats** 160. D daily 7-9.30, Set 5 course D €75. A la carte D also available; house wines from €28. SC.15% **Cullen's at The Cottage:** On Ashford's manicured lawns, a stone's throw from the Corrib and within sight of the castle, Cullen's at The Cottage is named after the late Peter Cullen, a much-loved former Maitre D', and offers a completely different experience: mid-priced dining, open to the public, with none of the pomp and ceremony associated with the grandeur of meals served in the castle itself. The kitchen is operated under Stefan Matz's direction, but functions independently from the main castle kitchen. Internally, the cottage has been transformed, with burgundy-coloured banquette seating, plain wood tables, tiled floors, and white walls. The menu, while leaning towards seafood, offers a varied selection of meat and vegetarian dishes, salads and side orders, also a daytime sandwich, pitta and panini section, and coffees, teas and desserts. Highlights include a platter of McGeough's cured hams (speciality meats from Connemara), grilled fillet of organic salmon, and char-grilled Irish rib-eye steak On a fine summer's day, dining al fresco here has a continental air - and, there's a short, fairly-priced wine list, with suggestions for food pairings. Well-trained staff give good service, while appearing to have all the time in the world to chat. **Seats** 65 (private room 48, outdoor seating 48). Open 12-9 daily high season; Fri-Tue, 12.30-9pm shoulder season (a phone call to check is advised, especially off-season). Reservations accepted. A la carte. Wines from about €20. Amex, Diners, MasterCard, Visa, Laser. **Directions:** 48km (30 m) north of Galway on Lough Corrib.

Cong
COUNTRY HOUSE

Ballywarren Country House

Cross Cong Co Mayo **Tel: 094 954 6989**
ballywarrenhouse@gmail.com www.ballywarrenhouse.com

Diane and David Skelton's hospitable country house is in a pleasant rural area of gentle farming countryside just a few minutes' drive east of Cong and Ashford Castle. Large and well-proportioned, it has a welcoming feeling from the minute you arrive through the door into the classic back and white tiled hall. Public rooms are furnished stylishly and include a spacious drawing room with a cosy open fire, and the lovely Garden Room dining room, where dinner is available to guests by arrangement - like a dinner party, it's a wholesome 5-course meal based on seasonal local ingredients, organic where possible, and all bread and rolls are home-made; a short but surprising wine list includes a choice of five bubblies. An oak staircase leads up to the three charming bedrooms, all with luxurious, well-finished bathrooms. This would make a very comfortable base for a few days spent in the area; the only slight downside is that the road is rather close, although it is not busy at night. **Rooms** 3 (all ensuite & no smoking); children over 14 and small babies welcome (under 1s free in parents' room, cot available free of charge); all-day room service; B&B €74pps, ss €50. Pets permitted in certain areas by prior arrangement. Residents' D at 8pm in the **Garden Room**; dining room **seats** 8; set D €42 (4 course); reservation required and should be ordered earlier in the day. House wine €16; No SC. Fishing, golf, lake cruising, horse riding, hill walking all nearby. Garden. Closed 1 week May, 1 week Oct. Amex, MasterCard, Visa. **Directions:** East of Cong, on the Headford road.

Cong
HOTEL•RESTAURANT

Lisloughrey Lodge

The Quay Cong Co Mayo **Tel: 094 954 5400**
lodge@lisloughrey.ie www.lisloughrey.ie

IRISH BREAKFAST AWARDS - NATIONAL WINNER
HOTEL BREAKFAST OF THE YEAR AWARD

Completing its second season in business as we go to press, this new hotel enjoys one of the most beautiful locations in Ireland, with views down Lough Corrib and Lisloughrey Quay adding interest in the foreground, with small boats in the harbour and its old stone buildings set against wooded hills. The heart of the hotel is a fine period house on a ten-acre site adjacent to Ashford Castle, and with access to its grounds; behind it, new accommodation has been added discreetly in two-bedroom units, built around an attractive landscaped courtyard (where civil wedding ceremonies may be held); to the side, a bright and airy function room is well-designed with direct access to a bar and other public areas, and also to the lawn at the front of the house, making a wonderful setting for weddings and other special occasions. A modern approach has been taken throughout the interior and, while it has its admirers, it is not to everyone's taste – notably the treatment of the beautiful old house which now sports a fashionable red and matt black colour scheme throughout the main public areas, bare wooden floors, lots of leather in the bars and some strange lighting. The best accommodation is in the old house, with views down Lough Corrib - one suite has a free-standing copper bath in the room; however, most rooms are in the new development, accessed by a wide corridor bizarrely featuring red wall lights and lamps. Bedrooms are not especially large but like those in the otherwise very different sister property, Wineport Lodge in County Westmeath - have big, very comfortable beds and tip-top quality pillows and bedding; wall-mounted flat screen TV is well placed for watching a film in bed, and a large wardrobe with trendy padded finish also conceals a good few bells and whistles. Fashion-led bathrooms are a good size but, with a frosted glass door compromising privacy, no bath in most rooms (power shower with rain dance shower head) and free-flow washbasins (designed to be plugless apparently), they may not be to everyone's taste; however, ten spacious junior suites with better bathrooms including full bath are available, and worth the premium. Lisloughrey has facilities for business meetings, with the first-floor Library in the main house suitable for meetings (or private dinners) of up to 30. Conferences/Banqueting (200/180); free-broadband wi/fi. Treatment rooms, masseuse, jacuzzi, sauna, fitness room, walking, boat trips, fishing (trout, salmon), golf & equestrian nearby. **Rooms 50** (26 suites, 10 family, 24 ground floor, 3 disabled). B&B from €125 pps, ss €75. Children welcome (under 10s free in parents room, cot available free of charge, baby sitting arranged); all day room service; lift. **Salt Restaurant:** Situated in two rooms on the first floor, with lovely views of the lough and quay, this is one of the most successful areas of the hotel. The red and black scheme is lifted by smart tables, classically-appointed with crisp white linen and, as the evening draws in, warm lighting softens the atmosphere. Head chef Wade Murphy, like General Manager Marc MacCloskey, came here from Four Seasons hotels, renowned for their high levels of service and here, as elsewhere in the hotel, staff are exceptionally well trained, friendly and helpful. Several variations of the dinner menu are offered, so you can have the full six courses (€69), one of two lighter combinations (€52 or €53), or main course only (€36); a good arrangement, not too complicated and offering good value, especially for the full menu. Excellent breads and iced water arrive promptly at your table, quickly followed by an amuse-bouche (a single seared scallop on a slice of black pudding, perhaps: magic); from a choice of seven starters, you might have a delicious signature dish of grilled baby calamari with white bean cassoulet and chilli oil – generous, perfectly cooked calamari rings, interestingly paired with quite toothsome butter beans, this is a smashing little dish – or try a new, very pretty, starter created for McGeough's of Oughterard to showcase their wonderful air-dried Connemara ham. Next a mini-course 'Soupçon' - a miniature of, say, roasted pepper soup: perfect for a special meal. From seven equally tempting main courses (including a strong vegetarian option), an impressive signature dish of pan-roasted beef tenderloin (fillet) with red onion purée, wild chanterelles, sautéed foie gras and lemon thyme jus will change your mind about the predictability of steak, or you might try one of several excellent fish dishes, an unusual polenta-crusted skate wing with orange and snap pea with citrus brown butter vinaigrette, for example. These imaginative variations on classics are perfectly cooked, beautifully presented – and taste divine; and, although each dish is individually garnished, seasonal side vegetables are also served, without a supplement. Finish with one of pastry chef Pauline Reilly's sinful creations (raspberry & dark chocolate tart with raspberry sorbet, perhaps) or an artisan Irish cheese platter with plum chutney & pain d'épice bread, but try to leave a little space for the gorgeous petits fours that come with coffee. Backed up by an interesting wine list (but without tasting notes) and solicitous, knowedgeable service, Wade Murphy's outstanding cooking makes for a special dining experience. And you may immediately look forward to your next meal here, as an exceptionally good breakfast is served in the restaurant each morning too. **Seats 56** (private room, 15); children welcome (high chair, children's menu, baby changing facilities); D daily 6.30-9.45pm; set D €70; house wine from €30; SC 12.5% on groups 8+. Bar food also served daily, 12.30-10pm. Closed 24-26 Dec. Amex, MasterCard, Visa, Laser. **Directions:** Just outside Cong, in the Ashford Castle estate.

FOXFORD

Nestling between the Ox and Nephin mountains, Foxford is situated on the River Moy, famous for its fishing. Foxford is synonymous with woollens, especially 'the Foxford blanket'; established in 1892, vistors today will find a newly revitalised business at Foxford Woollen Mills Visitor Centre (094 925 6104; www.museumsofmayo.com/foxford) which is very much the centre of the local community and hosts two art galleries, a jewellery workshop, Christmas Craft Fair and Saturday Farmers' Market as well as showcasing their own updated ranges of homewares and clothing. The first floor café, **It'so** (094 925 7280), offers a wide range of wholesome meals, notably salads and homebakes.

WWW.IRELAND-GUIDE.COM FOR ALL THE BEST PLACES TO EAT, DRINK & STAY

Foxford Area
HOTEL

Healys Hotel

Pontoon Foxford Co Mayo **Tel: 094 925 6443**
info@healyspontoon.com www.healyspontoon.com

This famous old hotel, loved by fisherfolk, landscape artists and those who seek peace and tranquillity, changed hands in 1998, and there has since been a plan of gradual renovation and refurbishment, both indoors and in the gardens, without spoiling the old-fashioned qualities that have earned this hotel its special reputation. Accommodation is modest but comfortable - and also moderately priced. The scale is small and it's an intimate place, and very relaxed; the hotel has lots of information on things to do in the area - including golf at around a dozen nearby courses, fishing, shooting, horse racing, and mountain climbing. The bar has character both here and in the restaurant; the food has always tended to be above-average for a country hotel, although recent restaurant visits have been disappointing and 'a good steak', cooked as requested, is the safest choice. Small conference/banqueting facilities (25/70); free broadband wi/fi. **Rooms 14** (all shower only & no smoking, 1 family); children welcome (under 3s free in parents' room; cots available at no charge, baby sitting arranged); room service (all day); B&B €35-45pps, ss €20. Dogs welcome (stay in outhouse/kennel). Packed lunches available. *Bar food available 12.30-9.30 daily (in restaurant); Dining Room L & D daily. Garden, fishing. Closed 25 Dec. Amex, Diners, MasterCard, Visa, Laser. **Directions:** R310 from Castlebar - 10 min drive; R318 from Foxford to junction R310; R310 from Ballina - 10 min drive.

Lahardane
PUB

Leonard's

Lahardane Ballina Co Mayo
Tel: 096 51003

This unspoilt roadside traditional pub & grocery shop was established in 1897 and the original owners would be proud of it today. Very much the centre of local activities, Leonard's has a large dining area behind the pub, where all the area's get-togethers take place – if only those walls could talk. And, if you get hungry, there's always the makings of a picnic on the shelves. Closed 25 Dec & Good Fri.

Lecanvey
BAR

T.Staunton

Lecanvey Westport Co Mayo
Tel: 098 64850/64891

Thérèse Staunton runs this great little pub near the beginning of the ascent to Croagh Patrick - genuinely traditional, with an open fire, it has the feeling of a real 'local'. Not really a food place, but home-made soup and sandwiches or plated salads are available every day until 9pm. Occasional traditional music sessions - and frequent impromptu sing-songs. Closed 25 Dec & Good Fri. **No Credit Cards. Directions:** 12.5km (8 m) from Westport on Louisburgh Road.

MULRANNY

This tranquil seaside village is located on the strip of land between Clew Bay and Blacksod Bay, home to colourful giant fuchsias and exotic plants - a rich natural heritage which is celebrated each summer during the Mulranny Mediterranean Heather Festival. Mulranny offers a Blue Flag sandy beach, which is ideal for swimming and shore fishing, whilst the Corraun Peninsula offers three mountain peaks with incredible views. Golfers will enjoy the links at Mulranny Golf Course (098 36262).

Mulranny
HOTEL•RESTAURANT

Park Inn Mulranny

Mulranny Westport Co Mayo **Tel: 098 36000**
info@parkinnmulranny.ie www.parkinnmulranny.ie

This landmark hotel, originally built by the Midland Great Western Railways, first opened for business in March 1897 and it became a famous destination during the lifetime of the railway between Westport and Achill Island. Situated on a 42-acre woodland estate, the hotel is now owned by Tom and Kathleen O'Keeffe, who have retained much of its original character and charm while developing a contemporary style. It now has 60 guest bedrooms, and an elegant dining room, a modern bar, relaxing lounges and a luxurious leisure centre with 20 metre pool - all of which, plus a Blue Flag beach, a golf course and wonderful walks nearby, make this a holiday haven for both Irish guests and visitors from other countries. Conference/banqueting (500/300); free broadband wi/fi; business centre. Children welcome (free cot available, baby sitting arranged, kids club). No pets. Leisure centre (pool, fitness room, jacuzzi, sauna, steam room); massage; beauty salon; pool table; golf (9), walking. Garden visits, equestrian and fishing nearby. **Rooms 60** (3 superior, 7 shower only, 23 family, 3 disabled, 56 no smoking). B&B €105 pps ss €25. Closed 18-26 Dec. **Nephin Restaurant:** The restaurant is an elegant room and it has the best view, overlooking the Atlantic. It is a formal room, as befits the dining experience offered here, and is set up comfortably but in no way ostentatiously, with good-sized square and round tables, traditional mahogany dining chairs and crisp white linen. Head chef Seamus Commons, who is from Bohola in East Mayo, is well-known in Ireland and has worked in some leading restaurants including L'Ecrivain, in Dublin, where he was head chef - now he is back, making his mark in this 'oasis in the west', where he has attracted a following and established the hotel as a destination for food lovers. Menus read well and offer many unusual ingredients and combinations: a snail and white pudding croquette with garlic coriander butter makes a delicious table d'hôte starter, for example, followed by choices between pan-fried veal, with tarragon scented sweetbread and a mushroom cream; seared red snapper with avocado and crab purée; or grilled cornfed chicken, with creamed leek & smoked bacon and a red onion jam. One is spoiled for choice with the à la carte menu which includes creatively cooked beef fillet, canon of lamb, monkfish and turbot, all around €35, while lobster is very much in the luxury bracket at €40. The cooking is accomplished, with everything having a lovely fine, fresh appearance and taste - and the Table d'Hôte is excellent value, especially when compared to nearby restaurants of a similar standard. Service is excellent and friendly under the supervision of the new French restaurant manager and sommelier, from Burgundy and Bordeaux respectively. A Tasting Menu is also offered at €85, or €128 including wine. **Seats 50**; D daily, 7-9.30pm; set 3 course D, €49; gourmet menu €85; also a la carte. Vegetarian menu. Waterfront Bistro: Seats 80; food served 12.30-9pm. Bar food also available, 12.30-9pm. MasterCard, Visa, Laser. **Directions:** In Mulranny village on the N59.

NEWPORT

This pleasant town on the Brown Oak River is well-known as an angling centre, and close to the attractive and unspoilt coastline of Clew Bay famous for its 365 islands. Anglers have a wide choice of lake and river fishing, (on Loughs Feegh and Furnace, the Newport River and Lough Beltra) and boats for deep sea fishing can be chartered from Clew Bay. Walkers will find varied trails over mountains and hills, including cultural/historical tours such as the Old Bangor Trail Walk (48km), which is regarded as one of the finest walks in the country. Golfers have the Westport championship 18-hole golf course (098 28262), or Clew Bay 9-hole course (098 41730) to choose from. Nearby Blue Flag beaches offer water sports including surfing and water skiing. And, in the town, foodies should head for the famous butchers shop, Kelly's (098 41149) on the main street, and stock up with some of their renowned puddings and sausages.

Newport
COUNTRY HOUSE•RESTAURANT

Newport House

Newport Co Mayo **Tel: 098 41222**
info@newporthouse.ie www.newporthouse.ie

For two hundred years, this distinctive creeper-clad Georgian House overlooking the river and quay, was the home of the O'Donnells, once the Earls of Tir Connell. Today it symbolises all that is best about the Irish country house, and has been especially close to the hearts of fishing people for many years. But, in the caring hands of the current owners, Kieran and Thelma Thompson, and their outstanding staff, the warm hospitality of this wonderful house is accessible to all its guests, not least in shared enjoyment of the club-fender cosiness of the little back bar. And, predating the current fashion by several centuries, pure spring water has always been piped into the house for drinking and ice-making. The house has a beautiful central hall, sweeping staircase and gracious drawing room, while bedrooms, like the rest of the house, are furnished in style with antiques and fine paintings. The day's catch is weighed and displayed in the hall - and the fisherman's bar provides the perfect venue for a reconstruction of the day's sport. *Newport was our Country House of the Year in 1999, and also selected for our annual Wine Award in 2004. Fishing, garden, walking, snooker. Riding, walking, diving and hang gliding nearby. **Rooms 18** (2 with private (non connecting) bathrooms, 2 with bath & separate shower, 4 ground floor, 2 disabled). Children welcome (under 2s free in parents' room; cots available, baby sitting arranged). Limited wheelchair access. Pets allowed in some areas. B&B €164pps, ss €26, no S.C. Closed mid Oct-mid Mar. **Restaurant:** High-ceilinged and elegant, this lovely dining room makes the perfect backdrop for "cooking which reflects the hospitable nature of the house" in fine meals made with home-produced and local foods. Home-smoked salmon is a speciality and some of the fruit, vegetables and herbs come from a walled kitchen garden that has been worked since 1720, and was established before the house was built, so that fresh produce would be on stream for the owners when they moved in. John Gavin has been head chef since 1983 and his 5-course menus feature fresh fish, of course - freshwater fish caught on local lakes and rivers, and also several varieties of fish delivered daily from nearby Achill Island; smoked salmon is prepared to a secret recipe, but carnivores will be equally delighted by charcoal-grilled local beef or roast spring lamb, and perhaps game in season. To finish, there are Irish farmhouse cheeses with fresh fruit, and classic desserts, often using fruit from the garden. Service, under the direction of restaurant manager Catherine Flynn and sommelier Cathal Murray, is warm, discreet and efficient. And then there is Kieran's renowned wine list that, for many, adds an extra magic to a meal at Newport. It includes classic French wines about 150 clarets from 1961-1996 vintages, a great collection of white and red burgundies, excellent Rhônes and a good New World collection too. The foundations of this cellar go back many decades to a time when Kieran was himself a guest at Newport; great wines are a passion for him and, while acknowledging that they are irreplaceable, he offers them to guests at far less than their current retail value. Great lists of this scale and quality are almost a thing of the past, so it is a matter of celebration that such a collection should belong to a generous spirit like Kieran, who takes pleasure in allowing others to share his passion. **Seats 38.** L daily, 12-2pm; D daily, 7-9. Set 6 course D €65; house wine from €24. Toilets wheelchair accessible. Non-residents welcome by reservation. House closed 10 Oct-18 Mar. Amex, MasterCard, Visa, Laser. **Directions:** In village of Newport.

WESTPORT

A great example of good town planning - Westport was designed by the Georgian architect James Wyatt - this charming town has high standards of accommodation and restaurants, making it a very agreeable base. It is a delightful place to spend some time: The Mall, with its lime trees flanking the Carrowbeg River, is especially pleasing to the eye, and it is pleasant town to browse; an interesting spot that's a little off the beaten track is **The Linenmill** (098 50546), an interiors shop near **Hotel Westport** (see entry) with daytime café and dinner on Fri & Sat in summer. There are two Farmers' Markets, off James Street car park (Thursdays, 8.30am-1pm) and, from March, on The Mall (Saturdays, 9am-5pm). Near the harbour, Westport House (098 27766) is open to the public in summer and well worth a visit, and nearby **Westport Woods Hotel** (098 25811; www.westportwoodshotel.com), conveniently situated between the town and the quay, has a well-earned reputation for friendly and helpful staff, and its environmental policies. Along the harbour front there are shops to browse and several pubs and cafes, including **The Creel** (098 26174) a relaxed restaurant that is a good choice for a daytime bite. Also in the harbour area, the well know **Quay Cottage Restaurant** (098 26412) changed ownership in 2008, check www.ireland-guide.com for updates. A visit to Clare Island makes an interesting day out and there are regular ferries (Clare Island Ferries, 098 28288). The famous pilgrimage mountain of Croagh Patrick, known locally as "the Reek" lies some 10km west of the town near the villages of Murrisk and Lecanvey. The mountain presents a striking backdrop to the town and the church on the summit can just be made out with the naked eye from Westport. The town is well-known as a sea fishing centre and its annual festival attracts many visitors. Other activities include swimming and watersports at the many nearby beaches and, for golfers, there is a championship golf course (Westport Golf Club, 098 28262) and 5km north of Westport there is a sailing centre at Glenans, Rosmoney (01 661 1481). The Clew Bay Heritage Centre (The Quays, 098 26852) depicts the maritime history of the area and local history and traditions; it also provides a genealogical service. Westport is an ideal base for touring Connemara, Sligo, Galway and Donegal, all of which are within easy driving distance. If you are driving out to Louisburgh, consider a meal at **Hudson's** (098 23747) on Longstreet, (on the left just before the Diamond in the centre of the town); run by Richard and Tricia Hudson, who will be remembered from their long-running restaurant in Navan, Co Meath, it is sure to be worth a visit.

WWW.IRELAND-GUIDE.COM FOR ALL THE BEST PLACES TO EAT, DRINK & STAY

Westport
HOTEL•RESTAURANT

Ardmore Country House Hotel
The Quay Westport Co Mayo **Tel: 098 25994**
ardmorehotel@eircom.net www.ardmorecountryhouse.com

Pat and Noreen Hoban's small family-run hotel is quietly located in immaculately maintained gardens near Westport harbour, with views over Clew Bay, and it offers warm hospitality, very comfortable accommodation and good food. Spacious, individually-decorated guest rooms are all furnished to a very high standard; the style is luxurious and the range of facilities - which includes an iron and ironing board and, in many rooms, a separate bath and shower - is impressive. Guests are given the choice of seaview or back of house rooms, allowing for a less expensive option; this also applies to short breaks offered. An outstandingly good breakfast includes (amongst other equally tempting items) a choice of freshly squeezed juices in generous glasses, fresh fruit (correctly prepared according to type, eg skinned grapefruit segments), delicious cafetière coffee, a perfectly-cooked, simple version of 'the full Irish', and a superb fish plate. Great details too - freshly-baked breads, home-made preserves and prompt service. [Ardmore was selected for our Best Hotel Breakfast Award in 2005.] Not suitable for children. No pets. Free broadband wi/fi. Garden, walking. **Rooms 13** (all superior; 2 ground floor; all no smoking). Room service (limited hours); turndown service. B&B €95 pps, ss €35. Closed Jan & Feb. **Restaurant:** Pat and Noreen have been overseeing the restaurant since the late '70s and must be the longest serving management team in fine-dining in the West of Ireland. The enduring popularity of Ardmore House is testament to the classical style of food cooked by Pat. The restaurant - a well-appointed room with some useful corners for tête-à-têtes and a sea view over the front gardens - is the heart of this house. Pat's menus make good reading over an aperitif in the comfortable bar, where nightly specials are listed and explained. Around nine starters are offered, including Kelly's black pudding with apple, pan-fried prawns, home-made paté or chowder; there is plenty of choice, including local lamb and duck, but locally-caught fish and shellfish feature strongly with scallops, lobster, black sole and monkfish among others to the fore - and Pat does his fine ingredients proud. Warm and friendly service together with accomplished cooking make dining here a very pleasant experience. The wine list features wines from around the world, a balance of old and new world and includes house wines at €24.50 and 6 half bottles in addition to the main list. **Seats 50**; not suitable for children under 12. D 7-9 (daily in summer, Tue-Sat low season); set 3 course D €55; also a la carte. House wine €22.50. Closed Sun (& Mon in low season), all Jan & Feb. Amex, MasterCard, Visa, Laser. **Directions:** 1.5 km from Westport town centre, on the coast road.

Westport
HOTEL•RESTAURANT

Carlton Atlantic Coast Hotel
The Quay Westport Co Mayo **Tel: 098 29000**
info@atlanticcoasthotel.com www.atlanticcoasthotel.com

Behind the traditional stone façade of an old mill on Westport harbour, this bright modern hotel has spacious public areas combining traditional and contemporary themes and materials, and creating a smart youthful tone that is continued through to good-sized bedrooms, with good facilities and stylish Italian bathrooms. Although it may seem like an impersonal city hotel in some ways, staff (including those in the excellent leisure centre, and spa) are exceptionally friendly and efficient. Conferences/banqueting (160/140). Business centre; secretarial services; video-conferencing. Children welcome (under 4s free in parents' room, cots available without charge, baby sitting arranged). Leisure centre, swimming pool; spa; fishing; discount at local golf club. Golf breaks; details on application. **Rooms 85** (1 suite, 2 junior suites, 10 superior, 55 no smoking, 3 for disabled). Lift. 24 hr room service. B&B about €135pps, ss about €25; SC incl. Closed 22-27 Dec. **Blue Wave Restaurant:** The restaurant is situated right up at the top of the building, which is a good idea, although the view is somewhat restricted by sloping roof windows and the room can be very warm in summer. But the hotel has always taken pride in its food and interesting, well-balanced contemporary menus offer a good choice of imaginative dishes, with a natural leaning towards seafood. Cooking is reliable and, as elsewhere in the hotel, friendly and helpful service adds to the occasion. Breakfast is also served in the Blue Wave Restaurant - and a very good start to the day it is. **Seats 90**; children welcome; reservations required; air conditioning. Lift. Toilets wheelchair accessible. D daily, 6.30-9.15. Set D about €36. House wine about €17.50. SC discretionary. Informal bar menu also offered, 12.30-9 daily. Amex, MasterCard, Visa, Laser. **Directions:** Located at Westport harbour, 1 mile from town centre on main Louisburgh and coast road.

Westport
RESTAURANT•CHARACTER PUB

Cronins Sheebeen

Rosbeg Westport Co Mayo **Tel: 098 26528**
info@croninssheebeen.com www.croninssheebeen.com

Just outside Westport, west of the harbour, this old-world thatched pub and restaurant overlooking Clew Bay enjoys an almost-waterside location just across from the foreshore on the Louisburgh road. Now run by the Cronin family, (well-known former owners of The Towers nearby on the harbour), it is one of Westport's busiest and most hospitable establishments. It's a relaxed and characterful place, with a number of rooms and hideaway corners in the downstairs bar, and a first floor restaurant with sloping ceiling, whitewashed walls, timber floors and oilcloth-covered tables giving a traditional and homely feel. The restaurant opens at weekends and other busy times and, whether eating here or in the bar, an all-day à la carte menu offers an extensive range of dishes, with lunch specials from 12.30pm and the evening specials from 5.30pm, when the emphasis is on seafood. Typically you may expect to find starters like fresh crab timbale and a very good chowder, while main courses include good fish dishes (pan-fried fillet of hake was the star of the show on a recent visit), but also a balanced mix of meat and poultry - which may include an outstanding wild venison pie, in season. Finish with home-made desserts (vanilla pannacotta with baked plums, perhaps) or a cheeseboard with local Carrowholly cheeses, which are made just along the road, and home-made chutney. Wines from a small list are served by the bottle and quarter bottle. Overall, The Sheebeen makes for a most enjoyable experience, with beautiful sea and mountain views and with the added interest of the red and green navigation lights of Clew Bay flashing in the distance as night draws in. Restaurant **Seats about 45**; children welcome (high chair, childrens menu); food served daily 12-9.30 high season (4-9.30 Nov-Mar); function room (50) at the rear of the building; a la carte; starters €5-10, approx, mains about €12.50 - €32; house wine €16. MasterCard, Visa, Laser.
Directions: Far side of Westport harbour.

Westport
HOTEL•RESTAURANT
V

Hotel Westport

Newport Rd Westport Co Mayo **Tel: 098 25122**
reservations@hotelwestport.ie www.hotelwestport.ie

Just a short stroll from Westport town centre, this large modern hotel offers excellent facilities for both leisure and business guests, numerous short breaks are offered and the conference and business centre provide a fine venue for corporate events. Constant refurbishment and upgrading is an ongoing feature of this well-managed hotel and, although all bedrooms are well-appointed and have all the usual amenities, 48 Premier rooms and bathrooms were enlarged and refurbished to a high standard in 2008, and 25 rooms were given additional balconies. The hotel's extensive leisure facilities include the white flag standard Ocean Spirit Spa, and there is also a year-round Cub's Corner for children (0-3). The whole hotel is unusually wheelchair-friendly, and staff are invariably helpful and friendly which, together with the quiet but almost-central location and outstanding facilities, make this a very pleasant place to stay. Conference/banqueting (500/250); free broadband wi/fi; laptop-sized safes in bedrooms. **Rooms 129** (6 suites, 48 premier, 74 family, 8 for disabled, 104 no smoking, 42 ground floor); children welcome (under 3s free in parents' room; cots available without charge, baby sitting arranged; children's playground, playroom & kids club). Lift. 24-hr room service. B&B €140 pps, ss €20. Leisure centre (swimming pool, fitness room, jacuzzi, sauna, steam room); spa, treatment rooms, massage, hairdressing, beauty salon. Garden. **Islands Restaurant:** A typical hotel dining room in many ways, this is where both breakfast and dinner are served. A sensible policy of seating people towards one end of the room and trying to seat couples facing the same way makes for a good atmosphere at quieter times, and - as elsewhere in the hotel - charming service from the mainly non-Irish staff is invariably friendly and caring. Guests are met promptly at the door and seated at tables simply set up with white linen cloths and napkins; a jug of water and basket of breads quickly follows, along with the winelist and upbeat traditional menus which are strong for a hotel, and may include organic salmon (from nearby Clare Island), and treats such as pheasant when in season, along with favourites like char-grilled Angus rib eye steaks and at least one imaginative vegetarian option. In the Guide's recent experience, predictable desserts may be the weak point in a meal here, but the offering overall is well above average hotel standard, and with enough daily changes to ensure that you look forward to your meal each evening on a short break. Breakfast is cooked to order off-season and there is a decent range of stewed fruits on offer, also a fish of the day. **Seats 140**; children welcome (high chair, childrens menu, baby changing facilities); D daily, 6-9.30pm; L Sun only 1-2.30pm; set Sun L €26; set D €41. House wine from €23. Bar food also served daily, 12-9.30pm. SC discretionary. Open all year. Amex, Diners, MasterCard, Visa, Laser.
Directions: From Castlebar Street, turn right onto north mall (do not go over the hump back bridge), then turn onto Newport Road, 1st left and at the end of the road.

Westport

HOTEL•RESTAURANT

Knockranny House Hotel & Spa

Knockranny Westport Co Mayo **Tel: 098 28600**

info@khh.ie   www.khh.ie

Set in landscaped grounds on an elevated site overlooking the town, this privately-owned Victorian-style hotel opened in 1997. A welcoming open fire and friendly staff at reception create an agreeably warm atmosphere: the foyer sets the tone for a hotel which has been built on a generous scale and is full of contrasts, with spacious public areas balanced by smaller ones - notably the library and drawing room - where guests can relax in more homely surroundings. Bedrooms are also large – a number of suites have four poster beds and sunken seating areas with views - and most are very comfortable (some with jacuzzi baths). 'Spa Salveo' health spa has nine treatment rooms, swimming pool, gym, and hair salon and, recent development has included a new conference and meeting area. Conferences/Banqueting (600/350); business centre; free broadband wi/fi; laptop-sized safes in bedrooms. Destination Spa. Fitness room, jacuzzi, sauna, steam room, beauty salon. Equestrian and fishing nearby. Children welcome (under 3s free in parents' room, cots available free of charge, baby sitting arranged). **Rooms 97** (9 suites, 41 grand deluxe, 4 junior suites, 3 shower only, all no smoking, 3 family, 4 for disabled.) Lift. 24 hr room service. B&B €125 pps, ss €50. Closed 22-27 Dec. **La Fougère:** Contemporary Irish cooking is offered in the hotel dining room, La Fougère ("the fern"), which is at the front of the hotel, with fine views across the town to Clew Bay and Croagh Patrick. Head chef David O'Donnell's menus are wide-ranging, in a classic/modern style; French rabbit may top the menu but there is pride in local produce, including the renowned organic Clare Island salmon, Achill scallops and Mayo lamb - specialities include an accomplished dish of roast loin of Ballinrobe lamb with cranberry & herb stuffing on aubergine caviar with baby vegetables, potato confit & rosemary jus. Even in a town with plenty of good restaurants to choose from, this can be a pleasant place for an outing – although recent experience suggests that it might be advisable to ensure that a private visit does not coincide with a wedding. An informative user-friendly wine list includes a good choice of mid-range wines, with plenty available by the glass, and an innovative feature of the restaurant is a walk-through wine cellar. **Seats 150**; children welcome (high chair, childrens menu, baby changing facilities); air conditioning; pianist. D 6.30-9.30. L 1-2.30. Set D €54; set Sun L €29.50. House wines from €22. SC discretionary. Hotel closed 22-27 Dec. Amex, MasterCard, Visa, Laser. **Directions:** Take N5/N60 from Castlebar. Hotel is on the left just before entering Westport.

Westport

RESTAURANT

The Lemon Peel

The Octagon Westport Co Mayo **Tel: 098 26929**

info@lemonpeel.ie   www.lemonpeel.ie

Proprietor-chef Robbie McMenamin returned to his town-centre restaurant on the Octagon in 2008, having spent a season in the Harbour area on the outskirts of Westport. His relocation back to town was welcomed and this small, simply furnished restaurant is as busy and popular as ever. The welcome from the friendly staff is warm, and Robbie makes a point of meeting diners and recommending a particular dish or special of the night. The emphasis as always is on the food, well-sourced ingredients including local seafood, Kelly's of Newport black pudding, McCormack's lamb steaks; all combine to make an interesting and moderately priced menu of seven starters, eight main courses and a list of five nightly specials, mostly fish. Other good dishes include a wild mushroom tartlet starter, turbot stuffed with crabmeat in a white wine cream sauce, or a moist stuffed pork fillet wrapped in Parma ham, which was enjoyed on a recent visit. Bread and butter pudding is a favourite among the homemade desserts or you might round off an excellent meal with fruit crumble and ice cream, with freshly brewed tea selected from a list of fourteen choices. A short well-balanced wine list with many around the €22 mark includes eight house wines served by the glass. The early dinner menu (€27, 6-7pm) is good value and offers a good choice including vegetarian options. **Seats 60**. D daily in summer 5.30/6-9/9.30.30pm. Early menu about €25 (5-7pm), also à la carte. House wines about €20; SC discretionary. Closed Sun & Mon off season (Telephone off-season to check opening times.) Amex, MasterCard, Visa, Laser. **Directions:** Centre of Wesport on the Octagon.

Westport
CHARACTER PUB

Matt Molloy's Bar
Bridge Street Westport Co Mayo
Tel: 098 26655

If you had to pick one pub in this pretty town, this soothingly dark atmospheric one would do very nicely - not least because it is owned by Matt Molloy of The Chieftains, a man who clearly has respect for the real pub: no TV (and no children after 9 pm). Musical memorabilia add to the interest, but there's also the real thing as traditional music is a major feature in the back room - or out at the back in fine weather. Matt is often away on tour, but he's a real local when he's back, and takes great pride in this smashing town. It's worth noting that normal pub hours don't apply, this is an afternoon into evening place, not somewhere for morning coffee. Closed 25 Dec & Good Fri. **Directions:** Town centre.

Westport
CAFÉ•RESTAURANT

McCormack's at The Andrew Stone Gallery
Bridge Street Westport Co Mayo
Tel: 098 25619

Go under the archway beside Kate McCormack's sixth generation butcher's shop and up the stairs, where you will find an art gallery on your right and, on your left, this small, unpretentious restaurant with an open counter displaying an array of good things, including home-baked cakes, quiches and patés - the product of generations of family recipes and particularly of Annette McCormack's table. Here, her two daughters, Katrina and Mary Claire, carry on the tradition - and the welcome. Treats especially worth trying include seafood chowder, leek and bacon quiche and, in season, fresh crab on home-made baps. Locally reared meats go into specialities like bacon and cabbage, and a casserole of spring lamb. And don't leave without one of the gloriously home-made desserts. Many of the deli dishes from the shop are on the menu, as well as farmhouse cheeses including the local Carrowholly cheese. Works by local artists hang in the restaurant and adjacent rooms: well worth a visit. **Seats 34**; children welcome. Open all day 10.15am-4.45pm, Thu-Sat and Mon. Closed Sun & Wed. MasterCard, Visa. **Directions:** Westport town centre - on the main street (the one with the clock tower at the top).

Westport
RESTAURANT
Ⓝ

Sol Rio Restaurant
Bridge Street Westport Co Mayo **Tel: 098 28944**
solrio@iol.ie www.solriowestport.com

Euro-Toques chef Jose Barroso from Portugal and his Westport-born wife Sinead Lambert run this lively restaurant on two floors over the Connemara Shop on Bridge Street. The tiled floor, light coloured decor and simple table settings of the first floor room contrast to the style upstairs, which has more of a party atmosphere and is in great demand over the weekends. The welcome is warm and friendly from the very helpful local staff. Menus offer a very wide range of popular dishes (starters and pasta dishes, pizzas and a selection of fish, poultry and meat dishes, with at least ten choices in each section) and is well-priced, with generous main courses ranging from €18 to €27. Daily specials could include mussels mariniere with excellent brown bread, local scallops and crab claws in a good beurre blanc, and roast duckling with an orange and cranberry sauce. Classic desserts include lemon torte, sticky toffee pudding and a moist, well-flavoured chocolate gateau. Lunch is a lighter affair with soups, chowder, wraps, panini and baguettes, and some pasta dishes for a continental flavour; main courses under €10. A balanced choice of wines from the old and new worlds includes 4 house wines at about €20, also served by the glass, and some half bottles. Try to get a window table and watch the comings and goings of night time Bridge Street. **Seats 75** (private room, 40); reservations recommended; children welcome (high chair, childrens menu); air conditioning. L&D Wed-Mon, 12-3pm & 6-10pm; a la carte L&D; house wine from €17.95. Closed Tue, 3 weeks middle Jan, 1st week Feb. MasterCard, Visa, Laser. **Directions:** In the heart of Westport opposite Matt Molloy's pub.

Westport
HOTEL•RESTAURANT

Westport Plaza Hotel
Castlebar Street Westport Co Mayo **Tel: 098 51166**
info@westportplazahotel.ie www.westportplazahotel.ie

Adjoining its larger sister property the Castlecourt Hotel, in the centre of Westport, this is a smart, contemporary hotel, with spacious stylishly-furnished public areas, including a comfortable bar, and impressive accommodation. Some rooms have balconies overlooking a rooftop garden and, with king-size beds, marbled bathrooms with jacuzzi, air conditioning, plasma screen TV with interactive services, minibar and safe all included as standard, this is a desirable place to stay. Guests have use of the C Club leisure facilities next door, in addition to the new 'Spa Sula' with 12 treatment rooms, which opened in 2008. Conferences/Banqueting (120/80); business centre; free broadband wi/fi.

Leisure centre (pool, fitness room, jacuzzi, steam room); beauty salon, hair dressing. Spa to open winter 07. Equestrian, golf, fishing and garden visits nearby. Children welcome (under 3s free in parents' room, cots available free of charge, baby sitting arranged, crèche, playroom). **Rooms 88** (1 suite, 2 junior suites, 5 shower only, 9 family, 5 for disabled); Lift; All day room service. B&B €125pps, ss €35. Open all year. **Restaurant Merlot:** Situated just inside the main entrance and overlooking the busy street, this attractive restaurant has three distinct areas decorated in contrasting styles; all are well-appointed with white linen, smart table settings and comfortable chairs, and the welcome is warm and efficient. Menus offer a good variety of modern international dishes, with some local ingredients named - organic Clare Island salmon, for example, and Newport lamb; pan-seared Clew Bay scallops with black pudding, cèpes and Madeira jus is a speciality. Food is well presented and enjoyable, although it is not a place to linger as this busy restaurant usually does two sittings each night. *An interesting and well-priced lunchtime menu is offered in the Plaza Bar. **Seats 120** (private room, 80); air conditioning; children welcome; reservations required; D daily, 6-9.30pm, set D €42.50; also à la carte; house wine from €22. Open all year. MasterCard, Visa, Laser. **Directions:** Approaching town from the N5, hotel is on the right hand side at first set of traffic lights.

Westport Area
RESTAURANT•PUB

The Tavern Bar & Restaurant

Murrisk Westport Co Mayo **Tel: 098 64060**
info@tavernmurrisk.com www.tavernmurrisk.com

Myles and Ruth O'Brien have been running this fine bar and restaurant just outside Westport, at the foot of Croagh Patrick, since 1999 and have built up an enviable reputation. The fine dining restaurant, Upstairs At The Tavern, offers several very attractive menus, including an early dinner, a mid-week special, and an à la carte; local seafood from Clew Bay is very much the speciality here, and menus also include named local and artisan foods such as air-dried Connemara lamb and meat from the renowned butchers McGeough's of Oughterard, Chris Smyth's organic leaves and Carrowholly cheeses. Bar menus are quite extensive, with a children's menu as well as a good choice of dishes for full meals, and a range of sandwiches. This is a fine well-run establishment, with caring hand-on owners, and standards are consistently good. Traditional Irish music on Wed. **Seats 75**; reservations required; toilets wheelchair accessible; children welcome (playground, playroom, high chair, childrens menu, baby changing facilities); beer garden; air conditioning; free broadband wi/fi. D served daily in summer, 6-10pm (D weekends only off-season, although bar food is served daily all year, 12-9.30pm), value D about €25 pp Mon-Fri, 6-7.30pm, also a la carte; house wine €17.50. Traditional Irish music on Wed. Restaurant closed during the week off-season. Establishment closed Good Fri, 25 Dec. Amex, MasterCard, Visa, Laser. **Directions:** At the foot of Croagh Patrick, 5 mins from Westport.

COUNTY MEATH

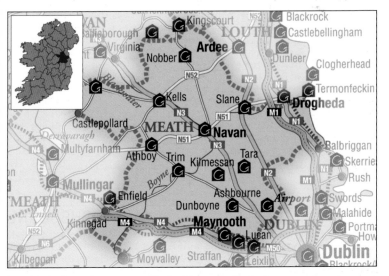

Royal Meath. Meath of the pastures. Meath of the people. Meath of many people.......Any recent Census has confirmed what had been expected. The population of Ireland may have increased by 8%, but Meath is one of the fastest-growing places of all, its increase clocking in at 22.1% and counting.

The numbers aren't huge in today's overcrowded and city-oriented world, perhaps, but nevertheless Meath is a county which finds itself living in interesting times. The proximity of Dublin - with the inevitable pressures of prosperity and population – can be challenging. But it also brings benefits. With an increasingly affluent and discerning population, Meath is able to support a wide variety of hospitable establishments, ranging from glossy restaurants of international quality to characterful pubs deep in the heart of the country.

And the inevitable changes – for instance, the need to find ways through the county for new major roads - are projects which you feel Meath can absorb. For this is a county which is comfortable and confident with itself, and rightly so. The evidence of a rich history is everywhere in Meath. But it's a history which sits gently on a county which is enjoying its own contemporary prosperity at a pace which belies the bustle of Dublin just down the road.

And anyone with an interest in the past will find paradise in Meath, for along the Boyne Valley the neolithic tumuli at Knowth, Newgrange and Dowth are awe-inspiring, Newgrange in particular having its remarkable central chamber which is reached by the rays of sun at dawn at the winter solstice.

Just 16 kilometres to the southwest is another place of fascination, the Hill of Tara. Royal Tara was for centuries the cultural and religious capital of pre-Christian Ireland. Its fortunes began to wane with the coming of Christianity, which gradually moved the religious focal point to Armagh, though Tara was a place of national significance until it was finally abandoned in 1022 AD.

Little now remains of the ancient structures, but it is a magical place, for the approach from the gently rising eastern flank gives little indication of the wonderful view of the central plain which the hill suddenly provides to the westward. It is truly inspiring, and many Irish people reckon the year is incomplete without a visit to Tara, where the view is to eternity and infinity, and the imagination takes flight.

Local Attractions and Information

Donore	Bru na Boinne Visitor Centre	041 988 0300
Dunboyne	Hamwood House & Gardens	01 825 5210
	Good Food Circle (Meath)	c/o 046 907 3426
Kells	Grove Gardens & Tropical Bird Sanctuary	046 923 4276
Laytown	Sonairte (National Ecology Centre)	041 982 7572
Navan	Tourism Information	046 907 3426
Navan	Navan Racecourse	046 902 1350
Newgrange	(inc Dowth & Knowth)	041 988 0300 / 982 4488
Oldcastle	Loughcrew Historic Gardens	049 854 1922
Oldcastle	Loughcrew Passage Tombs (3000BC)	049 854 2009
Ratoath	Fairyhouse Racecourse	01 825 6167
Summerhill	Larchill Arcadian Gardens	01 628 7354
Tara	Interpretive Centre	046 25903
Trim	Butterstream Garden	046 943 6017
Trim	Tourism Information	046 943 7111
Trim	Trim Castle (restored Norman stronghold)	046 943 8619

R # ASHBOURNE

Convenient to Dublin Airport and on the edge of countryside offering rural activities including horse riding and racing (Fairyhouse Racecourse, 01 825 6167), golf at Ashbourne Golf Club (01 835 2005) or the championship course at nearby Roganstown Golf & Country Club (Swords, 01 843 3118) as well as the historical sites of County Meath. There is a Farmers' Market each Saturday outside the council offices (10am-4pm). This fast-growing town is gradually acquiring much-needed amenities and the new Marriott Hotel (see entry) has been a welcome addition. Dining options in the town include the popular Chinese restaurant, **EatZen** (01 835 2110; www.eatzen.ie) in the town centre, a stylish modern restaurant that takes pride in presenting authentic Cantonese cuisine - with a twist.
WWW.IRELAND-GUIDE.COM FOR ALL THE BEST PLACES TO EAT, DRINK & STAY

Ashbourne

GUESTHOUSE

R

Broadmeadow Country House & Equestrian Centre

Bullstown Ashbourne Co Meath **Tel: 01 835 2823**
info@irishcountryhouse.com www.irishcountryhouse.com

The Duff family's country guesthouse is also home to a fine equestrian centre; an interest in horses is certainly an advantage here, but this well-located house also makes a good base for other activities in the area. Very much a family business, the house is set well back from the road and surrounded by landscaped gardens. The spacious bedrooms are all en-suite and furnished to hotel standards. Residential riding holidays are a speciality but, as there are 20 golf courses within easy reach, golfing breaks are almost equally popular and the location, close to Dublin Airport and a fairly short distance from the city centre, also makes this a convenient venue for meetings and seminars. A short all-day menu is available to residents (9am-9pm), with wine or beverages. Small conferences (20). **Rooms 8** (all en-suite, 1 executive with separate bath & shower, 5 with over-bath shower, 2 shower only, 3 family rooms; all no smoking); children welcome (under 5s free in parents' room, cot available without charge, baby sitting arranged). No pets. Garden, tennis, cycling, equestrian. Room service (all day). B&B €60 pps, ss €20. All day menu available 9am-9pm. No SC. *Short breaks offered (equestrian & golf). Closed 23 Dec-2 Jan. MasterCard, Visa, Laser. **Directions:** Off N2 at R125 towards Swords village.

Ashbourne

HOTEL

R

Marriott Ashbourne

The Rath Ashbourne Co Meath **Tel: 01 835 0800**
info@marriottashbourne.com www.marriottashbourne.com

A good choice for business travellers who need to be near Dublin city and the airport but prefer a less hectic location, this new hotel offers all the amenities and comfort required both on and off duty, with business facilities for meeting and events of all sizes, a high standard of accommodation and plenty to do after hours (including, believe it or not, karaoke in the Red Bar, where red-themed cocktails are a speciality and a bar menu is also available from noon daily). It is also providing much-needed facilities for the area and the Fitness & Leisure Club is open to local membership. Conferences/Banqueting

(300/350); business centre, laptop-sized safes in bedrooms, free broadband wi/fi; **Rooms 148** (4 suites, 4 junior suites, 8 executive, 49 family, 8 disabled); children welcome (under 12s free in parents room, cots available free of charge, baby sitting arranged). 24-hr room service, lift. Room rate from about €125. Fitness & Leisure Club (swimming pool, sauna, steam room, jacuzzi, gym.); Spa & Beauty Salon (massage, treatments, hairdressing). Special offers/short breaks available. Golf nearby. Ample parking. Closed 24-26 Dec **Directions:** 23km north of Dublin on main Dublin-Derry road.

Athboy
RESTAURANT•GUESTHOUSE

R

Frankville House

Frankville House O'Growney St Athboy Co Meath
Tel: 046 943 0028

degnangeraghty@eircom.net   www.bluedoorguesthouse.ie

Degnan and Josephine Geraghty's charming restaurant and guesthouse is in a fine 18th cenury house on the edge of the pretty town of Athboy, offering the grandeur of a large period house and the charm and attention of a smaller guest house. Their son, Donncha, is a chef and returned to his home town recently to open a restaurant here. Like the rest of the house, the bright restaurant is filled with interesting and carefully-chosen antique furniture, making a pleasing setting for the great flavours of Donncha's 7-course Tasting Menu; all ingredients are sourced locally. There is a comfortable lounge for the use of guests, and of the five individually-decorated bedrooms four are en-suite - including a master bedroom - and one has a private bathroom. In addition, an unusual dormitory room downstairs has four bunk beds and access to a showering area with under-floor heating, a boon for families. The Geraghtys enjoy catering for private functions as well as their regular guests and there are small conference/meeting facilities for approximately, with a projector and an organ available if required. There is also a sauna and outside hot-tub. *At the time of going to press Frankville House was closed as a result of flood damage; please contact the Geraghtys directly for an update. Small conferences/banqueting (30/25). **Rooms 5** (en-suite); children welcome (under 8s free in parents' room, cot available free of charge). B&B €40-45pps, ss €10. **Restaurant seats 25** (private room, 10; outdoors, 8); D should be booked in advance. Visa, Laser. **Directions:** North-west of Trim; at end of main street - on edge of town, opposite the church. ◈

R

CLONEE

The population of the Clonee/Dunboyne area has grown a lot in recent years, and many residents enjoy eating at the original **EatZen Chinese Restaurant** (01 801 3738) at Unit 1, Clonee Village; see also under Ashbourne, where their second restaurant is thriving. Garden lovers will find plenty of interest within a short drive, including Larchill Arcadian Gardens (01 628 7354, Kilcock), and Primrose Hill (Lucan) which are both nearby.

WWW.IRELAND-GUIDE.COM FOR ALL THE BEST PLACES TO EAT, DRINK & STAY

Dunboyne
CAFÉ•RESTAURANT

N R

As You Like It

Summerhill Road Dunboyne Co Meath
Tel: 01 801 3866

In a modern building in the centre of Dunboyne, this family friendly café is simple and colourful in style - clean lines, unfussy table settings and a high-ceilinged ground floor area which overlooks a large patio give it a light, bright atmosphere. The food is simple and good, and the menu and the staff are full of information on its preparation and origin. Various specials are offered, but we would recommend keeping it simple with, for example, the wholesome beef casserole, served with good homemade bread (offered in generous quantities before food arrives). Dinner is served in more traditional surroundings upstairs on the small balcony on Thursday to Saturday evenings, where more elaborate menu is offered - and this is where some of the excellent classics on the wine list come into their own (a few wines are offered by the glass on the downstairs menu, and the full wine list is also available during the day on request). The service is unfussy and family-friendly, and very fair prices make this a firm favourite with locals. **Seats 60** (private balcony area 22); children welcome. Cafe open Mon-Sat, 9.30-5.30pm. Restaurant D Thu-Sat, 6.30-9/9.30pm. House wine about €19. Closed Sun. Amex, MasterCard, Visa, Laser. **Directions:** Dunboyne village, through lights, 2nd building on left.

Dunboyne
HOTEL

R

Dunboyne Castle Hotel & Spa

Dunboyne Co Meath **Tel: 01 801 3500**
info@dunboynecastlehotel.com   www.dunboynecastlehotel.com

Set in 21 acres of woodland and gardens on the Meath-Dublin border, this 18th century mansion has been stylishly developed with the original building, a large 3-storey over-basement country house, very much the dominant feature in the overall design; the fine interior has been carefully restored and the two main reception rooms are impressive in scale and have many original features. However, most of the accommodation is in the new development, where spacious, high-ceilinged rooms reflect the proportions of the old house and are luxuriously furnished. This is an extensive development and includes a choice of restaurants, bars, conference and meeting facilities, a dedicated exhibition complex and spa. It is a very popular wedding venue. Conferences/Banqueting (400/300), business centre, video conferencing, free broadband wi/fi. **Rooms 145** (2 suites, 2 junior suites, 8 executive, 6 shower only, 106 no smoking, 39 ground floor, 8 for disabled); children welcome (under 12s free in parents' room, cot available at no charge, baby sitting arranged); 24-hr room service, Lift; B&B from €85 pps, ss €60. Destination Spa, fitness room; Equestrian and golf nearby. Open all year. Amex, MasterCard, Visa, Laser. Heli-pad. **Directions:** N3 into Dunboyne village, left at Slevin's pub, few hundred metres down the road on the left. ◇

R R R   ENFIELD

This small town to the west of Dublin is situated on the Royal Canal and was believed to have been on the main road to Tara, seat of the High Kings of Ireland. Since then, its history has been continuously interwined with roads, rail and the canal as transport requirements have changed over the years. Today, the canal is an attractive feature and, despite its close proximity to the motorway (which has relieved traffic in the town itself), the harbour area has been pleasantly developed as a public park. Nearby at Johnstownbridge, the O'Neill family's 30-room **Hamlet Court Hotel** (046 954 1200; www.thehamlet.ie) has earned a reputation for hands-on management and caring service, and it is especially popular for weddings. Garden lovers will find several properties of interest within 20km, including Ballindoolin House & Garden (Carbury, 046 973 2377), Williamstown Garden (Carbury, 046 955 2971) and Lodge Park Walled Gardens (Straffan, 01 628 8412). Golfers are spoilt for choice with several top championship courses nearby including The K Club (Straffan, 01 601 7200), Carton House (Maynooth, 0505 2000) and Palmerstown House PGA National (Johnstown, 045 906 901). **WWW.IRELAND-GUIDE.COM FOR ALL THE BEST PLACES TO EAT, DRINK & STAY**

Enfield
HOTEL
R R R

Marriott Johnstown House Hotel & Spa

Enfield Co Meath **Tel:** 046 954 0000
info@johnstownhouse.com   www.marriottjohnstownhouse.com

Although close to the motorway, this mainly modern hotel has a carefully restored mid-18th century house at its heart and something of its country house atmosphere lives on. The original house is only a small part of the hotel, but it is the focal point and an unusually fine feature is a drawing room with a ceiling by the Francini brothers, renowned for the beauty and skill of their decorative plasterwork. The hotel has a spa and leisure club and, in addition to rooms in the hotel, 'The Residences' offer additional 2-bedroom duplex accommodation (www.theresidences.ie). Johnstown House is very attractive for corporate events and business meetings, and has a dedicated outdoor events and corporate activity centre on site (Quest Corporate Events). It is also a pleasing and well-appointed hotel for private guests to stay, and is well-located west of Dublin, making it a good short break destination or a useful place to break a journey. Conferences/Banqueting (900/400); business centre; free broadband wi/fi; video conferencing. **Rooms 126** (7 suites, 4 junior suites, 20 family, 30 ground floor, 4 for disabled) ;children welcome (under 12s free in parents' room, cot available free of charge, baby sitting arranged, crèche, playroom); 24hr room service, lift. B&B about €100 pps, ss €45. Destination Spa; Leisure centre (fitness room, 'pool, jacuzzi, sauna, steam room); hair dressing; beauty salon. Equestrian and golf nearby. Amex, Diners, MasterCard, Visa, Laser. Heli-pad. **Directions:** Take M4 from Dublin - exit at Enfield. ◇

KELLS

Famously associated with the Book of Kells, this busy market town has much of historical interest to offer, including a Round Tower and High Crosses. The Kells Heritage Centre (046 924 7840, open all year) is located in the old Courthouse on the Navan Road and provides an interesting summary of Kells' ancient monastic history to visitors, who may also enjoy The Kells Heritage Trail, a walk of the town that takes in all the monastic sites. For those interested in rural and social history, Causey Farm (046 943 4135) gives presentations on activities such as ceili dancing, turf cutting and traditional bread baking, along with traditional meals and live music. Grove Gardens and tropical bird sanctuary (046 943 4276), an informal garden on 6 acres with exotic animals and fowl, walks, roses and clematis is well worth a visit and makes a great family outing. Golfers can enjoy a round at Headfort Golf Club (046 924 0146), which is one of Ireland's most scenic courses. The town includes some interesting craft shops and art studios, and visitors can buy the best of local farmhouse produce at the Farmers'

Market held every Saturday. If accommodation is needed in the area, **Headfort Arms Hotel** (0818 222800; www.headfortarms.ie) is the centre of local activities and has a spa.
WWW.IRELAND-GUIDE.COM FOR ALL THE BEST PLACES TO EAT, DRINK & STAY

Kells   # The Ground Floor Restaurant

RESTAURANT   Bective Square Kells Co Meath **Tel: 046 924 9688**

R   bookings@chuig.com

A bright and attractive contemporary restaurant in the centre of Kells, The Ground Floor is a sister of The Loft in Navan and The Side Door in Cavan (see entries), and has much in common with them: wacky paintings and a youthful buzzy atmosphere, plus interesting, colourful food at accessible prices. Popular dishes from around the world abound in starters like Greek feta cheese & sundried tomatoes and the House Combination, a selection of spicy wings, crispy skins, and lightly fried brie, with home-made dips, sauces & garlic bread. Equally cosmopolitan main courses range from Caesar salads, through sizzling fajitas and chicken New Orleans to a choice of pasta dishes and steaks. Vegetarian dishes are highlighted, and gluten-free options are given for some dishes - you can even get gluten free pizza on request. Interesting daily blackboard specials are often a good bet. Consistent cooking and exceptionally pleasant and helpful staff add to the relaxed ambience. The early dinner menu is particularly good value. **Seats 65**; children welcome (childrens menu); toilets wheelchair accessible; air conditioning. D Mon-Sat, 5.30-10.30 (to 11 Fri/Sat), Sun 4-9. Early D about €17.50 (Mon-Sat 5.30-7.30 & all day Sun); otherwise à la carte. House wine about €18. SC discretionary except 10% on parties of 4+. Closed 25-26 Dec. MasterCard, Visa, Laser. **Directions:** Centre of Kells on the Athboy/Mullingar Road, in Bective Square.

Kells   # Vanilla Pod Restaurant

RESTAURANT   Headfort Arms Hotel Kells Co Meath **Tel: 0818 222 800**

V R   info@headfortarms.ie www.headfortarms.ie

Although reached through an unappealing entrance just inside the foyer of the Headfort Arms Hotel and in common ownership, this attractive bistro-style restaurant is run as an independent entity. In contrast to the hotel, it is very modern, with lots of pale wood, recessed lighting and sleek informal table settings. Efficient staff show you straight to your table to choose from a well-structured contemporary menu, which offers quite a few dishes (including some vegetarian) which can be chosen as a starter or main course. Good quality, carefully-sourced ingredients are used, from named suppliers, many of them local. The cooking is excellent and the presentation delightful, without being at all fussy or over-decorated. Starters recently enjoyed included a delicious confit of duck with honeyed fig, rocket salad & orange essence, and a very different but well-received baked Glenboy organic goat's cheese, with a salad of Parma ham, red onion & corn salad. Similarly contrasting main courses might include a strong vegetarian choice – an impressive wild morel mushroom risotto with parmesan crisp, perhaps – and (as this is beef country) a really good steak, such as a perfectly-cooked fillet wrapped in Parma ham, served on a tomato bread crostini; with a topping of duck liver paté, this rather like beef Wellington without the pastry crust, and comes with a wild mushroom sauce. Desserts are home-made (the day's choices are on a blackboard) and quite homely; a popular choice which can be shared is chocolate fondue, with a plate of prepared seasonal fruits. There is an interest in wine - specials are offered from time to time, and there are sometimes wine evenings, perhaps matching a special menu (eg Spanish) from a particular food culture. The all-in price for these specials is particularly good value, as is the early bird menu. **Seats 80** (private room, 40); children welcome (childrens menu); air conditioning. D 5.30-10pm, L Sun only, 12.30-3. Early D €21.95 (5.30-7.30), set D €36; also à la carte; set Sun L €25.95. House wine €19.95. Closed 24-26 Dec. Amex, MasterCard, Visa, Laser. **Directions:** On main Dublin-Cavan road, left section of black &white building on right.

Kilmessan   # The Station House Hotel

HOTEL•RESTAURANT   Kilmessan Co Meath **Tel: 046 902 5239**

R   info@thestationhousehotel.com www.thestationhousehotel.com

The Slattery family's unique establishment is an old railway junction, which was closed in 1963, and all the various buildings were converted to a make an hotel of charm and character. It is an interesting and unusual place to visit, with lovely gardens, and makes a good base for business, or for exploring this fascinating county. It also makes a pretty wedding venue. **Rooms 20**. B&B from about €55pps. Open all year. **The Signal Restaurant:** The chintzy decor, piped Irish music and traditional fare haven't really dated and somehow it all works well, creating a relaxing place with a very warm feeling. The restaurant attracts diners from a wide area - their traditional Sunday lunch is especially renowned. The food is enjoyable in a no-nonsense way that is becoming all too rare, portions are generous and it is very family-friendly. Overall a really pleasant little place. **Seats 90**. (Private rooms; outdoor seating, 50); reservations advised; children welcome; toilets wheelchair accessible. L daily 12.30-3 (Sun to 5.30); D daily 7-10.30 (Sun to 9.30). Set D: Mon-Fri about €26; Sat about €50; Sun about €30. A la carte L & D also available, except Sat D. Bar Menu Mon-Sat, 11-6. House wine from about €18. Amex, Diners, MasterCard, Visa, Laser. **Directions:** From Dublin N3 to Dunshaughlin and follow signposts.

R R   # NAVAN

Situated on the banks of the River Boyne, Navan, is the main town and administrative capital of County Meath. The Blackwater River meets the River Boyne on the eastern side of the town at the ancient Poolbeg bridge and there are many attractive riverside walks. Famous for its fine furniture and carpets, it's a good shopping town and also hosts an open air market every Friday. There are plenty of places to drop into a break when shopping, and lovers of Indian food should enjoy Mahammad Kahlid's attractive, well-maintained and conveniently located **Shahi Tandoori** (Watergate Street; 046 902 8762), a welcoming traditional Indian restaurant offering good food and service at very fair prices. 10 minutes drive north of Navan, **Scanlons of Kilberry** (046 902 8330; www.scanlonspub.ie) is an old-world pub with a following for its traditional atmosphere and good food, especially steaks. Nearby gardens to visit include Grove Gardens (near Kells, 046 943 4276) which is an informal garden on 6 acres with exotic animals and fowl, walks, roses and clematis (especially good for a family day out) and Rockfield House (Drumconrath, 046 905 2135), a charming old walled garden with a stream and a collection of herbaceous plants. For sporting folk, there's Navan Racecourse (046 902 1350), and Headfort Golf Club (Kells, 046 928 2001) has championship golf over two 18-hole courses.

WWW.IRELAND-GUIDE.COM FOR ALL THE BEST PLACES TO EAT, DRINK & STAY

Navan   # The Loft Restaurant

RESTAURANT   26 Trimgate Street Navan Co Meath **Tel: 046 907 1755**

R R   bookings@chuig.com

Older sister to The Ground Floor in Kells, and the newer Side Door in Cavan (see entries), this thriving two-storey restaurant has much in common with them, notably strong modern decor (including some interesting original paintings by the Northern Ireland artist Terry Bradley), exceptionally pleasant, helpful staff and a lively global menu at reasonable prices that lays the emphasis on accessibility: this is a place for all ages and every (or no particular) occasion. The main menu is similar to The Ground Floor, also with daily blackboard specials. Downstairs the "Tapas Bar" serves a range of cold and hot tapas, with wine available by the glass and by the bottle. **Seats 90**; children welcome; air conditioning. D daily, 5.30-10.30 (Fri/Sat to 11). Early D about €16.50 (Mon-Sat 5.30-7.30, all Sun), otherwise à la carte. House wine about €17.95. 10% sc added to tables of 4+. Closed 25-26 Dec. MasterCard, Visa, Laser. **Directions:** Centre of Navan, corner of Trimgate Street and Railway Street.

Navan   # The Russell Restaurant

RESTAURANT   15-16 Ludlow Street Navan Co Meath

◐ ◉ N R R   **Tel: 046 903 1607**

On low-key Ludlow Street, just off Navan's Market Square, large windows, painted white frontage and a pair of smart topiary trees make an arresting statement at this new restaurant just across the road from Bermingham's lovely old bar. Inside lies The Russell, an ultra-glamorous restaurant that wouldn't look out of place in a chic boutique hotel. A glitzy bar fronts a generous reception area, which is curtained off from the large dining room. Here a palette of blacks, silvers, greys and dark woods lends an air of style and comfort. Curving banquettes, comfy bucket seats and well-spaced tables are illuminated by statement lampshades, and dressed in smart table linen and bud vases. The menu is intimidatingly long, yet - despite a seemingly disparate mix of crowd-pleasers - the food is consistently good. Starters of wild Irish smoked salmon or scallops might be offered alongside imaginative salads. Roast chicken and excellent steak are popular with locals, but there's plenty of lighter fare, including a good selection of seafood. Everything is made on the premises, including good breads, excellent pasta and impressive sorbets and ice cream. Stylish presentation suits the smart décor, and the pace of service is relaxed but informed. Unusually, most of the dishes can be ordered as tapas portions, and enjoyed in the main dining room, or taken at tables in the bar area. A thoughtful wine list offers good variety and there's a full spirits menu as well as beers on tap. **Seats 50**; D Tue-Sat 6-10pm (to 9pm Fri); Sun 5-9pm. MasterCard, Visa, Laser. **Directions:** Centre of town, off Market Square, parallel to N3. ◈

Navan
PUB

Ryan's Bar

22 Trimgate Street Navan Co Meath
Tel: 046 902 1154

This pleasant, well-run and very popular pub makes a good meeting place for a drink or at lunch-time, when contemporary light meals are offered: soups, hot panini bread, wraps (including a vegetarian option) and toasties (honey baked ham, perhaps, with a salad garnish). Apple pie and cream may be predictable but it's enjoyable nonetheless - and there's always a dessert among the daily specials. It's good value, the airy bar makes for a comfortable atmosphere and staff are friendly and efficient. Disc parking. Open from 11.30 am; L Mon-Sat. 12-4 (to 3pm Sat). Closed 25 Dec & Good Fri. MasterCard, Visa, Laser. **Directions:** Main Street Navan.

Navan Area
HOTEL•RESTAURANT

Bellinter House

Navan Co Meath **Tel: 046 903 0900**
info@bellinterhouse.com www.bellinterhouse.com

Not content with creating some of Dublin's most successful informal restaurants – Eden, The Market Bar and the Cafe-Bar-Deli chain among them – Jay Bourke turned his attention to hotels with his most lavish project to date. Bellinter House is an elegant Palladian gem that's been transformed into a chic Meath bolthole. Designed by Richard Castle (Carton, Russborough, Powerscourt, Leinster Houses) it's set on the banks of the River Boyne in 12 acres of parkland, less than an hour from Dublin and Dublin Airport. The interior has been restored with meticulous attention to the architectural integrity of the building, but with an original, contemporary twist. Public rooms include the fanciful Drawing Room tricked out with retro furnishings, worn floorboards, grand old fireplaces and huge windows commanding views of the rolling countryside. All-day dining is available there, including excellent afternoon tea, which is popular with the locals. The Games Room and Library are relaxing spaces packed with board games and books, while the small Bellinter Bar is perfect for 'pints and cocktails'; bar food available any time. A cosy Wine Bar in the basement, which is adjacent to the restaurant, offers an interesting, competitively priced wine-list. Outdoors, when the weather permits, the terraces and lawns are ideal for dining al fresco. Accommodation, in 34 individually styled rooms, is divided between the Main House (capacious and extravagant), East and West Wings (modest in size) and several restored outbuildings (charming and chic). Though all rooms feature luxurious Egyptian cotton sheets, goose down pillows, centrally controlled mood lighting, and Italian multi-media 40" plasma screens – and the complimentary cafetière coffee, selection of teas, bottle of milk and tea cakes is especially thoughtful - the eclectic mix of hand-made and old furniture doesn't always work in harmony. The bathrooms are spacious and beautiful but, while most have a full bath and/or power showers, some are shower only, so it's best to establish which you're being allocated when you book. The Voya certified organic seaweed toiletries are especially nice, and reflect the speciality seaweed baths on offer in the hotel's spa. The pool house is a glamorous contemporary add on, with a glass wall overlooking the countryside and a beautiful infinity pool. On the Guide's visit, the pool house needed a thorough spring-cleaning to match the pristine standards in the bedrooms. An outdoor hot tub beneath trees is an appealing facility, although the outdoor pool has never been in operation during the Guide's visits. The gardener does a good job outdoors but several pieces of sun-faded rubbish in the car park, and a broken glass on the driveway show more care should be taken with grounds maintenance. Fishing on adjoining Boyne; overlooks Royal Tara Golf Club grounds, spa, massage, indoor and outdoor 'pool, leisure centre, walking, cycling, fly-fishing, pool table. Small Conferences/Banqueting (50/70), secretarial services, free broadband wi/fi; children welcome (cots available, baby sitting arranged, crèche). **Rooms 34** (13 shower only, 1 family room, 10 ground floor); all day room service. B&B room rate €225-380. **Eden Restaurant:** Modelled on its iconic sister restaurant in Temple Bar, Eden is the most exciting thing to happen Meath's dining scene in recent years. The elegant restaurant in a vaulted basement with natural daylight has well-spaced tables, leather swivel chairs and an unusual mustard carpet with discrete graphics that evoke the nearby Hill of Tara. The menu reflects this modern decor, with quality fresh produce used imaginatively in contemporary combinations and an accessible, affordable wine list. Service is friendly and informed, ensuring both residents and non-residents have a relaxing experience. **Seats 90** (private rooms, 20, outdoors, 20); not suitable for children after 7pm; reservations required; food served all day, 11am-11pm in the drawing room; L Fri -Sun 12-3pm, D daily 6.30-10.30pm; set 2/3 course L Fri-Sun about €30/35; early 2/3 course D about €25/30, 5-7pm; also a la carte D; house wine €24. SC 12.5%. Restaurant closed 24-26 Dec. Amex, MasterCard, Visa, Laser. **Directions:** Off N3 near the Hill of Tara.

Navan Area | O'Brien's Good Food and Drink House
RESTAURANT•PUB | The Village Johnstown Navan Co Meath
R R | **Tel: 046 902 0555**

Located in a new development in the centre of Johnstown village, just five minutes' drive from Navan, this popular and fashionable gastro-pub is in the same ownership as Franzini O'Briens Restaurant in Trim, and worth a visit. Wood-panelling, red brick walls and candles on the tables combine to create a modern rustic feel, and the international-style menu has broad appeal, with starters like duck spring rolls, pan-fried black pudding and prawn won tons all under €10, and main dishes including pizzas, pastas, burgers and chicken dishes under €20, although fresh fish may rise a little above this level. There are tasty vegetarian choices too, including good salads, also appealing side dishes (eg stringy onions, spring onion mash and home-made fries) and a nice dessert menu - a light tangy ginger and honeycomb pudding, for example, with crème anglaise. Service is friendly and efficient, and a well-priced wine list offers a balanced range including a house champagne, two dessert wines and some decent wines by the glass. The weekday Early Bird dinner offers particularly good value. **Seats 110** (private room, 60); children welcome until 9pm; toilets wheelchair accessible. reservations not necessary; D Mon-Sat 5-10pm; Sun 1-9; Early D about €20, 5.30-7.30; also a la carte and vegetarian menu; SC 10%. Closed Good Fri, 25 Dec. Amex, Diners, MasterCard, Visa, Laser. **Directions:** 1km from Navan on Dublin road. ◇

Nobber | Turlough's Restaurant
RESTAURANT | Nobber Co Meath **Tel: 046 905 2244**
N | turloughs@iol.ie

Located in the centre of the sleepy village of Nobber in the rolling hills of north County Meath, this stylish restaurant is named after the legendary composer and harpist Turlough O'Carolan, who was born in Nobber in 1670. Just the sort of place every village would love to have, Turlough's is a great find for tourists as well as locals, as Nobber lies on a popular shortcut route from the North, and the long opening hours (including Sunday) make this a convenient stop. The welcome is genuine, and well-balanced menus are not overlong yet combine contemporary options with traditional Irish favourites, described simply and accurately. Dishes enjoyed on a recent visit include the house version of Caesar salad, and very tasty roast breast of guinea fowl with mash, buttered cabbage, mushroom & onion sauce. It's comfortable and relaxing and the food is well-sourced, carefully cooked and presented and served with attention, and a genuine concern that your visit will be an enjoyable one. **Seats 70** (private room, 40); children welcome (high chair), wheelchair accessible; L Sun only, 12.30-3pm; D Wed-Sat 5.30-9.30pm (to 10pm Sat), Sun 4-8pm. Early bird D Wed-Fri to 7.30pm. Closed Mon, Tue; 25/26 Dec, Good Fri. MasterCard, Visa, Laser. **Directions:** On the R162 (Navan to Kingscourt road); Turlough's is a natural stone building opposite the police station.

R | SLANE

This appealing village is well placed for visitors to the historic sites of the area and places ujseful to know about include **George's Patisserie**, a neat little deli-café in the centre of the village where chef/proprieter Georg Heise offers a delicious range of desserts and pastries, home-made breads, preserves and locally-grown organic fruit and veg - and also a small, interesting selection of wines including organic wines; always a good place for a snack (Tue-Sat), and a bigger café/restaurant **The Poet's Rest** (see below) opened next door in 2008. There are many historical sites in the area around Slane, notably the Brú na Báinne complex of Neolithic chamber tombs, which lies on the River Boyne 5km down river from the village. This includes Newgrange, a passage tomb built c. 3200 BC that is of special interest on the morning of the winter solstice. Garden lovers should consider a visit to Listoke Gardens (Drogheda, 041 983 2265), a 6-acre Edwardian garden with walled garden, herbaceous borders and woodland walks, or Beaulieu House, Gardens and Car Museum (Drogheda, 041 983 8557) a beautifully located three hundred year old walled garden with herbaceous borders, fruit and vegetables. Championship golf beckons at nearby Headfort Golf Club (Kells, 046 928 2001), County Louth Golf Club (Drogheda, 041 988 1530) and Seapoint Golf Club (Termonfeckin, 0982 2333).
WWW.IRELAND-GUIDE.COM FOR ALL THE BEST PLACES TO EAT, DRINK & STAY

The Millhouse

Slane
HOTEL

The Old Mill Slane Co Meath **Tel: 041 982 0723**
info@themillhouse.ie www.themillhouse.ie

Janey Quigley's unusual boutique hotel is scenically located right on the River Boyne and it is quite a place. The riverside setting is very beautiful and it's an interesting place. An ambitious renovation plan has begun on the big stone mill buildings beside the main house. Inside the hotel, dramatic contemporary décor contrasts with the old building and a series of public rooms draws you through the building as each area links enticingly to the next. The eleven very desirable bedrooms and their bathrooms are all individually designed, and a restaurant available for residents/events only at the time of going to press is expected to open to the public at a later stage. A very desirable venue for weddings and private parties, and for short breaks away from the city. Conferences/Banqueting (60/120, or 300 in marquee); free broadband wi/fi; **Rooms 11** (5 superior, 5 shower only, all no smoking); limited room service; B&B about €110pps, ss about €90; unsuitable for children. Jacuzzi, sauna, pool table, walking, massage. Visa, Laser. **Directions:** On main N2, on the bridge in Slane. ◈

The Poet's Rest

Slane
RESTAURANT

Chapel Street Slane Co Meath **Tel: 041 982 4493**
reservations@georgespatisserie.com www.georgespatisserie.com

In an attractive stone-fronted building in the village, George's Patisserie and Poet's Rest restaurant sit next to each other. Renowned for his baking and wedding cake creations, chef/owner Georg Heise's patisserie/café has a small amount of seating and offers a tempting daytime selection of freshly-baked breads, cakes, buns and speciality pastries alongside a range of tasty open sandwiches, homemade soups and a wide selection of tea and coffee, alongside a deli section selling fresh fruit and veg and an array of specialist food products, all Fairtrade or organic if possible. Next door, the adjoining Poet's Rest restaurant is in a slightly spartan dining room, with bare floor boards and tables and simple white or terracotta-washed walls; a free-standing stove adds a dash of warmth, however – and the focus is on the fine ingredients-led food that he is known for. Heise's menus are very well-balanced, offering plenty of light, fresh dishes and vegetarian options alongside heartier fare, with producers listed on the menu and an emphasis on organic ingredients and real flavour. A fresh-flavoured spicy crabmeat and avocado salad (€9.50) is perfectly complemented by a zingy citrus dressing, while a traditional Caesar salad (€8.50) is in a class of its own, with crunchy cos lettuce, fresh anchovies and homemade Parmesan-crusted croûtons setting it above the usual bland version. Main courses might include poached guinea fowl breast with herb tagliatelle (€19.50), roast poussin with herb crust and gratin potatoes (€18.50), grilled lamb cutlets with courgettes and cous cous (€22.50) - or, perhaps, a perfectly seasoned pan-fried sea bass with pickled lemon, green beans and new potatoes (€23.50); with a light crispy skin and succulent juicy flesh this is an excellent dish. And desserts, as you would expect, are a highlight: a slice of zesty lemon tart in buttery shortcrust pastry (€6.50) would finish any meal off perfectly. Knowledgable, discreet and friendly service adds to the pleasure of a meal here, and the wine list includes plenty available by the glass, and an interesting choice of organic wines. Open Tue-Sat, 12-3pm & 6-10pm; Sun 12-5pm; fully wheelchair accessible. Closed Mon. MasterCard, Visa, Laser. **Directions:** Heading north through the village, it's just past the crossroads, on the right. ◈

Rossnaree

Slane
HISTORIC HOUSE

Slane Co Meath **Tel: 041 982 0957**
rossnaree@eircom.net www.rossnaree.ie

Impressively perched on a promontory above the River Boyne, this handsome Victorian and Italianate house commands superb views across the fields to the famous megalithic passage tombs of Knowth, and, closest of all, the grass-topped Newgrange. The whole area is steeped in legend and folklore – and all 196 acres of the Rossnaree estate are part of that history. Not only does the property have significant links with one of the most important battles in Irish history, the Battle of the Boyne, but also with the monks of Mellifont Abbey, legendary Irish warrior Cuchullain, and the Salmon of Knowledge, caught and cooked here by Finn MacCumhail. The history doesn't stop outdoors either.

Inside this large family home, belonging to the Laws since 1925, you'll find a gorgeous interior tastefully styled with wonderful old portraits, family silver, crystal glass and antiques. Aisling and the late Robert Law set about refurbishing the house in 2000, preserving the family history and adding rare art and textile collections from their travels in Africa and, since Robert's death in 2004, Aisling has continued to welcome guests to this very special house. Each of the four bedrooms is individually themed, from the flamboyantly floral William Morris room, to the dreamy Bird Room, hand painted with Chinese-style birds and flowers by her nephew, artist Samuel Horler. Aisling is also an artist of some repute and enjoys an impressive lineage – her great grandmother was the revolutionary figure, Maud Gonne, her grandfather was the prolific writer Francis Stuart, and her parents were both celebrated sculptors. A converted loft studio on the estate is used for art courses throughout the year, and attracts guest teachers. First impressions of Rossnaree don't do it justice – the entrance is on a dangerous bend, with rusting gates, and pot-holed driveway; but then the encroaching trees part to reveal a real beauty of a house. A friendly donkey grazes on the lawn, country flowers brush against the windows, and the views of the countryside are breathtaking. Guests can arrange to fish the river, or simply borrow wellington boots to stroll along its banks, perhaps covered in blackberries or revealing a fishing heron. Breakfast is a grand affair, served in the elegant dining room in front of a crackling log fire. Fresh fruits, excellent brown bread, homemade muesli and conserves are followed by a short selection of cooked items. Dinner can be arranged a day in advance, provided there are 4 or more guests. (Slane is less than 10 minutes away, should you wish to dine out.) With an honesty bar, stacks of interesting books and magazines, and views across the valley to Newgrange, the drawing room is a lovely place to relax. The silence and sense of history here make Rossnaree an enchanting bolthole, ideal for a quick escape from Dublin - and this immaculately maintained house is ideal for taking over with a few friends. Small conferences/banqueting (30/30); broadband wi/fi; **Rooms 4** (some en-suite, some with private bathrooms); children welcome (under 4s free in parents' room, cot available free of charge). B&B €80pps, ss €40. Closed Jan-Apr. **Directions:** M1 north, exit for Bru na Boinne, through Donore, past Newgrange visitors' centre, entrance on sharp bend on left.

Slane

HISTORIC HOUSE

Tankardstown House

Rathkenny Slane Co Meath **Tel: 041 982 4621**
info@tankardstown.ie www.tankardstown.ie

Since buying this appealing period property near Slane in 2002, Trish and Brian Conroy have restored and renovated the house with consideration and taste – and, thank to their efforts, it also stands proud once again on the 80 acres of land that belonged to the original estate. The main house is available as a private venue for groups or events, and offers six splendid double bedooms, several elegant reception rooms, an exceptional dining room, huge kitchen, games room and more. No expense has been spared with fine antiques, splendid mirrors, attractive artwork, and only the very finest fabrics and furnishings featured in every room; the overall impression is one of immaculate taste and luxurious comfort. Each bedroom is beautifully decorated, with additional comforts including waffle cotton robes, slippers, Molton Brown toiletries – and, out on the landing, a dresser laden with home-made cakes, fine bone china and tea and coffee-making facilities. The 19th century stable yard has since been converted into seven elegant cottages, available for self-catering or B&B - breakfast is delivered to your door on request (from €15). The courtyard cottages offer luxurious accommodation for 24 guests in double or twin rooms as needed, complete with living room and fully fitted kitchen. All bedrooms are en-suite with bath and shower and, as in the main house, every room is elegantly decorated in a different style. The cottages lead out to a Garden Party Room, fitness studio and two treatment rooms. The house lends itself particularly well to small weddings (up to 60 guests can be catered for to dine in the house and a marquee can be arranged for larger numbers), and is also ideal for a family reunion or special birthday party. Arriving at dusk with the courtyard fountain, walled garden and sweeping grounds all romantically lit up, you could imagine you are pulling up to a grand Tuscan villa. *The main house is only available to rent in its entirety (from €3000). **Accommodation in the courtyard cottages costs €100 per person per night. Dinner by arrangement when available (about €45), otherwise Slane is only a short drive. Conferences/Banqueting (120/60); free broadband wi/fi; secretarial services. **Rooms 12;** children welcome (cots available, baby sitting arranged, play ground); B&B €120 pps. Pets welcome (stay in bedroom or outside in kennel). Fitness room, equestrian, tennis, archery, clay pigeon shooting, garden, massage, treatments. Fly fishing, golf, garden visits, & horse racing nearby. Open all year. Amex, MasterCard, Visa, Laser. **Directions:** Navan Road (N51) out of Slane; Right turn after back-gate to Slane Castel estate, follow signs.

O'Connell's

Tara Area
PUB
R

Skryne Nr. Tara Co Meath
Tel: 046 902 5122

Three generations of O'Connells have been caretakers of this wonderfully unspoilt country pub and the present owner, Mary O'Connell, has been delighting customers old and new for well over a decade now. It's all beautifully simple – two little bars with no fancy bits, lots of items of local interest, and a welcoming fire in the grate. What more could anyone want? Closed 25 Dec & Good Fri. **No Credit Cards. Directions:** just head for the tower beside the pub, which is visible for miles around.

TRIM

Most famous for its enormous Anglo-Norman Castle (restored and open to the public, 046 943 8619) and other medieval monuments, Trim is a small but - thanks to its location only 45km north-west of Dublin - fast-growing town. Well-located for visitors interested in the history of the area, it is also becoming a popular short break destination and has recently acquired two new hotels: **Trim Castle Hotel** (046 9483000; www.trimcastle.com) is located shockingly close to the castle and its dull, concrete exterior is at odds with the castle walls across the road; however, once inside, it is an exciting new establishment furnished in a contemporary, minimalist style and, in the Guide's experience, with friendly staff serving tasty food. A short distance away and well-signed in the area, is **Knightsbrook Hotel and Golf Resort** (see entry). **Brogan's Bar & Guesthouse** (046 943 1237; www.brogans.ie) on High Street, is also home to **The Beacon Restaurant**, a comfortable mid-range restaurant offering something to please everyone, with most dishes cooked to order and prompt service; open daily from 5.30, and bar food is also available. Gardens to visit in the area include Grove Gardens (near Kells, 046 943 4276) which is an informal garden on 6 acres with exotic animals and fowl, walks, roses and clematis – especially interesting for a family outing; Rockfield House (Drumconrath, 046 905 2135) which is a charming old walled garden with stream and a good collection of herbaceous plants and Ballinlough Castle (Clonmellon, 046 943 3234) which is a restored Edwardian garden in an 18th century demesne. Golfers will appreciate the championship golf at Headfort Golf Club (Kells, 046 928 2001).
WWW.IRELAND-GUIDE.COM FOR ALL THE BEST PLACES TO EAT, DRINK & STAY

Franzini O'Briens

Trim
RESTAURANT

French's Lane Trim Co Meath
Tel: 046 943 1002

Modern and spacious, this smart and very popular restaurant beside Trim Castle has well-trained staff who greet and seat arriving guests promptly and - by ensuring that everyone settles in comfortably from the start - setting a tone of relaxed efficiency that makes for an enjoyable outing. Space is attractively broken up around a central carpeted square with leather sofas to provide a variety of seating areas and simple, uncluttered table settings are modern and elegantly functional - tall water carafes, finger bowls for nachos and paper napkins. Light-hearted menus offer an excellent range of choices in the international style and, together with an informal, buzzy atmosphere, indicate that this is a place for a good night out. Service is excellent, even at very busy times. Interesting wine list (supplied by Jim Nicholson). *See also O'Briens Good Food & Drink House, Navan. **Seats 110**; reservations accepted; children welcome before 8.30; toilets wheelchair accessible; air conditioning. D Mon-Sat, 6.30-10, Sun: L 1-4, D 4-8.30. Early bird D Mon-Fri 6.30-7.30 about €21.95. Also A la carte. House wines from €16.95. SC 10% on groups 4+. Closed Mon off-season (Sept-May), 23-26 Dec, Good Fri. MasterCard, Visa, Laser. **Directions:** Beside Trim Castle.

Knightsbrook Hotel & Golf Resort

Trim
HOTEL
🏨

Trim Co Meath **Tel: 046 948 2100**
info@knightsbrook.com www.knightsbrook.com

Convenient to Dublin and also well-placed for visiting the many historical and cultural attractions in County Meath, this new hotel just outside Trim makes a luxurious destination for a short golf or leisure break, business conference, or wedding. Although the approach to it is unexpectedly suburban, the countryside around it is lovely and, once inside, palatial public areas are sure to impress. The tone is

Georgina Campbell's Ireland

welcoming, too, with mellow woods and warm-toned furnishings used throughout, and the hotel is notable for helpful and friendly staff. Bedrooms are large and luxuriously furnished, and excellent leisure facilities include a health club with 17m swimming pool and the River Spa as well as an 18-hole championship golf course - great for weekenders and also off-duty delegates attending conferences and meetings here. In addition to the hotel accommodation, guests can opt to stay in one of the 3-bedroom holiday homes which are rented out on a weekly-basis. Several dining options are offered - informal dining is available in the Golf Club and bars, whilst the well-appointed, high ceilinged Rococo Restaurant offers the hotel's formal dining experience. Conference/Banqueting (1,500/700), business centre, secretarial services, video conferencing, broadband wi/fi. Equestrian nearby, fly fishing nearby, golf (18), leisure centre with fitness room and 'pool, spa (beauty salon, massage), tennis, walking. Children welcome (under 3s free in parents' room, cots available at no charge, baby sitting arranged, crèche, playground). **Rooms 131** (4 suites, 8 junior suites, 12 executive, 6 family rooms, 8 for disabled, 80 no smoking); lift; 24 hr room service. B&B from €100pps; ss€50. Open all year. Helipad. **Directions:** About a mile from Trim town, on the Dublin Road.

COUNTY MONAGHAN

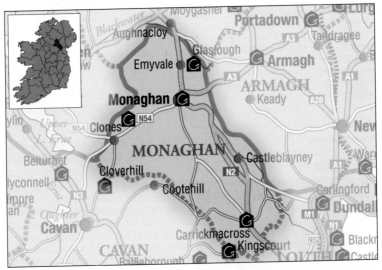

Of all Ireland's counties, it is Monaghan which is most centrally placed in the drumlin belt, that strip of rounded glacial hills which runs right across the country from Strangford Lough in County Down to Clew Bay in Mayo. Monaghan, in fact, is all hills. But as very few of them are over 300 metres above sea level, the county takes its name from Muineachain - "Little Hills". Inevitably, the actively farmed undulating country of the little hills encloses many lakes, and Monaghan in its quiet way is a coarse angler's paradise.

Much of the old Ulster Canal is in Monaghan, while the rest is in Armagh and Tyrone. Once upon a time, it connected Lough Erne to Lough Neagh. It has been derelict for a very long time, but with the success of the restored Shannon-Erne Waterway along the line of the old Ballinamore-Ballyconnell Canal bringing added vitality to Leitrim, Cavan and Fermanagh, the even more ambitious vision of restoring the Ulster Canal is now under way.

Vision of a different sort is the theme at Annaghmakerrig House near the Quaker-named village of Newbliss in west Monaghan. The former home of theatrical producer Tyrone Guthrie, it is a busy centre for writers and artists who can stay there to complete 'work in progress', or defer deadlines in congenial company. The dedicated eccentricity of the area is also celebrated at the Flat Lake Cultural Festival around the big house in Hilton Park around the third weekend in August, a remarkably high-powered gathering of poetry, literature, music and humour.

In the east of the county at Castleblayney, there's a particularly attractive lake district with forest park and adventure centre around Lough Mucko. Southwards of Castleblayney, we come to the bustling town of Carrickmacross, still famous for its lace, and a Tidy Towns awardee.

Monaghan's pretty village of Glaslough towards the north of the county is worth a visit, and at Clontibret in northeast Monaghan, there's gold in them thar little hills. Whether or not it's in sufficient quantities to merit mining is a continuing matter of commercial debate, but the fact that it's there at all is another of Monaghan's more intriguing secrets. Another is the county's uncrowded character. It has been confirmed in a recent census, but there seem to be plenty of folk about the place.

Local Attractions and Information

Carrickmacross	Carrickmacross Lace Gallery	042 966 2506
Carrickmacross	(Kingscourt Rd) Dun a Ri Forest Park	042 966 7320
Castleblayney	Lough Muckno Leisure Park	042 974 6356
Clones	Clones Lace Exhibits	047 51051
Glaslough	Castle Leslie Gardens	047 88109
Inniskeen	Patrick Kavanagh Centre	042 937 8560
Monaghan town	Tourism Information	047 81122
Monaghan town	Monaghan County Museum	047 82928
Monaghan town	(Newbliss Rd.) Rossmore Forest Park	047 81968
Newbliss	Annaghmakerrig (Tyrone Guthrie Centre)	047 54003

Carrickmacross
HOTEL•RESTAURANT
♛ ☆ ♈ Ⓥ Ⓡ

Nuremore Hotel & Country Club

Carrickmacross Co Monaghan **Tel: 042 966 1438**
info@nuremore.com www.nuremore.com

This fine owner-managed country hotel just south of Carrickmacross is set in a parkland estate, with its own 18-hole golf course, and serves the leisure and business requirements of a wide area very well. As you go over the little bridge ("Beware - ducks crossing") and the immaculately maintained hotel and golf club open up before you, worldly cares seem to recede - this is a place you can get fond of. The hotel invariably gives a good impression on arrival and this sense of care and maintenance is continued throughout. Spacious, comfortably arranged public areas and generous bedrooms with views over the gardens and lakes are regularly refurbished and it would make an excellent base to explore this little known area - and there is plenty to do on site. The superb country club has a full leisure centre and a wide range of related facilities - including a gymnasium and spa - and there are conference and meeting rooms for every size of gathering, with state-of-the-art audio-visual equipment available. Conference/banqueting (600/400); business centre, secretarial services on request, video conferencing; broadband wifi. Leisure centre, swimming pool, spa; beauty salon; golf (18), fishing, walking, tennis, garden; snooker. Children welcome (cots available, €13; baby sitting arranged). No pets. Heli-pad. **Rooms 72** (7 junior suites, 11 executive, 5 family, 42 no smoking, 1 disabled). 24 hr room service. B&B €130 pps, ss €50. *Short breaks offered, including spa and golf breaks; details on application. Open all year. **The Restaurant at Nuremore:** This is the leading restaurant in a wide area, and the head chef, Raymond McArdle, has earned a national reputation for the hotel, which is now on the must-visit destination list for discerning travellers in Ireland. Proprietress Julie Gilhooly has lent every possible support to this talented protegé since his arrival here in 2000, and his spacious, state-of-the art kitchen is the envy of chefs throughout the country. Unfortunately though, there has been a gap - the restaurant itself has long let the kitchen down, and promised refurbishment has been deferred several times; however, we are informed that this overdue renovation will finally be undertaken shortly after the Guide goes to press...the room is expected to retain its pleasant layout, with a couple of steps dividing the window area and inner tables, allowing everybody to enjoy the view over golf course and woodland. Raymond sources ingredients meticulously, using local produce as much as possible in top rank daily set lunch and dinner menus, a separate vegetarian menu, a 'grown-up' children's menu, an evening à la carte and an 8-course Prestige Menu (which, at just €88, offers remarkable value). Menus read fairly simply (notably the Prestige Menu, which names only the main ingredient on each course and so gives very little away) but everything, it seems, is equally impressive and difficult choices must be made on every course. But, whatever you choose, you may be sure of experiencing exceptional cooking and, under the supervision of restaurant manager Harry Gribbin, service is in line with the high standard of food. And sommelier Romain Guillot has many a treat in store on the extensive and well-organised wine list too, including a good house wine selection and a range of 'flights', i.e. a trio of 125ml glasses that follow a theme – and you can have a flight selected specially to match your particular food choices; there's also a good choice of dessert wines and half bottles, a fair number of magnums and a menu of Caterède armagnacs going back to 1948. This is a restaurant offering outstanding value for money, especially at lunch time. *Raymond McArdle was our Chef of the Year in 2005. **Seats 100** (private room, 50); air conditioning. L Sun-Fri, 12.30-2.30; D daily 6.30-9.30 (Sun to 9). Set 2/3 course L €19.50/25 (Set Sun L, €35); Set D €52 (vegetarian menu about €25, children's menu €17.50); prestige menu €85. House wine from €26; sc discretionary. Closed L Sat. Open all year. Amex, Diners, MasterCard, Visa, Laser. **Directions:** Just south of Carrickmacross, 88km (55 m) from Dublin on N2 ot take M1 from Dublin and turn off at Ardee/Derry exit.

Clones
COUNTRY HOUSE

Hilton Park

Clones Co Monaghan **Tel: 047 56007**
mail@hiltonpark.ie www.hiltonpark.ie

Once described as a "capsule of social history" because of their collection of family portraits and memorabilia going back 250 years or more, Johnny and Lucy Madden's wonderful 18th century mansion is set in beautiful countryside, amidst 200 acres of woodland and farmland. With lakes, Pleasure Grounds and a Lovers' Walk to set the right tone, the house is magnificent in every sense. Johnny and Lucy are natural hosts and, as the house and its contents go back for so many generations, there is a strong feeling of being a privileged family guest as you wander through grandly-proportioned, beautifully furnished rooms. Four-posters and all the unself-conscious comforts that make for a very special country house stay are part of the charm, but as visitors from all over the world have found, it's the warmth of Johnny and Lucy's welcome that lends that extra magic. Formal gardens have been restored and Lucy, an enthusiastic organic gardener and excellent cook, supplies freshly-harvested produce from the walled kitchen gardens for meals in the house, while other ingredients are carefully sourced from trusted suppliers. Dinner for residents is served in a beautiful dining room overlooking the gardens and lake - and memorable breakfasts are taken downstairs in the Green Room next morning. This is exceptional hospitality, with an Irish flavour and, in recognition, Hilton Park was selected for our International Hospitality Award in 1999. **Rooms 6** (all en-suite, with bath & no smoking). B&B from €125 pps, ss €40; not suitable for children under 8 yrs (except babies under 1 free with parents, cot available, 8-14 yrs, 50% disc). Residents D at 8 pm (Fri, 8.30) Tue-Sat about €55; please give 24 hours notice. Interesting short wine list; house wine about €20/22. SC discretionary. Pets allowed in some areas by arrangement. Gardens, boating, fishing (own lake), walking, cycling. Golf nearby. *Self-catering accommodation also available - details on inquiry. *Hilton Park is available for group bookings - family celebrations, small weddings and small conferences. Open all year by arrangement. MasterCard, Visa, Laser. **Directions:** 5km (3 m) south of Clones on Scotshouse Road.

Glaslough
HOTEL

The Hunting Lodge at Castle Leslie

Glaslough Co Monaghan **Tel: 047 88100**
info@castleleslie.com www.castleleslie.com

During the three centuries that this extraordinary place has been in the Leslie family it had changed remarkably little until recently - and its fascinating history has continually intrigued and beguiled both Irish and international guests. The castle recently ceased operations as an hotel and, following extensive refurbishment, has re-opened as a private venue for weddings, conferences etc. Guests now stay in the Hunting Lodge At Castle Leslie, which is a modern 4* hotel just inside the castle gates; built around an atmospheric stable courtyard, it is popular with riding enthusiasts participating at Castle Leslie's impressive Equestrian Centre, which offers miles of trekking, cross-country rides and jumps on the 1000-acre estate. The Hunting Lodge features all manner of horsey memorabilia with the newer bedrooms designed to appeal especially to horse lovers. A Victorian Spa specialises in organic treatments while Castle Leslie Cookery School, situated in the Castle's restored Victorian kitchens, offers a choice of evening, one- and two-day courses. Non-residents are welcome to dine at the bar or in the hotel's informal Conors Bar or Snaffles Brasserie, where Matthew King – head chef since 2008 (having practised on two American Presidents, Clinton & Bush, before arriving here) - cooks up a storm in a wood-burning stone oven.

Conferences/Banqueting (35/63); free broadband wi/fi. **Rooms 30** (all separate bath & shower, 2 family, 10 ground floor, all no smoking & equipped for disabled); children welcome (under 2s free in parents' room, cots available free of charge). Lift. B&B €95-115 pps, ss €45. Equestrian Centre, Victorian Spa & Cookery School. **Snaffles Brasserie: Seats 85**; children welcome; D daily 5.30-9.30pm; a la carte; L Sun only, 1-2.30pm; house wine from €18. Bar food served daily in Conor's Bar, 12.30-8.30pm. Amex, Diners, MasterCard, Visa, Laser. **Directions:** 10 mins from Monaghan Town: Monaghan-Armagh road-Glaslough.

Monaghan
BAR•RESTAURANT
R

Andy's Bar and Restaurant
12 Market Street Monaghan Co Monaghan **Tel: 047 82277**
www.andysmonaghan.com

Right in the centre of Monaghan, the Redmond family's bar is furnished and decorated in traditional Victorian style, with a lot of fine mahogany, stained glass and mirrors. Everything is gleaming clean and arranged well for comfort, with high-backed bar seats and plenty of alcoves set up with tables for the comfortable consumption of their good bar food. Substantial bar meals include a range of specials on a blackboard as well as a concise written menu. The restaurant upstairs, which has a pleasingly old-fashioned ambience, offers a much more extensive range of popular and classic dishes, including a good choice of prime fish and steaks various ways. This is good cooking based on quality ingredients and the results are extremely tasty, satisfying - and good value too. Traditional desserts like pavlova and home-made ices are served from a trolley. Members of the Redmond family keep a constant eye on everything, and service is charming and efficient. **Restaurant: Seats 50** (private room, 20); children welcome (high chair, childrens menu, baby changing facilities); D only, Tue-Sun, 4-10.15 (Sun 3.30-10). à la carte; house wine €17.70. Bar meals Tue-Sun, 4-10.15. Closed Mon, 25 Dec, Good Fri, bank hols & 1-11 Jul. MasterCard, Visa, Laser. **Directions:** Town centre, opposite the Market House.

Monaghan
HOTEL
R

Hillgrove Hotel
Old Armagh Rd Monaghan Co Monaghan **Tel: 047 81288**
info@hillgrovehotel.com www.hillgrovehotel.com

Overlooking the town from a fine hillside location, the Hillgrove is the leading hotel in the area; it has quite recently been smartly refurbished in a classic contemporary style and offers excellent business and leisure facilities. An impressive foyer sets the tone and the public areas around it are spacious and inviting, including the main bar, PK's, and the Toulouse-Lautrec lounge; the well-appointed restaurant, Vettriano, offers stylish informality and is open for lunch and dinner every day. Bedrooms are spacious and contemporary, all with pleasant views, a full range of facilities and smart en-suite bathrooms. Staff are friendly and very helpful. Conference/banqueting (1,500/900), business centre, secretarial services, video conferencing, free broadband wi/fi. **Rooms 87** (2 suites, 2 junior suites, 8 family rooms, 4 for disabled, 18 ground floor, 16 no smoking); children welcome (under 4s free in parents' room, cot available at no charge, baby sitting arranged, crèche, play room); Lift, 24-hr room service, no pets. B&B from €75-90 pps, ss €30. Leisure centre with 'pool, fitness room, Spa (including beauty salon, massage, hair dressing), garden.Closed 25 Dec. Amex, MasterCard, Visa, Laser. Helipad. **Directions:** Take N2 from Dublin to Monaghan town.

COUNTY OFFALY

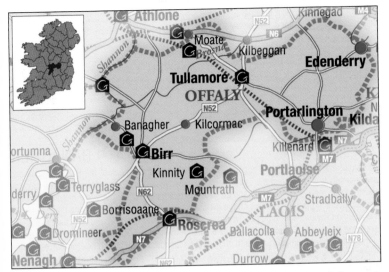

At the heart of the old Ely O'Carroll territory, Offaly is Ireland's most sky-minded county. In the grounds of Birr Castle, there's the Parsons family's famous restored 1845-vintage 1.83m astronomical telescope – rated one of the Seven Wonders of Ireland - through which the 3rd Earl of Rosse observed his discovery of the spiral nebulae. And in Tullamore, there's a thriving amateur Astronomical Society whose members point out that the wide clear skies of Offaly have encouraged the regular observation of heavenly bodies since at least 1057 AD, when astronomy was the province of moon-minded monks.

On a more modern note, the Tullamore Dew Heritage Centre is housed in the restored 1897 canal-side bonded warehouse, which formerly stored the famous local whiskey. The Centre explores Tullamore's distilling, canal and urban history with entertaining style. Style is also the theme of the new County Hall in Tullamore, which has been awarded the An Taisce Sustainable Building accolade.

Back in Birr meanwhile, the restored gardens of Birr Castle are an added attraction. And it's also in the heart of historic hunting country. Offaly is home to the Ormonde, which may not be Ireland's largest or richest hunt, "but it's the oldest and undoubtedly the best." Once upon a time, they invited the neighbouring County Galway Hunt for a shared meet, and afterwards the carousing in Dooly's Hotel in Birr reached such a hectic pitch that the hotel was joyously torched by the visitors. Dooley's was rebuilt to fulfill its central role in Birr, and the hunt from across the Shannon has been known as the Galway Blazers ever since.

The Grand Canal finally reaches the great river at Shannon Harbour in Offaly, after crossing Ireland from Dublin through Tullamore, and on the river itself, waterborne travellers find that Offaly affords the opportunity of visiting Clonmacnoise, where the remains of an ancient monastic university city give pause for thought. In the south of the county, the Slieve Bloom Mountains rise attractively above Offaly's farmland and bogs. These are modest heights, as they attain just 526m on the peak of Arderin. However, it is their understated charms which particularly appeal, and in the Slieve Blooms we find Ireland's first organised system of gites, the French concept whereby unused farmhouses have been restored to a comfortable standard for self-catering visitor accommodation.

Nestling in a valley of the Slieve Blooms is the unspoilt village of Kinnitty, where Offaly's quality of life is most in evidence. And in the far east of the county, where Offaly marches with Kildare, we find Clonbulloge, top title holder in Offaly in the Tidy Towns awards, a pretty place on the banks of the neat stream known as the Figile River. Yet in Offaly they're not afraid of life's more earthy joys – Annaharvey Farm at Tullamore has found itself a special niche in the annual national ploughing context.

Local Attractions and Information

Banagher	Cloghan Castle (15C Tower House)	0509 51650
Birr	Castle Demesne & Historic Science Centre	0509 20336 / 22154
Birr	Tourism Information	0509 20110
Clonmacnoise	Visitor & Interpretive Centre	090 967 4195
Edenderry	Canal Festival (June)	046 973 2071
Shannonbridge	Clonmacnoise & West Offaly Railway	090 967 4114
Slieve Bloom	Rural Development Society	0509 37299
Tullamore	Offaly Historical Society	0506 21421
Tullamore	Offaly Tourist Council	0506 52566
Tullamore	Tullamore Dew Heritage Centre	0506 25015
Tullamore	Tourism Information	0506 52617

BANAGHER

This small town on the western edge of County Offaly sits on the bank of the River Shannon and was originally built to protect a crossing point - impressive fortifications guarding the river crossing are still to be seen. Today, angling and all watersports are attractions; there is a marina and it is a popular stopping place for cruisers on the river, and boats can be hired here. Along the river banks, the Shannon Callows are home to a wealth of wild flowers and bird life, and river buses take visitors along the river to Clonmacnoise (Visitor & Interpretive Centre 090 967 4195) and other places of interest. The town provided a wealth of inspiration for author Anthony Trollope who wrote his first novels here. For those who seek the 'real Ireland' this is an interesting small town to be based, and Pat and Della Horan's small family-run **Brosna Lodge Hotel** (057 915 1350; www.brosnalodge.com) provides the genuine experience, offering good food and genuine hospitality. Good food is also offered at **Flynn's Bar and Restaurant** (057 915 1312) where the cosy bar has an open fire, and at **Heidi's Coffee Shop** (087 956 2680) - renowned for generous helpings of wholesome food and good value. If a B&B in a quiet and picturesque waterside setting with a pub serving good food only yards away takes your fancy, you won't do better than the charming and hospitable **Harbour Master House** (057 915 1532) at Shannon Harbour.

WWW.IRELAND-GUIDE.COM FOR ALL THE BEST PLACES TO EAT, DRINK & STAY

Banagher
CHARACTER PUB

J.J.Hough

Main Street Banagher Co Offaly **Tel: 057 915 1893**
johnhough@eircom.net

Hidden behind a thriving vine, which threatens to take over each summer, this charming 250-year old pub is soothingly dark inside, making a fine contrast to the cheerful eccentricity of the current owner, Michael Hough. A world famous music pub, it's authentic and unique, family-run and with a wealth of Irish art on the walls. It's a great local and also popular with people from the river cruisers, who come up from the harbour for pints, music and craic - for over thirty years, there's been traditional Irish music here every night from March to November, and on Friday, Saturday & Sunday in winter. Nothing ever changes much here, although they did add a beer garden when the no-smoking law came in. Children and pets welcome. Open 10.30 am - 1 am. No food. Traditional music nightly. Closed 25 Dec & Good Fri. **Directions:** Lower Main Street.

BIRR

Birr is a lovely old town steeped in history and it makes a good holiday centre, with plenty to do locally - Birr Castle, with its observatory and magnificently restored gardens to visit, also golfing, fishing, riding and river excursions. The charmingly old-fashioned **Dooly's Hotel** (Tel 057 912 0032 www.doolyshotel.com) is one of Ireland's oldest coaching inns, dating back to 1747 and is right on Emmet Square, the centre of Georgian Birr (food served all day); for those who like a little more space, the Georgian **County Arms Hotel** (Tel 057 912 0791; www.countyarmshotel.com) is set in its own grounds nearby, with gardens and glasshouses to supply the hotel, and also a leisure centre; the hotel has recently completed a major upgrade and renovation programme. There are a number of pleasant cafés and pubs in the town including the **Courtyard Café** at Birr Castle, **Emma's Café & Deli** (057 912 5678) on Main Street, **The Chestnut** (057 912 2011) an old pub on Green Street that now makes a stylish evening bar, and **The Stables** (see entry). Birr makes a good holiday centre, with plenty to do locally – Birr Castle (057 912 0336), with its observatory and magnificently restored gardens to visit, also golfing (Birr Golf Club, 057 912 0082), fishing, riding (Birr Equestrian Centre, 057 912 1961);

river excursions are available and Birr Outdoor Education Centre (057 912 0029) has a range of water-sports education courses including canoeing, sailing and board sailing.
WWW.IRELAND-GUIDE.COM FOR ALL THE BEST PLACES TO EAT, DRINK & STAY

Brambles Café & Deli

Birr
CAFÉ
Ⓝ

Mill Street Birr Co Offaly
Tel: 087 745 3359

Gillian Delahunt's inviting cafe in Birr is undoubtedly the best place in town to enjoy a really well-made cup of coffee and some excellent home baked produce. Gillian makes and sells her own soda bread, carrot cake, chocolate biscuit cake, scones and other sweet treats along with home-made soup and deep-filled pies which have regulars coming back for more every day. She also sells her own organic ducks eggs and organic butterleaf lettuce from her family farm alongside a range of quality local produce, including Williams' Bakery breads, Mossfield farm cheese and a choice of home-made jams and chutneys. Seating in the cafe is cosy and comfortable, newspapers are available for customers and the place is very child friendly. **Seats 21** (outdoors, 4); children welcome; open Mon-Sat, 9am-6pm. Closed Sun, Bank Hols, Christmas. **No credit cards. Directions:** From top of main square, go down the main street, take a right at the credit union, just down on the right, red shop front.

Spinners Town House

Birr
RESTAURANT•GUESTHOUSE

Castle Street Birr Co Offaly **Tel: 057 912 1673**
spinnerstownhouse@eircom.net www.spinnerstownhouse.com

Conveniently situated near Birr Castle, sympathetic renovation of a row of Georgian townhouses and an old woollen mill has created a restaurant and accommodation within the old stone walls, making it an interesting place to stay or have a meal. Several areas are used for dining, including the lobby and drawing room of what was once a substantial private house, which retains its Georgian features, including plasterwork - and red and blue stained glass in the large front door casts lovely shadows onto a wall; some well-known paintings have been added and, with subdued jazz, a covered terrace and a pretty garden with box hedges and wonderful climbing hydrangeas (and fresh flowers on all the carefully-appointed tables), it makes a very attractive dining venue. Early dinner and à la carte menus are offered, with the carte offering a much better choice at a fair price - and showcasing carefully sourced ingredients and good cooking. Competent, willing service and well-chosen, good value wines complete an attractive package. *****Accommodation** is also offered, in simple but comfortable bedrooms with ensuite or private showers. **Rooms 13**; B&B from €40pps. **Restaurant** Open: D Wed-Mon 6.30-9 (to 10pm Fri & Sat); L Sun only 12.30-2.30. Closed Tue. A la carte & set menus offered. MasterCard, Visa, Laser. **Directions:** Beside Birr Castle. ◇

The Stables Emporium & Tea Rooms

Birr
CAFÉ

6 Oxmantown Mall Birr Co Offaly **Tel: 057 912 0263**
cboyd@indigo.ie

The Boyd family's characterful establishment is in a lovely old Georgian house overlooking the tree-lined mall. It was renowned for many years as one of the area's favourite restaurants - now it is run by Caroline Boyd, who has transformed it into a high quality furniture and gift shop, Emporium at the Stables. The store, which is located in the atmospheric old coach house, stocks crystal and glassware, fine furniture, lighting, garden accessories, jewellery and giftware. (Worldwide delivery can be arranged). Meanwhile, in the main house, light lunches, snacks, wine, tea, coffee and home-made desserts are served in the elegant drawing room, complete with open fire and comfortable armchairs, also a rather nice little front garden for sitting out in fine weather. Open Tue-Sat, 10.30-5.30 and Sun 1-5.30 (Nov, Dec, Jun, Jul & Aug). Children welcome; air conditioning; toilets wheelchair accessible. Closed Dec 25-29. Amex, Diners, MasterCard, Visa, Laser. **Directions:** Town centre, between St Brendan's Church & private gates of Birr Castle.

The Thatch Bar & Restaurant

Birr
PUB•RESTAURANT

Crinkle Birr Co Offaly
Tel: 057 912 0682

This characterful little thatched pub and restaurant just outside Birr shows just how pleasing a genuine, well-run country pub can be. Des Connole, proprietor since 1991, has achieved a well-earned reputation for the immaculate maintenance and atmosphere of the pub, and both bar food and restaurant meals offer generous portions for a reasonable price. **Seats 50** (private room, 15-20); children welcome; parking; toilets wheelchair accessible. D Mon-Fri, 6.30-9pm; Sun & Mon, 5-7pm, Set D about €40, also à la carte; L Sun- two sittings (reservations essential) - 12.30 & 2.30; Set Sun L about €25; à la carte L&D; house wine about €20; SC discretionary. Bar meals Mon-Sat, 12.30-3 & 5-7.30. Restaurant closed D Sun, establishment closed 25 Dec, Good Fri. Diners, MasterCard, Visa, Laser. **Directions:** 1 mile from Birr (Roscrea side).

Kinnitty
COUNTRY HOUSE

Ardmore Country House

The Walk Kinnitty Co Offaly **Tel: 057 913 7009**
info@kinnitty.com www.kinnitty.com

Set back from the road in its own lovely gardens, Christina Byrne's stone-built Victorian house offers old-fashioned comforts: brass beds, turf fires and home-made bread and preserves for breakfast. Bedrooms are deliberately left without amenities, in order to make a visit to Ardmore a real country house experience and encourage guests to spend less time in their rooms and mix with each other - tea is available downstairs at any time. All bedrooms are decorated to a high standard - one with jacuzzi bath - and a ground floor room is wheelchair-friendly. Christina runs 1-7 day guided walking breaks in this beautiful and unspoilt area, with dinner in local restaurants, including Kinnitty Castle and Leap Castle - Ireland's most haunted castle (walking brochure available on request). There's usually a traditional Irish night on Friday nights, at nearby **Kinnitty Castle. Rooms 5** (4 en-suite, 3 shower only, 1 with private bathroom, 1 family room, 1 ground floor, 1 for disabled, all no smoking); children welcome (under 2s free in parents' room, cot available at no charge, baby sitting arranged); pets allowed in certain areas (stay in bedroom). B&B €45 pps, ss €10. Closed 23-27 Dec. **No Credit Cards. Directions:** In village of Kinnitty, 15km from Birr (R440).

Kinnitty
B&B•RESTAURANT

The Glendine Bistro

Kinnitty Co Offaly
Tel: 057 913 7973

Situated in a charming village at the foot of the Slieve Bloom mountains, the clean-lined simplicity of Percy and Phil Clendennan's attractive contemporary restaurant provides a welcome contrast to other, more traditional, dining options nearby, giving visitors to this unspoilt area a choice of styles. Wide-ranging menus suit the surroundings: this is steak country and prime Hereford beef is sure to feature in steaks various ways, but there are also many more international dishes - barbecued tiger prawns & king scallops with char-grilled peppers, perhaps - and sound cooking is backed up by friendly service. Vegetarian options, typically stir-fries and fresh pasta dishes, are always available. **Seats 60** (private room 15); children welcome; air conditioning. D Thu- Sun, 6.30-9. L Sun only, 12.30-2.30. D à la carte. Set Sun L about €20. House wine €18. Closed Mon-Wed; all Jan. **Accommodation:** Bright, comfortably furnished en-suite bedrooms are offered, all with direct dial phones, TV and tea/coffee-making facilities. Children under 8 free in parents' room (cot available without charge). **Rooms 5** (all shower-only & no smoking). Closed Jan. B&B €35 pps, ss €7. MasterCard, Visa, Laser **Directions:** 11 km from Birr, in centre of Kinnitty Village. ◇

Kinnitty
HOTEL

Kinnitty Castle

Kinnitty Co Offaly **Tel: 057 913 7318**
info@kinnittycastle.com www.kinnittycastle.com

Furnished in keeping with its dramatic history and theatrical character, this Gothic Revival castle in the foothills of the Slieve Bloom Mountains is at the centre of a very large estate with 650 acres of parkland and formal gardens. Public areas include a library bar, Georgian style dining room, Louis XV drawing room and an atmospheric Dungeon Bar. Bedrooms vary and the best are big and romantic, with great country views. Known as a successful wedding venue, it has atmospheric, medieval-style banqueting/conference facilities and also a small leisure centre (no swimming pool). The castle is haunted (of course) and at its best a stay here can be great fun, but make sure you don't leave your sense of humour at home. Olde-worlde character and interested staff who contribute to the overall sense of fun are the things that make a visit to this hotel worth considering, and it should come as no surprise that wacky events including a Ghost Fest are held from time to time. **Rooms 37** (10 suites, 11 junior suites); children welcome. No lift (long corridors and a lot of stairs). Room rate from about €215. **Restaurant:** D daily & L Sun. Tennis, fishing, equestrian, garden. Open all year. Amex, Diners, MasterCard, Visa, Laser. **Directions:** On the R422- Emo to Birr Road,off main N7 Limerick Road.

Shannonbridge
CHARACTER PUB
R

The Village Tavern
Main Street Shannonbridge Co Offaly
Tel: 090 967 4112

At J.J. Killeen's wonderful pub, shop-weary travellers can be restored, particularly by the house special of hot rum and chocolate - perfect after a damp day on the river. Meanwhile you can also top up on groceries, fishing bait and gas. Music nightly May-September; weekends only off-season. *See also Shannonbridge, Co Rscommon. **Directions:** On the main street of Shannonbridge, between Ballinasloe and Cloghan.

R

TULLAMORE

This thriving canalside town is perhaps best known for its most famous product, Tullamore Dew and, while it may no longer be made here, The Tullamore Dew Heritage Centre (057 9325015) on the banks of the Grand Canal focuses on the distilling, canal and urban history of the town (tours available daily). Nearby, the splendid Gothic Charleville Forest Castle stands in beautiful parkland - the Charleville oak is one of the biggest and oldest in the country and, botanically, an important survivor of primeval stock. Tullamore is also an ideal base for discovering the Slieve Bloom Mountains, with many beautiful walking and cycling trails, and picnic areas with panoramic views of the surrounding lowlands. Also nearby are the unique 'Lough Boora' parklands; the boglands habitat supports a wide range of flora and fauna and now also hosts some of the most innovative land and environmental sculptures in Ireland - the artists, inspired by the rich natural and industrial legacy of the boglands, have created a series of large-scale sculptures that are now part of the Parklands permanent collection. Garden lovers should make a point of visiting Birr Castle (057 912 0336), with its observatory and magnificently restored gardens, and might consider a trip to Belvedere House, Park & Gardens (Edenderry area, 044 934 9060) an historic 18th century house and park with a beautifully restored 2-acre walled garden. Meanwhile Headfort Golf Club (Kells, 046 928 2001) caters well for golfers, with championship golf over two 18-hole courses. Tullamore itself offers plenty for visitors, many of whom find it an excellent short break destination with everything in the compact town within walking distance. There is a country market on in the Millenium Square each Saturday (9-4pm). Well-established restaurants to check out include **Anatolia** (057 932 3669; www.anatolia.ie), on Harbour Street which is open for lunch and dinner, also **Acorn** (057 932 4700) another successful restaurant on the same steet which has recently re-opened following renovations; and the evening Italian restaurant, **Sirroco's** (057 935 2839), which is nearby. Several popular ethnic restaurants include **Shisar** (057 935 1439) on High Street, specialising in Thai/Indian cuisine. The main hotel in the area is the **Tullamore Court** (see entry), but the newer **Days Hotel** (057 932 0350; www.dayshoteltullamore.com) offers a moderately priced alternative likely to be of particular interest to business guests.
WWW.IRELAND-GUIDE.COM FOR ALL THE BEST PLACES TO EAT, DRINK & STAY

Tullamore
RESTAURANT
R

Jamie's Restaurant
Harbour Street Tullamore Co Offaly
Tel: 057 935 1529

Just the kind of place that every town needs, Jamie's is truly a local restaurant: welcoming, full of infectious enthusiasm, with a desire to please and serving good food at reasonable prices. The room is modern but homely, with tables dressed with white linen, and Jamie Owens (who trained at Adare Manor) runs the show from the kitchen with his mother Jeanette in charge out front ably assisted by daughters Ashling and Jessica. The early bird menu is great value, offering a choice of four starters and main courses, then selection of home-made desserts with tea or coffee - and a 7oz fillet steak served on champ with a mushroom, whiskey and cream sauce is a real winner. The à la carte menu offers a good variety of dishes, such as black pudding to start, then perhaps veal medallions with madeira, wild mushrooms and cream; dishes are well-presented and portions are generous. A compact wine list offers about 20 wines, including 2 house wines and, like the food, is well judged and fairly priced. **Seats 40**. D Wed-Sun, á la Carte 5.30- late, early D about €25, 5.30-7.30; L Sun only 12.30-2.15. Closed Mon & Tue. Major credit cards. **Directions:** Town centre, just across from the canal harbour. ◇

Tullamore

HOTEL

R

Tullamore Court Hotel

O'Moore Street Tullamore Co Offaly **Tel: 057 934 6666**
info@tullamorecourthotel.ie www.tullamorecourthotel.ie

An attractive building, set back from the road a little and softened by trees, this large modern hotel is welcoming, with an extensive foyer, and bright and cheerful public areas. It serves the local community very well, with an excellent leisure centre and fine banqueting facilities - and has become popular for short breaks, providing a comfortable and hospitable base within easy walking distance of the whole town. Bedrooms are pleasantly decorated in an easy modern style, using warm colours and unfussy fabrics - and the staff are exceptionally friendly and helpful. It makes an ideal base for visiting the area and, as the food is generally above the standard expected in hotels, this can be a refreshing place to break a journey. However, the hotel's greatest strength has always been its business and conference facilities and, following recent investment, state-of-the-art facilities include nine conference rooms, a business centre, 33 new executive bedrooms (including four suites) and a business centre. **Rooms 105** (1 suite, 4 junior suites, 8 family rooms, 90 no smoking, 6 for disabled); children welcome (under 4s free in parents room, cot available with no charge, baby sitting arranged). Lift. B&B about €105 pps, ss €20. Free Broadband, leisure centre, swimming pool, garden. Closed 24-26 Dec. Amex, MasterCard, Visa, Laser. **Directions:** South end of town. ◊

Tullamore Area

GUESTHOUSE

R

Annaharvey Farm

Tullamore Co Offaly **Tel: 057 934 3544**
info@annaharveyfarm.ie www.annaharveyfarm.ie

Henry and Lynda Deverell's restored grain barn, with pitch pine floors and beams, open fires and comfortable accommodation, provides a good base for a holiday offering all the pleasures of the outdoor life. Equestrian activities are the main attraction (including tuition in indoor and outdoor arenas), but walking, cycling and golfing also lay their claims - and, for the rest days, major sights including Clonmacnoise and Birr Castle are nearby. Good home cooking has always been a central feature here, and it has developed dramatically since Annaharvey Farm Foods became part of the 'Offaly Delicious' local food producers network and the kitchen. With Rachael Deverell now overseeing the operation, they produce even more delicious home-baking and preserves for the retail and catering trade – also on sale at their Saturday markets. Small conference/banqueting (40/20). **Rooms 7** (6 shower only, 1 with bath; all no-smoking); children welcome (under 2 free in parents' room; cot available without charge). No pets. B&B €45pps, ss €15. Meals available for residents only Mon-Sat, about €25 - details on application. Cookery school. Closed Dec & Jan. MasterCard, Visa, Laser. **Directions:** R420 Tullamore - Portarlington.

COUNTY ROSCOMMON

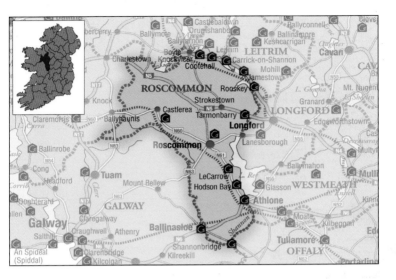

Irish villages are small places, but even by such standards, Keadue in north Roscommon is small indeed. It has just two shops, two pubs, a church and a health centre. The population is barely 150 people. But a third of them seem to be on the local Tidy Towns Committee. They keep their very Irish little village a neat as a new pin, and have celebrated the fact that Keadue (try pronouncing it "Kay-doo") has been the Tidy Towns Gold Medal holder for Roscommon, and for all Ireland.

And in August 2008 Roscommon acquired a further all-Ireland distinction. The national public health survey came up with the new that Roscommon has the highest life-expectancy figures for both men and women in the entire country. By the standards of some notably long-lived countries, the figures aren't particularly high – 76 years for men, and 82 for women – but nevertheless the emergence of Roscommon at the top was newsworthy, particularly as Leitrim next door was analysed as having the lowest lifespans.

It could be said that in times past, Roscommon was a county much put upon by the counties about it. Or, put another way, to the casual visitor it seemed that just as Roscommon was on the verge of becoming significant, it became somewhere else. In one notable example - the hotel complex at Hodson's Bay on the western shores of Lough Ree - the location is actually in Roscommon, yet the exigencies of the postal service have given it to Athlone and thereby Westmeath.

But Roscommon is a giving sort of county, for it gave Ireland her first President, Gaelic scholar Douglas Hyde (1860-1949), it was also the birthplace of Oscar Wilde's father, and as well the inimitable song-writer Percy French was a Roscommon man. Like everywhere else in the western half of Ireland, Roscommon suffered grievously from the Great Famine of the late 1840s, and at Strokestown, the handsome market town serving the eastern part of the county, Strokestown Park House has been sympathetically restored to include a Famine Museum. A visit to it will certainly add a thoughtful element to your meal in the restaurant.

Roscommon town itself has a population of 1,500, but it's growing, though the presence of extensive castle ruins and a former gaol tell of a more important past. The gaol was once noted for having a female hangman, today it has shops and a restaurant. Northwestward at Castlerea - headquarters for the County Council - we find Clonalis House, ancestral home of the O'Conor Don, and final resting place of O'Carolan's Harp.

In the north of the county, the town of Boyle near lovely Lough Key with its outstanding Forest Park is a substantial centre, with a population nearing the 2,000 mark. Boyle is thriving, and symbolic of this is the restored King House, a masterpiece from 1730. Reckoned to have been the most important provincial town house in Ireland, it is today filled with exhibits which eloquently evoke the past. Nearby, the impressive riverbank remains of Boyle Abbey, the largest Cistercian foundation in Ireland, date from 1148.

Lough Key is, of course, on one of the upper reaches of the inland waterways system, and a beautiful part it is too. In fact, all of Roscommon's eastern boundary is defined by the Shannon and its lakes, but as the towns along it tend to identify themselves with the counties on the other side of the river, Roscommon is left looking very thin on facilities. But it has much to intrigue the enquiring visitor. For instance, along the Roscommon shore of Lough Ree near the tiny village of Lecarrow, the remains of a miniature city going back to mediaeval times and beyond can be dimly discerned among the trees down towards Rindown Point. These hints of an active past serve to emphasise the fact that today, Roscommon moves at a gentler pace than the rest of Ireland.

Local Attractions and Information

Boyle	Boyle Abbey (12th C Monastery)	071 966 2604
Boyle	Frybrook House (18thC town hse)	071 966 2513
Boyle	King House (500 years of Irish life)	071 966 3242
Boyle	Lough Key Forest Park	071 966 2363
Boyle	Tourism Information	071 966 2145
Castlerea	Clonalis House	094 962 0014
Elphin	Restored windmill	071 963 5181
Frenchpark	Dr Douglas Hyde Interpretive Centre	0907 70016
Roscommon town	Arts Centre	090 662 5824
Roscommon town	County Museum	090 662 5613
Roscommon Town	Race Course	090 662 6231
Roscommon town	Tourism Information	090 662 6342
Strokestown	Park House, Garden & Famine Museum	071 963 3013
Strokestown	Roscommon County Heritage Centre	071 963 3380

Ballyfarnon
HOTEL

Kilronan Castle

Ballyfarnon Co Roscommon **Tel: 071 964 7771**
info@kilronancastle.ie www.kilronancastle.ie

Close by the very tidy village of Keadue and at the heart of a 40-acre estate overlooking Lough Meelagh, you will find this 5* sister establishment to **Lough Rynn Castle** in Co Leitrim (see entry), and the two properties have much in common, notably very beautiful natural surroundings and a romantic old-world atmosphere. The hotel was just opening at the time of the Guide's visit and, whilst it wasn't possible to view the new rooms, the original castle had been restored with style in both the public areas and also the accommodation, which is appealing and luxurious. The Douglas Hyde Restaurant (named after Ireland's first President, who was born at Castlerea) overlooks the grounds and is both beautifully appointed and intimate – a good combination, especially as early indications are that the standard of food and service matches the surroundings. When fully complete, the estate will have a spa, walled gardens and grounds designed by Diarmuid Gavin, a 9-hole Nick Faldo golf course (due to open in 2009) and - perhaps the estate's most unusual feature – a Supercar Museum. With its romantic setting and luxurious appointments, Kilronan Castle will be a popular wedding venue, and the restoration includes a chapel. Very reasonably priced special breaks are offered during the opening phase – and may well introduce many new visitors to this fascinating and unspoilt part of the country. **Directions:** R280/284 north from Carrick-on-Shannon. ◇

BOYLE

The attractive town of Boyle lies beneath the Curlew Mountains on the main pass connecting the plains of Connaught with the North and straddles the Boyle River. It has its own harbour, a mile from the town centre, where boats cruising the Shannon can overnight; there's a path into the town, which is known for its fine music pubs including **Kate Lavins** (071 96 62855), the **Abbey Bar** (071 96 63333) and **Clarke's** (071 96 62064), where there's also a restaurant. Across the bridge, **The Old Stone House** (086 155 2620) is a dramatically situated riverside daytime restaurant (Mon-Fri 9-6, Sat 10-6),

serving wholesome food and good coffee, while the characterful old **Royal Hotel** (071 96 62016), has a welcoming atmosphere, open fires and a riverside restaurant (Chinese). There is much of historical interest in the town, notably King House (500 years of Irish life, 071 966 3242), and it is a great place for fisherfolk, who will find plenty of trout or coarse fishing in the vicinity.
WWW.IRELAND-GUIDE.COM FOR ALL THE BEST PLACES TO EAT, DRINK & STAY

Carrick-on-Shannon
COUNTRY HOUSE•FARMHOUSE

Glencarne House

Ardcarne Carrick-on-Shannon Co Roscommon
Tel: 071 966 7013

On the border between Leitrim and Roscommon - Glencarne House is physically in Leitrim, but the postal address is Roscommon - the Harrington family's large Georgian house is set well back from the road, with a large garden in front and farmland behind, so it is easy to find, yet without intrusion from traffic. Spacious and elegantly furnished with antiques, this is very much a family home and Agnes Harrington has won many awards for hospitality and home-cooked food based on their own farm produce. Good-sized bedrooms all have en-suite bathrooms, and a fine breakfast, cooked to order, will set you up for the day. **Rooms 4** (all en-suite & no smoking); children welcome; pets permitted by arrangement. B&B €40 pps, ss €5. No meals other than breakfast. Garden. Closed Nov-Mar. **No Credit Cards. Directions:** On the N4,halfway between Carrick-on-Shannon and Boyle.

Castlecoote
HISTORIC HOUSE

Castlecoote House

Castlecoote Co Roscommon **Tel: 090 666 3794**
info@castlecootehouse.com www.castlecootehouse.com

This fine Georgian residence overlooking the beautiful River Suck was built in the enclosure of a medieval castle between 1690 and 1720, and is of considerable historic interest - not least as the birthplace of the Gunning sisters, who became the Duchess of Hamilton (and later, of Argyll) and Countess of Coventry; celebrated for their beauty, portraits of them by Sir Joshua Reynolds hang in the main hall. Having acquired the house as a ruin in 1997, the present owner, Kevin Finnerty, has painstakingly restored it to its former glory and, even if you cannot stay there, it is an exceptionally beautiful and interesting place to visit - guided tours of the house and grounds are offered from April to October (Tue-Sun, 2-6pm), and afterwards you can have afternoon tea with freshly-baked scones and home-made apple pie, apple juice and apple chutney in The Old Ballroom. The gardens are really lovely and include a walled orchard of rare apple trees (and none of the apples go to waste), three of the four towers of the ruined castle, a medieval bridge and even an ice house, all encircled by the river – a most romantic setting for the house, and soon to be seen to even better advantage as a new driveway is under construction, to create an appropriately dramatic entrance. An atmospheric cellar with a big open fire and snooker table is on a charmingly human scale, in contrast to the grand proportions of the reception rooms – which, Kevin feels, lend themselves especially well to group events; thus musical events, in particular, have become important to the life of the house, helped along by the arrival of a baby grand piano in 2008. The bright and airy guest rooms have marble fireplaces and stucco ceilings, and are beautifully furnished with four-poster beds and sumptuous bathrooms, making a wonderful place to stay for both individuals and groups. Conferences/Banqueting (120); business centre. **Rooms 5** (4 en-suite, 1 with private bathroom, 1 shower only. 1 family, 1 ground floor); children welcome (cot available, high chair); not suitable for wheelchairs. B&B €89pps, ss €30; D by arrangement €49-55 (book previous day); house wine from €19. Snooker, walking, garden, croquet, tennis, trout and coarse fishing on site; equestrian and golf nearby. Closed 31 Oct - 17 Mar. MasterCard, Visa. Heli-pad. **Directions:** Castlecoote is about 5km southwest of Roscommon, into village, cross bridge, bear right, gates are directly ahead.

Castlerea
COUNTRY HOUSE

Clonalis House

Castlerea Co Roscommon **Tel: 094 962 0014**
clonalis@iol.ie www.clonalis.com

Standing on the land that has been the home of the O'Conors of Connacht for 1,500 years, this 45-room Victorian Italianate mansion may seem a little daunting on arrival, but it's magic - and the hospitable owners, Pyers and Marguerite O'Conor-Nash, clearly relish sharing their rich and varied history with guests, who are welcome to browse through their fascinating archive. Amazing heirlooms include a copy of the last Brehon Law judgment (handed down about 1580) and also Carolan's Harp. Everything is on a huge scale: reception rooms are all very spacious, with lovely old furnishings and many interesting historic details, bedrooms have massive four poster and half-tester beds and bathrooms to match - and the dining room is particularly impressive, with a richly decorated table to enhance Marguerite's home cooking. Yet, despite the grandeur, there is a wonderfully warm and homely atmosphere at Clonalis House, which is set amid peaceful parklands and is well-placed for exploring County Roscommon, and the nearer parts of Galway, Mayo and Sligo – and, of course, it is very handy to Ireland West Airport at Knock, which is fast becoming an airport of choice for visitors wishing to avoid the hassle of larger airports. *Two attractive self-catering cottages are also offered, in the courtyard; details on application. **Rooms 4** (3 en-suite, 1 with private bathroom; all no smoking); unsuitable for children under 10 years. B&B €95-110 pps, ss €20. Residents D Tue-Sat, 8pm, €45 (24-hrs notice required); house wine from €20. (D not available Sun or Mon.) No pets. *A 10% reduction is offered for stays of three or more nights. Horse riding, fishing, shooting and golf (9) are all nearby. Garden, walking. Closed Oct-Apr. MasterCard, Visa, Laser. **Directions:** N60, west of Castlerea.

Cootehall
RESTAURANT
R

Cootehall Bridge Riverside Restaurant

Cootehall Boyle Co Roscommon
Tel: 071 966 7173

Cootehall is one of those places which can't decide which county it is in but, whether it is in Roscommon or Leitrim, this waterside restaurant provides a very complete service and it's the first port of call for many weekenders, as soon as they arrive in the area. After many years under the stewardship of Manfred Khan, the restaurant changed hands in 2006 and since then, the style is more rustic French/Italian food with Irish influences, although new owner Eric Cahill and his kitchen team kept on some of the old favourites like French onion soup. Menus based mainly on local and organic produce offer five starters, which usually include several salads (possibly including the house version of Chicken Caesar) and five main courses, which are strong on grills (char-grilled lamb cutlets, Chateaubriand steak) but also include imaginative vegetarian options, fish and daily specials, which are displayed on a blackboard, as are desserts, changed daily. And Manfred often drops in, as a customer, just to make sure everything is being done right; and he must be well pleased - judging by the way their good food and value for money have been sending many a customer happy into the night, they're doing a great deal of things absolutely right. **Seats 40**; children welcome (high chair, children's menu). L Sun only 12.30-5.30; D Thu-Sat 6-9.30. 3-course meal about €30-40. Dinner reservations recommended, especially at weekends. House wine €19.50. A phone call to check opening times is recommended, especially off-season. Closed Sun D, Mon, Tues, Wed and Nov & Jan. MasterCard, Visa, Laser. **Directions:** Right of the bridge as you approach the village.

Cootehall
CHARACTER PUB
R

M. J. Henry

Cootehall Boyle Co Roscommon
Tel: 071 966 7030

The more theme pubs and superpubs there are, the better everyone likes M J Henry's bar, which hasn't changed in at least 30 years and, in true country Irish fashion, is also a food store 'that caters for all your grocery needs'. A visit to Cootehall (the village of well-known writer, the late John McGahern) would be unthinkable without checking on this little gem They don't make them like this any more, alas, but this delightful old pub - complete with formica from the most recent renovation - is a one-off. Get in beside the fire with a hot whiskey and the world will do you no harm. No bar food, but there is sometimes music. Closed 25 Dec & Good Fri. **Directions:** 3km off N4 Sligo - Dublin road, between Boyle & Carrick-on-Shannon.

Knockvicar
RESTAURANT

Bruno's Restaurant

Knockvicar Boyle Co Roscommon **Tel: 071 966 7788**
brunoboe@eircom.net

Bruno Boe's attractively-located contemporary restaurant (previously known as Italia) is equally popular with local diners and boating visitors to the marina. The interior is well-designed on two levels to take full advantage of views over the river and Knockvicar marina, and the decor is colourful, comfortable and stylishly appointed - high-back chairs, classy tableware, fine glasses - an unusually cosmopolitan approach for a rural restaurant. Expect authentic Italian cooking - and fair prices. Hospitality is generally warm - when in top form you get the real Italian welcome and, although service can be slow, the overall package is attractive enough to keep people coming back. **Seats 70**; children welcome (high chair, childrens menu); toilets wheelchair accessible. D Tue-Sun 6-9.30pm, L Sun only 1-4pm. Set Sun L about €22; set D about €35; also a la carte. House wine about €17. No SC. (reservations required; advisable to ring and check opening hours, especially off-season.) Closed Mon & a few weeks Oct-Nov & Feb. Amex, MasterCard, Visa, Laser. **Directions:** Near Carrick-on-Shannon, on the Knockvicar-Cootehall road.

Lecarrow
RESTAURANT
Ⓝ 𝕍

The Yew Tree

Lecarrow Co Roscommon **Tel: 090 666 1255**
sal-aherne22@hotmail.com

A welcome sight for hungry travellers on the main Athlone-Roscommon road and just a short walk up from the attractive little harbour for those visiting Lecarrow by boat, Gerald and Sarah Aherne's smartly-presented restaurant is open from lunchtime onwards and makes a pleasing place to break a journey, or somewhere to head out to for a more leisurely meal in the evening. It's a friendly, welcoming restaurant, offering a short à la carte lunch menu during the afternoon - a good carrot & spring onion soup perhaps, served with home-made brown bread, or a crisp salad with bacon bits and a rich house dressing, followed by traditional Irish stew or goat's cheese crostini with crisp seasonal leaves. The evening menu offers more elaborate dishes – deep-fried Tournafulla black pudding (from west county Limerick) in a crunchy oatmeal crumb is a speciality starter, for example, served with basil mash and an apple and onion relish; also a main course of crisp half Silver Hill duckling on curried butternut, with a plum, blueberry and port wine glaze. Service is friendly and helpful, and the portions generous – some may find them too generous, in fact, especially with homely desserts like apple crumble. It is good to see the names of suppliers credited on the menu, especially as they are given under the relevant dish rather than simply listed at the end. All round, a welcome newcomer to Lecarrow. **Seats 65** (private room, 20); children welcome before 6pm (childrens menu); toilets wheelchair accessible. L & D daily, 12.30-5pm (from 1pm Sun) & 6-9pm (to 8pm Sun); a la carte. Closed 25-26 Dec, 1 Jan. MasterCard, Visa, Laser. **Directions:** From Athlone, N61 Roscommon road, about midway between two towns on the right hand side.

Roscommon
HOTEL

Abbey Hotel & Leisure Centre

Abbeytown Galway Road Roscommon Co Roscommon **Tel: 090 662 6240**
info@abbeyhotel.ie www.abbeyhotel.ie

The heart of this pleasing 4* hotel is an old manor house and, despite major developments, the atmosphere of the original building still prevails (and there's even a charmingly romantic honeymoon suite with a four-poster in the old house). Big changes have included the addition of a contemporary wing with spacious bedrooms, all designed and decorated to a high standard and with pleasant views. With good conference and business facilities, the hotel is the centre of local activities and a first choice for business guests staying in the area, but the high level of comfort, together with excellent leisure facilities and good value offered, also makes it appealing for short breaks. *Short/golfing breaks offered; details on application. Conference/banqueting (250/300); broadband wi/fi, laptop-sized safe in bedrooms. **Rooms 50** (all no smoking, 10 family, 10 ground floor, 4 disabled, 2 shower only); children welcome (under 12s free in parents' room; cots available without charge, baby sitting arranged). Garden. No pets. Lift. Room service (limited hours). B&B €120 pps, ss €20. Restaurant & Bar meals daily. House wines from €16.50, no SC. Leisure centre (20m swimming pool, sauna, steam room, gym, jacuzzi). Hotel closed 24-26 Dec. Amex, Diners, MasterCard, Visa, Laser. Heli-pad. **Directions:** N4 to Roscommon, Galway Road; next to the library, on the left.

Roscommon   # Gleeson's Townhouse and Restaurant

RESTAURANT WITH ROOMS   Market Square Roscommon Co Roscommon

Tel: 090 662 6954

info@gleesonstownhouse.com   www.gleesonstownhouse.com

Set right in the heart of Roscommon town, overlooking the square, Mary and Eamonn Gleeson's townhouse and restaurant provides just what every visitor requires: a warm welcome, comfortable rooms and first-class food. Over the last 15 years, they have made huge changes to their nineteenth century home. Having started out with just a coffee shop and four rooms, today there are 19 ensuite bedrooms, the original coffee shop and a restaurant. Bedrooms are comfortable, with all the usual facilities, including Internet access. There's a junior suite and an excellent executive suite with adjoining sitting-room that would make an ideal base for touring the area. The coffee shop opens for breakfast with home-made scones, bread and cakes, and then light lunches include delicious seafood chowder and beef and Guinness stew and lasagne. Small conferences/banqueting (80); free broadband wi/fi; video conferencing. **Rooms 19**. Children welcome (under 3s free in parents' room, 50% discount for under 14s in parents' room, baby sitting arranged, cot available). B&B €60 pps, ss €15.
Manse Restaurant: The Gleesons place great emphasis on food and buy local produce, organic when possible; the weekly Farmers' Market is held next door. An excellent residents' breakfast is served in the restaurant, until 11.30 - freshly-baked breads, croissants and brioche, fresh juices, cereals and porridge served with honey and cream, then hot dishes like the full Irish breakfast or toasted bagel with goat's cheese and onion marmalade. Dinner brings quite an extensive à la carte menu, maybe starting with that famous chowder, packed with fresh fish and served with home-made breads. Follow with Leitrim Organic Farmers' beefburger, served with Mossfield garlic herb cheese or Roscommon rack of lamb cooked with an apricot and pine nut crust. Finish with a very moreish tarte tatin, perhaps, or an organic cheeseboard and a good coffee. A good reasonably priced wine list includes some organic wines and a pair of half bottles. **Seats 55** (private room, 80, outdoors, 30); wheelchair access to restaurant & toilets; children welcome (high chair, childrens menu, baby changing facilities); air conditioning. L&D daily 12.30-6pm (Sun 12.30-5); 6.30-9.15pm (Sun to 8.45pm); a la carte. Also café open 8am-6pm daily; house wine €16.50. Closed 25-26 Dec. Amex, MasterCard, Visa, Laser. **Directions:** On Market Square, town centre. ◇

Shannonbridge   # The Old Fort

RESTAURANT   Shannonbridge Co Roscommon **Tel: 090 967 4973**

[V] [R]   info@theoldfortrestaurant.com   www.theoldfortrestaurant.com

In a pleasant and historically interesting site right beside the Shannon, this restaurant is in a restored fort and has oodles of character. The proprietor, Fergal Moran, grew up here and, having fulfilled a lifetime ambition to restore the fort, opened it as a restaurant in 2002. You arrive into a large and welcoming reception area and bar, which has lovely old timbers, a fine bar and comfortable sofas beside an open fire - and an extra dining space, which is useful at busy times or for guests who can't manage the stairs. The main dining room is upstairs and the ambience is lovely, with old wooden floors, well-spaced polished wood tables smartly laid with starched linen napkins and candles. Head chef Marie Haverty joined the restaurant in 2008, and house specialities are now exotic meats such as kangaroo, ostrich and crocodile. However, as ever, the simplest dishes are often best – a juicy local steak, cooked as ordered, makes a very good meal and, together with attentive service and lovely surroundings, can make for a memorable outing. **Seats 80** (private room, 30); children welcome (high chair, childrens menu); toilets wheelchair accessible; reservations advised. D Wed-Sun, from 5-9.30 (Sun, in summer only, 5-8); L Sun only 12.30-3. Value D €25 (Wed-Thu, 5-9.30 & Fri-Sat 5-7), Set 2/3 course D €27/40, also à la carte. Set Sun L, €23.50. House wine €18.50. Small weddings. Closed 3 weeks Jan. 1 week Nov. MasterCard, Visa, Laser. **Directions:** Beside the bridge in Shannonbridge.

Tarmonbarry

BAR•RESTAURANT•GUESTHOUSE

Keenans

Tarmonbarry (via Clondra) Co Roscommon

Tel: 043 26052 / 26098 info@keenans.ie www.keenans.ie

Just beside the bridge over the Shannon in Tarmonbarry, this well-run bar and restaurant is a favourite watering hole for river folk and makes a great place to break a journey between Dublin and the north-west. The bar is comfortably set up for food, and informal meals - mostly quite traditional, but with more international influences in the more expensive evening dishes - are served all day: open sandwiches on home-made wholemeal or soda bread, toasted sandwiches, salads and scones with jam & cream are typical, plus half a dozen daily specials (including specialities such as smoked fish casserole and bacon & cabbage at lunch, perhaps). A la carte bar menus are similar in tone but more extensive - wholesome, hearty fare that pleases all age groups; the steak sandwich (served with onions, chips, garlic butter & home-made horseradish sauce) is not to be missed. However it's been all change at the restaurant lately, with the recent opening of their lovely bright new dining room on the waterside corner of the building. It is really nicely done, with walnut flooring and tables, a minstrels' gallery, and a small bar. But fans will be glad to know that the hospitality's the same as ever and the food hasn't changed too much either. The à la carte offers seven or eight starters and main courses, including at least one vegetarian dish, a couple of steaks and the rest divided between poultry and fish. As ever, you'll find starters like garlic mushrooms or seafood chowder, main courses including the trademark honey roast duck, and desserts such as raspberry meringue roulade or apple crumble with walnut & cinnamon topping: good unpretentious food and cheerful, efficient service keep happy customers coming back. *****Accommodation** is offered, in 12 smart new en-suite rooms overlooking the Shannon; most have river views and some have balconies. **Rooms 12**; B&B €60 pps, single €85. Mid-week offers, Monday to Thursday €99 per room. **Restaurant seats 100**. Broadband wi/fi. Food served daily 12.30-8.30; L 12.30-2.30, D 6.30-8.30. Set D €40, also a la carte, Set Sun L €27.95. House wine €21. Restaurant closed D Sun. Establishment closed 24/25 Dec, Good Fri. Amex, MasterCard, Visa, Laser. **Directions:** On N5, west of Longford town.

Tarmonbarry

RESTAURANT•PUB

The Purple Onion Bar & Restaurant

Tarmonbarry (via Clondra) Co Roscommon **Tel: 043 59919**

info@purpleonion.ie www.purpleonion.ie

Paul Dempsey and Pauline Roe's village pub has an olde world feeling with dark wood, bric-à-brac and prints and, unusually, it doubles as an art gallery, so good original paintings add interest and charm. It can get very busy in the evening, with people waiting for tables, and there may be standing room only; however, watchful staff quickly bring menus to arriving diners, and even if you have to read while standing, the choice offered is impressive for a small restaurant, and may include some unusual dishes (grilled sardines, for example), also organic food including salmon and chicken; an early dinner menu is offered, also a separate children's menu and daily changing specials and desserts too. Sensibly, given the clientèle, there's a core of popular dishes, including sirloin and T-bone steaks, but also a fair sprinkling of suggestions to tempt more adventurous diners. Although some may find it dark and cramped (features that tend to go with the territory in old pubs), the restaurant has character and the dining experience overall is enjoyable - the food is interesting and offers something different from other choices in the area, and staff are attentive and genuinely caring. The wild boar sausage alone is reason enough to want to return to this restaurant. **Seats 55**; children welcome before 10pm (high chair, children's menu); air conditioning; L Sun only, 12.30-3.30pm; D Tue-Sun, 5.30-9.30pm (4.30-7.30 Sun). Good wine list; house wine €18.95. Closed Mon, one week Nov. MasterCard, Visa, Laser. **Directions:** 13km (8 miles) west of Longford on Dublin-Westport road.

COUNTY SLIGO

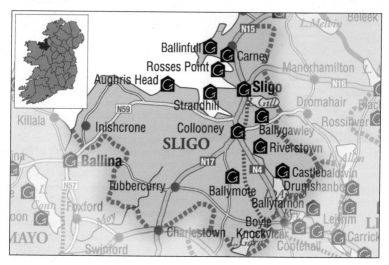

There's a stylish confidence to Sligo which belies its compact area as one of Ireland's smallest counties. Perhaps it's because they know that their place and their way of life have been immortalised through association with two of the outstanding creative talents of modern Ireland, W.B.Yeats and his painter brother Jack. The former's fame seems beyond question, while the latter's star was never higher than it is today.

The town and the county have many associations with Yeats, but few are more remarkable than Lissadell House, the former home of the Gore-Booths. Best known as the family of Constance Gore-Booth - who as Countess Markievicz was much involved with the Easter Rising of 1916 – the Gore-Booths were extraordinary people in several generations, and the sale in 2003 of Lissadell – which is now open to the public – was a timely reminder of this, and of Sligo's unique qualities.

But whatever the reason for Sligo's special quality, there's certainly something about it that encourages repeat visits. The town itself is big enough to be reassuring, yet small enough to be comfortable. And the countryside about Sligo town also has lasting appeal. Mankind has been living here with enthusiasm for a very long time indeed, for in recent years it has been demonstrated that some of County Sligo's ancient monuments are amongst the oldest in northwest Europe. Lakes abound, the mountains are magnificent, and there are tumbling rivers a-plenty.

Yet if you wish to get away from the bustle of the regular tourist haunts, Sligo can look after your needs in this as well, for the western part of the county down through the Ox Mountains towards Mayo is an uncrowded region of wide vistas and clear roads.

Local Attractions and Information

Carrowmore	Largest Megalithic Cemetry in Ireland	071 916 1534
Drumcliff	Drumcliffe Church & Visitor Centre (Yeats)	071 914 4956
Drumcliff	Lissadell House	071 916 3150
Inniscrone	Seaweed Bath House	096 36238
nr Drumcliff	Lissadell House	071 916 3150
Lough Gill	Waterbus Cruises	071 916 4266
Sligo	Discover Sligo Tours	071 914 7488
Sligo	Model Arts & Niland Gallery	071 914 1405
Sligo Abbey	(13thC Dominican Friary)	071 914 6406
Sligo	Sligo Airport, Strandhill	071 916 8280
Sligo	Sligo Art Gallery	071 914 5847
Sligo	Tourism Information	071 916 1201
Sligo	Yeats Memorial Building, Hyde Bridge	071 914 2693
Strandhill	Seaweed Baths, Maritime House	071 916 8686

AUGHRIS HEAD

Backing onto the Ox Mountains and facing the Atlantic Ocean, Aughris Head is situated in Sligo Bay, and is known for its cliffs and small sandy beaches. Walking enthusiasts may enjoy the rugged Ox Mountains or a gentler walk along the coast to the cliffs at Coragh Dtonn, where dolphins are regular visitors. The area is exposed to the powerful North Atlantic waves, making it a popular surfing spot, and the Irish Surfing Association (096 49428) headquarters is nearby in Easkey. Angling enthusiasts will find excellent shore fishing from Aughris Head, and there are many chartered deep sea trips provided by local fishermen.

Aughris Head
PUB•B&B

Beach Bar/Aughris House
Aughris Head Templeboy Co Sligo
Tel: 071 916 6703 / 071 917 6465

The McDermott family's picturesque and beautifully-located thatched pub seems too good to be true when you first find it in this quiet and unspoilt place, but there it has been since the 18th century when, apparently, it was a shibín known as Maggie Maye's. Today, after sensitive restoration, it has retained some of the best characteristics of the past and makes a lovely stopping place, with food served in the flag-stoned bar - and access to a beach just a hop across the wall from the car park. Wholesome, home-cooked meals are served here - creamy Atlantic seafood chowder, great steaks, bangers and mash, and delicious home-made desserts too. Bar food daily 1-8 in summer. Phone to check times off-season. **Accommodation:** In a neat bungalow just beside the pub and overlooking the Atlantic Ocean, the McDermotts also offer comfortable, inexpensive, family-friendly B&B accommodation, with neat shower rooms and TV. Complimentary tea and biscuits on arrival. Children welcome (under 2 free in parents' room, cot available, baby sitting arranged); pets allowed in some areas. Garden, scenic walks, sandy beach, boat trips and sea angling arranged. B&B €35 pps, single about €40. (Short breaks & family rates available). Open all year. MasterCard, Visa. **Directions:** Off N59 Sligo/Ballina Road, Coast road to Aughris Head/Pier.

Ballinfull
CAFÉ
🏛️ Ⓝ Ⓥ

Lissadell House Café
Lissadell Ballinfull Co Sligo **Tel: 071 916 3150**
info@lissadellhouse.com www.lissadellhouse.com

Lissadell is the former home of the Gore-Booths, of whom the best known was Constance Gore-Booth who, as Countess Markievicz, was closely involved with the Easter Rising of 1916. Since the sale of Lissadell in 2003, the stated aim of new owners Edward Walsh and Constance Cassidy was 'the restoration of this national treasure as a family home open to visitors, and the regeneration of the flower and pleasure gardens'. Already they have 'reversed the decline and neglect of the previous seventy years' and opened both the house and gardens to the public. It is an extraordinary place, and of interest at so many levels. Its generosity of spirit strikes the visitor immediately on arrival – passing by the lovely 2-acre seashore Alpine Rockery Garden, which is easily accessible from the road, with no entrance charge - and Edward and Constance planned well when they placed the tea rooms so near the entrance, as it must be obvious to even the most casual visitor that sustenance will be needed ahead of any visit here, there is just so much to see. The Tea Rooms serve wholesome country fare – quiches, scones, salads, fruit and vegetables (fresh produce comes from the Kitchen Gardens), and also oysters from their own oyster beds. As well as the tables indoors, there are seats for visitors around the courtyard – and the gift shop is well worth visiting, for Lissadell organic fruit and vegetables, their own home-made chutneys and jams, a range of French wines (by bottle or case) and many other quality gifts. It's a wonderful place – if you have to choose just one visitor attraction in Ireland to visit, make it Lissadell. And allow plenty of time. **Seats 100** (outdoors, 40); children welcome (high chair); open daily 10.30am-6pm. MasterCard, Visa, Laser. **Directions:** 7km off the N15 Sligo - Donegal road.

Ballygawley
HOTEL
Ⓡ

Castle Dargan Hotel - Estate Hotel & Golf Resort
Castle Dargan Estate Ballygawley Co Sligo **Tel: 071 911 8080**
info@castledargan.com www.castledargan.com

Named after the ruins of the ancient castle which remain within its Darren Clarke-designed championship golf course, Castle Dargan House makes a fine centrepiece for this contemporary hotel and is set amongst dramatic scenery on 170 acres of mature woodlands, with uninterrupted views over the countryside and golf course. A lovely period drawing room and meeting room within the original house sets the tone for the well-designed new section across a courtyard to the rear of the old house. A large reception area with high ceilings, warm colour schemes and log fires establish the warm, modern tone that prevails throughout the new areas - the bar is especially striking, featuring a mezzanine level with floor to ceiling windows overlooking a large decking area and the golf course. Alongside is an intimate restaurant, which shares the same views. **Accommodation** is mainly in the new area - all bedrooms are finished to a high standard, with the usual amenities, and have views of the golf course - but the suites are in the old house and enjoy a special atmosphere. Apartments separately located at the gate of the hotel are also available, each sleeping up to four people. The hotel would make a magnificent wedding venue and the function room, an L-shaped room with floor-to-ceiling windows on two sides and a private bar, is in a prime location on the first floor. Conferences/Banqueting (400/300), free broadband wi/fi, video conferencing. **Rooms 54** (16 junior suites, 4 executive, 14 ground floor, 1 for disabled); children welcome (under 4s free in parents' room, cot available at no charge, baby sitting arranged); wheelchair friendly; limited room service, Lift. B&B from €85pps, ss €35. **Hall Door Restaurant: seats 60**, D daily 6-9.30pm; L Sun only, 1-3pm. Bar food available all day, 10.30am-9pm. Championship golf (18), spa, jacuzzi, steam room, beauty salon, walking; Hunting/shooting, surfing and equestrian nearby. Open all year. Heli-pad. Amex, MasterCard, Visa, Laser. **Directions:** 10 minutes from Sligo town- take the R284 to Ballygawley. There is an alternative access from the Collooney By-pass roundabout via the Dromahair Road.

Ballymote

COUNTY HOUSE

Temple House

Ballinacarrow Ballymote Co Sligo **Tel: 071 918 3329**

enquiry@templehouse.ie   www.templehouse.ie

One of Ireland's most unspoilt old houses, this is a unique place - a Georgian mansion situated in 1,000 acres of farm and woodland, overlooking the original lakeside castle which was built by the Knights Templar in 1200 A.D. The Percevals have lived here since 1665 and the house was re-designed and refurbished in 1864 - some of the furnishings date back to that major revamp. Sandy and Deb Perceval first opened the doors of their home to guests in 1981 and it is now owned by their son Roderick and his wife Helena, who have brought their own brand of energy and enthusiasm to running this amazing house. The whole of the house has retained its old atmosphere and, in addition to central heating, has log fires to cheer the enormous rooms. Spacious bedrooms are furnished with old family furniture and bathrooms are gradually being upgraded. Guests have the use of an elegant sitting room with open fires, and evening meals are served in a very beautiful dining room - based on seasonal produce from the estate and other local suppliers, they are a treat to look forward to. You may expect homely treats like spinach soufflé, Temple House lamb, and desserts based on garden produce like rhubarb fool; there's always an Irish cheeseboard too - and home-made fudge with coffee in the Morning Room. Traditional Irish music and dancing sessions are often held nearby. **Rooms 6** (5 en-suite, 2 shower only, 1 with private bathroom, 2 family, all no smoking); free broadband wi/fi; children welcome (under 12s 60% discount, babies free in parents' room; cots available at no charge, baby sitting arranged). B&B from €80 pps, ss €25. Residents 4-course D €45, 7.30pm (book by 1pm, not available Sun); house wine €18. Children's tea 6.30pm; SC discretionary. Fishing (fly & coarse), hunting/shooting, walking, snooker. Garden visits nearby. *Golf nearby, at Rosses Point, Strandhill and Enniscrone - short breaks available. Closed Dec-Mar. MasterCard, Visa, Laser. Heli-pad. **Directions:** Signposted off N17, 0.5 km south of Ballinacarrow. 11km (7 m) south of N4/N17.

Carney

BAR•RESTAURANT

Laura's

Main Street Carney Co Sligo **Tel: 071 916 3056**

www.lauras.ie

Husband and wife team Ger and Geraldine Reidy will be well known to many from their time at The Parliament House in Kilkenny and then Hargadon's in Sligo. These days you will find them at this thriving pub and restaurant near Lissadell, which is pretty with flowers, creepers and climbing roses. Entrance to the restaurant area is through the pub, where home-made light meals (mussels, chicken wings, home-made spare ribs with home-made sweet & sour sauce, etc) are served in a traditional setting, or at picnic-style seating outside. If a restaurant atmosphere is preferable, there are some intimate tables downstairs, and more upstairs in a bright and airy high-windowed space; towards the back, the view takes in part of Ben Bulben, and a terrace offers the option of al fresco dining with a view of the sea – and plenty of room for restless children to let off steam. The restaurant has built its reputation largely on seafood, a theme that runs through starters (chowder, crab claws, mussels, warm tuna salad plate, Arctic char salad) and main dishes but, with dishes like chicken liver paté, lamb's kidneys, steaks, local pork, and organic chicken offered too, meat lovers are well catered for, and vegetarians also. All main courses come with a generous platter of very nicely cooked vegetables – and salad greens and vegetables are organic, from the nearby gardens of Lissadell. Ger owns a fish shop in Sligo and the Catch of the Day selection can include as many as 8 or 9 varieties of fish, including Arctic char, which is farmed nearby; the menu offers a variety of sauces and styles of preparation, but Ger's own philosophy is that fresh fish needs little or no dressing up; and simplest is best in the Guide's experience - half a dozen Lissadell oysters, perhaps, and perfectly cooked turbot with a light creamy sauce. With good home-made puddings too, and friendly, efficient service, this is a pleasant spot – but, while quality ensures value for money, don't expect fresh seafood to be inexpensive. Restaurant open evenings only (from 6 o'clock) weekdays, and from lunchtime on Sundays; bar food served daily. MasterCard, Visa, Laser. **Directions:** Follow N15 from Sligo-Donegal. Turn left just after Drumcliffe, following sign for Carney and Lissadell. Carney is about 1.5 km and Laura's is on the right, just at left turn off for Lissadell House.

Clevery Mill

Castlebaldwin
RESTAURANT WITH ROOMS•WINE BAR

Castlebaldwin Co Sligo **Tel: 071 912 7424**
cleverymill@eircom.net www.cleverymill.com

This charmingly converted old mill, complete with millwheel, is located in the countryside about 20 minutes' drive from Sligo. From the moment you push open the door of the old stone building, you get a sense of warmth and relaxation. Overnight guests will find six comfortable bedrooms with plenty of character - some rooms have four-poster beds and all are attractively furnished in a country style, with modern en-suite shower rooms. Both residents and people in for a meal will enjoy the old-world country ambience in the bar area or, perhaps, in the smaller snug room adjacent; log fires are an attractive feature and there's a pleasant feeling to the whole building. The main dining room overlooks the old waterwheel and is classically appointed with white linen and full of character; the menu tempts with a wide selection of dishes and lists sources, which are mostly local and organic. **Seats 54** (outdoors, 8); D Thu-Sat 6.30-9.30, L Sun only 12.30-4pm; set Sun L about €28; set D about €40. **Rooms 6**; B&B from €65 pps; midweek specials available on request. Closed D Sun, Mon-Wed; house closed Christmas & New Year. MasterCard, Visa, Laser **Directions:** 22.5km (14 m) from Sligo, N4 towards Dublin.

Cromleach Lodge

Castlebaldwin
HOTEL•RESTAURANT

Castlebaldwin via Boyle Co Sligo **Tel: 071 916 5155**
info@cromleach.com www.cromleach.com

Quietly situated in the hills just above Lough Arrow, Christy and Moira Tighe's very special hotel enjoys one of the finest views in Ireland - and it makes a luxurious retreat for the most discerning of guests. Cromleach is rightly renowned for its exceptionally high standards of both food and accommodation - and, most importantly, the Tighe family and their staff have the magic ingredient of genuine hospitality, doing everything possible to ensure comfort and relaxation for their guests. The hotel has grown dramatically recently – the new bedrooms were just opening at the time of the Guide's 2008 visit – but the hospitable philosophy is unchanged, and this remains a wonderful place to stay. Bedrooms vary more than formerly, and the choice in position, size and price will ensure that a suitable option is available to more guests. All are stylishly decorated and, as always, there is a welcome emphasis on comfort rather than fashion, and all rooms are thoughtfully furnished to make the most of their size and outlook. Many have seating areas overlooking the lough with easy chairs to relax in, and all have well-planned bathrooms with lots of luxurious little extras - and housekeeping and attention to detail are invariably outstanding. The area around Cromleach is beautiful and unspoilt, and the Tighes like nothing better than to introduce guests to the many places of interest and activities nearby but, for many, just being here is more than enough. In addition to the new accommodation, other recent additions include the first floor 'Diarmaid & Grainne' banqueting suite, where weddings for up to 200 can be held; also a smart little bar, Nuada's, where a light snack menu is available all day. *A new spa facility, making the most of the view over Lough Arrow, opened in Summer 2008. Conferences/Banqueting (220/200); free broadband wi/fi. Children welcome (under 3 free in parents' room, cot available (€10), baby sitting arranged). Pets permitted by arrangement (stay in bedroom, no charge). Spa, sauna, steam room, massage, treatments, hair dressing. Garden; walking; fishing. Golf, equestrian and garden visits nearby. **Rooms 68** (21 executive, 9 ground floor). Lift; Room service (limited hours). Turndown service. B&B €99 pps, single €125. Short breaks and off-season value breaks available. **Moira's:** This contemporary restaurant is elegant and calm - arranged to allow every table to take full advantage of the view, it is decorated in shades of cream and coffee, with black leather high-backed chairs and stylish long seats at each end of the room - stripes of lime green, pale mauve, moss green and grey fit beautifully with the voile curtains embroidered in golds and lined in silk. Moira Tighe (a former Chef of the Year) remains very involved with the kitchen, and works closely with her team; menus are based on meticulously sourced ingredients - and the many regular guests who have grown attached to Cromleach will be glad to know that the wonderful food has not changed too much - specialities created by Moira over the years will still feature, along with new dishes, as has always been the case. Everything, from the first little amuse-bouche to the last petit four with coffee is a treat - and, as in all aspects of this exceptional place, service is flawless. **Seats 100** (private room, 24); children welcome (high chair, childrens menu, baby changing facilities); toilets wheelchair accessible; reservations required. Light food served throughout the day. L & D daily, 12.30-6pm (to 4om Sun) & 6-9pm (Sun 6.30-8pm). Set Sun L €35, À la carte L&D; house wines from €19.95; sc discretionary. Open all year. Amex, MasterCard, Visa, Laser **Directions:** Signposted from Castlebaldwin on the N4.

Collooney

HOTEL•RESTAURANT

V **R**

Markree Castle

Collooney Co Sligo **Tel: 071 9167800**

info@markreecastle.ie www.markreecastle.ie

Sligo's oldest inhabited house has been home to the Cooper family for 350 years. Set in magnificent park and farmland, this is a proper castle, with a huge portico leading to a covered stone stairway that sweeps up to an impressive hall, where an enormous log fire always burns. Everything is on a very large scale, and it is greatly to the credit of the present owners, Charles and Mary Cooper, that they have achieved the present level of renovation and comfort since they took it on in a sad state of disrepair in 1989 - and they have always been generous with the heating. Ground floor reception areas include a comfortably-furnished double drawing room with two fireplaces (where light food, including after-noon tea, is served). There is a lift and also disabled toilets, but the layout of the castle makes it difficult for elderly people or wheelchair users to get around; a phone call ahead to ensure the (very willing) staff are available to help would be wise. The dining room is a very beautiful room and its Knockmuldowney Restaurant is open to non-residents for dinner, and lunch on Sunday. There are many idiosyncrasies - in bedrooms, for example – but this slightly eccentric place has got real heart; do, however, beware of times when very inexpensive offers are available, as it can be noisy and children are not always kept under control. Conferences/banqueting (110/170), free broadband wi/fi. **Rooms 30** (all en-suite, 4 executive rooms, 1 family, 3 ground floor, 1 disabled); children welcome (under 4s free in parents' room; cots available free of charge, baby sitting arranged). Pets permitted (stay in bedrooms free of charge). Lift. B&B from €97.50 pps, ss €12.50. **Restaurant seats 90** (private room, 40); non-residents are welcome (reservations recommended); children welcome (high chair, childrens menu); D 7-9pm daily; L Sun only 1-3pm. Set 2/3 course D €35/45, Set Sun L about €20; house wine €20; no sc. Horse riding, walking, fishing (coarse). Fly fishing, surfing. golf all nearby. Hotel closed 24-27 Dec. Amex, Diners, MasterCard, Visa. **Directions:** Just off the N4, take the Dromohair/R290 exit at Collooney roundabout.

Riverstown
COUNTRY HOUSE

Coopershill House

Riverstown Co Sligo **Tel: 071 916 5108**
ohara@coopershill.com www.coopershill.com

Undoubtedly one of the most delightful and superbly comfortable Georgian houses in Ireland, this sturdy granite mansion was built to withstand the rigours of a Sligo winter but it's a warm and friendly place. Peacocks wander elegantly on the croquet lawns (and roost in the splendid trees around the house at night) making this lovely place, home of the O'Hara family since it was built in 1774, a particularly perfect country house. In immaculate order from top to bottom, the house not only has the original 18th century furniture but also some fascinating features, notably an unusual Victorian free-standing rolltop bath complete with fully integrated cast-iron shower 'cubicle' and original brass rail and fittings, all in full working order. Luxurious rooms are wonderfully comfortable and have phones and tea/coffee-making facilities. Simon O'Hara has now taken over management of the house from his parents, Brian and Lindy, and the house runs with the seamless hospitality born of long experience; this includes the kitchen which is now in the capable hands of Cristina McCauley, who had worked alongside Lindy O'Hara since 2004. As well as their own neatly maintained vegetable garden, the O'Haras have a deer farm, so you may well find venison on the dinner menu – roast loin of Coopershill venison with red wine sauce is a favourite - along with other deliciously wholesome country house cooking. Donegal crab tart, spinach & rosemary soup (straight from the garden), baked Donegal cod with a herb crust, and Coopershill rhubarb compôte & meringues are all typical, served in their lovely dining room where the family silver is used with magnificent insouciance (even at breakfast). A surprisingly extensive wine list, which has many treats in store, offers four house wines and an exceptionally good choice of half bottles. Coopershill is well placed for exploring this unspoilt area - and makes a good base for golfers too, with several championship courses, including Rosses Point within easy range. **Rooms 8** (7 en-suite, 1 shower only, 1 private bathroom, 1 family room, all no smoking); children welcome (under 2 free in parents' room; cots available without charge, baby sitting arranged). Dogs may stay in outhouse/kennel. Turndown service. B&B €127 pps, ss €40. Dining Room Seats 34. D 8.15pm daily (non-residents welcome by reservation); Set D about €57, house wines from €24; sc discretionary. Free broadband wi/fi. Tennis, cycling, boating, fishing, garden, croquet, snooker room on site. Golf, hunting, sea angling, surfing and garden visits nearby. *10% discount on stays of 3+ days. Closed end Oct-1 Apr. (off-season house parties of 12-16 people welcome.) Amex, Diners, MasterCard, Visa, Laser. **Directions:** Signposted from N4 at Drumfin crossroads.

ROSSES POINT

This seaside village, a few minutes' drive from Sligo town, has views across to Oyster Island and Coney Island (after which the island off New York was named); Rosses Point is renowned for golf (County Sligo Golf Club, Rosses Point 071 917 7134) and has a lovely beach which is great for windsurfing, sailing and angling. There are several restaurants and bars to choose from: Joe Grogan's bar/restaurant **The Waterfront** (071 917 7122; from 5pm each evening) can be excellent at its best. There are many associations with the poet W.B. Yeats and his brother, the painter Jack Yeats - the most notable connection was with Lissadell House & Gardens (Ballinfull, 071 916 3150; see entry), the former home of the Gore-Booths, of whom the best known was Constance Gore-Booth who, as Countess Markievicz, was much involved with the Easter Rising of 1916. The nearby Enniscrone GC (096 36297) provide a tough test for golfers of all abilities.

WWW.IRELAND-GUIDE.COM FOR ALL THE BEST PLACES TO EAT, DRINK & STAY

SLIGO

A fascinating town, with a rich heritage, Sligo has a growing number of hotels: if business and leisure facilities convenient to the town are important, the **Sligo Park Hotel** (Tel 071 916 0291; www.leehotels.com) is a popular choice - this long-established hotel on the edge of the town has good facilities and ample parking; by contrast, a recent arrival is the shiny new town centre hotel **The Glasshouse** (071 919 4300; www.theglasshouse.ie), also with parking, which may appeal to modernists and is within walking distance of everything. There are plenty of popular coffee shops and cafés to sustain a day around the town: **Bistro Bianconi** (Tel 071 914 1744) on O'Connell Street continues to meet the informal family dining market well, and now has outlets in Dublin and Galway. For lovers of Indian

food, a branch of the long-established Dublin restaurant **Poppadom** (Tel 071 914 7171; www.poppadomsligo.com) is a few doors along, and there's another fine Indian restaurant, **Classic Indian** (formerly called Sher-E-Punjab; Tel 071 914 7700) on Market Street. Sligo has a rich cultural heritage and, in the town, the Model Arts & Niland Gallery is especially worth visiting (due to re-open in spring 2009, following redevelopment); there are many associations with the poet W.B. Yeats and his brother, the painter Jack Yeats - the most notable connection was with Lissadell House & Gardens (Ballinfull, 071 916 3150; see entry). The Atrium Café at Niland is not expected to re-open unfortunately, but you can find Brid Torrades' delicious food at her restaurants **Osta** and **Tobergal Lane** (see entries); and a chic newcomer to try is **Temptation** (071 915 2225), an authentic French patisserie at Quayside Shopping Centre. **The Silver Apple** (071 914 6770) is upstairs at the Gateway Bar, on Lord Edward Street; although not quite settled at the time of the Guide's visit, it offers promising ingredients-led French bistro cooking and is useful to know about. The nearby championship golf courses at Enniscrone (096 36297) & County Sligo (Rosses Point, 071 917 7134) provide a tough test for golfers of all abilities. There is a Farmers' Market in Sligo IT on Saturdays (9am -1pm).
WWW.IRELAND-GUIDE.COM FOR ALL THE BEST PLACES TO EAT, DRINK & STAY

Sligo	Clarion Hotel
HOTEL	Clarion Road Sligo Co Sligo **Tel: 071 911 9000**
info@clarionhotelsligo.com www.clarionhotelsireland.com

This large hotel in Sligo town actually dates back to 1848 but, following recent re-development, it has emerged as a modern classic with the contemporary style that is associated with the new Clarion hotels. The warm-toned reception area has a welcoming atmosphere and accommodation is well up to the usual standard, offering a high proportion of suites (including a penthouse suite) and good-sized rooms, all with high quality bedding, smart bathrooms, broadband, and irons & ironing board as standard. Dining options offer the now familiar choice between the well-appointed Sinergie restaurant (crisp white linen, international menu, attentive service) and casual dining Asian-style in the Kudos Bar. Leisure and pampering facilities include a 20m pool, gym and spa treatments. Business and conference facilities offer meeting rooms for groups of 4 to 400, and a business team to co-ordinate events if necessary. **Rooms 312** (91 suites); room rate from €99. Sinergie seats 160 (private room, 35); D daily 6-10; Sun: L 1-3, D 6-9.30; Set Sun L about €30; Set D about €35. House wine from €24. Food served in Kudos Bar & Rest 12.30-10 daily. Amex, Diners, MasterCard, Visa, Laser. **Directions:** Follow N16 signs for Enniskillen. ◈

Sligo	Coach Lane Restaurant @ Donaghy's Bar
RESTAURANT•PUB	1-2 Lord Edward Street Sligo Co Sligo
Tel: 071 916 2417

The restaurant over Orla and Andy Donaghy's pub is approached by an attractive side alley, with a menu board displayed on the street. It's a long narrow room, furnished in a comfortable mixture of traditional and contemporary styles, with well-appointed white-clothed tables, soft lighting and neatly uniformed waitresses in black polo shirts and trousers with white aprons all creating a good impression. Andy's menus are lively and attractive, the cooking is confident and, an active supporter of local produce, he does a great line in well-aged steaks, and seafood. There's also a wide choice of salads, pasta dishes and chicken - and the cooking style ranges from traditional (steak with home-made fries, crispy onion rings & HP sauce) to spicy (cajun chicken with a fresh fruit salsa). This attractive well-run restaurant has earned a well-deserved place as one of the best in the area. **Seats 120** (plus 40 on an outside terrace, weather permitting); children welcome; air conditioning. D daily from 5.30pm (from 4pm Sun); à la carte. Also bar food daily 3-10pm. House wine from €20.50; service discretionary except 10% on parties of 8+. Closed 25 Dec, Good Fri, 2nd week Feb. Amex, MasterCard, Visa, Laser. **Directions:** N4 to Sligo, left at Adelaide Street, right into Lord Edward Street.

Sligo	The Embassy Wine Bar & Grill
RESTAURANT•WINE BAR	JFK Parade Sligo Co Sligo **Tel: 071 916 1250**
Ⓝ	info@toffs.eu www.embassygrill.eu

Situated in the centre of Sligo's old town on the banks of the Garavogue River, the dark façade of this popular restaurant is not particularly inviting, although five arched windows in a stonework wall give it some character and attract attention to a stylishly well-appointed interior – and, from the inside, they allow a glimpse of the Garavogue. The decor has a gently modern feel in subtle browns and creams; a mix of high-back leather chairs and banquettes around bare-topped wooden tables contrast nicely with open stonework walls, and comfortable snugs add character and break groups up. Quite an extensive à la carte menu offers plenty of popular dishes, including starters like stuffed mushrooms house-style and crab claws in garlic butter; mains lead off with a choice of char-grilled steaks served with the signature Jameson Whiskey Sauce and include several poultry and fish dishes and one vegetarian. Desserts are home-made, including a hot chocolate fondant with basil ice cream – an unusual but successful combination. Generous servings of good quality food, served efficiently in a relaxed environment and giving good value for money, explain the Embassy's popularity – and the food is complemented by an appropriate choice of wines, including several half bottles. **Seats 60**; free broadband wi/fi; toilets wheelchair accessible; not suitable for children under 15; air conditioning; D Tue-Sat, 6-10pm, à la carte; L Sun only, 12.30-2pm, set 4 course Sun L €21.95; house wine €19. Closed Mon, Good Fri, 24-26 Dec. MasterCard, Visa, Laser. **Directions:** On the banks of the River Garavogue in the centre of Sligo town.

Sligo   # Lyons Café
CAFÉ   Quay Street Sligo Co Sligo
Ⓝ   **Tel: 071 914 2969**

Anyone visiting Sligo should make a point of calling into the magnificently traditional Lyons Department Store, in business since 1878 and still with its original shopfront; it's a joy to find a quirky owner-run store these days and, on the first floor, they have a café-restaurant serving fresh and wholesome locally-sourced food - Sligo's best kept secret, perhaps. 'Possibly the oldest café in Sligo town', Lyons Café opened in 1923 and has changed little since: casement window, cream panelling, wooden floor, bentwood chairs... There will be a couple of ladies putting the world to rights at a window table, as they have probably been doing for the last 30 years. You are immediately aware of the animated chatter and friendly feel – unlike so many smart modern places that could be anywhere, in Lyons's you really feel you are in Sligo. However, while retaining the best of older ways – especially the good scones and treats for those of sweet tooth, the food appeals also to the more contemporary palate. (Thai green curry, ciabatta, etc) there's a good selection of teas and coffees, sandwiches are made to order, a good salad bar to choose from and hot specials, such as roast stuffed Irish chicken with mushroom cream sauce. Enticing desserts are a strong point – definitely home-made - black cherry bakewell, tangy lemon and lime tart brownies... and the possibility of lashings of cream. Simply gorgeous. **Seats 125**; no reservations accepted; children welcome (high chair, baby changing facilities); free broadband wi/fi; toilets wheelchair accessible. Open Mon-Sat 9am-6pm. Closed Sun, Bank Hols, 25 Dec. MasterCard, Visa, Laser. **Directions:** On corner of Wine Street/Quay Street between town hall and post office.

Sligo   # Montmartre
RESTAURANT   1 Market Yard Sligo Co Sligo **Tel: 071 916 9901**
                       edelmckeon@eircom.net

French-run and staffed, this unpretentious place beside a carpark is the area's leading restaurant and has a strong local following, so reservations are strongly advised, especially at weekends. Although not big, there is a little bar area that doubles as reception with a bright and airy feeling, with potted palms, white crockery and smartly uniformed staff all emphasising the French style. Proprietor-chef Stéphane Magaud's varied menus offer imaginative French cuisine in a light, colourful style with local produce featuring in some dishes, especially seafood - Lissadell oysters and mussels, for instance, there may also be game in season, and there will always be imaginative vegetarian dishes. Sound cooking, attractive presentation and reasonable prices have brought this restaurant many friends; some say the service is slow, but to the French eating is a leisurely pastime. The wine list, which is mostly imported directly from France, includes an unusually good selection of half bottles and wines by the glass. An early dinner menu offers exceptional value. **Seats 50**; children welcome; air conditioning; toilets wheelchair accessible. D Tue-Sat, 5-11pm. Early D about €16 (5-7pm), D à la carte. House wines from €18. Closed Mon, 24-26 Dec. Amex, Diners, MasterCard, Visa, Laser. **Directions:** 200 yards from Hawks Well Theatre & Tourist Office. ◈

Sligo
Osta Café & Wine Bar

CAFÉ•WINE BAR

Garavogue Weir View (near Hyde Bridge) Stephen Street Sligo Co Sligo

V

Tel: 071 914 4639 www.osta.ie

The Garavogue River sweeps past this bright and airy café in the centre of Sligo town, and the floor-to-ceiling glass frontage makes it a delightful spot for coffee (organic and fairly traded) or a more substantial meal. Run by Brid Torrades, who is a leader in the Euro-Toques and Slow Food campaigns for better food, and well-known for her ardent support of local organic food and small producers, the food here has immediacy and real depth of flavour; breads and pastries from Brid's bakery at Ballinafad are a speciality, also Irish cheeses and charcuterie. Menus include modestly described soups which are very good indeed and come with home-made brown bread, quite complex in flavour and with a nice texture; Knockalara cheese & spinach quiche is a speciality and other interesting options include Tullynascreen herb goats' cheese with roasted vegetables & salad sandwich, and an exceptionally fresh and crunchy chicken and toasted almond salad with a light creamy dressing. Daily specials chalked up on a black board include panini and wraps - usually with a bit of a twist, such as chicken with jalepeno relish and cream cheese. And it would be difficult to leave without sampling something from a spectacular array of home-made cakes including coconut muffins, almond croissants, raspberry tarts, cream sponges and, of course, the famous Bakewell tart. A small bar area makes a good spot to sip wine from a well chosen list (all 13 offered on the café menu are available by the glass) and tapas are also on offer in the evening. **Seats 35** (outdoors, 10); no reservations; children welcome (high chair); toilets wheelchair accessible; air conditioning. Mon-Sat, 9am- 8.30pm (Thurs-Sat, to 9.30pm), Sun 12- 5pm. House wine €17. No sc. Closed Sun, Good Fri, Bank Hols, Christmas week. **No credit cards. Directions:** Near Hyde Bridge.

Sligo
Tobergal Lane Café

RESTAURANT•CAFÉ/BAR

Tobergal Lane Sligo Co Sligo **Tel: 071 914 6599**

N *V*

tobergallanecafe@eircom.net www.tobergallanecafe.com

Situated across the river from Osta, Brid Torrades' newest venture is in an excellent location, though a bit hard to find - tucked away up a shop-lined lane just off O'Connell Street, it would be easy to miss. The building follows the curve of the lane, which gives it a nice line outside – and a lovely curve to the space inside, with a series of sash style-windows on two sides following the curve. The first floor is used for functions and events like traditional music sessions whilst, downstairs in the simply set up restauraunt, soft background music brings an air of calm; patisserie (as served at Osta) is on display in a chill cabinet and tables are laid bistro-style. Daily-changed lunchtime menus are similar to Osta, and there's also a specials board with more in the way of plated lunches; starters might include treats like lobster salad (€10:50) and there will be some substantial mains like O'Hara's braised lamb shank (€19.95) - a good range of dishes and styles, with prices to match the variety offered. Dishes reflect Brid's dedication to using local specialities (notably cheeses, the excellent Noodle House pasta made near Sligo town, Lissadell vegetables and saladings, and Arctic char, which is farmed nearby) and also a sensitivity to special requirements, be it gluten free pasta or interesting vegetarian options. The dinner menu is also changed daily and includes interesting choices such as a starter of air-dried Connemara lamb with poached pear and rosemary and parsley oil (€7.50), and mains like Thornhill duck confit with puy lentils and spicy plum sauce (€16.95). And make sure you leave room for dessert – Alsace apple tartlet with vanilla ice cream, perhaps - all made by French pastry chef, Julien. The tone is a little more formal here than at Osta, so it might be the better choice for a more leisurely meal. Well-priced wine list and lovely service too: very nice all round. **Seats 70** (outdoors, 14; private room, 95); children welcome (high chair, childrens menu, baby changing facilities); toilets wheelchair accessible; air conditioning. Open daily 11am-10pm; à la carte; house wine €17. Closed Bank Hols (except 17 Mar); 3 weeks in Jan (tbc). MasterCard, Visa, Laser. **Directions:** Centre of Sligo, just off O'Connell Street on way to river.

Sligo Area
HOTEL

Radisson SAS Hotel & Spa

Ballincar Rosses Point Sligo Co Sligo **Tel: 071 914 0008**
info.sligo@RadissonSAS.com www.radissonsas.com

This fine contemporary hotel is out of town, towards Rosses Point; it is not especially attractive from the road but, once inside the door it has a huge welcoming flower arrangement in the large foyer, and a light and appealing atmosphere. Staff are keen to make guests feel at home, and clearly take pride in the hotel - and it's easy to see why. Simple lines and classy contemporary decor in quality materials and warm tones create a pleasing ambience, without distracting from the hotel's great attraction - the views over Sligo Bay. The good-sized bedrooms are very comfortable, with all the facilities now expected (TV options, voicemail, safe, mini bar, iron/ironing board as well as trouser press, and so on), and there are various room combinations offered, including family rooms. The Classiebawn Restaurant, which is an open-plan dining area along the front of the hotel (and the gains in smart design and, especially, views are greater than anything it loses in lack of privacy) is an especially pleasant place for a weekend lunch, or dinner on a long summer evening, when the views can be enjoyed to the full. Conference/banqueting (950/470); business centre, free broadband wi/fi. **Rooms 132** (7 junior suites, 3 executive rooms, 6 disabled); children welcome (under 16 free in parents' room; cots available without charge, baby sitting arranged). 24 hr room service, lift, turndown service offered. B&B about €80pps, ss €45. **Restaurant:** D daily 6.30-10.30, L sat & Sun 12.30-3. Set Sun L about €35. House wine, €21. Bar meals also available, 12-7 daily. No SC. Leisure centre, swimming pool, spa. Golf nearby. *Short breaks offered; golf breaks are a speciality (3 championship courses nearby). Open all year. Amex, MasterCard, Visa. **Directions:** From Sligo town, follow signs for Rosses Point; the hotel is on the right after 3km (2 m). ◈

Strandhill
BAR•RESTAURANT

Bella Vista Bar & Bistro

Shore Road Strandhill Co Sligo **Tel: 071 912 2222**
bellavistapizzeria@eircom.net www.bellavista.ie

Within view of the breakers on Strandhill's glorious shorefront, Bella Vista is well situated for the kind of all-day family trade it most appeals to. Benches and half barrel tables set up for outdoor dining in finer weather, while the atmosphere inside on the ground floor is cosy. It's basically a large pub offering a limited range of popular food at lunchtime, but that food – toasted sandwiches, pasta and pizza, for example - is unusually good. Soup has real home-made flavour and comes with dark, dense brown bread. A typical offering, a bacon, lettuce and tomato toasted sandwich, is served with a fresh salad accompaniment and ingredients are of really good quality. Best of all, the service is wonderfully cheerful and prompt, perhaps because of the bouncy attitude of the Australian host, who built up his business just a few doors down at the Bella Vista pizza outlet. In the evenings, the menu ranges more widely, with a focus on steaks and seafood and there is plenty of space upstairs to accommodate happy diners. **Seats 100** (outdoors, 20); reservations recommended at weekends, children welcome (high chair, childrens menu, baby changing facilties). Food served daily, 10am-10pm (from 12 Sun); L 12-5pm, D 5-10pm. House wine from €17.50; sc 10% on groups 10+. MasterCard, Visa, Laser. **Directions:** 50m from seashore in Strandhill.

Strandhill
PUB

Strand House Bar

Strandhill Co Sligo
Tel: 071 916 8140

Just ten minutes drive from Sligo, close to the airport and one of Europe's most magnificent surfing beaches, this well-known bar has a big welcoming turf fire, cosy snugs and friendly staff. No children after 9pm. [*The first floor restaurant is operated separately.] Bar meals served all day (12-4pm). Closed 25 Dec & Good Fri. MasterCard, Visa, Laser. **Directions:** Follow signs to Sligo airport (Strandhill). Strand House is situated at the end near the beach.

COUNTY TIPPERARY

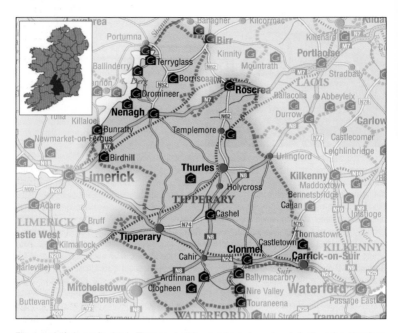

The cup of life is overflowing in Tipperary. In this extensive and wondrously fertile region, there's an air of fulfillment, a comfortable awareness of the world in harmony. And the place names reinforce this sense of natural bounty.

Across the middle of the county, there's the Golden Vale, with prosperous lands along the wide valley of the River Suir and its many tributaries, and westwards towards County Limerick across a watershed around Donohill. The Vale is so named because the village of Golden is at its heart, but then it could be the other way round - that's the kind of place it is.

The county's largest town, down in the far south under the Comeragh Mountains, is the handsome borough of Clonmel - its name translates as "Honey Meadow". Yet although there are many meadows of all kinds in Tipperary, there's much more to this largest inland county in Ireland than farmland, for it is graced with some of the most elegant mountains in the country.

North of the Golden Vale, the Silvermine Mountains rise to 694m on Keeper Hill, and beyond them the farming countryside rolls on in glorious profusion to Nenagh - a town much improved by by-passes on either side - and Tipperary's own riviera, the beautiful eastern shore of Lough Derg. Inevitably, history and historic monuments abound in such country, with the fabulous Rock of Cashel and its dramatic remains of ancient ecclesiastical buildings setting a very high standard for evoking the past.

But Tipperary lends itself every bit as well to enjoyment of the here and now. Tipperary is all about living life to the full, and they do it with style in a place of abundance.

Local Attractions and Information

Aherlow, Glen of	Glenbrook Trout Farm	062 56214
Birdhill	Tipperary Crystal Visitor Centre	061 379066
Cahir	Cahir Castle	052 41011
Cahir	Farmers Market Sats 9am-1pm	086 648 2044
Carrick-on-Suir	Ormond Castle	051 640787
Carrick-on-Suir	Tipperary Crystal Visitor Centre	051 641188
Cashel	Bru Boru Culture Centre	062 61122
Cashel	Rock of Cashel	062 61437

Cashel	Tourism Information	062 61333
Clonmel	Clonmel Racecourse	052 23422
Clonmel	Theatre & Arts Festival (July)	052 29339
Clonmel	Tourism Information	052 22960
Nenagh	Heritage Centre	067 32633
Nenagh	Tourism Information	067 31610
Roscrea	Roscrea Heritage - Castle & Damer House	0505 21850
Thurles	Holy Cross Abbey	0504 43241
Thurles	Race Course	0504 21040
Tipperary	Race Course (Limerick Junction)	062 51357
Tipperary Town	Tourism Information	062 51457

Ballinderry
RESTAURANT

Brocka-on-the-Water Restaurant
Kilgarvan Quay Ballinderry Nenagh Co Tipperary
Tel: 067 22038

Anthony and Anne Gernon's almost-waterside restaurant has attracted a following disproportionate to its size over the years and, although it has been extended at the back to include a high-ceilinged conservatory-style room which opens on to a garden patio, it is still basically carved out of the lower half of a family home that is by no means huge. The atmosphere is very much a "proper restaurant" - yet with all the warmth of welcome that the family situation implies. There's a reception room with an open fire, comfy chairs, interesting things to read and look at (Anthony's a dab hand at wood carving) - and aperitifs served in generous wine glasses, while you read a menu that promises good things to come in the adjoining dining room and conservatory. Guests arriving in daylight will notice hens clucking around a garden well-stocked with fruit and vegetables - promising the best of all possible beginnings for your dinner. Seasonal menus depend on availability, of course, but there are always some specialities retained by popular demand, including Cooleeney cheese croquettes with home-made chutney (Cooleeney is one of Ireland's finest cheeses, made by Breda Maher on the family farm near Thurles). **Seats 30** (private room, 30); air conditioning; toilets wheelchair accessible; reservations strongly advised. D 7-9pm Tue & Thu-Sat (call to check opening times off-season). Set D about €40, also à la carte & Vegetarian Menu. SC discretionary. House wine about €22. Closed Sun, Mon, Wed. **No Credit Cards. Directions:** Lough Derg drive, half way between Nenagh and Portumna.

CARRICK-ON-SUIR

This beautifully-located medieval town is set in the ancient Golden Vale (Gleann an Oir), with the Comeragh Mountains to the south and the Walsh Mountains to the southeast, making this unspoilt area a wonderful base for outdoor activities. The river has always been central to the life and development of the town, formerly for trade and now mainly for pleasure. Although tidal, Carrick-on-Suir is navigable from any part of Ireland's inland waterways and a landing pontoon allows access to the town by boat. The **Carraig Hotel** (051 641 455; www.carraighotel.com) on Main Street is the centre of community activities, and the new Blarney Woollen Mills/Meadows & Byrne development, Dove Hill Design Centre (5km outside town on the N24/Clonmel road), now brings shoppers to the area and refreshment is available there at **The Passionate Cook**, a large and attractively designed restaurant offering quality informal food. There is a farmers' market on Fridays in the Heritage Centre (Main St., 10am-2pm). Garden lovers are spoilt for choice in this area, several gardens of note nearby include Killurney Garden (Ballypatrick, 052 33155), a prize-winning informal garden in a gorgeous setting, Fairbook House Gardens & Museum of Contemporary Figurative Art (Kilmeaden, 051 384 657) which is an intriguing compartmental garden in an old mill complex and Mount Congreve (Kilmeaden, 051 384 115), an unforgettable massed planting of rhododendrons, shrubs and trees in a beautifully-located demesne. There is golf at Carrick Golf Club (051 640 047) while challenging championship golf is available in nearby Mount Juliet Golf Club (Thomastown, 056 777 3064).
WWW.IRELAND-GUIDE.COM FOR ALL THE BEST PLACES TO EAT, DRINK & STAY

Carrick-on-Suir Area

RESTAURANT

Kilkiernan Cottage Restaurant

Castletown Carrick-on-Suir Co Tipperary

Tel: 051 642 388

On an elevated site with views towards Carrick-on-Suir and to the Comeragh mountains, this pretty white cottage with its red half door enjoys a lovely rural setting and, with two stone-faced outhouses and a small cottage, it's a pleasing property with ample outside seating for al fresco dining when the weather allows. Chef-proprietor Michael Mee is well-known in the South-East – he moved here from Kilkenny in 2007 and quickly built up a following of diners who enjoy the location and the ambience as well as Michael's good food. There's a lot of pine, some modern paintings and light instrumental music playing in the background; an open door behind the reception area allows views into the kitchen where arriving guests see Michael at work preparing their meal, and in the restaurant, tables are set up classically with white linen. A friendly local waitress quickly brings iced water and warm breads along with a well-balanced à la carte menu: from a choice of half a dozen starters (€5-€12) and eight main courses (€18.50-€28) begin with perfectly pink lambs kidneys flamed in brandy with a wholegrain mustard sauce, perhaps, or an unusual salmon and crab twice-baked soufflé with a shellfish dressing. Kilkenny lamb and steaks are popular main courses, but you'll also find several fish dishes (whole black sole with capers & lemon butter, if you're lucky – good value at €26) and a vegetarian choice such as a vegetable curry. Michael Mee is a good chef and his well-sourced local ingredients produce fine dishes; smartly presented on modern white plates, the food is appealing, while classic desserts with a twist end an enjoyable meal well. Although side vegetables are charged separately, value is good overall, and a short but adequate wine list is also offered. The Sunday lunch menu offers outstanding value. Despite the out-of-the-way location, this is a popular restaurant and booking is advised. **Seats 50** (outdoors, 14); children welcome before 8.30pm (high chair); reservations recommended; ample car parking. D Wed-Sun, 6-9.30pm (to 8pm Sun); L Sun only 12.30-3.30pm. Set Sun L €22.50; set 3 course D €35, also à la carte D. House wine from €19. Closed Mon, Tue, Bank Hols, 5 Jan - 5 Feb. Amex, Diners, Mastercard, Visa, Laser. **Directions:** Castletown is a few km north of Carrick-on-Suir on the R697.

R # CASHEL

Visitors flock here to see the famous the Rock of Cashel, a site hosting a ruined church and fortifications, formerly the seat of the Irish kings of Munster; King Cormac built his superb Royal Chapel in the 12th century and it can be seen on the Rock - nearby were Cistercian, Dominican and Franciscan abbeys, two of which may still be viewed. And the town itself also has much to offer, including archaeology and architecture of great historical significance (information available at the Heritage Centre on Main Street), but also some of the best food and hospitality to be found in Ireland including - right beside the Rock - the renowned restaurant **Chez Hans** and its highly regarded informal younger brother, **Café Hans** (see entries). In the town, **The Spearman** (062 61143) bakery and café is a simple and charming old-style place to take a break and buy some home-bakes to take home. Lovers of food from the Indian sub-continent might enjoy **Rajput Indian & Pakistani Restaurant**, (062 65585) in Wesley Square, notable for very friendly staff and a pleasing ambience. Golfers will find a Philip Walton-designed 18-hole championship course nearby, at Dundrum House Hotel & Country Club (www.dundrumhousehotel.com).

WWW.IRELAND-GUIDE.COM FOR ALL THE BEST PLACES TO EAT, DRINK & STAY

Cashel

Bailey's Cashel

HOTEL•BAR•RESTAURANT

Main Street Cashel Co Tipperary **Tel: 062 61937**
info@baileys-ireland.com www.baileys-ireland.com

Set back from the road, with a very attractive planted plaza set up with seating and umbrellas in front, this fine early-18th century building in the heart of Cashel was previously a seven-bedroom guesthouse but a cleverly-concealed extension has allowed it to grow, gracefully, into a fully-fledged family-run hotel (with 14 new bedrooms, a spacious restaurant, a cosy cellar bar, and a lovely swimming pool and leisure centre). There's a comfortable residents' drawing room ('The Library') and, although the attractive contemporary bedrooms have no tea/coffee facilities (available in The Library), they tick all the right boxes otherwise: good lighting, quality furnishing, efficient air conditioning, windows that open, comfortable chairs, flat screen TV, irons and boards, hair-dryers, safes broadband and plenty of connection points for laptops, chargers and so on - and well-designed, if compact, bathrooms. Banqueting (80). Children welcome (under 3s free in parents' room, cot available free of charge); **Rooms 19** (1 suite, 1 for disabled, all no smoking); lift, room service (limited hours); B&B €75-90 pps, ss €15. **Restaurant Number 42:** Gently contemporary, with well-spaced tables and comfortable chairs, this is a pleasant place to relax and enjoy a good dinner. Chef Michael Doyle, who has been at the helm for a number of years, continues to cook Irish and Continental dishes showing his competent professional skills. His balanced menus feature some local ingredients and offer a wide choice; appealing dishes on the evening à la carte might include starters like twice-baked cheddar & chive soufflé or warm potato pancake with smoked salmon & chive crème fraîche, and main courses include excellent beef fillet or a tender rack of lamb with champ. The bar menu, which offers an extensive range of more casual dishes, provides a casual option and good value. This is a well-run place that delivers the goods in friendly Irish style... Free private parking in an underground car park makes this a particularly attractive all-purpose stop for business people and visitors alike. A lovely place to relax and enjoy good food. **Seats 80** (outdoors, 15); air conditioning; children welcome before 7pm; bar food served daily 12.30-9.30; Sun L 12.30-4, Sun D 6-9.30; set Sun L €25; also à la carte L&D; house wine €19. Establishment closed 23-27 Dec. Amex, MasterCard, Visa, Laser. **Directions:** Centre of town, on Main Street. ◊

Cashel

Café Hans

CAFÉ

Moor Lane Cashel Co Tipperary
Tel: 062 63660

Brother Hans and Stefan Matthia run this smashing little contemporary café, and it is the perfect complement to the parent establishment, Chez Hans, next door. A neat renovation job has been accomplished with clean-lined style, creating a bright and airy space out of very little – and the exterior now looks absolutely delightful, too. Bare-topped tables are laid café-style and a canny little menu offers just the kind of food that's needed during the day: colourful, sassy dishes including lots of salads - several versions of Caesar salad include a vegetarian one, and there's an irresistible house salad with pear Cashel Blue cheese (what else?) and Parma ham; open sandwiches come with home-made French fries and there are half a dozen hot dishes - grilled lamb cutlets with mushroom sauce, perhaps, or poached salmon with new potatoes, green beans and salsa verde. Good desserts and afternoon tea (2-5.30), lovely coffee; wine list. Well worth planning a journey around a break here - everyone travelling the Dublin-Cork route should make a note of this place and its hours. But get there early or be prepared to wait, as the secret about Café Hans is well and truly out. There is some menu overlap with Chez Hans, where, together with Jason Matthia, Stefan is also responsible for the early dinner. **Seats 30**; children welcome. Open Tue-Sat, 12-5pm (advisable to check off-season). Closed Sun & Mon. No reservations. No Credit Cards. **Directions:** Off N8 in Cashel, 50m in Rock of Cashel direction.

Cashel

HOTEL•RESTAURANT

Cashel Palace Hotel

Main Street Cashel Co Tipperary **Tel: 062 62707**

reception@cashel-palace.ie www.cashel-palace.ie

One of Ireland's most famous hotels, and originally a bishop's residence, Cashel Palace is a large, graciously proportioned Queen Anne-style house (dating from 1730), set well back from the road in the centre of Cashel town. Arrival here should be a very pleasant experience, with a friendly Irish reception complemented by charming porter service by John (who's been working at Cashel Palace for nearly 30 years), and beautifully served tea or coffee in your room or beside one of two log fires at reception. The lovely reception rooms and some of the spacious, elegantly furnished bedrooms overlook the gardens and the Rock of Cashel at the rear; rooms are furnished to a high standard, with maintenance and housekeeping to match. The present owners, Patrick and Susan Murphy, took over the hotel in 1998 and, since then, have been gradually renovating and refurbishing both public areas and bedrooms; the whole hotel has been re-decorated, and a new function room opened - but it still exudes that old fashioned atmosphere and hospitality that modern hotels simply cannot emulate. Conference/banqueting (85/130); free broad-band wi/fi. Children welcome (Under 3 free in parents' room, cot available, baby sitting arranged). No pets. Garden, walking. Equestrian, golf, fishing (fly & coarse) and horse racing nearby. **Rooms 23** (5 junior suites, 3 single, all no smoking). Lift. Room service (24 hr). B&B from €112.50, ss about €35. Closed 24-26 Dec. **The Bishop's Buttery:** Lunch and dinner are served every day in this atmospheric vaulted basement restaurant and bar, which successfully juggles the various demands of a mixed clien-tèle ranging from passing trade to local business people, corporate guests, families out for a treat - and, of course, residents; there is also a formal ground floor dining room, overlooking the gardens, which is used for breakfast (a little disappointing on the Guide's most recent visit) and Sunday lunch (interesting and good value). New head chef Shane McGonigle continues the house style, offering well-balanced and well-cooked meals that include the traditional choices like steak and chicken breast alongside more adventurous ones, and tasty bar fare - home-made lamb sausages with black pudding mash & red onion confit, for example; the cooking is quite modern and well-presented, with the generosity expected in country areas. Outdoor seating, 20; L & D daily, 12.30-2pm (to 2.30 Sun) & 6.30-9.30pm. Set 4 course Sun L €32; set D €55. House wine from €20. Live piano Fri/Sat night. *Food is also available in the Guinness Bar, 10am-8pm. Hotel closed 24-26 Dec. Amex, Diners, MasterCard, Visa, Laser. **Directions:** Exit N8 and take R639 which runs through Cashel, entrance to hotel just off Main Street.

Cashel

RESTAURANT

Chez Hans

Moore Lane Cashel Co Tipperary **Tel: 062 61177**

www.chezhans.net

ATMOSPHERIC RESTAURANT OF THE YEAR

Although many others have since followed suit, the idea of opening a restaurant in a church was highly original when Hans-Peter Matthia did so in 1968. The scale - indeed the whole style of the place - is superb and provides an unusual and atmospheric setting for the seriously fine food which people travel great distances to sample. Hans-Peter's son, Jason (who returned from working in some of London's finest kitchens) joined him in the busi-ness in 1998 and this - together with the opening in 2004 of their excellent daytime restaurant, Café Hans, next door (see entry) - brought renewed energy, confirming the status of Chez Hans as the leading restaurant in a wide area and assuring its future. Ably assisted by his wife, restaurant manager Louise Matthia, and a strong kitchen brigade (it is nice to note that he acknowledges his sous chefs, Barry Underwood and Julia O'Dwyer, on the menu) Jason offers menus that include an early dinner menu that represents some of the best value to be found in Ireland and an extensive à la carte, either of which is definitely worth a special journey. Guests are welcomed into the bar, to look at Jason's enticing menus over a drink: the à la carte offers an outstanding choice of nine excellent dishes on each course, including many specialities - their famous cassoulet of seafood (half a dozen varieties of fish and shellfish with a delicate chive velouté sauce), for example, imaginative vegetarian dishes - and, of course, the great lamb and beef for which the area is renowned. An inspired Tasting of Tipperary Lamb, for example, might be composed of braised shank, minted meatball and a herbed rack, and a classic beef dish with a twist could be char-grilled Angus sirloin, with béarnaise sauce, French fries, and rocket & parmesan salad. Finish perhaps with lemon tart & lime tart with raspberry sorbet or chocolate mousse with vanilla ice cream and candied oranges, then tea or coffee with home-made petits fours. Service, under Louise Matthia's direction, is quick and pleasant. An interesting, well described and fairly-priced wine list includes a good range of classic old world and international wines and varieties, and two pages of recommended wines under €40, some from Hans-Peter's sister's vine-yard in Germany. Booking ahead is essential. **Seats 70.** D Tue-Sat, 6-9.30. Early D 2/3 courses, €28.50/35 (6-7.15); also à la carte. House wines from about €25. Closed Sun, Mon, last 2 weeks Sept & last 2 weeks in Jan. MasterCard, Visa, Laser. **Directions:** First right from N8, 50m on left; at foot of Rock of Cashel.

Cashel | Hill House
B&B | Palmer Hill Cashel Co Tipperary **Tel: 062 61277**
 | hillhouse1@eircom.net www.hillhousecashel.com

Carmel Purcell's lovely Georgian house was built in 1710 and has great character. It is set well back from the road in large gardens, with plenty of parking and a magnificent view of the Rock of Cashel - and a welcoming hospitable atmosphere, noticeable immediately on arrival in the spacious entrance hall, which has fine Georgian features and fresh flowers. While Carmel shows guests to one of the large rooms (some with four posters), she gives the lowdown on local attractions and settles you in; rooms are very comfortable, with television, radio and tea/coffee facilities and good bathrooms. Breakfast is a high point, served at a large communal table very nicely set up with good linen, baskets of freshly-baked breads and scones and home-made preserves; a side table offers fruits and cereals, and the cooked breakfasts are delicious. **Rooms 5** (all shower only & no smoking, 1 family room); not suitable for children under 8 years; no pets. Free broadband wi/fi. B&B €50 pps, ss €25. Garden, walking. Fishing (fly & sea angling), equestrian and golf nearby. MasterCard, Visa, Laser. **Directions:** 2 minutes from Cashel town centre; from Dublin, bear left after the turn signed Rock of Cashel - Hill House is opposite the next junction.

Cashel Area | Carron House
FARMHOUSE | Carron Cashel Co Tipperary **Tel: 052 62142**
 | hallyfamily@eircom.net www.carronhouse.com

Mary Hally's country home is on an award-winning farm, in a peaceful location in the heart of the Golden Vale, yet only minutes from Cashel and just an hour from Kilkenny. Approached up a long, well-maintained drive, first impressions are very encouraging, as there's a lovely front garden in front of the large, modern house - and separate entrances for the house and farm. Large individually decorated bedrooms include one triple room (with double and twin beds) and are very comfortably furnished, with generous beds, television, tea/coffee facilities, hair dryers and neat en-suite shower rooms. Housekeeping throughout is immaculate and there's a guest sitting room with antique furniture and interesting books, which is always available to guests. Mary, who is a friendly, attentive and informa-tive hostess, gives guests a good send-off in the morning, with a generous, well-cooked and nicely presented breakfast in a large sun room overlooking the garden. **Rooms 4** (all with en-suite shower & all no smoking); not suitable for children. B&B €40pps, ss €20. Closed Sept- Apr. MasterCard, Visa, Laser. **Directions:** Take N8 south bound from Cashel for 4km (2.5 m), exit at sign for New Inn R639. After 3km (2m) signposted left at crossroads; follow signs.

Cashel Area | Dualla House
FARMHOUSE | Dualla Cashel Co Tipperary **Tel: 062 61487**
 | duallahse@eircom.net www.duallahouse.com

Set in 300 acres of rolling Tipperary farmland in the "Golden Vale", Martin and Mairead Power's fine Georgian manor house faces south towards the Slievenamon, Comeragh, Knockmealdown and Galtee Mountains. Just 3 miles from the Rock of Cashel, this is a convenient base for exploring the area but its special appeal is peace and tranquillity which, together with comfortable accommodation in large airy bedrooms (with tea/coffee trays), great hospitality and Mairead's home cooking, keep guests coming back time and again. An extensive breakfast menu includes local apple juice as well as other fresh fruits and juices, farmhouse cheeses, porridge with local honey, also free-range eggs and sausages from the local butcher in the traditional cooked breakfast - and home-made bread and preserves. **Rooms 4** (3 with en-suite shower, 1 with private bathroom, 1 family, all no smoking); children welcome (under 3s free in parents' room, cot available without charge). B&B €55 pps, ss €10. Closed Nov-Mar. MasterCard, Visa. **Directions:** 5km (3 miles) from Cashel on R691. Coming from Dublin signed from N8, 5 miles after Horse & Jockey. Sign on left. 2.5 miles to house.

Clogheen

GUESTHOUSE•RESTAURANT

The Old Convent Gourmet Hideaway

Mount Anglesby Clogheen Co Tipperary **Tel: 052 65565**
info@theoldconvent.ie www.theoldconvent.ie

Tellingly styled a 'gourmet hideaway', Dermot and Christine Gannon's restaurant with accommodation is in one of the most beautiful and unspoilt - yet relatively little known - parts of the country: just the place for couples 'seeking a short getaway from it all experience'. Emphatically not for 'family weekends' (bookings are not accepted for children under 12), it's an unusual, very comfortable, beautifully designed and decorated, country house with mountain views across the famously scenic 'Vee', and lovely gardens which are being developed and extended to provide as much home produce as possible for Dermot's kitchen, and as an interesting amenity for guests. A lofty double drawing room with large windows and a mixture of antiques and stylish modern furnishings makes a relaxing reception area, and the spacious, airy restaurant is in what was once the convent refectory and adjoining sacristy - now one large area, but still complete with stained glass windows. An unusual setting, for an exceptional meal: only a 9-course Tasting Menu is offered, plus an optional cheese platter of seven Irish cheeses with Trass Farm fruit and plum jam. Ingredients are sourced locally (and organic) when possible and, as anyone who has experienced a meal cooked by this talented chef will testify, the cooking is stunningly accurate - and everything is perfectly seasoned: there is no cheffy arrogance here and a (tiny) salt and pepper set is offered on tables, but Dermot has such a sure palate that it will almost certainly be unnecessary to use it. Many diners might be wary of the Tasting Menu, but servings are well-judged - it certainly isn't a marathon and, on the other hand, could never be described as 'grudging' or 'mean'; furthermore, in deference to Irish taste, the meat course is very generous indeed. Menus change daily and, although personal preferences will mean that you enjoy some even better than others, it is an ideal arrangement for guests staying for several nights. And at €60 it is exceptional value for a meal of this quality: skilfully cooked, generous and beautifully presented. **Seats 50**; children over 12 years welcome; D Thu-Sat (& Bank Hol Sun, also considering opening Wed D in 2009, call to check); set 8-course gourmet D €60. House wine from €22. SC 10% on groups 6+. **Accommodation** (ITB approval pending): The bedrooms, all individually styled, are sumptuously appointed and have wonderful views; bathrooms are also stylishly appointed, and have separate bath and shower. Although tea and coffee-making facilities are not provided in bedrooms, this is a very guest-focused place and a special area has been set aside on the first floor landing where guests can help themselves to all sorts of things from hot and cold drinks to DVDs. This is a lovely place that is definitely 'itself' - and you could very quickly become fond of it; everything they do at The Old Convent is not just done superbly well, but done differently - the wonderful breakfast that is a further treat in store for overnight guests, for example, begins with a beautiful Old Convent 'martini' with fruit, yogurt, honey & toasted pistachios, presented to your table in a martini glass on arrival - delightful; and everything that follows is equally special, including brown bread and beer bread baked in the Aga, Ballybrado eggs and Graham Roberts' organic smoked salmon. Simply superb. *Old Convent was selected for our Irish Breakfast Award in 2008 (country house category). Small conferences/banqueting (40). **Rooms 7** (4 suites, 1 shower only, all no smoking); not suitable for children; B&B from €75-90 pps, ss €40. Free Broadband wi/fi. Closed Christmas - end of Jan. MasterCard, Visa, Laser. **Directions:** From Clogheen take the Vee/Lismore road, 0.5km on right

CLONMEL

Clonmel derives its name form Cluain Meala, meaning the meadow of honey, and today it is a prosperous town on the River Suir, known especially for its apple orchards and cider production. Clonmel is rich in heritage: the town walls were built in the 14th century and the quays date back to medieval times; also of interest is the heritage site of St Patrick's Well which includes the remains of a 17th century church; and the White Memorial theatre which was formerly a Methodist church, built in 1843. Surrounded by the Comeragh and Knockmealdown Mountains, it is an excellent base for climbing and walking. Local attractions include the town's poppy field, which is best in July and August. Golfing enthusiasts can play the 18 holes at Slievenamon Golf Course (052 32213). Every Saturday the best of local produce is on display at the Clonmel Farmers' Market.

Clonmel

Befani's Mediterranean & Tapas Restaurant

RESTAURANT   6 Sarsfield Street Clonmel Co Tipperary **Tel: 052 77893**

v R   info@befani.com   www.befani.com

This stylish Mediterranean and tapas restaurant is in a recently restored listed building just up from the quays, and it's become a favourite spot for many people living in and around Clonmel. Co-owner and chef, Adrian Ryan, and business partner and restaurant manager, Fulvio Bonfiglio, are thorough professionals who quickly won the hearts of discerning diners in the locality after opening here in 2005. Spacious and simply furnished, the restaurant has a small bar, and a pleasant ambience; Adrian's appealing menus are deliberately restricted but you'll find flavoursome comfort food like cassoulet of duck leg confit, Toulouse sausage & pork belly as well as a tapas menu; vegetarians are well catered for, too – and look out for the 'fish of the day' as Adrian was formerly head chef at the renowned seafood restaurant, Doyle's of Dingle. Local organic ingredients are sourced where possible and the high quality of ingredients, cooking and service (and real value for money), has won them a lot of friends. The carefully chosen wine list includes a monthly special offer and, all round, Befani's is a delightful experience with a southern European atmosphere. The long opening hours are a great bonus too. **Seats 55** (outdoors, 15); children welcome; wheelchair access to courtyard only; air conditioning. Food served daily, 9am-9.30pm; L 12.30-3. D 6-9.30; set D about €31.50, set Sun L about €21.50, also à la carte L&D; house wine €18.50. Closed 25 Dec, 1 Jan. MasterCard, Visa, Laser. **Directions:** Town centre.

Clonmel

Hotel Minella

HOTEL   Coleville Road Clonmel Co Tipperary **Tel: 052 22388**

R   hotelminella@eircom.net   www.hotelminella.ie

Sparky, the Old English sheepdog, establishes a friendly tone from the outset as he welcomes arriving guests to this pleasant hotel, which is attractively located in its own grounds, overlooking the River Suir. The original house was built in 1863 and was purchased in 1961 by the current owners, the Nallen family. They've extended the hotel several times over the years, most recently to add a penthouse floor offering especially spacious and luxurious bedrooms and four suites with balconies. The existing rooms were also refurbished and upgraded; all are furnished to a high standard with smart bathrooms - and housekeeping is exemplary. This is the main hotel in the area, popular for weddings, with conference facilities and a fine leisure centre. The public areas in the old house include a cocktail bar, restaurant and lounge areas. **Rooms 90** (4 suites, 5 junior suites, 80 no smoking, 3 for disabled, 13 ground floor, 10 family rooms); children welcome (under 16 free in parents' room, cot available without charge, baby sitting arranged). B&B €80 pps. Broadband. Leisure centre with 20 metre swimming pool and outdoor Canadian hot tub, jacuzzi, steam room and gym; tennis, fishing, garden. Closed 23-29 Dec. Amex, MasterCard, Visa, Laser. **Directions:** Edge of Clonmel town. ◇

Clonmel

Sean Tierney

CHARACTER PUB   13 O'Connell Street Clonmel Co Tipperary

R   **Tel: 052 24467**

This tall, narrow pub is packed with "artefacts of bygone days", in short a mini-museum but, one with a giant screen which is discreetly hidden around the corner for watching matches. Upstairs (and there are a lot of them, this is a four-storey building) there's a relaxed traditional family-style restaurant. Expect hearty portions of popular, good value food like potato wedges, mushrooms with garlic, home-cooked lasagne, steaks and grills rather than gourmet fare; the evening restaurant menus are more ambitious, although it is unlikely there will be many surprises. This is a pub of character and toilets are at the very top, but grand when you get there. Children welcome before 8.30 pm (high chair, childrens menu); air conditioning. Food served daily, 12.30-9; set 2/3 course D €27.90/33.90. Closed 25 Dec, Good Fri. MasterCard, Visa, Laser. **Directions:** Situated half way down O'Connell St. on the left opposite Dunnes Stores.

Clonmel Area
FARMHOUSE

Kilmaneen Farmhouse

Ardfinnan Newcastle Clonmel Co Tipperary **Tel: 052 36231**
kilmaneen@eircom.net www.kilmaneen.com

As neat as a new pin, Kevin & Ber O'Donnell's delightfully-situated farmhouse is on a working dairy farm, surrounded by three mountain ranges - the Comeraghs, the Knockmealdowns and the Galtees - and close to the Rivers Suir and Tar, making it an ideal base for walking and fishing holidays. Trout fishing on the Suir and Tar on the farm is free (hut provided for tying flies, storing equipment and drying waders) and Kevin, who is trained in mountain skills, leads walking groups. It's an old house, but well restored to combine old furniture with modern comforts; the bedrooms are not especially big, but they are thoughtfully furnished (including tea/coffee facilities and iron/trouser press) and, like the rest of the house, immaculate. There's a great welcome and guests feel at home immediately - especially once they get tucked into Ber's delicious dinners. Don't expect any fancy menus or a wine list (you are welcome to bring your own wine), what you'll get here is real home cooking, based on fresh farm produce: home-produced beef, perhaps, or chicken stuffed with ricotta, spinach & parmesan and wrapped in cured ham, then apple pie for afters, perhaps - and breakfast are equally delicious, with stewed fruits from the garden and home-made breads and preserves as well as lovely porridge or the 'full Irish'. Genuinely hospitable hosts, homely comforts - including a log fire to relax beside after dinner and a large, well-maintained garden, where guests can enjoy the peaceful setting - all add up to a real country break. *Kilmaneen was our Farmhouse of the Year in 2005. *Self-catering also available. **Rooms 3** (2 shower only, all en-suite & no smoking); children welcome (under 2s free in parents' room, cots available without charge). B&B €45 pps, ss €10. Pets permitted by prior arrangement. Dining room seats 12. Residents' D 7pm except on Sun (must book in advance); Set D €27.50. No SC. Closed 1 Nov - 1 Mar. MasterCard, Visa, Laser. **Directions:** In Ardfinnan, follow signs at Ryan's Hill Bar.

R

DROMINEER

Dromineer is an appealing little place on Lough Derg, with a pretty harbour and lovely woodland walks. It's a popular destination for Shannon cruisers, sailing folk and families out for the day at weekends. Fishing is a popular activity on both the lake and the nearby Nenagh river. One of Dromineer's claims to fame is the Lough Derg Yacht Club, which is the third-oldest yacht club in the world. **The Whiskey Still** (067 24129), an attractive pub with a deck overlooking the harbour, offers good food. Unfortunately the hotel has closed but B&B/hostel type accommodation is available at the large stone building on the harbour, Lough Derg House (067 24958; info@loughderghouse.com). There is a Farmers' Market nearby in Nenagh on Saturdays (10am-2pm).
WWW.IRELAND-GUIDE.COM FOR ALLTHE BEST PLACES TO EAT, DRINK & STAY

Fethard
COUNTRY HOUSE

Mobarnane House

Fethard Co Tipperary **Tel: 052 31962**
info@mobarnanehouse.com www.mobarnanehouse.com

Approached up a stylish gravel drive with well-maintained grass verges, Richard and Sandra Craik-White's lovely 18th century home has been restored to its former glory and makes a wonderfully spacious retreat for guests: the aim is to provide peace and quiet in great comfort, with very personal attention to detail. A large, beautifully furnished drawing room has plenty of comfortable seating for everyone when there's a full house - and the dining room, where Richard's good country cooking is served (usually at a communal table, although separate tables can be arranged on request), is a lovely room; everything served for dinner is freshly prepared on the day, allowing for any preferences mentioned at the time of booking. Accommodation is of the same high standard: all rooms have restful country views and comfortable seating (two have separate sitting rooms), quality bedding and everything needed for a relaxing stay, including tea/coffee making facilities, phones and television - and fresh flowers from the garden.

Bathrooms vary somewhat (bedrooms without sitting rooms have bigger bathrooms), but all have quality towels and toiletries. An excellent breakfast gets the day off to a good start - and, as well as being well-placed to explore a large and interesting area blessed with beautiful scenery, fascinating history, local crafts and sports, there is tennis and croquet on site, and lovely lake and woodland walks in the grounds. **Rooms 4** (2 junior suites, 2 superior, all no smoking); not suitable for children under 5 except babies (cot available without charge), children aged 5-10 stay free in parents room. B&B €75 pps, ss €30. Pets by arrangement. Residents' 4-course D 8pm, €45; advance reservation essential. House wine €15. SC discretionary. Closed Nov-Mar. MasterCard, Visa. **Directions:** From Fethard, take Cashel road for 6km (3.5 m); turn right, signed Ballinure and Thurles; 2.5km (1.5 m) on left.

Garrykennedy
PUB

Larkins Bar & Restaurant

Garrykennedy Portroe Nenagh Co Tipperary **Tel: 067 23232**
info@larkinspub.com www.larkinspub.com

You can't miss this pretty white cottage pub with its cheerful red paintwork, at Garrykennedy's charming little harbour. Maura and Cormac Boyle have done a little gentle modernisation since they took over ownership of Larkins in 2006; thankfully, the atmosphere has not changed too much, and they are still renowned for good steaks. Lunch menus are fairly predictable – home-made soup, seafood chowder, chicken wings and steak sandwich, for example, plus a roast of the day which, on the Guide's most recent visit, offered a choice of beef or lamb: a hearty country portion of good meat with stuffing, plain vegetables and a brown gravy. Beef is the backbone of the evening menu, which gears up somewhat to offer the famous range of Irish Hereford steaks and home-made burgers – and also choices like stuffed pork fillet, honey roast duckling, and cajun chicken kebab, plus two or three fish dishes and something for vegetarians. Cheerful, friendly service matches the country mood of this attractive pub, which makes a pleasant outing if you are in the area. Music at weekends and every Wed in summer (with Irish dancing). Food available 10.30 am- 9.30 pm daily (12.30-9.30 Sun); set Sun L about €25. Closed Good Fri, 25 Dec. MasterCard, Visa, Laser. **Directions:** 12km (7 m) from Nenagh.

R # NENAGH

This thriving town in the heart of Ireland's best farmland can provide a convenient base within easy reach of many attractions in the mid-west, including Lough Derg. Chief amongst the town's attractions is Nenagh Castle, constructed by the Fitzwalter (also known as Butler) family in the 13th Century, and one of the finest of its kind in Ireland. Nenagh makes a handy place to break a journey, the modern **Abbey Court Hotel** (067 41111; www.abbeycourt.ie) is located on the edge of town, with ample parking and good facilities. Interesting places in the town that might be handy to know about include **Roots** (19a Pearse Street 067 42444), a quirky casual restaurant with a chess set for customers, newspapers and a selection of books on alternative healing and therapy to browse through, and **Café Q** (067 37445) on Pearse Street, the headquarters of a small chain of quality ingredients-led cafés connected with Quigley's bakery, who supply all the baked goods (*Also at: Limerick, Roscrea, Thurles, Tullamore). Near Nenagh, an unusual and hospitable farm B&B with 'cows, trees and total quiet' is **Bayly Farm** (067 31499; www.baylyfarm.ie) at Ballinaclough. And, between Cloughjordan and Nenagh, locals are warming to **The Fairways Bar & Orchard Restaurant** (see entry), in new ownership. There is a farmers' market in Nenagh each Saturday (10am-2pm).
WWW.IRELAND-GUIDE.COM FOR ALL THE BEST PLACES TO EAT, DRINK & STAY

Nenagh
CAFÉ

Country Choice Delicatessen & Coffee Bar

25 Kenyon Street Nenagh Co Tipperary **Tel: 067 32596**
info@countrychoice.ie www.countrychoice.ie

Food-lovers from all over the country plan journeys around a visit to Peter and Mary Ward's unique shop. Old hands head for the little café at the back first, fortifying themselves with simple home-cooked food that reflects a policy of seasonality - if the range is small at a particular time of year, so be it. Meats, milk, cream, eggs, butter and flour: "The economy of Tipperary is agricultural and we intend to demonstrate this with a finished product of tantalising smells and tastes." Specialities developed over the years include Cashel Blue and broccoli soup served with their magnificent breads, savoury and sweet pastry dishes and tender, gently-cooked meat dishes like Irish stew and Hereford beef (from their own farm) and Guinness casserole. The shop carries a very wide range of the finest Irish artisan produce, plus a smaller selection of specialist products from further afield, such as olive oil and a range of superb dried and glacé fruits that are in great demand for Christmas baking. Specialities that make this place so special include a great terrine, made from the family's saddleback pigs; the preserves - jam (Mary Ward makes 12,000 pots a year!) and home-made marmalade, based on oranges left to caramelise in the Aga overnight, producing a runny but richly flavoured preserve; then there is Peter's passion for cheese. He is one of the country's best suppliers of Irish farmhouse cheeses, which he minds like babies as they ripen and, unlike most shops, only puts on display when they are mature: do not leave without buying cheese. As well as all this, they run regular art exhibitions in the shop, wine courses and poetry readings. Definitely worth a detour. [*Country Choice was the winner of our Natural Food Award in 2004]. **Seats 35**; children welcome; picnic service available. Open all day (9-5.30). L 12.30-3.30 daily, à la carte; house wine - any bottle in the shop + €5 corkage; Vegetarian Menu available. Closed Sun. MasterCard, Visa, Laser. **Directions:** Centre of town, on left half way down Kenyon Street.

Nenagh

The Pantry

CAFÉ
N **R**

12 Qunetin's Way Nenagh Co Tipperary **Tel: 067 31237**
info@thepantrycafe.ie www.thepantrycafe.ie

Right in the heart of this thriving town, on a corner of a small but select shopping precinct, you'll find an Illy coffee sign alerting you to the presence of The Pantry, long a favourite eating place for young and old, but now housed in bright and attractive new premises. Somehow managing to combine selling home-baked bread, quiches, cakes and gateaux alongside providing hot lunches, breakfasts, brunches and afternoon teas, The Pantry is a buzzing hive of activity at all times. In good weather, you can sit outside beside a paved courtyard, away from the traffic, otherwise you find a table inside, which is bright and cheerful with a mural on one wall. Aside from the hot specials of the day (typically roast beef, salmon in a white wine and chive sauce, roast chicken), you can choose from a range of warm salads (pear, goats' cheese, pine nuts, beetroot and salad leaves, for example), or go for something quaintly called the 'hot belly' experience, where you choose a roll or a bagel and then wait for it to be filled to bursting with all kinds of goodies. Vegetarians are always catered for – pasta with freshly-made tomato and basil sauce liberally sprinkled with parmesan, perhaps – and those with a sweet tooth will be happy with the wide range of home-made pavlovas, coffee cakes, tarts and crumbles. Offering simple, quality food at modest prices, this a really enjoyable place to take a break. Open Mon-Sat, 8.30am-6.30pm. **Directions:** Town centre, in shopping precinct.

Nenagh

The Pepper Mill

RESTAURANT
W **E** **R**

27 Kenyon Street Nenagh Co Tipperary **Tel: 067 34598**
robert@thepeppermill.ie www.thepeppermill.ie

Mairead and Robert Gill's popular restaurant lies behind an elegant grey-green frontage, you'll find a smart but comfortable lunch venue/wine bar downstairs and a fine contemporary restaurant on the first floor. A giant crystal chandelier lights the wide atrium beside the stairs; elsewhere in the elegantly appointed soft brown and cream restaurant, lighting is discreet and soothing. With a mixture of banquette seating and upholstered chairs, a vase of fresh flowers on each bare-topped table and light modern jazz playing softly in the background, the scene is set for an enjoyable evening. Excellent breads arrive with a slab of fresh butter on a glass plate, and tap water is brought to the table in bottles. Refreshingly straightforward menus offer about eight choices on each course; there are world influences, but there's a welcome leaning towards Irish themes and, although this is definitely meat country there's an emphasis on fish, delivered daily from Union Hall in Co Cork – the tasty and accurately cooked fish dishes offered might typically include roast cod with a potato crust, and halibut with couscous and a lime crème fraiche. Meat and poultry choices might include chicken in a creamy cider sauce, served on apple mash with Clonakilty black pudding and caramelised apples; new season lamb shank comes with colcannon mash & red wine jus; and Irish Hereford fillet beef has an Irish whiskey and mushroom cream sauce; vegetables, served separately, are also good (and more varied than most Irish restaurants). Gorgeous puddings are another highlight, including home-made ice cream, strawberry cheesecake, or vanilla pannacotta served with balsamic raspberries. A well-chosen wine list is reasonably priced and includes wines by the glass. With interesting, well-sourced food, good cooking and combining value with a sense of occasion, it's no wonder The Peppermill is so popular. **Seats 75** (private room, 50; outdoors, 10); children welcome before 8pm; reservations recommended; air conditioning; toilets wheelchair accessible. L Tue-Sat, 12-3pm; D Tue-Sun, 6-10 (Sun 4-10). House wine €18.50. Closed Mon, 24-26 Dec & Good Fri. Amex, Diners, MasterCard, Visa, Laser. **Directions:** Nenagh town centre.

Nenagh Area

Ashley Park House

COUNTRY HOUSE

Ardcronney Nenagh Co Tipperary **Tel: 067 38223**
margaret@ashleypark.com www.ashleypark.com

From the moment you turn off the busy Nenagh-Borrisokane road, you enter a time warp. Margaret and P J Mounsey's home, Ashley Park, is one of those beautiful 18th century houses where all is elegance and comfort. This old house breathes an old-fashioned order, comfort and charm, with stunning views of Lough Ourna and the distant Slieve Bloom Mountains. You can walk down to the lakeshore or through the walled garden; the house is surrounded by 76 acres of woodland and walks are being created through it. Whichever room you stay in, you are guaranteed a fine view, a good night's rest, and a hearty breakfast the next morning in the splendour of the double dining room and dinner can be booked by arrangement in advance. Recommended if you want peace and comfort in really splendid surroundings. **Rooms 5** (all with private bathrooms, 2 shower only, 2 family, 4 no smoking, 1 for disabled). B&B about €60, ss €10. Residents L&D available by prior arrangement only, €30-38.45. Open all year. **No Credit Cards. Directions:** On the N52, 7km (4 miles) north of Nenagh. Heading north, look for the lake on the left and go through the stone archway, past the gatehouse.

Nenagh Area

Coolbawn Quay Lakeshore Spa

HOTEL

Coolbawn Nenagh Co Tipperary **Tel: 067 28158**
info@coolbawnquay.com www.coolbawnquay.com

Spas and retreats are appearing all over Ireland at the moment, but few could rival the beauty of this magic place. This unique resort on the eastern shores of Lough Derg is modelled on the lines of a 19th century Irish village with quietly understated luxurious accommodation scattered throughout the cottages in the village. The shoreside situation is truly lovely and there is a sense of being very close to the changing moods of nature, partly because the main building - which has a small traditional bar and a country style dining room - is only a few feet from the water. Rooms do vary considerably, but all are simple in style and furnished well, and - a very nice touch this - many have a turf-burning stove which is set up in advance, matches at the ready, so you can have your own real fire whenever you like. The contrasts are wonderful here: whether you want to pamper yourself at the mini spa, hold a small conference - or simply unwind with style - this unusual village could be the ideal destination. Excellent cooking is provided by chef, Rob Oosterbaan. This is a romantic location for weddings, which are held in a luxurious banqueting marquee set by the water's edge in summer; in winter, small weddings are possible in the main buildings. [*Coolbawn Quay was our Hideaway of the Year in 2005.] Small conference/banqueting (40/190). **Rooms 48** (9 suites, 7 shower only, 1 family room, 20 ground floor, 1 for disabled, all no smoking); children welcome (under 2s free in parents room, baby sitting arranged). No pets. Wheelchair accessible. Room service (all day). B&B €115 pps, ss €35. *Short / off-season breaks offered. **Restaurant Seats 35** (private room, 30; outdoors, 20). Non-residents welcome by reservation if there is room (not suitable for children after 7pm). D Tue-Sat, 7-9; Set D about €50, also small à la carte menu. Bar food daily in high season, 12.30-2.30 (residents & members only); also barbecues. House Wine from €18.95. Spa, sauna, steam room; beauty treatments. Walking, fishing, garden. *Luxury 3 & 4 bed cottages available with hotel-style service. Amex, Diners, MasterCard, Visa, Laser. **Directions:** From N7, Nenagh, N52 heading to Borrisokane for approximately 1.5km (1 mile) until you reach a factory on the right. Take the turn left (opposite the AIBP factory) onto the Lake Drive Route through the village of Puckane & Coolbawn village, located exactly 3.2km (2 miles) past Coolbawn village.

Nenagh Area
The Fairways Bar & Orchard Restaurant

CHARACTER PUB•RESTAURANT

Kilruane Nenagh Co Tipperary **Tel: 067 41444**
thefairwaysbar@eircom.net   www.thefairwaysbar.ie

Situated just a short distance outside Nenagh, this country pub is useful to know about because it offers lunch and evening meals every day of the week. The well-stocked bar area is decorated old-style, with old pub mirrors, enamel signs for plug tobacco, sit-up-and-beg bikes and so forth, and most people lunching will settle here, although there is a snug - and those who prefer more room can move into the adjacent **Orchard Restaurant**. At lunch, the menu of the day is presented, with six or more choices of first and main courses as well as desserts, although curiously there are no prices. (At the time of visiting, these turned out to be €4.95 for both first and last courses and €9.95 for main meals.) Amongst the starters you might be pleasantly surprised to find lobster and blue mussel salad, or a mince and chilli tartlet, as well as more mainstream egg, red onion and tomato salad. Main courses always include a roast or two – roast beef, roast pork, say – and fish is something they like to offer daily. Portions are hearty and, unusually, teas and coffees are complimentary after pudding (raspberry and custard flan or tiramisu are popular). Evening menus are more sophisticated, and may include game in season. The wine list offers over 20 bottles, with a couple of reds and whites available by the glass, and prices are moderate. Being a pleasant and laid-back venue, the Fairways has built up a loyal following locally, and it is certainly useful for travellers going through a part of Ireland that offers remarkably little in the way of journey breaks. **Seats 55** (outdoors, 16); toilets wheelchair accessible; children welcome (high chair, children's menu, baby changing facilities); L Mon-Fri, 12-2.30pm; D 5.30-8.30pm; Sun L 12-3pm. Set 3 course L €35. Closed Good Fri, 25 Dec. MasterCard, Visa, Laser. **Directions:** Three minutes drive from Nenagh town on the Cloughjordan Road, one minute from Nenagh Golf Club.

ROSCREA

Roscrea (Ros Cré - "wood of Cré") is a small town in the south midlands where, in ancient times, the five main routes in Ireland, or the Slighe Dhála, converged, and is quite near the Slieve Bloom Mountains. Designated a Heritage Town, it has many architectural features of note, including the Round Tower, Roscrea Castle and Damer House Complex (050 521 850). The town grew around its monastery and The Round Tower, on Church Street, has a doorway 15 feet from the ground and is the oldest surviving part of the ancient monastery. A Heritage Trail, with accompanying booklet in three languages, is freely available to help you explore this historic town (Roscrea Heritage - Castle & Damer House, 050 521 850). There are some exceptional gardens nearby: Birr Castle Demesne (Birr, 057 912 0336) is a large demesne with important collections of trees, lake, walks, and formal garden while Gash Gardens (Portlaoise, 057 873 2247) is a garden for plant enthusiasts that will inspire those making new gardens.

Roscrea Area
Fiacrí Country House Restaurant & Cookery School

RESTAURANT

Boulerea Knock Roscrea Co Tipperary **Tel: 0505 43017**
fiacrihouse@eircom.net   www.fiacrihouse.com

Enda & Ailish Hennessy's lovely country house-style restaurant and cookery school is not the easiest place to find (it is sensible to get directions when booking) but, once discovered, what a welcome sight their neat pink-painted farmhouse presents. Enda will be at hand to welcome guests, offering an aperitif beside the fire in the comfortably furnished bar, where you can look over Ailish's five-course menus, which are based on carefully sourced ingredients and credit suppliers on the first page. Menus are balanced, to include fish, poultry and vegetarian choices, but local meats are especially good, and generous portions of seasonal vegetables are served separately. Like the bar, the restaurant has an open fire and, with red walls, white ceiling, mahogany furniture and crisp white linen, it is cosy and pleasingly traditional, making a special yet relaxed setting to enjoy a good meal. House specialities include lovely breads, a delicious starter salad of baked Clonakilty black pudding & caramelised apple, and fairly traditional main courses like rack of Tipperary lamb, the ever-popular grilled sirloin steak Diane or a speciality dish of pan-fried medallions of veal with celeriac and Madeira cream sauce. If a long list of tempting desserts makes decisions difficult, you could try the excellent Assorted Dessert Plate or farmhouse cheeses. Ailish's cooking is excellent and, under Enda's supervision, caring service makes it a special experience; and a compact, informative wine list offers good value and includes some half bottles. Ailish also offers cookery classes throughout the year. This is a very popular restaurant and advance booking is essential. *Fiacri was selected for our Féile Bia Award in 2004. **Seats 70**; toilets wheelchair accessible; reservations required; not suitable for children under 12. D Wed-Sat, 7-9.15. Set 5 course D €55. House wine €20. Full bar licence. Closed Sun, Mon, Tue and 25 Dec, Good Fri. *Cookery classes held Tue night, over a 5 week period (€140pp). 1 day courses (c. €100) are also held at other times such as Christmas and Easter. **Directions:** Roscrea 10.5km, Erril 7km, Templemore 13km. Signed from Dublin-Limerick Road (N7). Dublin side of Roscrea.

Templemore Area

Saratoga Lodge

COUNTY HOUSE

Barnane Templemore Co Tipperary **Tel: 0504 31886**
saratogalodge@eircom.net www.saratoga-lodge.com

In a particularly unspoilt and peaceful part of the country, just below the famous Devil's Bit in the Silvermine mountain range, Valerie Beamish's lovely classically-proportioned house on a working stud farm is well-situated on an open, sunny site looking out over the hills. A large, pleasing garden with lovely trees and hedges, is well planted and beautifully maintained. Expect to enjoy fruit from the garden in season. A greeting by Valerie and a friendly Irish wolfhound sets the tone for a very relaxing and peaceful stay in this lovely country house, where large traditionally furnished reception rooms open off a spacious hall, and good equestrian paintings reflect the family interest. Bedrooms are very comfortably furnished and peaceful, with no TV - and all have lovely en-suite bathrooms. Valerie enjoys giving guests a good breakfast, and she's also willing to cook 4-course dinners on request, and make picnics - this is an extremely hospitable house all round. For guests wishing to dine out, however, Valerie Beamish recommends Sheehy's in Borrisoleigh. **Rooms 3** (all en-suite, 1 shower only, 1 family room, all no smoking). B&B €40-50 pps, no ss; children welcome (under 3s free in parents' room, cots available free of charge, baby-sitting arranged, play ground). Pets by arrangement - be assured that pets and pet lovers get a very warm welcome (no charge - stay in bedroom or in outhouse/kennel). Residents' D €30, daily 7-10pm (on request). House wine €15-20. Garden, walking. Golf, fishing, horse riding, hiking, racing (horses, greyhounds), cheesemakers and garden visits all nearby. Closed 23 Dec-3 Jan. No credit cards. **Directions:** From Templemore, take the Nenagh road for 3km (2 m); take 2nd turn right at the B&B sign. Take left at next junction (2.5km/1.5m); house is on the left.

Terryglass

The Derg Inn

PUB•RESTAURANT

Terryglass Co Tipperary **Tel: 067 22037**
sales@derginn.ie www.derginn.ie

Tables set up outside Michael and Joyce Soden's popular Derg Inn please the summer crowd, and a crackling fire is a welcome sight on a cold day - like many country pubs this is, perhaps, a place seen at its best off-season. This is one of the area's best pubs for food and the sight of tables set up for the comfortable enjoyment of a good meal quickly gets hungry guests into a relaxed mood (especially boating visitors, after the walk up from the harbour). Everything is sourced with care, using the best of local produce including organic food when possible; sea fish is more prominent on the menu than might be expected in a river and lakeland area, and traditional Irish dishes like bacon & cabbage and beef & Guinness pie are always a treat here. Evening menus are quite wide-ranging with a choice that usually includes delicious house specialities like home-made paté with Derg Inn mango chutney & garlic bread, and salmon in filo pastry with lemon & caper sauce - and maybe fillet steak with wholegrain mustard sauce - along with more-ish desserts like praline parfait with cinnamon syrup. Sunday lunch is also quite a speciality, but you don't have to eat to experience the Derg - there's an interesting little wine list to enjoy with or without food, and a very pleasant bar. Music in summer - Friday, Saturday and Sunday, various styles; Sunday night is the one for traditional music enthusiasts. **Seats 150** (private function room, 70+); toilets wheelchair accessible. Open daily: food available 11-10. Breakfast from 11 am, L 12-5, D 6-10. A la carte. House wine €19. SC discretionary. Closed Good Fri, 25 Dec. Amex, MasterCard, Visa, Laser. **Directions:** In the heart of Terrryglass Village. ◇

Terryglass Area

Kylenoe House

COUNTRY HOUSE

Ballinderry Terryglass Nenagh Co Tipperary **Tel: 067 22015**
ginia@eircom.net

Virginia Moeran's lovely old stone house on 150 acres of farm and woodland offers homely comfort and real country pleasures close to Lough Derg. The farm is home to an international stud and the woodlands are a haven for wildlife, including deer, stoats, red squirrels, badgers, rabbits and foxes as well as many varieties of birds and flowers. With beautiful walks, riding (with or without tuition), golf and water sports available on the premises or close by, this is a real rural retreat. Spacious, airy bedrooms are furnished in gentle country house-style, with antiques and family belongings, and overlook beautiful rolling countryside; recent refurbishment has included new super-comfortable beds. Downstairs there's a delightful guests' sitting room and plenty of interesting reading. Virginia enjoys cooking, her breakfasts are a speciality and dinner is available to residents by arrangement. Importantly for people who like to travel with their dogs, this is a place where man's best friend is also made welcome and Kylenoe was our Pet Friendly Establishment of the Year in 1999. **Rooms 4** (3 ensuite, 1 with private bathroom, all no-smoking); B&B €60 pps, ss €10; children welcome (under 8 free in parents' room; cot available free of charge, baby sitting arranged). Pets welcome. Garden, walking. Residents D 7-8pm, about €40 (book by noon). Wines from about €18. Closed 15, Dec - 15 Jan. MasterCard, Visa. **Directions:** N7 to Moneygall, Cloughjordan, Borrisokane, leave Egans shop on right and straigt 10km (6.5m) on right.

THURLES

In the heart of the Suir Valley - a beautiful area renowned for its world class farmland - Thurles is the largest town in North Tipperary. There are many castles and monastic settlements in the surrounding and area and, with the Silvermines mountains to the north-west and the Slieveadagh Hills to the south-east, it has much to offer walkers and trekkers. In the town, **Mitchell House Restaurant** (0504 90776), on Mitchell Street, is an attractive, spacious, comfortable restaurant with friendly and efficient service; open for lunch and dinner seven days a week.

WWW.IRELAND-GUIDE.COM FOR ALL THE BEST PLACES TO EAT, DRINK & STAY

Thurles Area   # Inch House Country House & Restaurant

COUNTRY HOUSE•RESTAURANT   Bouladuff Thurles Co Tipperary **Tel: 0504 51348**

R   mairin@inchhouse.ie www.inchhouse.ie

Built in 1720 by John Ryan, one of the few landed Catholic gentlemen in Tipperary, this magnificent Georgian house managed to survive some of the most turbulent periods in Irish history and to remain in the Ryan family for almost 300 years. John and Norah Egan, who farm the surrounding 250 acres, took it over in a state of dereliction in 1985 and began the major restoration work which has resulted in the handsome, comfortably furnished period house which guests enjoy today. Reception rooms on either side of a welcoming hallway have period fireplaces with big log fires, and include an unusual William Morris-style drawing room with a tall stained glass window, a magnificent plasterwork ceiling (and adjoining library bar) and a fine dining room, which is used for residents' breakfasts and is transformed into a restaurant at night. The five bedrooms are quite individual and are furnished with antiques. Small weddings. Equestrian, golf, fishing (coarse) and hunting/shooting all nearby. Walking. Children welcome (under 10 free in parents' room; cot available without charge). No Pets. **Rooms 5** (all en-suite, 1 shower only, 1 family room). B&B €65 pps, ss €10. Closed Christmas & New Year. **Restaurant:** The restaurant, which is open to non-residents by reservation, has polished wood floors, classic country house decor and tables laid with crisp white linen and fresh flowers, which provide a pleasing setting for dinner, especially when the ambience is softened by firelight and candles. Dinner menus offer a well-balanced choice of about six dishes on each course, in a fairly traditional style that combines French country cooking and Irish influences, and makes good use of local produce. Dishes like Cooleeney cheese parcel, for example (local cheese in filo pastry, with grape chutney), for example, and the ever-popular entrecôte steak with mushroom & whiskey sauce, illustrate the style. Anyone with special dietary needs, including vegetarians, should mention this on booking to allow for preparation of extra dishes. **Seats 50**; not suitable for children after 7 pm. D Tue-Sat 7-9; Set D €50-55; house wine €17; sc discretionary. Restaurant closed Sun & Mon; house closed 2 weeks Christmas, 1 week Easter. MasterCard, Visa, Laser. **Directions:** Four miles from Thurles on Nenagh Road.

COUNTY WATERFORD

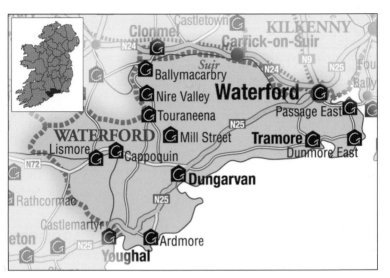

On the quays of Waterford city, we are witness to a trading and seafaring tradition which goes back at least 1,150 years. But this sense of history also looks to the future, as Waterford – traditionally the city of crystal and quality glassware – is popular as a Tall Ships assembly port. Today's larger commercial ships may be berthed downstream on the other side of the river at Belview, but the old cityside quays on the south bank retain a nautical flavour which is accentuated by very useful marina berthing facilities in the heart of town.

This fine port was founded in 853 AD when the Vikings - Danes for the most part - established the trading settlement of Vadrefjord. Its strategic location in a sheltered spot at the head of the estuary near the confluence of the Suir and Barrow rivers guaranteed its continuing success under different administrators, particularly the Normans, so much so that it tended to overshadow the county of Waterford, almost all of which is actually to the west of the city.

But for many years now, the county town has been Dungarvan, which is two-thirds of the way westward along Waterford's extensive south coast, which includes the attractive Copper Coast - between Fenor and Stradbally - in its midst. This spreading of the administrative centres of gravity has to some extent balanced the life of the Waterford region. But even so, the extreme west of the county is still one of Ireland's best kept secrets, a place of remarkable beauty between the Knockmealdown, Comeragh and Monavullagh mountains, where fish-filled rivers such as the Bride, the Blackwater, and the Nire make their way seawards at different speeds through valleys of remarkable variety and beauty, past pretty towns and villages such as romantic, castle-bedecked Lismore which has been an overall winner in the Tidy Towns awards, and is architecturally all of a piece.

West Waterford is a place of surprises. For instance, around the delightful coastal village of Ardmore, ancient monuments suggest that the local holy man, St Declan, introduced Christianity to the area quite a few years before St Patrick went to work in the rest of Ireland. And across the bay from Ardmore, the Ring neighbourhood is a Gaeltacht (Irish-speaking) area with its own bustling fishing port at Helvick.

Dungarvan itself is enjoying the fruits of an attractive revival. It has relinquished its role as a commercial port, but is enthusiastically taking to recreational boating and harbourside regeneration instead. Along the bluff south coast, secret coves gave smugglers and others access to charming villages like Stradbally and Bunmahon. Further east, the increased tempo of the presence of Waterford city is felt both at the traditional resort of Tramore, and around the fishing/sailing harbour of Dunmore East.

Local Attractions and Information

Ballymacarbry	Nire Valley & Comeraghs on Horseback	052 36147
Cappoquin	Mount Melleray Activity Centre	058 54322
Cappoquin	Tourism Information	058 53333
Dungarvan	Tourism Information	058 41741
Kilmeaden	Old School House Craft Centre	051 853 567
Lismore	Lismore Castle & Gardens	058 54424
Passage East	Car Ferry (to Ballyhack, Co Wexford)	051 382 480
Tramore	Tramore House Gardens	051 386 303
Waterford	Airport	051 875 589
Waterford	Christ Church Cathedral (18c Neoclassical)	051 858 958
Waterford	Waterford Crystal Glass Centre	051 332 500
Waterford	Heritage Museum	051 871 227
Waterford	Int. Festival of Light Opera (Sept)	051 375 437
Waterford	Reginald's Tower 13th C Circular Tower	051 304 220
Waterford	Theatre Royal	051 874 402
Waterford	Tourism Information	051 875 823
Waterford	Waterford Treasures at the Granary	051 304 500

ARDMORE

This picturesque village and popular seaside resort (with Blue Flag beach) overlooking Ardmore Bay was originally a 5th century monastic settlement; founded by St. Declan in 316 AD, it is reputed to be the first such settlement in Ireland. Today, the Ardmore Round Tower and Cathedral still attract visitors, as they always did, and St. Declan's Way, a 94km long-distance pilgrim's way walk to Cashel, follows the old routes as faithfully as possible. Ardmore is on the Gaeltacht & Galltacht Scenic Drive and there's a lovely 5km circular cliff walk, which takes about an hour. A highlight of the village is Ardmore Pottery and Craft Shop (024 94152) which is just below the Cliff House Hotel, looking down to the pier and boat cove; Ardmore's charming trademark blue and white pottery is made here, and they also stock a range of quality Irish crafts. In the village, **The Old Forge Restaurant** (024 94750) has recently re-opened under common management with **The Cliff House Hotel** (see entry); very useful to know about they have outdoor seating with a children's play area, and offer an appealing menu of snacks, tea time bites and desserts; a small choice of main courses includes black Angus steaks, plus an attractive wine/beer list to accompany (open 10am to 10pm Thu-Mon, closed Tue & Wed; times may vary in winter; credit cards accepted.)

WWW.IRELAND-GUIDE.COM FOR ALL THE BEST PLACES TO EAT, DRINK & STAY

Ardmore
HOTEL•RESTAURANT

The Cliff House Hotel

Ardmore Co Waterford **Tel: 024 87800**
info@thecliffhousehotel.com www.thecliffhousehotel.com

NEWCOMER OF THE YEAR AWARD

Built into steep cliffs beside the pretty village of Ardmore and overlooking Ardmore Bay and the Irish Sea, this boutique hotel opened to some acclaim and, with its fresh contemporary style, ambitious cooking and emphasis on service, it has brought a new focus to an area of outstanding hospitality and unspoilt natural beauty which has somehow remained a well-kept secret until now. The arrival of Adriaan Bartels as General Manager – one of Ireland's most respected hoteliers, well-known for his exceptional dedication to discreet customer care – sent a frisson of happy expectation around the hospitality world, giving this new property a well deserved leg-up for its opening season. On arrival from the Dungarvan side, the hotel is impossible to miss - pretty with twinkling lights at night, its rather obvious daytime persona will mellow as the natural 'grass' roofing grows in – and very easy to find, as the drive through the quaint little village is short. At the door, staff are keen to help and generally make you feel as welcome as possible. The entrance into the reception area is stunning, with smart contemporary design, a dramatic spiral staircase leading down to the bar and restaurant, striking colours, a welcoming open

fire - but the star is the sea, seen through the huge back window. The building has a unique lay out, which can make it hard to get your bearings; a ball of string could be your most useful accessory, but cheerful staff are always at the ready to rescue anyone who goes missing. The rooms are gorgeous: all have sea views, and many have a private balcony with table and chairs for al fresco dining. Décor, in several schemes, is bold and modern with wifi, flat screen TV etc as standard, yet with classic touches and an emphasis on comfort; the boldest is in a strong pink, which works well against dark wood furniture, subdued carpet, original artwork and feature bedheads – one is a 'cat's cradle' of coloured wools strung behind glass. Generous bathrooms take up perhaps a tad too much of the available space but, with free standing bath and separate shower seen against soft natural light from a frosted glass window on the bedroom side and a combination of natural slate and iridescent mosaic tiling, they are impressive - and, while a little short on practical shelf space, have loads of fluffy white towels, robes, slippers and lovely toiletries to pamper. And, when it comes to pampering, they're no slouches here, with The Well spa offering a stunningly positioned outdoor infinity pool - and a jacuzzi, sauna, steam room and gym, all overlooking the bay. And, better still perhaps, there are steps down to a natural rock pool. Events and meetings – details on inquiry. Small conferences/banqueting (66/50); business centre, secretarial services, video conferencing, free broadband wi/fi. Children welcome (under 5s free in parents room, baby sitting arranged, play room). Leisure Centre (swimming pool, fitness room, jacuzzi, sauna, steam room); Spa (treatment rooms, massage); beauty salon. Fishing, golf, equestrian, scuba diving, surfing & watersports all nearby. **Rooms 39**. Average room rate €200. 24 hr room service; lift. Dogs permitted (staying in outhouse/kennel). Closed 2 Jan - 13 Feb. **House Restaurant:** The attractive bar and restaurant are on the floor below reception, opening onto an extensive terrace. Head Chef Martijn Kajuiter has moved from his native Holland and settled his family in the area – showing a level of commitment that is also seen in his kitchen and, already, he is making a mark on the culinary scene well beyond the immediate locality. The simply-worded menu speaks volumes for his philosophy – organic Clare Island salmon, Irish free-range pork, local Suffolk lamb, Helvick turbot, hake and monkfish and Skeaghanore duck (from nearby County Cork) all feature. Yet, for all the strong simplicity of ingredients, they appear in a highly sophisticated international cuisine featuring foams and smokes aplenty, and with many original touches. Be sure to leave some room for desserts, which are a highlight – as are the petits fours which end the meal with éclat. **Seats 36** (private room, 18; outdoors, 20); children welcome (high chair, childrens menu, baby changing facilities); air conditioning; reservations required; toilets wheelchair accessible. L & D Mon-Sat, 1-5pm & 7-10pm. Sun D only, 7-10pm. Set 3 course L €35; set 2/3 course D €57/62.50; gourmet D €75; also à la carte; house wine from €18. Food served in the bar daily, noon - 9pm. Hotel closed first six weeks of the year. Amex, MasterCard, Visa, Laser. **Directions:** Hotel is located at the end of Ardmore village (N25-R673) via the Middle Road.

Ardmore
RESTAURANT

White Horses Restaurant
Ardmore Co Waterford **Tel: 024 94040**
whitehorses@eircom.net

Christine Power and Geraldine Flavin's delightfully bright and breezy café-restaurant on the main street of this famous seaside village is one of those places that changes its character through the day but always has style. They're open for all the little lifts that visitors need through the day - morning coffee, afternoon tea - as well as imaginative lunches (plus their traditional Sunday lunch, which runs all afternoon) and a more ambitious à la carte evening menu. Vegetarian dishes feature on both menus - a pasta dish during the day perhaps, and spinach & mushroom crêpe with toasted brie in the evening - and there's a good balance between traditional favourites like steaks and more adventurous fare: a daytime fish dish could be deep-fried plaice with tartare sauce, for example, while its evening counterpart might be grilled darne of Helvick salmon on asparagus, with a wine & cream sauce. Attractive and pleasant to be in - the use of pretty local Ardmore pottery is a big plus on the presentation side, and emphasises the sense of place - this is a friendly, well-run restaurant and equally good for a reviving cuppa and a gateau or pastry from the luscious home-made selection on display, or a full meal. Even at its busiest, service is well-organised and efficient. **Seats 50**; air conditioning. In summer (May-Sep) open: Tue-Sun 11-'late'; L 12.30-3.30, D 6.30-8.30/9pm. In winter (Oct-Apr) open weekends only: Fri from 6 pm, Sat 11-11 & Sun 12-6. A la carte except Sun - Set L about €27. Licensed; House Wine €18.50; sc discretionary. Closed Mon all year, except bank hols (bank hol opening as Sun), 1 Jan-13 Feb. MasterCard, Visa, Laser. **Directions:** Centre of village.

BALLYMACARBRY

This small village is beautifully situated between the Knockmealdown and Comeragh Mountains, an unspoilt area with terrain to suit every level of walker; the Comeragh Mountain Walking Festival is held here every October, with graded walks led by very experienced guides. Anglers will enjoy Clonanav Farmhouse (053 913 6141), which provides tuition for game angling, whilst horseriding can be arranged by Nire Valley Equestrian Trail-Riding & Trekking (052 36147), with treks through some of the most beautiful scenery in Waterford. Golfers will find that many pleasing Co Waterford courses are convenient to Ballymacarbry, including the Eddie Hackett-designed Williamstown Golf Club (051 853131), Waterford Golf Club (051 876 748), Dunmore East Golf Club (051 383 151), and Tramore Golf Club (051 386 170).

Ballymacarbry Glasha

FARMHOUSE Glasha Ballymacarbry via Clonmel Co Waterford **Tel: 052 36108**

  glasha@eircom.net www.glashafarmhouse.com

 Paddy and Olive O'Gorman's spacious farmhouse is set in its own gardens high up in the hills and makes a very comfortable and hospitable base for a relaxed rural break. Fishing is a major attraction (the Nire runs beside the farmhouse and permits are available locally), also walking (Glasha links the Comeragh and Knockmealdown sections of the famous Munster Way), pony trekking, golf (available locally), and painting this beautiful area. Olive thinks of everything that will help guests feel at home and bedrooms - which are extremely luxurious for a farm stay - have lots of little extras including TV/radio, hair dryers, electric blankets, tea/coffee-making, spring water and magazines; most rooms have king-size beds, all are en-suite, and the newer ones have lovely bathrooms with jacuzzi baths. There's plenty of comfortable lounging room for guests' use, too, including a conservatory - and the nearest pub is just 3 minutes' walk from the house. Olive makes a delicious home-cooked dinner for guests, by arrangement, and it is served in a comfortable big dining room; her 3-course menus change daily and you might begin with something that showcases local seafood, like Dungarvan mussels in a creamy basil sauce, then a main course of Comeragh lamb - a rack, perhaps, served with apple & mint chutney and a rosemary sauce - and finish with rhubarb & strawberry crumble, or warm apple fudge cake, then tea or coffee and chocolates in the conservatory, or in beside the fire on chilly evenings. The food is gorgeous with its farmhouse simplicity, and you'll get a really good breakfast to set you up for the day too. This is a lovely place to stay, and a perfect antidote to the stresses of urban life. **Rooms 6** (4 with jacuzzi bath, 2 shower only, 1 family room, 2 ground floor, all no-smoking); Children welcome (cots available). B&B about €60 pps, ss €10. Residents' D Mon-Sat, 7.30 by arrangement (short à la carte), €25-35. Closed D Sun, 20-27 Dec. MasterCard, Visa, Laser. **Directions:** Off 671 road between Clonmel and Dungarvan, 3.5km (2 m) from Ballymacarbry; signed on 671.◇

Ballymacarbry Hanora's Cottage

GUESTHOUSE•RESTAURANT Nire Valley Ballymacarbry Co Waterford **Tel: 052 36134**

  hanorascottage@eircom.net www.hanorascottage.com

 Although the Wall family's gloriously remote country guesthouse is now a very substantial building, the spirit of the ancestral home around which Hanora's is built remains a strong presence. This a very special place - equally wonderful for foot-weary walkers, or desk-weary city folk in need of some clear country air and real comfort - and the genuine hospitality of the Wall family is matched by the luxurious accommodation and good food they provide. Comfortably furnished seating areas have sofas and big armchairs, giving plenty of room to relax, and the spacious thoughtfully furnished bedrooms all have jacuzzi baths (one especially romantic room is perfect for honeymooners); there's also a spa tub in a conservatory overlooking the garden, with views of the mountains. Overnight guests begin the day with Hanora's legendary breakfast buffet, which was the National Winner of our Irish Breakfast Awards in 2002; it takes some time

to get the measure of this feast, so make sure you get up in time to make the most of it. Local produce and exotics jostle for space on the beautifully arranged buffet: fruits and freshly squeezed juices (also luscious Crinnaghtaun Apple Juice from Lismore), home-made muesli and porridge... freshly-baked breads, including organic and gluten-free varieties... local farmhouse cheeses, smoked salmon, home-made jams - and all the cooked breakfast options you could wish for. This is truly a gargantuan feast, designed to see you many miles along the hills before you stop for a little packed lunch (prepared that morning), and ultimately return for dinner... Small weddings/corporate hospitality (currently 40, but venue due to be extended to seat 80). **Rooms 10** (1 suite, 3 junior suites, all no smoking). Not suitable for children. No pets. B&B from €85 pps. Closed Christmas week. **Restaurant:** One of the best things about Hanora's is that people travel from far and wide to dine here, which adds to the atmosphere. It is pleasant for evening guests to mingle with residents at the fireside, have an aperitif and ponder on Eoin and Judith Wall's imaginative, well-balanced menus - then, difficult choices made, you move through to the restaurant, which overlooks a secluded garden and riverside woodland. Enthusiastic supporters of small suppliers, Eoin and Judith use local produce whenever possible and credit them on the menu - fresh fish from Dunmore East, free-range chickens from Stradbally and local cheeses, for example. There's a separate vegetarian dinner menu on request as well as an à la carte which offers about seven dishes on each course, usually including some vegetarian options. Popular dishes include starters of sautéed lambs kidneys on a croustade with mushroom cream, and stuffed mushrooms with walnuts, blue cheese & garlic mayonnaise; main courses include beautifully fresh and accurately cooked fish and, as lamb is so abundant locally, the all-time favourite is roast rack of lamb (served, perhaps, with a delicious mint hollandaise). Desserts include well-made classics like lemon tart with crème anglaise and good home-made ice creams - and, of course, there's always an Irish cheese selection. *Hanora's is now also open during the day for morning coffee and afternoon tea – a lovely place for a break when exploring the area. **Seats 40**; not suitable for children under 12. D Mon-Sat, 7-9, Set D about €40, also à la carte. House wine about €16. Closed Sun. MasterCard, Visa, Laser. **Directions:** Take Clonmel/Dungarvan (R671) road, turn off at Ballymacarbry.

Cappoquin

COUNTRY HOUSE•RESTAURANT

Richmond House

Cappoquin Co Waterford **Tel: 058 54278**

info@richmondhouse.net www.richmondhouse.net

Genuine hospitality, high standards of comfort, caring service and excellent food are all to be found in the Deevy family's fine 18th century country house and restaurant just outside Cappoquin - no wonder this is a place so many people like to keep as a closely guarded secret. For returning guests, there's always a sense of pleasurable anticipation that builds up as you approach through parkland along a well-maintained driveway, which is lit up at night; after a brief pause to admire the climbing plants beside the door, you're into the fine high-ceilinged hall with its warming stove and catch the scent of log fires burning in the well-proportioned, elegantly furnished drawing room and restaurant opening off it. Claire or Jean Deevy will usually be there to welcome arriving guests, and show you to one of the nine individually-decorated bedrooms; they vary in size and appointments, as is the way with old houses - some guests love the smallest cottagey bedroom, while others may prefer the larger ones - but all are comfortably furnished in country house style with full bathrooms, and four were renovated in 2008. As well as serving wonderful dinners in the restaurant (see below), the Deevys make sure that you will have a memorable breakfast to see you on your way - it is a wonderful area to explore, and Richmond House makes an excellent base. Children welcome (under 3 free in parents' room, cot available without charge, baby sitting arranged). No pets. Garden; walking. Golf, garden visits nearby. **Rooms 9** (1 junior suite, all with full bathrooms & no smoking). B&B €75 pps, ss €20. Closed 22 Dec-10 Jan. **Restaurant:** The restaurant is the heart of Richmond House and non-residents usually make up a high proportion of the guests, which makes for a lively atmosphere. Warm and friendly service begins from the moment menus are presented over aperitifs - in front of the drawing room fire, or in a conservatory overlooking the garden. Paul is an ardent supporter of local produce and sources everything with tremendous care: Quality Assured meats (beef, lamb, bacon and sausages) come from his trusted local butcher, fresh seafood is from Dunmore East and Dungarvan, while herbs, fruit and vegetables are home grown where possible, and extra organic produce is grown nearby. There is a sureness of touch in Paul's kitchen, and his menus balance traditional country house cooking and more adventurous dishes inspired by international trends; dinner menus offering about five choices on each course are changed daily, and a slightly shorter separate vegetarian menu is also offered. House specialities include Helvick prawns (tempura, perhaps) and -

a dish it would be hard to resist at Richmond House - roast rack of delicious West Waterford lamb, a memorable dish presented on braised puy lentils and buttered green beans, with home-made mint jelly and rosemary & garlic jus; vegetables, served separately, are invariably imaginative and perfectly cooked. Classic desserts are always a treat too, including plenty of imaginative and beautifully executed fruit-based choices to balance the richness of a fine meal here - orange pannacotta with orange segments, perhaps - and, of course, there will always be Irish farmhouse cheeses with home-made biscuits. Service, under Claire's direction, is attentive and discreet. A carefully selected and fairly-priced wine list includes about twenty offered by the glass, several wines of the month, and a good choice of half bottles. The early dinner menu offers particularly good value. *Richmond House was selected for the Féile Bia Award in 2006. **Seats 45** (private room, 14); children welcome. D 6.30-9.30 daily; Set D about €50, early bird about €35 (vegetarian menu also avail); house wine €20; sc 10% on groups 6+. Closed 22 Dec-10 Jan. Amex, Diners, MasterCard, Visa, Laser. **Directions:** 1km (0.5 mile) outside Cappoquin on N72.

Cheekpoint
RESTAURANT

The Cottage Bistro

Cheekpoint Village Co Waterford **Tel: 051 380 854**
cottagebistro@eircom.net www.cottagebistro.com

Aidan and Marian McAlpin's neat cottagey restaurant is spick and span and the style is pleasingly simple, with a small bar area and plain, handsomely-laid tables softened by warm lighting and fresh flowers. Freshly-baked brown bread and iced water are served promptly, along with attractive hand-written menus that offer plenty of choice, including steaks, chicken and a tempting speciality vegetarian shepherd's pie; but local seafood is the speciality, and some dishes – a smoked salmon salad, for example, and a hot dish of prawns in garlic, coriander & chilli butter – are offered as either starters or main courses. What you get here is Marian McAlpin's sound home cooking, simply presented - and prices are reasonable, especially for seafood, including an excellent Seafood Platter which could include ten different fish and shellfish and is good value at about €24. An interesting, informative and well-priced wine list includes unusual house wines and an equally carefully selected choice of half bottles. **Seats 45** (+10 outside); children welcome before 7pm; reservations required; toilets wheelchair accessible. D Tue-Sat, 6-9.30. A la carte. House wine €19. SC discretionary. Closed Sun, Mon, last week Sept, all Jan. Amex, MasterCard, Visa, Laser. **Directions:** 7 miles east of Waterford city; in village, above the harbour.

Cheekpoint
RESTAURANT

The Suir Inn

Cheekpoint Co Waterford **Tel: 051 382 220**
frances@mcalpins.com www.mcalpins.com

This immaculately maintained black-and-white painted inn is 300 years old and has been run by the McAlpin family since 1972. It's a characterful, country style place with rustic furniture, cottagey plates and old prints decorating the walls - more like a traditional bar than a restaurant. Seasonal menus offer a choice of about six starters (mostly seafood) and ten main courses, including several cold dishes and two vegetarian ones, again all moderately priced - specialities include a generous and reasonably priced seafood platter and home-made seafood pie. All meals come with brown soda bread and butter, and a side salad - and a nice little wine list includes a choice of eight moderately priced wines. **Seats 62**; no children after 9pm. D Mon-Sat, 5.30-9.30; à la carte; sc discretionary. House wine from about €15. SC discretionary. Closed Sun. MasterCard, Visa, Laser **Directions:** 7 miles east of Waterford, on harbour front. ◊

DUNGARVAN

This is the county's main town outside Waterford city and is beautifully located on Dungarvan Harbour (renowned for its wildlife), with much of interest nearby: the Gaeltacht of Ring is just a few miles away, for example, and the lovely Nire Valley (walking, pony trekking) runs deep into the Comeragh Mountains north of the town. West of Dungarvan, the Heritage Town of Lismore, with its fairytale castle and gardens, is just a short drive. Garden lovers should allow time to visit Lismore Castle Garden (Lismore, 058 54424) which is a historic garden dating back in parts to the 17th century, and Cappoquin House Garden (Cappoquin, 058 54290), a four-acre garden surrounding a Georgian country house. The main hotel in Dungarvan is the Flynn family's **Park Hotel** (058 42899; www.flynnhotels.com), which is just on the edge of town overlooking the Colligan River estuary; it is spacious and comfortable, with leisure centre/swimming pool. There is a Farmers' Market on the Square on Thursdays (9.30am-2pm). Championship golf is available at West Waterford Golf Club (Dungarvan, 058 41475).
WWW.IRELAND-GUIDE.COM FOR ALL THE BEST PLACES TO EAT, DRINK & STAY

Dungarvan
B&B•COUNTRY HOUSE

Cairbre House

Strandside North Abbeyside Dungarvan Co Waterford **Tel: 058 42338**
cairbrehouse@eircom.net www.cairbrehouse.com

Brian Wickham's fine old house is just across the bridge from Dungarvan town centre - it is of great historical interest, and set in wonderful gardens, right on the water. The house has a homely feel with lots of local information, a lounge and fire for guests, and also a lovely new all-year conservatory with views over the gardens and harbour. The very traditionally furnished bedrooms are spacious and comfortable, with beautiful views out over the water; they include rooms for families or groups and, as well as en-suite facilities, there's an extra communal bathroom. Breakfast is a high point - and includes a hot vegetarian special, with the option of bacon for non-vegetarians! In fine weather, Brian is happy to serve breakfast in the back garden, where there are some wooden tables and benches. The gardens, which enjoy a micro-climate that allows many 'impossible' plants to survive here, are Brian's greatest love and a source of great pleasure to guests. **Rooms 4** (all shower only, 3 en-suite, 1 with private bathroom, 1 family room, 3 no smoking, 1 ground floor); children welcome (under 4s free in parents' room, cot available free of charge); free broadband wi/fi. B&B €40-45 pps, ss €6. Garden visits, golf and sea angling nearby. Closed Nov-mid Feb. Amex, Diners, MasterCard, Visa. **Directions:** From Waterford, take right exit off N25 at Strandside roundabout, house 200m up on the left.

Dungarvan
GUESTHOUSE

Powersfield House

Ballinamuck West Dungarvan Co Waterford **Tel: 058 45594**
powersfieldhouse@cablesurf.com www.powersfield.com

You could be forgiven for thinking that Edmund and Eunice Power's fine guesthouse has been here for a long time - although quite new, the garden has matured well and this, together with traditional country house style of both the house and furnishing, gives it an unexpected sense of age. Antiques and interesting fabrics create a soothing and relaxing atmosphere throughout the house, including a comfortable, homely sitting room as well as bedrooms which have been individually decorated and finished to a high standard, with smart bathrooms and all the necessary comforts. Eunice is an enthusiastic professional cook and offers dinner to residents by arrangement; her menus are based on local produce and, as a new vegetable garden is well under way, Eunice aims to be self-sufficient in seasonal produce during the summer. This is a lovely, friendly place to stay and would make a good base for exploring the area. **Rooms 4** (all en-suite, no smoking & shower only, 1 family); children welcome (under 4 free in parents' room; cot available without charge; children's playground, baby sitting arranged); B&B €55 pps, ss €10. Dogs allowed in some areas by arrangment (kennel in garden); Room service (limited hours). Residents' D by arrangement about €25-35; house wine €20-30; sc discretionary. *Cookery Courses available, details on application. Amex, MasterCard, Visa, Laser. **Directions:** Take the Killarney road R672 from Dungarvan at Kilrush roundabout; second turn left, first house on right.

Dungarvan
CAFE/BAR

Quealy's Café Bar

82 O'Connell Street Dungarvan Co Waterford **Tel: 058 24555**
info@quealys.com www.quealys.com

Just off the main square in Dungarvan town, Quealy's is a friendly buzzy place with simple, good quality table settings in the smart bar, and food that is well above the usual expectation of "bar food" in terms of sourcing, cooking and presentation. They offer a modern menu of good dishes at very reasonable prices, many of them available either as starters or as main courses, and there is always a good traditional "specials of the day" menu on blackboards - mixed seafood platter, perhaps, or St Tola goat's cheese salad with pine nuts & piquillo peppers. Well-turned out staff are efficient, ensuring relaxed ambience even at busy times. Toilets & bar wheelchair accessible; children welcome before 8/9pm (high chair, childrens menu in bar); air conditioning; Bar meals: Mon-Sun, 12-5pm (from 12.30 Sun); à la carte D menu from 5-9pm (to 8.30pm Sun). House wines €20-25; SC 10% on groups 6+. MasterCard, Visa, Laser. **Directions:** Town centre, west of the main square.

Dungarvan

RESTAURANT WITH ROOMS

The Tannery

10 Quay Street Dungarvan Co Waterford **Tel: 058 45420**

info@tannery.ie www.tannery.ie

Discerning diners from all over Ireland (and beyond) make a beeline for Paul and Maire Flynn's stylish contemporary restaurant, which is in an old leather warehouse - the tannery theme is echoed throughout the light, clean-lined interior, giving a sense of historic continuity to the modern setting. Arriving guests can see Paul and his team at work in the open kitchen on their way upstairs to the first-floor dining area, which is bright and welcoming, with dramatic paintings, fresh flowers and smart, simple table settings. Over ten years after opening, both the style and the room itself feel fresh, which is rarely the case with minimalism. Menus are also wonderfully simple but the food tastes very exciting; while inspired to some extent by global trends and regional cooking, particularly of the Mediterranean countries, menus have a strongly Irish feeling and are based mainly on local ingredients, which Paul supports avidly and sources with care - notably local seafood of course (and often including less-used fish, such as pollock), also meats including pork and bacon supplied by renowned local butcher JD Power. Simplicity is of the essence here, and (in line with international trends) there are no amuse bouches; what is certain to be an outstanding meal cuts straight to the chase with superb starters (stout-cured sea trout perhaps – a delicious variation on gravadlax – served with buckwheat blini and sour cream; one of many classics revisited). Even hardened food critics are continually surprised by Paul Flynn's cooking which, as one fellow chef put it, "makes dishes which one thought one knew the taste of, as if one was eating them for the first time". Presentation is good and all the better for being plain - not too much height, and not too many useless drops about the plate; occasionally a dish may look a little bizarre - a lasagne of rabbit shredded like rillettes, for example - but you can be sure that it will taste extremely good. An Irish farmhouse cheese platter is invariably a highlight, and the dessert menu offers plenty of treats - but, here too, the maverick genius is at work and you will find novelty alongside the conventional chocolate confections. And giving good value has always been a notable feature of The Tannery: the à la carte is very fairly priced for food of this quality, but the lunch and early evening menus (both changed daily) are outstandingly good value. Attentive and efficient service, an interesting and kindly-priced wine list (which offers lots of cheaper choices for this style of restaurant, also a welcome page of half bottles) and, above all, Paul's exceptional cooking, make for memorable meals. A recent introduction is the Chef's Table Menu, available for parties of 12-30 and, with the emphasis on informality – shared plates of meat or fish antipasti to start, for example – it would be great fun for a group of friends or colleagues. *Paul was our Chef of the Year in 2008, and The Tannery was our Restaurant of the Year in 2004. **Seats 60** (+ 30 downstairs, private room, 30); children welcome (mini Sun L menu €10). L Fri & Sun only, 12.30-2.15 (Sun to 2.30); D Tue-Sat, 6.30-9.30 (from 6.30 Sat). Early D €30 (Tue-Fri, 6-7.15); Set Sun L €30; house wine €23; sc discretionary (10% on parties of 6+). Closed Mon, D Sun, L Mon-Thurs & L Sat; annual closure 2 weeks end Jan, 1 week Sept. **Rooms:** Comfortable and very convenient accommodation is offered in a boutique guesthouse just around the corner, in Church Street. Public areas of the house are very bright and funky but, while also contemporary, the seven double rooms and a self-catering apartment are furnished more calmly; a continental breakfast is organised so that you can have it in your room. *The Tannery Cookery School and seven new rooms are due to open shortly after going to press. **Rooms 7** (all en-suite, 2 shower only), children welcome (under 4s free in parents' room, cots available at no charge); B&B €60 pps or €80 pps for superior room, ss €10. Amex, Diners, MasterCard, Visa, Laser **Directions:** End of lower main street beside old market house.

Dungarvan Area

B&B

An Bohreen

Killineen West Dungarvan Co Waterford **Tel: 051 291 010**

mulligans@anbohreen.com www.anbohreen.com

Just a few miles outside Dungarvan, off the Waterford road, Jim and Ann Mulligan's striking contemporary house has panoramic mountain and coastal view. You'll get a warm welcome from Jim, who will show you to a compact bedroom with an antique bedstead (with modern mattress), old-style furniture and neat en-suite shower room. Guests also have use of a patio for warm weather, and the spacious, open plan sitting room has an open fire, television, radio, CDs, books and a comfortable seating area; a couple of steps up from it, the dining room has wall-to-wall windows overlooking the garden to the sea at Helvick Head, a fine setting for Ann's good cooking. Dinner is by arrangement and meals are cooked to order: preferring to concentrate on one set of guests at a time, you are asked when booking to agree a time and choose, from a short menu, what you would like for a main course at dinner as ingredients are bought freshly each day. Ann takes pride in sourcing local ingredients and a typical dinner might include a home-made seasonal soup (an unusual leek and pear, perhaps), a simple salad, lamb chops with a wine sauce, barbary duck breast or fillet of salmon and, to finish, the superb house dessert of New York cheesecake and good coffee. For breakfast (you agree a suitable time on arrival), a good menu includes fresh fruit and juice, freshly baked scones and bread and, in addition to the more usual offerings, crêpes with a strudel-style apple filling. **Rooms 4** (all shower only, no smoking and ground floor). B&B €45-50 pps, ss about €20. Not suitable for children under 12. Free broadband wi/fi. Residents D €40, 6.30-8.30pm daily. Fishing, golf and walking nearby. Closed Oct 31-Mar 21. MasterCard, Visa **Directions:** Off N25. Look for town of Lemybrien; look for resume speed sign, 5km later there is a right turn; house signed after 220m.

Dungarvan Area   Gortnadiha Lodge

FARMHOUSE   Ring Dungarvan Co Waterford

      Tel: 058 46142

Eileen and Thomas Harty's house is west of Dungarvan in the Ring Gaeltacht (Irish speaking) area, and it is in a lovely quiet setting, with woodland gardens and wonderful land and sea views. Accommodation in the family home is spacious, furnished with quality and style, and very comfortable. Eileen is a warm and interested host, and delicious breakfasts offer a very wide selection of local and home produce, including fresh fish in season. **Rooms 3** (2 shower only, 1 ground floor). B&B room rate €90. Children welcome (under 5 free in parents' room, cot available without charge, baby sitting arranged). Pets permitted. Closed 21 Dec - 21 Jan. Visa. **Directions:** N25 Rosslare to Cork, 3 km from Dungarvan: follow the sea.

DUNMORE EAST

Dunmore East is a picturesque village, known for its pretty well-maintained thatched cottages, and it is a major fishing port. Local historic sites include the 12th century Anglo Norman castle and the Church of St Andrew built in 1815. Above the town is a lovely wooded park with pleasant walks, and there is also a protected EU blue flag beach, Counsellor's Strand, which is an ideal spot for swimming and sea angling. The harbour is popular for boating, and Dunmore East Adventure Centre (051 383 783) offers both land and water-based activities, such as sea kayaking, which is a fun way to explore the coast. Golfers may play the 18-hole seaside course at Dunmore East Golf Club (051 383 151), while championship standard golf is nearby in Faithlegg Golf Club (Waterford, 051 382 000) and Waterford Castle Golf Club (Waterford, 051 871 633). Garden lovers might consider a visit to Sion Hill House & Gardens (Ferrybank, 051 851 558) nearby in Waterford, a hillside garden with roses, daffodils and rhododendrons a special feature.

Dunmore East   Beach Guesthouse

GUESTHOUSE   1 Lower Village Dunmore East Co Waterford **Tel: 051 383316**

      beachouse@eircom.net   www.dunmorebeachguesthouse.com

Breda Battles' smart modern guesthouse has easy accessibility to the beach, and offers a moderately-priced base for exploring the area. Rooms to the front - including the pleasant breakfast room and lounge, as well as some of the bedrooms - have a sea view. Everything is very clean and well-maintained and, although hard flooring throughout can be noisy, bedrooms have plenty of hanging space and a writing desk as well as TV/radio and tea/coffee making. Tasty breakfasts include lovely scones and preserves, well-made traditional Irish and some other options, such as scrambled egg with smoked salmon. Free broadband wi/fi; not suitable for children under 6. No pets. **Rooms 7** (1 suite, 2 shower only, 1 family room, 1 ground floor, 1 for disabled, all no smoking). B&B €45, ss €10. Closed 1 Nov - 1 Mar. Amex, MasterCard, Visa, Laser. **Directions:** First left after pertol station in village; house facing sea wall.

Dunmore East
PUB•RESTAURANT WITH ROOMS

Strand Inn
Dunmore East Co Waterford **Tel: 051 383 174**
strandin@iol.ie www.dunmoreeast.com

Right on the beach, and with sea views out towards the Hook Lighthouse, The Strand goes back a good few hundred years but today it is the first choice for many when it comes to seafood. 'Fish, fish, fish' is how they describe their menu, and so it is - up to a point: non-seafood eaters will be glad to know that there are some concessions, including a roast perhaps, or poultry such as traditional duck with orange sauce. But it is mainly for the seafood that people head for the Strand - and it couldn't be fresher as much of it comes from the nearby harbour, which is one of Ireland's main fishing ports. **Seats 120** (outdoor, 40); children welcome before 8pm; toilets & restaurant wheelchair accessible. L daily in summer, 12.30-4.30, set L €23.50; D daily all year, 6.30-10; early D €23.50, 6.30-7.30; House wine from €19.50; SC 10% on parties 8+. Restaurant closed all of Jan and Mon-Tue in Nov-Mar. Amex, Diners, MasterCard, Visa, Laser. **Directions:** Left after petrol station in village; beachside building.

Dunmore East Area
HISTORIC HOUSE

Gaultier Lodge
Woodstown Co Waterford **Tel: 051 382 549**
gaultierlodge@yahoo.ie www.gaultier-lodge.com

Beautifully located right beside the beach at Woodstown Strand and snugged down in sand dunes for shelter, Sheila Molloy's early 19th century lodge is built on the mezzanine plan, with reception rooms on the upper floor and bedrooms beneath - and it has wonderful views from the upper windows right across the Suir estuary, to Duncannon and the Hook Peninsula in County Wexford. Set in large and very private gardens, it has the feeling of a secret place - on arrival you almost wonder if you are in the right place at all and, although Sheila describes it modestly as 'comfortably furnished' it has great style and, like Sheila herself - who is an artist and a warmly hospitable person - this lovely house will lift the spirits. Reception rooms and bedrooms are all large and well-proportioned, providing a good framework for her inspired modern classical décor and guests will be pleased to find that, along with other interests including gardening and horses, she enjoys cooking and entertaining. Dinner is available on most nights by arrangement (book 24 hours in advance); when unavailable you can go to Dunmore East, just three miles away. On site there is swimming and beach or coastal walks, and other activities like sea fishing, sailing, riding and golf are all available nearby. **Rooms 3** (all en-suite and no smoking, 1 shower only); Not suitable for children under 4; B&B €75 pps, ss €20. Dogs permitted by arrangement; equestrian, fishing, hunting and golf all nearby. Walking, cookery courses, art courses. D €50 by arrangement (book 24 hours in advance; not always available Sun or Thu). Closed mid Oct - mid Apr. MasterCard, Visa, Laser. **Directions:** From Waterford, take R684, Dunmore East road. Take left for Woodstown after 4km. Right at beach, last house on left behind high wall.

LISMORE
Designated a Heritage Town, this attractive place is most famous for its castle and gardens, although there is much more of historic interest to be discovered at Lismore Heritage Centre and Tourist Information Office (058 54975/54855;www.discoverlismore.com), which are well signed (black and gold signs) as you enter the town. Situated in a panoramic position overlooking the Blackwater Valley, Lismore Castle (058 54424) is perhaps Ireland's most romantic fairytale castle, and has been the Irish home of the Dukes of Devonshire since 1753; it has views over rolling, wooded hills to the Knockmealdown Mountains beyond, and the gardens are very beautiful. Other gardens nearby that merit a visit are Cappoquin House Garden (Cappoquin, 058 54290) and Ballyvolane House (appointment only, Fermoy, 025 36349). The restored 29-room **Lismore House Hotel** (058 72966; www.lismorehousehotel.com) in the centre of the town is particularly popular for weddings. Golfers may play the local nine hole golf course (058 54026) and championship golf is available in nearby West Waterford Golf Club (Dungarvan, 058 41475). For fisherfolk the Blackwater River offers excellent trout and salmon fishing. There are several craft shops in the town, including the pretty Summer House (058 54148; www.thesummerhouse.ie) home and gift shop (with a very nice café, Tue- Sun, 10-5.30), and the Heritage Centre which showcases fine examples of Irish pottery; visitors may also enjoy visiting Glencairn Pottery (058 56694) to learn the pottery process. A Farmers' Market is held every Sunday offering the best in local farmhouse produce.

The Glencairn Inn & Pastis Bistro

Lismore Area
RESTAURANT WITH ROOMS•BAR

Glencairn Lismore Co Waterford **Tel: 058 56232**
info@glencairninn.com www.glencairninn.com

Husband-and-wife team Stéphane and Fiona Tricot's pretty pub just outside Lismore has earned a well-deserved following for the restaurant - which they named Pastis French Bistro. Three delightful old-world dining rooms ooze charm and cosiness and, just off the small bar, there is an alcove for intimate dining for four. Fiona manages front-of-house while Stéphane produces wonderful food using plenty of local produce, and offering menus with about five choices on each course, plus a weekly special on the board. Well-chosen starters may include a flavoursome salad like pear & roquefort cheese salad with roasted walnuts and balsamic & honey vinaigrette or a crispy confit of duck spring roll with a mint orange dip, while delicious speciality main courses include pan-seared seabass provençale and ever-popular slow-roasted lamb shank. A very nice dessert menu includes classics like tarte tatin and crêpes suzettes, offered with liqueur coffees, dessert wine or a digestif. A compact, carefully-chosen wine list, offers a surprisingly wide range and includes some real treats, also half a dozen wines by the glass. Service is excellent, with friendly and knowledgeable staff - a rare treat. *A sun room dining area has recently been added and can accommodate small private parties; weddings and larger private parties can now be catered for in a marquee. **Seats 45** (private room, 30/15, outdoors, 24); not suitable for children under 5 after 8pm. L Sun only, 1-3pm, set Sun L €30 & D Wed-Sun high season 7-9pm (6.30-8.30 Sun), à la carte; house wine from €21; SC disc. **Accommodation:** Upstairs, there are four delightful en-suite rooms, all no smoking. **Rooms 4** (all en-suite, 1 shower only, all no smoking). Dogs may be permitted to stay in bedrooms by prior arrangement (free). Free broadband wi/fi; lawn bowls; walking; equestrian, fishing (fly & coarse), golf and garden visits all nearby. *Weddings catered for in marquee (150). Closed Mon & Tues (& Wed Oct-Apr), Christmas period & 2 weeks Nov, 2 weeks Jan. MasterCard, Visa, Laser. **Directions:** 3.5km (2 m) from Lismore off N72 Lismore/Tallow Road.

The Castle Country House

Millstreet
FARMHOUSE•CASTLE

Millstreet Dungarvan Co Waterford **Tel: 058 68049**
castlefm@iol.ie www.castlecountryhouse.com

Set in several acres of landscaped gardens encompassing a circular walk overlooking the River Finisk, the Nugent family's unusual and wonderfully hospitable house is a substantial 18th century farmhouse built around the remains of a 16th century castle. Although most of the house seems quite normal inside, it blends into the original building in places - so, for example, the dining room has walls five feet deep and an original castle archway. Outside, you can visit the cellar of the original castle and, on the other side, view the rock on which the house and castle are built; and, as befits a farmhouse, you may watch the milking and whatever other farm activities are in season. The spacious, exceptionally comfortably-appointed rooms not only have king-size beds, television, tea/coffee facilities and neat shower rooms well-equipped with a selection of toiletries - but also easy chairs, good lighting, lots of books and the full history of the house in an information pack. (And there is also a full bathroom available for any guest who prefers a bath). Meticulous housekeeping, a very pleasant guests' sitting room (more books, games, an open fire), interesting pictures and fresh flowers everywhere all add up to a very appealing farmhouse indeed and, together with her daughter and daughter-in-law, Joan provides excellent breakfasts including home-grown fresh fruit, fruit compôtes and fruit juices, porridge and home-baked bread. In addition to the traditional Irish breakfast you may choose from dishes like smoked salmon and scrambled free-range eggs, French toast with bacon and maple syrup. Dinner is served at separate tables in the lovely dining room, set up with crisp white linen and silver, more like a small restaurant than a farmhouse dining room; it is only available by arrangement so you must book when making a reservation, when you will be asked about your likes and dislikes. The menu changes daily and might include home-made soups with freshly-baked bread, poached salmon with hollandaise sauce and a rhubarb, ginger and orange crumble followed by good coffee; some well-chosen wines are available, around €19. Improvements to the house are constant - decorating, renewing furniture and linen and re-doing bathrooms; it is a wonderful place to stay. *Castle Country House was our Farmhouse of the Year in 2008. **Rooms 5** (all en-suite, shower only and no smoking); B&B €50pps, ss €20; children welcome (under 5s free in parents' room, cot available without charge, baby sitting arranged). Pets permitted by arrangement. Garden, walking, fishing (fly). **Dining Room:** Seats 20 (+5 outside); Residents D 7pm €30, House wine €16. Closed 1 Nov-31 Mar. MasterCard, Visa, Laser. **Directions:** Off N25 on R671.

Passage East
COUNTRY HOUSE

Parkswood Country House

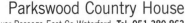

Parkswood Lower Passage East Co Waterford **Tel: 051 380 863**
info@parkswood.com www.parkswood.com

Roger and Terrie Pooley's lovely house is very near the car ferry linking Waterford and Wexford and is beautifully situated in six acres of grounds overlooking the River Suir. The house has been fully refurbished since the Pooleys took it on in 2002, and four of the very pleasing guest rooms have estuary views, three of them with walk-out balconies; all have power showers except one family room, with a private bathroom. Part of the house dates back to the early 17th century, and later additions have been made in keeping with the house; some are hundreds of years old, more recently a sunroom was added to the front of the house, allowing guests to enjoy the view fully whatever the weather and making a lovely dining room. Breakfast and evening meals for residents (including those in a self-catering cottage in the grounds) are served here, and local residents are welcome too, on request - and, although they do not consider themselves a restaurant, they're open for afternoon teas and light refreshments during the day in summer. They make their own jams and cakes, which are also for sale, and use local, preferably organic produce as much as possible. As if all this is not enough, they also undertake small functions (weddings, parties), and have plans to convert a 200-year old barn in the grounds to create more self-catering accommodation. Parkswood is a lovely, welcoming place, and a stay here should be very relaxing. **Rooms 4** (all en-suite, shower only & no smoking, 2 ground floor, 1 family); B&B €80pps, ss €10; children welcome (under 2s free in parents room). Pets permitted in certain areas (stay in outhouse/kennel). Walking. Equestrian, fishing (coarse & sea angling), golf and garden visits nearby. Discounts available for stays longer than one night. Closed Christmas. **Directions:** R684 from Waterford City (Dunmore East road); 5km left to Passage East; 5km on left hand side. ◇

Tallowbridge
RESTAURANT•PUB

The Brideview Bar & Restaurant

Tallowbridge Tallow Co Waterford **Tel: 058 56522**
info@brideviewbar.com www.brideviewbar.com

Noel and Annmarie Costello's attractive roadside bar and restaurant is in a beautiful setting just outside Tallow, beside an old stone bridge over the River Bride and with wonderful views from a stylishly informal dining area and a spacious deck overlooking the river and bridge. Ongoing renovations in recent years have made big improvements and brought a gently contemporary tone through most of the building; however, they have been careful to retain the character in the older bar (which is along the road side of the building, and has a welcoming open fire) and have also added a snug-like after-dinner lounge beside the restaurant, with original artwork, and library. Whether you call in for an informal bite in the bar or go for the full dining experience, food will be carefully sourced and prepared, and the fairly contemporary menus include a great selection of local seafood (there's a lobster tank, and the seafood platters are very popular), and home-grown fruit and vegetables. To complement the food, a short but carefully-selected wine list offers a balanced choice, and lists a selection of lesser-known wines including Thomas Walks red wine, from Kinsale. One big recent change is very noticeable on arrival, as two of the old stables have been converted to make a shop, which opens at the same time as the restaurant so people dining can browse before or after their meal; they sell as much local produce as possible including their own excellent brown bread and hampers based on their own food range, Bride View Foods. Noel and Annmarie's dedication and hard work over the last decade has transformed this bar into a fine establishment that is offering something different from others in the area - including an exceptional location, of course, as well as good food and very long opening hours all year round. *An on-site cottage is being converted to offer self-catering accommodation. **Seats 45** (outdoors, 28); toilets wheelchair accessible; children welcome (baby changing facilities); lifestyle gift shop (home-ware, food, wine). Food available Mon-Sat, 12.30-9pm (to 9.30pm Fri/Sat; no food 2.30-5.30pm Mon-Thurs off-season). Set Sun L, 12.30-2.30pm; then à la carte 2.30-8.30pm. House wine from €18.95. Closed 22-27 Dec & Good Fri. Amex, MasterCard, Visa, Laser. **Directions:** Near Tallow on N72; 20Km (12 m) east of Fermoy - 3 from Lismore.

Touraneena
FARMHOUSE

Sliabh gCua Farmhouse

Touraneena Ballinamult Dungarvan Co Waterford **Tel: 058 47120**
breedacullinan@sliabhgcua.com www.sliabhgcua.com

Breeda Cullinan's lovely creeper-clad farmhouse is in a beautiful area for lovers of the rural life; it is not as old or as large as it looks, but it was built with the classical proportions that create handsome, light-filled rooms, and has a happy atmosphere. There's a delightful drawing room (completely refurbished recently) and the bedrooms, which are all individually furnished and decorated with great care by Breeda, are very comfortable and have tea/coffee-making facilities. Dinner is not offered (there are plenty of good restaurants within a short drive) but at breakfast time, wholesome food, based on fresh farm produce, is served in a lovely dining room overlooking the garden; there are home-made cereals, fruit salads, freshly-baked breads, local cheeses and hot cooked dishes to set guests up for the day. The garden is charming, with plenty of well-planned paths for guests to enjoy and, just beyond the hedge, a seat set up to take full advantage of the unspoilt country view and the peace. People love this place, and it is easy to see why. **Rooms 4** (all en-suite, shower-only & no smoking, 1 family); children welcome (under 3 free in parents' room, cot available without charge, baby sitting arranged, playground). B&B €45 pps, ss €5. Dogs permitted. Walking; garden. Fishing, golf & hunting all nearby. Closed Nov-Mar. **No Credit Cards. Directions:** 16km off the N25, signposted on main Dungarvan-Clonmel Road (R672). ◊

Tramore
CHARACTER PUB•RESTAURANT

Rockett's of The Metal Man

Westown Tramore Co Waterford **Tel: 051 381 496**
rockettsofthemetalman@eircom.net

Open fires and a friendly, welcoming atmosphere will always draw you into this unusual pub but it's the speciality of the house, Crubeens (pig's trotters) which has earned it fame throughout the land. Crubeens (cruibíns) were once the staple bar food in pubs everywhere in Ireland but, as they've been supplanted by crisps, peanuts and lasagne & chips, Rockett's is one of the few places to keep up the old tradition. Two bars are set up with tables for the comfortable consumption of these porcine treats, served with cabbage and colcannon. Other traditional foods like boiled bacon & cabbage, spare ribs, colcannon and apple pie are also very much on the menu at Rockett's - and all prepared freshly. **Seats 150** (outdoors, 20); children welcome (high chair, childrens menu, baby changing facilities); toilets wheelchair accessible; air conditioning. Food served daily 12.30-9pm (Sun to 8pm). A phone call is advised to check times off-season. Closed 25 Dec & Good Fri. MasterCard, Visa, Laser. **Directions:** From Waterford, straight through Tramore, 1.5km (1 m) far side. ◊

WATERFORD

Known around the world as the home of the Waterford Crystal Glass Centre (051 33 2500), which is certainly worth visiting, Waterford City has many other attractions too, including the Waterford Christ Church Cathedral (051 858 958), the Waterford Heritage Museum (051 876 123), the 13th century Reginald's Tower (051 304 220) and Waterford Treasures at the Granary (051 304500, open all year), which houses gold, silver and bronze treasures, along with historical documents and a treasure trail that takes you through 1000 years of Waterford's history and is well worth a visit. Only recently designated a city, its centre is now developing attractively around the river - which, with a marina and walkways along the quays, is a pleasant place to explore. Of its many cultural events, the most famous is the Waterford International Festival of Light Opera, which is held in the autumn. There is a Farmers' Market each Saturday in Jenkin's Lane (10am-4pm), and hospitality is very much alive and well in the city - notably, with a number of French restaurants providing healthy competition, there is an unusually good choice of eating places offering quality and value for money. (Other Irish towns and cities might take note.) A useful pub to know about in the old Norman area of the city, which is also the central shopping area, is **The Gingerman** (051 879522) on Arundel Lane; a pleasant place, with welcoming open fires in several bars and a good-humoured hands-on owner with a commitment to serving wholesome food. And, when 'a good steak' is what's called for, head to **The Munster Bar** (051 874656, Baileys New Street behind Reginalds Tower), their rib-eye with garlic butter is the business. While there, make a point of seeing their stunning Victorian panelled Oak Room, used in the filming of Maeve Binchy's "Echoes". Travellers requiring spacious modern accommodation outside the city at a reasonable room rate may be interested in the **Ramada Viking Hotel** (051 336 933; www.vikinghotel.ie) on the Cork road, which has business facilities and family/interconnecting rooms. Gardens of note in the area include Sion Hill House & Gardens (Ferrybank, 051 851 558) a hillside garden with roses, daffodils and rhododendrons a special feature, Fairbrook House Gardens & Museum of Contemporary Figurative Art (Kilmeaden, 051 384657), an intriguing compartmental garden in an old mill complex and Mount Congreve (Kilmeaden, 051 384 115), an unforgettable massed planting of rhododendrons, shrubs and trees in a beautifully located demesne. There are two championship golf courses in the city area, Waterford Castle Golf Club (051 871 633) and Faithlegg (Faithlegg, 051 382 000). The River Blackwater offers excellent game angling for wild salmon and brown trout. The surrounding area offers beautiful scenic drives through routes such as The Comeragh Mountains, or the Dungarvan and Copper coast routes, providing panoramic views of the sea. Other activities include horse riding and pony trekking, provided by the four stables within easy reach of Waterford and walking along the breathtaking coast or local mountain and valley trails.

WWW.IRELAND-GUIDE.COM FOR ALL THE BEST PLACES TO EAT, DRINK & STAY

Waterford	Arlington Lodge

HOTEL   John's Hill Waterford Co Waterford **Tel: 051 878 584**
        info@arlingtonlodge.com   www.arlingtonlodge.com

Originally the home of the Paul family, prominent merchants in Waterford, and then the Bishop's Palace for 200 years, Arlington Lodge is now owned by local man Maurice Keller, who converted it into the four star boutique hotel that it is today. Surrounded by gardens and walls that give it complete privacy from the hustle and bustle of the city outside, it's a two-storey building with a terrace for fine weather and a covered area for Friday night barbecues. Public areas include a classy Drawing Room, which is perfect for afternoon tea or morning coffee, or just relaxing with the papers, and the William Morris bar, which is cosy and intimate, with a good bar menu. Accommodation is predictably luxurious, in spacious traditionally furnished rooms, junior suites, and full suites overlooking the courtyard; some rooms have four-posters and all have either queen or king-sized beds. Meals are served in the tastefully-decorated Robert Paul Restaurant, where à la carte and set dinner menus are based on local fresh produce, particularly fish from Dunmore East. The pièce de resistance at breakfast is the famous Waterford Bla, not available anywhere else: this fluffy roll is halved, a freshly poached egg placed on each side and covered with Kilmeaden cheddar that melts and combines all the ingredients into a delicious meal. Complimentary broadband in bedrooms. Meeting facilities available. **Rooms 20.** B&B from about €75pps. Closed 24-27 Dec. Amex, MasterCard, Visa, Laser. **Directions:** Over bridge in Waterford city, turn left down quay. After Tower Hotel go through to 3rd set of traffic lights and turn left. Go straight to next set, Arlington Lodge Hotel is up hill on left.

Waterford	Athenaeum House Hotel

HOTEL   Christendom Waterford Co Waterford **Tel: 051 833 999**
       info@athenaeumhousehotel.com   www.athenaeumhousehotel.com

Guests feel very much at home in this 4* boutique hotel, which is set amidst 10 acres of parkland overlooking the River Suir, just outside Waterford city - and owner-managed by Stan Power, a former General Manager of Mount Juliet House in County Kilkenny, and his wife Mailo. Chic contemporary decor, luxurious suites and deluxe rooms and a welcome emphasis on service are the characteristics that will appeal most to discerning travellers. The restaurants of Waterford city are just a short taxi ride away, but you can dine in-house at the hotel's Zaks Restaurant, where you should get an enjoyable meal and good service. **Rooms 28**. B&B from €60. Restaurant seats 65 (private room, 40; also outdoor area, 20); toilets accessible by wheelchair; Live Music Sat pm. Food served all day 7.30-9.30; set D daily, €23; also à la carte; L Sun, 12.30-3; Set Sun L €23. House Wine from €22. Rest closed Mon, House closed 25-27 Dec. MasterCard, Visa, Laser. **Directions:** Leaving railway station on N25 in the direction of Wexford, take the first right after the traffic lights on to Abbey Road, half a mile later take the first right. ◇

Waterford
PUB•RESTAURANT

Becketts Bar & Restaurant

Dunmore Road Waterford Co Waterford
Tel: 051 873 082

A well-maintained garden with plenty of seating make a good impression on arrival at this large pub on the outskirts of the city; inside it is big and airy - the décor is very simple, with some black and white photos and quotations from Irish authors on the walls, and high tables with tall chairs and minimal pub-style place settings (knife and fork in a paper napkin). Pleasant staff make you feel very welcome and immediately offer menus which, with about a dozen main courses, are perhaps too long for the kitchen to handle well; however, there is also a set menu with a very short choice (about €12.50 for main courses) which is great value for a family tea and, on the à la carte, it is a pleasant surprise to find a dish like lamb's liver and lamb's kidneys as a starter, also a huge bowl of mussels in tomato & scallion sauce. Main courses include staples like cod in beer batter with mushy peas, pasta dishes and, although perhaps less successful than the starters, prices are very reasonable and, with very good staff and pleasing surroundings, this is a useful place to know about. Toilets wheelchair accessible. Children welcome (high chair, childrens menu, baby changing facilities); Food served daily 12.30-9.30pm (to 8.30pm Sun). House wine €19.95. Closed 25 Dec, Good Fri. Visa, Laser. **Directions:** Follow Dunmore East signs out of city.

Waterford
RESTAURANT•WINE BAR

Bodéga!

54 John Street Waterford Co Waterford **Tel: 051 844 177**
info@bodegawaterford.com www.bodegawaterford.com

With its warm Mediterranean colours, this place would bring the sun out on the darkest of days: interesting artwork, pine tables covered with the occasional oilcloth, a mix'n'match collection of seating; and, now firmly established as a Waterford restaurant that delivers quality and value, it is always busy. The chef is French and you will find many favourites like beef bourguinon, Toulouse sausage with choucroûte and moules frites mingling with the international dishes. A written menu offers everything from lunchtime dishes like soup of the day and quiche of the day, to Bodega fish pie and steaks, to dinner specialities such as roast magret & confit de canard with sweet red cabbage & apple. But, although menus are quite extensive and offer a wide range, their particular strength lies in their strong selection and skilled cooking of fish; there may be eight or more local fish available on the menu, possibly including an excellent Kilmore fish cake and delicious mains of crisply-fried John Dory fillets successfully married with a mango garnish, and tuna served correctly rare with a marinade of soy and ginger adding flavour and moisture to this difficult fish. There are also blackboard specials, which are likely to be a good bet - and friendly staff are well-informed to advise. At lunchtime, the place fills up with young people, some with children - who are made especially welcome - and there are lots of regulars. Dinner is a little more structured and the prices heat up a bit too, but it's still good value - and at about €21/26 for 2/3 courses, the early dinner is a snip. Regular live music too, with big names including Mary Coughlan, Freddie White, Eleanor McCoy. **Seats 80**; children welcome (high chair). L Sun-Fri, 12-5pm & D Mon-Sun 5-10pm (to 10.30pm Fri/Sat). Early D 2/3 course, about €21/26, Mon-Fri 5.30-7pm. Also à la carte. House wines from €20. SC discretionary. Closed Sat L, bank hol Mons, Good Fri, 25/26 Dec, 1 Jan. Amex, MasterCard, Visa, Laser. **Directions:** A few doors down from the Applemarket, in city centre. ◊

Waterford
GUESTHOUSE

Diamond Hill Country House

Slieverue Waterford Co Waterford **Tel: 051 832 855**
info@stayatdiamondhill.com www.stayatdiamondhill.com

The Smith-Lehane family's long-established and moderately-priced guesthouse just outside Waterford city is set in one and a half acres of landscaped gardens; it would make a good base for exploring the area, and will appeal to anyone who wants to be quietly located yet handy to the city. The house has been completely refurbished recently, and most of the well-equipped bedrooms have king-size beds as well as power showers and all the other usual amenities (phone, TV, tea/coffee facilities etc). With ten courses, including Mount Juliet, within half an hour's drive, it's ideal for golfing breaks; other sporting activities nearby include fishing and horse riding. **Rooms 17** (14 shower only, all no smoking); children welcome (under 5s free in parents' room, cot available without charge). No pets. B&B €45pps, ss €5. Gardens. Closed Dec. MasterCard, Visa, Laser. **Directions:** Off the N25 - 0.8km outside Waterford.

Waterford
COUNTRY HOUSE

Foxmount Country House

Passage East Road Waterford Co Waterford **Tel: 051 874 308**
info@foxmountcountryhouse.com www.foxmountcountryhouse.com

For those who prefer a country house atmosphere, rather than an hotel, the Kent family's 17th century home on the edge of Waterford city is a haven of peace and tranquillity. The house is lovely, with classically proportioned reception rooms, and accommodation in four very different rooms which are all thoughtfully, and very comfortably, furnished - but, as peace and relaxation are the aim at Foxmount, don't expect phones or TVs in bedrooms, or a very early breakfast. However, Margaret Kent is a great cook and she loves baking, as guests quickly discover when offered afternoon tea in the drawing room - or in the morning, when freshly-baked breads are presented at breakfast. David and Margaret celebrated forty years in business in 2007 and say they are "delighted to have survived through the era of tax incentives, venture capital, leisure centres & spas, and still have guests coming from all parts of the world to enjoy the homely comforts and experiences of a family-run country house on a working farm." They are right - it is a very special place and no amount of investment in new developments can recreate what Foxmount, and others like them, do so well. No evening meals are offered, but the restaurants of Waterford and Cheekpoint are quite close - and guests are welcome to bring their own wine and enjoy a glass at the log fire before going out for dinner. **Rooms 4** (all with en-suite or private bathrooms, all no-smoking, 1 family room); children welcome (under 2s free in parent' room, cot available without charge). B&B €65 pps, ss€10. No pets. Garden. Closed Nov-mid Mar. **No Credit Cards. Directions:** From Waterford city, take Dunmore Road - after 4 km, take Passage East road for 1.5km.

Waterford
HOTEL

Granville Hotel

The Quay Waterford Co Waterford **Tel: 051 305 555**
stay@granville-hotel.ie www.granville-hotel.ie

One of the country's oldest hotels, this much-loved quayside establishment in the centre of Waterford has many historical connections - with Bianconi, for example, who established Ireland's earliest transport system, and also Charles Stuart Parnell, who made many a rousing speech here. Since 1979, it's been owner-run by the Cusack family, who have overseen significant restoration and are continuously renewing the old building, and it has that indefinable ambience of the well-run privately-owned hotel, the sense of being cosseted in an old fashioned way unlike the slick informality of modern "concept" establishments. It's a large hotel, bigger than it looks perhaps, with fine public areas including a spacious bar/lounge where both residents and locals congregate, and well-appointed if, perhaps, slightly dated bedrooms (all with well-designed bathrooms, with both bath and shower). This is a good choice for business guests and would also make a comfortable and friendly base for touring the area - how many hotels today would inspire comments like this: "I loved the Granville; having tea and a sandwich in the afternoon I was asked by a caring local bar lady: 'more tea dear?'." And, aside from being very conveniently situated for exploring this interesting city on foot, the many activities available locally include boating, fishing, golf, walking and horse riding. Off-season value breaks available. Conference/banqueting (200). **Rooms 98** (3 junior suites, 60 executive rooms, 90 no-smoking); children welcome (under 3s free in parents' room; cots available without charge). Parking nearby. No pets. Lift. B&B €60-75 pps, ss €35 (winter rate from about €55pps, ss €20). Meals: D daily, L Sun-Fri (except bank hol Mons); bar meals 10.30-6 daily. Closed 25-27 Dec. Amex, Diners, MasterCard, Visa. **Directions:** In city centre, on the quays opposite Clock Tower. ◊

Waterford
CAFÉ•WINE BAR
Ⓝ

Harlequin Café & Winebar
37 Stephen Street Waterford Co Waterford Tel: **051 877 552**
www.harlequin-cafe.com

Run by two cheerful and energetic young Italian men, Simone and Allesandro, who interchange between chef and waiter and greet all their customers in Italian, this tiny café serves remarkably authentic Italian food at very reasonable prices; it has only been open for about a year at the time of going to press, but has already become a favourite with the people of Waterford. The menu, like the proprietors, is very Italian - you feel immediately transported to a back street in Rome or Venice; You might have the Antipasto Misto to start – a generous plate overflowing with Italian goodies: braesola, mortadella, Parma ham and various salamis, with salad and crisp slices of toasted Italian bread dribbled with fruity olive oil; and a vegetarian version has dried porcini and tomatoes, with good mozzarella instead of the meats. For many, this would be enough on its own, but the very hungry might follow with mains such as gnocchi carne (little potato dumplings with minced beef and courgette sauce) or tortelloni pomodori (tortelloni stuffed with spinach and ricotta and a good creamy tomato sauce). You could wash it down with a cheap and very cheerful bottle of Pino Grigio, finish off with a tiny, intense espresso and come away with a bill under €65 for two. This is a delightful addition to eating out in Waterford, and is open and serving all sorts of meals and snacks from morning to night - it is a particular hit for its Italian croissant and cappuccino for breakfast. **Seats 20**; children welcome (childrens menu); toilets wheelchair accessible. Open Mon-Sat, 8.30am-10.30pm (from 9.30am Sat). Closed Sun, Bank Hols, 23 Dec - 7 Jan. MasterCard, Visa, Laser. **Directions:** On Stephen Street.

Waterford
CHARACTER PUB

Henry Downes
8-10 Thomas Street Waterford Co Waterford
Tel: 051 874 118

Established in 1759, and in the same (eccentric) family for six generations, John de Bromhead's unusual pub is one of the few remaining houses to bottle its own whiskey. Although not the easiest of places to find, once visited it certainly will not be forgotten. Large, dark and cavernous with a squash court on the premises as well as the more predictable billiards and snooker, it consists of a series of bars of differing character, each with its own particular following. It achieves with natural grace what so-called Irish theme pubs would dearly love to capture, and friendly, humorous bar staff enjoy filling customers in on the pub's proud history and will gladly sell you a bottle of Henry Downes No.9 to take away. Not suitable for children. Open from 5pm to normal closing time. No food. Closed 25 Dec & Good Fri. **No Credit Cards. Directions:** Second right after Bridge Hotel, halfway up Thomas Street on right.

Waterford
RESTAURANT
Ⓝ

Il Veliero
20-22 William Street Waterford Co Waterford
Tel: 051 844 180

Authentic Italian fine dining is a rarity in Ireland and the recently opened Il Veliero is a welcome addition. Located just off The Mall (in the premises formerly occupied by Chez K's), it is spacious and elegant with dark wood, linen-clad tables, comfortable tall-backed chairs and some interesting artwork on the walls. The atmosphere has a distinct European feel and the professional welcome from well-trained Italian staff inspires confidence. The menu (promptly presented along with a basket of good bread and chilled water) is written in Italian with English translations, and reveals a Tuscan emphasis with some northern Italian influences; it is not overlong, and a page of Specials of the Day is offered separately which may include some treats like lobster (with home-made spaghetti or, Mediterranean style, as a main course, reasonably priced at around €16/28 respectively). Dishes are divided Italian-style into first, second and third plates, then sub-divided into dishes from the land or sea. You might begin, as the Guide did on a recent visit, with an antipasta of richly-flavoured Pecorino mousse with a rocket salad garnished with crisp strips of onion, or a salmon and prawn tartare with a green salad. Next, you could choose between traditional pasta dishes like tomato, basil and olives, or a wild mushroom risotto. Main courses offer a choice of simply-cooked and elegantly-presented seafoods; or meat dishes such as classic Tuscan lamb accompanied with peppers, onion and courgettes. The bread is authentic, service of both food and wine knowledgeable and helpful, the wine list favours Italian wines, and the prices are very fair for the quality and expertise offered. Unusually for an Italian restaurant, desserts are very good, and may include a mille feuille of chewy dried pears with a wine mousse - strange, but delicious. A very welcome newcomer to Waterford. **Seats 90**; children welcome; reservations advised; toilets wheelchair accessible. D daily 5.30-10 (Sun 4-9). Early D about €25 (Mon-Fri, 5.30-7). D also à la carte. House wine about €20. Open all year. MasterCard, Visa, Laser. **Directions:** Left at traffic lights at Tower Hotel - on the left 400m.

Waterford

RESTAURANT

L'Atmosphère

19 Henrietta Street Waterford Co Waterford **Tel: 051 858 426**

latmosphererestaurant@hotmail.com   www.restaurant-latmosphere.com

The closely-packed tables in Arnaud Mary and Patrice Garreau's well-named French restaurant don't matter too much - the decor is basic, with pine tables, paper napkins, and menus that double as paper mats, and it all adds up to a cheerful bistro atmosphere. Three menus are offered, an early bird, an à la carte and the day's specials – a large selection (6 starters and 6 mains) is offered on the blackboard as well as the place mat à la carte; the early dinner menu (5.30 to 7) is extremely good value, and even includes a glass of house wine, which is unusually generous. Expect typical French bistro and 'gran'mère' cooking at its best: for starters, there are good soups (fish, perhaps) and excellent breads (Arnaud has a French bakery in the town), then maybe silky foie gras with wild mushrooms, accompanied by a little shot glass of liver foam with diced mushrooms and some onion marmalade (an ambitious dish that comes off beautifully), or delicious interleaved potato and melt-in-the-mouth ox tongue with diced vegetables. Main courses could include a nicely timed John Dory with tiny spring vegetables – or a masterful dish of 6-hour lamb, which still keeps its shape but is as tender as butter; accompanied by crisp French beans and carrots and a very intense jus, it is a triumph. The offering is different from other restaurants in the area - there is a high level of skill here and a good old fashioned sense that cheaper cuts of meat will be used and properly; menus may also offer luxurious items like foie gras, or lobster, but the same philosophy applies. Finish, perhaps with a classic hot chocolate soufflé (wonderful liquid chocolate insides, served with vanilla ice cream) or a Temptation Plate sampler of delicious desserts. Impeccable presentation on big square white plates shows off the food well, so it looks as good as it tastes. With delicious, keenly priced, food and friendly service from French and Irish waiting staff, the whole impression is of eating in a really good French bistro, rare today even in France. **Seats 48**; air conditioning; children welcome; Open for L&D Mon-Fri, 12.30-2pm & 5.30-9.30/10pm; D only Sat, Sun; early D €20, 5.30-7; also à la carte; House wine about €18, Closed Sat L, Sun and Bank Hol Mons. MasterCard, Visa, Laser. ◊

Waterford

RESTAURANT

La Bohème

2 George Street Waterford Co Waterford **Tel: 051 875 645**

labohemerestaurant@eircom.net

Christine and Eric Thèze's restaurant in the basement of Waterford's Chamber of Commerce building is cleverly flooded in light, with white arched ceilings giving the room a wonderful feeling of height. The feeling is certainly France: French waiters are warm and friendly as you are shown to the bar for your aperitif - no cold French professionalism here, but they give one a feeling of being in expert hands. The shining glass, silver, and crisp white linen are perfect in this room, which has plenty of flowers, some nicely restrained art on the walls, French music in the background, and - a nice touch - mismatched old crockery. Seasonally changed menus are not overlong but offer plenty of choice and good value for the quality of food and service; an early Table d'Hôte offers remarkable value at €29, and includes excellent dishes like a superb crab brulée, a chargrilled sirloin steak with green peppercorn & cognac cream sauce, and a Sheridan's French farmhouse cheese plate among the options. The cooking style is modern classic French and menus offer a strong seafood section including fish landed nearby at Dunmore East, Irish lamb and beef, the rabbit and veal dishes that typify French restaurants and a list of daily specials, including a vegetarian dish and the soup, pinned on the menu. An excellent amuse bouche of whipped goats' cheese on a tomato concassé sets the tone for the cooking, and seafood offered includes a speciality of Dunmore East lobster, flambéed in cognac and smothered in a herbed beurre blanc sauce (not available on the Guide's most recent visit, alas); other luxurious treats may include foie gras. Pleasingly, for Irish tastes, main courses are accompanied by some good mashed potatoes and vegetables, and in addition to the all-French cheese board, there are excellent classic desserts. Good wines - strongly French, as you would expect, but including some cheaper regional French wines - and very good service. This is a restaurant that is serious about its food and is a great asset to Waterford city. **Seats 70** (private room, 10 & 20); toilets wheelchair accessbile, see note below); not suitable for children under 8 years. air conditioning; reservations recommended; D Tue-Sat (& Bank Hol Sun), 5.30-10pm; Value D €29-35, all evening Tue-Fri; gourmet menu €75; also à la carte; house wine from €26; SC 10%

on groups 6+. *Wheelchair users should call to reserve wheelchair lift & table. Closed Sun (except on Bank Hol weekends), Mon; 27 Jul - 4 August. MasterCard, Visa, Laser. **Directions:** Across from the Bank Bar on O'Connell Street, parallel to the quays.

Waterford
RESTAURANT

La Palma on the Mall

20 The Mall Waterford Co Waterford **Tel: 051 879 823**
info@lapalma.ie www.lapalma.ie

Claudio, Rachel and Dario Cavieleri's popular Italian restaurant is in a graceful Georgian building on Waterford's Mall. The restaurant is downstairs in a series of pleasant high-ceilinged Georgian rooms, with reception upstairs in a tall navy and beige drawing room, now working as a cocktail bar; here guests are greeted and seated, and offered a drink while you look at the menu - mainly an à la carte, but there's also a very good value midweek "Treat" menu offered. The tone is rustic - dishes might include hearty bruschetta, pasta or confit of duck, and classic tiramisu -and meals begin generously, with a little amuse bouche and a choice of breads. Service is very pleasant and attentive, and the wine waiter is happy to give a good recommendation for the perfect bottle to accompany your meal. Good coffee to finish, and an agreeably reasonable bill. [The old Palma is now called the Espresso and serves pizzas and pasta.] **Seats 75** (private room, 35, outdoors, 10); children welcome; toilets wheelchair accessible; D only Mon-Sat, 5.30-10.30pm; early D about €25, 5.30-7pm Mon-Sat; house wine from €19. Closed Sun and 25-26 Dec. Amex, Diners, MasterCard, Visa, Laser. **Directions:** In city centre opposite Bishop's Palace & Theatre Royal.

Waterford
HISTORIC HOUSE

Sion Hill House & Gardens

Sion Hill Ferrybank Waterford Co Waterford **Tel: 051 851 558**
info@sionhillhouse.com www.sionhillhouse.com

George and Antoinette Kavanagh have been welcoming guests to their lovely hillside house above Waterford city since 1996 and the story of how they came to be here is an interesting one. The Kavanagh family were devastated when their three acre garden in Waterford city was compulsorily purchased some years ago, and this house on the opposite hill became the focus of their dreams; it was built in 1746 and is one of five houses built by the Pope family, who made their fortune as wine merchants during the Napoleonic embargo. George and Antoinette managed to buy it in 1995 and moved in, transplanting 2,000 plants from their previous garden. They also planted 20,000 daffodils and over 400 species of roses and - thanks to a map in the National Archives - rediscovered the original paths in the upper part of the garden, which lies in Kilkenny. And they have been restoring and replanting ever since. So this is more a garden with a house in it, rather than a house with a garden attached - but what a house, all the same. Immaculately maintained and with classically-proportioned rooms furnished with fine antiques, anyone who enjoys beautiful old things will find this a wonderful place to stay and George and Antoinette are great hosts, who really enjoy sharing their home and garden with visitors. Their many plans for the house include restoring the ballroom, and adding a spa in the basement. Magic. **Rooms 4** (all en-suite & no smoking, 2 shower only, 3 family); B&B €58 pps, ss €12; children welcome (under 8s free in parents' room, cot available free of charge, baby sitting arranged). Gardens; walking. Equestrian, fishing & hunting all nearby. Closed 18 Dec - 5 Jan. MasterCard, Visa. **Directions:** 300 metres from Waterford Bridge roundabout and rail station on the N25 to Wexford/Rosslare.

Waterford
HOTEL

Tower Hotel Waterford

The Mall Waterford Co Waterford **Tel: 051 875801**
reservations@thw.ie www.towerhotelwaterford.com

A central location within easy walking distance of everything in the city, ample secure private parking, large conference/banqueting capacity and excellent on-site leisure facilities are all reasons for staying at this big hotel, which is the flagship hotel of the Tower Hotel Group and a sister property to the beautifully located Faithlegg House Hotel (see entry). Considerable investment over the last few years has seen an improvement in standards throughout the hotel: the lobby and reception area have been refurbished (and make a handy meeting place), there's a state-of-the-art conference centre, a smart bistro and a carvery restaurant. Bedrooms have been renovated too, but do ensure you're getting a refurbished room when booking as there's a big difference between old and new rooms; free internet access in all bedrooms. Conference/banqueting facilities (450/350). **Rooms 136** (3 suites, 6 junior suites, 15 executive, 38 no smoking, 3 for disabled); children welcome (cots available free of charge). Lift. B&B from €60-90 pps, ss €20. Leisure centre, indoor swimming pool. Own parking. No pets. Closed 24-26 Dec. Amex, Diners, MasterCard, Visa, Laser. **Directions:** Waterford city centre overlooking the marina.

Waterford
HOTEL•RESTAURANT

Waterford Castle Hotel & Golf Club

The Island Ballinakill Waterford Co Waterford **Tel: 051 878 203**
info@waterfordcastle.com www.waterfordcastle.com

This beautiful hotel dates back to the 15th century, and is situated on its own 310-acre wooded island (complete with 18-hole golf course), reached by a private ferry. The hotel combines the elegance of earlier times with modern comfort, service and convenience - and the location is uniquely serene; its quietness (and the golf facility for off-duty relaxation) makes the castle a good venue for small conferences and business meetings, but it is also a highly romantic location and perfect for small weddings. All guest rooms have been refurbished recently and, although they inevitably vary in size and outlook (and may have some of the little quirks that are typical of old buildings), all are very comfortably furnished in a luxurious country house style, and discreet, well-trained staff look after guests magnificently. And you may be sure of an excellent breakfast, offering a well presented buffet with fresh juices and prepared fruit, yoghurts, muffins, smoked salmon, local cheeses, Waterford Blas (the local bread rolls), and cooked offerings of Flavahan's porridge, excellent dry-cured bacon and sausages in a full breakfast, or other hot dishes including omelettes and scrambled eggs & smoked wild Irish salmon and breakfast service is excellent too. *Waterford Castle was the winner of our Irish Breakfast Awards in 2008: Best Hotel Breakfast category, and also the National Winner. Conference/banqueting (30/80). Golf, archery, clay pigeon shooting, fishing, tennis, walking, gardens. Pool table. Children welcome (under 4 free in parents' room; cots available; baby sitting arranged). **Rooms 19** (5 suites, 3 junior suites, 2 family, 4 ground floor, all no smoking). Lift. 24 hr room service. Turndown service. Room rate from about €195. Closed 2 Jan - 8 Feb. **Munster Dining Room:** It is always a very special event to go across on the little car ferry to this island hotel, where the peaceful grounds and the Victorian Gothic Pile which is the Castle work as an aperitif for Michael Quinn's beautiful natural food. The staff are friendly and welcoming, even the pianist raises a hand of welcome in the handsome and atmospheric dining room with its richly panelled interior. Appointed to the highest standard, it makes a magnificent setting for outstanding food which displays in every course Michael's Euro Toques and Slow Food background, is intelligently sourced and spankingly fresh and local. A set dinner menu offers outstanding value for the quality of the experience, and is also considerately-priced by course, allowing for a semi à la carte selection; it is not long, with just half a dozen choices on each course, but each concisely-worded dish tells the story of its origins: O'Flynn's beef tongue and cheek salad; seared Kilmore Quay scallops; tian of Mrs Bate's crab; Paul Crotty's organic chicken breast; local cheeses, including Knockalara Sheep's and Crozier Blue... Dishes especially admired on a recent visit included a starter of scallops, seared to a caramel crisp on the outside and meltingly soft in the centre, the garnishes (hot tomato salsa, orange segments, avocado purée, hazelnut oil) a delicious, unobtrusive foil to their sweetness...a little chef's treat was an Irish twist on the French rillette: shredded beef tongue and cheek, but held together only by its natural gelatine rather than by fat; with a nice bite of horseradish and salsa verde on the side, it was a beautiful local success. A main course of turbot with asparagus was simplicity itself, the asparagus allowing the turbot, sea fresh and cooked à point, to shine through. But it was the Chocolate Plate, however, that stole the show, so do not miss this treat. ("It even surpassed a chocolate plate eaten in Arzac's 3-Star establishment in San Sebastian...") Wow.) Good coffees and petits fours round off a meal here and, with warmly professional service and a good wine list to match the superb food, the experience is sure to be memorable. **Seats 60**; children welcome. D daily, 7-9 (to 8.30 Sun), L Sun only (12.30-2); Set D about €65, à la carte and vegetarian menu also available; Set Sun L about €30. House wines from €34. SC 10%. Pianist at dinner. Amex, Diners, MasterCard, Visa, Laser. **Directions:** Outskirts of Waterford City just off Dunmore East road.

Waterford Area
HOTEL

Faithlegg House Hotel

Faithlegg Co Waterford **Tel: 051 382 000**
reservations@fhh.ie www.faithlegg.com

Set in wooded landscape with magnificent views over its own golf course and the Suir estuary, this lovely 18th century house has a splendid Waterford Crystal chandelier to set the tone in the foyer, and public areas are elegant throughout. Accommodation is shared between really lovely, large, graciously-proportioned rooms and suites in the old house, and more practical modern hotel rooms in a discreetly positioned new wing, but all are comfortably furnished to a high standard. (Self-catering accommodation is also offered in the grounds.) Aside from golf, the range of activities available on site includes a swimming pool, and numerous health and beauty treatments. There is a choice of restaurants nearby (Waterford city, or Cheekpoint, both of which are only a few minutes' drive), and the hotel's fine dining restaurant, The Roseville Rooms, offers classical cuisine. The restaurant is shared between two lovely classical, formally-appointed dining rooms and it is a very pleasant place to enjoy an evening meal. **Rooms 82**. B&B from €60-95 pps. Restaurant seats 90 (private room 40). Not suitable for children after 8.30pm. D daily, 6.30-9.30; L Sun only, 12.30-2.30. Set D about €50, Set Sun L about €30. House wines from €18. Amex, MasterCard, Visa, Laser. **Directions:** Off Dunmore East Road 10km outside Waterford city. ◇

COUNTY WESTMEATH

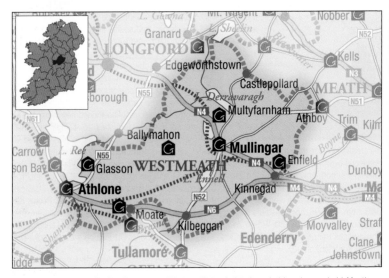

As its name suggests, in the distant past Westmeath tended to be ruled by whoever held Meath, or perhaps it was the other way around But today, Westmeath is a county so cheerfully and successfully developing its own identity that they should find a completely new name for the place. For this is somewhere that makes the very best of what it has to hand.

Its highest "peak" is only the modest Mullaghmeen of 258m, 10 kilometres north of Castlepollard. But this is in an area where hills of ordinary height have impressive shapes which make them appear like miniature mountains around the spectacularly beautiful Lough Derravaragh, famed for its association with the legend of the Children of Lir, who were turned into swans by their wicked step-mother Aoife, and remained as swans for 900 years until saved by the coming of Christianity.

Westmeath abounds in lakes to complement Derravaragh, such as the handsome expanses of Lough Owel and Lough Ennell on either side of the fine county town of Mullingar, where life has been made even more watery in recent years with the continuing work to restore the Royal Canal, which loops through the town on its way from Dublin to the north Shannon.

Meanwhile, Athlone to the west is confidently developing as one of Ireland's liveliest river towns, its Shannonside prosperity based on its riverside location, and a useful manufacturing mixture of electronics, pharmaceuticals and the healthcare industry. Following a period of riverside development, Athlone's waterfront has become a mixture of old and new, with the traditional quayside area below the bridge on the west providing a haven from modern buildings.

Despite modernity, this remains a very rural place - immediately south of the town, you can hear the haunting call of the corncrake coming across the callows (water meadows). Athlone itself has a real buzz, and north of it there's the wide lake expanse of Lough Ree in all its glory, wonderful for boating in an area where, near the delightful village of Glasson, the Goldsmith country verges towards County Longford, and they have a monument to mark what some enthusiasts reckon to be the true geographical centre of all Ireland. You really can't get more utterly rural than that.

Local Attractions and Information

Athlone	All Ireland Amateur Drama Festival (May)	090 647 3358
Athlone	Athlone Castle Visitor Centre	090 649 2912
Athlone	River Festivals	090 649 4981
Athlone	Tourism Information	090 649 4630
Ballykeeran	MV Goldsmith Lake & River Cruises	090 648 5163
Castlepollard	Tullynally Castle & Gardens	044 49060
Clonmellon	Ballinlough Castle Gardens	046 943 3135

Glasson	Glasson Rose Festival (August)	090 648 5677
Kilbegggan	Locke's Distillery Museum	0506 32134
Kilbeggan	Race Course	0506 32176
Moate	Dun na Si Folk Park	090 648 1183
Mullingar	Belvedere House, Gardens & Park	044 49060
Mullingar	Tourism Information	044 48761
Mullingar	Westmeath Tourism Council	044 48571

ATHLONE

R

Athlone makes a perfect break for anyone crossing the country, but it's much more than a handy stop-over: it is now a destination town for weekend breaks, especially since the recent opening of the big new town centre shopping centre. This bustling, youthful centre town of Ireland has much of historical interest to offer - and, although other towns along the mighty Shannon will no doubt be keen to mount a challenge, Athlone is presently seen as the culinary capital of the inland waterways, with a cluster of good eating places in the town itself and surrounding area. And there's a growing supply of quality accommodation in and around the town too: **The Prince of Wales Hotel** (090 647 7246; www.the princeofwales.ie) is reinstated in the centre of the town again, after a complete re-build; just out of town on the Roscommon side, the (very) large and beautifully located waterside **Hodson Bay Hotel** (090 644 2000) serves the area well by offering an extensive conference venue and exceptional leisure facilities - and it gets bigger all the time; bar food at the hotel is standard fare, but – although the tables are tightly packed together in this large restaurant - visitors may be very pleasantly surprised with both the service and the high standard of food in **L'Escale** restaurant. The town is gaining a reputation for good ethnic restaurants too: lovers of spicy foods should check out the authentic **Saagar Indian Restaurant** (090 647 0011) on Lloyds Street; and followers of the popular Lebanese restaurant, **Al Mezza** (090 649 8765) formerly of Jamestown, Co Leitrim, will be delighted to find that it has moved to Bastion Street, Athlone. There are two Farmers' Markets in Athlone, Fridays (North Gate Street, 10am-3pm) and Saturdays (Market Square 10am-3pm). Popular local attractions for visitors include the award-winning Glendeer Open Farm (090 6437 147) and the Viking Cruise (090 647 3383) of the Shannon. Lakeside championship golf is found nearby, at the beautifully located Glasson Golf Hotel (Glasson, 090 648 5120).

WWW.IRELAND-GUIDE.COM FOR ALL THE BEST PLACES TO EAT, DRINK & STAY

Athlone

RESTAURANT

Kin Khao Thai Restaurant
1 Abbey Lane Athlone Co Westmeath **Tel: 090 649 8805**
kinkhaothai@eircom.net www.kinkhaothai.ie

You can't miss this restaurant on the western side of Athlone, near the castle - its vivid yellow exterior walls on two sides of a street corner and red doors and windows mark it out very easily. The reception has recently been moved downstairs, allowing room for seating more happy diners upstairs. It's a pleasant room in soft tones and warm colours, with simple but very neat table settings (although only paper napkins), and large working ceiling fans adding to the atmosphere - you may not quite have been transported to Thailand, but it's a good try and, once you start eating, you might actually be convinced. Kin Khao Thai is run by Irishman Adam Lyons and his Thai wife Janya - Janya's family is steeped in the restaurant and food tradition, with recipes and techniques passed from generation to generation. The choice is enormous, neatly broken down into the various headings such as curry, soups, starters etc and with each dish accompanied by a short but useful explanation of the dish - the best initial choice is a starter platter for two of various finger items, and perhaps ask one of the attentive and charming staff for their recommendations, or select from the list of Janya's Favourites. Desserts include ice creams and, more unusually, sticky rice with coconut custard, which is interesting and tasty. All the dishes are perfectly cooked and presented by really friendly staff. Authenticity is their mantra, and the chefs are from several regions in Thailand so whether you're looking for a creamy coconut curry from the south or a sharp spicy dish from the north, you'll find it here; with the exception of Adam, all the waiters, chefs, and managers are Thai - in fact, the kitchen is a real family affair with Head Chef Num and his little sister Song working side by side. An extensive wine list is also offered. This is undoubtedly one of the best Thai restaurants in Ireland, and good value for money too (estimate around €20 for a main course); it is deservedly popular; and reservations are strongly advised. D daily 5.30-10.30; L Wed-Fri, 12.30-2.30 & Sun all day 2.30-10.30pm. MasterCard, Visa, Laser. **Directions:** Behind Athlone Castle, west side of the Shannon.

Athlone

RESTAURANT

The Left Bank Bistro

Fry Place Athlone Co Westmeath **Tel: 090 649 4446**

info@leftbankbistro.com www.leftbankbistro.com

A growing number of people now see Athlone as a destination for holidays or short breaks and, for many, it would be unthinkable to visit the area or even pass through it without a visit to Annie McNamara and Mary McCullough's elegantly informal contemporary restaurant, where architectural salvage materials and interesting, subtle colours combine well with the simplicity of bare tables and paper napkins to suit the lively modern food. Short, keenly-priced menus - plus specials chalked up on a blackboard - offer a wide range of delicious-sounding dishes with a multi-cultural stamp which, together with carefully-sourced ingredients and snappy cooking, make this a top choice for an informal meal in Athlone. Focaccia, big salads and pasta are typical lunch-time dishes, and vegetables are colourful and full of zing. Fresh fish has always had its own separate menu here, and vegetarians can choose between blackboard specials and dishes from the regular menu, including favourites like Left Bank Salad and vegetable spring rolls. Dinner menus are more extensive and tend to be based on more expensive ingredients, but the style is similar; delicious desserts are a high point (anyone for layered ice cream bombe with blackcurrant coulis?), and all home-made - and, of course, there's a farmhouse cheese plate too. A concise, well-chosen wine list offers a fair choice of half bottles and several champagnes. For the quality of food and cooking, not to mention the style of the place, a meal here is always good value. *A range of speciality products is sold at the Left Bank: salamis, pestos, house dressing, oils, olives, pastas, and coffee are just a few examples - and breads, dressings, chutneys and desserts from the restaurant too. **Seats 60**; air conditioning; toilets wheelchair accessible; children welcome. Open Tue-Sat L 12-5 & D 5.30-9.30; Early bird D €25 (5.30-7.30), also à la carte; house wine about €19. SC 10% on groups 8+. Closed Sun & Mon, bank hols & 10 days Christmas/New Year. Amex, MasterCard, Visa, Laser. **Directions:** Behind Athlone Castle, west side of the Shannon.

Athlone

RESTAURANT

The Olive Grove Restaurant

Custume Pier Athlone Co Westmeath **Tel: 0902 76946**

info@theolivegrove.ie www.theolivegrove.ie

Garry Hughes and Gael Bradbury celebrated a decade in their charming Custume Place restaurant in 2007 - and then moved into these spanking modern waterfront premises just a few yards away in 2008. Overlooking the castle and with plate glass windows all along the riverside, The Olive Grove may well have the best location of any restaurant on the Shannon. A major feature is the riverside deck which seats 50 people and is partially covered by an awning, although it is sometimes closed due to bad weather. The main reception area is on a higher level than the restaurant (there is another entrance via the deck) and smartly furnished with comfortable sofas which are ideal for coffee, scones and using the free Wifi which is available for customers' use. The main restaurant is long, spacious, and chic, and friendly staff are quick to greet and seat arriving guests, and offer the menu and an extensive wine & cocktail list. The menu is international and youthful, as always, but has changed direction somewhat with exotics like fillet of antelope appearing on the special menu and the former house speciality of char-grilled steak now replaced by slow-cooked Morroccan spiced whole roast chicken. Food is stylishly presented and dessert was the highlight of a recent visit, with a delicious chocolate amaretto biscuit cake and a selection of ice creams (especially the mint flavour) attracting praise. Overall, this is a great place, and especially worth knowing about for its oustanding location, friendly staff and long opening hours. **Seat 140** (private room 40; outdoors 50); children welcome (high chair, children's menu, baby changing facilities); L & D daily, 12-4pm (to 5 Sun) & 5.30-10pm (5-9pm Sun). 3 course early bird D €25, 5.30-7.30pm. House wine €18.50. Closed 25 Dec, 1 Jan. Amex, MasterCard, Visa, Laser. **Directions:** Town centre, on the river opposite the castle (beside bridge).

Athlone

HOTEL

Radisson SAS Hotel

Northgate Street Athlone Co Westmeath **Tel: 090 644 2600**

Info.Athlone@RadissonSAS.com www.athlone.radissonsas.com

Magnificently located right on the river and bang in the middle of town, this hotel has impressive public areas and great style: an expansive foyer leads off to an informal split-level restaurant one side, conference and meeting rooms on the other - and opens out on to a huge riverside deck; overlooking the marina and set up with teak furniture, umbrellas and patio heaters, this is a great asset to a town centre hotel. The usual Radisson attributes of contemporary chic and eco-awareness apply throughout the hotel, and also a choice of room styles - Urban if you like warm tones, Ocean if you prefer a cooler, watery theme; all rooms have excellent facilities, including mini-bar, hospitality tray and broadband internet access - and some have great views of the River Shannon and the town. Athlone has character and is well-placed to explore an interesting area that deserves to be better known; for those who like a town centre location, this would be hard to beat as a short break destination. Conference/banqueting (600/380); business centre, secretarial services, free broadband wi/fi, laptop-sized safe in bedrooms. **Rooms 124** (8 junior suites, 4 executive, 11 family suites, 7 disabled); children welcome (1 x under 16 free in parents' room, cots available free of charge, baby sitting arranged, playroom). No pets. Lift. 24 hr room service. B&B from €105 pps (various packages and offers available). Meals available all day. Synergie health & leisure club on site (16.5m pool). Golf nearby (golf breaks offered). Open all year. **Directions:** Town centre, east side of the bridge.

Athlone

RESTAURANT

Restaurant Le Chateau

St. Peter's Port The Docks Athlone Co Westmeath **Tel: 090 649 4517**

lechateau@eircom.net

Steven and Martina Linehan's quayside restaurant is in a converted Presbyterian Church, and it makes a two-storey restaurant of character which complements their well-earned reputation for good food and hospitality. Designed around the joint themes of church and river, the upstairs section has raised floors at each end, like the deck of a galleon, while the church theme is reflected in the windows, notably an original "Star of David". Having been open for very long hours in recent years, and perhaps a little stretched, food service times have been reduced recently, which seems to have brought a corresponding improvement in standards although service can be rather slow. The current menus make a point of offering great value - fine dining is still offered, both on the à la carte and their renowned Candlelight Dinners (which are very good value at €35), but the early dinner, Sunday lunch and children's menus are exceptionally reasonable. Local and speciality produce is very much in evidence - notably Blue organic goat's cheese, Cloonacool Arctic char, certified Irish Angus beef and roast rack of Midland lamb – although there is a supplement on some dishes. Early dinner and Sunday lunch menus are popular, and offer especially good value. **Seats 90** (private room, 25, outdoor, 8); broadband wi/fi; children welcome; air conditioning. D Tue-Sat, 4.30-10pm; Sun all day 12.30-9.30pm; set 4-course Sun L €20; early D €20 (4.30-7pm only); also à la carte; house wines from €22; SC10%. Full bar. Closed Mon, 25-26 Dec. Amex, MasterCard, Visa, Laser. **Directions:** Heading west through Athlone, over Shannon and left at castle, left again and onto bank of Shannon.

Athlone

CHARACTER PUB

Sean's Bar

13 Main Street Athlone Co Westmeath

Tel: 090 649 2358

West of the river, in the interesting old town near the Norman castle (which has a particularly good visitors' centre for history and information on the area, including flora and fauna of the Shannon), Sean Fitzsimons' seriously historic bar lays claim to being the pub with the longest continuous use in Ireland, all owners since 900 AD are on record. (It has actually been certified by the National Museum as the oldest pub in Britain and Ireland - and the all-Europe title is under investigation.) Dimly-lit, with a mahogany bar, mirrored shelving, open fire and an enormous settle bed, the bar has become popular with the local student population and is very handy for visitors cruising the Shannon. The sloping floor is a particularly interesting feature, cleverly constructed to ensure that flood water drained back down to the river as the waters subsided. A glass case containing a section of old wattle wall original to the building highlights the age of the bar, but it's far from being a museum piece. Food is restricted to sandwiches (Mon-Sat), and they serve a good pint. Closed 25 Dec & Good Fri. **Directions:** On the west quayside, just in front of the castle.

Athlone

HOTEL

🏭 Ⓝ 🆁

Sheraton Athlone Hotel

Athlone Co Westmeath **Tel: 090 645 1000**

info.athlone@sheraton.com www.sheratonathlonehotel.com

No need to seek directions for Athlone's newest hotel, as the glazed 12-storey tower soaring high above the new town centre shopping complex makes finding this landmark building an easy matter. Views from the tower take in the mighty Shannon and four surrounding counties (Westmeath, Roscommon, Longford and Offaly) as well as the town itself and, although the vast street level foyer is impressive enough, it is in the upper floors that this unusual hotel excels. In addition to a smart contemporary restaurant, there is a casual café-style restaurant which opens onto a particularly appealing rooftop garden at the base of the tower, and has direct access to the shops - a useful feature that bonds this shiny newcomer to the town. Although it will also appeal to leisure guests, this hotel's key offering is exceptional conference, business and leisure facilities, and a very large banqueting capacity, which will make it an attractive venue for a wide range of events. A double-height Presidential Suite ups the ante when it comes to impressive accommodation, which is luxuriously appointed throughout (although, strangely, curtains bundle untidily against the floor-to-ceiling glass in the tower, spoiling its pristine perfection), and an exclusive club lounge is available to all club level bedrooms. Off-duty delegates will enjoy the Fitness Centre, with swimming pool and several feature pools among the facilities, and a Stephen Pearce-designed Urban Spa offers seven treatment rooms. **Rooms 167**. From €120 per room. **Directions:** Athlone town centre.

Athlone Area

HOTEL

😋 👁 🆁

Glasson Golf Hotel

Glasson Athlone Co Westmeath **Tel: 090 648 5120**

info@glassongolf.ie www.glassongolf.ie

Beautifully situated in an elevated position overlooking Lough Ree, the Reid family's impressive hotel has been developed around their fine old family home; although the golfing dimension has earned an international reputation as one of Ireland's premier inland courses, the hotel is equally geared to business guests and non-golfers, and it is a lovely place to stay. Bright and contemporary, with a welcoming atmosphere, it has grown a lot of late, and each addition has been carefully designed to enhance the property. The spacious, gently contemporary bedrooms are thoughtfully furnished and most have balconies to make the most of excellent views of the lough or over the golf course at the back; the new Master Suites have separate sitting rooms and, allowing for all weathers, a fire and a private terrace. Both the bar and restaurant have been recently refurbished, and in these areas the style is warmly traditional. Conference/banqueting (100/130); free broadband wi/fi, secretarial services, video conferencing. **Rooms 65** (3 suites, 6 junior suites, 13 executive, 3 disabled, 25 ground floor, 15 family rooms, all no smoking); children welcome (under 5 free in parents' room, cots available without charge, baby sitting arranged). Pets by arrangement. Lift. Room service (all day). B&B €85-100pps, ss€40. Walking, fishing, golf (18), garden. Special breaks offered. *Golf breaks are offered - details on application. Closed 25 Dec. Amex, Diners, MasterCard, Visa, Laser. **Directions:** 10km (6 m) north of Athlone, off the N55 Cavan-Longford road.

GLASSON

Originally built as an estate, the poet Goldsmith's "village of the roses" has old world charm, and (once you get away from the main Athlone-Cavan road) peacefulness - Glasson is surrounded by beautiful countryside on the shores of Lough Ree, where visitors can enjoy lakeshore or forest walks and anglers can take full advantage of some of Ireland's finest brown trout and pike fishing. Golfers will enjoy the Glasson Golf Club (090 6485120), whilst other activities available include pony trekking, cruises on the River Shannon or on Lough Ree. Historic buildings include an old schoolhouse built in 1844 and the village is blessed with two good good pubs - **Grogan's** (see entry) and **Farrell's** (090 648 5208). Local historical attractions include Athlone Castle (090 649 2912) and Fore Abbey (044 936 1780), which are the only Benedictine remains in Ireland, dating back to 630AD.

WWW.IRELAND-GUIDE.COM FOR ALL THE BEST PLACES TO EAT, DRINK & STAY

Glasson

RESTAURANT

Glasson Village Restaurant

Glasson Co Westmeath **Tel: 090 648 5001**

michaelrosebrooks@gmail.com

In an attractive stone building which formerly served as an RIC barracks, chef-proprietor Michael Brooks opened the Village Restaurant in 1986, making his mark as a culinary pioneer in the area; there's a real country atmosphere about the place, with a pleasant conservatory overlooking fields. The style is imaginative - traditional French meets modern Irish perhaps; unusually for the area (especially in 1986) fresh fish has always featured strongly, and wide-ranging seasonal menus include treats like lobster and scallops – even the Sunday lunch menu may include grilled black sole on the bone and grilled Clare Island organic salmon, which is remarkable value on a €25 menu. He often offers less usual dishes too, such as roast wild rabbit and game, in season, and there are always popular dishes like Midland lamb and a couple of interesting vegetarian dishes. There is a true love of food which, together with caring service under the direction of Michael's sister, Marie Brooks, and good value, has earned a loyal following. A balanced and informative wine list includes seven house recommendations (€20-28) and nearly a dozen half bottles. **Seats 60** (private room, 16); toilets wheelchair accessible; parking (25); children welcome. D Tue -Sat 6-9.30; L Sun only 12.30-2.30. Set D €42, also à la carte; early D €30 (Tue-Fri, 6-7pm). Set Sun L €25. House wines €20-28; SC discretionary. Closed D Sun, all Mon, 3 weeks mid Oct, 3 days Christmas. Amex, MasterCard, Visa, Laser. **Directions:** 8 km (5 m) from Athlone on Longford/Cavan road (N55).

Glasson

PUB

R

Grogan's Pub

Glasson Co Westmeath

Tel: 090 648 5158

It's hard to cross the Midlands without being drawn into at least a short visit to this characterful pub in Goldsmith's "village of the roses". It's one of those proudly-run, traditional places with two little bars at the front (one with a welcome open fire in winter) and everything gleaming; it was established in 1750 and feels as if the fundamentals haven't changed too much since then. Good food is served in the back bar and, on Wednesday nights, there's traditional music when three generations of the same family play and visiting musicians are also welcome. Food served Mon-Sat 12-9pm, Sun 2-5pm. Closed 25 Dec, Good Fri. **Directions:** Centre of village.

Glasson

GUESTHOUSE•RESTAURANT

Wineport Lodge

Glasson Co Westmeath **Tel: 090 643 9010**

lodge@wineport.ie www.wineport.ie

Ray Byrne and Jane English's lovely lakeside lodge styles itself 'Ireland's first wine hotel' and, although it is not an hotel but a four star-guesthouse, the accommodation - which now offers thirty beautiful rooms, a hot tub and treatment rooms - is nothing less than stunning. A covered lakeside boardwalk leads to the front door: you enter your guest key card and step into a different world. A lofty residents' lounge with a stove and its own bar simply oozes style and comfort, a hint of the high pamper quota waiting above in spacious suites and guest rooms, all with private balconies overlooking the lake. Superbly comfortable beds with goose down duvets and extra large pillows face the view, and seriously luxurious bathrooms have separate double-ended bath and walk-in shower. Wineport has a huge amount to offer discerning guests and has quickly become a hot choice for business and corporate events. Luxurious, romantic, beautiful, businesslike, this is a place of many moods: Wineport has everything. *Ray and Jane were the Guide's Hosts of the Year in 1999, and Wineport was our Hideaway of the Year in 2003. Conference /banqueting 100/150. Free broadband wi/fi, laptop-sized safes in bedrooms. Children welcome (under 2 free in parents room, cot available free of charge, baby sitting arranged). Walking; fishing; garden; jacuzzi; treatment rooms; relaxation room. No pets. Helipad. **Rooms 29** (5 suites, 8 junior suites, 3 superior, 2 family, 15 ground floor, 2 disabled, 2 shower only, all no smoking). B&B €117.50pps; SC discretionary. Lift. Turndown service. All day room service. Closed 24-26 Dec. **Restaurant:** Wineport Lodge began life as a restaurant, and faithful fans continue to beat a path to the door at the slightest excuse, to be treated to a fine meal, served with style and professionalism in this lovely contemporary restaurant - and what a setting! Regular guests find the combination of the view, the company and a good meal irresistible, and many return bearing additions to the now famous Wineport collections (nauticalia, cats...) Current head chef Cathal Moran offers well-balanced and strongly seasonal menus which are quite international in tone but based on Quality Assured and local ingredients including game in season, eels, home-grown herbs and wild mushrooms; a tasting plate of McGeough's turf-smoked ham is an unusual starter, served with honey roast figs stuffed with Cashel blue cheese, and signature dishes include slow roast confit of pork belly and seared King scallops with buttered spring onions, smoked paprika and apple cream. A lovely dessert menu is teamed with a list of pudding wines and a very inform-ative cheese section offers seven ports, all offered by the glass even a Graham's 40-year Tawny, at €250 per bottle (glass, €27.50). An impressive and informative wine list charts a wine connection with the area going right back to 542AD, and makes very interesting reading; improvements are constantly made to the list, which offers special treats and many more affordable wines, and includes a good selection of wines by the glass and six well chosen half bottles. **Seats 120** (private room, 50; outdoor seating, 50); toilets wheelchair accessible; children welcome. Food service: Mon-Sat, 6-10pm; Sun 3-5pm & 6-10pm; set Sun L €45; set D €75, gourmet menu €85; otherwise à la carte; wines from about €30. Closed 24-26 Dec. Amex, Diners, MasterCard, Visa, Laser. **Directions:** Mid-way between Dublin and Galway: take the Longford/Cavan exit off the Athlone relief road; fork left after 4km at the Dog & Duck; 1.6km, on the left.

KILBEGGAN

Kilbeggan is a handy place to break a journey across the country, and famous for its old distillery, which is now returning to whiskey production again after a long lapse. Even if you do not wish to do the tour, Locke's Distillery (0506 32134) is a useful place to stop for a bite to eat in the café, which is open during the day.

WWW.IRELAND-GUIDE.COM FOR ALL THE BEST PLACES TO EAT, DRINK & STAY

Moate
COUNTRY HOUSE•RESTAURANT

Temple Country Retreat & Spa
Horseleap Moate Co Westmeath **Tel: 057 933 5118**
reservations@templespa.ie www.templespa.ie

Declan and Bernadette Fagan's well known well-being retreat is on its own farmland in the unspoilt Westmeath countryside, where guests are welcome to walk close to peat bogs, lakes and historical sites, and outdoor activities such as walking, cycling and riding are all at hand. Wellbeing programmes and healthy eating have been avail-able at Temple since 1987, but the magnificent new facility which they opened some twenty years later has made it possible for many more people to enjoy and benefit from their philosophy of calm relaxation, which is unchanged and, despite the much larger scale of the operation, the essence of its origins in their charming and immaculately maintained 200 year-old farmhouse next door remains at its heart. Impressive spa facilities include18 treatment rooms with over 80 restorative treatments; a hydrotherapy pool, steam room, sauna and relaxation room; stress management and guided relaxation; yoga; personal training centre with fully equipped gym and on-site personal trainer. But Temple is not just a spa - it also well equipped for business meetings, training programmes and seminars (up to 48 delegates), and you do not in fact need any special reason to come here: it is a lovely place to stay, with very comfortable accommodation, and there is no obligation to take part in activities. However, once there, casual guests tend to be drawn in to the spirit of the place, and many return as soon as possible to enrol in specific activities. An atmosphere of calm, good food, comfortable surroundings, gentle exercise and pampering therapies all contribute to a relaxing experience here - and the wide range of programmes offered include pampering weekends, 24-hour escape breaks, mother & daughter breaks, maternity breaks, and his & her weekends. Small Conferences/Banqueting (48/60). Destination Spa (hair dressing, massage, fitness room, jacuzzi, sauna, steam room etc), garden, cycling, equestrian nearby. **Rooms 23** (all en-suite, 1 shower only, 1 junior suite, 1 suite, 1 for disabled, all no-smoking). B&B about €115 pps, ss €50. Spa Package about €235 pps, (min 2-night stay at weekends). Spa weekends from about €300 pps (ss about €40). Garden Room **Restaurant:** Temple is a member of the Health Farms of Ireland Association, which means that special attention is given to healthy eating guidelines, and vegetarian, vegan and other special diets are catered for. However, French head chef David Godin has much more than healthy eating in mind when creating the wonderful menus which make this lovely contemporary restaurant a dining destination for non-residents, as well as an experience for spa or corporate guests to look forward to at the end of each day. Top quality ingredients, local and organic where possible - including lamb from the farm, garden vegetables, organic Midland beef, cheese and yoghurts - are the sound foundation on which seriously tasty and beautifully presented meals are based. As one reader put it "The food was fantastic; what impressed us most was that there were so many low-fat options, and yet this was beautiful and substantial - 'real' food". It may seem strange to dine in a spa, but you would need to travel a long way before finding a restaurant to match it. Organic wines. Special dining events are held from time to time, eg Traditional French Cuisine Menu, offered with or without accommodation. **Seats 60** (outdoors, 20); reservations essential; not suitable for children; air conditioning. L & D Tue-Sat 12.30-2.30 & 7-9.30; Sun L only, 12.30-2.30. Set L €32.50; set 2/3 course D €39/48, also à la carte; house wine from €24; sc 8% on groups 8+. Closed Sun D, Mon (seasonal, please call to check off season); Establishment closed Christmas. Amex, MasterCard, Visa, Laser. **Directions:** Signed off N6, 1.6km (1 m) west of Horseleap.

R R   # MULLINGAR

This thriving Midlands town beside the Royal Canal is dominated by the cathedral, an imposing renaissance-style structure dedicated in 1939. The attractive old town-centre hotel, the **Greville Arms Hotel** (Tel 044 934 8563) continues to be the hub of local activities although, with the opening of both **Mullingar Park Hotel** and, more recently, the town centre **Annebrook House Hotel** (see entries), the choice of facilities has grown dramatically of late which is good news for the growing number of city folk who find the town is a perfect short break destination. In the town centre, **Canton Casey's** (044 939 0171) pub is a place for those who appreciate traditional bars (at its best at quiet times - it can get very busy); upstairs, over the bar, **Fat Cats Brasserie** (044 934 9969) offers informal dining. For those who enjoy a good traditional pub, **Con's Bar** (044 934 0925) on Dominick Street is the place head for, and they serve reliable, wholesome fare. The informal, mid-range **Zest Restaurant and Café** (044 933 3816) opened on Oliver Plunkett Street recently, and new restaurants - including several ethnic ones - are opening all the time, so it's worth taking a browse around the town. Lovers of Indian food should check out **Saagar** (044 934 0911) which is near the Dublin Bridge and is the parent restaurant of the highly-regarded Saagar in Dublin (see entry). Mullingar is also known for the neighbouring lakes, Lough Owel and Lough Ennell, which attract many anglers, as well as Lough Derravaragh, which is best known for its connection with the Irish legend of the Children of Lir. Having being turned into swans, the four children of King Lir spent three hundred years on Lough Derravaragh before moving to other locations around Ireland. Nearby Belvedere House and Gardens (044 934 9060) is a lovely place to spend a few hours, while a testing round of golf is available in Mullingar Golf Club (044 934 8366). It is also a great area for cycling. There is a Farmers' Market every Sunday (probably at Fairgreen, adjacent to Penneys but venue subject to change) 10.30a.m to 2.30 p.m. **WWW.IRELAND-GUIDE.COM FOR ALL THE BEST PLACES TO EAT, DRINK & STAY**

Mullingar   # Annebrook House Hotel

HOTEL   Pearse Street Mullingar Co Westmeath **Tel: 044 935 3300**
R R   info@annebrook.ie   www.annebrook.ie

If you haven't been to Mullingar for a while, this fine town centre hotel will be a pleasant surprise, just off the main street and yet built around a beautiful old house situated elegantly in spacious surroundings, with the town park on the doorstep and the River Brosna flowing through the grounds - it's all distinctly fairytale. The original house has an interesting history, having been built around 1810 as a residence for the County Surgeon and, surprisingly perhaps, was still lived in as a family home for its original use until recently; however, its most famous historical connection is with the author Maria Edgworth, who is said to have stayed here in the early 19th century. The old house is now used mainly for its impressive public rooms, including the atmospheric Brook Restaurant (good food and service, lovely ambience), the Old House Bar, and also a very pleasant reading room and drawing room. Accommodation is in the new part of the hotel, entered over a little bridge into reception, and bedrooms are very comfortably furnished in an easy modern style and soothing colours that won't date too quickly. Popular for weddings and business/conferences, it's also an ideal destination for a weekend away. Staff are friendly and helpful and there's a welcome emphasis on service. Conferences/Banqueting (350/260), free broadband wi/fi. **Rooms 111** (2 suites, 26 executive, +36 apart-hotel suites, 3 disabled); children welcome (cot available free of charge, baby sitting arranged); B&B about €75-95 pps, ss €20-30. **Brook Restaurant:** L & D Tue-Sat, 12-3pm & 6-9.30; Sun L only, 12-3pm; set L €29.50; early D €25, Tue-Thurs, 6-7pm. Brosna Bar: food served all day 9am-8.30pm; carvery L daily, à la carte bar meals every evening. Restaurant closed Sun D, Mon. Amex, MasterCard, Visa, Laser. **Directions:** On main street.

Mullingar
RESTAURANT
👁 R R

The Belfry Restaurant

Ballynegall Mullingar Co Westmeath **Tel: 044 934 2488**
info@thebelfryrestaurant.ie www.belfryrestaurant.com

The tall spire will lead you to this well known restaurant in a magnificently converted church near Mullingar. The design is brilliant, with (excellent) toilets near the entrance, perfect for a quick freshen up before heading up thickly carpeted stairs to a mezzanine lounge which is luxuriously furnished. A second staircase descends to the striking dining area, which is extremely atmospheric, especially when seen in candle light, with background music from the grand piano where the altar used to be. Everything has been done to the highest specifications, and colour schemes are subtle and elegant. After a short closure, the restaurant re-opened in summer 2008, following a change of management. Executive chef Marco Heinrich was formerly at Inchydoney Lodge & Spa in West Cork, and is familiar with the quality of native Irish produce - although it would be nice to see reference to the provenance of ingredients and their suppliers. His menus are quite contemporary, offering with a mix of European dishes such as chicken, potato gnocchi & oyster mushrooms, or slow roast belly pork with scallop and puréed peas, and Irish traditions like the (very popular) Westmeath Hereford beef and Yorkshire pudding. Imaginative desserts were the highlight of a recent visit – a delicious roasted walnut parfait with raspberry sauce, for example, and – inspired no doubt by the local connection with the Children of Lir - Swan Lake Meringue with blood orange sorbet and Curacao jelly and walnuts. The front of house, and friendly and efficient service is in the capable hands of proprietor Lorraine Gavigan. **Seats 65** (private room, 16); children welcome before 7.30pm; L & D Wed-Sat, 12.30-2.30 & 6-9.30pm; Sun 12-5.30pm. Set Sun L €30. Early D Wed-Thurs, 6-7pm. Closed Mon, Tues, 25-26 Dec. MasterCard, Visa, Laser. **Directions:** Castlepollard road, off the Mullingar by-pass.

Mullingar
CAFÉ
R R

Gallery 29 Café

16 Oliver Plunkett Street Mullingar Co Westmeath **Tel: 044 49449**
corbetstown@eircom.net

Although now only open three days a week, Ann & Emily Gray's smart, black-painted, traditionally-fronted premises is bright and welcoming – and is a good place for any time of day, including breakfast (with freshly-squeezed juice). They're great bakers, and the buzz of an open kitchen and freshly-cooked food on display draws people in. You'll find good soups, salads, savoury tart of the day, and "tailor-made" sandwiches, and also hot main courses like oven-baked salmon with sweet chilli sauce, champ & salad, and steak sandwich on ciabatta, with spicy salsa & mixed salad. Outside catering, picnics and freshly-made dishes for home freezing are also offered. **Seats 50**; children welcome. Open Thu-Sat 9am-6pm. All à la carte. Wine licence. Closed Sun-Wed, Christmas/New Year. **No Credit Cards. Directions:** From Dublin through traffic lights at Market Square in town centre. About 60m on right hand side.

Mullingar
CAFÉ
R R

Ilia A Coffee Experience

28 Oliver Plunkett Street Mullingar Co Westmeath **Tel: 044 934 0300**
juliekenny@eircom.net www.ilia.ie

Julie Kenny's delightful 2-storey coffee house and informal restaurant in the centre of Mullingar is attractively set up - the first floor area is particularly pleasing, with a seating area of sofas, low tables and plants at the top of the stairs setting a relaxed tone. The rest is more conventionally furnished in café style - and a more comfortable height for eating a real meal. Menus cater for all the changing moods though the day, beginning with an extensive breakfast, including the full traditional, then there are the mid-day bites like home-made soup, panini, steak baguettes, and much more. More predictably, there's a nice little drinks menu offering everything from big glasses of freshly-squeezed orange juice through iced teas, smoothies, teas - and, of course, coffees (Java Republic), any way you like, including flavoured coffees. Everything is deliciously fresh and wholesome, staff are charming and efficient, with reasonable prices. Takeaway also available. Wine licence. *"Ilia Gourmet" specialist food store (also offering hampers and outside catering) is across the road, and the new Ilia Tapas & More. **Seats 60**; children welcome; toilets wheelchair accessible; air conditioning. Open Mon-Sat 9am-5.30pm. Closed Sun, Christmas & bank hols. Amex, MasterCard, Visa, Laser. **Directions:** Centre of Town.

Mullingar
RESTAURANT
N R R

Ilia Tapas & More

37 Dominick Street Mullingar Co Westmeath **Tel: 044 934 5947**
juliekenny@eircom.net www.iliatapasandmore.ie

A younger sister establishment to the Ilia Gourmet fine food store and the original café, Ilia A Coffee Experience (see entry), this stylish tapas bar-cum-restaurant has proved such a hit locally that reservations are always essential, even early in the evening. Bearing little resemblance to a typical standing room-only Spanish tapas bar, it's a pleasing contemporary restaurant, in a room well-designed to create interesting shapes and break up the space into more intimate areas - and (one case where lack of authenticity is welcome) the seating is very comfortable indeed. Although it's the sort of place where you can eat as much or as little as you like, the point of tapas here seems to be mainly its sociability; servings are of the generously-sized rather than a small nibble variety, making them particularly well-suited to groups sharing, and in the Guide's experience they like you to order the full meal at the start, as in other restaurants. The menu, which may prove a little confusing, is made up of two pages of tapas, i.e. International tapas (including some traditional Spanish items like platters of Spanish meats, or olives), and Tapas to share (a mixture of beautifully presented and fully garnished starters), then main courses ('More') offer a balanced range of popular fish, meat, poultry and vegetarian dishes, not specifically Spanish. The sharing theme returns at the end of the meal, with the option of 'Ilia Delight', a fondue with strawberries and marshmallows to dip, or a shared cheeseboard. A reasonably priced international wine list includes some by the glass. This is a fun and relaxing place to dine out with family or friends, the food is clearly carefully sourced and tasty dishes are cooked with flair and served efficiently – and, once you get the hang of the way the menu works, it offers a good value too: no wonder it's always full. Open Wed-Sat 6.30pm-10.30pm; Sun 10am-6pm. Closed Mon & Tue. MasterCard, Visa, Laser. **Directions:** Centre of Town.

Mullingar
HOTEL
R R

Mullingar Park Hotel

Dublin Road Mullingar Co Westmeath **Tel: 044 934 4446**
info@mullingarparkhotel.com www.mullingarparkhotel.com

This large hotel on the Dublin side of Mullingar contributes quality accommodation and welcome facilities to the town - and (providing you can find the entrance, which is not easy due to confusing signage off the N4) it makes a convenient journey break when travelling across the country. Although not especially appealing from the road, it is a spacious and friendly place - and has an unexpectedly pleasant outlook at the back, where the bar and conference areas open on to a large and sheltered courtyard style 'garden' with neatly kept lawns and paths, well away from the road. **The Terrace Restaurant** offers more than the usual hotel fare, and attracts diners from the town and beyond; the highly regarded chef Michael Rath joined the hotel shortly before the Guide went to press, and he offers appealing and attractively priced contemporary à la carte menus, including unusually strong vegetarian choices. Conference/banqueting (1000/700); secretarial services, video conferencing, free broadband wi/fi. **Rooms 95** (1 junior suites, 2 disabled, 67 no smoking). 24 hr room service. B&B €100 pps, ss €30; children welcome (under 2s free in parents' room, cot available without charge, baby sitting arranged). No pets. Garden, walking; leisure centre, swimming pool, spa, beauty salon.*Short breaks offered. Closed 25-26 Dec. Amex, Diners, MasterCard, Visa, Laser. **Directions:** Off the N4 - take exit no. 9.

Mullingar
RESTAURANT
V R R

Oscars Restaurant

21 Oliver Plunkett Street Mullingar Co Westmeath
Tel: 044 934 4909

This smartly-painted, centrally-located restaurant enjoys enduring popularity locally, pleasing people of all ages with its lively atmosphere and mix of traditional and contemporary favourites at reasonable prices. This is beef country, so a section of the menu given over to steaks should come as no surprise, but there's much else besides, ranging from '80s' classics like deep-fried mushrooms with garlic & cucumber dip, through spicy chicken wings to simple smoked salmon. Main courses include steaks various ways, honey-glazed lamb shanks, chicken Oscar's style and crispy Silver Hill duckling. Pastas and pizzas too - this is popular food, well executed at fair prices - and with cheerfully efficient service to match. Oscar's offers an affordable outing with something for everyone, and wines (from an accessible and informative list, with details on grape varieties as well as a well-balanced selection) starting at under €20. **Seats 70**; air conditioning. D daily, 6-9.30 (to 10 Fri/Sat, to 8.15 Sun), L Sun only, 12.30-2.15. A la carte D. Set Sun L €29. House wine €18.50. Closed 25/26 Dec, first 2 weeks Jan. MasterCard, Visa, Laser. **Directions:** Centre of town opposite town mall.

Mullingar Area

Mary Lynch's Pub

PUB
R R

MacNead's Bridge Coralstown Nr. Mullingar Co Westmeath
Tel: 044 937 4501

John and Mary Moriarty's charming old-world pub a short distance east of Mullingar is tucked between the N4 and the Royal Canal, with a grandstand view of the new harbour works from the back of the bar. A blackboard menu offers traditional home-cooked dishes like soup of the day, fish pie, roast of the day and steak sandwiches, and there's likely to be live music at weekends too. It's a popular destination for locals, and a useful place for travellers to know about. Meals from noon daily. **Directions:** Between the N4 and the canal.

R R

MULTYFARNHAM

Set in lovely unspoilt rolling countryside, this is a very attractive village with stone buildings and a pretty river, and it is rich in history, with a Franciscan monastery which was founded in 1268 and is still in use; today it is the site of one of the finest outdoor shrines in Ireland, with 14 life-size Stations of the Cross on the monastery lawns, around the church and college. Horse-riding facilities are also available near by. It is a lovely area for a short break and is close to Lough Derravaragh, with activities including horesriding, hill walking, boating, and fishing (with authorised permits) all nearby. Garden lovers staying in the area should make a point of visiting Tullynally Castle & Gardens (Castlepollard, 044 966 1159) especially in spring as they are bulb specialists. In the village itself, **Weirs Bar & Restaurant** (044 937 1111); with lots of character, and a full restaurant at the back, this welcoming country pub is a place well worth knowing about.

WWW.IRELAND-GUIDE.COM FOR ALL THE BEST PLACES TO EAT, DRINK & STAY

Multyfarnham

Mornington House

COUNTRY HOUSE•HISTORIC HOUSE
👑 👁 *V* **R R**

Mornington Multyfarnham Co Westmeath
Tel: 044 937 2191 stay@mornington.ie www.mornington.ie

Warwick and Anne O'Hara's gracious Victorian house is surrounded by mature trees and is just a meadow's walk away from Lough Derravarragh where the mythical Children of Lir spent 300 years of their 900-year exile - the lough is now occupied by a pleasing population of brown trout, pike, eels and other coarse fish. This has been the O'Hara family home since 1858, and is still furnished with much of the original furniture and family portraits - and, although centrally heated, log fires remain an essential feature. Bedrooms are typical of this kind of country house - spacious and well-appointed, with old furniture (three have brass beds) but with comfortable modern mattresses. Anne is well-known for her skills in the kitchen, and cooks proper country breakfasts and country house dinners for residents, using fresh fruit and vegetables from the walled garden and local produce (Westmeath beef cooked in Guinness is a speciality), while Warwick does the honours front-of-house. There is a wealth of wildlife around the house, and there are gardens and archaeological sites to visit nearby - this is a tranquil and restorative place for a short break. **Rooms** 5 (4 en-suite, 1 with private bathroom, 2 shower only, 1 family room, all no smoking); children welcome (under 3s free in parents' room, cot available without charge). Turndown service. Pets allowed by arrangement. B&B €75 pps, ss €20. Set residents D €45, at 8pm (book by 2pm). House wine about €16. Garden, croquet, fishing. Canoes, boats & bicycles can be hired. Equestrian: trekking & a cross-country course and Golf nearby. *Short breaks offered: 3-day stay (3 DB&B) from €275pps. Closed Nov-Mar. Amex, Diners, MasterCard, Visa, Laser. **Directions:** Exit N4 for Castlepollard.

COUNTY WEXFORD

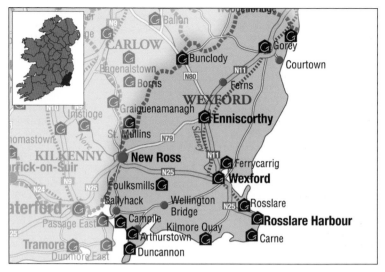

The popular view of Wexford is beaches, sunshine and opera. The longest continuous beach in all Ireland runs along the county's east coast, an astonishing 27 kilometres from Cahore Point south to Raven Point, which marks the northern side of the entrance to Wexford town's shallow harbour. As for sunshine, while areas further north along the east coast may record marginally less rainfall, in the very maritime climate of the "Sunny Southeast" around Wexford, the clouds seem to clear more quickly, so the chances of seeing the elusive orb are much improved.

And opera.....? Well, the annual Wexford Opera Festival is a byword for entertaining eccentricity - as international enthusiasts put it, "we go to Wexford town to enjoy operas written by people we've never heard of, and we have ourselves a thoroughly good time."

But there's much more to this intriguing county than sun, sand and singing. Wexford itself is but one of three substantial towns in it, the other two being the market town of Enniscorthy, and the river port of New Ross. While much of the county is relatively low-lying, to the northwest it rises towards the handsome Blackstairs Mountains. There, the 793m peak of Mount Leinster may be just over the boundary in Carlow, but one of the most attractive little hill towns in all Ireland, Bunclody, is most definitely in Wexford.

In the north of the county, Gorey is a pleasant and prosperous place, while connoisseurs of coastlines will find the entire south coast of Wexford a fascinating area of living history, shellfish-filled shallow estuaries, and an excellent little harbour at the much-thatched village of Kilmore Quay inside the Saltee Islands.

Round the corner beyond the intriguing Hook Head, the peninsula marked by Ireland's oldest light-house, Wexford County faces west across its own shoreline along the beauties of Waterford estuary. Here, there's another fine beach, at Duncannon, while nearby other sheltered little ports of west Wexford - Arthurstown and Ballyhack - move at their own sweet and gentle pace.

In New Ross, the authentic re-creation of a 19th Century emigrant ship - the impressive Dunbrody - is proving to be a very effective focal point for the revival of the picturesque waterfront. It's a fitting place for the lovely River Barrow to meet ships in from sea in an area with strong historical links to President John F Kennedy – his great-grandparents sailed from New Ross to America on the original Dunbrody.

Local Attractions and Information

Ballygarrett	Shrule Deer Farm	055 27277
Ballyhack	Ballyhack Castle	051 389 468
Campile	Kilmokea Gardens	051 388 109
Dunbrody	Abbey & Visitor Centre	051 388 603
Duncannon	Duncannon Fort	051 388 603
Enniscorthy	National 1798 Visitor Centre	054 37596
Enniscorthy	Tourism Information	054 34699
Enniscorthy	Wexford County Museum	054 46506
Ferrycarrig	National Heritage Park	053 20733
Gorey (Coolgreany)	Ram House Gardens	0402 37238
Hook Head	Hook Head Lighthouse	051 397 055
Johnstown	Castle Demesne & Agricultural Museum	053 42888
Kilmore Quay	Saltee Island Ferries	053 29684
New Ross	Dunbrody - re-creation of 19th C ship	051 425 239
New Ross	Galley River Cruises	051 421 723
New Ross	John F Kennedy Arboretum	051 388 171
New Ross	John F Kennedy Homestead, Dunganstown	051 388 264
New Ross	Tourism Information	051 421 857
Rosslare	Ferry Terminal	053 33622
Tintern	Abbey (nr Saltmills)	051 562 650
Wexford	North Slobs Wildfowl Reserve	053 23129
Wexford	Opera Festival (October)	053 22144
Wexford	Tourism Information	053 23111

ARTHURSTOWN

This seaside village is a popular family holiday destination on the spectacular Hook Peninsula, home to many sandy coves, and historical sites such as Tintern Abbey (051 562650, open June to October), Dunbrody Abbey & Visitor Centre (051 388603, open May to September) and the Hook Lighthouse (051 397055/4, open all year). Tintern Abbey is a Cistercian Abbey set in a beautiful woodland area alongside a small riverside estuary, and Dunbrody Abbey dates back to 1210 AD, and is one of the most striking Cistercian ruins in the country. Visitors can take guided tours of Hook Head Lighthouse, which also dates back to the early 13th century and, although automated in 1996, is one of the oldest operational lighthouses in the world. Other local attractions include Ballyhack Castle (051 389 468) and Duncannon Fort (051 388 603). Garden lovers will enjoy the beautiful Kilmokea Gardens (Campile, 051 388 109), and the John F. Kennedy Aboretum (051 388171) is within a short drive; it covers an area of 252 hectares and contains a visitor centre with an audio-visual show. For shopping, the nearby towns of Waterford and Wexford have much to offer including crafts, designer knitwear and the world famous Waterford Crystal.

Arthurstown

HOTEL•RESTAURANT

Dunbrody Country House Hotel & Cookery School

Arthurstown Co Wexford **Tel: 051 389 600**
dunbrody@indigo.ie www.dunbrodyhouse.com

Set in twenty acres of parkland and gardens on the Hook Peninsula, just across the estuary from Waterford city, Catherine and Kevin Dundon's elegant Georgian manor was the ancestral home of the Chichester family and the long tradition of hospitality at this tranquil and luxurious retreat is very much alive and well. Well-proportioned public rooms, which include an impressive entrance hall and gracious drawing room, are all beautifully furnished and decorated with stunning flower arrangements and the occasional unexpectedly modern piece that brings life to a fine collection of antiques. Spacious bedrooms, including those in a newer wing which blends perfectly with the original building, generally have superb bathrooms and offer all the comforts expected of such a house - and fine views over the gardens. Converted outbuildings house what must be Ireland's most stylish cookery school and, alongside it, a beautiful spa. An outstanding breakfast offers a magnificent buffet - fresh juices, fruit compôtes, cheeses - as well as hot dishes from a tempting menu - and was the national winner of our Irish Breakfast Awards in 2004. While Dunbrody provides a wonderfully relaxing place for a leisure break, they also cater for business meetings, small conferences, product launches and incentive programmes (full details available on request). Conference/banqueting (30/110). Secretarial services; video conferencing. Cookery school. Spa & beauty salon. Garden, walking. Children welcome (under 5s free in parents' room; cot available without charge, baby sitting arranged). No pets. **Rooms 22** (7 suites, 7 junior suites, 7 superior). B&B about €135 pps; ss €25. *A range of special breaks is offered (weekend, midweek, cookery, New Year); details on application. Open all year except Christmas. **The Harvest Room at Dunbrody:** The restaurant looks out on to a beautifully maintained pleasure garden and, beyond, to a promisingly productive organic vegetable and fruit garden. The dining room is a lovely well-proportioned room, with an open fire in winter and stunning flower arrangements all the time; it presents a striking blend of classic and contemporary style. Likewise, Kevin Dundon and his head chef, Neil McEvoy (formerly of L'Ecrivain), offer a tempting à la carte and a Full On Irish Tasting Menu (named after his successful cookbook, Full On Irish) that combine classical and international influences with local produce and Irish themes; the 8-course Tasting Menu can be adjusted to accommodate dietary requirements, including a vegetarian option, and it is excellent value (€80; with wine, €110). And suppliers are given full credit: fresh fish is delivered daily from nearby Duncannon harbour, and shellfish from Kilmore Quay, and meats are supplied by Wallace's butchers, of Wellington Bridge - and organic fruit, vegetables and herbs are, as far as possible, home grown. Starters - which tend to be pretty and richly flavoured yet light – might include a lovely terrine of foie gras with honey-glazed fig, toasted brioche and raspberry coulis (a rich dish, but the portion is petite), and beautifully caramelised Dunmore East scallops with an unusual accompaniment of creamed sweetcorn with mustardcress & truffle shavings. Kevin Dundon's 'eat local' philosophy comes through on all his menus, and local meats like rack of Wexford lamb often top the bill - in a terrific house speciality, roast rack of lamb with a confit of shoulder (the slow-cooked meat shredded and served crispy), for example, which is a modern twist on a very traditional theme. And meals at Dunbrody always end on a high note, so make sure you save a little space for a spectacular dessert – a duo of fruit jellies (raspberry and loganberry) with a minty tea granita went down a storm on a recent visit... Catherine leads a well-trained and efficient dining room staff with the charm and panache that typifies all aspects of the hospitality at this exceptional country house. The care and attention to detail seen in every dish is truly admirable, and presentation is masterly, adding to the enjoyment. An informative wine list which leans towards the classics includes a nice selection of half bottles and wines by the glass. The early dinner menu and Sunday lunch offer particularly good value. *At the all-day **Dundon's Champagne Seafood Bar & Terrace** - a stylish contemporary area with a temperature controlled wine cellar and another drawing room off it, and a lovely outside eating area under a white canopy – a smart menu offers 16 items, many served in starter-sized portions, plus desserts and cheese; the food is delicious and served with the usual Dundon style: Hook Head haddock smokies come with grilled bread; fish and skinny chips with tartare sauce and a pea shot, and a trilogy of pannacotta is served in large shot glasses. This stylish and reasonably-priced casual food will introduce many new guests to this lovely house. **Harvest Room Seats 70** (private room, 18; outdoors, 20); children welcome before 8pm; reservations required; toilets wheelchair accessible. D Mon-Sat 6.30-9.15. L Sun only 1.30-2.30. Set 2/3 course D €52/€65; 'Full On Irish' Tasting Menu €80, changes daily, offered with or without matching wines (€110 with wine). House wines from €25. SC discretionary. Dundon's Champagne Seafood Bar Seats 20; food served daily 2-10pm. Closed 22-26 Dec. Amex, Diners, MasterCard, Visa, Laser. **Directions:** N11 to Wexford, R733 from Wexford to Arthurstown.

Arthurstown

B&B•FARMHOUSE

Glendine Country House

Arthurstown New Ross Co Wexford **Tel: 051 389 500**
glendinehouse@eircom.net www.glendinehouse.com

Ann and Tom Crosbie's large nineteenth century farmhouse is approached up a driveway off the main road to Arthurstown, and has magnificent views across the estuary. It is a spacious house and makes a very comfortable and hospitable place to stay at a reasonable price; it would be ideal for a family holiday as there are sandy beaches nearby and there's a safe, enclosed playground for children beside the house - and they also enjoy the highland cows, Jacob sheep and horses which the Crosbies keep in paddocks around the house. A pleasant guest drawing room has plenty of comfortable seating with excellent views down to the harbour and across the estuary, and the immaculately maintained bedrooms are very large, as are the en-suite bathrooms. Guest rooms are of two types: the newer ones are bright and individually decorated in quite a contemporary style, with smart bathrooms; the original rooms are more traditional, with a cosy atmosphere - and all nine rooms have sea views. Service is a priority: the Crosbies take pride in giving their guests personal attention and lots of advice on local amenities, and a full dinner menu, with a choice of three dishes on each course, is offered on some nights; this includes local seafood, of course - but also, in true farmhouse tradition, their own lamb and beef, eggs and vegetables. And the Crosbies also believe in sending everyone off well-fed for the day after a really good breakfast that offers home-baked breads, fresh and cooked fruits, organic porridge and the range of hot dishes includes smoked salmon & scrambled eggs and French toast as well as the full Irish. *Glendine House was our Farmhouse of the Year in 2006. **Rooms 6** (1 suite, 2 family rooms, all no smoking); turndown service offered; B&B €65 pps, ss €15; children welcome (under 1s free in parents room, cot available, baby sitting arranged; children's playground), but not in dining room after 8.30pm; room service (limited hours); pets allowed by arrangement (stay in bedrooms, no charge); free broadband wi/fi. Light meals (soup & home-baked bread, open sandwiches) available all day. Residents D €35. Equestrian, fishing & golf all nearby. Garden, walking. *Off-season breaks offered. 2 self-catering cottages are also available - details on application. Closed Nov-Jan. MasterCard, Visa, Laser. **Directions:** From Wexford, turn right before Talbot Hotel, onto R733; 35km (22 m) to Arthurstown; entrance on right before village.

Arthurstown

B&B

Marsh Mere Lodge

Arthurstown New Ross Co Wexford **Tel: 051 389 186**
info@marshmerelodge.com www.marshmerelodge.com

The McNamaras' friendly almost-waterside bed and breakfast is beautifully located just outside Arthurstown and has lovely views out toward the Hook Head lighthouse. When you see the sign beside the car parking spaces that fresh eggs are for sale - and you see the chickens running around the yard - you know that you are in for something special, so just enjoy Maria McNamara's warm welcome and let yourself relax in this beautiful part of Wexford. There's a cosy and relaxing sitting room, with DVDs and books for guests' use; the spacious, individually decorated en-suite rooms are very comfortably furnished, and you'll get a lovely breakfast too. Everything is cooked to order and you can mix and match from a varied menu including fresh fruit and yoghurts, smoked trout and salmon, excellent sausages, bacon, tomatoes and those fresh home-produced eggs any way you want, including crisp and tasty French toast. Then excellent home-made breads and jams to finish off. With a lovely, well-kept cottage garden and a comfortably-furnished veranda overlooking the bay, Marsh Mere complements other accommodation in the area - and, as some rooms are suitable for families, this warm and welcoming place would make a relaxing base for a family break. **Rooms 4** (all en suite, shower only). B&B €50-55 pps; single €60; family rooms from €90. Children welcome (under 10s free in parents room, no cot available). Garden. Pets permitted. Open all year. MasterCard, Visa, Laser. **Directions:** From Wexford, R733 to Arthurstown via Wellingtonbridge; from Waterford, take Passage East-Ballyhack car ferry - coming off ferry turn right. House 1km on left.

BUNCLODY

Situated seven miles from Enniscorthy, the picturesque town of Bunclody is set in wonderful rolling countryside on the edge of the Hall-Dare estate, with magnificent parkland and riverside walks along the River Slaney. Quietly located at the base of Mount Leinster, away from the bigger towns, with walking, fishing and a number of equestrian centres nearby which offer countryside treks for all standards, it is a place to enjoy the unspoilt countryside. The town is well known for the Eileen Aroon Festival during the months of July and August, and the wonderful Altamont Gardens (059 915 9444) are only a few miles away; officially open 9-7.30 daily, but a phone call to check is advised. Golfers will not have too far to travel to Enniscorthy Golf Club (053 923 3191), which is 18 holes, par 72-and is known for the high standard of its greens. At the top of main street, next to the Millrace Hotel, the contemporary **Bia Alainn Wine Pub & Brasserie** (053 9377725) is owned by the nearby Redmond's Pub and wine merchants (lovely old bar); a large, impressively appointed bar with a spacious dining area, it offers country portions of quality fare well cooked to order, including good fish. L&D daily.

Bunclody
HOTEL
R

Carlton Millrace Hotel

Carrigduff Bunclody Co Wexford **Tel: 053 937 5100**
info@millrace.ie www.millrace.ie

Ideally located for a break to explore this beautiful area, Bunclody is not much more than an hour's drive from either Dublin or Rosslare. This large hotel offers a wide range of facilities and, despite its size, is tucked quite neatly into a wooded site and does not dominate the village too much. Individually furnished guest rooms, suites and family apartments are spacious and comfortably furnished for leisure and business guests, and there are full spa facilities. A modern bar on the ground floor attracts local people as well as hotel guests, and there is an impressive restaurant at the top of the building, which overlooks the town and opens on to a balcony - very pleasant on a summer evening, and handy for smokers. There's salmon fishing on site, walking in parkland and the nearby hills, and a number of championship golf courses are within an hour's drive. **Rooms 60**. B&B from €39-99pps. Business facilities. Spa. Midweek specials from €129 (3 nights). Closed 24-27 Dec. MasterCard, Visa. **Directions:** On the N80 between Carlow and Enniscorthy. ◈

CAMPILE

The interest that will bring many to this attractive village is Kilmokea Gardens (051 388109), which are situated on the joint estuary of the Nore and the Barrow and cover almost three hectares; originally started in 1947, they include walled gardens designed as a series of rooms around the house, and host a wide selection of rare and tender trees and shrubs in the very different lower garden. Other local attractions include Duncannon Fort (051 389454, open June to September), and Ballyhack Castle (051 389 468); within a short drive you will also find many other places of historical and cultural interest. The village holds a Farmers' Market every Sunday.

Campile
COUNTRY HOUSE•CAFÉ

Kilmokea Country Manor & Gardens

Great Island Campile Co Wexford **Tel: 051 388 109**
kilmokea@eircom.net www.kilmokea.com

Mark and Emma Hewlett's peaceful and relaxing late Georgian country house is set in 7 acres of Heritage Gardens, including formal walled gardens. The house is elegantly and comfortably furnished, with a drawing room overlooking the Italian Loggia, an honesty library bar, and a restaurant in the dining room. The individually-designed and immaculately maintained bedrooms command lovely views over the gardens and towards the estuary beyond and in an adjoining coach house there are newer rooms and self-catering suites, with some offering a contemporary atmosphere. Mark and Emma continue with their ongoing programme of improvements to the property - there is now a tennis court and an indoor swimming pool, plus a gym and aromatherapy treatment rooms. And work continues on a large organic vegetable garden, planted in the traditional potager design. Dinner is cooked by Emma and served in the **Peacock Dining Room**, overlooking the lovely gardens at the back, and an unusually extensive wine list includes some real treats. Conferences/banqueting (60/55). **Rooms 6** (5 en-suite, 1 with private bathroom; 1 suite, 1 junior suite, 1 shower only, 2 ground floor, 1 family room, 1 disabled, all no smoking); children welcome (under 2s free in parents' room, cots available without charge; baby sitting arranged, playground, high chair, children's menu). Pets allowed in some areas by arrangement. B&B €95 pps; ss €30. Self-catering also available. Light meals in conservatory Pink Teacup Café, 10-5 daily when house and gardens are open; light lunch menu 12-3; gift shop. Open weekends only 5 Nov- 1 Feb. Gardens, fishing, tennis, croquet, walking; swimming pool, gym, mini-spa, aromatherapy. Amex, MasterCard, Visa, Laser. **Directions:** Take R733 south from New Ross to Ballyhack, signposted for Kilmokea Gardens.

Campile
RESTAURANT

The Shelburne
Main Street Campile New Ross Co Wexford
Tel: 051 593 030

Chef Denise Bradley, already well known in the area from her time as head chef at Sqigl in Duncannon, took over this neat restaurant in Campile village in 2007, and has continued to please her loyal following with its hospitable atmosphere and good cooking. It's a simple enough place: a rectangular room broken up by low room dividers has a little bar, tiled floor, white tablecloths and napkins, nightlights and plain good quality cutlery and glasses; but there's a speedy greeting on arrival, excellent breads served with pesto and a welcoming amuse-bouche, such as salmon & potato cake. Quite an extensive and wide ranging menu is offered and, of course, the seafood for which the area is well known is well respresented, and fish dishes are especially attractive: a dish of pan-fried Duncannon sea bass with fennel, in a crisp parmesan cheese crust with an aniseed cream sauce is a notable example – and there is plenty else to choose from including good steaks, tasty stuffed pork fillet, guinea fowl and duck. Presentation, on modern white plates of various shapes, is attractive - but portions are generous, so remember to save a little space for dessert: summer berry pudding, perhaps, or a very good chocolate fondant, and there are petits fours with the coffee too. **Seats 40** (private room 20); reservations advised; children welcome; air conditioning; toilets wheelchair accessible. D Wed-Sat, 5-9pm. Early bird D 5-6.55pm; also à la carte; house wine about €18. Closed Sun. MasterCard, Visa, Laser. **Directions:** In centre of Campile. ◇

Carne
RESTAURANT•CHARACTER PUB

The Lobster Pot
Ballyfane Carne Co Wexford
Tel: 053 913 1110

SEAFOOD BAR OF THE YEAR

Near Carnsore Point and just over 5 miles from Rosslare ferry port, Ciaran and Anne Hearne's handsome country pub, in elegant dark green with lots of well-maintained plants, is a welcome sight indeed. Inside the long, low building several interconnecting bar areas are furnished in simple, practical style, with sturdy furniture designed for comfortable eating. For fine summer days, there are picnic tables outside at the front. One room is a slightly more formal restaurant, but the atmosphere throughout is very relaxed and the emphasis is on putting local seafood to good use, providing good value and efficient service. Daily deliveries ensure fresh fish supplies and, the catch dictates daily specials. Simple but carefully prepared meals are served all day in the bar, typically including an outstanding seafood chowder (salmon, crab, prawns, cod, cockles & mussels in a rich fish base), a wild Irish smoked salmon platter and delicious fresh crab salad. An extensive laminated evening menu (with the names of 21 fish listed in eight different languages) offers treats like River Rush oysters and lobsters from the sea tank, crab mornay and, for non-seafood lovers, crispy duckling and various steaks, pork fillet and ever-popular rack of lamb. Friendly service, a relaxing atmosphere and carefully-prepared fresh food should ensure an enjoyable visit here - and, on Wednesday nights off-season (Sep-May), a special dinner menu offers great value. No reservations in high season (Jun-Aug) or bank hol weekends, so avoid busy times if possible. **Seats 100** (private rooms 16/28; outdoor seating, 20); children welcome, but not under 10 after 5pm; no reservations in high season (Jun-Aug) or bank hol weekends, so avoid busy times if possible. Bar menu Tue-Sat, 12-9 (to 8.30 Sun, 7.30 off-season). A la carte menu 6-9 (to 8.30 Sun, 7.30 off-season). Closed Mon except bank hols, 25 Dec, first 5 weeks of the year. Good Fri. MasterCard, Visa, Laser. **Directions:** 8km (5 m) south of Rosslare port; follow route to Carnsore Point.

Carne Area
RESTAURANT

Castleview Heights

Our Lady's Island Broadway Co Wexford
Tel: 053 913 1140

Set on a hill overlooking the old castle ruins and the pretty inlet around Our Lady's Island, this family-run restaurant is worth a stop on the way to or from Rosslare Harbour - not only is the food good, but the views are wonderful too. You can sit at a window table in the bright, spacious dining room, or on one of the outdoor seats, and watch the golfers while sipping a glass of wine or choosing from the tempting menu. Seafood features strongly, as you would expect, usually including a good house chowder, and a wide variety of fish and shellfish, including mussels, calamari, smoked salmon, sea bass and cod. Seafood salad includes a generous quantity of prawns, smoked salmon and an unusual hickory smoked trout. Home-made lasagne topped with Wexford Cheddar, steak, duckling and char-grilled chicken are the kind of non-fish meals you can expect, and there's a vegetarian option, a children's menu and a variety of freshly-made sandwiches. A short wine list includes some quarter bottles, also bottled beer. As well as the restaurant, there's a good craft shop - and crazy golf and an 18-hole Par-3 golf course are part of the business, so if you have time to spare before your ferry, you could happily while away an afternoon here. In good weather, there is a trampoline and bouncing castle to keep children amused too. **Seats 56** (outdoors, 16); toilets wheelchair accessible; children welcome (high chair, children's menu, baby changing facilities). Food served all day, 10-8.45pm (to 7.45pm Sun & Mon); à la carte. Set Sun L about €20; house wine about €18.50. Closed Mon-Thurs off-season. MasterCard, Visa, Laser. **Directions:** N25 Wexford to Rosslare, take right after Tagoat, to Our Lady's Island. 300m on right after village.

DUNCANNON

This small seaside town and fishing port is famous for its excellent fresh fish and seafood and, with a beautiful Blue Flag beach, it is a popular family holiday destination. It is dominated by Duncannon Fort (051 389454, open June to September), a star-shaped fort which was built in 1588 in expectation of an attack by the Spanish Armada. Cruises along the coast are available from the little harbour.

Duncannon
RESTAURANT WITH ROOMS

Aldridge Lodge

Duncannon New Ross Co Wexford **Tel: 051 389116**
info@aldridgelodge.com www.aldridgelodge.com

Euro-Toques chef Billy Whitty and his partner Joanne Harding's modern stone-fronted dormer home overlooks the picturesque fishing village of Duncannon, with lovely views of the beach and mountains - and has earned a well-deserved reputation for excellence in fine modern Irish cooking. The restaurant is bright and airy, with patio doors out onto a deck area, tables smartly set up with white linen runners and comfortable high-backed leather chairs. Billy's fine training shows through in the many delightful dishes on dinner menus which are changed daily and offer six or eight appealing dishes on each course, including steak, poultry and some imaginative vegetarian options, although the emphasis is on seafood. First-class ingredients are cooked with skill: a moist, flavourful and deliciously crumbly Hook Head crab cake with curried crème fraîche could make a wonderful starter, for example, and lobster is a treat of a main course, perfectly baked and served with pomme duchesse & a shot of lobster bisque; it is also very good value, attracting a mere €5 supplement on the (very reasonable) dinner menu. Soups, breads and side vegetables are all lovely, and a tasting plate of half a dozen desserts rounds off a meal here nicely. The wine list is sensibly limited and offers good value. **Seats 32** (outdoors, 12; private room, 14); reservations required. Children welcome before 7pm. D daily in summer, 6-9.30 (to 9pm Sun). Set D €38.50; à la carte; vegetarian menu also available. SC discretionary. Closed Mon (& Tues Sept-Jun), 24-28 Dec, 6-14 Jan. **Accommodation:** Three well-appointed bedrooms (one with full bath and shower, the others with shower only) are quiet and comfortable, with a residents' lounge area on the landing. *Aldridge Lodge was our Newcomer of the Year in 2006. Small conferences/banquets (30/34). **Rooms 3** (all en-suite, 2 shower only, 1 junior suite, all no smoking, 1 family room); not suitable for children under 7; turndown service; no pets. B&B €50 pps, no ss. Garden. Closed Mon (& Tues Sept-Jun), 24-28 Dec, 6-14 Jan. MasterCard, Visa, Laser. **Directions:** 1/4 mile outside Duncannon, overlooking beach on Fethard-on-Sea road.

Duncannon
RESTAURANT•BAR

Sqigl Restaurant & Roches Bar

Quay Road Duncannon New Ross Co Wexford **Tel: 051 389 188**
info@sqiglrestaurant.com www.rochesbar.com

Bob and Eileen Roche's fine traditional bar in the centre of Duncannon village serves the local community (and discerning visitors) well. There's an old bar at the front, pleasingly free of improvements, and it gradually develops more towards the back, which keeps the younger crowd and the oldies in their preferred spaces. The bar food menu offers a selection of starters, salads open sandwiches and popular hot dishes, plus some daily specials. There is something for everyone - and if the weather is fine, you can enjoy it out in the beer garden. Bar Food served 12.30-6 daily (to 7 Sun). Pub closed 25 Dec, Good Fri, 3-4 weeks Jan. **Restaurant:** Sqigl (pronounced Squiggle) is located in a converted barn beside the pub and is run by Bob and Eileen's daughter Cindy Roche, supported by head chef Aidan Kelly, who is cooking interesting dishes with confidence - his fish dishes, especially, are accurately cooked, flavoursome and nicely presented, and local seafood is the star here: a lovely summer dish, for example, might be seared monkfish wrapped in Seranno ham, with marjoram, summer greens and parmesan butter. Sqigl aims to make the most of local produce and does it well with a sensibly limited menu (with full credit to suppliers), featuring not only the white fish landed at the harbour round the corner, but also Wexford beef and lamb – and a short vegetarian menu is also offered. Decor is light, bright and modern and the cooking style is modern too, except that portions are aimed at hearty Wexford appetites: flavoursome Duncannon seafood chowder with crème fraîche, for example, makes a substantial starter. An early dinner menu offers really good value, and the à la carte dinner menu is also very fairly priced. Well-made classic desserts will round off a good meal nicely and, together with good cooking and caring service from a friendly and efficient front of house team under Cindy's supervision, Sqigl offers a very attractive package. The wine list is not overlong but offers quality and value to match the food, and includes a fair choice of half bottles and wines by the glass. **Seats 36** (outside seating, 12); reservations advised. D Tue-Sat, 7-9.30; 2/3 course early D €24/28, Tue-Wed 7-8pm; house wines from €17.50. Bar food served daily, 12.30-6pm (to 7pm Sun). Restaurant closed Sun (except bank hol Suns), Mon (& Tue off-season), 24-27 Dec & 3-4 weeks in Jan. MasterCard, Visa, Laser. **Directions:** R733 from Wexford & New Ross. Centre of village.

R # ENNISCORTHY

The aptly named **Riverside Park Hotel** (Tel 053 92 37800; www.riversideparkhotel.com) has a pleasant riverside path in a linear park beside the hotel, this can be a useful place to break a journey to stretch the legs and have a bite. If you enjoy finding an unusual place to stay, **Woodbrook** (053 925 5114; www.woodbrookhouse.ie) is a large late Georgian house a few miles from Enniscorthy which is open for guests in the summer months; set in its own parkland under the Blackstairs Mountains, it is owned by the FitzHerbert family and is known for its spectacular 'flying' spiral staircase. The Irish Green Gathering (www.irishgreengathering.com) is held at Woodbrook House (in August, and the Blackstairs Opera is also held there, in July. There is a particularly good Farmers' Market every Saturday (the Abbey Square Carpark, 9am-2pm). Nearby, The Bay Garden (Camolin, 053 938 3349) is a series of contrasting gardens, each beautifully conceived and wonderfully planted, and well worth a visit.
WWW-IRELAND-GUIDE.COM FOR ALL THE BEST PLACES TO EAT, DRINK & STAY

Enniscorthy
COUNTRY HOUSE

Ballinkeele House

Ballymurn Enniscorthy Co Wexford **Tel: 053 913 8105**
john@ballinkeele.com www.ballinkeele.com

Set in 350 acres of parkland, game-filled woods and farmland, this historic house is a listed building; designed by Daniel Robertson, it has been the Maher family home since it was built in 1840 and remains at the centre of their working farm. It is a grand house, with a lovely old cut-stone stable yard at the back and some wonderful features, including a lofty columned hall with a big open fire in the colder months, and beautifully proportioned reception rooms with fine ceilings and furnishings which have changed very little since the house was built. Nevertheless, it is essentially a family home and has a refreshingly hospitable and down-to-earth atmosphere. Large bedrooms are furnished with antiques and have wonderful countryside views - all are large and comfortably furnished but one has been upgraded to a more luxurious standard, and now has a bath and shower. Margaret, who is a keen cook and a member of Euro-Toques, enjoys preparing 4-course dinners for guests (nice little wine list to accompany too). There's croquet on the lawn, a long sandy beach nearby at Curracloe, and bicycles (and wellingtons!) are available for guests' use; horse riding, fishing and golf can be organised nearby - and work continues in the leisure grounds: two walled gardens are under restoration (the smaller for flowers and the larger one the orchard and vegetables), and a recently completed lake is to be stocked for coarse fishing. **Rooms 5** (all en-suite, 2 shower only, 1 family, all no smoking); children welcome (cot available, €15). No pets. B&B €85 pps; ss €20. Residents Set D €45 at 7.30 (book by 11am); house wine from €19.50. Private parties up to 14. Garden. Closed 30 Nov - 1 Feb. MasterCard, Visa, Laser. **Directions:** From Wexford N11, north to Oilgate Village, turn right at signpost, follow to next signpost.

Enniscorthy
RESTAURANT

Via Veneto

58 Weafer Street Enniscorthy Co Wexford **Tel: 053 923 6929**
reservations@viaveneto.ie www.viaveneto.ie

Just off the main square in Enniscorthy, you'll encounter the unexpected - an authentic Italian restaurant, run by Paolo Fresilli, who is President of the Irish Delegation of the Italian Chefs' Federation, no less. It's buzzy and homely Italian in style, and with the ingredients they prize, wines and Italian liqueurs all on shelves open to view; the welcome is warm and efficient, white clothed tables are simply laid and a generous basket of good bread is left on the table throughout the meal, along with two carafes of home-flavoured olive oils to dress your salad to taste. As you'd expect, the menu is divided into antipasti, pasta, main dishes, pizza, and also an intriguing page of house specials for each course, all written in Italian, with accurate descriptions in English; you'll find dishes here that rarely feature on Irish/Italian menus, and top quality Italian cheese, salami, cured hams and other speciality foods feature. With seating for over 60, it's broken up into 3 areas by a central bar and semi-open kitchen. This is a hive of good-humoured activity and the three chefs cook everything to order. Dishes are prepared and served Italian-style without fussy presentation: a salami selection with marinated olives comes simply but stylishly on a wooden platter, for example, and the emphasis is on good cooking and real flavour; gnocchi comes with delicious gorgonzola cheese, sage & cream, and jump in the mouth veal rolls with sage and parma ham are cooked in a rich white wine and olive oil sauce, then served with mashed potatoes - wonderful. The dessert menu offers home-made traditional delights like ice creams, tiramisu, Italian meringues, gateaux, biscotti and amaretti. An all-Italian wine list offers over 120 wines, including some special bottles and many more affordable wines. The locals have taken this place (which is very family friendly) to heart, so it's wise to make a reservation - especially if you want to dine after 7.30 or 8.00 pm. *A sister retaurant Il Veliero (see entry) has recently opened in Waterford. **Seats 72** (private room, 20); children welcome (high chair, baby changing facilities); toilets wheelchair accessible; D Wed-Mon, 5.30-10pm (from 5pm Sun). Closed Tue. MasterCard, Visa, Laser. **Directions:** Enniscorthy centre, market square.

Enniscorthy Area Monart Destination Spa

HOTEL•RESTAURANT The Still Enniscorthy Co Wexford **Tel: 053 923 8999**

info@monart.ie www.monart.ie

Arriving at Monart's imposing gates, you get a sense that something quite special lies inside this private estate. From the welcome you receive through the intercom to the porter awaiting your arrival at the main house, the valet parking, front desk hospitality and personal tour, checking in is one immense pleasure. The handsome facade of the original house, completed in 1740, belies the magnificent architectural feat of glass and wood that snakes behind it into the surrounding woodlands. Despite the striking contemporary design, the hotel and spa marries seamlessly with the wonderful old trees and cleverly landscaped areas that succeed in bringing nature up close to every window. A leaf motif features subtly throughout the hotel - from the ornate bedroom balconies to the table lamps, and the bedroom prints to the faux topiary balls that stand sentinel on the ground floor - reflecting the mature 100-acre estate outdoors. Monart is a destination spa and guests are encouraged to lounge in fluffy gowns during the day. Despite the spa being large, therapist treatments must be booked well in advance, especially at weekends where guests are limited to two each. Access to the impressive thermal suite, which includes nine unique experiences, including a caldarium, hammam and salt grotto, is complimentary for all guests however, as is the relaxation room with juices, fruit and newspapers. Away from the spa, the old house retains its elegant proportions and is accessed from the main hotel through a bold glass corridor. Its reception rooms have all been tricked out in dramatic décor and guests are encouraged to enjoy the space, whether taking afternoon tea in the conservatory, reading papers in the drawing room or playing chess in the library. Upstairs, two private suites enjoy extra grand proportions, although Monart's standard bedrooms, all in the new extension, are extremely roomy and spacious. Request the back bedrooms and you'll enjoy glorious views of the trees and lake, all of which are imaginatively lit by night. The rooms feature a curious blend of French-influenced furniture and more modern pieces while Egyptian cotton sheets, stacks of pillows, a flat screen TV, DVD and CD players and individual balconies and a pale palette make for a comfy, relaxing space. Extra large bathrooms are impressive with good mirrors, a large shower, separate double-ended bath, bespoke local Kiltrea pottery washbasins and lovely Damana herbal toiletries. Breakfast, served in the rather lavish formal dining room, is an impressive affair - the egg dishes especially worthy of praise. A bistro-style menu is offered all day in the Garden Lounge, where guests may eat outdoors enjoying the lakeside setting and resident cheeky ducks. By night, this space becomes an intimate lounge for casual dining or a relaxing nightcap. The casual Spa Café serves lighter fare, and a more limited menu, although it is conveniently located next to the relaxation rooms. The estate boasts miles of marked walks, allowing you take in the fresh country air and tranquillity of the area. **Rooms 70** (2 suites, all executive & no smoking); not suitable for children; broadband wi/fi; lift; B&B about €230 pps, ss €40. Garden, fitness room, destination spa, indoor 'pool, walking, hairdressing, massage. **The Restaurant:** Special attention has been paid to Monart's elegant fine dining restaurant which opens each evening for dinner, as well as for Sunday lunch, and welcomes non-residents. Opulent chandeliers, crisp linen, large tables and a curving organic roof make this a glamorous space for the sophisticated cooking. Good breads and an exciting amuse bouche - perhaps a smoked eel raviolo - alert diners to Brendan Byrne's creative approach in the kitchen, where quality seasonal produce is imaginatively prepared. Seasonal meat and seafood dishes are given a classic twist, with Spa dishes highlighted for those looking for lighter, healthier options. Food is beautifully presented, service is smooth and informed, and though the wine list is expensive, there is value to be found from a dozen house wines. **Seats 105**; non residents welcome by reservation; L&D daily. Closed 24-27 Dec. Amex, MasterCard, Visa, Laser. **Directions:** N11 from Dublin, then right on to N80, first left and follow the signs.

Foulksmills Horetown House

HISTORIC HOUSE Foulksmills Co Wexford **Tel: 051 565 633**

info@horetownhouse.ie www.horetownhouse.ie

Situated in beautiful unspoilt rolling pastures about 20 minutes from Wexford town (and half an hour from Waterford), this 18th century house has recently undergone extensive restoration and refurbishment. Untidy grounds and a rather bleak exterior may make a bad first impression, so a spacious, comfortable hallway, with fine reception rooms off it and a genuine period feel, will come as a pleasant surprise. Having been thoroughly renovated, furnished and decorated with some style, the interior now offers a good level of comfort. Public rooms, which include a drawing room and a private dining room, are well furnished in period style and arriving guests are shown into a large comfortable sitting-room and made welcome with tea and home-made bonne bouches. The ten bedrooms, which vary considerably according to their position in the house, are individually decorated rooms and named after historic figures associated with the house; accommodation includes some suites, with jacuzzi bath and sitting room. **The Cellar** restaurant offers both lunch and dinner but it would be advisable to check as, in the Guide's experience, meals, including dinner, may instead be served in a ground floor dining room overlooking the rural landscape. Ongoing work is being undertaken to develop a garden. Small conferences/banqueting (50/75); free broadband wi/fi; **Rooms 10** (3 suites, 3 executive, 2 family, 3 shower only, 5 ground floor, 4 disabled); children welcome (under 5s free in parents room, cot available free of charge, baby sitting arranged); No lift; Limited room service; B&B €160 pps, ss €40. dogs permitted, staying in outhouse/kennel. Equestrian, fishing and golf nearby. Garden, walking, massage, beauty treatments. MasterCard, Visa, Laser. **Directions:** N25 from Wexford, turn for Taghmon, in Taghmon take turn for Foulksmills, approx. 4km turn right immediately after bridge.

R # GOREY

Conveniently situated mid-way between Dublin and Wexford, and now by-passed which makes it a much more enjoyable place to be, Gorey is an attractive town with many interesting old shop fronts and good shopping. It is handy to the many sandy beaches for which the area is famous, and close to the fishing village of Courtown, where swimming and other watersports are available. The **Ashdown Park Hotel** (053 948 0500; www.ashdownparkhotel.com) offers quality accommodation and good facilities including a Leisure Centre; a smart sister hotel **Amber Springs Hotel & Health Spa** (053 948 4000; www.ambersspringshotel.ie) has more recently opened on the edge of Gorey; within easy walking distance of the town centre, it makes a very comfortable place to stay. Nearby, Courtown Harbour is a popular family resort with an attractive harbour, and walks in the surrounding countryside. Near Gorey, **Seafield Hotel & Spa** (053 942 4000; www.seafieldhotel.com) has golf, good facilities and frequent special offers. Gorey has a vibrant cultural life and their Summer Theatre (www.GoreyTheatre.com) is among the many events taking place each year, with twice weekly performances at Gorey Little Theatre in July and August. Molumney Art Centre is open daily in summer. Numerous other activities available locally include championship standard golf, walking, watersports, horse riding and angling. For garden lovers, there is a Garden Festival in June, and the Ram House Gardens at Coolgreany (0402 37238) are a 'must visit'; The Ram family were responsible for the layout of Gorey, and the remains of Bishop Thomas Ram are buried in the Old Cemetery in the Market Square.
WWW-IRELAND-GUIDE.COM FOR ALL THE BEST PLACES TO EAT, DRINK & STAY

Gorey
COUNTRY HOUSE•RESTAURANT

Marlfield House
Courtown Road Gorey Co Wexford **Tel: 053 942 1124**
info@marlfieldhouse.ie www.marlfieldhouse.com

Often quoted as 'the luxury country house hotel par excellence', this impressive house was once the residence of the Earls of Courtown, and is now an elegant oasis of unashamed luxury offering outstanding hospitality and service, where guests are cosseted and pampered in sumptuous surroundings. It was first opened as an hotel in 1978 by Mary and Ray Bowe who have lavished care and attention on this fine property ever since - imposing gates, a wooded drive, antiques and glittering chandeliers all promise guests a very special experience - and their daughters Margaret and Laura Bowe now continue the family tradition of hospitality. The interior is luxurious in the extreme, with accommodation including six very grand state rooms, but the gardens are also a special point of interest: there is a lake and wildfowl reserve, a formal garden, kitchen garden, and beautiful woodland with extensive woodland walks - and a number of gardens open to the public are within easy access, including Ram House, Mount Usher, Powerscourt, Altamont and Kilmokea. Conference/banqueting (30/40); broadband wi/fi; secretarial services. Dogs may be permitted by arrangement. Children welcome by prior arrangement (under 2s free in parents room, cots available without charge, baby sitting arranged). Tennis, cycling, walking, croquet, garden. Golf nearby. Heli-pad. **Rooms 20** (6 state rooms, 14 superior, 8 ground floor, all no smoking). B&B €140pps, ss €17.50. Room service (limited hours). Closed Jan & Feb. **Restaurant:** Dining is always an exceptional experience in Marlfield's fine restaurant, where the graceful dining room and Turner-style conservatory merge into one, allowing views out across the gardens, including a fine kitchen garden that is a delight to the eye and provides a wide range of fresh produce for the restaurant. The conservatory, with its hanging baskets, plants and fresh flowers (not to mention the occasional statue), is one of the most romantic spots in the whole of Ireland, further enhanced at night by candlelight, a wonderful setting in which to enjoy chef Colin Byrne's accomplished cooking. His strongly seasonal menus are changed daily and outline the produce available in the kitchen garden (which remains Ray Bowe's particular point of pride, even though he has officially retired), and the origin of other ingredients used. Although contemporary in style and presentation, there is a strong classical background to the cooking, and it is all the better for that. Specialities that indicate the style include a delicious starter of quail with poached beans and apple butter, or Marlfield's classic chicken liver parfait with apple and tarragon jelly and toasted brioche; the aged Wexford rib-eye of beef is served with a fine béarnaise sauce, a deliciously-herbed mash and perfectly cooked seasonal vegetables from the garden (crunchy sugar snap peas, tiny sautéed white turnips and baby leeks). Fish lovers should be delighted with dishes like a perfectly cooked and crisp (skin-side breaded) cod fillet, served on a pea and potato purée and accompanied by tiny braised Little Gem lettuces. The ready supply of fresh garden produce inspires imaginative vegetarian choices too, and lovely puds tend to reflect the best fruit in season at the time; alternatively, a cheese selection from Sheridan's cheesemongers is served with a delectable little salad, caramelised walnuts and apple cider jelly. Then it's off to the drawing room for coffee and petits fours to round off the feast. Very professional service is a match for this fine food and an informative wine list, long on burgundies and clarets, offers a wine of the month, a page of special recommendations and a very good selection of half bottles. Although not inexpensive, a meal here is always a treat and good value for the quality of food and service; the early dinner menu and Sunday lunch offer outstanding value. **Seats 90** (private room, 20; outdoor,20); not suitable for children under 8 at D; reservations advised; air conditioning; toilets wheelchair accessible. D daily, 7-9 (Sat to 10, Sun to 8); L Sun only 12.30-2. Value D €45 (Sun-Thu, 7-8pm), also à la carte; Set Sun L €45. House wine €31. SC 12.5% for parties 6+. Light à la carte lunches are served daily in Library, 12.30-5. Amex, Diners, MasterCard, Visa, Laser. **Directions:** 2km outside Gorey - exit 23 N11, left at Courtown roundabout and follow signs.

Gorey
CAFÉ
R

Partridges Artisan Café & Fine Food Shop

93 Main Street Gorey Co Wexford **Tel: 053 948 4040**
christian@partridgelodge.com www.partridgelodge.com

A culinary focul point in the bustling town of Gorey, this centrally located daytime café is a buzzy place, popular with locals and visitors alike. It is located at the back of a speciality food shop selling artisan foods from Ireland and beyond, and there will be plenty to tempt you on your way in and out - ingredients used in the café are on sale in the shop, which is useful for picking up a picnic. The menu features simple, unpretentious dishes that allow the high quality of the ingredients to take pride of place - enjoy, amongst other treats, good soups served with freshly home-baked bread, unusual pasta dishes, tasty savoury tarts, flavoursome salads, an excellent farmhouse cheese and oatcake plate, and an enticing selection of home-baked cakes and tarts. There is a coffee menu and a short "by the glass" wine list. It does get busy (especially at lunchtime), but service is friendly and willing. Good value considering the high quality of the food. **Seats 30**; children welcome (high chair); no reservations accepted; open all day Mon-Sat, 10am-7pm (to 9pm Fri/Sat); D Fri-Sat only, 7-9pm; house wine from €6 per glass. Closed Sun. MasterCard, Visa, Laser. **Directions:** Main Street Gorey town.

Gorey
RESTAURANT
N R

Portofino

18 Main Street Gorey Co Wexford **Tel: 053 948 0808**
www.portofinorestaurant.ie

This pleasant, casual, family-friendly restaurant offers Italian style, a real Italian menu, and authentic ingredients, together with genuine home cooking and good service. You arrive up the stairs into a bar area dressed up to look like an Italian street (complete with an Italian grandmother overlooking all from a little balcony high over the tables); a bit kitsch but it's all good fun and it's the sort of place where you can drop in for a quick bite or linger a while over the wine list, which is devoted to Italian wine. The long opening hours are bonus for travellers, but street parking is difficult until after 6pm (nearby supermarket carparks are the alternative). Open 7 days 12 noon -10.30 (Sat 11pm). Early dinner menu 4-7 pm. MasterCard, Visa, Laser. **Directions:** Well signed (above Malocca's café) on the main street of Gorey, with separate entrance.

Gorey Area

Seafield Hotel & Oceo Spa

HOTEL

Ballymoney Gorey Co Wexford **Tel: 053 942 4000**
sales@seafieldhotel.com www.seafieldhotel.com

Set in lush parkland adjacent to Seafield Golf Club with its 18-hole Peter McAvoy-designed course, this modern hotel enjoys a fine location with views of Irish Sea. It is a stylish property with extensive facilities, including a spa, and luxurious contemporary accommodation; some rooms have terraces and all are furnished to a high standard with very comfortable beds and many extras, including complimentary WiFi, and well-designed bathrooms with bath and monsoon shower. Although a very popular short break destination (it is only about an hour from south Dublin), it is also well equipped for business and conferences. **Rooms 265**. B&B from about €85pps. Spa, golf (18), walking. Amex, MasterCard, Visa, Laser. **Directions:** On coast north of Gorey, signed from N11. ◊

Gorey Area

Woodlands Country House

COUNTRY HOUSE

Killineirin Gorey Co Wexford **Tel: 040 237 125**
info@woodlandscountryhouse.com www.woodlandscountryhouse.com

John and Philomena O'Sullivan's charming creeper-clad mid-19th country house between Inch and Gorey is surrounded by two acres of mature gardens and, with woodlands, a river, a small lake and lots of seated areas to relax in, it is ideal for a quiet break. Once the home of a prominent Wexford miller, there is also has a fine cut-stone courtyard and the house has retained its period features; now, with antique furnishings and big log fires, it is a delightful place to be – and the O'Sullivans are hospitable people who like nothing better than to share the history of their home with interested guests, and to help them to plan outings and get the best out of their time exploring the surrounding area. The six en-suite bedrooms are all very comfortably furnished, with power showers and toiletries, electric blankets for chilly nights and tea/coffee trays among the facilities. And you'll enjoy good food here too – tea or coffee and home-made scones are offered on arrival, and a good breakfast is served in the sunny dining room, overlooking the back garden. With woodland and river walks and a tennis court on site, and hill walking and beaches only a short drive, this is a lovely place to relax. **Rooms 6** (all en suite & no smoking, 1 single); children welcome (under 2s free in parents room, cot available free of charge); free broadband wi/fi; no dogs permitted in house but may stay in outhouse/kennel. B&B €55 pps; ss €15. Garden, walking, tennis, pool table. Horse racing, fishing (fly) and equestrian nearby. Closed 1 Oct - 1 May. MasterCard, Visa, Laser. **Directions:** 1.5km (1 mile) off the N11 north of Gorey (N11).

KILMORE QUAY

This picturesque fishing village is noted for its thatched cottages, as a base for sea angling and for the Maritime Museum (053 912 9655) in the harbour, which is housed in a lightship - the Guillemot - previously used by Irish Lights, and still with all the original cabin furniture and fittings. It is a popular place for family holidays, and accommodation in the village includes the **Hotel Saltees** (053 912 9601; www.hotelsaltees.ie) a modest, friendly, two-star hotel, offering comfortable accommodation at moderate prices; lovers of Thai food should enjoy it here as Lek Phikhrohkan took over the kitchen shortly before going to press, and she is an authentic Thai chef. There are several attractive pubs and restaurants in the village, notably the characterful **Kehoe's Pub & Maritime Heritage Centre** (053 912 9830), which is home to many fascinating marine artefacts. The area around Kilmore Quay has many unspoilt beaches which offer miles of the finest sand dunes in the south-east, and the nearby Saltee Islands are home to Ireland's largest bird sanctuary.
WWW-IRELAND-GUIDE.COM FOR ALL THE BEST PLACES TO EAT, DRINK & STAY

Kilmore Quay

Kilmore Quay Guest House

GUESTHOUSE

Quay Road Kilmore Quay Co Wexford **Tel: 053 912 9988**
quayhome@iol.ie www.quayhouse.net

Siobhan McDonnell's pristine guesthouse is centrally located in the village and is especially famous for its support of sea angling and diving; an annexe is especially geared for anglers with drying/storage room, fridges and freezers, live bait and tackle sales. Packed lunches can be provided and non-residents are welcome for breakfast The overall tone is practical: the whole place is ship shape, with attractive, slightly nautical bedrooms ("a place for everything and everything in its place"), practical pine floors and neat en-suite rooms (most shower only). **Rooms 7** (all en-suite, 4 shower-only). B&B €50 pps. Children welcome (under 2s free in parents' room, cots available without charge). Pets by arrangement. Garden. Walking; cycling. *Self-catering also available. Open all year. MasterCard, Visa, Laser. **Directions:** Wexford 14 miles, Rosslare Ferry route.

Kilmore Quay

RESTAURANT

Le Poisson D'Or

Kilmore Quay Co Wexford **Tel: 053 914 8853**
www.lepoissondor.ie

Although it is not inspiring from the outside, this new restaurant over the Seaview Fish Shop is well worth investigation - and those who know Dominic Dayot's cooking, with its subtle flavourings and well-chosen combinations, will soon be beating a path to the door. Once inside, it is quite small and narrow, but dark wood and light coloured walls, soft music and local paintings for sale give it an unexpected feeling of luxury; pristine white-clothed tables, with classy settings and leather chairs set the tone for a serious restaurant - and, with the sea and the beautiful Saltees Islands framed in two large porthole windows, a restaurant with one of the best views of any in Ireland. Friendly local staff show you to your table, where iced water, bread and butter balls are quickly served. The menu may surprise fans on first reading but, like the restaurant itself, the food on the plate will come up trumps. A wide-ranging choice includes a good few crowd-pleasers and there is something to please all palates, but the star turn is local fish cooked perfectly and at a reasonable price. You might start with a delicious special of belly of pork with champ mash & shallot jus, or mussels in cream with shallot and spices, as fresh as could be. A main course of Slaney Valley fillet of beef, with foie gras, onion marmalade, aubergine caviar and brandy cream will be excellent, if expensive, but a quaintly named and beautifully presented "rendezvous of the sea" is more kindly priced and comes with salmon, cod, lemon sole, and prawns in a basil cream sauce; a dish to remember with each fish perfectly cooked. Side dishes of fresh vegetables and, perhaps, Lyonnaise potatoes, accompany and you could finish with a classic chocolate bavarois or carrot cake and toffee sauce. The wine list covers all major regions of the world, and wines by the glass are served in dinky little decanters. Get there before the crowds. **Seats 40**; children welcome before 7.30pm (high chair, childrens menu); open for L & D Tue-Sun, 12-5pm & 6-9.15pm; ample car parking across the road. Closed Mon, 25-26 Dec; 2 weeks in mid-Jan. MasterCard, Visa, Laser. **Directions:** Above Seaview Fish Shop.

Kilmore Quay

RESTAURANT

The Silver Fox Seafood Restaurant

Kilmore Quay Co Wexford **Tel: 053 912 9888**
info@thesilverfox.ie www.thesilverfox.ie

This well-known restaurant was originally established in 1991 and, has been under the direction of proprietors Shane Carroll and Gopal Kawendar since 2006. Gopal is the head chef, and he is serving interesting local fish dishes with flavourings from South East Asia. The three rooms are simply decorated, with cream walls allowing an uncluttered background for nautical paintings by local artist Ivan Sutton (all for sale). An extensive (perhaps over-extensive) à la carte menu is offered and, although fresh fish is the main focus, steaks, lamb, duck and chicken dishes also feature, so there is something for everyone. The cooking is reliable and, except for the Asian flavourings in some dishes which set this restaurant apart, food is quite straightforward: crab with Marie Rose sauce, cod fillet with chive cream sauce, and pan-fried fillet of plaice are all typical. Prices tend to be on the high side considering the easy availability of fresh fish, but the early bird menu is interesting and it represents good value. Staff are very pleasant and knowledgable, and there is a short wine list of 10 whites and 10 reds appropriate for the style of food (with plans to increase the list). Private room (30); children welcome (high chair, children's menu, baby changing facilities); toilets wheelchair accessible; air conditioning. Open daily, 12.30-9.30pm. Sun L €24.95; early bird D €25, 12.30-7pm. House wine €19.95; sc discretionary. Closed Feb. Diners, MasterCard, Visa, Laser. **Directions:** 20 min. drive from Rosslare ferry, Wexford Town and Ballyhack ferry.

NEW ROSS

This old town on the estuary of the River Barrow has much of interest to the visitor - especially, of course, its key attraction, the recreation of the nineteenth century sailing ship the SS Dunbrody (South Quay, 051 425 239). For good food and good value (even if the exterior and carpark are a little rough), head to **The Hillside Bar** (051 421 155) Camblin, which serves hearty carvery lunches that regulars are happy to queue for, and more sophisticated evening menus. For comfortable accommodation in a pleasant environment, the **Brandon House Hotel** (Tel 051 421 703; www.brandonhousehotel.ie), just outside the town, is on a hillside site with river views; it has been developed around a house of character and offers some surprises (including an interesting art collection) as well as much-needed facilities (conference; leisure centre; new spa). Signage from the road can be a little off-putting, but it is worth going up the drive to take a closer look. The Kennedy Centre and Arboretum (051 388 171) just a few miles from the centre of New Ross are well worth a visit; you can picnic in the gardens or just stroll around many acres of parkland. New Ross is an ideal base for taking in a drive around the scenic Ring of Hook which features many historical sites including Dunbrody Abbey, Tintern Abbey and The Hook Lighthouse. The famous and reputedly haunted Loftus Hall is also located nearby. There are also many fine beaches and many other activities such as angling and charters, diving and snorkelling, canoeing, windsurfing, golf and river cruises (Galley River Cruises; 051 421723). Possible outings for garden lovers include Kilmokea Gardens (Campile, 051 388 109), which is made up of seven acres of Heritage Gardens There is a Farmers' Market every Saturday (The Quay, 9am-2pm). **WWW-IRELAND-GUIDE.COM FOR ALL THE BEST PLACES TO EAT, DRINK & STAY Directions:**

New Ross	Café Nutshell
CAFÉ	In A Nutshell 8 South Street New Ross Co Wexford **Tel: 051 422 777**
	inanutshell8@gmail.com

A walk through the town to find Philip and Patsy Rogers' Emporium will be very rewarding for lovers of good food. The concept is a natural evolution from Philip's background in farming, and Patsy's love of cooking: traditional country methods, handed down recipes and a respect for fresh produce are at the heart of this delightful shop and café, where everything is freshly made every day - and 'chemically treated or pre-prepared foods are not welcome'. Choose from a wide range of delicious freshly-prepared dishes beginning with delicious breakfasts and fresh bakes for elevenses, then moving on to soups, panini, wraps and ciabattas, warm salads, quiche of the day, and classic platters (fresh seafood, charcuterie, Irish farmhouse cheese) - and lots of other seasonal produce - and, perhaps, a perfectly brewed Illy coffee - then take time to browse around the shop, which has a vast range of goodies to take home, including complimentary medicines like homeopathic and herbal remedies. Anyone staying in self-catering accommodation in the area should also check out the food to go, which offers the same high standards of genuinely home-cooked foods that Patsy serves in the café. A little treasure. **Seats 50**; air conditioning; no reservations; children welcome (supervised). Open Mon-Sat 9-5.30, L 12.30-3.30pm; house wine €20. Closed Sun, (& Mon Oct-May), 1 week May, Oct & Jan. MasterCard, Visa, Laser. **Directions:** Town centre.

New Ross	Greenpark
B&B	Creakan New Ross Co Wexford **Tel: 051 421 028**
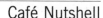	creakan@hotmail.com

Greenpark is an immaculately maintained family-run B&B in a quiet rural location two miles outside New Ross, and convenient to a number of the area's tourist attractions. You'll receive a warm welcome from John and Annette Kinsella, and it makes a good choice for anyone seeking the genuine experience of staying in a family home and enjoying the peace of the countryside. Bedrooms are compact, but well-equipped, warm, and comfortable and there's a guest sitting room; the gardens are sheltered, well-planted and maintained, making a good spot for relaxing in summer. Breakfast, offering variations on the traditional Irish, is freshly cooked and generous. **Rooms 3** (2 en-suite, 1 with private bathroom). B&B from €33pps, ss €12. **Directions:** Leave N25 at New Ross; onto R733, Greenpark is 4km on left. Well signed.

ROSSLARE & AREA

Ireland's Euro Port (ferry terminal, 053 916 1560) is also a seaside resort, with a magnificent beach and a 27-hole links golf course (053 913 2203). The Rosslare area is well-placed for exploring the southeast coast, and is within easy reach of Carne and Kilmore Quay. Local activities include golf, fishing, watersports and horse riding along miles of sandy beaches. Local attractions include Yola Farmstead Folk Park (091 32610, open March to November), Our Lady's Island (053 913 1167), and Tacumskin Windmill.

Rosslare Area
COUNTRY HOUSE

Churchtown House

Tagoat Rosslare Co Wexford **Tel: 053 913 2555**

info@churchtownhouse.com www.churchtownhouse.com

Although situated very near the coast, Patricia and Austin Cody's fine Georgian house is set in about eight and a half acres of wooded gardens and makes an ideal destination for anyone seeking rural tranquillity. The house dates back to 1703 but it has been completely renovated and elegantly furnished by the Codys, to make a comfortable country house retreat: spacious sitting rooms have antique furniture and open fires, and the large bedrooms are equally pleasing, with generous beds, phones, TV and well-finished bathrooms... it would make a beautifully relaxing base for a few days exploring the area, and there is no shortage of things to do. Golfers have no less than six championship links and parkland courses to choose from (two are only a few minutes' drive away), for example, sea and shore angling are a big attraction, also walking the long sandy beaches, and horse riding - there's a choice of equestrian centres nearby. And there's so much to visit too - the great Victorian revival Johnstown Castle and demesne is not to be missed, for example, also unspoilt Hook Head and the Hook Lighthouse which are just a short drive away, and there's much more besides. The Codys are renowned for their hospitality and, if you're lucky enough to arrive at this well-run house at around teatime, you'll be served delicious home-made cake and tea in the drawing room - other edible highlights include the fine Irish breakfast served in the bright dining room, also home-cooked dinners, which are available to residents by arrangement. Mid-week breaks, weekends and golf breaks all offer very good value. **Rooms 12** (2 junior suite, 3 executive, 6 shower only, all no smoking, 1 family room); children welcome (under 3s free in parents' room, cot available, €15). Pets permitted in certain areas (dog run); free broadband wi/fi. Garden. Dining room closed Sun-Mon. House closed Nov - Mar. MasterCard, Visa, Laser. **Directions:** On R736, 1km (half mile) from N25, at Tagoat.

Rosslare Strand
HOTEL•RESTAURANT

Kelly's Resort Hotel & Spa

Rosslare Co Wexford **Tel: 053 913 2114**

info@kellys.ie www.kellys.ie

With its special brand of relaxed professionalism, the Kelly family's renowned beachside hotel sums up all that is best about the sunny south-east for many regular visitors. Perhaps it's because its history in the same family spans three centuries, so there's not a lot they don't know about keeping guests happy - quite simply, the hotel has everything, for both individuals and families. Its special qualities are so wide-ranging that it's hard to know where to begin - will it be with the stunning art collection they have built up over the years, the exceptional leisure and pampering facilities (constantly updated), or perhaps the unusual amount of 'personal space' offered in a series of comfortable lounging areas around the hotel; for some, the highlight of the hotel is the two excellent restaurants (see below). It's known as the 'hotelier's hotel' because so many others in the hospitality industry choose to come here to relax (praise indeed!) and, along with exceptional hospitality (and a no conference/event policy), its key appeal is that there is genuinely something for everybody, so people with different interests can do their own thing (or nothing at all) then meet up with friends and family over dinner to chat about their day. In summer it's the in-place for family holidays - there's a crèche, playroom and a children's playground - but people travelling without children will be glad to know that the number permitted at any one time is limited, to prevent creating an imbalance. Many of the bedrooms have sea views (the best have balconies), and even now, when so there is so much competition between hotels to offer the best leisure facilities, Kellys remains right up there at the top, with two indoor swimming pools, a 'SeaSpa' well-being centre (11 treatment rooms, seawater vitality pool, steam room, rock sauna and much else besides), indoor tennis, and - a bit of fun for Francophiles - boules. Lots to do nearby too, including golf, of course. Outside the summer holiday season (end June-early Sept), ask about special breaks (including special interest breaks), when rates are reduced. No conferences or functions are accepted. Free broadband wi/fi. Fishing (sea). Snooker, pool table. Hair dressing. Children welcome (under 3 months free in parents' room, cot available without charge, baby sitting arranged). Supervised playroom & children's playground. Destination Spa; Leisure centre ('pool, fitness room, sauna, steam room, jacuzzi); Walking, cycling, croquet, lawn bowls, tennis, pitch & putt. Garden. No pets. **Rooms 118** (2 suites, 2 junior suites, 2 superior, 20 ground floor, 2 disabled). Lift. Room service (limited hours). Turndown service offered. B&B €95, ss €10; SC10%. Hotel closed mid Dec - mid Feb. **Beaches Restaurant:** This L-shaped room, which has been run under the eagle eye of Pat Doyle since 1971, has a sense of traditional opulence yet with a fresh, almost gallery-esque approach - an ideal home for some favourites from the hotel's famous art collection. Executive Chef Jim Aherne has been pleasing guests with his classic cuisine for over thirty years now - and his menus reflect the value placed on fresh local produce, with ingredients like Wexford beef, Rosslare mackerel, Slaney salmon and locally sourced vegetables used in daily-changing menus. The hotel's renowned wine list is meticulously sourced, always changing, and excellent value. Highly informative, most wines are directly imported and there are many treats in the collection, which includes organic and bio-dynamic wines, and an exceptional choice of half bottles - and a page of magnums (2 bottles), jeraboams (4 bottles) and imperials (8 bottles), which are ideal for big parties and special celebrations and often represent exceptional value too. **Seats 200** (private room 40); air conditioning. L &D daily: 1-2.15pm, 7.30-9pm; Set L €28; Set D €50. House wine from €20; SC discretionary. **La Marine:** This informal restaurant has its own separate entrance and offers a relaxed alternative to the dining experience in Beaches Restaurant. A zinc bar imported from France is the focal point of the rather pubby bar, where you can have an aperitif - although the turnover in La Marine is brisk and it is better to go directly to your table if it is ready. Fashionably sparse tables have fresh flowers, good quality cutlery and paper napkins, but space is at a premium. Head chef Eugene Callaghan's ingredients are carefully sourced, using local seasonal produce as much as possible, and a finely judged balancing act between traditional and contemporary fare is achieved on menus offering plenty of choice: a starter of goats' cheese 'truffles' with black olive crostini rubs shoulders with classic grilled Bannow Bay mussels with garlic & parsley butter, while main courses may include an interesting variation on Wexford rib eye steak (with Burgundy snails, garlic & red wine jus) and also offer upbeat comfort food like veal liver with champ and sweet & sour onions. Desserts are deliciously updated-classics – chocolate truffle cake with candied kumquats perhaps - and there's always a carefully selected trio of Irish cheeses. Service is swift and friendly and Sunday lunch, which is very good value, tends to be a little more traditional. Booking strongly advised, especially at weekends. A light bar menu is also available every afternoon, 12.30-5.30. Well chosen wines reflecting the style of food are fairly priced. **Seats 70**. L daily, 12.30-2pm; D 6.30-9pm. Closed mid Dec - mid Feb, Good Fri. Amex, MasterCard, Visa, Laser. **Directions:** Take the signs for Wexford/Rosslare/Southeast. 20km from Wexford Town alongside Rosslare Strand beach.

WEXFORD

Wexford is a fascinating old town and offers much of interest, notably the annual Opera Festival which takes place every autumn; the exciting redevelopment of the Theatre Royal was completed in time for the 30th festival in October 2008. The new building is on the site of the old theatre, and it has been conceived as a secret opera house, nestling into Wexford's medieval street setting. It has a larger capacity main auditorium (750 seats) with excellent acoustics, a second theatre and many other greatly enhanced facilities and, although focused on the autumn festival, the new building will operate as a year-round arts venue for both additional Wexford Festival productions and visiting companies. Guided walking tours of the town are available to take visitors through its narrow meandering streets and old town walls which originate from early Celtic and Nordic heritage. Wexford has much to offer the visitor including the striking spires of the Twin Churches. Nearby attractions include Johnstown Castle Gardens & Irish Agricultural Museum (053 917 1200), the Wexford Wildfowl Reserve which is Ireland's premier wildfowl reserve (North Slob, 091 912 3129) and Selskar Abbey. Also popular is the Irish National Heritage Park (053 912 0733, open all year), which allows visitors to experience 9000 years of Irish history in picturesque settings of woodland, riverbanks and historic dwellings. On a more workaday note, anyone who is looking for moderately-priced good quality accommodation with leisure facilities and does not want to be in the town, might try the re-branded **Maldron Hotel & Leisure Club** (053 917 2000) on the edge of town, with rooms from €79 and good facilities, including a swimming pool. Local activities include angling, horse riding and pleasure cruises. Wexford town offers many craft centres, art galleries and every Friday at Mallin Street car park there is a Farmers' Market from 9am to 2pm. A pleasing recent newcomer to Wexford Town is the attractive **Stable Diet Café** (053 914 9012) on Main Street South; Stable Diet are winners of an Irish Food Writers Guild award for their baked goods, which you'll find here in the shop, there's a daytime café too (closed Sun). Also, in the former La Riva premises off Crescent Quay, you'll now find an Italian fine dining restaurant, **Amalfi Coast** (053 9124330; www.amalfifinedining.com).

WWW.IRELAND-GUIDE.COM FOR ALL THE BEST PLACES TO EAT, DRINK & STAY

Wexford
RESTAURANT

Forde's Restaurant
Crescent Quay Wexford Co Wexford
Tel: 053 912 3832

Happy customers and good lighting create a good atmosphere at this informal restaurant in a reno-vated building near the Ballast Office; on the first floor, overlooking the harbour, it has mirrors reflecting lots of candles and, as darkness falls, lights twinkling across the harbour are highly atmos-pheric. Although set up in the pared-down modern style, fresh flowers and candles on well-spaced polished tables create a caring feeling, and Liam Forde's varied seasonal set and à la carte menus offer value and a wide choice, with vegetarian (and vegan) options listed although there's an understand-able leaning towards local seafood. Steaks and Wexford mussels are popular options and servings are generous. Everything is made on the premises and well-trained, knowledgeable staff are courteous and efficient, and there's an interesting, informative wine list. Sunday lunch and the short dinner menu offer especially good value. [*Now also at the fast-growing suburb of Castlebridge (053 9159767); open daily 12.00-9.30.] **Seats 80**; reservations advised; air conditioning; children welcome. D daily, 6-9.30, L Sun only, 12-6pm. Early D €24.95 (2-course), 6-7pm; Set Sun L about €24.95. Also à la carte. House wine from €18.50; SC discretionary. Closed 22-25 Dec. Diners, MasterCard, Visa, Laser. **Directions:** On the quay front, opposite statue.

Wexford
CAFÉ•RESTAURANT

La Dolce Vita
6/7 Trimmers Lane Wexford Co Wexford
Tel: 053 917 0806

In a wide side street that creates an unexpected oasis just off bustling North Main Street, one of Ireland's favourite Italian restaurateurs has a daytime restaurant and deli that is so popular with the locals that lunchtime hopefuls must arrive early, or be prepared for a long wait. You'll spot the trademark striped awning (and tables outside, in summer) and, through the big window, see a bright spacious eating area set up with smart tables and chairs, surrounded by shelves stacked with Italian goodies. Good glasses and elegant tableware heighten the sense of anticipation - and so to Roberto Pons's seriously tempting menus, in Italian with English translations, including home-made Italian bread with oil, fresh soup of the day, or risotto of the day. Excellent salads are offered and a range of pasta dishes. Then there are some more 'serious' dishes, like grilled seabass with salmoriglio dressing or Italian sausage with lentils. Don't leave without tasting at least one of Roberto's lovely desserts too - a perfect pannacotta, orange & lemon tart perhaps and, of course, a classic tiramisu, with a really good coffee. But, anyway, there's still the shopping to do - all sorts of Italian treats, including wines (with plenty offered by the glass) are imported directly by Roberto and, should you be lucky enough to live nearby (or staying in self-catering accommoda-tion), there's even a short takeaway menu. **Seats 45** (outdoors, 20); toilets wheelchair accesible; Open Mon-Sat; Mon-Thurs 9-5.30pm; Fri-Sat all day, 9am-9.30pm; L 12-4pm. Set L about €15; House Wine from about €15. Closed Sun, Bank Hols & 4 days Christmas. MasterCard, Visa, Laser. **Directions:** Off the northern end of the main street - look out for the big green, red & white canopy.

Wexford
RESTAURANT

Mange 2
@ Crown Bar Monck Street Wexford Co Wexford
Tel: 053 914 4033

A real taste of France awaits you in this first-floor restaurant above The Crown pub, which has two entrances, one from the quayside (close to the Admiral Barry statue), the other on an adjoining side street. Decorated in a simple but elegant manner with very comfortable tables, good tableware and glasses and a relaxing atmosphere, this is a place with the confidence not to court fashion but to do their own thing, and do it well. A fairly brief but well-constructed menu offering French cooking with a creative contemporary spin, is delivered with simple style. Expect interesting starters, good lamb and beef with intense sauces and well chosen accompaniments, classic fresh fish dishes and excellent breads and desserts. A la carte, plus an early bird set menu that is good value for the quality of food and cooking. Service is attentive and professional, and there's a short but carefully chosen wine list. L & D Tue-Sun, 12.30-2.30pm & 6pm-'late'. Early bird D, 6-7.30pm (to 7pm Sat) €27.95. Closed Mon. MasterCard, Visa, Laser. **Directions:** Just off Custom House quay, west of Wexford bridge.

Wexford
B&B

McMenamin's Townhouse

6 Glena Terrace Spawell Road Wexford Co Wexford **Tel: 053 914 6442**
mcmem@indigo.ie www.wexford-bedandbreakfast.com

Seamus and Kay McMenamin's B&B has been one of the most highly-regarded places to stay in this area for many years, making a useful first or last night overnight stop for travellers on the Rosslare ferry (15 minutes), as a base for the Wexford Opera, or for a short break exploring this fascinating corner of Ireland. This hospitable duo recently moved around the corner to this beautiful Victorian terrace house, which was completely restored and beautifully furnished, with quality beds and bedding, and everything that you need to be comfortable away from home, including TV and tea/coffee-making facilities. The McMenamins' considerable local knowledge is generously passed on to guests and this, together with a really good breakfast, gets you off to a good start and helps to make the most of every day: quite extensive menus include a range of fruits and juices, home-made yoghurts, old-fashioned treats like kippers and also fresh local fish such as delicious fillets of plaice, lambs' kidneys in sherry sauce, omelettes or pancakes - all served with a choice of several freshly baked breads and home-made preserves, including an excellent marmalade and unusual jams such as loganberry. A McMenamin breakfast is always beautifully prepared and presented, and cooked dishes served piping hot: you will want to return as soon as possible. *McMenamin's was our B&B of the Year in 2008. **Rooms 4** (2 family rooms, all en-suite, shower only & no smoking, 1 ground floor, 1 disabled). B&B €50 pps; ss €10; children welcome (under 2s free in parents' room, cots available without charge). No pets. Private parking. Hunting, shooting, fishing & walking all nearby. Also scenic drives, historic walks, racing, boating, swimming & tennis. Closed 10 Dec - 28 Feb. MasterCard, Visa, Laser. **Directions:** In town centre, opposite county hall.

Wexford
HOTEL

Riverbank House Hotel

The Bridge Wexford Co Wexford **Tel: 053 912 3611**
info@riverbankhousehotel.com www.riverbankhousehotel.com

Away from the bustle of the town, this pleasant hotel just across the bridge has an encouraging approach, with well-tended gardens and a welcoming reception area with lovely flower arrangements and candles. An attractive Victorian-style bar and restaurant enjoys views of the river, and an adjacent conservatory area has character and interesting plants. Renovations have been done with deference to the character of the building so, although comfortable, guest rooms tend to be a little small (making a good choice for business guests requiring single occupancy). A very nice breakfast is served in Windows restaurant - a good range of juices, excellent coffee, lovely breads and good hot dishes. This hotel offers a pleasingly personal style of hospitality and food service. Conference/banqueting 350/260); business centre. **Rooms 23** (14 shower only, 1 disabled, 8 no smoking, 6 family rooms, 8 ground floor); children welcome (under 4s free in parents' room, cot available free of charge, baby sitting arranged). 24 hr room service, Lift. No pets. B&B about €50-85pps, ss €25. No SC. Restaurant open Fri/Sat (daily Jul, Aug, Dec) L 12.30-2.30, D 6.30-9.30 (Sun to 9). Bar meals available 12-10 daily. Garden, walking. *Short breaks, including golf breaks, offered. Closed 25 Dec. Amex, Diners, MasterCard, Visa, Laser. **Directions:** Directly across the bridge in Wexford town. ◊

Wexford
B&B

Rosemount House

Spawell Road Wexford Co Wexford **Tel: 053 912 4609**
info@rosemounthouse.ie www.wexfordbedandbreakfast.ie

Having run their B&B on Auburn Terrace for many years, Carol and Tim Kelly agreed to the local council's request to relocate to allow for road expansion there, and have now opened Rosemount House on Spawell Road. The new premises is an 18th century period residence, on a quiet road, within walking distance of the town centre. All the original features have been retained, allowing for bright, spacious and comfortable rooms, which are beautifully decorated and furnished with antique furniture throughout. Work has now been fully completed, making this a lovely place to stay. **Rooms 3** (all en-suite & no smoking, 2 shower only); not suitable for children under 3. B&B €60 pps, ss €10. Closed 18 Dec - 2 Jan. MasterCard, Visa, Laser. **Directions:** Follow N25 into town centre, on Spawell Road (signed).

Talbot Hotel

Wexford
HOTEL

On the Quay Wexford Co Wexford **Tel: 053 912 2566**
sales@talbotwexford.ie www.talbotwexford.ie

A sister establishment to the Stillorgan Park Hotel in Dublin, this 1960s' hotel originally dates back to 1905 and has recently undergone major renovation, including an exterior facelift. It is well-located on the harbour-front, and also convenient to the town centre - indeed, so many activities revolve around it that many would say the Talbot is the town centre. A warm welcome from friendly staff, plus the contented crowd that always seems to be milling around the foyer, immediately sets arriving guests at ease - and one is immediately struck by the range and quality of original paintings, which is a feature of special interest throughout the hotel. Bedrooms are inevitably somewhat limited by the age and style of the building, but are pleasant and comfortable, with phone, TV and tea/coffee trays as standard. The basement leisure centre is an unexpectedly characterful area, confirming the feeling that the Talbot will always spring a few surprises. Conference/banqueting (450/400); free broadband wi/fi, business centre, secretarial services). **Rooms 109** (1 suite, 2 junior suites, 8 family, 4 disabled); children welcome (under 4s free in parents room, cot available free of charge, baby sitting arranged, crèche, playroom). B&B €100 pps, ss €20; wheelchair access; own parking. No pets. Lift. Limited room service. Leisure centre ('pool, jacuzzi, sauna, steam room); Spa (massage, beauty salon). Short breaks offered. Closed 24-25 Dec. Amex, Diners, MasterCard, Visa, Laser. **Directions:** On quay front.

Westgate Design

Wexford
RESTAURANT

22 North Main Street Wexford Co Wexford **Tel: 053 912 3787**
info@westgatedesign.ie www.westgatedesign.ie

Locals know how to find this popular daytime café - the entrance is through Westgate Design and downstairs. It's a big bustling self-service café, with plenty of rustic but comfortable seating and a friendly atmosphere. Food quality is very good and the menu wide-ranging, from home-made soups and a varied selection of salads (20 per day) to hot dishes of the day - lasagne and braised lamb shank with chive champ, or fish pie are all typical. It's contemporary Irish home cooking, but with international favourites taking their place alongside traditional Irish dishes. The baking is exceptionally good, with delicious cakes and desserts. Everything is served in generous portions and it's family-friendly. Take-away dishes are available and outside catering is also on offer for parties. Good food at very reasonable prices is a winning combination for daytime meals. **Seats 150**; air conditioning; children welcome; Open Mon-Sat, Food served all day, 8.30am-5.30pm; Wine from €4.50 per glass. Closed Sun, Bank Hols, 25/6 Dec. Visa, Laser. **Directions:** Accessible from the main street or, through the lower level, at the back. ◇

Whites of Wexford

Wexford
HOTEL

Abbey Street Wexford Co Wexford **Tel: 053 912 2311**
info@whitesofwexford.ie www.whitesofwexford.ie

Wexford's most famous hotel, Whites, re-opened fairly recently following a total reconstruction and you certainly won't miss it as it is a very large building, with obvious signage which can be seen from all around the town. Very different from the higgledy-piggledy building we had all grown fond of, this new development does not have quite the character expected of an hotel that goes back to 1795, but it is comfortable, and the unbroken tradition of hospitality lives on. The consolation is that what is now a very large hotel has excellent facilities in all areas, including on-site leisure activities and pampering treatments; White's now has the first Cryotherapy Clinic in Ireland, and an impressive swimming pool and Spa. Smart contemporary guest rooms and suites have all the bells and whistles: in addition to the usual facilities, all rooms have plasma screen television, in-house movie & satellite channels, broadband, in-room safe and minibar. There's also a choice of bars and restaurants, and extensive conference facilities. Conference/banqueting (1,000/800); broadband; secretarial services. **Rooms 157** (all en-suite); children welcome (under 4s free in parents' room, cots available free of charge, baby sitting arranged). Lift, 24hr room service. B&B €95 pps; ss €25. Parking. Leisure Centre (swimming pool, fitness room, sauna, steam room); Spa; beauty salon; walking; no pets. Closed 24-26 Dec. Amex, Diners, MasterCard, Visa, Laser **Directions:** Follow signs when leaving N25 or N11.

Wexford Area
HOTEL•RESTAURANT

Ferrycarrig Hotel

Ferrycarrig Wexford Co Wexford **Tel: 053 912 0999**
info@ferrycarrighotel.com www.ferrycarrighotel.ie

This stylish modern hotel is in a lovely location overlooking the Slaney estuary and has excellent amenities, including a superb health and fitness club. Public areas include an appealing contemporary bar, the Dry Dock, which has a large riverside deck where you can relax and enjoy the view and also lunchtime barbecueing at the Courtyard Grill (Mon-Sat); it is a popular meeting place for local people as well as residents, and appeals to all ages. Good food is served here - real beef burgers, steak, ribs, pasta and fish, and desserts like pear and almond tart and rhubarb & mascarpone fool, also an excellent cheese board with John Hempenstall's Blue Brie and Wicklow Bán cheeses; a separate children's menu includes spaghetti bolognese and chicken curry as well as old favourites. Alternatively Reeds (see below) offers a fine dining option which is more appropriate for adults. Accommodation is contemporary in style, and very comfortable - unusually, all of the well-appointed bedrooms have splendid views across the water, and some also have balconies with wooden loungers; well-equipped family rooms have bunk beds or adjoining rooms, depending on your requirements, and there's a private baby-station room for guests. It's a very family-friendly and child-friendly hotel, especially in July and August when children between four and 12 can enjoy 'Crazy Clubbers' facilities in the leisure centre, which offers a programme of daytime activities and evening entertainment but it is not a babysitting service, as an adult must be on the hotel premises at all times; there's an excellent swimming pool for younger swimmers, with its own fountain and jacuzzi jets, and a separate room for 'baby clubbers' where parents can entertain babies and toddlers. Staff are exceptionally welcoming and friendly, and special breaks are offered. Conference/banqueting (400/320); broadbandwi/fi; business centre. Leisure centre (swimming pool, jacuzzi, fitness room, sauna, steam room), beauty salon. Garden, walking. Fishing and golf nearby. Children welcome (cots available, baby sitting arranged; playroom, kids club & crèche - limited hours). No pets. Heli-pad. **Rooms 102** (5 junior suites, 4 executive, 2 for disabled, all no smoking). Lift. 24hr room service. B&B about €120 pps; ss €40. Open all year. *Ferrycarrig was our Family Friendly Hotel of the Year in 2008. **Reeds Restaurant:** Good food has always been a strong point at the Ferrycarrig, and Reeds offers adult guests accomplished modern cooking in the atmosphere of an independent restaurant rather than an hotel dining room. It has its own reception/bar area, and formally-appointed tables are arranged to make the most of the waterside position. Imaginative and well-balanced à la carte menus are interesting and, although the style is international, there is real emphasis on local foods - Killurin lamb, fresh fish from Duncannon or Kilmore Quay, and speciality cheeses from Wexford and Wicklow are likely to be among the produce named, for example. Food presentation is fashionable but not over the top, and service is pleasant and professional, ensuring a relaxing evening. **Seats 160**; toilets wheelchair accessible; air conditioning; children welcome. D daily 6.00-9.45pm (to 9.15pm Sun; limited opening in winter); early D €23, 6-7pm; also à la carte. House wines from about €20 sc discretionary. Amex, Diners, MasterCard, Visa, Laser. **Directions:** Located on N11, 3km north of Wexford Town.

Wexford Area
FARMHOUSE

Killiane Castle

Drinagh Wexford Co Wexford **Tel: 053 915 8885**
killianecastle@yahoo.com www.killianecastle.com

The past and present mix effortlessly in Killiane Castle, the Mernagh family's farm B&B: the farmhouse and Towerhouse are 17th century and some of the 13th century Norman Castle still stands. Inside there's a spacious entrance hall, an elegant, comfortably furnished residents' sitting-room with an open fire, and there's a small room down a few steps used as a TV room. Climb up the 17th century staircase to the second and third floors, where individually-designed bedrooms have comfortable beds, en-suite facilities and great views over the countryside. This friendly family always have plans for further improvements and they are hoping to repair the castle, with a view to restoration in time. The working farm allows visitors to see a modern dairy in action and their own hens supply the eggs for the delicious breakfasts that Kathleen Mernagh serves here in a warm, cosy dining-room, buffet-style. No dinners are offered but the restaurants of Wexford are very close, or Kathleen will advise guests on the best local choices. Killiane is just a few miles from Wexford town so it's ideal for an overnight on the way to or from Rosslare Harbour (about 10 minutes), although it's unlikely that you'll want to leave after one night here. **Rooms 8** (1 shower only, 2 family rooms, all no smoking); children welcome (cots available free of charge). B&B about €50 pps, ss €15. 10 bay driving range, croquet, cycling, tennis, garden, walking. Golf and equestrian nearby. *Self-catering also available in 3 courtyard apartments. MasterCard, Visa, Laser. **Directions:** Off N11 approx 7km from central Wexford. Left at Drinagh Garden Centre.

COUNTY WICKLOW

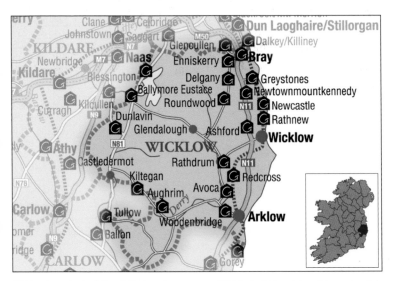

Wicklow is a miracle. Although the booming presence of Dublin is right next door, this spectacularly lovely county is very much its own place, an away-from-it-all world of moorland and mountain, farmland and garden, forest and lake, seashore and river. It's all right there, just over the nearest hill, yet it all seems so gloriously different.

In times past, the official perception of Wicklow – as seen from the viewpoint of the authorities in Dublin Castle – was the complex story of mountain strongholds where rebels and hermits alike could keep their distance from the capital. But modern Wicklow has no need to be in a state of rebellion, for it is an invigorating and inspiring place which captivates everyone who lives there, so much so that while many of its citizens inevitably work in Dublin, they're Wicklow people first, and associate Dubs - if at all - an extremely long way down the line.

Their attitude is easily understood, for even with today's traffic, it is only a short drive on notably handsome roads to transform your world from the crowded city streets right into the heart of some of the most beautiful scenery in all Ireland. This building of roads into Wicklow was a Dublin thing. One of the most scenic in the country – the old Military Road along the top of the hills to the Sally Gap – was originally built for the enforcement of rule from Dublin Castle Today, it is one of Wiklow's assets, as is the elegant dual carriageway sweeping through the Glen of the Downs, a masterpiece in itself which improves life in the county, and augments the scenery.

Such scenery generates its own strong loyalties and sense of identity, and Wicklow folk are rightly and proudly a race apart. Drawing strength from their wonderful environment, they have a vigorous local life which keeps metropolitan blandness well at bay. Thus the hill town of Aughrim in southeast Wicklow has so much community spirit that it has topped the Tidy Towns awards.

While being in a place so beautiful is almost sufficient reason for existence in itself, they're busy people too, with sheep farming and forestry and all sorts of light industries, while down in the workaday harbour of Arklow in the south of the county - a port with a long and splendid maritime history - they've been so successful in organising their own seagoing fleet of freighters that there are now more cargo ships registered in Arklow than any other Irish port.

Local Attractions and Information

Arklow	Tourism Information	0402 32484
Ashford	Mount Usher Gardens	0404 40116
Avoca	Tourism Information	0402 35788
Blessington	Russborough House & Gardens	045 865 239
Bray	Kilruddery House & Gardens	01 286 3405
Bray	National Sealife Centre	01 286 6939
Derrynamuck	Dwyer McAllister Traditional Cottage	0404 45325
Enniskerry	Powerscourt House & Gardens	01 204 6000
Glendalough	Farm Market (second Suns)	0404 43885
Glendalough	Tourism Information	0404 45688
Glendalough	Visitor Centre	0404 45325
Kilmacanogue	Avoca Handweavers Garden	01 286 7466
Kilquade	Nat. Garden Exhibition Centre	01 281 9890
Macreddin	Organic Market (first Suns month)	0402 36444
Rathdrum	Avondale House	0404 46111
Rathdrum	Kilmacurragh Arboretum	01 647 3000
Wicklow County	Gardens Festival (May-July)	0404 20100
Wicklow Mountains	National Park	0404 45425
Wicklow Town	Wicklow Historic Gaol	0404 61599
Wicklow Town	Tourism Information	0404 69117

Arklow
COUNTRY HOUSE

Plattenstown House

Coolgreaney Road Arklow Co Wicklow **Tel: 0402 37822**
mcdpr@indigo.ie www.plattenstownhouse.com

About halfway between Dublin and Rosslare and overlooking parkland, this quiet, peaceful place is set in 50 acres of land amidst its own lovely gardens close to the sea - and Margaret McDowell describes her period farmhouse well as having "the soft charm typical of the mid-19th century houses built in scenic Wicklow". The garden is lovely (a new fernery and waterfall were added last year) and there is plenty to do in the area, with the sea, golf, riding stables and forest walks all nearby, and places such as Glendalough and Avondale House to visit. There's a traditional drawing room furnished with family antiques overlooking the front garden, a TV lounge and a lovely dining room where breakfast is served - and evening meals are also offered by arrangement. Comfortable bedrooms vary in size and outlook according to their position in the house and have interestingly different characters. **Rooms 4** (3 ensuite with shower only, 1 with private bathroom, all no smoking); children welcome (under 3s free in parents' room, cot available without charge); no pets; limited room service. B&B €42-49 pps, ss €8. Garden, walking, croquet. Equestrian, fishing, golf & garden visits all nearby. French spoken. Weekend/mid-week breaks - details on application. Closed 23 Dec-2 Jan. MasterCard, Visa, Laser.
Directions: Top of Arklow town, small roundabout, straight on to Coolgreaney Road. 5km on left.

Ashford
FARMHOUSE

Ballyknocken House & Cookery School

Gleanealy Ashford Co Wicklow **Tel: 0404 44627**
info@ballyknocken.com www.ballyknocken.com

Perfectly placed for walking holidays in the Wicklow Hills, playing golf, or simply for touring the area, Catherine Fulvio's charming Victorian farmhouse provides comfort, cosiness, home-cooked food and hospitality. The farm has been in the Byrne family for three generations and they have welcomed guests for over thirty years - Catherine took over in 1999, and she has since refurbished the house throughout in old country style. A gently Victorian theme prevails: the charming bedrooms (all renovated in 2008) have antique furniture and very good beds - and pretty bathrooms, five of which have Victorian baths. The dining room, parlour and sitting room are in a similar style and her energetic quest for perfection also extends to the garden, where new fruit tree, roses and herbs were planted, and her cookery school -

which is in a renovated milking parlour in the grounds. Catherine cooks four-course dinners for guests, based on local produce, including vegetables and herbs from the Ballyknocken farm (with wine list, including some specially imported wines). The cooking style is modern Irish. All this, plus extensive breakfasts and great picnics - and a relaxing atmosphere ensure guests keep coming back for more. Short breaks are offered, also self-catering accommodation; details on these, and Ballyknocken Cookery School, on application. *Ballyknocken was our Farmhouse of the Year in 2004. **Rooms 7** (all en-suite, 1 shower only, 1 family room, all no smoking). B&B €69 pps, ss €26. Residents D Tue-Sat, at 7.30. Set 4-course D about €42.00; Lighter suppers also served midweek; houses wines €21.95. No D on Sun, Mon or Wed. Closed Mid Dec & Jan. MasterCard, Visa, Laser. **Directions:** From Dublin turn right after Texaco Petrol Station in Ashford. Continue for 5.5km (3 m). House on right.

Ashford

The Garden Café @ Avoca

CAFÉ

Mount Usher Gardens Ashford Co Wicklow **Tel: 0404 40205**

R

info@mountushergardens.ie www.mount-usher-gardens.com

The River Vartry is the central feature of these magnificent gardens planted in the Robinsonian (informal) manner, and it's a veritable garden of Eden where, throughout 20 acres, visitors are treated to a series of glorious prospects and to a magnificent collection of trees, plants and shrubs in sylvan settings - a place to revisit in celebration of the changing seasons. And, although the Jay family continue to live at Mount Usher, the stewardship of these wonderful gardens was recently taken on by Avoca (see entries); despite fears that a rush of commercialisation would follow, it is widely acknowledged that the Pratt family are managing the garden with care, and that the Garden Café @ Avoca is an asset, enhancing the experience of a visit to these wonderful gardens. Food served daily, 10am-4.30pm; B menu 10-12; L menu 12-4.30pm. **Directions:** Mount Usher Gardens are in the centre of Ashford, just off the N11.

Avoca

Avoca Handweavers

CAFÉ

Avoca Village Co Wicklow **Tel: 0402 35105**

R

info@avoca.ie www.avoca.ie

Avoca handweavers, established in 1723, is Ireland's oldest business. It's a family-owned craft design company which now has half a dozen branches throughout Ireland (most of which feature in this Guide) and the business originated here, at Avoca village, where you can watch the hand-weavers who produce the lovely woven woollen rugs and fabrics which became the hallmark of the company in its early days. Today, the appeal of Avoca shops is much broader, as they are known not only for the high standard of crafts sold (and their beautiful locations) but also for their own ranges of clothing, restaurants with a well-earned reputation for imaginative, wholesome home-cooked food - and delicious deli products and speciality foods to take home. **Seats 75**. Open all day (10-5) Mon-Sun. House wine about €12.50. No service charge. Wheelchair access. Garden. Parking. Children welcome. Pets allowed in some areas. Closed 25-26 Dec. Amex, Diners, MasterCard, Visa, Laser. **Directions:** Leave N11 at Rathnew and follow signs for Avoca.

Blessington

Grangecon Café

CAFÉ

Kilbride Road Blessington Co Wicklow **Tel: 045 857 892**

grangeconcafe@eircom.net

Wholesome aromas will draw you into Jenny and Richard Street's smashing cafe, which retained its name when re-locating from the charming village of Grangecon to the bustle of Blessington. Here they are in an old building that has been given new life by a lovely renovation job, with gentle modern decor and natural materials that should never date. But the fundamentals remain unchanged: the stated aim has always been "to provide you with a really good food stop", and this they continue to do brilliantly. Everything on the menu is made on the premises, including the breads, pastries and ice cream; the ham hocks for the quiche lorraine are cooked here, the pork meat used in the sausage rolls is organic, fruit and vegetables come from Castleruddery organic farm, and all other ingredients are of the very best quality, many of them also organic and/or free range. The menu is fairly brief, but that's the beauty of it, allowing the cooking to be this good, and flavours superb: the quiche, for example, is a little classic and comes with a scrumptious salad; similarly moist, freshly-baked brown bread arrives with home cooked ham, farmhouse cheese (Sheridan's) and home-made chutney, also garnished with salad: simple and excellent - not for the first time, we say: why aren't there more places like this? Delicious chilled Crinnaughton apple juice from Cappoquin, is offered, and B-Y-O wine is fine. Luscious Illy coffee to finish and maybe a slice of chocolate cake. This is not cheap food - how could it be when the ingredients are of such high quality - but is extremely good value for money. **Seats 30**; toilets wheelchair accessible; children welcome (high chair, baby changing facilities). Open all day Mon-Wed, 9am-4pm; Thu-Sat, 9am-5pm; party service. Closed Sun, Bank Hols & 25 Dec - 1 Jan. MasterCard, Visa, Laser. **Directions:** Centre of Blessington village, just off main street (Kilbride turning).

Bray

RESTAURANT

Ⓝ

Campo de' Fiori

1 Albert Avenue Bray Co Wicklow **Tel: 01 276 4257**

campodefioribray@msn.com www.campodefioribray.com

An unassuming exterior on a quiet lane opens into the cosy dining area of this small, family-run and authentically Italian restaurant; with newspaper-covered walls, old wine cases and fishing nets creating an informal atmosphere, and menus that are extensive without sacrificing quality, the restaurant is likely to be busy most evenings. Wide-ranging choices include a good selection of seafood, although unlikely that all options will be unavailable at any one time, and vegetarians are well catered for in the pasta selection. All the meat is sourced from a local butcher, and is of exceptional quality: the grigliata mista, a plate of grilled beef fillet, lamb and Italian sausage is particularly recommended. There are also blackboard specials, a good selection of pizza, and the home-made dessert specials are a good choice. The wine list is exclusively Italian and features some excellent wines, some by the glass. Service is informal but the Italian staff are clearly passionate about food and wine and keen to make suggestions. This unassuming restaurant has a well-deserved following, merited by the excellent quality of the food, the large choice of wine, and the enticing atmosphere. *Shortly before the Guide went to press, an all-day sister café/shop, **Pinocchio**, opened at the Luas Kiosk in Ranelagh, Dublin 6 (Tel: 01 497 0111; e-mail: info@pinocchio.ie www.pinocchiodublin.com). Wed-Sat & Mon 5-10.30pm (to 11pm Fri/Sat); Sun 2pm-9pm. Closed Tue. Amex, MasterCard, Visa, Laser. **Directions:** Albert Avenue is roughly half way down the seafront road, Strand Road.

Delgany

HOTEL

Ⓡ

Glenview Hotel

Glen O' The Downs Delgany Co Wicklow **Tel: 01 287 3399**

pkavanagh@glenviewhotel.com www.glenviewhotel.com

Famous for its views over the luxuriantly green and leafy Glen O'The Downs, this well-located four-star hotel has all the advantages of a beautiful rural location, yet is close to Dublin and offers a wide range of facilities, including an excellent Health and Leisure Club and a state-of-the-art conference centre. All bedrooms are attractively furnished in warm colours and an undemanding modern style. Public areas include a comfortably furnished conservatory bar, which is well-situated for a casual meal (Conservatory Bistro menu, international cooking, 12.30-9), and Woodlands Restaurant offers quite ambitious, formal cooking. All this, together with special breaks offering good value, make the hotel a valuable asset to the area. Conference/banqueting (250/180). Secretarial services, ISDN lines, video conferencing. **Rooms 70** (all en-suite, 1 suite, 12 executive rooms); children welcome (under 2s free in parents' room, cots available without charge, play room). Lift. B&B €55-100pps, ss about €40. No pets. Open all year. Leisure centre (indoor swimming pool); beauty salon. Snooker room (adults only). Garden, woodland walks. Amex, Diners, MasterCard, Visa, Laser. **Directions:** On N11, turn left 2 miles southbound of Kilmacanogue. ◇

Dunlavin   Rathsallagh House, Golf & Country Club

COUNTRY HOUSE•RESTAURANT   Dunlavin Co Wicklow **Tel: 045 403 112**

info@rathsallagh.com   www.rathsallagh.com

Situated just on the Wicklow side of the border with County Kildare, the O'Flynn family's large, rambling country house is just an hour from Dublin, but it could be in a different world. Although it's very professionally operated, they insist it is not a hotel and - although there is an 18-hole golf course with clubhouse in the grounds - the gentle rhythms of life around the country house and gardens ensure that the atmosphere is kept decidedly low-key. Day rooms are elegantly furnished in classic country house style, with lots of comfortable seating areas and open fires. Bedrooms, as in all old houses, do vary - some are spacious with lovely country views, while other smaller, simpler rooms in the stable yard have a special cottagey charm; and there are newer rooms, built discreetly behind the main courtyard, which are very big and finished to a high standard, with luxurious bathrooms. Rathsallagh is renowned for its magnif-icent Edwardian breakfast buffet which was, for the second time, the overall national winner of our Irish Breakfast Awards in 2005. Breakfast at Rathsallagh offers every conceivable good thing, including silver chafing dishes full of reminders of yesteryear. A large sideboard display offers such an array of temptations that it can be hard to decide where to start - fresh juices, fruits and home-bakes, local honey and home-made jams and chutneys... Irish farmhouse cheeses, Rathsallagh ham on the bone, salamis and smoked salmon... then there are the hot dishes, including the full Irish - and then some less usual dishes, like smoked salmon kedgeree, and Kay's devilled kidneys, are specialities worth travelling for; and, if that is not enough, there's even another whole menu devoted to the Healthy Option Breakfast. If golf is not your thing, there are plenty of other ways to work off this remarkable meal - the Wicklow Hills beckon walkers of all levels, for example, or you could at least fit in a gentle stroll around the charming walled gardens. Great food and service, warm hospitality, and surroundings that are quiet or romantic to suit the mood of the day - Rathsallagh has it all. Conference/banqueting (130), free broadband wi/fi. Swimming pool, jacuzzi, steam room. Golf (18), gardens, tennis, cycling, walking. Pool table. Beauty salon. Pets allowed by arrangement. Helipad. **Rooms 29** (1 suite, 9 ground floor, 2 shower only, 2 for disabled, all no smoking). B&B about €135 pps, single €195. *Short breaks (incl golf breaks) offered, details on application. Closed 6 Jan - 9 Feb. **Restaurant:** Have an aperitif in the old kitchen bar while considering daily-changing menus based on local and seasonal produce, much of it from Rathsallagh's own farm and gardens. Head Chef John Kostuik clearly relishes every-thing that is going on at Rathsallagh; his menus, which are interesting and change daily, are based on local and seasonal produce, much of it from Rathsallagh's own farm and walled garden. Menus are not over-complicated but offer a well-balanced range of about five dishes on each course, changed daily: ravioli of Dublin Bay prawns and salmon with prawn bisque makes a lovely starter, for example, while main courses will usually include Wicklow lamb from Doyle's butchers - a roast rack, perhaps, sometimes served with unusual accompaniments such as red rice, black trumpet mushrooms and orange clove sauce. Choices made, settle down in the graciously-furnished dining room overlooking the gardens and the golf course, to enjoy a series of dishes that are well-conceived and visually tempting but especially memorable for flavour. Leave room for luscious desserts, often based on fruit from the garden, which are served (generously) from a traditional trolley, or Irish farmhouse cheeses, before relaxing with coffee and petits fours in the drawing room or bar. An informative wine list offers many interesting bottles, notably in the Rathsallagh Cellar Collection, and includes a good choice of recom-mended wines under about €35. **Seats 120** (private room, 55). Reservations essential. D daily, 7-9.30. Gourmet D menu €65; house wine €25; SC discretionary. *Not suitable for children under 12. Non-residents welcome for dinner, by reservation. Lunch is available only for residents (12-4), but food is served at Rathsallagh Golf Club, 9-9 daily (to 7pm in winter). House closed 6 Jan - 9 Feb. Amex, Diners, MasterCard, Visa, Laser. **Directions:** 24km (15 m) south of Naas off Carlow Road, take Kilcullen Bypass (M9), turn left 3km (2 m) south of Priory Inn, follow signposts.

ENNISKERRY

Lying in a wooded hollow among the hills west of Bray, this pretty riverside village is close to the Powerscourt Demesne (01 204 6000, open all year). There's a traditional bar at the **Powerscourt Arms Hotel** and visitors will also find teas and meals across the square at **Poppies** (01 2828869), which is open every day from early morning to late afternoon. Nearby, the world-famous Powerscourt House and Gardens, built between 1731 and 1740, offers 47 acres of formal gardens, ornamental lakes, scenic walks and excellent views of Sugar Loaf Mountain. Other nearby attractions include the picturesque Glen of Dargle, and Coolakay House (01 286 2423), where there is an agricultural heritage display centre. The area is a favourite destination for walkers of all abilities, and golfers will enjoy the Powerscourt Golf Club (01 2046033) with a clubhouse in Georgian style, echoing Powerscourt House. Horse riding is on offer at Oakfield Equestrian Centre (01 282 9296), and anglers of all types are well catered for with the many local river, lake and sea fishing opportunities, with some excellent fly fishing for sea trout and sometimes salmon available at Tinnehinch Fishery (01 286 8652).

Enniskerry | # Powerscourt Terrace Café
CAFÉ•RESTAURANT | Powerscourt House Enniskerry Co Wicklow **Tel: 01 204 6070**
👁 Ⓡ | simon@avoca.ie www.avoca.ie

In a stunning location, overlooking the famous gardens and fountains of Powerscourt House, the Pratt family of Avoca Handweavers operate this appealing self-service restaurant. It is a delightfully relaxed space, with a large outdoor eating area as well as the café, and the style and standard of food is similar to the original Avoca restaurant at Kilmacanogue: everything is freshly made, using as many local ingredients as possible including organic herbs and vegetables with lots of healthy food. Avoca cafés are renowned for interesting salads, home-bakes and good pastries, and also excellent vegetarian dishes, many of which, such as oven-roasted vegetable and goat's cheese tart, have become specialities. **Seats 160** (indoors; additional 140 outside terrace; private room 20-90); children welcome; toilets wheelchair accessible. Parking (some distance from the house). Open daily 10-5 (Sun to 5.30). House wine about €15. Closed 25-26 Dec. Amex, Diners, MasterCard, Visa, Laser. **Directions:** 2 miles from Enniskerry Village.

Enniskerry | # The Ritz Carlton Powerscourt
HOTEL•RESTAURANT | Powercourt Estate Enniskerry Co Wicklow **Tel: 01 274 8888**
🛏🏛🏛👁 Ⓡ | www.ritzcarlton.com/resorts

A short drive south of Dublin city, in one of Ireland's most scenic locations in the beautiful Wicklow Hills, this deluxe hotel set in the 47-acre Powerscourt Estate has brought new facilities to the area. Reminiscent of a formally-iced wedding cake when seen from across the hills, the crescent shaped building is, in fact, designed to sit as neatly as possible into its forested site. Entry is on the first floor, where palatial public areas are designed to make the most of the wonderful location overlooking formal landscaped gardens and the Sugarloaf mountain beyond; informal meals are served in these areas, and open fires and the scent of woodsmoke add a human dimension. Accommodation, in quite traditionally-furnished suites and rooms, is to a predictably luxurious level throughout, with items like signature linens and marble bathrooms as standard and the hotel lays a special emphasis on service, including details like twice-daily housekeeping and evening turndown service; and then there is the Ritz-Carlton Club Level, with separate lounge, dedicated concierge staff and a range of complimentary refreshments offered throughout the day. Resort amenities include the existing 36-hole championship-quality Powerscourt Golf Club golf complex, and a new 30,000 square foot spa with VIP suites, 20 treatment rooms and beauty salon, and an equally impressive Fitness Centre and a children's activity programme and babysitting services. With such an exceptional location and state-of-the-art meeting and event amenities, this is a sought-after venue for a wide range of events, both corporate and private, including weddings. The dining experiences offered range from Afternoon Tea or casual meals in The Pub bar or the foyer lounge area, to fine dining on the terrace. But what has really interested everyone is Gordon Ramsay's first Irish venture – see below (and visit www.ireland-guide.com for updates). Conferences/Banqueting; broadband wi/fi; business centre, secretarial services, video conferencing, laptop-sized safes in bedrooms. Golf (36), walking, gardens, leisure centre ('pool, fitness room, steam room, jacuzzi); Destination Spa (treatment rooms, massage etc); Equestrian, fishing (fly, coarse & sea), garden visits & hunting/shooting all nearby. Children welcome (under 5s free in parents room, cot available, baby sitting arranged). Wheelchair friendly. **Rooms 200. Gordon Ramsay at Powerscourt:** The formal dining room is surprisingly low-ceilinged, but large tables are generously spaced and in fine weather the large terrace is particularly appealing, offering diners the chance to absorb the breathtaking mountain views al fresco. Indoors a pale green palette has been used in an understated way, with floral rugs in camouflage colours the main features in this low-key room. Like Ramsay's other culinary outposts around the world, the Scottish chef isn't cooking here (he was very upfront about this from the outset), and the kitchen was initially manned by Dubliner Paul Carroll, who worked with Ramsay for almost six years in London; however, at the time of going to press, Paul Carroll has moved to The Lyons Demesne, Celbridge (see entry), and his former sous chef Jonathan McIver has been appointed Chef de Cuisine. The menu to date has been high on luxury ingredients and seafood, and the welcome prevalence of items like Wickow venison or Tipperary lamb has demonstrated a policy of using use local seasonal produce. Especially good breads and a cheese trolley, comprising over 20 Irish and French cheeses in prime condition, merit special mention. A tasting menu (to be ordered by the whole table) is designed to showcase many of Ramsay's signature dishes, although those choosing à la carte should be equally spoiled with plenty of delicious complimentary morsels between courses. Adjoining the dining room is a classy looking bar packed with large armchairs and, although it is not always in use, it is a pleasant spot for aperitifs or digestifs. Restaurant open for L & D daily; 11.30-2pm, 6-10pm. Children welcome (high chair, children's menu, baby changing facilities). Bar food also available from 4pm daily in McGills pub. Open all year. Amex, Diners, MasterCard, Visa, Laser. Heli-pad. **Directions:** M50/N11 from Dublin, turn for Enniskerry, go through village following signs to Powerscourt. ◊

GLENDALOUGH

The Glen of the two lakes, Glendalough is a valley distinguished for its beauty and its historical and archaeological interest, notably the atmospheric monastic site established by St Kevin in the 6th century. The site includes the finest surviving example of a round tower in Ireland, a cathedral, St Kevin's Church and other stone churches dating back to the 8th and 12th centuries; there is also a Visitor Centre (0404 45325, open all year) with an exhibition explaining the history of the site. The Wicklow Mountains National Park (0404 45425) covers an area of 20,000 hectares, which includes the beautiful upper lake at Glendalough and most of the glaciated valley in which the lake is set. This is prime walking or driving country, and some of the most beautiful in Ireland - it is easy to see why Wicklow is known as 'Ireland's garden county.' The Wicklow Way is a popular route which covers 130km from Marlay Park in Dublin to Clonegal in County Carlow. There is a market at Glendalough carpark on the second Sunday of each month, including arts, crafts and farmhouse produce.

Greystones | A Caviston

CAFÉ•CAFE/BAR   1 Westview Church Road Greystones Co Wicklow **Tel: 01 287 7637**

N **R**   info@acaviston.ie www.acaviston.ie

 This new venture for the renowned Caviston family (see Dun Laoghaire entry) is run by Amy Caviston and her partner Shane Willis – and, like the original south Dublin establishment, it incorporates an excellent deli as well as an informal restaurant. It's a casual, charming, daytime self-service seafood café, with friendly staff and a warm welcome for children. You can sit inside or in the pretty partly-covered courtyard at the rear, or watch the world go by at a pavement table. Freshness is of the essence here, and the blackboard menu changes daily to take account of fish catches and seasonal vegetables and salads - but will always include a couple of hot dishes like smoked fish roulade, chowder, and organic chicken casserole, as well as open sandwiches like crab or shrimp, served with excellent brown bread and a choice of three salads from an enticing selection: cous cous, pasta, potato, courgette and tomato, and green salads a plenty. Treats among the specials might include a richly flavoured prawn bisque, very reasonably priced half lobster with garlic butter, or Dublin Prawns with garlic mayonnaise, while non-fish options might be a tasty lamb casserole or hearty Toulouse sausage & chickpea stew. Save a little room for the lovely home-made cakes and desserts, offered with a wide selection of teas and coffees to accompany. The wine list mirrors what is available in the shop and offers some very nice bottles from around €22. **Seats 25** (+ 24 outdoors); children welcome (high chair); fully wheelchair accessible. Open Tue-Sat, 9am-5pm. House wine €19.50. Closed Sun, Mon, 25 Dec - 3 Jan. MasterCard, Visa, Laser. **Directions:** At the top end of the town. From DART station, take a right and continue up the road.

Greystones | Backstage @ Bels

RESTAURANT   Church Road Greystones Co Wicklow **Tel: 01 201 6990**

V **R**   backstage@bels.ie www.bels.ie

Jeff and Tara Nolans' theatrical theme for Bels is seen in objets d'art on the walls, menus that are organised like the acts of a play - and special pre- and post- theatre meals planned in conjunction with the new local theatre. The restaurant has large windows looking out onto outdoor tables and the busy street outside, which diners can watch from window tables; the front room is elegant and relaxing, and a few steps lead down to the back room and the open kitchen where Jeff (who was formerly head chef at Roly's in Dun Laoghaire) presides. Menus that reassuringly carry Euro-Toques logos also state that dishes are adaptable for both coeliac and vegetarian diets - very down to earth, and considerate and the general cooking style, of fresh variations on old favourites, is appealing. Good breakfast and light lunch/terrace menus are offered but, like the theatre, the kitchen really comes into its own in the evening. 'Act One' offers a good choice of eight promising starters including, for example, duck lover paté with spice plum chutney, and while catch of the day for 'Act Two' could be classic Dover sole on the bone, you may also find rump of Wicklow lamb with garlic mash, spring carrots, olive and rose-mary jus - and a vegetarian dish of Ardsallagh goat's cheese, tomato, courgette and aubergine tart with baby spinach & gazpacho is always a contender for best dish of the night. Luscious 'Act Three' desserts offer very seasonal dishes such as Wexford strawberries, or rhubarb crumble with Chantilly cream, or there's an Irish farmhouse cheese selection. On Sunday nights, it's all change at Bel's, however, as Jeff puts on a loively anti pasti / tapas menu – accompanied by live Spanish music. A nice wine list offers daily wine specials as well as house wines, but no tasting notes. Staff, under Tara Nolan's direc-tion, are particularly warm, friendly and knowledgeable. It's little wonder that Backstage@Bel's has carved out a well-deserved niche in the Greystones dining scene. **Seats 60** (outdoors, 18); reservations recommended; toilets wheelchair accessible; children welcome (high chair, childrens menu, baby changing facilities); Food served daily 9am-10pm (12-9pm Sun); B 9-12pm, L 12-4pm, D 5-9pm. Value D €22, 5-7pm; house wine from €20. SC 10% on groups 10+. Closed Mon, 25 Dec, Good Fri. MasterCard, Visa, Laser. **Directions:** Middle of Greystones.

Greystones   # Chakra by Jaipur
RESTAURANT   1st Floor Meridian Point Church Road Greystones Co Wicklow
R   **Tel: 01 201 7222**   info@jaipur.ie   www.chakra.ie

This delightful sister to the other successful Jaipur restaurants in Dalkey, Dublin & Malahide (see entries) occupies a custom-designed restaurant space in, and overlooking, a modern shopping mall just off the main street of Greystones. It has a comfortable bar/reception within a spacious and very attractive high-ceilinged dining room, with lovely subdued warm-toned décor and, from the moment of arrival, service is unobtrusively attentive and charmingly friendly. The cooking maintains Jaipur's crisp, modern contemporary take on traditional Indian food - colourful, delicious, well-flavoured dishes with a lot of eye-appeal. The vegetarian choices are numerous and appealing, and old favourites like tandoori prawns and succulent biryanis are served with splendid breads and delicious sauces. Unusually for an Indian restaurant, even the dessert menu is worth exploring and, like all the restau-rants in the group, a fairly-priced wine list has been carefully selected to complement Indian food. The shopping mall car park is available free for diners. **Seats 95** (private room, 12); toilets wheelchair accessible; children welcome (high chair); air conditioning; D daily, 5-11pm; Early D €22, 5.30-7pm; Set D €30-45. House wine €18-20. Closed 25-26 Dec. MasterCard, Visa, Laser. **Directions:** Just off main street in new shopping centre, 2 minutes from DART station.

Greystones   # Diva Restaurant and Piano Bar
BAR•RESTAURANT   The Harbour Greystones Co Wicklow
R   **Tel: 01 201 7151**

Tara O'Grady's harbourside Italian restaurant has had to contend with construction work associated with the new marina recently, but will once again enjoy a prime location once it comes on-stream. At the top of the stairs, double doors open into the pleasant bar with comfortable sofas, where a fire blazes in winter. The two rooms that make up the restaurant are usually busy, with tables full of contented diners, often including young families; the back room is where the pianist plays and sings while you dine. The menu has all the Italian favourites, including pizza and a choice of chicken dishes - and, unusually, gluten-free pasta is available and there is no flour in any of the sauces. Bruschetta, authentic minestrone soup, or mussels on the half shell make good starters, and main courses include classics like lasagne al forno, and spaghetti bolognese, alongside less usual dishes like scallopine Anna Bolena (sautéed scallops in fresh pasta, with a white wine sauce with sundried tomatoes). And do leave space for dessert - a chocolate and orange mousse, perhaps, profiteroles, tiramisu or a seasonal strawberry mascarpone cheesecake. The wine list is shortish, with good value house wines. With excellent mid-range food, a lively atmosphere and friendly, welcoming staff, Diva has all the ingre-dients that make for a good night out. **Seats 120**; Open Mon-Fri 5-"late"; Sat-Sun 12-"late". MasterCard, Visa, Laser. **Directions:** At the harbour. ◊

The Happy Pear

Greystones
CAFÉ•RESTAURANT
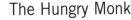

Church Road Greystones Co Wicklow **Tel: 01 287 3655**
info@thehappypear.ie   www.thehappypear.ie

Twins David and Stephen Flynn run this cheerfully ethical vegetable shop, with smoothie bar, café and an evening tapas bar with wine and beer available. If that all sounds a lot for a vegetable shop, it is, but the food is simple and tasty. Try the house salad, for example, with sprouted mung bean, watercress, radicchio in a pumpkin seed & parsley dressing: very good. Although the shop itself is very small, a restaurant has recently been opened upstairs on Friday and Saturday nights, with live guitar. A telling detail about this pair – they run their van on local rapeseed oil. Now that is walking the walk. **Seats 40** (outdoors, 30); children welcome (high chair); toilets wheelchair accessible. Vegetarian; food served daily 9-6pm (from 11am Sun); house wine about €17. MasterCard, Visa, Laser. **Directions:** Main Street, Greystones.

The Hungry Monk

Greystones
RESTAURANT

Church Road Greystones Co Wicklow **Tel: 01 287 5759**
info@thehungrymonk.ie   www.thehungrymonk.ie

Well-known wine buff Pat Keown celebrated 20 years of running this hospitable first floor restaurant on the main street in 2008, and his warmth and enthusiasm are undimmed. Pat is a great and enthusiastic host; his love of wine is infectious, the place is spick and span and the monk-related decor is a bit of fun - and a combination of hospitality, great wines and interesting, good quality food at affordable prices are at the heart of this restaurant's success. Seasonal menus offered include a well-priced all-day Sunday lunch and an evening à la carte menu, with fish the speciality in summer, and game in winter. Blackboard specials guaranteed to sharpen the appetite include the day's seafood dishes, any special wine offers - and, perhaps, a special treat like suckling pig. Menus give a slight nod to current trends, but there is no pretence at cutting edge style and you will also be pleased find faithful renditions of old favourites, like lambs kidneys Madeira and roast fillet of Irish pork. Vegetarian dishes are highlighted on the menu and there is emphasis on high quality ingredients, including Angus steaks and Wicklow lamb as well as seafood, both local and from Castletownbere. The famous wine list ('The Thirsty Monk') is clearly a labour of love and, in turn, gives great pleasure to customers, especially as prices are very fair; affordable favourites include a whole page of house wines listed by category, and of course, offers many special bottles for connoisseurs. Two pages of half bottles too, and a couple of dozen pudding wines. Restaurant **Seats 35**; children welcome; reservations advised; air conditioning. Food served Wed-Sun 12.30-9. Á la carte; also Vegetarian Menu; Set Sun L about €27. House wines from €19, SC 10%. Restaurant closed Mon & Tue. Closed 24-26 Dec. *Downstairs, The Hungry Monk Wine Bar offers an informal menu of bistro-style dishes (Monk's famous burger, Dublin Bay prawn scampi & chips...) and a carefully selected short wine list. Wine Bar open daily, 5-12. Closed 25-26 Dec. Amex, MasterCard, Visa, Laser. **Directions:** Centre of Greystones village beside DART.

The Three Q's

Greystones
RESTAURANT

Gweedore Church Road Greystones Co Wicklow **Tel: 01 287 5477**
thethreeqs@gmail.com

This small, stylish restaurant on the main street is run by three brothers, Brian, Paul and Colin Quinn, who bring together local foods and international inspiration to create innovative menus with real style. The dinner menu has a smart edge, perhaps including dishes such as a speciality saddle of rabbit with sage and black pudding stuffing, while the lunch and brunch menus are more relaxed, offering tasty, fresh-tasting combinations like a dish of corn fritters with crispy pancetta, avocado and tomato. Attention to detail is seen in good side orders, including proper, freshly-cut chips. The flavours of North Africa and Arab cooking may be seen in some dishes, perhaps including a delicious dessert like Medjoul dates soaked in espresso, star anise and cinnamon, and served with vanilla mascarpone and shortbread. There's welcome originality here, also well-informed service and fair pricing on both food and wine. **Seats 30** (outdoors, 8); not suitable for children after 6pm; food served daily 9am-10pm (Sun to 9pm); L 12-4 (brunch on Sun), D 5.30-10 (from 6pm Fri/Sat). Early bird D €25 Tue-Thu 5.30-7pm & all night Sun; also à la carte; house wine about €19. Closed Mon, Christmas week. Amex, MasterCard, Visa, Laser. **Directions:** Main street Greystones, 100m from the DART station. ◇

Greystones   # Vino Pasta
RESTAURANT   Church Road Greystones Co Wicklow **Tel: 01 287 4807**
                                            www.vinopasta.ie

Attractive red awnings, clear signage and outside seating make a good impression at this popular restaurant serving Mediterranean-style cuisine. Past a tiny reception/bar area – with seats for just two – you'll find a warmly decorated room with bistro style settings. Featuring plenty of pasta dishes (gluten-free available) as well as steaks, lamb, veal, chicken and prawns, the menu is augmented with many daily fish specials listed on chalkboards: brill with chorizo and lime butter, plump mussels in an aromatic garlic and white wine broth, plaice with a herb dressing or perhaps hake with olives, tomatoes and capers – all fish-fresh from Dunmore East. Moderately-priced wine list including half bottles. Generous portions, home-made bread and desserts together with good cooking, efficient friendly service and good value keep people coming back. **Seats 60** (outdoors, 10); children welcome before 7.30pm; reservations recommended; air conditioning. L & D daily, 12-3pm & 5-10pm (Sun 3-9pm). Value D 5-7pm. House wine €20; sc 12.5% on groups 6+. Closed Bank Hols. Amex, MasterCard, Visa, Laser. **Directions:** End of Main Street beside DART station. ◈

Kilmacanogue   # Avoca Handweavers
CAFÉ   Kilmacanogue Bray Co Wicklow **Tel: 01 286 7466**
                        reception@avoca.ie   www.avoca.ie

This large shop and restaurant, off the N11 south of Dublin, is the flagship premises of Ireland's most famous group of craft shops and they have become almost equally well-known for the quality of their food - people come here from miles around to shop, and to tuck into wholesome home-cooked food, which is based as much as possible on local and artisan produce. The style at Avoca is eclectic and, although they are especially well-known for great baking and traditional dishes like beef and Guinness casserole, their salads and vegetables are also legendary. In addition to the large self-service area (recently renovated and now with covered verandah seating, there is also a wide range of excellent delicatessen fare for sale in the shop. **The Fernhouse Café:** This delightful new table service café is located in a large and spacious orangerie-style conservatory with a terrace, and is open for breakfast, lunch and afternoon snacks; like the self-service area, it is very popular, but you can reserve a table and enjoy a rather more extensive menu than the café including specials of the day, such as osso bucco and couscous, cheese plates, imaginative salads and delicious desserts, making this an even more attractive destination.*Also at: Avoca, Powerscourt, Mount Usher Gardens, Rathcoole & Suffolk Street, Dublin 2 (see entries). Self-service café seats 160 (+outdoor dining, 100); verandah, 60; toilets wheelchair accessible; children welcome; air conditioning. Open daily, 9.30-5 (Sun 10-5). House wine from €20. Fernhouse Cafe: **Seats 100;** open 10am-5.30pm. No s.c. Closed 25-26 Dec. Amex, Diners, MasterCard, Visa, Laser. **Directions:** On N11 sign posted before Kilmacanogue Village.

Kiltegan   # Barraderry Country House
COUNTRY HOUSE   Barraderry Kiltegan Co Wicklow **Tel: 059 647 3209**
     jo.hobson@oceanfree.net   www.barraderrycountryhouse.com

Olive and John Hobson's delightful Georgian house is in a quiet rural area close to the Wicklow Mountains and, once their family had grown up, the whole house was extensively refurbished and altered for the comfort of guests. Big bedrooms with country views are beautifully furnished with old family furniture and have well-finished shower rooms - and there's a spacious sitting room for guests' use too. Barraderry would make a good base for exploring the lovely counties of Wicklow, Kildare, Carlow and Wexford and there's plenty to do nearby, with six golf courses within a half hour drive, several hunts and equestrian centres within easy reach and also Punchestown, Curragh and Naas racecourses - and, of course, walking in the lovely

Wicklow Mountains. **Rooms 4** (all en-suite, shower only & no smoking). B&B €50 pps; ss €5; children welcome (cot available); pets permitted in certain areas by arrangement. Garden; walking. Closed 14 Dec-14 Jan. MasterCard, Visa. **Directions:** N81 Dublin-Baltinglass; R 747 to Kiltegan (7km).

Macreddin
HOTEL•RESTAURANT

The BrookLodge Hotel
Macreddin Village Co Wicklow **Tel:** 0402 36444
brooklodge@macreddin.ie   www.brooklodge.com

Built on the site of a deserted village in a Wicklow valley, this extraordinary food, drink and leisure complex exists thanks to the vision of three brothers, Evan, Eoin and Bernard Doyle. Below we outline the various strands that make up this very complex operation – but, as you will sense from the bright helpful staff and an atmosphere of care about the place, this very special operation is more than the sum of its parts. The driving force is Evan, a pioneer of the new organic movement when he ran The Strawberry Tree restaurant in Killarney. Here in Wicklow, their hotel and restaurant has earned national recognition for its strong position on organic food (BrookLodge won the Guide's Natural Food Award in association with Euro-Toques, in 2003); and their little "street" is thriving, with an olde-worlde pub (Acton's), a café, a micro-brewery, gift shops selling home-made produce and related quality products and - most recently- the opening of **La Taverna Armento**. This alternative dining choice for guests is the result of a continuing collaboration between Evan and the towns of Armento and Basilicata in southern Italy; décor, food, and wines are all influenced by sources and personalities from that area, and the result is an authentic casual dining experience offering really good artisan food and an intimate ambience. Organic food markets, held on the first Sunday of the month (first and third in summer) have also proved a great success. The hotel itself is spacious and welcoming, with elegant country house furnishings, open fires and plenty of places to sit quietly or meet for a sociable drink - and there are accommodation choices between the original rooms, which are furnished with quite traditional free-standing furniture, and state-of-the-art mezzanine suites, which will please those who relish very modern high-tech surroundings. A luxurious spa centre, The Wells, features an indoor-to-outdoor swimming pool, gym, juice bar and a wide variety of exclusive beauty and health treatments. Mid-week, weekend and low-season special offers are good value, and staff are friendly and helpful. *Recent developments include the addition of **Brook Hall**, which is effectively a separate 24-bedroom hotel used for weddings and events, allowing the original BrookLodge Hotel to operate as a dedicated food and spa hotel; the River Room at Brook Hall is a beautiful banqueting room for up to 200, with French windows, a patio and mezzanine bar. Brook Hall also has a separate swimming pool and gym, for the use of all guests.*Macreddin Golf Club, a beautifully situated 18-hole par-72 championship course, the first to be designed by Irish Ryder Cup hero Paul McGinley, is now open. Conference/banqueting (350/190); business centre, free broadband wi/fi, secretarial services, video conferencing (by arrangement). Equestrian centre, archery, clay pigeon shooting, falconry, golf (18), snooker, garden, walking, lawn bowls, leisure centre (fitness room, swimming pool, sauna, steam room, hot tub), Spa (massage, beauty treatments). Children welcome (under 3s free in parents' room, cot available without charge, baby sitting arranged). Pets allowed in some areas by arrangement. Heli-pad. **Rooms 66** (13 suites, 3 junior suites, 4 ground floor, 27 family, 4 disabled, 27 no smoking). Lift. 24 hr room service; B&B €130 pps; ss €50. Open all year. **Strawberry Tree:** Ireland's only certified organic restaurant reflects the BrookLodge philosophy of sourcing only from producers using slow organic methods and harvesting in their correct season. Menus are not too long or too fussy: dishes have strong, simple names and, except when indicated on the menu as wild, everything offered is organic; the wine list also offers an exceptional range of organic wines, all priced at a very reasonable €30. There's a great buzz associated with the commitment to organic production at BrookLodge, and it makes a natural venue for meetings of like-minded groups such as Euro-Toques and Slow Food, especially on market days. Dining at the Strawberry Tree is a unique experience - and good informal meals can be equally enjoyable at The Orchard Café and Acton's pub (both open noon-9pm daily) and, more recently, La Taverna Armento (see above). Given the quality of ingredients used and the standard of cooking, all meals at BrookLodge represent very good value. **Seats 145** (private room, 60, outdoor, 10); children welcome; air conditioning; toilets wheelchair accessible. D daily 7-9.30pm. Set D €65. House wines €30. SC discretionary. *William Acton's Pub - Bar food daily, 12.30-9; La Taverna Armento, Italian food Thurs-Sat 7-9.30 pm and 1-6pm Sun. Amex, Diners, MasterCard, Visa, Laser. **Directions:** Signed from Aughrim.

Newcastle

RESTAURANT

Main Street Newcastle Co Wicklow **Tel: 01 201 8980**
info@theoldcandle.ie www.theoldcandle.ie

Located in a stone building on the main street of Newcastle village, this recently opened restaurant has clearly filled a need for both local residents and visitors taking the Wicklow coastal drive between Kilcoole and Rathnew. Behind a deceptively narrow frontage you'll find a good-sized restaurant in an atmospheric, genuinely old room with open stone walls, simple wooden tables and ladder-back chairs – and many candles. Leading off with ubiquitous tiger prawns – modern menus are carefully planned to please a wide market – and local seafood features too, while good local steaks and lamb are a point of pride. Dishes enjoyed on a recent visit included perfectly cooked pan-seared scallops (with coral) and spanking fresh crab salad; and, although fish of the day disappointed, pan-fried breast of duck was cooked exactly as requested - and a fruit salad was willingly produced, although not on the menu. Ingredients are sourced from named local and quality assured providers, and pleasant, efficient (unobtrusive) local staff make dining here a pleasure. The wine list is well chosen to suit the menu and, although with no vintages and little to choose from under €25, includes an organic choice and a handful of half bottles. All menus offer a vegetarian option and children are offered half portions of any main course at half price. Booking ahead is advisable. **Seats 60**; reservations recommended; children welcome (high chair, childrens menu); wheelchair accessible; air conditioning; parking (40). D daily 6-10pm; L Sun only 1-6pm. Set 2/3 value D €25/30 Mon-Thurs 6-8pm; set Sun L €30; also à la carte. House wine €25. SC 10% on groups 8+. Closed Good Fri, 24-25 Dec. MasterCard, Visa, Laser. **Directions:** Newcastle is off the N11, 3 mins after Greystones exit.

Newtownmountkennedy

CAFÉ

Newtownmountkennedy Co Wicklow **Tel: 01 281 9955**
www.fishers.ie

Anyone familiar with Fisher's of Newtownmountkennedy - a shop of character on the old schoolhouse at the end of the village, well known for quality country clothing - tends to make a detour to take in a visit here when in the area, as they sell lots of things you won't find anywhere else. And, by a happy chance, they also have a very nice café offering wholesome fare. You'll find home-made soups and freshly baked breads, generous shepherd's/cottage or fisherman's pie (using local Wicklow lamb, beef or seafood), honey-baked ham on the bone, stuffed pancakes, quiches, salads and much else besides. Three hot dishes offered at lunch time are good value, at around €8-9 complete with vegetables. And the home-made desserts and lovely cakes to have with your tea or coffee are particularly good. A nice place to know about. **Seats 60** (outdoors, 20); children welcome (high chair); toilets wheelchair accessible. Open Mon-Sat 10am-5pm; Sun & bank hols 12.30-5.30pm. L 12-3.30pm. Sun L €14. House wine from €5 per glass. SC discretionary. Closed 25-27 Dec, 1 Jan, Easter Sun. MasterCard, Visa, Laser. **Directions:** In Fisher's Shop in the heart of Newtownmountkennedy.

Newtownmountkennedy

HOTEL•RESTAURANT

Newtownmountkennedy Co Wicklow **Tel: 01 287 0800**
mhrs.dubgs.reservations@marriotthotels.com www.marriottdruidsglen.com

Just over 30km south of Dublin, in a stunning location between the sea and the mountains and adjacent to Druids Glen Golf Club, this luxurious hotel has a feeling of space throughout - beginning with the marbled foyer and its dramatic feature fireplace. Suites and guest rooms, many of them "double/doubles" (with two queen-sized beds), are all generously-sized, with individual 'climate control' (heating and air conditioning), and all bathrooms have separate bath and walk-in shower. A wide range of recreational facilities on site includes the hotel's spa and health club (recently refurbished and extended), and two championship golf courses; nearby you'll also find horse riding, archery, quad biking - and, of course, the gentler attractions of the Wicklow Mountains National Park are on the doorstep. When dining in, choose between Flynn's Steakhouse (see below) and the bigger Druid's Restaurant (where breakfast, carvery lunch and dinner are served daily). Bar meals also available in 'The Thirteenth' bar or, in fine weather, on a sheltered deck outside the two restaurants. *Druids Glen Marriott was our Business Hotel of the

Year in 2003 - and this is a place to relax and unwind, as well as do business. Conference/banqueting 250/220; business centre, secretarial services. Golf (2x18); leisure centre, swimming pool; spa, beauty/treatment rooms, walking, garden. **Rooms 148** (11 suites, 137 executive, 6 disabled). Lift. Children welcome (under 12s free in parents' room, cots available without charge; baby sitting arranged). 24 hr. room service, turndown service, laundry/valet service. B&B about €115, ss €30.

Flynn's Steakhouse: Quite small and intimate, with an open log fire and candlelight, Flynn's has more atmosphere than the bigger daytime Druids Restaurant, and reservations are essential. American-style steaks and grills are the speciality but, demonstrating a welcome commitment to using Irish produce, a supply of Certified Irish Angus is contracted for the hotel; just remember that American-style means big - 24oz porterhouse and ribeye, for example... Rack of Wicklow lamb is another speciality and there's a sprinkling of other dishes with an Irish flavour which might not be expected in an international hotel, like Dingle crab cakes, Guinness-braised mussels - and an Irish cheese platter. **Seats 75** (private room 16); reservations essential; not suitable for children after 8. D daily, 6-10.30. Set D about €40/50 2/3 course, also à la carte. House wine, from about €22; SC discretionary. *The larger **Druid's Restaurant** serves breakfast, lunch & dinner daily; L carvery, Druids Irish D Menu à la carte. Bar meals also available in 'The Thirteenth' bar or, in fine weather, on a sheltered deck outside the two restaurants. Amex, Diners, MasterCard, Visa, Laser. **Directions:** 36km (20 miles) south of Dublin on N11, at Newtownmountkennedy. ◊

Newtownmountkennedy

HOTEL

R

Parkview Hotel

Main Street Newtownmountkennedy Co Wicklow **Tel: 01 201 5600**

info@parkviewhotel.ie www.parkviewhotel.ie

This quietly contemporary privately-owned hotel is a useful addition to the accommodation options in this beautiful area. Public areas include an attractive modern bar, where informal food is served, and facilities for small business meetings of up to 20 people are available. The spacious and pleasingly furnished bedrooms include four suites and four family rooms, and this would make a very comfortable base for exploring the area, golfing, or any of the many other activities available locally. Staff are extremely helpful and friendly and smart. Conferences/Banqueting (400/250); laptop-sized safe in bedrooms; jacuzzi, walking; children welcome (under 2s free in parents' room, cot available free of charge, baby sitting arranged); **Rooms 60** (4 executive, 4 family, 3 disabled); Lift; all day room service; B&B from €47.50 pps, ss €40. MasterCard, Visa, Laser. **Directions:** N11, Newtownmountkennedy, in village on Main Street. ◊

Rathdrum

RESTAURANT

N V R

Bates Restaurant

3 Market Street Market Square Rathdrum Co Wicklow

Tel: 040 429 988

Located in a tourist-focused but pleasant laneway just off Rathdrum's main street, which is also home to a cosy café/pub and has been used as a location for many Irish films (the restaurant walls feature stills from the various productions) and, this attractive Italian restaurant is in the simple whitewashed interior of a long cottage, with the dining area divided by an open wood stove and a view into the raised kitchen at one end. It has lots of atmosphere and people travel long distances to eat here for its relaxed ambience and excellent food, made with simple, quality ingredients in genuine Italian style – perfectly cooked pastas in simple sauces and beef and lamb dishes centred on superb meat. The well organised wine list is exclusively Italian and ranges from two good house wines for €18 to excellent bottles for over €100. The service is very good and possible minor linguistic difficulties only add to the genuine Italian feel of the establishment. **Seats 46** (outdoors, 12); reservations recommended; children welcome (high chair); wheelchair accessible. D Tue-Sun 6.30-10pm (to 9pm Sun); L Sun only 12.30-2pm; à la carte; house wine €18.95; sc 10% on groups 6+. Closed Mon, Bank Hols. MasterCard, Visa, Laser. **Directions:** Near Cartoon Inn pub.

Rathnew

HOTEL•RESTAURANT

Hunter's Hotel

Newrath Bridge Rathnew Co Wicklow **Tel: 0404 40106**
reception@hunters.ie www.hunters.ie

A rambling old coaching inn set in lovely gardens alongside the River Vartry, this much-loved hotel has a long and fascinating history - it's one of Ireland's oldest coaching inns, with records indicating that it was built around 1720. In the same family now for five generations, the colourful Mrs Maureen Gelletlie takes pride in running the place on traditional lines, with her sons Richard and Tom. This means old-fashioned comfort and food based on local and home-grown produce with the emphasis very much on 'old fashioned' which is where its charm and character lie. There's a proper little bar, with chintzy loose-covered furniture and an open fire, a traditional dining room with fresh flowers from the riverside garden where their famous afternoon tea is served in summer - and comfortable country bedrooms. There is nowhere else in Ireland like it. *Hunter's Hotel was our Atmospheric Establishment of the Year in 2008. Conference (30). Garden. Parking. Children welcome. No pets. **Rooms 16** (1 junior suite, 1 shower only, 1 disabled). Wheelchair access. B&B from about €95 pps, ss about €20. **Restaurant:** In tune with the spirit of the hotel, the style is traditional country house cooking: simple food with a real home-made feeling about it - no mean achievement in a restaurant and much to be applauded. Seasonal lunch and dinner menus change daily, but you can expect classics such as chicken liver paté with melba toast, soups based on fish or garden produce, traditional roast rib beef with Yorkshire pudding or old-fashioned roast stuffed chicken with bacon and probably several fish dishes, possibly including poached salmon with hollandaise and chive sauce. Desserts are often based on what the garden has to offer, and baking is good, so fresh raspberries and cream or baked apple and rhubarb tart could be wise choices. Delightful. **Seats 50**. Toilets wheelchair accessible. L daily, 1-3 (Sun 2 sittings: 12.45 & 2.30). D daily 7.30-9. Set D about €40. Set L about €22. No s.c. House wine about €16. Afternoon tea about €7.50. Closed 3 days at Christmas. Amex, Diners, MasterCard, Visa. **Directions:** Off N11 at Ashford or Rathnew. ◊

Redcross

FARMHOUSE

Kilpatrick House

Redcross Co Wicklow **Tel: 040 447 137**
info@kilpatrickhouse.com www.kilpatrickhouse.com

Just about one hour's drive south of Dublin and north of Rosslare ferryport, this handsome 18th century farmhouse is clearly signed from the landmark Jack White's pub and, with its beautifully kept gardens and an immaculate working farmyard, it creates a good impression from the outset. Extensively renovated in 2003, it has been the Kingston family home for three generations and open to guests since 1941. The influential Austrian philosopher Ludwig Wittgenstein stayed here for a year (1947-48) working on his classic "Philosophical Investigations". The four comfortable bedrooms (3 en-suite, the 4th has a bathroom across a landing) have television and radio, tea and coffee-making facilities, and there is a private sitting room for guests. A good breakfast menu (with home-made breads, scones, jams and marmalades and fruits from the garden), and a genuine family welcome, make Kilpatrick a great base for exploring Wicklow – and nothing is too much trouble when it comes to helping guests plan their day. Three miles from Brittas Bay beach, it offers a tennis court and is close to several fine golf courses and well situated for visiting many of Co. Wicklow's scenic and historic attractions including Avoca, Glendalough, Avondale House and Forest Park and the Wicklow Hills. **Rooms 4** (3 en-suite shower only, 1 with private bathroom, 1 family, all no smoking); children welcome (under 1s free in parents room, cots available free of charge, high chair); parking (20); dogs permitted by arrangement (stay in outhouse/kennel). B&B €47.50 pps; ss €12.50. Garden, walking, tennis. Fishing (coarse & sea angling), hunting, garden visits and equestrian all nearby. Closed Nov-May. MasterCard, Visa, LAser. **Directions:** From Dublin south on N11; turn right opposite Jack Whites pub, take immediate left, 1 km further on the right hand side.

Roundwood
PUB•RESTAURANT

Roundwood Inn
Roundwood Co Wicklow
Tel: 01 281 8107

Jurgen and Aine Schwalm have owned this atmospheric 17th century inn in the highest village in the Wicklow Hills for over 25 years and, during that time, caring hands-on management backed up by dedicated long-serving staff have earned this unique bar and restaurant a lot of friends. There's a public bar at one end with a snug and an open fire and, in the middle of the building, the main bar food area has an enormous open fireplace with an ever-burning log fire, and is furnished in traditional style. Together with head chef Paul Taube, who has also been in the kitchen here for over 20 years, the style that the Schwalms have developed is their own unique blend of Irish and German influences: excellent bar food includes Hungarian goulash, fresh crab bisque, Galway oysters, smoked Wicklow trout, and hearty meals, notably the delicious house variation on Irish stew. The food has always had a special character and this, together with the place itself and its own special brand of hospitality, has earned the Roundwood Inn an enviable reputation. Bar meals 12-9.30 daily. Bar closed 25 Dec, Good Fri. **Restaurant:** The restaurant is in the same style, only slightly more formal than the main bar, with fires at each end of the room, and is open by reservation. The menu choice leans towards more substantial dishes such as rack of Wicklow lamb, roast wild Wicklow venison, venison ragout, pheasant and other game in season. German influences are again evident in long-established specialities such as smoked Westphalian ham and wiener schnitzel, but there are also classic specialities such as roast stuffed goose on winter menus, and meltingly delicious roast suckling pig. An interesting mainly European wine list favours France and Germany, with many special bottles from Germany. *Roundwood Inn was our Pub of the Year in 2007. **Seats** 45 (private room, 25); not suitable for children after 6.30. D Fri & Sat, 7.30-9; à la carte. L Sun only, 1-2. (children welcome for lunch). House wine from about €16; SC discretionary; reservations advised. No SC. Restaurant closed L Mon-Sat, D Sun-Thu. Amex, MasterCard, Visa, Laser. **Directions:** N11, follow sign for Glendalough.

WICKLOW

Wicklow town has character and merits a visit when exploring the area. **The Grand Hotel** (Tel: 0404 67337 www.grandhotel.ie) was redeveloped and greatly extended in 2004; while it has as lost its old-fashioned charm, accommodation would be comfortable. Restaurants to check out include **The Bakery** (Tel 0404 66770), an interesting old place in Church Street which still has the original ovens in situ, and **Rungantino's River Café** (Tel 0404 61900), which is on the river in the centre of the town and specialises in seafood. **Tinakilly House Hotel** (0404 69274; www.tinakilly.ie) is outside Wicklow town at Rathnew, and is popular for weddings and events.
WWW.IRELAND-GUIDE.COM FOR ALL THE BEST PLACES TO EAT, DRINK & STAY

Woodenbridge
HOTEL

Woodenbridge Hotel
Vale of Avoca Arklow Co Wicklow **Tel: 0402 35146**
info@woodenbridgehotel.com www.woodenbridgehotel.com

This pleasant country hotel lays claim to the title of Ireland's oldest hotel, with a history going back to 1608, when it was first licensed as a coaching inn on the old Dublin-Wexford highway - and later came to prominence when gold and copper were mined in the locality. Today, it is very popular for weddings and golf, and makes a friendly and relaxing base for a visit to this beautiful part of County Wicklow. Older bedrooms in the hotel have all been refurbished and are comfortably furnished, and many of them overlook Woodenbridge golf course; Woodenbridge Lodge offers forty newer en-suite rooms overlooking the River Aughrim. As well as a more formal restaurant, food – possibly including some fine old traditional Irish dishes in honour of the hotel's 400th anniversary - is available in the lively bar (traditional Irish music in summer). *Golf breaks are a speciality and discounted green fees are offered on a number of local golf courses, with other activities for non-golfing partners if required. Conferences/Banqueting (200/180); free broadband wi/fi, secretarial services. **Rooms** 62 (8 family rooms, 45 no smoking, 3 for disabled); B&B €50pps, ss €20; children welcome (under 12s free in parents' room; cots available without charge, baby sitting arranged). No pets. Food available 12.30-9. Amex, Diners, MasterCard, Visa, Laser. **Directions:** N11 to Arklow; turn off - 7km (4 m).

BELFAST

The origins of the cities of Ireland are usually found in 5th Century monastic centres which were overrun by the Vikings some four hundred or so years later to become trading settlements that later "had manners put on them" by the Normans. But Belfast is much newer than that. When the Vikings in 823AD raided what is now known as Belfast Lough, their target was the wealthy monastery at Bangor, and thus their beach-heads were at Ballyholme and Groomsport further east along the lough's southern shore. Then, when the Normans held sway in the 13th Century, their main stronghold was at Carrickfergus on the northern shore of the wide sea inlet which was known for several centuries as Carrickfergus Bay. And in the tumult of the 17th Century, with the Plantation of Ulster, the Cromwellian campaign, and the Williamite Wars, Carrickfergus with its powerful Norman Castle continued as a major historical focus.

But at the head of Carrickfergus Bay beside the shallow River Lagan, the tiny settlement of beal feirste - the 'town at the mouth of the Farset or the sandspit' - wasn't noted on maps at all until the late 15th Century. But Belfast proved to be the perfect greenfield site for rapid development as the Industrial Revolution got under way. Its rocketing growth began with linen manufacture in the 17th Century, and this was accelerated by the arrival of skilled Huguenot refugees after 1685.

There was also scope for ship-building on the shorelines in the valleymouth between the high peaks crowding in on the Antrim side on the northwest, and the Holywood Hills to the southeast, though the first shipyard of any significant size wasn't in being until 1791, when William and Hugh Ritchie opened for business. The Lagan Valley gave convenient access to the rest of Ireland for the increase of trade and commerce to encourage development of the port, while the prosperous farms of Down and Antrim fed a rapidly expanding population.

So, at the head of what was becoming known as Belfast Lough, Belfast took off in a big way, a focus for industrial ingenuity and manufacturing inventiveness, and a magnet for entrepreneurs and innovators from all of the north of Ireland, and the world beyond. Its population in 1600 had been less than 500, yet by 1700 it was 2,000, and by 1800 it was 25,000. The city's growth was prodigious, such that by the end of the 19th Century it could claim with justifiable pride to have the largest shipyard in the world, the largest ropeworks, the largest linen mills, the largest tobacco factory, and the largest heavy engineering works, all served by a greater mileage of quays than anywhere comparable. And it was an essentially Victorian expansion - the population in 1851 was 87,062, but by 1901 it was 349,l80 - the largest city in Ireland.

Growth had become so rapid in the latter half of the 19th Century that it tended to obliterate the influence of the gentler intellectual and philosophical legacies inspired by the Huguenots and other earlier developers, a case in point being the gloriously flamboyant and baroque Renaissance-style City Hall, which was completed in 1906. It was the perfect expression of that late-Victorian energy and confidence in which Belfast shared with conspicuous enthusiasm. But its site had only become available because the City Fathers authorised the demolition of the quietly elegant White Linen Hall, which had been a symbol of Belfast's less strident period of development in the 18th Century.

However, Belfast Corporation was only fulfilling the spirit of the times. And in such a busy city, there was always a strongly human dimension to everyday life. The City Hall may be on the grand scale, but it was nevertheless right at the heart of town. Equally, while the gantries of the shipyard may have loomed overhead, they did so near the houses of the workers in a manner which somehow softened their sheer size. Admittedly this theme of giving great projects a human dimension seems to have been forgotten in the later design and location of the Government Building (completed 1932) at Stormont, east of the city. But back in the vibrant heart of Belfast, there is continuing entertainment and accessible interest in buildings as various as the Grand Opera House, St Anne's Cathedral, the Crown Liquor Saloon, Sinclair Seamen's Church, the Linenhall Library, Smithfield Market, and some of the impressive Victorian and Edwardian banking halls, while McHugh's pub on Queen's Square, and Tedford's Restaurant just round the corner on Donegall Quay, provide thoughtful reminders of the earlier more restrained style.

Today, modern technologies and advanced engineering have displaced the old smokestack industries in the forefront of the city's work patterns, with the shipyard ceasing to build ships in March 2003. Shorts' aerospace factories are now the city's biggest employer, while parts of the former shipyard are being redeveloped as the Titanic Quarter in memory of the most famous ship built in Belfast, although it's a moot point if all the people of Belfast wish to be reminded on a daily basis of the Titanic disaster, which occured as recently as 1912.

The energy of former times has been channeled into impressive urban regeneration along the River Lagan. Here, the flagship building is the Waterfront Hall, a large concert venue which has won international praise, and is complemented by the Odyssey Centre on the other side of the river. In the southern part of the city, Queen's University (founded 1845) is a beautifully balanced 1849 Lanyon building at the heart of a pleasant university district which includes the respected Ulster Museum & Art Gallery, while the university itself is particularly noted for its pioneering work in medicine and engineering.

There's a buzz to Belfast which is expressed in its cultural and warmly sociable life, and reflected in the internationally-minded innovative energy of its young chefs. Yet in some ways it is still has marked elements of a country town and port strongly rooted in land and sea. The hills of Antrim can be glimpsed from most streets, and the farmland of Down makes its presence felt.

They are quickly reached by a developing motorway system, relished by those in a hurry who also find the increasingly busy and very accessible Belfast City Airport a convenient boon, while access to the International Airport to the west beside Lough Neagh is being improved. So although Belfast may have a clearly defined character, it is also very much part of the country around it, and is all the better for that. And in the final analysis, Belfast is uniquely itself.

Local Attractions and Information

Arts Council of Northern Ireland	028 90 385200
Belfast Castle & Zoo	028 90 776277
Belfast Crystal	028 90 622051
Belfast Festival at Queens (late Oct-early Nov)	028 90 665577
Belfast Welcome Centre	028 90 246609
City Airport	028 90 457745
City Hall	028 90 270456
Citybus Tours	028 90 458484
Fernhill House: The People's Museum	028 90 715599
Grand Opera House	028 90 241919
International Airport	028 94 484848
Kings Hall (exhibitions, concerts, trade shows)	028 90 665225
Lagan Valley Regional Park	028 90 491922
Linenhall Library	028 90 321707
Lyric Theatre	028 90 381081
National Trust Regional Office	028 97 510721
Northern Ireland Railways	028 90 899411
Odyssey (entertainment & sports complex)	028 90 451055
St Anne's Cathedral	028 90 328332
Sir Thomas & Lady Dixon Park (Rose Gardens)	028 90 320202
Tourism Information	028 90 246609
Ulster Historical Foundation (genealogical res.)	028 90 332288
Ulster Museum & Art Gallery	028 90 383000
Waterfront Hall (concert venue)	028 90 334455
West Belfast Festivals	028 90 313440

BELFAST

Ireland's fastest changing city has a huge buzz about it and, whatever your reason for visiting, you'll be glad to find plenty of great places to eat, drink and chill out. Belfast abounds with bars, coffee shops and informal eating places and, as well as those listed, some worth keeping an eye open for include the smart **Clements Cafés** throughout the city, which are well known for quality and ethical standards they use Fairtrade coffee in their trademark cappuccinos, make their own crisps and let the staff choose the music (Donegall Square West, Castle Street, Royal Avenue & Rosemary Street, all open all day; and Botanic Avenue, Stranmillis Road and Lisburn Road, also open at night). In the city centre **The Linen Hall Library** on Donegall Square North (Tel: 028 9032 1707; www.linenhall.com) is a hidden gem, and it has a coffee shop overlooking the City Hall with an old world feeling and serene, restorative atmosphere and **Waterstones**, almost next door on Fountain Street, has more substantial fare on offer and you can browse the books, and have a quick read over coffee. A promising newcomer that burst onto the Belfast dining scene shortly before going to press is **Drennans Restaurant** (028

Georgina Campbell's Ireland

9020 4556) at 43, University Road; smart and atmospheric, with lots of foliage, white linen and a (rather loud) pianist some nights, this up and coming place hit the ground running and (although no wine licence or credit card facility at the time of going to press) weekend reservations are strongly advised. Meanwhile, lovers of spicy food might head to **Jharna Indian** (028 9038 1299) on the first floor at 133 Lisburn Road; since recent refurbishment has raised the game, this long-established restaurant has been attracting renewed attention and is open for lunch and dinner; alternatively, on nearby Stranmillis Road, **Indie Spice** (028 9066 8100) offers a stylish take on Indian cuisine, and offers lighter options and European dishes (see also under Swords, Co Dublin). For wholesome fast food in the city centre, the crêperie **Flour** (028 9033 9966) at 46 Upper Queen Street offers 45 sweet & savoury crêpes and filled baguettes too. And, if attending an event at The Waterfront Hall, it may be useful to know that pre-theatre menus are available at their **Arc Brasserie** (028 9024 4966; www.waterfront.co.uk), from 5pm until 30 minutes before curtain up (also open for lunch). Food lovers visiting the city will of course want to go to **St George's Market**, which is one of Belfast's oldest attractions; since its refurbishment in 1997, the Friday (variety, including clothes, books and antiques) and Saturday (food and garden) markets held in this atmospheric Victorian building are among the most interesting things to visit in Belfast. In 2002 the Saturday Market won the Irish Food Writers' Guild Supreme Award for Contribution to Food in Ireland; Portavogie fish, venison and pheasant in season, local beef and pork, local organic vegetables, herbs and fruit, and farmhouse. Garden centres are often great places for a bite to eat, and Belfast is no exception; two to consider are the huge **Hillmount Garden Centre** (028 9044 8822; www.hillmount.co.uk), Gilnahirk, is well worth a visit for many reasons, including its café, **The Gardeners Rest**, where you'll find wholesome home cooked food every day (Mon-Fri 10-7.30, Sat 10-5, Sun 12.30-4.45); and Cameron Landscapes & Ballylesson Garden Centre (028 9082 6467; www.cameronlandscapes.com) on Ballylesson Road, Belfast 8, which is a Taste of Ulster member; open all day daily, plus evening meals on the last Fri & Sat of the month. Garden lovers are spoilt for choice when it comes to visits, as there are many outstanding gardens within 20km or so, including Redcot (appointment only, Kings Road, 028 9079 6614) a large town garden with herbaceous and grass borders, woodland and wild garden, Glenmount (appointment only, Dundonald, 028 9048 6324) a child friendly hillside garden with mixed planting of shrubs herbaceous plants and herbs and Guincho (appointment only, Helen's Bay, 028 9048 6324) which is an informal 12 acre garden with rare shrubs and trees, and stream and woodland area. cheeses are among the delicious things you'll find here. Visitors seeking other activities near Belfast will find plenty to do, including championship golf at the waterside Royal Belfast Golf Club (Craigavad, 028 9042 8165).
WWW.IRELAND-GUIDE.COM FOR THE BEST PLACES TO EAT, DRINK & STAY

Belfast

RESTAURANT

Aldens Restaurant

229 Upper Newtownards Road Belfast Co Antrim BT4 3JF
Tel: 028 9065 0079
info@aldensrestaurant.com www.aldensrestaurant.com

Fresh, bright, friendly and relaxed, Jonathan Davis's smart neighbourhood restaurant provides an antidote to all that is formal and stuffy. Recently renovated, Aldens proudly announced "a new look with new ideas, new menus and new opening times", yet some things won't be changed: it remains a destination address for food lovers visiting Belfast, as well as a favourite with residents - and its proximity to the government buildings at Stormont is a big plus. Despite recently spreading his wings to launch Aldens in the City (see entry) the ever present Mr Davis keeps his finger on the pulse and this continues to be an especially hospitable restaurant, with comfortable seating and pleasing details - fresh flowers, choice of olives, newspapers and food guides to browse over a drink in the welcoming bar/reception area, and warm service throughout. The style is lively and admirably simple, and rather more relaxed since the recent renovations, taking on a less formal brasserie feel. After more than two years at the helm of this busy kitchen, head chef Denise Hockey's policy is to allow quality fresh ingredients express themselves naturally through straightforward preparation, and giving good value is also a point of honour here, with several daily changing menus offered, including an extremely reasonable midweek menu and great lunch specials. Quality coffees and freshly baked pastries are now served in the afternoon, and also evening charcuterie and mezze plates. Menus include some luxurious dishes - roast squab pigeon with soft polenta and truffle jus perhaps; updated classics, like chicken liver paté with hot toast & red onion marmalade and steamed mussels with white wine, parsley and garlic sit happily alongside prime fish and meats (roast hake, ribeye steak), and simpler everyday foods like twice-baked spinach soufflé with parmesan cream (one of several mainstream vegetarian choices), served with imaginative side dishes. Consistency at this level over a decade is not an easy thing to achieve and, although the cooking was a little less impressive than formerly on a recent visit, Jonathan Davis's personal direction of a fine team should safeguard Aldens' longterm place at the top of Northern Ireland's dining scene. A well selected, fairly priced and informative wine list includes a good range of house wines and half bottles. *A range of Aldens gift items, including tapenade, red onion marmalade and Caesar salad dressing, is available. **Seats 70**; children welcome; air conditioning. L Mon-Fri,12-2.30; D Mon-Thu 5.30-9.30, Fri & Sat 6-11; Set 2/3 course D £18/22 (Mon-Thu), à la carte. House wines from about £12.95; sc discretionary. Closed L Sat, all Sun, Public Holidays, 2 weeks July. Amex, Diners, MasterCard, Visa, Switch. **Directions:** On the Upper Newtownards Road at junction with Sandown Road. ◊

Belfast   # Aldens in the City
CAFÉ•DELI

8-14 Callendar Street, Belfast BT1 5BN
Tel: 028 9024 5385   www.aldensinthecity.com

Very centrally situated in the former Skandia site just a few paces from the City Hall, this smart new offshoot of the well known fine dining restaurant, Aldens, has really taken off. A mirror along the length of one wall opens up the rather narrow space and a striking green soft leather bench running under it sounds a fresh note amid the contemporary cream tables and chairs and white paintwork. A row of window seats faces out onto the street, backed by a couple of inviting dark leather couches offering lower level tables, and shelves of tempting non-perishables line the walls. Queues frequently form at the neat deli servery, where there's an excellent and varied choice - over 20 very different dishes, plus a choice of ten sandwiches - including a few things that may be remembered from Aldens, such as bread with tapenade, and Aldens caesar salad, with or without anchovies. An outstanding seafood chowder has lots of finely diced fish and shellfish and truly lovely taste, served with very fresh bread - tomato with fennel, perhaps - and butter. Desserts displayed in a chill cabinet might include chocolate mousse with a profiterole on top, chocolate cake, tiramisu - and a lovely delicately made lemon tart with a fine pastry base and good lemon flavour, served with whipped cream and garnish. (There's a dedicated bread and patisserie chef on the staff here, and it shows.) The only downside here is a high noise level, but it's a great spot to drop into at any time during the day - and their 'coffee and scone £1.75' offer would be hard to beat. **Seats 50**. Table service L available. Open all day Mon-Sat, from 8am. **Directions:** Near back entrance to Marks and Spencers Royal Avenue store. ◊

Belfast   # An Old Rectory
GUESTHOUSE   148 Malone Road Belfast Co Antrim BT9 5LH **Tel: 028 90 66 7882**
info@anoldrectory.co.uk   www.anoldrectory.co.uk

Conveniently located near the King's Hall, Public Records Office, Lisburn Road and Queen's University, Mary Callan's lovely late Victorian house is set well back from the road in mature trees, with private parking. A former Church of Ireland rectory, it has the benefit of being in the Malone conservation area and retains many original features, including stained glass windows. There's a lovely drawing room with books, sofas, comfortable armchairs with cosy rugs over the arms - and a very hospitable habit of serving hot whiskey in the drawing room at 9 o'clock each night. Accommodation is on two storeys, every room is individually decorated (and named) and each has both a desk and a sofa, magazines to browse, also beverage trays with hot chocolate and soup sachets as well as the usual tea and coffee; better still there's a fridge on each landing with iced water and fresh milk, helpful advice on eating out locally is available (including menus) and, although they don't do evening meals, pride is taken in providing a good breakfast with an emphasis on using organic produce where possible. Children welcome (under 5 free in parents' room). Garden, walking. No pets. **Rooms 5** (3 en-suite, 2 with private bathrooms - 2 shower only, all no smoking). B&B £37.50 pps, ss £11.50. Closed Christmas-New Year & Easter. **No Credit Cards.** **Directions:** 2 miles (3km) from city centre, between Balmoral Avenue and Stranmillis Road.

Belfast   Avoca Café Belfast

CAFÉ   41 Arthur Street Belfast Co Antrim BT1 4GB **Tel: 028 9027 9955**
Ⓝ   b633elfast@shop.avoca.ie www.avoca.ie

Open since late 2007, the Belfast city centre branch of Avoca is the ninth store in Ireland for the
renowned Wicklow-based homeware, fashion and food company, who also have a US outlet in
Annapolis, Maryland. The Belfast store is in the former Habitat building in Arthur House on Arthur
Street, between Donegall Place and the new Victoria Square Shopping Centre; as elsewhere, it offers
all of the classy clothes, giftware, books and household items Avoca is famous for (including some of
the beautiful handwoven rugs from the looms in their original mill at Avoca village), and there is a
kitchen shop, food hall, café and bakery, which is in operation from 6am daily. Although slightly bigger,
it will feel very familiar to anyone who knows the flagship Dublin store. The restaurant is on the first
floor, with the usual pleasant décor and well spaced tables, but also a highly unusual feature - a glass-
walled cheese room, which is tempered for the cheeses, making a practical and very interesting
addition. The style at Avoca is eclectic and, although they are especially well-known for great baking
and traditional dishes like beef and Guinness casserole, their salads and vegetables are also legendary.
Quality ingredients-led menus follow the established formula here, with special strengths in breads
and baking, along with a wide range of wholesome dishes, possibly including a tasty lamb pie with
green beans, and a bean cassoulet with chorizo, served with nicely crusted bread, salsa verde and
créme fraiche. Rounded off with a homely dessert such as good baked cheesecake, this makes a
perfect shopping break - and, with enthusiastic young staff keen to please, service is good. Open 7
days a week - mon, tues, wed, fri & sat - 9.30am to 6pm (cafe closes at 5pm) thurs - 9.30am to 8pm
(cafe closes at 7pm) sun - 12.30pm to 6pm (cafe closes at 5pm). **Directions:** Between Donegall Place
and the new Victoria Square Shopping Centre.

Belfast   The Bank Gallery @ The Edge

RESTAURANT   The Edge May's Meadow Belfast Co Antrim BT1 3PH
                                                                                Tel: 028 9032 2000

Right on the Lagan and just a short stroll along a walkway from the Waterfront (and only 10 minutes
walk from Royal Avenue), this popular establishment known as The Edge operates on three levels,
with the smart Port Bar at lower ground level, a gently contemporary restaurant The Bank Gallery
above it, and a function/hospitality area on the top floor; food is served at all levels and, at busy times
in summer, people tend to migrate from one to another - and there are tables set up outside, and
even in the car park in good weather. With views of the famous Harland & Wolff cranes, Samson &
Goliath, and doors opening onto a small outside seating area on both bar and restaurant levels it a
pleasant spot which, thanks to consistently good cooking, has earned a following. The decor is
appealing: portholes in the double doors are repeated on chair backs and, with lightwood everywhere,
recessed wall lights and dusky pinks and beiges used in voile curtains and upholstery, there's a soft-
ness that offsets the industrial exterior. Tables are set up smartly with black rubber mats and simply
folded damask napkins, and professional black-aproned servers move speedily to bring delicious
warm breads with tapenade (about £2.50). As well as snacks and light lunches in the Port Bar,
Scottish head chef Duncan Millar's Bank Gallery menus offer a range of options at for lunch, early
evening meals and dinner; the style is modern , with a leaning towards Asian flavours although
appealing dishes with a more traditional influence may include wild Irish venison with Clonakilty
black pudding, creamed celeriac & caramelised red onion, or roast cod with mash, confit of tomato
& saffron. This is a super place, where good food combines with caring service and value for money.
Open L Mon-Fri 12-2.30; D Tue-Sat, 5.30-9.30; early 2/3 course D £14/17 5.30-7pm; D reservations advised; disabled access; lift. Pianist - baby grand (Fri & Sat from 9pm). Parking (8). Closed
Sun. MasterCard, Visa. **Directions:** Laganside. ◈

Belfast   Beatrice Kennedy

RESTAURANT   44 University Road Belfast Co Antrim BT7 1NJ **Tel: 028 9020 2290**
Ⓔ   www.beatrice.kennedy.co.uk

Named after the lady whose home it once was, the dining area of this unusual restaurant begins in
what would have been her front room and extends into adjoining areas towards the back, retaining
something of the authentic lived-in feeling of a private period residence; although now furnished with
white damask covered tables, it has a Victorian atmosphere with a small open fireplace and mantel-
piece and a few books and leftover personal effects: softly-lit, atmospheric, intimate, it exudes an
atmosphere of calm in which to enjoy proprietor-chef Jim McCarthy's accomplished cooking.
Ingredients are carefully sourced, and you may find some unusual dishes here - starters of slow cooked

duck tortellini with caramelised apples & shallots, perhaps, or seared foie gras on toasted malt loaf with five spiced apricots. Mains may include ever-popular steak, but it will come with a twist - a char-grilled ribeye of beef may be served with marinated red peppers, cocotte potatoes, salsa verde & pea shoots, for example. Desserts are very special, particularly the homemade icecreams (unlike many restaurants, the breads, desserts and ice creams are all home-made). Presentation is very special, especially the desserts, but the best thing about Beatrice Kennedy is that everything tastes as good as it looks. An understandably popular early evening menu offers excellent choices at a reasonable price, and Sunday lunch will also see the throngs arriving as the cost of a three-course meal is realistic. Staff are constantly friendly and helpful and this delightful place is very much itself, offering a welcome contrast to the mainly contemporary restaurants of the city. **Seats 80** (private room 25). D Tue-Sun, 5-10.15 (Sun to 8.15pm); L Sun only 12.30-2.15. Early D (5-7), Set Sun L £17.95. Closed Mon, 24-26 Dec, 11-14 Jul. Amex, MasterCard, Visa, Switch. **Directions:** Adjacent to Queen's University.

Belfast
HOTEL

Benedict's Hotel Belfast

7-21 Bradbury Place Belfast Co Antrim BT7 IRQ **Tel: 028 9059 1999**
info@benedictsHotel.co.uk www.benedictshotel.co.uk

Very conveniently located in Bradbury Place, just off Shaftesbury Square, this reasonably priced city centre hotel is situated in the heart of Belfast's "Golden Mile", and a wide range of attractions, including the Botanic Gardens, Queen's University, Queen's Film Theatre and Ulster Museum, are within a few minutes walk. Benedicts combines comfort and a degree of contemporary style with very moderate prices; the comfortable beds invariably come in for special praise, as do the warm and friendly staff; on the downside, it can sometimes be noisy and there is no on-site parking, although the hotel has an arrangement with a nearby carpark. Fusion/modern Irish the cooking style at the Bistro, where they offer a 'beat the clock' menu instead of the usual early brid; available 5.30-7 daily, the time you order is the price you pay. **Rooms 32** (12 executive rooms, 2 for disabled, all no smoking); children welcome (under 8s free in parents room; cot available without charge). No private parking (arrangement with nearby car park); no pets; free broadband WI/FI. Lift; all day room service. B&B from £40 pps, ss £30. Closed 24-25 Dec. Amex, Diners, MasterCard, Visa, Switch. **Directions:** City centre hotel situated in Bradbury Place - just off Shaftesbury Square in the heart of Belfast's "Golden Mile."

Belfast
RESTAURANT

Bourbon

60 Great Victoria Street Belfast Co Antrim BT2 7BB **Tel: 028 9033 2121**
info@bourbonrestaurant.com www.bourbonrestaurant.com

Behind an unassuming entrance lies an amazingly theatrical interior: totally at home alongside neighbouring buildings like the Crown Liquor Saloon and the Grand Opera House, it features pillars, palms, ornate plaster work and wrought iron, chandeliers and statues - everything, in short, to convey sumptuousness. Not to everybody's taste, to be sure, but it works, and this 'taste of New Orleans' is one of Belfast's most popular restaurants. But don't expect pristine white linen, silver and crystal: what you actually get is bare table tops, the ubiquitous black rubber place mats, and paper napkins. So it should come as no surprise that menus are modern, written in a no-nonsense style and offering a wide range of mainly international contemporary crowd pleasers: starters of spicy chicken wings and an extensive selection of main courses includes several poultry dishes, pasta, dry aged Aberdeen Angus steaks various ways, and homemade burgers. But vegetarians do get some choice too - pasta dishes for example and, perhaps, a Moroccan vegetable couscous with roast almonds and dates - and there will be several main course fish dishes, including a grilled whole fish with traditional parsley & caper butter. Helpful staff, competent cooking and an amazing atmosphere make this a place worth visiting. Open daily; air con. L Mon-Fri 12-2.3; D Mon-Sat 5-10 (to 11pm Fri/Sat); set menu and à la carte. House wine about £15. Closed Sat L & Sun L; 25-26 Dec. MasterCard, Visa, Switch **Directions:** City centre. ◊

Belfast
RESTAURANT

Café Conor

11A Stranmillis Road Belfast Co Antrim BT9 5AF
Tel: 028 9066 3266

Just across the road from the Ulster Museum, Manus McConn's unusual high-ceilinged room was originally the William Conor studio (1944-1959) and is bright with natural light from a lantern roof. The art theme is carried through to having original work always on show - there's a permanent exhibition of Neill Shawcross's bold and colourful work. Open for breakfast and brunch, through coffee, lunch, afternoon tea and eventually dinner, this is a casual place with a distinctive style - light wood booths along the walls and a long refectory-style table down the centre. Good coffee, home-baked scones, informal food such as warm chicken salad, hot panini with mozzarella, modern European dishes including lots of pastas, comfort food and classic dishes such as steak & Guinness pie are all worth dropping in for. Popular with locals, this place is a real find for those visiting the Museum (especially on Sundays); the only downside is that background music is sometimes too loud, which can make it difficult to converse. **Seats 50**. Open daily 9am-10pm (to 11pm Fri/Sat), L menu from noon, D specials from 5pm. A la carte. Licensed. Closed July fortnight. MasterCard, Visa, Switch. **Directions:** Opposite Ulster Museum. ◇

Belfast ㅤㅤㅤㅤㅤㅤㅤㅤㅤㅤㅤㅤㅤㅤㅤㅤㅤㅤㅤ Café Paul Rankin

CAFÉ ㅤㅤㅤㅤㅤㅤㅤㅤㅤㅤㅤㅤ 27-29 Fountain Street Belfast Co Antrim BT1 5EA

Tel: 028 9031 5090

Café Paul Rankin offers informal quality food (notably their speciality baking) throughout the day - be it for a quick cup of coffee or a more leisurely bite with a glass of wine, this is an in place for a shopping break. The breakfast menu is available all day and includes Jeanne's toasted muesli & yoghurt, while a wider range of hot food on offer after 11am includes the Rankin club sandwich and a range of quiches and salads. Smart pavement tables for fine weather - and food to go too. **Seats 50** (outside seating, 12); no reservations. Shop open 7.30-5.30; kitchen open 8am-5pm. Closed Sun; 25 Dec, 1 Jan, 12 Jul. MasterCard, Visa, Switch. **Directions:** Town centre, near City Hall. ◇

Belfast ㅤㅤㅤㅤㅤㅤㅤㅤㅤㅤㅤㅤㅤㅤㅤㅤㅤㅤㅤㅤㅤ Café Renoir

CAFÉ•RESTAURANT ㅤㅤㅤㅤㅤㅤㅤㅤ 95 Botanic Avenue Belfast Co Antrim BT7 1JN

Tel: 028 9031 1300

Husband and wife team Lindsay and Karen Loney's Café Renoir restaurant and shop have a great local following, especially among young professionals, for wholesome homemade food, both in this stylishly informal premises and in the original Queen Street daytime café in the city's main shopping area, which has been in business since 1991. Here on Botanic Avenue, European bistro is the stated style and they've earned respect for their support of local and organic produce as well as for delicious cooking with real home flavour. Open throughout the day with varying offerings, the café begins early with a breakfast menu and is open right through until late at night. Home baking is a speciality and their cakes, tray bakes and scones are popular for in-between times; lunchtime is busy and the menu includes a wide selection of vegetarian dishes, then at night it takes on a bistro atmosphere and menu. Beside it, the pizzeria (with wood fired pizza oven) offers keenly priced informal evening meals. Private rooms available; outside catering also offered. Private rooms available; outside catering also offered. Cafe/Bistro: **Seats 100**. Licensed. Open 8am -11pm. Pizzeria: Seats 100. Unlicensed (BYO). Open 5pm 'late'; early bird 5-7pm; on Mon & Tue all pizzas are about £8. *Also at: 5-7 Queen Street. MasterCard, Visa. **Directions:** Near Botanic Gardens, at back of Queen's University. ◇

Belfast ㅤㅤㅤㅤㅤㅤㅤㅤㅤㅤㅤㅤㅤㅤㅤㅤㅤㅤㅤㅤㅤ Cargoes Café

CAFÉ ㅤㅤㅤㅤㅤㅤㅤ 613 Lisburn Road Belfast Co Antrim BT9 7GT **Tel: 028 9066 5451**

Ⓔ ㅤㅤㅤㅤㅤㅤㅤㅤㅤㅤㅤㅤㅤㅤ info@cargoescafe.com www.cargoescafe.com

Radha Patterson's very special little delicatessen and café has maintained a great reputation over more than a decade in business - fine produce for the delicatessen side of the business is meticulously sourced, and the same philosophy applies to the food served in the café. Modern European cooking works well with some Thai and Indian influences here, and simple preparation and good seasonal ingredients dictate menus. Smoked & fresh salmon terrine, Mediterranean tapas selection and beef & Guinness are regulars, also vegetarian dishes such as goat's cheese & tarragon tart. There are classic desserts like lemon tart or apple flan, also delicious bakes like cinnamon scones and Moroccan orange cake and a range of stylish sandwiches. Very nice friendly and helpful staff, too. Children welcome; toilets wheelchair accessible; air conditioning. Seats 36 (+ outdoor seating area, 12). Open Mon-Sat 9 am-4.15 pm, L 12-3.30; Sun 10-3pm. A la carte; sc discretionary. MasterCard, Visa, Switch. Directions: On the Lisburn Road. **Seats 36** (new outdoor seating area, 12); children welcome; toilets wheelchair accessible; air conditioning. Open Mon-Sat 9 am-4.30 pm (to 5pm Sat), L 12-3.30; Sun 10-3.30pm. A la carte; sc discretionary. MasterCard, Visa, Switch. **Directions:** On the Lisburn Road. ◇

Belfast   Cayenne

RESTAURANT   7 Ascot House Shaftesbury Square Belfast Co Antrim BT2 7DB

🏆 ☆   **Tel: 028 9033 1532**

belinda@rankingroup.co.uk www.rankingroup.co.uk

After two decades as pioneers of Northern Ireland's food culture, Paul and Jeanne Rankin's flagship restaurant continues to offer Belfast diners a mix of interesting and fashionable food in a cool urban atmosphere. While perhaps no longer at the cutting edge of the city's food scene, this large, funky restaurant still does what it has always done: cooking well sourced food skilfully, and presenting it with style at affordable prices. Yet, although both well known and well located, it seems to be less busy than it used to be, probably because - largely thanks to the efforts of the Rankins themselves - the city now offers so much choice; also, perhaps, because you could easily walk past it without knowing it was a restaurant, so that casual diners unfamiliar with the legend try their luck elsewhere. They may, however, be missing a bargain, especially at lunchtime when 2/3 course menus at £12/15 are a steal. The dark brown and spicy cayenne interior is a pleasing mix of smart contemporary décor and old fashioned comfort; round tables down one side of the restaurant have classic white linen, while rectangular ones opposite are bare, but both have very comfortable chairs - and friendly, smartly uniformed staff are quick to settle arriving guests in and offer menus. At lunch a choice of three dishes is offered on each course and very nice they are too, although perhaps a little too restrictive as the jump to à la carte prices is discouragingly significant for lunchtime. Fish cooking is a strength at Cayenne, and other especially enjoyable choices could include an interesting and tasty rare breed pork belly with crubeen sausage, thyme and flageolet beans and - from a separate vegetarian menu - a simple, fresh-tasting ricotta and spinach ravioli, with tomatoes and olive oil. The à la carte menu is likely to feature many of the Cayenne signature dishes - the ever-popular salt'n'chilli squid with chilli jam and aioli, for example, or - striking a more more European tone - a delectable combination of pan seared foie gras with toasted brioche and roast nectarines; but nothing stands still here, and even the most popular dishes are under constant review. Desserts offer a combination of innovative (crispy fried strawberry & marshmallow strudel with blackcurrant sauce and crème fraîche) and familiar (Bramley apple & blackberry crumble with blackberry ripple ice cream), and portions may be unexpectedly large. The cooking can be really exciting, and is generally backed efficiently up by smart, well-trained young staff who work tirelessly to ensure guests receive first class service. A very good wine list, organised by grape variety and style, offers a wide choice in both range and price, and includes plenty of wines by the glass and half bottles, also some fine wines; extensive drinks menu too. **Seats 120** (private room, 16); reservations advised; children welcome; air conditioning; toilets wheelchair accessible. L Tue-Fri 12-2.15; set 2/3 course L £12/15.50. D Mon-Sun 5-10/10.30pm (to 8.45pm Sun); early bird 2/3 course D 5-7pm £15.50/19.50; also la carte & vegetarian menu. House wine from about £17 sc discretionary (except 10% recommended on parties of 6+). Closed L Sat-Mon, 25-26 Dec, 1 Jan, 12 July. Amex, Diners, MasterCard, Visa, Switch. **Directions:** 5 mins from Europa Hotel at top of Great Victoria St. ◊

Belfast   The Crescent Townhouse

HOTEL•RESTAURANT   13 Lower Crescent Belfast Co Antrim BT7 1NR **Tel: 028 9032 3349**

info@crescenttownhouse.com www.crescenttownhouse.com

This is an elegant 19th century listed building on the corner of Botanic Avenue, just a short stroll from the city centre and is a good choice for business visitors. The reception lounge is on the first floor and the ground floor is taken up by the Metro Brasserie and a stylish club-like bar, Bar Twelve, that is particularly lively and popular at night - so noise could be a problem in front bedrooms. Spacious bedrooms include suites and superior rooms, that are more elaborate and have luxurious bathrooms (some with Victorian roll top baths and walk-in showers), but all are comfortably furnished, with neat bathrooms. Breakfast is taken in the contemporary Metro Brasserie on the lower ground floor (see below), which is open for all meals. Children welcome before 7pm (under 14s free in parents' room, cots available without charge, baby sitting arranged). No pets.*Weekend breaks offer good value. **Rooms 17** (1 suite, 2 junior suites, 5 superior, 6 shower only, 1 disabled, 2 no smoking); children welcome before 7pm (under 14s free in parents' room, cots available without charge, baby sitting arranged). No pets.Wheelchair lift. Room service (limited hours). B&B £45-55 pps, ss £45. **Metro Brasserie:** This popular restaurant has a following for its good value contemporary cooking, and the atmosphere is welcoming and pleasant. The main restaurant is split level, classy and elegant, with an audible buzz and comfortable seating including banquettes around the walls. Menus offer well-sourced, often local, ingredients and accomplished cooking - sometimes in unusual combinations, such as lavender and goat's cheese terrine, with fig & port chutney and toasted brioche, or Finnebrogue venison, with wild mushroom strudel, butternut squash purée, spinach and Madeira jus. The 2/3 course Early Bird menu is especially popular and very reasonable at £16.95 / £19.50. **Rooms 17** (1 suite, 2 junior suites, 5 superior, 6 shower only, 1 disabled, 2 no smoking); children welcome before 7pm (under 14s free in parents' room, cots available without charge, baby sitting arranged). No pets.Wheelchair lift. Room service (limited hours). B&B £45-55 pps, ss £45. Metro Brasserie **Seats 70.** D daily from 5.45 (Sat from 5.30, Sun from 5pm). Early D & Vegetarian menus available. Lunch also at BarTwelve: Mon-Sat 12-3. *Weekend breaks offer good value. Amex, MasterCard, Visa, Switch. **Directions:** Opposite Botanic Railway Station. ◇

Belfast   Crown Liquor Saloon
CHARACTER PUB   46 Great Victoria Street Belfast Co Antrim BT2 7 BA
                                               Tel: 02890 279 901

Belfast's most famous pub, The Crown Liquor Saloon, was perhaps the greatest of all the Victorian gin palaces which once flourished in Britain's industrial cities. Although now owned by the National Trust (and run by Bass Leisure Retail) the Crown is far from being a museum piece and attracts a wide clientèle of locals and visitors. A visit to one of its famous snugs for a pint and half a dozen oysters served on crushed ice, or a bowl of Irish Stew, is a must. The upstairs restaurant section, "Flannigans Eaterie & Bar", is built with original timbers from the SS Britannic, sister ship to the Titanic. Crown: bar food served Mon-Sat 12-3. Flannigans: 11-9. Closed 25-16 Dec. Diners, MasterCard, Visa. Directions: City centre, opposite Europa Hotel. Bar food served Mon-Sat 12-3. Flannigans: 11-9. Closed 25-16 Dec. Diners, MasterCard, Visa. **Directions:** City centre, opposite Europa Hotel.

Belfast   Deanes at Queens
BAR•RESTAURANT   36-40 College Gardens Belfast Co Antrim BT **Tel: 028 9038 2111**
                                               www.michaeldeane.co.uk

With its stylish contemporary interior enhanced by original work from local artist Oliver Jeffers and an alfresco eating area overlooking 'Methody' (as the school, Methodist College, is known locally), this all day bar and grill is a relatively recent addition to the Deane empire - and, as well as Deane's trademark good food, it brings a refreshing contrast to the mainly traditional atmosphere that the fine Victorian architecture of the university gives to the area. Menus through the day begin with casual brunch fare, then light food in the afternoon and follow with more structured evening meals; many of the dishes are Deanes classics that will be familiar to anyone who has visited Deanes Deli in the city centre. It's child friendly (children's menu available up to 7pm) with the outside seating area being non-smoking. An accessible wine list includes a good choice by the glass and a high proportion of half bottles. The Common Rooms are available for private parties, either singly or together. Open daily 1-10 (except: Sun 11.30-3; Mon & Tue 11.30-9). L Menu 12-3; Afternoon Specials 3-5; D from 5pm. **Directions:** Just up from Queen's University and to the right, Deane's at Queens is at the QUB Common Rooms on College Gardens, overlooking Methodist College. ◇

Belfast   Deanes Deli
RESTAURANT   44 Bedford Street Belfast Co Antrim BT2 7FF **Tel: 028 9024 8800**
                               info@michaeldeane.co.uk www.michaeldeane.co.uk

Just around the corner from Deanes Restaurant, this smashing New York style all day deli-dining experience is a smart-casual venue serving great bistro food and given an extra twist by the sumptuous retail deli store adjacent to the restaurant. Walter's smoked salmon with cucumber, lemon crème fraich, capers & cress, Salt & chilli squid with Asian salad and Portavogie fish'n'chips with tartare sauce & mushy peas are all typical dishes, and although the evening menu gears up a bit, it's still very informal. And there are loads of tempting things to take home from the deli, of course, including Deanes own label range. Well chosen drinks list to match, including beer and cocktails, as well as accessible wines. **Seats 80** (outdoors, 10); reservations advised; children welcome (high chair, baby changing facilities); toilets wheelchair accessible; air conditioning. Open all day Mon-Sat, 11.30-9pm (to 10pm Wed-Sat); L 11.30-3, D 5.30-9; à la carte. SC 10%. Live music weekend evenings. Closed Sun; 25 Dec; 12-13 Jul. Amex, MasterCard, Visa, Switch. **Directions:** City centre, near Ulster Hall.

Belfast

RESTAURANT

💬 🍷 ★★

Deanes Restaurant

36-40 Howard Street Belfast Co Antrim BT1 6PF **Tel: 028 9033 1134**

info@michaeldeane.co.uk www.michaeldeane.co.uk

Following the recent makeover of Northern Ireland's most exceptional dining experience, Michael Deane's city centre hot spot continues to fly ever higher. For not only has the prolific chef's hard working team been flamboyantly flying the flag of quality food but, with the dynamic duo of Derek Creagh and Alain Kerloc'h, in the kitchen and restaurant respectively, they have fashioned an outstanding all round package. Diners can enjoy pre-dinner drinks in the elegant bar and lounge area before exploring the brightly lit, minimalist dining room. The smart, attentive and knowledgeable staff are plentiful and always on hand, providing unobtrusive professional service while, behind the open kitchen service hatch, Donegal born Creagh works his magic, and what magic! An evening à la carte menu offers six choices on each course and reads deceptively simply, yet it is anything but basic and offers many luxury ingredients, artistically prepared in dishes of great refinement. Homemade breads come with tapenade, olive oil and balsamic vinegar, leading you into a meal that is sure to be a memorable experience and is, if anything, enhanced by the limited choice and simple menu offering. Typically, you will find creative, perfectly judged starters like pan-fried local scallops with pickled carrot & watercress salad, orange and aniseed emulsion, or carpaccio of Oisin venison, with pan-fried sweetbreads and summer mushrooms, baby leaves & almond butter vinaigrette, and a flavour-packed speciality of saddle back pork belly with roast langoustine, Savoy cabbage, black pudding & apple caramel which proved to be a sublime encounter on a recent visit by the Guide. Main courses may include a stunningly tender cannon of new season lamb, confit lamb breast, St Tola goat's cheese gnocchi, fennel purée & sauce niçoise, executed to perfection with seemingly effortless precision; and, perhaps, a much-loved French classic with a modern twist - saddle of rabbit with smoked bacon, macaroni gratin, roast cèpes, salsify & verjus reduction. Every dish is brilliantly accomplished, perfectly judged, eye-catching and - something which is missing in too many restaurants - has real depth of flavour. Dynamic pastry chef Monto Mansour ensures that you will conclude your Deane's experience on a high. Accomplished treats such as warm pistachio tart with a sublime blood orange & rose water sorbet, and a Granny Smith tart fine with frangelico ice-cream and hazelnut praline are testament to this young man's talent. Lunch menus offer a good range of more informal dishes, but the same high standards apply. An appropriate wine list includes a champagne menu and many classic treats, as well as some more accessible bottles and a page of wines available by the glass and, as always, the discreet advice given to match wines with the food is outstanding. Deane and his team have for many years been the pioneers of modern food in Belfast and further afield, and have been exceptionally courageous and tireless in advancing this cause, providing serious diners with a world class cuisine choice on their doorsteps. Deane's has set the standard for the local scene, and few will equal it. The first floor restaurant is available by arrangement for private parties. *Deanes Restaurant was the Guide's Restaurant of the Year in 2008. **Seats 80** (private room, 40); air conditioning; toilets wheelchair accessible; children welcome. L Mon-Sat 12-3, D Mon-Sat 6-10. Set L £17.50; also A la carte L&D; SC 10%. Closed Sun, Bank Hols; 24-26 Dec, Jul 12-14. *'Deanes Deli', a New York style all day deli dining experience is around the corner at 44 Bedford Street (see entry). Amex, MasterCard, Visa, Switch. **Directions:** From back of City Hall, about 150m towards M1, on left.

Belfast

RESTAURANT

💬 🄴

Ginger

7-8 Hope Street Belfast Co Antrim BT12 5EE **Tel: 028 9024 4421**

www.gingerbistro.com

A flyer proclaims "Where there is life there is Hope Street, where there is Hope Street there is the Ginger Bistro" and that nicely sums up the attitude at redhead Simon 'Ginger' McCance's chic and cheerful bistro just off Great Victoria Street. Far from grand - except for a lovely mahogany floor and a tall window beautifully dressed with softly smoky leather trimmed voile - it's a quirky place with two dining spaces, a partially visible kitchen, and décor 'a bit like home' with a mix'n'match of furniture and light fittings and acid green and deep mauve/purple accents. Carefully sourced ingredients have always been at the centre of this likeable chef's philosophy and, although you will find wide ranging influences on his constantly changing menus, you can be sure that the food that tastes so good will be local if possible. Menus are balanced, offering a good choice of vegetarian dishes alongside appealing meat dishes like braised pork belly with creamy mash & rosemary jus, but seafood is what he likes to cook best: grilled sardines, for example or beautifully cooked crisp-skinned seabass with an unusual celeriac and pea casserole. And, although they don't take themselves too seriously (there's a light-hearted tone on blackboard notices etc), there's no doubt that this is a place that is serious about the quality of both food and wine. Finish with a classic dessert (crème brulée with raspberry compôte, perhaps) or an Irish cheese selection. Prices are reasonable and lunch/pre-theatre menus offer especially good value. In addition to carefully-chosen wines, there's a full bar list. **Seats 60**; children welcome; reservations required. L Tue-Sat, 12-3pm; D Mon-Sat 5-10pm; A la carte L&D; house wine £13.50. Closed Sun, L Mon, 2 weeks Jul, 2 weeks Christmas. MasterCard, Visa, Switch. **Directions:** Off Great Victoria street, 5 mins from Europa Hotel. ◇

Belfast   # Harbour View Teppanyaki
RESTAURANT   1 Lanyon Quay Belfast Co Antrim BT1 3LG **Tel: 028 9023 8823**
                               booking@harbourviewbelfast.co.uk www.harbourviewbelfast.co.uk

At this scenic Lagan side location beside the Waterfront Hall, the ever popular Japanese dining experience, Teppanyaki, is alive and well. Very friendly professional staff greet customers arriving at the spacious lounge and reception area overlooking the river and, after choosing from the extensive Japanese menu, one is led to the Teppan and seated comfortably to watch the chef's deft displays, as he cuts, stirs and flambés various seafood and meat dishes on the Teppan. The menu offers an excellent selection of superbly fresh seafood, sushi and sashimi, with some meat dishes such as duck, beef and chicken also available, all served with wonderfully fluffy fried rice and Japanese noodles. After such an impressively cooked meal, the desserts are somewhat less appealing (although the idea of flambé ice cream might be entertaining), so you could find yourself returning to the lounge to relax, enjoy the view and finish drinks. Teppanyaki is an entertaining night out and is especially suited to larger parties, but be warned: it does come at a premium. Toilets wheelchair accessible; open for food all day; L 12-2.30; à la carte from 2.30 to 11pm; house wine £16. Closed Christmas Day only. Amex, MasterCard, Visa, Switch. **Directions:** By the Waterfront Hall. ◇

Belfast   # Hastings Europa Hotel
HOTEL   Great Victoria Street Belfast Co Antrim BT2 7AP **Tel: 028 9027 1066**
                               res@eur.hastingshotels.com www.hastingshotels.com

This landmark 1970s city centre building is the largest hotel in Northern Ireland and particularly striking when illuminated at night. It has undergone many changes since first opening in the '70s and has been renovated and refurbished to a high standard, including the addition of executive rooms. Off the impressive tall-columned entrance foyer is an all-day brasserie and the lobby bar featuring live musical entertainment; and upstairs, on the first floor, you'll find the Gallery Lounge and a cocktail bar. However, perhaps the hotel's greatest assets are the function suites and the staff, who are excellent, ensuring high standards of service, housekeeping and maintenance. Nearby parking can be added to your account. Conference/banqueting (750/600); business centre, bradband wi/fi. **Rooms 275** (1 presidential suite, 4 junior suites, 56 executive rooms, 7 family, 90 single, 90 shower only, 240 no smoking, 2 for disabled); children welcome (under 14s free in parents' room; cots available without charge). No pets. Lifts. B&B £121 pps, ss £35. **Piano Bar Restaurant:** D Mon-Sat (closed 24 Dec-2 Jan); Brasserie open all day 6am-11pm (Sun from 7 am). *Short breaks offered - details on application. Hotel closed 24-25 Dec. Amex, Diners, MasterCard, Visa, Switch. **Directions:** Located in the heart of Belfast.

Belfast   # Hastings Stormont Hotel
HOTEL   Upper Newtownards Road Belfast Co Antrim BT4 3LP **Tel: 028 9067 6012**
                               res@stor.hastingshotels.com www.hastingshotels.com

A few miles east of the city centre, the hotel is directly opposite the imposing gates leading to Stormont Castle and Parliament Buildings and it suits the business guest well. There's a huge entrance lounge, with stairs up to a more intimate mezzanine area overlooking the castle grounds, and the main restaurant and informal modern bistro are both pleasantly located. Spacious, practical bedrooms have good workspace and offer the usual facilities; several rooms are designated for female executives, and there is a relatively new executive floor. The hotel also has eight self-catering apartments with their own car parking area, featuring a twin bedroom, lounge and kitchen/dinette, available for short stays or long periods. The self-contained Confex Centre, comprising ten trade rooms, complements the function suites in the main building. Weekend rates and short breaks are good value. Conference/banqueting (500/350); business centre, broadband wi/fi. **Rooms 110** (1 suite, 5 junior suites, 23 executive, 2 family, 25 ground floor, 1 for disabled, all no smoking). Own parking (255). Wheelchair accessible. No pets. Lift. B&B £106 pps, ss £50. Fitness room. Golf nearby. Open all year. Amex, Diners, MasterCard, Visa, Switch. Directions: 3 miles east of Belfast city centre; take A20 towards Newtownards - directly opposite Stormont Parliament Buildings.

Belfast   # Hawthorne Coffee Shop & Espresso Bar
CAFÉ•RESTAURANT   Fulton's Fine Furnishings Balmoral Plaza Boucher Road
Belfast Co Antrim BT2 6HU **Tel: 028 9038 4705**

Not only did The Hawthorne café/restaurant retain pride of place on the first floor when Fulton's relocated to the Balmoral Plaza development on Boucher Road, but a downstairs espresso bar was included too, with splendid leather seats where you can have a restorative coffee and something to tempt the sweet tooth. The shop's stairwell - of cathedral proportions, like the shop itself - incorporates a double escalator leading to the first floor where the Hawthorne has floor to ceiling windows and a number of pleasant seating areas, some with elevated views over the Boucher Road and beyond to the Black Mountain. If you're shopping or have business in the area (generous parking) this is a great place to know about as, thanks to the personal attention of Sylvia Fulton, there's a pride in real home cooking - and the art of scone making is alive and well. There's nothing flashy about the food: expect lovely flavoursome dishes like home-made soup with wheaten bread, quiches - asparagus & salmon, vegetable - seafood pie and steak & mushroom hot-pot and several casseroles daily. There's always a large selection of salads, and home-made desserts like banoffee and lemon meringue pie - and free refills of coffee. An added attraction, between 12 and 2, is the resident pianist playing on a Steinway baby grand. **Seats 160** (private room, 60); children welcome (high chair, baby changing facilities); toilets wheelchair accessible. Open Mon Sat 9.15-5.15. A la carte. Espresso bar open to 8 pm Thu, for late night shoppers. Master Card, Visa, Switch. **Directions:** Off M1, take Stockman's Lane exit off roundabout, left into Boucher Road. (At Fultons Fine Furnishings Store).

Belfast   # Hilton Belfast
HOTEL   4 Lanyon Place Belfast Co Antrim BT1 3LP **Tel: 028 9027 7000**
hilton_belfast@hilton.com

Occupying a prominent position on a rise beside the Waterfront Hall, the interior of this landmark hotel is impressive: the scale is grand, the style throughout is of contemporary clean-lined elegance - the best of modern materials have been used and the colour palette selected is delicious - and, best of all, it makes the best possible use of its superb waterside site, with the Sonoma Restaurant and several suites commanding exceptional views. Outstanding conference and business facilities include the state-of-the-art Hilton Meeting service tailored to individual requirements, and three executive floors with a Clubroom. All rooms have air-conditioning, in-room movies, and no-stop check-out in addition to the usual facilities, and recreational facilities are also excellent; however, although there is a multi-storey carpark next door, it is not owned by the hotel. Conference/banqueting (400/260); secretarial services; business centre; video conferencing; broadband. **Rooms 195** (6 suites, 7 junior suites, 38 executive rooms, 68 no-smoking, 10 for disabled); children welcome (cots available). Lifts. Room rate (max. 2 guests) from about £100. Leisure centre; indoor swimming pool; beauty salon. Open all year. Amex, Diners, MasterCard, Visa, Switch **Directions:** Belfast city centre, beside Waterfront Hall. ◇

Belfast   # Holiday Inn Belfast
HOTEL   22 - 26 Ormeau Avenue Belfast Co Antrim BT2 8HS **Tel: 028 9032 8511**
belfast@ichotelsgroup.com   www.belfast.holiday-inn.com

Conveniently located near most of the main city centre attractions, this contemporary hotel offers luxurious modern accommodation, with excellent business and health and leisure facilities. The style is classy and spacious; bedrooms are designed particularly with the business guest in mind - the decor is unfussy and warm, with comfort and relaxation in mind to match its use as a workbase; superior rooms all have air conditioning, modem points, fridge, interactive TV with on-screen checkout facility and Sky Sports, trouser press, power shower, cotton bathrobe and quality toiletries, while suites have their own hallway as well as a separate sitting/dining room. 'The Academy' offers state-of-the-art conference and training facilities, and business support. Conference/banqueting (120/100); business centre, secretarial services, video-conferencing. **Rooms 170** (2 suites, 36 executive, 102 no smoking, 10 for disabled); children welcome (under 16s free in parents' room, cot available without charge). Lift. 24 hour room service. B&B from about £85pps. Special weekend rates available. No private parking (NCP car park behind hotel). Leisure centre; swimming pool; beauty salon. Open all year. Amex, Diners, MasterCard, Visa, Switch. **Directions:** Opposite BBC, 2 minutes walk from City Hall via Bedford Street. ◇

Belfast

James Street South

RESTAURANT   21 James Street South Belfast Co Antrim BT2 7GA **Tel: 028 9043 4310**

info@jamesstreetsouth.co.uk   www.jamesstreetsouth.co.uk

In a narrow side street behind Belfast's City Hall, Niall and Joanne McKenna's bright and stylish restaurant has tall arched windows overlooking James Steet South and, with its crisp white linen, fresh flowers, contemporary Irish artwork and smart mirrors, it conveys a welcoming sense of confidence. Since opening in 2004 Niall McKenna has stamped his own authority on the Northern food scene, and this gem of a restaurant has earned a loyal following for refined cooking which can be truly memorable. McKenna, who has worked for respected names like Gary Rhodes, Marco Pierre White and Nico Ladenis, heads a first-rate team, effortlessly combining natural charm with focus. His exuberant modern cooking is innovative, yet takes care to maintain harmony and balance; menus make interesting reading, with seasonal and local produce very prevalent and a good balance of fresh flavours - seen, perhaps in a tomato terrine with wild rocket vinaigrette that is choc-a-bloc with summery Mediterranean flavours - and full on dishes with richer

flavours, such as crispy pork belly with calamari, asparagus and red pepper dressing. Fish and seafood are skilfully handled and, on a recent visit by the guide, a main dish of roast turbot with razor clam and lobster bouillabaisse was a triumph; strikingly presented, perfectly executed, and full of flavour - what a delight. Vegetarians are thoughtfully catered for too - you may find a seasonal white onion and asparagus galette with fig and red wine reduction, for example, packed with flavour yet fresh and lively. Utterly irresistible desserts include reworked classics such as, strawberry Melba and warm pear tarte tatin with vanilla bean ice cream. This is, in a sense, simple food; using only the best of fresh, local ingredients it is cooked with an assured elegance and a merciful absence of fusion influences. The dining room has an exciting lively ambience, with friendly staff going about their business in a quietly efficient manner - and it is never difficult to catch their eye. The wine list is one of the best in town and includes numerous regional varieties; although mainly under £30, there is also a short selection of fine wines. Lunch and pre-theatre menus offer exceptional value, and gourmet wine evenings are sometimes held. **Seats 70**; reservations advised; air conditioning; children welcome. L Mon-sat, 12-2.45; D daily, 5.45-10.45 (Sun 5.30-9.30). Set L about £15. Pre theatre D Mon-Thu 5.45-6.45 about £16, also à la carte. Closed 25-26 Dec, 1 Jan, 11-12 July. Amex, MasterCard, Visa, Switch. **Directions:** City centre: located behind Belfast City Hall, between Bedford Stree and Brunswick street.

Belfast

The John Hewitt Bar & Restaurant

BAR•RESTAURANT•PUB   51 Donegall Street Belfast Co Antrim BT1 2FH

Tel: 028 9023 3768

info@thejohnhewitt.com   www.thejohnhewitt.com

The in-place pub for discerning Belfast people, who like the combination of traditional interior and good quality sassy modern food, The John Hewitt is owned by the Unemployment Resource Centre next door, which was originally opened by the poet and socialist John Hewitt in the 1980s. Some years ago they decided to open the premises as a bar, and all profits go back to that worthy cause. High-ceilinged, with a marble bar, a snug and an open fire, there's a pleasing preference for conversation and civilised relaxation. It operates more or less as a restaurant by day - they serve lunch every day except Sunday, and offer a light afternoon 'Talking Bowls' snack menu on Friday & Saturday afternoons. There are traditional music sessions three nights a week (Tue, Wed & Sat), live music every Thursday and jazz on Fridays - which leaves Mondays free for exhibition launches. The day's menu is posted on their website. A short wine list includes two wines of the month, four by the glass and two bubblies. Children welcome before 4pm; toilets wheelchair accessible. Open daily; food served Mon-Thur 12-3pm; Fri-Sat, 3.30-6pm. Closed Sun. MasterCard, Visa, Switch. **Directions:** Belfast city centre; 3 doors from St Ann's Cathedral.

Belfast
HOTEL

Jurys Inn Belfast

Fisherwick Place Great Victoria Street Belfast Co Antrim BT2 7AP
Tel: 028 9053 3500
jurysinnbelfast@jurysinns.com www.jurysinns.com

Located in the heart of the city, close to the Grand Opera House and City Hall and just a couple of minutes walk from the major shopping areas of Donegall Place and the Castlecourt Centre, Jurys Belfast Inn offers comfortable accommodation in a central location at very reasonable prices. The high standards and good value of all Jurys Inns applies here too: all rooms are en-suite (with bath and shower) and spacious enough to accommodate two adults and two children (or three adults) at a fixed price. Rooms are well-designed and regularly refurbished, with good amenities for a hotel in the budget class. **Rooms 190** (all no smoking, 1 for disabled); children welcome (under 12s free in parents room, cot available free of charge). Room rate from £74, (max 3 guests w/o b'fst). Lift. Small conferences (30). Restaurant. Closed 24-26 Dec. Amex, Diners, MasterCard, Visa. **Directions:** City centre, next to Opera House. ◇

Belfast
HOTEL

Malhaison Hotel

34-38 Victoria Street Belfast Co Antrim BT1 3GH **Tel: 028 9022 0200**
belfast@malmaison.com www.malmaison-belfast.com

This beautiful building (especially striking when lit up at night) is now owned by the stylish UK group Malmaison who introduced a new wow factor to Belfast accommodation choices, beginning with the reception area where everything is black and white, with opulent drapes and large church candles. Although it may seem a bit overwhelming (notably the bar, which can be very noisy), friendly, efficient staff at reception set arriving guests at their ease and guest accommodation - spacious, contemporary, luxurious, with all the technical gizmos you could possibly want - is given a human dimension with the offer of early morning delivery of a quarter pint of fresh milk. The two suites aptly-named Samson and Goliath (after the famous Harland & Wolff cranes) sport nine foot beds, and one of them even has its own purple baize pool table. The Brasserie offers simple wholesome fare (steaks from The Duke of Baccleuch's Scottish Estate, for example), and good breakfasts are smartly served here too. The bar, with extensive cocktail menu, flat screen television, huge leather sofas, flickering lights, and loud music, is an in-place at night. Multi storey car park nearby, but check details when booking as it is may not be possible to access your car at certain times. Multi storey car park nearby. **Rooms 62**; Room rate from about £140. Brasserie: L & D daily. Amex, MasterCard, Visa, Switch. **Directions:** Centre of Belfast. ◇

Belfast
HOTEL

Malone Lodge

60 Eglantine Avenue Malone Road Belfast Co Antrim BT9 6DY **Tel: 028 9038 8000**
info@malonelodgehotel.com www.malonelodgehotel.com

This reasonably priced townhouse hotel near Queen's University is very pleasantly located if you like to be in a quiet area, yet convenient to the city centre. It offers comfortable accommodation in spacious well-maintained en-suite rooms, with all the facilities required by business guests, both in-room and in the hotel itself. There are good conference and meeting facilities and plenty of parking space, and yet it is within walking distance of city centre restaurants and entertainment. Conferences/Banqueting (140). **Rooms 51** (standard or executive), B&B £52.50-60; ss £25; suites from about £150; ample parking (access to back of hotel from carpark), fitness suite, broadband. Weekend specials from £99. Open all year. *Malone Lodge also has 22 apartments comprising of one, two and three bedroom suites. MasterCard, Visa, Switch. **Directions:** Between the Lisburn and Malone Roads in South Belfast.

Belfast
RESTAURANT•PUB

McHugh's Bar & Restaurant

29-31 Queen's Square Belfast Co Antrim BT1 3FG **Tel: 028 9050 9999**
info@mchughsbar.com www.mchughsbar.com

This remarkable pub near the Odyssey Arena is in one of Belfast's few remaining 18th century buildings; built in 1711, it is the city's oldest listed building. It has been extensively and carefully renovated allowing the original bar (which has many interesting maps, photographs and other memorabilia of old Belfast) to retain its character while blending in a new café-bar and restaurant. It is worth a visit for its historical interest, and the modern food offered includes an interesting lunch menu ('open flame' wok cooking is a speciality), a slightly more formal evening menu and light food through the day. **Seats 75** (private room, 35); children welcome (high chair, childrens menu); toilets wheelchair accessible; air conditioning. L Thu/Fri only, 12-3pm; D daily from 5pm; set 2/3 course D £16/23, also à la carte. Bar food 12-7 daily. House wine from £12.95. Parking in nearby carpark. SC 10% on groups 8+. Closed 25 Dec, 1 Jan, 12/13 Jul. Amex, MasterCard, Visa, Switch. **Directions:** Turn right at Albert Clock.

Belfast

HOTEL•RESTAURANT

The Merchant Hotel

35-39 Waring Street Belfast Co Antrim BT1 2DY **Tel: 028 9023 4888**
info@themerchanthotel.com www.themerchanthotel.com

The grandeur of a larger than life Victorian banking building is a fit setting for Belfast's most dramatic and beautiful hotel. The exterior of the building is Italianate in style, with sculptures depicting Commerce, Justice and Britannia, looking down benignly from the apex of the magnificent façade. The entrance is up two flights of steps, through tall mahogany and glass revolving doors and then into a room of epic proportions with high ceilings, a central glassed dome with Tyrone crystal and brass chandelier, Corinthian columns, very tall doors painted black with bevelled glass panes and lovely windows with stained glass features at the back (where chunky bamboo plants give at least the appearance of garden outside). The lobby - furnished with comfortable sofas and chairs, rich autumnal fabrics, antiques and curiosities - sets the tone for the whole hotel, which has an authentic period feeling throughout and, although very luxurious, is not ostentatious. The adjacent cocktail bar is equally beautifully furnished in the same style, with red velvet and deep fringing and more of that autumnal velvet too on soft chairs; here, there are two beautiful windows overlooking the street. (On the other side of the front door, also with two beautiful windows, a residents' bar with modern furnishings seems less successful.) The bedrooms and suites are all named after a literary figure with Belfast associations (MacNeice, Heaney, Brian Friel, C.S. Lewis, Larkin etc); the geography of the building means there are features like lovely marble fireplaces with comfy chairs in lobbies and quaint corners en route to somewhere else - a world away from purpose built hotel accommodation with long corridors of doors. All guest rooms are elegantly and opulently appointed and offer air conditioning, black out curtains, WiFi, flat screen television, and spacious marbled bathrooms with many extras. Everything at the hotel is about luxury and indulgence - including the offer of The Merchant Bentley, which you can book to collect you from the airport or elsewhere. Meeting rooms (18); free broadband wi/fi. Children welcome (under 4s free in parents' room, cot available free of charge). **Rooms 26** (5 suites, 2 junior suites, 19 executive, 2 shower only, 7 ground floor, 2 disabled, all no smoking). Room rate from £160-220. 25 hr room service; lift; laundry service. SC 10%. **The Great Room Restaurant:** Three central steps take you from the lobby up to the restaurant, where a small antique reception desk and menu signal the transition; here, despite the great height and scale, low dividers give a sense of more intimate spaces without interrupting the view - and a bold choice, carried throughout the hotel, is the striped carpet. Menus offered at various times include set, vegetarian and à la carte, and a 7-course Tasting Menu is also available; it offers good value, and is available with suggested wines with each course at only £20 extra. The house style is upbeat classic and, typically, you might expect to find starters like foie gras terrine with local plums, star anise & pistachio toast, and dressy main courses including local Finnebrogue venison - smoked saddle, perhaps, served with red cabbage, bacon gnocchi, and vanilla & coco butter. Desserts include house versions of many favourites and there's an informatively described French and Irish cheeseboard. Coffee is beautifully served in art deco style silver pot with wicker handles and matching bowls. An outstanding wine list is compiled in consultation with Jane Boyce, MW. *A traditional Afternoon Tea, with all the trimmings, is also served in The Great Room. **Seats 65** (private room, 18); air conditioning; open daily, L 12-2.30pm; D 6-10.30pm; open all day Sun, 12-9pm; value menu £25; also à la carte; house wine from £18; SC 10%. Bar food also available in the hotel and in the Cloth Ear pub-bar nearby. Parking on site (35); valet parking offered. Closed 25 Dec. Amex, Diners, MasterCard, Visa, Switch. **Directions:** City centre.

Belfast
RESTAURANT

Molly's Yard

1 College Green Mews Botanic Avenue Belfast Co Antrim BT7 1LW
Tel: 028 9032 2600 www.mollysyard.co.uk

This atmospheric restaurant on two floors - informal ground floor bistro with a more elegant dining room above - is in the former stables of College Green House and there is nothing clichéd about it, giving an intriguing feeling that this place is a 'find'. There have been several changes of chef since this unusual place opened in December 2005, but menus include local produce and have a pleasingly down to earth tone - casual bistro fare downstairs with more 'grown up' versions upstairs. And it is always a place worth visiting: Molly's Yard is the site of Belfast's first (and Ireland's smallest) micro-brewery, and an interesting drinks list is a key attraction here. **Seats 45** (outdoors, 20; reservations recommended; children welcome before 6pm; toilets wheelchair accessible. Food served Mon-Sat 12-9.pm (to 9.30pm Fri/Sat); set D 2/3 course £22/27; house wine £13/13.50; sc 10% on groups 6+. Closed Sun, 25-26 Dec, 1 Jan, 12-13 Jul. MasterCard, Visa, Switch. **Directions:** Beside Dukes hotel at back of Queen's University.

Belfast
RESTAURANT

Mourne Seafood Bar Belfast

34-36 Bank Street Belfast Co Antrim BT1 1HL
Tel: 028 9024 8544

This informal restaurant and fish shop is owned by Andy Rae, formerly head chef with Paul Rankin at Roscoff and Cayenne, and business partner Bob McCoubrey, of the original Mourne Seafood Bar in Dundrum, Co Down (see entry), who have their own shellfish beds on Carlingford Lough. Passing a well-stocked display of fish (including lobster, oysters etc), you go through a dark brown painted door which opens onto a long bar with an authentic Belfast feel; a world away from your designer bar concept, the old walls are a mixture of red brick and black areas acting as large chalkboards for the menu and cocktail list, floorboards have been roughly painted black, tables are simply set and there's more of the same upstairs for overflow at weekends. Andy's passion for seafood is evident - starting with the sourcing; he uses less popular local fish rather than trendy imports and, of course, mussels and oysters from Carlingford - everything is homemade and the menu, which offers a mix of dishes at varying prices, changes daily according to the catch (a steak option is also offered). A daily specials board might offer 15 dishes, including potted herrings, seafood casserole or roast hake. Nice desserts, good coffee to finish and lovely service. **Seats 75** (private room, 30); air conditioning; children welcome; toilets wheelchair accessible. Food served Mon-Sat, 12-9.30pm, Sun, 1-6pm; à la carte; house wine about £12.95. SC 10% added to groups 6+. Closed 25-26 Dec, 1 Jan. MasterCard, Visa, Switch. **Directions:** Near Kelly's Bar - turn off Royal Avenue onto Bank Street. 100 yards on left. ◇

Belfast
RESTAURANT

Nick's Warehouse

35-39 Hill Street Belfast Co Antrim BT1 2LB **Tel: 028 9043 9690**
info@nickswarehouse.co.uk www.nickswarehouse.co.uk

Nick and Kathy Price's long established restaurant was originally a whiskey warehouse (built for Bushmills Whiskey in 1832), and when they opened here over 150 years later they were very much the culinary pioneers in this now popular area of Belfast. It's a clever conversion on two floors, with interesting lighting and an open kitchen, which is intended to be theatrical and adds to the buzz. This was Belfast's first wine bar and, although the layout has changed a little, wine is an even more important element these days, as they now have their own wine business. Both lunch and dinner are served on the informal ground floor (Anix) and also the restaurant upstairs, which is slightly more formal; menus change daily in both areas, depending on the fresh produce available from a network of trusted suppliers. The style is lively and contemporary, with menus offering a wide range of dishes which are consistently interesting and often include unusual local items, and game in season; there's always an imaginative selection of vegetarian dishes, and menus are considerably marked with symbols indicating dishes containing nuts or oils and also shellfish. Consistency is a special feature (head chef Sean Craig has been at Nick's since 1996), and Nick Price does a lot for the food scene in Belfast, including being generous with his time; he supports numerous food initiatives, and is Chairman of the Taste of Ulster group. There's a sense of fun about this place ("Why not try one of our 'Seductive Money Saving Offers'" pudding and a glass of dessert wine or cheese with port") so it's no wonder that Nick's has a loyal clientèle who love the good food, attentive, friendly service and the buzz. A well-priced and entertaining wine list offers a carefully selected range of house/by the glass wines, a small selection of (very good value) fine wines, and a special Spanish list. **Seats 130** downstairs (+ 55 upstairs, available as private room at night); children welcome before 9 pm; toilets wheelchair accessible; air conditioning. L Mon-Fri 12-3, D Tue-Sat 6-9.30 (Fri & Sat to 10); set 2/3 course L £16.50/19.50. House wines from about £12.95. Closed Sat L, all Sun, Mon D; 25-26 Dec, 1 Jan, Easter Mon/Tue, May Day, 12 July. Amex, Diners, MasterCard, Visa, Switch. **Directions:** Behind St.Anne's Cathedral, off Waring St.

Belfast   # Northern Whig
BAR   2 Bridge Street Belfast Co Antrim BT1 1LU **Tel: 028 9050 9888**
                                        info@thenorthernwhig.com www.thenorthernwhig.com

Located in the former offices of the Northern Whig newspaper and convenient to the city's now fash-ionable Cathedral Quarter, this is an impressive bar of grand proportions. The high ceilings of the old press hall have been retained - and now look down on several gigantic statues salvaged from Eastern Europe that are in keeping with the scale of the building. A long bar has comfortable contemporary seating in coffee and cream, where Belfast's trend-setters meet for drinks or a bite to eat - or you can take a pavement table on a sunny afternoon and watch the world go by, sipping cocktails or sampling something from a reasonably priced menu which is designed to please a varied clientele - the Northern Whig is very popular with people of all ages and backgrounds, including the local business fraternity who come here for lunch and for a relaxing drink after work. With a short tapas menu also available, a decent wine list starting from £14 and excellent, knowledgeable and efficient staff, The Northern Whig stands out in a city with a plethora of good eating establishments. **Seats 160** (private room 40); air conditioning; toilets wheelchair accessible; children welcome. Open 10am-1am; bar food 12-9 (to 8pm Sun). MasterCard, Visa, Switch. **Directions:** From front of City Hall: walk to 2nd set of traffic lights, turn right, left at next lights; cross road - Northern Whig is on the corner. ◊

Belfast   # Number 27
RESTAURANT   27 Talbot Street BT1 2LD **Tel: 028 9031 2884**
Ⓝ   info@no27.co.uk www.no27.co.uk

This recent addition to Belfast's Cathedral Quarter dining scene was quick to make an impact after opening in December 2007 - which should come as no surprise since the man behind the project is Adrian Lowry, a former manager in Nick's Warehouse. It's a bright modern space, but with references to the building's redbrick industrial past as a linen mill: the white walls have panels of red brick and contemporary art works, recesses in a mauve ceiling reveal the original girders, now painted white; oak floor boards soften the effect of contemporary tables and chairs and big windows to the front have high tables and stools looking across to the side of St. Anne's Cathedral. By day, it's a bright, airy space; by night, lights are dimmed for a softer effect; while not an obvious choice for an intimate meal (acoustics could be improved to absorb the dining chatter), there is the promise of imaginative modern European cooking from chefs Jason More (ex Roscoff and Shanks) and Alan Higginson. Their frequently changed à la carte menus are well designed to please a wide clientèle, notably at lunch time when 'Light and Tasty' and 'Hot and Filling' options are offered. Begin, perhaps, with a substantial and beautifully cooked starter of chargrilled squid with rocket and basil pesto (£5.50), followed by a 'Light and Tasty' rare beef salad with blue cheese walnut vinaigrette and rocket (£7.95), or a 'Hot and Filling' pork belly with creamy champ, broccoli, five spice thyme jus, or confit chicken with Mediterranean vegetables and polenta (each £7.25). The dinner menu, also à la carte, offers a very good range of dishes - seared lamb salad, spaghetti with Portavogie prawns and ingredients like rabbit and mackerel, are all possible starters, for example, and main courses offer upbeat renditions of many favourites including chargrilled steaks and honey roast duck. Appealing mainstream vegetarian choices are offered, and vegetarian dishes and those containing nuts, seeds or shellfish are indicated on menus. Finish with an Irish and continental cheeseboard or homemade desserts, possibly including a rich but beautiful glazed chocolate terrine, excellent apple crumble and a selection of ices and sorbets. With friendly professional service to match the accomplished cooking, a good wine list (including 12 wines by the glass) and reasonable prices it is not difficult to see why this restaurant has found a niche. Opening hours: Lunch - Mon-Fri Noon-3.00 pm D Tue-Sat from 6pm, last orders 10 p.m. A la carte. Cards accepted.

Belfast
CAFÉ

The Olive Tree Company

353 Ormeau Road Belfast Co Antrim BT7 3GL **Tel: 028 9064 8898**
www.olivetreecompany.com

This unique delicatessen/café specialises in freshly marinated olives, handmade cheeses and salamis - and also sells an exclusive range of French specialities, notably from Provence. The café offers authentic French patisserie and food with a Mediterranean flavour, mainly based on the best of local Irish produce: think sandwiches with tapenade (olive paté with vine-ripened tomatoes & spring onions, or dolmades (vine leaves) salad with organic natural yoghurt and ciabatta bread and you'll get the flavour. Hot dishes include specialities like 'brodetto' a traditional Italian fish stew, or contemporary dishes such as warm duck salad with chilli & lime dressing. **Seats 26**. Shop open daily: Mon-Sat 9am-6pm (café to 4.30pm), Sun 11-5. Hot food available Mon-Fri, 8.30-3.45pm, Sat, 8-3.45pm; (no wine but BYO allowed.) Closed 8-15 July, 24 Dec-2 Jan. **No Credit Cards. Directions:** From Belfast City Centre, take the direction for Newcastle/Downpatrick, cross the Ormeau Bridge - spot the Ormeau Bakery landmark and The Olive Tree Company is on the right. ◇

Belfast
RESTAURANT

Oxford Exchange

1st floor St George's Market Oxford Street Belfast Co Antrim BT1 3NQ
Tel: 028 9024 0014
info@oxfordexchange.co.uk www.oxfordexchange.co.uk

Dining in an historically interesting building has a certain cachet at any time, but this stylish venue over the renovated glass-roofed St. George's Market is particularly fascinating The market is a redbrick listed Victorian building and Paul Horshcroft's successful conversion has created a pleasing restaurant with views of either the daytime market scene below or, at night, the attractively lit Laganside area. There's a small bar area, with comfortable seating, and a large restaurant with some striking features where menus reflecting the produce available in the market below are offered; interesting good-value lunches are served and, later, a more ambitious dinner menu takes over it's quite convenient to the Waterfront Hall for pre-theatre meals. Interesting wine list. **Seats 110**. Opening hours: L Mon-Sat 12-2.30; D Mon-Sat from 5pm; Express D Menu, 5-7pm, 2/3 course £15.95/18.95; Breakfast on the balcony Fri & Sat 10am-midday; also à la carte. House wine £11.95. SC discretionary (except 10% on parties of 8+). Closed Sun; 25 Dec, 1 Jan, public holidays. MasterCard, Visa, Laser, Switch. **Directions:** Opposite Waterfront Hall. ◇

Belfast
HOTEL

Radisson SAS Hotel Belfast

The Gasworks 3 Cromac Place Ormeau Road Belfast Co Antrim BT7 2JB
Tel: 028 9043 4065 www.radissonsas.com

The hard red brick high-rise exterior may not be immediately pleasing, but you are in for a pleasant surprise on entering this uncompromisingly modern hotel. Most strikingly, seen through a glass wall, a highly original water feature has been created from the old 'grave dock' that was once a turning space for the boats coming up to the gasworks to deliver coal; both restaurant and bar overlook this extraordinary feature, and it is worth a journey to see this alone. Accommodation is designed and finished to the high standard that is usual in Radisson hotels; suites and rooms have everything that the modern traveller could need, and more - and the friendly ad helpful staff clearly take great pride in this hotel. Conference/banqueting (150/40); secretarial services. **Rooms 120**. (1 suite, 7 junior suites, 18 executive, 94 no smoking, 6 disabled); children welcome (cot available without charge, baby sitting arranged). No pets. Lift. 24 hour room service. B&B about £95pps, ss about £20. *Special offers / short breaks available. **Filini Restaurant:** L Mon-Sat, 12.30-2.30; D Mon-Sat, 6-10. Closed Sun. Bar meals 12-9 daily. Hotel open all year (not L 25 Dec). Parking (60). MasterCard, Visa, Switch. **Directions:** Belfast city centre, in the Cromac Wood Business Park development. ◇

Belfast
HOTEL

Ramada Hotel Belfast

117 Milltown Road Shaws Bridge Belfast Co Antrim BT8 7XP **Tel: 028 9092 3500**
mail@ramadabelfast.com www.ramadabelfast.com

This modern four star hotel near Shaws Bridge enjoys a beautiful setting in the Lagan Valley Regional Park, overlooking the River Lagan. Bedrooms are decorated in a fairly neutral modern style and have all the facilities expected of a contemporary hotel, including in-room safes, TV with satellite and movie channels, telephone with voicemail and either a king-size bed or two singles. There are also executive suites available, intended mainly for business guests, and good conference and banqueting facilities. **Rooms 120** (4 suites, 62 family, 90 no smoking, 44 ground floor, 6 disabled); children welcome, (under 16s free in parents' room, cot available without charge, creche). No pets. Lift. 24 hour room service. Room rate from £99. Belfast Bar & Grill, L&D daily. Parking (300). Garden, walking, pool table, snooker. Open all year. Amex, Diners, MasterCard, Visa, Switch. **Directions:** In Lagan Valley Regional Park, near Shaws Bridge.

Belfast
GUESTHOUSE

Ravenhill House

690 Ravenhill Road Belfast Co Antrim BT6 0BZ **Tel: 028 9020 7444**
info@ravenhillhouse.com www.ravenhillhouse.com

Although it is beside a busy road, mature trees, the Nicholson family's late Victorian redbrick house has some sense of seclusion, with private parking and a quiet tree-lined street alongside. A comfortable ground floor lounge has an open fireplace, a big sofa, lots of books and a PC for guests who want to use the internet (at a modest charge). Bedrooms, which are a mixture of single, twin and double rooms, are comfortably furnished with style - beds and other furniture have been specially commissioned from an Islandmagee craftsman; all are en-suite, with tea/coffee making facilities and TV. After a good night's sleep, breakfast is sure to be the highlight of a visit here: served in a bay-windowed dining room with white-damasked tables, the breakfast buffet is displayed on the sideboard in a collection of Nicholas Mosse serving bowls - a feel for craft objects that is reflected elsewhere in the house. A printed breakfast menu shows a commitment to using local produce of quality and includes a vegetarian cooked breakfast; the Nicholsons buy all their fresh goods from local framers/producers who they deal with directly via the weekly St George's Farmers' Market, and they make what they can on the premises, including marmalade and wheaten bread for breakfasts. All these good things, plus a particularly helpful attitude to guests, make this an excellent, reasonably priced base for a stay in Belfast. **Rooms 5** all en-suite, 3 shower only, all no smoking). B&B £35 pps, single room £50; children welcome (under 2s free in parents' room, cot available without charge); free broadband wi/fi. No pets. Garden. Open all year. MasterCard, Visa, Switch. **Directions:** Follow signs for A24 to Newcastle. 2 miles from city centre, located on corner of Ravenhill Road and Rosetta Park, close to junction with Ormeau Road (A24). ◊

Belfast
RESTAURANT

Roscoff Brasserie

7-11 Linenhall Street Belfast Co Antrim BT2 8AA **Tel: 028 9031 1150**
belinda@rankingroup.co.uk www.rankingroup.co.uk

Modelled on Paul and Jeannie Rankins' original flagship restaurant which deservedly earned them great critical acclaim, Roscoff Brasserie opened some 4 years ago to the delight of many who admired the Rankins' fine cooking but were less keen on the style of the newer restaurants. With white linen-clad tables, soft neutral toned furnishings, effective lighting and artwork by Peter Anderson, the decor is timelessly classic: the overall effect is attractively subdued and low key. A little reception bar is the perfect place to sip aperitifs and choose from à la carte or set menus which are basically classic French, although head chef Paul Waterworth also allows local influence; you may find a (very generous) salad of poached lobster tail, with new potatoes, tomato, avocado & basil, among the starters, and also a Rankin classic of Irish goats cheese with beetroot carpaccio, walnut pesto and beetroot crisps. Deciding between the eight equally appealing main courses plus specials may not be easy: a bowl of pan roast turbot with crab risotto, spinach & red wine jus, for example, is bursting with flavours, while chargrilled sirloin with smoked chilli butter, crispy onion rings & chargrilled Mediterranean vegetables is a vibrant version of an often unexciting cut. A vanilla crème brulée, so frequently a victim of over elaboration and poor execution, is a simple triumph perfectly partnered by some poached seasonal peaches. The recent decision to open for Sunday lunch allows for excellent value at £19.50 for 3 courses, especially considering the menu is mainly composed of dishes directly from their evening menu. The wine list offers a large well selected range from around the world with several excellent 'by the glass options' and interesting half bottles. **Seats 86**; toilets wheelchair accessible; children welcome. L Mon-Fri 12-2.15pm & Sun 1-5pm; D Mon-Sat 6-10pm (to 11.15 Fri/Sat). Set 2/3 course L £15.50/19.50. Set D Mon-Thu £24.50; otherwise à la carte; separate vegetarian à la carte menu available. Closed Jan 1, Jul 12, Dec 25/26, Easter Sun/Mon. Amex, Diners, MasterCard, Visa. **Directions:** Near the City Hall. ◊

Belfast
RESTAURANT

Shu

253 Lisburn Road Belfast Co Antrim BT9 7EN **Tel: 028 9038 1655**
eat@shu-restaurant.com www.shu-restaurant.com

Set back somewhat from the main road, tall arched windows and a smartly painted Victorian frontage exude warmth, providing a vivid contrast to the stainless steel efficiency of the bar and de rigeur 'on view' kitchen of Alan Reid's increasingly admired restaurant. After a courteous welcome, guests are led into a large and atmospheric L shaped room, which is light and airy, with shiny metal softened by terracotta pillars and discreet coverings. Headed up by the fervent Brian McCann since 2004, a seriously talented team of chefs are in serious pursuit of gastronomic excellence here - McCann's past experiences with culinary greats both home and away, coupled with his unique unwavering enthusiasm for uncomplicated quality food are unmistakable in the menus at Shu. Olives with chilli and pickles offer a small taste of what is to follow, in menus that really do have something to suit every taste and pocket. A choice of à la carte and set menus at lunch and dinner offer exceptional value, and illustrate this chef's dedication to seasonal provenance. In season you may start with a light and perfectly executed risotto of summer vegetables, with mascarpone, basil, extra virgin olive oil, or Shu's legendary duck confit packed with flavour and falling off the bone, perfectly paired with tangy mango salsa and a light jus. Main courses such as curry dusted yellow fin tuna with avocado purée, coriander cress and sauce vierge (served rare) or roast corn-fed chicken, with mash, ragoût of peas, bacon and baby gem is testament to McCann's ability to effectively combine the classics with brassiere favourites. To finish, a refreshing dessert of Dunleath estate strawberries, mint and soft vanilla ice cream (simple perfection - a high point of a recent visit by the guide) or, for the sweeter tooth perhaps a Valrhona chocolate tart, coffee foam and vanilla ice cream may win the day. Under the supervision of restaurant manager Julian Henry, an enthusiastic, friendly restaurant team offer a very professional service - and, to match the food, a well-researched wine list iincludes many choices available by the glass. Downstairs, Shubar is a good place to enjoy pre or post dinner drinks, and an upstairs room is available for private parties. With great food, service and atmosphere Shu continues to provide the Belfast restaurant scene with a good value, quality choice. **Seats 80** (private room, 24); children welcome; air conditioning. L Mon-Sat, 12-2.30, D Mon-Sat 6-9 (Sat to 9.30). L £7-13 for 1-3 courses; value D £19.50, Mon-Thu, 6-10pm (also available in Shu Bar Fri, Sat 6-10pm); set 2/3 course D £19.50/26; also à la carte; house wine from £17; s.c. discretionary (10% on parties of 6+). Bar open Fri & Sat 7-1. Closed Sun, 24-26 Dec, 11-13 Jul. Amex, MasterCard, Visa, Switch. **Directions:** Half mile south on Lisburn Road. ◊

Belfast
RESTAURANT

Sun Kee Restaurant

42-47 Donegall Pass Belfast Co Antrim BT7 1BS
Tel: 028 9031 2016

The Lo family's restaurant just off Shaftesbury Square has earned widespread recognition as one of Ireland's most authentic Chinese restaurants and, as it became more famous, it became almost impossible to get a table so they moved to bigger premises across the road. Old hands may miss the squeeze, but what you still get here is the classic Chinese dishes which are already familiar - but created in uncompromising Chinese style, without the usual "blanding down" typical of most oriental restaurants in Ireland. They also offer more unusual dishes, which offer a genuine challenge to the jaded western palate: be prepared to be adventurous. Open for food daily, 12-10.45pm; children welcome; house wine £11.50; MasterCard, Visa, Switch. **Directions:** Opposite Police Station. ◊

Belfast
CAFÉ

Swantons Gourmet Foods

639 Lisburn Road Belfast Co Antrim BT9 7GT **Tel: 028 9068 3388**
swantonsh@aol.com www.swantons.com

Run by husband and wife team Stewart and Gloria Swanton, this speciality food store and café has earned a following amongst discerning Belfast people - even in an area that is especially well served with good places to shop and eat, it stands out for dedication to quality and value. As well as offering a carefully selected (and ever growing) range of deli fare, the food freshly cooked on site is delicious. You can see the chefs at work in the kitchen at the back, and a changing selection through the day begins with breakfasts that include lovely options such as fruits with yoghurt and so on then, from late morning the lunch menu offers really good home made soups, custom made sandwiches in a variety of good breads, salads, hot dishes like quiches and spinach & filo pastry layer, plus one or two specials. Baking is a speciality - beautiful home baked desserts and tarts - and tray bakes with tea and their exclusive Café Mokarabia (Italy's favourite coffee) on the afternoon menu. It's a small place, so you may have to wait for a table at peak times, but you are not hurried or hassled once you get served. **Seats 24** (+ outdoors, 10); toilets wheelchair accessible. Open Mon-Sat, 9-5; L 11.30-3. D Thurs-Fri in summer only; set 2 course L £10.95. Closed Sun, 1 week 12 Jul, 1 week Christmas. Amex, MasterCard, Visa, Switch. **Directions:** On the Lisburn Road.

Belfast
RESTAURANT

Tedfords Restaurant

5 Donegall Quay Belfast Co Antrim BT1 3EF **Tel: 028 9043 4000**
www.tedfordsrestaurant.com

Sailing folk may remember this listed building as a ship's chandlers and, although the maritime theme is now less pronounced than formerly (and it has lost its landmark blue frontage), there are still reminders of its history. Since Alan and Sharon Foster took over several years ago, the interior has been refurbished and the ground floor now has a more contemporary feeling to match the more sophisticated private dining room upstairs - and, although seafood is still the star here, it is now a seafood restaurant and steakhouse; there's plenty to choose from - especially speciality fish and seafood dishes, of course (pan roast turbot & scallops, perhaps, with crab crushed new potatoes, buttered asparagus and hollandaise) and their certified Irish angus steaks, but also creative vegetarian options (chestnut mushroom, blue cheese & broccoli samosas, with tomato & basil chutney and basil oil, for example). Tedfords is earning a growing following for imaginative and well cooked food, and caring service - and, as it is close to the Waterfront Hall and Odyssey Area, it is a particularly good choice for a pre-theatre meal. An extensive and reasonably priced wine list includes half a dozen house wines. **Seats 45**; children welcome; toilets wheelchair accessible; reservations required. L Wed-Fri, 12-2.30; D Tue-Sat, 5-9.30. Pre-theatre D Tue-Sat, about £20 (5-6.30). House wine from £14.95; sc discretionary. Parking in multi-storey carpark next door. Closed Sun-Mon, Tue L, July fortnight, 1 week Christmas. Amex, MasterCard, Visa, Switch. **Directions:** 3 minute walk from Waterfront Hall, next to multi storey car park.

Belfast
HOTEL•RESTAURANT

Ten Square Hotel

10 Donegall Square South Belfast Co Antrim BT1 5JD
Tel: 028 9024 1001
reservations@tensquare.co.uk www.tensquare.co.uk

Situated in a particularly attractive listed Victorian building - just opposite the City Hall, and within walking distance of the whole city centre area - this boutique hotel has established a special niche for discerning visitors to Belfast. The interior is contemporary, and accommodation - in generous high-windowed rooms, theatrically decorated in an uncompromisingly modern style - is simple yet very luxurious; even the most dyed-in-the-wool traditionalist would be won over by the sheer style of these rooms and they have wonderful bathrooms to match. *The hotel changed ownership shortly before the Guide went to press. Conference/banqueting 100/150. **Rooms 22** (13 junior suites, 2 executive, 2 for disabled). Lift. 24 hour room service. Turndown service. Air conditioning, safe, ISDN, TV/DVD/video channel, tea/coffee-making facilities, iron & trouser press. B&B room rate £175 (max 2 guests). Closed 24-25 Dec. The Grill Room & Bar: This stylishly informal area, which occupies the whole of the ground floor, has become one of Belfast's most popular restaurants and meeting places, and is always busy with non-residents, which gives the hotel a great buzz. Live music Wed & Sun. Food served daily 12-10pm (Sun, 1-10pm); L 12-3, D 6-10. A la carte. SC discretionary. **Seats 120** (private room, 30, outdoor, 72); Live music Wed & Sun. Food served daily 12-10pm (Sun, 1-10pm); L 12-3, D 6-10. A la carte. SC discretionary. Amex, MasterCard, Visa, Switch. **Directions:** Corner of Linenhall Street at rear of City Hall.

Belfast
RESTAURANT

The Water Margin
159-161 Donegall Pass Belfast Co Antrim BT7 1DP
Tel: 028 9032 6888

This 200-seater emporium in a converted church at the bottom of the Ormeau Road is the biggest Chinese restaurant in Ireland. Inside, East meets West - a comfortable reception lounge with red leather sofas leads into the large open dining space with tables of various sizes, lots of artificial plants and garish stained glass windows. An open bar runs the length of the inside wall and the dining area is divided between the ground floor and a gallery with a purple painted vaulted ceiling and an adjoining opaque glass walled function room. The menu is massive and it pays to either know Chinese food really well, or have inside information to find your way about. An extensive Dim Sum menu offers authentic Chinese dishes, but also includes set banquets with familiar dishes - at this level, the food is pretty average (and by no means cheap), but there is plenty of noisy atmosphere to experience. [The original sister restaurant is in Coleraine, Co. Londonderry (see entry).] **Seats 200**. Open daily, 12-11pm (to 9pm Sun). Set menus £20-25 per person. House wine £11.95. Open all year. MasterCard, Visa, Laser. [*The original sister restaurant is in Coleraine, Co. Londonderry (see entry).] **Directions:** Bottom of Ormeau Road. ◇

Belfast
HOTEL

The Wellington Park Hotel
21 Malone Road Belfast Co Antrim BT9 6RU **Tel: 028 9038 1111**
info@wellingtonparkhotel.com www.wellingtonparkhotel.com

Located in the fashionable Malone Road area close to the University, this friendly, family-owned and managed hotel is a Belfast institution. It is well located near most of the city's cultural attractions and is also a popular choice for business guests and as a conference venue, with up to date audio-visual equipment and facilities. The spacious foyer and public areas are comfortably furnished, as are the refurbished bedrooms, featuring the usual facilities. A new patio area and restaurant 'Wellie Bar & Grill' (reflecting the affectionate local nickname for the hotel) were recently added, and all the ground floor public areas have been refurbished. Guests have free use of Queen's University sports centre, a few minutes from the hotel. *The Dunadry Hotel & Country Club, a fifteen minute drive from the city, is in the same ownership, also the Armagh City Hotel (see entries). Conference/banqueting (300/130); business centre, broadband wi/fi, secretarial services; video conferencing. **Rooms 75** (all en-suite, 3 suites, 30 no smoking, 2 for disabled); children welcome (under 12 free in parents' room; cots available without charge, baby sitting arranged). Parking. Lift. 24 hour room service. B&B from £65 pps. No pets. Restaurant open for L&D daily. *Short breaks offered. Closed 24-26 Dec. Amex, Diners, MasterCard, Visa, Switch. **Directions:** Near Queen's University.

Belfast
RESTAURANT

Zen
55-59 Adelaide Street Belfast Co Antrim BT2 8FE
Tel: 028 9023 2244

It would be interesting to know what the original owners of this 19th centry redbrick mill would make of its recent transformation by proprietor Eddie Fung into an ultra modern, stunningly cool Japanese restaurant. To call it spectacular would be an understatement - with acres of glass and mirror to contend with if you wish to eat in the upstairs area, where you can dine in booths or hunkered down Japanese style, traditionalists may opt instead to try the downstairs dining area, where you can choose your food at the sushi bar if you wish. In keeping with its setting, this is a place where they talk about 'food design', although more familiar Asian food is offered as well as cutting edge Japanese cuisine. Now one of Belfast's most popular ethnic restaurants, Zen offers a unique dining experience and is especially known for the authenticity of their fresh sushi and sashimi. L Mon-Fri, 12-2.30pm; D daily 5-11pm (Sat from 6). Closed L Sat, L Sun. Amex, MasterCard, Visa. **Directions:** Behind City Hall. ◇

BELFAST INTERNATIONAL AIRPORT

Although dining out at airport restaurants was once all the rage, airports and good food have not often been seen together recently - but Paul & Jeanne Rankin have done their best ensure that passengers going through Belfast can look forward to something a cut above the rest at **Café Paul Rankin** (028 9445 4992), which is in the Departure Lounge and offers wide range of quiches, salads, gourmet sandwiches and pasta dishes, and an upmarket all-day breakfast menu: Eggs Benedict, home-made pancakes, free range scrambles egg & toast, as well as their version of the traditional fry. For accommodation near the airport, **Hilton Templepatrick** (028 944 3500; www.templepatrickhilton.com) is nearby, on the Castle Upton Estate; it has excellent facilities, including golf; see also **Ballyrobin Country House**, Crumlin, Co Antrim.

COUNTY ANTRIM

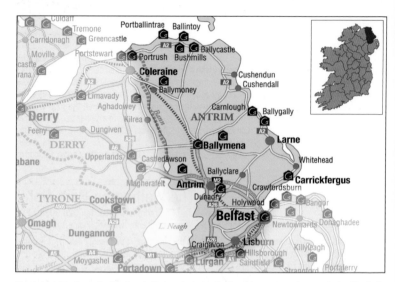

The Antrim Coast may be timeless in its beauty, but today its picturesque ports are enjoying the fruits of restoration and development at places as various as Ballycastle, Glenarm and Carrickfergus.

With its boundaries naturally defined by the sea, the River Bann, the extensive lake of Lough Neagh, and the River Lagan, County Antrim has always had a strong sense of its own clearcut geographical identity. This is further emphasised by the extensive uplands of the Antrim Plateau, wonderful for the sense of space with the moorland rising to heights such as Trostan (551m) and the distinctive Slemish (438m), famed for its association with St Patrick.

The plateau eases down to fertile valleys and bustling inland towns such as Ballymena, Antrim and Ballymoney, while the coastal towns ring the changes between the traditional resort of Portrush in the far north, the ferryport of Larne in the east, and historic Carrickfergus in the south.

In the spectacularly beautiful northeast of the county, the most rugged heights of the Plateau are softened by the nine Glens of Antrim, havens of beauty descending gently from the moorland down through small farms to hospitable villages clustered at the shoreline, and connected by the renowned Antrim Coast Road. Between these sheltered bays at the foot of the Glens, the sea cliffs of the headlands soar with remarkable rock formations which, on the North Coast, provide the setting for the Carrick-a-Rede rope bridge and the Giant's Causeway. From the charming town of Ballycastle, Northern Ireland's only inhabited offshore island of Rathlin is within easy reach by ferry, a mecca for ornithologists and perfect for days away from the pressures of mainstream life.

Local Attractions and Information

Antrim town	Lough Neagh cruises	028 94 481312
Antrim town	Shanes Castle	028 94 428216
Antrim town	Tourism Information	028 94 428331
Ballycastle	Carrick-a-Rede Rope Bridge	028 20 731582
Ballymena	Tourism Information	028 25 660300
Ballymoney	(Dervock) Benvarden Garden	028 20 741331
Ballymoney	Leslie Hill Open Farm	028 27 666803
Bushmills	Antrim Coast and Glens	028 20 731582
Bushmills	Irish Whiskey-World's Oldest Distillery	028 20 731521
Carnlough	Always Ireland Activity Holidays	028 28 885995
Carrickfergus	Castle	028 93 351273
Carrickfergus	Waterfront	028 93 366455
Carrickfergus	Andrew Jackson Centre	028 93 366455
Dunluce	Castle Visitor Centre	028 20 731938

Giants Causeway		028 20 731855
Giants Causeway & Bushmills Railway		028 20 741157
Glenariff	Forest Park	028 21 758232
Larne	Carnfunnock Country Park	028 28 270451
Larne	Ferryport	028 28 872100
Larne	Tourism Information	028 28 260088
Lisburn	Irish Linen Centre & Lisburn Museum	028 92 663377
Lisburn	Tourism Information	028 92 660038
Portrush	Tourism Information	028 70 823333
Rathlin Island	Ferries	028 20 769299
Rathlin Island	Visitor Centre	028 20 763951
Templepatrick	Patterson's Spade Mill	028 94 433619

Ballintoy

B&B

Whitepark House

150 Whitepark Road Ballintoy Ballycastle Co Antrim BT54 6NH

Tel: 028 2073 1482

bob@whiteparkhouse.com   www.whiteparkhouse.com

A warm welcome from chatty and well-informed hosts Bob and Siobhán Isles awaits visitors to this pretty old house which is tucked away in well-maintained gardens and has stunning views of Whitepark Bay, and a path down to a beautiful beach just across the road. Arriving guests, welcomed to the cosy sitting room - furnished with couches, easy chairs and an extraordinary array of antiques and Asian mementos - could easily lose themselves in hours of relaxation at the open fire while indulging in home-made pastries and bottomless cups of perfect tea. The bedrooms have recently been redesigned to allow for en-suite bathrooms (which are gorgeous, some with bath and separate shower, and some have views - in one you can lie in the bath and soak in the beauty of the garden); one front bedroom is exceptionally large and another has windows on three sides. You may be lucky enough to have a four-poster bed and seating area, but all are beautifully decorated with distinctive colour themes and lots of exotic touches to give each its special personality, and there is that warm feeling of being surrounded by a well-loved garden. There is also a huge conservatory at the back, where breakfast is served, and there are comfy couches to relax on. Bob likes to see guests well prepared for the day ahead - there is much to explore, notably of course, the beautiful north coast and the Glens of Antrim - and, as a vegetarian, he's well placed to make a great vegetarian breakfast in addition to a perfect rendition of the traditional Ulster Fry. Bob and Siobhán are exceptional hosts, giving guests plenty of space to relax but ensuring they never want for anything - and they have apparently unlimited local knowledge of the area, attractions and restaurants to help you enjoy your stay. A treasure indeed. *Whitepark House was our Guesthouse of the Year in 2008. **Rooms 3** (all en-suite & no smoking). B&B about £70 pps, ss £25; not suitable for children under 12. No pets. Garden, walking. Beach, fishing (fly, sea angling) & golf all nearby. 5% surcharge on credit card payments. MasterCard, Visa. Open all year. **Directions:** On Antrim coast road A2, 6 miles (9km) East of Bushmills; on east side of Whitepark Bay. ◊

BALLYCASTLE

Ballycastle, a friendly market town on the beautiful north-eastern corner of Co Antrim, has a museum (028 207 62942) on Castle Street which will be of interest to visitors who are curious about the folk and social history of the Glens of Antrim (open daily Jul-Aug, otherwise by arrangement; free entry), and a growing number of restaurants and bars. **The Central Bar & Restaurant** (028 2076 3877), on Ann Street, is friendly and very popular, with chef Paul Deaney offering a simple lunch menu in both the traditional bar and a large brasserie-style restaurant above, and much more adventurous evening menus with plenty of choice, several fish dishes, shank of lamb, steaks, chicken, etc. With high quality food at fair prices, reservations are advised upstairs, particularly at weekend. Across the road you'll find **O'Connors** (028 207 62123), an old bar that has been restored, keeping some of its old charm and with friendly staff and a good atmosphere; attracts a young crowd (folk nights on Thursdays). On the Diamond, **The Cellar Restaurant** (028 2076 3037; www.thecellarrestaurant.co.uk), with barrel vaulted roof and cosy snugs separated by traditional etched glass dividers, is known for its atmosphere; expect traditional cooking with good fish and surf'n'turf. **Quay 26 Restaurant** (028 2076 1133) on Bayview Road overlooking the marina, with lovely views towards Fairhead – offers interesting menus and local seafood. The best golf to be found in this region is at Royal Portrush (028 7082 2311) and Portstewart Golf Clubs (028 7083 2015). For garden lovers, Benvarden (Ballymoney, 028 2074 1331; www.benvarden.com) is a beautifully reinterpreted old walled garden.

WWW.IRELAND-GUIDE.COM FOR ALL THE BEST PLACES TO EAT, DRINK & STAY

Ballycastle

The House of McDonnell

CHARACTER PUB   71 Castle Street Ballycastle Co Antrim BT54 6AS **Tel: 028 2076 2975**

toms1744@aol.com www.houseofmcdonnell.com

The House of McDonnell has been in the caring hands of Tom and Eileen O'Neill since 1979 and in Tom's mother's family for generations before that, they can even tell you not just the year, but the month the pub first opened (April 1766). Tom and Eileen delight in sharing the history of their long, narrow premises with its tiled floor and mahogany bar: it was once a traditional grocery-bar, and is now a listed building. The only real change in the last hundred years or so, says Tom, was the addition of a toilet block. They have a good traditional music session every Friday and love to see musicians coming along and joining in. As Tom and Eileen rightly take pride in the fact that this is the only old bar in Ballycastle to have resisted 'refurbishment and makeover', you can rest assured that any changes will be completed with a very light touch. Not suitable for children after 8pm. They're usually open from 11 am until "late" at weekends, but only in the evenings mid-week, although times might vary in winter; it's worth checking out at weekends anyway, all year. **Directions:** Town centre, near the Diamond.

Ballyclare

Oregano

RESTAURANT   29 Ballyrobert Road Ballyrobert Ballyclare Co Antrim BT39 9RY

Tel: 028 9084 0099

oregano.rest@btconnect.com www.oreganorestaurant.co.uk

A Victorian house in the small village of Ballyrobert is the setting for this rural restaurant. It's run by Dermot and Catherine Reagan, a young couple whose passion for good food is evident from the moment you enter their delightful, spacious, high-ceilinged dining room: with three white walls and one in warm raspberry, and classic wooden tables perfectly set off by smart white leather seats, it's clear that a lot of thought has gone into the décor - but it's the menu that takes centre stage. Dermot offers both à la carte and set menus (lunch and early dinner), based mainly on locally sourced foods including fish, duck, beef and venison, which he cooks to perfection. Two lunch menus are offered during the week, a short à la carte or a Business Lunch of one to three courses; there will be home-made soup and a couple of other appealing starters - a well made Caesar salad with char-grilled chicken, perhaps, or pretty goats' cheese with mixed leaves and a toasted hazelnut, chilli & herb dressing. Main courses may include a good mainstream vegetarian dish such as penne pasta with parmesan, cherry tomatoes, spinach & basil, and popular local minute steaks with chunky chips. Evening à la carte menus offer more luxurious options, with an emphasis on seafood, including treats such as crab & chilli crème brûlée, and you'll also find dishes based on local beef, rack of Northern Irish lamb and local chicken. Desserts feature favourites chocolate tart with vanilla ice cream alongside more unusual offerings. The set menus – early evening and all day Sunday – are especially good value. A global wine list includes excellent house wines, also available by the glass. **Seats 60** (private room, 20; outdoors, 6); children welcome. L&D Tue-Sat, 12-2.30 & 5.30-9.30pm; Sun all day 12-7pm; business L 1-3 course, £7-13, Tue-Fri 12-2.30pm; value 2/3 course D £15.95/18.95 Tue-Fri 5.30-7.30; also à la carte; Sun 2/3 courses £16.95/19.95. House wine £14.50. SC 10% on groups 6+. Garden. Parking. Closed Mon, 25-26 Dec, 1-2 Jan, 1 week around 12 Jul. **Directions:** M2 north from Belfast, then A6 to Sandyknowes roundabout; take Larne exit to Corrs Corner roundabout; turn left to Ballyclare. Oregano is 1.5 miles on the right.

Hastings Ballygally Castle Hotel

Ballygally
HOTEL

Coast Road Ballygally Co Antrim BT40 2QZ **Tel: 028 2858 1066**
res@bgc.hastingshotels.com www.hastingshotels.com

This coastal hotel really has got a (very) old castle at the heart of it - and they've even got a ghost (you can visit her room at the top of the castle). The whole thing is quite unlike any of the other Hastings hotels and, although recent investment has improved standards dramatically, the hotel still has character; some of the older rooms are literally shaped by the castle itself, and are quite romantic. Cosy chintzy wing chairs and open fires make welcoming lounge areas to relax in - and the beach is just a stone's throw away, across the road. Conference/banqueting (200/120). **Rooms 44** (2 junior suites, 9 executive, 6 family rooms, all no smoking, 1 for disabled); children welcome; (under 14 free in parents' room; cots available without charge). Wheelchair accessible. Parking. No pets. B&B £82.50pps, ss £37.50; no SC. **Meals:** Rest D, 5-9; buffet L 12.30-2.30. *Short breaks offered - details on application. Open all year. Amex, Diners, MasterCard, Visa, Switch. **Directions:** Situated on the coast road between Larne and Glenarm (5km /3 miles from Larne on A2).

Galgorm Manor Hotel

Ballymena
HOTEL

136 Fenaghy Road Ballymena Co Antrim BT42 1EA **Tel: 028 2588 1001**
sales@galgorm.com www.galgorm.com

Set amidst beautiful scenery, with the River Maine running through the grounds, this former gentleman's residence is now a country house hotel. Approaching through well-tended parkland, guests pass the separate banqueting and conference facilities to arrive at the front door of the original house, which is a mere 100 yards from the river. The hotel has been greatly extended recently but the original house still has a very pleasant atmosphere, with a welcoming fire in the foyer, an elegant drawing room and characterful socialising spaces in Gillie's Pub & Bollinger Garden and Gillies Bar & Grill (where meals are also served). Accommodation includes 48 contemporary deluxe bedrooms in the old walled garden area, and some suites and rooms in the old house; most of these have views over the river. Conference/banqueting (500). **Rooms 75** (9 suites, 6 junior suites, 2 disabled); children welcome (under 4s free in parents room, cot £10, babysitting arranged). B&B from about £70 pps. golf (9/18); spa; fishing; horse-riding; walking; garden. Wheelchair accessible. No pets. L &D available daily. Open all year. Amex, Diners, MasterCard, Visa. **Directions:** From the Galgorm roundabout, take the third exit for Cullybackey (Fenaghy road). About 2 miles, on the left.

Marlagh Lodge

Ballymena
COUNTRY HOUSE

71 Moorfields Road Ballymena Co Antrim BT42 3BU
Tel: 028 2563 1505
info@marlaghlodge.com www.marlaghlodge.com

Robert and Rachel Thompson took on this neglected early Victorian house on the edge of Ballymena in 2003 and then painstakingly restored it to make an unusual and very comfortable haven for guests and, although close to the main road, the result is truly impressive. Originally built as the Dower House for the O'Hara family of nearby Crebilly House, the Lodge is a classic of its era, double fronted with spacious, high-ceilinged reception rooms on either side of the entrance hall, and bedrooms which have lent themselves remarkably well to the architectural gymnastics needed to provide en-suite bathrooms in an old house. The three rooms - The Blue Room, The Chintz Room and The Print Room - are all large and comfortably furnished with interesting antiques, but otherwise very different. Robert and Sarah also offer dinner for residents - and non-residents are welcome too, by reservation. The repertoire is quite extensive, and a 6-course menu uses local and artisan produce in some unusual ways; special gourmet evenings are sometimes held, with wine paired with each course. Marlagh Lodge is within easy reach of the main airports and ferry ports, and all the attractions of the north Antrim coast. Banqueting (20). **Rooms 3** (2 en-suite, 1 with private bathroom, all no smoking); children welcome (under 3s free in parents' room, cot available, free of charge). B&B £45 pps, no ss. No pets. D Mon-Sat, 8pm (book by noon); non-residents welcome on Fri-Sat by reservations; Set D £32.50; wines from about £15. Golf, equestrian & fishing all nearby. "Closed occasionally," and D Sun; please ring ahead off-season. MasterCard, Visa, Switch. **Directions:** On A36, 0.6 miles (1km) from Larne Road roundabout and visible from the road.

BUSHMILLS

Most people visiting Bushmills do so to see the world's oldest licensed whiskey distillery - and this interesting and immaculately maintained distillery and visitor attraction is certainly worth a detour. The village is also well-placed for a break when exploring the beautiful North Coast, and you will find "old-fashioned home-style of the highest order" at **Bushmills Garden Centre** (028 2073 2225; www.creativegardens.net) on Ballyclough Road. Famous for their scones and home baking, this busy place is open Mon-Sat 10am-5pm, Sun 12.30-5 and, in summer they stay open to 7pm and offer evening meals; (see also their Garden Centre at Donaghadee, Co Down).

Bushmills | **Bushmills Inn**
HOTEL•RESTAURANT | 9 Dunluce Rd Bushmills Co Antrim BT57 8QG **Tel: 028 2073 3000**
| mail@bushmillsinn.com www.bushmillsinn.com

Originally a 19th-century coaching inn, developments here have been done well, improving amenities without loss of character. The traditional tone is set by the turf fire and country seating in the hall and public rooms - bars, the famous circular library, the restaurant, even the Pine Room conference room carry on the same theme. Bedrooms are individually furnished in a comfortable cottage style, and even have "antiqued" bathrooms, but it's all very well done and avoids a theme park feel. Although quite expensive, it's hard to think of a better base for a holiday playing the famous golf courses of the area (Royal Portrush is just four miles away) - or simply exploring this beautiful coastline and its hinterland; taking the Magilligan-Greencastle ferry, day trips can comfortably include a visit to the beautiful Inishowen peninsula in Co. Donegal. Garden. Fishing (fly). Broadband wi/fi; children welcome (cot available, £10). No pets. **Rooms 32**: 22 in Mill House, 10 in Coaching Inn; (6 superior, 7 shower only, all no smoking, 2 family, 1 for disabled) B&B from £89 pps.*Short breaks offered. **Restaurant:** The Inn is known for its wholesome food and it makes a good place to plan a break when touring, as it offers both day and evening menus in cosy surroundings (although be warned that coaches often make a lunchtime stop here for the same reasons, so it can be very busy). Pride in Irish ingredients is seen in A Taste of Ulster menus that offer a range of traditional dishes with a modern twist: an unusual speciality, for example, is Dalriada cullen skink, a 'meal in a soup bowl' based on smoked haddock and topped with an (optional) poached egg; another is onion & Guinness soup, which is topped with a cheese croûton like the French soup that inspired it - and, of course 'Bushmills coffee', which is better than a dessert any day. **Seats 110** (private room, 40, outdoor, 14); not suitable for children after 6pm; wheelchair accessible; reservations advised. L&D à la carte; D daily 6-9.30; L daily, Day Menu 12-6.00; (Sun: carvery from 12.30-2.30pm and day menu to 6pm); bar food Sun only 12-4 (soup & sandwiches). House wines from £15; SC discretionary. Closed 24/25 Dec. MasterCard, Visa. **Directions:** On the A4 Antrim coast road, in Bushmills village, as it crosses the river.

Bushmills | **The Distillers Arms**
BAR•RESTAURANT | 140 Main Street Bushmills Co Antrim BT57 8QE **Tel: 028 2073 1044**
V | simon@distillersarms.com www.distillersarms.com

In a stylishly renovated 18th century building which was once the home of the distillery owners, Simon Clarke's modern bar has smart modern lightwood bar stools with comfortable curved backs, comfy sofas, and table lamps lending a warm atmosphere; beyond it, the restaurant is more rustic by comparison, with open stonework and a fireplace. As much as half of the menu could be seafood, including a speciality starter of salmon cured with Old Bushmills whiskey; main courses also offer a good choice of seafood, including a Moyle Seafood Platter with Ballycastle lobster and crab among the offerings; other good dishes may include Moycraig Wood venison, local lamb and mainstream vegetarian dishes. Lunch (weekends) and early evening menus offer particularly good value and the wine list, which offers many bottles sourced directly from auction and sold with only a small mark-up, includes a fair choice of house wines and half bottles. **Seats 80** (outdoor seating, 6, private room, 25); toilets wheelchair accessible; children welcome before 8.30pm (high chair, childrens menu). Open daily in summer, D 5.30-9 (to 9.30 Fri/Sat); L Fri & Sat only. Closed Mon-Tue off-season (Oct-Mar); 25 Dec. MasterCard, Visa, Switch. **Directions:** 300 yards from Old Bushmills Distillery. ◇

Bushmills
RESTAURANT
Ⓝ

Sixteenoeight
66 Main Street Bushmills Co Antrim BT57 8QD
Tel: 028 2073 2040

This popular contemporary restaurant, bistro & café takes its name from the historic event when King James 1st granted a licence to distill 'uisce beatha' (water of life, or whiskey as it is known today) within the territory called the Rowte (Bushmills) in Co Antrim, in 1608. The bright, airy restaurant has two dining areas - a café downstairs, and split-level restaurant upstairs where you can dine in comfortable relaxed surroundings while watching the chefs busily preparing your tasty dishes in the open kitchen. The atmosphere is lively, décor is warm and modern, and the menu offers well-balanced food combinations using many local ingredients. Tempting dishes offered may include the 1608 Fisherman's Pie, a wholesome and generous selection of salmon, cod, crab and prawns poached in a white wine creamy sauce and topped with a generous portion of creamed potatoes, and appealing vegetarians choices such as baked butternut squash stuffed with vegetable couscous, and drizzled with spiced basil oil. Finish, perhaps, with traditional desserts such as apple & rhubarb crumble – served, appropriately enough, with Bushmills Malt-scented custard. And, of course, you couldn't leave without having an Irish coffee made with the famous 1608 brand. Children are also welcome and evening reservations are essential. Tempting modern menus, good cooking, friendly staff and good value make this a very popular spot with local residents and visitors alike. L daily,12-4; early D 4-6.30pm; D 6.45-9pm (reservations essential). Closed Mon. MasterCard, Visa, Switch. **Directions:** On the main street. ◇

Carnlough
HOTEL
♛ ◉ Ⓥ

Londonderry Arms Hotel
20 Harbour Road Carnlough Co Antrim BT44 0EU **Tel: 028 2888 5255**
lda@glensofantrim.com   www.glensofantrim.com

The Londonderry Arms Hotel, built by the Marchioness of Londonderry in 1848 as a coaching inn, was inherited by her great grandson, Sir Winston Churchill, in 1921 and retains great character to this day. Since 1948, it has been in the caring hands of the O'Neill family, and they do good home-made bar meals, or afternoon tea, which you can have in the bar or beside the fire in an old-fashioned lounge; as well as dinner, High Tea is still served in the restaurant on Sunday afternoons. Bedrooms are comfortable and well-furnished; many of the older rooms have sea views and it is worthwhile discussing the type and location of your room when booking, as some have been refurbished recently and one or two are badly positioned for a restful night's sleep. This is a delightful place in a lovely old-fashioned village, and a refreshing contrast to today's streamlined new hotels. Conferences/banqueting (100/80); secretarial services. **Rooms 35** (all en-suite, 4 executive, 6 family, 1 for disabled); children welcome (under 2s free in parents' room; cots available without charge). Wheelchair accessible. No pets. Lift; limited room service. B&B £55 pps, ss £15. **Restaurant:** D 7-9 (5-8 Sun), L Sun only, 12-3. Bar food served daily, 12.30-8.30pm (to 9.15 pm weekends). Parking. Walking. *Off season short breaks offered - details on application. Closed 24-25 Dec. Amex, MasterCard, Visa, Switch. **Directions:** On the A2 Antrim coast road, 14 miles (24km) north of Larne.

Carrickfergus
HOTEL

Clarion Hotel
75 Belfast Road Carrickfergus Co Antrim BT38 8BX **Tel: 028 9336 4556**
info@clarioncarrick.com   www.clarioncarrick.com

Conveniently located to Belfast Airport (10 miles) and the scenic attractions of the Antrim coast, this modern hotel makes a comfortable base for business and leisure visitors. It has good conference facilities (600), meeting rooms (max. 60) and in-room amenities (desk, fax/modem line) for business guests. Bedrooms include three suitable for disabled guests, two suites, two junior suites and 20 non-smoking rooms; all are furnished to a high standard with well-finished en-suite bathrooms (all with bath and shower). **Rooms 68**. B&B £130 per room. Open all year except Christmas. Amex, MasterCard, Visa, Switch. **Directions:** Main Coast Road exit Belfast North (8 miles). ◊

Crumlin
RESTAURANT•COUNTRY HOUSE

Ballyrobin Country House

144 - 146 Ballyrobin Road Aldergrove
Crumlin Co Antrim BT29 4EG **Tel: 028 9442 2211**
jkenny@ballyrobin.com www.ballyrobin.com

Literally two minutes drive from Belfast International Airport's terminal building and nestled between fields of barley, this lovingly restored 200-year old country house makes a welcome haven for travellers who will find good realistically-priced food (open to non-residents), or a bed for the night in one of the four individually-themed en-suite bedrooms. Built from local field stones, "The Ballyrobin", as it is affectionately called, has old-fashioned charm, with a turf fire, household memorabilia everywhere, and nooks and crannies for intimate dining in cosy surroundings. The menu, too, has been carefully chosen to match the atmosphere: you could travel a long way before finding a starter as interesting and flavoursome as their asparagus, poached duck egg and crispy Fermanagh streaky bacon with hollandaise. Local Dundrum crab is popular – in, for example, the intriguingly named 'Crab, Crab, Crab'; alternatively, if you are looking for something simple, try the soda stack with rare breed pork sausages, free-range egg and brown sauce. Reasonably priced wines are offered to match the menu, and service is casual and friendly as would be expected in the relaxed atmosphere of this amiable property. Restaurant open daily: B 7-12 (Open to non residents); Mon - Sat 12-9pm (to 10pm Fri & Sat); Sun 12-8.30pm. MasterCard, Visa, Switch. **Directions:** From Belfast International Airport - take the A57 to Belfast. By car, they are literally two minutes from the Main Terminal Building. ◊

Dunadry
HOTEL

Dunadry Hotel & Country Club

2 Islandreagh Drive Dunadry Co Antrim BT41 2HA **Tel: 028 9443 4343**
info@dunadry.com www.dunadry.com

This attractive riverside hotel is well-located close to Belfast International Airport and only about 15 minutes from the city centre. It was formerly a mill and it succeeds very well in combining the character of the old buildings with the comfort and efficiency of an international hotel. It has excellent facilities and stylish, spacious bedrooms include three suites and eleven executive rooms; all have good amenities. There's a choice of dining in The Linen Mill Restaurant or the informal Mill Race Bistro, which makes the most of its situation over-looking the river. Leisure facilities within the grounds include a professional croquet lawn, fun bowling, trout fishing and cycling, as well as a leisure centre with beauty therapies. *Sister hotel to the **Wellington Park Hotel** in Belfast city and the **Armagh City Hotel** (see entries). Conference/banqueting 350/300. **Rooms 83** (all en-suite, 2 for disabled); children welcome (under 12s free in parents' room cot available without charge, baby sitting arranged). No pets. B&B £52.50-60pps; room-only rate also available; ss £20-38. Garden, walking, fishing, cycling; leisure centre, beauty salon. *Short breaks offered. Linen Mill Restaurant (fine dining): D Sat only, 7.30-10.30. Bistro: open all day. Closed 24-26 Dec. Amex, Diners, MasterCard, Visa, Switch. **Directions:** Near Belfast Airport; look for signs to Antrim/Dunadry. ◊

GLENARM

Glenarm (in Irish: Gleann Airm, i.e. Glen of the Army) is a village on the North Channel coast and a popular port of call for sailors (visitors are welcome at the marina). The first of the Nine Glens of Antrim, Glenarm claims to be the oldest town in Ulster, having been granted a charter in the 12th Century. Glenarm Castle, ancestral home of the Earls of Antrim, offers much of interest including The Walled Garden (open 10-6 daily, May-Sep); **The Tea Rooms**, in the old Mushroom House overlooking the kitchen garden, are open to the public and would make a lovely stopping-off place when touring on the coast road. They offer tasty snacks, such as an all-day breakfast bagel with organic scrambled egg and local bacon; seafood chowder; home-made bruschetta; Tuscan tart dressed with olives & pesto; and a dish called the hot goat: marinated chicken breast topped with goat's cheese, chorizo sausage and chilli jam. Also sandwiches, and home-made cream tea, with organic teas and various coffees.

Portballintrae
HOTEL

Bayview Hotel

2 Bayhead Road Portballintrae Bushmills Co Antrim BT57 8RZ
Tel: 028 2073 4100
info@bayviewhotelni.com   www.bayviewhotelni.com

This well maintained hotel on the seafront of the attractive village of Portballintrae has great Atlantic views and offers a tranquil and reasonably priced base for exploring the beautiful north Antrim coast. Comfortable, spacious bedrooms are well-appointed, and have a small seating area and a work station; interconnecting rooms are available for families and, while more expensive, superior and premier rooms have magnificent sea views. The Porthole, a modern air-conditioned bar and restaurant with an open fire, offers casual dining at affordable prices in a lively environment; fresh local Portballintrae lobster (when available) grilled with a warm lemon butter sauce and a fresh summer leaf salad is a popular choice here. Close to the Old Bushmills Distillery and the Giant's Causeway, this would make an ideal base for leisure and business (conference/business facilities available); short breaks offered. **Rooms 25**. B&B £40-60 pps (off season breaks from £55). Open all year. **Directions:** On the seafront. ◇

Portballintrae
BAR•RESTAURANT

Sweeney's Public House & Wine Bar

Seaport Avenue Portballintrae Co Antrim BT57 8SB
Tel: 028 2073 2405   seaport@freeuk.com

Seymour Sweeney's bar is in an attractive stone building on the sea side of the road as you drive into Portballintrae, and is very handy to both the Royal Portrush Golf Club and the Giant's Causeway. Formerly a coaching stable for the Leslie estate, it is one of the oldest surviving domestic buildings in the village and listed as being of architectural and historic significance. Now restored to capture its former character, it's a pleasant place with a welcoming open fire in the bar and a choice of places to drink or have a bite to eat. Unpretentious food is in the modern international café/bar style; the lunchtime offering is casual fare – steak sandwich, chicken Caesar, steak & Guinness pie, panini etc – and a roast lunch is available on Sunday in addition to the normal menu. On the evening menu, you'll find steak and chicken dishes, also rack of Irish lamb on colcannon, some fish (typically grilled plaice or salmon and battered cod) and a couple of vegetarian dishes. Although likely to suit all age groups during the day, it can get very busy during the evening, especially on live music nights (folk & country; there is a late licence to 1 am on Friday and Saturday). A useful place to break a day exploring the area, although a phone call is advised. **Seats 120** (+50 outside, +32 private room); children welcome, wheelchair accessible; air conditioning. L & D daily, 12-3pm & 5-9pm (to 8.30pm Sun); A la carte. Closed 25 Dec. Amex, Diners, MasterCard, Visa, Switch. **Directions:** Centre of village overlooking bay & harbour. ◇

PORTRUSH

Portrush is a popular seaside holiday resort, golfing destination and a good base for exploring the beautiful Antrim coast. The most spectacularly located hotel in the area is the **Royal Court** (028 7082 2236; www.royalcourthotel.co.uk) on the coast road, and it is open for snacks and daytime meals. In the town, those in the know head for the smart **Ramada Hotel Portrush** (028 782 6100; www.ramadaportrush.com), formerly Comfort Hotel. Nearby, the popular family-run **'55 North'** (028 7082 2811; www.55-north.com) is in an attractive modern building with sea views, offering a useful all-day café on the ground floor and a restaurant with beautiful views serving eclectic food above it. The three main golf courses in the area are Royal Portrush (028 7082 2311), Portstewart (028 7083 2015) and Castlerock Golf Clubs (028 7084 8314). Garden lovers might also wish to visit Benvarden (028 2074 1331; www.benvarden.com), a beautifully reinterpreted old walled garden in nearby Ballymoney.

Portrush
RESTAURANT
⏣

The Ramore Oriental Restaurant

6 The Harbour Road Portrush Co Antrim BT56 8BN **Tel: 028 7082 6969**
www.ramorerestaurants.co.uk

The wonderful Ramore Restaurant was once the leading light of cosmopolitan fine dining in Northern Ireland and, after a long spell concentrating exclusively on quality fast food, George and Jane McAlpin promised to being back something of the spirit of the old Ramore in an 80-seater restaurant that now complements their three existing casual eating places (The Wine Bar, Coast Pasta & Pizza and Harbour Bistro). Things are not quite what they were, of course; although the smart modern design is perhaps in tune with the hopes of longtime followers, the fact that the name has been changed to 'Oriental Restaurant' indicates how different the current Ramore really is. On the top floor, above the wine bar, the new restaurant is in two areas - one large square room overlooking the harbour, which is very noisy, and a quieter area in a room along the bar. The very long menus offer a wide range of broadly oriental dishes and would sound a warning note in any but the most accomplished hands - but here the cooking is as good as ever, presentation is very attractive and service is quick and attentive. Wine service, especially, is impressive and the drinks menu includes a tempting range of cocktails. This is a fun place, with many of the dishes designed for sharing, and it is executed with flair. NB: There are two sittings each evening and reservations are essential. **The Wine Bar:** This informal restaurant is on the first floor, underneath Ramore Oriental, and above Coast, the pasta restaurant; it remains very popular with the holiday market and with the young who appreciate the fun and friendly atmosphere, the speed and reasonable prices. Menus offer a wide selection of contemporary dishes ranging from home-baked breads with nuts, olives and dips, through bang bang chicken, or chilli steak in pitta, to roast fillet of salmon with champ. Prices are very accessible – although the downside is noise, discomfort and scanty service. *The famous old Harbour Bar nearby is in the same ownership; the front section retains its original character and, behind it the Harbour Bistro & Wine Bar offers mainly contemporary food, and roasts for Sunday lunch. (L&D served daily). Ramore Wine Bar **Seats 300**. L&D daily: L12.15-2.15pm, D 5-10 (Sun,12.30-3 & 5-9); early bird D £7.95, 5-6.30pm; house wine from £9.95. Coast Italiano Seats 90 (Mon-Sat 4-10.30, Sun 3-9.30). Wine bar & toilets on ground floor wheelchair accessible. Harbour Bistro - Mon-Sat, 5-10pm, Sun 4-9pm. Closed 25 Dec. MasterCard, Visa, Switch. **Directions:** This complex of four linked establishments is at the harbour in Portrush.

Portrush

FARMHOUSE•B&B

Maddybenny Farmhouse

Loguestown Road Portrush Coleraine Co Antrim BT52 2PT

Tel: 028 7082 3394

beds@maddybenny.com www.maddybenny.com

Just two miles from Portrush, the White family's Plantation Period farmhouse was built before 1650. Since extended, and now modernised, it makes a very comfortable and exceptionally hospitable place to stay, with a family-run equestrian centre nearby (including stabling for guests' own horses). There is also snooker, a games room and quiet sitting places, as well as a garden and an outdoor area for children's games. The accommodation is just as thoughtful. The bedrooms are all en-suite and there are all sorts of useful extras electric blankets, a comfortable armchair, hospitality tray complete with tea cosy, a torch and alarm clock beside the bed, trouser press, hair dryer and, on the landing, an ironing board, fridge and pay phone for guests' use. Across the yard there are six self-catering cottages, open all year (one wheelchair friendly). No evening meals, but Karen White guides guests to the local eating places that will suit them best - and the breakfasts here are legendary, so make sure you allow plenty of time to start the day with a feast the like of which you are unlikely to encounter again. *Maddybenny was the Guide's Farmhouse of the Year in 2000. **Rooms 3** (all en-suite, all family rooms & all no smoking) B&B £32.50pps, single £47 (children £10). Children welcome (cot available £2 charge). No pets. Equestrian, garden, walking; snooker. Golf, fishing, tennis and pitch & putt nearby. Closed 25-26 Dec. MasterCard, Visa, Switch. **Directions:** Signposted off A29 Portrush/Coleraine road.

RATHLIN ISLAND

This island off the north-east corner of County Antrim is accessible by ferry from Ballycastle (details from Ballycastle TIO 028 207 62024). Popular with walkers and birdwatchers, it is a Special Area of Conservation and home to vast colonies of seabirds; the RSPB Rathlin Island Seabird Centre (028 2076 0062; open early Apr-end Aug), is at the West Lighthouse. Accommodation on the island includes the National Trust owned **Manor House Guesthouse** (028 2076 3964), an 1870s' Gentleman's Residence that was renovated in the early 1990s and now offers 12 bedrooms and evening meals. **McCuaig's** bar and restaurant (028 2076 3974), is near the ferry terminal and serves lunch, snacks and evening meals; a shop also offers basics for campers and picnics.

WWW-IRELAND-GUIDE.COM FOR ALL THE BEST PLACES TO EAT, DRINK & STAY

COUNTY ARMAGH

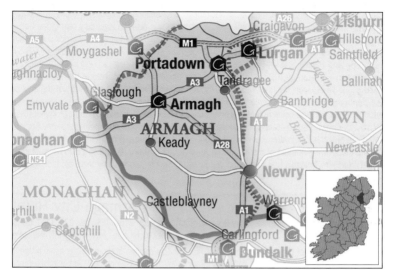

Mention Armagh, and most people will think of apples and archbishops. In the more fertile northern part of the county, orchards are traditionally important in the local economy, with the lore of apple growing and their use a part of County Armagh life. And the pleasant cathedral city of Armagh itself is, of course, the ecclesiastical capital of all Ireland, and many a mitre is seen about it.

But, in fact, Armagh city's significance long pre-dates Christian times. Emhain Macha - Navan Fort - to the west of the town, was a royal stronghold and centre of civilisation more than 4,000 years ago. Marking the county's northern coastline, the inland freshwater sea of Lough Neagh provides sand for the construction industry, eels for gourmets, and recreational boating of all sorts. In times past, it was part of the route which brought coal from the mines in Coalisland in Tyrone to Dublin, the main link from Lough Neagh to the seaport of Newry being the canal from Portadown which, when opened in 1742, was in the forefront of canal technology.

That County Armagh was a leader in canal technology is only one of its many surprises. The discerning traveller will find much of interest, among the undulating farmland and orchards, the pretty villages, or the handsome uplands rising to Carrigatuke above Newtownhamilton, and on towards the fine peak of Slieve Gullion in the south of the county, down to Forkhill and Crossmaglen and the Gaelic football heartlands.

Local Information and Attractions

Annaghmore	(nr Portadown) Ardress (NT house)	028 38 851236
Armagh	County Museum	028 37 523070
Armagh	Planetarium	028 37 523689
Armagh	Astronomical Observatory	028 37 522928
Armagh	Palace Stables Heritage Centre	028 37 529629
Armagh	St Patrick's Trian Visitor Centre	028 37 521801
Bessbrook	Derrymore House	028 30 830353
Forkhill	(Slieve Gullion) Ti chulainn Cultural Centre	028 30 888828
Loughgall	Loughgall Country Park	028 38 892900
Lough Neagh	Discovery Centre, Oxford Island	028 38 322205
Markethill	Gosford Forest Park	028 37 551277
Moy	The Argory (NT Mansion)	028 87 784753
Newry	Derrymore House	028 30 830353
Portadown	Moneypenny's Lock (Newry Canal)	028 37 521800
Scarva	Newry Canal Visitor Centre	028 38 832163
Slieve Gullion	Forest Park	028 30 848226

ARMAGH

Elegant Georgian buildings surround this city's impressive oval tree lined mall, and turn any corner and you will be sure to see superb examples of Georgian terraced houses. Ireland's religious centre for 1,500 years and the seat of both Protestant and Catholic Archbishops, the city of Armagh predates Canterbury as a Christian religious site. Armagh was also the legendary seat of the Celtic Kings of Ulster. Local visitor attractions include the Armagh Cathedral, St Patrick's Anglican Church, the county museum (028 3752 3070, open all year), the Armagh Observatory (028 37 522928), and Palace Stables Heritage Centre (028 3752 1801, open all year) and the impressive Armagh Planetarium (028 3752 3689). Other places of interest include the Navan Centre (028 3752 1801), which allows visitors to discover the archaeology and mythology of the area or the Benburb Valley Heritage Centre (028 3754 9885, open March to September), which houses a former linen mill and collection of machinery used in linen making. Nearby Carnagh Forest (028 3755 1277) has many picturesque walking trails, with fishing lakes and an angler's inn. Anglers will also enjoy the Blackwater River, which is one of the most famous rivers in Ireland for salmon. Among the growing number of restaurants in Armagh city is **Uluru** (028 3751 8051), on Market Street; Northern Ireland's first Australian restaurant, is specialises in using local produce with an Australian twist.

Armagh   ## Armagh City Hotel
HOTEL   2 Friary Road Armagh Co Armagh BT60 4FR **Tel: 028 3751 8888**
info@armaghcityhotel.com   www.armaghcityhotel.com

Located at the heart of the "orchard county" of Armagh, this modern hotel is a sister establishment to the Dunadry Inn, Co. Antrim and Wellington Park Hotel, Belfast (see entries). Although the functional lines of the building are disappointingly out of place in this historic location, it has brought welcome facilities to the area, notably contributing Northern Ireland's largest hotel conference facility. A cafeteria-style 'deli' and informal dining area located in the foyer give a poor impression on arrival - but the bar and more formal restaurant areas at the back of the hotel look out onto pleasant landscaped gardens, and there is a beer garden, 'The Balcony'. Bedrooms are practical and well-equipped for business guests, with good amenities. Conference/banqueting (1,200/700); business centre, secretarial services, broadband wi/fi. **Rooms 82** (10 executive, 30 no smoking, 4 for disabled). B&B from £52 pps; single £89; children welcome (under 10s free in parents' room, cot available without charge, baby sitting arranged). Leisure centre with swimming pool, steam room, jacuzzi. *Special breaks offered - details on application. Closed 24-26 Dec. Amex, Diners, MasterCard, Visa, Switch. **Directions:** From Dublin, take A28 to Armagh City; when the police station is in sight, follow the road round to the left to the hotel. From Belfast, take M1 to Junction 11, then M12 on to A3; hotel is situated just before Palace Stables.

Armagh   ## Manor Park Restaurant
RESTAURANT   2 College Hill The Mall Armagh Co Armagh BT61 9DF
Tel: 028 3751 5353   manorparkrestaurant@yahoo.ie

An attractive early nineteenth century stone-fronted building beside the entrance to the Observatory is home to this well known French restaurant; it is a building of character - low-ceilinged, with a period fireplace and antique furnishings. Arriving guests are greeted by the French staff, and may have an aperitif in the bar, or go straight to their table. Several different menus are offered at various times, and they make a good read - ingredients are good quality and include local seafood, beef and lamb, and also Blacklion duck. The main dinner menu – quite a grand à la carte choice, including game in season - can seem expensive, although the lunch and early dinner menus generally offer good value for money. An extensive wine list includes a wide selection of half bottles. **Seats 60** (private room 26); children welcome; reservations required. Open for L&D daily: L 12.30-2.30, D 5.30-10. Carvery L £7.50; early D £19.95 (Mon-Fri, 5-6.30); also à la carte. House wines from about £15. Closed 24 & 26 Dec & 1 Jan. MasterCard, Visa, Laser, Switch. **Directions:** On the mall, beside the Courthouse. ◊

Craigavon
COUNTRY HOUSE

Newforge House

58 Newforge Road Magheralin Craigavon Co Armagh BT67 0QL
Tel: 028 9261 1255
enquiries@newforgehouse.com   www.newforgehouse.com

John and Louise Mathers' fine Georgian country house is less than half an hour's drive south-west of Belfast, and handy to both Belfast International and City Airports and Ferry Terminal - yet, in a wonderful setting of mature trees, gardens and green fields on the edge of the quiet village of Magheralin, it feels like worlds away. The property - which is substantial - was built around 1785 and has been in the Mathers family for six generations. Following major renovations, the Mathers opened John's former family home as a guesthouse in 2005, and it now offers luxurious accommodation in stylish, individually-decorated rooms (all with beautiful bathrooms, five of which have separate bath and shower), a period drawing room with an open log fire, and a fine dining room where John takes pride in presenting meals based mostly on local and organic produce - which can be taken at separate tables or as a group. It is a lovely spot for a short break (various special offers are available) and makes a perfect setting for special occasions, including weddings (which can be in a marquee in the garden for larger numbers), smaller celebrations, or corporate events. **Rooms 6** (5 with separate bath & shower, 1 shower only, all no smoking). B&B £65 pps, ss £15. Free Broadband Wi/FI. Wheelchair accessible on ground floor, including toilet facilities; bedrooms are upstairs & not wheelchair accessible. Dining Room seats 22. D daily 7-8.30 (to 9 Fri/Sat); Sun & Mon light dinner only; Set 2/3 course D £25/29.50; Vegetarian meals on request; House wine £14. No smoking house. Croquet, garden. Fishing (fly & coarse), golf, garden visits and watersports nearby. Closed 24 Dec - 8 Jan. MasterCard, Visa, Switch. **Directions:** M1 from Belfast to Craigavon until junction for A3 to Moira; through Moira to Magheralin then turn left at Byrnes Pub (on the corner) onto Newforge Road. Continue for 2 minutes until the National Speed Limit signs; black and white sign for Newforge House on the left. Next left through entrance in stone wall; take first right turn and park in front of the house.

CROSSMAGLEN

Crossmaglen (Irish: Crois Mhic Lionnáin Lennon's Cross) is the largest village in South Armagh and has a reputation for, among other things, horse breeding and hand-made lace. It is not far from Newry and convenient to areas of natural beauty, including the lovely Slieve Gullion Forest Park (028 3755 1277); after a walk there, refreshment at the charming **Slieve Gullion Inn** at Forkhill is recommended. Accommodation in Crossmaglen, is offered at the Carragher family's modern **Cross Square Hotel** (028 30860505; www.crosssquarehotel.com) on O'Fiaich Square. This is an area that has not been much visited in recent years but there is growing interest and, shortly before going to press, **Garveys** (028 3088 8220 www.garveysbar.com), a well known country pub nearby at Silverbridge, was purchased by a group that includes Bill Wolsey of The Merchant Hotel in Belfast – so watch this space.
WWW-IRELAND-GUIDE.COM FOR ALL THE BEST PLACES TO EAT, DRINK & STAY

Lurgan
RESTAURANT

The Brindle Beam Tea Rooms

House of Brindle 20 Windsor Avenue Lurgan Co Armagh BT67 9BG
Tel: 028 3832 1721

This in-store self-service restaurant is a real one-off. Nothing is bought in and the kitchen team, puts the emphasis firmly on real home cooking. There are two freshly-made soups each day and hot dishes like beef stew, made with well trimmed fat-free chump steak - with no onions. None of the pies or casseroles contain onions as some customers don't like them, but they're still full of flavour. Their salad cart is a special attraction, with anything up to 30 different salads served each day, and several different hot dishes including baked or grilled chicken breasts, salmon and always some vegetarian dishes too. There's also a huge variety of tray bakes and desserts - and only real fresh cream is used. Scrupulously clean, with reasonable prices (not cheap, but good value for the quality) and real home cooking, this place is a gem. **Seats 110** (private room 50). Open Mon-Sat, 10-5, L 12-2.30, Afternoon Tea 2-4pm. A la carte self-service except special set menus, e.g. Christmas. Unlicensed. Closed Sun, 25-26 Dec, Easter, 12-13 Jul. MasterCard, Visa. **Directions:** Town centre; located in The House of Brindle Store. ◇

Portadown   # Seagoe Hotel

HOTEL   Upper Church Lane Portadown Co Armagh BT63 5JE **Tel: 028 3833 3076**

R   info@seagoe.com www.seagoe.com

Attractively situated in its own grounds on the edge of Portadown, this fine hotel has been in the same ownership for many years but underwent a complete makeover a few years ago. The design is innovative and exceptionally easy on the eye, once inside, the tone of the whole development is set by stylish public areas; an outstanding feature is the comprehensive and well-planned wheelchair friendliness, which allows easy access and use of facilities throughout the building. In the smart contemporary bedrooms, warm, rich fabrics are teamed with good work space for business guests; executive rooms also have modem and fax facilities. Business/conference facilities are also impressive; a separate function entrance has its own dramatic lobby/reception area - and there are two superb honeymoon suites. Bar and restaurant areas are designed with equal care, looking on to a pleasant courtyard garden. Conferences/Banqueting (600/450); business centre. **Rooms 34** (all en-suite, 2 junior suites, 2 executive, 2 family, 17 ground floor, 2 disabled); children welcome (under 5s free in parents' room, cot available free of charge). B&B £65 pps; room only £104. Lift. Limited room service. Restaurant open for lunch and dinner daily. 12-2.30 & 5-9.30 (Sun 6-9) and bar meals (panini, ciabatta, steak etc.) are available at the same times. Own parking. Garden. Closed 25 Dec. Amex, Diners, MasterCard, Visa, Switch. **Directions:** Off A27 (Old Lurgan Road).

Portadown   # Yellow Door Deli, Bakery & Café

CAFÉ   74 Woodhouse Street Portadown Co Armagh BT62 1JL **Tel: 028 3835 3528**

♨ € R   info@yellowdoordeli.co.uk www.yellowdoordeli.co.uk

The energetic and talented Simon Dougan is one of the luminaries of the Northern Ireland food scene, and his Yellow Door Deli celebrated a decade of success in 2008. His in-house bakery produces some of the finest bread in Northern Ireland (an area renowned for good home baking) and, as well as retailing a wide selection of the best speciality foods from Ireland and abroad, they also have a number of home-made specialities, including patés, terrines, chutneys, salads and ice cream, which are sold in the shop and served in the café - discerning customers from all over the north home in on this smashing shop, to top up with goodies and have a tasty bite of lunch. Hot smoked Irish salmon with grilled soda bread, wild rocket and lemon dill cream is a house speciality - go for it! There is a also an extensive, very interesting and keenly priced wine list, and a soft seating area, complete with cookery book library, where customers can relax. *Outside catering is now a speciality – and, true to form, the food is all honest local and 100% home-made. Café **seats 75**. Breakfast from 9am, L 12-2.45pm, otherwise food from deli all day until 5pm; house wine about £10. Closed Mon, 12-13 Jul, 25-26 Dec, "some" Bank Hols. MasterCard, Visa, Switch. **Directions:** Off Main St. on left; only street on left as the traffic flows one way. ◇

COUNTY DOWN

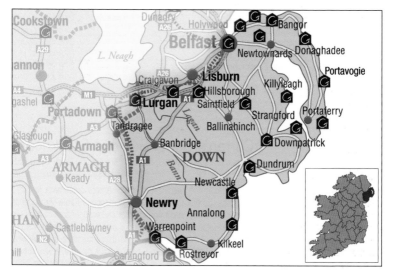

County Down rings the changes in elegant style, from its affluent shoreline along Belfast Lough - the "Gold Coast" - through the rolling drumlin country which provides Strangford Lough's many islands, and on then past the uplands around Slieve Croob, with the view southward being increasingly dominated by the purple slopes of the Mountains of Mourne.

The Mournes soar to Northern Ireland's highest peak of Slieve Donard (850m), and provide excellent hill-walking and challenging climbing. When seen across Down's patchwork of prosperous farmland, however, they have a gentleness which is in keeping with the county's well-groomed style. In the same vein, Down is home to some of Ireland's finest gardens, notably Mount Stewart on the eastern shore of Strangford Lough, and Rowallane at Saintfield, while the selection of forest and country parks is also exceptional.

Within the contemporary landscape, history is much in evidence. St Patrick's grave is in Downpatrick, while the Ulster Folk and Transport Museum at Cultra near Holywood provides an unrivalled overview of the region's past. The coastline is much-indented, so much so that, when measured in detail, County Down provides more than half of Northern Ireland's entire shoreline. Within it, the jewel of Strangford Lough is an unmatched attraction for naturalists and boat enthusiasts, while Portaferry has one of Ireland's longest-established saltwater aquariums in Exploris.

In the south of the county, the increasingly prosperous town of Newry on the river inland from Carlingford Lough is – with Lisburn in County Antrim – one of Ireland's two newest cities under a re-designation of 2003. Newry is responding with enthusiasm to its enhanced status, and the urban regeneration of this interesting canalside centre is intriguing to watch, while the Ship Canal down to the sea has been restored and was re-opened in 2006.

Local Attractions and Information

Bangor	Events Office	028 91 278051
Bangor	Tourism Information	028 91 270069
Bangor	North Down Heritage Centre	028 91 271200
Castle Espie	Wildfowl and Wetlands Centre	028 91 874146
Cultra	Ulster Folk & Transport Museum	028 90 428428
Downpatrick	Down Cathedral	028 44 614922
Downpatrick	St Patrick Centre	028 44 619000
Dromore	Kinallen Craft Centre	028 97 533733
Dundrum	Murlough National Nature Reserve	028 43 751467
Greyabbey	Mount Stewart House	028 42 788387

Hillsborough	Hillsborough Castle Gardens	028 92 681300
Kilkeel	Nautilus Centre	028 41 765555
Millisle	Ballycopeland Windmill	028 91 861413
Mourne Mountains	Guided Wildlife Walks	028 43 751467
Newcastle	Tollymore Forest Park	028 43 722428
Newtownards	Kingdoms of Down Tourism	028 91 822881
Portaferry	Exploris Aquarium	028 42 728062
Rathfriland	Bronte Interpretive Centre	028 40 631152
Saintfield	Rowallane Gardens	028 97 510131
Strangford	Castle Ward	028 44 881204
Strangford Lough	Wildlife Centre	028 44 881411

Ardglass

RESTAURANT•PUB

Ⓥ

Curran's Bar & Seafood Steakhouse

83 Strangford Road Chapeltown Ardglass Co Down BT30 7SB

Tel: 028 4484 1332 www.curransbar.net

Originally the Curran family home, this popular and well-located establishment dates back to 1791 and, in recent times, has earned a reputation for fine food, under the guidance of Paula Mahon, (née Curran). Today, it not only has a 60-seater restaurant, a comfortable bar and outdoor area to offer but the premises also holds a licence for civil weddings, with an outdoor arch used for the ceremony; receptions are held in the restaurant - which has a large fireplace as its centrepiece, with original family photographs and memorabilia. Outside, there's a covered, heated smoking area, a walled beer garden and barbecue area, and a play area for children - and the old milking parlour has been converted into The Stables Bar and function room. Seafood has always played a central role here, of course, and menus - which are written in French and Spanish as well as English - offer a wide range including the ever-popular Seafood Platter (a splendid collection of clams, smoked mackerel, mussels, crabcakes, prawns, dressed crabs and langoustine, served with home-made wheaten bread) along with other delights such as Ardglass prawns, crab claws, poached salmon, Dundrum Bay mussels, and crayfish risotto. Alternatively, there's a daily roast dinner, prime sirloin or fillet from local butchers and home-made steakburger. Children are well catered for and the wine list, although short, is well chosen. **Seats 100** (outdoors, 44); reservations recommended; toilets wheelchair accessible; children welcome (high chair, childrens menu, baby changing facilities; playground); free broadband wi/fi. Food served all day, 7 days, 12.30-9pm; set Sun L £14.95; value L £4.95, 12.30-5pm; also à la carte; house wine from £11. Live music (trad & modern) Fri/Sat, 9.30-1; Sun from 7.30pm. Closed 25 Dec. MasterCard, Visa, Switch. **Directions:** Main road between Ardglass (2 miles) and Strangford (6 miles).

Banbridge

CAFÉ

Ⓡ

Greenbean Coffee Roasters

11 Townsend Street Banbridge Co Down BT32 3LF **Tel: 028 4062 9096**

info@greenbeanroasters.com www.greenbeanroasters.com

Hidden behind a stylish frosted glass frontage and contemporary logo in the relative calm of Banbridge's Townsend Street, a treat awaits famished shoppers and caffeine addicts alike. Since opening their Greenbean Coffee Shop and Barista training school here in August 2006, the renowned coffee roasters Deirdre and Pat Grant, long celebrated for supplying quality coffees to the catering trade, have already built up a loyal following of discerning locals. A comfortable and well spaced mixture of high and low level seats at round and oval tables provide the perfect resting place to re-fuel and watch the world go by. Coffee is, of course, their speciality and very much in evidence, with glass topped tables and casks filled with beans, and freshly roasted coffee delivered twice daily - it doesn't get much fresher than this! Greenbean offers a rich or smooth option with all coffees, to suit varying tastes. The food is unfussy and homely: delicious French toast with crispy bacon and maple syrup is a speciality on the inviting breakfast menu, and lunch specials include freshly prepared quiches, soups, salads, sandwiches and pastas. A large selection of home-made desserts and sweet and savoury pastries is on display, and just too good to resist. Deirdre is very much hands-on, along with the other friendly staff, providing cheerful, informal but efficient service. This reasonably priced and consistent gem is the perfect spot for a brunch, lunch, snack or caffeine hit, and children are welcome. Children welcome (high chair); toilets wheelchair accessible; MasterCard, Visa, Switch. **Directions:** Centre of Banbridge town, go down Rathfriland Street; take right turn up Townsend Street.

Banbridge
RESTAURANT

Simply Deanes

Unit 1 The Outlet Bridgewater Park Banbridge Co Down BT32 4GJ
Tel: 028 4062 7220
info@michaeldeane.co.uk www.michaeldeane.co.uk

🆁

Located just outside Banbridge on the main Belfast-Dublin Road, The Outlet discount designer centre is billed as 'the ultimate shopping destination' and here you will find the an outpost of the Deanes portfolio (see Belfast entries). Seasonal, locally sourced ingredients are used for a carefully constructed all day menu and daily blackboard specials that offer everything from snacks, salads and sandwiches 'to go'. Children welcome (high chair, childrens menu, baby changing facilities); toilets wheelchair accessible. Open: B Mon-Sat, 9.30 11.30; L Mon-Sat, 11.30 5.30; D Thu-Sat , 6-9pm (Sat to 9.30pm); Sun L only, 1-6pm; set Sun L £15. Closed Easter Sun, 25 Dec. Amex, MasterCard, Visa, Switch. **Directions:** Well-signed on the main Dublin-Belfast road.

BANGOR

A thriving shopping town and popular seaside resort easily accessible from Belfast, Bangor has a three-mile seafront with extensive promenades, and a large marina. For a pleasing informal dining experience, head for **Coyle's Bar & Bistro** (028 9127 0362) on High Street, where you will find appealing food in a stylish environment, whether for mid-day bar food or more structured meals in the evening. At the top of High Street, on Holborn Avenue, **Back Street Bistro** (028 9145 4741) offers modern cooking during the day and evening every day except Sunday. For those who prefer quality family-run accommodation in a more intimate environment rather than an hotel, **Hebron House** (see entry) is a 5* B&B on Princetown Road, near the marina. Apart from water-based activities such as sailing and fishing, it is garden lovers who are are spoilt for choice for garden visits in this part of Down – Guincho (by appointment only, Helen's Bay, 028 9048 6324), Glenmount (by appointment only, Dundonald, 028 9048 6324), Mountstewart House & Gardens (Newtownards, 028 4278 8387) and Redcot (by appointment only, Belfast, 028 9079 6614) are all within 10 miles. For golfers, the famous waterside fairways of The Royal Belfast Golf Club (Craigavad, 028 9042 8165) beckon.
WWW-IRELAND-GUIDE.COM FOR ALL THE BEST PLACES TO EAT, DRINK & STAY

Bangor
B&B
🅽

Hebron House

68 Princetown Road Bangor Co Down BT20 3TD **Tel: 028 9146 3126**
reception@hebron-house.com www.hebron-house.com

The Maddock family's substantial redbrick house is an exceptionally convenient and appealing place to stay in Bangor, offering the space and comfort associated with the leafy suburbs and a remarkably central location that is within easy walking distance of both the town centre shops and the harbour area. The three guest rooms include two on the first floor, with a pleasant outlook (one overlooks the marina); both have 5' beds (one with a traditional brass and iron bedstead) and comfortable seating, also power showers, bathrobes and Molton Brown toiletries. The third room is on the ground floor and overlooks the marina; it is particularly spacious and has zip-and-link beds also a whirlpool bath, as well as a power shower and all the extras provided upstairs - the flexible layout will appeal especially to older guests, anyone with mobility problems and those travelling with young children. All the comfy beds have goose down and feather anti-allergy duvets and pillows, and every room has fresh flowers, tea tray, TV/DVD, radio, magazines, hairdryer, iron and ironing board, making this a real home-from-home. Guests have use of a comfortable sitting room too, and an imaginative breakfast menu is served at a communal table in the traditional dining room. Ilona Maddock really wants her guests to make the best of their stay and provides lots of information about the area, including nearby Pickie Park (perfect for families), the North Down Heritage centre and the Folk & Transport Museum, as well as places of interest further afield. **Rooms 3** (all en-suite, 2 shower only); children welcome (under 2s free in parents room, cot available free of charge); free broadband wi/fi. B&B £40 pps (single occupancy £40-80). No smoking house. Closed 22 Dec - 1 Jan. MasterCard, Visa, Switch **Directions:** Arriving from Belfast direction on B2 (Crawfordsburn) road, you will pass a Maxol garage on the right hand side. At the first roundabout after the garage (top of Gray's Lane), take the first exit left into Maxwell Road, which leads directly into Princetown Road. Hebron House is a large red brick detached property on the left hand side of the road. Parking is allowed across the road from the house.

Jeffers by the Marina

Bangor
RESTAURANT   7 Grays Hill Bangor Co Down BT20 2BB   **Tel: 028 9185 9555**
V
www.jeffersbythemarina.com

Although not large, clever use of mirrors creates a feeling of space in Stephen Jeffers' smart harbour front restaurant overlooking the marina - bare tables, café chairs and uncurtained windows make for an uncluttered look too, although the downside is that there's not a lot to absorb noise. Friendly staff are quick to settle new arrivals in with the wine list (informative, interesting, good value) and everything is very relaxed, with unstructured menus offering an eclectic choice of modern dishes. Although there are constants through the year, there's always a seasonal twist, such as a winter dish of richly flavoured Portavogie Estate game sausage, with creamy colcannon, or risotto of new season asparagus in spring. Menus change throughout the day - there's an afternoon tea menu, with a good choice of teas and coffees and treats like Victoria sponge - and a proper children's menu, offering real food. Sunday brunch is especially popular here, but this really is an any-time place. **Seats 60**; children welcome (high chair, childrens menu); air conditioning; free broadband wi/fi. Open daily; Mon-Sat, 10am-10pm, Sun, 11-8pm. A la carte D. House wine £13.95. SC 10% on groups 6+. Closed Mon off season; 25-26 Dec, 1 Jan. MasterCard, Visa, Switch. **Directions:** At the bottom of Grays Hill, overlooking the marina.

Marine Court Hotel

Bangor
HOTEL   18-20 Quay Street Bangor Co Down BT20 5ED   **Tel: 028 9145 1100**
marinecourt@btconnect.com   www.marinecourthotel.net

Excellent leisure facilities at the Marine Court's Oceanis Health & Fitness Club are this hotel's greatest asset, and these include an 18-metre pool, steam room, whirlpool and sunbeds, plus a well-equipped, professionally-staffed gym. The hotel overlooks the marina (beyond a public carpark) but the first-floor Lord Nelson's Bistro restaurant is the only public room with a real view. Only a few bedrooms are on the front - most overlook (neatly maintained) service areas - but all rooms are regularly refurbished and they are spacious, with plenty of worktop and tea/coffee tray, hair dryer and trouser press as standard in all rooms.Conference/banqueting (350/220). **Rooms 51** (3 junior suites, 15 executive, 3 family, 29 no smoking, 1 for disabled); children welcome (cots available without charge; baby sitting arranged). Private parking 30. No Pets. Lift. 24 hour room service. B&B £50pps, ss £20. Leisure centre (steam room, fitness room, swimming pool); yoga (Mon eve.). *Short/off-season breaks offered - details on application. Closed 25 Dec. Amex, Diners, MasterCard, Visa, Switch. **Directions:** 14 miles (23km) from Belfast/ 10 miles (16km) Belfast City Airport, A2.

Royal Hotel

Bangor
HOTEL   26/28 Quay Street Bangor Co Down BT20 5ED   **Tel: 028 9127 1866**
royalhotelbangor@aol.com   www.the-royal-hotel.com

This old hotel near the marina is family-run and has old-fashioned charm. There's a warm personal welcome and a clear willingness to help guests in any way possible and, although, alas, the early 20th century lift with folding grille doors and a mind of its own, has long since been replaced by a sleek new early 21st century one, the building has some endearing idiosyncrasies. Rooms vary, but all have been refurbished quite recently - the best are the new ones on the front, overlooking the marina. Public areas include The Crown Bar pub, with original coal fire, photographs of old Bangor and access to a landscaped garden area, a cosy oak-lined Library Bar, (also with open fire) and a new modern cocktail bar, The Windsor. This is a characterful place to stay and there is a large public carpark just across at the marina. Small conferences (40); **Rooms 50** (7 executive, 8 shower only, 1 for disabled); children welcome (under 5s free in parents' room; cots available). No Pets. Lift. B&B about £30-40pps, ss about £15. Special offers sometimes available. Nearby parking. Closed 25-26 Dec. Amex, Diners, MasterCard, Visa. **Directions:** A2 from Belfast, at bottom of Main Street turn right (keeping in left lane). Hotel is 300 yards on right facing marina. ◈

Clandeboye Lodge Hotel

Bangor Area
HOTEL   10 Estate Road Clandeboye Bangor Co Down BT19 1UR   **Tel: 028 9185 2500**
info@clandeboyelodge.co.uk   www.clandeboyelodge.com

Quietly set in woodland on the edge of the Clandeboye estate, this comfortable modern four-star hotel fits in well with its rural surroundings and offers a pleasing alternative for those who do not need to stay in town. With a welcoming fire and plentiful seating areas, the large foyer creates a good impression that carries throughout the hotel. Following recent refurbishment, the spacious bedrooms are smartly furnished in a clean-lined modern style, with plenty of work space, complimentary wireless internet access and an express check-out service among the features appealing to business guests, and in-room entertainment including LCD wide screen TV with satellite stations and a DVD library. Well-finished bathrooms sport Gilchrist and Soames toiletries, and suites have whirlpool baths. The range of rooms offered includes executive, with extras such as complimentary newspapers; more luxurious and spacious junior suites, and family rooms. The hotel is a popular wedding venue but events take place in separate conference and banqueting centre, so other hotel guests are not disturbed. Meals are available in the lobby bar, and the adjoining Lodge Restaurant, where breakfast is also served. Conference/banqueting (450/350); free broadband wi/fi, business centre, secretarial services. **Rooms 43** (all en-suite & no smoking, 2 junior suites, 13 executive, 2 family, 13 ground floor, 2 disabled); children welcome (under 12s free in parents' room; cots available at no charge, baby sitting arranged). No Pets. Parking. Lift; 24-hr rooms service. B&B from £55 pps, ss £25. Credit card numbers are taken when booking - and the deduction may be made before your arrival. Closed 24-26 Dec. Amex, Diners, MasterCard, Visa, Switch. **Directions:** 15 minutes from Belfast, on outskirts of Bangor off A2. ◇

Bangor Area
RESTAURANT•BAR

Thyme

Blackwood Golf Club 150 Crawfordsburn Rd Bangor
Co Down BT19 1GB **Tel: 028 9185 3394**

Smart signage at the Golf Club entrance, and frosted glass doors with the name in elegant black capitals, create a sense of anticipation that should not be disappointed at this unusually located restaurant. Formerly Shanks, it was for many years a landmark in Irish gastronomic circles and is now run successfully by the affable young Conor McCann, formerly head chef at Roscoff in Belfast, whose temperate, natural and unobtrusive style has established it as a major asset to the North Down/Belfast food scene. Upstairs, a grill bar offers informal meals, downstairs you will find the more serious fine dining on white linen in an elegantly-appointed room which has recently been improved with new artwork; in the restaurant, which is managed by partner, Nicola, and separated from the kitchen by a soundproof glass screen, nothing is out of place and everything runs sweetly throughout a meal of impressively consistent quality and apparently effortless endeavour, with the staff appearing to enjoy the experience as much as the diners. At Thyme, one senses a gifted cook at work and absorbed in his craft. Descriptions of his creations are succinct and simple, yet have a capacity to amaze through flawless and mature cookery, each dish expressing its natural flavours with uncomplicated style. Top quality produce is used, much of it local, and the well-balanced menu presents luxury ingredients in perfectly judged dishes, possibly including a starter of lightly cured salmon gravadlax with lemon dressing and rocket, main course dishes like Trio of Pork (a confit belly, braised shoulder and roast loin of Tamworth rare breed pork with sautéed apples and calvados) and, on a recent Sunday lunch visit, a very successful, classic roast sirloin of dry-aged beef with Yorkshire pudding and horseradish cream. Great flavour and appealingly simple presentation are the key characteristics - and this applies equally to delicious desserts - a Valrhona chocolate mousse with home-made sablé biscuits, perhaps, and the now signature dessert of pineapple carpaccio with pink peppercorn syrup and passionfruit sorbet. The lively, cheerful ambience adds to the experience, as does an extensive and well chosen wine list, and it offers good value for the quality of food and culinary skill. Sunday lunch and a recently introduced early evening supper menu offer outstanding value. **Seats 60**. L Wed-Fri 12-3, D Wed-Sat 5-10pm; Sun all day 12-7. Closed Mon & Tue. Mastercard, Visa, Maestro. **Directions:** 2km off main Belfast-Bangor road, opposite Clandeboye Estate. ◇

Comber

B&B

Anna's House

35 Lisbarnett Road Comber Newtownards Co Down BT23 6 AW
Tel: 028 9754 1566
anna@annashouse.com www.annashouse.com

Anna and Ken Johnson's charming house near Strangford Lough looks over their own ten-acre wildfowl lake to the rolling North Down countryside, and it makes a wonderfully comfortable and hospitable base for exploring this beautiful area. The original two roomed cottage has been extended to provide four en-suite guestrooms, one wheelchair-friendly which opens out onto a private terrace, and two with large sitting rooms which open out onto the mezzanine floor. All are modestly yet tastefully decorated with a cottage feel. Beds are luxuriously dressed with Irish linen and all rooms have a hospitality tray, WiFi internet, mini-fridge, hairdryer and a wide selection of reading material. However, it is unlikely that guests will spend long in the bedrooms when a splendid Music Room with views of the Mourne Mountains to the south is available for guest use: heated by a geo-thermal central heating system from a field in front of the house and with a 45ft x 15ft window and polished granite floor, this comfortably furnished haven even has a concert grand piano which guests are encouraged to play. However, it is the warmth of the hosts and the quality of the food (they have committed to serving at least 75% organic food) which is the most striking aspect of one stay in this charming home. Breakfast is the only meal available and the hosts are passionate about the quality of the food served. Anna bakes all her own bread and scones, jams and preserves are made with home-grown fruit as far as possible and, while a traditional cooked breakfast is available, how could you resist ordering Anna's organic porridge with Irish Mist followed by a smoked salmon omelette? (Some choices have to be ordered the evening before.) After a leisurely breakfast, guests are encouraged to stroll around the large garden (which is now not as carefully nurtured as Anna would like), before departing to explore the Peninsula area. **Rooms 4** (all en-suite and no-smoking, 2 suites, 2 shower only, 1 ground floor, 1 equipped for disabled); children welcome (under 2s free in parents room, cot available free of charge, high chair); free broadband wi/fi. B&B from £40 pps, ss about £10. Closed Christmas & New Year. MasterCard, Visa. **Directions:** From Lisbane, follow the brown B&B signs.

Crawfordsburn

HOTEL•RESTAURANT•PUB

The Old Inn

11-15 Main Street Crawfordsburn Co Down BT19 1JH
Tel: 028 9185 3255 info@theoldinn.com www.theoldinn.com

The pretty village setting of this famous and hospitable 16th century inn - the oldest in continuous use in all Ireland - belies its convenient location close to Belfast and the City Airport, and also the Ulster Folk & Transport Museum and the Royal Belfast Golf Club which are both nearby. Oak beams, antiques and gas lighting emphasise the natural character of the building, an attractive venue for business people and private guests alike. A welcoming fire and friendly staff in the cosy reception area set the tone for the whole hotel, which is full of charm, very comfortable - and always smartly presented. Bedrooms are individually decorated and, due to the age of the building, vary in size and style - most have antiques, some have romantic four-posters and a few have private sitting rooms; 12 new junior suites are soon to be added. There are several dining options in the hotel: '1614' (see below) is the fine dining restaurant, informal evening meals are served in the Churn Bistro, and food is also served in the Parlour Bar during afternoon and early evening. Conference/banqueting (120/125); broadband wi/fi, business centre, secretarial services. Ample parking. Garden, walking. Golf, fishing (sea angling, coarse) & equestrian all nearby. Children welcome (cot available, £10, baby sitting arranged). Dogs permitted by prior arrangement. Rooms 31 (7 junior suites, 18 executive, 6 family, 8 ground floor, 1 disabled, all no smoking). Limited room service. B&B from £52.50 pps. *Short breaks offered. Open all year except 25 Dec. **Restaurant '1614':** The Old Inn is one of the busiest establishments in North Down, and a stalwart in the area – with assured cooking from Alex Taylor in Restaurant 1614 undoubtedly contributing to its popularity. After an aperitif in the bar or the large and comfortable residents' lounge, a meal in this characterful old-world dining room should be very enjoyable. Alex Taylor's interesting updated classic menus offer plenty of choice and might typically include dishes like chicken liver parfait or a tian of local smoked salmon to start, followed perhaps by a speciality main course of pan-fried seabass with spring vegetables and lobster & chive velouté or an unusual and attractively presented dish of local Finnebrogue venison, served pink, with savoy cabbage, bacon & morel cream. A nice dessert menu offers more refreshing fruit-based dishes than is usual, and coffee is served in the lounge. An informative wine list is organised by country and includes a well-selected page of house wines and half a dozen half bottles. **Seats 64** (private room, 25, outdoors, 50); toilets wheelchair accessible; children welcome (high chair, childrens menu, baby changing facilities); D Mon-Sat, 7-9.30, D Sun 5-10, L Sun only 12.30-2.30. Set Sun L £18.75; set 2/3 course D £26/30; house wine £13.75. Bar meals: 12 noon-7pm daily. Closed 25 Dec. Amex, MasterCard, Visa, Switch **Directions:** Off A2 Belfast-Bangor, 6 miles after Holywood (exit B20 for Crawfordsburn).

DONAGHADEE

A charming seaside town on the Ards Peninsula, about five miles south-east of Bangor and 18 miles from Belfast, Donaghadee is best known for its attractive little harbour and lighthouse. According to the Guinness Book of Records, **Grace Neills** (see entry) claims to be Ireland's oldest public house, opened in 1611 as the 'King's Arms'. Another pub of character is the Waterworth family's **Pier 36** (028 9188 4466), a lively place with a welcoming fire in winter, a good buzz and friendly staff; known for its food, especially local seafood, it is atmospheric in the evening. And garden lovers in search of a wholesome bite to eat will be delighted with the food at **Creative Gardens** at Donaghadee Garden Centre (028 9188 3237; www.creativegardens.net) on Stockbridge Road, between Bangor and Donaghadee (and also at Bushmills, Co Antrim; 028 2073 2225); the range of wholesome home-made fare offered in their coffee shop is impressive, and the opening hours are long (Mon, Tue, Sat 9.30-5; Wed, Thu, Fri 9.30-8, and Sun 12.30-5). And there are many great gardens to visit within 18 miles of Donaghadee, including Mountstewart House & Gardens (Newtownards, 028 4278 8387), Guincho (by appointment only, Helen's Bay, 028 9048 6324) and Glenmount (by appointment only, Dundonald, 028 9048 6324). For golfers, the famous waterside fairways of the nearby Royal Belfast Golf Club (Craigavad, 028 9042 8165) beckon.

WWW-IRELAND-GUIDE.COM FOR ALL THE BEST PLACES TO EAT, DRINK & STAY

Donaghadee
CHARACTER PUB•RESTAURANT

Grace Neill's

33 High Street Donaghadee Co Down BT21 0AH
Tel: 028 9188 4595
info@graceneills.com www.graceneills.com

Dating back to 1611, Grace Neill's lays a fair claim to be one of the oldest inns in all Ireland; Grace Neill herself was born when the pub was more than two hundred years old and died in 1916 at the age of 98. Extensions and improvements in recent ownership have been completed with due sensitivity to the age and character of the original front bar, which has been left simple and unspoilt; this is one of Ireland's best-loved pubs and, even without serving as much as soup and sandwiches, it would be on the must-visit list for visitors to Donaghadee. However, there is also a stylish informal restaurant with nautically-inspired decor in a bright, high-ceilinged contemporary area at the back of the old pub, and it is popular for its easy-going food and relaxed atmosphere. Sunday Brunch is a speciality, with live jazz. **Seats 80**; children welcome before 8pm. L & D daily 12-3pm & 5.30-9pm, food served all day Fri-Sun 12-9.30pm (12.30-8 Sun); à la carte; house wine from £12.95; sc discretionary. Live jazz Sundays 2-6pm. Closed 25 Dec, 12 Jul. MasterCard, Visa, Switch. **Directions:** Centre of Donaghadee.

Downpatrick
CHARACTER PUB•B&B

Denvirs

14 English Street Downpatrick Co Down BT30 6AB
Tel: 028 4461 2012

What a gem this ancient place is. Established in 1642, it's a wonderful pub with two old bars and an interesting informal restaurant, genuinely olde-worlde with an amazing original fireplace and chimney discovered during renovations. Accommodation is offered in six charmingly updated rooms, and there's a first floor room with some remarkable original features, suitable for meetings or private parties. Good food and genuinely friendly service too. Go and see it - there can't be another place in Ireland quite like it. **Seats 40**; toilets wheelchair accessible; children welcome before 7pm (high chair, childrens menu). L & D daily, 12-4pm & 5-9pm; Sun 12.30-5 & 5-8pm; value L £6.95, 12-5pm. House wine from £11.95. Accommodation offered (B&B £35 pps). Bar/Restaurant: Food served L daily & D Mon-Fri. Closed 25 Dec. Amex, Diners, MasterCard, Visa. **Directions:** On same street as the Cathedral and Courthouse in Downpatrick.

Downpatrick
COUNTRY HOUSE

Pheasants Hill Farm

37 Killyleagh Road Downpatrick Co Down BT30 9BL
Tel: 028 4461 7246
info@pheasantshill.com www.pheasantshill.com

Pheasants' Hill was a small Ulster farmstead for over 165 years until it was rebuilt in the mid-'90s - and is now a comfortable country house on a seven-acre organic small-holding within sight of the Mourne Mountains. The property is in an area of outstanding natural beauty and, although very close to the road, it is otherwise an idyllic spot. The bedrooms differ in character and outlook but are all comfortably furnished with generous beds and modern facilities; rooms at the back are quieter. Breakfast is a major event and worth factoring in as a main meal in your day, including dry-cured bacon and home-made sausages made with their own free-range Tamworth pork; vegetarians are also well catered for. *Farm shop: rare breed free-range pork, bacon, lamb, beef & organic poultry, fruit, vegetables sold. Open Mon-Sat 9-6 & Sun 12-6. Delivery service available. Also farm shop and butchers' shop in Comber, Mon-Sat 9-6. **Rooms 5** (2 en-suite & 1 with private bathroom, 1 ground floor, 1 family room, 3 shower-only, all no smoking); children welcome (cot available free of charge). B&B about £35. Garden, fishing, walking. Golf & equestrian nearby. Closed 1 Nov-16 Mar. Amex, MasterCard, Visa, Switch. **Directions:** On A22, 2.5 miles (4km) north of Downpatrick, 2.5 miles south of Killyleagh. ◇

Dundrum
RESTAURANT•BAR

The Buck's Head Inn

77 Main Street Dundrum Co Down BT33 0LU **Tel: 028 4375 1868**
buckshead1@aol.com www.thebucksheaddundrum.com

In recent years, Michael and Alison Crothers have developed this attractive, welcoming place from a pub with bar food and a restaurant, to its present position as a restaurant with bar - and it is probably the most popular destination in the whole Mourne area for anyone who appreciates quality food. Alison is in charge of the kitchen and sources local produce, especially seafood, including oysters from Dundrum Bay, which might be baked with a garlic & cheddar crust and Kilkeel cod, with mushy peas and chips. Well-balanced and interesting menus have a pleasing sense of place - aside from the seafood, County Down beef is used for the Sunday roast sirloin and steaks on the dinner menu, lamb is from the Mournes, and the famous butchers McCartneys of Moira supply sausages for the traditional bangers & champ; many tempting dishes are offered, also a short but imaginative vegetarian menu - and the range of styles ensures there is something to please all tastes. At lunchtime there's a shortish à la carte (often including excellent salads - try the fresh Dublin Bay prawns...) and daily blackboard specials - and they are open for high tea as well as dinner. Cooking is consistently good (and continues to become more interesting) and service under the direction of the proprietor Michael Crothers, is friendly and efficient. The atmosphere is always relaxed and each dining space has its own personality and is quite intimate - a dining room at the back (formerly a conservatory) overlooks a walled garden and is particularly pleasant. This is a fine restaurant, providing an exceptionally comprehensive service: well worth planning a journey around. Interesting wines are supplied by the highly respected Co Down wine merchant James Nicholson. **Seats 80** (private room, 50); children welcome. L 12-2.30, High Tea 5-6.30, D7-9.30 (Sun to 8.30). Set Sun L £18.50; Set D £28.50, otherwise à la carte. House wine from £11; sc discretionary. Closed Mon off-season (Oct-Apr); 25 Dec. Amex, MasterCard, Visa, Switch. **Directions:** On the main Belfast-Newcastle road, approx 3 miles from Newcastle. ◇

Dundrum
B&B

The Carriage House

71 Main St Dundrum Co Down BT33 0LU **Tel: 028 437 51635**
inbox@carriagehousedundrum.com www.carriagehousedundrum.com

Maureen Griffith, a former owner of The Buck's Head Inn, offers well-hidden bed and breakfast accommodation in her unusual house, which is next door to the Inn. Her home has great style, and is furnished mainly with antiques but she has an eye for unusual items and you will find modern pieces amongst them, and also quirky decorative little bits and pieces among the lovely paintings and prints

- and some not so little too, as a full-size horse sculpture at the back of the house is the item that guests find most fascinating. The three guest rooms include one away from the road at the back of the house, and all are quietly luxurious with beautiful bedding and delightful details. No dinner is offered (and it's only a few steps to the best in the area) but a lovely breakfast is served in a sun room overlooking a walled garden, prettily planted with wild flowers and herbs. **Rooms 3** (all en-suite and no smoking); B&B £35 pps, ss £10. Broadband wi/fi. Fishing, equestrian, garden visits, walking and golf nearby (Royal County Down Golf Club). **No Credit Cards. Directions:** A24 from Belfast, Dundrum. The violet blue house next to The Bucks Head (no sign: name etched in glass on top of front door).

Dundrum
RESTAURANT

Mourne Seafood Bar

10 Main Street Dundrum Co Down BT33 0LU **Tel: 028 4375 1377**
bob@mourneseafood.com www.mourneseafood.com

A prominent black and white 19th century terrace building in the centre of Dundrum, Robert and Joanne McCoubrey's lively and informal two-storey seafood restaurant and fish shop is the best bet for seafood in the Mourne area - and much appreciated by the many happy punters who relish the ultra-fresh fish and seafood offered. They specialise in fresh fish from the local ports of Keel and Annalong, and mussels, oysters and cockles from their own shellfish beds on Carlingford Lough - and, like the sister restaurant run by Andy Rae in Belfast (see entry), they use local fish that is not under threat such as gurnard and ling, helping to take the pressure off species like cod, so their extensive menu changes according to what is caught. Very friendly, family-tolerant staff deserve special mention, and the wine list is short and interesting - and (always an interesting choice) the sparkling water offered is San Pelligrino. *Also now at the smart modern **Mourne Café** (028 437 26401 at 107 Central Promenade, Newcastle. *The McCoubreys also run Mourne Coastal Tours (www.mournecoastaltours.com), offering boat trips of 15 minutes -1 hour along this beautiful coast. **Seats 45** (private room, 20, outdoors, 20); children welcome before 8pm (high chair, childrens menu); toilets wheelchair accessible. Food served daily, 12-9.30pm; à la carte; house wine £12.95. Closed Mon & Tue in winter, 25 Dec. Amex, MasterCard, Visa, Switch. **Directions:** Main Street of village.

Hillsborough
PUB•RESTAURANT•CAFE/BAR

The Plough Inn

3 The Square Hillsborough Co Down BT26 6AG
Tel: 028 9268 2985 www.barretro.com

Established in 1752, this former coaching inn is owned by the Patterson family who have built up a national reputation for hospitality and good food, especially seafood. Somehow they manage to run three separate food operations each day, so pleasing customers looking for a casual daytime meal and more serious evening diners. The evening restaurant is in the old stables at the back of the pub, and renowned for seafood and fine steaks; booking is required. There's a characterful old bar, where fairly traditional bar food is available, and the original **Plough Restaurant**, which has a separate entrance from the carpark, is also traditional in style. However, the rest of the pub is now stylishly contemporary, including the adjacent building where you will find the trendy **Barretro Café & Bistro**, which is open most of the day. In the main building, a stylish bistro above the old bar offers quite substantial international dishes; bookings are taken there for business lunches, although not in the evening. While there is obvious youth appeal, people of all ages feel comfortable here and the staff, who are clearly very proud of it, are friendly and helpful. It is very extensive, so allow yourself time to have a good look around and get your bearings before settling down to eat. [The Plough Inn was our Pub of the Year in 2004]. *The Pheasant Inn at Annahilt is a sister establishment (see entry). **Seats 40** (private room, 28, outdoors, 60); toilets wheelchair accessible; restaurant not suitable for children, but they are welcome in the bistro (high chair, childrens menu, baby changing facilities); value L £10.95, 12-2pm; set L £12.95; value 2 course D £14.95, 5-7pm; set 2 course D £19.50. Sun terrace. Parking. L daily, 12-2.30; D 5-9.30 daily (to 8pm Sun). **Bar Retro Bistro/Café: Seats 150**; food served all day, daily. Closed 25 Dec. Amex, Diners, MasterCard, Visa, Switch. **Directions:** Off the main Dublin-Belfast road, turn off at Hillsborough roundabout; in village square.

Hillsborough Area

PUB•RESTAURANT

The Pheasant

410 Upper Ballynahinch Road Annahilt Hillsborough
Co Down BT26 6NR **Tel: 028 9263 8056**

A sister to the well known **The Plough Inn** (see entry) in Hillsborough, this welcoming cottage style bar and restaurant is discreetly tucked away in the green County Down countryside and has earned a following locally for its tasty food served at very reasonable prices. Everyone loves an old world pub, and this one has a pleasant country charm, with old carts and rural memorabilia beside the excellent parking facilities. Inside, there's a traditional, relaxed feeling in the busy and atmospheric restaurant, where friendly and efficient staff greet guests and quickly take orders from an extensive à la carte menu with daily specials. Starters such as a trio of skewers (tiger prawn, Hoi sin pork & teriyaki chicken) or barbeque dusted calamari with Asian slaw, chilli & mint mayo and lime avocado salsa are typical of an Asian influence, while a house main course speciality of suckling hog medallions with bramley apple mash & sprouting broccoli demonstrates a more Irish feel; there's a separate menu section dedicated to dry-aged local beef, and also very attractive vegetarian, gluten-free and children's menus offered, so there really is something for everybody – and regular special events include Game Nights. All food is local, very freshly prepared and generous, and even the most basic dishes are packed with flavour and well executed. A low to mid-priced wine selection also offers great value; all this plus good service and a children's play area makes this a excellent place for a family outing. A private function room on the first floor is available for parties. **Seats 75** (private room, 16, outdoors, 40); reservations recommended; fully wheelchair accessible; children welcome before 9pm (high chair, childrens menu, baby changing facilities, playground); food served all day Tue-Sun, 12-9pm; L 12-2.30 (to 3pm Sun), D 5-9 (to 8pm Sun). Value L £7, value D £24, 5-7pm. Set 2 course L £10; Sun L £13.95; set 2/3 course D £19.95/23.95; also à la carte; house wine £12. Closed Mon (restaurant); 25-26 Dec; 12-13 Jul. Amex, Diners, MasterCard, Visa, Switch. **Directions:** 4 miles (7km) from the A1 Hillsborough.

Holywood

CAFÉ•RESTAURANT

Bay Tree Coffee House & Restaurant

118 High Street Holywood Co Down BT18 9HW **Tel: 028 9042 1419**
suefarmer@utvinternet.com

Since 1988, The Bay Tree has been attracting customers from miles around to its delightful restaurant and coffee house on the main street. Baking is a strength, especially the cinnamon scones which are a house speciality, and there's quite a strong emphasis on vegetarian dishes and organic salads, especially in summer, when you can also eat out on a patio in fine weather. No reservations for lunch, but they are required on busy evenings. *Sue Farmer has published a book of Bay Tree Recipes, available directly from the restaurant. **Seats 55** (outdoors, 8); children welcome. wheelchair accessible (not to toilets). Open all day Mon-Sat & D Mon & Wed-Sat; Sun brunch 9am-3pm. House wine about £12.50. SC 10% on Fri D. Parking. Closed D Tue & D Sun. Christmas 4 days, Easter 3 days & 12 July 4 days. MasterCard, Visa, Switch. **Directions:** Opposite the police station. ◊

Holywood

RESTAURANT

Fontana Restaurant

61A High Street Holywood Co Down BT18 9AE
Tel: 028 9080 9908

A first floor restaurant over a classy kitchen shop, Fontana is fresh and bright - perfectly in tune with the lovely zesty cooking that proprietor-chef Colleen Bennett offers. Starters and main courses tend to overlap on her interesting and loosely structured menus, with small and large portions of some dishes offered; a popular dish like Caesar salad with char-grilled chicken might come in two sizes, for example, and appear on both the lunch and dinner menus. Imaginative use of fresh produce is a striking characteristic of the food at Fontana: vegetables and salads are used with great panache and seafood is usually strongly represented - consistently accomplished cooking, stylishly simple presentation and clear flavours make an appealing combination. **Seats 54**; outside eating area; toilets wheelchair accessible; children welcome. L Tue-Fri 12-2.30 (Sun brunch 11-3), D Tue-Fri 5-9.30, D Sat, 6-10pm. Set 2/3 course D £14/17.50, otherwise à la carte; house wine about £12.50; SC discretionary, except 10% added on tables of 6+. On street parking. Closed L Sat, D Sun, all Mon, 25-26 Dec & 1 Jan. MasterCard, Visa, Switch. **Directions:** Three doors from Maypole flag pole. ◊

Holywood
HOTEL•RESTAURANT

Hastings Culloden Estate & Spa
Bangor Road Holywood Co Down BT18 0EX **Tel: 028 9042 1066**
res@cull.hastingshotels.com www.hastingshotels.com

Formerly the official palace for the Bishops of Down, Hastings Hotels' flagship property is a fine example of 19th-century Scottish Baronial architecture with plasterwork ceilings, stained glass windows and an imposing staircase. It is set in beautifully maintained gardens and woodland overlooking Belfast Lough and the County Antrim coastline. Period furniture and fine paintings in spacious high ceilinged rooms give a soothing feeling of exclusivity, and comfortable drawing rooms overlook the lough. Spacious, lavishly decorated guest rooms include a large proportion of suites and a Presidential Suite, with the best view; all are lavishly furnished and decorated with splendid bathrooms and details such as bathrobes, a welcoming bowl of fruit, and nice touches like ground coffee and a cafetière on the hospitality tray. Wireless internet access is available in all areas, and there are video/DVD players in suites. 26 new bedrooms were completed in 2008, and major changes are planned for the reception area and bar at the time of going to press. The hotel has an association with The Royal Belfast Golf Club, four minutes away by car (book the complimentary hospitality limousine) also a fine health club; the 'Cultra Inn', a bar and restaurant in the grounds, offers an informal alternative to The Mitre Restaurant. The hotel is licensed to hold weddings on the premises. Conference/banqueting (1,000/600); business centre, broadband wi/fi. Leisure centre (swimming pool, steam room, sauna, jacuzzi, fitness room; spa). Garden. Children welcome (under 14s free in parents' room; cot available without charge). No pets. **Rooms 105** (1 suite, 21 junior suites, 35 executive, 7 family, 2 disabled, all no-smoking). Lift. 24 hr room service. B&B £138 pps, ss £70.* Short breaks offered. Parking (400). Helipad. Open all year. **The Mitre Restaurant:** The fine dining restaurant is in a long room overlooking the lough, with a discreet and luxurious ambience - and, with very comfortable and well-padded upholstered chairs, conducive to lingering. Tables are beautifully appointed in classic style, and extensive menus that live up to their promise may include a speciality main course of tender saddle of venison from nearby Clandeboye Estate, with crushed root vegetables and buttered greens. Classic cooking, lovely surroundings and correct, attentive service all make this a restaurant with a sense of occasion. Extensive wine list to match. **Seats 110** (private room, 50); reservations required; children welcome; toilets wheelchair accessible. D daily, 7-9.30, Set D about £32.50; L Sun only, 12.30-2.30. Set Sun L about £28. House wine £17. Amex, Diners, MasterCard, Visa, Switch. **Directions:** 6 miles (10km) from Belfast city centre on A2 towards Bangor. ◇〉

Holywood
COUNTRY HOUSE

Rayanne Country House
60 Demesne Road Holywood Co Down B18 9EX **Tel: 028 9042 5859**
rayannehouse@hotmail.com www.rayannehouse.com

Situated almost next to the Holywood Golf Club and Redburn Country Park, and with views across Belfast Lough, the McClellands' family-run country house is a tranquil spot in which to unwind, and a fine alternative to impersonal hotels. It has a long-standing reputation as a relaxing place, known for its friendly staff and extensive breakfasts (including a 'healthy house grill', with nothing fried), and the restful option of dining in the restaurant here rather than having to go out in the evening. However the ante has well and truly been upped recently, with extensive refurbishment and the addition of a new wing, which has been carefully designed to blend with the period features of the original house. Some bedrooms have views of Belfast Lough, and all are individually decorated to a high standard with phones, television, hospitality tray and many little extras. Conor McClelland cooks for up to 30 guests in the restaurant, which is also open to non-residents by reservation. He offers an impressive, mainly classical, dinner menu with about half a dozen choices on each course. Friendly staff are helpful and make families with children most welcome; beach, shops and restaurants are all just a few minutes' walk away. Small conferences/banqueting (15/34); free broadband wi/fi. Parking (14). **Rooms 11** (4 shower only, 2 family, 1 ground floor, 1 disabled, all no smoking); children welcome (under 2s free in parents room, cot available without charge, baby sitting arranged). B&B £55pps, single £80. No pets. D £48, by reservation. Short breaks offered. Garden, walking. Closed 24/25 Dec, 31 Dec, 1 Jan. MasterCard, Visa, Switch. **Directions:** Take A2 out of Belfast towards Holywood 6 miles (10km), up to top of My Lady's Mile; turn right; 200 yards.

Sullivans Restaurant

Holywood
RESTAURANT

2 Sullivan Place Holywood Co Down BT18 9JF **Tel: 028 9042 1000**
www.sullivansrestaurant.co.uk

Simon Shaw's bright, friendly and informal restaurant is now well over a decade in business - and consistently excellent food, varied menus, a good atmosphere and fair prices are the secret of his success. Lively lunch and sandwich menus are offered, based on the quality ingredients which have always been the building blocks of his cooking, and he seeks out interesting produce from trusted suppliers like Helen's Bay Organics, McKee's Farm (beef) and Finnebrogue (venison); vegetarians do well here, too, with interesting choices on the regular menus as well as a separate vegetarian menu. Menus are refreshingly down-to-earth and keenly priced, and the cooking never disappoints. The wine list is not very informative (no tasting notes) but is well chosen and good value. **Seats 60**; children welcome (high chair). L daily 12-2.30, D Tue-Sun, 6-9.30 (from 5pm Fri-Sun, to 8.30pm Sun); à la carte; house wine from £13; sc 10%, on parties of 8+. Closed D Mon, 2 days Christmas,12-13 Jul. MasterCard, Visa, Switch. **Directions:** Just off main Belfast-Bangor dual carriageway.

Beech Hill Country House

Holywood Area
B&B•COUNTRY HOUSE
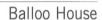

23 Ballymoney Road Craigantlet Holywood Co Down BT23 4TG
Tel: 028 9042 5892
info@beech-hill.net www.beech-hill.net

Victoria Brann's attractive Georgian-style house is set in the peaceful Holywood Hills. It has great style - and the benefit of an exceptionally hospitable hostess, who does everything possible to ensure that guests have everything they need. Ground floor bedrooms have panoramic views over the North Down countryside and are furnished with antique furniture - and, believe it or not, the beds are made up with fine Irish linen; all also have good in-room facilities including laptop-size safes - and lovely en-suite bathrooms with lots of special little extras. Breakfast is a meal worth allowing time to enjoy - and it is served in a spacious conservatory overlooking a croquet lawn. **Rooms 3** (all en-suite, 1 shower only, all no smoking, all ground floor). B&B £50.00pps. ss £15.00. Dogs permitted by arrangement (stay in bedroom, no charge); free broadband wi/fi. Open all year. *Self-catering accommodation or B&B also offered in The Colonel's Lodge (£280-£380 per week self-catering, £70 per night B&B). Amex, MasterCard, Visa, Switch. **Directions:** A2 from Belfast; bypass Holywood; 1.5 miles (3km) from bridges at Ulster Folk Museum, turn right up Ballymoney Road signed Craigantlet - 1.5 miles (3km) miles on left.

Balloo House

Killinchy
RESTAURANT•PUB

1 Comber Road Killinchy Co Down BT23 6PA **Tel: 028 9754 1210**
info@balloohouse.com www.balloohouse.com

PUB OF THE YEAR

This famous old 19th century coaching inn fell into great hands when Ronan and Jennie Sweeney took it over in 2004. With extensive experience in the hospitality industry behind them, they were determined to restore Balloo's reputation as one of the finest country dining pubs in Northern Ireland - and this they are now achieving very successfully. Downstairs operates as a full licensed bar daily and it is extremely busy all week; the place has oodles of genuine character and the old kitchen bar, with its flagstones and traditional range, makes a great setting for excellent bistro fare like fresh Kilkeel scampi & chips, dry-aged locally reared steaks, homemade burgers and some less usual dishes such as Finnebrogue venison shepherd's pie. **Restaurant:** A separate entrance from the bar leads up to the first floor, which resembles a quaint and cosy converted loft, and has a snug reception area with open fire and comfy seats, beside a well stocked bar with many liqueurs on display. The décor is quite traditional in style, with beautiful exposed stone walls the main feature; the restaurant is beautifully laid out with tall-backed chairs around white linen clad tables with sparkling crystal wine glasses - and despite the cosy appearance, there's plenty of space between tables. Head chef **Danny Millar** is a well known advocate of local seasonal produce and this is reflected in his menus, typically in dishes such as smoked Lough Neagh eel with apple, beetroot, horseradish & micro salad; grilled Strangford Lough prawns with garlic, parsley and lemon butter; rump of Finnebrogue venison with spiced apple & sweet potato purée, watercress & wild mushrooms - and a house speciality of Balloo House chocolate tart – served, perhaps, with fresh berries and crème fraîche. The cooking is accomplished, as would be expected of this highly regarded chef, and he is producing stunning food. Every dish has a wow factor, but the real skill is in allowing the quality of ingredients to shine through, and this beautifully presented food has real flavour. Service, under the supervision of Restaurant Manager Didier Nyceront, is excellent in the Guide's experience - professional, helpful and efficient; however, food of this quality does take time to prepare, and the popularity of this restaurant can sometimes bring the kitchen under pressure, especially at weekends. An impressive wine list includes a good choice of wines by glass and a page of 'Didier's recent tasting favourites'. Overall, the lovely relaxed ambience and outstanding food at very reasonable prices are a credit to all involved, and Balloo's growing reputation is well earned. Booking in advance is essential for the restaurant. Downstairs bistro **seats 80** (private room, 40, outdoors, 12); children welcome; wheelchair access to downstairs only; free broadband WI/FI; air conditioning; reservations recommended. Live music (Blue Grass) Wed 9pm & trad Thurs 9pm. Bistro: Food served daily 12-9 (to 8.30pm on Sun, Mon); house wine from £12.95. Restaurant seats 30; open Tue-Sat, 6-9pm (to 9.30 Fri-Sat), also available for functions and private dining. SC 10% on groups 6+. Closed 25 Dec. MasterCard, Visa, Switch. **Directions:** At Balloo crossroads on main road from Comber to Killyleagh.

Killinchy
PUB

Daft Eddies

Sketrick Island Whiterock Killinchy Co Down BT23 6QB
Tel: 028 9754 1615

A scenic coastal drive along Strangford Lough brings you to a causeway that curves behind trees to reach this unassuming but beautifully located pub, which has lovely views of Sketrick Castle, Whiterock marina and the lough, and is a popular summer destination. A comfortable old world bar leads into a cosy restaurant decorated with maritime memorabilia, where well-balanced menus offer plenty of choice with, as would be expected, particular strength in local seafood. Descriptions on the menu may seem more adventurous than they turn out on the plate, but the simpler choices are probably best in any case: battered fillets of cod with mushy peas and tartare sauce, for example, is large, fresh and crispy, while the Daft Eddy's burger with bacon and cambazola never fails to please the hungry diner. A nice flavoursome home-made light Irish Mist pannacotta with berries could be the perfect end to a generous meal, and there's a reasonably priced wine list available too. Wholesome food, cheery staff and a beautiful location make this a popular casual dining destination. Open Mon-Fri 12-2.30 & 5-9; Sat 12-9.30. Sun 12.30-9 . Weekday Bistro Menu; Fri & Sat night à la carte; set Sun L £16.95. MasterCard, Visa, Switch. **Directions:** From Killinchy drive to shore and turn left for 1/2 mile - pub is on island over causeway. ◇

KILLYLEAGH

This charming village in north County Down is best known for its castle, which is built in the style of a Loire valley chateau and believed to be the oldest inhabited castle in the country. Just beside the castle, **Picnic** (028 4482 8525) is a smashing little deli and café which is well worth knowing about: lovely simple daytime food to enjoy while you're there - and a great range of carefully sourced goodies to take home. (Open Mon-Fri 7am-6.30pm (last orders 5.30), Sat 10-4; closed Sun off season). And, nearby, the 200-year old **Dufferin Arms** (028 4482 1182; www.dufferincoachinginn.com) is an inn in the true sense of the word, offering food, drink and shelter to travellers. It's full of old-world character, and known for music too. For golfers, the nearest recommended championship course is Royal County Down (Newcastle, 028 4372 3314), and as with most of County Down, the main issue for garden lovers will be getting the time to see all of the wonderful gardens in the area, the closest being Anna's House Garden (Comber, 028 9754 1566), Rowallane Garden (Saintfield, 028 9751 0131), Seaforde Gardens (Downpatrick, 028 4481 1225) and Mountstewart House & Gardens (Newtownards, 028 4278 8387).

WWW-IRELAND-GUIDE.COM FOR ALL THE BEST PLACES TO EAT, DRINK & STAY

Kircubbin
RESTAURANT WITH ROOMS

Paul Arthurs Restaurant
62-66 Main Street Kircubbin Newtownards
Co Down BT22 2SP **Tel: 028 4273 8192**
www.paularthurs.com

Located above the family chip shop on the main street of his home town, the warmly lit staircase sets a welcoming tone for customers into Paul Arthurs' small first floor dining room. With a hexagonal window into the kitchen the focal point for diners, and work by Belfast artist Terry Bradley adding splashes of gusto, it exudes character and has an informal atmosphere. Friendly staff quickly make customers feel at home and offer a short, enticing menu. Local produce, including seafood, features strongly and there is always a catch of the day; but, unusually for the area, the wide range of dishes usually favours meat, and there will also be local game in season. However, vegetarians are not over-looked, with options listed separately, and there's even a vegan choice. Homely desserts are accompanied by excellent Lavazza coffee. Fresh local produce, accurate cooking and deep, well-balanced flavours make for a memorable dining experience here, enhanced by an accessible, well priced wine list that includes a Chef's Selection and a short list of higher end bottles. Both the excel-lent food and its setting reflect not only the character of the chef, but the unique character of this beautiful part of the world. **Accommodation:** Seven simply furnished en-suite bedrooms are offered, including 2 for disabled guests. **Seats 55** (outdoor, 20), air conditioning. L & D Tue-Sat, 12-2.30 & 5-9.30. A la carte. House wine about £12.95. **Rooms 7** (all en-suite, 3 ground floor, 2 disabled); B&B about £35pps, ss about £15.Closed Sun, Mon, 25 Dec & Jan. Amex, MasterCard, Visa, Switch. **Directions:** On main street, 1st floor, opposite supermarket. ◇

Newcastle
HOTEL

Burrendale Hotel & Country Club
51 Castlewellan Road Newcastle Co Down BT33 0JY **Tel: 028 4372 2599**
reservations@burrendale.com www.burrendale.com

Just outside the traditional seaside holiday town of Newcastle, and close to the championship links of the Royal County Down golf course, this friendly hotel on the edge of the Mourne mountains has a pleasingly remote atmosphere and spacious public areas, including the homely Cottage Bar with an open log fire, welcome on chilly days. Well-appointed accommodation includes some family rooms and some newer superior rooms that have lovely views and are furnished to a higher standard, including air conditioning, but all rooms are well-equipped with the usual amenities. The Burrendale has recently been attracting attention for good food, served in both the informal Cottage Kitchen Restaurant and the evening restaurant, Vine. Well-trained, courteous staff are efficient in all areas of the hotel, making this a pleasant place to stay. Golf is a major attraction to the area, and the hotel is also a popular conference venue. Conference/banqueting (350 /250); business centre, secretarial serv-ices; video conferencing available, broadband WI/Fi. **Rooms 69** (3 suites, 18 executive, 6 family, 20 no smoking, 19 ground floor, 10 disabled); children welcome (under 4s free in parents' room; cots available without charge, baby sitting arranged). Lift. 24-hour room service. B&B £60 pps, ss £20. Bar and restaurant meals available daily (phone to check restaurant times). Garden, walking, cycling, pool table. Leisure centre (swimming pool, steam room, jacuzzi, sauna, fitness room); Spa (beauty salon, treatment rooms, massage). Open all year. Amex, Diners, MasterCard, Visa, Switch. **Directions:** On A50 Castlewellan Road.

Newcastle
HOTEL

Hastings Slieve Donard Hotel
Downs Road Newcastle Co Down BT33 0AH **Tel: 028 4372 1066**
res@sdh.hastingshotels.com www.hastingshotels.com

This famous hotel stands beneath the Mountains of Mourne in six acres of public grounds, adjacent to the beach and the Royal County Down Golf Links. The Victorian holiday hotel par excellence, the Slieve Donard first opened in 1897 and has been the leading place to stay in Newcastle ever since. Hastings Hotels are renowned for their high standards – including regular refurbishment, immaculate maintenance and good housekeeping - and this 'grand old lady' of the group has recently been treated to a major makeover, which has brought a freshness while always having respect for the old building. Both public areas and guest rooms are furnished with style and finished to a high standard - and all the bathrooms still sport one of the famous yellow Hastings' ducks! The hotel is perfectly positioned for exploring the Mournes or a golfing holiday (Royal County Down Golf Club is adjacent to the prop-erty) and is well known for its wide range of special short breaks, which can be very good value - excellent on-site facilities include the hotel's Elysium health club and Spa, and the nearby Tollymore Forest Park provides excellent walking. Conference/banqueting (825/440); business centre; secretarial services; broadband wi/fi. **Rooms 179** (6 suites, 12 executive, 29 family, 6 disabled, all no smoking).

2 Lifts; room service (limited hours). B&B £100 pps, ss £65; children welcome (under 14s free in parents' room; cots available without charge). No pets. Leisure centre (swimming pool, jacuzzi, fitness room, sauna, steam room); spa (massage, treatments). Ample parking. Golf (18) and beach nearby. Open all year. Helipad. Amex, Diners, MasterCard, Visa, Laser, Switch. **Directions:** Situated on the coast 32 miles (50km) south-east of Belfast.

Mourne Café

Newcastle
CAFÉ
Ⓝ

107 Central Promenade Newcastle Co Down BT33 0EU **Tel: 028 4372 6401**
mournecafe@hotmail.co.uk www.mourneseafood.com

A recent offshoot of the Mourne Seafood Bars in Dundrum and Belfast (see entries), this smart modern café offers an informal way to experience the great seafood that the McCoubrey family has made their niche. As in their other restaurants, they specialise in fresh fish from the local ports of Keel and Annalong, and mussels, oysters and cockles from their own shellfish beds on Carlingford Lough – and, whenever possible, use local fish that is not under threat. No-nonsense menus read refreshingly simply - hake fillet with minted pea cream; mussels in garlic white wine cream, or Thai style – and there's a 14oz dry-aged sirloin steak with chunky chips & pepper sauce for anyone not in the mood for fish. A separate children's menu is all one price (£4.95) and they hold a Lobster Fest every Thursday night, which is great value at only £11.99 for a whole grilled lobster (+£1 with thermidor sauce). This place should do very well. Open Sun- Thu, 11.30am-8.30pm, Fri & Sat 11.30-10. L 12-5pm and evening menu from 5pm onwards. *The McCoubreys also run Mourne Coastal Tours (www.mournecoastal-tours.com), offering boat trips of 15 minutes - 1 hour along this beautiful coast. **Directions:** On Central Promenade, at entrance to Donard car park.

Sea Salt Delicatessen & Bistro

Newcastle
CAFÉ•RESTAURANT

51 Central Promenade Newcastle Co Down BT33 0HH
Tel: 028 4372 5027

A good meal will add greatly to your enjoyment of a visit to this traditional holiday town on the sea edge of the Mountains of Mourne, so make a point of seeking out this unusual and rather special seafront restaurant. Sea Salt has recently found renewed energy under proprietor Aidan Small, who is unperturbed by vagaries of the Irish summer weather, as loyal regulars continue to support his honest venture. Having reduced the number of choices to focus more on quality and local produce, Aidan has concentrated on offering simple quality dishes cooked with flair and an attention to flavour: certain menu items feature an "FU" symbol, which means 'flavours unleashed' and applies to particularly tasty dishes. On Friday and Saturday, as well as being open all day, they do a Tapas evening to 9.30-10pm; other theme nights are held too, eg World Cuisine. Aidan is very passionate about what he is doing and the shelves are packed with interesting deli goods, many produced locally - and, although they are competing with an ice cream parlour on one side and chip shop/café on the other, an interested middle market, seeking quality, continues to find them here. **Seats 30**; air conditioning; booking is essential. Open daily 10am-5pm (from 9am Sat/Sun); also D Thu-Sat, 7-9/10pm (Fri & Sat only in winter). MasterCard, Visa, Switch. **Directions:** Seafront Newcastle, foot of Mournes. ◈

Glassdrumman Lodge

Newcastle Area
COUNTRY HOUSE•RESTAURANT

85 Mill Road Annalong Co Down BT34 4RH
Tel: 028 4376 8451
info@glassdrummanlodge.com www.glassdrummanlodge.com

In a dramatic hillside location just outside the coastal village of Annalong, and close to the great forest parks of Tollymore and Castlewellan, Glassdrumman Lodge is in the heart of one of Ireland's most picturesque mountain districts, the ancient 'Kingdom of Mourne'. Graeme and Joan Hall have developed their former farmhouse into an unusual country house, where comfortable guest rooms and suites offer a peaceful base for golfers wishing to play the Royal County Down Golf Course - and for fishing folk, who may prefer casting for trout on the well-stocked lake, to other more energetic outdoor activities like walking and climbing. The fine dining restaurant is also open to non-residents, by reservation, and fresh produce for dinner comes from their own gardens, and local seafood from nearby ports. **Rooms 10** (all en-suite, 2 junior suites, 2 suites, 1 ground floor); children welcome (cots avail free of charge); B&B £62.50 pps, ss about £30. Memories Restaurant seats 45 (private room, 20); D Daily at 8pm £45 (also à la carte menu at the weekend). Small conferences/banqueting (16/50). Amex, Diners, MasterCard, Visa, Switch. **Directions:** A2 coast road between Newcastle and Kilkeel. Take right at Halfway House pub, 1 mile (1.6km) up Mill road. ◈

NEWRY

Newry - now a city - has a canal as its central feature, and **Canal Court Hotel** (028 3025 1234; www.canalcourt.com) is the leading establishment of the area. An interesting dining option in the town is **The Graduate Restaurant** (reservations: 028 3025 9611) at Newry College (now the Southern Regional College, Newry Campus), hospitality and tourism department. Experienced lecturers all with quality industry backgrounds run the restaurant on different days of the week, and the whole operation is a realistic training environment for student chefs and waiters. Open during the college term only: L Mon-Fri, 12.30 (about £6.95 for 4 courses), D Tue only, 7pm is about £10 for a 6 course dinner. An interesting newcomer to the town is **Copper Café** (028 4175 3047; www.copperrestaurant.co.uk), an offshoot of the highly regarded Warrenpoint restaurant **'Copper'** (see entry); located at the Newry Museum in Bagenal's Castle, on the site of the famous McCann's Bakery, this daytime café with easy parking nearby is open daily, Mon-Sat 9-5, Sun 1-4.30, and offers varying menus through the day, all with the trademark Copper stamp of quality. A welcome newcomer for the town.

Newtownards

B&B•COUNTRY HOUSE

Edenvale House

130 Portaferry Road Newtownards Co Down BT22 2AH

Tel: 028 9181 4881

edenvalehouse@hotmail.com www.edenvalehouse.com

Diane Whyte's charming Georgian house is set peacefully in seven acres of garden and paddock, with views over Strangford Lough to the Mourne mountains and a National Trust wildfowl reserve. The house has been sensitively restored and modernised, providing a high standard of accommodation and hospitality. Guests are warmly welcomed and well fed, with excellent traditional breakfasts and afternoon tea with home-made scones. For evening meals, Diane directs guests to one of the local restaurants. Edenvale is close to the National Trust property Mount Stewart, renowned for its gardens, and also convenient to Rowallane and Castle Ward. **Rooms 3** (all en-suite, 1 junior suite, 1 superior, 1 shower only, 1 family room, all no-smoking); children welcome (under-5s free in parents' room; cots available without charge). Pets permitted by arrangement. B&B £50 pps, ss £10. Garden. Closed Christmas. MasterCard, Visa. **Directions:** 2 miles (3.5 km) from Newtownards on A20 going towards Portaferry. ◊

Portaferry

HOTEL•RESTAURANT

Portaferry Hotel

The Strand Portaferry Co Down BT22 1PE **Tel: 028 4272 8231**

info@portaferryhotel.com www.portaferryhotel.com

This 18th-century waterfront terrace presents a neat, traditional exterior overlooking the lough towards the attractive village of Strangford, and the National Trust property, Castleward. The inn is now one of the most popular destinations in Northern Ireland - not least for its reputation for good food, including their excellent lunchtime bar meals. The ground floor bar, a comfortable sitting room, and the restaurant all have a cosy, well-kept old-fashioned feeling to them and, while not luxurious, accommodation is comfortable and most of the individually decorated en-suite bedrooms have views of the water - those on the front attract a small supplement. The hotel is beautifully kept and maintained, a lovely place with personality, and friendly, helpful staff. Small conference/private parties (35/80); parking. Children (Under 16s free in parents' room; cots available at no charge). No pets. **Rooms 14** (all en-suite, 2 shower only, 4 family rooms, all no-smoking) B&B from £55 pps, ss £20. *Mid-week deals often available. **Restaurant:** A slightly cottagey feeling provides the perfect background for good unpretentious food. Local produce features prominently in prime Ulster beef, Mourne lamb and game from neighbouring estates but it is, of course, the seafood that takes pride of place. Well-balanced table d'hôte lunch and dinner menus are offered, plus a short à la carte, providing plenty of choice although majoring on local seafood. Excellent breakfasts are served in the restaurant - a particularly good menu is offered, giving plenty of choice including fresh and smoked fish as a feature. This may not be the gargantuan spread that some country houses lay on for guests, but it is all freshly cooked to order and really delicious - and efficiently served by friendly staff: exactly what the perfect hotel breakfast should be. **Seats 65**; children welcome. L daily, 12.30-2.30; D daily 5.30-9 (to 8.30 Sun). D Value Menu nightly 5.30-6.30. Set menu; Sun L about £18.50. à la carte and children's menu also available; house wine from about £10.50; sc discretionary. Toilets wheelchair accessible. Open all year except Christmas. Amex, Diners, MasterCard, Visa. **Directions:** On Portaferry seafront. ◊

Portavogie
BAR•RESTAURANT

The Quays

81 New Harbour Road Portavogie Co Down BT22 1EB
Tel: 028 4277 2225
info@quaysrestaurant.co.uk www.quaysrestaurant.co.uk

Way down the Ards peninsula, in the fishing village of Portavogie, you'll find an authentic fishing village experience at The Quays, a pub and seafood restaurant in a picturesque location overlooking the harbour and the Irish Sea. Inside the brightly painted yellow exterior visitors are immediately immersed in a fun, colourful maritime setting, with marine blues, wooden beam features and the odd lobster pot hanging from the wall. This welcoming family-friendly atmosphere is complemented by warm staff, who serve up skilfully cooked, honest food with an emphasis on the spanking fresh locally caught seafood. At The Quays they're clearly proud of the precious raw product that is landed on their doorstep and treat it with endearing respect, offering simply cooked, unfussy food, with a focus on fresh ingredients, and changing the seafood menu regularly to reflect seasonality. Who could resist a classic prawn cocktail, for example, made with big, fat, juicy Portavogie prawns? Or fish & chips made with very thinly battered hake, perfectly cooked to be crunchy crisp on the outside and the fish just flaking apart? Non-seafood lovers are well catered for too, however, as you'll also find some tempting meat dishes and a handful of appetising vegetarian options on the menu. The Quays is the kind of place where you can have a pint and a plate of beautifully cooked fresh seafood, with two of the best seasonings in the world: fresh sea air and the sight of moored fishing boats gently rocking in the harbour as you eat. Delightful. Restaurant: L&D Mon–Fri, 12-2.30pm & 5-8.30pm, Sat & Sun all day 12-9pm (to 8pm Sun). Bar: Mon-Sat 11:30am - 11:30 pm, Sun 12-10pm. MasterCard, Visa, Switch.
Directions: Overlooking the harbour. ◇

Saintfield
RESTAURANT

Edgars Restaurant

11-15 Main Street Saintfield Co Down BT24 7AA
Tel: 028 9751 1755

In an attractive traditional terrace at the centre of Saintfield, Colin and Emma Edgar's smart contemporary café-style restaurant is in a lovely double-height room simply furnished with wooden tables, and comfortable café-style chairs. Depending on the day of the week, you can order anything from fry-ups and other breakfast dishes, through an interesting lunchtime selection including open sandwiches, and salads; a bistro menu offers dishes such as fresh cod, scampi, home-made burgers, rib-eye steak and chicken, all served with thick-cut home-made chips. Then, for evening meals, it shifts up a gear when an enticing contemporary à la carte dinner menu comes on stream - starters like shellfish linguini, perhaps, and mains including slow-roasted Mourne lamb. Edgar's is a charming place (the kind every small town deserves) and run by an enthusiastic young couple who offer good quality, freshly prepared and correctly cooked food - with friendly service to match. **Seats 30**; children welcome before 8pm; reservations recommended; L & D Tue-Sat, 10am-2.30pm; 6-8.30pm (to 9.30pm Fri/Sat); Sun 10am-6pm; value D about £30, Tue-Thur 6-8.30pm, also à la carte; house wine from about £12. Closed Mon, 25 Dec, 12-13 Jul. MasterCard, Visa **Directions:** 11 miles (18km) south of Belfast on the A7. ◇

Strangford Village
PUB•GUESTHOUSE

The Cuan Licensed Guest Inn

6-10 The Square Strangford Village Co Down BT30 7ND
Tel: 028 4488 1222 info@thecuan.com www.thecuan.com

On the square, just up from the car ferry that goes over to Portaferry, Peter and Caroline McErlean's friendly village inn presents a neat, inviting face to the world. Over a century old, it has character with open fires, cosy lounges and a homely bar where food is available every day. Bedrooms, including two family rooms, are comfortably furnished with television and tea/coffee-making facilities, and most of the bathrooms have bath and shower. Short breaks offered. Small conferences/banqueting (60/80); free broadband wi/fi. **Rooms 9** (3 shower only, all no smoking, 3 family); children welcome (under 2s free in parents' room, cots available without charge). Limited room service (on request). B&B £42.50 pps, ss £10. Short breaks offered; SC discretionary. Closed 25 Dec. MasterCard, Visa, Switch
Directions: 7 miles (11km) from Downpatrick on the A25; on the square, near the ferry.

Warrenpoint
RESTAURANT

Copper Restaurant

4 Duke Street Warrenpoint Co Down BT34 3JY **Tel: 028 4175 3047**
info@copperrestaurant.co.uk www.copperrestaurant.co.uk

Just off the diamond in the centre of Warrenpoint, Neil Bradley and Sarah Meaney's appealing restaurant lies behind a smart understated façade. Inside, there's a bar and a fine high-ceilinged dining room, with tables welcomingly set up with classic white linen and all the nice little touches that convey a quality feeling. Neil is an extremely strong advocate of local food: his fish is bought straight off the boat at Kilkeel Harbour, his herbs and vegetables are from Lurganconary Organic Farm at Kilkeel, and naturally-reared beef and pork for the restaurant come from the nearby Narrow Water Castle Farm... thus the building blocks of good food are in place and, if you add the magic ingredient of seriously good cooking by a talented and dedicated chef, it is no surprise that this delightful restaurant should be on so many customers' list of favourites. A range of imaginative but admirably concise set menus is offered (lunch, early dinner, vegetarian) as well as a more extensive à la carte; typically delicious summer offerings might include starters using vegetables, herbs and local fish in season such as fresh pea risotto with local ham & mint or spiced mackerel fillets with orange & rhubarb salad, possibly followed by a great meat dish like char-grilled Narrow Water sirloin with dauphinoise potatoes & chilli butter, or cumin roast lamb with potato gnocchi & aubergine. Finish, perhaps, with an unusual dessert like vanilla mousse with crushed strawberries and vanilla sherbert... The vegetarian menu is equally appealing, and also an 8-course Tasting Menu (£35) available for whole tables, which offers exceptional value. Everything served here is delicious, but the underlying reason for this restaurant's success is that it is so customer-friendly – all menus offer extremely good value and, where possible, flexibility too; an interesting wine list is very fairly priced and, not only is service charming and efficient under Sarah's direction, but she keeps in constant contact with customers throughout the year, offering special dining deals that entice people back. And, once through the door, Neil and Sarah ensure an enjoyable – perhaps memorable - experience, at a fair price. Well worth a detour. * A daytime Copper Cafe is now open at the Newry Museum. **Seats 42**; toilets wheelchair accessible; air conditioning; children welcome. L Tue-Fri, 12-3pm; D Tue-Sat 5.30-9.30pm (to 10.30 Fri/Sat); Sun all day, 12-8.30pm. Set L £16; set 2/3 course D £19.50/23.50, also à la carte L&D. House wine from £13. SC 10% on groups 6+. Closed Sat L, Mon & 25-26 Dec. Amex, MasterCard, Visa, Switch. **Directions:** Just off main square in Warrenpoint.

Warrenpoint
RESTAURANT
R

The Duke Restaurant

7 Duke Street Warrenpoint Co Down BT34 3JY **Tel: 028 4175 2084**
www.thedukerestaurant.com

Seafood straight from Kilkeel harbour, and most other produce also sourced with a ten mile radius, is the foundation for Ciaran Gallagher's success at his popular restaurant, which occupies the whole of the first floor over a pleasantly traditional pub, The Duke. There's a comfortable mixture of traditional and modern styles which, together with the busy atmosphere and friendly service, all add up to a relaxed ambience. Like the surroundings, menus are balanced and well-tailored to the clientèle; crowd pleasers like surf'n'turf and chicken kiev take their regular places alongside some more ambitious dishes for discerning diners, notably local seafood. **Seats 65**; air conditioning. D Wed-Sun, 6-9pm. Special set D Wed/Thu £14.95, also à la carte. House wine from about £12. No SC. Closed Mon, Tue. Amex, MasterCard, Visa, Switch. **Directions:** Just off town square. ◇

Warrenpoint
RESTAURANT

Restaurant 23

23 Church St Warrenpoint Co Down BT34 3HN **Tel: 028 4175 3222**
restaurant23@btconnect.com www.restaurant-23.co.uk

In the busy town centre of Warrenpoint, a long L-shaped room that was once part of a very large traditional pub now serves as a remarkable contemporary restaurant. There's a great team at work here – the proprietors are Raymond McArdle (renowned head chef at the Nuremore Hotel, Carrickmacross, see entry) and his wife, Andrea, and heading up the kitchen team is one of Northern Ireland's most talented chefs, Trevor Cunningham. Despite the stylish surroundings and accomplished cooking, it's an accessible place and enticing menus designed to please all tastes are based on carefully-sourced, quality ingredients. The style is broadly upbeat modern classical (which allows for some of the currently fashionable Asian influences), to include tasty lunchtime food like smoked salmon Caesar salad or comforting Cumberland sausage & champ, and more sophisticated evening dishes such as a house speciality of pressed confit foie gras, or mussels with chilli, ginger & white wine, or lovely crisp spiced belly of pork. Excellent attention to detail is seen in delicious freshly baked breads, tempting desserts and home-made petit fours with your after-dinner coffee. The same care is reflected in a well chosen wine list, and – although not perhaps a match for the exceptional skill in the kitchen - the service brings an easy blend of Northern friendliness and professional skill. With such a talented and confident chef in the kitchen, a relaxed ambience and good value, this is a restaurant that should do well. **Seats 60** (private room, 30); toilets wheelchair accessible; air conditioning. Open Wed-Sat, L 12.30-3, D 6.30-9.30 (to 10 Fri/Sat), Sun 12.30-8. Value L £8; set Sun L £16; value D £18 Wed-Fri; set 2/3 course D £22/30; also à la carte; House wine £14-16. Closed Mon, Tue, 25 Dec, 3rd week Jan. Amex, MasterCard, Visa, Switch.

COUNTY FERMANAGH

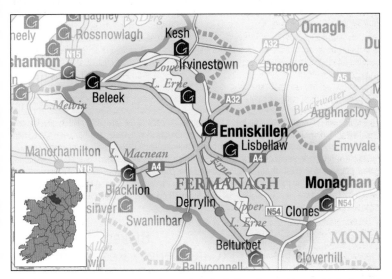

Ireland is a watery place of many lakes, rivers and canals. So it's quite an achievement to be the most watery county of all. Yet this is but one of Fermanagh's many claims to distinction. It is the only county in Ireland through which you can travel the complete distance between its furthest extremities entirely by boat.

Rivers often divide one county from another, but Fermanagh is divided - or linked if you prefer - throughout its length by the handsome waters of the River Erne, both river and lake. Southeast of the historic county town of Enniskillen, Upper Lough Erne is a maze of small waterways meandering their way into Fermanagh from the Erne'e source in County Cavan.

Northwest of characterful Enniskillen, the river channels open out into the broad spread of Lower Lough Erne, a magnificent inland sea set off against the spectacular heights of the Cliffs of Magho. Through this broad lake, the River Erne progresses to the sea at Ballyshannon in Donegal by way of a rapid descent at Belleek in Fermanagh.

It's a stunningly beautiful county with much else of interest, including the Marble Arch caves, and the great houses of Castle Coole and Florence Court, the latter with its own forest park nestling under the rising heights of Cuilcagh (667m) – beyond it, the River Shannon emerges to begin its long journey south.

For those who think lakes are for fishing rather than floating over, in western Fermanagh the village of Garrison gives access to Lough Melvin, an angler's heaven which is noted particularly for its unique sub-species of salmon, the gillaroo. You just can't escape from water in this county, and Fermanagh is blessed as much of the rest of the world contemplates water shortages.

Local Attractions and Information

Belleek	Porcelain and Explore Erne Exhibition	028 68 659300
Bellanaleck	Sheelin Lace Museum	028 66 348052
Enniskillen	Ardhowen Lakeside Theatre	028 66 325440
Enniskillen	Castle Coole House & Parkland	028 66 322690
Enniskillen	Enniskillen Castle	028 66 325000
Enniskillen	Florence Court	028 66 348249
Enniskillen	Lakelands Tourism	028 66 346736
Enniskillen	Lough Erne Cruises	028 66 322882
Enniskillen	Tourism Information	028 66 323110
Enniskillen	Waterways Ireland	028 66 323004
Florence Court	House and garden	028 66 348249

Florence Court	Marble Arch Caves	028 66 348855
Garrison	Lough Melvin Activity Holiday Centre	028 68 658142
Kesh	Ardess Craft Centre	028 68 631267
Kesh	Castle Archdale Country Park	028 68 621588
Newtownbutler	Crom Castle	028 67 738174

Belleek
CAFÉ

The Thatch
Belleek Co Fermanagh BT93 3SY
Tel: 028 6865 8181

This coffee shop is really special: a listed building dating back to the late 18th century, it's the only originally thatched building remaining in County Fermanagh. Home-made food has been served here since the early 1900s and the tradition is being well-maintained today, with home-made soups, a range of freshly made sandwiches and toasted sandwiches all made to order, hot specials like stuffed baked potatoes and (best of all) delicious bakes like chocolate squares, carrot cake and muffins. Drinks include a coffee menu and, more unusually, you can also buy fishing tackle, hire a bike - or even a holiday cottage here. Open Mon-Sat. 9-5 (from 10 off-season). Closed Sun. **Directions:** On the main street.

Enniskillen
CHARACTER PUB•RESTAURANT

Blakes of the Hollow
(Café Merlot / Restaurant No 6)
6 Church Street Enniskillen Co Fermanagh BT74 6JE
Tel: 028 6632 0918

One of the great classic pubs of Ireland, Blakes has been in the same family since 1887 and, up to recently, was always one of the few places that could be relied upon to be unchanged. Not a food place, a pub; maybe a sandwich, but mainly somewhere to have a pint and put the world to rights. The original Victorian front bar still remains untouched after 120 years, but relatively recent changes elsewhere in this historic establishment include the addition of the Café Merlot (serving reliable informal, bistro-style food) on the lower ground floor, and The Atrium, a gothic-style bar spread over two floors. And, right up at the top of the house, there is an elegantly-appointed fine dining restaurant, **Number 6**, which brings together the talents of two personalities well known in the hospitality of the area, head chef Gerry Russell and front-of-house manager Johnny Donnelly. As a team, they present ambitious cooking, a relaxed fine dining atmosphere and caring, knowledgeable service with all the little extra that gives guests that pampered feeling all of which adds up to something very special. Wine is Johnny Donnelly's passion, and this is reflected in both an interesting list, and interested guidance and service; Wine & Food evenings are held regularly, and always a sell-out; otherwise Number 6 is open on Friday & Saturday nights when there is enough demand. Otherwise diners are directed to Café Merlot, which is very popular, not least at lunchtime and for their pre-theatre menu (from 5.30 Mon-Sat), which is good value at £14.95 for two course; a Saturday night Blues and Jazz disco is also a great hit. **Café Merlot** (casual dining), L daily 12-3.30; D daily 5-9.30; à la carte, also 2-course early D about £12 (5.30-7.30). No 6: D Fri-Sat 6-10; A la carte; will open any day for parties 12+. Open all year. MasterCard, Visa, Laser, Switch. **Directions:** Town centre. ◇

Enniskillen
RESTAURANT

Dollakis Restaurant
23 Cross Street Enniskillen Co Fermanagh BT74 7DX
Tel: 028 6634 2616
mail@dollakis.com www.dollakis.com

This cheerfully cosmopolitan little restaurant burst onto the Enniskillen dining scene in 2008 and, with an experienced team of various nationalities who all arrived here via Café Merlot, it immediately found a niche. Although quite small, the décor has a pleasantly contemporary airy feel, and a very large window looks out towards Cole's Monument with lots of mature trees. Tightly packed tables are laid bistro-style, music including the odd rendering of Zorba the Greek puts customers in a light mood and menus, simply worded in the continental style, reflect the various national identities involved and offer something new for Enniskillen. As well as an obvious Greek influence in dishes like spanakopita, tzatziki, Greek pitta burger, Greek salad and Dollakis pikilia platter, there are also northern European dishes like gravadlax and wiener schnitzel (and speciality beers, too from Spain, Madeira and Germany, in addition to the wine list). But these people know their market and you'll find plenty of standards too, especially on the evening menu and for Sunday lunch; things such as pan-fried black sole, mixed grill of the day, (though this has a twist, with the meats served on a skewer), traditional aged sirloin steak (or as a roast on Sunday), and soup served with welsh rarebit. Vegetarian tastes are well enough catered for with salads, and mains such as filled courgette, stuffed with rice and Mediterranean vegetables. Skilful service is a special feature (eg filleting whole fish on hot plates in the restaurant, adding a bit of theatre too) and, outside of the main lunch and dinner times, they cater for early callers with freshly squeezed orange juice (proper continental press) and coffees and teas with freshly baked croissants. A blackboard outside also advertises tapas in the afternoon too. With tasty cooking, great service and very good value too, this place is sure to succeed. **Seats 40** (outdoors, 6); children welcome (high chair, childrens menu, baby changing facilities); air conditioning. Open L & D Tue-Sat, 12-4pm & 5.30-10pm; Sun L only 12-4pm; set Sun L £17.95; otherwise à la carte. House wine £12. Closed Mon, 26 Jan- 9 Feb; 1 Sept-14 Sept. MasterCard, Visa, Switch. **Directions:** Town centre, down side of town hall.

Enniskillen
RESTAURANT
R

Franco's Restaurant

Queen Elizabeth Road Enniskillen Co Fermanagh BT74 7DY
Tel: 028 6632 4424

If what you want is buzz and relaxed bustle, this is the place for you - there is no other restaurant in town that can even begin to match the ambience. You get a fair hint of this on arrival, as the exterior facing the Queen Elizabeth Road is always attractively maintained, with a pleasing mix of red brick and glass, and an eye-catching display of plants and creepers - and all expertly lit after dark too. Informal meals, including pizzas, pastas and barbecues, are the order of the day - and it's all done with great style, using quality ingredients. More sophisticated items include seafood, lamb and dry-aged beef. No side vegetables, except potato dishes, alas, but vegetarians have plenty to choose from in every section of the menu. Smart staff, efficient service and fairly reasonable prices keep this place busy, all the time. Popular wine list too (mainly under about £15). **Seats 140** (private room, 60). Toilets wheelchair accessible. Children welcome. Open Mon-Sat, 12-11 (Sun to 10.30 pm); open from 5pm Mon/Tue in Sept/Oct. A la carte. Houses wines from about £10. Closed 25 Dec Amex, MasterCard, Visa, Switch. **Directions:** East side of town, by river (in centre). ◊

Enniskillen
HOTEL

Killyhevlin Hotel

Killyhevlin Enniskillen Co Fermanagh BT74 6RW **Tel: 028 6632 3481**
info@killyhevlin.com www.killyhevlin.com

Just south of Enniskillen, on the A4, this spacious four-star hotel on the banks of the Erne is a popular choice for business guests and would make a comfortable and relaxing base from which to explore this fascinating and unspoilt area. Big windows running right along the back of the main building make the most of a wonderful view of the lake and the mountains beyond, and there are comfortable sofas in the windows where you can have coffee. The view is shared by many of the bedrooms and the Boathouse Grill, where informal meals are available. Recent developments have added 27 new rooms and a state-of-the art health and beauty spa with gymnasium & fitness suite, indoor swimming pool, hot tub, hydro therapy pool, treatment suites, sauna, and steam room. Fishing and river cruising are particular attractions and the hotel gardens reach down to the riverbank and their own pontoon, where visiting cruisers can berth. Golf and horse riding nearby. Lakeshore self-catering chalets also available, with private jetties and full use of hotel facilities. Conference/banqueting facilities (400/300); secretarial services; broadband wi/fi. **Rooms 70** (4 suites, 3 junior suites, 22 ground floor, 2 for disabled, 50 no smoking); children welcome (under 12s free in parents' room; cots available (£10); baby sitting arranged). B&B £75 pps, ss £30;. Wheelchair accessible; pets permitted by arrangement. No SC. Garden, cycling, walking, leisure centre ('pool, jacuzzi, sauna, fitness room); Spa (massage & treatments). Ample parking. Closed 24-25 Dec. Amex, Diners, MasterCard, Visa, Switch. **Directions:** On the A4 just south of Enniskillen.

Enniskillen

HOTEL•RESTAURANT

👑 🏛 👁 Ⓝ Ⓡ

Lough Erne Golf Resort

Belleek Road Enniskillen Co Fermanagh BT93 7ED

Tel: 028 6632 3230

info@loughergolfresort.com www.loughergolfresort.com

With the opening of the Lough Erne Golf Resort, proprietors Jim and Eileen Treacy have achieved a lifetime ambition to create a golf resort of international standards in the stunning setting of County Fermanagh's rolling lakelands. The property, located between two lakes on its own bridge-linked island, offers sweeping panoramic views of the water and the undulating greens of the golf course from every room. When complete, there will be two championship golf courses, the premier course designed by Nick Faldo, and in addition to the hotel's 120 bedrooms and suites, there are 25 luxury lodges. Rooms are generous and very comfortable – replete with every mod con including free WiFi, minibar, tea and coffee station, free-standing bath and rain shower; for added luxury an impressive Thai spa offers eight treatment rooms, a tranquil relaxation room, thermal suite and a beautiful mosaic 14m swimming pool (open to children from 8-10am and 3-5pm). Under the eye of general manager, Jonathan Stapleton, the hotel is notably well run: service is attentive, warm and courteous, and everything is extremely well kept with log fires blazing, brasses gleaming and cutlery polished to a high shine. The Drawing Room and Blaney Bar serve tasty bar food, afternoon tea and refreshments, while the Catalina restaurant (see below) offers fine dining in the evening and Sunday lunch; surprisingly, breakfast is not cooked to order but hot dishes are set up in chafing dishes - and no sign of the renowned Fermanagh black bacon.
Catalina Restaurant: A tone of elegant, understated luxury pervades the restaurant which, like every other room in the hotel, enjoys lovely views. The kitchen is now under the leadership of renowned Irish chef Noel McMeel, who earned his culinary stripes working in some of the world's best restaurants and was Executive Head Chef at nearby Castle Leslie for over seven years before joining Lough Erne Golf Resort. In keeping with McMeel's philosophy, the food is unpretentious with the emphasis on quality ingredients, locally sourced where possible – and, with time, he plans to introduce more local flavours. Meanwhile, a typical menu might tempt you with a pre-starter of chilled crab & lemongrass bisque followed, perhaps, by a sophisticated terrine of guinea fowl and foie gras. Main courses may include char-grilled medallions of beef fillet with celeriac purée and parmesan crisps, or roast fillet of monkfish wrapped in Parma ham with saffron potato purée, and black grape jus. Finish with a deliciously upbeat classic dessert such as an orange and thyme scented crème brûlée, or dark chocolate torte with calvados-soaked prunes. Premium ingredients are cooked with flair and presented with style - which, together with attentive service and a fair wine list, makes for a very enjoyable dining experience. **Directions:** Northside of Enniskillen, a few miles outside town. ◇

Enniskillen

CAFÉ

Ⓝ Ⓡ

Russell & Donnelly

28 Darling Street Enniskillen Co Fermanagh BT74 7EW

Tel: 028 6632 0111

From the Cafe Merlot and Number 6 partnership Gerry Russell and John Donnelly, this new café and deli in the centre of Enniskillen hit the ground running when it opened early in 2008. The food and the concept have clearly found a niche as the town's foodies weren't long in discovering the place, which offers a really good deli counter with lots of goodies equally suitable for home or picnics. There's a great selection of Irish and continental cheeses, dishes like home-made hummus and tapenade, pesto, seafood salad, potato and sweet potato salad with garlic, orzo, couscous, selection of olives, stuffed peppers, cured meats... Home-smoked chicken is a house speciality and a favourite for salads and sandwiches, and an Iberico ham on the bone is given pride of place on the deli counter. Elsewhere, shelves display oils and vinegars, tinned specialities, gourmet biscuits and so on. Drawing on John's expertise, there is a really extensive selection of wines, well displayed on sectioned shelves, and they do a line in foodie gifts and bespoke hampers. Customers opting to eat in sit at barrels with round glass tops and high stools, or at a bench along the big front window facing the street (favoured for people watching). With space at a premium, a small element of discomfort keeps people moving; there's room for seating outside at the back in fine weather too – still to be developed at the time of going to press. Favourite lunch options are soup and sandwich (made to order in freshly made bread – e.g. olive or sundried tomato) or the antipasti platter (small or large) served with Gerry's fresh bread. Although sometimes under pressure, the staff are very pleasant – and, with such good things on offer, people seem prepared to queue if necessary. Open 9 till 9, Mon-Sat; Sun open 1-6 for coffee (though no food served to eat in) and deli stock to take away. **Directions:** On Darling Street. ◇

Enniskillen
RESTAURANT•WINE BAR
R

Scoffs Restaurant & Uno Wine Bar
17 Belmore Street Enniskillen Co Fermanagh BT74 6AA
Tel: 028 6634 2622
info@scoffsuno.com www.scoffsuno.com

Just a few minutes walk from the town centre, proprietor-chef Gavin Murphy's popular two-storey bistro-style restaurant and wine bar has now been pleasing a wide range of customers for eight years. Early evening opening and Gavin's wide-ranging menus - offering everything from inexpensive pastas to more serious (but still moderately priced) 'dinner' dishes such as pan-fried Blacklion duck breast - partly explain the wide appeal, but consistent cooking, friendly, attentive staff and an atmosphere of relaxed informality are equally attractive. Although menus may include some choices from afar, such as kangaroo, local produce features and there are some interesting vegetarian options and plenty of seafood, usually on the daily specials. Modern classics like fillet steak with dauphinoise potato, grilled plum tomato & béarnaise sauce are well cooked and stylishly presented, and the only down-side is that side dishes charged extra can add significantly to the cost of a meal. **Seats 147** (private room, 57); reservations accepted; toilets wheelchair accessible; children welcome. D only daily, 5-'late'. D à la carte. House wine about £12. Closed 24-26 Dec. Diners, MasterCard, Visa, Laser. **Directions:** Access from main shopping centre. ◊

ENNISKILLEN AREA

Beautifully situated between two channels of the river joining Upper and Lower Lough Erne, Enniskillen has developed as a holiday centre in recent years, and is especially popular with fisherfolk and anyone with an interest in life on the river. Enniskillen is also famously associated with Oscar Wilde, who attended Portora Royal School, and the town has celebrated this cultural connection ever since - **Picasso's** (028 6632 2226), however, opts to develop a different artistic theme. In Belcoo village, between Enniskillen and Blacklion, the nine-room **Customs House Country Inn** (028 6638 6285; www.customshouseinn.com) offers moderately priced accommodation and popular cooking. An exciting new golf course designed by Nick Faldo is due to open fully in summer 2009 at the Lough Erne Golf Resort (028 6632 3230, see story) and the Castle Hume (028 6632 7077) course is right next door. While in Enniskillen, a visit to the gardens and house of the National Trust properties Florence Court (028 6634 8249) & Castle Coole (028 6632 2690) and the Marble Arch Caves (028 66348855) are highly recommended.
WWW-IRELAND-GUIDE.COM FOR ALL THE BEST PLACES TO EAT, DRINK & STAY

Enniskillen Area
FARMHOUSE

Arch House
Tullyhona Florencecourt Enniskillen Co Fermanagh BT92 1DE
Tel: 028 6634 8452
info@archhouse.com www.archhouse.com

Located near Marble Arch Caves and Florence Court House, Rosemary Armstrong's friendly farm guesthouse has six pretty en-suite bedrooms and a big comfortably furnished sitting room with lots of room for guests to relax. Good food is important at Arch House - a varied breakfast is served in the large dining room, and quite an extensive à la carte evening menu is offered too (also available to non-residents by arrangement). And, not only does Rosemary do meals for guests, but she also has scone and bread making demonstrations in her kitchen - and home produce is on sale in their own shop as well. A good place for a family stay as children are very welcome, and there's a children's menu and high chair available. **Rooms 6** (3 family rooms, 2 twin, 1 double, all en-suite), children welcome (play ground, toys & games, baby listening); B&B about £25 pps, £10ss. Broadband wi/fi. Farm shop, walking, table tennis; fishing (fly & coarse), golf, tennis, equestrian, boating and Marble Arch Caves nearby. Open all year. MasterCard, Visa, Switch. **Directions:** From Enniskillen follow the A4 (Sligo Road) for 4km (2.5 m) on to A32 (Swanlinbar road). Follow signs for the Marble Arch Caves. Turn right at posting for National Trust Property at Florence Court, 2 miles (3km) further on. ◊

The Sheelin Tea Shop

Enniskillen Area
CAFÉ
178b Derrylin Road Bellanaleck Enniskillen Co Fermanagh BT92 2BA
👁 Ⓝ
Tel: 028 6634 8232

Bedecked with window boxes and hanging baskets, this picturesque thatched house in the village centre houses the Sheelin Lace Shop and Museum, the latter displaying probably the most comprehensive collection of Irish lace anywhere in Ireland or beyond. Visitors seeking refreshment will now be pleased to find the adjoining teashop, prettily refurbished and reopened in 2008 after a closure. Run by Julie Snoddy, who has built up a reputation for her superb baking since coming to Fermanagh, the tea shop is now a light and airy space with some outside tables in an attractive paved area, complete with fountain. Julie's speciality scones (e.g.blueberry and white chocolate, apple and cinnamon) are popular with morning coffee, and there is always an array of baked goodies on display - honeymoon bites, paradise squares, yum yums, mile-high lemon meringue pie, peach & raspberry frangipane tart, chocolate gateaux; and how nice to see an old-fashioned Victoria sandwich cake, filled with jam and butter cream. **Seats 36** (outdoors, 12); children welcome (high chair, childrens menu, baby changing facilities); toilets wheelchair accessible. Open daily 10am-5.30pm (to 6pm Sun). Closed 10 days at Christmas. MasterCard, Visa, Switch. **Directions:** Centre of village, opposite petrol station.

Lough Erne Hotel

Kesh
HOTEL
Main Street Kesh Co Fermanagh BT93 1TF **Tel: 028 6863 1275**
info@loughernehotel.eu www.loughernehotel.eu

In a very attractive location on the banks of the Glendurragh River, this pleasantly old-fashioned and friendly hotel in the centre of the little town has comfortable accommodation in rooms that are not large but have everything you need including en-suite bath/shower rooms, TV and tea/coffee facilities. The hotel is understandably popular for weddings, as the bar and function rooms overlook the river and have access to a paved riverside walkway and garden. Wholesome fare is available in the bar for most of the day and helpful staff, good value and a soothing view make this a relaxing place to break a journey. Popular for fishing holidays, it would also make a good base for a family break; there is plenty to do in this lovely, unspoilt area, including golf, watersports and horse-riding. Conference/banqueting(200/180). **Rooms 12** (all en-suite). B&B £35pps, ss £10; sc discretionary; children welcome; pets permitted in some areas; limited wheelchair access. Bar L Mon-Sat, 12.30-2; Grill Menu daily 2.30-8 (Sun 5-8). Restaurant D only except L Sun. Light snacks available all day. Fishing, cycling, garden. Off-season breaks and self-catering accommodation in one and two bedroom cottages (from about £250 pw) also on offer. Own parking. Closed 25 Dec. Amex, Diners, MasterCard, Visa, Switch. **Directions:** From Dublin N3 to Belturbet, A509 to Enniskillen, A35 to Kesh. ◈

Lusty Beg Island

Kesh
B&B•RESTAURANT•PUB
Boa Island Kesh Co Fermanagh BT93 8AD
Tel: 028 6863 3300
info@lustybegisland.com www.lustybegisland.com

You can call in by boat, of course, and if you arrive by road, a little ferry takes you over to the island. It's an unusual place and worth a visit, if only to call into the pleasant waterside pub for a drink, a cup of tea or an informal bite. However, you could stay much longer as accommodation is available in lodges, chalets and a motel, all spread relatively inconspicuously around the wooded island. Conferences, corporate entertaining and management training are specialities, and all sorts of activity breaks are offered. Visiting boats are welcome; phone ahead for details of barbecues and other theme nights; music Saturday nights. Bar food available daily in summer, may be weekends only off season (phone ahead for details). Conference/banqueting (300/200). **Rooms 40** (all shower only, 23 family rooms, 10 ground floor, 2 for disabled, all no smoking); children welcome (under 5s free in parents' room; cot available £5). B&B £45 pps; ss £20. Bar food available daily in summer, may be weekends only off-season (phone ahead for details). Leisure centre: swimming pool, sauna, tennis, pool table. Football pitch, canoes, bike hire, archery, clay pigeon shooting, equestrian & fly fishing nearby. Closed Christmas week. MasterCard, Visa, Switch. **Directions:** Located off the main Kesh - Belleek Road A47. ◈

Killadeas
HOTEL•RESTAURANT

Manor House Resort Hotel

Killadeas Co Fermanagh BT94 1NY **Tel: 028 6862 2211**
info@manor-house-hotel.com www.manor-house-hotel.com

This impressive lakeside period house makes a fine hotel, and the scale of the Victorian architecture and the style of furnishings and decor lean very much towards the luxurious in both public areas and accommodation. Recent changes have included extensive refurbishments, most noticeably in the foyer and adjacent areas, and the addition of an impressive new conference and banqueting area with its own separate entrance, which has been discreetly added to the side and rear of the original building and, despite its large size and more contemporary approach, in no way detracts from the appeal of the old house. Spacious bedrooms range from interconnecting family rooms to deluxe doubles and romantic suites with canopied four-poster beds, and front rooms have stunning views. The hotel's air conditioned cruiser, Lady of the Lake, offers catering and bar facilities for up to 56 for tours, corporate events, conferences and parties. Conference/banqueting. Leisure centre, indoor swimming pool; beauty salon. Children under 3 free in parents' room. No pets. **Rooms 81** (all en-suite, 6 suites) B&B £65pps, single £105. Special breaks offered. **The Belleek Restaurant:** Newly refurbished in 2008, the restaurant is beautifully appointed and well positioned to make the most of the lovely view. Quite classical dinner menus are offered and, while not aiming to be cutting edge, cooking is accomplished and presentation well-judged (simple but attractive). Service from a well-trained team is exemplary and, like the food, in tune with the grand surroundings, making this a good choice for a special evening out. **Seats 65** (private room 30). Air Conditioning. L&D daily 12.30-2.45 and 6.30-9.30. Bar meals available 12.30-9 pm daily. [*Information on the nearby Inishclare restaurant, bar & marina complex is available from the hotel, which is in common ownership.] Open all year. Amex, MasterCard, Visa. **Directions:** 6 miles from Enniskillen on the B82. ◊

Lisbellaw
COUNTRY HOUSE•CASTLE

Belle Isle Castle

Belle Isle Estate Lisbellaw Co Fermanagh BT94 5HG
Tel: 028 6638 7231
accommodation@belleisle-estate.com www.belleislecastle.com

Belle Isle is owned by the Duke of Abercorn, and magically situated on one of eleven islands on Upper Lough Erne that are owned by the Estate; the original castle dates back to 1680 and has mid-19th century additions, including a courtyard and coach house which have been converted to make appealing self-catering accommodation. The castle itself has a delightfully exclusive away-from-it-all country house atmosphere and is impressively furnished with antiques, striking paintings and dramatic colour schemes (the work of the internationally-renowned interior designer, David Hicks); in addition to the eight romantic bedrooms, which all have their special character, guests have use of a magnificent drawing room and also the Grand Hall, complete with minstrels' gallery, where dinner is served. Under the eagle-eyed supervision of hosts Charles and Fiona Plunket, maintenance and housekeeping are immaculate throughout - and full central heating has recently been installed in the dining room and the four bedrooms above it. This romantic place could be the perfect choice for a small wedding: they are licensed to hold civil weddings and the courtyard accommodation is available to guests. There are many wonderful things to do in this idyllically beautiful area - fishing is an obvious first choice but there are also golf courses nearby, field sports can be arranged and there are historic houses and gardens to visit. But, most tempting of all, perhaps, might be a course at the very successful Belle Isle School of Cookery, which is operated with impressive professionalism and offers an extensive range of courses of varying lengths throughout the year. [Cookery School: Tel 028 6638 7231; www.irishcookeryschool.com] Small weddings (30). **Rooms 8** (1 en-suite, 7 with private bathrooms, 1 shower only, all no smoking). B&B £70 pps, ss £15; children welcome (under 5s free in parents' room, cot available without charge; playground). Pets allowed in some areas. No SC. Residents D daily, 8pm, £28/30; wines from £10.45. Garden, walking, fishing, tennis. *Self-catering also offered in 10 apartments & 3 cottages, with 1-3 bedrooms; larger groups may use both castle & apartments. Open all year. Amex, Diners, MasterCard, Visa, Laser, Switch. **Directions:** From Belfast, take A4 to Lisbellaw - follow signs to Carrybridge.

COUNTY LONDONDERRY

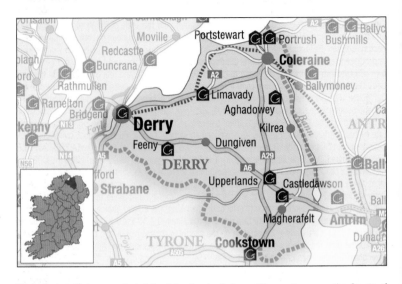

When its boundaries were first defined for "modern" times, this was known as the County of Coleraine, named for the busy little port on the River Bann a few miles inland from the Atlantic coast. It was an area long favoured by settlers, for Mountsandel - on the salmon-rich Bann a mile south of Coleraine - is where the 9,000-year old traces of the site of some of the oldest-known houses in Ireland have been found.

Today, Coleraine is the main campus of the University of Ulster, with the vitality of student life spreading to the nearby coastal resorts of Portstewart and Portrush in the area known as the "Golden Triangle", appropriately fringed to the north by the two golden miles of Portstewart Strand. South-westward from Coleraine, the county - which was re-named after the City of Derry became Londonderry in 1613 - offers a fascinating variety of places and scenery, with large areas of fine farmland being punctuated by ranges of hills, while the rising slopes of the Sperrin Mountains dominate the County's southern boundary.

The road from Belfast to Derry sweeps through the Sperrins by way of the stirringly-named Glenshane Pass, and from its heights you begin to get the first glimpses westward of the mountains of Donegal. This is an appropriate hint of the new atmosphere in the City of Derry itself. This lively place could reasonably claim to be the most senior of all Ireland's contemporary cities, as it can trace its origins directly back to a monastery of St Colmcille, otherwise Columba, founded in 546AD. Today, the historic city, its ancient walls matched by up-dated port facilities on the River Foyle and a cheerfully restored urban heart, is moving into a vibrant future in which it thrives on the energy drawn from its natural position as the focal point of a larger catchment area which takes in much of Donegal County to the west in addition to County Londonderry to the east.

The area eastward of Lough Foyle is increasingly popular among discerning visitors, the Roe Valley through Dungiven and Limavady being particularly attractive. The re-establishment of the ferry between Magilligan Point and Greencastle in Donegal across the narrow entrance to Lough Foyle has added a new dimension to the region's infrastructure, as does the up-grading of the increasingly busy City of Derry Airport at Eglinton.

COUNTY LONDONDERRY

Local Attractions and Information

Bellaghy	Bellaghy Bawn (Seamus Heaney centre)	028 79 386812
Castlerock	Hezlett House	028 70 848567
City of Derry	Airport	028 71 810784
Coleraine	Guy L Wilson Daffodil Garden	028 70 344141
Coleraine	Tourism Information	028 70 344723
Derry City	The Fifth Province - Celtic culture	028 71 373177
Derry City	Foyle Cruises (year round)	028 71 362857
Derry City	Foyle Valley Railway Centre	028 71 265234
Derry City	The Guildhall	028 71 377335
Derry City	Harbour Museum	028 71 377331
Derry City	Millennium Forum Theatre	028 71 264426
Derry City	Orchard Gallery	028 71 269675
Derry City	The Playhouse	028 71 268027
Derry City	St Columb's Cathedral	028 71 267313
Derry City	Tourism Information	028 71 267284
Derry City	Tower Museum	028 71 372411
Downhill	Mussenden Temple & Gardens	028 70 848728
Draperstown	Plantation of Ulster Visitor Centre	028 79 627800
Garvagh	Museum & Heritage Centre	028 29 558216
Limavady	Roe Valley & Ness Wood Country Parks	028 77 722074
Limavady	Tourism Information	028 77 760307
Magherafelt	Tourism Information	028 79 631510
Magilligan	Lough Foyle Ferry (to Donegal) (ROI t.n.)	077 81901
Moneymore	Springhill (NT house)	028 86 748210
Sperrin Mountains	Sperrins Tourism	028 79 634570

Aghadowey
HOTEL•RESTAURANT

The Brown Trout Golf & Country Inn
209 Agivey Road Aghadowey Co Londonderry BT51 4AD
Tel: 028 7086 8209
jane@browntroutinn.com www.browntroutinn.com

Golf is one of the major attractions at this lively family-run country inn, both on-site and in the locality, but it's a pleasant and hospitable place for anyone to stay. Golfers and non-golfers alike will soon find friends in the convivial bar, where food is served from noon to 10 pm every day - and outside in a pleasant barbecue area too, in fine weather. Accommodation is not especially luxurious, but very comfortable, in good-sized en-suite rooms which are all on the ground floor, arranged around the main courtyard, and have plenty of space for golfing gear. Newer cottage suites overlooking the golf course (just 100 yards from the main building) were the first of this standard to be completed in Northern Ireland. As well as bar food, there's an evening restaurant up a steep staircase (with chair lift for the less able), overlooking the garden end of the golf course. A dedicated kitchen team produces good home cooking with local fresh ingredients for daytime food (soups, freshly-made sandwiches and open sandwiches, baked potatoes, pasta) and evening meals like hot garlic Aghadowey mushrooms or ribeye steak with a Bushmills whiskey sauce. Small conference/private parties (50); free broadband wi/fi. **Rooms 15** (all en-suite; 1 for disabled & most wheelchair friendly); children welcome (under 4s free in parents' room; cots available without charge, baby sitting arranged). Stair lift; toilets wheelchair accessible. No smoking house. Pets permitted. B&B £50 pps, ss £20. Bar meals, 12-9.30 daily (to 10 in summer). Traditional music in bar (Sat, 9.30pm). Restaurant D only, 5-9.30. A la carte; house wine £11.95; sc discretionary. Garden, walking, tennis, horse-riding, golf (9), fishing. Gym. Open all year. Amex, Diners, MasterCard, Visa, Switch. **Directions:** Intersection of A54/B66, 7 miles (11km) south of Coleraine.

Aghadowey
FARMHOUSE

Greenhill House

24 Greenhill Road Aghadowey Coleraine Co Londonderry BT51 4EU
Tel: 028 7086 8241
greenhill.house@btinternet.com www.greenhill-house.co.uk

Framed by trees with lovely country views, the Hegarty family's fine Georgian farmhouse is at the centre of a large working farm. In true Northern tradition, Elizabeth Hegarty is a great baker and greets guests in the drawing room with an afternoon tea which includes a vast array of home-made teabreads, cakes and biscuits - and home baking is also a highlight of wonderful breakfasts that are based on tasty local produce like bacon, sausages, mushrooms, free-range eggs, smoked salmon, strawberries and preserves. There are two large family rooms and, although not luxurious, the thoughtfulness that has gone into furnishing bedrooms makes them exceptionally comfortable; everything is in just the right place to be convenient - and Elizabeth is constantly maintaining and improving the decor and facilities. Bedrooms have direct dial telephones, and little touches - like fresh flowers, a fruit basket, After Eights, tea & coffee-making facilities, hair dryer, bathrobe, good quality clothes hangers and even a torch - are way above the standard expected of farmhouse accommodation. There's also broadband internet access, a safe, fax machine, iron and trouser press available for guests' use on request. Guests have been welcomed to Greenhill House since 1980 and, wonderfully comforting and hospitable as it is, Elizabeth constantly seeks ways of improvement, big and small: this lovely house and the way it is run demonstrate rural Irish hospitality at its best. [Greenhill House was our Farmhouse of the Year in 2003.] **Rooms 6** (all en-suite, 2 shower only, 2 bath only, 2 family rooms, all no smoking); free broadband wi/fi. B&B £30 pps, ss £10; children welcome (under 2s free in parents' room, cot available). No pets. Garden. Fishing (coarse) & golf nearby. Closed Nov-Feb. Amex, MasterCard, Visa, Switch. **Directions:** On B66 Greenhill Road off A29, 7 miles (10.5km) south of Coleraine, 3 miles (5km) north of Garvagh.

Castledawson
CAFÉ

Ditty's

44 Main Street Castledawson Co Londonderry BT45 8AB
Tel: 028 7946 8243

Renowned throughout the Ireland for their excellent home baking, this great craft bakery has received widespread recognition through the years (including a Good Food Award from the Irish Food Writers' Guild) for the quality of their products. Their bakeries in both Castledawson and Magherafelt are great places for a journey break and you can pick up a few loaves of their speciality breads and other treats to take home, or to your self-catering accommodation. The in-store café serves a range of baked treats to have with a cup of tea or coffee - and several hot dishes are offered every day. Ditty's baked products, most famously the delicious oatcakes that are so good with cheese (now sold at Waitrose stores throughout England), are also widely available in good food stores, and appear on many restaurant menus. Also at: 33 Rainey Street, Magherfelt (028 7963 4644). Food served Mon-Sat, 6.30am-5.30pm. Closed Sun. **Directions:** On the Main Street.

Castledawson
RESTAURANT•GUESTHOUSE

The Inn at Castledawson

47 Main Street Castledawson Co Londonderry BT45 8AA
Tel: 028 7946 9777
info@theinnatcastledawson.co.uk www.theinnatcastledawson.co.uk

Built around the 200-year old Castledawson House, Simon Toye and Kathy Tully's latter day inn is a delightful place - and, thanks to Simon's excellent cooking and their 'nothing is too much trouble' policy, a visit here is sure to be memorable and relaxed. The Inn is most attractive, with a modern bar where smart informal dining is offered at neat round darkwood tables with cream leather armchairs and banquettes and, beyond it, a lovely tiered light-filled restaurant with a huge arched window looking over the garden to the River Moyola and has doors leading out to a decked balcony. The deceptively simple restaurant menu offers seven or eight choices on each course and Simon's philosophy to use only locally sourced organic produce certainly pays off, as food is beautifully cooked and simply presented; the slow-cooked crispy pork belly with cauliflower puree & cider soaked raisins, for example, oozes with flavour and is a favourite with the many returning guests. Desserts lean towards the traditional, typically a nice baked cheesecake with toasted pecans and maple syrup. A light bite menu, which always features a roast of the day, is available in the bar during lunch service. This restaurant delivers what it promises – good fresh food at reasonable prices served by friendly efficient staff. And it is a true inn, offering food, drink and a (very relaxing) place to lay your head: there are twelve chic contemporary bedrooms with river or courtyard views, including a suite with its own riverside balcony. With a spa next door, and golf, equestrian and fishing all nearby, this is a very appealing place for a short break. Small conferences/banqueting (90/80); secretarial services, video conferencing. **Rooms 12** (6 shower only, 6 ground floor, all no smoking, 2 disabled); children welcome (under 5s free in parents' room, cot available free of charge); wheelchair accessible. B&B £39.50pps, ss about £10. **Restaurant Seats 80** (+20 outside). L & D daily 12-2.30 & 5-9.30pm. House wine about £11.95. Establishment closed 12 Jul. MasterCard, Visa, Switch. **Directions:** On main street of Castledawson, on the main Belfast-Derry road (M2-M22-A6). ◇

Coleraine
RESTAURANT

Water Margin

The Boat House Hanover Place Coleraine Co Londonderry BT52 1EB
Tel: 028 7034 2222

An impressive first-floor restaurant above the Boat Club, this magnificently located Chinese restaurant predated its famous Belfast sister (the largest Chinese restaurant in Ireland) by many a year and, with its fine river views, plush bar and a rather luxuriously-appointed dining room to enhance cooking which has enjoyed a great reputation in the area over a long period, it has all the ingredients for a special meal out. Extensive menus offer all the familiar set 'banquets' and western favourites like aromatic duck, sesame toast, sweet & sours and sizzling dishes, but the more adventurous diner will find that there are many unusual dishes available too - and made all the more enjoyable by good service, provided by helpful, smartly-dressed staff. L & D daily 12.30-2.30pm & 5-11pm. MasterCard, Visa, Switch. **Directions:** Above the boat club in Coleraine. ◇

LIMAVADY

An attractive Georgian town in the leafy Roe Valley, a few miles east of Derry city, the main focus of interest for visitors is the beautiful Roe Valley Country Park. Also of interest to visitors will be the smart new bistro on Catherine Street, **50 Restaurant and Wine Bar** (028 7776 6250) which is open through the day from about 11 onwards, and for lunch and dinner.
WWW.IRELAND-GUIDE.COM FOR ALL THE BEST PLACES TO EAT, DRINK & STAY

Lime Tree Restaurant

Limavady
RESTAURANT

60 Catherine Street Limavady Co Londonderry BT49 9DB
Tel: 028 7776 4300
info@limetreerest.com www.limetreerest.com

Loyal customers come from far and wide for the pleasure of dining at Stanley and Maria Matthews' restaurant on the handsome, wide main street of this attractive town. And no wonder, as Stanley is a fine chef and Maria a welcoming and solicitous hostess. Ingredients are carefully sourced, many of them local; menus are generous, with a classical base that Stanley works on to give popular dishes a new twist. Specialities include their own home-made wheaten bread, which is the perfect accompaniment for a chowder of Atlantic fish & local potatoes, while main course favourites include Sperrin lamb (with classic onion white sauce) fillet or sirloin steak (from the award-winning local butcher, Hunters) and seafood thermidor (Stanley's selection of fresh fish with a mild cheese & brandy sauce). Menus are not over-extensive, but change frequently to suit different occasions - there's an attractive early dinner menu which is exceptional value, followed by a dressier (and more adventurous) à la carte for the main evening menu; "Our version of Osso Bucco", a dish of slow-cooked shin of Sperrin lamb cooked on the bone with wine and fresh herbs, is now a big hit with diners and modestly priced at £15.50. Stanley's cooking is refreshingly down-to-earth - new dishes are often introduced, but if it's on the menu it's because it works: there are no gimmicks. Good cooking and good value go hand-in-hand with warm hospitality here, and it is always a pleasure to visit The Lime Tree - indeed, many discerning guests enjoy it so much that they plan journeys around a meal here. A concise, interesting wine list also offers predictably good value. **Seats 30**; children welcome (high chair, childrens menu); toilets wheelchair accessible. D Tue-Sat, 6-9 (Sat to 9.30). Early D £15.95 (6-7pm, Tue-Fri); also à la carte; house wine £13.50; sc discretionary. Closed Sun & Mon, 25/6 Dec, 1 week around 12 July. Amex, MasterCard, Visa, Switch Directions: On the outskirts of town, main Derry-Limavady road.

Radisson SAS Roe Park Resort

Limavady
HOTEL

Roe Park Limavady Co Londonderry BT47 2AH **Tel: 028 7772 2222**
reservations@radissonroepark.com www.radissonroepark.com

Built on rising ground in lovely rolling countryside, this imposing hotel dates back to the eighteenth century when a Captain Richard Babington built the original house from which today's extensive hotel has grown. There is a pleasant air of relaxed luxury - the tone is set in an impressive foyer, with columns and a curved gallery overlooking a seating area smartly set up with comfortable sofas and armchairs. Conferences play a major part in present-day business - and the surrounding greensward provides relaxation for delegates, along with many others who come here specifically to enjoy the excellent leisure facilities. Spacious bedrooms are designed in the modern classic mode, with double and single beds and all the features expected of this type of hotel (all have desk areas, some with computers) and well-finished bathrooms - and all look out over the golf course or a courtyard garden. Dining options allow for different moods: formal dining in Greens Restaurant (dinner daily and lunch on Sunday) or a more relaxed style in The Coach House Brasserie; healthy options and dishes suitable for vegetarians or coeliacs are highlighted on menus. Conferences/banqueting (450/275). **Rooms 118** (7 suites, 3 junior suites, 108 executive, 15 family, 2 disabled); children welcome (under 5 free in parents' room; cot available, baby sitting arranged, playroom). No pets. Lift. 24 hr room service. B&B £55-70 pps, ss £25. Greens Restaurant: Seats 150; air conditioning; children welcome; D Tue-Sat, 6.30-9.30; L Sun only, 12-2.30. Closed for D Sun & Mon. Leisure centre (indoor swimming pool, spa). Golf (18 hole), fishing, garden, walking, cycling. *Wide range of special breaks offered. Open all year. Amex, Diners, MasterCard, Visa, Laser, Switch. **Directions:** On the A2 L'Derry-Limavady road, 1 mile from Limavady (Derry City 16 miles).

LONDONDERRY / DERRY CITY

The City of Londonderry, also known as Derry, is the economic centre for the northwest of Ireland and a vibrant modern city with a fascinating history and rich cultural life. It is a very hospitable place and, for a city of its size, it has an exceptionally wide range of hotels, cafés, restaurants and pubs to suit every taste, budget and occasion. In addition to the recommendations below, other establishments which are useful to know about include the popular **Ramada Da Vinci's Hotel** (see entry), about a mile from the city centre on the Culmore Road; it has private car parking and a pleasant riverside walkway into the city from the hotel. If you are attending an event at The Millennium Forum (Theatre and Conference Centre), you will be very glad to find the Derry Theatre Trust's stylish **Encore Brasserie** (028 7137 2492; www.encorebrasserie.com), which offers interesting, fairly-priced food and a well-chosen wine list and is open for lunch and dinner; its location between the city's two main shopping centres widens the appeal, especially as children are very well catered for. Lovers of Italian food will find authentic Italian cooking at **La Sosta Ristorante** (028 7137 4817; www.lasostarestaurant.com) which is one of Derry's most popular restaurants: just a few minutes walk from the city centre, you go through an archway off Carlisle Road to find this little bit of the Mediterranean which offers an excellent choice of all the usual pasta dishes, fresh salads and good meat dishes with sauces made from authentic Italian recipes; modestly-priced dinners in a friendly, relaxed atmosphere. With the rejuvenation of the Strand Road area attracting new restaurants, it is quickly becoming a Mecca for diners; a very stylish newcomer with outside seating and a very modern restaurant and bar interior is **Timber Quay Restaurant and Wine Bar** (028 71 370020; www.timberquay.com) on the edge of the River Foyle, offering light international lunch choices, with a mixture of traditional more exotic dishes in the evening. The city offers great shopping, including a craft village in the city centre, and local attractions include the award-winning Tower Museum (028 7137 2411, open all year), which gives visitors an insight into the city's history, the Foyle Valley Railway Centre (028 7126 5234), the Harbour Museum (028 71 377331), and St Columb's Cathedral (028 7126 7313). Local activities include an 18 hole championship golf course at the City of Derry Golf Club (028 7143 6369), and anglers will enjoy the Foyle river system famous for its salmon or a trip to the Oaks Trout Fishery (028 8224 4932), a 15-acre spring fed lake with a healthy stock of rainbow trout. The nearby Ness Wood Country Park is a beautiful spot for walking, offering 50 hectares of mixed woodland and includes a spectacular waterfall.

WWW.IRELAND-GUIDE.COM FOR ALL THE BEST PLACES TO EAT, DRINK & STAY

Londonderry
HOTEL•RESTAURANT

Beech Hill Country House Hotel

32 Ardmore Road Londonderry Co Londonderry BT47 3QP
Tel: 028 7134 9279
info@beech-hill.com www.beech-hill.com

Beech Hill is just a couple of miles south of Londonderry, beautifully set in 42 acres of peaceful woodland, waterfalls and gardens. Built in 1729, the house has retained many of its original details and proprietor Patsy O'Kane makes an hospitable and caring hostess. Comfortable bedrooms vary in size and outlook - many overlook the gardens, but all are thoughtfully and attractively furnished with Mrs O'Kane's ever-growing collection of antiques. Public rooms include a good-sized bar, a fine restaurant (in what was originally the snooker room, now extended into a conservatory overlooking the gardens) and, unusually, a private chapel, now used for meetings, private parties or small weddings. All the main public areas have recently been refurbished, but changes are always undertaken sensitively, in keeping with the building. American visitors, especially, will be interested to know that US Marines had their headquarters here in World War II and an informative small museum of the US Marine Friendship Association is housed within the hotel. Facilities include picnic areas in the grounds for fine weather and a fitness suite with sauna, steam room, jacuzzi and weight room.*Beech Hill is understandably popular for weddings; private guests are advised to check if there is a wedding expected during their stay, as it may affect dining arrangements and the atmosphere in the hotel. Conference/banqueting (300); business centre, broadband wi/fi, secretarial services. Beauty salon, massage & treatments, walking, tennis, garden. Golf, fishing & equestrian nearby. Children welcome (under 3s free in parents' room cot available without charge, babysitting arranged). Pets allowed by arrangement. **Rooms 27** (2 suites, 3 junior suites, 10 executive rooms, 10 shower only, 1 for disabled, all no smoking). Lift. B&B £67.50pps, ss £22.50; SC discretionary. Closed 24/25 Dec. **Ardmore Restaurant:** The restaurant is a particularly attractive feature of this charming hotel; it is elegantly appointed and well-positioned overlooking gardens (which is a particularly pleasant outlook at breakfast time). Menus are a hymn to quality ingredients, citing use of local seafood, dry-aged local meats, free-range pork and Thornhill duck, award-winning cheeses; similarly, the ingredients of the dishes themselves are described in detail, all of which is interesting and confidence-inspiring. At the time of going to press, a new head chef is due to be appointed, but the house style is modern classic, with a strong Irish twist, and a separate vegetarian menu is offered, and also an early dinner menu, which is very good value. An informative, well chosen wine list includes tasting notes and a good choice of wines by the glass. **Seats 100**. Reservations accepted; children welcome; toilets wheelchair accessible. L daily, 12-2; D daily 6.30-9. Set L about £20, Set Sun L about £20. Set 2/3 course D about £25/30. A la carte and vegetarian menu also available. House wines from £14.95. SC discretionary. Amex, MasterCard, Visa, Switch. **Directions:** Main Londonderry road A6.

Londonderry
RESTAURANT

Browns Restaurant, Bar & Brasserie
1-2 Bonds Hill Londonderry Co Londonderry BT47 6DW
Tel: 028 7134 5180
eat@brownsrestaurant.com www.brownsrestaurant.com

The city's leading contemporary restaurant has a devoted local following. Always immaculate, inside and out, it's a relaxed space with subtle blends of natural colours, textures and finishes - proprietor-chef Ivan Taylor's cool cooking keeps them coming back for more; his approach to food never stands still, and the cooking is consistently creative. Wide-ranging menus offer a range of fresh-flavoured dishes, including delicious starters like spiced crumbled beef served in a light vegetable broth with pecorino, and a perfectly judged main dish of char-grilled rare-breed sirloin steak on a fine balsamic onion gravy with a horesradish Yorkshire pudding & pea purée and braised root vegetables - one of several examples of classics that have been modernised without forgetting the basics. Desserts also ring some changes with the classics - or espresso, vin santo & home-made biscotti might make a pleasing alternative. All round, there's imagination, a certain amount of style, dedication and consistency - not bad after more than 20 years in business. *Browns2Go service offered, for boardroom lunches and corporate entertaining. L Tue-Fri, 12-2; D Tue-Sat, 5.30-Late. Early 2/3 course D Tue-Fri, £11.50/14.50 (5.30-6.45). House wine about £15. Closed Sun & Mon, 1st 2 weeks Aug. Amex, MasterCard, Visa, Laser, Switch. **Directions:** In a cul-de-sac opposite the old Waterside railway station: Belfast-Derry road (A6), turn left at Melrose Terrace & branch right at sign. (Or park at station and walk across). ◇

Londonderry
HOTEL

City Hotel
Queens Quay Londonderry Co Londonderry BT48 7AS **Tel: 028 7136 5800**
res@derry-gsh.com www.gshotels.com

Centrally located on a quayside site overlooking the River Foyle, this modern hotel is bright and contemporary, and would make an equally attractive base for a leisure visit or for business - executive rooms have a workstation with modem/PC connections, voice mail, interactive TV systems and mini-bar and there's a business centre providing secretarial services for guests. Well-located close to the old city, business districts and main shopping areas, it also has free private parking for guests and on-site leisure facilities. Conference/banqueting (450/350). **Rooms 145** (1 suite, 4 junior suites); children welcome (under 2s free in parents' room, cot available without charge). Lift. 24-hour room service. B&B about £50pps. Room rate about £100 (max 3 guests). Leisure centre: swimming pool, Jacuzzi, steam room, sauna, dance suite, gym, hydrotherapy). Amex, Diners, MasterCard, Visa, Laser. **Directions:** In Derry city centre, overlooking River Foyle. ◇

Londonderry
RESTAURANT

Exchange Restaurant & Wine Bar
Queens Quay Londonderry Co Londonderry BT48 7AY
Tel: 028 7127 3990

Just outside the walled city, the contemporary design of this popular bar and restaurant makes a great contrast to the age of nearby landmarks. Although seriously modern, this is a friendly and welcoming place that appeals to all age groups and their colourful, fresh-flavoured food suits the mood perfectly.

They seem to have a winning formula here as prices are reasonable, ingredients are sourced locally as far as possible and the cooking hits the mark. At first glance, the menu seems very international but close examination reveals plenty to please traditionalists too and blackboard specials reflect the same desire to please a wide range of customers. Service is helpful and speedy. **Seats 120**; toilets wheelchair accessible; children welcome; air conditioning. L Mon-Sat, 12-2.30; D daily 5-10 (Sun 4-9pm). A la carte. House wine about £12. SC discretionary. Closed L Sun, 25 Dec. Amex, MasterCard, Visa, Laser, Switch. **Directions:** Opposite City Hotel. ◊

Londonderry   # Fitzroys Restaurant
RESTAURANT•WINE BAR   2-4 Bridge Street 3 Carlisle Road Londonderry
                                    Co Londonderry BT48 6JZ **Tel: 028 7126 6211**
                          info@fitzroysrestaurant.com www.fitzroysrestaurant.com

This large modern restaurant beside the Foyle Shopping Centre is on two floors and very handy for shoppers, visitors or pre- and post-theatre meals. Refurbishment has revamped the interior, but the central philosophy of providing good quality, reasonably priced food in enjoyably informal surroundings - and with quick service from the very friendly staff - remains unchanged. Menus change through the day and offer a wide range of food in the current international fashion, ranging from soup of the day (a very good chowder, perhaps, full of a variety of smoked and unsmoked fish and shell fish, attractively presented with home-made wheaten bread) and designer sandwiches (roast vegetables & goats' cheese baguette), to house favourites like spicy chicken tagliatelle, or a 10 oz sirloin steak. A conveniently located, family-friendly restaurant - handy to know about. The wine list includes a useful flavour key, indicating style. **Seats 80**; reservations accepted. Open daily, L&D Mon-Sat, 12-4pm & 5-10pm; Sun all day 1-8pm, all à la carte. House wine from about £13. Closed 25 Dec. MasterCard, Visa, Switch. **Directions:** City centre, opposite main entrance to Foyleside Shopping Centre. ◊

Londonderry   # Hastings Everglades Hotel
HOTEL   Prehen Road Londonderry Co Londonderry BT47 2NH **Tel: 028 7132 1066**
                          res@egh.hastingshotels.com www.hastingshotels.com

Situated on the banks of the River Foyle, close to City of Derry airport and quite convenient to the city, this blocky modern hotel is well located for business and pleasure. Warm and welcoming staff are very hospitable and helpful and, as at all the Hastings Hotels, an on-going system of refurbishment and upgrading pays off as the spacious public areas never feel dated. The well-maintained bedrooms have all recently been through their regular refurbishment programme and are all very comfortable, with good amenities; most of the bathrooms have also been renewed. The hotel is quietly situated which, together with a high standard of accommodation and friendly staff, makes it a very pleasant place to stay and they do a particularly good breakfast (from 7am). Although probably most popular for business guests, it is well located for golf, with the City of Derry course just a couple of minutes away and six other courses, including Royal Portrush, within easy driving distance. * The Everglades is the only hotel in Derry city open on Christmas Day. Conference/banqueting (400/320); broadband wi/fi. **Rooms 64** (2 suites, 1 junior suite, 3 executive, 12 family, all no-smoking, 1 disabled); children under 14 free in parents' room; cots available; baby sitting arranged. No pets. Lift. Room service (all day). B&B £75 pps, ss £35; no sc. Wheelchair accessible. Own parking (200). *Short breaks & golfing breaks offered. Open all year. Amex, Diners, MasterCard, Visa, Switch **Directions:** From Belfast follow M2; hotel is on A5 approx 1 mile (2km) from city.

Londonderry   # Mange 2
RESTAURANT   110-115 Strand Road Londonderry Co Londonderry BT48 7NR
                                              Tel: 028 7136 1222
                          dine@mange2derry.com www.mange2derry.com

John O'Connell and Kieran McGuinness have recently moved to bright and spacious new premises on the Strand Road, with a great view over the River Foyle. An outside seating area attracts attention as you approach, but it is only as you enter that you are really drawn in to this stylish contemporary restaurant with seating on two levels: an open kitchen is clearly visible as you enter, providing a perfect backdrop for enjoying Kieran's creative cooking. Frequently changed menus are refreshingly unpretentious, with old favourites such as his classic 5 onion soup and Donegal bacon and cabbage remaining as popular as ever with lunchtime diners, as they are always reliably good, generous and reasonably priced. Evening menus move up a gear and include an especially appealing house speciality of fillet of Finnebrogue venison, with sweet potato purée, pan-seared spinach & redcurrant jus is a not-to-be-missed; local seafood's and meats also feature, of course, and vegetarians are well catered for too, with tempting dishes such as gorgonzola and walnut ravioli, served with a choice of sauces and dressings. Friendly staff are always willing to give advice, but are not in any way intrusive. A limited but well priced wine menu is offered. Bright by day and candlelit at night, the atmosphere in this chic and stylish restaurant is romantic and relaxed; the food is as good as it looks, and good value too – no wonder it is so popular. **Seats 120** (outdoors, 50); reservations recommended; toilets wheelchair accessible; children welcome. Open daily, all day 12-10pm: L, 12-3, D, 5.30-10. A la carte; set Sun L £11.95; house wines £12.95; sc discretionary. Closed 3 days Christmas. Amex, MasterCard, Visa, Switch. **Directions:** By the River Foyle, within the walled city.

Londonderry

Ramada Da Vinci's Hotel

HOTEL   15 Culmore Road Londonderry Co Londonderry BT48 8JB **Tel: 028 7127 9111**
Ⓝ   reservations@davincishotel.com www.davincishotel.com

This very popular hotel is about a mile from the city centre; it has private car parking and there is a pleasant riverside walkway into the city from the hotel. Public areas include a large traditional bar which tends to be very busy; also The Style Bar - a trendy little bar used as part of the attractive Grillroom Restaurant (with walk-in wine room to one side), a stand-alone room for private functions or the late night residents' bar at the weekend. and the very popular Spirit bar which opens on Friday & Saturday nights from 10.30pm onwards for over-23s. Conference facilities available. Complimentary broadband internet access. Guests have complimentary use of Fitness First (located half mile from hotel). **Rooms 70.** Room rates from £49.95 Closed 24-26 Dec. MasterCard, Visa, Switch. **Directions:** Located 5 minutes from City Centre. ◊

Londonderry

Tower Hotel Derry

HOTEL   Off The Diamond Londonderry Co Londonderry BT48 6HL **Tel: 028 7137 1000**
                                                reservations@thd.ie www.towerhotelderry.com

This attractive hotel has the distinction of being the only one to have been built inside the city walls and, while this does have its disadvantages (the constraints of the site restricted the amount of parking provided, for example), these are offset by wonderful views over the river and a real sense of being at the real heart of the city. Accommodation and facilities have obvious appeal for both leisure and business visitors - the style throughout is bright and sassy, and rooms are pleasingly decorated, with all the necessary modern facilities, including phones/ISDN, hospitality trays, TV, trouser press etc (also a safe in suites). An attractive bistro restaurant off the lobby has the potential to appeal to non-residents as well as hotel guests. A fitness suite with gym and sauna has a great view across the city. Conference/banqueting 250/180). Parking (limited). **Rooms 90** (3 suites, 4 disabled). Lift. Room service (limited hours). Children welcome (cot available without charge). Room rate about £85-109. Closed 24-27 Dec. Amex, Diners, MasterCard, Visa, Laser. **Directions:** City centre - old town. ◊

Magherafelt

Gardiners G2

RESTAURANT   7 Garden Street Magherafelt Co Londonderry BT45 5DD
            Tel: 028 7930 0333 gardiners2000@hotmail.com www.gardiners.net

Local man Sean Owens opened this impressive restaurant with his wife Helen in 1999, with a redesign of the original premises creating a smart and atmospheric dining room, with a proper bar. It has been a great success and, having seen many a good night enjoyed here, they decided after nearly a decade in business to give it a complete revamp - and, following major refurbishment, it has recently re-emerged with a lot more than just a new name. But some things are better left unchanged, and the stated aim - to bring quality local food and service to the people of the area - is one of them. This is achieved remarkably well, through accessible menus that offer really good variations of many popular dishes: ever-popular prawn cocktail, for example, deep fried Ulster button mushrooms with garlic aoili and (who could resist?) a range of juicy local steak dishes... Sean is a committed supporter of local produce and suppliers, and you may find some unusual specialities here too - Lough Neagh smoked eel, for example (a parfait, perhaps, on roasted soda bread), and dishes inspired by traditional rural products. All menus are good value (including a Celebrations Menu, offered occasionally to give the kitchen a good stretch, which is also keenly priced), and an early dinner menu offering plenty of choice is a snip. But it's not just good food that attracts people to Gardiners - it's a good night out. Gardiners is a great neighbourhood restaurant - and plenty come from other neighbourhoods to enjoy a night out here, especially at weekends. A carefully selected (and thoroughly tasted) wine list is also well priced. Children welcome; toilets wheelchair accessible; air conditioning. **Seats 90** (private room, 105); D Tue-Sun, 5.30-10pm; Sun L about £15, value D about £15, 5.30-7pm, set D about £20, also à la carte; house wine from £11.95. Closed Mon, 25-26 Dec, 12-13 Jul. MasterCard, Visa, Switch. **Directions:** To diamond in Magherafelt, down Rainey St., first right into Garden Street.

Magherafelt
GUESTHOUSE
Ⓝ

Laurel Villa

60 Church Street Magherafelt Co Londonderry BT45 6AW
Tel: 028 7963 2238
info@laurel-villa.com www.laurel-villa.com

Situated in the heart of Northern Ireland, Gerardine and Eugene Kielt's Victorian townhouse exudes charm and instils a sense of curiosity within the many guests who travel here from far and wide to experience not only the warmth and enthusiasm of the owners, but also to enjoy their permanent exhibition of internationally-renowned award-winning poet Seamus Heaney, who was born only a few kilometres from this fine old residence. The five individually decorated en-suite bedrooms have period furniture and all the modern comforts, and there's a cosy reading room where guests are invited to relax - or alternatively to research family history, using the vast array of resources available and the wide-ranging local knowledge of the owners. Heritage and cultural tours are available on request, taken by Eugene who is a professional guide, or you may be lucky enough to combine your stay with one of the Laurel Villa special poetry reading evenings. Breakfast is served in the wood-panelled dining room where tasty cooked breakfasts using local produce are garnished with fresh herbs picked from the kitchen garden; freshly baked wheaten bread and Gerardine's fresh fruit salad are popular with guests, many of whom return often to relax in these comfortable surroundings. This is an unusual place to stay, and an asset to the area. **Rooms 5** (all en-suite); children welcome (under 5s free in parents room, over 5s £10); B&B £35-40 pps, ss £5; reading room. MasterCard, Visa. **Directions:** Church Street is on the main Castledawson Road (A31). ◇

PORTSTEWART

Probably best-known for its sandy beach, this popular seaside resort is popular with surfers and golfers - and generally regarded as a quieter version of neighbouring Portrush. **Cromore Halt Inn** (028 7083 6888; www.cromore.com) is a friendly, family-owned 12-room guesthouse and restaurant on Station Road and would make an equally good base for a business or leisure visit, as the rooms are furnished to hotel standard and prices are reasonable. The 'Blue Flag' strand at Portstewart is the main attraction for visitors, and offers excellent surf fishing for bass as well as the traditional family beach holiday. Other local attractions include Agherton Old.Church (028 7083 3277), Portstewart's original church dating from the 1300s, and the Flowerfield Arts Centre (028 7083 1400), which is a venue for arts and crafts courses, and also houses exhibitions and provides art lectures. The nearby Mussenden Temple and Gardens (028 70 848728), at Downhill, is well worth a visit; originally built as a library by the Bishop of Derry, it is now owned by the National Trust. Golfers will enjoy a round at the 18-hole championship links course at Portstewart Golf Club (028 7083 2015), which provides magnificent views of the Atlantic and Donegal.

WWW.IRELAND-GUIDE.COM FOR ALL THE BEST PLACES TO EAT, DRINK & STAY

Portstewart
B&B

Strand House

105 Strand Road Portstewart Co Londonderry BT55 7LZ **Tel: 028 7083 1000**
enquiries@strandguesthouse.com www.strandguesthouse.com

Ernestine and Claire McKeever's family-run B&B has lovely views and offers a stylish alternative to hotel accommodation on the Causeway Coast. With lovely décor in subtle creams and beiges, it has generous lounging space for guests in a comfortable sitting room and a library area, with big windows to take advantage of the sea views, across to Greencastle in Donegal (complimentary WiFi on the ground floor). Pleasingly uncluttered bedrooms have tea and coffee facilities and well finished bathrooms with shower/Jacuzzi baths. Claire serves home-made scones when guests arrive, and breakfast is lovely, with freshly-squeezed orange juice and organic porridge. Storage and drying facilities for golfing guests. Ample parking. *Frequent special offers, including special interest breaks; details on inquiry. **Rooms 7** (all en-suite, 3 shower only, 5 suites, 1 disabled, all no smoking). B&B £45-50pps, ss £20, single room £45. Not suitable for children. Championship golf 3 minutes walk away; walking; massage. Free broadband wi/fi. Closed mid Dec-mid Jan. MasterCard, Visa, Switch. **Directions:** On Strand Road (from first road coming from Strand & Golf Course).

Upperlands
COUNTRY HOUSE•RESTAURANT

Ardtara Country House

8 Gorteade Road Upperlands Maghera
Co Londonderry BT46 5SA **Tel: 028 7964 4490**
valerie_ferson@ardtara.com www.ardtara.com

Former home to the Clark linen milling family, Ardtara is now an attractive, elegantly decorated Victorian country house and, in the caring hands of manager Valerie Ferson, has a genuinely hospitable atmosphere. Well-proportioned reception rooms include a proper bar which has access to the recently renovated conservatory and garden, and there are antique furnishings and fresh flowers everywhere. All the large, luxuriously furnished bedrooms enjoy views of the garden and surrounding countryside and have king size beds, original fireplaces and LCD TV and DVDs, while bathrooms combine practicality with period details, some including free-standing baths and fireplaces; a room conversion in 2008 has allowed for the addition of an extra bedroom, on the ground floor. Breakfast should be a high point, so allow time to enjoy it. Ardtara would make an excellent base for exploring this beautiful and unspoilt area. Tennis, golf practice tee. Pets allowed by arrangement. Garden, woodland walk. Conferences/Banqueting (50). **Rooms 8** (3 suites) B&B about £75pps, ss about £10. *Short breaks offered. **Restaurant:** Although meals may also be served in the conservatory or bar, the main dining room was previously a snooker room and still has the full Victorian skylight and original hunting frieze, making an unusual setting for fine dining. Daily-changed menus offer three or four choices on each course, typically including starters like pheasant terrine, or smoked salmon with avocado, and main courses like rack of lamb, or fillet of McKee's beef, served with champ. A selection of Irish cheeses is offered (with the famous locally-made Ditty's biscuits) as well as classic desserts like Armagh apple tatin. The food is excellent, and guests enjoy the intimacy of the small house which allows the time to build up a rapport with staff. Seats 65 (private room,30). Reservations required. Children welcome. Toilets wheelchair accessible. L Daily 12-2.30, Sun L 12-4. Set L about £25, Set Sun L about £25. D daily 6.30-9.30 (to 9 Sun). Set D about £33. House wines from about £12. Amex, MasterCard, Visa, Switch. **Directions:** M2 from from Belfast to A6. A29 to Maghera. B75 to Kilrea.

COUNTY TYRONE

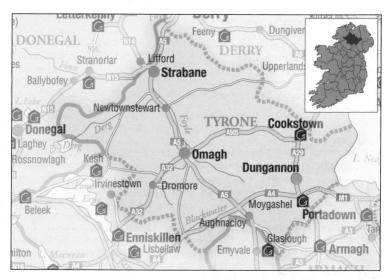

People in Ireland identify strongly with their counties. This is as it should be. The county boundaries may have evolved in many ways over a very long period, often in obscure ways. But in the 21st Century, Irish counties – for all that they vary enormously in size – seem to provide their people with a sense of place and pride which survives modern efforts to create newer administrative structures.

Tyrone is Northern Ireland's largest county, so it is something of a surprise for the traveller to discover that its geography appears to be dominated by a range of mountains of modest height, and nearly half of these peaks seem to be in the neighbouring county of Londonderry.

Yet such is the case with Tyrone and the Sperrins. The village of Sperrin itself towards the head of Glenelly may be in Tyrone, but the highest peak of Sawel (678m), which looms over it, is on the county boundary. But much of the county is upland territory and moorland, giving the impression that the Sperrins are even more extensive than is really the case.

In such a land, the lower country and the fertile valleys gleam like jewels, and there's often a vivid impression of a living - and indeed, prosperity - being wrested from a demanding environment. It's a character-forming sort of place, so it's perhaps understandable that it was the ancestral homeland of a remarkable number of early American Presidents, and this connection is commemorated in the Ulster American Folk Park a few miles north of the county town of Omagh.

Forest parks abound, while attractive towns like Castlederg and Dungannon, as well as villages in the uplands and along the charming Clogher Valley, provide entertainment and hospitality for visitors refreshed by the wide open spaces of the moorlands and the mountains.

Local Attractions and Information

Ardboe	Kinturk (Lough Neagh) Cultural Centre	028 86 736512
Benburb	Benburb Castle and Valley Park	028 37 548241
Castlederg	Visitor Centre (Davy Crockett links)	028 81 670795
Clogher	Clogher Valley Rural Centre	028 85 548872
Coagh	Kinturk Cultural Centre	028 86 736512
Cookstown	Drum Manor Forest Park	028 86 762774
Cookstown	Wellbrook Beetling Mill (Corkhill)	028 86 748210
Cranagh	(Glenelly) Sperrin Heritage Centre	028 81 648142
Creggan	(nr Carrickmore) Visitor Centre	028 80 761112
Dungannon	Heritage Centre	028 87 724187
Dungannon	Tourism Information	028 87 767259

Dungannon	Tyrone Crystal	028 87 725335
Dungannon	Ulysses S Grant Ancestral Homestead	028 85 557133
Fivemiletown	Clogher Valley Railway Exhibition	028 89 521409
Gortin	Ulster History Park	028 81 648188
Newtownstewart	Baronscourt Forest Park	028 81 661683
Newtownstewart	Gateway Centre & Museum	028 81 662414
Omagh	Ulster-American Folk Park	028 82 243292
Omagh	Tourism Information	028 82 247831
Strabane	Gray's Printing Press (US Independence)	028 71 884094
Strabane	Tourism Information	028 71 883735
Strabane	President Wilson Ancestral Home	028 71 384444

Dungannon   Grange Lodge

COUNTRY HOUSE   7 Grange Road Dungannon Co Tyrone BT71 7EJ **Tel: 028 8778 4212**

 stay@grangelodgecountryhouse.com www.grangelodgecountryhouse.com

Norah and Ralph Brown's renowned Georgian retreat offers comfort, true family hospitality and good food. The house is on an elevated site just outside Dungannon, with about 20 acres of grounds; mature woodland and gardens (producing food for the table and flowers for the house) with views over lush countryside. Improvements over the years have been made with great sensitivity and the feeling is of gentle organic growth, culminating in the present warm and welcoming atmosphere. Grange Lodge is furnished unselfconsciously, with antiques and family pieces throughout; bedrooms (and bathrooms) are exceptionally comfortable and thoughtful in detail. Norah is well known for her home cooking and they will cater for groups of 10-30. Dinner menus change daily (in consultation with guests) and residents' dinner (from about £32) must be pre-booked, especially if you want to dine on the day of arrival. Breakfasts are also outstanding, so allow time to indulge: a fine buffet, beautifully set out on a polished dining table, might typically include a large selection of juices, fruit and cereals - and porridge is a speciality, served with a tot of Bushmills whiskey, brown sugar and cream - and that's before you've even reached the cooked breakfast menu, served with lovely fresh breads and toast and home-made preserves. *"Cook with Norah" cookery classes have been running since 2002, and are very successful; details on application. Conferences/banqueting (20/30). **Rooms 5** (3 shower only, all no smoking); not suitable for children under 12. Pets allowed by arrangement. Room service (limited hours). Turndown service. B&B £42.50 pps, ss £22.50. Residents D Mon-Sat, 7.30pm, by arrangement; Set D from £32. Garden, walking, snooker. Closed 15 Dec-1 Feb. MasterCard, Visa, Switch. **Directions:** 1 mile from M1 junction 15. On A29 to Armagh, follow "Grange Lodge" signs.

Dungannon   Stangmore Town House

RESTAURANT WITH ROOMS   24 Killyman Road Dungannon Co Tyrone BT71 6DH

                                         Tel: 028 8772 5600

info@stangmoretownhouse.com www.stangmoretownhouse.com

Anne and Andy Brace will be remembered by many visitors to Dungannon from their previous business, Stangmore Country House. Now they are about a mile and a half away, and it didn't take their followers very long to catch up with them as both their new rooms and the restaurant are always busy. Guests will find very comfortable accommodation here, with Anne's trademark hospitality and immaculate housekeeping - and, of course, Andy's cooking. They are members of A Taste of Tyrone and quite extensive menus are offered, always based on local produce wherever possible, including steaks from award-winning Cloughbane Farm, 5 miles away; there's also a carefully chosen and fairly priced wine list to accompany. Small conferences/meetings (20); free broadband wi/fi; wheelchair access to restaurant & toilet; children welcome (high chair, childrens menu, baby changing facilities; under 12s free in parents' room, cot available); **Seats 50**; D Mon-Sat, 6.30-8.30pm; early D £15, 6.30-7.30pm; set D £25; also à la carte; house wine £13.50. **Rooms 5** (all en-suite & no smoking, 1 shower only); limited room service; B&B £40pps; ss £25. Restaurant closed Sun; house closed 1 week Jul & 1 week Christmas. Amex, MasterCard, Visa, Switch. **Directions:** Junction 15 off M1, 2nd set of traffic lights take a right down Gortmellon Links road. At the end of the road take a left, 1.5 miles (3km) on the right.

Moygashel
RESTAURANT
R

Deli on the Green

The Linen Green Moygashel Co Tyrone BT71 7HB **Tel: 028 8775 1775**
info@delionthegreen.com www.delionthegreen.com

Across the yard from The Loft @ The Linen Green (see entry), the stylish Deli on the Green offers table service and a slightly more leisurely pace. Glasgow-born chef Bob McDonald, highly respected in Ulster food circles, is head chef and ideas man. Besides a classy deli (choose your lunch or pick up the makings of a picnic from the selection of quality local and more exotic foodstuffs) there are sofas and café-style seating, inside and out, for coffees and snacks, and a brasserie, where the contemporary cuisine is reflected in a stylish combination of bare stone and glass, blond wood tables and high-backed cream leather chairs. Changed daily, the menus reflect Bob's commitment to profiling quality local produce including Kettyle's dry-aged beef, Moyallon sausages, Ditty's oatcakes and Tickety Moo Jersey Ice Cream - and there's a guarantee of no GM foods. Breakfast includes organic porridge and freshly-squeezed orange juice, then lunch can be as simple as you want to make it, from the salad and cooked meats display (including Bob's home-made corned beef), or wholesome hot dishes. Then, in the evening, the tea lights and relaxing music herald a mood move: an ambitious menu, stylish presentation, comprehensive wine list and good service from well-trained, smartly turned out staff all create a sense of occasion. Begin with deli breads with home-made soup, or steamed mussels with leeks & cider cream, perhaps, then follow with rack of Lough Erne lamb with spiced couscous, classic Kettyle dry-aged char-grilled steaks (char-grills are a speciality), or seared scallops with black pudding & chive hollandaise, baby new potatoes & asparagus, with interesting side orders. Finish with a delicious dessert such as caramelised lemon tart with raspberries & sorbet or Irish cheeses with Ditty's Oatcakes. Nice wine list includes an interesting Deli House Selection, a handful of half bottles and some mini-bottles too. **Seats 45**; children welcome (high chair, children's menu, baby changing facilities); fully wheelchair accessible. Open all day Mon-Sat 8.30 am to 5.30 pm, D Thu, Fri & Sat 6-9.30 (booking advisable). Early Bird Thu & Fri, 5.30-7. 2/3 courses £13.50/ £16.50. House wine £11.50. SC 10% on groups 6+. Closed Sun, 1 Jul, 12-13 Jul, 25-26 Dec. Amex, Diners, MasterCard, Visa, Switch. **Directions:** Just off main Belfast road, follow signs to Moygashel.

Moygashel
CAFÉ
R

The Loft @ The Linen Green

Moygashel Co Tyrone BT71 7HB
Tel: 028 8775 3761

In the heart of Ulster, near the Dungannon end of the M1 motorway and just three minutes off the main Belfast road (look for the sign to Moygashel village) is The Linen Green discount designer outlet and retail park, its phenomenal success testimony to the lure of retail therapy in its most pleasurable guise. Developed on the site of a former textile mill, the complex retains an historic feel and hosts names such as Paul Costelloe, Foxford, Helen McAlinden and Ann Storey as well as shops offering luxury lingerie, textiles and treats for the house and garden. Add to that generous parking and a choice of two contrasting restaurants, The Loft, and Deli on the Green (see entry), both run by Claire Murray, and it makes an attractive refuelling stop. Upstairs in the main building, The Loft is an attractive café with high ceilings, lots of light and some memorabilia from Moygashel's days as a textile mill. Head up the stairs (lift access too) for a pick-me-up cappuccino and, perhaps, a generous scone, a tray bake or lemon meringue, or a quick lunch - sandwiches on good bread made to order from the salads and meats selection, or a tasty panini, with a good choice of hot and cold drinks too. Open Mon-Sat, 10am-5pm. **Directions:** Just off main Belfast road, follow signs to Moygashel. ◇

JOURNEY PLANNER - WITH SUGGESTED PLACES FOR A BREAK...

e – EAT   d – DRINK   s – STAY

Dublin - Belfast

Travel Time (approx):
2 Hours

Distance:
166 km (103 miles)

Roads:
M1 / N1 / A1

DUBLIN

25%   50%   75%

	Town	County	Road	Km from Dublin	Km from Road	Category
1	Malahide	Dublin	M1	12	5	e d s
	Swords	Dublin	M1	12	3	e d s
2	Skerries	Dublin	M1	18	15	e d s
3	Drogheda	Louth	M1	46	3	s
	Termonfeckin	Louth	M1	46	10	e
4	Clogherhead	Louth	M1	53	16	e
5	Collon	Louth	M1	60	8	e
6	Dunleer	Louth	M1	70	2	e

BELFAST

	Town	County	Road	Km from Dublin	Km from Road	Category
7	Ardee	Louth	M1	75	9	e d
8	Blackrock	Louth	M1	80	5	e d s
9	Dundalk	Louth	M1	90	2	e d s
10	Warrenpoint	Down	A1	106	11	e
	Rostrevor	Down	A1	106	15	e
11	Portadown	Armagh	A1	125	17	e d s
12	Hillsborough	Down	A1	150	3	e d

JOURNEY PLANNER - WITH SUGGESTED PLACES FOR A BREAK...

ⓔ – EAT ⓓ – DRINK ⓢ – STAY

Dublin – Derry

Travel Time (approx):
3.5 Hours

Distance:
231 km (145 miles)

Roads:
N2 / A5

DUBLIN ➞ ------ 25% | ------ 50% | ------ 75% | ------ DERRY

❷ ❷ ❸ ❹ ❺   ❻   ❼

	Town	County	Road	Km from Dublin	Km from Road	Category
1	Ashbourne	Meath	N2	22	2	ⓔ ⓢ
2	Navan	Meath	N2	47	13	ⓔ ⓓ ⓢ
	Slane	Meath	N2	47.5	0	ⓔ ⓓ ⓢ
3	Collon	Louth	N2	56	0	ⓔ
4	Ardee	Louth	N2	66	0	ⓔ ⓓ
5	Carrickmacross	Monaghan	N2	86	1	ⓔ ⓓ ⓢ

	Town	County	Road	Km from Dublin	Km from Road	Category
6	Monaghan	Monaghan	N2	123	2	ⓔ ⓓ ⓢ
	Clones	Monaghan	N2	123	25	ⓢ
	Glaslough	Monaghan	N2	124	10	ⓔ ⓢ
7	Dungannon	Tyrone	A5	167	7	ⓢ
	Moygashel	Tyrone	A5	167	9	ⓔ

JOURNEY PLANNER - WITH SUGGESTED PLACES FOR A BREAK...

ⓔ – EAT   ⓓ – DRINK   ⓢ – STAY

Dublin - Donegal

Travel Time (approx):
4 Hours

Distance:
235 km (146 miles)

Roads:
N3 / A509 / N3 / N15

DUBLIN ➡ 25% | 50% | 75% | DONEGAL

	Town	County	Road	Km from Dublin	Km from Road	Category
1	Dunboyne	Meath	N3	14	10	ⓔ ⓓ ⓢ
	Kilmessan	Meath	N3	16	22	ⓢ
2	Navan	Meath	N3	50	0	ⓔ ⓓ ⓢ
	Athboy	Meath	N3	50	19	ⓔ ⓢ
3	Tara	Meath	N3	61	0	ⓓ
4	Kells	Meath	N3	66	0	ⓔ
5	Virginia	Cavan	N3	85	0	ⓔ ⓓ ⓢ
	Mount Nugent	Cavan	N3	85	20	ⓢ
	Bailieborough	Cavan	N3	85	13	ⓔ

	Town	County	Road	Km from Dublin	Km from Road	Category
6	Cavan	Cavan	N3	113	2	ⓔ ⓓ ⓢ
7	Cloverhill	Cavan	N3	122	3	ⓔ ⓓ ⓢ
8	Belturbet	Cavan	N3	130	0	ⓔ ⓓ ⓢ
	Ballyconnell	Cavan	N3	130	12	ⓔ ⓓ ⓢ
9	Blacklion	Cavan	N3	162	16	ⓔ ⓓ ⓢ
10	Enniskillen	Fermanagh A509		166	0	ⓔ ⓓ ⓢ
11	Belleek	Fermanagh A509		204	0	ⓔ
12	Ballyshannon	Donegal	N3	212	0	ⓔ ⓓ

JOURNEY PLANNER - WITH SUGGESTED PLACES FOR A BREAK...

ⓔ – EAT   ⓓ – DRINK   ⓢ – STAY

Dublin - Sligo

Travel Time (approx): 3.25 Hours

Distance: 208 km (130 miles)

Roads: M4 / N4

DUBLIN ➝ SLIGO

	Town	County	Road	Km from Dublin	Km from Road	Category
1	Lucan	Dublin	M4	15	2	ⓔ ⓢ
2	Leixlip	Dublin	M4	16.5	2	ⓔ ⓢ
	Celbridge	Kildare	M4	16.5	8	ⓔ
	Clane	Kildare	M4	16.5	20	ⓔ
3	Maynooth	Kildare	M4	24	3	ⓔ ⓓ ⓢ
	Straffan	Kildare	M4	24	11	ⓔ ⓢ
4	Enfield	Kildare	M4	37	9	ⓢ
	Moy Valley	Kildare	M4	37	2	ⓔ ⓓ ⓢ
5	Mullingar	Westmeath	N4	76	3	ⓔ ⓓ ⓢ
6	Multyfarnham	Westmeath	N4	86	5	ⓢ
7	Granard	Longford	N4	106	12	ⓢ
8	Longford	Longford	N4	119	3	ⓔ ⓓ ⓢ
	Tarmonbarry	Roscommon	N4	119	9	ⓔ ⓓ

	Town	County	Road	Km from Dublin	Km from Road	Category
9	Rooskey	Leitrim	N4	137	3	ⓢ
10	Jamestown	Leitrim	N4	146	3	ⓔ
11	Carrick on Shannon	Leitrim	N4	153	0	ⓔ ⓓ ⓢ
	Drumshanbo	Leitrim	N4	153	15	ⓢ
	Leitrim	Leitrim	N4	153	7	ⓔ ⓓ
	Keshcarrigan	Leitrim	N4	153	15	ⓔ
12	Knockvicar	Roscommon	N4	158	3	ⓔ ⓓ
13	Cootehall	Roscommon	N4	165	3	ⓔ ⓓ
14	Castlebaldwin	Sligo	N4	181	0	ⓔ ⓓ ⓢ
15	Riverstown	Sligo	N4	189	2	ⓢ
16	Collooney	Sligo	N4	195	0	ⓢ
	Ballygawley	Sligo	N4	195	5	ⓔ ⓢ

JOURNEY PLANNER - WITH SUGGESTED PLACES FOR A BREAK...

e – EAT   d – DRINK   s – STAY

Dublin – Westport

Travel Time (approx):
4 Hours

Distance:
253 km (157 miles)

Roads:
M4 / N4 / N5

DUBLIN →

	Town	County	Road	Km from Dublin	Km from Road	Category
1	Lucan	Dublin	M4	15	2	e s
	Leixlip	Dublin	M4	16.5	2	e s
	Celbridge	Kildare	M4	16.5	8	e
	Clane	Kildare	M4	16.5	20	e
2	Maynooth	Kildare	M4	24	3	e d s
	Straffan	Kildare	M4	24	11	e s
3	Enfield	Kildare	M4	37	9	s
	Moy Valley	Kildare	M4	37	2	e d s

WESTPORT

	Town	County	Road	Km from Dublin	Km from Road	Category
4	Mullingar	Westmeath	N4	76	3	e d s
5	Multyfarnham	Westmeath	N4	86	5	s
6	Granard	Longford	N4	106	12	s
7	Longford	Longford	N4	119	0	e d s
8	Tarmonbarry	Roscommon	N5	128	0	e d s
9	Turlough	Mayo	N5	227	5	e
10	Castlebar	Mayo	N5	234	0	e d s

Dublin

Westport

JOURNEY PLANNER - WITH SUGGESTED PLACES FOR A BREAK...

☺ – EAT 🍸 – DRINK ☺ – STAY

Dublin - Galway

Travel Time (approx): 3 Hours

Distance: 215 km (133 miles)

Roads: M4 / N6

DUBLIN ➞ ➞ ➞ GALWAY

№	Town	County	Road	Km from Dublin	Km from Road	Category
1	Lucan	Dublin	M4	15	2	☺ ☺
	Leixlip	Dublin	M4	16.5	2	☺ ☺
	Celbridge	Kildare	M4	16.5	8	☺
	Clane	Kildare	M4	16.5	20	☺
2	Maynooth	Kildare	M4	24	3	☺ 🍸 ☺
	Straffan	Kildare	M4	24	11	☺ ☺
3	Enfield	Kildare	M4	37	9	☺
	Moy Valley	Kildare	M4	37	3	☺ 🍸 ☺
4	Tullamore	Offaly	N6	93	10	☺ 🍸 ☺

№	Town	County	Road	Km from Dublin	Km from Road	Category
5	Moate	Westmeath	N6	100	0	☺
6	Glasson	Westmeath	N6	120	10	☺ 🍸 ☺
7	Athlone	Westmeath	N6	123	2	☺ 🍸 ☺
8	Shannonbridge	Offaly	N6	146	10	☺ 🍸
9	Ballinasloe	Galway	N6	150	2.5	☺ 🍸 ☺
10	Loughrea	Galway	N6	176	0	☺ ☺
11	Athenry	Galway	N6	191	3	☺
12	Clarinbridge	Galway	N6	206	6	☺

JOURNEY PLANNER - WITH SUGGESTED PLACES FOR A BREAK...

ⓔ – EAT   ⓓ – DRINK   ⓢ – STAY

Dublin - Limerick - Killarney

Travel Time (approx):
4.5 Hours

Distance:
305 km (190 miles)

Roads:
N7 / M7 / N20 / N21 / N23

DUBLIN ➞ KILLARNEY

1 2 3 4 5 6 7 8 9 10 11 12 13 14 15

25%   50%   75%

	Town	County	Road	Km from Dublin	Km from Road	Category
1	Red Cow R/about	Dublin	N7	9	0	ⓢ
2	Newlands Cross	Dublin	N7	12	0	ⓢ
	Liffey Valley	Dublin	N7	12	0	ⓔ ⓢ
3	Saggart	Dublin	N7	17	1	ⓢ
4	Naas	Kildare	M7	30	3	ⓔ ⓓ ⓢ
5	Newbridge	Kildare	M7	47	3	ⓢ
6	Killenard	Laois	M7	60	13	ⓔ ⓢ
7	Portlaoise	Laois	M7	80	5	ⓔ ⓢ
8	Mountrath	Laois	N7	100	0	ⓢ
9	Roscrea	Tipperary	N7	123	2	ⓔ
10	Nenagh	Tipperary	N7	151	6	ⓔ ⓓ ⓢ
	Garrykennedy	Tipperary	N7	151	11	ⓔ ⓓ ⓢ
11	Dromineer	Tipperary	N7	162	18	ⓔ ⓓ
12	**LIMERICK**	Limerick	N7	197	3	ⓔ ⓓ ⓢ
13	Adare	Limerick N20/N21		212	0	ⓔ ⓓ ⓢ
	Ballingarry	Limerick	N21	212	11	ⓔ ⓢ
14	Listowel	Kerry	N21	257	16	ⓔ ⓢ
15	Tralee	Kerry	N23	280	17.5	ⓔ ⓓ ⓢ

JOURNEY PLANNER - WITH SUGGESTED PLACES FOR A BREAK...

(e) – EAT   (d) – DRINK   (S) – STAY

Dublin - Cork

Travel Time (approx):
4 Hours

Distance:
257 km (167 miles)

Roads:
N7 / M7 / N8 / M8

DUBLIN → → → → ... → → **CORK**

Town	County	Road	Km from Dublin	Km from Road	Category
1 Red Cow R/about	Dublin	N7	9	0	(S)
2 Newlands Cross	Dublin	N7	12	0	(S)
Liffey Valley	Dublin	N7	12	0	(e)(S)
3 Saggart	Dublin	N7	17	1	(S)
4 Naas	Kildare	M7	30	3	(e)(d)(S)
5 Newbridge	Kildare	M7	47	3	(S)
6 Killenard	Laois	M7	60	13	(e)(S)
7 Portlaoise	Laois	N8	87	1	(e)(S)
8 Abbeyleix	Laois	N8	98	0	(e)(d)(S)

Town	County	Road	Km from Dublin	Km from Road	Category
9 Durrow	Laois	N8	107	0	(e)(S)
10 Thurles	Tipperary	N8	137	15	(e)(S)
11 Cashel	Tipperary	N8	156	3	(e)(d)(S)
12 Clonmel	Tipperary	N8	176	20	(e)(d)(S)
Clogheen	Tipperary	N8	176	15	(e)(S)
13 Mitchelstown	Cork	M8	203	1	(e)
Doneraile	Cork	M8	203	23	(S)
14 Fermoy	Cork	M8	218	2	(e)(S)

JOURNEY PLANNER - WITH SUGGESTED PLACES FOR A BREAK...

ⓔ – EAT   ⓓ – DRINK   ⓢ – STAY

Dublin - Kilkenny - Waterford

Travel Time (approx):
2.5 Hours

Distance:
160 km (100 miles)

Roads:
N7 / M7 / M9 / N9

25% | 50% | 75% |

DULLIN →

❶ ❷ ❸   ❹   ❺   ❻

	Town	County	Road	Km from Dublin	Km from Road	Category
1	Red Cow R/about	Dublin	N7	9	0	ⓢ
2	Newlands Cross	Dublin	N7	12	0	ⓢ
	Liffey Valley	Dublin	N7	12	0	ⓔ ⓢ
3	Saggart	Dublin	N7	17	1	ⓢ
4	Naas	Kildare	M7	30	3	ⓔ ⓓ ⓢ
	Ballymore Eustace	Kildare	M7/M9	30	11	ⓔ ⓓ
5	Dunlavin	Wicklow	N9	54	3	ⓔ ⓓ ⓢ
6	Castledermot	Kildare	N9	73	5	ⓢ
	Athy	Kildare	N9	73	15	ⓔ ⓓ ⓢ

❼   ❽ ❾ ❿   ⓫

→ WATERFORD

	Town	County	Road	Km from Dublin	Km from Road	Category
7	Carlow	Carlow	N9	83	3	ⓔ ⓓ ⓢ
8	Leighlinbridge	Carlow	N9	97	1.5	ⓔ ⓓ ⓢ
9	Bagenalstown	Carlow	N9	100	2	ⓢ
	Borris	Carlow	N9	100	15	ⓔ ⓓ ⓢ
10	Maddoxtown*	Kilkenny	N9*	105	14	ⓢ
	KILKENNY CITY*	Kilkenny	N9*	105	18	ⓔ ⓓ ⓢ
11	Inistioge	Kilkenny	N9	125	9	ⓔ
	Thomastown	Kilkenny	N9	125	0	ⓔ ⓢ

* Turn on to N10 for Kilkenny

ⓔ – EAT ⓓ – DRINK Ⓢ – STAY

Dublin - Wexford

Travel Time (approx): 2 Hours

Distance: 138 km (58 miles)

Roads: M11 / N11

DUBLIN → **WEXFORD**

25% — 50% — 75%

	Town	County	Road	Km from Dublin	Km from Road	Category
1	Enniskerry	Wicklow	N11	23	3	ⓔ ⓓ Ⓢ
	Kilmacanogue	Wicklow	N11	24	2	ⓔ
2	Greystones	Wicklow	N11	29	4	ⓔ ⓓ
	Delgany	Wicklow	N11	29	0	Ⓢ
3	N/twnmtkennedy	Wicklow	N11	32	3	ⓔ Ⓢ
4	Ashford	Wicklow	N11	40	3	ⓔ Ⓢ
5	Rathnew	Wicklow	N11	43	2	ⓔ Ⓢ
	Rathdrum	Wicklow	N11	43	15	Ⓢ
6	Avoca	Wicklow	N11	55	10	ⓔ
7	Woodenbridge	Wicklow	N11	66	10	Ⓢ
	Arklow	Wicklow	N11	66	10	ⓔ
8	Gorey	Wexford	N11	86	2	ⓔ ⓓ Ⓢ
9	Bunclody	Wexford	N11	100	15	ⓔ Ⓢ
10	Enniscorthy	Wexford	N11	114	0	ⓔ ⓓ Ⓢ

90 MINUTES
... from the Red Cow

Work-weary Dubliners... find revitalising short breaks in recommended accommodation within 110km of the Red Cow Roundabout:

County	Town	Establishment	Category	Distance*
Kildare	Leixlip	Courtyard Hotel	Hotel	7
Kildare	Leixlip	Leixlip House Hotel	Hotel	7
Dublin	Leixlip	Becketts Country House Hotel	Hotel	12
Dublin	Lucan	Finnstown Country House Hotel	Hotel	12
Kildare	Maynooth	Glenroyal Hotel	Hotel	16
Kildare	Maynooth	Maynooth Campus	Accommodation	16
Kildare	Maynooth	Carton House Hotel	Hotel	16
Meath	Dunboyne	Dunboyne Castle Hotel & Spa	Hotel	20
Kildare	Naas	Osprey Hotel & Spa	Hotel	21
Kildare	Naas	Killashee House Hotel & Villa Spa	Hotel	21
Kildare	Naas	Keadeen Hotel	Hotel	21
Dublin	Killiney	Fitzpatrick Castle Hotel	Hotel	22
Dublin	Dun Laoghaire	Royal Marine Hotel	Hotel	25
Meath	Ashbourne	Broadmeadow Country House	Guesthouse	25
Dublin	Portmarnock	Portmarnock Hotel	Hotel	26
Kildare	Straffan	Barberstown Castle	Hotel	26
Kildare	Straffan	K Club	Hotel	26
Kildare	Moyvalley	Moyvalley Estate	Hotel	27
Dublin	Swords	Roganstown Golf & Country Club	Hotel	28
Kildare	Clane	Westgrove Hotel	Hotel	29
Dublin	Howth	King Sitric Fish Restaurant & Acc	Restaurant with rooms	30
Wicklow	Enniskerry	Ritz Carlton Powerscourt	Hotel	31
Wicklow	Delgany	Glenview Hotel	Hotel	34
Wicklow	Newtnmkedy.	Marriott Druids Glen Hotel	Hotel	38
Wicklow	Newtnmkedy.	Parkview Hotel	Hotel	38
Meath	Enfield	Marriott Johnstown House Hotel	Hotel	39
Meath	Kilmessan	The Station House Hotel	Hotel	39
Dublin	Skerries	Red Bank House & Restaurant	Guesthouse/Restaurant	40
Kildare	Curragh	Martinstown House	Country House	40
Wicklow	Dunlavin	Rathsallagh House	Country House	41
Meath	Trim	Trim Castle Hotel	Hotel	43
Meath	Trim	Knightsbrook Hotel & Golf Resort	Hotel	43
Meath	Navan	Bellinter Country House	Country House	45
Wicklow	Rathnew	Hunter's Hotel	Hotel	48
Wicklow	Ashford	Ballyknocken House & Cookery Sch.	Farmhouse	50
Meath	Slane	Rossnaree	Historic House	52
Meath	Slane	The Millhouse	Hotel	52
Meath	Slane	Tankardstown House	Historic House	52
Louth	Collon	Forge Gallery Restaurant	Restaurant with rooms	58
Louth	Drogheda	Boyne Valley Hotel & Country Club	Hotel	58
Louth	Drogheda	D Hotel	Hotel	58
Kildare	Athy	Carlton Abbey Hotel	Hotel	61

*Distance in kilometres.

County	Town	Establishment	Category	Distance*
Kildare	Athy	Coursetown Country House	Country House	61
Wicklow	Redcross	Kilpatrick House	Farmhouse	62
Wicklow	Kiltegan	Barraderry Country House	Country House	62
Wicklow	Rathdrum	Avonbrae	Guesthouse	62
Meath	Athboy	Frankville House - The Blue Door	B&B	64
Kildare	Castledermot	Kilkea Castle	Hotel	65
Laois	Killenard	The Heritage Golf & Spa Resort	Hotel	65
Carlow	Carlow	Barrowville Townhouse	Guesthouse	73
Wicklow	Arklow	Plattenstown Country House	Country House	73
Carlow	Tullow	Mount Wolseley Hilton Hotel	Hotel	76
Carlow	Tullow	Ballyderrin House	B&B	76
Laois	Portlaoise	Ivyleigh House	Guesthouse	76
Laois	Portlaoise	Portlaoise Heritage Hotel	Hotel	76
Westmeath	Mullingar	Annebrook House Hotel	Hotel	80
Westmeath	Mullingar	Mullingar Park Hotel	Hotel	80
Wicklow	Woodenbridge	Woodenbridge Hotel	Hotel	80
Carlow	Leighlinbridge	Lord Bagenal Inn	Hotel	84
Wexford	Gorey	Woodlands Country House	Country House	85
Cavan	Kingscourt	Cabra Castle Hotel & Golf Club	Hotel	86
Westmeath	Multyfarnham	Mornington House	Country House	87
Carlow	Ballon	Ballykealey Manor Hotel	Hotel	88
Carlow	Ballon	Sherwood Park House	Country House	88
Laois	Abbeyleix	Sandymount House	Country House/B&B	90
Louth	Dundalk	Crowne Plaza Hotel	Hotel	90
Carlow	Bagenalstown	Kilgraney House	Country House	90
Carlow	Bagenalstown	Lorum Old Rectory	Country House	90
Monaghan	Carrickmacross	Nuremore Hotel & Country Club	Hotel	90
Louth	Dundalk	Ballymascanlon House Hotel	Hotel	92
Louth	Dundalk	Rosemount	B&B	92
Wicklow	Macreddin	BrookLodge	Hotel	95
Offaly	Tullamore	Tullamore Court Hotel	Hotel	96
Offaly	Tullamore	Annaharvey Farm	Farmhouse	96
Laois	Durrow	Castle Durrow	Hotel	99
Cavan	Mountnugent	Ross House	Farmhouse	100
Laois	Mountrath	Roundwood House	Country House	100
Westmeath	Moate	Temple Country Retreat & Spa	Country House	103
Carlow	Borris	The Step House Hotel	Hotel	104
Offaly	Kinnity	Ardmore Country House	Country House	110
Offaly	Kinnity	Glendine Bistro	B&B	110
Offaly	Kinnity	Kinnitty Castle	Hitel	110

Georgina Campbell's Ireland

Georgina Campbell's Ireland

Georgina Campbell's Ireland

Georgina Campbell's Ireland

Georgina Campbell's Ireland

INDEX

Georgina Campbell's Ireland

How to Use the Guide

Location /Establishment name

- Cities, towns and villages are arranged in alphabetical order within counties, with the exception of Dublin, Cork, Belfast, Galway and Limerick where the city comes ahead of other towns
- Establishments arranged alphabetically within location
- In Dublin city, postal codes are arranged in numerical order. Even numbers are south of the River Liffey, and uneven numbers on the north, with the exception of Dublin 8 which straddles the river. Dublin 1 and 2 are most central; Dublin 1 is north of the Liffey, Dublin 2 is south of it (see map). Within each district, establishments are listed in alphabetical order.

Telephone numbers

- Codes are given for use within the Republic of Ireland / Northern Ireland. To call ROI from outside the jurisdiction, the code is +353 (or +44 for NI), then drop the first digit (zero) from the local code.
- To call Northern Ireland from the Republic, replace the 028 code with 048.

Reading the text

Our aim is to lead readers to the best places in Ireland, to suit their needs, allowing for regional variations in standards - and differing requirements, depending on the occasion. Please read the text for each establishment and consider what it is about them that we are recommending. The longer narratives tend to be for the better establishments as they have more positive and interesting things to say about them e.g. if we only highlight the business and conference facilities about a particular hotel then this may not be the best choice for those seeking a romantic break.

Categories

We have multiple categories including Hotel, Restaurant, Café etc, and we highlight the aspects of a particular establishment that we recommend. Where only one category is highlighted, that is the main recommendation, for example 'Hotel' is recommended as a place to stay. If there is a restaurant and it is recommended, the category becomes 'Hotel/Restaurant'.

Abbreviations

SC	Service Charge
SC incl	Service Charge Included
B	Breakfast
L	Lunch
D	Dinner (evening meal)
PP	Per Person
PPS	Per Person Sharing
PN	Per Night
Power Shower	A shower that has an electric pump that increases the water flow
Double	A bedroom with a bed that sleeps two people
Twin	A bedroom that has two separate beds
Family Room	Contains multiple beds suitable for a family, contact establishment for more information

Rating for outstanding cooking, accommodation or features

- 👑 - Best Establishment: selected for overall excellence and/or specific special qualities - e.g. 'Outstanding Location'
- ☆ - Demi-star: for cooking and service well above average
- ★ - Restaurants offering consistent excellence overall
- ★★ - One of the best restaurants in the land
- ★★★ - The highest restaurant grade achievable
- 🏛 - Outstanding accommodation of its type
- 🏛🏛 - Deluxe hotel
- 🍺 - Pub star: good food and atmosphere
- ⬤ - Identifies inclusion in the BIM Seafood Circle programme
- Ⓥ - Indicates that establishment accepts the Guide's discount voucher (€5/£5)
- € - 'Best Budget' denotes moderately priced establishment (max approx €50 pps for accommodation, €35 for 3-course meal without drinks)
- 👁 - Outstanding location, building or atmosphere
- Ⓔ - Editor's Choice; a selection of establishments outside the standard categories that should enhance the discerning travellers experience of Ireland
- Ⓝ - Establishments that are new to this edition of the Guide
- ♔ - Previous award winner in earlier editions of our guides
- ◇ - Times/prices not received from establishment at time of going to press (were confirmed by phone)

Route indicators:

Throughout the Guide, we have highlighted establishments which are on or close to National Primary routes, to or from Dublin. Further details are contained within the Route Planning Section towards the back of this book. Each colour denotes a route as follows:

R – Dublin to Belfast   R – Dublin to Derry
R – Dublin to Donegal   R – Dublin to Sligo
R – Dublin to Westport   R – Dublin to Galway
R – Dublin to Limerick / Killarney   R – Dublin to Cork
R – Dublin to Kilkenny / Waterford   R – Dublin to Wexford

Maps are intended for reference only: Ordnance Survey maps are recommended when travelling; available from Tourist Information Offices.

PRICES & OPENING HOURS
PLEASE NOTE THAT PRICES AND OPENING HOURS ARE GIVEN AS A GUIDELINE ONLY, AND MAY HAVE CHANGED; CHECK BEFORE TRAVELLING OR WHEN MAKING A RESERVATION.

Prices in the Republic of Ireland are given in Euro (€) and those in Northern Ireland in pounds Sterling (£).

Don't forget...

you can always check

ireland-guide.com

for all our latest
recommendations
and news!